McDougal Littell

CLASSZONE

MW01691983

Visit classzone.com and get connected.

ClassZone resources provide instruction, practice and learning support for students and parents.

Literature and Reading Center

- Selection-specific content includes vocabulary practice, research links, and extension activities for writing and critical thinking
- Author Online provides information about each author, as well as in-depth author studies on selected writers
- English Learner support for a variety of languages includes audio summaries of selections and a Multi-Language Academic Glossary

Vocabulary and Spelling Center

- Vocabulary practice and games
- Spelling lessons

Writing and Grammar Center

- Quick-Fix Editing Machine provides grammar help in a student-friendly format
- Writing Templates and graphic organizers promote clear, orderly communication

Media Center

- Media Analysis Guides encourage critical thinking skills
- Project Ideas, Storyboards, and Production Templates inspire creative media projects

Access the online version of your textbook at **classzone.com**

Your complete text is available for immediate use!

McDougal Littell

Where Great Lessons Begin

ALABAMA

McDougal Littell

LITERATURE

ACKNOWLEDGMENTS

STUDENT GUIDE

From *The War of the Worlds* by H. G. Wells. Reprinted by permission of A. P. Watt Ltd.

INTRODUCTORY UNIT

The Barbara Hogenson Agency: Excerpt from *A Young Lady of Property* by Horton Foote. Copyright © 1955, 1983 by Horton Foote. Reprinted by arrangement with Horton Foote and The Barbara Hogenson Agency.

KidsHealth: Excerpt from "Stress" by the Memours Foundation, from KidsHealth.com. Copyright © by KidsHealth.com. Reprinted with permission.

Atheneum Books for Young Readers: Excerpt from "Shells," from *Every Living Thing* by Cynthia Rylant. Copyright © 1985 by Cynthia Rylant. Reprinted by permission of Atheneum Books for Young Readers, an imprint of Simon & Schuster Children's Publishing Division.

Continued on page R147

ART CREDITS

COVER, TITLE PAGE

Untitled (1986), Jerry N. Uelsmann. © 2003 Jerry N. Uelsmann.

Continued on page R151

Copyright © 2009 by McDougal Littell, a division of Houghton Mifflin Company. All rights reserved.

Warning: No part of this work may be reproduced or transmitted in any form or by any means, electronic or mechanical, including photocopying and recording, or by any information storage or retrieval system without the prior written permission of McDougal Littell unless such copying is expressly permitted by federal copyright law. With the exception of not-for-profit transcription in Braille, McDougal Littell is not authorized to grant permission for further uses of copyrighted selections reprinted in this text without the permission of their owners. Permission must be obtained from the individual copyright owners as identified herein. Address inquiries to Supervisor, Rights and Permissions, McDougal Littell, P.O. Box 1667, Evanston, IL 60204.

ISBN 13: 978-0-618-90141-8 ISBN 10: 0-618-90141-8

Printed in the United States of America.

1 2 3 4 5 6 7 8 9—VJM—12 11 10 09 08 07

SENIOR PROGRAM CONSULTANTS

JANET ALLEN Reading and Literacy Specialist; creator of the popular "It's Never Too Late"/"Reading for Life" Institutes. Dr. Allen is an internationally known consultant who specializes in literacy work with at-risk students. Her publications include *Tools for Content Literacy; It's Never Too Late: Leading Adolescents to Lifelong Learning; Yellow Brick Roads: Shared and Guided Paths to Independent Reading; Words, Words, Words: Teaching Vocabulary in Grades 4–12;* and *Testing 1, 2, 3 . . . Bridging Best Practice and High-Stakes Assessments.* Dr. Allen was a high school reading and English teacher for more than 20 years and has taught courses in both subjects at the University of Central Florida. She directed the Central Florida Writing Project and received the Milken Foundation National Educator Award.

ARTHUR N. APPLEBEE Leading Professor, School of Education at the University at Albany, State University of New York; Director of the Center on English Learning and Achievement. During his varied career, Dr. Applebee has been both a researcher and a teacher, working in institutional settings with children with severe learning problems, in public schools, as a staff member of the National Council of Teachers of English, and in professional education. Among his many books are *Curriculum as Conversation: Transforming Traditions of Teaching and Learning; Literature in the Secondary School: Studies of Curriculum and Instruction in the United States;* and *Tradition and Reform in the Teaching of English: A History.* He was elected to the International Reading Hall of Fame and has received, among other honors, the David H. Russell Award for Distinguished Research in the Teaching of English.

JIM BURKE Lecturer and Author; Teacher of English at Burlingame High School, Burlingame, California. Mr. Burke is a popular presenter at educational conferences across the country and is the author of numerous books for teachers, including *School Smarts: The Four Cs of Academic Success; The English Teacher's Companion; Reading Reminders; Writing Reminders;* and *ACCESSing School: Teaching Struggling Readers to Achieve Academic and Personal Success.* He is the recipient of NCTE's Exemplary English Leadership Award and was inducted into the California Reading Association's Hall of Fame.

DOUGLAS CARNINE Professor of Education at the University of Oregon; Director of the Western Region Reading First Technical Assistance Center. Dr. Carnine is nationally known for his focus on research-based practices in education, especially curriculum designs that prepare instructors of K-12 students. He has received the Lifetime Achievement Award from the Council for Exceptional Children and the Ersted Award for outstanding teaching at the University of Oregon. Dr. Carnine frequently consults on educational policy with government groups, businesses, communities, and teacher unions.

YVETTE JACKSON Executive Director of the National Urban Alliance for Effective Education. Nationally recognized for her work in assessing the learning potential of underachieving urban students, Dr. Jackson is also a presenter for the Harvard Principal Center and is a member of the Differentiation Faculty of the Association for Supervision and Curriculum Development. Dr. Jackson's research focuses on literacy, gifted education, and cognitive mediation theory. She designed the Comprehensive Education Plan for the New York City Public Schools and has served as their Director of Gifted Programs and Executive Director of Instruction and Professional Development.

ROBERT T. JIMÉNEZ Professor of Language, Literacy, and Culture at Vanderbilt University. Dr. Jiménez's research focuses on the language and literacy practices of Latino students. A former bilingual education teacher, he is now conducting research on how written language is thought about and used in contemporary Mexico. Dr. Jiménez has received several research and teaching honors, including two Fulbright awards from the Council for the International Exchange of Scholars and the Albert J. Harris Award from the International Reading Association. His published work has appeared in the *American Educational Research Journal, Reading Research Quarterly, The Reading Teacher, Journal of Adolescent and Adult Literacy,* and *Lectura y Vida.*

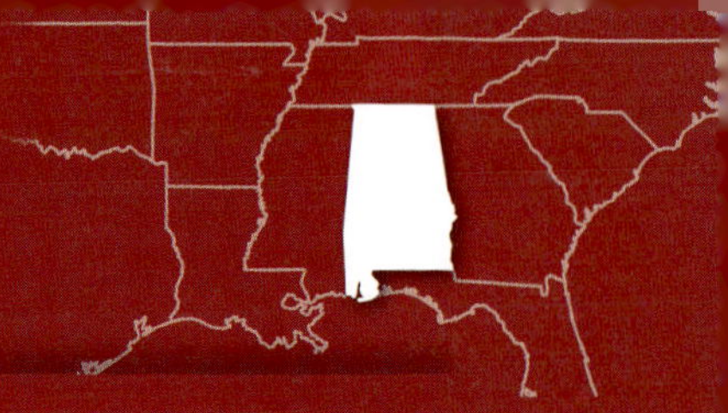

ALABAMA

McDougal Littell

LITERATURE

Janet Allen
Arthur N. Applebee
Jim Burke
Douglas Carnine
Yvette Jackson
Robert T. Jiménez
Judith A. Langer
Robert J. Marzano
Mary Lou McCloskey
Donna M. Ogle
Carol Booth Olson
Lydia Stack
Carol Ann Tomlinson

Alabama State House, Montgomery, Alabama © Dave Newman / iStockphoto

McDougal Littell
EVANSTON, ILLINOIS • BOSTON • DALLAS

JUDITH A. LANGER Distinguished Professor at the University at Albany, State University of New York; Director of the Center on English Learning and Achievement; Director of the Albany Institute for Research in Education. An internationally known scholar in English language arts education, Dr. Langer specializes in developing teaching approaches that can enrich and improve what gets done on a daily basis in classrooms. Her publications include *Getting to Excellent: How to Create Better Schools* and *Effective Literacy Instruction: Building Successful Reading and Writing Programs.* She was inducted into the International Reading Hall of Fame and has received many other notable awards, including an honorary doctorate from the University of Uppsala, Sweden, for her research on literacy education.

ROBERT J. MARZANO Senior Scholar at Mid-Continent Research for Education and Learning (McREL); Associate Professor at Cardinal Stritch University in Milwaukee, Wisconsin; President of Marzano & Associates. An internationally known researcher, trainer, and speaker, Dr. Marzano has developed programs that translate research and theory into practical tools for K-12 teachers and administrators. He has written extensively on such topics as reading and writing instruction, thinking skills, school effectiveness, assessment, and standards implementation. His books include *Building Background Knowledge for Academic Achievement; Classroom Management That Works: Research-Based Strategies for Every Teacher;* and *What Works in Schools: Translating Research Into Action.*

DONNA M. OGLE Professor of Reading and Language at National-Louis University in Chicago, Illinois; Past President of the International Reading Association. Creator of the well-known KWL strategy, Dr. Ogle has directed many staff development projects translating theory and research into school practice in middle and secondary schools throughout the United States and has served as a consultant on literacy projects worldwide. Her extensive international experience includes coordinating the Reading and Writing for Critical Thinking Project in Eastern Europe, developing integrated curriculum for a USAID Afghan Education Project, and speaking and consulting on projects in several Latin American countries and in Asia. Her books include *Coming Together as Readers; Reading Comprehension: Strategies for Independent Learners; All Children Read;* and *Literacy for a Democratic Society.*

CAROL BOOTH OLSON Senior Lecturer in the Department of Education at the University of California, Irvine; Director of the UCI site of the National Writing Project. Dr. Olson writes and lectures extensively on the reading/writing connection, critical thinking through writing, interactive strategies for teaching writing, and the use of multicultural literature with students of culturally diverse backgrounds. She has received many awards, including the California Association of Teachers of English Award of Merit, the Outstanding California Education Research Award, and the UC Irvine Excellence in Teaching Award. Dr. Olson's books include *Reading, Thinking, and Writing About Multicultural Literature* and *The Reading/Writing Connection: Strategies for Teaching and Learning in the Secondary Classroom.*

CAROL ANN TOMLINSON Professor of Educational Research, Foundations, and Policy at the University of Virginia; Co-Director of the University's Institutes on Academic Diversity. An internationally known expert on differentiated instruction, Dr. Tomlinson helps teachers and administrators develop effective methods of teaching academically diverse learners. She was a teacher of middle and high school English for 22 years prior to teaching at the University of Virginia. Her books on differentiated instruction have been translated into eight languages. Among her many publications are *How to Differentiate Instruction in Mixed-Ability Classrooms* and *The Differentiated Classroom: Responding to the Needs of All Learners.*

ENGLISH LEARNER SPECIALISTS

MARY LOU McCLOSKEY Past President of Teachers of English to Speakers of Other Languages (TESOL); Director of Teacher Development and Curriculum Design for Educo in Atlanta, Georgia. Dr. McCloskey is a former teacher in multilingual and multicultural classrooms. She has worked with teachers, teacher educators, and departments of education around the world on teaching English as a second and foreign language. She is author of *On Our Way to English, Voices in Literature, Integrating English,* and *Visions: Language, Literature, Content*. Her awards include the Le Moyne College Ignatian Award for Professional Achievement and the TESOL D. Scott Enright Service Award.

LYDIA STACK International ESL consultant. Her areas of expertise are English language teaching strategies, ESL standards for students and teachers, and curriculum writing. Her teaching experience includes 25 years as an elementary and high school ESL teacher. She is a past president of TESOL. Her awards include the James E. Alatis Award for Service to TESOL (2003) and the San Francisco STAR Teacher Award (1989). Her publications include *On Our Way to English; Wordways: Games for Language Learning;* and *Visions: Language, Literature, Content.*

CURRICULUM SPECIALIST

WILLIAM L. McBRIDE Curriculum Specialist. Dr. McBride is a nationally known speaker, educator, and author who now trains teachers in instructional methodologies. A former reading specialist, English teacher, and social studies teacher, he holds a Masters in Reading and a Ph.D. in Curriculum and Instruction from the University of North Carolina at Chapel Hill. Dr. McBride has contributed to the development of textbook series in language arts, social studies, science, and vocabulary. He is also known for his novel *Entertaining an Elephant,* which tells the story of a burned-out teacher who becomes re-inspired with both his profession and his life.

MEDIA SPECIALISTS

DAVID M. CONSIDINE Professor of Instructional Technology and Media Studies at Appalachian State University in North Carolina. Dr. Considine has served as a media literacy consultant to the U.S. government and to the media industry, including Discovery Communications and Cable in the Classroom. He has also conducted media literacy workshops and training for county and state health departments across the United States. Among his many publications are *Visual Messages: Integrating Imagery into Instruction,* and *Imagine That: Developing Critical Viewing and Thinking Through Children's Literature.*

LARKIN PAULUZZI Teacher and Media Specialist; trainer for the New Jersey Writing Project. Ms. Pauluzzi puts her extensive classroom experience to use in developing teacher-friendly curriculum materials and workshops in many different areas, including media literacy. She has led media literacy training workshops in several districts throughout Texas, guiding teachers in the meaningful and practical uses of media in the classroom. Ms. Pauluzzi has taught students at all levels, from Title I Reading to AP English IV. She also spearheads a technology club at her school, working with students to produce media and technology to serve both the school and the community.

LISA K. SCHEFFLER Teacher and Media Specialist. Ms. Scheffler has designed and taught media literacy and video production curriculum, in addition to teaching language arts and speech. Using her knowledge of mass communication theory, coupled with real classroom experience, she has developed ready-to-use materials that help teachers incorporate media literacy into their curricula. She has taught film and television studies at the University of North Texas and has served as a contributing writer for the Texas Education Agency's statewide viewing and representing curriculum.

ALABAMA MIDDLE SCHOOL LITERATURE REVIEWERS

Patricia Beale
Liberty Middle School
Madison City, AL

Diane Emerson
Monroria Middle School
Huntsville, AL

Kimberly L. Green
Hudson K-8 School
Birmingham, AL

Janie S. Mohajerin
Georgia Washington Junior High School
Montgomery, AL

Dr. Janet L. Reese
Montgomery Public Schools
Director of Public Development
Montgomery, AL

Julee F. Rodgers
Shades Valley High School
Irondale, AL

NATIONAL TEACHER ADVISORS

These are some of the many educators from across the country who played a crucial role in the development of the tables of contents, the lesson design, and other key components of this program:

Virginia L. Alford
MacArthur High School
San Antonio, Texas

Yvonne L. Allen
Shaker Heights High School
Shaker Heights, Ohio

Dave T. Anderson
Hinsdale South High School
Darien, Illinois

Kacy Colleen Anglim
Portland Public Schools District
Portland, Oregon

Beverly Scott Bass
Arlington Heights High School
Fort Worth, Texas

Jordana Benone
North High School
Torrance, California

Patricia Blood
Howell High School
Farmingdale, New Jersey

Marjorie Bloom
Eau Gallie High School
Melbourne, Florida

Edward J. Blotzer
Wilkinsburg Junior/Senior High School
Wilkinsburg, Pennsylvania

Stephen D. Bournes
Evanston Township High School
Evanston, Illinois

Barbara M. Bowling
Mt. Tabor High School
Winston-Salem, North Carolina

Kiala Boykin-Givehand
Duval County Public Schools
Jacksonville, Florida

Laura L. Brown
Adlai Stevenson High School
Lincolnshire, Illinois

Cynthia Burke
Yavneh Academy
Dallas, Texas

Hoppy Chandler
San Diego City Schools
San Diego, California

Gary Chmielewski
St. Benedict High School
Chicago, Illinois

Delorse Cole-Stewart
Milwaukee Public Schools
Milwaukee, Wisconsin

L. Calvin Dillon
Gaither High School
Tampa, Florida

Dori Dolata
Rufus King High School
Milwaukee, Wisconsin

Jon Epstein
Marietta High School
Marietta, Georgia

Helen Ervin
Fort Bend Independent School District
Sugarland, Texas

Sue Friedman
Buffalo Grove High School
Buffalo Grove, Illinois

Chris Gee
Bel Air High School
El Paso, Texas

Paula Grasel
The Horizon Center
Gainesville, Georgia

Christopher Guarraia
Centreville High School
Clifton, Virginia

Rochelle L. Greene-Brady
Kenwood Academy
Chicago, Illinois

Michele M. Hettinger
Niles West High School
Skokie, Illinois

Elizabeth Holcomb
Forest Hill High School
Jackson, Mississippi

Jim Horan
Hinsdale Central High School
Hinsdale, Illinois

James Paul Hunter
Oak Park-River Forest High School
Oak Park, Illinois

Susan P. Kelly
Director of Curriculum
Island Trees School District
Levittown, New York

Beverley A. Lanier
Varina High School
Richmond, Virginia

Pat Laws
Charlotte-Mecklenburg Schools
Charlotte, North Carolina

Diana R. Martinez
Treviño School of Communications & Fine Arts
Laredo, Texas

Natalie Martinez
Stephen F. Austin High School
Houston, Texas

Elizabeth Matarazzo
Ysleta High School
El Paso, Texas

Carol M. McDonald
J. Frank Dobie High School
Houston, Texas

Amy Millikan
Consultant
Chicago, Illinois

Terri Morgan
Caprock High School
Amarillo, Texas

Eileen Murphy
Walter Payton Preparatory High School
Chicago, Illinois

Lisa Omark
New Haven Public Schools
New Haven, Connecticut

Kaine Osburn
Wheeling High School
Wheeling, Illinois

Andrea J. Phillips
Terry Sanford High School
Fayetteville, North Carolina

Cathy Reilly
Sayreville Public Schools
Sayreville, New Jersey

Mark D. Simon
Neuqua Valley High School
Naperville, Illinois

Scott Snow
Sequin High School
Arlington, Texas

Jane W. Speidel
Brevard County Schools
Viera, Florida

Cheryl E. Sullivan
Lisle Community School District
Lisle, Illinois

Anita Usmiani
Hamilton Township Public Schools
Hamilton Square, New Jersey

Linda Valdez
Oxnard Union High School District
Oxnard, California

Nancy Walker
Longview High School
Longview, Texas

Kurt Weiler
New Trier High School
Winnetka, Illinois

Elizabeth Whittaker
Larkin High School
Elgin, Illinois

Linda S. Williams
Woodlawn High School
Baltimore, Maryland

John R. Williamson
Fort Thomas Independent Schools
Fort Thomas, Kentucky

Anna N. Winters
Simeon High School
Chicago, Illinois

Tonora D. Wyckoff
North Shore Senior High School
Houston, Texas

Karen Zajac
Glenbard South High School
Glen Ellyn, Illinois

Cynthia Zimmerman
Mose Vines Preparatory High School
Chicago, Illinois

Lynda Zimmerman
El Camino High School
South San Francisco, California

Ruth E. Zurich
Brown Deer High School
Brown Deer, Wisconsin

ALABAMA

OVERVIEW

Alabama Student's Edition

Alabama State House, Montgomery, Alabama © Dave Newman / iStockphoto

ALABAMA CONTENTS IN BRIEF

STUDENT GUIDE TO ADAW & ARMT SUCCESS

- Understanding the Alabama Course of Study
- Embedded Assessment Practice
- Preparing for the ADAW & ARMT
- ADAW & ARMT Strategies and Preparation

INTRODUCTORY UNIT

The Power of Ideas

LITERARY GENRES WORKSHOP

- Fiction
- Poetry
- Drama
- Nonfiction and Informational Texts
- Types of Media

READING STRATEGIES WORKSHOP

- Preview
- Set a Purpose
- Connect
- Use Prior Knowledge
- Predict
- Visualize
- Monitor
- Make Inferences

WRITING PROCESS WORKSHOP

- Writing Process Review
- Key Traits

PART 1: LITERARY ELEMENTS

WEAVING A STORY

UNIT 1 Plot, Conflict, and Setting

READER'S WORKSHOP: Plot, Conflict, Setting
WRITING WORKSHOP: Descriptive Essay

PERSONALITY TESTS

UNIT 2 Analyzing Character and Point of View

READER'S WORKSHOP: Point of View, Narrator, Methods of Characterization
WRITING WORKSHOP: Comparison-Contrast Essay

LESSONS TO LEARN

UNIT 3 Understanding Theme

READER'S WORKSHOP: Theme
WRITING WORKSHOP: Short Story

PART 2: LANGUAGE AND CULTURE

FINDING A VOICE

UNIT 4 Mood, Tone, and Style

READER'S WORKSHOP: Mood, Tone, Author's Style
WRITING WORKSHOP: Interpretive Essay

PICTURE THE MOMENT

UNIT 5 Appreciating Poetry

READER'S WORKSHOP: Form, Speaker, Sound Devices, Imagery, Figurative Language
WRITING WORKSHOP: Personal Response to a Poem

SHARING OUR STORIES

UNIT 6 Myths, Legends, and Tales

READER'S WORKSHOP: Traditional Literature
WRITING WORKSHOP: Cause-and-Effect Essay

PART 3: NONFICTION WITH PURPOSE

WRITING A LIFE

UNIT 7 Biography and Autobiography

READER'S WORKSHOP: Characteristics of Biographies and Autobiographies

WRITING WORKSHOP: Personal Narrative

FACE THE FACTS

UNIT 8 Information, Argument, and Persuasion

READER'S WORKSHOP: Text Features, Preview, Main Idea and Supporting Details, Take Notes, Outline

WRITING WORKSHOP: Persuasive Essay

INVESTIGATION AND DISCOVERY

UNIT 9 The Power of Research

RESEARCH STRATEGIES WORKSHOP: Reference Materials and Technology, Evaluate Sources

WRITING WORKSHOP: Research Report

STUDENT RESOURCE BANK

READING HANDBOOK

WRITING HANDBOOK

GRAMMAR HANDBOOK

VOCABULARY AND SPELLING HANDBOOK

SPEAKING AND LISTENING HANDBOOK

MEDIA HANDBOOK

TEST-TAKING HANDBOOK

GLOSSARIES

Online LITERATURE CLASSZONE.COM

LITERATURE AND READING CENTER
- Author Biographies
- Additional Selection Background
- Literary Analysis Frames
- Power Thinking Activities

WRITING AND GRAMMAR CENTER
- Writing Templates and Graphic Organizers
- Publishing Options
- Quick-Fix Editing Machine

VOCABULARY AND SPELLING CENTER
- Vocabulary Strategies and Practice
- Multi-Language Academic Vocabulary Glossary
- Vocabulary Flash Cards
- Spelling Lessons

MEDIA CENTER
- Production Templates
- Analysis Guides

RESEARCH CENTER
- Web Research Guide
- Citation Guide

ASSESSMENT CENTER
- ADAW/ARMT Practice and Test-Taking Tips
- SAT/ACT Practice and Tips

MORE TECHNOLOGY

eEdition
- Interactive Selections
- Audio Summaries

WriteSmart
- Writing Prompts and Templates
- Interactive Student Models
- Interactive Graphic Organizers
- Interactive Revision Lessons
- Rubric Generator

MediaSmart DVD
- Media Lessons
- Interactive Media Studies

UNIT 1

ALABAMA

Weaving a Story
PLOT, CONFLICT, AND SETTING

• IN FICTION • IN NONFICTION • IN POETRY • IN DRAMA • IN MEDIA

CONTENT STANDARDS

VOCABULARY STRATEGIES

UNIT 2

ALABAMA

Personality Tests
ANALYZING CHARACTER AND POINT OF VIEW

• IN FICTION • IN NONFICTION • IN POETRY

CONTENT STANDARDS

UNIT 3

ALABAMA

Lessons to Learn
UNDERSTANDING THEME

• IN FICTION • IN POETRY • IN DRAMA • IN MEDIA

CONTENT STANDARDS

FICTION

UNIT 4

ALABAMA

Finding a Voice

MOOD, TONE, AND STYLE

• IN FICTION • IN NONFICTION • IN POETRY • IN MEDIA

CONTENT STANDARDS

UNIT 5

ALABAMA

Picture the Moment
APPRECIATING POETRY

CONTENT STANDARDS

UNIT 6

ALABAMA

Sharing Our Stories
MYTHS, LEGENDS, AND TALES

CONTENT STANDARDS

UNIT 7

ALABAMA

Writing a Life
BIOGRAPHY AND AUTOBIOGRAPHY

• IN NONFICTION • IN MEDIA • IN DRAMA • IN POETRY

CONTENT STANDARDS

UNIT 8
ALABAMA

Face the Facts
INFORMATION, ARGUMENT, AND PERSUASION

• IN NONFICTION • IN MEDIA

CONTENT STANDARDS

UNIT 9

ALABAMA

Investigation and Discovery
THE POWER OF RESEARCH

CONTENT STANDARDS

Use Reference Materials and Technology, Evaluate Sources

Research, Synthesis

FICTION

SHORT STORIES

ORAL TRADITION

NOVELS

NONFICTION

AUTOBIOGRAPHY/MEMOIR

BIOGRAPHY

ESSAYS

INFORMATIONAL NONFICTION

NARRATIVE NONFICTION

POETRY

DRAMA

Features

READER'S WORKSHOPS

LITERATURE CENTER at ClassZone.com

WRITING WORKSHOPS

WriteSmart

VOCABULARY STRATEGIES

SPEAKING, LISTENING, AND VIEWING

MEDIA CENTER at ClassZone.com

MEDIA STUDY

MediaSmart DVD

GRAMMAR AND WRITING

STUDENT GUIDE TO ADAW & ARMT SUCCESS

Alabama State House, Montgomery, Alabama © Dave Newman / iStockphoto

Understanding the Alabama Course of Study

What is the Alabama Course of Study?

The Alabama Course of Study is a list of content standards that outlines what you should know and be able to do at each grade level. Your teacher uses the content standards to create a course of instruction that will help you develop the skills and knowledge you are expected to have by the end of grade 7. The Alabama Course of Study prepares you not only for success on tests such as the ARMT and ADAW, but also for everyday life and the workplace.

How will I learn the Alabama Course of Study?

Your textbook is closely aligned to the Alabama Course of Study for English Language Arts, so that every time you learn new information or practice a skill, you are mastering one of the content standards. Each unit, each reading selection, and each workshop in the textbook connects to one or more of the standards. The standards covered in each section of your textbook are listed on the opening page of the section.

For a complete listing of the Alabama Course of Study for English Language Arts, see page S1.

The Alabama Course of Study for English Language Arts for grade 7 is divided into five subject areas called strands:

- Reading
- Literature
- Writing and Language
- Research and Inquiry
- Oral and Visual Communication

Each of the strands is broken down into content standards. Some content standards are further broken down into bullets that point out specific skills that you need to learn in order to master the standard. Alabama uses a special code to identify the grade level, the content standard, and the bullet.

ALABAMA CONTENT STANDARD DECODER

7 . 6 . a

Indicates a grade 7 standard

Identifies the standard:
6. Analyze nonfiction, science fiction, mystery or suspense, fantasy, and adventure for distinguishing characteristics.

Identifies the bullet:
a. Classifying plot elements as exposition or hook, conflict, rising action, climax, falling action, or resolution

Embedded Assessment Practice

Each unit has a formatted practice test that covers specific standards-based skills.

ASSESSMENT PRACTICE LOCATOR

UNIT 1 page 166
Plot, Conflict, and Setting

- Plot Stages
- Setting
- Sequence
- Cause and Effect
- Latin Roots
- Prefixes
- Suffixes
- Possessives
- Pronoun-Antecedent Agreement
- Run-On Sentences

UNIT 2 page 294
Analyzing Character and Point of View

- Character Traits
- Characterization
- Point of View
- Make Inferences
- Idioms
- Similes
- Verb Tenses
- Comparative and Superlative Forms

UNIT 3 page 428
Understanding Theme

- Theme
- Symbol
- Make Inferences
- Cause and Effect
- Compare and Contrast
- Context Clues
- Connotation and Denotation
- Independent and Dependent Clauses
- Coordinating Conjunctions

UNIT 4 page 532
Mood, Tone, and Style

- Mood
- Style
  - Word Choice
  - Sentence Structure
  - Tone
- Summarize
- Synonyms
- Literal and Figurative Meanings
- Subject-Verb Agreement

UNIT 5 page 616
Appreciating Poetry

- Imagery
- Figurative Language
- Sound Devices
- Make Inferences
- Connotation
- Sentence Type
- Active Voice

UNIT 6 page 744
Myths, Legends, and Tales

- Characteristics of Myths and Tales
- Cultural Value
- Chronological Order
- Cause and Effect
- Compound Words
- Homographs
- Compound Sentences
- Complex Sentences

UNIT 7 page 858
Biography and Autobiography

- Biography
- Chronological Order
- Make Inferences
- Summarize
- Latin Words and Roots
- Base Words
- Proper Nouns
- Italics and Quotation Marks

UNIT 8 page 956
Information, Argument, and Persuasion

- Elements of an Argument
- Fact and Opinion
- Text Features
- Main Idea and Supporting Details
- Idioms
- Prefixes and Latin Roots and Words
- Commas
- Colons

UNIT 9 page 963
The Power of Research

Research Strategies page 966
Writing Research Reports page 984

Preparing for the ADAW & ARMT

What is the ADAW?

ADAW stands for the Alabama Direct Assessment of Writing. All grade 7 students must take the ADAW in early spring. The ADAW is a test that assesses your ability to compose essays. It consists of a single writing prompt for either a descriptive, narrative, expository, or persuasive essay. You will have sixty minutes to respond to the prompt.

What is the ARMT?

ARMT stands for the Alabama Reading and Mathematics Test. The ARMT is given to all grade 7 students in spring. The ARMT is a test that measures your understanding of the Alabama Course of Study for every grade you have completed. For example, the ARMT you take in the spring of grade 7 measures your mastery of the Alabama Course of Study through grade 7. The reading portion of the ARMT includes multiple-choice and open-ended items.

How can I be successful on the ADAW and ARMT?

Use the passages, questions, and sample writing prompts on the following pages to prepare for the ADAW and the reading portion of the ARMT. This section will familiarize you with the kinds of questions and writing prompts you can expect on the actual tests. The tips and strategies highlighted in blue will guide you as you read the passages and answer the questions.

- Read the passages and prompts carefully, as well as the tips in the blue boxes. The tips help you to focus on important ideas and details in the reading so you will be better prepared to respond to the prompts and answer the reading questions.

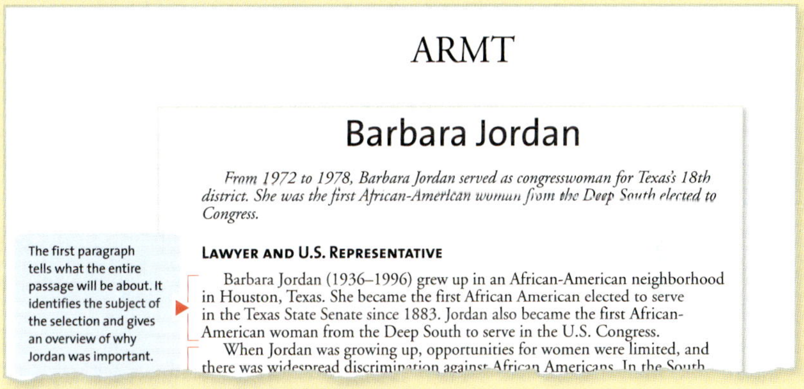

ARMT

Barbara Jordan

From 1972 to 1978, Barbara Jordan served as congresswoman for Texas's 18th district. She was the first African-American woman from the Deep South elected to Congress.

LAWYER AND U.S. REPRESENTATIVE

Barbara Jordan (1936–1996) grew up in an African-American neighborhood in Houston, Texas. She became the first African American elected to serve in the Texas State Senate since 1883. Jordan also became the first African-American woman from the Deep South to serve in the U.S. Congress.

When Jordan was growing up, opportunities for women were limited, and

The first paragraph tells what the entire passage will be about. It identifies the subject of the selection and gives an overview of why Jordan was important.

- Each question tests a particular content standard. Strategies highlighted in blue suggest ways to approach the different types of questions.

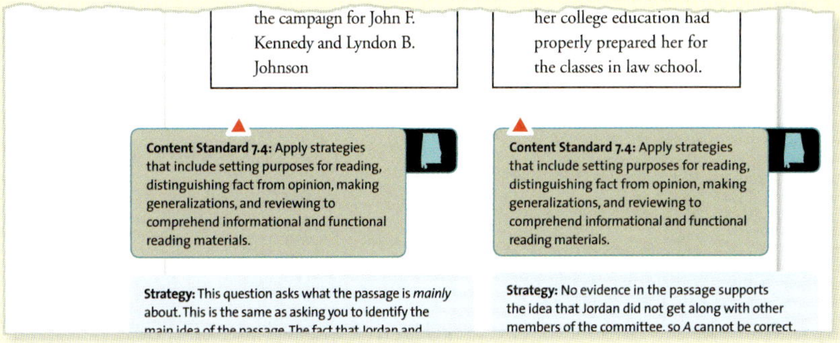

the campaign for John F. Kennedy and Lyndon B. Johnson

her college education had properly prepared her for the classes in law school.

Content Standard 7.4: Apply strategies that include setting purposes for reading, distinguishing fact from opinion, making generalizations, and reviewing to comprehend informational and functional reading materials.

Content Standard 7.4: Apply strategies that include setting purposes for reading, distinguishing fact from opinion, making generalizations, and reviewing to comprehend informational and functional reading materials.

Strategy: This question asks what the passage is *mainly* about. This is the same as asking you to identify the

Strategy: No evidence in the passage supports the idea that Jordan did not get along with other members of the committee, so *A* cannot be correct.

ADAW & ARMT Strategies and Preparation

The following section introduces you to how the ADAW and the reading portion of the ARMT will look and what kinds of questions you may encounter. Look for tips and strategies in blue boxes throughout this section.

ADAW

On the grade 7 ADAW, you will have sixty minutes to respond to a single prompt. The following pages include examples of each type of prompt you may encounter on the ADAW, followed by an explanation of how your response will be scored.

Persuasive Prompt

Your social studies class is working on a project to convince the families and businesses in your community to begin recycling their newspapers, cans, and bottles. Your job is to write a persuasive essay for your townspeople in which you present your argument.

Strategy: You are being asked to write an essay that persuades someone to agree with your position or opinion. To help focus on your topic, repeat part of the prompt when you begin to write. Here, your first sentence could indicate that you are writing to your townspeople about the importance of recycling. Decide on three ideas that strongly support your argument. Write one paragraph for each example. Then write a final paragraph that gives a summary of your main argument. Be sure to vary the types of sentences you use in your essay and make effective word choices that present your points clearly.

Expository Prompt

You read a story about someone who has achieved great success. Think about what factors help people become successful. Do you think success is mostly due to good luck, personal courage, or natural talent? Write a paper to share with your class. In it, explain what factor or factors you think lead to success.

Strategy: Think about someone you know whom you consider successful. Make a list of factors that helped that person succeed. For instance, under the heading "Good Luck," you might list being in the right place at the right time. Under "Personal Courage," you might write a list of obstacles that person overcame. Under "Natural Talent," you can list other strengths that helped the person achieve success. Then ask yourself if one of these factors is more important than the others in becoming successful. Can you think of any additional factors that contribute to success? Your answers to these questions will help you find your main idea. When you write your essay, support your ideas with the examples you listed.

Narrative Prompt

Imagine a time when you ran into someone you did not expect to see. It could be a friend, a relative, or someone famous. Write a narrative essay describing what happened when you met with this person.

Strategy: This prompt asks you to write a narrative essay. When you write a narrative essay, you are trying to tell your readers about a series of events or a situation in which something happened. For this essay, you will describe an unexpected meeting. Where were you? Who did you meet? Why was it unexpected? How did it end? Describe the sights, sounds, and smells that you remember from the meeting. Use sensory details to describe the scene as clearly as possible. Be careful not to spend so much time describing the setting that you rush through the action.

Descriptive Prompt

Everyone has a favorite object that they treasure. Think of an object in your room that you really like. It could be a toy, a game, a stuffed animal, a book, or something else. What does it look, feel, smell, and sound like? Now, describe this object to your reader so that he or she will be able to picture it clearly.

Strategy: This is a descriptive writing prompt. Unlike other writing prompts, descriptive prompts ask you to focus only on describing sensory details. You are not trying to persuade anyone to agree with you, nor are you imagining a story. Because of this, it is important to include as many details about the object as possible. Include descriptions for as many of the senses as possible. Though you want to describe the object as accurately as possible, you may also want to use creative language to describe why the object is special to you.

ALABAMA DIRECT ASSESSMENT OF WRITING RUBRICS

The rubrics on this page and the next provide a way to evaluate your writing. The rubrics outline how well your writing demonstrates your ability to develop ideas; organize information logically; make appropriate word choices; and show mastery of grammar, usage, and mechanics. Your writing will be compared to the rubrics and scored appropriately. Read the rubrics to see what a teacher reading your essay might look for. See pages S3–S6 in the back of your textbook for complete descriptions of each performance level.

Alabama Analytic Rubric

	Writing Mechanics	Sentence Formation	Grammar and Usage
Level IV	• Few if any errors in mechanics • Success with use of advanced techniques	• Few if any errors in sentence formation • Success in use of varied and advanced sentence structure or formation	• Few if any errors in grammar and usage • Expressive, powerful, creative word choice
Level III	• Few errors in mechanics • Some use of advanced techniques	• Few errors in sentence formation • Some use of varied and/or advanced sentence structure or formation	• Few errors in grammar and usage • Meaningful, precise word choice
Level II	• Some or no errors in mechanics • No use of advanced techniques	• Some or no errors in sentence formation • No variety in sentence structure or formation	• Some or no errors in grammar and usage • Appropriate, basic-functional word choice
Level I	• Frequent, serious errors in mechanics • No use of advanced techniques	• Frequent, serious errors in sentence formation • No variety in sentence structure or formation	• Frequent and/or serious errors in grammar and usage • Inappropriate, repetitive, vague word choices

KEY

Level IV: Exceeds Standard

Level III: Meets Standard

Level II: Partially Meets Standard

Level I: Does Not Meet Standard

FOCUSED HOLISTIC SCORES	
LEVEL 1 Not Rated	Level 1 (Not Rated) Responses are • NR1 = Blank • NR2 = Insufficient • NR3 = Off Topic / Off Mode • NR4 = Refusal / Illegible / Incomprehensible / Foreign Language • NR5 = Invalidated
LEVEL I 2 points	A response at Level I indicates little understanding of the writing task. There is little or no sense of audience and purpose. The writer exhibits little or no organizational plan and gives little or no attention to topic development.
LEVEL II 3 points **LEVEL II 4 points**	A response at Level II indicates some understanding of the writing task. The writer may drift off mode and/or off topic. The writer displays some sense of audience and purpose but more author involvement than author control. Some success is evident with an organizational plan, but ideas are loosely organized. The writer introduces the topic but may wander from it or may develop it minimally with basic/functional vocabulary.
LEVEL III 5 points **LEVEL III 6 points**	A response at Level III indicates a good understanding of the writing task. A sense of audience and purpose is evident. The writer displays a sense of author control, using one controlling idea with only minimal wandering from it. The organization of this sufficiently developed response and the use of meaningful, precise vocabulary set this Level III response apart from the Level II responses.
LEVEL IV 7 points **LEVEL IV 8 points**	A response at Level IV indicates a thorough understanding of the writing task. The writer successfully addresses and controls the writing task with a strong sense of audience and purpose. This thoroughly developed response is precise, consistent, and elaborated. The response displays clear and coherent ideas that flow smoothly. The use of vivid and precise vocabulary sets this Level IV response apart from the Level III responses.

NOTE: A score of "1" on the Focused Holistic Scale is not possible because of the scoring guidelines.

Barbara Jordan

From 1972 to 1978, Barbara Jordan served as congresswoman for Texas's 18th district. She was the first African-American woman from the Deep South elected to Congress.

The first paragraph tells what the entire passage will be about. It identifies the subject of the selection and gives an overview of why Jordan was important.

Lawyer and U.S. Representative

Barbara Jordan (1936–1996) grew up in an African-American neighborhood in Houston, Texas. She became the first African American elected to serve in the Texas State Senate since 1883. Jordan also became the first African-American woman from the Deep South to serve in the U.S. Congress.

The writer includes facts about Jordan's early life to help the reader understand why she made the decisions she did later in life.

When Jordan was growing up, opportunities for women were limited, and there was widespread discrimination against African Americans. In the South, segregation by race was still sanctioned by law. From grade school through college, Jordan received her education at all African-American schools. The ambitious young Texan doubted that the system would change any time soon. Even so, at Phillis Wheatley High School, Jordan decided she wanted to become a lawyer—though at the time she "had no fixed notion of what that was."

Entering the White World

In 1954, Jordan was in her junior year at Texas Southern University. That year, the Supreme Court decided, in the case *Brown v. Board of Education of Topeka*, that separate was not equal when it came to education. But change came slowly.

A concrete example of conditions at the time helps the reader understand how bad the situation was and why Jordan and others wanted to do something about it.

When traveling in the South, Jordan's college debate team had to pack their own food and stay at black motels. Her coach recalled that in the North "we didn't eat at any fancy restaurants…But we could at least go in front doors to get something to eat."

Jordan left Texas to attend Boston University Law School. Jordan and Issie Shelton, a fellow Texan, were the only two black women among six first-year women students. Breaking into the white, male world of law school was not easy. Jordan realized that "the best training available in an all-black…university was not equal." Jordan and Shelton rose to the challenge. Within three years, they had won their law degrees.

A Career in Politics

The facts tell about Jordan's life and her accomplishments, but the quotes help the reader learn something about her personality. She was not just intelligent but also had a sense of humor.

After graduating, Jordan returned to Texas. In 1960, she volunteered to work for the election campaign of Democrats John F. Kennedy and Lyndon B. Johnson. At first, she addressed envelopes and licked stamps. But one night, Jordan had to fill in for a speaker who was ill. Jordan was a gifted speaker. "Right after that," she recalled, "they took me off licking and addressing."

After her work on the Kennedy campaign, Jordan entered politics. In 1966, she was elected state senator. Reporters were curious to see how an African-American woman would manage in this white-male stronghold. "As it turned out," Jordan said, "the Capitol stayed on its foundations and the star didn't fall off the top."

Jordan won a seat in the U.S. House of Representatives in 1972. Just as she had once campaigned for him, former President Lyndon B. Johnson now returned the favor. LBJ said, "Wherever [Barbara Jordan] goes she is going to be at the top."

Jordan served on the House Judiciary Committee that held hearings on the impeachment of President Richard M. Nixon. In the course of the 1974 hearings, she delivered a speech on the Constitution that drew the world's admiration.

Context clues in the sentences after the one containing *multiple sclerosis* help readers understand this illness if they are not familiar with it.

After serving three terms in the U.S. House of Representatives, Jordan returned to Texas. She later suffered from multiple sclerosis. Even so, she refused to let the crippling disease keep her from public service. Instead, she spoke from a wheelchair.

As head of the U.S. Commission on Immigration Reform in 1995, Jordan asked Congress not to deny citizenship to children born in the United States to illegal immigrants. "It was immigration that taught us that, in this country, it does not matter where you came from, or who your parents were. What counts is who you are." Barbara Jordan died in January 1996.

Dates help the reader understand the sequence of events.

1. What is this passage *mainly* about?

A How Barbara Jordan became an important government official despite obstacles in her path

B The way Barbara Jordan and Issie Shelton were pioneering students at Boston University Law School

C Barbara Jordan's informed and opinionated view of the leaders who wrote the Constitution

D How Barbara Jordan's interest in politics was sparked by her volunteer work on the campaign for John F. Kennedy and Lyndon B. Johnson

2. Which of the following is suggested by evidence in the passage?

A Jordan did not get along well with the other members of the House Judiciary Committee.

B When she was young, Jordan believed that segregation by race would be quickly eliminated.

C Jordan felt that the Constitution should be completely ignored because it called for the unfair treatment of certain people.

D Jordan did not believe that her college education had properly prepared her for the classes in law school.

Content Standard 7.4: Apply strategies that include setting purposes for reading, distinguishing fact from opinion, making generalizations, and reviewing to comprehend informational and functional reading materials.

Strategy: This question asks what the passage is *mainly* about. This is the same as asking you to identify the main idea of the passage. The fact that Jordan and Shelton were students in law school is not the main idea, so *B* is incorrect. *D* is not correct because the information about Jordan's work with Kennedy and Johnson supports the main idea, but it is not the main idea. Based on the information in the last section, you could draw the conclusion that *C* is correct, but the whole passage is not about this idea. The passage describes events in Jordan's life and her eventual success in Congress. Therefore, *A* is the correct answer.

Content Standard 7.4: Apply strategies that include setting purposes for reading, distinguishing fact from opinion, making generalizations, and reviewing to comprehend informational and functional reading materials.

Strategy: No evidence in the passage supports the idea that Jordan did not get along with other members of the committee; eliminate *A*. The passage states that the young Jordan believed the opposite of *B*; it says she "doubted that the system would change any time soon." There is no evidence for *C*, either. Though Jordan was concerned about part of the Constitution, she worked within the system to try to solve problems. *D* is supported by information in the passage. The passage includes a quote about Jordan's belief that college had not prepared her for law school. Therefore, *D* is correct.

3. This passage would *most likely* be found in—

A a book of fables
B a book about important people
C a science fiction magazine
D a book written by Barbara Jordan

Content Standard 7.3: Distinguish among the major genres, including poetry, short stories, novels, plays, biographies, and autobiographies, and subgenres, such as folktales, myths, parables, fables, and science fiction, based on their characteristics.

Strategy: For this question, you must decide what genre this passage belongs to. The passage is about a real person, Barbara Jordan, and it gives you facts about her life; therefore, it is nonfiction and biographical. You can eliminate *A* and *C* because fables and science fiction are types of fiction. *B* is the correct answer because Barbara Jordan is famous, and a book about important people would have biographical information about those people. *D* is incorrect because the passage is not an autobiography—it is not written by Barbara Jordan about herself.

4. From the information in the passage, we know that Jordan's speech in Nixon's impeachment hearings was received with—

A equality
B disapproval
C admiration
D debate

Content Standard 7.4: Apply strategies that include setting purposes for reading, distinguishing fact from opinion, making generalizations, and reviewing to comprehend informational and functional reading materials.

Strategy: Find the paragraph in the passage that mentions the hearings on the impeachment of President Richard Nixon. It says that her speech "drew the world's admiration," so *C* is correct. *A* does not make sense. *B* is not correct; Jordan's speech was not met with disapproval. *D* is not correct; the passage does not tell us if Jordan's speech was met with debate.

5. According to the passage, Barbara Jordan was ambitious in setting goals for her education.

Identify at least *two* details from the passage that support this statement.

Content Standard 7.2: Relate literary elements and devices to each other, including main idea and supporting details, climax, point of view, and imagery.

Strategy: For this question, you must be able to recognize what details from the passage act as supporting details for the statement that Barbara Jordan was ambitious about her education. Pay close attention to details in the paragraphs that describe how and where she earned her education. It is important to choose details for your answer that strongly support the statement. For each detail you choose, ask yourself, "How does this support the fact that Barbara Jordan was ambitious in setting goals for her education?"

Score Point	The response should
3	The response demonstrates the student's understanding of the idea that Barbara Jordan was ambitious and overcame great obstacles to become an important government official. The response must use two details from the passage for support. Examples could include, but are not limited to, the following: • In high school, she decided that she wanted to become a lawyer. • She left her home in Texas to enroll in a Northern law school. • She dared to enroll in a mostly male, mostly white law school. • She saw that her university had not prepared her, yet still she "rose to the challenge" and succeeded in law school.
2	The response demonstrates a general understanding of Barbara Jordan's ambitions and obstacles and includes two details for support. However, the answer lacks the depth and completeness of a score point 3 response.
1	The response shows a limited understanding of Barbara Jordan's ambitions and obstacles OR The response does not identify any details to support the response.
0	The response demonstrates no attempt to address the prompt.

Excerpted from *The War of the Worlds*

by H.G. Wells

This is just an excerpt, or part of a book. The first paragraph of the excerpt introduces what the story will be about. The words *Martians* and *trouble* make the reader wonder what kind of trouble the Martians may have caused. The title provides a further hint. The beginning of the story is a good time to make some predictions about what may happen.

The Martians seem to have calculated their descent with amazing subtlety—their mathematical learning is evidently far in excess of ours—and to have carried out their preparations with a well-nigh perfect unanimity. Had our instruments permitted it, we might have seen the gathering trouble far back in the nineteenth century. Men like Schiaparelli watched the red planet—it is odd, by-the-bye, that for countless centuries Mars has been the star of war—but failed to interpret the fluctuating appearances of the markings they mapped so well. All that time the Martians must have been getting ready.

During the opposition of 1894 a great light was seen on the illuminated part of the disk, first at the Lick Observatory, then by Perrotin of Nice, and then by other observers. English readers heard of it first in the issue of NATURE dated August 2. I am inclined to think that this blaze may have been the casting of the huge gun, in the vast pit sunk into their planet, from which their shots were fired at us. Peculiar markings, as yet unexplained, were seen near the site of that outbreak during the next two oppositions.

The storm burst upon us six years ago now. As Mars approached opposition, Lavelle of Java set the wires of the astronomical exchange palpitating with the amazing intelligence of a huge outbreak of incandescent gas upon the planet. It had occurred towards midnight of the twelfth; and the spectroscope, to which he had at once resorted, indicated a mass of flaming gas, chiefly hydrogen, moving with an enormous velocity towards this earth. This jet of fire had become invisible about a quarter past twelve. He compared it to a colossal puff of flame suddenly and violently squirted out of the planet, "as flaming gases rushed out of a gun."

A singularly appropriate phrase it proved. Yet the next day there was nothing of this in the papers except a little note in the DAILY TELEGRAPH, and the world went in ignorance of one of the gravest dangers that ever threatened the human race. I might not have heard of the eruption at all had I not met Ogilvy, the well-known astronomer, at Ottershaw. He was immensely excited at the news, and in the excess of his feelings invited me up to take a turn with him that night in a scrutiny of the red planet.

This part of the story introduces a new character, a scientist who studies the stars and planets.

This paragraph gives the time setting of the 1800s. The phrase "their shots were fired at us" also helps confirm the original prediction about trouble and gives the reader more information about the kind of trouble that might be.

This paragraph paints a picture of where Ogilvy studied the stars and planets. It describes the sights and sounds the narrator experienced when he visited the scientist. It also describes what he saw when he looked through the telescope at Mars. Creating a mental picture from the words will help you understand this part of the story.

In spite of all that has happened since, I still remember that vigil very distinctly: the black and silent observatory, the shadowed lantern throwing a feeble glow upon the floor in the corner, the steady ticking of the clockwork of the telescope, the little slit in the roof—an oblong profundity with the stardust streaked across it. Ogilvy moved about, invisible but audible. Looking through the telescope, one saw a circle of deep blue and the little round planet swimming in the field. It seemed such a little thing, so bright and small and still, faintly marked with transverse stripes, and slightly flattened from the perfect round. But so little it was, so silvery warm—a pin's-head of light! It was as if it quivered, but really this was the telescope vibrating with the activity of the clockwork that kept the planet in view.

As I watched, the planet seemed to grow larger and smaller and to advance and recede, but that was simply that my eye was tired. Forty millions of miles it was from us—more than forty millions of miles of void. Few people realise the immensity of vacancy in which the dust of the material universe swims.

This last paragraph of the excerpt hints at, or foreshadows, things that will happen in the rest of the story. What kind of mood do these words create? What predictions come to your mind about what the "Thing" might be and how it might bring struggle, calamity, and death? As you read, keep in mind the title of the story.

Near it in the field, I remember, were three faint points of light, three telescopic stars infinitely remote, and all around it was the unfathomable darkness of empty space. You know how that blackness looks on a frosty starlight night. In a telescope it seems far profounder. And invisible to me because it was so remote and small, flying swiftly and steadily towards me across that incredible distance, drawing nearer every minute by so many thousands of miles, came the Thing they were sending us, the Thing that was to bring so much struggle and calamity and death to the earth. I never dreamed of it then as I watched; no one on earth dreamed of that unerring missile.

6. In this excerpt, the author implies that—

A only a few people are intelligent enough to worry about the future

B people are sometimes unaware of major life-changing events that may occur in the future

C people should live every day to its fullest

D things are seldom what they appear to be

Content Standard 7.7: Interpret the author's message in various literary, informational, and functional texts.

Strategy: The answer to this question will not be directly stated in the text. Instead, you must use context clues to determine the author's message. There is nothing in the excerpt to support *A*. *C* is certainly an idea that many people would agree with, but it is not the strongest response to this question. The narrator describes how Mars looks from a distance, "a little thing," which is not really true, so there is some evidence for *D*. The strongest answer choice, however, is *B*. The beginning of the story hints at something happening in the world that people did not predict. The last sentence of the excerpt also foreshadows an event that people were not aware of.

7. The description of the puff of flame from Mars "as flaming gases rushed out of a gun" is an example of—

A personification

B metaphor

C onomatopoeia

D simile

Content Standard 7.2: Relate literary elements and devices to each other, including main idea and supporting details, climax, point of view, and imagery.

Strategy: Personification is attributing human qualities to a non-human thing. The author is not doing that here, so *A* is incorrect. Onomatopoeia means using words that imitate sounds, such as *buzz*. However, this is not what the author does in this sentence, so you can eliminate *C*. Metaphor is a comparison of two things by saying that one is another, such as "the jet of fire was a colossal puff of flame." This is not exactly what the author does in this particular sentence. A simile is a comparison of two things using the words *like* or *as*. Therefore, *D* is correct.

8. In the excerpt, Ogilvy invites the narrator to "take a turn with him that night in a *scrutiny* of the red planet." The word *scrutiny* means—

A fight
B inspection
C protest
D tour

Content Standard 7.1.c: Using specific context clues to determine meaning of unfamiliar words.

Strategy: Review the part of the excerpt where this phrase appears. Ogilvy is an astronomer—a scientist who studies planets and stars. Ogilvy and the narrator look at the planet through a telescope. The sixth paragraph begins with "As I watched," which confirms the idea that a scrutiny is "a watch" or "an observation." Ask yourself which of the answer choices means almost the same thing. *A* does not make sense because the narrator and Ogilvy do not fight. They do not protest the planet, nor do they tour it, as they remain on Earth. Ogilvy and the narrator inspect the planet through a telescope, so *B* is correct.

9. Looking at the universe, the narrator feels—

A terrified
B angry
C bored
D thrilled

Content Standard 7.1.e: Drawing conclusions to interpret unstated intent in text.

Strategy: Use clues from the story to draw conclusions about how the narrator feels. Review the story. The narrator says he will always remember the night he spent watching Mars. He describes the universe as "profound" and Mars as "silvery warm." He is struck by the "immensity of vacancy" of the universe. He does not sound terrified or angry, so *A* and *B* can be eliminated. He seems excited, not bored, so *C* is incorrect. He sounds thrilled by the experience, so *D* is the correct answer.

10. Who does the narrator admire more, the Martians or the astronomers, such as Schiaparelli, Lavelle of Java, and Ogilvy?

Use details from the excerpt to support your response.

Content Standard 7.5: Recognize the use of textual elements, including main idea and supporting details, and gain information from various text formats, including graphs.

Strategy: Decide whom the narrator seems to admire. What is his tone when he describes the Martians? What is his tone when he mentions the various astronomers? What kinds of words does he use to describe each? Be sure to support your response with evidence from the excerpt.

Score Point	The response should
3	The response demonstrates the student's understanding of the narrator's admiration for the Martians or the astronomers. In the response, the student takes a position and includes details from the story to support his or her position. Examples could include, but are not limited to, the following: **The Martians:** • They "calculated their descent with amazing subtlety." • The narrator describes the Martians' mathematical learning as "evidently far in excess of ours." • Men like Schiaparelli watched Mars but "failed to interpret" what they saw. • No humans dreamed that a missile was going to crash into Earth. **The astronomers:** • Men like Schiaparelli watched Mars. • Various observers noticed a "great light" on Mars in 1894. • Lavelle of Java announced an outbreak of gases upon Mars, using a spectroscope. • Ogilvy was very excited at the news and watched Mars from his observatory.
2	The response demonstrates a general understanding of the narrator's admiration for the Martians or the astronomers and includes some detail from the story to support the position taken. However, the answer lacks the depth and completeness of a score point 3 response.
1	The response shows a limited understanding of the narrator's admiration for the Martians or the astronomers OR The response does not include support for the position taken.
0	The response demonstrates no attempt to address the prompt.

Fire in the Sky

The topic of this paragraph is people's ideas about lightning. As you read, the author wants you to picture each example.

Transition words tell you that the topic is changing. Instead of telling you about old beliefs, this paragraph will describe facts that we now know to be true about lightning.

Flash! Crack! Rumble! As you read these words, lightning struck the earth more than a hundred times. There are thousands of lightning strikes every day—every one different and every one possibly very dangerous.

People have always been awed and frightened by the power of lightning and have tried to explain it in many different ways. Some Native Americans believed that lightning was reflected from the feathers of a mystical bird, the thunderbird, whose flapping wings created thunder. The Vikings of Scandinavia thought that lightning was produced by their god Thor. As he rode his rumbling chariot across the sky, he hit a hammer against an anvil to create lightning. The Greeks attributed lightning to the gods, too. They believed that Zeus, the king of the gods, threw lightning bolts when he got angry.

We now know, though, that lightning is an electrical discharge that is one of the strongest forces in nature. Lightning begins when opposite electrical charges build up in different parts of clouds and on the ground. Sparks shoot down from the clouds and meet similar sparks shooting upward from the ground. When the sparks meet, they form a lightning bolt. The flash that you see is actually rising from the ground, not descending from the sky.

As lightning strikes, the atmosphere in the lightning channel is heated to 30,000 degrees Celsius, five times hotter than the surface of the sun. The heat causes the air to expand, producing the sound waves we call thunder. Because light travels almost a million times faster than sound, it seems to us that lightning happens first. In fact, though, lightning and thunder occur at the same time.

As you read, consider how the writer has organized the safety rules into two lists.

There are four main types of lightning: intracloud (within a single cloud), intercloud (between clouds), cloud-to-air, and cloud-to-ground. All lightning is made up of zigzag strokes, but it can look like sheets, ribbons, beads, or even balls, depending on conditions in the atmosphere.

In spite of all we now know about lightning, we should, like ancient people, treat it with awe and respect. Follow these safety rules during a thunderstorm.

If you are outside:

- Move at least 15 feet away from other people.
- Stay away from water.
- Stay away from hilltops and open fields.
- Try to find shelter in a large building or in an enclosed car, truck, or van with the windows rolled up.
- Avoid metal objects.

If you are inside:

- Stay away from electrical sockets and appliances, televisions, and telephones.
- Do not touch water.
- Avoid doors and windows.
- Unplug electrical appliances.

Once you have taken these precautions, sit back and enjoy nature's light show!

11. Based on the information in "Fire in the Sky," the reader can conclude that—

A metal cannot conduct electrical energy

B electrical charges are not present in every type of lightning

C lightning only appears to happen before thunder

D the ancient Greeks and Native Americans worshipped the same gods

Content Standard 7.4: Apply strategies that include setting purposes for reading, distinguishing fact from opinion, making generalizations, and reviewing to comprehend informational and functional reading materials.

Strategy: The passage lists metal things that you should stay away from, so *A* is not correct. The passage states that lightning is an electrical discharge, so *B* is also incorrect. You can eliminate *D* because the details in the passage do not support this conclusion. Information in the fourth paragraph shows that *C* is correct.

12. What do the four main types of lightning have in common?

A They all resemble beads.

B They are all incredibly rare.

C They all have the same stroke pattern.

D They are all cooler than the surface of the sun.

Content Standard 7.4: Apply strategies that include setting purposes for reading, distinguishing fact from opinion, making generalizations, and reviewing to comprehend informational and functional reading materials.

Strategy: Review important details in the passage. It says that lightning can take many shapes other than beads, so *A* is incorrect. *B* is also incorrect because lightning is not rare. The passage states that lightning is much hotter than the surface of the sun, so *D* is incorrect. *C* is the correct answer because it is supported by information in the passage.

13. Which is the *best* way to summarize the second paragraph of the passage?

A Different cultures have different types of lightning.
B Different cultures have different ways to explain lightning.
C Lightning is an electrical discharge whose flash rises from the ground.
D The heat of lightning causes thunder.

Content Standard 7.7: Interpret the author's message in various literary, informational, and functional texts.

Strategy: Review the second paragraph of the passage. It describes how different cultures explained lightning. Therefore, *B* is correct. The second paragraph does not say that different cultures have different types of lightning, so you can eliminate *A*. The third paragraph says that lightning is an electrical discharge, and the fourth paragraph says that the heat of lightning causes thunder, so both *C* and *D* are incorrect.

14. The passage "Fire in the Sky" uses bulleted lists to—

A describe four main types of thunder and its causes
B provide guidelines for safety during a thunderstorm
C tell where lightning usually strikes
D describe what causes lightning

Content Standard 7.5: Recognize the use of textual elements, including main idea and supporting details, to gain information from various text formats, including graphs.

Strategy: The passage describes lightning, not thunder, so *A* is incorrect. The passage does not give information about where lightning usually strikes, so you can also eliminate *C*. Notice the structure of the passage. While one paragraph describes what causes lightning, the information does not appear in a bulleted list. Therefore, *D* is not correct. The bulleted lists at the end of the passage give safety information, so *B* is the correct answer.

15. Why does the author describe lightning as "one of the strongest forces in nature"?

Use at least two details from the passage to support your response.

Content Standard 7.4: Apply strategies that include setting purposes for reading, distinguishing fact from opinion, making generalizations, and reviewing to comprehend informational and functional reading materials.

Strategy: First, find this statement in the context of the passage. Read or skim the text before and after the statement. Does the author give details to support this conclusion? Find sentences that describe what causes lightning, what its effects are, and how powerful lightning can be. Try to find as many details as you can and include them in your response. Reread your response to be sure it makes sense.

Score Point	The response should
3	The response demonstrates the student's understanding of the effects of lightning that lead the author to conclude it is "one of the strongest forces in nature." The response contains two details from the passage to support this conclusion. Examples could include, but are not limited to, the following: • Lightning strikes thousands of times every day. • Every lightning strike is possibly dangerous. • Lightning heats the atmosphere up to five times hotter than the surface of the sun. • Lightning produces sound waves that we call thunder.
2	The response demonstrates a general understanding of the effects of lightning that lead the author to conclude it is "one of the strongest forces in nature" and includes at least one detail. However, the answer lacks the depth and completeness of a score point 3 response.
1	The response shows a limited understanding of the effects of lightning that lead the author to conclude it is "one of the strongest forces in nature" OR The response does not include any details to support the response.
0	The response demonstrates no attempt to address the prompt.

Life

by Paul Laurence Dunbar

A crust of bread and a corner to sleep in,
A minute to smile and an hour to weep in,
A pint of joy to a peck of trouble,
And never a laugh but the moans come double;
And that is life!

A crust and a corner that love makes precious,
With a smile to warm and the tears to refresh us;
And joy seems sweeter when cares come after,
And a moan is the finest of foils for laughter;
And that is life!

Poets use sound to emphasize words and ideas and to create a musical quality. The repetition of initial consonant sounds is called alliteration. Notice the repetition of the hard *c* sound in this line.

To understand the language and sentence structure in poetry, paraphrase each line, or restate it in your own words.

Prose writers use sentences and paragraphs in the same way that poets use lines and stanzas.

Use context clues to help you determine the meaning of unfamiliar words, such as *foils*. Poets may use synonyms, antonyms, or comparisons to help readers with these words.

Poets use figurative language, or language that means something other than what it says, to convey old ideas in new ways. It is difficult to measure emotions such as joy or hardships such as trouble. Take a moment to notice how the poet conveys the amounts of these things.

16. What conclusion can be drawn from the first stanza?

A Life is easy if we work hard.
B There are more good things than bad things in life.
C Life is full of struggles.
D Love erases the pain of life.

Content Standard 7.7: Interpret the author's message in various literary, informational, and functional texts.

Strategy: To answer this question, you must decide what the poet is trying to say in the first stanza. Paraphrase each line in the stanza. Then, think about what these lines have in common. You can eliminate *A*, *B*, and *D* because the poet describes life's hardships or struggles. The poet does not mention working hard, nor does he say that there are more good things than bad things in life. In fact, he says the opposite is true. He also does not imply that love erases the pain of life. Therefore, *C* is the correct answer.

17. Read this line from the poem.

A pint of joy to a peck of trouble

What is the meaning of this line?

A Life contains more unhappiness than happiness.
B Life contains more happiness than unhappiness.
C There is no way to measure life's happiness or unhappiness.
D There are equal amounts of happiness and unhappiness in life.

Content Standard 7.7: Interpret the author's message in various literary, informational, and functional texts.

Strategy: Paraphrase the line from the poem. Decide what you think the poet means. The poet uses creative imagery to make a point. If you do not know what a pint or a peck is, use the context of the poem to help you understand the imagery. The lines that surround this line all talk about there being more bad than good. So, you can conclude that a peck of trouble would be more than a pint of joy—that is, a peck is bigger than a pint. Therefore, the correct answer is *A*.

18. The poet repeats the phrase "And that is life!" at the end of each stanza to—

A persuade the reader that the speaker is correct
B clarify any misinterpretation of a line
C express excitement at the opportunities that await us
D emphasize the unchanging nature of the human condition

Content Standard 7.1.e: Drawing conclusions to interpret unstated intent.

Strategy: Think about what the speaker says in each stanza and paraphrase it in your own words. You may think something such as, "Though there may be joy in life, it is outweighed by hardship." By delivering the same message in each stanza and repeating the last line, the poet is emphasizing the constant hardship we face in life. Therefore, *D* is correct.

19. In the poem, the speaker states that "a moan is the finest of *foils* for laughter." The word *foils* means—

A contrasts
B metals
C similarities
D remedies

Content Standard 7.1.c: Using specific context clues to determine meaning of unfamiliar words.

Strategy: Use context clues to help you figure out what *foils* means in the line. Look at the line immediately before this one. The speaker says that "... joy seems sweeter when cares come after." He is saying that joy would not be as sweet if it could not be compared to cares or worries. With this in mind, a moan and laughter probably have a similar relationship in the context of the poem. Replace the word *foils* with each of the answer choices. Then, pick the one that best illustrates the original meaning. *B* and *C* do not make sense in the line. *D* is not correct because laughter does not need a remedy. Therefore, *A* is the correct answer.

20. Some critics believe this poem means that hardships cause people to appreciate the pleasures of life.

Using details from the poem as support, explain why you agree or disagree with this interpretation.

Content Standard 7.7: Interpret the author's message in various literary works.

Strategy: Here, you are asked to interpret the meaning of the poem. The question tells you what some critics believe. You can infer that other critics may interpret the poem differently. Reread the poem and decide if you agree or disagree with the interpretation given in the question. Any interpretation is acceptable as long as you can support it with details from the poem. Remember to check your answer for spelling and grammar errors.

Score	The response should
3	The response demonstrates the student's understanding of the speaker's message in the poem. In the response, the student takes a position (agreeing or disagreeing with the message) and includes details from the poem to support his or her position. Examples could include, but are not limited to, the following: **Agree:** • Love makes "the crust of bread" and "the corner to sleep in" precious. • Tears are refreshing. • Joy "seems sweeter" when trouble follows it. • Moans are a great contrast to laughter. **Disagree:** • We end up with only "a crust" to eat and "a corner" to sleep in. • We cry much more than we laugh. • We have a lot more trouble than joy. • We moan (in pain, in grief) twice as much as we laugh.
2	The response demonstrates a general understanding of the speaker's message in the poem and a position is taken, including some detail from the poem to support that position. However, the answer lacks the depth and completeness of a score point 3 response.
1	The response shows a limited understanding of the speaker's message OR The response does not include support for the position taken.
0	The response demonstrates no attempt to address the prompt.

DIRECTIONS:

The following questions are not related to any passage you have read. Read each question and decide which is the best answer to the question.

1. A message given in a text about life or human nature that the writer shares with the reader is called—

A imagery
B theme
C symbolism
D plot

Content Standard 7.2: Relate literary elements and devices to each other, including main idea and supporting details, climax, point of view, and imagery.

Strategy: Recall what you know about each of the four literary elements and devices given as answer choices. *A* is incorrect. Imagery gives the reader a clear picture of a setting or object, and consists of words and phrases that appeal to the reader's five senses. *D* is incorrect. Plot is the series of events in a story. While this series of events may lead to a message about life or human nature, that message is separate from the series of events as a whole. *B* and *C* both look like good answer choices, but one of them can be eliminated. Symbolism is the use of a person, place, object, or activity in a text that stands for something else. Symbolism may contribute to the overall message of a text, but alone it does not communicate the message. *B* is correct.

2. A fable could *best* be described as having—

A imaginary creatures and made-up worlds
B factual accounts of real people and events
C a setting, plot, and characters who go on a journey
D a setting, plot, and characters who learn a lesson or moral

Content Standard 7.6: Analyze nonfiction, science fiction, mystery or suspense, fantasy, and adventure for distinguishing characteristics.

Strategy: Think about what characteristics fables have. Though the characters and settings may be strange, they are not usually part of imaginary or made-up worlds. Therefore, you can rule out *A*. On the other hand, fables do not involve real people or events, so *B* is also incorrect. Both *C* and *D* look like good answers, but only *D* involves learning a lesson or moral, which is one of the major characteristics of a fable. It is the correct answer.

3. Read the example in the box.

> When the three brothers returned, they were greeted as heroes by all the people. The king granted them great riches. And they lived happily ever after that because they had found out two important things: together they could do more than apart, and there is nothing better than a good brother.

Which of these does this example *most likely* represent?

A An epic poem
B Autobiography
C A fable
D Science fiction

Content Standard 7.3:
Distinguish among the major genres, including poetry, short stories, novels, plays, biographies, and autobiographies, and subgenres, such as folktales, myths, parables, fables, and science fiction, based on their characteristics.

Strategy: While this example does mention that the brothers were "greeted as heroes," the text does not appear to be in the form of an epic poem, so you can eliminate *A*. *B* is also incorrect; it is clear from such phrases as "The king granted them great riches" and "they lived happily ever after" that this is not an autobiography. While the example does appear to be a part of the fiction genre, it does not include any scientific information. What it does include is a lesson that the writer shares with his or her readers; therefore, *C* is correct.

4. Science fiction is unlike other types of fiction because it—

A includes a setting, characters, and a plot
B is set in the real, modern world
C blends scientific information with a real or imagined world
D includes a setting and a plot, but not characters

Content Standard 7.3:
Distinguish among the major genres, including poetry, short stories, novels, plays, biographies, and autobiographies, and subgenres, such as folktales, myths, parables, fables, and science fiction, based on their characteristics.

Strategy: This question asks you to determine which answer best explains how science fiction is *unlike* other fiction. It is very important that you read questions like this one carefully to avoid making a mistake. You can immediately rule out *A* and *D* because all subgenres of fiction include settings, characters, and plots. If you read the question carefully, it is clear that *C* is the correct answer. Science fiction blends scientific information with either real or imaginary settings and characters.

5. Read the sentence below.

> Every source of information is available to the public, we can get the information free of charge.

What is the *best* way to revise this sentence?

A Every source of information is available to the public. We can get the information; free of charge.

B Every source of information is available to the public, we can get the information; free of charge.

C Every source of information is available to the public; we can get the information free of charge.

D Every source of information is available to the public; we can get the information. Free of charge.

6. Read the sentences below.

> Polar bears can weigh as much as one ton. Weighing up to one ton, the polar bear is the largest bear in the world.

What is the *best* way to combine these sentences?

A Being a polar bear, it weighs up to one ton, the largest bear in the world.

B Weighing up to one ton, polar bears are the largest bears in the world.

C The largest bear in the world, weighing up to one ton: the polar bear.

D In the world, the largest bear is the polar bear, which weighs up to one ton.

Content Standard 7.10.b: Using semicolons, conjunctive adverbs, and commas to join two independent clauses or to correct run-on sentences.

Strategy: *A* is incorrect; while separating the independent clauses with a period is a good revision, the dependent clause modifying *information* should not be set off with a semicolon. *B* is not correct because the independent clauses should not be separated with a comma, and a semicolon should not come before the dependent clause. *C* is correct. A semicolon separates the two independent clauses. *D* is not correct; "free of charge" should not be a fragment.

Content Standard 7.10.e: Using commas to set off nonessential clauses and appositives.

Strategy: To answer this question correctly, review the two sentences. Look for the clearest way to state the information. *A* is not correct because the first clause creates confusion. *C* puts the subject at the end of the sentence, which also creates confusion. In *D*, the subject, the polar bear, is too far from the prepositional phrase *in the world*. *B* is the best answer because it keeps the subject, polar bears, next to the verb and predicate.

The Power of Ideas

INTRODUCING THE ESSENTIALS

- Literary Genres Workshop
- Reading Strategies Workshop
- Writing Process Workshop

The Power of Ideas

What Are Life's Big Questions?

We all wrestle with the big questions in life, including the ones shown here. That's because such questions prompt us to think about key ideas—for example, love, growing up, and loss—that affect all our lives, no matter who we are or where we come from. Through our experiences, we come closer to answering these questions, making sense of the world, and understanding ourselves. But powerful literature holds some answers too.

What is COURAGE?

Courage helps people face big challenges, such as protecting their families or fighting life-threatening illnesses. It can also take courage to do something small, like talk to someone who intimidates you. This book is filled with brave characters—among them a pet mongoose and a shy seventh grader—who can teach you what true courage is.

Is life always FAIR?

If you've ever single-handedly lost a team championship or gotten blamed for something that wasn't your fault, you've probably realized that life can feel completely unfair. Read Ernest Lawrence Thayer's poem "Casey at the Bat" or Chaim Potok's story "Zebra," and you'll discover that you're not alone in feeling this way.

Where is HOME?

"Home is where the heart is," as the old saying goes. The place you call home doesn't have to be the house where you live. Rather, home can be wherever you feel most comfortable and secure. Think about all the places that people might call home—for example, a certain country or a hiding place that nobody else knows about. Then ask yourself: Where is home?

Can we achieve the IMPOSSIBLE?

In many Hollywood action movies, the hero emerges victorious despite impossible odds. Some stories in this book star real-life heroes whose astonishing achievements can make us believe that anything is possible. However, tales as ancient as Greek myths warn us about what can happen if we set our sights too high. Is the impossible really within our reach?

Literary Genres Workshop

Exploring Ideas in Literature

The big questions in life are not easy to answer, but that doesn't stop people from trying. For centuries, writers have searched for answers to such questions, exploring their ideas through stories, poems, and plays. As readers, we turn to literature to understand how others see the world and to learn about ourselves.

ALABAMA STANDARDS

READING & WRITING STANDARDS

1 Apply strategies appropriate to the reading material

3 Distinguish among the major genres

9 Compose in various modes

The Genres

Literature includes a variety of genres, including the ones shown here. Some are meant to be read; others are meant to be performed. Formats such as blockbuster movies and advertisements are not what you would expect to find in a literature book. They are important to analyze, though, since they communicate many ideas and messages in today's world.

In this book you will explore questions and ideas in many genres. By reading everything from dramas and newspaper articles to poetry and short stories, you will be able to discuss and write about such key ideas as survival and happiness. First, review the characteristics of each genre.

GENRES AT A GLANCE

FICTION

Fiction refers to made-up stories about characters and events.

- short stories
- novels
- novellas
- folk tales

POETRY

Poetry is a type of literature in which words are chosen and arranged in a compact, precise way to create specific effects.

- haiku
- limericks
- narrative poems

DRAMA

Dramas are stories that are meant to be performed.

- comedies
- historical dramas
- teleplays

NONFICTION

Nonfiction tells about real people, places, and events.

- autobiographies
- biographies
- essays
- speeches
- news articles
- feature articles

TYPES OF MEDIA

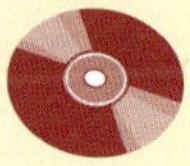

The word *media* refers to communication that reaches many people.

- feature films
- advertising
- news media

FICTION

Whether it is a book by your favorite author or a story that your friend invented, a work of fiction starts as an idea in someone's imagination. Sometimes fiction is also inspired by real people and events.

A good work of fiction keeps readers interested by weaving together many elements. These elements include **plot** (the action of the story), **characters** (the persons or animals involved in the action), **setting** (where and when the action takes place), and **theme** (the big idea behind the story—what the story is *really* about). Three types of fiction are short stories, novels, and novellas.

- A **short story** is a brief work of fiction that can usually be read in one sitting. It often focuses on a single event or a few main characters.
- A **novel** is a much longer work of fiction that can take several days or even weeks to read. Because they are longer than short stories, novels have room to develop more complex characters and plots.
- A **novella** is longer than a short story but shorter than a novel.

Read the Model In the novel *The Cay,* a young boy named Phillip and his mother flee their home in the Caribbean. After their ship is attacked, Phillip goes blind from an injury and gets lost at sea. Soon he finds himself stranded on a remote island. His only companions are an island man named Timothy and a cat. Notice the elements of fiction that the author uses to explore the **key idea** of survival.

ACADEMIC VOCABULARY FOR FICTION

- plot
- conflict
- character
- setting
- theme
- point of view

from

The Cay

Novel by **Theodore Taylor**

The palm fronds above me rattled in the breeze, and there were other noises from the underbrush. I knew Stew Cat was around somewhere, but it didn't sound like him.

I wondered if Timothy had checked for snakes. There were also scorpions on most Caribbean islands, and they were deadly. I wondered if there were any on our cay.

During those first few days on the island, the times I spent alone were terrible. It was, of course, being unable to see that made all the sounds so frightening. I guess if you are born blind, it is not so bad. You grow up knowing each sound and what it means.

Suddenly, the tears came out. I knew it was not a manly thing to do, something my father would have frowned on, but I couldn't stop.

Close Read

1. Using terms from the Academic Vocabulary list, describe what's happening in this scene.

2. **Key Idea: Survival** Phillip will probably have to overcome his fear if he wants to **survive.** What qualities might help him stay alive on this solitary island?

POETRY

Poetry is all around you—in the nursery rhymes you learned as a child, in the lyrics of the songs you listen to, in greeting-card messages, and in this book. You already know that poetry is very different from fiction, starting with the way words are arranged on the page. In poetry, ideas are expressed through a series of **lines,** which are often grouped into **stanzas.**

Many poems are meant to be heard, not just read. For that reason, the way a poem sounds is as important as the way it looks on the page. Poets often experiment with sound devices, including **rhythm** and **rhyme,** to emphasize important words and create musical effects.

Read the Model A powerful poem can make readers look at something ordinary—a thumbprint, for example—in a new way. Read this poem aloud so that you can hear its rhythm and rhyme. What is the poet saying about the **key idea** of individuality?

ACADEMIC VOCABULARY FOR POETRY

- form
- line
- stanza
- rhythm
- rhyme
- speaker
- imagery

Thumbprint

Poem by **Eve Merriam**

On the pad of my thumb
are whorls, whirls, wheels
in a unique design:
mine alone.
What a treasure to own!
My own flesh, my own feelings.
No other, however grand or base,
can ever contain the same.
My signature,
thumbing the pages of my time.
My universe key,
my singularity.
Impress, implant,
I am myself,
of all my atom parts I am the sum.
And out of my blood and my brain
I make my own interior weather,
my own sun and rain.
Imprint my mark upon the world,
whatever I shall become.

Close Read

1. How can you tell that "Thumbprint" is a poem? Cite specific details to support your answer.

2. **Key Idea: Individuality** A thumbprint is one of many things that distinguishes one person from another. What other qualities or characteristics make an **individual** unique?

DRAMA

At the heart of both fiction and drama are good stories. Unlike fiction, though, drama is meant to be performed before an audience. As a result, a drama does not include long descriptions of settings or characters' thoughts. Instead, the story is developed through **dialogue** and actions—what the characters say and do. The structure of a drama is also different from that of a short story or novel. A drama is made up of **scenes** and **acts,** rather than chapters and parts.

A drama also includes notes to help the actors and the director perform it as the writer intended. These instructions, or **stage directions,** describe the setting and how the characters should look, talk, and act. Stage directions are often printed in *italic* type.

Read the Model *A Young Lady of Property* is about Wilma, a teenager who dreams of leaving her home and becoming a movie star. Wilma also wants to leave so that she doesn't have to deal with Mrs. Leighton, her father's girlfriend. In this excerpt Wilma reveals her plan to her father. As you read, think about the **key idea** of ambition.

ACADEMIC VOCABULARY FOR DRAMA

- plot
- character
- act
- scene
- dialogue
- stage directions

from

A Young Lady of Property

Drama by **Horton Foote**

Lester. Say hello to Mrs. Leighton.

Wilma (*most ungraciously*). Hello, Mrs. Leighton.

Mrs. Leighton (*most graciously*). Hello, Wilma.

Lester. What are you doing hanging around the streets, Wilma?

Wilma. Waiting to see if I have a letter.

Lester. What kind of letter, Wilma?

Wilma. About getting into the movies. Arabella and I saw an ad in the *Houston Chronicle* about a Mr. Delafonte who is a famous Hollywood director.

Lester. Who is Mr. Delafonte?

Wilma. The Hollywood director I'm trying to tell you about. He's giving screen tests in Houston to people of beauty and talent, and if they pass they'll go to Hollywood and be in the picture shows.

Lester. Well, that's all a lot of foolishness, Wilma. You're not going to Houston to take anything.

Wilma. But, Daddy . . . I . . .

Lester. You're fifteen years old and you're gonna stay home. . . .

Close Read

1. How does Wilma treat Mrs. Leighton? How does Mrs. Leighton act toward Wilma? Explain how you can tell.
2. **Key Idea: Ambition** Wilma's desire to become a movie star is an **ambition** that many other teens may share. What other ambitions do young people have? Explain why such ambitions are appealing.

NONFICTION AND INFORMATIONAL TEXT

Through **literary nonfiction,** such as autobiographies and speeches, you can learn about historic events, inspiring people, and groundbreaking topics. **Informational text,** such as instruction manuals, magazine articles, and other writing that conveys factual information, is also an important source for learning about the world. For these reasons, you need to become a critical reader of all types of nonfiction.

ACADEMIC VOCABULARY FOR NONFICTION

- purpose
- organization
- main idea
- argument

TYPE OF NONFICTION	CHARACTERISTICS
AUTOBIOGRAPHY/ BIOGRAPHY The true story of a person's life, told by that person (autobiography) or by someone else (biography)	• Helps readers learn about events and experiences in a person's life • Is told from the first-person point of view (autobiography) or the third-person point of view (biography)
ESSAY A short piece of writing about a single, focused subject	• Has one or more of the following purposes: to express feelings, to inform, to entertain, to persuade • Uses either formal or informal language
SPEECH An oral presentation of the speaker's ideas or beliefs	• Is intended to express feelings, to inform, to entertain, or to persuade • Achieves its power through well-chosen language as well as the speaker's voice and gestures
NEWS/FEATURE ARTICLES Informational writing in newspapers and magazines. News articles report on recent events. Feature articles provide in-depth coverage of interesting people, topics, and trends.	• Are primarily intended to inform or entertain • Often use examples, statistics, quotations from sources, and graphic aids to present information
CONSUMER DOCUMENTS Printed materials that usually accompany products and services	• Are intended to inform consumers about how to use a product or service • Often include illustrations, diagrams, and step-by-step directions

Homeless

Anna Quindlen

TheHoriz

DO PROFESSIONAL ATHLETES GET PAID TOO MUCH?

JUSTIN HJELM

Staff Reporter

MODEL 1: AUTOBIOGRAPHY

As you read this excerpt from an autobiography by author Walter Dean Myers, notice how he describes his feelings. Through his descriptions, what do you learn about the **key idea** of overcoming obstacles?

from BAD BOY

Autobiography by **Walter Dean Myers**

I knew in my heart that I would have some difficulties in life because of my speech problems, and I also knew that I wouldn't always be able to solve them by punching somebody out. But I didn't want to make my speech the focus of my life. If I couldn't speak well, I could still communicate by writing. If the words didn't come easily from my mouth, they would, I hoped, eventually come from my writing.

I never understood my speech problem. The words I spoke sounded clear to me. When a teacher or classmate asked me to say something more clearly, I didn't know what to do. Reading aloud in front of an audience was especially difficult for me. After a while I dreaded reading even a sports page to my friends. My stomach would tighten up, and I would become so nervous I could hardly read at all.

Close Read

1. What challenges did young Myers face because of his speech problem? Look for descriptions of his feelings.
2. **Key Idea: Overcoming Obstacles** Myers realized early on that he had to deal with his problem. Do you think that all **obstacles** can be **overcome** with enough effort? Why or why not?

MODEL 2: FEATURE ARTICLE

Stress, the **key idea** in this article, is something that many people experience. How does the article help you understand the reactions that Myers describes in his autobiography?

HEALTH WATCH

Stress

Everyone experiences stress at times—adults, teens, and even kids. But there are things you can do to minimize stress and manage the stress that's unavoidable.

What Is Stress? Stress is a feeling that's created when we react to particular events. It's the body's way of rising to a challenge and preparing to meet a tough situation with focus, strength, stamina, and heightened alertness.

The events that provoke stress are called *stressors,* and they cover a whole range of situations—everything from outright physical danger to making a class presentation. . . .

Close Read

1. How are the boxed details in this article different from the kinds of details that Myers uses to describe the stress he felt as a child?
2. **Key Idea: Stress** Life is full of stressful situations. What other events or factors in life can cause **stress?**

TYPES OF MEDIA

Movies allow you to experience everything from time travel to heroic adventures. The news informs you about what's happening in the world. Ads promise that your life will improve if you buy certain products. Media messages like these influence your life in many ways. That's why you need to become **media literate**—that is, learn how to "read" the media as carefully as you would a work of literature.

ACADEMIC VOCABULARY FOR MEDIA

- medium
- message
- purpose
- target audience

TYPE OF MEDIA	CHARACTERISTICS
FEATURE FILMS Motion pictures that tell stories	• Are meant to entertain and to make a profit • Use camera shots, sound effects, music, actors, and sets to tell stories • Are at least one hour long
NEWS MEDIA Reports of recent events in newspapers and magazines and on TV, the radio, and the Web	• Are intended to inform and to create a loyal audience • Medium (TV, radio, or print) affects how information is presented • Need to be closely examined for accuracy and bias
TV SHOWS Dramas, sitcoms, and other programs broadcast on television	• Are meant to inform and entertain • Use visuals, sound effects, and music to create entertaining stories • Are usually 30 to 60 minutes long
ADVERTISING The promotion of products, services, and ideas using print and broadcast media	• Is designed to persuade a target audience to buy a product or agree with an idea • Uses persuasive techniques, visuals, and sounds to convey a message
WEB SITES Collections of pages on the World Wide Web	• Use text, graphics, audio, and video to present information • Include hyperlinks and menus that allow users to navigate to the information they are looking for

Strategies That Work: Literature

1 Ask Yourself the Right Questions

One skill that can help you analyze any work of literature is the ability to ask good questions. This book will show you what good questions are, so that you can begin to craft them yourself.

Kinds of Questions	Where to Look
Big questions about key ideas ▶	**Before Reading** pages (at the beginning of every selection)
Questions about literary elements and analysis ▶	Side notes (alongside each selection) and **After Reading** pages (following each selection)
Questions to ask when reading different genres ▶	**Analysis Frames (Literature Center at Classzone.com)**

2 Make Connections

For literature to have real meaning for you, you have to make connections. Here are some ways to do just that:

- **Connect to Your Life** What does it take to survive? What makes an individual unique? Consider how experiences in your own life can help you explore big questions like these and the key ideas at the heart of them.
- **Connect to Other Subjects** Surviving on an island, managing stress, living in ancient times—the subjects you read about can help you learn about the world. If a subject interests you, research it on the Web.

3 Record Your Reactions

Jot down your thoughts and impressions in a **Reader's Notebook,** both while and after you read. Consider using these formats.

JOURNAL

Capture your thoughts as you read.

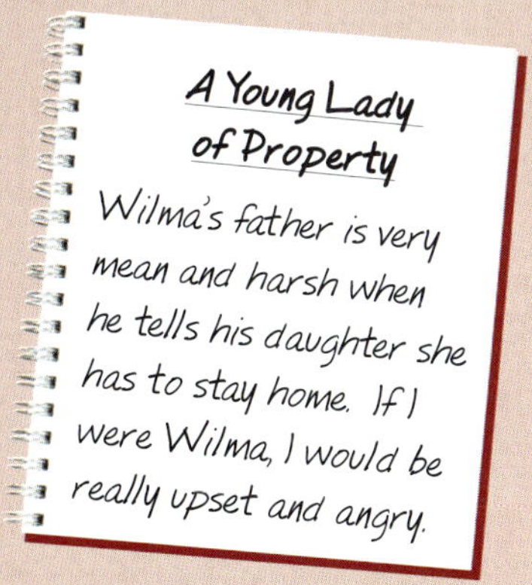

GRAPHIC ORGANIZER

After reading, create a graphic organizer to help you understand characters and events.

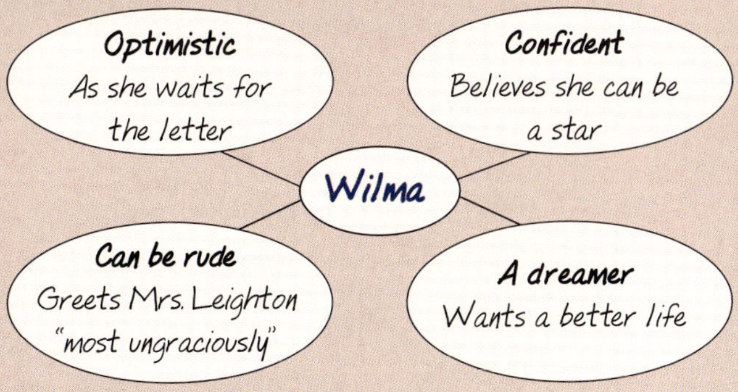

Reading Strategies Workshop

Becoming an Active Reader

A science fiction story, a biography of an athlete, a news article about a faraway country—every kind of text offers a world of ideas for you to explore. Active reading skills and strategies can help you tap into those ideas. Most of the skills and strategies you will practice throughout this book are already familiar to you. Which ones do you recognize?

SKILLS AND STRATEGIES FOR ACTIVE READING

Preview
Get your bearings before you read.
- Scan the title, graphics, and subheadings.
- Skim the first paragraph to get a sense of what the text is about.

Set a Purpose
Think about *why* you are reading a text.
- Ask: Am I reading to learn, to be entertained, or for another reason?
- Decide how this purpose affects your reading. Pay close attention or simply enjoy?

Connect
Take the text personally.
- Think about whether any situations described remind you of experiences in your own life.
- Ask: If I were this character, how would I feel?

Use Prior Knowledge
Recall what you already know about a topic.
- Jot down any facts, descriptions, and impressions before you read.
- Use your notes to help you connect what you know to what you're learning.

Predict
Guess what will happen next.
- Note details that hint at where the story is going.
- Read on to find out if you guessed correctly.

Visualize
Picture in your mind what is being described.
- Note descriptions of characters and settings.
- Use these details to help you form a clear mental image.

Monitor
Check your understanding as you read.
- **Question** what is happening and why.
- Reread difficult parts or ask for help to **clarify** your understanding.
- **Evaluate** yourself as a reader. Ask: How well am I understanding the text?

Make Inferences
Make logical guesses based on details in the text and your own experiences.
- Record important details about characters, settings, and events.
- Ask: How can what I know help me "read between the lines"? (This chart shows how one student made an inference about a character in the story on the next page.)

Details in "Shells"	*What I Know*	*My Inference*
Both of Michael's parents died six months ago.	*It takes time for people to deal with loss.*	*Michael's anger and sadness won't last forever.*

MODEL: SHORT STORY

This story is about a boy named Michael who goes to live with his aunt Esther after his parents die. Will Michael ever break out of his lonely shell and overcome his anger toward Esther? As you read this excerpt, use the **Close Read** questions to practice the skills and strategies you just learned.

from

Shells

Short story by **Cynthia Rylant**

"I can't make you happy, Michael. You just refuse to be happy here. And you punish me every day for it."

"*Punish* you?" Michael gawked at her. "I don't punish you! I don't care about you! I don't care what you eat or how you dress or where you go or what you think. Can't you just leave me alone?"

He slammed down the glass, scraped his chair back from the table and ran out the door.

"Michael!" yelled Esther.

They had been living together, the two of them, for six months. Michael's parents had died and only Esther could take him in—or, only she had offered to. Michael's other relatives could not imagine dealing with a fourteen-year-old boy. They wanted peaceful lives.

Esther lived in a condominium in a wealthy section of Detroit. Most of the area's residents were older (like her) and afraid of the world they lived in (like her). They stayed indoors much of the time. They trusted few people.

Esther liked living alone. She had never married or had children. She had never lived anywhere but Detroit. She liked her condominium.

But she was fiercely loyal to her family, and when her only sister had died, Esther insisted she be allowed to care for Michael. And Michael, afraid of going anywhere else, had accepted.

Oh, he was lonely. Even six months after their deaths, he still expected to see his parents—sitting on the couch as he walked into Esther's living room, waiting for the bathroom as he came out of the shower, coming in the door late at night. He still smelled his father's Old Spice somewhere, his mother's talc.

Sometimes he was so sure one of them was somewhere around him that he thought maybe he was going crazy. His heart hurt him. He wondered if he would ever get better.

Close Read

1. **Set a Purpose** People often read short stories for enjoyment. Here, you also have another purpose—to practice active reading skills and strategies. Have a notebook ready in which you can record your observations.

2. **Monitor** Reread the boxed text. Why did Esther insist on taking care of Michael?

And though he denied it, he did hate Esther. She was so different from his mother and father. Prejudiced—she admired only those who were white and Presbyterian. Selfish—she wouldn't allow him to use her phone. Complaining—she always had a headache or a backache or a stomachache.

He didn't want to, but he hated her. And he didn't know what to do except lie about it.

Michael hadn't made any friends at his new school, and his teachers barely noticed him. He came home alone every day and usually found Esther on the phone. She kept in close touch with several other women in nearby condominiums.

Esther told her friends she didn't understand Michael. She said she knew he must grieve for his parents, but why punish her? She said she thought she might send him away if he couldn't be nicer. She said she didn't deserve this.

But when Michael came in the door, she always quickly changed the subject.

One day after school Michael came home with a hermit crab. He had gone into a pet store, looking for some small, living thing, and hermit crabs were selling for just a few dollars. He'd bought one, and a bowl.

Esther, for a change, was not on the phone when he arrived home. She was having tea and a crescent roll and seemed cheerful. Michael wanted badly to show someone what he had bought. So he showed her.

Esther surprised him. She picked up the shell and poked the long, shiny nail of her little finger at the crab's claws.

"Where is he?" she asked.

Michael showed her the crab's eyes peering through the small opening of the shell.

"Well, for heaven's sake, come out of there!" she said to the crab, and she turned the shell upside down and shook it.

"Aunt Esther!" Michael grabbed for the shell.

"All right, all right." She turned it right side up. "Well," she said, "what does he do?"

Michael grinned and shrugged his shoulders.

"I don't know," he answered. "Just grows, I guess."

His aunt looked at him.

"An attraction to a crab is something I cannot identify with. However, it's fine with me if you keep him, as long as I can be assured that he won't grow out of that bowl." She gave him a hard stare.

"He won't," Michael answered. "I promise." . . .

Close Read

3. **Make Inferences** Why do you think Michael treats his aunt the way he does? Explain how the details in lines 22–34 help you to understand his behavior at the beginning of the story.

4. **Visualize** Reread lines 51–64 and try to picture the scene in your mind. Cite specific details that helped you to see the characters, the setting, and the action.

5. **Predict** Do you think Michael and his aunt will ever find a way to get along? Try to guess what will happen to their relationship.

Strategies That Work: Reading

1 Know Your Purpose

Before you delve into any selection, make sure you know *why* you are reading. Then choose the strategy that best suits your purpose. Consider these strategies.

Purpose	Strategy
For enjoyment	▶ Take your time and read at your own pace.
To learn or become informed	▶ Take notes on the main ideas and supporting details to help you remember what you've learned.
For research	▶ Use text features, such as subheadings and graphic aids, to help you locate the information you're looking for.
To follow directions	▶ Follow each step carefully, using any photographs or illustrations as your guide.

2 Take Notes

Recording your observations as you read can help you better understand a selection. Try creating a two-column chart. In one column, record details or quotations from the selection. In the other, write your thoughts and impressions.

"Shells"	My Thoughts
Esther likes living by herself, and she never had children of her own.	No wonder Esther is frustrated with Michael. She can't seem to make him feel better, and she's not used to taking care of someone else.

3 Create a Personal Word List

Keep track of new words you encounter as you read. This is a good habit to continue to practice.

- **Pick your words.** You may decide to list the vocabulary words for each selection, as well as any other words you find particularly challenging.
- **Don't stop with the definitions.** Write synonyms, antonyms, and sentences to help the words really stick in your mind.
- **Practice makes perfect.** Visit the **Vocabulary Center** at **ClassZone.com** for interactive exercises.
- **Use them or lose them.** Weave new words into your speaking and writing before you forget what you learned.

Word	Meaning
gawked (v.) "Shells," line 3	**Definition:** stared at long and hard in amazement **Synonym:** gaped **Antonym:** glanced **Sentence:** As they entered the lobby, the family gawked at the magnificent hotel.

Writing Process Workshop

Expressing Ideas in Writing

Writing is a way of sharing your ideas with others and learning more about what you really think. Whether you're writing a diary entry for your eyes alone or creating a Web site intended for millions of visitors, the power of words is in your hands.

Consider Your Options

All writers must make some important choices *before* they start giving shape to their ideas. You might want to describe a hilarious incident, write a letter of complaint about a damaged CD, or post a movie review to an online database. No matter what your topic is, you should begin by considering your **purpose, audience,** and **format.**

PURPOSE

Why am I writing?

- to entertain
- to inform or explain
- to persuade
- to describe
- to express thoughts and feelings

AUDIENCE

Who are my readers?

- classmates
- teachers
- friends
- myself
- community members
- Web users
- customer service at a company

FORMAT

Which format will best suit my purpose and audience?

- essay
- letter
- poem
- short story
- review
- speech
- journal entry
- research paper
- script
- power presentation
- Web site

Continue the Process

There is no single right way to write. Every writer does it a little differently. The **Writing Workshops** in this book will help you discover the process that works best for you. First, though, familiarize yourself with the basic process. Then you can move forward according to your own working style.

THE WRITING PROCESS

What Should I Do?	*What Does It Look Like?*
PREWRITING Explore your ideas and decide what you want to write about. Once you have considered the options on the preceding page, try some of these strategies: **freewriting, brainstorming,** and **questioning.** See page 19 for more strategies.	**FREEWRITING** *The Cay* *It must be terrifying to be stranded on an island. This scenario is often shown as being exciting (on TV, at least). Maybe I will write about what it takes to keep going in that situation.*
DRAFTING Turn your ideas into a rough draft. If you are doing some informal or personal writing, you might **draft to discover**—jump in without a formal outline to guide you. If you are writing an essay for school, you may want to **draft from an outline.** If you are writing a short story, create a **story map.**	**OUTLINE** *I. Survival depends on both physical and emotional strength.* *A. Phillip has a serious physical problem—can't see* *B. Needs to get his emotions under control*
REVISING AND EDITING Review what you've written. Think about how you might improve the ideas, style, and structure of your writing. • Use a **rubric** to make sure you are on track (page 18). • Have a classmate review your draft. • **Proofread** for errors in spelling and grammar.	**PEER SUGGESTIONS** *It's all about survival. Phillip in The Cay is in a terribel position. Luckily, he has the qualities he needs to pull through.* ***Suggestion:*** *Could you make the first sentence clearer? Also, it is too informal. Try: "What does it take to survive when your life is threatened?"*
PUBLISHING Get your writing out where it can be read. Choose a publishing option suited to your **purpose, audience,** and **format.** Visit the **Writing Center** at **Classzone.com** for specific publishing options.	**PUBLISHING OPTIONS**  

Do a Self-Check

Knowing the key traits of effective writing can help you at every step of the process. Stay on track by checking your draft against this rubric.

KEY TRAITS RUBRIC

	Strong	Average	Weak
Ideas 1	• has a clear topic • supports statements with relevant details	• has a topic that needs more focus • includes some details but not enough	• has no clear topic • lacks details or includes ones that are unrelated to the topic
Organization 2	• begins with an interesting introduction and ends with a satisfying conclusion • uses transitions between ideas	• has an introduction and a conclusion, but they could be more interesting • needs more transitions to connect ideas	• has no introduction or conclusion • presents a confusing jumble of unrelated ideas
Voice 3	• reflects the writer's unique personality • has a tone that fits the audience and purpose	• shows a lack of interest in the topic • sounds too formal or informal at times	• has no life • uses a completely inappropriate tone
Word Choice 4	• uses vivid words • expresses ideas in a way that sounds natural	• uses words that are correct, but ordinary • sounds forced or awkward at times	• uses words that are too general or incorrect • fails to make the meaning clear
Sentence Fluency 5	• includes sentences of varying length and type	• varies sentence length and type somewhat, but not enough	• includes mostly short or overly long sentences
Conventions 6	• has few errors in grammar, usage, and mechanics	• includes some errors, but readers can still follow the ideas	• has so many errors that the writing is hard to understand

Strategies That Work: Writing

❶ Use Prewriting Strategies

Try different strategies to help you get a strong start.

- **Freewrite.** Jot down whatever pops into your head.
- **Picture it.** Use a graphic organizer to capture your ideas.
- **Brainstorm with classmates.** Generate topics and supporting details with others.
- **Observe your surroundings.** Venture into the world with your notebook. Write notes about interesting people, events, and places.
- **Question yourself.** "What if I were president?" The answer to a silly or serious "what if" question could be your topic.

❷ Get Friendly Feedback

You can ask other writers for help at any stage of the writing process. Keep these guidelines in mind.

When You're the Writer	When You're the Reader
• Be clear about the feedback you want. Should readers comment on your ideas or proofread for errors? • Listen politely to readers' comments and suggestions. • Ask your readers to clarify suggestions that you find confusing.	• Be respectful and positive when you talk about the writer's work. • Support your opinions with reasons, and try to give specific suggestions for improvement. • Don't rewrite the work yourself. Let the writer make the final changes.

❸ Read, Read, Read

Reading other people's writing can help you develop your own style. Here are some sources.

LITERATURE
Take advantage of the literature in this book. Also, don't forget about novels, magazines, and newspapers that interest you.

WRITING COMMUNITY
Form a writing group with other students to share your writing processes and products.

ONLINE RESOURCES
Visit the Writing Center at ClassZone.com for links to blogs and student publication sites.

UNIT 1

Weaving a Story

PLOT, CONFLICT, AND SETTING

- In Fiction
- In Nonfiction
- In Poetry
- In Drama
- In Media

UNIT 1

Share What You Know

What makes a STORY *unforgettable?*

Whether it's a spellbinding mystery, a heartwarming true story, or a tale from your grandmother's past, an **unforgettable story** has a certain "something" that sets it apart from other tales. The story might have a riveting plot, a mysterious setting, or a powerful ending, but whatever that certain something is, an unforgettable story stays with you long after you've read or heard it.

ACTIVITY Think of an unforgettable story that you've read or heard. It might be a classic piece of fiction, such as *The Black Stallion,* or a family story that has been passed down for generations. With a group of classmates, discuss the following questions:

- What makes the story unforgettable?
- What do your reasons have in common?
- After your discussion, how would you answer the original question: What makes a story unforgettable?

Online LITERATURE CLASSZONE.COM

Literature and Reading Center
Writing Center
Vocabulary and Spelling Center

ALABAMA STANDARDS

Preview Unit Goals

LITERARY ANALYSIS
- Identify stages of plot; analyze plot development
- Identify and analyze setting
- Identify conflict, flashback, and foreshadowing

READING
- Use reading strategies, including connecting and predicting
- Identify sequence and cause-and-effect relationships
- Identify patterns of organization, including chronological order

WRITING AND GRAMMAR
- Write a description
- Avoid sentence fragments and run-on sentences
- Punctuate possessives correctly
- Maintain pronoun-antecedent agreement in number

SPEAKING, LISTENING, AND VIEWING
- Identify and analyze visual and sound elements in film
- Analyze film techniques that establish plot and setting
- Compare personal opinions with a reviewer's opinion
- Produce a radio dramatization

VOCABULARY
- Understand and use prefixes, suffixes, and word roots

ACADEMIC VOCABULARY
- plot
- conflict
- setting
- sequence
- foreshadowing
- flashback
- cause and effect
- prefix, suffix, word root

UNIT 1

Reader's Workshop

ALABAMA STANDARDS

READING & LIT STANDARDS

2 Relate literary elements to each other, including climax

6.a Classifying plot elements

Parts of a Story

What makes you willing to spend two hours at the movie theater or a week finishing a book? Is it the thrill of action-packed events or a connection to the characters? Is it a fascination with the setting, such as a faraway galaxy? Setting, characters, conflict, and plot all play a role in holding your interest in a story. Looking closely at these parts can help you understand what makes a story worthwhile.

Part 1: What Drives a Story?

Even the best-built car doesn't cruise on its own. A car needs an engine and a good set of wheels. In the same way, a writer can invent an interesting story, but without the following key parts, that story would sputter to a stop.

- **Setting** is the time and place of the action. The time might be the historical era, the season, or the time of day. The place might be a country, a neighborhood, or a room. In many stories, setting affects the action and the characters' feelings.
- **Characters** are the people, animals, or imaginary creatures that take part in a story. The characters' behavior directly affects what happens.
- **Conflict** is a struggle between different forces. It is the fuel that keeps the action moving forward. A conflict can be external or internal.

TYPE OF CONFLICT	EXAMPLE
 ***External Conflict*** is a struggle between a character and an outside force. This force might be another character, a group of characters, or nature.	A sea captain attempts to guide his boat to shore in the middle of a deadly storm. **(sea captain vs. nature)** *Other Examples* • A boxer faces an opponent. • A girl has a fight with friends.
 ***Internal Conflict*** is a struggle within a character's mind. This kind of conflict happens when a character must deal with opposing thoughts or feelings.	A girl strongly disagrees with her friends, but she wants them to like her. Should she speak her mind or stay silent? **(girl vs. herself)** *Other Examples* • Admit needing help or do it alone? • Take a risk or play it safe?

MODEL 1: SETTING

This author draws you into the story by providing specific details about the setting. How might the setting affect what happens?

from The Clay Marble

Novel by **Minfong Ho**

The last rays of afternoon sun were filtering through the forest as we approached the Border. Gradually the trees thinned out and the path widened. Several trails merged into ours. It seemed as if all the paths out of Cambodia were converging on this one spot on the Thai border.

I could barely contain my excitement. I imagined mountains of rice lining the horizon, and piles of tools and fishnets everywhere. Perhaps there would even be mounds of sweet moist coconut cakes and banana fritters. "Hurry," I urged my brother.

Yet, as we finally emerged from the forest, all we could see was a vast barren plain dotted with shrubs and scraggly trees, flat and desolate.

Close Read

1. What details about the setting do you find in lines 1–4? One detail has been boxed.
2. Describe what the narrator expects to see when she crosses the border. Then describe what she actually sees. How might the actual setting affect the narrator and the story?

MODEL 2: CONFLICT

Here, a girl watches from the deck of a ship as her brother is left on a deserted island. What do you learn about the conflict in this excerpt?

from Island of the Blue Dolphins

Novel by **Scott O'Dell**

Against my will, I screamed.

Chief Matasaip grasped my arm.

"We cannot wait for Ramo," he said. "If we do, the ship will be driven on the rocks."

"We must!" I shouted. "We must!"

"The ship will come back for him on another day," Matasaip said. "He will be safe. There is food for him to eat and water to drink and places to sleep."

"No," I cried.

Matasaip's face was like stone. He was not listening.

Close Read

1. Describe the conflict the girl experiences.
2. Is the girl's conflict internal or external? Explain how you know.

Part 2: Stages of Plot

No matter who the characters are, where the action takes place, or what conflicts occur, a story has a plot. A **plot** is the series of events in a story. Usually a story begins by introducing a main character who has a conflict. As the story moves on, the conflict becomes more complicated, and the character must find a solution. Once the problem is solved, the character adjusts, and the story ends.

A typical plot can be broken down into five stages. By understanding these stages, you can follow a story more closely and know what to look for at all times. For example, at the beginning—or **exposition**—of a story, pay attention to the details that tell you about the characters, the setting, and any potential conflicts that may arise.

PLOT AT A GLANCE

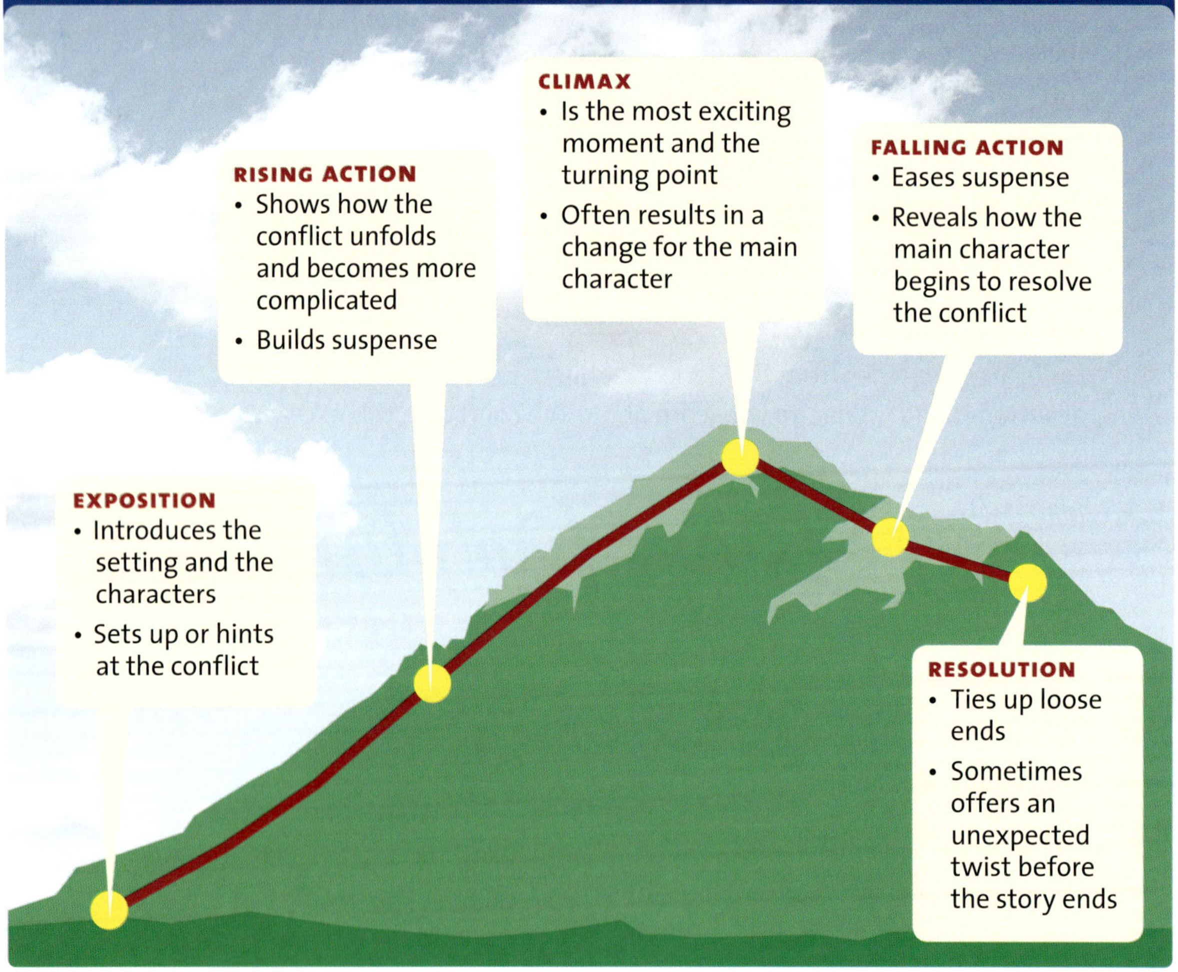

MODEL 1: EXPOSITION

What do you learn about the setting and the conflict in the exposition of this story?

from Last Cover

Short story by **Paul Annixter**

I'm not sure I can tell you what you want to know about my brother; but everything about the pet fox is important, so I'll tell all that from the beginning.

It goes back to a winter afternoon after I'd hunted the woods all day for a sign of our lost pet. I remember the way my mother looked up as I came into the kitchen. Without my speaking, she knew what had happened. For six hours I had walked, reading signs, looking for a delicate print in the damp soil or even a hair that might have told of a red fox passing that way—but I had found nothing.

Close Read

1. What can you tell about the setting in which the main character lives? Find specific details that describe the setting.
2. Review the boxed details. Describe the conflict that the main character faces. What does this conflict suggest the story will be about?

MODEL 2: RISING ACTION

At the beginning of this story, lonely Mr. Peters is granted three wishes. He uses his first wish to ask for a wife. In the rising action, what do you learn about the conflict that results from this wish?

from THE THIRD WISH

Short story by **Joan Aiken**

One evening he was returning home along the river path when he saw Leita in front of him, down by the water. A swan had sailed up to the verge and she had her arms round its neck and the swan's head rested against her cheek. She was weeping, and as he came nearer he saw that tears were rolling, too, from the swan's eyes.

"Leita, what is it?" he asked, very troubled.

"This is my sister," she answered. "I can't bear being separated from her."

Now he understood that Leita was really a swan from the forest, and this made him very sad because when a human being marries a bird it always leads to sorrow.

Close Read

1. Reread the boxed text. What conflict is Mr. Peters facing?
2. The rising action leads toward the climax. What decision or action might this situation be building toward?

Part 3: Analyze the Literature

In this story, an elegant dinner party turns dangerous when an uninvited "guest" makes an appearance. As you read, use what you've just learned about plot, conflict, and setting to analyze the story.

The Dinner Party

Short story by
Mona Gardner

The country is India. A large dinner party is being given in an up-country station by a colonial official[1] and his wife. The guests are army officers and government attachés[2] and their wives, and an American naturalist.[3]

At one side of the long table a spirited discussion springs up between a young girl and a colonel. The girl insists women have long outgrown the jumping-on-a-chair-at-the-sight-of-a-mouse era, that they are not as fluttery as their grandmothers. The colonel says they are, explaining that women haven't the actual nerve control of men. The other men at the table agree with him.

"A woman's unfailing reaction in any crisis," the colonel says, "is to scream. And while a man may feel like it, yet he has that ounce more of control than a woman has. And that last ounce is what counts!"

The American scientist does not join in the argument, but sits watching the faces of the other guests. As he looks, he sees a strange expression come over the face of the hostess. She is staring straight ahead, the muscles of her face contracting slightly. With a small gesture she summons the native boy standing behind her chair. She whispers to him. The boy's eyes widen: he turns quickly and leaves the room.

---

1. **colonial official:** a person holding a position in the British government ruling India.
2. **attachés** (ăt'ə-shāz'): people who assist an ambassador.
3. **naturalist:** a person who studies living things by observing them directly.

Close Read
Exposition (Lines 1–13)

1. What do you learn about the setting in the exposition?
2. What are the young girl and the colonel arguing about in lines 5–13?

Close Read
Rising Action (Lines 14–36)

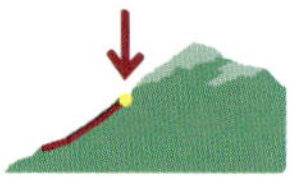

3. Find two details in lines 14–19 that hint at a possible conflict. One detail has been boxed.

No one else sees this, nor the boy when he puts a bowl of milk on the verandah[4] outside the glass doors.

The American comes to with a start. In India, milk in a bowl means only one thing. It is bait for a snake. He realizes there is a cobra in the room.

He looks up at the rafters[5]—the likeliest place—and sees they are bare. Three corners of the room, which he can see by shifting only slightly, are empty. In the fourth corner a group of servants stand, waiting until the next course can be served. The American realizes there is only one place left—under the table.

His first impulse is to jump back and warn the others. But he knows the commotion will frighten the cobra and it will strike. He speaks quickly, the quality of his voice so arresting that it sobers everyone.

"I want to know just what control everyone at this table has. I will count three hundred—that's five minutes—and not one of you is to move a single muscle. The persons who move will forfeit 50 rupees.[6] Now! Ready!"

The 20 people sit like stone images while he counts. He is saying ". . . two hundred and eighty . . ." when, out of the corner of his eye, he sees the cobra emerge and make for the bowl of milk. Four or five screams ring out as he jumps to slam shut the verandah doors.

"You certainly were right, Colonel!" the host says. "A man has just shown us an example of real control."

"Just a minute," the American says, turning to his hostess, "there's one thing I'd like to know. Mrs. Wynnes, how did you know that cobra was in the room?"

A faint smile lights up the woman's face as she replies. "Because it was lying across my foot."

4. **verandah:** a long porch, usually roofed, along the side of a building.
5. **rafters:** wooden beams that support a roof.
6. **rupees** (ro͞o-pēz′): Indian units of money.

4. Reread lines 22–24. What is the main conflict? Explain whether it is internal or external.

Close Read
Climax (Lines 37–40)

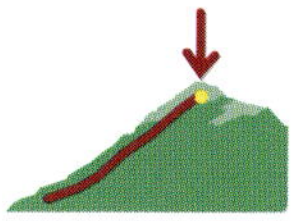

5. What happens at the climax, or the most exciting moment?

Close Read
Falling Action and Resolution (Lines 41–47)

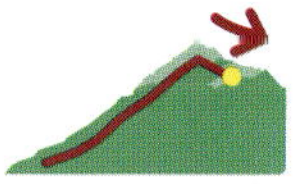

6. At what point in the falling action does the tension begin to ease? Explain.
7. What surprise is revealed in the resolution?

Seventh Grade

Short Story by Gary Soto

How do you make a good IMPRESSION?

ALABAMA STANDARDS

READING & LIT STANDARDS

1.d Applying self-monitoring strategies

6.a Classifying plot elements

KEY IDEA All of us have times when we're eager to make a good **impression**—to win the approval of parents, teachers, or friends. But influencing how others see us isn't always easy. In "Seventh Grade," a boy finds that trying to make a good impression can lead to some embarrassing moments.

LIST IT What tips have you heard about how to make a good impression? Create a list of the suggestions you think are most effective.

LITERARY ANALYSIS: PLOT

A **plot** is what happens in a story, and usually consists of five stages.

- The **exposition** introduces the characters, the setting, and often the conflict, or struggle between forces.
- The **rising action** shows how the conflict gets more complicated.
- The **climax** is the moment of greatest interest.
- The **falling action** and **resolution** reveal the outcome.

As you read "Seventh Grade," notice how the events in the story lead up to the climax.

READING STRATEGY: CONNECT

In almost any story, you can find some common ground with the characters by relating your knowledge and experiences to theirs. This is called **connecting,** and it helps you enter into the story. As you read the selection, use a chart like the one shown to connect what is happening in "Seventh Grade" to your own life.

What's Happening in the Story	*Connection to My Life*
Victor is daydreaming about traveling to France.	*I daydream about the world outside my neighborhood too.*

VOCABULARY IN CONTEXT

The boldfaced words help tell the story of a day in the life of a seventh grader. After reading the sentences, write the definitions of the boldfaced words with which you are familiar.

1. A student may **quiver** when tests are handed back.
2. Feel free to **linger** after class if you have a question.
3. Sam loves to eat; he is rather **portly.**
4. The athlete's **ferocity** was praised.
5. She smiled **sheepishly** as she admitted to staying up late.
6. The class recited poems in **unison.**

Author Online

A Neighborhood's Influence

Gary Soto
born 1952

Gary Soto fills his fiction and poetry for young adults with lively details of his upbringing in a Mexican-American neighborhood. Soto wants his work to help others appreciate his old neighborhood's values. But, he says, "I am really writing about the feelings and experiences of most American kids: having a pet, going to the park for a family cookout . . . getting a bee sting!"

The Power of Reading Soto has said that as a child he never thought about being a writer. Today, though, he meets with young people to encourage their curiosity about reading and writing. The award-winning author explains, "I believe in literature and the depth it adds to all our lives."

MORE ABOUT THE AUTHOR
For more on Gary Soto, visit the **Literature Center** at **ClassZone.com.**

Background

Fresno, California "Seventh Grade" is set in Fresno, California, where Gary Soto grew up. Fresno is located southeast of San Francisco. Its dry, hot summers and cool, humid winters are excellent for growing grapes. A large number of Latinos, whose families are originally from Spanish-speaking countries, are employed in Fresno's vineyards.

Seventh Grade

Gary Soto

On the first day of school, Victor stood in line half an hour before he came to a wobbly card table. He was handed a packet of papers and a computer card on which he listed his one elective, French. He already spoke Spanish and English, but he thought some day he might travel to France, where it was cool; not like Fresno, where summer days reached 110 degrees in the shade. There were rivers in France, and huge churches, and fair-skinned people everywhere, the way there were brown people all around Victor. (A)

Besides, Teresa, a girl he had liked since they were in catechism classes[1] at Saint Theresa's, was taking French, too. With any luck they would be in the same class. Teresa is going to be my girl this year, he promised himself as he left the gym full of students in their new fall clothes. She was cute. And good in math, too, Victor thought as he walked down the hall to his homeroom. He ran into his friend, Michael Torres, by the water fountain that never turned off.

ANALYZE VISUALS
What might you **infer** about the girl from her expression?

(A) PLOT: EXPOSITION
What background information do you learn about Victor in the first paragraph?

1. **catechism** (kăt′ĭ-kĭz′əm) **classes:** formal classes in religious instruction.

They shook hands, *raza*-style,[2] and jerked their heads at one another in a *saludo de vato*.[3] "How come you're making a face?" asked Victor. **B**

"I ain't making a face, *ese*.[4] This *is* my face." Michael said his face had changed during the summer. He had read a GQ[5] magazine that his older brother had borrowed from the Book Mobile and noticed that the male models all had the same look on their faces. They would stand, one arm around a beautiful woman, and *scowl.* They would sit at a pool, their rippled stomachs dark with shadow, and *scowl.* They would sit at dinner tables, cool drinks in their hands, and *scowl.*

"I think it works," Michael said. He scowled and let his upper lip **quiver.** His teeth showed along with the **ferocity** of his soul. "Belinda Reyes walked by a while ago and looked at me," he said.

Victor didn't say anything, though he thought his friend looked pretty strange. They talked about recent movies, baseball, their parents, and the horrors of picking grapes in order to buy their fall clothes. Picking grapes was like living in Siberia,[6] except hot and more boring.

"What classes are you taking?" Michael said, scowling.

"French. How 'bout you?"

"Spanish. I ain't so good at it, even if I'm Mexican."

"I'm not either, but I'm better at it than math, that's for sure."

A tinny, three-beat bell propelled students to their homerooms. The two friends socked each other in the arm and went their ways, Victor thinking, man, that's weird. Michael thinks making a face makes him handsome.

On the way to his homeroom, Victor tried a scowl. He felt foolish, until out of the corner of his eye he saw a girl looking at him. Umm, he thought, maybe it does work. He scowled with greater conviction. **C**

In homeroom, roll was taken, emergency cards were passed out, and they were given a bulletin to take home to their parents. The principal, Mr. Belton, spoke over the crackling loudspeaker, welcoming the students to a new year, new experiences, and new friendships. The students squirmed in their chairs and ignored him. They were anxious to go to first period. Victor sat calmly, thinking of Teresa, who sat two rows away, reading a paperback novel. This would be his lucky year. She was in his homeroom, and would probably be in his English and math classes. And, of course, French.

The bell rang for first period, and the students herded noisily through the door. Only Teresa **lingered,** talking with the homeroom teacher.

B CONNECT
How do you greet your friends when you see them in the hall?

quiver (kwĭv′ər) *v.* to shake with a slight, rapid movement

ferocity (fə-rŏs′ĭ-tē) *n.* fierceness; extreme intensity

C PLOT: EXPOSITION
Reread lines 25–27 and lines 39–41. When the boys scowl, they see girls look at them. What might the girls be thinking?

linger (lĭng′gər) *v.* to continue to stay; delay leaving

---

2. ***raza*** (rä′sä)**-style** *Spanish*: in the manner that Mexican Americans greet each other.
3. ***saludo de vato*** (sä-lo͞o′dō dĕ bä′tō) *Spanish:* greeting between Mexican-American friends.
4. ***ese*** (ĕ′sĕ) *Spanish:* a slang term used in addressing someone, as in "Hey, man."
5. ***GQ:*** *Gentleman's Quarterly,* a magazine of men's styles and fashions.
6. **Siberia:** a cold, isolated region of northern Russia.

"So you think I should talk to Mrs. Gaines?" she asked the teacher. "She would know about ballet?"

"She would be a good bet," the teacher said. Then added, "Or the gym teacher, Mrs. Garza."

Victor lingered, keeping his head down and staring at his desk. He wanted to leave when she did so he could bump into her and say something clever.

He watched her on the sly. As she turned to leave, he stood up and hurried to the door, where he managed to catch her eye. She smiled and said, "Hi, Victor."

He smiled back and said, "Yeah, that's me." His brown face blushed. Why hadn't he said, "Hi, Teresa," or "How was your summer?" or something nice?

As Teresa walked down the hall, Victor walked the other way, looking back, admiring how gracefully she walked, one foot in front of the other. So much for being in the same class, he thought. As he trudged to English, he practiced scowling.

In English they reviewed the parts of speech. Mr. Lucas, a **portly** man, waddled down the aisle, asking, "What is a noun?"

"A person, place, or thing," said the class in **unison.**

"Yes, now somebody give me an example of a person—you, Victor Rodriguez."

"Teresa," Victor said automatically. Some of the girls giggled. They knew he had a crush on Teresa. He felt himself blushing again.

"Correct," Mr. Lucas said. "Now provide me with a place."

Mr. Lucas called on a freckled kid who answered, "Teresa's house with a kitchen full of big brothers."

After English, Victor had math, his weakest subject. He sat in the back by the window, hoping he would not be called on. Victor understood most of the problems, but some of the stuff looked like the teacher made it up as she went along. It was confusing, like the inside of a watch.

After math he had a fifteen-minute break, then social studies, and, finally, lunch. He bought a tuna casserole with buttered rolls, some fruit cocktail, and milk. He sat with Michael, who practiced scowling between bites.

Girls walked by and looked at him.

portly (pôrt'lē) *adj.* stout or overweight

unison (yo͞o'nĭ-sən) *n.* harmony or agreement; as with one voice

"See what I mean, Vic?" Michael scowled. "They love it."

"Yeah, I guess so."

They ate slowly, Victor scanning the horizon for a glimpse of Teresa. He didn't see her. She must have brought lunch, he thought, and is eating outside. Victor scraped his plate and left Michael, who was busy scowling at a girl two tables away. D

The small, triangle-shaped campus bustled with students talking about their new classes. Everyone was in a sunny mood. Victor hurried to the bag lunch area, where he sat down and opened his math book. He moved his lips as if he were reading, but his mind was somewhere else. He raised his eyes slowly and looked around. No Teresa.

He lowered his eyes, pretending to study, then looked slowly to the left. No Teresa. He turned a page in the book and stared at some math problems that scared him because he knew he would have to do them eventually. He looked to the right. Still no sign of her. He stretched out lazily in an attempt to disguise his snooping. E

Then he saw her. She was sitting with a girlfriend under a plum tree. Victor moved to a table near her and daydreamed about taking her to a movie. When the bell sounded, Teresa looked up, and their eyes met. She smiled sweetly and gathered her books. Her next class was French, same as Victor's.

D PLOT: RISING ACTION
What obstacles are getting in the way of Victor making Teresa "his girl"?

E CONNECT
What experiences have you had that help you understand how Victor might be feeling as he looks for Teresa?

They were among the last students to arrive in class, so all the good desks in the back had already been taken. Victor was forced to sit near the front, a few desks away from Teresa, while Mr. Bueller wrote French words on the chalkboard. The bell rang, and Mr. Bueller wiped his hands, turned to the class, and said, *"Bonjour."*[7]

"Bonjour," braved a few students.

"Bonjour," Victor whispered. He wondered if Teresa heard him. **F**

Mr. Bueller said that if the students studied hard, at the end of the year they could go to France and be understood by the populace.

One kid raised his hand and asked, "What's 'populace'?"

"The people, the people of France."

Mr. Bueller asked if anyone knew French. Victor raised his hand, wanting to impress Teresa. The teacher beamed and said, *"Très bien. Parlez-vous français?"*[8]

Victor didn't know what to say. The teacher wet his lips and asked something else in French. The room grew silent. Victor felt all eyes staring at him. He tried to bluff his way out by making noises that sounded French.

"La me vave me con le grandma," he said uncertainly. **G**

Mr. Bueller, wrinkling his face in curiosity, asked him to speak up.

Great rosebushes of red bloomed on Victor's cheeks. A river of nervous sweat ran down his palms. He felt awful. Teresa sat a few desks away, no doubt thinking he was a fool. Without looking at Mr. Bueller, Victor mumbled, "Frenchie oh wewe gee in September."

Mr. Bueller asked Victor to repeat what he said.

"Frenchie oh wewe gee in September," Victor repeated.

Mr. Bueller understood that the boy didn't know French and turned away. He walked to the blackboard and pointed to the words on the board with his steel-edged ruler.

"Le bateau," he sang.

"Le bateau," the students repeated.

"Le bateau est sur l'eau,"[9] he sang.

"Le bateau est sur l'eau."

Victor was too weak from failure to join the class. He stared at the board and wished he had taken Spanish, not French. Better yet, he wished he could start his life over. He had never been so embarrassed. He bit his thumb until he tore off a sliver of skin.

The bell sounded for fifth period, and Victor shot out of the room, avoiding the stares of the other kids, but had to return for his math book. He looked **sheepishly** at the teacher, who was erasing the board, then

F PLOT: RISING ACTION
Why does the tension increase now that Victor and Teresa are in the same class together?

G CONNECT
Think of a time when you said you knew something that you really didn't. **Compare and contrast** how it made you feel with how Victor is feeling now.

sheepishly (shē'pĭsh-lē) *adv.* with a bashful or embarrassed look

---

7. ***Bonjour*** (bôn'zhōōr) *French:* Good day.
8. ***Très bien. Parlez-vous français?*** (trĕ byăn pär'lā vōō frän'sĕ) *French:* Very good. Do you speak French?
9. ***Le bateau est sur l'eau*** (lə bä'tō ĕ sür lō) *French:* The boat is on the water.

widened his eyes in terror at Teresa who stood in front of him. "I didn't know you knew French," she said. "That was good." **H**

Mr. Bueller looked at Victor, and Victor looked back. Oh please, don't say anything, Victor pleaded with his eyes. I'll wash your car, mow your lawn, walk your dog—anything! I'll be your best student, and I'll clean your erasers after school.

Mr. Bueller shuffled through the papers on his desk. He smiled and hummed as he sat down to work. He remembered his college years when he dated a girlfriend in borrowed cars. She thought he was rich because each time he picked her up he had a different car. It was fun until he had spent all his money on her and had to write home to his parents because he was broke. **I**

Victor couldn't stand to look at Teresa. He was sweaty with shame. "Yeah, well, I picked up a few things from movies and books and stuff like that." They left the class together. Teresa asked him if he would help her with her French.

"Sure, anytime," Victor said.

"I won't be bothering you, will I?"

"Oh no, I like being bothered."

"Bonjour," Teresa said, leaving him outside her next class. She smiled and pushed wisps of hair from her face.

"Yeah, right, *bonjour*," Victor said. He turned and headed to his class. The rosebushes of shame on his face became bouquets of love. Teresa is a great girl, he thought. And Mr. Bueller is a good guy.

He raced to metal shop. After metal shop there was biology, and after biology a long sprint to the public library, where he checked out three French textbooks.

He was going to like seventh grade. **J**

H PLOT: CLIMAX
Why is this the moment of greatest interest in the story?

I PLOT: FALLING ACTION
How do Mr. Bueller's actions affect the plot at this point?

J PLOT: RESOLUTION
How has Victor's life changed by the end of the day?

Comprehension

ALABAMA STANDARDS

LITERATURE STANDARD
6.a Classifying plot elements

1. **Recall** What is the main reason Victor wants to take French?
2. **Recall** How does Victor respond when Teresa talks to him after homeroom?
3. **Summarize** Explain the events that happen after Victor tells Mr. Bueller that he speaks French.

Literary Analysis

4. **Connect** Review the chart you created as you read. How do the connections you made help you understand the characters and events that take place in the story? Note specific examples.
5. **Compare and Contrast** Compare and contrast Michael's efforts to impress girls with Victor's efforts to impress Teresa. Give examples from the story. How do their efforts give the story tension—and humor?
6. **Make Inferences** The French teacher, Mr. Bueller, realizes that Victor is faking his knowledge of French. Why does he keep the truth to himself?
7. **Analyze Plot** The plot of "Seventh Grade" centers on Victor's attempts to win Teresa over. Go back through the story and make a list of the important events. Then use a diagram like the one shown, and fill in what happens at each stage of the plot.

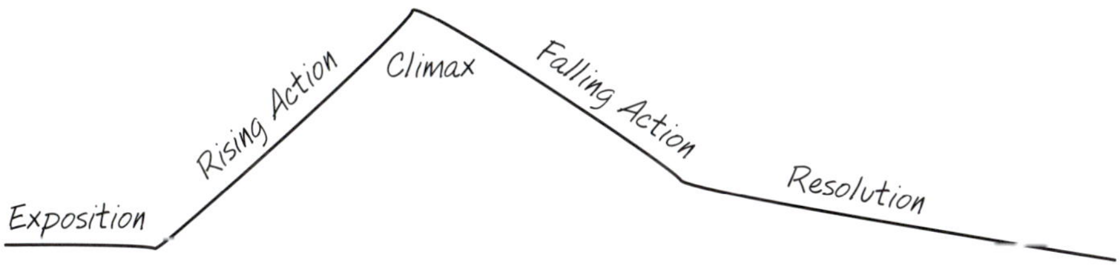

8. **Make Judgments** Victor is finally able to impress Teresa. Do you think it matters that this **impression** is based on something that isn't true? Explain your answer.

Extension and Challenge

9. **Readers' Circle** In a group, discuss what Teresa might be thinking at each stage in the plot. Draw a diagram like the one shown in question 7, and note on it the thoughts and feelings your group identifies for her.
10. **Creative Project: Writing** Imagine that Victor and Michael both work as personalities on a radio talk show. A boy calls in, asking for their opinions about how to impress girls. Write the response each of the boys would give.

Vocabulary in Context

VOCABULARY PRACTICE

Choose the word in each group that is most nearly opposite in meaning to the boldfaced word.

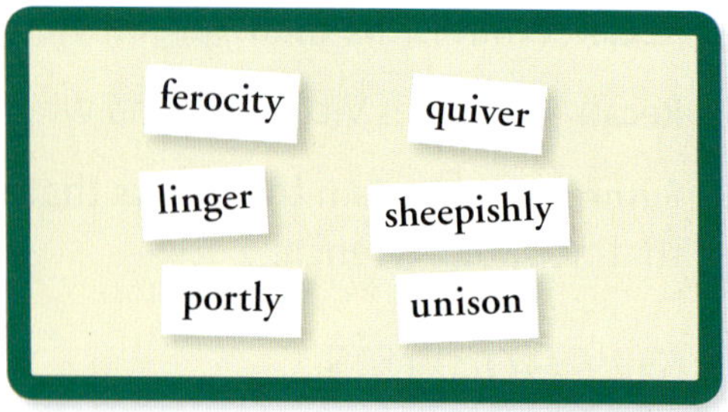

1. **ferocity:** (a) fear, (b) bravery, (c) gentleness
2. **quiver:** (a) tremble, (b) vibrate, (c) stiffen
3. **sheepishly:** (a) shyly, (b) boldly, (c) easily
4. **linger:** (a) struggle, (b) hurry, (c) prolong
5. **portly:** (a) fluid, (b) heavy, (c) thin
6. **unison:** (a) separation, (b) company, (c) time

VOCABULARY IN WRITING

Write a paragraph about what things were like for you during your first few days of seventh grade. Include at least three vocabulary words. Here is a sample of how you might begin your paragraph.

EXAMPLE SENTENCE

*As I walked up the school steps that first day, I just wanted to **linger** outside the door forever.*

ALABAMA STANDARDS

READING STANDARD
1.c Using context clues to determine meaning of words

VOCABULARY STRATEGY: THE LATIN ROOT *uni*

The vocabulary word *unison* contains the Latin root *uni,* which means "one." *Uni* is combined with base words and other roots in a number of English words. To understand the meaning of a word containing *uni,* use context clues—the words and sentences around the word—as well as your knowledge of the root.

VOCABULARY PRACTICE
For more practice, go to the **Vocabulary Center** at **ClassZone.com.**

PRACTICE Choose the word from the web that best completes each sentence. Be ready to explain how *uni* helps give meaning to each word.

1. The _____, a creature with one horn, exists only in fairy tales.
2. The clown rode in circles, balanced unsteadily on a _____.
3. Each team member stood out from the crowd in his bright purple _____.
4. The colonists banded together to form a new _____.
5. She claims her ring is _____, but I've seen others like it.

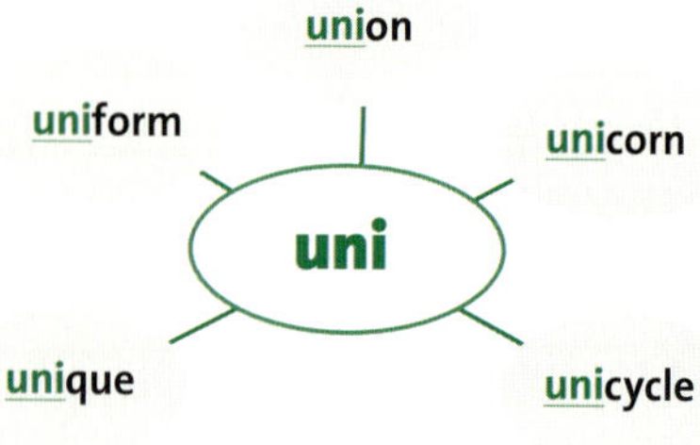

SKILLS PRACTICE

Reading-Writing Connection

Increase your understanding of "Seventh Grade" by responding to these prompts. Then complete the **Grammar and Writing** exercise.

WRITING PROMPTS	SELF-CHECK
A. Short Response: Describe an Expression Victor's friend Michael has some interesting opinions about what kind of facial expression **impresses** girls. Write a **one-paragraph description** of Michael's scowl.	***A strong description will . . .*** • include details about Michael's facial expression • use words and phrases that appeal to the sense of sight
B. Extended Response: Write a Journal Entry What would Victor write in a journal about his first day of seventh grade? Write a **two- or three-paragraph journal entry** from Victor's point of view.	***A creative journal entry will . . .*** • relate events and feelings described in the story • use words that Victor would use

GRAMMAR AND WRITING

ALABAMA STANDARDS

WRITING/LANGUAGE STANDARD
10 Apply mechanics in writing

AVOID SENTENCE FRAGMENTS Every complete sentence has a subject and a predicate. The complete subject includes all the words that tell whom or what the sentence is about. The complete predicate includes the verb and all the words that go with it. If a sentence is missing a subject, a predicate, or both, then it is a **sentence fragment.** The missing part(s) must be added in order to make the sentence complete.

Original: I had French class today. In Mr. Bueller's room.
("In Mr. Bueller's room" is a sentence fragment because it is missing a subject and a predicate.)

Revised: I had French class today. It was in Mr. Bueller's room.
(This is now a complete sentence because it contains the subject "It" and the predicate "was in Mr. Bueller's room.")

PRACTICE Decide whether the following sentence fragments (in bold) are missing a subject, a predicate, or both. Then insert the missing parts.

1. I went to homeroom. **Then to English class.**
2. **Saw Teresa in the hall.** She walked the other way.
3. After English class, I had math. **My weakest subject.**
4. Teresa and I get along well. **In most ways.**

For more help with sentence fragments, see page R64 in the ***Grammar Handbook.***

The Last Dog

Short Story by Katherine Paterson

Why are pets good COMPANIONS?

ALABAMA STANDARDS

READING & LIT STANDARDS

1.b Determining sequence of events

6.a Classifying plot elements

KEY IDEA For many of us, pets are an important part of our lives. We feed them and care for them and often consider them to be a part of the family, but what do we get in return? Some would say that pets reward us with their **companionship**—their affection, loyalty, and good company. In "The Last Dog," a boy's powerful bond with a puppy helps teach him an important lesson.

LIST IT In a small group, make a list of reasons pets are good companions. To get started, use a list like the one shown. Then share your list with other groups.

● LITERARY ANALYSIS: SETTING

Setting is where and when a story happens. Sometimes the setting of a story is obvious. In the story you're about to read, however, you will need to look for details to help you understand the setting. Here are some details to look for:

- details about scenery and weather
- details about buildings, clothing, culture, and technology

As you read, note these and other details about where and when the story takes place.

Review: **Plot**

■ READING SKILL: IDENTIFY SEQUENCE

A plot is made up of many events. The **sequence,** or order, of the events is important to understanding the story. These words and phrases are often clues to the sequence of events:

first **then** **later** **in the past**

While events are often presented in the order in which they occur, sometimes the action is interrupted to present a scene from an earlier time. This is called a **flashback.** When you come across a flashback, notice any new information.

As you read, keep track of the sequence by recording important events on a sequence chart like the one shown.

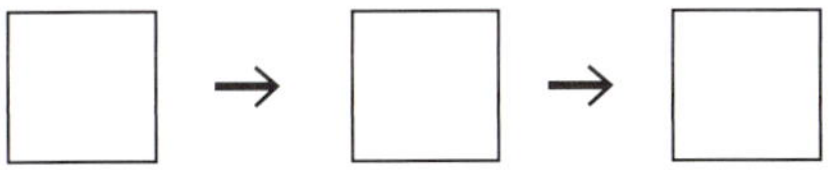

Review: **Compare and Contrast**

▲ VOCABULARY IN CONTEXT

Katherine Paterson uses the following words in her story about a futuristic world. See how many you know. Make a chart like the one shown, and put each vocabulary word in the appropriate column.

WORD LIST			
	copious	foray	posterity
	disembodied	foresighted	reproof
	evasive	languish	

Know Well	*Think I Know*	*Don't Know at All*

Author Online

"A Weird Little Kid"

Katherine Paterson
born 1932

Sometimes an outsider has an interesting way of looking at things. Katherine Paterson is convinced that as the child of U.S. missionaries in China, she learned valuable lessons about life. But being an outsider wasn't always easy. After returning to the United States at the age of five, Paterson and her family moved 18 times. She remembers feeling "small, poor, and foreign" on the playground. She was, in her own words, "a weird little kid," but she states today that "there are few things, apparently, more helpful to a writer than having once been a weird little kid."

MORE ABOUT THE AUTHOR
For more on Katherine Paterson, visit the **Literature Center** at **ClassZone.com.**

Background

Science Fiction In a work of science fiction, a writer combines real scientific information with elements from his or her imagination to create an altered universe. Science fiction stories typically take place in the distant future—in outer space or on a changed Earth. Plots often center on challenges characters face in these unusual settings.

THE LAST DOG

KATHERINE PATERSON

Brock approached the customs gate. Although he did not reach for the scanner, a feeling it might have labeled "excitement" made him tremble. His fingers shook as he punched in his number on the inquiry board. "This is highly irregular, Brock 095670038," the **disembodied** voice said. "What is your reason for external travel?"

Brock took a deep breath. "Scientific research," he replied. He didn't need to be told that his behavior was "irregular." He'd never heard of anyone doing research outside the dome—actual rather than virtual research. "I—I've been cleared by my podmaster and the Research Team. . . ."

"Estimated time of return?" So, he wasn't to be questioned further.

"Uh, 1800 hours."

"Are you wearing the prescribed dry suit with helmet and gloves?"

"Affirmative."[1]

"You should be equipped with seven hundred fifty milliliters of liquid and food tablets for one day travel."

"Affirmative." Brock patted the sides of the dry suit to be sure. **A**

"Remember to drink sparingly. Water supply is limited." Brock nodded. He tried to lick his parched lips, but his whole mouth felt dry. "Is that understood?"

"Affirmative." Was he hoping customs would stop him? If he was, they didn't seem to be helping him. Well, this was what he wanted, wasn't it? To go outside the dome.

"Turn on the universal locator, Brock 095670038, and proceed to gate."

Why weren't they questioning him further? Were they eager for him to go? Ever since he'd said out loud in group speak that he wanted to go outside the dome, people had treated him strangely—that session with the podmaster and then the interview with the representative

ANALYZE VISUALS
How would you describe the **setting** shown in this painting?

disembodied
(dĭs'ĕm-bŏ'dēd)
adj. separated from or lacking a body
disembody *v.*

A SETTING
Reread lines 1–16. What does the unusual technology in the dome suggest about the time in which the story takes place?

1. **affirmative** (ə-fûr'mə-tĭv): formal or scientific word for *yes.*

It was then, in the middle of post-*pecnec* satisfaction, that he heard the new sound. Like that programmed into a robopet, yet different. He struggled to his feet. The dry suit from storage was certainly awkward when you wanted to stand up or sit down. Nothing on the scanner indicated danger, so he went into the scrubby woods toward the sound. And stopped abruptly.

Something was lying under the shadow of a tree. Something about a meter long. It was furred and quite still. The sound was not coming from it. And then he saw the small dog—the puppy. He was sure it was a puppy, nosing the stiff body of what must once have been its mother, making the little crying sounds that he'd heard from the brook. Later, much later, he realized that he should have been wary. If the older dog had died of some extradomal disease, the puppy might have been a carrier. But at the time, all he could think of was the puppy, a small creature who had lost its mother. **G**

He'd found out about mothers from the Virtuals. Mothers were extinct in the dome. Children were conceived and born in the lab and raised in units of twelve in the pods, presided over by a bank of computers and the podmaster. Nuclear families, as everyone knew, had been wasteful of time, energy, and space. There was an old proverb: The key to survival is efficiency. So though Brock could guess the puppy was "sad" (like that fictions person, Jo, whose podmate expired), he didn't know what missing a mother would feel like. And who would whimper for a test tube?

Brock had never seen a dog, of course, but he'd seen plenty of dog breed descriptions on the science/history virtuals. Dogs had been abundant once. They filled the ancient fictions. They even had names

ANALYZE VISUALS
What do the details in the painting tell you about the **setting?**

G COMPARE AND CONTRAST
How has Brock's attitude about his adventure and his safety changed since he left the dome?

there—Lassie, Toto, Sounder. But now dogs were extinct, gone during the dark ages when the atmosphere had become warm and poisonous. The savages who had not had the intelligence or wealth to join the **foresighted** dome crafters had killed all animals wild or domesticated for food before they had eventually died out themselves. It was all in one of the very first virtual lessons. He had seen that one many times. He never confessed to anyone how, well, sad it made him feel.

foresighted (fôr′sī′tĭd) *adj.* having the ability to anticipate the future and prepare for it

But obviously, dogs were not quite extinct. Cautiously, he moved toward the small one.

"Alert. Alert. Scanning unknown object."

Brock pushed the off button. "Are you sure you want to turn off scanner?"

"Affirmative." He stuck the scanner into his pouch.

The puppy had lifted its head at the sound of his voice. It looked at him, head cocked, as though deciding whether to run or stay.

"It's all right, dog," Brock said soothingly. "I won't hurt you." He stayed still. He didn't want to frighten the little beast. If it ran, he wasn't sure he'd be able to catch it in his clumsy dry suit.

Slowly he extended his gloved hand. The dog backed away anxiously, but when Brock kept the hand extended, the puppy slowly crept toward him and sniffed, making whimpering sounds. It wasn't old enough to be truly afraid, it seemed. The pup licked his glove tentatively, then backed away again. It was looking for food, and plasticine gloves weren't going to satisfy.

Brock looked first at the dead mother whose source of nourishment must have long dried up, then around the landscape. What would a dog eat? A puppy on its own? He took off his glove and reached through his pouch into the inside pocket that held his pellet supply. Making every move slow and deliberate so as not to startle the dog, he held out a pellet. The dog came to his hand, licked it, then the pellet. It wrinkled its nose. Brock laughed. He didn't need the scanner now to tell him that what he felt was "pleasure." He loved the feel of the rough tongue on his palm and the little furred face, questioning him.

"It's all right, fellow. You can eat it." **H**

H SEQUENCE
What sequence of events leads to Brock's touching the puppy?

As though understanding, the pup gulped down the pellet. Then looked around for more, not realizing that it had just bolted down a whole meal. When the dog saw there was no more coming, it ran over to the brook. Brock watched in horror as it put its head right down into the poisonous stream and lapped noisily.

"Don't!" Brock cried.

The puppy turned momentarily at the sound, then went back to drinking, as though it was the most normal thing in the world. Well, it was, for the dog. Where else would a creature in the wild get liquid? If the streams were not all dried up, they must have learned to tolerate the water. But then, it was breathing the poisoned atmosphere, wasn't it?

Why hadn't it hit Brock before? This was a fully organic creature on the outside *without any life support system.* What could that mean? Some amazing mutation[8] must have occurred, making it possible for at least some creatures to breathe the outside atmosphere and drink its poisoned water. Those who couldn't died, those who could survived and got stronger. Even the ancient scientist Darwin[9] knew that. And Brock had come upon one of these magnificent mutants!

SETTING
Reread lines 209–220. How is finding the puppy changing what Brock has always believed about the outside?

The puppy whimpered and looked up at Brock with large, trusting eyes. How could he think of it as a mutant specimen? It was a puppy. One who had lost its mother. What would it eat? There was no sign of food for a carnivore.[10] Perhaps way back in the mountains some small mammals had also survived, keeping the food chain going, but the puppy would not live long enough to find its way there, much less know how to hunt with its mother gone. For the first time in his life something deep inside Brock reached out toward another creature. The thought of the puppy **languishing** here by the side of its dead parent until it, too . . .

languish (lăng'gwĭsh) *v.* to remain unattended or be neglected

"Your name is Brog, all right?" The ancient astronomers had named stars after themselves. He had discovered something just as wonderful. Didn't he have the right to name it sort of after himself while preserving the puppy's uniqueness? "Don't worry, Brog. I won't let you starve."

Which is why Brock appeared at the customs portal after dark, the front of his dry suit stained, carrying a wriggling *Canis familiaris*[11] of uncertain breed.

If there had been any way to smuggle the dog in, Brock would have. But he couldn't for the life of him figure out how. As it was, every alarm in the area went off when he stepped into the transitional cubicle.[12] The disembodied voice of the monitor queried him:

"Welcome back, Brock 095670038. You're late."

"Affirmative."

"And you are carrying contraband."

"I pulled a leaf."

"Deposit same in quarantine bins."

"Affirmative."

"Sensors denote warm-blooded presence not on official roster."

"I found a dog," Brock mumbled.

---

8. **mutation** (myo͞o-tā'shən): a change within a creature's genes that results in a new trait or characteristic.
9. **Darwin:** Charles Darwin (1809–1882) was a British naturalist who founded the theory of evolution based on natural selection.
10. **carnivore** (kär'nə-vôr'): a flesh-eating animal.
11. ***Canis familiaris*** (kă'nĭs fə-mĭl-ē-âr'əs): the scientific name for the domesticated, or household, dog.
12. **transitional cubicle:** a small compartment where one is examined before moving from one environment into the next.

"Repeat."

"A dog."

"*Canis familiaris* is extinct."

"Well, maybe it's just a robopet that got out somehow."

"Correction. Robopets are bloodless. Leave dry suit for sterilization and proceed to quarantine inspection."

The officials in quarantine inspection, who rarely had anything to inspect, were at first nervous and then, as they watched the puppy happily licking Brock's face, interested despite themselves. An actual dog! None of them had ever seen one, of course, and Brock's dog was so much, well, more vital than a robopet. And although, on later reflection, they knew they should have terminated or expelled it, they couldn't quite bring themselves to do so that night.

"It will have to go to Research," the chief inspector finally declared.

"Permission requested to hand carry the dog known as Brog to Research," Brock said. There was a bit of an argument about that. Several inspectors sought the honor, but the chief declared that Brock, having shed his dry suit and being already contaminated, should be placed with the dog in a hermetically sealed air car and transported to Research. **J**

The scientists in Research were predictably amazed to see a live *Canis familiaris.* But being scientists and more objective than the lower-grade quarantine inspectors, they kept a safe distance both physically and psychically[13] from the creature. Only the oldest scientist, dressed in proper protective clothing, came into the laboratory with Brock and the dog.

ANALYZE VISUALS
Look at the boy's expression. What can you **infer** about his feelings toward the puppy?

J SEQUENCE
What events happen after Brock finds the puppy? As you read, record the sequence on your chart.

13. **psychically** (sī′kĭk-lē): in a manner related to the mind or spirit.

He scanned and poked and prodded the poor little fellow until it began to whimper in protest.

"Brog needs to rest," said Brock, interrupting the scientist in the midst of his inspection. "She's (for by this time gender had been indisputably established) had a hard day. And if there's some actual food available—she's not used to pellets."

"Of course, of course," said one of the researchers through the speaker in the observation booth. "How thoughtless. Send someone out for a McLike burger without sauce. She may regard it as meat. Anyhow, it will seem more like food to her than a pellet, affirmative, Brock?"

The scientists, Brock soon realized, were looking to him for advice. He was, after all, the discoverer of the last dog. It gave him sudden scientific status. Brock had sense enough to take advantage of this. After Brog had swallowed the McLike burger in three quick gulps, Brock insisted that he be allowed to stay with Brog, so that he might interact and sleep with her. "She's not like us," he explained. "She's used to tumbling about and curling up with other warm bodies. In the old myths," he added, "puppies separated from their litters cried all night long. She will need constant interaction with another warm-blooded creature or she might well die of," he loved using his new vocabulary, "'loneliness.'"

The scientists agreed. After all, research was rather like quarantine, and since Brock had touched the dog ungloved and unprotected, he might well have picked up some germ from her. It was better to keep them both isolated in the research lab where proper precautions would be taken.

For nearly a week, Brock lived with Brog in the research center, eating McLike burgers, playing "fetch," teaching Brog to "sit," "heel," "come"—all the commands he could cull from the ancient texts. The dog quickly learned to obey Brock's commands, but it wasn't the automatic response of a robopet. Brog delighted in obedience. She wanted to please Brock, and those few times when she was too busy nosing about the lab and failed to obey instantly, those times when Brock's voice took on a sharp tone of **reproof,** the poor little thing put her tail between her legs, looked up at him with sorrowful eyes, begging to be forgiven. Brock was tempted to speak sharply to her even when there was no need, for the sight of her drooping ears and tail, her mournful eyes was so dear to him that he did what Travis Coates had done to Old Yeller.[14] He hugged her. There was no other way to explain it. He simply put his arms around her and held her to his chest while she beat at him with her tail and licked his face raw. Out of the corner of his eye he was aware that one of the scientists was watching. Well, let him watch. Nothing was as wonderful as feeling this warmth toward another creature.

reproof (rĭ-pro͞of') *n.* criticism for a fault

14. **Travis Coates . . . Old Yeller:** In the novel *Old Yeller,* Old Yeller is a stray dog who becomes friends with 14-year-old Travis.

For the first week, the researchers seemed quite content to observe dog and boy from their glass-paneled observation booth and speak **copious** notes into their computers. Only the oldest of them would come into the lab and actually touch the alien creature, and he always wore a sterile protective suit with gloves. The others claimed it would interfere with objectivity if they got close to the dog, but they all seemed to behave positively toward Brog. No mention was made to Brock of his own less than objective behavior. So Brock was astounded to awake in the middle of the night to the sounds of an argument. Someone had forgotten to turn off the communication system. K

copious (kō′pē-əs) *adj.* more than enough; plentiful

K SEQUENCE How long have Brock and Brog been living in the dome when the argument occurs?

"Cloning[15]—it's the only thing to do. If she's the last, we owe it to **posterity** to keep the line going."

posterity (pŏ-stĕr′ĭ-tē) *n.* future generations

"And how are we going to raise a pack of dogs in a dome? One is nearly eating and drinking us out of test tube and petri dish. We can't go on this way. As drastic as it may seem, we have to be realistic. Besides, no one has had the chance to do actual experiments since the dark ages. Haven't you ever, just once, yearned to compare virtual research with actual?"

"What about the boy? He won't agree. Interfacing daily with the dog, he's become crippled by primal urges."

"Can you think what chaos might ensue if a flood of primordial emotions[16] were to surface in a controlled environment such as ours?" another asked. "Apparently, emotions are easily triggered by interactions with primitive beasts, like dogs."

"Shh. Not now. The speaker is—" The system clicked off. L

L SEQUENCE What are the scientists planning to do to Brog? As you read, note on your chart the events that follow.

But Brock had already heard. He knew he had lost anything resembling scientific objectivity. He was no longer sure objectivity was a desirable trait. He rather enjoyed being flooded by "primordial emotions." But he was more worried for Brog than for himself. It wasn't hard to figure out what the scientists meant by "actual experiments." Cloning would be bad enough. Ten dogs who looked just like Brog so no one would know how special, how truly unique Brog was. But experiments! They'd cut her open and examine her internal organs, the way scientists had in the dark ages. They'd prod her with electric impulses and put chips in her brain. They'd try to change her personality or modify her behavior. They'd certainly try to make her eat and drink less!

In the dark, he put his arm around Brog and drew her close. He loved the terrible smell of her breath and the way she snored when she slept. They'd probably fix that, too.

The next day he played sick. Brog, faithful dog that she was, hung around him whimpering, licking his face. The scientists showed no

15. **cloning:** the scientific process of creating several identical plants or animals from a single ancestor.

16. **primal urges . . . primordial** (prī-môr′dē-əl) **emotions:** feelings or desires that have existed from the beginning of humankind.

particular concern. They were too busy plotting what they might do with Brog.

Brock crept to the nearest terminal in the lab. It was already logged in. The scientists had been doing nothing but research on *Canis familiaris.* COMMON CANINE DISEASES. Brock scrolled down the list with descriptions. No, *distemper* wouldn't do. The first symptom was loss of appetite. He couldn't make Brog fake that. On and on it went—no, *heartworms* wouldn't do. What he needed was a disease that might affect *Homo sapiens*[17] as well as *Canis familiaris.* Here it was! "Rabies: A viral disease occurring in animals and humans, esp. in dogs and wolves. Transmitted by bite or scratch. The early stages of the disease are most dangerous, for an otherwise healthy and friendly appearing animal will suddenly bite without provocation."

Rabies was it! Somehow he would have to make Brog bite him. There was no antirabies serum in the dome, he felt sure. There were no animals in the dome. Why would they use precious space to store an unneeded medication? So they'd have to expel him as well as Brog for fear of spreading the disease. He shivered, then shook himself. No matter what lay on the outside, he could not stand to go back to the life he had lived in the dome before he met Brog. Ⓜ

Ⓜ **SETTING**
How does the setting inside the dome help Brock make his decision?

He crept back to bed, pulling the covers over Brog. When one of the scientists came into the observation booth, Brock pinched Brog's neck as hard as he could. Nothing. He pinched again, harder. Brog just snuggled closer, slobbering on his arm.

Disgusted, Brock got out of bed. Brog hopped down as well, rubbing against his leg. Pinching obviously was not going to do it. While the scientist on duty in the booth was bending over a computer terminal, Brock brought his foot down on Brog's paw. A tiny *yip* was all he got from that cruel effort—not enough sound even to make the man look up.

"Feeling better, Brock 095670038?" The oldest researcher had come into the lab.

"Affirmative," Brock answered.

"And how are you, puppy-wuppy?" The old man tickled Brog under her chin with his gloved hand. *If I were a dog, I'd bite someone like that,* thought Brock, but Brog, of course, simply licked the researcher's glove and wagged her tail.

That was when he got his great idea. He waited to execute it until the proper moment. For the first time, all the scientists had gathered in the lab, all of them in protective garb, some of them twitching nervously in their chairs. They were sitting in a circle around Brock and Brog, explaining what must be done.

---

17. ***Homo sapiens*** (hō'mō sā'pē-ənz): the scientific name for the species of human beings now on Earth.

"It has to be done for the sake of science," they began. Then they went on to, "For the sake of the dome community, which is always, as you well know, short on food, and particularly short on water." Brock listened to their arguments, nodding solemnly, pretending to agree. "It won't be as if she'll really be gone, you know. We've made virtuals of her—a special series just for you to keep. You can virtually play with her whenever you like."

That was the cue. Brock turned and bit Brog on the tail so hard that the blood started. Brog, surprised and enraged, spun around and bit Brock on the nose.

There was a shocked silence. Every scientist leaned backward, body pressed hard against his or her chair back. Every eye was on the two of them.

"I—I don't know what got into me," Brock said. "I've been feeling very weird." The scientists continued to stare. "I was checking the historical records. . . ."

All of the scientists fled the room. Someone ran to a computer terminal. When Brock offered to take Brog out of the dome and let her loose in the mountains, no one argued. Neither did they say, "Hurry back," or even, "Take care." No one came close as he loaded his pouch with water and food pellets. The customs gate monitor asked no questions. N

Out of sight of the dome, Brog was delirious with joy, jumping and running about in circles around Brock's boots. Why wasn't the

N SEQUENCE
How does Brock get the scientists to release him and Brog?

ONLINE ARTICLE Robotic pets, such as the ones in the dome, are not just futuristic fantasy. This news article describes a contemporary project that is testing whether robotic dogs can bring joy to senior citizens.

BACK FORWARD STOP REFRESH HOME PRINT

E-mail This | Print This | Save This | Subscribe

'Spot' Goes High-Tech

Researchers Try Robotic Pets as Companions for the Elderly

Researchers in Indiana are trying to find out if robots —which no one has to feed or walk—can do the same job as flesh and blood animals.

Rosewalk Common is an assisted living community for seniors in Lafayette, Indiana. Rose Lawson, 90, has lived at Rosewalk for four years and recently joined other residents to meet "Aibo" (pronounced "I-bo"), a frisky, silver and black robotic dog.

Aibo made its way around a circle of seated residents, playing fetch, responding to spoken commands, sitting in laps to be petted—and winning friends.

"Do you like me? Do you like me?" Lawson asked Aibo. The robot responded with an electronic "Ohhh," winning a big smile from Lawson. . . .

Can Robots Make People Happier?

The robotic dogs were brought to Rosewalk by researchers at Indiana's Purdue University as part of a **project** to determine whether robots can make people happier.

Alan M. Beck, a professor at Purdue and director of the **Center for Human-Animal Bond** at the university's veterinary school, said one possible benefit may be better socialization.

"We find people who in nursing home settings might be socially isolated and don't routinely chat with each other have something to talk about together, to have fun, to have reminiscences," said Beck. . . .

Programmed to Generate Human Feelings

Robotic dogs are programmed to respond to commands, to wag their tails if told they are "good." All of this is supposed to lull humans into feeling . . . attached—to a robot.

The very concept of robots that seduce people into thinking they are real is just too much for sociologist Sherry Turkle, director of the **Initiative on Technology and Self** at the Massachusetts Institute of Technology.

"I think we should take it as a wake-up call and really say, 'Now, why are we giving robot pets to old people?' And the answer, I think, is that we really have been struggling to figure out how to give enough people to old people."

Assistant professor Nancy Edwards, of the Purdue School of Nursing, acknowledges the preference of human contact. But she still sees value in the Aibo study. "We know human interaction is best, we know human-animal [interaction] is probably second, but if these people are having no interaction, what we're saying is, will some interaction with a robot help in some way?"

"You can see smiling, laughing, remembering of good things, and talking among each other," said Beck. "This is more than just diversion. This is kind of a therapeutic event, where people really, I think, benefit from the experience."

Thank You, M'am

Short Story by Langston Hughes

Who sees the BEST *in you?*

ALABAMA STANDARDS

READING & LIT STANDARDS
1.d Applying self-monitoring strategies
6.a Classifying plot elements including conflict

KEY IDEA Have you ever gone through a time when it seemed like you couldn't do anything right? If so, then you know how important it is to have someone have faith in you. When a friend, a family member, or a teacher believes you can do better, it can help you try harder instead of giving up. In "Thank You, M'am," a woman sees **potential**—or possibility—where others might see a problem.

QUICKWRITE Create a web of people you know who see the best in you. Then explain why you have included these people. In what ways do they show their belief in you?

LITERARY ANALYSIS: CONFLICT

There is no story without plot, and there is no plot without **conflict.** A story's plot centers on conflict, or the struggle between opposing forces.

- An **external conflict** is a character's struggle against an outside force. For example, a character may struggle against nature or against another character.
- An **internal conflict** takes place inside the character. For example, a character may struggle between wanting something and knowing that taking it is wrong.

Stories often contain more than one conflict. As you read "Thank You, M'am," look for examples of both types of conflict.

READING SKILL: MAKE INFERENCES

When you make an **inference,** you use your reason and experience to guess at what a writer doesn't say directly. Combining clues in a passage with your own knowledge helps you understand what characters are feeling and thinking. As you read "Thank You, M'am," make inferences to better understand the characters. Record your inferences on a chart like the one shown.

Detail About Character	*What I Infer*
Mrs. Jones holds Roger but lets him stoop to pick up her purse.	*Mrs. Jones is trying to decide whether to trust Roger.*

VOCABULARY IN CONTEXT

The following words helped Langston Hughes write a story about a boy facing a serious conflict. To see how many words you already know, use them to complete the sentences.

WORD LIST barren frail mistrust presentable

1. Don't _____ him; he will keep his promise.
2. Because he was _____, the hard work tired him.
3. The _____ room was a source of loneliness.
4. He wanted to look _____ for the assembly.

Author Online

A Fascinating Journey As a child being raised by his grandmother in Lawrence, Kansas, Langston Hughes began a lifelong exploration of literature and blues music. He later went to Columbia University, worked in hotels, and traveled the world as a cook's assistant on freighters. Hughes was first recognized as a poet while working as a busboy. He left his poems at a table where the poet Vachel Lindsay was dining. Lindsay promoted the young poet's work, and Hughes's career was launched. Langston Hughes went on to become an influential writer of the 20th century.

Langston Hughes
1902–1967

The People's Poet After being discovered, Hughes went on to write novels, short stories, and plays as well as poems. Hughes's work shows a special understanding of everyday people—people who may not be famous or rich but whose lives are inspiring and valuable nonetheless.

MORE ABOUT THE AUTHOR
For more on Langston Hughes, visit the **Literature Center** at **ClassZone.com.**

Background

Harlem "Thank You, M'am" takes place in Harlem, a section of New York City. In the early 1900s, Harlem attracted many African-American writers. The stimulating community had a deep influence on their work.

Thank You, M'am

Langston Hughes

She was a large woman with a large purse that had everything in it but hammer and nails. It had a long strap, and she carried it slung across her shoulder. It was about eleven o'clock at night, and she was walking alone, when a boy ran up behind her and tried to snatch her purse. The strap broke with the single tug the boy gave it from behind. But the boy's weight and the weight of the purse combined caused him to lose his balance so, instead of taking off full blast as he had hoped, the boy fell on his back on the sidewalk, and his legs flew up. The large woman simply turned around and kicked him right square in his blue-jeaned sitter. Then she reached down, picked the boy up by his shirt front, and shook him until his teeth rattled. **A**

After that the woman said, "Pick up my pocketbook, boy, and give it here."

She still held him. But she bent down enough to permit him to stoop and pick up her purse. Then she said, "Now ain't you ashamed of yourself?"

Firmly gripped by his shirt front, the boy said, "Yes'm."

The woman said, "What did you want to do it for?"

The boy said, "I didn't aim to."

She said, "You a lie!"

By that time two or three people passed, stopped, turned to look, and some stood watching.

"If I turn you loose, will you run?" asked the woman.

A CONFLICT
Who is in conflict and why?

ANALYZE VISUALS
Look at the woman in the painting. What might you **infer** about her personality?

Faith Ringgold (1977), Alice Neel. Oil on canvas, 48″ × 36″. Private collection. © 2004 Estate of Alice Neel/Courtesy Robert Miller Gallery, New York/Philadelphia Museum of Art, Special Exhibition.

LITERARY ANALYSIS: SUSPENSE

When you feel growing tension and excitement as you read or watch a movie, that feeling is called **suspense.** Sometimes writers build suspense by using **foreshadowing,** hints or clues about events that will happen later. Foreshadowing can occur when a character makes an unusual statement or issues a strong warning. As you read "Rikki-tikki-tavi," notice how the author builds suspense and makes you want to keep reading. Also notice examples of foreshadowing.

Review: **Conflict**

READING STRATEGY: PREDICT

A **prediction** is a reasonable guess about what will happen over the course of a story. Predicting helps you stay involved as you read. To make predictions, ask yourself:

- What do I already know about the setting and plot?
- On the basis of their words and actions, what might characters do in the future? What events might result?

As you read, write predictions in a chart like the one shown.

Clues from the Story	*Predictions*
Teddy's mother takes Rikki-tikki home.	*Rikki-tikki will become a part of Teddy's family.*

Review: **Cause and Effect**

VOCABULARY IN CONTEXT

Rudyard Kipling uses the following boldfaced words in telling his tale of bravery. Restate each sentence, using a different word or phrase for the boldfaced word.

1. She made a **valiant** effort to overcome hardship.
2. She tried to **revive** the unconscious woman.
3. He **cunningly** outsmarted the other contestants.
4. Do not **cower** in scary situations.
5. The dog had a peculiar limping **gait.**
6. The **fledgling** made its first trip outside the nest.
7. We offered them **consolation** in their sorrow.
8. Be careful not to **singe** the hair on your arms.

Author Online

A Man of Two Countries When Rudyard Kipling was five, he left India, where he had been born, to go to school in England. India, however, would always be a powerful attraction for Kipling; he lived there again for a while as an adult, and many of his stories take place there. In works such as *The Jungle Book,* Kipling introduced a vivid cast of animal and human characters. Kipling's adventure stories gained worldwide popularity. In 1907, he received the Nobel Prize in literature.

Rudyard Kipling
1865–1936

MORE ABOUT THE AUTHOR
For more on Rudyard Kipling, visit the **Literature Center** at **ClassZone.com.**

Background

The Mongoose and the Cobra The mongoose and the cobra are a pair of natural enemies—a pair that will fight to the death. The mongoose, a mammal growing to a length of only 16 inches, seems hardly a match for the poisonous cobra, a snake that averages six feet in length. But the mongoose's speed and agility make it a powerful fighter.

Life in Colonial India This story is set in India during the late 1800s, when Great Britain ruled India. Many British families lived in bungalows—open, airy houses that permitted snakes to enter easily. In such an environment, mongooses were valuable assets.

Rikki-*tikki*-tavi

Rudyard Kipling

This is the story of the great war that Rikki-tikki-tavi fought single-handed, through the bathrooms of the big bungalow in Segowlee cantonment.[1] Darzee, the tailorbird, helped him, and Chuchundra,[2] the muskrat, who never comes out into the middle of the floor but always creeps round by the wall, gave him advice; but Rikki-tikki did the real fighting.

He was a mongoose, rather like a little cat in his fur and his tail but quite like a weasel in his head and his habits. His eyes and the end of his restless nose were pink; he could scratch himself anywhere he pleased with any leg, front or back, that he chose to use; he could fluff up his tail till it looked like a bottle-brush, and his war cry as he scuttled through the long grass was: *Rikk-tikk-tikki-tikki-tchk!* **A**

One day, a high summer flood washed him out of the burrow where he lived with his father and mother and carried him, kicking and clucking, down a roadside ditch. He found a little wisp of grass floating there and clung to it till he lost his senses. When he **revived,** he was lying in the hot sun on the middle of a garden path, very draggled indeed, and a small boy was saying, "Here's a dead mongoose. Let's have a funeral."

"No," said his mother, "let's take him in and dry him. Perhaps he isn't really dead."

ANALYZE VISUALS
What might you **infer** about the people who live in this house?

A PREDICT
Recall the information in the **Background** section on page 73. Whom will Rikki-tikki go to war with? Record this and other predictions in your chart as you read.

revive (rĭ-vīv′) *v.* to return to life or consciousness

1. **Segowlee** (sə-gou′lē) **cantonment:** area in India that was home to a British military base.
2. **Chuchundra** (chə-cho͝on′drə).

Illustrations © 1997 by Jerry Pinkney.

They took him into the house, and a big man picked him up between his finger and thumb and said he was not dead but half choked; so they wrapped him in cotton wool and warmed him over a little fire, and he opened his eyes and sneezed. "Now," said the big man (he was an Englishman who had just moved into the bungalow), "don't frighten him, and we'll see what he'll do."

It is the hardest thing in the world to frighten a mongoose, because he is eaten up from nose to tail with curiosity. The motto of all the mongoose family is "Run and Find Out"; and Rikki-tikki was a true mongoose. He looked at the cotton wool, decided that it was not good to eat, ran all round the table, sat up and put his fur in order, scratched himself, and jumped on the small boy's shoulder.

"Don't be frightened, Teddy," said his father. "That's his way of making friends."

"Ouch! He's tickling under my chin," said Teddy.

Rikki-tikki looked down between the boy's collar and neck, snuffed at his ear, and climbed down to the floor, where he sat rubbing his nose.

"Good gracious," said Teddy's mother, "and that's a wild creature! I suppose he's so tame because we've been kind to him."

"All mongooses are like that," said her husband. "If Teddy doesn't pick him up by the tail or try to put him in a cage, he'll run in and out of the house all day long. Let's give him something to eat."

They gave him a little piece of raw meat. Rikki-tikki liked it immensely; and when it was finished, he went out into the veranda and sat in the sunshine and fluffed up his fur to make it dry to the roots. Then he felt better.

"There are more things to find out about in this house," he said to himself, "than all my family could find out in all their lives. I shall certainly stay and find out." **B**

He spent all that day roaming over the house. He nearly drowned himself in the bathtubs, put his nose into the ink on a writing table, and burnt it on the end of the big man's cigar, for he climbed up in the big man's lap to see how writing was done. At nightfall he ran into Teddy's nursery to watch how kerosene lamps were lighted, and when Teddy went to bed, Rikki-tikki climbed up too; but he was a restless companion, because he had to get up and attend to every noise all through the night and find out what made it. Teddy's mother and father came in, the last thing, to look at their boy, and Rikki-tikki was awake on the pillow.

"I don't like that," said Teddy's mother; "he may bite the child."

"He'll do no such thing," said the father. "Teddy is safer with that little beast than if he had a bloodhound to watch him. If a snake came into the nursery now—" **C**

But Teddy's mother wouldn't think of anything so awful.

VISUAL VOCABULARY

veranda *n.* a long, open porch, usually with a roof

B CAUSE AND EFFECT
How does Rikki-tikki come to live in the bungalow?

C SUSPENSE
What might the father's words be **foreshadowing?**

Early in the morning Rikki-tikki came to early breakfast in the veranda, riding on Teddy's shoulder, and they gave him banana and some boiled egg; and he sat on all their laps one after the other, because every well-brought-up mongoose always hopes to be a house mongoose some day and have rooms to run about in; and Rikki-tikki's mother (she used to live in the general's house at Segowlee) had carefully told Rikki what to do if ever he came across white men.

Then Rikki-tikki went out into the garden to see what was to be seen. It was a large garden, only half-cultivated, with bushes, as big as summerhouses, of Marshal Niel roses, lime and orange trees, clumps of bamboos, and thickets of high grass. Rikki-tikki licked his lips. "This is a splendid hunting ground," he said, and his tail grew bottlebrushy at the thought of it; and he scuttled up and down the garden, snuffing here and there till he heard very sorrowful voices in a thorn bush. It was Darzee, the tailorbird, and his wife. They had made a beautiful nest by pulling two big leaves together and stitching them up the edges with fibers and had filled the hollow with cotton and downy fluff. The nest swayed to and fro, as they sat on the rim and cried.

"What is the matter?" asked Rikki-tikki.

"We are very miserable," said Darzee. "One of our babies fell out of the nest yesterday, and Nag ate him."

"H'm!" said Rikki-tikki, "that is very sad—but I am a stranger here. Who is Nag?"

Darzee and his wife only **cowered** down in the nest without answering, for from the thick grass at the foot of the bush there came a low hiss—a horrid, cold sound that made Rikki-tikki jump back two clear feet. Then inch by inch out of the grass rose up the head and spread hood[3] of Nag, the big black cobra, and he was five feet long from tongue to tail. When he had lifted one-third of himself clear of the ground, he stayed, balancing to and fro exactly as a dandelion tuft balances in the wind; and he looked at Rikki-tikki with the wicked snake's eyes that never change their expression, whatever the snake may be thinking of.

"Who is Nag?" said he. "*I* am Nag. The great god Brahm[4] put his mark upon all our people when the first cobra spread his hood to keep the sun off Brahm as he slept. Look, and be afraid!"

SOCIAL STUDIES CONNECTION

From 1858 to 1947, Britain ruled India. India gained its independence after decades of fighting for it.

cower (kou'ər) *v.* to crouch or shrink down in fear

3. **hood:** an expanded part on or near the head of an animal.
4. **Brahm** (bräm): another name for Brahma, creator of the universe in the Hindu religion.

ANALYZE VISUALS
Notice how the mongoose and the snake hold their bodies. Does either of these **characters** look particularly brave or scared?

He spread out his hood more than ever, and Rikki-tikki saw the spectacle mark on the back of it that looks exactly like the eye part of a hook-and-eye fastening. He was afraid for the minute, but it is impossible for a mongoose to stay frightened for any length of time; and though Rikki-tikki had never met a live cobra before, his mother had fed him on dead ones, and he knew that all a grown mongoose's business in life was to fight and eat snakes. Nag knew that too, and at the bottom of his cold heart, he was afraid.

"Well," said Rikki-tikki, and his tail began to fluff up again, "marks or no marks, do you think it is right for you to eat **fledglings** out of a nest?"

fledgling (flĕj′lĭng) *n.* a young bird that has recently grown its flight feathers

Nag was thinking to himself and watching the least little movement in the grass behind Rikki-tikki. He knew that mongooses in the garden meant death sooner or later for him and his family; but he wanted to get Rikki-tikki off his guard. So he dropped his head a little, and put it on one side.

"Let us talk," he said. "You eat eggs. Why should not I eat birds?"

"Behind you! Look behind you!" sang Darzee.

Rikki-tikki knew better than to waste time in staring. He jumped up in the air as high as he could go, and just under him whizzed by the head of

Nagaina,[5] Nag's wicked wife. She had crept up behind him as he was talking, to make an end of him; and he heard her savage hiss as the stroke missed. He came down almost across her back, and if he had been an old mongoose, he would have known that then was the time to break her back with one bite; but he was afraid of the terrible lashing return stroke of the cobra. He bit, indeed, but did not bite long enough; and he jumped clear of the whisking tail, leaving Nagaina torn and angry. **D**

"Wicked, wicked Darzee!" said Nag, lashing up as high as he could reach toward the nest in the thorn bush; but Darzee had built it out of reach of snakes, and it only swayed to and fro.

Rikki-tikki felt his eyes growing red and hot (when a mongoose's eyes grow red, he is angry), and he sat back on his tail and hind legs like a little kangaroo and looked all around him and chattered with rage. But Nag and Nagaina had disappeared into the grass. When a snake misses its stroke, it never says anything or gives any sign of what it means to do next. Rikki-tikki did not care to follow them, for he did not feel sure that he could manage two snakes at once. So he trotted off to the gravel path near the house and sat down to think. It was a serious matter for him. **E**

D SUSPENSE
Reread lines 111–125. Which details of Nagaina's attack on Rikki-tikki create tension?

E PREDICT
As you read, check the predictions you make. Was the prediction you made on page 74 correct?

If you read the old books of natural history, you will find they say that when the mongoose fights the snake and happens to get bitten, he runs off and eats some herb that cures him. That is not true. The victory is only a matter of quickness of eye and quickness of foot—snake's blow against mongoose's jump—and as no eye can follow the motion of a snake's head when it strikes, this makes things much more wonderful than any magic herb. Rikki-tikki knew he was a young mongoose, and it made him all the more pleased to think that he had managed to escape a blow from behind.

It gave him confidence in himself, and when Teddy came running down the path, Rikki-tikki was ready to be petted. But just as Teddy was stooping, something wriggled a little in the dust, and a tiny voice said, "Be careful. I am Death!" It was Karait,[6] the dusty brown snakeling that lies for choice on the dusty earth; and his bite is as dangerous as the cobra's. But he is so small that nobody thinks of him, and so he does the more harm to people.

Rikki-tikki's eyes grew red again, and he danced up to Karait with the peculiar rocking, swaying motion that he had inherited from his family. It looks very funny, but it is so perfectly balanced a **gait** that you can fly off from it at any angle you please; and in dealing with snakes this is an advantage.

gait (gāt) *n.* a manner of walking or moving on foot

If Rikki-tikki had only known, he was doing a much more dangerous thing than fighting Nag; for Karait is so small and can turn so quickly,

5. **Nagaina** (nä′gə-ē′nə).
6. **Karait** (kə-rīt′).

that unless Rikki bit him close to the back of the head, he would get the return stroke in his eye or his lip. But Rikki did not know: his eyes were all red, and he rocked back and forth, looking for a good place to hold. Karait struck out. Rikki jumped sideways and tried to run in, but the wicked little dusty gray head lashed within a fraction of his shoulder, and he had to jump over the body, and the head followed his heels close. **F**

Teddy shouted to the house, "Oh, look here! Our mongoose is killing a snake"; and Rikki-tikki heard a scream from Teddy's mother. His father ran out with a stick, but by the time he came up, Karait had lunged out once too far, and Rikki-tikki had sprung, jumped on the snake's back, dropped his head far between his forelegs, bitten as high up the back as he could get hold, and rolled away.

That bite paralyzed Karait, and Rikki-tikki was just going to eat him up from the tail, after the custom of his family at dinner, when he remembered that a full meal makes a slow mongoose; and if he wanted all his strength and quickness ready, he must keep himself thin. He went away for a dust bath under the castor-oil bushes, while Teddy's father beat the dead Karait. "What is the use of that?" thought Rikki-tikki; "I have settled it all."

And then Teddy's mother picked him up from the dust and hugged him, crying that he had saved Teddy from death; and Teddy's father said that he was a providence,[7] and Teddy looked on with big scared eyes. Rikki-tikki was rather amused at all the fuss, which, of course, he did not understand. Teddy's mother might just as well have petted Teddy for playing in the dust. Rikki was thoroughly enjoying himself. **G**

F SUSPENSE
Reread lines 156–163. What doesn't Rikki-tikki realize about Karait?

G CONFLICT
Which characters in this story have conflicts with the snakes in the garden?

That night at dinner, walking to and fro among the wineglasses on the table, he might have stuffed himself three times over with nice things; but he remembered Nag and Nagaina, and though it was very pleasant to be patted and petted by Teddy's mother and to sit on Teddy's shoulder, his eyes would get red from time to time, and he would go off into his long war cry of *"Rikk-tikk-tikki-tikki-tchk!"*

Teddy carried him off to bed and insisted on Rikki-tikki sleeping under his chin. Rikki-tikki was too well-bred to bite or scratch, but as soon as Teddy was asleep, he went off for his nightly walk around the house; and in the dark he ran up against Chuchundra, the muskrat, creeping around by the wall. Chuchundra is a brokenhearted little beast. He whimpers and cheeps all the night, trying to make up his mind to run into the middle of the room; but he never gets there.

"Don't kill me," said Chuchundra, almost weeping. "Rikki-tikki, don't kill me!"

"Do you think a snake killer kills muskrats?" said Rikki-tikki scornfully.

---

7. **providence:** blessing; something good given by God.

"Those who kill snakes get killed by snakes," said Chuchundra, more sorrowfully than ever. "And how am I to be sure that Nag won't mistake me for you some dark night?"

"There's not the least danger," said Rikki-tikki; "but Nag is in the garden, and I know you don't go there."

"My cousin Chua,[8] the rat, told me—" said Chuchundra, and then he stopped.

"Told you what?"

"H'sh! Nag is everywhere, Rikki-tikki. You should have talked to Chua in the garden."

"I didn't—so you must tell me. Quick, Chuchundra, or I'll bite you!"

Chuchundra sat down and cried till the tears rolled off his whiskers. "I am a very poor man," he sobbed. "I never had spirit enough to run out into the middle of the room. H'sh! I mustn't tell you anything. Can't you *hear,* Rikki-tikki?"

Rikki-tikki listened. The house was as still as still, but he thought he could just catch the faintest *scratch-scratch* in the world—a noise as faint as that of a wasp walking on a windowpane—the dry scratch of a snake's scales on brickwork. **H**

"That's Nag or Nagaina," he said to himself, "and he is crawling into the bathroom sluice.[9] You're right, Chuchundra; I should have talked to Chua."

He stole off to Teddy's bathroom, but there was nothing there, and then to Teddy's mother's bathroom. At the bottom of the smooth plaster wall, there was a brick pulled out to make a sluice for the bath water, and as Rikki-tikki stole in by the masonry curb where the bath is put, he heard Nag and Nagaina whispering together outside in the moonlight.

"When the house is emptied of people," said Nagaina to her husband, "*he* will have to go away, and then the garden will be our own again. Go in quietly, and remember that the big man who killed Karait is the first one to bite. Then come out and tell me, and we will hunt for Rikki-tikki together."

"But are you sure that there is anything to be gained by killing the people?" said Nag.

"Everything. When there were no people in the bungalow, did we have any mongoose in the garden? So long as the bungalow is empty, we are king and queen of the garden; and remember that as soon as our eggs in the melon bed hatch (as they may tomorrow), our children will need room and quiet." **I**

"I had not thought of that," said Nag. "I will go, but there is no need that we should hunt for Rikki-tikki afterward. I will kill the big man and his

H SUSPENSE
Reread lines 203–216. What details make the conversation between Chuchundra and Rikki-tikki suspenseful?

I PREDICT
Think about what Nag and Nagaina are planning to do. How do you think Rikki-tikki might respond?

---

8. **Chua** (cho͞o′ə).

9. **bathroom sluice** (slo͞os): an opening in a wall through which the water in a bathtub can be drained outdoors.

wife, and the child if I can, and come away quietly. Then the bungalow will be empty, and Rikki-tikki will go."

Rikki-tikki tingled all over with rage and hatred at this, and then Nag's head came through the sluice, and his five feet of cold body followed it. Angry as he was, Rikki-tikki was very frightened as he saw the size of the big cobra. Nag coiled himself up, raised his head, and looked into the bathroom in the dark, and Rikki could see his eyes glitter.

"Now, if I kill him here, Nagaina will know; and if I fight him on the open floor, the odds are in his favor. What am I to do?" said Rikki-tikki-tavi.

Nag waved to and fro, and then Rikki-tikki heard him drinking from the biggest water jar that was used to fill the bath. "That is good," said the snake. "Now, when Karait was killed, the big man had a stick. He may have that stick still, but when he comes in to bathe in the morning, he will not have a stick. I shall wait here till he comes. Nagaina—do you hear me?—I shall wait here in the cool till daytime."

There was no answer from outside, so Rikki-tikki knew Nagaina had gone away. Nag coiled himself down, coil by coil, around the bulge at the bottom of the water jar, and Rikki-tikki stayed still as death. After an hour he began to move, muscle by muscle, toward the jar. Nag was asleep, and Rikki-tikki looked at his big back, wondering which would be the best place for a good hold. "If I don't break his back at the first jump," said Rikki, "he can still fight; and if he fights—O Rikki!" He looked at the thickness of the neck below the hood, but that was too much for him; and a bite near the tail would only make Nag savage. **J**

J SUSPENSE
Why is the outcome of Rikki-tikki's fight with Nag uncertain?

"It must be the head," he said at last; "the head above the hood. And, when I am once there, I must not let go."

Then he jumped. The head was lying a little clear of the water jar, under the curve of it; and, as his teeth met, Rikki braced his back against the bulge of the red earthenware to hold down the head. This gave him just one second's purchase,[10] and he made the most of it. Then he was battered to and fro as a rat is shaken by a dog—to and fro on the floor, up

10. **purchase:** an advantage, such as a firm hold, to be used when applying power.

and down, and round in great circles; but his eyes were red, and he held on as the body cart-whipped over the floor, upsetting the tin dipper and the soap dish and the flesh brush, and banged against the tin side of the bath. **K**

As he held, he closed his jaws tighter and tighter, for he made sure he would be banged to death; and, for the honor of his family, he preferred to be found with his teeth locked. He was dizzy, aching, and felt shaken to pieces when something went off like a thunderclap just behind him; a hot wind knocked him senseless, and red fire **singed** his fur. The big man had been awakened by the noise and had fired both barrels of a shotgun into Nag just behind the hood.

Rikki-tikki held on with his eyes shut, for now he was quite sure he was dead; but the head did not move, and the big man picked him up and said, "It's the mongoose again, Alice; the little chap has saved *our* lives now." **L**

Then Teddy's mother came in with a very white face and saw what was left of Nag, and Rikki-tikki dragged himself to Teddy's bedroom and spent half the rest of the night shaking himself tenderly to find out whether he really was broken into forty pieces, as he fancied.

When morning came, he was very stiff but well pleased with his doings. "Now I have Nagaina to settle with, and she will be worse than five Nags, and there's no knowing when the eggs she spoke of will hatch. Goodness! I must go and see Darzee," he said.

Without waiting for breakfast, Rikki-tikki ran to the thorn bush where Darzee was singing a song of triumph at the top of his voice. The news of Nag's death was all over the garden, for the sweeper had thrown the body on the rubbish heap.

"Oh, you stupid tuft of feathers!" said Rikki-tikki angrily. "Is this the time to sing?"

"Nag is dead—is dead—is dead!" sang Darzee. "The **valiant** Rikki-tikki caught him by the head and held fast. The big man brought the bang stick, and Nag fell in two pieces! He will never eat my babies again."

"All that's true enough; but where's Nagaina?" said Rikki-tikki, looking carefully round him.

"Nagaina came to the bathroom sluice and called for Nag," Darzee went on; "and Nag came out on the end of a stick—the sweeper picked him up on the end of a stick and threw him upon the rubbish heap. Let us sing about the great, the red-eyed Rikki-tikki!" And Darzee filled his throat and sang.

"If I could get up to your nest, I'd roll your babies out!" said Rikki-tikki. "You don't know when to do the right thing at the right time. You're

K PREDICT
Thinking about how the **plot** has unfolded so far, predict what will happen next.

singe (sĭnj) *v.* to burn lightly

L CAUSE AND EFFECT
What happens because of Rikki-tikki's tight hold on Nag?

valiant (văl′yent) *adj.* brave; courageous

safe enough in your nest there, but it's war for me down here. Stop singing a minute, Darzee."

"For the great, the beautiful Rikki-tikki's sake I will stop," said Darzee. "What is it, O Killer of the terrible Nag?"

"Where is Nagaina, for the third time?"

"On the rubbish heap by the stables, mourning for Nag. Great is Rikki-tikki with the white teeth."

"Bother my white teeth! Have you ever heard where she keeps her eggs?"

"In the melon bed, on the end nearest the wall, where the sun strikes nearly all day. She hid them there weeks ago."

"And you never thought it worthwhile to tell me? The end nearest the wall, you said?"

"Rikki-tikki, you are not going to eat her eggs?"

"Not 'eat' exactly, no. Darzee, if you have a grain of sense, you will fly off to the stables and pretend that your wing is broken and let Nagaina chase you away to this bush. I must get to the melon bed, and if I went there now, she'd see me." **M**

M SUSPENSE
Why does Rikki-tikki's impatience with Darzee lend suspense to this scene?

Darzee was a featherbrained little fellow who could never hold more than one idea at a time in his head; and just because he knew that Nagaina's children were born in eggs like his own, he didn't think at first that it was fair to kill them. But his wife was a sensible bird, and she knew that cobra's eggs meant young cobras later on; so she flew off from the nest and left Darzee to keep the babies warm and continue his song about the death of Nag. Darzee was very like a man in some ways.

She fluttered in front of Nagaina by the rubbish heap and cried out, "Oh, my wing is broken! The boy in the house threw a stone at me and broke it." Then she fluttered more desperately than ever.

Nagaina lifted up her head and hissed, "You warned Rikki-tikki when I would have killed him. Indeed and truly, you've chosen a bad place to be lame in." And she moved toward Darzee's wife, slipping along over the dust.

"The boy broke it with a stone!" shrieked Darzee's wife.

"Well! It may be some **consolation** to you when you're dead to know that I shall settle accounts[11] with the boy. My husband lies on the rubbish heap this morning, but before night the boy in the house will lie very still. What is the use of running away? I am sure to catch you. Little fool, look at me!"

consolation
(kŏn′sə-lā′shən) *n.*
a comfort

Darzee's wife knew better than to do *that,* for a bird who looks at a snake's eyes gets so frightened that she cannot move. Darzee's wife fluttered on, piping sorrowfully, and never leaving the ground, and Nagaina quickened her pace. **N**

N CONFLICT
How do Darzee and his wife differ in their approach to the conflict with Nagaina?

Rikki-tikki heard them going up the path from the stables, and he raced for the end of the melon patch near the wall. There, in the warm litter above

11. **settle accounts:** even things out by getting revenge.

the melons, very **cunningly** hidden, he found twenty-five eggs, about the size of a bantam's eggs[12] but with whitish skins instead of shells.

"I was not a day too soon," he said, for he could see the baby cobras curled up inside the skin, and he knew that the minute they were hatched they could each kill a man or a mongoose. He bit off the tops of the eggs as fast as he could, taking care to crush the young cobras, and turned over the litter from time to time to see whether he had missed any. At last there were only three eggs left, and Rikki-tikki began to chuckle to himself when he heard Darzee's wife screaming.

"Rikki-tikki, I led Nagaina toward the house, and she has gone into the veranda and—oh, come quickly—she means killing!"

Rikki-tikki smashed two eggs and tumbled backward down the melon bed with the third egg in his mouth and scuttled to the veranda as hard as he could put foot to the ground. Teddy and his mother and father were there at early breakfast; but Rikki-tikki saw that they were not eating anything. They sat stone still, and their faces were white. Nagaina was coiled up on the matting by Teddy's chair, within easy striking distance of Teddy's bare leg; and she was swaying to and fro, singing a song of triumph.

"Son of the big man that killed Nag," she hissed, "stay still. I am not ready yet. Wait a little. Keep very still, all you three! If you move, I strike, and if you do not move, I strike. Oh, foolish people who killed my Nag!"

Teddy's eyes were fixed on his father, and all his father could do was to whisper, "Sit still, Teddy. You mustn't move. Teddy, keep still." O

Then Rikki-tikki came up and cried, "Turn round, Nagaina; turn and fight!"

"All in good time," said she, without moving her eyes. "I will settle my account with you presently. Look at your friends, Rikki-tikki. They are still and white. They are afraid. They dare not move, and if you come a step nearer, I strike."

"Look at your eggs," said Rikki-tikki, "in the melon bed near the wall. Go and look, Nagaina!"

The big snake turned half round and saw the egg on the veranda. "Ah-h! Give it to me," she said.

cunningly (kŭn′ĭng-lē) *adv.* in a clever way that is meant to trick or deceive

O SUSPENSE
At this point in the story, what questions are you waiting to have answered?

---

12. **bantam's eggs:** the eggs of a small hen.

Rikki-tikki put his paws one on each side of the egg, and his eyes were blood-red. "What price for a snake's egg? For a young cobra? For a young king cobra? For the last—the very last of the brood? The ants are eating all the others down by the melon bed."

Nagaina spun clear round, forgetting everything for the sake of the one egg; and Rikki-tikki saw Teddy's father shoot out a big hand, catch Teddy by the shoulder, and drag him across the little table with the teacups, safe and out of reach of Nagaina. **P**

P CAUSE AND EFFECT
Reread lines 395–406. What does Rikki-tikki do to save Teddy?

"Tricked! Tricked! Tricked! *Rikk-tck-tck!*" chuckled Rikki-tikki. "The boy is safe, and it was I—I—I that caught Nag by the hood last night in the bathroom." Then he began to jump up and down, all four feet together, his head close to the floor. "He threw me to and fro, but he could not shake me off. He was dead before the big man blew him in two. I did it! *Rikki-tikki-tck-tck!* Come then, Nagaina. Come and fight with me. You shall not be a widow long."

Nagaina saw that she had lost her chance of killing Teddy, and the egg lay between Rikki-tikki's paws. "Give me the egg, Rikki-tikki. Give me the last of my eggs, and I will go away and never come back," she said, lowering her hood.

"Yes, you will go away, and you will never come back, for you will go to the rubbish heap with Nag. Fight, widow! The big man has gone for his gun! Fight!"

Rikki-tikki was bounding all round Nagaina, keeping just out of reach of her stroke, his little eyes like hot coals. Nagaina gathered herself together and flung out at him. Rikki-tikki jumped up and backwards. Again and again and again she struck, and each time her head came with a whack on the matting of the veranda, and she gathered herself together like a watch spring. Then Rikki-tikki danced in a circle to get behind her, and Nagaina spun round to keep her head to his head, so that the rustle of her tail on the matting sounded like dry leaves blown along by the wind.

He had forgotten the egg. It still lay on the veranda, and Nagaina came nearer and nearer to it, till at last, while Rikki-tikki was drawing breath, she caught it in her mouth, turned to the veranda steps, and flew like an arrow down the path, with Rikki-tikki behind her. When the cobra runs for her life, she goes like a whiplash flicked across a horse's neck. Rikki-tikki knew that he must catch her, or all the trouble would begin again. **Q**

Q SUSPENSE
Reread lines 429–434. How does the suspense increase at this point?

She headed straight for the long grass by the thorn bush, and as he was running, Rikki-tikki heard Darzee still singing his foolish little song of triumph. But Darzee's wife was wiser. She flew off her nest as Nagaina came along and flapped her wings about Nagaina's head. If Darzee had helped, they might have turned her; but Nagaina only lowered her hood and went on. Still, the instant's delay brought Rikki-tikki up to her, and as she plunged into the rat hole where she and Nag used to live, his little white teeth were clenched on her tail, and he went down with her—and very few mongooses, however wise and old they may be, care to follow a cobra into its hole. **R**

R PREDICT
What problem does Rikki-tikki now face? On the basis of the details you've learned, what do you predict?

It was dark in the hole; and Rikki-tikki never knew when it might open out and give Nagaina room to turn and strike at him. He held on savagely and stuck out his feet to act as brakes on the dark slope of the hot, moist earth.

Then the grass by the mouth of the hole stopped waving, and Darzee said, "It is all over with Rikki-tikki! We must sing his death song. Valiant Rikki-tikki is dead! For Nagaina will surely kill him underground."

So he sang a very mournful song that he made up on the spur of the minute;[13] and just as he got to the most touching part, the grass quivered again, and Rikki-tikki, covered with dirt, dragged himself out of the hole leg by leg, licking his whiskers. Darzee stopped with a little shout. Rikki-tikki shook some of the dust out of his fur and sneezed. "It is all over," he said. "The widow will never come out again." And the red ants that live between the grass stems heard him and began to troop down one after another to see if he had spoken the truth.

Rikki-tikki curled himself up in the grass and slept where he was—slept and slept till it was late in the afternoon, for he had done a hard day's work. **S**

S CONFLICT
How is the conflict between Rikki-tikki and the cobras resolved?

"Now," he said, when he awoke, "I will go back to the house. Tell the coppersmith, Darzee, and he will tell the garden that Nagaina is dead."

The coppersmith is a bird who makes a noise exactly like the beating of a little hammer on a copper pot; and the reason he is always making it is because he is the town crier to every Indian garden and tells all the news to everybody who cares to listen. As Rikki-tikki went up the path, he heard his "attention" notes like a tiny dinner gong, and then the steady *"Ding-dong-tock!* Nag is dead—*dong!* Nagaina is dead! *Ding-dong-tock!"* That set all the birds in the garden singing and the frogs croaking, for Nag and Nagaina used to eat frogs as well as little birds.

When Rikki got to the house, Teddy and Teddy's mother (she looked very white still, for she had been fainting) and Teddy's father came out and almost cried over him; and that night he ate all that was given him till he could eat no more and went to bed on Teddy's shoulder, where Teddy's mother saw him when she came to look late at night.

"He saved our lives and Teddy's life," she said to her husband. "Just think, he saved all our lives."

Rikki-tikki woke up with a jump, for the mongooses are light sleepers.

"Oh, it's you," said he. "What are you bothering for? All the cobras are dead; and if they weren't, I'm here."

Rikki-tikki had a right to be proud of himself; but he did not grow too proud, and he kept that garden as a mongoose should keep it, with tooth and jump and spring and bite, till never a cobra dared show its head inside the walls.

13. **on the spur of the minute:** on a sudden impulse, without previous thought or planning.

Comprehension

ALABAMA STANDARDS

READING STANDARD
1.f Analyzing predictions

1. **Recall** Why is Rikki-tikki grateful to Teddy's family?
2. **Recall** Why does Rikki-tikki destroy Nagaina's eggs?
3. **Represent** At first, Teddy's mother doesn't want the mongoose too close to Teddy. Use a timeline to show the events that help Rikki-tikki prove himself.

Literary Analysis

4. **Predict** Check the predictions you wrote in your chart against what happened. What details helped you guess correctly or misled you?
5. **Analyze Suspense** Go back through the story and write down clues that **foreshadow** Rikki-tikki's ultimate victory. Then write down details that led you to believe Rikki might be defeated. How did the combination of the two kinds of details help create suspense?
6. **Compare Literary Works** Both "Rikki-tikki-tavi" and "The Last Dog" have exciting plots and **brave** main characters. How else are the two stories similar? How are they different? To present your answer, add details to a Venn diagram like the one shown.

7. **Make Judgments** "Rikki-tikki-tavi" is regarded as one of the great adventure stories. Does it deserve this reputation? Explain your answer.

Extension and Challenge

8. **Creative Response: Drama** Plan an oral reading of a scene from the story. Some students can perform the parts of the characters and the narrator, while other students provide sound effects. Rehearse your performance and tape-record it for other classes.
9. **SOCIAL STUDIES CONNECTION** This story takes place in colonial India. With a partner, do research to find out more about India under British rule, from 1858 to 1947. What are two long-lasting effects that resulted from Britain's control of India? Present your findings to the class.

RESEARCH LINKS
For more on colonial India, visit the **Research Center** at **ClassZone.com.**

Vocabulary in Context

VOCABULARY PRACTICE

Choose the vocabulary word that makes the most sense in each sentence.

1. After Rikki-tikki almost drowned, the family put him by the fire to _____ him.
2. The fire accidentally began to _____ his fur, and he quickly woke up.
3. Nag would not hesitate to eat a _____.
4. Though Darzee would _____ in fear at the sight of Nag, Rikki was not afraid.
5. He walked with a proud _____ that showed how brave he felt.
6. Rikki's killing Nag was a great _____ to the frightened family.
7. Rikki also _____ discovered Nagaina's eggs hidden among the melons.
8. Because of his _____ actions, everyone admired Rikki's courage.

consolation
cower
cunningly
fledgling
gait
revive
singe
valiant

VOCABULARY IN WRITING

Using three or more vocabulary words, write a paragraph to describe how Rikki killed Nag. Here is a sample of how you might begin.

EXAMPLE SENTENCE

Rikki ***cunningly*** *waited until Nagaina had left her husband alone.*

ALABAMA STANDARDS

READING STANDARD
1.c Using context clues to determine meaning of words

VOCABULARY STRATEGY: THE LATIN ROOTS *viv* AND *vit*

The vocabulary word *revive* contains the Latin root *viv*, which means "live." Another Latin root, *vit*, has the same meaning. *Viv* and *vit* occur in a number of English words. To understand the meaning of words with *viv* or *vit*, use context clues and your knowledge of what these roots mean.

VOCABULARY PRACTICE
For more practice, go to the **Vocabulary Center** at **ClassZone.com.**

PRACTICE Choose the word from the web that best completes each sentence. Then tell how *viv* or *vit* helps give meaning to each word.

1. People cannot _____ without food and water.
2. She was a _____ hostess who threw lively parties.
3. _____ can provide some of the substances our bodies need to be healthy.
4. He lost much of his _____ after the accident.
5. The artist used _____ colors in her painting.

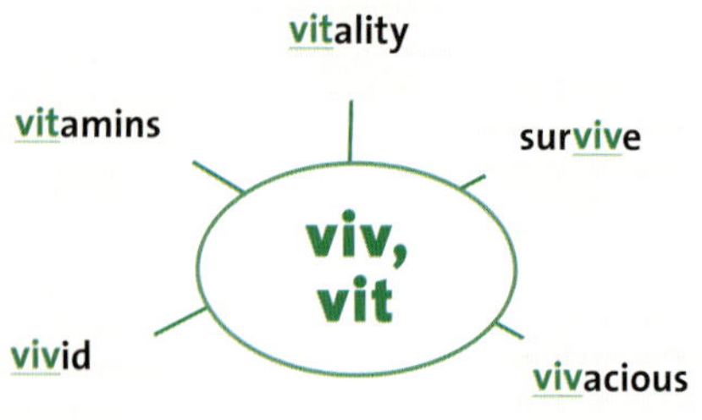

SKILLS PRACTICE

Reading-Writing Connection

Deepen your understanding of "Rikki-tikki-tavi" by responding to these prompts. Then complete the **Grammar and Writing** exercise.

WRITING PROMPTS	SELF-CHECK
A. Short Response: Write a Scene Most of the characters, but not all, consider Rikki-tikki to be a hero. In **one paragraph,** write a scene from the story from Nagaina's perspective. What does she think and feel about Rikki-tikki?	***A creative scene will . . .*** • include details about events in the story • include a convincing portrait of Nagaina
B. Extended Response: Give an Evaluation Is Rikki-tikki the **bravest** character in this story? Choose a brave character. Decide whether the character shows more or less bravery than Rikki. Write **two or three paragraphs** to evaluate the bravery of your chosen character and of Rikki.	***An effective evaluation will . . .*** • describe scenes that show each character's bravery • show similarities and differences between Rikki-tikki and the other character

GRAMMAR AND WRITING

MAINTAIN PRONOUN–ANTECEDENT AGREEMENT You may recall that an antecedent is the noun or pronoun that a pronoun refers to. For example, in the following sentence, notice how the plural pronoun *their* refers to the plural antecedent *friends: My friends grabbed their bags.* Be especially careful when using antecedents like *each, someone,* and *no one*. These words should always be paired with singular pronouns. In the revised sentence, notice how the pronouns (in yellow) and the antecedent (in green) **agree in number.**

Original: Someone had to take control. They would need to kill the snakes.

Revised: Someone had to take control. He or she would need to kill the snakes.

PRACTICE Correct the pronoun-antecedent error in each sentence.

1. Each snake wants the garden for themselves.
2. No one in the family wants to have their life threatened by the snakes.
3. Rikki-tikki stands up to the snakes and gets rid of its eggs.
4. Each person has their own space again!

For more help with pronoun-antecedent agreement, see pages R52–R53 in the ***Grammar Handbook.***

ALABAMA STANDARDS

WRITING/LANGUAGE STANDARD
11 Apply grammar conventions to pronoun-antecedent agreement

Great Reads

Holes

Novel by Louis Sachar

Louis Sachar
born 1954

Other Books by Louis Sachar

- *The Boy Who Lost His Face*
- *Dogs Don't Tell Jokes*
- *Sixth Grade Secrets*
- *Someday Angeline*

Meet Louis Sachar

Louis Sachar knows what it's like to be a kid. As a writer, he tries to share with his readers the thoughts and feelings he had when he was their age. "When I write," he says, "I'm always putting myself in the shoes of the character and always reacting to how I would feel about something if I were that character." Sachar also says that as he writes, he's "constantly doing it in fear that the reader is going to close the book at any second." Fearing that his readers might get bored inspires Sachar to keep his plots interesting.

Sachar worked as a teacher's aide at an elementary school while he was in college, and that gave him the idea to try writing books for young readers. He even used the names of his students in the first stories he wrote. He went to law school after college, but he found that he was more interested in writing than in practicing law.

Try an Adventure Novel

Holes is an example of an **adventure novel.** This type of fiction focuses on a main character who is usually on a mission and is facing many challenges and choices. There is often physical danger involved. In *Holes,* the main character and his friend face what seem at times to be overwhelming obstacles, but they do so with great courage.

Read a Great Book

Stanley Yelnats, the main character in *Holes,* gets teased in school, has no friends, and lives in a smelly apartment. He also has some unfortunate family history. Stanley is suffering from a curse dating back to the time of his great-great-grandfather, a "no-good-dirty-rotten-pig-stealing" character whose reputation continues to haunt Stanley. In an episode of bad luck, Stanley lands at Camp Green Lake, "a camp for bad boys." And so the adventure begins.

from HOLES

There is no lake at Camp Green Lake. There once was a very large lake here, the largest lake in Texas. That was over a hundred years ago. Now it is just a dry, flat wasteland.

There used to be a town of Green Lake as well. The town shriveled and dried up along with the lake, and the people who lived there.

During the summer the daytime temperature hovers around ninety-five degrees in the shade—if you can find any shade. There's not much shade in a big dry lake.

The only trees are two old oaks on the eastern edge of the "lake." A hammock is stretched between the two trees, and a log cabin stands behind that.

The campers are forbidden to lie in the hammock. It belongs to the Warden. The Warden owns the shade.

Out on the lake, rattlesnakes and scorpions find shade under rocks and in the holes dug by the campers.

Here's a good rule to remember about rattlesnakes and scorpions: If you don't bother them, they won't bother you.

Usually.

Being bitten by a scorpion or even a rattlesnake is not the worst thing that can happen to you. You won't die.

Usually.

Sometimes a camper will try to be bitten by a scorpion, or even a small rattlesnake. Then he will get to spend a day or two recovering in his tent, instead of having to dig a hole out on the lake.

But you don't want to be bitten by a yellow-spotted lizard. That's the worst thing that can happen to you. You will die a slow and painful death.

Always.

If you get bitten by a yellow-spotted lizard, you might as well go into the shade of the oak trees and lie in the hammock.

There is nothing anyone can do to you anymore.

The reader is probably asking: Why would anyone go to Camp Green Lake?

Most campers weren't given a choice. Camp Green Lake is a camp for bad boys.

If you take a bad boy and make him dig a hole every day in the hot sun, it will turn him into a good boy.

That was what some people thought.

Stanley Yelnats was given a choice. The judge said, "You may go to jail, or you may go to Camp Green Lake."

Stanley was from a poor family. He had never been to camp before.

Stanley Yelnats was the only passenger on the bus, not counting the driver or the guard. The guard sat next to the driver with his seat turned around facing Stanley. A rifle lay across his lap.

Stanley was sitting about ten rows back, handcuffed to his armrest. His backpack lay on the seat next to him. It contained his toothbrush, toothpaste, and a box of stationery his mother had given him. He'd promised to write to her at least once a week.

He looked out the window, although there wasn't much to see—mostly fields of hay and cotton. He was on a long bus ride to nowhere. The bus wasn't air-conditioned, and the hot, heavy air was almost as stifling as the handcuffs.

Stanley and his parents had tried to pretend that he was just going away to camp for a while, just like rich kids do. When Stanley was younger he used to play with stuffed animals, and pretend the animals were at camp. Camp Fun and Games he called it. Sometimes he'd have them play soccer with a marble. Other times they'd run an obstacle course, or go bungee jumping off a table, tied to broken rubber bands. Now Stanley tried to pretend he was going to Camp Fun and Games. Maybe he'd make some friends, he thought. At least he'd get to swim in the lake.

He didn't have any friends at home. He was overweight and the kids at his middle school often teased him about his size. Even his teachers sometimes made cruel comments without realizing it. On his last day of school, his math teacher, Mrs. Bell, taught ratios. As an example, she chose the heaviest kid in the class and the lightest kid in the class, and had them weigh themselves. Stanley weighed three times as much as the other boy. Mrs. Bell wrote the ratio on the board, 3:1, unaware of how much embarrassment she had caused both of them.

Stanley was arrested later that day.

He looked at the guard who sat slumped in his seat and wondered if he had fallen asleep. The guard was wearing sunglasses, so Stanley couldn't see his eyes.

Stanley was not a bad kid. He was innocent of the crime for which he was convicted. He'd just been in the wrong place at the wrong time.

It was all because of his no-good-dirty-rotten-pig-stealing-great-great-grandfather!

He smiled. It was a family joke. Whenever anything went wrong, they always blamed Stanley's no-good-dirty-rotten-pig-stealing-great-great-grandfather.

Supposedly, he had a great-great-grandfather who had stolen a pig from a one-legged Gypsy, and she put a curse on him and all his descendants. Stanley and his parents didn't believe in curses, of course, but whenever anything went wrong, it felt good to be able to blame someone.

Things went wrong a lot. They always seemed to be in the wrong place at the wrong time.

He looked out the window at the vast emptiness. He watched the rise and fall of a telephone wire. In his mind he could hear his father's gruff voice softly singing to him.

"If only, if only," the woodpecker sighs,
"The bark on the tree was just a little bit softer."
While the wolf waits below, hungry and lonely,
He cries to the moo—oo—oon,
"If only, if only."

It was a song his father used to sing to him. The melody was sweet and sad, but Stanley's favorite part was when his father would howl the word "moon."

The bus hit a small bump and the guard sat up, instantly alert.

Stanley's father was an inventor. To be a successful inventor you need three things: intelligence, perseverance, and just a little bit of luck.

Stanley's father was smart and had a lot of perseverance. Once he started a project he would work on it for years, often going days without sleep. He just never had any luck.

Every time an experiment failed, Stanley could hear him cursing his dirty-rotten-pig-stealing-great-grandfather.

Stanley's father was also named Stanley Yelnats. Stanley's father's full name was Stanley Yelnats III. Our Stanley is Stanley Yelnats IV.

Everyone in his family had always liked the fact that "Stanley Yelnats" was spelled the same frontward and backward. So they kept naming their sons Stanley. Stanley was an only child, as was every other Stanley Yelnats before him.

All of them had something else in common. Despite their awful luck, they always remained hopeful. As Stanley's father liked to say, "I learn from failure."

But perhaps that was part of the curse as well. If Stanley and his father weren't always hopeful, then it wouldn't hurt so much every time their hopes were crushed.

"Not every Stanley Yelnats has been a failure," Stanley's mother often pointed out, whenever Stanley or his father became so discouraged that they actually started to believe in the curse. The first Stanley Yelnats, Stanley's great-grandfather, had made a fortune in the stock market. "He couldn't have been too unlucky."

At such times she neglected to mention the bad luck that befell the first Stanley Yelnats. He lost his entire fortune when he was moving from New York to California. His stagecoach was robbed by the outlaw Kissin' Kate Barlow.

If it weren't for that, Stanley's family would now be living in a mansion on a beach in California. Instead, they were crammed in a tiny apartment that smelled of burning rubber and foot odor.

If only, if only . . .

The apartment smelled the way it did because Stanley's father was trying to invent a way to recycle old sneakers. "The first person who finds a use for old sneakers," he said, "will be a very rich man."

It was this latest project that led to Stanley's arrest.

The bus ride became increasingly bumpy because the road was no longer paved.

Actually, Stanley had been impressed when he first found out that his great-grandfather was robbed by Kissin' Kate Barlow. True, he would have preferred living on the beach in California, but it was still kind of cool to have someone in your family robbed by a famous outlaw.

Kate Barlow didn't actually kiss Stanley's great-grandfather. That would have been really cool, but she only kissed the men she killed. Instead, she robbed him and left him stranded in the middle of the desert.

"He was *lucky* to have survived," Stanley's mother was quick to point out.

The bus was slowing down. The guard grunted as he stretched his arms.

"Welcome to Camp Green Lake," said the driver.

Stanley looked out the dirty window. He couldn't see a lake.

And hardly anything was green.

Keep Reading

Now you have a sense of the bad situation Stanley is in. Which part of the description of the camp surprised you most? To find out how Stanley will handle the situation, read the rest of the story. As the plot of *Holes* unfolds, Stanley experiences many challenges and obstacles, some because of the harsh setting and others because of some harsh people. Through it all, he learns a few things about himself.

from Exploring the *Titanic*

Narrative Nonfiction by Robert D. Ballard

What can we learn from DISASTERS?

ALABAMA STANDARDS

READING & LIT STANDARDS
4.a Determining sequence of events
6 Analyze nonfiction for distinguishing characteristics

KEY IDEA Have you ever learned a lesson the hard way? Unfortunately, sometimes it takes a **disaster** to teach us to properly plan for danger. In the selection you're about to read, people on an "unsinkable" ship encounter terrible danger at sea—without enough lifeboats for everyone.

CHART IT When a disaster happens, we try to find out what went wrong so that we know how to be better prepared in the future. Using a chart like the one shown, list different types of disasters and things we can learn from them. Compare your chart with those of your classmates.

Disasters	What We Can Learn from Them
Fires	*We can learn to build safer buildings.* *More fire drills will help people know what to do in emergencies.*

LITERARY ANALYSIS: NARRATIVE NONFICTION

Narrative nonfiction uses literary elements, such as plot, setting, and conflict, to tell a story. Unlike fiction, though, narrative nonfiction tells a true story about events that really happened. To be accurate, narrative nonfiction relies on source material, such as quotations from real people, facts from reliable accounts, and photographs. As you read *Exploring the* Titanic, notice how literary elements and source material help create a compelling narrative.

Review: **Suspense**

READING SKILL: USE CHRONOLOGICAL ORDER

When writers use **chronological order,** or time order, they present events in the order in which they happened. To help you recognize time order, look for

- calendar dates, such as *Wednesday, April 10, 1912*
- clock time, such as *shortly after noon* and *8:03 P.M.*
- words and phrases that show time order, such as *before, later, around lunchtime,* and *for the next ten months*

Use a timeline to track the events of the *Titanic*'s final day.

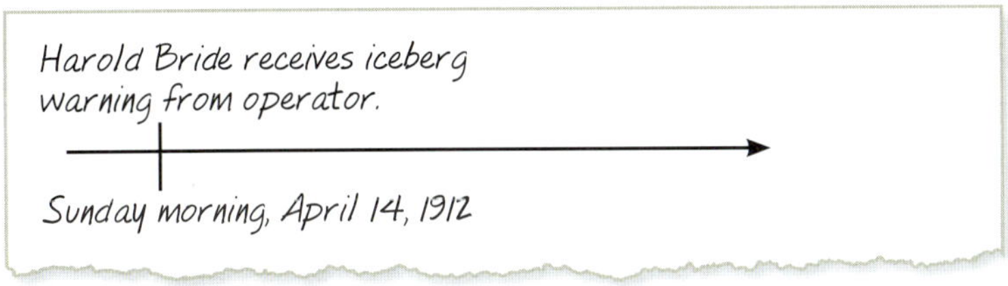

Review: **Make Inferences**

VOCABULARY IN CONTEXT

The boldfaced words help tell the story of this disaster. Use context clues to give a definition for each word.

1. The elegant **accommodations** thrilled the passengers.
2. **Adjoining** rooms kept families together.
3. There were **moderate** prices for less luxurious rooms.
4. Travelers enjoyed the **novelty** of the ship's first voyage.
5. Some believed they had heard a **prophecy** of tragedy.
6. The crews worked **feverishly** to avoid a collision.
7. They were unable to prevent a **ghastly** disaster at sea.
8. Rescue ships were delayed **indefinitely.**

Author Online

Underwater Explorer

Robert D. Ballard
born 1942

Robert D. Ballard, a pioneer of deep-sea exploration, traces his interest in the ocean to childhood walks on the beach in San Diego. He was so fascinated by sea lore and by the crabs washed in by the tide that he decided to spend his life by the water. Ballard is trained as a marine geologist, a geophysicist (a mapper of land and oceans), and a Navy commander. After years of searching, he found one of the most important shipwrecks in history—the remains of the *Titanic.*

A World Beneath the Water

The oxygen-poor water at the bottom of the ocean keeps shipwrecks in excellent condition. "There's probably more history now preserved underwater than in all the museums of the world combined," Ballard has observed. To help excavate that history, Ballard organizes expeditions to areas rich in shipwrecks. He explores the depths with the help of robots and submersibles, or minisubmarines.

Mysteries Solved Ballard's discovery solved many mysteries about the *Titanic*'s last hours. For instance, pieces on the ocean floor reveal that the ship broke in two before sinking.

MORE ABOUT THE AUTHOR
For more on Robert D. Ballard, visit the **Literature Center** at **ClassZone.com.**

Exploring the TITANIC

Robert D. Ballard

The story of the *Titanic* began before anyone had even thought about building the great ship. In 1898, fourteen years before the *Titanic* sank, an American writer named Morgan Robertson wrote a book called *The Wreck of the* Titan.[1] In his story, the *Titan,* a passenger ship almost identical to the *Titanic,* and labeled "unsinkable," sails from England headed for New York. With many rich and famous passengers on board, the *Titan* hits an iceberg in the North Atlantic and sinks. Because there are not enough lifeboats, many lives are lost.

The story of the *Titan* predicted exactly what would happen to the *Titanic* fourteen years later. It was an eerie **prophecy** of terrible things to come. **A**

In 1907, nearly ten years after *The Wreck of the* Titan was written, two men began making plans to build a real titanic ship. At a London dinner party, as they relaxed over coffee and cigars, J. Bruce Ismay, president of the White Star Line of passenger ships, and Lord Pirrie, chairman of Harland & Wolff shipbuilders, discussed a plan to build three enormous

ANALYZE VISUALS
What **details** in the poster emphasize the *Titanic*'s huge size?

prophecy (prŏf′ĭ-sē) *n.* a prediction of the future

A CHRONOLOGICAL ORDER
Why do you think Ballard begins his narrative with a reference to *The Wreck of the* Titan?

1. ***Titan:*** In Greek mythology, the Titans were a race of giants. The word *titanic* has come to be applied to any person or thing of great size or power.

Titanic, Olympic, White Star Line (1912), Montague B. Black. Christie's Images/Corbis.

WHITE STAR LINE.
"OLYMPIC."
45,000 TONS.
AND
"TITANIC."
45,000 TONS.
THE LARGEST STEAMERS IN THE WORLD.

ocean liners. Their goal was to give the White Star Line a competitive edge in the Atlantic passenger trade with several gigantic ships whose **accommodations** would be the last word in comfort and elegance.

The two men certainly dreamed on a grand scale.[2] When these floating palaces were finally built, they were so much bigger than other ships that new docks had to be built on each side of the Atlantic to service them. Four years after that London dinner party, the first of these huge liners, the *Olympic,* safely completed her maiden voyage.[3]

On May 31, 1911, the hull of the *Titanic* was launched at the Harland & Wolff shipyards in Belfast, Ireland, before a cheering crowd of 100,000. Bands played, and people came from miles around to see this great wonder of the sea. Twenty-two tons of soap, grease, and train oil were used to slide her into the water. In the words of one eyewitness, she had "a rudder as big as an elm tree . . . propellers as big as a windmill. Everything was on a nightmare scale." **B**

For the next ten months the *Titanic* was outfitted and carefully prepared down to the last detail. The final size and richness of this new ship was astounding. She was 882 feet long, almost the length of four city blocks. With nine decks, she was as high as an eleven-story building.

Among her gigantic features, she had four huge funnels, each one big enough to drive two trains through. During construction an astonishing three million rivets had been hammered into her hull. Her three enormous anchors weighed a total of thirty-one tons—the weight of twenty cars. And for her maiden voyage, she carried enough food to feed a small town for several months.

As her name boasted, the *Titanic* was indeed the biggest ship in the world. Nicknamed "the Millionaires' Special," she was also called "the Wonder Ship," "the Unsinkable Ship," and "the Last Word in Luxury" by newspapers around the world. **C**

The command of this great ocean liner was given to the senior captain of the White Star Line, Captain Edward J. Smith. This proud, white-bearded man was a natural leader and was popular with both crew members and passengers. Most important, after thirty-eight years' service with the White Star Line, he had an excellent safety record. At the age of fifty-nine, Captain Smith was going to retire after this last trip, a perfect final tribute to a long and successful career.

On Wednesday, April 10, 1912, the *Titanic's* passengers began to arrive in Southampton for the trip to New York. Ruth Becker was dazzled as she boarded the ship with her mother, her younger sister, and two-year-old brother, Richard. Ruth's father was a missionary in India. The rest of the

accommodations (ə-kŏm'ə-dā'shənz) *n.* rooms and food, especially in a hotel or on a ship or train

B NARRATIVE NONFICTION
What details help you picture the **setting** of the *Titanic*'s launch?

C NARRATIVE NONFICTION
What do the newspaper quotations add to your understanding?

---

2. **on a grand scale:** in a large or impressive way.
3. **maiden voyage:** very first trip.

Illustration of grand staircase © Ken Marschall, from *On Board the Titanic,* a Hyperion/Madison Press Book.

Ruth Becker

Jack Thayer

family was sailing to New York to find medical help for young Richard, who had developed a serious illness in India. They had booked second-class tickets on the *Titanic.*

Twelve-year-old Ruth was delighted with the ship. As she pushed her little brother about the decks in a stroller, she was impressed with what she saw. "Everything was new. New!" she recalled. "Our cabin was just like a hotel room, it was so big. The dining room was beautiful—the linens, all the bright, polished silver you can imagine."

Meanwhile, seventeen-year-old Jack Thayer from Philadelphia was trying out the soft mattress on the large bed in his cabin. The first-class rooms his family had reserved for themselves and their maid had thick carpets, carved wooden panels on the walls, and marble sinks. As his parents were getting settled in their **adjoining** stateroom,[4] Jack decided to explore this fantastic ship. **D**

On A Deck, he stepped into the Verandah and Palm Court and admired the white wicker furniture and the ivy growing up the trellised walls. On the lower decks, Jack discovered the squash court,[5] the swimming pool, and the Turkish bath[6] decorated like a room in a sultan's palace. In the gymnasium, the instructor was showing passengers the

ANALYZE VISUALS
The photographs of Ruth Becker and Jack Thayer are **source material.** How does seeing the faces of these young passengers affect the way you read the selection?

adjoining (ə-joiʹnĭng) *adj.* next to or in contact with **adjoin** *v.*

D NARRATIVE NONFICTION
What details about the **setting** do you learn from firsthand observations of people on the ship?

4. **stateroom:** a private cabin on a ship.
5. **squash court:** a walled court or room for playing squash, in which a rubber ball is hit off the walls.
6. **Turkish bath:** steam bath.

Illustration © Ken Marschall, from *On Board the Titanic,* a Hyperion/Madison Press Book.

latest in exercise equipment, which included a mechanical camel you could ride on, stationary bicycles, and rowing machines.

Daylight shone through the huge glass dome over the Grand Staircase as Jack went down to join his parents in the first-class reception room. There, with the ship's band playing in the background, his father pointed out some of the other first-class passengers. "He's supposed to be the world's richest man," said his father of Colonel John Jacob Astor, who was escorting the young Mrs. Astor. He also identified Mr. and Mrs. Straus, founders of Macy's of New York, the world's largest department store. Millionaire Benjamin Guggenheim was aboard, as were Jack's parents' friends from Philadelphia, Mr. and Mrs. George Widener and their son, Harry. Mr. Widener had made a fortune building streetcars. Mr. and Mrs. William Carter were also friends of the Thayers. Stowed in one of the holds below was a new Renault car that they were bringing back from England.

J. Bruce Ismay, president of the White Star Line, moved about the room saying hello to people. He wanted to make sure that his wealthy passengers were comfortable, that they would feel relaxed and safe aboard his floating palace.

ANALYZE VISUALS
Identify which parts of the boat are dedicated to the first-, second-, and third-class passengers. What differences do you note?

Indeed, when Ruth Becker's mother had asked one of the second-class staff about the safety of the ship, she had been told that there was absolutely nothing to worry about. The ship had watertight compartments that would allow her to float **indefinitely.** There was much talk among the passengers about the *Titanic* being unsinkable.

In 1912, people were divided into social classes according to background, wealth, and education. Because of these class lines, the *Titanic* was rather like a big floating layer cake. The bottom layer consisted of the lowly manual workers sweating away in the heat and grime of the boiler rooms and engine rooms. The next layer was the third-class passengers, people of many nationalities hoping to make a new start in America. After that came the second class—teachers, merchants, and professionals of **moderate** means like Ruth's family. Then, finally, there was the icing on the cake in first class: the rich and the aristocratic. The differences between these groups were enormous. While the wealthy brought their maids and valets[7] and mountains of luggage, most members of the crew earned such tiny salaries that it would have taken them years to save the money for a single first-class ticket. (E)

indefinitely (ĭn-dĕf′ə-nĭt-lē) *adv.* for an unlimited length of time

moderate (mŏd′ər-ĭt) *adj.* not excessive or extreme; average

(E) **NARRATIVE NONFICTION**
Why is it important to understand the way social class influenced the people on the ship?

7. **valets** (vă-lāz′): gentlemen's personal servants.

At noon on Wednesday, April 10, the *Titanic* cast off. The whistles on her huge funnels were the biggest ever made. As she began her journey to the sea, they were heard for miles around.

Moving majestically down the River Test,[8] and watched by a crowd that had turned out for the occasion, the *Titanic* slowly passed two ships tied up to a dock. All of a sudden, the mooring ropes holding the passenger liner *New York* snapped with a series of sharp cracks like fireworks going off. The enormous pull created by the *Titanic* moving past her had broken the *New York*'s ropes and was now drawing her stern toward the *Titanic*. Jack Thayer watched in horror as the two ships came closer and closer. "It looked as though there surely would be a collision," he later wrote. "Her stern could not have been more than a yard or two from our side. It almost hit us." At the last moment, some quick action by Captain Smith and a tugboat captain nearby allowed the *Titanic* to slide past with only inches to spare.

It was not a good sign. Did it mean that the *Titanic* might be too big a ship to handle safely? Those who knew about the sea thought that such a close call at the beginning of a maiden voyage was a very bad omen. **F**

Jack Phillips, the first wireless operator on the *Titanic,* quickly jotted down the message coming in over his headphones. "It's another iceberg warning," he said wearily to his young assistant, Harold Bride. "You'd better take it up to the bridge." Both men had been at work for hours in the *Titanic*'s radio room, trying to get caught up in sending out a large number of personal messages. In 1912, passengers on ocean liners thought it was a real **novelty** to send postcard-style messages to friends at home from the middle of the Atlantic.

Bride picked up the iceberg message and stepped out onto the boat deck. It was a sunny but cold Sunday morning, the fourth day of the *Titanic*'s maiden voyage. The ship was steaming at full speed across a calm sea. Harold Bride was quite pleased with himself at having landed a job on such a magnificent new ship. After all, he was only twenty-two years old and had just nine months' experience at operating a "wireless set," as a ship's radio was then called. As he entered the bridge area, he could see one of the crewmen standing behind the ship's wheel steering her course toward New York. **G**

Captain Smith was on duty in the bridge, so Bride handed the message to him. "It's from the *Caronia,*[9] sir. She's reporting icebergs and pack ice ahead." The captain thanked him, read the message, and then posted it on the bulletin board for other officers on watch to read. On his way

SCIENCE CONNECTION

An important technological advancement used on the *Titanic* was the wireless. A wireless telegraph is a machine used for transmitting and receiving messages.

F SUSPENSE
Reread lines 116–130. How does the author use **foreshadowing** to create suspense?

novelty (nŏv′əl-tē) *n.* something new, original, or unusual

G CHRONOLOGICAL ORDER
Reread lines 139–141. What day does Bride pick up the iceberg warning from the operator? Begin your timeline by recording this event. As you read on, record each major event that follows.

8. **the River Test:** a river flowing into the English Channel at Southampton, the city in England from which the *Titanic* set sail.

9. ***Caronia*** (kə-rō′nē-ə).

Harold Bride

Illustration © Ken Marschall, from *On Board the Titanic,* a Hyperion/Madison Press Book.

back to the radio room, Bride thought the captain had seemed quite unconcerned by the message. But then again, he had been told that it was not unusual to have ice floating in the sea lanes during an April crossing. Besides, what danger could a few pieces of ice present to an unsinkable ship?

Elsewhere on board, passengers relaxed on deck chairs, reading or taking naps. Some played cards, some wrote letters, while others chatted with friends. As it was Sunday, church services had been held in the morning, the first-class service led by Captain Smith. Jack Thayer spent most of the day walking about the decks getting some fresh air with his parents.

Two more ice warnings were received from nearby ships around lunch time. In the chaos of the radio room, Harold Bride only had time to take one of them to the bridge. The rest of the day passed quietly. Then, in the late afternoon, the temperature began to drop rapidly. Darkness approached as the bugle call announced dinner.

Jack Thayer's parents had been invited to a special dinner for Captain Smith, so Jack ate alone in the first-class dining room. After dinner, as he was having a cup of coffee, he was joined by Milton Long, another passenger going home to the States. Long was older than Jack, but in the easy-going atmosphere of shipboard travel, they struck up a conversation and talked together for an hour or so. **H**

H CHRONOLOGICAL ORDER
Reread lines 160–170. About how much time passes between these iceberg warnings and Jack's conversation?

At 7:30 P.M., the radio room received three more warnings of ice about fifty miles ahead. One of them was from the steamer *Californian* reporting three large icebergs. Harold Bride took this message up to the bridge, and it was again politely received. Captain Smith was attending the dinner party being held for him when the warning was delivered. He never got to see it. Then, around 9:00 P.M., the captain excused himself and went up to the bridge. He and his officers talked about how difficult it was to spot icebergs on a calm, clear, moonless night like this with no wind to kick up white surf around them. Before going to bed, the captain ordered the lookouts to keep a sharp watch for ice.

After trading travel stories with Milton Long, Jack Thayer put on his coat and walked around the deck. "It had become very much colder," he said later. "It was a brilliant, starry night. There was no moon, and I have never seen the stars shine brighter . . . sparkling like diamonds. . . . It was the kind of night that made one feel glad to be alive." At eleven o'clock, he went below to his cabin, put on his pajamas, and got ready for bed. **I**

I NARRATIVE NONFICTION
How does the inclusion of **primary source material**—Jack Thayer's firsthand observation—help you better understand what it must have been like on the ship that night?

In the radio room, Harold Bride was exhausted. The two operators were expected to keep the radio working twenty-four hours a day, and Bride lay down to take a much-needed nap. Phillips was so busy with the passenger messages that he actually brushed off the final ice warning of the night. It was from the *Californian.* Trapped in a field of ice, she had stopped for the night about nineteen miles north of the *Titanic.* She was so close that the message literally blasted in Phillips's ears. Annoyed by the loud interruption, he cut off the *Californian*'s radio operator with the words, "Shut up, shut up. I'm busy."

The radio room had received a total of seven ice warning messages in one day. It was quite clear that floating icebergs lay ahead of the *Titanic.* **J**

J SUSPENSE
Reread lines 187–197. What details in these lines create a sense of worry and dread?

High up in the crow's nest on the forward mast, Fred Fleet had passed a quiet watch. It was now 11:40 P.M., and he and his fellow lookout were waiting to be relieved so they could head below, perhaps for a hot drink before hopping into their warm bunks. The sea was dead calm. The air was bitterly cold.

Suddenly, Fleet saw something. A huge, dark shape loomed out of the night directly ahead of the *Titanic.* An iceberg! He quickly sounded the alarm bell three times and picked up the telephone.

Illustration by Ken Marschall © 1992 from *Titanic: An Illustrated History.* Hyperion/Madison Press Books.

"What did you see?" asked the duty officer.

"Iceberg right ahead," replied Fleet.

Immediately, the officer on the bridge ordered the wheel turned as far as it would go. The engine room was told to reverse the engines, while a button was pushed to close the doors to the watertight compartments in the bottom of the ship.

The lookouts in the crow's nest braced themselves for a collision. Slowly the ship started to turn. It looked as though they would miss it. But it was too late. They had avoided a head-on crash, but the iceberg had struck a glancing blow along the *Titanic's* starboard bow. Several tons of ice fell on the ship's decks as the iceberg brushed along the side of the ship and passed into the night. A few minutes later, the *Titanic* came to a stop. **K**

Many of the passengers didn't know the ship had hit anything. Because it was so cold, almost everyone was inside, and most people had already gone to bed. Ruth Becker and her mother were awakened by the dead silence. They could no longer hear the soothing hum of the vibrating engines from below. Jack Thayer was about to step into bed when he felt himself sway ever so slightly. The engines stopped. He was startled by the sudden quiet.

Sensing trouble, Ruth's mother looked out of the door of their second-class cabin and asked a steward[10] what had happened. He told her that nothing was the matter, so Mrs. Becker went back to bed. But as she lay there, she couldn't help feeling that something was very wrong.

Jack heard running feet and voices in the hallway outside his first-class cabin. "I hurried into my heavy overcoat and drew on my slippers. All excited, but not thinking anything serious had occurred, I called in to my father and mother that I was going up on deck to see the fun."

On deck, Jack watched some third-class passengers playing with the ice that had landed on the forward deck as the iceberg had brushed by. Some people were throwing chunks at each other, while a few skidded about playing football with pieces of ice.

Down in the very bottom of the ship, things were very different. When the iceberg had struck, there had been a noise like a big gun going off in one of the boiler rooms. A couple of stokers[11] had been immediately hit by a jet of icy water. The noise and the shock of cold water had sent them running for safety. **L**

Twenty minutes after the crash, things looked very bad indeed to Captain Smith. He and the ship's builder, Thomas Andrews, had made a rapid tour below decks to inspect the damage. The mail room was filling up with water, and sacks of mail were floating about. Water was also pouring into some of the forward holds and two of the boiler rooms.

K CHRONOLOGICAL ORDER
What is the time order of the events that happen after Fleet spots the iceberg? Record the events on your timeline.

L NARRATIVE NONFICTION
In lines 218–240 the author describes how the passengers react after the collision. **Compare and contrast** the responses of the passengers and the workers in different areas of the ship.

---

10. **steward:** a worker on a ship who attends to the needs of the passengers.

11. **stokers:** workers who tended the boilers that powered steamships.

Captain Smith knew that the *Titanic*'s hull was divided into a number of watertight compartments. She had been designed so that she could still float if only the first four compartments were flooded, but not any more than that. But water was pouring into the first five compartments. And when the water filled them, it would spill over into the next compartment. One by one all the remaining compartments would flood, and the ship would eventually sink. Andrews told the captain that the ship could last an hour, an hour and a half at the most. **M**

Harold Bride had just awakened in the radio room when Captain Smith stuck his head in the door. "Send the call for assistance," he ordered.

"What call should I send?" Phillips asked.

"The regulation international call for help. Just that." Then the captain was gone. Phillips began to send the Morse code[12] "CQD" distress call, flashing away and joking as he did it. After all, they knew the ship was unsinkable.

Five minutes later, the captain was back. "What are you sending?" he asked.

"CQD," Phillips answered. Then Bride cut in and suggested that they try the new SOS[13] signal that was just coming into use. They began to send out the new international call for help—it was one of the first SOS calls ever sent out from a ship in distress.

Ruth and her family had stayed in their bunks for a good fifteen minutes or so after the room steward had told them nothing was wrong. But Ruth's mother couldn't stop worrying as she heard the sound of running feet and shouting voices in the hallway. Poking her head out of the cabin, she found a steward and asked what the matter was.

"Put on your things and come at once," said the steward.

"Do we have time to dress?" she asked.

"No, madam. You have time for nothing. Put on your life jackets and come up to the top deck."

Ruth helped her mother dress the children quickly. But they only had time to throw their coats over their nightgowns and put on their shoes and stockings. In their rush, they forgot to put on their life jackets.

Just after midnight, Captain Smith ordered the lifeboats uncovered. The ship's squash court, which was thirty-two feet above the keel,[14] was now completely flooded. Jack Thayer and his father came into the first-class lounge to try to find out exactly what the matter was. When Thomas Andrews, the ship's builder, passed by, Mr. Thayer asked him what was going on. He replied in a low voice that the ship had not much more than an hour to live. Jack and his father couldn't believe their ears. **N**

M NARRATIVE NONFICTION
What **conflict** do the people aboard the ship now face?

N MAKE INFERENCES
What can you infer about how Thomas Andrews, the ship's builder, might have felt as he passed through the passenger lounge?

12. **Morse code:** a system used in wireless telegraphy in which numbers and letters are represented by sets of long and short sounds or flashes of light.
13. **CQD . . . SOS:** standard international distress calls used by ships at sea.
14. **keel:** the main timber or steel piece that extends the whole length of the bottom of a ship.

Illustration © Ken Marschall from *Titanic, an Illustrated History*, a Hyperion/Madison Press Book.

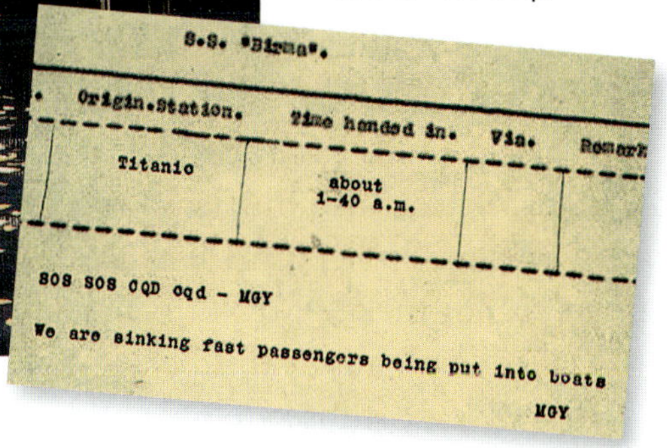

S.S. "Birma".

Origin Station.	Time handed in.	Via.	Remarks
Titanic	about 1-40 a.m.		

SOS SOS CQD CQD - MGY

We are sinking fast passengers being put into boats

MGY

This telegraph message was sent by Bride and Phillips as a call for help.

From the bridge of the *Titanic,* a ship's lights were observed not far away, possibly the *Californian*'s. Captain Smith then ordered white distress rockets fired to get the attention of the nearby ship. They burst high in the air with a loud boom and a shower of stars. But the rockets made no difference. The mystery ship in the distance never answered.

In the radio room, Bride and Phillips now knew how serious the accident was and were **feverishly** sending out calls for help. A number of ships heard and responded to their calls, but most were too far away to come to the rescue in time. The closest ship they had been able to reach was the *Carpathia,*[15] about fifty-eight miles away. Immediately, the *Carpathia* reported that she was racing full steam to the rescue. But could she get there in time? O

feverishly (fē′vər-ĭsh-lē) *adv.* in a way marked by intense emotion or activity

O SUSPENSE
Given what you already know about the *Titanic,* what details help create suspense?

Not far away, the radio operator of the *Californian* had gone to bed for the night and turned off his radio. Several officers and crewmen on the deck of the *Californian* saw rockets in the distance and reported them to their captain. The captain told them to try to contact the ship with a Morse lamp. But they received no answer to their flashed calls. No one thought to wake up the radio operator. P

P CHRONOLOGICAL ORDER
Record the *Californian*'s response on your timeline. At this point, how might disaster still have been minimized?

On board the *Titanic,* almost an hour after the crash, most of the passengers still did not realize the seriousness of the situation. But Captain Smith was a very worried man. He knew that the *Titanic* only carried lifeboats for barely half the estimated twenty-two hundred people on board. He would have to make sure his officers kept order to avoid any panic among the passengers. At 12:30 Captain Smith gave the orders

15. ***Carpathia*** (kär-pā′thē-ə).

to start loading the lifeboats—women and children first. Even though the *Titanic* was by now quite noticeably down at the bow and listing[16] slightly to one side, many passengers still didn't want to leave the huge, brightly lit ship. The ship's band added to a kind of party feeling as the musicians played lively tunes.

About 12:45 the first lifeboat was lowered. It could carry sixty-five people, but left with only twenty-eight aboard. Indeed, many of the first boats to leave were half empty. Ruth Becker noticed that there was no panic among the crowds of passengers milling about on the decks. "Everything was calm, everybody was orderly." But the night air was now biting cold. Ruth's mother told her to go back to their cabin to get some blankets. Ruth hurried down to the cabin and came back with several blankets in her arms. The Beckers walked toward one of the lifeboats, and a sailor picked up Ruth's brother and sister and placed them in the boat.

"That's all for this boat," he called out. "Lower away!"

"Please, those are my children!" cried Ruth's mother. "Let me go with them!" Q

Q NARRATIVE NONFICTION
How does Ruth's mother's pleading with the sailor add to the **conflict?**

The sailor allowed Mrs. Becker to step into the lifeboat with her two children. She then called back to Ruth to get into another lifeboat. Ruth went to the next boat and asked the officer if she could get in. He said, "Sure," picked her up, and dumped her in.

Boat No. 13 was so crowded that Ruth had to stand up. Foot by foot it was lowered down the steep side of the massive ship. The new pulleys shrieked as the ropes passed through them, creaking under the weight of the boat and its load of sixty-four people. After landing in the water, Ruth's lifeboat began to drift. Suddenly Ruth saw another lifeboat coming down right on top of them! Fearing for their lives, the men in charge of her boat shouted, "Stop!" to the sailors up on the deck. But the noise was so great that nobody noticed. The second lifeboat kept coming down, so close that they could actually touch the bottom of it. All of a sudden, one of the men in Ruth's boat jumped up, pulled out a knife, and cut them free of their lowering ropes. Ruth's boat pushed away from the *Titanic* just as boat No. 15 hit the water inches away from them.

Below, in the third-class decks of the ship, there was much more confusion and alarm. Most of these passengers had not yet been able to get above decks. Some of those who did finally make it out had to break down the barriers between third and first class. R

R MAKE INFERENCES
Given the lifeboat situation, what do delays in getting above decks mean for the third-class passengers?

By 1:30 the bow was well down, and people were beginning to notice the slant of the decks. In the radio room, Bride and Phillips were still desperately sending out calls for help: "We are sinking fast . . . women and children in boats. We cannot last much longer." The radio signal

16. **listing:** tilting; leaning.

Reading-Writing Connection

Deepen your understanding of the excerpt from *Exploring the* Titanic by responding to these prompts. Then complete the **Grammar and Writing** exercise.

WRITING PROMPTS	SELF-CHECK
A. Short Response: Write a Description How would you describe the state of mind of the passengers and crew when the *Titanic* first set sail? Write **one paragraph,** describing how people felt that day. Include details from the selection.	***An effective description will . . .*** • include passengers' impressions of the ship • include quotations from eye-witnesses or newspapers
B. Extended Response: Give an Evaluation What was your opinion of the behavior of the *Titanic*'s builder, captain, and crew before and during the **disaster?** Could more lives have been saved if responses to warnings or evacuation efforts had been conducted differently? Write **two or three paragraphs,** giving your evaluation.	***A convincing evaluation will . . .*** • make a judgment about whether more lives could have been saved • give reasons and evidence why or why not

GRAMMAR AND WRITING

USE CORRECT PRONOUN CASE People often confuse the **subject** and **object cases** of personal pronouns. If a pronoun is functioning as a subject, then you should use a **subject pronoun,** such as *I, she, he, we,* or *they.* If a pronoun is functioning as an object, then you should use an **object pronoun,** such as *me, her, him, us,* or *them.* (*You* and *it* function as both subject and object pronouns.)

Original: Him and his crew should have been more careful.

Revised: He and his crew should have been more careful. (*The pronoun is a subject, so it should be* he, *not* him.)

PRACTICE Choose the correct pronouns in the following sentences.

1. The crew knew about the icebergs. The captain had warned (they, them) about the possibility of floating ice.
2. Despite everything, the crew didn't pay attention to (he, him).
3. The radio operator was especially to blame. (Him, He) and his assistant didn't pass on messages to the captain.
4. (They, Them) should've communicated better with each other.

*For more help with pronoun cases, see page R53 in the **Grammar Handbook.***

ALABAMA STANDARDS

WRITING/LANGUAGE STANDARD
11 Apply grammar conventions in writing

from An American Childhood

Memoir by Annie Dillard

When do you feel most ALIVE?

ALABAMA STANDARDS

READING & LIT STANDARDS
4.c Applying self-monitoring strategies
6 Analyze nonfiction

KEY IDEA We all have something that makes us appreciate the wonder and excitement of life. It might be a tense basketball game, a rocky roller-coaster ride, or the **thrill** of an unexpected snowstorm. The author Annie Dillard has said that nothing makes her feel alive like facing a tough challenge. This selection is about one of the most exciting challenges she ever faced.

QUICKWRITE When do you feel most alive? Reflect on this question in a journal entry. Other questions you might ask yourself are these: When do I feel the happiest? What makes me feel great about my life? When am I glad to be me? Explain your answers.

LITERARY ANALYSIS: SETTING IN NONFICTION

In the memoir you're about to read, Annie Dillard tells a true story from her childhood. The **setting,** the time and place in which events occur, is the 1950s in suburban Pittsburgh, Pennsylvania, where Dillard grew up.

As you read, look for details that help you understand and picture where the selection takes place.

We were standing up to our boot tops in snow on a front yard on trafficked Reynolds Street . . .

Then look for ways the setting affects events.

READING SKILL: RECOGNIZE CAUSE AND EFFECT

Events are often related as **cause and effect:** one event brings about the other. The event that happens first is the cause; the one that follows is the effect. Often an effect becomes the cause of another effect, forming a chain of causes and effects.

As you read "An American Childhood," record causes and effects in a chain like the one shown.

Cause:
↓
Effect/Cause:
↓
Effect:

Review: **Make Inferences**

VOCABULARY IN CONTEXT

The following words help Annie Dillard tell about her exciting experience. How many of the words do you know? Create a chart like the one shown, and place each word in the appropriate column. As you read the selection, look for definitions of words that you've listed in the third column.

WORD LIST

improvise, perfunctorily, redundant, revert, righteous, simultaneously, spherical, translucent

Know Well	Think I Know	Don't Know at All

Author Online

Childhood Memories Pulitzer Prize–winner Annie Dillard frequently writes about events in her life when she was growing up. Her parents shared with her and her sisters their favorite books and music and told stories and jokes. The young Dillard, full of curiosity, spent hours studying small pond creatures with her microscope. But despite a childhood filled with happy memories, as Dillard reached her late teens, she began to rebel and yearned to get away.

Annie Dillard
born 1945

A Fulfilling Life Dillard got her wish for a new adventure when she went away to college and began to focus on writing. Since then, she has written essays, a memoir, poetry, and a Western novel. Dillard spends a great deal of time alone in the wilderness, and she frequently writes about nature. One might think a nature writer would tend to be serious, but Dillard loves to laugh. She keeps an "index of jokes" and says that ". . . irony has the highest place . . ." in literature.

MORE ABOUT THE AUTHOR
For more on Annie Dillard, visit the **Literature Center** at **ClassZone.com.**

An American Childhood

Annie Dillard

Some boys taught me to play football. This was fine sport. You thought up a new strategy for every play and whispered it to the others. You went out for a pass, fooling everyone. Best, you got to throw yourself mightily at someone's running legs. Either you brought him down or you hit the ground flat out on your chin, with your arms empty before you. It was all or nothing. If you hesitated in fear, you would miss and get hurt: you would take a hard fall while the kid got away, or you would get kicked in the face while the kid got away. But if you flung yourself wholeheartedly at the back of his knees—if you gathered and joined body and soul and pointed them diving fearlessly—then you likely wouldn't get hurt, and you'd stop the ball. Your fate, and your team's score, depended on your concentration and courage. Nothing girls did could compare with it.

Boys welcomed me at baseball, too, for I had, through enthusiastic practice, what was weirdly known as a boy's arm. In winter, in the snow, there was neither baseball nor football, so the boys and I threw snowballs at passing cars. I got in trouble throwing snowballs, and have seldom been happier since. A

ANALYZE VISUALS
Why is it interesting to see the snowballs flying through the air but not see who threw them?

A CAUSE AND EFFECT
What effect does the snow have on the children's activities? Begin creating your chain here.

On one weekday morning after Christmas, six inches of new snow had just fallen. We were standing up to our boot tops in snow on a front yard on trafficked Reynolds Street, waiting for cars. The cars traveled Reynolds Street slowly and evenly; they were targets all but wrapped in red ribbons, cream puffs. We couldn't miss.

I was seven; the boys were eight, nine, and ten. The oldest two Fahey boys were there—Mikey and Peter—polite blond boys who lived near me on Lloyd Street, and who already had four brothers and sisters. My parents approved Mikey and Peter Fahey. Chickie McBride was there, a tough kid, and Billy Paul and Mackie Kean, too, from across Reynolds, where the boys grew up dark and furious, grew up skinny, knowing, and skilled. We had all drifted from our houses that morning looking for action, and had found it here on Reynolds Street.

It was cloudy but cold. The cars' tires laid behind them on the snowy street a complex trail of beige chunks like crenellated[1] castle walls. I had stepped on some earlier; they squeaked. We could have wished for more traffic. When a car came, we all popped it one. In the intervals between cars we **reverted** to the natural solitude of children. B

I started making an iceball—a perfect iceball, from perfectly white snow, perfectly **spherical,** and squeezed perfectly **translucent** so no snow remained all the way through. (The Fahey boys and I considered it unfair actually to throw an iceball at somebody, but it had been known to happen.)

I had just embarked on the iceball project when we heard tire chains come clanking from afar. A black Buick was moving toward us down the street. We all spread out, banged together some regular snowballs, took aim, and, when the Buick drew nigh, fired.

A soft snowball hit the driver's windshield right before the driver's face. It made a smashed star with a hump in the middle.

Often, of course, we hit our target, but this time, the only time in all of life, the car pulled over and stopped. Its wide black door opened; a man got out of it, running. He didn't even close the car door.

He ran after us, and we ran away from him, up the snowy Reynolds sidewalk. At the corner, I looked back; incredibly, he was still after us. He was in city clothes: a suit and tie, street shoes. Any normal adult would have quit, having sprung us into flight and made his point. This man was gaining on us. He was a thin man, all action. All of a sudden, we were running for our lives. C

Wordless, we split up. We were on our turf; we could lose ourselves in the neighborhood backyards, everyone for himself. I paused and

revert (rĭ-vûrt') *v.* to return to a former condition

B SETTING
How do you think the tire tracks look on the snowy street? Referring to the footnote might help you **visualize** the scene.

spherical (sfîr'ĭ-kəl) *adj.* having the shape of a sphere or round ball

translucent (trăns-lo͞o'sənt) *adj.* allowing light to pass through

C CAUSE AND EFFECT
What happens when the children hit the Buick? Record the effect in your chain.

---

1. **crenellated** (krĕn'ə-lā'tĭd): notched at the top.

considered. Everyone had vanished except Mikey Fahey, who was just rounding the corner of a yellow brick house. Poor Mikey—I trailed him. The driver of the Buick sensibly picked the two of us to follow. The man apparently had all day.

He chased Mikey and me around the yellow house and up a backyard path we knew by heart: under a low tree, up a bank, through a hedge, down some snowy steps, and across the grocery store's delivery driveway. We smashed through a gap in another hedge, entered a scruffy backyard, and ran around its back porch and tight between houses to Edgerton Avenue; we ran across Edgerton to an alley and up our own sliding woodpile to the Halls' front yard; he kept coming. We ran up Lloyd Street and wound through mazy backyards toward the steep hilltop at Willard and Lang. **D**

He chased us silently, block after block. He chased us silently over picket fences, through thorny hedges, between houses, around garbage cans, and across streets. Every time I glanced back, choking for breath, I expected he would have quit. He must have been as breathless as we were. His jacket strained over his body. It was an immense discovery, pounding into my hot head with every sliding, joyous step, that this ordinary adult evidently knew what I thought only children who trained at football knew: that you have to fling yourself at what you're doing, you have to point yourself, forget yourself, aim, dive. **E**

Mikey and I had nowhere to go, in our own neighborhood or out of it, but away from this man who was chasing us. He impelled us forward; we compelled him to follow our route. The air was cold; every breath tore my throat. We kept running, block after block; we kept **improvising,** backyard after backyard, running a frantic course and choosing it **simultaneously,** failing always to find small places or hard places to slow him down, and discovering always, exhilarated, dismayed, that only bare speed could save us—for he would never give up, this man—and we were losing speed.

He chased us through the backyard labyrinths of ten blocks before he caught us by our jackets. He caught us and we all stopped. **F**

We three stood staggering, half blinded, coughing, in an obscure hilltop backyard: a man in his twenties, a boy, a girl. He had released our jackets, our pursuer, our captor, our hero: he knew we weren't going anywhere. We all played by the rules. Mikey and I unzipped our jackets. I pulled off my sopping mittens. Our tracks multiplied in the backyard's new snow. We had been breaking new snow all morning. We didn't look at each other. I was cherishing my excitement. The man's lower pant legs were wet; his cuffs were full of snow, and there was a prow of snow beneath them on his shoes and socks. Some trees bordered the little flat

D SETTING
Reread lines 63–71. In what way does the children's familiarity with the neighborhood help them?

E MAKE INFERENCES
Dillard uses the word *joyous* to describe the difficulty of the chase. What does this choice of words suggest about her?

improvise (ĭm'prə-vīz') *v.* to make up on the spur of the moment, without preparation

simultaneously (sī'məl-tā'nē-əs-lē) *adv.* at the same time

F CAUSE AND EFFECT
What happens because the children lose speed? List the effect in your chain.

backyard, some messy winter trees. There was no one around: a clearing in a grove, and we the only players.

It was a long time before he could speak. I had some difficulty at first recalling why we were there. My lips felt swollen; I couldn't see out of the sides of my eyes; I kept coughing.

"You stupid kids," he began **perfunctorily.**

We listened perfunctorily indeed, if we listened at all, for the chewing out was **redundant,** a mere formality, and beside the point. The point was that he had chased us passionately without giving up, and so he had caught us. Now he came down to earth. I wanted the glory to last forever.

perfunctorily (pər-fŭngk'tə-rĭ-lē) *adv.* in a mechanical or unconcerned way

redundant (rĭ-dŭn'dənt) *adj.* not needed; more than necessary

But how could the glory have lasted forever? We could have run through every backyard in North America until we got to Panama. But when he trapped us at the lip of the Panama Canal, what precisely could he have done to prolong the drama of the chase and cap its glory? I brooded about this for the next few years. He could only have fried Mikey Fahey and me in boiling oil, say, or dismembered us piecemeal, or staked us to anthills. None of which I really wanted, and none of which any adult was likely to do, even in the spirit of fun. He could only chew us out there in the Panamanian jungle, after months or years of exalting pursuit. He could only begin, "You stupid kids," and continue in his ordinary Pittsburgh accent with his normal **righteous** anger and the usual common sense. G

If in that snowy backyard the driver of the black Buick had cut off our heads, Mikey's and mine, I would have died happy, for nothing has required so much of me since as being chased all over Pittsburgh in the middle of winter—running terrified, exhausted—by this sainted, skinny, furious redheaded man who wished to have a word with us. I don't know how he found his way back to his car.

righteous (rī'chəs) *adj.* based on one's sense of what is right

G MAKE INFERENCES
Reread lines 111–122. Why does Dillard say that the man's response would have been the same even if he had finally caught them in Panama?

Comprehension

ALABAMA STANDARDS

LITERATURE STANDARD
6 Analyze nonfiction

1. **Recall** Why did the man chase Dillard and her friend?
2. **Recall** What happened when he caught up with them?
3. **Represent** Reread the paragraph that begins at line 51 on page 122. Using details from the paragraph, sketch the scene.

Literary Analysis

4. **Recognize Cause and Effect** Look over the chain you created as you read. What was the most important effect in the story? Why?
5. **Connect** What do you learn about Dillard from her reaction to being chased? Do you understand this reaction? Explain your answer.
6. **Make Inferences** What do you think the man who chased Dillard might be like? Use details from the selection and your own knowledge to fill out a chart like the one shown.

The Man	Details	Inference
What work might the man do?		
What might he have been like as a kid?		
What might he be like now?		

7. **Evaluate Setting** Go through the selection and find passages that describe Dillard's neighborhood and the weather there on the day of the chase. Which details are especially effective at conveying setting? Explain your answer.
8. **Analyze the Ending** Reread lines 111–128. Why do you think Dillard ended the piece this way, rather than just ending at line 110? Explain what information the last section provides and why Dillard included it.

Extension and Challenge

9. **Big Question Activity** Survey a small group of people to find out when they feel most alive. Then combine your findings with those of your classmates to create a master list of answers. What experiences **thrill** people? What generalizations can you make about these experiences, on the basis of your survey results?
10. **Inquiry and Research** In the first paragraph, Dillard says that when she was growing up, nothing girls did could compare with playing football. Do research to find out how women's sports have changed and grown over the last 50 years. What team sport might Dillard play if she were growing up today? Share your findings with the class.

RESEARCH LINKS
For more on women's sports, visit the **Research Center** at **ClassZone.com.**

Vocabulary in Context

VOCABULARY PRACTICE

Show that you understand the vocabulary words by deciding if each statement is true or false.

1. A **redundant** explanation is one that's already been given.
2. You can expect a **spherical** object to roll.
3. A tightly woven wool scarf is **translucent.**
4. If two events occur **simultaneously,** they happen one after the other.
5. If you clean your room **perfunctorily,** you do a very careful job.
6. If I **revert** to telling lies, I am going back to an old habit.
7. A speaker following carefully prepared notes will **improvise.**
8. A **righteous** person tends to act in a moral way.

improvise
perfunctorily
redundant
revert
righteous
simultaneously
spherical
translucent

VOCABULARY IN WRITING

What is your opinion of the end of this selection? Write a one-paragraph answer, using two or more vocabulary words. You could start like this.

EXAMPLE SENTENCE

*I was surprised at the end of the chase when the man reacted so **perfunctorily**.*

VOCABULARY STRATEGY: SUFFIXES THAT FORM ADJECTIVES

A **suffix** is a word part that appears at the end of a root or base word to form a new word. Some suffixes, such as those in *righteous* and *spherical,* can be added to nouns to form adjectives. If you can recognize the noun that a suffix is attached to, you can often figure out the meaning of the adjective formed from it. See the chart for common suffixes and their meanings.

Suffixes	Meanings
-ate, -ous, -eous, -ial, -ical	like; having to do with; showing

PRACTICE Identify the noun in each boldfaced word. Then define the adjective.

1. The science experiment produced a **gaseous** cloud.
2. Their pet dog is gentle and **affectionate.**
3. Many famous people write **autobiographical** books or articles.
4. Pollution has a **ruinous** effect on our environment.
5. His **facial** features included a long, thin nose.

VOCABULARY PRACTICE
For more practice, go to the **Vocabulary Center** at **ClassZone.com.**

Casey at the Bat

Poem by Ernest Lawrence Thayer

Do sports FANS *care too much?*

ALABAMA STANDARDS

READING STANDARDS
1 Apply strategies appropriate to the reading material
3 Distinguish among subgenres based on characteristics

KEY IDEA Sports **fans** love their teams. They dress in the teams' colors, cheer wildly when great plays are made, and boo when things don't go their way. Is this a good thing, or do sports fans care too much about winning? In "Casey at the Bat," the fans expect only the best from their mighty hitter.

WEB IT Create an idea web of what can happen when fans care too much. List things you have read about or witnessed happening at sporting events.

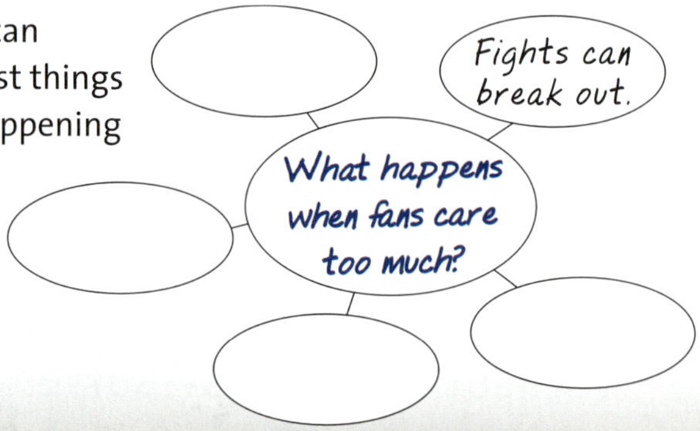

LITERARY ANALYSIS: NARRATIVE POETRY

Like fiction, poetry can tell stories. Poems that do so are called **narrative poems.** Just as any other story, a narrative poem has characters, a plot, and a setting. It presents a conflict and might also include suspense.

As you read "Casey at the Bat," identify its setting, characters, and main plot events in a diagram like the one shown. Also note the suspense that builds as you read the story.

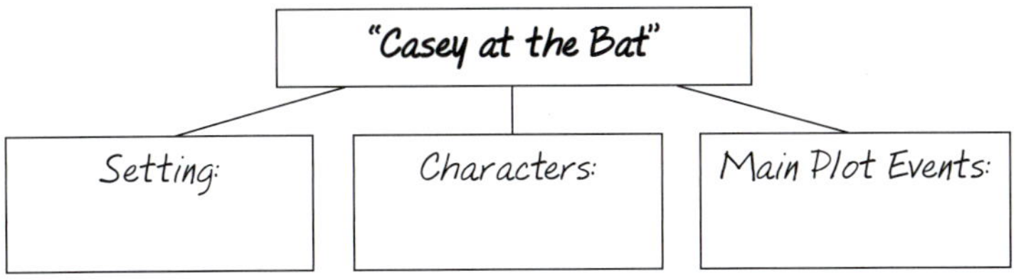

READING STRATEGY: READING POETRY

In addition to the elements that all stories have, narrative poems include poetic elements that add meaning and interest. Much of the energy and excitement of "Casey at the Bat" comes from the poet's use of **sound devices,** such as repetition, rhyme, and rhythm.

- **Repetition** is the repeating of a sound, word, phrase, or line to emphasize something in a poem.

  For <u>Casey</u>, mighty <u>Casey</u>, was advancing to the bat.

- **Rhyme** is the repetition of sounds at the ends of words.

  It looked extremely rocky for the Mudville nine that <u>day</u>;
  The score stood two to four, with but an inning
  left to <u>play</u>.

- **Rhythm** is a pattern of stressed (´) and unstressed (˘) syllables in a line of poetry.

  Thĕn frórn thĕ gláddenĕd múltitúde wĕnt úp ă
  jóyoŭs yéll—

As you read the poem, pay attention to the sound devices. Reading the poem aloud may help you.

Review: **Make Inferences**

Author Online

One-Hit Wonder Although Ernest Lawrence Thayer wrote many poems for newspapers, he is remembered for just one: "Casey at the Bat." Thayer was educated at Harvard University. Being known among his classmates as a very funny person probably helped him become editor, and later president, of the university's humor magazine, the *Lampoon.*

Ernest Lawrence Thayer
1863–1940

Crowd Pleaser After graduation, Thayer joined the staff of the *San Francisco Examiner,* where in 1887 he began writing a poem for each Sunday issue. "Casey at the Bat" was first printed in the paper in 1888. By the time of Thayer's death in 1940, "Casey at the Bat" had become an American favorite.

MORE ABOUT THE AUTHOR
For more on Ernest Lawrence Thayer, visit the **Literature Center** at **ClassZone.com.**

Background

America's Sport Baseball began in the United States in the mid-1800s. Small towns and large cities formed teams and clubs. The first baseball game with set rules was played in 1846 between Cartwright's Knickerbockers and the New York Baseball Club. By the early 1900s, going to baseball games was a favorite pastime of people throughout the United States.

Casey at the Bat

ERNEST LAWRENCE THAYER

It looked extremely rocky for the Mudville nine that day;
The score stood two to four, with but an inning left to play.
So, when Cooney died at second, and Burrows did the same,
A pallor wreathed the features of the patrons of the game. **A**

A straggling few got up to go, leaving there the rest,
With that hope which springs eternal within the human breast.
For they thought: "If only Casey could get a whack at that,"
They'd put even money now, with Casey at the bat.

But Flynn preceded Casey, and likewise so did Blake,
And the former was a pudd'n, and the latter was a fake.
So on that stricken multitude[1] a deathlike silence sat;
For there seemed but little chance of Casey's getting to the bat.

But Flynn let drive a "single," to the wonderment of all.
And the much-despised Blakey "tore the cover off the ball."
And when the dust had lifted, and they saw what had occurred,
There was Blakey safe at second, and Flynn a-huggin' third.

Then from the gladdened multitude went up a joyous yell—
It rumbled in the mountaintops, it rattled in the dell;[2]
It struck upon the hillside and rebounded on the flat;
For Casey, mighty Casey, was advancing to the bat. **B**

A NARRATIVE POETRY
What is the **setting** of this poem? How do you know?

ANALYZE VISUALS
Look at the picture. What can you **infer** about the baseball player's attitude?

B READING POETRY
Reread line 20. Why do you think Casey's name is repeated?

1. **stricken multitude:** a crowd of people affected by great trouble.
2. **dell:** valley.

There was ease in Casey's manner as he stepped into his place,
There was pride in Casey's bearing and a smile on Casey's face;
And when responding to the cheers he lightly doffed his hat,
No stranger in the crowd could doubt 'twas Casey at the bat. **C**

Ten thousand eyes were on him as he rubbed his hands with dirt,
Five thousand tongues applauded when he wiped them on his shirt;
Then when the writhing pitcher ground the ball into his hip,
Defiance glanced in Casey's eye, a sneer curled Casey's lip.

And now the leather-covered sphere came hurtling through the air,
And Casey stood a-watching it in haughty grandeur[3] there.
Close by the sturdy batsman the ball unheeded sped;
"That ain't my style," said Casey. "Strike one," the umpire said.

From the benches, filled with people, there went up a muffled roar,
Like the beating of the storm waves on the stern and distant shore.
"Kill him! Kill the umpire!" shouted someone on the stand;
And it's likely they'd have killed him had not Casey raised his hand. **D**

With a smile of honest charity great Casey's visage[4] shone;
He stilled the rising tumult, he made the game go on;
He signaled to the pitcher, and once more the spheroid[5] flew;
But Casey still ignored it, and the umpire said, "Strike two."

"Fraud!" cried the maddened thousands, and the echo answered "Fraud!"
But one scornful look from Casey and the audience was awed;
They saw his face grow stern and cold, they saw his muscles strain,
And they knew that Casey wouldn't let the ball go by again. **E**

The sneer is gone from Casey's lips, his teeth are clenched in hate,
He pounds with cruel vengeance his bat upon the plate;
And now the pitcher holds the ball, and now he lets it go,
And now the air is shattered by the force of Casey's blow.

Oh, somewhere in this favored land the sun is shining bright,
The band is playing somewhere, and somewhere hearts are light;
And somewhere men are laughing, and somewhere children shout,
But there is no joy in Mudville: Mighty Casey has struck out.

C MAKE INFERENCES
What inferences can you make about Casey from what you've read so far?

D NARRATIVE POETRY
What is the **conflict** in this poem?

E READING POETRY
Reread lines 37–44. How does the poet's use of **rhyme** and **rhythm** increase the suspense in the poem?

---

3. **haughty grandeur:** proud majesty and splendor.
4. **visage** (vĭz'ĭj): face.
5. **spheroid** (sfîr'oid'): in this instance, another name for a baseball.

Comprehension

ALABAMA STANDARDS

READING STANDARD
3 Distinguish among subgenres based on characteristics

1. **Recall** What events occur to allow Casey a final turn at bat?
2. **Recall** How does Casey approach the last pitch?
3. **Represent** Review the poem and figure out what some of the game statistics are in the ninth inning. Include the score for each team and the number of hits and men left on base for "the Mudville nine."

	Score	*Hits*	*Men Left on Base*
Home			
Visitor			

Literary Analysis

4. **Draw Conclusions** How would you describe Casey's overall response to his team's situation? Consider his interactions with his **fans,** the pitcher, and the umpire.
5. **Make Judgments About a Character** What is your opinion of Casey by the end of the poem? Explain.
6. **Analyze Narrative Poetry** Review the notes about setting, characters, and plot that you included in your diagram as you read. How does the setting affect the characters' actions and emotions?
7. **Analyze Repetition** A **stanza** is a group of lines that form a unit within a poem. Reread the last stanza and notice the word that is repeated in lines 50–51. What idea does the repeated word seem to emphasize?
8. **Evaluate the Poem** Why do you think this poem has remained popular for so many years?

Extension and Challenge

9. **Speaking and Listening** With a small group, practice reading the poem aloud in a way that captures the excitement and suspense of the game. Then discuss how the sound devices help you add drama to your oral reading.
10. **Inquiry and Research** Choose a famous baseball player—such as Babe Ruth, Lou Gehrig, or Hank Aaron—whose accomplishments have made history. Research the player to find out what team he played for and when, what records he broke, and what his fans and teammates had to say about him.

Babe Ruth
1895–1948

The Monsters Are Due on Maple Street

Teleplay by Rod Serling

What turns a crowd into a MOB?

ALABAMA STANDARDS

READING & LIT STANDARDS

1 Apply strategies appropriate to the reading material

6.a Classifying plot elements including conflict

KEY IDEA People in a crowd often act differently than they do when they're alone. In a big group, people might laugh louder, feel braver, or get angrier. Sometimes a crowd can even become dangerous. When it does—as in the teleplay you're about to read—it becomes a **mob.**

DISCUSS With a small group, share stories you may have heard about crowds turning into mobs. Think about how some fans react after a favorite sports team wins a championship or about what can happen when frustrated people take the law into their own hands. Continue your discussion by creating a list of things that can turn a crowd into a mob.

What Can Turn a Crowd into a Mob?

1. Feeling of victory
2.
3.
4.

LITERARY ANALYSIS: CONFLICT IN DRAMA

Like any story, a drama has a plot that centers on a **conflict.** Since drama is meant to be performed by actors, a drama's conflict usually unfolds through dialogue (conversation between characters) and action that you picture taking place on a stage or screen.

As you read "The Monsters Are Due on Maple Street," make notes about the story's conflict in a conflict map like the one shown.

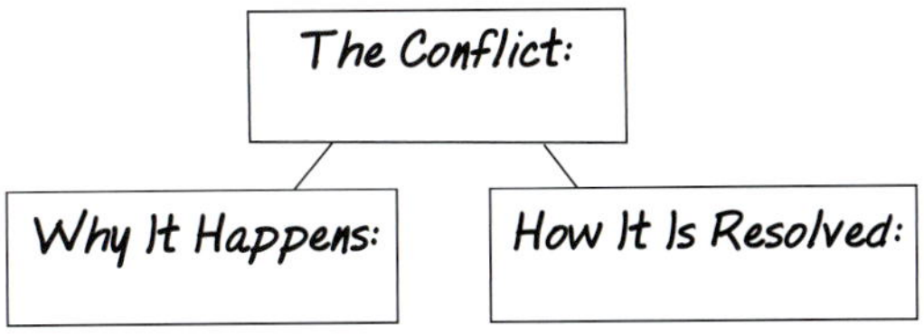

READING STRATEGY: READING A TELEPLAY

To best understand the dialogue and action in a drama, it's important to read the **stage directions.** Stage directions are instructions for the actors, the director, and the reader. They often appear in italics within parentheses. In a **teleplay,** a drama written specifically for television, stage directions also include directions for the camera, such as the following:

The camera moves slowly across the various porches . . .

As you read this teleplay, use all the stage directions to help you imagine the story as it might be presented on television.

VOCABULARY IN CONTEXT

Rod Serling uses these words to help show the conflict unfolding. See how many of them you can match with their numbered definitions.

WORD LIST	assent	converging	optimistic
	antagonism	defiant	revelation
	contorted	incriminate	

1. hopeful about the future; confident
2. willing to stand up to opposition; bold
3. hostility
4. something made known
5. agreement
6. to cause to appear guilty
7. twisted or pulled out of shape
8. moving toward one point

Author Online

Social Issues

Rod Serling
1924–1975

During his extraordinary career, Rod Serling won six Emmy awards, the highest honors given to those in the television industry. Known to the public as a creator of exciting television shows, Serling was sometimes referred to by his friends and business associates as "the angry young man of television." Serling wanted to write teleplays about important social issues, but television executives often thought his topics were too controversial.

Science Fiction Frustrated by this lack of support, Serling turned to writing science fiction and fantasy. He created an eerie series called *The Twilight Zone,* which became one of the most popular shows in television history during its 1959–1964 run. Because the teleplays for this series were not realistic, Serling had more freedom to deal with issues such as prejudice and intolerance. "The Monsters Are Due on Maple Street" first appeared in 1960 as an episode of *The Twilight Zone.*

MORE ABOUT THE AUTHOR
For more on Rod Serling, visit the **Literature Center** at **ClassZone.com.**

THE MONSTERS ARE DUE ON MAPLE STREET

ROD SERLING

CHARACTERS

Narrator
Tommy
Steve Brand
Don Martin
Myra Brand, Steve's wife
Woman
Voice One
Voice Two
Voice Three
Voice Four
Voice Five
Pete Van Horn
Charlie
Sally, Tommy's mother
Man One
Les Goodman
Ethel Goodman, Les's wife
Man Two
Figure One
Figure Two

Empire of Lights (1954), René Magritte. Oil on canvas, 146 cm × 114 cm. Musée d'Art Moderne, Brussels. © 2008 C. Herscovici, Brussels/Artists Rights Society (ARS), New York.

Voice Three. Can't get a thing on the radio.

Voice Four. My power mower won't move, won't work at all.

Voice Five. Radio's gone dead!

(Pete Van Horn, *a tall, thin man, is seen standing in front of his house.)*

Pete. I'll cut through the back yard to see if the power's still on, on Floral Street. I'll be right back!

(He walks past the side of his house and disappears into the back yard. The camera pans[2] *down slowly until we are looking at ten or eleven people standing around the street and overflowing to the curb and sidewalk. In the background is* Steve Brand*'s car.)*

Steve. Doesn't make sense. Why should the power go off all of a sudden and the phone line?

Don. Maybe some kind of an electrical storm or something.

Charlie. That don't seem likely. Sky's just as blue as anything. Not a cloud. No lightning. No thunder. No nothing. How could it be a storm?

Woman. I can't get a thing on the radio. Not even the portable.

(The people again begin to murmur softly in wonderment.)

Charlie. Well, why don't you go downtown and check with the police, though they'll probably think we're crazy or something. A little power failure and right away we get all flustered and everything—

Steve. It isn't just the power failure, Charlie. If it was, we'd still be able to get a broadcast on the portable.

(There is a murmur of reaction to this. Steve *looks from face to face and then at his car.)*

Steve. I'll run downtown. We'll get this all straightened out.

(He gets in the car and turns the key. Looking through the open car door, we see the crowd watching Steve *from the other side. He starts the engine. It turns over sluggishly and then stops dead. He tries it again, and this time he can't get it to turn over. Then very slowly he turns the key back to "off" and gets out of the car. The people stare at* Steve*. He stands for a moment by the car and then walks toward them.)*

2. **pans:** turns.

Steve. I don't understand it. It was working fine before—

Don. Out of gas?

Steve (*shakes his head*). I just had it filled.

Woman. What's it mean?

Charlie. It's just as if (*pause*) as if everything had stopped. (*Then he turns toward* Steve.) We'd better walk downtown.

(*Another murmur of* ***assent*** *to this.*)

Steve. The two of us can go, Charlie. (*He turns to look back at the car.*) It couldn't be the meteor. A meteor couldn't do this.

(*He and* Charlie *exchange a look. Then they start to walk away from the group.* Tommy *comes into view. He is a serious-faced young boy in spectacles. He stands halfway between the group and the two men, who start to walk down the sidewalk.*)

Tommy. Mr. Brand—you'd better not!

Steve. Why not?

Tommy. They don't want you to.

(Steve *and* Charlie *exchange a grin, and* Steve *looks back toward the boy.*)

Steve. *Who* doesn't want us to?

Tommy (*jerks his head in the general direction of the distant horizon*). Them!

Steve. Them?

Charlie. Who are them?

Tommy (*intently*). Whoever was in that thing that came by overhead.

(Steve *knits his brows for a moment, cocking his head questioningly. His voice is intense.*)

Steve. What?

Tommy. Whoever was in that thing that came over. I don't think they want us to leave here.

(Steve *leaves* Charlie, *walks over to the boy, and puts his hand on the boy's shoulder. He forces his voice to remain gentle.*)

Steve. What do you mean? What are you talking about?

Tommy. They don't want us to leave. That's why they shut everything off.

Steve. What makes you say that? Whatever gave you that idea?

Woman (*from the crowd*). Now isn't that the craziest thing you ever heard?

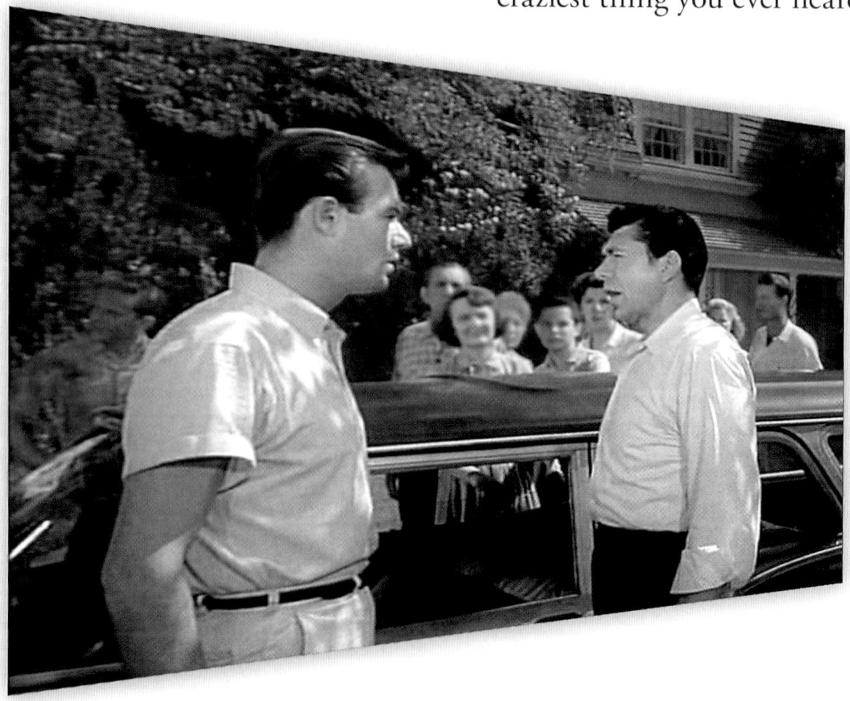

Tommy (*persistent but a little frightened*). It's always that way, in every story I ever read about a ship landing from outer space.

Woman (*to the boy's mother,* Sally, *who stands on the fringe of the crowd*). From outer space yet! Sally, you better get that boy of yours up to bed. He's been reading too many comic books or seeing too many movies or something!

Sally. Tommy, come over here and stop that kind of talk.

Steve. Go ahead, Tommy. We'll be right back. And you'll see. That wasn't any ship or anything like it. That was just a . . . a meteor or something. Likely as not— (*He turns to the group, now trying very hard to sound more* ***optimistic*** *than he feels.*) No doubt it did have something to do with all this power failure and the rest of it. Meteors can do some crazy things. Like sunspots.

Don (*picking up the cue*). Sure. That's the kind of thing—like sunspots. They raise Cain[3] with radio reception all over the world. And this thing being so close—why, there's no telling the sort of stuff it can do. (*He wets his lips and smiles nervously.*) Go ahead, Charlie. You and Steve go into town and see if that isn't what's causing it all.

(Steve *and* Charlie *walk away from the group down the sidewalk as the people watch silently.* Tommy *stares at them, biting his lips, and finally calls out again.*)

Tommy. Mr. Brand!

(*The two men stop.* Tommy *takes a step toward them.*)

Tommy. Mr. Brand . . . please don't leave here.

(Steve *and* Charlie *stop once again and turn toward the boy. In the crowd there is a murmur of irritation and concern, as if the boy's words—even though they didn't make sense—were bringing up fears that shouldn't be brought up.* Tommy *is both frightened and* ***defiant.***)

Tommy. You might not even be able to get to town. It was that way in the story. Nobody could leave. Nobody except—

Steve. Except who?

Tommy. Except the people they sent down ahead of them. They looked just like humans. And it wasn't until the ship landed that—

(*The boy suddenly stops, conscious of the people staring at him and his mother and of the sudden hush of the crowd.*)

Sally (*in a whisper, sensing the* ***antagonism*** *of the crowd*). Tommy, please son . . . honey, don't talk that way—

Man One. That kid shouldn't talk that way . . . and we shouldn't stand here listening to him. Why this is the craziest thing I ever heard of. The kid tells us a comic book plot, and here we stand listening—

(Steve *walks toward the camera and stops beside the boy.*)

Steve. Go ahead, Tommy. What kind of story was this? What about the people they sent out ahead?

Tommy. That was the way they prepared things for the landing. They sent four people. A mother and a father and two kids who looked just like humans . . . but they weren't.

(*There is another silence as* Steve *looks toward the crowd and then toward* Tommy. *He wears a tight grin.*)

Steve. Well, I guess what we'd better do then is to run a check on the neighborhood and see which ones of us are really human.

(*There is laughter at this, but it's a laughter that comes from a desperate attempt to lighten the*

3. **raise Cain:** cause trouble; create a disturbance. (In the Bible, Adam and Eve's son Cain becomes the first murderer when he kills his brother Abel.)

atmosphere. The people look at one another in the middle of their laughter.)

Charlie (*rubs his jaw nervously*). I wonder if Floral Street's got the same deal we got. (*He looks past the houses.*) Where is Pete Van Horn anyway? Isn't he back yet?

(*Suddenly there is the sound of a car's engine starting to turn over. We look across the street toward the driveway of* Les Goodman's *house. He is at the wheel trying to start the car.*)

Sally. Can you get started, Les?

(Les Goodman *gets out of the car, shaking his head.*)

Les. No dice.[4]

(*He walks toward the group. He stops suddenly as, behind him, the car engine starts up all by itself.* Les *whirls around to stare at the car. The car idles roughly, smoke coming from the exhaust, the frame shaking gently.* Les's *eyes go wide, and he runs over to his car. The people stare at the car.*)

Man One. He got the car started somehow. He got *his* car started!

(*The people continue to stare, caught up by this* ***revelation*** *and wildly frightened.*)

Woman. How come his car just up and started like that?

Sally. All by itself. He wasn't anywheres near it. It started all by itself.

(Don Martin *approaches the group and stops a few feet away to look toward* Les's *car.*)

Don. And he never did come out to look at that thing that flew overhead. He wasn't even interested. (*He turns to the group, his face taut and serious.*) Why? Why didn't he come out with the rest of us to look?

Charlie. He always was an oddball. Him and his whole family. Real oddball.

Don. What do you say we ask him?

(*The group starts toward the house. In this brief fraction of a moment, it takes the first step toward changing from a group into a mob. The group members begin to head purposefully across the street toward the house.* Steve *stands in front of them. For a moment their fear almost turns their walk into a wild stampede, but* Steve's *voice, loud, incisive, and commanding, makes them stop.*)

Steve. Wait a minute . . . wait a minute! Let's not be a mob!

(*The people stop, pause for a moment, and then, much more quietly and slowly, start to walk across the street.* Les *stands alone facing the people.*)

Les. I just don't understand it. I tried to start it, and it wouldn't start. You saw me. All of you saw me.

(*And now, just as suddenly as the engine started, it stops, and there is a long silence that is gradually intruded upon by the frightened murmuring of the people.*)

Les. I don't understand. I swear . . . I don't understand. What's happening?

Don. Maybe you better tell us. Nothing's working on this street. Nothing. No lights, no power, no radio, (*then meaningfully*) nothing except one car—yours!

(*The people's murmuring becomes a loud chant filling the air with accusations and demands for action. Two of the men pass* Don *and head toward* Les, *who backs away from them against his car. He is cornered.*)

Les. Wait a minute now. You keep your distance —all of you. So I've got a car that starts by itself—well, that's a freak thing—I admit it. But does that make me a criminal or something? I don't know why the car works—it just does!

(*This stops the crowd momentarily, and* Les, *still backing away, goes toward his front porch. He goes up the steps and then stops, facing the mob.*)

4. **no dice:** no success.

Les. What's it all about, Steve?

Steve (*quietly*). We're all on a monster kick, Les. Seems that the general impression holds that maybe one family isn't what we think they are. Monsters from outer space or something. Different from us. Aliens from the vast beyond. (*He chuckles.*) You know anybody that might fit that description around here on Maple Street?

Les. What is this, a gag? (*He looks around the group again.*) This a practical joke or something?

(*Suddenly the car engine starts all by itself, runs for a moment, and stops. One woman begins to cry. The eyes of the crowd are cold and accusing.*)

Les. Now that's supposed to **incriminate** me, huh? The car engine goes on and off, and that really does it, doesn't it? (*He looks around at the faces of the people.*) I just don't understand it . . . any more than any of you do! (*He wets his lips, looking from face to face.*) Look, you all know me. We've lived here five years. Right in this house. We're no different from any of the rest of you! We're no different at all. . . . Really . . . this whole thing is just . . . just weird—

Woman. Well, if that's the case, Les Goodman, explain why— (*She stops suddenly, clamping her mouth shut.*)

Les (*softly*). Explain what?

Steve (*interjecting*). Look, let's forget this—

Charlie (*overlapping him*). Go ahead, let her talk. What about it? Explain what?

Woman (*a little reluctantly*). Well . . . sometimes I go to bed late at night. A couple of times . . . a couple of times I'd come out here on the porch, and I'd see Mr. Goodman here in the wee hours of the morning standing out in front of his house . . . looking up at the sky. (*She looks around the circle of faces.*) That's right, looking up at the sky as if . . . as if he were waiting for something, (*pauses*) as if he were looking for something.

(*There's a murmur of reaction from the crowd again as* Les *backs away.*)

Les. She's crazy. Look, I can explain that. Please . . . I can really explain that. . . . She's making it up anyway. (*Then he shouts.*) I tell you she's making it up!

(*He takes a step toward the crowd, and they back away from him. He walks down the steps after them, and they continue to back away. Suddenly he is left completely alone, and he looks like a man caught in the middle of a menacing circle as the scene slowly fades to black.*)

ACT 2 Scene One

(*Fade in on Maple Street at night. On the sidewalk, little knots of people stand around talking in low voices. At the end of each conversation they look toward Les Goodman's house. From the various houses, we can see candlelight but no electricity. The quiet that blankets the whole area is disturbed only by the almost whispered voices of the people standing around. In one group* Charlie *stands staring across at the Goodmans' house. Two men stand across the street from it in almost sentrylike*[5] *poses.*)

Sally (*in a small, hesitant voice*). It just doesn't seem right, though, keeping watch on them. Why . . . he was right when he said he was one of our neighbors. Why, I've known Ethel Goodman ever since they moved in. We've been good friends—

Charlie. That don't prove a thing. Any guy who'd spend his time lookin' up at the sky early in the morning—well, there's something wrong with that kind of person. There's something that ain't legitimate. Maybe under normal circumstances we could let it go by, but these aren't normal circumstances. Why, look at this street! Nothin' but candles. Why, it's like goin' back into the Dark Ages[6] or somethin'!

(Steve *walks down the steps of his porch, down the street to the Goodmans' house, and then stops at the foot of the steps.* Les *is standing there;* Ethel Goodman *behind him is very frightened.*)

Les. Just stay right where you are, Steve. We don't want any trouble, but this time if anybody sets foot on my porch—that's what they're going to get—trouble!

Steve. Look, Les—

Les. I've already explained to you people. I don't sleep very well at night sometimes. I get up and I take a walk and I look up at the sky. I look at the stars!

5. **sentrylike:** resembling those of guards.

6. **Dark Ages:** a period from about A.D. 400 to 1000, when learning and culture in Western Europe were decreasing.

Ethel. That's exactly what he does. Why, this whole thing, it's . . . it's some kind of madness or something.

Steve (*nods grimly*). That's exactly what it is—some kind of madness.

Charlie's Voice (*shrill, from across the street*). You best watch who you're seen with, Steve! Until we get this all straightened out, you ain't exactly above suspicion yourself.

Steve (*whirling around toward him*). Or you, Charlie. Or any of us, it seems. From age eight on up!

Woman. What I'd like to know is—what are we gonna do? Just stand around here all night?

Charlie. There's nothin' else we *can* do! (*He turns back, looking toward* Steve *and* Les *again.*) One of 'em'll tip their hand. They got to.

Steve (*raising his voice*). There's something you can do, Charlie. You can go home and keep your mouth shut. You can quit strutting around like a self-appointed judge and climb into bed and forget it.

Charlie. You sound real anxious to have that happen, Steve. I think we better keep our eye on you, too!

Don (*as if he were taking the bit in his teeth, takes a hesitant step to the front*). I think everything might as well come out now. (*He turns toward* Steve.) Your wife's done plenty of talking, Steve, about how odd you are!

Charlie (*picking this up, his eyes widening*). Go ahead, tell us what she's said.

(Steve *walks toward them from across the street.*)

Steve. Go ahead, what's my wife said? Let's get it all out. Let's pick out every idiosyncrasy[7] of every single man, woman, and child on the street. And then we might as well set up some kind of citizens' court. How about a firing squad at dawn, Charlie, so we can get rid of all the suspects. Narrow them down. Make it easier for you.

Don. There's no need gettin' so upset, Steve. It's just that . . . well . . . Myra's talked about how there's been plenty of nights you spent hours down in your basement workin' on some kind of radio or something. Well, none of us have ever seen that radio—

(*By this time* Steve *has reached the group. He stands there defiantly.*)

Charlie. Go ahead, Steve. What kind of "radio set" you workin' on? I never seen it. Neither has anyone else. Who do you talk to on that radio set? And who talks to you?

Steve. I'm surprised at you, Charlie. How come you're so dense all of a sudden? (*He pauses.*) Who do I talk to? I talk to monsters from outer space. I talk to three-headed green men who fly over here in what look like meteors.

(Myra Brand *steps down from the porch, bites her lip, calls out.*)

Myra. Steve! Steve, please. (*Then looking around, frightened, she walks toward the group.*) It's just a ham radio[8] set, that's all. I bought him a book on it myself. It's just a ham radio set. A lot of people have them. I can show it to you. It's right down in the basement.

Steve (*whirls around toward her*). Show them nothing! If they want to look inside our house—let them go and get a search warrant.

Charlie. Look, buddy, you can't afford to—

Steve (*interrupting him*). Charlie, don't start telling me who's dangerous and who isn't and who's safe and who's a menace. (*He turns to the group and shouts.*) And you're with him, too—all of you! You're standing here all set

7. **idiosyncrasy** (ĭd′ē-ō-sĭng′krə-sē): personal way of acting; odd mannerism.

8. **ham radio:** a two-way radio with which an amateur broadcaster communicates with other amateurs.

to crucify—all set to find a scapegoat[9]—all desperate to point some kind of a finger at a neighbor! Well now, look, friends, the only thing that's gonna happen is that we'll eat each other up alive—

(*He stops abruptly as* Charlie *suddenly grabs his arm.*)

Charlie (*in a hushed voice*). That's not the only thing that can happen to us.

(*Down the street, a figure has suddenly materialized in the gloom. In the silence we hear the clickety-clack of slow, measured footsteps on concrete as the figure walks slowly toward them. One of the women lets out a stifled cry.* Sally *grabs her boy, as do a couple of other mothers.*)

Tommy (*shouting, frightened*). It's the monster! It's the monster!

(*Another woman lets out a wail, and the people fall back in a group staring toward the darkness and the approaching figure. The people stand in the shadows watching.* Don Martin *joins them, carrying a shotgun. He holds it up.*)

Don. We may need this.

Steve. A shotgun? (*He pulls it out of* Don*'s hand.*) No! Will anybody think a thought around here! Will you people wise up. What good would a shotgun do against—

(*The dark figure continues to walk toward them as the people stand there, fearful, mothers clutching children, men standing in front of their wives.*)

Charlie (*pulling the gun from* Steve*'s hands*). No more talk, Steve. You're going to talk us into a grave! You'd let whatever's out there walk right over us, wouldn't yuh? Well, some of us won't!

(Charlie *swings around, raises the gun, and suddenly pulls the trigger. The sound of the shot explodes in the stillness. The figure suddenly lets out a small cry, stumbles forward onto his knees, and then falls forward on his face.* Don, Charlie, *and* Steve *race forward to him.* Steve *is there first and turns the man over. The crowd gathers around them.*)

Steve (*slowly looks up*). It's Pete Van Horn.

Don (*in a hushed voice*). Pete Van Horn! He was just gonna go over to the next block to see if the power was on—

Woman. You killed him, Charlie. You shot him dead!

Charlie (*looks around at the circle of faces, his eyes frightened, his face* ***contorted***). But . . . but I didn't know who he was. I certainly didn't know who he was. He comes walkin' out of the darkness—how am I supposed to know who he was? (*He grabs* Steve.) Steve—you know why I shot! How was I supposed to know he wasn't a monster or something? (*He grabs* Don.) We're all scared of the same thing. I was just tryin' to . . . tryin' to protect my home, that's all! Look, all of you, that's all I was tryin' to do. (*He looks down wildly at the body.*) I didn't know it was somebody we knew! I didn't know—

(*There's a sudden hush and then an intake of breath in the group. Across the street all the lights go on in one of the houses.*)

Woman (*in a hushed voice*). Charlie . . . Charlie . . . the lights just went on in your house. Why did the lights just go on?

Don. What about it, Charlie? How come you're the only one with lights now?

Les. That's what I'd like to know.

(*Pausing, they all stare toward* Charlie.)

Les. You were so quick to kill, Charlie, and you were so quick to tell us who we had to be careful of. Well, maybe you had to kill. Maybe Pete there was trying to tell us something. Maybe he'd found out something and came

9. **scapegoat:** a person or thing made to bear the blame for the mistakes of others.

back to tell us who there was amongst us we should watch out for—

(Charlie *backs away from the group, his eyes wide with fright.*)

Charlie. No . . . no . . . it's nothing of the sort! I don't know why the lights are on. I swear I don't. Somebody's pulling a gag or something.

(*He bumps against* Steve, *who grabs him and whirls him around.*)

Steve. A gag? A gag? Charlie, there's a dead man on the sidewalk, and you killed him! Does this thing look like a gag to you?

(Charlie *breaks away and screams as he runs toward his house.*)

Charlie. No! No! Please!

(*A man breaks away from the crowd to chase* Charlie. *As the man tackles him and lands on top of him, the other people start to run toward them.* Charlie *gets up, breaks away from the other man's grasp, and lands a couple of desperate punches that push the man aside. Then he forces his way, fighting, through the crowd and jumps up on his front porch.* Charlie *is on his porch as a rock thrown from the group smashes a window beside him, the broken glass flying past him. A couple of pieces cut him. He stands there perspiring, rumpled, blood running down from a cut on the cheek. His wife breaks away from the group to throw herself into his arms. He buries his face against her. We can see the crowd* ***converging*** *on the porch.*)

Voice One. It must have been him.

Voice Two. He's the one.

Voice Three. We got to get Charlie.

(*Another rock lands on the porch.* Charlie *pushes his wife behind him, facing the group.*)

Charlie. Look, look, I swear to you . . . it isn't me . . . but I do know who it is . . . I swear to you, I do know who it is. I know who the monster is here. I know who it is that doesn't belong. I swear to you I know.

Don (*pushing his way to the front of the crowd*). All right, Charlie, let's hear it!

(Charlie*'s eyes dart around wildly.*)

Charlie. It's . . . it's . . .

Man Two (*screaming*). Go ahead, Charlie.

Charlie. It's . . . it's the kid. It's Tommy. He's the one!

(*There's a gasp from the crowd as we see* Sally *holding the boy.* Tommy *at first doesn't understand and then, realizing the eyes are all on him, buries his face against his mother.*)

Sally (*backs away*). That's crazy! He's only a boy.

Woman. But he knew! He was the only one! He told us all about it. Well, how did he know? How could he have known?

(*Various people take this up and repeat the question.*)

Voice One. How could he know?

Voice Two. Who told him?

Voice Three. Make the kid answer.

(*The crowd starts to converge around the mother, who grabs* Tommy *and starts to run with him. The crowd starts to follow, at first walking fast, and then running after him. Suddenly Charlie's lights go off and the lights in other houses go on, then off.*)

Man One (*shouting*). It isn't the kid . . . it's Bob Weaver's house.

Woman. It isn't Bob Weaver's house, it's Don Martin's place.

Charlie. I tell you it's the kid.

Don. It's Charlie. He's the one.

(*People shout, accuse, and scream as the lights go on and off. Then, slowly, in the middle of this nightmarish confusion of sight and sound, the camera starts to pull away until, once again, we have reached the opening shot looking at the Maple Street sign from high above.*)

Scene Two

(*The camera continues to move away while gradually bringing into focus a field. We see the metal side of a spacecraft that sits shrouded in darkness. An open door throws out a beam of light from the illuminated interior. Two figures appear, silhouetted against the bright lights. We get only a vague feeling of form.*)

Figure One. Understand the procedure now? Just stop a few of their machines and radios and telephones and lawn mowers. . . . Throw them into darkness for a few hours, and then just sit back and watch the pattern.

Figure Two. And this pattern is always the same?

Figure One. With few variations. They pick the most dangerous enemy they can find . . . and it's themselves. And all we need do is sit back . . . and watch.

Figure Two. Then I take it this place . . . this Maple Street . . . is not unique.

Figure One (*shaking his head*). By no means. Their world is full of Maple Streets. And we'll go from one to the other and let them destroy themselves. One to the other . . . one to the other . . . one to the other—

Scene Three

(*The camera slowly moves up for a shot of the starry sky, and over this we hear the* Narrator's *voice.*)

Narrator. The tools of conquest do not necessarily come with bombs and explosions and fallout. There are weapons that are simply thoughts, attitudes, prejudices—to be found only in the minds of men. For the record, prejudices can kill and suspicion can destroy. A thoughtless, frightened search for a scapegoat has a fallout all its own for the children . . . and the children yet unborn, (*a pause*) and the pity of it is . . . that these things cannot be confined to . . . The Twilight Zone!

(*Fade to black.*)

Comprehension

ALABAMA STANDARDS

LITERATURE STANDARD
6.a Classifying plot elements including conflict

1. **Recall** When do the neighbors first sense something is wrong?
2. **Clarify** How is Pete Van Horn killed?
3. **Clarify** Why do the neighbors become suspicious of Tommy?

Literary Analysis

4. **Identify Conflict** Review the conflict map you created as you read. Then explain what you think is the main conflict in the story. What do their reactions to the conflict reveal about the characters?
5. **Analyze the Teleplay** How did the stage directions help you **visualize** the teleplay? Record your answers on a chart like the one shown.

Stage Direction	*Its Effect*
Fade in on a shot of the night sky.	*It makes you focus on outer space.*

6. **Analyze Foreshadowing** Foreshadowing is a technique a writer uses to hint at something that will occur later in a story. Reread what the narrator says in lines 51–54 of Act 1. How does this example of foreshadowing affect you as a reader?
7. **Draw Conclusions** At various points in the teleplay, the **mob** thinks different people are the monsters in their midst. Make a list of these people, and consider the moments when the mob turns on them. What conclusions can you draw about how the mob picks its victims?
8. **Make Judgments** In your opinion, who are the monsters referred to in the title? Give reasons for your answer.

Extension and Challenge

9. **Creative Project: Drama** With a small group, review the information about Rod Serling on page 135. Then act out a part of the teleplay that your group thinks communicates a message about prejudice and fear. Remember to follow stage directions as you act out your scene. After your performance, explain why your group chose that particular scene.
10. **Big Question Activity** Look again at the big question on page 134. Not all of the characters in this teleplay are equally quick to go along with the crowd. Identify a character who urges people to think calmly and reasonably, and write three paragraphs describing his or her efforts. Include a sentence that tells why the character isn't successful in preventing the crowd from becoming a mob.

Media Study

from Back to the Future

Film Clip on *MediaSmart* DVD

What makes your IMAGINATION *soar?*

ALABAMA STANDARDS

COMMUNICATION STANDARD
15 Demonstrate listening skills

KEY IDEA One of the keys to a good story is how it is told. Storytellers of all kinds know how satisfying a story can be when it taps into your sense of wonder and your willingness to believe in fantastic happenings and places. To explore how a movie can bring an unusual plot and setting to life, you'll watch a scene from a movie that has captured the **imagination** of millions of people.

Background

From Time to Time The movie *Back to the Future* is a science fiction adventure about time travel. Seventeen-year-old Marty McFly has a scientist friend, Dr. Emmett L. Brown, who has been experimenting with ways to travel across time. Doc, as Marty calls him, has invented a time machine that looks like a stylish, specially equipped car.

To escape sudden danger, Marty leaps into the car and speeds 30 years into the past—to 1955. He soon learns that having the power to control time comes with certain risks.

Media Literacy: Plot and Setting in Movies

Moviemakers tell stories by using visual and sound techniques. These techniques are used to help viewers follow the events of a plot. In addition, the techniques help to make the setting and the actions within it seem very real.

MOVIE TECHNIQUES	STRATEGIES FOR VIEWING
Visual Techniques A movie director uses carefully chosen camera shots to support important elements of the plot. A **shot** is the continuous recording of a scene or image.	Watch for carefully chosen **camera shots.** • A **close-up shot** is a close view of a person or an object. It is often used to show a character's emotions or reactions. • A **reaction shot** shows a character responding in some way to what he or she sees. • A **low-angle shot,** in which the camera looks up at the subject, can help create the impression of height or distance.
Editing The careful selection and arrangement of shots is called **editing.** Moviemakers put shots together in ways that help you follow the action of a story or show relationships between place and events.	• Single shots, when put together, can form a **sequence.** For example, a shot of someone tossing a ball, a shot of the same ball in mid-air, and then a shot of someone catching the ball fit together to form a complete action. • Look for shots that set up a cause-and-effect sequence. In movies with lots of actions, these shots add excitement.
Sound Techniques Moviemakers use sound to make a setting or action believable. In addition, sound techniques can affect the audience's emotions as events unfold.	• Listen to the **sounds,** which in a movie consist of **music, sound effects,** and **dialogue.** • Be aware of what **sound effects** add to images. Seeing a flash of lightning is one thing, but hearing the clap of thunder helps viewers experience the setting and react to it.

MediaSmart DVD

- **Film Clip:** *Back to the Future*
- **Director:** Robert Zemeckis
- **Rating:** PG
- **Genre:** Sci-fi adventure
- **Running Time:** 8 minutes

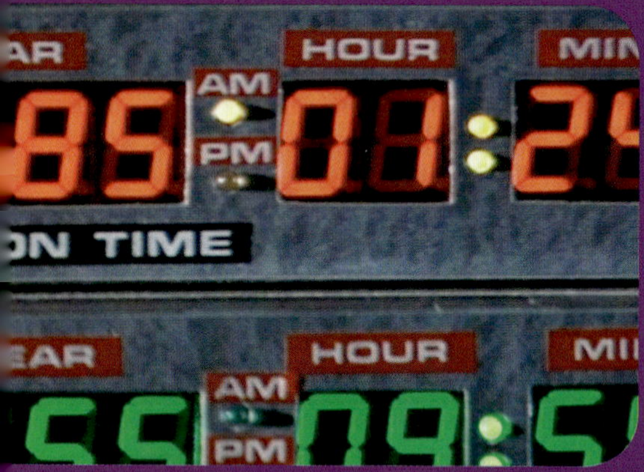

Viewing Guide for

Back to the Future

At this point in the movie, Marty has realized that his presence in the past has caused a disturbance in time. He has found Dr. Brown, who is 30 years younger, and convinced the inventor to help. If Marty can't leave the year 1955 within the next few minutes, his family will lose its place in the future. He and Doc make speedy preparations in the middle of a lightning storm. As they say their goodbyes, Marty feels he must take a moment to share some important information.

Watch the clip several times. Take as much time as you need to see the events unfold and to spot different visual and sound techniques. Use these questions to help you.

NOW VIEW

FIRST VIEWING: **Comprehension**

1. **Summarize** What has to happen for the time machine to leave 1955?
2. **Recall** What does Doc do with the information from Marty?

CLOSE VIEWING: **Media Literacy**

3. **Analyze Camera Shots** The director uses many **low-angle shots** to show Doc at work at the top of the clock tower. How do the low-angle shots help you believe Doc is in danger?
4. **Analyze Sound** Identify at least three **sound effects** that add excitement to the scene.
5. **Analyze Techniques** The clip from *Back to the Future* includes many shots of clocks—both old-fashioned and digital. Why do you think the director uses so many shots that focus on the time?

Write or Discuss

Evaluate the Film Clip In this lesson, you've explored several moviemaking techniques that are used to spark an audience's imagination. Consider the clip from *Back to the Future*. How close did you come to believing the amazing events? Give at least two reasons for your response. Think about

- how you reacted to the events at your first viewing
- how well the moviemakers use such techniques as camera shots and music and other sounds to create excitement

Produce Your Own Media

Storyboard a Race Against Time A **storyboard** is a device used to plan the shooting of a movie. A storyboard is made up of drawings and brief descriptions of what is happening in each shot of a scene. The drawings of a storyboard help moviemakers visualize how a finished scene might look before the scene is filmed. Create a storyboard for a part of the *Back to the Future* clip that you think shows a tense moment. Work with a partner to decide what part of the clip to present.

HERE'S HOW Here are two suggestions for making the storyboard:

- Show what happens in four to six individual frames.
- Show Marty and Doc's race against time. Include a shot or two that includes their quick actions.

MEDIA TOOLS

For help with creating a storyboard, visit the **Media Center** at **ClassZone.com.**

STUDENT MODEL

Shot 1
Marty is speeding down the street.

Shot 2
The hand moves on the clock.

Shot 3
Lightning strikes the tower.

Shot 4
An electrical current moves down the cable.

Shot 5
Doc connects the cables in time.

Shot 6
The car and the current make contact!

Tech Tip

Try using a computer drawing program to make the frames for the storyboard.

The Unnatural Course of Time

Movie Review

Use with the *Back to the Future* Media Study, page 150.

ALABAMA STANDARDS

LIT & WRITING STANDARDS
7 Interpret author's message in informational texts
9 Compose in expository mode

What's the Connection?

Did you enjoy the film clip from *Back to the Future?* Find out what Daniel Briney thought of the entire film by reading his movie review, "The Unnatural Course of Time."

Skill Focus: Analyze a Writer's Position

If someone were to say, "That was a great movie! Go see it!" you might ask, "What makes it so good?" and "What's it about?"

When you run across a movie review, read to find out the reviewer's opinion of the film. But don't stop there. Read on to learn specific reasons and evidence for the reviewer's opinion. Then you can decide whether you might agree.

You can usually find the writer's opinion, or **position,** stated in the first paragraph. In the following review, Daniel Briney uses the first paragraph to express his position on the film. He writes

> *Back to the Future* is a thoughtful, beautifully crafted fantasy that maintains a joyous momentum from beginning to end. The movie succeeds so magnificently in everything it sets out to do as to be an absolutely perfect motion picture.

Now you know Briney's position. As you read the rest of his review and learn more about his position, complete the chart.

Briney's Position	*Specific Reasons and Evidence*
The movie is "thoughtful."	*"Fox's Marty McFly is a genuine kid, with genuine fears for his future."*
The movie is a "beautifully crafted fantasy."	*All the characters and events affect one another in important ways.*
The movie "maintains a joyous momentum from beginning to end."	
The movie succeeds "magnificently in everything it sets out to do."	
The movie is "an absolutely perfect motion picture."	

BACK FORWARD STOP REFRESH HOME PRINT

The Unnatural Course of Time

Review by **Daniel Briney**

Back to the Future is a thoughtful, beautifully crafted fantasy that maintains a joyous momentum from beginning to end. The movie succeeds so magnificently in everything it sets out to do as to be an absolutely perfect motion picture. **A**

Its hero is Marty McFly (Michael J. Fox), an average American 17-year-old of the '80s—filled with youthful hopes for his future, and fearful that they may not come to pass. . . . One night, an encounter with his friend Dr. Emmett L. Brown's (Christopher Lloyd) time machine throws Marty into a struggle for his very existence. . . . He's deposited in the year 1955, where his home town Hill Valley is cleaner and brighter, Doc Brown is a younger man only beginning to probe the fourth dimension, and Marty's own parents are high school students with their whole lives before them. . . . But by coming to the past, Marty has accidentally altered something with profound ramifications for his future: his parents' first meeting. A photo of Marty and his siblings, whose images are fading away one by one, is an ominous sign of what this turn of events means. Of course, if his parents never meet and fall in love, he can never be born. . . . Marty has exactly a week to somehow bring them together, or be erased for all time. **B**

Fox's Marty McFly is a genuine kid, with genuine fears for his future—and as we are introduced to the other members of his family, failures all, his otherwise-normal teenage anxieties take on a greater urgency. . . . It's in this context that his friendship with Doc Brown makes such perfect sense.

Fox and Lloyd both turn in outstanding performances here—the personalities of these two and the excellent comic and dramatic chemistry

FOCUS ON FORM "The Unnatural Course of Time" is a **movie review,** a short essay in which a writer presents and supports his or her opinions about a movie.

A ANALYZE A WRITER'S POSITION Judging by his opening paragraph, what do you expect Daniel Briney to discuss in the rest of the review?

B MOVIE REVIEW A movie review usually gives a short description of the movie's main plot and conflict. Briefly summarize Briney's description of *Back to the Future.*

BACK FORWARD STOP REFRESH HOME PRINT

C ANALYZE A WRITER'S POSITION

Reread lines 22–28. What observations does Briney make to support his opinion that the film is "an absolutely perfect motion picture"? Add these to your chart.

between them are crucial to *Back to the Future*'s great appeal. . . . **C**

The characters' relationship is best communicated by the major conflict that erupts between them: that of future knowledge. Doc is adamant that *no one* should be allowed information about his own future, lest that knowledge endanger the same future—just as Marty's has been endangered. Marty faces a heart-rending decision over whether to heed the scientist's warnings or ignore them. . . . And even if there were an easy way to tell him, Doc won't listen. . . . In this, one of the movie's most touching scenes, Doc rebuffs his friend's attempt to save him:

DOC: Marty, I'm going to be really sad to see you go. You've made a real difference in my life; you've given me something to shoot for. Just *knowing* that I'm going to be around to see *1985,* that I'm going to succeed in *this,* that I'm going to have a chance to travel through time . . . It's going to be really hard waiting thirty years before I can talk to you about everything that's happened in the past few days. I'm really going to miss you, Marty.

MARTY: I'm really going to miss you. (*a beat*) Doc, *about* the future . . .

DOC: *No!* Marty, we've already agreed that having information about the future can be extremely dangerous! Even if your intentions are *good,* it can backfire drastically. Marty, whatever you have to tell me, I'll find out through the natural course of *time.*

Of course, the film deserves a great deal of praise for its action sequences, most of which feature the bizarrely modified, impossibly cool DeLorean time machine. There is a great deal of excitement in Marty's . . . pursuit through the town square by an enraged bully, and a superbly realized, adrenaline-fueled climax in which Doc Brown dangles precipitously from the courthouse clock tower. . . . **D**

D ANALYZE A WRITER'S POSITION

Part of Briney's position is that the film maintains momentum. Reread lines 49–54. What does Briney say in this paragraph that supports this idea? Add your answer to your chart. What words and phrases support this idea? Record them in your chart.

But it is *Back to the Future*'s ultimate message—that we can change our lives for the better—that is at the very heart of its enormous success. . . .

Back to the Future is a unique coming-of-age story that hits every mark in spectacular fashion and leaves us not only thoroughly entertained, but heartened. We don't need to believe in real-life time machines for it to successfully remind us that all things are possible—and that we are our own second chances.

Comprehension

1. **Recall** What does Daniel Briney say is the main message of *Back to the Future?*
2. **Summarize** In his movie review, Briney includes a touching scene between Doc and Marty. Summarize what happens in this scene.

Critical Analysis

3. **Examine a Movie Review** Reread the notes next to the movie review. Besides providing a writer's opinions of a movie and support for those opinions, what else does a movie review usually provide? Tell why you think this might be helpful to a reader.
4. **Analyze a Writer's Position** Review the chart you completed. Does Briney support each part of his position?

Read for Information: Compare and Contrast

WRITING PROMPT

In the review you just read, Daniel Briney describes the clock-tower scene as "a superbly realized, adrenaline-fueled climax" (lines 52–53). Do you agree with his opinions of this scene? In a paragraph, compare and contrast your opinions of this scene with Briney's.

To answer this prompt, first decide on your own opinions of the clock-tower scene by jotting them down. Then follow these steps:

1. Use a Venn diagram to record your opinions and Daniel Briney's.
2. Look at your diagram to see whether there are more similarities or more differences.
3. In a sentence, tell whether your opinions and Briney's are very similar or quite different. Then support the sentence by pointing out the specific similarities and differences.
4. If your opinion of the clock-tower scene is very different from Briney's, consider explaining the reasons for your opinion.

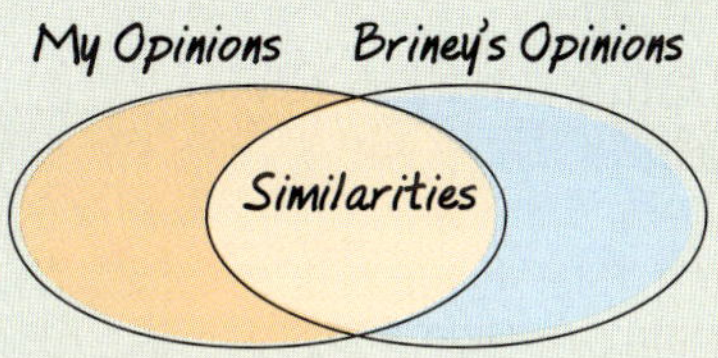

ALABAMA STANDARDS

LIT & WRITING STANDARDS
7 Interpret author's message in informational texts
9 Compose in expository mode

Writing Workshop

Descriptive Essay

The literature in this unit includes vivid descriptions that make you feel as if you're right there with the characters. Now you have a chance to describe the world as you see it. Check out the **Writer's Road Map** for details on writing a focused description—a detailed explanation of what a certain place is like.

WRITER'S ROAD MAP

Describing People and Places

WRITING PROMPT 1

Writing from Your Life Write a focused description of a special place. Your description should be richly detailed and should explain why the place is important to you.

Places to Consider

- an unusual or special place you have visited
- a place in your everyday life, such as a park or mall
- a place that was important in your past

WRITING PROMPT 2

Writing from Literature Choose a place from a story you have read. Describe the place in that story from a character's point of view. You may invent details about the place, as long as they make sense in the story. Be sure to explain which story and character you chose and why you chose them.

Places to Consider

- Mrs. Jones's room from the point of view of Roger ("Thank You, M'am")
- Victor's school, from his point of view ("Seventh Grade")

WRITING TOOLS

For prewriting, revision, and editing tools, visit the **Writing Center** at **ClassZone.com.**

KEY TRAITS

1. IDEAS

- Identifies the **place**
- Explains why the place is **significant**

2. ORGANIZATION

- Follows a clear **organizational pattern,** with an introduction, a body, and a conclusion
- Uses **transitions** to connect ideas
- Provides **background information** for the reader, if it is needed

3. VOICE

- Shows the writer's or the character's personality and **style**

4. WORD CHOICE

- Uses **sensory details** to show the reader what the place is like

5. SENTENCE FLUENCY

- Holds reader interest by using different **sentence lengths**

6. CONVENTIONS

- Uses **correct grammar, spelling, and punctuation**

WRITING/LANGUAGE STANDARD
9 Compose in descriptive mode

Part 1: Analyze a Student Model

Online INTERACTIVE MODEL CLASSZONE.COM

Rico Alvarez
Draper School

Sammy's: My Special Place

If you ask friends to name a special place, they'll probably say some fancy spot that costs a lot of money to visit. I'm different. One of my special places is a tiny little diner with peeling paint and small, crowded tables. For four years, I went to Sammy's Place every day after school to wait for my mom and to see my grandma. For about five hours a week almost every week, Sammy's Place was my place.

The first thing I'd notice on my way to Sammy's was the smells. Sammy's was known for its fried chicken, hamburgers, and pizza. It was also known for gyros, which is a kind of sandwich made with lamb. As I got close to the diner, the smell of meat on the grill would always greet me first. Before I entered the door, my nose would tell me if lamb was roasting in the oven. I could usually smell peppers and onions frying. Sometimes, I knew something sizzling and crispy had just come out of the deep fryer. On Fridays, the smells of garlic, sauce, and fresh pizza crust drifted onto the street from the pizza oven.

When I stepped inside the door, the same scene always greeted me. I'd see the line of tables, some filled with diners. At that time of day, though, most sat like empty boxes, waiting for people to fill them. There was always some music playing, too—some old '90s stuff, only the violin version. The best part of walking in, though, was the people who greeted me. "Rico!" Sammy's voice would sing out. She'd say it like a song, with a long *REEEE* and a short, short *ko,* the way she'd learned it from my grandma. A huge smile would crack her face from cheek to cheek. Sammy was really Samantha Stavros, the owner and the cook.

KEY TRAITS IN ACTION

Introduction identifies the **place** and explains why it is **significant** to the writer.

Description includes **transitions** and has a clear **organization**—on the way to the diner, at the diner, leaving the diner. **Background information** (the explanation of gyros) helps the reader understand.

Sensory details involving sound and sight give the reader a "you are there" feeling.

Better than hearing Sammy, though, was seeing my grandma. Even if she was in the middle of waiting on a customer, her face would brighten, and she'd always come over and give me a hug. "How's my little man?" she'd ask. As I hugged her back, her apron, with its coffee spills or sauce stains, would tell me part of the story of her day.

Then I'd sit down. I always sat at the right end of the counter on a tall silver stool with a soft, red leather seat. That was close to where Sammy flipped burgers. I'd almost always order my favorite, a gooey tuna melt, with cheese dripping out of the toasted bread. I loved the slightly salty taste of the tuna. Yum! I'd eat the sour pickle last and wash it all down with cold milk. As long as it wasn't busy, my grandma would take her break then and sit with me. She'd ask me about my day and tell me about customers. Then my mom would arrive. I'd hug Grandma goodbye, and Sammy would call out, "Take care of your mama!" It was always the same.

Different **sentence lengths** help keep the description lively and interesting.

I don't go to Sammy's Place anymore. I'm old enough to be on my own now, and besides, I have track or math club most days. The strange thing is how much I miss that old diner, though. I can still see that counter and smell the cooking smells. Maybe that's because, for a few years, Sammy's Place was the next best thing to home.

Entire description has a relaxed, informal **style** that shows the writer's personality.

2

WRITING/LANGUAGE STANDARD
9.a Using transitional words and phrases

Part 2: Apply the Writing Process

PREWRITING

What Should I Do?	What Does It Look Like?

1. Generate ideas.
List places that are special to you. Try to see, hear, or otherwise experience each one in your mind. Which one comes to life best? Put an asterisk next to it.

TIP **Are you short on ideas? Look through old photo albums, scrapbooks, post cards, or souvenirs.**

the beach near Uncle Dave's house
- *hot sand, cold water, big waves*

the baseball field in the park
- *shouts, cheers, dust*

**Sammy's Place, where I went after school*
- *food, smells of cooking*

2. Decide on your focus.
Now ask yourself how you can make your topic interesting to your reader.

Sammy's Place

I went there every school day for four years! Sammy is really Samantha. Lots of great smells and tastes.

3. Think about sensory details.
Make a cluster of details related to sights, sounds, smells, tastes, and textures.

TIP **Some memories don't include certain senses, such as taste. However, if you can't come up with plenty of sensory details, choose a new topic.**

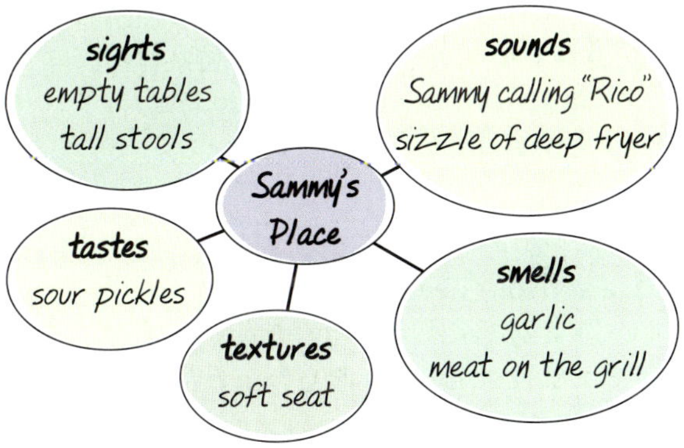

4. Freewrite as you observe your topic or picture it in your mind.
If you can, observe the place again, or try studying pictures of your subject. Otherwise, call your subject to mind. Then just start writing.

I can smell the garlic and pizza crust baking before I even go in. Peppers frying, too. Hamburgers on the grill, lamb roasting. Grandma smiling!

DRAFTING

What Should I Do?	What Does It Look Like?
1. Get organized. There are many ways to organize a description. Here are two: • **Spatial Order** Describes qualities in the order they appear, such as top to bottom, left to right, inside to outside • **Order of Impression** Discusses details in the order in which the writer experiences them	**SPATIAL ORDER**: *Left—grill area and kitchen (smell meat on grill, hear sizzle) Middle—tables (see empty tables, hear old 1990s music) Right—doorway and cash register (see people coming in, hear beeps of register)* **ORDER OF IMPRESSION**: *Outside the door (smell meat, onions, pizza crust) When I come in (see people, hear Sammy and Grandma) When I sit down (feel soft seat, taste tuna melt)*
2. Start out strong. Start your description with a "hook" to interest your reader. You can do that with emotion, surprise, humor, a question, a contrast, or vivid details. TIP **If you have trouble writing your introduction, write your body and conclusion first.**	*Vivid details* *I can still smell the roasting meat and hear the sizzling peppers of Sammy's Place.* *A contrast* *If you ask friends to name a special place, they'll probably say some fancy spot that costs a lot of money to visit. I'm different.*
3. Use sensory details. Don't stop with how something looks. Tell how it smells, tastes, sounds, or feels. Use language that lets your reader share the experience. **See page 164:** Avoid Clichés	*My nose would tell me if lamb was roasting in the oven. I could usually smell peppers and onions frying.* — *Sensory details: smell*
4. Wrap it up. Is there a final detail or thought that could help your reader understand why this subject matters to you?	*The strange thing is how much I miss that old diner. Maybe that's because, for a few years, Sammy's Place was the next best thing to home.* — *Why it matters*

REVISING AND EDITING

What Should I Do?	What Does It Look Like?
1. Check your organization. • Underline transitional words and phrases. Transitions include *first, next, then, when, after, on the right, on the left, at the top, next to,* and *below,* and any other words and phrases that link ideas. • Do you have enough transitions to help your reader move easily from detail to detail and idea to idea? **See page 292:** Add Transitions	*As I got close to the diner, the smell of meat on the grill would always greet me first.* *Before I entered the door,* *~~M~~y nose would tell me if lamb was roasting in the oven.*
2. Add background information. • Ask a peer reader to [bracket] words or references that are confusing or unfamiliar. • Add details or explanations that make your description clear. **See page 164:** Ask a Peer Reader	*It was also known for [gyros.] That's a kind of sandwich made with lamb.*
3. Make your voice heard. • Because this is personal writing, you want your reader to get a sense of your **voice**—your style and personality. (If you chose prompt 2, you want your reader to get a sense of the character's voice.) • Read your description aloud. Does it sound like a textbook? If so, add details that put you (or the character) in the picture.	*For four years, I went to Sammy's Place every day after school to wait for my mom and to see my grandma. For about five hours a week almost every week, Sammy's Place was my place.*
4. Add variety to your sentences. • Are all your sentences about the same length? • Try mixing in some short and long sentences for a change of pace.	*~~I'd almost always order my favorite. It was a gooey tuna melt. It had cheese dripping out of the toasted bread. I really liked it.~~* *I'd almost always order my favorite, a gooey tuna melt, with cheese dripping out of the toasted bread. Yum!*

Preparing to Publish

Descriptive Essay

Apply the Rubric

A strong description of a place . . .

- ☑ identifies the place being described
- ☑ tells why the place matters
- ☑ is well organized, with an introduction, a body, and a conclusion
- ☑ uses transitions to connect ideas
- ☑ uses details that appeal to the senses
- ☑ varies the lengths of sentences
- ☑ explains information that might be unclear to the reader
- ☑ has a style that shows the writer's or character's personality

Ask a Peer Reader

- What is my subject, and why is it important to me?
- As you read, what can you see? hear? taste? touch? smell?
- Is anything unclear? What do I need to explain?

Avoid Clichés

Cliché	Replacement
home sweet home	my place
like night and day	as different as waking and dreaming
dry as a bone	dry as dune grass in the sun
as tough as nails	steely, strong, unyielding

Check Your Grammar

- Use commas to separate items in a series.

garlic, sauce, and fresh pizza crust

- Use a comma after an introductory phrase or clause.

For four years, I went to Sammy's Place every day after school.

See page R49: Quick Reference: Punctuation

Writing Online

PUBLISHING OPTIONS
For publishing options, visit the **Writing Center** at **ClassZone.com.**

ASSESSMENT PREPARATION
For writing and grammar assessment practice, go to the **Assessment Center** at **ClassZone.com.**

COMMUNICATION STANDARD
15 Demonstrate listening skills

PUBLISHING WITH TECHNOLOGY

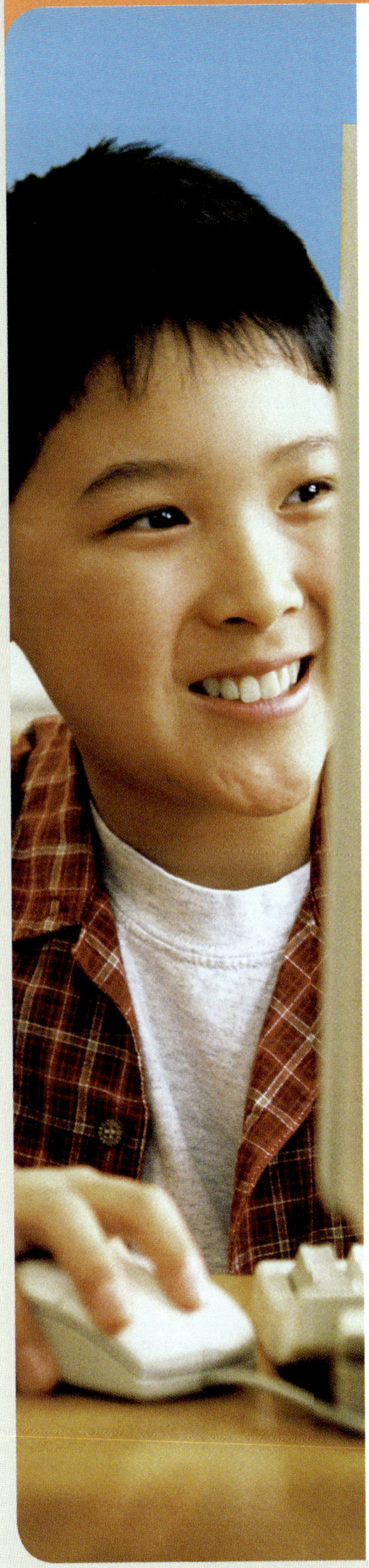

Producing a Radio Dramatization

To turn all or part of your description into a radio segment, all you need is a tape recorder, sound effects, and imagination.

Preparing the Dramatization

1. **Sound it out.** A radio segment needs words, sound effects, and, usually, a narrator. To get started, try making a chart.

Narrator	Words	Sound Effects
Rico tells own story	"I walk into Sammy's Place."	dishes clinking, pop music playing (violin version)
	"Sammy always says hello."	Sammy's voice saying "REEEEko"
	"It's not very busy now."	background voices of diners

2. **Write a script.** A radio script is more than words and sound effects. It includes information on emotions, pauses, interruptions, and sensory details. It also tells how—for example, loud or soft, fast or slow.

> RICO: Grandma would always come over and give me a hug.
> GRANDMA (cheerfully): How's my little man?
> (Sound effects: glasses and silverware clinking, people talking in background)

Presenting the Dramatization

1. **Cast your segment.** Choose your actors and narrator. Put some other classmates in charge of sound effects.
2. **Rehearse.** Run through the presentation. Look for ways to make it more interesting, more dramatic, and more entertaining. Add or change sounds and words.
3. **Record and air your segment.** Record your segment on audiotape. Then play it for your classmates or for family members. Get their feedback on your descriptive powers.

Assessment Practice

Reading Comprehension

ASSESS
The practice test items on the next few pages match skills listed on the Unit Goals page (page 23) and addressed throughout this unit. Taking this practice test will help you assess your knowledge of these skills and determine your readiness for the Unit Test.

REVIEW
After you take the practice test, your teacher can help you identify any skills you need to review.

- Plot Stages
- Setting
- Sequence
- Cause and Effect
- Latin Roots
- Prefixes
- Suffixes
- Possessives
- Pronoun-Antecedent Agreement
- Run-On Sentences

ASSESSMENT ONLINE
For more assessment practice and test-taking tips, go to the **Assessment Center** at **ClassZone.com.**

DIRECTIONS *Read this selection and answer the questions that follow.*

Papa's Parrot

Cynthia Rylant

Though his father was fat and merely owned a candy and nut shop, Harry Tillian liked his papa. Harry stopped liking candy and nuts when he was around seven, but, in spite of this, he and Mr. Tillian had remained friends and were still friends in the year Harry turned twelve.

For years, after school, Harry had always stopped in to see his father at work. Many of Harry's friends stopped there, too, to spend a few cents choosing penny candy from the giant bins or to sample Mr. Tillian's latest batch of roasted peanuts. Mr. Tillian looked forward to seeing his son and his son's friends every day. He liked the company.

When Harry entered junior high school, though, he didn't come by the candy and nut shop as often. Nor did his friends. They were older and they had more spending money. They went to a burger place. They played video games. They shopped for records. None of them were much interested in candy and nuts anymore.

A new group of children came to Mr. Tillian's shop now. But not Harry Tillian and his friends.

The year Harry turned twelve was also the year Mr. Tillian got a parrot. He went to a pet store one day and bought one for more money than he could really afford. He brought the parrot to his shop, set its cage near the sign for maple clusters and named it Rocky.

Harry thought this was the strangest thing his father had ever done, and he told him so, but Mr. Tillian just ignored him.

Rocky was good company for Mr. Tillian. When business was slow, Mr. Tillian would turn on a small color television he had sitting in a corner, and he and Rocky would watch the soap operas. Rocky liked to scream when the romantic music came on, and Mr. Tillian would yell at him to shut up, but they seemed to enjoy themselves.

The more Mr. Tillian grew to like his parrot, and the more he talked to it instead of to people, the more embarrassed Harry became. Harry would stroll past the shop, on his way somewhere else, and he'd take a quick look inside to see what his dad was doing. Mr. Tillian was always talking to the bird. So Harry kept walking.

At home things were different. Harry and his father joked with each other at the dinner table as they always had—Mr. Tillian teasing Harry about his smelly socks; Harry teasing Mr. Tillian about his blubbery stomach. At home things seemed all right.

But one day, Mr. Tillian became ill. He had been at work, unpacking boxes of caramels, when he had grabbed his chest and fallen over on top of the candy. A customer had found him, and he was taken to the hospital in an ambulance.

Mr. Tillian couldn't leave the hospital. He lay in bed, tubes in his arms, and he worried about his shop. New shipments of candy and nuts would be arriving. Rocky would be hungry. Who would take care of things?

Harry said he would. Harry told his father that he would go to the store every day after school and unpack boxes. He would sort out all the candy and nuts. He would even feed Rocky.

So, the next morning, while Mr. Tillian lay in his hospital bed, Harry took the shop key to school with him. After school he left his friends and walked to the empty shop alone. In all the days of his life, Harry had never seen the shop closed after school. Harry didn't even remember what the CLOSED sign looked like. The key stuck in the lock three times, and inside he had to search all the walls for the light switch.

The shop was as his father had left it. Even the caramels were still spilled on the floor. Harry bent down and picked them up one by one, dropping them back in the boxes. The bird in its cage watched him silently.

Harry opened the new boxes his father hadn't gotten to. Peppermints. Jawbreakers. Toffee creams. Strawberry kisses. Harry traveled from bin to bin, putting the candies where they belonged.

"Hello!"

Harry jumped, spilled a box of jawbreakers.

"Hello, Rocky!"

Harry stared at the parrot. He had forgotten it was there. The bird had been so quiet, and Harry had been thinking only of the candy.

"Hello," Harry said.

"Hello, Rocky!" answered the parrot.

Harry walked slowly over to the cage. The parrot's food cup was empty. Its water was dirty. The bottom of the cage was a mess.

Harry carried the cage into the back room.

"Hello, Rocky!"

GO ON

"Is that all you can say, you dumb bird?" Harry mumbled. The bird said nothing else.

Harry cleaned the bottom of the cage, refilled the food and water cups, then put the cage back in its place and resumed sorting the candy.

"Where's Harry?"

Harry looked up.

"Where's Harry?"

Harry stared at the parrot.

"Where's Harry?"

Chills ran down Harry's back. What could the bird mean? It was like something from *The Twilight Zone.*

"Where's Harry?"

Harry swallowed and said, "I'm here. I'm here, you stupid bird."

"You stupid bird!" said the parrot.

Well, at least he's got one thing straight, thought Harry.

"Miss him! Miss him! Where's Harry? You stupid bird!"

Harry stood with a handful of peppermints.

"*What?*" he asked.

"Where's Harry?" said the parrot.

"I'm *here,* you stupid bird! I'm here!" Harry yelled. He threw the peppermints at the cage, and the bird screamed and clung to its perch.

Harry sobbed, "I'm here." The tears were coming.

Harry leaned over the glass counter.

"Papa." Harry buried his face in his arms.

"Where's Harry?" repeated the bird.

Harry sighed and wiped his face on his sleeve. He watched the parrot. He understood now: someone had been saying, for a long time, "Where's Harry? Miss him."

Harry finished his unpacking, then swept the floor of the shop. He checked the furnace so the bird wouldn't get cold. Then he left to go visit his papa.

Comprehension

DIRECTIONS *Answer these questions about the story "Papa's Parrot."*

1. Most of the story takes place at the

A Tillian home **C** hospital
B candy shop **D** pet store

2. The conflict in the story begins when

A Harry is seven years old
B Rocky screams at the television
C Harry turns twelve years old
D Rocky says, "Where's Harry?"

ARMT/ADAW SKILLS PRACTICE

3. The author probably begins the story when Harry is seven to show that
   - **A** Harry liked visiting his father at the shop for many years
   - **B** Mr. Tillian became less talkative at that time
   - **C** Harry's friends did not like the shop
   - **D** Rocky changed Harry's feelings about the shop

4. Which conflict does Mr. Tillian struggle with in the story?
   - **A** His parrot argues with him.
   - **B** He does not like birds.
   - **C** His store is losing money.
   - **D** He misses his son's company.

5. When does Mr. Tillian buy the parrot?
   - **A** when Harry and his school friends visit the nut shop
   - **B** when he first buys the candy and nut shop
   - **C** after he gets sick and has to go to the hospital
   - **D** after Harry stops visiting the shop every day

6. Which of the following is the cause of Harry's conflict?
   - **A** He is embarrassed by his father.
   - **B** He does not like candy.
   - **C** He is unhappy with his friends.
   - **D** He cannot work after school.

7. The climax of the story occurs when
   - **A** Harry and his friends stop visiting the store
   - **B** Mr. Tillian buys a parrot
   - **C** the parrot watches television
   - **D** Harry realizes that his father has been lonely

Open-Ended

SHORT ANSWER

Write two or three sentences to answer each question.

8. Why are Harry's friends less interested in the shop after they turn twelve?

9. Why can Harry and his father joke together at home but not at the store?

ESSAY

Write two or three paragraphs to answer this question.

10. Discuss how the parrot brings about the climax of the story. What does Harry learn about his father when he takes care of the shop and Rocky?

GO ON

Vocabulary

DIRECTIONS *Use your knowledge of Latin word roots to answer the following questions.*

1. The Latin word *ambulare* means "to go about." Which word in the story most likely comes from the word *ambulare?*

   A business

   B caramels

   C ambulance

   D customer

2. The Latin word *hospes* means "guest." Which word in the story most likely comes from the word *hospes?*

   A company

   B home

   C hospital

   D friends

3. The Latin word *fornax* means "oven." Which word in the story most likely comes from the word *fornax?*

   A forward

   B furnace

   C afford

   D food

DIRECTIONS *Use your knowledge of prefixes and suffixes to answer the following questions.*

4. The word *round* means "circle." What is the most likely meaning of the prefix *a-*, which is used to form *around* in line 3?

   A in **C** without

   B not **D** under

5. The word *pack* means "to put into a container." What is the most likely meaning of the prefix *un-*, which is used to form *unpacking* in line 37?

   A the opposite of **C** again

   B not done **D** away

6. Which suffix can be added to the noun *music* in line 26 to form an adjective that means "skilled in music"?

   A *-al* **C** *-ial*

   B *-able* **D** *-eous*

7. Which suffix can be added to the noun *room* in line 68 to form an adjective that means "having plenty of room"?

   A *-ate* **C** *-ly*

   B *-ial* **D** *-y*

ARMT/ADAW SKILLS PRACTICE

Writing & Grammar

DIRECTIONS *Read this passage and answer the questions that follow.*

(1) Nature can do some amazing things, sometimes, people even get to watch. (2) In 1995, a new island formed as part of the Tonga Islands. (3) An active volcano erupted at Metis Shoal this eruption caused a heavy flow of lava. (4) As the volcanos lava bubbled up, it built a new island. (5) Fortunately, someone used their video camera to record this event. (6) According to many scientists accounts, Metis Shoal had erupted before with similar results. (7) The volcano produced new islands when they erupted in 1968 and 1979.

1. Choose the correct way to rewrite sentence 1 so that it is no longer a run-on sentence.

A Nature can do some amazing things, sometimes people. Even get to watch.

B Nature can do some amazing things sometimes people even get to watch.

C Nature can do some amazing things sometimes, people; even get to watch.

D Nature can do some amazing things; sometimes, people even get to watch.

2. Choose the correct way to rewrite sentence 3 so that it is no longer a run-on sentence.

A An active volcano erupted at Metis Shoal, and this eruption caused a heavy flow of lava.

B An active volcano erupted at Metis Shoal this eruption. Caused a heavy flow of lava.

C An active volcano erupted but at Metis Shoal this eruption caused a heavy flow of lava.

D An active volcano; erupted at Metis Shoal this eruption caused a heavy flow of lava.

3. Choose the correct way to write the possessive form of the underlined word in sentence 4.

A volcano's' **C** volcano's

B volcanos' **D** volcanos's

4. To maintain pronoun-antecedent agreement in sentence 5, change "their" to

A her **C** its

B they **D** theirs

5. Choose the correct way to write the possessive form of the underlined word in sentence 6.

A scientists's **C** scientist's

B scientists' **D** scientist's'

6. To maintain pronoun-antecedent agreement in sentence 7, change "they" to

A he **C** theirs

B them **D** it

STOP

UNIT 1

More Great Reads

Ideas for Independent Reading

Which questions from Unit 1 made an impression on you? Continue exploring them with these books.

How do you make a good impression?

The Ghost in the Tokaido Inn
by Dorothy Hoobler

What do you long to be? Seikei wants to be a samurai, but he knows that as a merchant's son, the chances are slim. Will Seikei achieve his life's dream? Read this award-winning book and find out.

The Great Turkey Walk
by Kathleen Karr

It is 1860. Fifteen-year-old Simon likes and respects his teacher. One day she tells him it's time he left her class to venture out into the real world. But what will become of him in the rough world of this frontier setting?

No Man's Land
by Susan Bartoletti

Fourteen-year-old Thrasher lies about his age, joins the Confederate Army, and begins his courageous adventure. Along the way, Thrasher comes to know that enemies are people too.

Who sees the best in you?

Bearstone
by Will Hobbs

A troubled Native American teen is sent to work on a ranch in the mountains of Colorado. There the elderly owner provides the steadying influence the boy needs, but complications arise.

Good Night, Mr. Tom
by Michelle Magorian

Young Willie is among thousands of children evacuated from London because of the bombing raids at the brink of World War II. When a wise old man named Mr. Tom adopts him, Willie learns to trust his world again.

Nobody's Daughter
by Susan Pfeffer

Eleven-year-old Emily is packed off to an orphanage but dreams of finding her sister, who has been adopted. Harsh reality greets her in the form of Miss Browne, the director. Whom can she turn to?

What makes you brave?

North by Night
by Katherine Ayres

This story centers on the 1850 Fugitive Slave Act. Through her letters and journal entries, 16-year-old Lucinda tells of her family's attempts to turn their Ohio farm into an Underground Railroad station.

The Dark Is Rising
by Susan Cooper

Eleven-year-old Will Stanton struggles to overcome the powers of the Dark. Will must search for the six magical signs needed in the great battle between the Dark and the Light. Can he find them in time?

The Clay Marble
By Minfong Ho

After fleeing war-torn Cambodia in 1980, Dara, her older brother, and her mother find sanctuary on the Thailand border in a refugee camp. Then fighting erupts, and Dara is separated from her family.

ACT 1

(*Fade in*[1] *on a shot of the night sky. The various heavenly bodies stand out in sharp, sparkling relief. The camera moves slowly across the heavens until it passes the horizon and stops on a sign that reads "Maple Street." It is daytime. Then we see the street below. It is a quiet, tree-lined, small-town American street. The houses have front porches on which people sit and swing on gliders, talking across from house to house.* Steve Brand *is polishing his car, which is parked in front of his house. His neighbor,* Don Martin, *leans against the fender watching him. An ice-cream vendor riding a bicycle is just in the process of stopping to sell some ice cream to a couple of kids. Two women gossip on the front lawn. Another man is watering his lawn with a garden hose. As we see these various activities, we hear the* Narrator*'s voice.*)

Narrator. Maple Street, U.S.A., late summer. A tree-lined little world of front-porch gliders, hopscotch, the laughter of children, and the bell of an ice-cream vendor.

(*There is a pause, and the camera moves over to a shot of the ice-cream vendor and two small boys who are standing alongside just buying ice cream.*)

Narrator. At the sound of the roar and the flash of the light, it will be precisely six-forty-three P.M. on Maple Street.

(*At this moment* Tommy, *one of the two boys buying ice cream from the vendor, looks up to listen to a tremendous screeching roar from overhead. A flash of light plays on the faces of both boys and then moves down the street and disappears. Various people leave their porches or stop what they are doing to stare up at the sky.* Steve Brand, *the man who has been polishing his car, stands there transfixed, staring upwards. He looks at* Don Martin, *his neighbor from across the street.*)

Steve. What was that? A meteor?

Don. That's what it looked like. I didn't hear any crash though, did you?

Steve. Nope. I didn't hear anything except a roar.

Myra (*from her porch*). What was that?

Steve (*raising his voice and looking toward the porch*). Guess it was a meteor, honey. Came awful close, didn't it?

Myra. Too close for my money! Much too close.

(*The camera moves slowly across the various porches to people who stand there watching and talking in low conversing tones.*)

Narrator. Maple Street. Six-forty-four P.M. on a late September evening. (*He pauses.*) Maple Street in the last calm and reflective moment (*pause*) before the monsters came!

(*The camera takes us across the porches again. A man is replacing a light bulb on a front porch. He gets off his stool to flick the switch and finds that nothing happens. Another man is working on an electric power mower. He plugs in the plug, flicks the switch of the mower off and on, but nothing happens. Through a window we see a woman pushing her finger up and down on the dial hook of a telephone. Her voice sounds far away.*)

Woman. Operator, operator, something's wrong on the phone, operator! (Myra Brand *comes out on the porch and calls to* Steve.)

Myra (*calling*). Steve, the power's off. I had the soup on the stove, and the stove just stopped working.

Woman. Same thing over here. I can't get anybody on the phone either. The phone seems to be dead.

(*We look down again on the street. Small, mildly disturbed voices are heard coming from below.*)

Voice One. Electricity's off.

Voice Two. Phone won't work.

---

1. **fade in:** cause the television image to appear gradually.

UNIT 2

Personality Tests

ANALYZING CHARACTER AND POINT OF VIEW

- In Fiction
- In Nonfiction
- In Poetry

UNIT 2 Share What You Know

What makes a great CHARACTER?

An eccentric inventor, an orphaned boy, and a spider—hard to imagine what these three characters have in common, isn't it? But once you know their names—Willy Wonka, Harry Potter, and Charlotte—the connection becomes clearer. All three are examples of **great characters**—figments of authors' imaginations that are so lifelike they seem to pop off the page and into our own world.

ACTIVITY With a partner, brainstorm a list of great characters from stories, TV shows, and movies. Then discuss the following questions:

- Why did you choose these characters? Next to each name, jot down what makes him or her (or it!) great.
- What similarities do you notice about your reasons for selecting these characters?
- On the basis of your discussion, what advice would you give a first-time author about how to create great characters?

ALABAMA STANDARDS

Preview Unit Goals

LITERARY ANALYSIS

- Recognize character traits
- Identify and analyze characterization
- Recognize point of view, including first person, limited third person, and omniscient
- Identify and compare characters

READING

- Use reading strategies, including visualizing, predicting, and connecting
- Make inferences, draw conclusions, and synthesize
- Identify cause-effect relationships

WRITING AND GRAMMAR

- Write a comparison-contrast essay
- Correctly use present, past, and future verb tenses
- Correctly use comparative and superlative forms of adjectives and adverbs

SPEAKING, LISTENING, AND VIEWING

- Conduct an interview

VOCABULARY

- Use context clues to determine the meaning of words and idioms

ACADEMIC VOCABULARY

- character traits
- characterization
- first-person point of view
- omniscient point of view
- inferences
- context clues

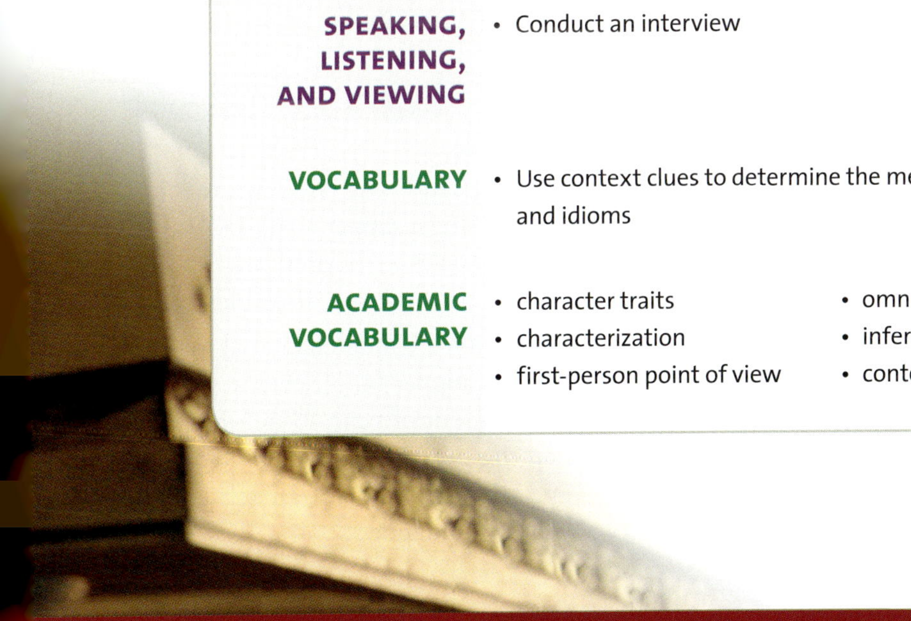

UNIT 2

Reader's Workshop

Character and Point of View

Bossy and loud, sensitive and shy, athletic and adventurous—what qualities make you admire one person and dislike another? When you meet characters in literature, you are likely to form strong impressions, just as you do with people in real life. By looking closely at character and point of view, you can understand your reactions to the people you meet on the page.

ALABAMA STANDARDS

READING STANDARD
2 Relate literary elements to each other, including point of view

Part 1: Point of View

Imagine watching three videotapes of a soccer game. One was taken from the sidelines; you can see all the players in action. The second was taped by someone running alongside one player. The third was taken *by* a player; you can see the game through her eyes. In literature, the **narrator** holds the camera—that is, tells the story. A writer's choice of narrator is referred to as **point of view.**

Just how much can point of view affect a story? Find out by examining these examples from a comical take on the familiar tale "Cinderella."

FIRST-PERSON POINT OF VIEW

The Narrator

- is a character in the story
- uses the pronouns *I* and *me* to refer to himself or herself
- describes his or her own thoughts, feelings, and impressions
- does not know what other characters are thinking and feeling

Example

Cinderella was the last girl in the world I would want to marry. I mean, who wears glass slippers to a ball? I only picked up that lost slipper because it was a safety hazard. And it seemed like a princely thing to do.

THIRD-PERSON POINT OF VIEW

The Narrator

- is not a character in the story
- is called **limited** if he or she tells the thoughts and feelings of only one character
- is called **omniscient,** or all-knowing, if he or she reveals the thoughts and feelings of all the characters

Examples

Limited: Cinderella ran down the steps, losing a slipper along the way. The prince thought to himself, "She's going to break an ankle."

Omniscient: Cinderella hated to lose her slipper but knew she was running out of time. Watching her, the prince shook his head and thought, "There's an accident waiting to happen!"

MODEL 1: FIRST-PERSON POINT OF VIEW

This story is told by a teenage boy. What do you learn about him from what he says and thinks?

from

An Hour with Abuelo

Short story by **Judith Ortiz Cofer**

My grandfather is in a nursing home in Brooklyn, and my mother wants me to spend some time with him, since the doctors say that he doesn't have too long to go now. *I* don't have much time left of my summer vacation, and there's a stack of books next to my bed I've got to read if I'm going to get into the AP English class I want. I'm going stupid in some of my classes, and Mr. Williams, the principal at Central, said that if I passed some reading tests, he'd let me move up.

Besides, I hate the place, the old people's home, especially the way it smells like industrial-strength ammonia and other stuff I won't mention, since it turns my stomach.

Close Read

1. Copy any sentence, then circle the pronouns that show the first-person point of view.
2. Describe two things you learn about the narrator from what he tells you about himself.

MODEL 2: THIRD-PERSON POINT OF VIEW

In a story told from the third-person limited point of view, the narrator reveals the thoughts of one character. Here, the character is a dog named Buck.

from

The Call of the Wild

Novel by **Jack London**

Dazed, suffering intolerable pain from throat and tongue, with the life half throttled out of him, Buck attempted to face his tormentors. But he was thrown down and choked repeatedly, till they succeeded in filing the heavy brass collar from off his neck. Then the rope was removed, and he was flung into a cagelike crate.

There he lay for the remainder of the weary night, nursing his wrath and wounded pride. He could not understand what it all meant. What did they want with him, these strange men? Why were they keeping him pent up in this narrow crate? He did not know why, but he felt oppressed. . . .

Close Read

1. Find two places where the narrator reveals Buck's thoughts. One example has been boxed.
2. What more might an omniscient narrator be able to tell you?

Part 2: Methods of Characterization

When you meet people, how do you figure out what they are like? You might make judgments based on how they look or how they behave. You may also find out information from others. In literature, these kinds of details are clues to a character's personality. As a reader, you can use these clues to infer a character's **traits**, or qualities, such as sloppiness or bravery. By knowing what to look for, you can get to know the **main characters,** or the most important ones. You may even learn something about the **minor characters,** or less important ones, too.

Writers use four **methods of characterization** to bring their characters to life. What do you learn about Cinderella's fairy godmother from each example?

METHOD OF CHARACTERIZATION	EXAMPLE
 **PHYSICAL APPEARANCE** **Appearances can tell you a great deal about a character. Ask:** • What does the character look like? • What are his or her expressions, gestures, or body language?	The fairy godmother was wearing greasy overalls with a rusty garden fork sticking out of one back pocket. She brushed some dirt off her hands and smiled.
 **THOUGHTS, SPEECH, AND ACTIONS** **A character's words and actions can reveal his or her personality. Ask:** • What does the character think, say, or do? • How does he or she treat others? • What kinds of things are important to him or her?	The fairy godmother thought to herself, "I'd better get to work! I have only eight hours to get Cinderella ready for the ball. And from what I've seen of her, I'll need every second of it."
 **OTHER CHARACTERS** **Other characters' reactions to a character can also serve as clues. Ask:** • What do others say about the character? • How do they treat him or her?	Cinderella's wicked stepsister shrieked when she saw the fairy godmother. "What is this disgusting woman doing in my home? Have her removed at once!"
 **NARRATOR'S COMMENTS** **Sometimes the narrator tells you directly about a character. Ask:** • What does the narrator say about the character? • Does the narrator respect the character or criticize him or her?	The fairy godmother knew how to handle wicked people! In fact, she was frighteningly clever.

METHOD 1: PHYSICAL APPEARANCE

In this novel, a girl finds herself abandoned with her younger siblings in a car outside a shopping mall. What do you learn about their mother from this one brief glimpse?

from

Homecoming

Novel by **Cynthia Voigt**

The woman put her sad moon-face in at the window of the car. "You be good," she said. "You hear me? You little ones, mind what Dicey tells you. You hear?"

"Yes, Momma," they said.

"That's all right then." She slung her purse over her shoulder and walked away, her stride made uneven by broken sandal thongs, thin elbows showing through holes in the oversized sweater, her jeans faded and baggy. When she had disappeared into the crowd of Saturday morning shoppers entering the side doors of the mall, the three younger children leaned forward onto the front seat.

Close Read

1. Find three details that describe the mother's appearance. One example has been boxed for you.
2. What do you learn about the mother from these details?

METHOD 2: THOUGHTS, SPEECH, AND ACTIONS

Here, a girl at her piano lesson notices an umbrella that was left behind by Eugenie, an older student she admires and envies.

from

The White Umbrella

Short story by **Gish Jen**

I stared at the umbrella. I wanted to open it, twirl it around by its slender silver handle; I wanted to dangle it from my wrist on the way to school the way the other girls did. I wondered what Miss Crosman would say if I offered to bring it to Eugenie at school tomorrow. She would be impressed with my consideration for others; Eugenie would be pleased to have it back; and I would have possession of the umbrella for an entire night. I looked at it again, toying with the idea of asking for one for Christmas. I knew, however, how my mother would react.

"Things," she would say. "What's the matter with a raincoat? All you want is things, just like an American."

Close Read

1. The boxed text suggests that the girl wants to fit in at school. What do her other thoughts tell you about her?
2. What do the girl's thoughts in lines 7–10 reveal about her relationship with her mother?

METHOD 3: OTHER CHARACTERS

In this excerpt, a girl named Cassie walks into her classroom and faces her classmates and her teacher. As you read, observe how others react to Cassie. Does she seem to be well liked?

from

ROLL OF THUNDER, HEAR MY CRY

Novel by
Mildred Taylor

I hurried to the rear of the building, turned to the right, and slid into a third-row bench occupied by Gracey Pearson and Alma Scott.

"You can't sit here," objected Gracey. "I'm saving it for Mary Lou."

I glanced back at Mary Lou Wellever depositing her lunch pail on a shelf in the back of the room and said, "Not any more you ain't."

Miss Daisy Crocker, yellow and buckeyed, glared down at me from the middle of the room with a look that said, "Soooooooo, it's you, Cassie Logan."

Close Read

1. Does Gracey Pearson like Cassie? Explain.
2. Reread the boxed sentence about Miss Crocker, Cassie's teacher. How does Miss Crocker feel about Cassie?
3. What impression do you get of Cassie from other characters' reactions to her?

METHOD 4: NARRATOR'S COMMENTS

Here, the narrator tells you directly about a character named Mack. What do you learn about Mack from the narrator's comments?

from

Kitty and Mack: A Love Story

Short story by
Walter Dean Myers

He was eighteen and one newspaper article about him said that he could be in the major leagues by the time he was nineteen. That's how good he was. Naturally the baseball coach loved him. That was the thing about Mack, the people who liked him usually liked him because he was a star. Mack had an attitude problem. He thought he could just show up and everybody was supposed to fall down and go crazy or something.

He was pretty smart, too, but he made this big show of not caring about grades.

Close Read

1. On the basis of the narrator's comments, how would you describe Mack?
2. Do you think the narrator admires Mack? Support your opinion with evidence.

Part 3: Analyze the Literature

In this story, a girl named Katie spends her birthday visiting her dying mother in the hospital. Among her presents is one from her mother. It's a box—a beautiful, empty box. Katie is upset by the present and by her mother's last words to her: "It's you." As you read, use what you have learned to analyze both Katie and her mother.

from

Birthday Box

Short story by **Jane Yolen**

. . . For about a year I cried at anniversaries, like Mama's birthday or mine, at Thanksgiving, on Mother's Day. I stopped writing. I stopped reading except for school assignments. I was pretty mean to my half brothers and totally rotten to my stepmother and Dad. I felt empty and angry, and they all left me pretty much alone.

And then one night, right after my first birthday without Mama, I woke up remembering how she had said, "It's you." Not, "It's for you," just "It's you." Now Mama had been a high school English teacher and a writer herself. She'd had poems published in little magazines. She didn't use words carelessly. In the end she could hardly use any words at all. So—I asked myself in that dark room—why had she said, "It's you"? Why were they the very last words she had ever said to me, forced out with her last breath?

I turned on the bedside light and got out of bed. The room was full of shadows, not all of them real.

Pulling the desk chair over to my closet, I climbed up and felt along the top shelf, and against the back wall, there was the birthday box, just where I had thrown it the day I had moved in with my dad.

I pulled it down and opened it. It was as empty as the day I had put it away.

"It's you," I whispered to the box.

And then suddenly I knew.

Mama had meant *I* was the box, solid and sturdy, maybe even beautiful or at least interesting on the outside. But I had to fill up the box to make it all it could be. And I had to fill me up as well. She had guessed what might happen to me, had told me in a subtle way. In the two words she could manage.

I stopped crying and got some paper out of the desk drawer. I got out my fountain pen. I started writing, and I haven't stopped since.

Close Read

1. From what point of view is this story told? Explain how you can tell.
2. Reread the boxed paragraph. How does Katie react to her mother's death?
3. What do you learn about Katie's mother from what Katie tells you in lines 6–13?
4. Reread lines 23–27. Given what you know about the characters, why do you think Katie's mother would have chosen to deliver her message in this way?
5. How would you describe the character of Katie? Support your answer.

Zebra

Short Story by Chaim Potok

What has the power to HEAL?

ALABAMA STANDARDS

READING STANDARDS
1.d Applying self-monitoring strategies
2 Relate literary elements to each other

KEY IDEA You never know what kind of wounds will cause the greatest damage. An argument with a friend can cause as much pain as a broken leg. Likewise, a physical injury can also scar the spirit. In "Zebra," you will read about a boy your age who needs to **heal** both his body and his mind.

LIST IT With a partner, create two lists. In the first, list three to five ways people cope with physical injuries or disabilities. In the second, identify at least three ways that people deal with emotional pain.

LITERARY ANALYSIS: CHARACTER

The people who appear in stories are called **characters.** A short story usually focuses on one or two **main characters.** To identify who they are, ask yourself:

- Who are the most important characters in the story?
- Who changes or grows over the course of the story?

Minor characters help the reader learn more about the main characters. As you read, notice each character's role.

READING STRATEGY: VISUALIZE

How would you like to view every story in this book as a movie? If you **visualize** while you read, you might come close. To visualize, use descriptions from the selection and your knowledge and imagination to form mental pictures. As you read, record these descriptions in a chart and then sketch the mental pictures they help you form.

Descriptions	*Mental Picture*
"They were odd-looking creatures, like stubby horses, short-legged, thick-necked, with dark and white stripes."	

Review: **Make Inferences**

VOCABULARY IN CONTEXT

Chaim Potok uses the boldfaced words to help tell a story of pain and healing. To see how many you know, substitute a different word or phrase for each one.

1. He tried not to **grimace** in pain.
2. It was hard to unwrap the **intricate** bandage.
3. She is a firm **disciplinarian.**
4. The animal looked **gaunt** and underfed.
5. They skipped **jauntily** down the path.
6. He **winced** when he got a flu shot.
7. A cast might **chafe** your skin.
8. We saw the **contour** of the jagged mountain.
9. She appeared **somber** when she heard the bad news.
10. They applauded our team **exuberantly.**

Author Online

Early Days While growing up in New York City, Chaim Potok lived the strict life of a Hasidic Jew. His parents wanted him to be a religious scholar. But by the time he was 16, Potok had started reading literature other than traditional Jewish texts. The more he read, the more he struggled between religious learning and the call to become a creative artist.

Chaim Potok
1929–2002

Coming to Terms Potok eventually left the Hasidic community for the Conservative movement of Judaism. He became a rabbi and published his first novel in 1967. Much of Potok's writing centers on characters who try to live in both the spiritual world and the secular world of everyday life.

MORE ABOUT THE AUTHOR
For more on Chaim Potok, visit the **Literature Center** at **ClassZone.com.**

Background

Vietnam War One of the characters in this story is a veteran of the Vietnam War. U.S. troops fought in Vietnam from 1965 until 1973. Approximately 58,000 Americans died there, and more than 300,000 were wounded. In 1982, the Vietnam Veterans Memorial was unveiled in Washington, D.C., to honor the men and women who served in the war. A black granite wall bears the names of those who died.

ZEBRA

CHAIM POTOK

He couldn't remember when he began to be called by that name. Perhaps they started to call him Zebra when he first began running. Or maybe he began running when they started to call him Zebra.

He loved the name and he loved to run.

When he was very young, his parents took him to a zoo, where he saw zebras for the first time. They were odd-looking creatures, like stubby horses, short-legged, thick-necked, with dark and white stripes.

Then one day he went with his parents to a movie about Africa, and he saw zebras, hundreds of them, thundering across a grassy plain, dust rising in boiling brown clouds. **A**

ANALYZE VISUALS
Examine the photograph. What images can you identify?

A VISUALIZE
Reread lines 8–10. What words help you picture the scene in the movie?

Was he already running before he saw that movie, or did he begin to run afterward? No one seemed able to remember.

He would go running through the neighborhood for the sheer joy of feeling the wind on his face. People said that when he ran he arched his head up and back, and his face kind of flattened out. One of his teachers told him it was clever to run that way, his balance was better. But the truth was he ran that way, his head thrown back, because he loved to feel the wind rushing across his neck.

Each time, after only a few minutes of running, his legs would begin to feel wondrously light. He would run past the school and the homes on the street beyond the church. All the neighbors knew him and would wave and call out, "Go, Zebra!" And sometimes one or two of their dogs would run with him awhile, barking.

He would imagine himself a zebra on the African plain. Running. **B**

There was a hill on Franklin Avenue, a steep hill. By the time he reached that hill, he would feel his legs so light it was as if he had no legs at all and was flying. He would begin to descend the hill, certain as he ran that he needed only to give himself the slightest push and off he would go, and instead of a zebra he would become the bird he had once seen in a movie about Alaska, he would swiftly change into an eagle, soaring higher and higher, as light as the gentlest breeze, the cool wind caressing his arms and legs and neck.

B CHARACTER
Reread lines 13–24. How does Zebra feel about running?

Then, a year ago, racing down Franklin Avenue, he had given himself that push and had begun to turn into an eagle, when a huge rushing shadow appeared in his line of vision and crashed into him and plunged him into a darkness from which he emerged very, very slowly. . . .

"Never, never, *never* run down that hill so fast that you can't stop at the corner," his mother had warned him again and again.

His schoolmates and friends kept calling him Zebra even after they all knew that the doctors had told him he would never be able to run like that again. **C**

C MAKE INFERENCES
What happened to Zebra a year ago? What details tell you this?

His leg would heal in time, the doctors said, and perhaps in a year or so the brace would come off. But they were not at all certain about his hand. From time to time his injured hand, which he still wore in a sling, would begin to hurt. The doctors said they could find no cause for the pain.

One morning, during Mr. Morgan's geography class, Zebra's hand began to hurt badly. He sat staring out the window at the sky. Mr. Morgan, a stiff-mannered person in his early fifties, given to smart suits and dapper bow ties, called on him to respond to a question. Zebra stumbled about in vain for the answer. Mr. Morgan told him to pay attention to the geography inside the classroom and not to the geography outside.

"In this class, young man, you will concentrate your attention upon the earth, not upon the sky," Mr. Morgan said.

Later, in the schoolyard during the midmorning recess, Zebra stood near the tall fence, looking out at the street and listening to the noises behind him.

His schoolmates were racing about, playing **exuberantly,** shouting and laughing with full voices. Their joyous sounds went ringing through the quiet street.

exuberantly (ĭg-zo͞o′bər-ənt-lē) *adv.* in a manner showing enthusiasm or joy

Most times Zebra would stand alongside the basketball court or behind the wire screen at home plate and watch the games. That day, because his hand hurt so badly, he stood alone behind the chain-link fence of the schoolyard. **D**

D CHARACTER
Why does Zebra stand alone and watch the other students run and play?

That's how he happened to see the man. And that's how the man happened to see him.

One minute the side street on which the school stood was strangely empty, without people or traffic, without even any of the dogs that often roamed about the neighborhood—vacant and silent, as if it were already in the full heat of summer. The red-brick ranch house that belonged to Mr. Morgan, and the white clapboard two-story house in which Mrs. English lived, and the other homes on the street, with their columned front porches and their back patios, and the tall oaks—all stood curiously still in the warm golden light of the mid-morning sun. **E**

E VISUALIZE
Reread lines 66–73. What descriptions help you see the street in your mind? Record them in your chart.

Then a man emerged from wide and busy Franklin Avenue at the far end of the street.

Zebra saw the man stop at the corner and stand looking at a public trash can. He watched as the man poked his hand into the can and fished about but seemed to find nothing he wanted. He withdrew the hand and, raising it to shield his eyes from the sunlight, glanced at the street sign on the lamppost.

He started to walk up the street in the direction of the school.

He was tall and wiry, and looked to be about forty years old. In his right hand he carried a bulging brown plastic bag. He wore a khaki army jacket, a blue denim shirt, blue jeans, and brown cowboy boots. His **gaunt** face and muscular neck were reddened by exposure to the sun. Long brown hair spilled out below his dark-blue farmer's cap. On the front of the cap, in large orange letters, were the words LAND ROVER.[1]

gaunt (gônt) *adj.* thin and bony

He walked with his eyes on the sidewalk and the curb, as if looking for something, and he went right past Zebra without noticing him.

Zebra's hand hurt very much. He was about to turn away when he saw the man stop and look around and peer up at the red-brick wall of

1. **Land Rover:** British automaker known for producing four-wheel-drive vehicles.

the school. The man set down the bag and took off his cap and stuffed it into a pocket of his jacket. From one of his jeans pockets he removed a handkerchief, with which he then wiped his face. He shoved the handkerchief back into the pocket and put the cap back on his head. F

Then he turned and saw Zebra.

He picked up the bag and started down the street to where Zebra was standing. When the man was about ten feet away, Zebra noticed that the left sleeve of his jacket was empty.

The man came up to Zebra and said in a low, friendly, shy voice, "Hello."

Zebra answered with a cautious "Hello," trying not to look at the empty sleeve, which had been tucked into the man's jacket pocket.

The man asked, with a distinct Southern accent, "What's your name, son?"

Zebra said, "Adam."

"What kind of school is this here school, Adam?"

"It's a good school," Zebra answered.

"How long before you-all begin your summer vacation?"

"Three days," Zebra said.

"Anything special happen here during the summer?"

"During the summer? Nothing goes on here. There are no classes."

"What do you-all do during the summer?"

"Some of us go to camp. Some of us hang around. We find things to do."

Zebra's hand had begun to tingle and throb. Why was the man asking all those questions? Zebra thought maybe he shouldn't be talking to him at all. He seemed vaguely menacing in that army jacket, the dark-blue cap with the words LAND ROVER on it in orange letters, and the empty sleeve. Yet there was kindness in his gray eyes and ruddy features.

The man gazed past Zebra at the students playing in the yard. "Adam, do you think your school would be interested in having someone teach an art class during the summer?"

That took Zebra by surprise. "An *art* class?"

"Drawing, sculpting, things like that."

Zebra was trying *very hard* not to look at the man's empty sleeve. "I don't know. . . ."

"Where's the school office, Adam?"

"On Washington Avenue. Go to the end of the street and turn right."

"Thanks," the man said. He hesitated a moment. Then he asked, in a quiet voice, "What happened to you, Adam?"

"A car hit me," Zebra said. "It was my fault."

The man seemed to **wince.**

F **CHARACTER**
Reread lines 74–95. What are your first impressions of this new character?

wince (wĭns) *v.* to draw back, as in pain or distress

For a flash of a second, Zebra thought to ask the man what had happened to *him*. The words were on his tongue. But he kept himself from saying anything.

The man started back up the street, carrying the brown plastic bag.

Zebra suddenly called, "Hey, mister."

The man stopped and turned. "My name is John Wilson," he said softly.

"Mr. Wilson, when you go into the school office, you'll see signs on two doors. One says 'Dr. Winter,' and the other says 'Mrs. English.' Ask for Mrs. English."

Dr. Winter, the principal, was a **disciplinarian** and a grump. Mrs. English, the assistant principal, was generous and kind. Dr. Winter would probably tell the man to call his secretary for an appointment. Mrs. English might invite him into her office and offer him a cup of coffee and listen to what he had to say.

ANALYZE VISUALS
What might you **infer** from this figure's body language?

disciplinarian
(dĭs′ə-plə-nâr′ē-ən) *n.* someone who enforces strict discipline, or rules

The man hesitated, looking at Zebra.

"Appreciate the advice," he said. **G**

Zebra watched him walk to the corner.

Under the lamppost was a trash can. Zebra saw the man set down the plastic bag and stick his hand into the can and haul out a battered umbrella.

The man tried to open the umbrella, but its metal ribs were broken. The black fabric dangled flat and limp from the pole. He put the umbrella into the plastic bag and headed for the entrance to the school.

A moment later, Zebra heard the whistle that signaled the end of recess. He followed his classmates at a distance, careful to avoid anyone's bumping against his hand.

G CHARACTER
Why did Zebra give Mr. Wilson advice?

He sat through his algebra class, copying the problems on the blackboard while holding down his notebook with his left elbow. The sling **chafed** his neck and felt warm and clumsy on his bare arm. There were sharp pains now in the two curled fingers of his hand.

chafe (chāf) *v.* to irritate by rubbing

Right after the class he went downstairs to the office of Mrs. Walsh, a cheerful, gray-haired woman in a white nurse's uniform.

She said, "I'm sorry I can't do very much for you, Adam, except give you two Tylenols."

He swallowed the Tylenols down with water.

On his way back up to the second floor, he saw the man with the dark-blue cap emerge from the school office with Mrs. English. He stopped on the stairs and watched as the man and Mrs. English stood talking together. Mrs. English nodded and smiled and shook the man's hand.

The man walked down the corridor, carrying the plastic bag, and left the school building.

Zebra went slowly to his next class.

The class was taught by Mrs. English, who came hurrying into the room some minutes after the bell had rung.

"I apologize for being late," she said, sounding a little out of breath. "There was an important matter I had to attend to."

Mrs. English was a tall, gracious woman in her forties. It was common knowledge that early in her life she had been a journalist on a Chicago newspaper and had written short stories, which she could not get published. Soon after her marriage to a doctor, she had become a teacher.

This was the only class Mrs. English taught.

Ten students from the upper school—seventh and eighth grades—were chosen every year for this class. They met for an hour three times a week and told one another stories. Each story would be discussed and analyzed by Mrs. English and the class.

Mrs. English called it a class in the *imagination.*

Zebra was grateful he did not have to take notes in this class. He had only to listen to the stories.

That day, Andrea, the freckle-faced, redheaded girl with very thick glasses who sat next to Zebra, told about a woman scientist who discovered a method of healing trees that had been blasted apart by lightning.

Mark, who had something wrong with his upper lip, told in his quavery[2] voice about a selfish space cadet who stepped into a time machine and met his future self, who turned out to be a hateful person, and how the cadet then returned to the present and changed himself.

Kevin talked in blurred, high-pitched tones and often related parts of his stories with his hands. Mrs. English would quietly repeat many of his sentences. Today he told about an explorer who set out on a journey through a valley filled with yellow stones and surrounded by red mountains, where he encountered an army of green shadows that had been at war for hundreds of years with an army of purple shadows. The explorer showed them how to make peace. **H**

When it was Zebra's turn, he told a story about a bird that one day crashed against a closed windowpane and broke a wing. A boy tried to heal the wing but couldn't. The bird died, and the boy buried it under a tree on his lawn.

When he had finished, there was silence. Everyone in the class was looking at him.

"You always tell such sad stories," Andrea said.

The bell rang. Mrs. English dismissed the class.

In the hallway, Andrea said to Zebra, "You know, you are a very gloomy life form."

"Andrea, get off my case," Zebra said. **I**

H MAKE INFERENCES
What do all the students in Mrs. English's class have in common with Zebra? Cite details to support your answer.

I CHARACTER
What does Andrea's comment tell you about Zebra?

He went out to the schoolyard for the midafternoon recess. On the other side of the chain-link fence was the man in the dark-blue cap. Zebra went over to him.

"Hello again, Adam," the man said. "I've been waiting for you."

"Hello," said Zebra.

"Thanks much for suggesting I talk to Mrs. English."

"You're welcome."

"Adam, you at all interested in art?"

"No."

2. **quavery** (kwā'vər-ē): quivering or trembling.

"You ever try your hand at it?"

"I've made drawings for class. I don't like it."

"Well, just in case you change your mind, I'm giving an art class in your school during the summer."

"I'm going to camp in August," Zebra said.

"There's the big long month of July."

"I don't think so," Zebra said.

"Well, okay, suit yourself. I'd like to give you something, a little thank-you gift."

He reached into an inside pocket and drew out a small pad and a pen. He placed the pad against the fence.

"Adam, you want to help me out a little bit here? Put your fingers through the fence and grab hold of the pad."

Extending the fingers of his right hand, Zebra held the pad to the fence and watched as the man began to work with the pen. He felt the pad move slightly.

"I need you to hold it real still," the man said.

He was standing bent over, very close to Zebra. The words LAND ROVER on his cap shone in the afternoon sunlight. As he worked, he glanced often at Zebra. His tongue kept pushing up against the insides of his cheeks, making tiny hills rise and fall on his face. Wrinkles formed **intricate** spidery webs in the skin below his gray eyes. On his smooth forehead, in the blue and purple shadows beneath the peak of his cap, lay glistening beads of sweat. And his hand—how dirty it was, the fingers and palm smudged with black ink and encrusted with colors.

Then Zebra glanced down and noticed the plastic bag near the man's feet. It lay partly open. Zebra was able to see a large pink armless doll, a dull metallic object that looked like a dented frying pan, old newspapers, strings of cord, crumpled pieces of red and blue cloth, and the broken umbrella.

ANALYZE VISUALS
How does the sketch in this photo **compare** with your mental image of Zebra?

intricate (ĭn'trĭ-kĭt) *adj.* arranged in a complex way; elaborate

"One more minute is all I need," the man said.

He stepped back, looked at the pad, and nodded slowly. He put the pen back into his pocket and tore the top page from the pad. He rolled up the page and pushed it through the fence. Then he took the pad from Zebra.

"See you around, Adam," the man said, picking up the plastic bag.

Zebra unrolled the sheet of paper and saw a line drawing, a perfect image of his face. J

He was looking at himself as if in a mirror. His long straight nose and thin lips and sad eyes and gaunt face; his dark hair and smallish ears and the scar on his forehead where he had hurt himself years before while roller skating.

In the lower right-hand corner of the page the man had written: "To Adam, with thanks. John Wilson."

Zebra raised his eyes from the drawing. The man was walking away.

Zebra called out, "Mr. Wilson, all my friends call me Zebra."

The man turned, looking surprised.

"From my last name," Adam said. "Zebrin. Adam Martin Zebrin. They call me Zebra."

"Is that right?" the man said, starting back toward the fence. "Well, in that case you want to give me back that piece of paper."

He took the pad and pen from his pocket, placed the page on the pad, and, with Zebra holding the pad to the fence, did something to the page and then handed it back.

"You take real good care of yourself, Zebra," the man said.

He went off toward Franklin Avenue.

Zebra looked at the drawing. The man had crossed out Adam and over it had drawn an animal with a stubby neck and short legs and a striped body.

A zebra!

Its legs were in full gallop. It seemed as if it would gallop right off the page.

A strong breeze rippled across the drawing, causing it to flutter like a flag in Zebra's hand. He looked out at the street.

The man was walking slowly in the shadows of the tall oaks. Zebra had the odd sensation that all the houses on the street had turned toward the man and were watching him as he walked along. How strange that was: the windows and porches and columns and front doors following intently the slow walk of that tall, one-armed man—until he turned into Franklin Avenue and was gone. K

J MAKE INFERENCES
Why do you think Mr. Wilson drew the picture of Zebra?

K VISUALIZE
Reread lines 300–305. What images do you see in your mind?

The whistle blew, and Zebra went inside. Seated at his desk, he slipped the drawing carefully into one of his notebooks.

From time to time he glanced at it.

Just before the bell signaled the end of the school day, he looked at it again.

Now *that* was strange!

He thought he remembered that the zebra had been drawn directly over his name: the head over the A and the tail over the M. Didn't it seem now to have moved a little beyond the A?

Probably he was running a fever again. He would run mysterious fevers off and on for about three weeks after each operation on his hand. Fevers sometimes did that to him: excited his imagination.

He lived four blocks from the school. The school bus dropped him off at his corner. In his schoolbag he carried his books and the notebook with the drawing.

His mother offered him a snack, but he said he wasn't hungry. Up in his room, he looked again at the drawing and was astonished to discover that the zebra had reached the edge of his name and appeared poised to leap off.

It *had* to be a fever that was causing him to see the zebra that way. And sure enough, when his mother took his temperature, the thermometer registered 102.6 degrees.

She gave him his medicine, but it didn't seem to have much effect, because when he woke at night and switched on his desk light and peered at the drawing, he saw the little zebra galloping across the page, along the **contours** of his face, over the hills and valleys of his eyes and nose and mouth, and he heard the tiny clickings of its hooves as cloudlets of dust rose in its wake.

contour (kŏn′tŏŏr′) *n.* the outline of a figure or body

He knew he was asleep. He knew it was the fever working upon his imagination.

But it was so real.

The little zebra running . . .

When he woke in the morning the fever was gone, and the zebra was quietly in its place over ADAM.

Later, as he entered the school, he noticed a large sign on the bulletin board in the hallway:

SUMMER ART CLASS

The well-known American artist Mr. John Wilson will conduct an art class during the summer for students in 7th and 8th grades. For details, speak to Mrs. English. There will be no tuition fee for this class.

During the morning, between classes, Zebra ran into Mrs. English in the second-floor hallway.

"Mrs. English, about the summer art class . . . is it okay to ask where—um—where Mr. Wilson is from?"

"He is from a small town in Virginia. Are you thinking of signing up for his class?"

"I can't draw," Zebra said.

"Drawing is something you can learn."

"Mrs. English, is it okay to ask how did Mr. Wilson—um—get hurt?"

The school corridors were always crowded between classes. Zebra and Mrs. English formed a little island in the bustling, student-jammed hallway.

"Mr. Wilson was wounded in the war in Vietnam," Mrs. English said. "I would urge you to join his class. You will get to use your imagination."

For the next hour, Zebra sat impatiently through Mr. Morgan's geography class, and afterward he went up to the teacher.

"Mr. Morgan, could I—um—ask where is Vietnam?"

Mr. Morgan smoothed down the jacket of his beige summer suit, touched his bow tie, rolled down a wall map, picked up his pointer, and cleared his throat.

"Vietnam is this long, narrow country in southeast Asia, bordered by China, Laos, and Cambodia.[3] It is a land of valleys in the north, coastal plains in the center, and marshes in the south. There are barren mountains and tropical rain forests. Its chief crops are rice, rubber, fruits, and vegetables. The population numbers close to seventy million people. Between 1962 and 1973, America fought a terrible war there to prevent the south from falling into the hands of the communist north. We lost the war."

"Thank you."

"I am impressed by your suddenly awakened interest in geography, young man, though I must remind you that your class is studying the Mediterranean," said Mr. Morgan.

During the afternoon recess, Zebra was watching a heated basketball game, when he looked across the yard and saw John Wilson walk by, carrying a laden plastic bag. Some while later, he came back along the street, empty-handed.

Over supper that evening, Zebra told his parents he was thinking of taking a summer art class offered by the school.

His father said, "Well, I think that's a fine idea."

"Wait a minute. I'm not so sure," his mother said.

SOCIAL STUDIES CONNECTION

In 1976 North Vietnam and South Vietnam were reunited into one country, the Socialist Republic of Vietnam

3. **Laos** (lous) . . . **Cambodia** (kăm-bō'dē-ə): countries in southeast Asia.

"It'll get him off the streets," his father said. "He'll become a Matisse[4] instead of a lawyer like his dad. Right, Adam?"

"Just you be very careful," his mother said to Adam. "Don't do anything that might injure your hand."

"How can drawing hurt his left hand, for heaven's sake?" said his father.

That night, Zebra lay in bed looking at his hand. It was a dread and a mystery to him, his own hand. The fingers were all there, but like dead leaves that never fell, the ring and little fingers were rigid and curled, the others barely moved. The doctors said it would take time to bring them back to life. So many broken bones. So many torn muscles and tendons. So many injured nerves. The dark shadow had sprung upon him so suddenly. How stupid, stupid, *stupid* he had been! **L**

L VISUALIZE Reread lines 389–395. Notice the description of Zebra's hand. What words help you visualize how it looks?

He couldn't sleep. He went over to his desk and looked at John Wilson's drawing. The galloping little zebra stood very still over ADAM.

Early the following afternoon, on the last day of school, Zebra went to Mrs. English's office and signed up for John Wilson's summer art class.

"The class will meet every weekday from ten in the morning until one," said Mrs. English. "Starting Monday."

Zebra noticed the three plastic bags in a corner of the office.

"Mrs. English, is it okay to ask what Mr. Wilson—um—did in Vietnam?"

"He told me he was a helicopter pilot," Mrs. English said. "Oh, I neglected to mention that you are to bring an unlined notebook and a pencil to the class." **M**

M CHARACTER What does Mrs. English tell Zebra about Mr. Wilson?

"That's all? A notebook and a pencil?"

Mrs. English smiled. "And your imagination."

When Zebra entered the art class the next Monday morning, he found about fifteen students there—including Andrea from his class with Mrs. English.

The walls of the room were bare. Everything had been removed for the summer. Zebra noticed two plastic bags on the floor beneath the blackboard.

He sat down at the desk next to Andrea's.

She wore blue jeans and a yellow summer blouse with blue stripes. Her long red hair was tied behind her head with a dark-blue ribbon. She gazed at Zebra through her thick glasses, leaned over, and said, "Are you going to make gloomy drawings, too?"

Just then John Wilson walked in, carrying a plastic bag, which he put down on the floor next to the two others.

He stood alongside the front desk, wearing a light-blue long-sleeved shirt and jeans. The left shirtsleeve had been folded back and pinned to the shirt.

---

4. **Matisse** (mə-tēs') (1869–1954): a French painter who was one of the best-known artists of the 20th century.

The dark-blue cap with the words LAND ROVER sat **jauntily** on his head.

"Good morning to you-all," he said, with a shy smile. "Mighty glad you're here. We're going to do two things this summer. We're going to make paper into faces and garbage into people. I can see by your expressions that you don't know what I'm talking about, right? Well, I'm about to show you."

He asked everyone to draw the face of someone sitting nearby.

Zebra hesitated, looked around, then made a drawing of Andrea. Andrea carefully drew Zebra.

He showed Andrea his drawing.

"It's awful." She **grimaced.** "I look like a mouse."

Her drawing of him was good. But was his face really so sad? N

John Wilson went from desk to desk, peering intently at the drawings. He paused a long moment over Zebra's drawing. Then he spent more than an hour demonstrating with chalk on the blackboard how they should not be thinking *eyes* or *lips* or *hands* while drawing, but should think only *lines* and *curves* and *shapes*; how they should be looking at where everything was situated in relation to the edge of the paper; and how they should not be looking *directly* at the edges of what they were drawing but at the space *outside* the edges.

jauntily (jôn′tə-lē) *adv.* in a light and carefree way

grimace (grĭm′ĭs) *v.* to twist one's face to show pain or disgust

N **CHARACTER**
How does Andrea's drawing affect Zebra?

Zebra stared in wonder at how fast John Wilson's hand raced across the blackboard, and at the empty sleeve rising and falling lightly against the shirt.

"You-all are going to learn how to *see* in a new way," John Wilson said.

They made another drawing of the same face.

"Now I look like a horse," Andrea said. "Are you going to add stripes?"

"You are one big pain, Andrea," Zebra said.

Shortly before noon, John Wilson laid out on his desk the contents of the plastic bags: a clutter of junked broken objects, including the doll and the umbrella.

Using strips of cloth, some lengths of string, crumpled newspaper, his pen, and his one hand, he swiftly transformed the battered doll into a red-nosed, umbrella-carrying clown, with baggy pants, a tattered coat, a derby hat, and a **somber** smile. Turning over the battered frying pan, he made it into a pedestal, on which he placed the clown.

somber (sŏm'bər) *adj.* serious; gloomy

"That's a sculpture," John Wilson said, with his shy smile. "Garbage into people."

The class burst into applause. The clown on the frying pan looked as if it might take a bow.

"You-all will be doing that, too, before we're done," John Wilson said. "Now I would like you to sign and date your drawings and give them to me."

When they returned the next morning the drawings were on a wall.

Gradually, in the days that followed, the walls began to fill with drawings. Sculptures made by the students were looked at with care, discussed by John Wilson and the class, and then placed on shelves along the walls: a miniature bicycle made of wire; a parrot made of an old sofa cushion; a cowboy made of rope and string; a fat lady made of a dented metal pitcher; a zebra made of glued-together scraps of cardboard.

"I like your zebra," Andrea said.

"Thanks," Zebra said. "I like your parrot."

One morning John Wilson asked the class members to make a contour drawing of their right or left hand. Zebra felt himself sweating and trembling as he worked.

"That's real nice," John Wilson said, when he saw Andrea's drawing.

He gazed at the drawing made by Zebra.

"You-all were looking at your hand," he said. "You ought to have been looking at the edge of your hand and at the space outside."

Zebra drew his hand again. Strange and ugly, the two fingers lay rigid and curled. But astonishingly, it looked like a hand this time.

One day, a few minutes before the end of class, John Wilson gave everyone an assignment: draw or make something at home, something very special that each person *felt deeply* about. And bring it to class.

Zebra remembered seeing a book titled *Incredible Cross-Sections* on a shelf in the family room at home. He found the book and took it into his room.

There was a color drawing of a rescue helicopter on one of the Contents pages. On pages 30 and 31, the helicopter was shown in pieces, its complicated insides displayed in detailed drawings. Rotor blades, control rods, electronics equipment, radar scanner, tail rotor, engine, lifeline, winch—all its many parts.

Zebra sat at his desk, gazing intently at the space outside the edges of the helicopter on the Contents page.

He made an outline drawing and brought it to class the next morning.

John Wilson looked at it. Was there a stiffening of his muscular neck, a sudden tensing of the hand that held the drawing?

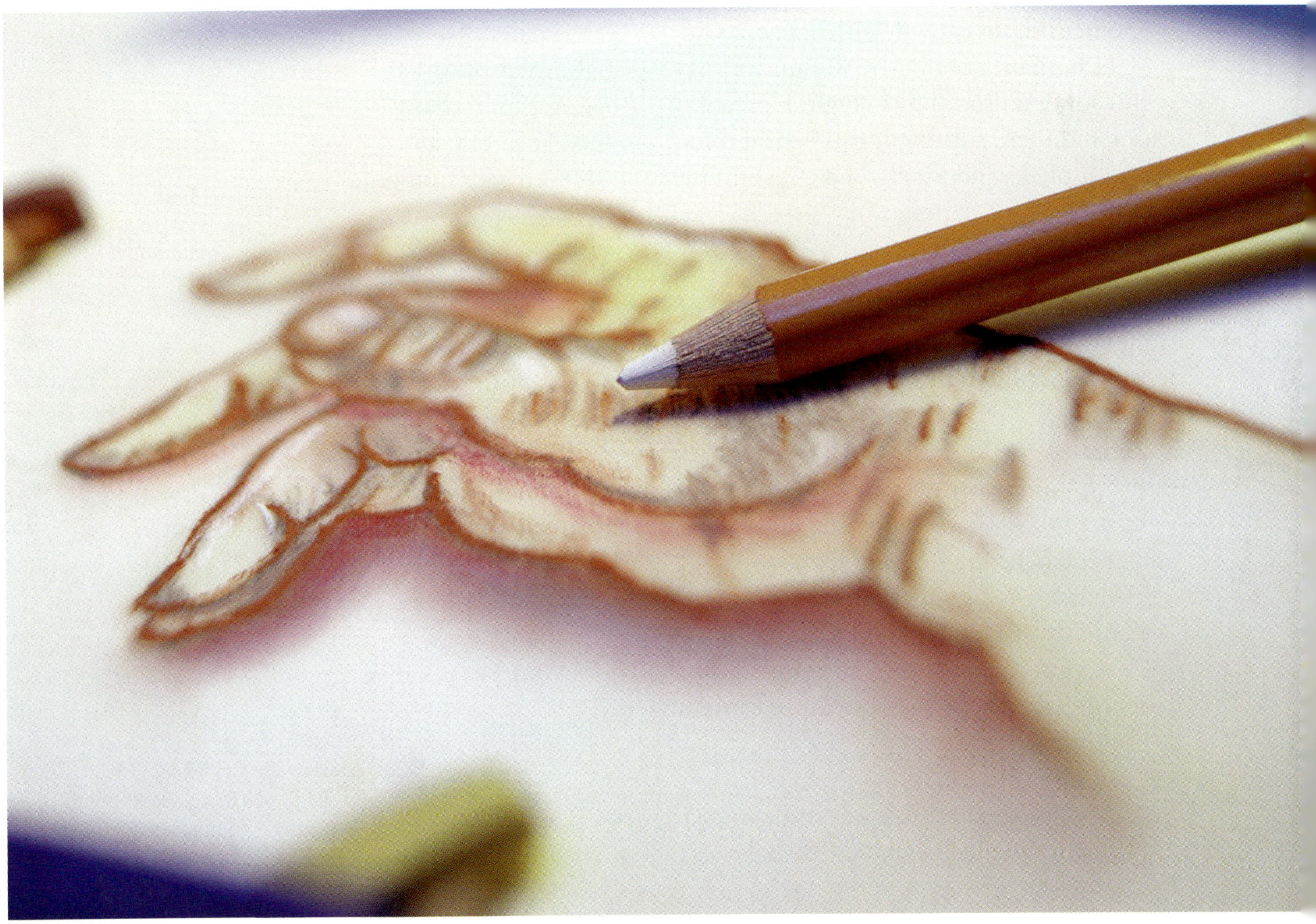

He took the drawing and tacked it to the wall.

The next day he gave them all the same home assignment: draw or make something they *felt very deeply* about.

That afternoon, Zebra went rummaging through the trash bin in his kitchen and the garbage cans that stood near the back door of his home. He found some sardine cans, a broken eggbeater, pieces of cardboard, chipped buttons, bent bobby pins, and other odds and ends.

With the help of epoxy glue, he began to make of those bits of garbage a kind of helicopter. For support, he used his desktop, the floor, his knees, the elbow of his left arm, at one point even his chin. Struggling with the last piece—a button he wanted to position as a wheel—he realized that without thinking he had been using his left hand, and the two curled fingers had straightened slightly to his needs. **O**

O CHARACTER
What effect is John Wilson's art class having on Zebra?

His heart beat thunderously. There had been so many hope-filled moments before, all of them ending in bitter disappointment. He would say nothing. Let the therapist or the doctors tell him. . . .

The following morning, he brought the helicopter to the class.

"Eeewwww, what is *that*?" Andrea grimaced.

"Something to eat you with," Zebra said.

"Get human, Zebra. Mr. Wilson will have a laughing fit over that."

But John Wilson didn't laugh. He held the helicopter in his hand a long moment, turning it this way and that, nodded at Zebra, and placed it on a windowsill, where it shimmered in the summer sunlight.

The next day, John Wilson informed everyone that three students would be leaving the class at the end of July. He asked each of those students to make a drawing for him that he would get to keep. Something to remember them by. All their other drawings and sculptures they could take home.

Zebra lay awake a long time that night, staring into the darkness of his room. He could think of nothing to draw for John Wilson.

In the morning, he sat gazing out the classroom window at the sky and at the helicopter on the sill.

"What are you going to draw for him?" Andrea asked.

Zebra shrugged and said he didn't know.

"Use your imagination," she said. Then she said, "Wait, what am I seeing here? Are you able to move those fingers?"

"I think so."

"You *think* so?"

"The doctors said there was some improvement."

Her eyes glistened behind the thick lenses. She seemed genuinely happy. **P**

P CHARACTER
How have Andrea's feelings toward Zebra changed?

He sat looking out the window. Dark birds wheeled and soared. There was the sound of traffic. The helicopter sat on the windowsill, its eggbeater rotor blades ready to move to full throttle.

Later that day, Zebra sat at his desk at home, working on a drawing. He held the large sheet of paper in place by pressing down on it with the palm and fingers of his left hand. He drew a landscape: hills and valleys, forests and flatlands, rivers and plateaus. Oddly, it all seemed to resemble a face.

Racing together over that landscape were a helicopter and a zebra.

It was all he could think to draw. It was not a very good drawing. He signed it: "To John Wilson, with thanks. Zebra." **Q**

Q CHARACTER
Why does Zebra thank John Wilson?

The next morning, John Wilson looked at the drawing and asked Zebra to write on top of the name "John Wilson" the name "Leon."

"He was an old buddy of mine, an artist. We were in Vietnam together. Would've been a much better artist than I'll ever be."

Zebra wrote in the new name.

"Thank you kindly," John Wilson said, taking the drawing. "Zebra, you have yourself a good time in camp and a good life. It was real nice knowing you."

He shook Zebra's hand. How strong his fingers felt!

"I think I'm going to miss you a little," Andrea said to Zebra after the class.

"I'll only be away a month."

"Can I help you carry some of those drawings?"

"Sure. I'll carry the helicopter."

Zebra went off to a camp in the Adirondack Mountains.[5] He hiked and read and watched others playing ball. In the arts and crafts program he made some good drawings and even got to learn a little bit about watercolors. He put together clowns and airplanes and helicopters out of discarded cardboard and wood and clothing. From time to time his hand hurt, but the fingers seemed slowly to be coming back to life.

"Patience, young man," the doctors told him when he returned to the city. "You're getting there."

One or two additional operations were still necessary. But there was no urgency. And he no longer needed the leg brace.

On the first day of school, one of the secretaries found him in the hallway and told him to report to Mrs. English.

"Did you have a good summer?" Mrs. English asked.

"It was okay," Zebra said.

---

5. **Adirondack** (ăd'ə-rŏn'dăk') **Mountains:** mountains covering a large area of northeast New York State.

"This came for you in the mail."

She handed him a large brown envelope. It was addressed to Adam Zebrin, Eighth Grade, at the school. The sender was John Wilson, with a return address in Virginia.

"Adam, I admit I'm very curious to see what's inside," Mrs. English said.

She helped Zebra open the envelope.

Between two pieces of cardboard were a letter and a large color photograph.

The photograph showed John Wilson down on his right knee before a glistening dark wall. He wore his army jacket and blue jeans and boots, and the cap with the words LAND ROVER. Leaning against the wall to his right was Zebra's drawing of the helicopter and the zebra racing together across a facelike landscape. The drawing was enclosed in a narrow frame.

The wall behind John Wilson seemed to glitter with a strange black light. **R**

R VISUALIZE
Reread lines 585–592. Sketch the photo Zebra found in the envelope.

Zebra read the letter and showed it to Mrs. English.

Dear Zebra,

One of the people whose names are on this wall was among my very closest friends. He was an artist named Leon Kellner. Each year I visit him and leave a gift—something very special that someone creates and gives me. I leave it near his name for a few hours, and then I take it to my studio in Virginia, where I keep a collection of those gifts. All year long I work in my studio, but come summer I go looking for another gift to give him.

Thank you for your gift.

Your friend,
John Wilson

P.S. I hope your hand is healing.

Mrs. English stood staring awhile at the letter. She turned away and touched her eyes. Then she went to a shelf on the wall behind her, took down a large book, leafed through it quickly, found what she was searching for, and held it out for Zebra to see.

Zebra found himself looking at the glistening black wall of the Vietnam Memorial in Washington, D.C. And at the names on it, the thousands of names. . . .

Later, in the schoolyard during recess, Zebra stood alone at the chain-link fence and gazed down the street toward Franklin Avenue. He thought how strange it was that all the houses on this street had seemed to turn toward John Wilson that day, the windows and porches and columns and doors, as if saluting him.

Had that been only his imagination?

ANALYZE VISUALS
Look carefully at this photograph. How do you think it was taken? What feelings was the photographer trying to show?

Maybe, Zebra thought, just maybe he could go for a walk to Franklin Avenue on Saturday or Sunday. He had not walked along Franklin Avenue since the accident; had not gone down that steep hill. Yes, he would walk carefully down that hill to the corner and walk back up and past the school and then the four blocks home.

Andrea came over to him.

"We didn't get picked for the story class with Mrs. English," she said. "I won't have to listen to any more of your gloomy stories."

Zebra said nothing.

"You know, I think I'll walk home today instead of taking the school bus," Andrea said.

"Actually, I think I'll walk, too," Zebra said. "I was thinking maybe I could pick up some really neat stuff in the street."

"You are becoming a pleasant life form," Andrea said. S

S CHARACTER
Reread lines 618–631. How has Zebra changed since the beginning of the story?

The Rider

Naomi Shihab Nye

A boy told me
if he rollerskated fast enough
his loneliness couldn't catch up to him,

the best reason I ever heard
for trying to be a champion.

What I wonder tonight
pedaling hard down King William Street
is if it translates to bicycles.

A victory! To leave your loneliness
panting behind you on some street corner
while you float free into a cloud of sudden azaleas,
luminous pink petals that have never felt loneliness,
no matter how slowly they fell.

Comprehension

ALABAMA STANDARDS

READING STANDARD
2 Relate literary elements to each other, including point of view

1. **Recall** How does Zebra get his name?
2. **Recall** What does John Wilson do with Zebra's drawing?
3. **Represent** On the basis of the description in the story, sketch Zebra's drawing of a helicopter and a zebra racing together over a landscape.

Literary Analysis

4. **Visualize** Choose three sketches from the chart you made while reading "Zebra." Which of the author's words helped you draw these sketches?
5. **Identify Static and Dynamic Characters** A static character doesn't change throughout a story. A dynamic character changes as a result of events in a story. Do you think John Wilson is a static or dynamic character? Give examples to support your answer.
6. **Analyze Characters** Complete a chart like the one shown by classifying each character as a main character or a minor character.

Characters	Main or Minor	Explanation
Zebra		
John Wilson		
Mrs. English		
Andrea		

7. **Analyze Point of View** When a story is told from third-person limited point of view, the narrator tells us what only one character sees, thinks, and feels. "Zebra" is told from third-person limited point of view. Find a place in the story where the narrator reveals Zebra's thoughts and feelings.
8. **Compare Literary Works** Consider the character Zebra and the speaker in "The Rider" on page 204. How are they alike? How are they different?

Extension and Challenge

9. **Creative Project: Art** Choose three characters from this story and decide what everyday things you would use to make a "sculpture" of each of them. For each character, list the objects and tell why you chose them.
10. **SOCIAL STUDIES CONNECTION** What challenges did Vietnam veterans like John Wilson face when they came home? Research what aid and resources were available to them as they sought help in the **healing** process. Share your findings with the class.

RESEARCH LINKS
For more on the aid and resources available to Vietnam veterans, visit the **Research Center** at **ClassZone.com.**

Downhearted by Janine Hilder is an example of a found objects sculpture.

Vocabulary in Context

VOCABULARY PRACTICE

For each set, choose the word that differs most in meaning from the other words. Refer to a dictionary if you need help.

1. (a) elaborate, (b) ornate, (c) intricate, (d) plain
2. (a) joyously, (b) glumly, (c) delightedly, (d) exuberantly
3. (a) thick, (b) fat, (c) gaunt, (d) full
4. (a) smile, (b) grimace, (c) grin, (d) laugh
5. (a) somber, (b) dreary, (c) angry, (d) depressing
6. (a) cringe, (b) flinch, (c) approach, (d) wince
7. (a) disciplinarian, (b) counselor, (c) advisor, (d) guide
8. (a) jauntily, (b) slowly, (c) lightheartedly, (d) cheerfully
9. (a) outline, (b) contour, (c) color, (d) shape
10. (a) scrape, (b) chafe, (c) rub, (d) bless

chafe
grimace
contour
intricate
disciplinarian
jauntily
exuberantly
somber
gaunt
wince

VOCABULARY IN WRITING

What role did John Wilson play in Zebra's healing process? Write a paragraph about this, using three or more vocabulary words. You could start like this.

EXAMPLE SENTENCE

*Before meeting John Wilson, Zebra's injury made him **somber** and sad.*

VOCABULARY STRATEGY: SIMILES

Writers sometimes use **similes** to compare two things (using the words *like* or *as*) that are not alike. In this story, Zebra's fingers are said to be "rigid and curled," "**like** dead leaves that never fell." This simile helps you see his fingers in a new way.

Similes can also provide context clues to help you figure out the meaning of unknown words. If you can visualize dead leaves, you can understand the meaning of *rigid.*

PRACTICE Use the simile in each sentence as a context clue to help you define the boldfaced word.

1. Teresa felt as **emancipated** as a prisoner recently released from jail.
2. Like a dam bursting, the **impasse** between the enemies was finally broken.
3. The sight of his destroyed home made him **recoil** like a snake.
4. The clues to the robbery were as **enigmatic** as unidentified ruins found in a desert.
5. Tom was as **tenacious** in business as a survivor hanging on to a lifeboat.

ALABAMA STANDARDS

READING STANDARD
1.c Using context clues to determine meaning of words

VOCABULARY PRACTICE
For more practice, go to the **Vocabulary Center** at **ClassZone.com.**

SKILLS PRACTICE

Reading-Writing Connection

Demonstrate an understanding of the characters in "Zebra" by responding to these prompts. Then complete the **Grammar and Writing** exercise.

WRITING PROMPTS	SELF-CHECK
A. Short Response: Write a Character Sketch When Zebra and John Wilson first notice each other, the author gives a long description of John Wilson. Now it's your turn. Describe Zebra in **one paragraph.**	***A strong description will . . .*** • include details about how Zebra looks, acts, and talks • use specific details from the story
B. Extended Response: Write a Letter Write a **two- or three-paragraph letter** that Zebra might send in response to John Wilson's letter. It should include a description of how the art class and their friendship helped **heal** his hand and spirits.	***An interesting letter will . . .*** • respond to details in John Wilson's letter • include descriptions that Zebra would be likely to make

GRAMMAR AND WRITING

USE CORRECT VERB TENSE **Verb tense** indicates the time that an action takes place. The three basic verb tenses are **present, past,** and **future.** In your writing, be sure to use the same verb tense when describing actions that happen at the same time. Only make a change in verb tense if actions are happening at different times.

Original: I am grateful for your encouragement. I looked forward to seeing you again. (Am *is present tense, and* looked *is past tense.*)

Revised: I am grateful for your encouragement. I look forward to seeing you again. (*Since both actions are happening in the present, both verbs should be present tense.*)

PRACTICE Choose the correct verb tense to complete the sentence.

1. I feel good when I work on my art. It (reflected, reflects) my creativity.
2. Art inspires me. It (helps, helped) me to focus my energy.
3. After the accident, I never thought my hand would get better. Now I (knew, know) I'll be fine.
4. I will always remember you and (will try, tried) to keep in touch.

For more help with verb tenses, see pages R56–R57 in the ***Grammar Handbook.***

ALABAMA STANDARDS

WRITING/LANGUAGE STANDARD
11 Apply grammar conventions in writing

Reading for Information

The Legacy of the Vietnam War

- Feature Article, page 209
- Letter, page 212
- Timeline, page 214

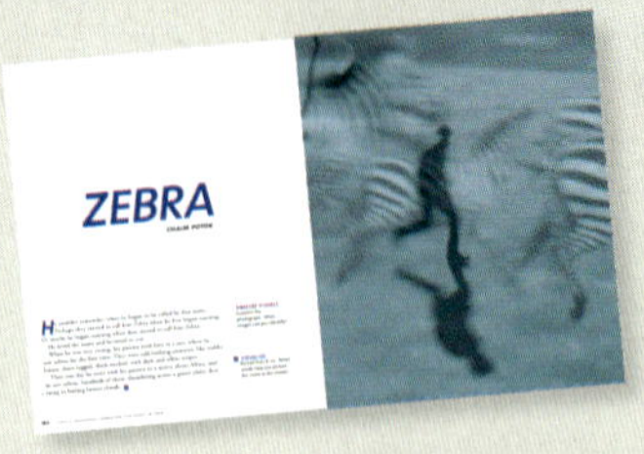

Use with "Zebra," page 184.

ALABAMA STANDARDS

READING & RESEARCH STANDARDS
4.d Drawing conclusions
13.a Taking notes to gather, summarize information

What's the Connection?

In "Zebra" you read about a veteran of the Vietnam War. In the following selections, you will learn more about the war and the Vietnam Veterans Memorial.

Skill Focus: Synthesize

Have you ever seen a movie about something—knights, for example—and then read about that topic in a textbook? What happened? Chances are you put together what you learned from the movie with what you learned from your book and wound up understanding knights even better than before.

When you put together information from different sources to get a fuller understanding of a topic, you are **synthesizing.** You probably synthesize information automatically all the time, but now you're going to practice doing it more purposefully. Here's how:

- Summarize what you learned about the Vietnam War and the Vietnam Veterans Memorial from reading "Zebra."
- Read the following three selections, and note any new information you learn from each one.
- Jot down any particular details or information you especially want to remember.

To help you in synthesizing, record this information in a chart like the one started here. As you read, add the titles of the other selections to the chart.

Source	*Ideas and Information About the Vietnam War and the Memorial*
"Zebra"	*Some veterans lost limbs in the war. Some veterans bring gifts to friends whose names are written on the Wall.*
"The Collected Grief of a Nation"	

The Collected Grief of a Nation

An Exhibit of Mementos from the Vietnam Wall

by Judith Weinraub

At 19 Duery Felton Jr. was drafted and sent to Vietnam.

At 20 the D.C. native, assigned to the 1st Infantry Division, was badly wounded—so badly he refuses to discuss the details. "I was almost a name on the Wall," he says simply.

Decades later, Felton has made the Vietnam Wall—or more properly, the tens of thousands of objects that have been left there since it was dedicated in 1982—the center of his life. From dog tags to combat boots, letters to prayers, he looks after them, he researches them, he speaks for them.

And the objects have become a collection of war memorabilia unlike any other.

"It's a living collection," says Felton. "People are leaving keepsakes at a public site—things normally passed on to their children.". . . **A**

No one would have predicted the memorial would engender such an outpouring of feeling.

Focus on Form

"The Collected Grief of a Nation" is a **feature article,** a nonfiction article found in a newspaper or magazine that gives readers information about an interesting topic. Unlike news articles, feature articles do not need to focus on current events.

A SYNTHESIZE

In "Zebra" you learned that a veteran brought a boy's drawing to the Vietnam Veterans Memorial. Now you're learning about gifts people have actually brought to the memorial. In your chart, jot down these items, along with your thoughts about what each might represent.

In 1981 Maya Lin's proposed design—two long walls of black granite meeting in a V, with the names of the dead chiseled in chronological order, set into the gradual incline of a site near the Lincoln Memorial—ignited a hue and cry.

But over the years, as millions of visitors viewed their reflections in the polished granite and left behind their tributes to the dead, the black gash has become a mirror of America. . . .

It was that way with the Vietnam Veterans Memorial almost from the start. In the first two years, according to Donna Donaldson, chief of visitor services for the National Park Service, some 600 tokens of remembrance were left. As time went on, the number grew. It is still growing. "It became obvious that we couldn't just leave them sitting there," says Donaldson. "Something different was happening at this memorial."

And the offerings weren't just flags and flowers. . . . A wooden cross with a crown of thorns made of barbed wire. Wedding rings. Purple Hearts. A varsity letter. A replica of a POW "tiger" cage. . . . POW-MIA bracelets. An IV bag. A menorah. **B**

B SYNTHESIZE
Add to the list of gifts you started in your chart. If any item is unfamiliar, circle it and make a note to find out what it is some other time.

"The objects were different from anything else we'd ever collected," says Pamela West, the regional curator for the Park Service's National Capital region. "It took on its own momentum. We decided to keep these things as a museum collection and treat it as such." . . .

Felton got involved one day while visiting the Lanham warehouse where the objects were stored. A reporter also there that day asked about certain objects. Only Felton knew what they were. . . .

By 1984, the collection had become overwhelming, and someone in the Park Service remembered Duery Felton. He began as a volunteer, working a couple of hours a day. Felton assumed responsibility for the collection in 1988. **C**

Felton now has a small staff and an army of volunteers. He has witnessed the changing American reaction to the war from the time he was evacuated to Walter Reed Army Medical Center in 1968 until today. "I feel the memorial meets a felt need," he says. "It has become America's bulletin board, a protest site—whatever you want to say, you can say at that site." . . . **D**

When asked what single object left at the Wall shocked him the most, he points to a black beret from the 101st Airborne Division reconnaissance unit ambushed in November 1967. "It was left by the sole surviving member of a 12-man unit some 20 years after the fact," he says, shaking his head.

At the Wall, the Capitol and the Washington Monument look postcard-perfect in the distance. And as Lincoln—the symbol of this country's other divisive war—looks down from his majestic perch nearby, people are still bringing offerings to the Wall.

This black beret (*left*) and purple heart (*right*), along with the other items shown were all left at the Wall.

C SYNTHESIZE
In your chart, jot down the service Duery Felton performs at the Wall.

D FEATURE ARTICLE
Reread Felton's thoughts about the Wall. Then reread **Focus on Form** on page 209. What makes the Wall such a good topic for a feature article?

A Mother's Words

Mrs. Eleanor Wimbish of Glen Burnie, Maryland, is the mother of William R. Stocks, who died in the Vietnam War. For years she left letters to her son under his name on the Vietnam Veterans Memorial in Washington, D.C.

Dear Bill,

Today is February 13, 1984. I came to this black wall again to see and touch your name, and as I do I wonder if anyone ever stops to realize that next to your name, on this black wall, is your mother's heart. A heart broken 15 years ago today, when you lost your life in Vietnam. **E**

E SYNTHESIZE
Why do you think Bill's mother comes to the Wall? Note her purpose for coming in your chart.

And as I look at your name, William R. Stocks, I think of how many, many times I used to wonder how scared and homesick you must have been in that strange country called Vietnam. And if and how it might have changed you, for you were the most happy-go-lucky kid in the world, hardly ever sad or unhappy. And until the day I die, I will see you as you laughed at me, even when I was very mad at you, and the next thing I knew, we were laughing together.

But on this past New Year's Day, I had my answer. I talked by phone to a friend of yours from Michigan, who spent your last Christmas and the last four months of your life with you. Jim told me how you died, for he was there and saw the helicopter crash. He told me how you had flown your quota and had not been scheduled to fly that day. How the regular pilot was unable to fly and had been replaced by someone with less experience. How they did not know the exact cause of the crash. . . .

He told me how, after a while over there, instead of a yellow streak, the men got a mean streak down their backs.

Each day the streak got bigger and the men became meaner. Everyone but you, Bill. He said how you stayed the same, happy-go-lucky guy that you were when you arrived in Vietnam. How your warmth and friendliness drew the guys to you. How your lieutenant gave you the nickname of "Spanky," and soon your group, Jim included, were all known as "Spanky's gang." How when you died it made it so much harder on them for you were their moral support. And he said how you of all people should never have been the one to die. F

How it hurts to write this. But I must face it and then put it to rest. I know after Jim talked to me, he must have relived it all over again and suffered so. Before I hung up the phone I told Jim I loved him. Loved him for just being your close friend, and for being there with you when you died. How lucky you were to have him for a friend, and how lucky he was to have had you. . . .

They tell me the letters I write to you and leave here at this memorial are waking others up to the fact that there is still much pain left, after all these years, from the Vietnam War. G

But this I know. I would rather have had you for 21 years, and all the pain that goes with losing you, than never to have had you at all.

Mom

F SYNTHESIZE
Reread lines 24–30. **Clarify** what Bill's friend said about the effects that fighting in Vietnam had on the soldiers.

G SYNTHESIZE
In what way do you think Bill's mother benefits from writing letters to her son?

Timeline: U.S. Involvement in Vietnam

The seeds of the Vietnam War were planted in 1858 when France attacked Vietnam for control of the government. After decades of frustration under foreign rule, many Vietnamese began supporting the Communist movement against the French. Meanwhile, the United States struggled against the spread of communism worldwide.

	USA	VIETNAM
1950s	**1950** The United States sends economic aid to the French forces in Vietnam.	**1954** The French are defeated. Vietnam divides into Communist North and non-Communist South. **1957** Communist rebels (the Viet Cong) fight for control of South Vietnam.
1960s	**1965** Antiwar protests become widespread. **1968** U.S. citizens begin to think the war cannot be won.	**1965** The United States bombs North Vietnam. The first U.S. combat troops arrive in South Vietnam. **1968** The number of U.S. troops in Vietnam reaches its peak. The North Vietnamese and the Viet Cong launch the Tet offensive, a series of surprise attacks.
1970s	**1970** Four students are killed at an antiwar demonstration in Ohio. **H**	**1973** All U.S. troops leave Vietnam. **1975** South Vietnam surrenders to the Communists. The U.S. Embassy in Vietnam is evacuated. **1978** Thousands of refugees flee Vietnam to escape poverty and punishment for aiding the United States during the war.
1980s	**1982** The Vietnam Veterans Memorial is dedicated in Washington, D.C.	**1986** The Vietnamese government begins economic restructuring.
1990s	**1995** The United States and Vietnam restore full diplomatic relations.	

H SYNTHESIZE
While the Vietnam War was being fought, how were U.S. citizens at home responding to the conflict? Note the information you learn about the war in your chart.

Comprehension

1. **Recall** When did the last U.S. combat troops leave Vietnam?
2. **Clarify** What kind of person was Bill Stocks?
3. **Summarize** In general, how would you describe the "tokens of remembrance" people leave at the Wall?

Critical Analysis

4. **Analyze** In the feature article, the Wall is described as a "black gash," a "mirror of America," a "bulletin board," and a "protest site." Pick one of these phrases and explain what it suggests about the Wall.
5. **Synthesize** Review your chart. What information did you get from reading the selections that you had not learned from reading "Zebra"?

Read for Information: Draw Conclusions

WRITING PROMPT

In a paragraph, state and support a **conclusion** you have reached about one of the following topics:

- the importance of the Vietnam Veterans Memorial to those who visit it
- the effects of the Vietnam War on veterans and their friends and family
- how people heal after suffering a loss

A **conclusion** is a judgment or belief about something. To reach a solid conclusion, you need sound reasoning, evidence, and experience to support it. The steps below can help you state and support a conclusion.

1. Choose a topic and jot down ideas or information about it. Ask yourself what this information leads you to conclude about your topic.
2. From two or more selections, pick out details that support your conclusion. If you can't find enough support, you might need to revisit your conclusion.
3. State your conclusion in a topic sentence. Then present the reasons and evidence that led you to this conclusion.

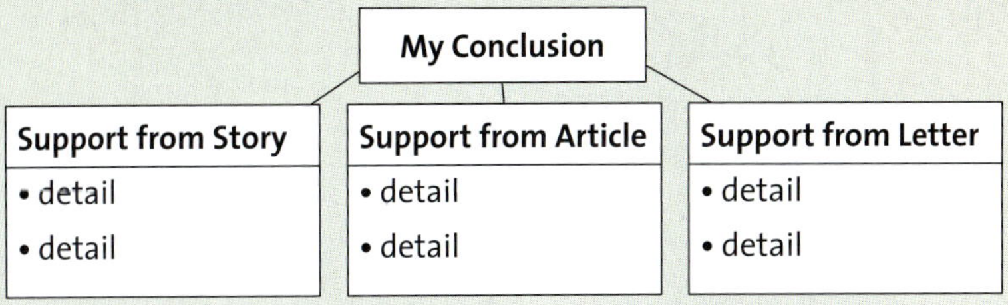

ALABAMA STANDARDS

READING & RESEARCH STANDARDS
4.d Drawing conclusions
13.a Taking notes to gather, summarize information

The Scholarship Jacket

Short Story by Marta Salinas

What stands in the way of your DREAMS?

ALABAMA STANDARDS

READING STANDARDS

1.d Applying self-monitoring strategies

2 Relate literary elements to each other, including point of view

KEY IDEA Your dream may be to go to camp, to be a star on the basketball court, to be class president, or to go to college someday. Whatever it is, hard work and luck can help you fulfill that dream. But, like the narrator of "The Scholarship Jacket," you may encounter **obstacles** that block your progress.

QUICKWRITE With a small group of classmates, discuss your dream for the future. What obstacles might you encounter while working to make your dream come true? Then, in your journal, write one or two ways to overcome each obstacle.

LITERARY ANALYSIS: FIRST-PERSON POINT OF VIEW

When you listen to a friend talk, you can learn a great deal about him or her. Your friend's personality, experiences, and opinions all come through. The same is true when you read a story from one character's point of view. When a story is told from the **first-person point of view,** the narrator

- is a character in the story
- tells the story using the pronouns *I, me, we,* and *us*
- tells the story as he or she experiences it

As you read "The Scholarship Jacket," notice how the information you receive is limited to what the narrator sees, hears, thinks, and feels.

READING SKILL: MAKE INFERENCES

One way to get the most out of what you read is to make logical guesses, or **inferences,** about things that are not directly stated. Base your inferences on details in the story and on your own knowledge and experiences. As you read "The Scholarshic Jacket," record each inference you make in an equation like the one shown.

Details from the Text		My Experiences		Inference
Martha couldn't play sports because of cost.	+	I couldn't go to playoffs because of expense.	=	Martha's grand-parents don't have extra money.

VOCABULARY IN CONTEXT

These words help tell the story of a girl facing obstacles. Write the word that best completes each sentence.

WORD LIST			
	agile	dismay	falsify
	despair	eavesdrop	vile

1. She unhappily swallowed the _____ medicine.
2. He would often _____ on his parents' conversations.
3. He tried not to _____ over the terrible news.
4. She climbed the tree in a very _____ manner.
5. There was a look of _____ when she received the news.
6. Don't _____ the records to hide the truth.

Author Online

California Native
Marta Salinas was born in Coalinga, California, and received a degree in creative writing from the University of California at Irvine. "The Scholarship Jacket" is one of several short stories Salinas has published in journals and collections.

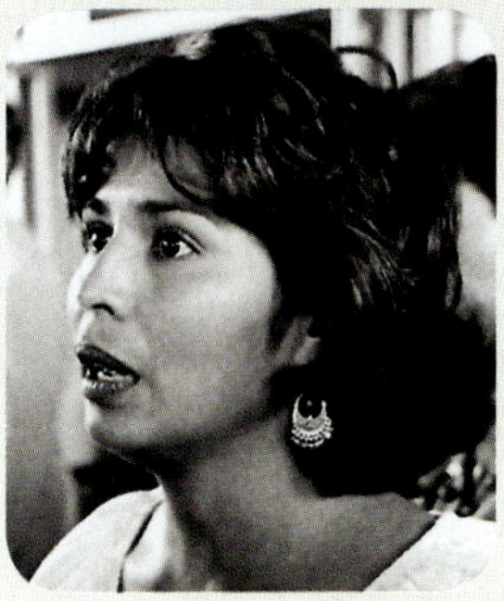

Marta Salinas
born 1949

Background

Texas History The main character in "The Scholarship Jacket" is a Mexican-American girl who lives in Texas. The history of Tejanos, or Texas Mexicans, dates back more than 200 years. As early as 1731, Tejanos established a ranch community in what was then northeastern Mexico. About 100 years later, Mexico invited immigrants from the United States to settle in the region. The Tejanos and the immigrants eventually joined forces to fight for their independence from Mexico, and in 1845, Texas became part of the United States. Mexicans continued migrating to Texas, but they often faced discrimination. Today, over seven million residents of Texas are Mexican Americans.

MORE ABOUT THE AUTHOR AND BACKGROUND
To learn more about Marta Salinas and Tejano history and culture, visit the **Literature Center** at **ClassZone.com.**

The Scholarship Jacket

Marta Salinas

The small Texas school that I went to had a tradition carried out every year during the eighth-grade graduation: a beautiful gold and green jacket (the school colors) was awarded to the class valedictorian, the student who had maintained the highest grades for eight years. The scholarship jacket had a big gold S on the left front side and your name written in gold letters on the pocket.

My oldest sister, Rosie, had won the jacket a few years back, and I fully expected to also. I was fourteen and in the eighth grade. I had been a straight A student since the first grade and this last year had looked forward very much to owning that jacket. My father was a farm laborer who couldn't earn enough money to feed eight children, so when I was six I was given to my grandparents to raise. We couldn't participate in sports at school because there were registration fees, uniform costs, and trips out of town; so, even though our family was quite **agile** and athletic there would never be a school sports jacket for us. This one, the scholarship jacket, was our only chance. **A**

In May, close to graduation, spring fever had struck as usual with a vengeance.[1] No one paid any attention in class; instead we stared out the windows and at each other, wanting to speed up the last few weeks of

ANALYZE VISUALS
On the basis of the **details** in the painting, how do you think the girl is feeling?

agile (ăj'əl) *adj.* quick and light in movement

A FIRST-PERSON POINT OF VIEW
Who is the narrator? What have you learned from her so far?

1. **with a vengeance** (vĕn'jəns): to an extreme degree.

Bernadita (1922), Robert Henri. Oil on canvas, 24 1/8" × 20 1/8". Gift of the San Diego Wednesday Club. © San Diego Museum of Art (1926:138).

ROBERT HENRI

school. I **despaired** every time I looked in the mirror. Pencil thin, not a curve anywhere. I was called "beanpole" and "string bean," and I knew that's what I looked like. A flat chest, no hips, and a brain; that's what I had. That really wasn't much for a fourteen-year-old to work with, I thought, as I absent-mindedly wandered from my history class to the gym. Another hour of sweating in basketball and displaying my toothpick legs was coming up. Then I remembered my P.E. shorts were still in a bag under my desk where I'd forgotten them. I had to walk all the way back and get them. Coach Thompson was a real bear if someone wasn't dressed for P.E. She had said I was a good forward and even tried to talk Grandma into letting me join the team once. Of course Grandma said no.

despair (dĭ-spâr') *v.* to lose hope

I was almost back at my classroom door when I heard voices raised in anger as if in some sort of argument. I stopped. I didn't mean to **eavesdrop,** I just hesitated, not knowing what to do. I needed those shorts and I was going to be late, but I didn't want to interrupt an argument between my teachers. I recognized the voices: Mr. Schmidt, my history teacher, and Mr. Boone, my math teacher. They seemed to be arguing about me. I couldn't believe it. I still remember the feeling of shock that rooted me flat against the wall as if I were trying to blend in with the graffiti written there.

eavesdrop (ēvz'drŏp') *v.* to listen secretly to a private conversation of others

"I refuse to do it! I don't care who her father is, her grades don't even begin to compare to Martha's. I won't lie or **falsify** records. Martha has a straight A-plus average and you know it." That was Mr. Schmidt and he sounded very angry. Mr. Boone's voice sounded calm and quiet.

falsify (fôl'sə-fī') *v.* to make false by adding to or changing

"Look. Joann's father is not only on the Board, he owns the only store in town: we could say it was a close tie and—"

The pounding in my ears drowned out the rest of the words, only a word here and there filtered through. " . . . Martha is Mexican . . . resign . . . won't do it . . . . " Mr. Schmidt came rushing out and luckily for me went down the opposite way toward the auditorium, so he didn't see me. Shaking, I waited a few minutes and then went in and grabbed my bag and fled from the room. Mr. Boone looked up when I came in but didn't say anything. To this day I don't remember if I got in trouble in P.E. for being late or how I made it through the rest of the afternoon. I went home very sad and cried into my pillow that night so Grandmother wouldn't hear me. It seemed a cruel coincidence that I had overheard that conversation. **B**

B FIRST-PERSON POINT OF VIEW
Reread lines 46–55. How does the argument between Mr. Schmidt and Mr. Boone make Martha feel?

The next day when the principal called me into his office I knew what it would be about. He looked uncomfortable and unhappy. I decided I wasn't going to make it any easier for him, so I looked him straight in the eyes. He looked away and fidgeted with the papers on his desk. **C**

C MAKE INFERENCES
Why is the principal unhappy?

"Martha," he said, "there's been a change in policy this year regarding the scholarship jacket. As you know, it has always been free." He cleared his throat and continued. "This year the Board has decided to charge fifteen dollars, which still won't cover the complete cost of the jacket."

I stared at him in shock, and a small sound of **dismay** escaped my throat. I hadn't expected this. He still avoided looking in my eyes.

dismay (dĭs-mā') *n.* distress caused by trouble or something unexpected

"So if you are unable to pay the fifteen dollars for the jacket it will be given to the next one in line." I didn't need to ask who that was.

Standing with all the dignity I could muster, I said, "I'll speak to my grandfather about it, sir, and let you know tomorrow." I cried on the walk home from the bus stop. The dirt road was a quarter mile from the highway, so by the time I got home, my eyes were red and puffy.

"Where's Grandpa?" I asked Grandma, looking down at the floor so she wouldn't ask me why I'd been crying. She was sewing on a quilt as usual and didn't look up.

"I think he's out back working in the bean field."

I went outside and looked out at the fields. There he was. I could see him walking between the rows, his body bent over the little plants, hoe in hand. I walked slowly out to him, trying to think how I could best ask him for the money. There was a cool breeze blowing and a sweet smell of mesquite[2] fruit in the air, but I didn't appreciate it. I kicked at a dirt clod. I wanted that jacket so much. It was more than just being a valedictorian and giving a little thank you speech for the jacket on graduation night. It represented eight years of hard work and expectation. I knew I had to be honest with Grandpa; it was my only chance. He saw my shadow and looked up.

He waited for me to speak. I cleared my throat nervously and clasped my hands behind my back so he wouldn't see them shaking. "Grandpa, I have a big favor to ask you," I said in Spanish, the only language he knew. He still waited silently. I tried again. "Grandpa, this year the principal said the scholarship jacket is not going to be free. It's going to cost fifteen dollars, and I have to take the money in tomorrow, otherwise it'll be given to someone else." The last words came out in an eager rush. Grandpa straightened up tiredly and leaned his chin on the hoe handle. He looked out over the field that was filled with the tiny green bean plants. I waited, desperately hoping he'd say I could have the money.

He turned to me and asked quietly, "What does a scholarship jacket mean?"

I answered quickly; maybe there was a chance. "It means you've earned it by having the highest grades for eight years and that's why they're giving it to you." Too late I realized the significance of my words.

---

2. **sweet smell of mesquite** (mĕ-skēt'): Mesquite, a small tree or shrub native to hot, dry regions of North America, has small flowers and large super-rich pods that give off a sweet smell.

Portrait of Patience Escalier (1888), Vincent van Gogh. Oil on canvas. Private collection. © Lefevre Fine Art Ltd., London/Bridgeman Art Library.

ANALYZE VISUALS
How does the man shown **compare** with your image of Martha's grandfather?

Grandpa knew that I understood it was not a matter of money. It wasn't that. He went back to hoeing the weeds that sprang up between the delicate little bean plants. It was a time-consuming job; sometimes the small shoots were right next to each other. Finally he spoke again as I turned to leave, crying.

"Then if you pay for it, Marta, it's not a scholarship jacket, is it? Tell your principal I will not pay the fifteen dollars." D

D MAKE INFERENCES
Why won't Martha's grandfather pay the money for the jacket?

I walked back to the house and locked myself in the bathroom for a long time. I was angry with Grandfather even though I knew he was right, and I was angry with the Board, whoever they were. Why did they have to change the rules just when it was my turn to win the jacket? Those were the days of belief and innocence.

It was a very sad and withdrawn girl who dragged into the principal's office the next day. This time he did look me in the eyes.

"What did your grandfather say?"

I sat very straight in my chair.

"He said to tell you he won't pay the fifteen dollars."

The principal muttered something I couldn't understand under his breath and walked over to the window. He stood looking out at something outside. He looked bigger than usual when he stood up; he was a tall, gaunt man with gray hair, and I watched the back of his head while I waited for him to speak. **E**

E FIRST-PERSON POINT OF VIEW
Reread lines 118–122. How does the first-person point of view limit your understanding of what the principal is thinking?

"Why?" he finally asked. "Your grandfather has the money. He owns a two-hundred acre ranch."

I looked at him, forcing my eyes to stay dry. "I know, sir, but he said if I had to pay for it, then it wouldn't be a scholarship jacket." I stood up to leave. "I guess you'll just have to give it to Joann." I hadn't meant to say that, it had just slipped out. I was almost to the door when he stopped me.

"Martha—wait."

I turned and looked at him, waiting. What did he want now? I could feel my heart pounding loudly in my chest and see my blouse fluttering where my breasts should have been. Something bitter and **vile** tasting was coming up in my mouth; I was afraid I was going to be sick. I didn't need any sympathy speeches. He sighed loudly and went back to his big desk. He watched me, biting his lip.

vile (vīl) *adj.* disgusting; unpleasant

"Okay. We'll make an exception in your case. I'll tell the Board, you'll get your jacket." **F**

F MAKE INFERENCES
Why do you think the principal changed his mind?

I could hardly believe my ears. I spoke in a trembling rush. "Oh, thank you, sir!" Suddenly I felt great. I didn't know about adrenalin[3] in those days, but I knew something was pumping through me, making me feel as tall as the sky. I wanted to yell, jump, run the mile, do something. I ran out so I could cry in the hall where there was no one to see me.

At the end of the day, Mr. Schmidt winked at me and said, "I hear you're getting the scholarship jacket this year."

His face looked as happy and innocent as a baby's, but I knew better. Without answering I gave him a quick hug and ran to the bus. I cried on the walk home again, but this time because I was so happy. I couldn't wait to tell Grandpa and ran straight to the field. I joined him in the row where he was working, and without saying anything I crouched down and started pulling up the weeds with my hands. Grandpa worked alongside me for a few minutes, and he didn't ask what had happened. After I had a little pile of weeds between the rows, I stood up and faced him.

"The principal said he's making an exception for me, Grandpa, and I'm getting the jacket after all. That's after I told him what you said."

Grandpa didn't say anything; he just gave me a pat on the shoulder and a smile. He pulled out the crumpled red handkerchief that he always carried in his back pocket and wiped the sweat off his forehead.

"Better go see if your grandmother needs any help with supper."

I gave him a big grin. He didn't fool me. I skipped and ran back to the house whistling some silly tune.

3. **adrenalin** (ə-drĕn′ə-lĭn): a hormone that speeds up the heartbeat and increases bodily energy. The body produces adrenalin when a person experiences emotions such as excitement or fear.

Comprehension

1. **Recall** Why does Martha call the scholarship jacket "our only chance"?
2. **Clarify** What do Mr. Boone and Mr. Schmidt argue about?
3. **Clarify** How does the principal respond when Martha says her grandfather will not pay for the jacket?
4. **Summarize** Tell why the scholarship jacket is so important to Martha. Cite evidence from the story.

Literary Analysis

5. **Make Inferences** Review the inferences that you recorded in equations. Have any of your inferences changed after reading the entire story? If necessary, write a revised inference next to the equation. Be prepared to explain your reasons for changing an inference or keeping the original.
6. **Interpret** Reread lines 47–48. During the teachers' argument, one of the teachers says, "Martha is Mexican." What could he mean by this?
7. **Analyze Character** Martha is the main character in the story. Use a web to describe how the minor characters interact with Martha and what effect they have on the story.

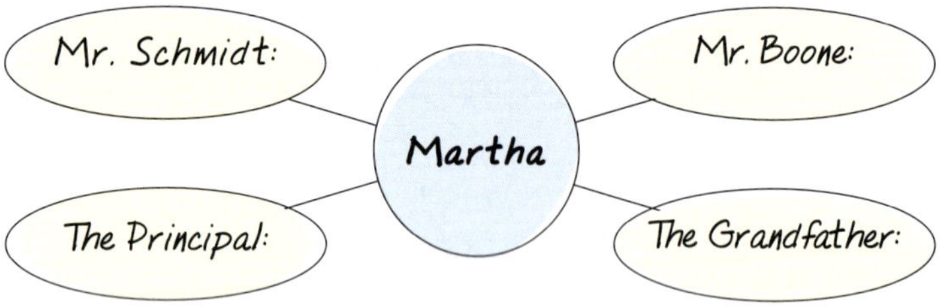

8. **Draw Conclusions** Martha's grandfather says little, but his words and actions mean much to Martha. What does Martha learn from him? Explain how you came to this conclusion.
9. **Evaluate First-Person Point of View** Think about how the story might change if you knew everyone's thoughts and feelings. In what ways would the story be different?

Extension and Challenge

10. **Big Question Activity** How would Martha answer the Big Question on page 216? Write a thank-you speech for Martha to give when she receives her scholarship jacket. In the speech, mention the **obstacles** Martha had to overcome in order to achieve this award.

ALABAMA STANDARDS

READING STANDARD
2 Relate literary elements to each other, including point of view

Vocabulary in Context

VOCABULARY PRACTICE

Answer each question to show your understanding of the vocabulary words.

1. Which is a way to **falsify**—forging a signature or correcting an error?
2. Would an **agile** person be more likely to sing well or run quickly?
3. If I began to **despair,** would I more likely mingle with others or keep to myself?
4. Which is the more **vile** material—rotting garbage or rose petals?
5. Would losing one's glasses or having lunch with friends more likely cause **dismay?**
6. If you were going to **eavesdrop,** would you talk on the phone or listen behind a door?

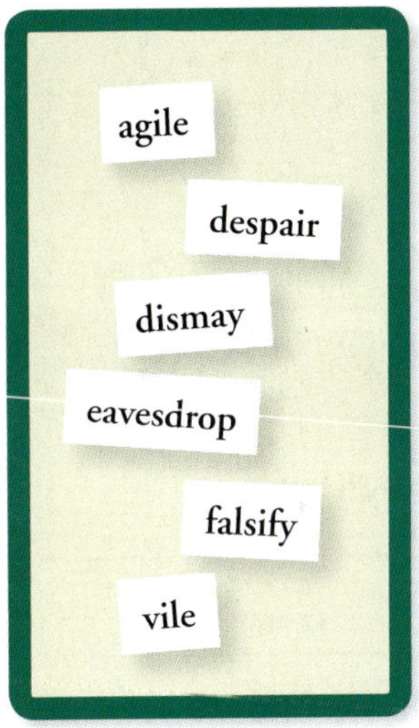

VOCABULARY IN WRITING

If someone asked you to summarize this story, what would you say? Use at least three vocabulary words in your account of the story's events. Here is a sample beginning.

EXAMPLE SENTENCE

Martha did not mean to ***eavesdrop****, but she overheard an argument.*

VOCABULARY STRATEGY: CONTEXT CLUES

Sometimes writers tell you directly what difficult words mean. This kind of context clue, a **definition,** usually follows the difficult word. It is set off by commas or dashes or by expressions like *that is.* Look for a definition of *valedictorian* on page 218 of this story.

Sometimes the definition might be in the form of a **synonym,** a word that has the same or similar meaning. Look for *falsify* and its synonym in the same sentence on page 220 of this story.

PRACTICE Define the boldfaced words. Identify context clues that helped you understand the meaning of the word.

1. Loretta is a **polyglot**—that is, someone who knows several languages.
2. The hurricane began as an **amorphous** mass—a shapeless group of clouds.
3. When I **disparaged** him, he put me down in the same way.
4. She was not simply happy to receive the gift; she was **euphoric.**
5. The sleep clinic treats **somnambulists,** people who walk in their sleep.

ALABAMA STANDARDS

READING STANDARD
1.c Using context clues to determine meaning of words

VOCABULARY PRACTICE
For more practice, go to the **Vocabulary Center** at **ClassZone.com.**

A Retrieved Reformation

Short Story by O. Henry

Who deserves a second CHANCE?

ALABAMA STANDARDS

READING STANDARDS
1.f Analyzing predictions
2 Relate literary elements to each other, including point of view

KEY IDEA Everybody makes mistakes—sometimes bad ones. But some people, if they're lucky, are given a **chance** to redeem themselves. In "A Retrieved Reformation," a man has the opportunity to change his scheming ways. Will he take it?

DISCUSS With a small group, think of one or two individuals who could have used a second chance. Perhaps it's a coach who had a losing season. Maybe it's someone who betrayed a friend's secret. What criteria could be used to determine whether that person deserves another chance?

LITERARY ANALYSIS: OMNISCIENT POINT OF VIEW

What would it be like to know what all your friends are thinking? The feeling would be similar to reading a story written in the **third-person omniscient point of view.** An omniscient, or all-knowing, narrator

- tells the story using the pronouns *he, she, it,* and *they*
- is aware of what all the characters in the story are thinking and doing

As you read "A Retrieved Reformation," notice when you have more information than the characters do.

READING STRATEGY: PREDICT

One way to make reading a story even more interesting is to **predict** what will happen next. Your predictions won't always be correct, but finding out whether they are correct or not can be fun. As you read "A Retrieved Reformation," record your predictions in a chart like the one shown.

My Prediction	*Reason for Prediction*
Jimmy will keep cracking safes.	

Review: **Make Inferences**

VOCABULARY IN CONTEXT

The boldfaced words help tell the story of a man who is given another chance. Figure out the meaning of each word by using the context clues in each of the phrases.

1. **saunter** casually through the park
2. might **balk** and change his mind at the last minute
3. friendly neighbors chatting **genially**
4. an upright, **virtuous** individual
5. **compulsory** attendance with no excuses allowed
6. slipped away like an **elusive** butterfly
7. tried to **rehabilitate** the injured man
8. honored to have such an **eminent** guest
9. a suitcase in the corner **unperceived** by anyone
10. promised **retribution** if the offender was caught

Author Online

An Early Reader How could one of the most famous short story writers of all time die with only 23 cents in his pocket? That is what happened to William Sydney Porter, better known as O. Henry. Porter's adventures began in the home of his aunt, who raised him. She encouraged the young boy's love of reading, writing, and drawing caricatures, which are comically exaggerated representations of people. The sense of humor seen in his drawings often appears in his writing.

O. Henry
1862–1910

No Ordinary Life Porter continued writing and illustrating throughout his adult life in addition to working as a pharmacist, ranch hand, cook, and bank teller. Several years after leaving his position at the First National Bank of Austin, Texas, he was convicted of stealing money from the bank. He published several short stories from jail, using the pen name O. Henry in order to conceal his criminal record.

A Real Character Porter's vast experiences serve as the inspiration for most of his stories. The main character in "A Retrieved Reformation" is based on a safecracker (someone who breaks into safes) who Porter met in prison.

MORE ABOUT THE AUTHOR
For more on O. Henry, visit the **Literature Center** at **ClassZone.com.**

A *Retrieved* REFORMATION

O. Henry

A guard came to the prison shoe shop, where Jimmy Valentine was assiduously stitching uppers,[1] and escorted him to the front office. There the warden handed Jimmy his pardon, which had been signed that morning by the governor. Jimmy took it in a tired kind of way. He had served nearly ten months of a four-year sentence. He had expected to stay only about three months, at the longest. When a man with as many friends on the outside as Jimmy Valentine had is received in the "stir"[2] it is hardly worthwhile to cut his hair. (A)

"Now, Valentine," said the warden, "you'll go out in the morning. Brace up, and make a man of yourself. You're not a bad fellow at heart. Stop cracking safes, and live straight."

"Me?" said Jimmy, in surprise. "Why, I never cracked a safe in my life."

"Oh, no," laughed the warden. "Of course not. Let's see, now. How was it you happened to get sent up on that Springfield job? Was it because you wouldn't prove an alibi for fear of compromising somebody in extremely high-toned society? Or was it simply a case of a mean old jury that had it in for you? It's always one or the other with you innocent victims."

ANALYZE VISUALS
What do the details in the painting help you **infer** about this man?

(A) OMNISCIENT POINT OF VIEW
Writers sometimes use the omniscient point of view to make general comments about life. Reread lines 6–8. What does this comment mean?

---

1. **assiduously** (ə-sĭj'o͞o-əs-lē) **stitching uppers:** carefully and industriously sewing together the top portions of shoes.
2. **"stir":** a slang term for prison.

Detail of *Tides of Memory* (1936), Norman Rockwell. Oil on board, 18¾″ × 15¼″.

"Me?" said Jimmy, still blankly **virtuous.** "Why, warden, I never was in Springfield in my life!"

"Take him back, Cronin," smiled the warden, "and fix him up with outgoing clothes. Unlock him at seven in the morning, and let him come to the bull-pen. Better think over my advice, Valentine."

At a quarter past seven on the next morning Jimmy stood in the warden's outer office. He had on a suit of the villainously fitting, ready-made clothes and a pair of the stiff, squeaky shoes that the state furnishes to its discharged **compulsory** guests.

The clerk handed him a railroad ticket and the five-dollar bill with which the law expected him to **rehabilitate** himself into good citizenship and prosperity. The warden gave him a cigar, and shook hands. Valentine, 9762, was chronicled[3] on the books "Pardoned by Governor," and Mr. James Valentine walked out into the sunshine.

Disregarding the song of the birds, the waving green trees, and the smell of the flowers, Jimmy headed straight for a restaurant. There he tasted the first sweet joys of liberty in the shape of a broiled chicken and a bottle of white wine—followed by a cigar a grade better than the one the warden had given him. From there he proceeded leisurely to the depot. He tossed a quarter into the hat of a blind man sitting by the door, and boarded his train. Three hours set him down in a little town near the state line. He went to the café of one Mike Dolan and shook hands with Mike, who was alone behind the bar.

"Sorry we couldn't make it sooner, Jimmy, me boy," said Mike. "But we had that protest from Springfield to buck against, and the governor nearly **balked.** Feeling all right?"

"Fine," said Jimmy. "Got my key?"

He got his key and went upstairs, unlocking the door of a room at the rear. Everything was just as he had left it. There on the floor was still Ben Price's collar-button that had been torn from that **eminent** detective's shirt-band when they had overpowered Jimmy to arrest him.

Pulling out from the wall a folding-bed, Jimmy slid back a panel in the wall and dragged out a dust-covered suitcase. He opened this and gazed fondly at the finest set of burglar's tools in the East. It was a complete set, made of specially tempered steel, the latest designs in drills, punches, braces and bits, jimmies, clamps, and augers, with two or three novelties invented by Jimmy himself, in which he took pride. Over nine hundred dollars they had cost him to have made at ___________, a place where they make such things for the profession.

virtuous
(vûr′cho͞o-əs) *adj.*
morally good; honorable

compulsory
(kəm-pŭl′sə-rē) *adj.*
forced; required

rehabilitate
(rē′hə-bĭl′ĭ-tāt′) *v.* to restore to useful life, as through therapy and education

balk (bôk) *v.* to refuse to move or act

eminent (ĕm′ə-nənt) *adj.* famous; well-respected

3. **chronicled** (krŏn′ĭ-kəld): written down in a record book or ledger book.

In half an hour Jimmy went downstairs and through the café. He was now dressed in tasteful and well-fitting clothes, and carried his dusted and cleaned suitcase in his hand. **B**

"Got anything on?" asked Mike Dolan, **genially.**

"Me?" said Jimmy, in a puzzled tone. "I don't understand. I'm representing the New York Amalgamated Short Snap Biscuit Cracker and Frazzled Wheat Company."

This statement delighted Mike to such an extent that Jimmy had to take a seltzer-and-milk on the spot. He never touched "hard" drinks.

A week after the release of Valentine, 9762, there was a neat job of safe-burglary done in Richmond, Indiana, with no clue to the author. A scant eight hundred dollars was all that was secured. Two weeks after that a patented, improved, burglar-proof safe in Logansport was opened like a cheese to the tune of fifteen hundred dollars, currency; securities and silver untouched. That began to interest the rogue catchers.[4] Then an old-fashioned bank safe in Jefferson City became active and threw out of its crater an eruption of banknotes amounting to five thousand dollars. The losses were now high enough to bring the matter up into Ben Price's class of work. By comparing notes, a remarkable similarity in the methods of the burglaries was noticed. Ben Price investigated the scenes of the robberies, and was heard to remark: "That's Dandy Jim Valentine's autograph. He's resumed business. Look at that combination knob—jerked out as easy as pulling up a radish in wet weather. He's got the only clamps that can do it. And look how clean those tumblers were punched out! Jimmy never has to drill but one hole. Yes, I guess I want Mr. Valentine. He'll do his bit next time without any short-time or clemency foolishness."[5]

Ben Price knew Jimmy's habits. He had learned them while working up the Springfield case. Long jumps, quick get-aways, no confederates,[6] and a taste for good society—these ways had helped Mr. Valentine to become noted as a successful dodger of **retribution.** It was given out that Ben Price had taken up the trail of the **elusive** cracksman, and other people with burglar-proof safes felt more at ease. **C**

One afternoon Jimmy Valentine and his suitcase climbed out of the mailhack in Elmore, a little town five miles off the railroad down in the blackjack country of Arkansas. Jimmy, looking like an athletic young senior just home from college, went down the board sidewalk toward the hotel.

B PREDICT
On the basis of Jimmy's actions in this paragraph, what do you predict he will do?

genially (jēn′yəl-lē) *adv.* in a pleasant, friendly manner

retribution (rĕt′rə-byo͞o′shən) *n.* punishment for bad behavior

elusive (ĭ-lo͞o′sĭv) *adj.* tending to elude capture

C OMNISCIENT POINT OF VIEW
Reread lines 84–89. What information does the narrator share with you that the main character, Jimmy, doesn't know?

4. **rogue** (rōg) **catchers:** people who chase after criminals.
5. **He'll do his bit . . . foolishness:** He'll serve his full term in prison without anyone shortening the length of it or pardoning him.
6. **confederates** (kən-fĕd′ər-ĭts): accomplices or associates in crime.

A young lady crossed the street, passed him at the corner, and entered a door over which was the sign "The Elmore Bank." Jimmy Valentine looked into her eyes, forgot what he was, and became another man. She lowered her eyes and colored slightly. Young men of Jimmy's style and looks were scarce in Elmore.

Jimmy collared a boy that was loafing on the steps of the bank as if he were one of the stockholders, and began to ask him questions about the town, feeding him dimes at intervals. By and by the young lady came out, looking royally unconscious of the young man with the suitcase, and went her way.

"Isn't that young lady Miss Polly Simpson?" asked Jimmy, with specious guile.[7]

"Naw," said the boy. "She's Annabel Adams. Her pa owns this bank. What'd you come to Elmore for? Is that a gold watch-chain? I'm going to get a bulldog. Got any more dimes?" **D**

Jimmy went to the Planters' Hotel, registered as Ralph D. Spencer, and engaged a room. He leaned on the desk and declared his platform to the clerk. He said he had come to Elmore to look for a location to go into business. How was the shoe business, now, in the town? He had thought of the shoe business. Was there an opening? **E**

The clerk was impressed by the clothes and manner of Jimmy. He, himself, was something of a pattern of fashion to the thinly gilded youth of Elmore, but he now perceived his shortcomings. While trying to figure out Jimmy's manner of tying his four-in-hand[8] he cordially gave information.

Yes, there ought to be a good opening in the shoe line. There wasn't an exclusive shoe store in the place. The dry-goods and general stores handled them. Business in all lines was fairly good. Hoped Mr. Spencer would decide to locate in Elmore. He would find it a pleasant town to live in, and the people very sociable.

D PREDICT
What do you think will happen now that Jimmy and the bank owner's daughter have noticed each other?

E MAKE INFERENCES
Reread lines 110–114. Why does Jimmy change his name and say he's going into the shoe business?

Eleanor (1907), Frank Weston Benson. Oil on canvas, 64.13 cm × 76.83 cm. The Hayden Collection–Charles Henry Hayden Fund. © Museum of Fine Arts, Boston (08.326).

7. **specious guile** (spē'shəs gīl): innocent charm masking real slyness.
8. **four-in-hand:** a necktie tied in the usual way, that is, in a slipknot with the ends left hanging.

Mr. Spencer thought he would stop over in the town a few days and look over the situation. No, the clerk needn't call the boy. He would carry up his suitcase, himself; it was rather heavy.

Mr. Ralph Spencer, the phoenix[9] that arose from Jimmy Valentine's ashes—ashes left by the flame of a sudden and alterative attack of love—remained in Elmore, and prospered. He opened a shoe store and secured a good run of trade. **F**

F OMNISCIENT POINT OF VIEW
Who in the story knows that Ralph Spencer is also Jimmy Valentine?

Socially he was also a success and made many friends. And he accomplished the wish of his heart. He met Miss Annabel Adams, and became more and more captivated by her charms.

At the end of a year the situation of Mr. Ralph Spencer was this: he had won the respect of the community, his shoe store was flourishing, and he and Annabel were engaged to be married in two weeks. Mr. Adams, the typical, plodding, country banker, approved of Spencer. Annabel's pride in him almost equaled her affection. He was as much at home in the family of Mr. Adams and that of Annabel's married sister as if he were already a member.

One day Jimmy sat down in his room and wrote this letter, which he mailed to the safe address of one of his old friends in St. Louis:

Dear Old Pal:

I want you to be at Sullivan's place, in Little Rock, next Wednesday night, at nine o'clock. I want you to wind up some little matters for me. And, also, I want to make you a present of my kit of tools. I know you'll be glad to get them—you couldn't duplicate the lot for a thousand dollars. Say, Billy, I've quit the old business—a year ago. I've got a nice store. I'm making an honest living, and I'm going to marry the finest girl on earth two weeks from now. It's the only life, Billy—the straight one. I wouldn't touch a dollar of another man's money now for a million. After I get married I'm going to sell out and go West, where there won't be so much danger of having old scores brought up against me. I tell you, Billy, she's an angel. She believes in me; and I wouldn't do another crooked thing for the whole world. Be sure to be at Sully's, for I must see you. I'll bring along the tools with me. **G**

Your old friend,
Jimmy

G PREDICT
Do you think Jimmy will ever crack another safe? Why or why not?

---

9. **phoenix** (fē′nĭks): a mythological bird that lived for 500 years and then burned itself to death, only to rise from its own ashes to live another long life.

Hill, Main Street, Gloucester (1916), John Sloan. Oil on canvas, 25¾″ × 39⅞″. Littlejohn Collection, The Parrish Art Museum, Southampton, New York, 1961.3.208.

On the Monday night after Jimmy wrote this letter, Ben Price jogged unobtrusively into Elmore in a livery buggy.[10] He lounged about town in his quiet way until he found out what he wanted to know. From the drugstore across the street from Spencer's shoe store he got a good look at Ralph D. Spencer.

"Going to marry the banker's daughter are you, Jimmy?" said Ben to himself, softly. "Well, I don't know!"

ANALYZE VISUALS
What **mood** do the colors in the painting suggest?

The next morning Jimmy took breakfast at the Adamses. He was going to Little Rock that day to order his wedding suit and buy something nice for Annabel. That would be the first time he had left town since he came to Elmore. It had been more than a year now since those last professional "jobs," and he thought he could safely venture out. **H**

After breakfast quite a family party went down together—Mr. Adams, Annabel, Jimmy, and Annabel's married sister with her two little girls,

H OMNISCIENT POINT OF VIEW
What do you know that Jimmy doesn't know at this point?

10. **livery** (lĭv′ə-rē) **buggy:** a hired horse and carriage.

aged five and nine. They came by the hotel where Jimmy still boarded, and he ran up to his room and brought along his suitcase. Then they went on to the bank. There stood Jimmy's horse and buggy and Dolph Gibson, who was going to drive him over to the railroad station.

All went inside the high, carved oak railings into the banking room—Jimmy included, for Mr. Adams's future son-in-law was welcome anywhere. The clerks were pleased to be greeted by the good-looking, agreeable young man who was going to marry Miss Annabel. Jimmy set his suitcase down. Annabel, whose heart was bubbling with happiness and lively youth, put on Jimmy's hat and picked up the suitcase. "Wouldn't I make a nice drummer?"[11] said Annabel. "My! Ralph, how heavy it is. Feels like it was full of gold bricks."

"Lot of nickel-plated shoehorns in there," said Jimmy, coolly, "that I'm going to return. Thought I'd save express charges by taking them up. I'm getting awfully economical."

The Elmore Bank had just put in a new safe and vault. Mr. Adams was very proud of it, and insisted on an inspection by everyone. The vault was a small one, but it had a new patented door. It fastened with three solid steel bolts thrown simultaneously with a single handle, and had a time lock. Mr. Adams beamingly explained its workings to Mr. Spencer, who showed a courteous but not too intelligent interest. The two children, May and Agatha, were delighted by the shining metal and funny clock and knobs. **I**

While they were thus engaged Ben Price **sauntered** in and leaned on his elbow, looking casually inside between the railings. He told the teller that he didn't want anything; he was just waiting for a man he knew.

Suddenly there was a scream or two from the women, and a commotion. **Unperceived** by the elders, May, the nine-year-old girl, in a spirit of play, had shut Agatha in the vault. She had then shot the bolts and turned the knob of the combination as she had seen Mr. Adams do.

The old banker sprang to the handle and tugged at it for a moment. "The door can't be opened," he groaned. "The clock hasn't been wound nor the combination set."

Agatha's mother screamed again, hysterically.

"Hush!" said Mr. Adams, raising his trembling hand. "All be quiet for a moment. Agatha!" he called as loudly as he could. "Listen to me." During the following silence they could just hear the faint sound of the child wildly shrieking in the dark vault in a panic of terror.

"My precious darling!" wailed the mother. "She will die of fright! Open the door! Oh, break it open! Can't you men do something?"

I MAKE INFERENCES
Why does "Mr. Spencer" show a "courteous but not too intelligent interest" in the new safe and vault?

saunter (sôn′tər) *v.* to stroll in a casual manner

unperceived (ŭn-pər-sēvd′) *adj.* not seen or noticed

11. **drummer:** an old-fashioned word for traveling salesman.

"There isn't a man nearer than Little Rock who can open that door," said Mr. Adams, in a shaky voice. "My God! Spencer, what shall we do? That child—she can't stand it long in there. There isn't enough air, and, besides, she'll go into convulsions from fright." **J**

Agatha's mother, frantic now, beat the door of the vault with her hands. Somebody wildly suggested dynamite. Annabel turned to Jimmy, her large eyes full of anguish, but not yet despairing. To a woman nothing seems quite impossible to the powers of the man she worships.

"Can't you do something, Ralph—try, won't you?"

He looked at her with a queer, soft smile on his lips and in his keen eyes.

"Annabel," he said, "give me that rose you are wearing, will you?"

Hardly believing that she had heard him aright, she unpinned the bud from the bosom of her dress, and placed it in his hand. Jimmy stuffed it into his vest pocket, threw off his coat and pulled up his shirt sleeves. With that act Ralph D. Spencer passed away and Jimmy Valentine took his place. **K**

"Get away from the door, all of you," he commanded, shortly.

He set his suitcase on the table, and opened it out flat. From that time on he seemed to be unconscious of the presence of anyone else. He laid out the shining, queer implements swiftly and orderly, whistling softly to himself as he always did when at work. In a deep silence and immovable, the others watched him as if under a spell.

In a minute Jimmy's pet drill was biting smoothly into the steel door. In ten minutes—breaking his own burglarious record—he threw back the bolts and opened the door.

Agatha, almost collapsed, but safe, was gathered into her mother's arms.

Jimmy Valentine put on his coat, and walked outside the railings toward the front door. As he went he thought he heard a faraway voice that he once knew call "Ralph!" But he never hesitated. At the door a big man stood somewhat in his way.

"Hello, Ben!" said Jimmy, still with his strange smile. "Got around at last, have you? Well, let's go. I don't know that it makes much difference, now."

And then Ben Price acted rather strangely.

"Guess you're mistaken, Mr. Spencer," he said. "Don't believe I recognize you. Your buggy's waiting for you, ain't it?"

And Ben Price turned and strolled down the street. **L**

J PREDICT
On the basis of everything you know about Jimmy, what do you think he will do?

K MAKE INFERENCES
What is Jimmy preparing to do? How does he expect it to affect his relationship with Annabel?

L MAKE INFERENCES
Why does Ben Price let Jimmy go free?

Comprehension

ALABAMA STANDARDS

READING STANDARD
1.f Analyzing predictions

1. **Recall** What successes does Jimmy achieve in Elmore?
2. **Recall** How does Ben Price react when Jimmy cracks the safe?
3. **Summarize** How has Jimmy changed?

Literary Analysis

4. **Predict** Review the prediction chart you made as you read. How close were your predictions to what actually happens to Jimmy?
5. **Analyze Omniscient Point of View** Skim the story from lines 196–236. Use a graphic organizer like the one shown to note the information the reader knows that Jimmy does not.

6. **Identify Irony** Irony is a contrast between what is expected and what actually happens. What is ironic about the turn of events in this story?
7. **Make Judgments** At the end of the story, it's not clear how Annabel and her family will react to Jimmy's safecracking tools and skills. How do you think they should react? Support your opinion with details from the story.
8. **Evaluate the Title** A reformation is a change for the better. The word *retrieve* means "to rescue or regain something." Think about what the title refers to. Do you think it is a good title for this story? Why or why not?

Extension and Challenge

9. **Speaking and Listening** Do you agree with Ben Price's decision to let Jimmy go free? Hold a classroom trial to decide Jimmy's fate. Choose who will be Jimmy's defense lawyer, the prosecutor, the judge, the witnesses, the jury, the audience, and the court reporter. The defense will argue that Jimmy be granted a second **chance** and the prosecution will argue that he should be sent back to prison. The closing arguments should be presented to the classroom jury. Your arguments must be supported with evidence from the text.

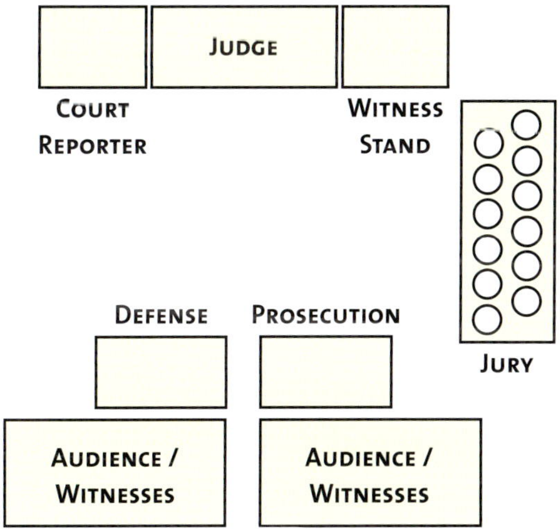

Typical courtroom layout

Vocabulary in Context

VOCABULARY PRACTICE

Synonyms are words that have the same meaning, and **antonyms** are words that have the opposite meaning. Decide whether the words in each pair are synonyms or antonyms.

1. compulsory—voluntary
2. elusive—slippery
3. virtuous—honorable
4. saunter—stroll
5. balk—agree
6. retribution—punishment
7. eminent—unknown
8. rehabilitate—restore
9. unperceived—unnoticed
10. genially—disagreeably

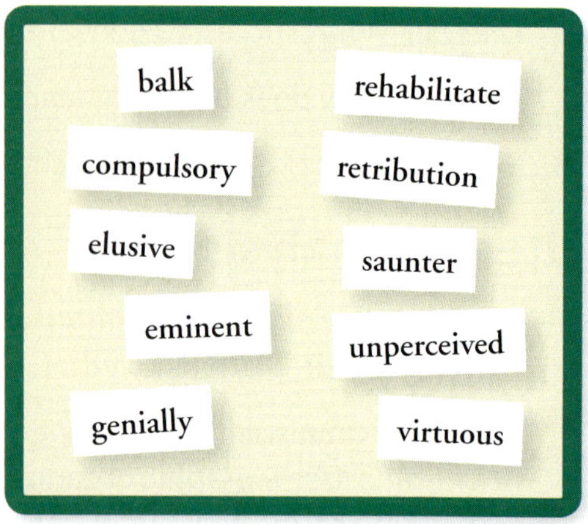

VOCABULARY IN WRITING

What were some of Ben Price's qualities? Write a paragraph describing Ben, using four or more vocabulary words. You could start like this.

EXAMPLE SENTENCE

*Ben Price often spoke **genially**, but he always took his job seriously.*

VOCABULARY STRATEGY: WORDS WITH MULTIPLE MEANINGS

Many English words have more than one meaning. For example, you might know that *compromising* can mean "giving in by both sides to reach an agreement." But you might not be familiar with its meaning in this story (line 15), "putting someone into a bad position or situation."

If a word does not make sense to you, look at the words around it for clues to other possible meanings. For further help, check a dictionary. For example, which of these meanings of *balk* would you expect to find in a baseball article?

balk (bôk) *v.* **1.** to refuse to move or act: *The horse balked at jumping the fence.* **2.** to make an illegal motion as a pitcher, especially to start a throw and not finish it.

PRACTICE Define the boldfaced words using context clues or a dictionary.

1. Shipping is one of the city's **key** industries.
2. He floated down the stream with the **current.**
3. Several town officials helped to **frame** the new law.
4. The stars stood out in sharp **relief** against the sky.
5. What numbers must you multiply to figure out the **volume** of a room?

ALABAMA STANDARDS

READING STANDARD
1.c Using context clues to determine meaning of words

VOCABULARY PRACTICE
For more practice, go to the **Vocabulary Center** at **ClassZone.com.**

SKILLS PRACTICE

Reading-Writing Connection

Demonstrate an understanding of the characters in "A Retrieved Reformation" by responding to these prompts. Then complete the **Grammar and Writing** exercise.

WRITING PROMPTS	SELF-CHECK
A. Short Response: Compare Characters Jimmy Valentine and Ben Price both make surprising decisions at the end of "A Retrieved Reformation." Using details and examples from the text, write **one paragraph** in which you compare the two characters.	***A strong comparison will . . .*** • use transition words and phrases such as *like* and *similarly* • conclude with a clear statement about the characters
B. Extended Response: Write a Personal Letter How will Jimmy Valentine explain his actions to Annabel? Write a **two- or three-paragraph letter** to Annabel in which Jimmy describes his past and asks for a second **chance.**	***A successful letter will . . .*** • show an understanding of Jimmy Valentine's character • be written in personal letter format

GRAMMAR AND WRITING

COMPARE CORRECTLY When making comparisons, follow these guidelines:

- To compare only two people or things, use the **comparative form** (stronger; more quickly). Never use *more* and *-er* together.
- To compare three or more people or things, use the **superlative form** (strongest; most quickly). Never use *most* and *-est* together.

PRACTICE Choose the comparative or superlative form to correctly complete each sentence.

1. Of the two men, Jimmy is the (smarter, smartest).
2. Annabel is the (sweeter, sweetest) person in the world to him.
3. Jimmy must decide what he wants (more, most)— the life of a safecracker or the life of a family man.
4. Ben Price can see that Jimmy has become the (more, most) reformed of all the crooks he has known.

*For more help with comparative and superlative forms, see page R58 in the **Grammar Handbook.***

ALABAMA STANDARDS

WRITING/LANGUAGE STANDARD
11.b Using degrees of comparison

Comparing Characters

The Three-Century Woman

Short Story by Richard Peck

Charles

Short Story by Shirley Jackson

Why do people MISBEHAVE?

ALABAMA STANDARDS

READING & LIT STANDARDS

1 Apply strategies, including setting purposes for reading

8 Compare selections and their characteristics

KEY IDEA No one's **behavior** is always perfect. When we misbehave, sometimes we do so for a reason—although that doesn't mean it's a good one. In the stories you are about to read, an elderly woman and a young boy misbehave at important milestones in their lives.

LIST IT Make a list of ways you've seen people misbehave. Did someone make a face in a yearbook picture? Did someone disrupt a serious ceremony? After making your list, discuss with classmates why you think those individuals may have acted as they did.

● LITERARY ANALYSIS: CHARACTERIZATION

Literary characters have personalities just as real people do. How a writer creates and develops these personalities is known as **characterization.** For example, a writer may

- describe a character's physical appearance
- present a character's thoughts, words, and actions
- present the thoughts, words, and reactions of other characters
- make direct comments about a character's personality

As you read the following two stories, note what the characters say and do and what is said about them.

● READING STRATEGY: SET A PURPOSE FOR READING

When you **set a purpose** for reading, you choose specific reasons for reading one or more works. Your purpose for reading "The Three-Century Woman" and "Charles" is to find similarities and differences between the two main characters. After the first story, begin filling in the chart.

	Great-Grandma	*Laurie*
What does each character look like?		
How does each character behave?		
How do others see each character?		
How would you describe each character's personality?		

Review: **Make Inferences**

▲ VOCABULARY IN CONTEXT

The listed words help reveal the characters' personalities. For each word, choose the numbered term closest in meaning.

WORD LIST			
	cynically	insolently	renounce
	incredulously	raucous	venerable

1. noisy
2. disrespectfully
3. sarcastically
4. skeptically
5. well-respected
6. give up

Author On|ine

Richard Peck: Inspired Teacher

Richard Peck
born 1934

Teaching high school English brought out the writer in Richard Peck. As he says, "I found my future readers right there in the roll book." Although Peck has written novels for adults, he is best known and loved for his young-adult fiction.

Shirley Jackson: Rebel with a Cause

Shirley Jackson
1919–1965

From an early age, Shirley Jackson rebelled against what she considered her wealthy family's selfish lifestyle. Instead of taking part in social events, she would disappear into her journals. After she married, Jackson moved to a small town in Vermont and adopted a much different way of life. She wrote many novels, essays, and short stories. Jackson's friends and critics described the reclusive author as the "Madame of Mystery," referring to the dark humor and strange twists found in her stories. Sadly, Jackson died at 45 from a heart attack.

MORE ABOUT THE AUTHOR
For more on the authors, visit the **Literature Center** at **ClassZone.com.**

The Three-Century *Woman*

Richard Peck

"I guess if you live long enough," my mom said to Aunt Gloria, "you get your fifteen minutes of fame."

Mom was on the car phone to Aunt Gloria. The minute Mom rolls out of the garage, she's on her car phone. It's state of the art and better than her car.

We were heading for Whispering Oaks to see my Great-Grandmother Breckenridge, who's lived there since I was a little girl. They call it an Elder Care Facility. Needless to say, I hated going.

The reason for Great-Grandma's fame is that she was born in 1899. Now it's January 2001. If you're one of those people who claim the new century begins in 2001, not 2000, even you have to agree that Great-Grandma Breckenridge has lived in three centuries. This is her claim to fame.

We waited for a light to change along by Northbrook Mall, and I gazed fondly over at it. Except for the Multiplex, it was closed because of New Year's Day. I have a severe mall habit. But I'm fourteen, and the mall is the place without homework. Aunt Gloria's voice filled the car. **A**

"If you take my advice," she told Mom, "you'll keep those Whispering Oaks people from letting the media in to interview Grandma. Interview her my foot! Honestly. She doesn't even know where she is, let alone how many centuries she's lived in. The poor old soul. Leave her in peace. She's already got one foot in the—"

"Gloria, your trouble is you have no sense of history." Mom gunned across the intersection. "You got a C in History."

"I was sick a lot that year," Aunt Gloria said.

"Sick of history," Mom murmured.

ANALYZE VISUALS
What can you **infer** about the personality of the woman in the red hat on the basis of her appearance?

A CHARACTERIZATION
Reread lines 14–17. What do you learn about the narrator here?

Red Hat (2003), Deidre Scherer
Fabric and thread. © Deidre Scherer.

"I heard that," Aunt Gloria said.

They bickered on, but I tuned them out. Then when we turned in at Whispering Pines, a sound truck from IBC-TV was blocking the drive.

"Good grief," Mom murmured. "TV."

"I told you," Aunt Gloria said, but Mom switched her off. She parked in a frozen rut.

"I'll wait in the car," I said. "I have homework."

"Get out of the car," Mom said.

If you get so old you have to be put away, Whispering Oaks isn't that bad. It smells all right, and a Christmas tree glittered in the lobby. A real tree. On the other hand, you have to push a red button to unlock the front door. I guess it's to keep the inmates from escaping, though Great-Grandma Breckenridge wasn't going anywhere and hadn't for twenty years.

When we got to her wing, the hall was full of camera crews and a woman from the suburban newspaper with a notepad.

Mom sighed. It was like that first day of school when you think you'll be okay until the teachers learn your name. Stepping over a cable, we stopped at Great-Grandma's door, and they were on to us.

"Who are you people to Mrs. Breckenridge?" the newspaperwoman said. "I want names."

These people were seriously pushy. And the TV guy was wearing more makeup than Mom. It dawned on me that they couldn't get into Great-Grandma's room without her permission. Mom turned on them.

"Listen, you're not going to be interviewing my grandmother," she said in a quiet bark. "I'll be glad to tell you anything you want to know about her, but you're not going in there. She's got nothing to say, and . . . she needs a lot of rest."

"Is it Alzheimer's?"[1] the newswoman asked. "Because we're thinking Alzheimer's."

"Think what you want," Mom said. "But this is as far as you get. And you people with the camera and the light, you're not going in there either. You'd scare her to death, and then I'd sue the pants off you." **B**

They pulled back.

But a voice came wavering out of Great-Grandma's room. Quite an eerie, echoing voice.

"Let them in!" the voice said.

B CHARACTERIZATION
Reread lines 41–59. What do you learn about the narrator's mother from how she talks to the reporters?

1. **Alzheimer's** (älts'hī-mərz): a disease of the brain that causes confusion and may lead to total loss of memory.

It had to be Great-Grandma Breckenridge. Her roommate had died. "Good grief," Mom murmured, and the press surged forward.

Mom and I went in first, and our eyes popped. Great-Grandma was usually flat out in the bed, dozing, with her teeth in a glass and a book in her hand. Today she was bright-eyed and propped up. She wore a fuzzy pink bed jacket. A matching bow was stuck in what remained of her hair.

"Oh for pity's sake," Mom murmured. "They've got her done up like a Barbie doll."

Great-Grandma peered from the bed at Mom. "And who are you?" she asked.

"I'm Ann," Mom said carefully. "This is Megan," she said, meaning me.

"That's right," Great-Grandma said. "At least you know who you are. Plenty around this place don't." **C**

The guy with the camera on his shoulder barged in. The other guy turned on a blinding light.

Great-Grandma blinked. In the glare we noticed she wore a trace of lipstick. The TV anchor elbowed the woman reporter aside and stuck a mike in Great-Grandma's face. Her claw hand came out from under the covers and tapped it.

"Is this thing on?" she inquired.

"Yes, ma'am," the TV anchor said in his broadcasting voice. "Don't you worry about all this modern technology. We don't understand half of it ourselves." He gave her his big, five-thirty news smile and settled on the edge of her bed. There was room for him. She was tiny.

"We're here to congratulate you for having lived in three centuries—for being a Three-Century Woman! A great achievement."

Great-Grandma waved a casual claw. "Nothing to it," she said. "You sure this mike's on? Let's do this in one take."

The cameraman snorted and moved in for a closer shot. Mom stood still as a statue, wondering what was going to come out of Great-Grandma's mouth next. **D**

"Mrs. Breckenridge," the anchor said, "to what do you attribute your long life?"

"I was only married once," Great-Grandma said. "And he died young."

The anchor stared. "Ah. And anything else?"

"Yes. I don't look back. I live in the present."

The camera panned around the room. This was all the present she had, and it didn't look like much.

"You live for the present," the anchor said, looking for an angle, "even now?"

C CHARACTERIZATION
Consider Great-Grandma's appearance and words. What is your first impression of her?

D MAKE INFERENCES
Reread lines 77–94. How do you think Megan feels about the reporters?

Great-Grandma nodded. "Something's always happening. Last night I fell off the bed pan."

Mom groaned.

The cameraman pulled in for a tighter shot. The anchor seemed to search his mind. You could tell he thought he was a great interviewer, though he had no sense of humor. A tiny smile played around Great-Grandma's wrinkled lips.

"But you've lived through amazing times, Mrs. Breckenridge. And you never think back about them?" **E**

Great-Grandma stroked her chin and considered. "You mean you want to hear something interesting? Like how I lived through the San Francisco earthquake—the big one of oh-six?"

Beside me, Mom stirred. We were crowded over by the dead lady's bed. "You survived the 1906 San Francisco earthquake?" the anchor said.

Great-Grandma gazed at the ceiling, lost in thought.

"I'd have been about seven years old. My folks and I were staying at that big hotel. You know the one. I slept in a cot at the foot of their bed. In the middle of the night, that room gave a shake, and the chiffonier walked right across the floor. You know what chiffonier is?"

"A chest of drawers?" the anchor said.

"Close enough," Great-Grandma said. "And the pictures flapped on the walls. We had to walk down twelve flights because the elevators didn't work. When we got outside, the streets were ankle-deep in broken glass. You never saw such a mess in your life."

Mom nudged me and hissed: "She's never been to San Francisco. She's never been west of Denver. I've heard her say so."

"Incredible!" the anchor said.

"Truth's stranger than fiction," Great-Grandma said, smoothing her sheet.

"And you never think back about it?"

Great-Grandma shrugged her little fuzzy pink shoulders. "I've been through too much. I don't have time to remember it all. I was on the Hindenburg when it blew up, you know."

Mom moaned, and the cameraman was practically standing on his head for a close-up.

"The Hindenburg?"

"That big gas bag the Germans built to fly over the Atlantic Ocean. It was called a zeppelin. Biggest thing you ever saw—five city blocks long. It was in May of 1937, before your time. You wouldn't remember. My husband and I were coming back from Europe on it. No, wait a minute."

Great-Grandma cocked her head and pondered for the camera.

E MAKE INFERENCES
Why do you think the reporter wants Great-Grandma to talk about her memories?

SOCIAL STUDIES CONNECTION

On April 18, 1906, an earthquake devastated San Francisco, California. It is still considered one of the worst natural disasters in the history of the United States.

"My husband was dead by then. It was some other man. Anyway, the two of us were coming back on the Hindenburg. It was smooth as silk. You didn't know you were moving. When we flew in over New York, they stopped the ball game at Yankee Stadium to see us passing overhead."

Great-Grandma paused, caught up in memories.

"And then the Hindenburg exploded," the anchor said, prompting her.

She nodded. "We had no complaints about the trip till then. The luggage was all stacked, and we were coming in at Lakehurst, New Jersey. I was wearing my beige coat—beige or off-white, I forget. Then whoosh! The gondola[2] heated up like an oven, and people peeled out of the windows. We hit the ground and bounced. When we hit again, the door fell off, and I walked out and kept going. When they caught up with me in the parking lot, they wanted to put me in the hospital. I looked down and thought I was wearing a lace dress. The fire had about burned up my coat. And I lost a shoe."

"Fantastic!" the anchor breathed. "What detail!" Behind him the woman reporter was scribbling away on her pad.

"Never," Mom muttered. "Never in her life."

"Ma'am, you are living history!" the anchor said. "In your sensational span of years you've survived two great disasters!"

"Three." Great-Grandma patted the bow on her head. "I told you I'd been married."

"And before we leave this **venerable** lady," the anchor said, flashing a smile for the camera, "we'll ask Mrs. Breckenridge if she has any predictions for this new twenty-first century ahead of us here in the Dawn of the Millennium."

"Three or four predictions," Great-Grandma said, and paused again, stretching out her airtime. "Number one, taxes will be higher. Number two, it's going to be harder to find a place to park. And number three, a whole lot of people are going to live as long as I have, so get ready for us."

"And with those wise words," the anchor said, easing off the bed, "we leave Mrs. Breck—"

venerable (vĕn′ər-ə-bəl) *adj.* deserving respect because of age, character, or importance

ANALYZE VISUALS
What do you notice about the fabric patterns used in this quilt of the Hindenburg?

2. **gondola** (gŏn′dl-ə): a car that hangs under an airship and contains equipment and controls.

"And one more prediction," she said. "TV's on the way out. Your network ratings are already in the basement. It's all websites now. Son, I predict you'll be looking for work." **F**

And that was it. The light went dead. The anchor, looking shaken, followed his crew out the door. When TV's done with you, they're done with you. "Is that a wrap?" Great-Grandma asked.

F MAKE INFERENCES
How does Great-Grandma feel about the anchorman?

But now the woman from the suburban paper was moving in on her. "Just a few more questions, Mrs. Breckenridge."

"Where you from?" Great-Grandma blinked pink-eyed at her.

"*The Glenview Weekly Shopper.*"

"You bring a still photographer with you?" Great-Grandma asked.

"Well, no."

"And you never learned shorthand either, did you?"

"Well . . . no."

"Honey, I only deal with professionals. There's the door."

So then it was just Mom and Great-Grandma and I in the room. Mom planted a hand on her hip. "Grandma. Number one, you've never been to San Francisco. And number two, you never *saw* one of those zeppelin things."

Great-Grandma shrugged. "No, but I can read." She nodded to the pile of books on her nightstand with her spectacles folded on top. "You can pick up all that stuff in books."

VISUAL VOCABULARY

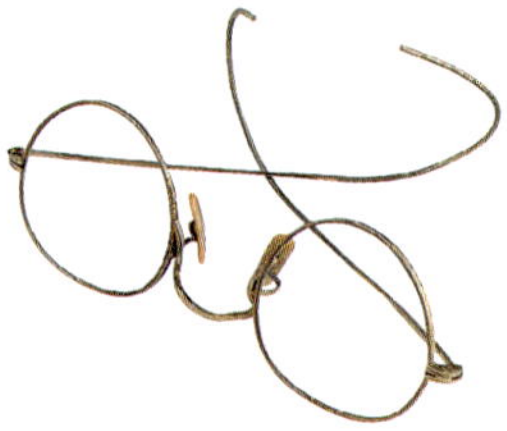

spectacles (spĕk'tə-kəls) *n.* eyeglasses

"And number three," Mom said. "Your husband didn't die young. I can *remember* Grandpa Breckenridge."

"It was that TV dude in the five-hundred-dollar suit who set me off," Great-Grandma said. "He dyes his hair, did you notice? He made me mad, and it put my nose out of joint.[3] He didn't notice I'm still here. He thought I was nothing but my memories. So I gave him some."

Now Mom and I stood beside her bed.

"I'll tell you something else," Great-Grandma said. "And it's no lie."

We waited, holding our breath to hear. Great-Grandma Breckenridge was pointing her little old bent finger right at me. "You, Megan," she said. "Once upon a time, I was your age. How scary is that?"

Then she hunched up her little pink shoulders and winked at me. She grinned and I grinned. She was just this little withered-up leaf of a lady in the bed. But I felt like giving her a kiss on her little wrinkled cheek, so I did.

"I'll come to see you more often," I told her. **G**

G CHARACTERIZATION
How has Megan's opinion of Great-Grandma changed?

"Call first," she said. "I might be busy." Then she dozed.

---

3. **put my nose out of joint:** got me into a bad mood.

ALABAMA STANDARDS

LITERATURE STANDARD
8 Compare selections and their characteristics

Comprehension

1. **Recall** Where does Great-Grandma live?
2. **Recall** Why are the reporters interviewing Great-Grandma?
3. **Clarify** Why does Great-Grandma make up the stories?

Literary Analysis

4. **Examine the Main Character** How would you describe Great-Grandma to someone who hasn't read "The Three-Century Woman"?
5. **Analyze Minor Characters** Even though the anchorman is a minor character, he plays an important role in the story. How do his interactions with Great-Grandma affect the plot?
6. **Evaluate the Main Character** In line 99, Great-Grandma says, "I don't look back. I live in the present." Is this true? Support your opinion with examples from the story.
7. **Make Judgments** Skim "The Three-Century Woman" and look for examples where each of the characters **misbehaves.** Who misbehaves the most in this story?

Comparing Characters

Now that you know more about Great-Grandma, start filling in your chart. Add information that helps you understand Great-Grandma's character.

	Great-Grandma	*Laurie*
What does each character look like?		
How does each character behave?	*She makes up stories for the news anchor.*	
How do others see each character?		
How would you describe each character's personality?		

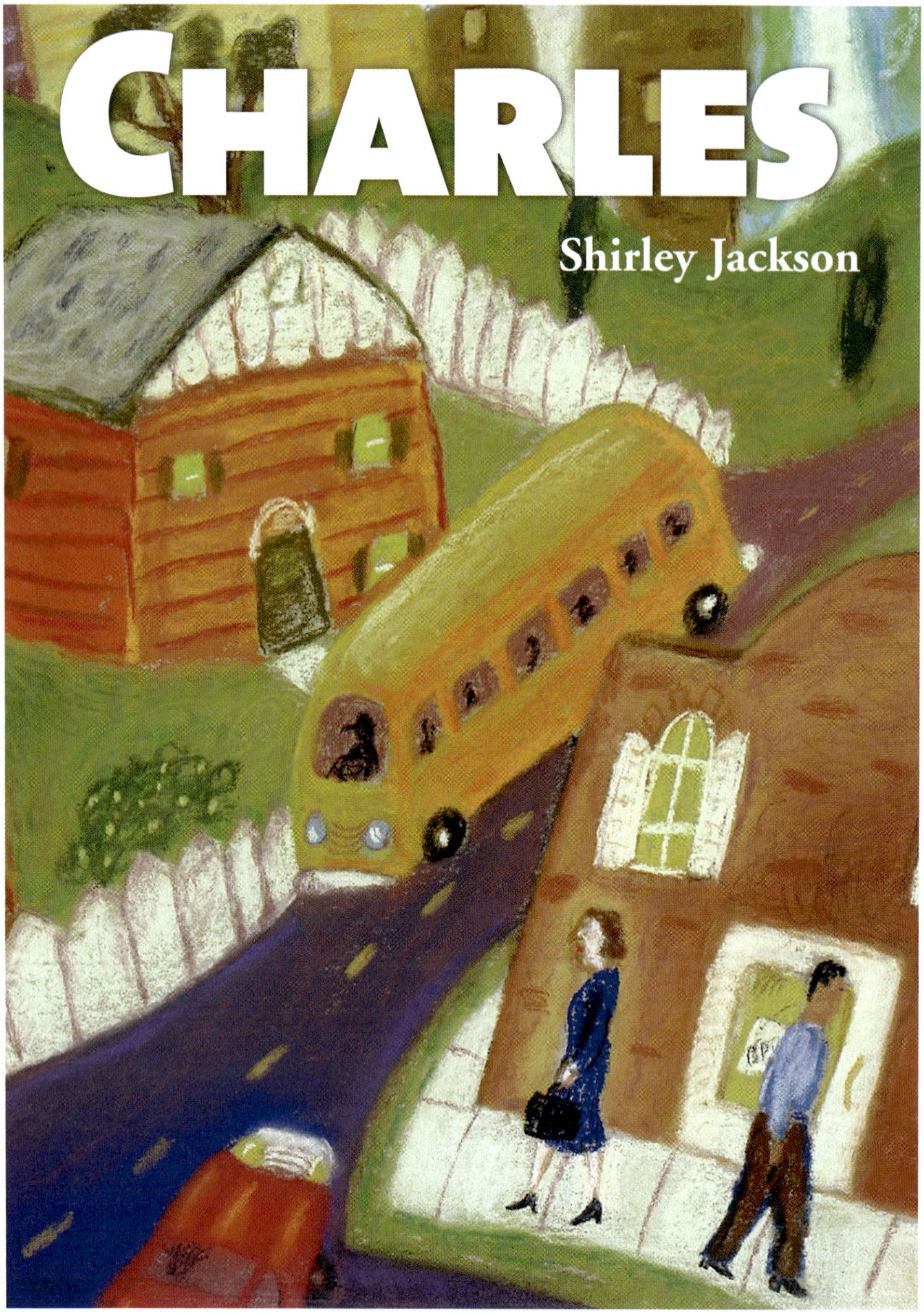

ANALYZE VISUALS
Make an **inference** about what kind of people live in this neighborhood. What details support your inference?

The day my son Laurie started kindergarten he **renounced** corduroy overalls with bibs and began wearing blue jeans with a belt; I watched him go off the first morning with the older girl next door, seeing clearly that an era of my life was ended, my sweet-voiced nursery-school tot replaced by a long-trousered, swaggering character who forgot to stop at the corner and wave goodbye to me. A

renounce (rĭ-nouns') *v.* to give up

A **CHARACTERIZATION**
What does the narrator imply about how Laurie's personality has changed recently?

He came home the same way, the front door slamming open, his cap on the floor, and the voice suddenly become **raucous** shouting, "Isn't anybody *here?*"

At lunch he spoke **insolently** to his father, spilled his baby sister's milk, and remarked that his teacher said we were not to take the name of the Lord in vain.

"How *was* school today?" I asked, elaborately casual.

"All right," he said.

"Did you learn anything?" his father asked.

Laurie regarded his father coldly. "I didn't learn nothing," he said.

"Anything," I said. "Didn't learn anything."

"The teacher spanked a boy, though," Laurie said, addressing his bread and butter. "For being fresh," he added, with his mouth full.

"What did he do?" I asked. "Who was it?"

Laurie thought. "It was Charles," he said. "He was fresh. The teacher spanked him and made him stand in a corner. He was awfully fresh."

"What did he do?" I asked again, but Laurie slid off his chair, took a cookie, and left, while his father was still saying, "See here, young man."

The next day Laurie remarked at lunch, as soon as he sat down, "Well, Charles was bad again today." He grinned enormously and said, "Today Charles hit the teacher."

"Good heavens," I said, mindful of the Lord's name, "I suppose he got spanked again?"

"He sure did," Laurie said. "Look up," he said to his father.

"What?" his father said, looking up.

"Look down," Laurie said. "Look at my thumb. Gee, you're dumb." He began to laugh insanely. **B**

"Why did Charles hit the teacher?" I asked quickly.

"Because she tried to make him color with red crayons," Laurie said. "Charles wanted to color with green crayons so he hit the teacher and she spanked him and said nobody play with Charles but everybody did."

The third day—it was Wednesday of the first week—Charles bounced a see-saw onto the head of a little girl and made her bleed, and the teacher made him stay inside all during recess. Thursday Charles had to stand in a corner during story-time because he kept pounding his feet on the floor. Friday Charles was deprived of blackboard privileges because he threw chalk.

On Saturday I remarked to my husband, "Do you think kindergarten is too unsettling for Laurie? All this toughness, and bad grammar, and this Charles boy sounds like such a bad influence."

"It'll be all right," my husband said reassuringly. "Bound to be people like Charles in the world. Might as well meet them now as later."

raucous (rô'kəs) *adj.* loud and harsh-sounding

insolently (ĭn'sə-lənt-lē) *adv.* boldly and insultingly

B CHARACTERIZATION
What do you learn about Laurie from how he treats his parents?

On Monday Laurie came home late, full of news. "Charles," he shouted as he came up the hill; I was waiting anxiously on the front steps. "Charles," Laurie yelled all the way up the hill, "Charles was bad again."

"Come right in," I said, as soon as he came close enough. "Lunch is waiting."

"You know what Charles did?" he demanded, following me through the door. "Charles yelled so in school they sent a boy in from first grade to tell the teacher she had to make Charles keep quiet, and so Charles had to stay after school. And so all the children stayed to watch him."

"What did he do?" I asked.

"He just sat there," Laurie said, climbing into his chair at the table. "Hi, Pop, y'old dust mop."

"Charles had to stay after school today," I told my husband. "Everyone stayed with him."

"What does this Charles look like?" my husband asked Laurie. "What's his other name?"

"He's bigger than me," Laurie said. "And he doesn't have any rubbers[1] and he doesn't ever wear a jacket."

Monday night was the first Parent-Teachers meeting, and only the fact that the baby had a cold kept me from going; I wanted passionately to meet Charles's mother. On Tuesday Laurie remarked suddenly, "Our teacher had a friend come to see her in school today." **C**

C MAKE INFERENCES
Why do you think Laurie's mother wanted to meet Charles's mother?

"Charles's mother?" my husband and I asked simultaneously.

"Naaah," Laurie said scornfully. "It was a man who came and made us do exercises, we had to touch our toes. Look." He climbed down from his chair and squatted down and touched his toes. "Like this," he said. He got solemnly back into his chair and said, picking up his fork, "Charles didn't even do exercises."

"That's fine," I said heartily. "Didn't Charles want to do exercises?"

"Naaah," Laurie said. "Charles was so fresh to the teacher's friend he wasn't *let* do exercises."

"Fresh again?" I said.

"He kicked the teacher's friend," Laurie said. "The teacher's friend told Charles to touch his toes like I just did and Charles kicked him."

"What are they going to do about Charles, do you suppose?" Laurie's father asked him.

Laurie shrugged elaborately. "Throw him out of school, I guess," he said.

1. **rubbers:** low-cut overshoes once commonly worn when it rained.

Wednesday and Thursday were routine; Charles yelled during story hour and hit a boy in the stomach and made him cry. On Friday Charles stayed after school again and so did all the other children.

With the third week of kindergarten Charles was an institution in our family;[2] the baby was being a Charles when she cried all afternoon; Laurie did a Charles when he filled his wagon full of mud and pulled it through the kitchen; even my husband, when he caught his elbow in the telephone cord and pulled the telephone and a bowl of flowers off the table, said, after the first minute, "Looks like Charles."

During the third and fourth weeks it looked like a reformation in Charles; Laurie reported grimly at lunch on Thursday of the third week, "Charles was so good today the teacher gave him an apple."

"What?" I said, and my husband added warily, "You mean Charles?"

"Charles," Laurie said. "He gave the crayons around and he picked up the books afterward and the teacher said he was her helper."

"What happened?" I asked **incredulously.**

"He was her helper, that's all," Laurie said, and shrugged.

"Can this be true, about Charles?" I asked my husband that night. "Can something like this happen?"

"Wait and see," my husband said **cynically.** "When you've got a Charles to deal with, this may mean he's only plotting." He seemed to be wrong. For over a week Charles was the teacher's helper; each day he handed things out and he picked things up; no one had to stay after school.

"The PTA meeting's next week again," I told my husband one evening. "I'm going to find Charles's mother there."

"Ask her what happened to Charles," my husband said. "I'd like to know."

"I'd like to know myself," I said.

On Friday of that week things were back to normal. "You know what Charles did today?" Laurie demanded at the lunch table, in a voice slightly awed. "He told a little girl to say a word and she said it and the teacher washed her mouth out with soap and Charles laughed."

"What word?" his father asked unwisely, and Laurie said, "I'll have to whisper it to you, it's so bad." He got down off his chair and went around to his father. His father bent his head down and Laurie whispered joyfully. His father's eyes widened.

"Did Charles tell the little girl to say *that?*" he asked respectfully.

"She said it *twice,*" Laurie said. "Charles told her to say it *twice.*" D

"What happened to Charles?" my husband asked.

"Nothing," Laurie said. "He was passing out the crayons."

incredulously (ĭn-krĕj'ə-ləs-lē) *adv.* in a way that shows doubt or disbelief

cynically (sĭn'ĭ-kəl-lē) *adv.* in a way that shows mistrust in the motives of others

D CHARACTERIZATION
Reread lines 112–121, paying close attention to how Laurie describes Charles's antics. How does Laurie feel about Charles?

2. **an institution in our family:** something that has become a significant part of family life.

Monday morning Charles abandoned the little girl and said the evil word himself three or four times, getting his mouth washed out with soap each time. He also threw chalk.

My husband came to the door with me that evening as I set out for the PTA meeting. "Invite her over for a cup of tea after the meeting," he said. "I want to get a look at her."

"If only she's there," I said prayerfully.

"She'll be there," my husband said. "I don't see how they could hold a PTA meeting without Charles's mother."

At the meeting I sat restlessly, scanning each comfortable matronly face, trying to determine which one hid the secret of Charles. None of them looked to me haggard enough. No one stood up in the meeting and apologized for the way her son had been acting. No one mentioned Charles.

After the meeting I identified and sought out Laurie's kindergarten teacher. She had a plate with a cup of tea and a piece of chocolate cake; I had a plate with a cup of tea and a piece of marshmallow cake. We maneuvered up to one another cautiously, and smiled.

"I've been so anxious to meet you," I said. "I'm Laurie's mother."

"We're all so interested in Laurie," she said.

"Well, he certainly likes kindergarten," I said. "He talks about it all the time."

"We had a little trouble adjusting, the first week or so," she said primly, "but now he's a fine little helper. With occasional lapses, of course."

"Laurie usually adjusts very quickly," I said. "I suppose this time it's Charles's influence."

"Charles?"

"Yes," I said, laughing, "you must have your hands full in that kindergarten, with Charles."

"Charles?" she said. "We don't have any Charles in the kindergarten." E

E MAKE INFERENCES
Who is Charles?

Comprehension

1. **Recall** Who is the narrator of the story?
2. **Recall** Reread lines 25–45. Why does Laurie's mother think kindergarten is "unsettling" for Laurie?
3. **Clarify** According to Laurie, do the other students tend to side with Charles or the teacher?

ALABAMA STANDARDS

LITERATURE STANDARD
8 Compare selections and their characteristics

Literary Analysis

4. **Examine Characterization** What have you learned about Laurie's mother from how she behaves, what she thinks, and what she says?
5. **Make Inferences** Why doesn't Laurie's mother realize that he is Charles?
6. **Analyze the Main Character** Why do you think Laurie **misbehaves?** Support your opinion with details from the story.
7. **Make Judgments** How do you think Laurie's parents should have responded to the "toughness" Laurie displayed around his family and to the tales he told about school?

Comparing Characters

Now that you have read the second short story, finish filling in your chart. Add the final questions and answer them.

	Great-Grandma	Laurie
What does each character look like?		He wears blue jeans and a belt.
How does each character behave?	She makes up stories for the news anchor.	
How do others see each character?		
How would you describe each character's personality?		

In what ways are the characters similar? In what ways are they different?

Vocabulary in Context

VOCABULARY PRACTICE

Show that you understand the boldfaced words. Decide if each statement is true or false.

1. At a **raucous** party, most guests sit quietly and talk.
2. You will most likely get in trouble if you speak **insolently** to the principal.
3. A **venerable** individual is usually between the ages of 9 and 12.
4. Dressing **cynically** is a good way to be safe on a long hike.
5. If you **renounce** your bad habits, you plan to continue them.
6. People respond **incredulously** to things they do not believe.

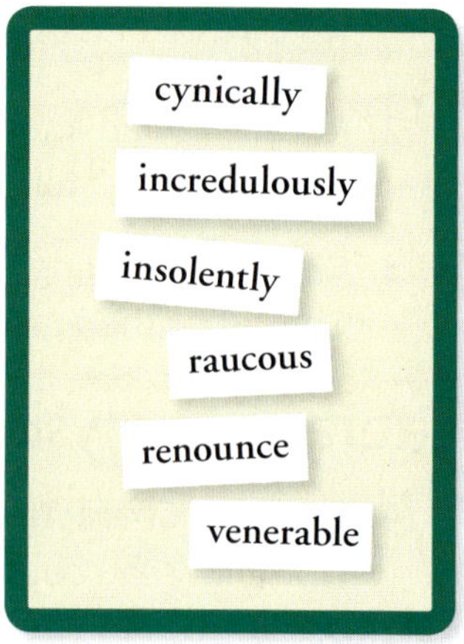

VOCABULARY IN WRITING

Which character in these stories was most surprising to you? Write an explanation, using three or more vocabulary words. Here is a sample beginning.

EXAMPLE SENTENCE

*I expected that Great-Grandma would talk like a **venerable** old lady.*

ALABAMA STANDARDS

READING STANDARD
1.c Using context clues to determine meaning of words

VOCABULARY STRATEGY: THE LATIN ROOT *cred*

The Latin root *cred* means "believe." This root is combined with various prefixes and suffixes to form a number of English words. For example, you already know that the vocabulary word *incredulously* means "in a way that shows doubt or disbelief." To understand the meaning of other words with *cred,* use context clues and your knowledge of what this root means.

VOCABULARY PRACTICE
For more practice, go to the **Vocabulary Center** at **ClassZone.com.**

PRACTICE Choose a word from the web that best completes each sentence.

1. If the witness is not _____ , the jury will not believe her.
2. The opposition tried to _____ the candidate by making false statements about him.
3. Many banks offer customers a _____ , which allows them to buy things without using cash.
4. When you come to the job interview, please bring all your _____ with you.
5. She gossips so much that it is hard to put any _____ in what she says.

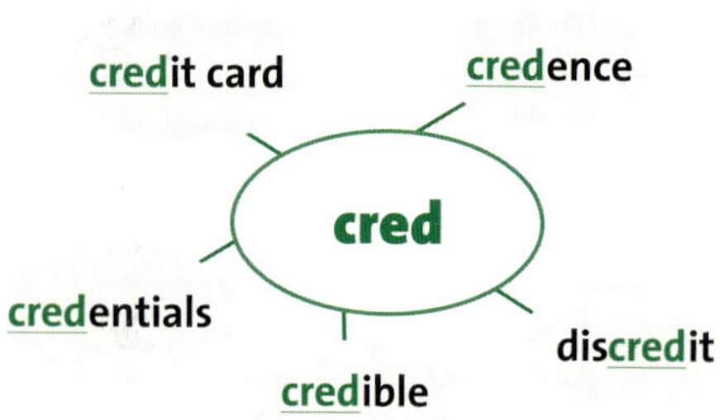

Writing for Assessment

1. READ THE PROMPT

In writing assessments, you will often be asked to compare and contrast two works that are similar in some way, such as two short stories with similar **characters.**

PROMPT

In four or five paragraphs, compare and contrast Great-Grandma from "The Three-Century Woman" and Laurie from "Charles." Identify the characters' similarities and differences, citing details from the two stories to support your ideas. Then state whether you think the characters are more alike than they are different.

STRATEGIES IN ACTION

1. I have to **tell** the **similarities and differences** between the characters.
2. I need to **give examples** that show how the characters are **alike** and how they are **different.**
3. I need to **decide** whether the characters are more alike than they are different.

2. PLAN YOUR WRITING

Using your chart, identify the ways in which the characters are alike and the ways they are different. Then think about how to best present these similarities and differences.

- Write a position statement that presents your main idea.
- Review the stories to find quotations and details that support the similarities and the differences you have identified.
- Create an outline to organize your ideas. This sample outline shows one way to organize your paragraphs.

I. Introduction
II. Differences between characters
III. Similarities between characters
IV. Conclusion

3. DRAFT YOUR RESPONSE

Introduction Introduce the characters you are comparing, the titles of the stories in which the characters appear, and your reason for comparing the characters. Also include your position statement.

Body Present the characters' similarities and differences, using your outline as a guide. Make clear whether you think the similarities or differences are more important.

Conclusion State whether you think the characters are more alike than different. Leave your readers with a final thought about the two characters.

Revision Make sure each point of your comparison is supported by an example .

Encounter with Martin Luther King Jr.

Autobiography by Maya Angelou

What if you could meet your HERO?

ALABAMA STANDARDS

READING STANDARDS

2 Relate literary elements and devices to each other

4.c Applying self-monitoring strategies

KEY IDEA You see them on TV, read about them in magazines and newspapers, and even watch movies that tell the stories of their accomplishments. But for most of us, meeting our famous **heroes** in person is something that only happens in daydreams. In this selection, Maya Angelou recounts an unforgettable private meeting with her larger-than-life hero, Martin Luther King Jr.

QUICKWRITE If a hero of yours walked into your home tomorrow, what would you say to him or her? In your journal, note whom you would like to meet in this way. Then write five questions you would ask if you had the chance.

LITERARY ANALYSIS: CHARACTERIZATION IN NONFICTION

To help her readers understand what Martin Luther King Jr. was like, Maya Angelou uses methods of **characterization** that fiction writers use. She reveals King's personality by

- making direct statements about his personality
- describing his appearance and actions
- showing how others acted toward him
- sharing what he said and what others said about him

As you read the selection, notice the ways in which Angelou conveys what King was like in person.

READING STRATEGY: CONNECT

Whenever you find similarities between your life and someone else's, you are connecting with that person. You can **connect** with what you are reading by comparing the events described with experiences you are familiar with. As you read, keep a log to record connections between you and Angelou.

Angelou	*Me*
Angelou was so surprised to see King that she didn't shake his hand right away	*When I saw my teacher at the grocery store, I was so surprised that I didn't say hello right away.*

VOCABULARY IN CONTEXT

The boldfaced words help Angelou convey the African-American experience in the 1960s. To see how many of them you know, restate each sentence, using a different word or words for the boldfaced term.

1. He did not allow his bitterness to **fester** and ruin his life.
2. For King, nonviolence was the key to winning the **fray.**
3. She is **punctual** and in her seat before the bell rings.
4. His kindness helped to **redeem** her from sadness.
5. For some, a **shanty** was the only affordable housing.

Author Online

An Early Activist At age 16, Maya Angelou wanted to become a streetcar conductor in San Francisco. However, the railway would not hire female or African-American drivers. Supported by organizations that backed her cause, Angelou went to the railway office every day. After three weeks, she became San Francisco's first female African-American streetcar driver.

Maya Angelou
born 1928

Renaissance Woman Angelou eventually moved on to many other pursuits. She has been a dancer, an actor, a mother, a poet, and a songwriter as well as the author of six autobiographies, each covering a different time in her life.

MORE ABOUT THE AUTHOR
For more on Maya Angelou, visit the **Literature Center** at **ClassZone.com.**

Background

Civil Rights Supporter Under the leadership of Rev. Martin Luther King Jr., the Southern Christian Leadership Conference (SCLC) promoted nonviolent protest as a way to gain civil rights for African Americans. In 1960, Angelou wrote and co-produced a musical to raise funds for the organization. She later became the Northern coordinator for the group. King was just becoming famous when Maya Angelou met him at the SCLC office.

Encounter with Martin Luther King Jr.

Maya Angelou

I returned from lunch. In the outer office Millie Jordan was working over a table of papers. Hazel was busy on the telephone. I walked into my office and a man sitting at my desk, with his back turned, spun around, stood up and smiled. Martin Luther King said, "Good afternoon, Miss Angelou. You are right on time."

The surprise was so total that it took me a moment to react to his outstretched hand.

I had worked two months for the SCLC, sent out tens of thousands of letters and invitations signed by Rev. King, made hundreds of statements in his name, but I had never seen him up close. He was shorter than I expected and so young. He had an easy friendliness, which was unsettling. Looking at him in my office, alone, was like seeing a lion sitting down at my dining-room table eating a plate of mustard greens. **A**

"We're so grateful for the job you all are doing up here. It's a confirmation for us down on the firing line."[1]

ANALYZE VISUALS
What might you **infer** about the expression on King's face?

A CHARACTERIZATION
Reread lines 10–13. What do you learn about King from Angelou's description of him?

1. **a confirmation . . . line:** proof to us in the middle of the struggle that we are doing the right thing.

WE MARCH FOR
INTEGRATED SCHOOLS NOW!
WE DEMAND
DECENT HOUSING NOW!
I.U.E
ASBURY

I was finally able to say how glad I was to meet him.

"Come on, take your seat back and tell me about yourself."

I settled gratefully into the chair and he sat on the arm of the old sofa across the room.

"Stanley says you're a Southern girl. Where are you from?" His voice had lost the church way of talking and he had become just a young man asking a question of a young woman. I looked at him and thought about the good-looking . . . school athlete, who was invariably the boyfriend of the . . . cheerleader.

I said, "Stamps, Arkansas. Twenty-five miles from Texarkana."

He knew Texarkana and Pine Bluff, and, of course, Little Rock. He asked me the size and population of Stamps and if my people were farmers. I said no and started to explain about Mamma and my crippled uncle who raised me. As I talked he nodded as if he knew them personally. When I described the dirt roads and **shanties** and the little schoolhouse on top of the hill, he smiled in recognition. When I mentioned my brother Bailey, he asked what he was doing now.

The question stopped me. He was friendly and understanding, but if I told him my brother was in prison, I couldn't be sure how long his

shanty (shăn′tē) *n.* a rundown house; a shack

understanding would last. I could lose my job. Even more important, I might lose his respect. Birds of a feather and all that, but I took a chance and told him Bailey was in Sing Sing.[2]

He dropped his head and looked at his hands.

"It wasn't a crime against a human being." I had to explain. I loved my brother and although he was in jail, I wanted Martin Luther King to think he was an uncommon criminal. "He was a fence. Selling stolen goods. That's all." **B**

He looked up. "How old is he?"

"Thirty-three and very bright. Bailey is not a bad person. Really."

"I understand. Disappointment drives our young men to some desperate lengths." Sympathy and sadness kept his voice low. "That's why we must fight and win. We must save the Baileys of the world. And Maya, never stop loving him. Never give up on him. Never deny him. And remember, he is freer than those who hold him behind bars." **C**

Redemptive[3] suffering had always been the part of Martin's argument which I found difficult to accept. I had seen distress **fester** souls and bend

B CONNECT
Have you ever felt the need to explain or defend the actions of someone you love? Why do you think Angelou might have done this?

C CHARACTERIZATION
Reread lines 45–49. What does King's statement suggest about him?

fester (fĕs'tər) *v.* to become an increasing source of irritation or poisoning

2. **Sing Sing:** a prison in New York State.
3. **redemptive:** earning freedom or salvation.

peoples' bodies out of shape, but I had yet to see anyone **redeemed** from pain, by pain.

There was a knock at the door and Stanley Levison entered.

"Good afternoon, Maya. Hello, Martin. We're about ready."

Martin stood and the personal tenderness disappeared. He became the fighting preacher, armed and ready for the public **fray.**

He came over to my desk. "Please accept my thanks. And remember, we are not alone. There are a lot of good people in this nation. White people who love right and are willing to stand up and be counted." His voice had changed back to the mellifluous Baptist cadence[4] raised for the common good. **D**

We shook hands and I wondered if his statement on the existence of good whites had been made for Stanley's benefit.

At the door, he turned. "But we cannot relax, because for every fair-minded white American, there is a Bull Connor[5] waiting with his shotgun and attack dogs."

I was sitting, mulling over the experience, when Hazel and Millie walked in smiling.

"Caught you that time, didn't we?"

I asked her if she had set up the surprise. She had not. She said when Martin came in he asked to meet me. He was told that I was due back from lunch and that I was fanatically **punctual.** He offered to play a joke by waiting alone in my office.

Millie chuckled. "He's got a sense of humor. You never hear about that, do you?"

Hazel said, "It makes him more human somehow. I like a serious man to be able to laugh. Rounds out the personality." **E**

Martin King had been a hero and a leader to me since the time when Godfrey and I heard him speak and had been carried to glory on his wings of hope. However, the personal sadness he showed when I spoke of my brother put my heart in his keeping forever, and made me thrust away the small constant worry which my mother had given me as a part of an early parting gift: Black folks can't change because white folks won't change. **F**

redeem (rĭ-dēm') *v.* to set free

fray (frā) *n.* a fight; a heated dispute

D CHARACTERIZATION
Reread lines 56–62. Describe the shift in King's attitude. What can you **infer** about why he is different in private than he is in public?

punctual (pŭngk'cho͞o-əl) *adj.* on time; prompt

E CHARACTERIZATION
What do you learn about King through Millie's and Hazel's words?

F CONNECT
Think about how Angelou feels toward King. Who has touched your heart or mind in a similar way?

4. **mellifluous** (mə-lĭf'lo͞o-əs) **Baptist cadence** (kād'ns): the smooth rhythms of speech characteristic of Baptist preachers.

5. **Bull Connor:** an official in Birmingham, Alabama, best known for ordering police officers to use fire hoses and police dogs to break up a civil rights demonstration in 1963.

Comprehension

ALABAMA STANDARDS

READING STANDARD
4.c Applying self-monitoring strategies

1. **Recall** What joke does King play on Maya Angelou?
2. **Recall** Why is Angelou afraid to tell King about her brother?
3. **Clarify** Why did King want to meet Angelou?

Literary Analysis

4. **Examine Connections** Review the notes you made in your log. What events were you able to connect with? Note which connection surprised you the most.
5. **Interpret Meaning** Reread lines 12–13. When Angelou enters her office and sees King, she describes her **hero** as a "lion sitting down at my dining-room table eating a plate of mustard greens." What does she mean by this?
6. **Analyze Characterization** What three words or phrases would you use to describe King's personality? Write them in a chart like the one shown. Below each word or phrase, cite several details from the selection to support it.

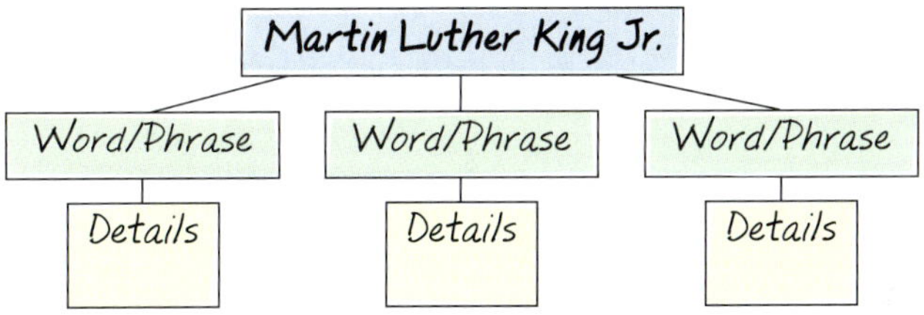

7. **Make Inferences** Reread the last paragraph. Why do you think King's comments about Angelou's brother helped Angelou stop worrying so much, or, in her words, "thrust away the small constant worry" she had felt since her mother left her?
8. **Draw Conclusions** Which side of King, the "fighting preacher" or the tender young man, do you think meant the most to Angelou? Give examples from the text to support your answer.

Extension and Challenge

9. **Speaking and Listening** If King were to give a speech to persuade people not to give up on family members who made mistakes like Angelou's brother, Bailey, what would he say? Prepare a short speech and present it to the class.
10. **SOCIAL STUDIES CONNECTION** Read the memorandum from Martin Luther King Jr. on page 267. Why were King and the SCLC concerned about the African-American vote in the South? What was the result of their efforts? Research the Voting Rights Act of 1965 to find the answers. Also note how the law changed voting practices.

RESEARCH LINKS
For more on the Voting Rights Act of 1965, visit the **Research Center** at **ClassZone.com.**

Vocabulary in Context

VOCABULARY PRACTICE

Choose the letter of the term that is most closely related to the boldfaced word.

1. **shanty:** (a) mansion, (b) abode, (c) hut
2. **fester:** (a) improve, (b) disturb, (c) go away
3. **redeem:** (a) rescue, (b) enslave, (c) preserve
4. **fray:** (a) conflict, (b) converse, (c) sew
5. **punctual:** (a) lazy, (b) on time, (c) late

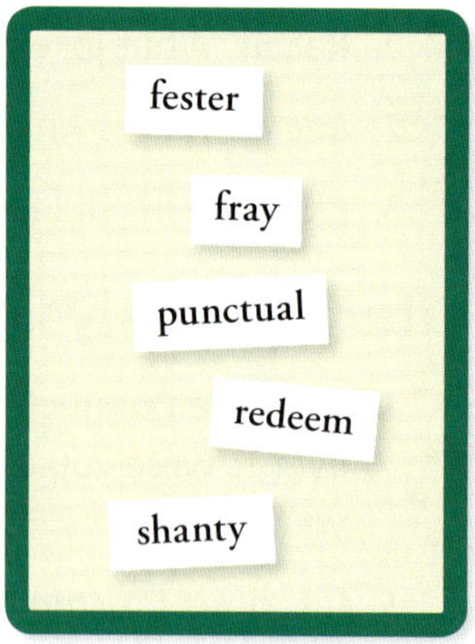

VOCABULARY IN WRITING

Using two or more vocabulary words, write a paragraph describing how Maya Angelou's encounter with Dr. King affected her. You might start like this.

EXAMPLE SENTENCE

*Maya Angelou was always **punctual**.*

VOCABULARY STRATEGY: USING REFERENCE AIDS

To express ideas clearly and accurately, you need to choose just the right words. Reference aids, or resources of information, can improve your writing by providing synonyms for words you already know. **Synonyms** are words with similar meanings. For example, a synonym for *shanty* is *shack*. To find a synonym for a word, look in a reference aid.

- A **thesaurus** is a reference book of synonyms. Also, many word processing programs contain an electronic thesaurus tool.

  shanty *noun* hovel, hut, lean-to, shack

- A **dictionary** lists synonyms after the definitions of some words.

  shanty (shăn'tē) *n., pl.* **-ties** a rundown house: *The shanty collapsed after years of neglect.* **syn** HOVEL, HUT, LEAN-TO, SHACK

PRACTICE Use a reference aid to find a synonym for each word. Note the synonym and the reference aid you used to find it. Then use each synonym in a sentence that matches its shade of meaning.

1. abolish
2. extricate
3. monopolize
4. voracious

VOCABULARY PRACTICE
For more practice, go to the **Vocabulary Center** at **ClassZone.com.**

MEMORANDUM Following is a memo that Dr. King sent to the people organizing the opening-day rallies for the Crusade for Citizenship, a drive to register African Americans to vote. Notice the phrases that reflect Dr. King's fairness and leadership.

FROM: M. L. King Jr., President
TO: Speakers, Local Contacts, Participants in S. C. L. C.
RE: Crusade for Citizenship Mass Meeting, February 12, 1958

UNITY OF EMPHASIS

At our executive committee meeting on Thursday, Jan. 30, 1958, many expressed the hope that all persons would leave the Mass Meetings with a clear picture of the aims and purposes of the Southern Christian Leadership Conference, with a firm determination to register and vote, and with a sense of being part of a southwide "crusade."

To help achieve this unity of aim and direction, we are urging you to make certain that the following points are clearly and simply made from the platform by some responsible person during the mass meeting:

1. The Crusade for Citizenship is a southwide movement. These meetings express this. The list should be read. It should be clear that this is the opening step in a long and hard, but necessary and glorious struggle.
2. The Crusade has two aims:
   (a) to double the number of Negroes who vote in the South
   (b) and thus, to help liberate all Southerners, Negro and white, to extend democracy in our great nation. When Negroes can vote, white people will have greater economic and political freedom. The South can have a real two party system—a necessity for real democracy.
3. The Crusade will place emphasis on preparing spiritually and tactically for registration prior to the 1958 and 1960 elections.
4. The Crusade is non-partisan. Its major purpose is to get men and women to realize that voting is a "moral" and "political" duty to God, to the nation, to themselves, and to their children; then to help them learn how to register and to want to vote. The Crusade will not engage in partisan politics. We urge people to vote: we do not want to influence them to vote for any particular party. We believe in the people. When they are aroused to vote, they will vote intelligently. No one need tell them where their political interest lies. This is morally the right approach.
5. The right to vote is related to all other rights. When Negroes have won and fully exercise their right to vote many changes can then occur:
   (a) segregated buses will disappear
   (b) wages will be increased
   (c) police brutality will be a thing of the past
   (d) men who believe in justice will be sent to congress
   (e) "mob violence" will fade away
   (f) justice will be established in the courts.

These things will come about because the mayors, city councilmen, police commissioners, the governors, congressmen and even the President will know that they must do the right things or be turned out of office when the people go to the ballot box. . . .

Dirk the Protector

Memoir by Gary Paulsen

What do you need to SURVIVE?

ALABAMA STANDARDS

READING STANDARDS
2 Relate literary elements to each
4.c Applying self-monitoring strategies, including point of view

KEY IDEA Hunger, fear, injury, turmoil—it's amazing what people can withstand when they must. But there's a limit. Every human being needs certain things to **survive.** In "Dirk the Protector," a chance encounter provides a young Gary Paulsen with what he needs to survive life alone on the streets.

LIST IT What if you woke up tomorrow and all the adults had vanished? Brainstorm a list of items you would need to survive. Remember, no one would know how to operate electrical plants, manufacture products in factories, or purify drinking water. You may use the list that is shown to get started. When you're finished, compare your list with those of your classmates.

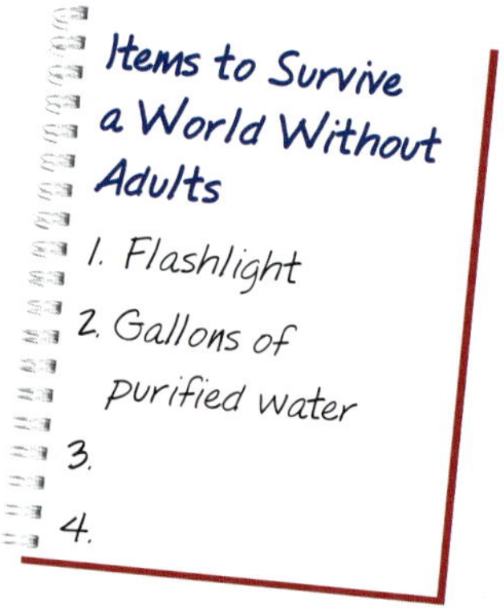

LITERARY ANALYSIS: POINT OF VIEW IN A MEMOIR

In a **memoir,** the writer gives a true account of experiences in his or her life. Because the writer has participated in the events, he or she writes from the **first-person point of view,** using the pronoun *I.* However, that doesn't mean the writer states everything directly. As you read "Dirk the Protector," note when Gary Paulsen says something openly about himself and when he only hints at his true meaning.

READING SKILL: IDENTIFY CAUSE AND EFFECT

To fully understand what you read, you need to know why things happen. Often, a writer tells you that one event (the **cause**) made another event (the **effect**) happen. In this example, Paulsen directly states that troubles with his parents caused him to leave home:

For a time in my life I became a street kid. It would be nice to put it another way but what with the drinking at home and the difficulties it caused with my parents I couldn't live in the house.

Other times you have to infer cause-and-effect relationships on the basis of clues in the text and your knowledge.

As you read "Dirk the Protector," note other cause-and-effect relationships and record them in a diagram like the one shown.

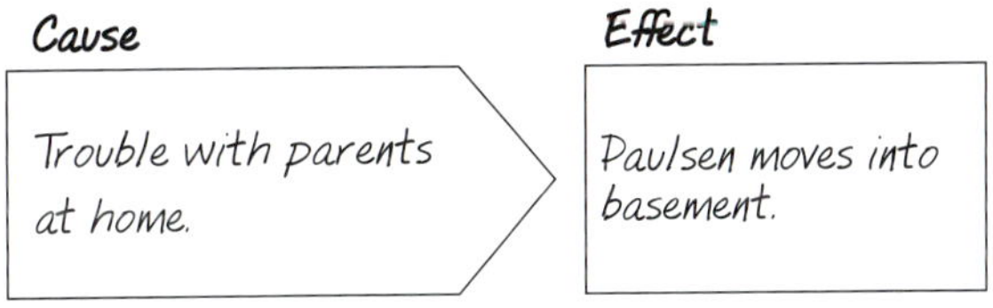

VOCABULARY IN CONTEXT

Make a chart like the one shown. Put each vocabulary word in the appropriate column, and then write a brief definition of each word you are familiar with.

WORD LIST

cohort
conventional
decoy
forerunner
hustle
impasse
predatory
puny

Know Well	Think I Know	Don't Know at All

Author On|ine

A Young Survivor Gary Paulsen was born to a family that faced many problems. As a boy, Paulsen often had to work and take care of himself. While delivering newspapers one cold evening, he went into a library to warm up. The librarian offered him a book and a library card. Paulsen recalls, "The most astonishing thing happened. This silly little card with my name on it gave me an identity." In the library, it did not matter what he wore, who liked him, or how much money he had.

Gary Paulsen
born 1939

Reader and Writer Paulsen still reads a lot, and he is a very hardworking writer. He has published more than 150 books for children, young adults, and adults. His childhood experiences and outdoor adventures are frequent subjects in his writing.

Devoted to Dogs "Dirk the Protector" is from Paulsen's memoir *My Life in Dog Years.* He gives the reader a peek into his own life by sharing memories of his dogs. Paulsen has said, "I've always thought of dogs as people. . . . They have personalities and likes and dislikes and humor and anger and great heart and spirit."

MORE ABOUT THE AUTHOR
For more on Gary Paulsen, visit the **Literature Center** at **ClassZone.com.**

Dirk the PROTECTOR

GARY PAULSEN

For a time in my life I became a street kid. It would be nice to put it another way but what with the drinking at home and the difficulties it caused with my parents I couldn't live in the house.

I made a place for myself in the basement by the furnace and hunted and fished in the woods around the small town. But I had other needs as well—clothes, food, school supplies—and they required money.

I was not afraid of work and spent most of my summers working on farms for two, three and finally five dollars a day. This gave me enough for school clothes, though never for enough clothes or the right kind; I was never cool or in. But during the school year I couldn't leave town to work the farms. I looked for odd jobs but most of them were taken by the boys who stayed in town through the summer. All the **conventional** jobs like working in the markets or at the drugstore were gone and all I could find was setting pins in the small bowling alley over the Four Clover Bar. **A**

It had just six alleys and they were busy all the time—there were leagues each night from seven to eleven—but the pay for truly brutal

ANALYZE VISUALS
Examine this painting. What can you **infer** about the boy's life?

conventional
(kən-vĕn′shə-nəl) *adj.* usual; traditional

A CAUSE AND EFFECT
What causes Paulsen to take the job at the bowling alley? Keep reading to find an effect of working this job.

Boy with Orange, Murray Kimber.
© Murray Kimber/Illustrationworks.com.

HOTEL

work was only seven cents a line. There weren't many boys willing to do the work but with so few alleys, it was still very hard to earn much money. A dollar a night was not uncommon and three was outstanding. To make up the difference I started selling newspapers in the bars at night. This kept me up and out late, and I often came home at midnight. But it added to my income so that I could stay above water.[1]

Unfortunately it also put me in the streets at a time when there was what might be called a rough element. There weren't gangs then, not exactly, but there were groups of boys who more or less hung out together and got into trouble. They were the **forerunners** of the gangs we have now, but with some singular differences. They did not have firearms—but many carried switchblade knives.

These groups were **predatory,** and they hunted the streets at night. I became their favorite target in this dark world. Had the town been larger I might have hidden from them, or found different routes. But there was only a small uptown section and it was impossible for me to avoid them. They would catch me walking a dark street and surround me and with threats and blows steal what money I had earned that night.

forerunner (fôr′rŭn′ər) *n.* person or thing that came before

predatory (prĕd′ə-tôr′ē) *adj.* given to stealing from or hurting others for one's own gain

I tried fighting back but there were usually several of them. I couldn't win. Because I was from "the wrong side of the tracks"[2] I didn't think I could go to the authorities. It all seemed hopeless. **B**

And then I met Dirk.

B POINT OF VIEW
Reread lines 35–37. What does Paulsen tell the reader about his attitude toward himself and his situation?

The bowling alley was on a second floor and had a window in back of the pit area. When all the lanes were going, the heat from the pin lights made the temperature close to a hundred degrees. Outside the window a ladder led to the roof. One fall evening, instead of leaving work through the front door, I made my way out the window and up the ladder onto the roof. I hoped to find a new way home to escape the boys who waited for me. That night one of the league bowlers had bowled a perfect game—300—and in celebration had bought the pit boys hamburgers and Cokes. I had put the burger and Coke in a bag to take back to my basement. The bag had grease stains and smelled of toasted buns, and my mouth watered as I moved from the roof of the bowling alley to the flat roof over the hardware store, then down a fire escape that led to a dark alcove[3] off an alley.

There was a black space beneath the stairs and as I reached the bottom and my foot hit the ground I heard a low growl. It was not loud, more a rumble that seemed to come from the earth and so full of menace that it stopped me cold, my foot frozen in midair.

---

1. **stay above water:** survive.
2. **"the wrong side of the tracks":** the less desirable part of town.
3. **alcove** (ăl′kōv′): a small hollow space in a wall.

I raised my foot and the growl stopped.

I lowered my foot and the growl came again. My foot went up and it stopped.

I stood there, trying to peer through the steps of the fire escape. For a time I couldn't see more than a dark shape crouched back in the gloom. There was a head and a back, and as my eyes became accustomed to the dark I could see that it had scraggly, scruffy hair and two eyes that glowed yellow. **C**

We were at an **impasse.** I didn't want to climb up the ladder again but if I stepped to the ground it seemed likely I would be bitten. I hung there for a full minute before I thought of the hamburger. I could use it as a **decoy** and get away.

The problem was the hamburger smelled so good and I was so hungry.

I decided to give the beast under the stairs half a burger. I opened the sack, unwrapped the tinfoil and threw half the sandwich under the steps, then jumped down and ran for the end of the alley. I was just getting my stride, legs and arms pumping, pulling air with a heaving chest, when I rounded the corner and ran smack into the latest group of boys who were terrorizing me.

There were four of them, led by a thug—he and two of the others would ultimately land in prison—named, absurdly, "Happy" Santun.

Happy was built like an upright freezer and had just about half the intelligence but this time it was easy. I'd run right into him.

"Well—lookit here. He came to us this time. . . ."

Over the months I had developed a policy of flee or die—run as fast as I could to avoid the pain, and to hang on to my hard-earned money. Sometimes it worked, but most often they caught me.

This time, they already had me. I could have handed over the money, taken a few hits and been done with it, but something in me snapped and I hit Happy in the face with every ounce of strength in my **puny** body.

He brushed off the blow easily and I went down in a welter of blows and kicks from all four of them. I curled into a ball to protect what I could. I'd done this before, many times, and knew that they would stop sometime—although I suspected that because I'd hit Happy it might take longer than usual for them to get bored hitting me. **D**

Instead there was some commotion that I didn't understand and the kicks stopped coming. There was a snarling growl that seemed to come from the bowels of the earth, followed by the sound of ripping cloth, screams, and then the fading slap of footsteps running away.

For another minute I remained curled up, then opened my eyes to find that I was alone.

But when I rolled over I saw the dog.

C CAUSE AND EFFECT
Reread lines 52–62. Make an **inference** about what kind of beast is under the stairs. What's causing the beast to growl?

impasse (ĭm′păs′) *n.* a situation in which no progress can be made; a deadlock

decoy (dē′koi′) *n.* a person or thing used to distract others or lead them in a different direction

puny (pyo͞o′nē) *adj.* weak and small

D POINT OF VIEW
Reread lines 79–89. As Paulsen describes the attack, what else does the reader learn about him?

It was the one that had been beneath the stairs. Brindled, patches of hair gone, one ear folded over and the other standing straight and notched from fighting. He didn't seem to be any particular breed. Just big and rangy, right on the edge of ugly, though I would come to think of him as beautiful. He was Airedale crossed with hound crossed with alligator.

Alley dog. Big, tough, mean alley dog. As I watched he spit cloth—it looked like blue jeans—out of his mouth.

"You bit Happy, and sent them running?" I asked.

He growled, and I wasn't sure if it was with menace, but he didn't bare his teeth and didn't seem to want to attack me. Indeed, he had saved me.

"Why?" I asked. "What did I do to deserve . . . oh, the hamburger."

I swear, he pointedly looked at the bag with the second half of hamburger in it.

"You want more?" **E**

He kept staring at the bag and I thought, Well, he sure as heck deserves it. I opened the sack and gave him the rest of it, which disappeared down his throat as if a hole had opened into the universe.

He looked at the bag.

"That's it," I said, brushing my hands together. "The whole thing."

A low growl.

"You can rip my head off—there still isn't any more hamburger." I removed the Coke and handed him the bag, which he took, held on the ground with one foot and deftly ripped open with his teeth.

"See? Nothing." I was up by this time and I started to walk away. "Thanks for the help . . ."

He followed me. Not close, perhaps eight feet back, but matching my speed. It was now nearly midnight and I was tired and sore from setting pins and from the kicks that had landed on my back and sides.

"I don't have anything to eat at home but crackers and peanut butter and jelly," I told him. I kept some food in the basement of the apartment building, where I slept near the furnace.

He kept following and, truth be known, I didn't mind. I was still half scared of him but the memory of him spitting out bits of Happy's pants and the sound of the boys running off made me smile. When I arrived at the apartment house I held the main door open and he walked right in. I opened the basement door and he followed me down the steps into the furnace room.

I turned the light on and could see that my earlier judgment had been correct. He was scarred from fighting, skinny and flat sided and with patches of hair gone. His nails were worn down from scratching concrete.

"Dirk," I said. "I'll call you Dirk." I had been trying to read a detective novel and there was a tough guy in it named Dirk. "You look like somebody named Dirk."

VISUAL VOCABULARY

brindled (brĭn′dld): *adj.* light brownish yellow or grayish with streaks or spots of a darker color

E CAUSE AND EFFECT
Reread lines 105–110. What is the cause-and-effect relationship Paulsen explains here?

And so we sat that first night. I had two boxes of Ritz crackers I'd **hustled** somewhere, a jar of peanut butter and another one of grape jelly, and a knife from the kitchen upstairs. I would smear a cracker, hand it to him—he took each one with great care and gentleness—and then eat one myself. We did this, back and forth, until both boxes were empty and my stomach was bulging; then I fell asleep on the old outdoor lounge I used for furniture.

Street Corner (1991), Daniel Bennett Schwartz. Oil on canvas, 91.4 cm × 71.1 cm. Private collection. © Bridgeman Art Library.

The next day was a school day. I woke up and found Dirk under the basement stairs, watching me. When I opened the door he trotted up the steps and outside—growling at me as he went past—and I started off to school.

He followed me at a distance, then stopped across the street when I went into the front of the school building. I thought I'd probably never see him again.

But he was waiting when I came out that afternoon, sitting across the street by a mailbox. I walked up to him.

"Hi, Dirk." I thought of petting him but when I reached a hand out he growled. "All right—no touching."

I turned and made my way toward the bowling alley. It was Friday and sometimes on Friday afternoon there were people who wanted to bowl early and I could pick up a dollar or two setting pins.

Dirk followed about four feet back—closer than before—and as I made my way along Second Street and came around the corner by Ecker's Drugstore I ran into Happy. He had only two of his **cohorts** with him and I don't think they had intended to do me harm, but I surprised them and Happy took a swing at me.

Dirk took him right in the middle. I mean bit him in the center of his stomach, hard, before Happy's fist could get to me. Happy screamed and doubled over and Dirk went around and ripped into his rear and kept tearing at it even as Happy and his two companions fled down the street.

It was absolutely great. Maybe one of the great moments in my life. F
I had a bodyguard.

hustle (hŭs′əl) *v.* to gain by energetic effort

cohort (kō′hôrt′) *n.* a companion or associate

F **POINT OF VIEW**
On the basis of what you know about Paulsen, why does he say it was "one of the great moments in my life"?

It was as close to having a live nuclear weapon as you can get.

I cannot say we became friends. I touched him only once, when he wasn't looking—I petted him on the head and received a growl and a lifted lip for it. But we became constant companions. Dirk moved into the basement with me, and I gave him a hamburger every day and hustled up dog food for him and many nights we sat down there eating Ritz crackers and he watched me working on stick model airplanes.

He followed me to school, waited for me, followed me to the bowling alley, waited for me. He was with me everywhere I went, always back three or four feet, always with a soft growl, and to my great satisfaction every time he saw Happy—every time—Dirk would try to remove some part of his body with as much violence as possible.

He caused Happy and his mob to change their habits. They not only stopped hunting me but went out of their way to avoid me, or more specifically, Dirk. In fact after that winter and spring they never bothered me again, even after Dirk was gone. **G**

G CAUSE AND EFFECT
What is the long-term effect Dirk has on the young Paulsen's life?

Dirk came to a wonderful end. I always thought of him as a street dog—surely nobody owned him—and in the summer when I was hired to work on a farm four miles east of town I took him with me. We walked all the way out to the farm, Dirk four feet in back of me, and he would trot along beside the tractor when I plowed, now and then chasing the hundreds of seagulls that came for the worms the plow turned up.

The farmer, whose name was Olaf, was a bachelor and did not have a dog. I looked over once to see Dirk sitting next to Olaf while we ate some sandwiches and when Olaf reached out to pet him Dirk actually—this was the first time I'd seen it—wagged his tail.

He'd found a home.

I worked the whole summer there and when it came time to leave, Dirk remained sitting in the yard as I walked down the driveway. The next summer I had bought an old Dodge for twenty-five dollars and I drove out to Olaf's to say hello and saw Dirk out in a field with perhaps two hundred sheep. He wasn't herding them, or chasing them, but was just standing there, watching the flock.

"You have him with the sheep?" I asked Olaf.

He nodded. "Last year I lost forty-three to coyotes," he said. "This year not a one. He likes to guard things, doesn't he?"

I thought of Dirk chasing Happy down the street, and later spitting out bits of his pants, and I smiled. "Yeah, he sure does."

Comprehension

1. **Recall** What keeps Paulsen out late at night?
2. **Recall** What does Paulsen do to take care of Dirk?
3. **Clarify** What are two challenges that Paulsen faces?

Literary Analysis

4. **Analyze Point of View** On the left side of a two-column chart, list information you know about Paulsen because he states it directly. On the right, list the questions you have about Paulsen after reading the memoir.

What I Know About Paulsen	Questions I Have About Paulsen
He lived by himself in a basement.	Did his parents know he was there?

5. **Analyze Cause and Effect** Compare the cause-and-effect relationships you recorded with those recorded by another classmate. With that classmate, choose the one cause-and-effect relationship that you think influenced Paulsen's life the most, and explain why you think so.
6. **Analyze Character** Writers often give animals character traits that appear human. On the basis of the details Paulsen provides about Dirk, describe the dog's "personality."
7. **Compare and Contrast** Reread the first two paragraphs of "Dirk the Protector" and then the last three. How is Paulsen's life the same in the end, and how has it changed?
8. **Draw Conclusions** Dirk's protection ended the attacks against Paulsen. Why don't the attacks start up again after Dirk stays at the farm?

Extension and Challenge

9. **Big Question Activity** Now that you've read "Dirk the Protector," think about the advice Paulsen might give you to enable you to survive in the world without the help of adults. If necessary, revise the list you made in the activity on page 268. Then create a **survival** manual based on your new list.
10. **Readers' Circle** One way to think about the complexity of a cause-and-effect relationship is to ask, What if . . . ? For example, what if the man had not bowled a perfect game? In a group discussion, talk about how the story might have turned out differently. Then, create another what-if question for another group to answer.

ALABAMA STANDARDS

READING STANDARD
2 Relate literary elements to each other, including point of view

Vocabulary in Context

VOCABULARY PRACTICE

Choose the vocabulary word that best completes each sentence.

1. The boy tried to get a(n) _____ job but could only find an unusual one.
2. He was frequently beaten up by members of a(n) _____ gang.
3. Unlike the big, strong gang members, he was _____.
4. He had to _____ all day for one solid meal.
5. There he met Dirk, and they stared each other down into a(n) _____.
6. The boy used his hamburger as a(n) _____ to distract the dog.
7. Dirk became the boy's protector and _____.
8. Is Dirk the ____ of other protectors in the boy's future?

cohort
conventional
decoy
forerunner
hustle
impasse
predatory
puny

VOCABULARY IN WRITING

Were you surprised that Dirk stayed with Olaf? Using two or more vocabulary words, write a paragraph to explain how you thought the memoir might have ended. Here is an example of how you might begin.

EXAMPLE SENTENCE

*I thought that Dirk would always want to remain the boy's **cohort**.*

VOCABULARY STRATEGY: IDIOMS

An **idiom** is an expression in which the overall meaning of the words in it is different from the meanings of the individual words. For example, in this story, Paulsen says that working at a certain job helped him "stay above water." *Stay above water* is an idiomatic expression because Paulsen was never in fear of drowning. We know Paulsen means that the job helped him survive.

Language is full of idioms. If you encounter an unfamiliar one, you can often use context clues to figure out its meaning. Otherwise, consult a dictionary.

PRACTICE Identify the idiom in each sentence and give a definition for it.

1. They kicked around a few ideas about how to make scenery for the play.
2. She changed her tune once she found out the cost of the project.
3. I don't trust Jackson, but his friend seems on the level.
4. Will you take me under your wing if I decide to join the chorus?
5. Getting all this work done will be tough, but hang in there and we'll finish it.

ALABAMA STANDARDS

READING STANDARD
1.c Using context clues to determine meaning of words

VOCABULARY PRACTICE
For more practice, go to the **Vocabulary Center** at **ClassZone.com.**

SKILLS PRACTICE

Reading-Writing Connection

Deepen your understanding of "Dirk the Protector" by responding to these prompts. Then complete the **Grammar and Writing** exercise.

WRITING PROMPTS	SELF-CHECK
A. Short Response: Analyze Cause and Effect Paulsen **survived** many things in addition to attacks from Happy and his friends. Use details from the text to describe in **one paragraph** how Paulsen's choices made his survival possible.	***A strong analysis will . . .*** • include more than one choice • explain how each choice made a difference
B. Extended Response: Explore Point of View In the memoir, we learn only as much about Dirk as Paulsen knows. If Dirk could talk, what kind of story might he tell? In **two or three paragraphs,** retell a part of the story from Dirk's point of view.	***An interesting response will . . .*** • use the pronouns *I, me, we,* and *us* • reveal something about the boy and the dog

GRAMMAR AND WRITING

AVOID MISPLACED MODIFIERS A **prepositional phrase** is a group of words that begins with a preposition, such as *from, in, on, under,* or *with,* and ends with a noun or pronoun. A prepositional phrase is used to modify, or give information about, another word in the sentence. When you use this kind of phrase in your writing, place it close to the word it modifies. Otherwise, you may end up with something confusing or unintentionally funny.

Original: He ran into the boys who had been terrorizing him with a hamburger in each hand. (*Were the boys terrorizing him with hamburgers?*)

Revised: With a hamburger in each hand, he ran into the boys who had been terrorizing him. (*It is the boy, himself, who has the hamburgers.*)

PRACTICE Move each misplaced prepositional phrase to the correct place.

1. While some waited, others punched him in his stomach on the sidewalk.
2. I bit one of the boys on the leg with blond hair.
3. I spit out pieces onto the sidewalk of his jeans.
4. I pulled a piece of hamburger from the bag with ketchup on it.

For more help with prepositional phrases, see page R60 in the ***Grammar Handbook.***

ALABAMA STANDARDS

WRITING/LANGUAGE STANDARD
11 Apply grammar conventions in writing

It Was a Long Time Before

Poem by Leslie Marmon Silko

Abuelito Who

Poem by Sandra Cisneros

What do we learn from our ELDERS?

ALABAMA STANDARDS

READING STANDARDS

1 Apply strategies appropriate to the reading material

2 Relate literary elements and devices to each other

KEY IDEA Between you, your parents, and your grandparents, the **generations** of your family may span a hundred years or more. As you move into the future, what will you take with you from the past? What will you take with you from the present? In the poems "It Was a Long Time Before" and "Abuelito Who," memories and more connect the generations.

LIST IT Think of someone in another generation who spends time with you. Brainstorm a list of the activities you do together. Reread the list, then write one way that person has affected your life or one thing that person has taught you.

UNIT 3

Lessons to Learn

UNDERSTANDING THEME

- In Fiction
- In Poetry
- In Drama
- In Media

UNIT 3 **Share What You Know**

What's the BIG IDEA?

"Things are not always what they seem." "There's no place like home." These are examples of **themes,** or messages about life and human nature that writers convey to their readers. Often, these ideas are what remain with you long after you've read the last page.

ACTIVITY Pick two or three of your all-time favorite books or movies. For each, reflect on what message the writer or director is trying to express about life and human nature. Get together with a small group and talk about your choices and your responses to these questions:

- What lessons do the characters learn?
- What message did you take away from the book or movie?
- How do you see this big idea, or message, apply to your own life?

Online LITERATURE CLASSZONE.COM

Literature and Reading Center
Writing Center
Vocabulary and Spelling Center

ALABAMA STANDARDS

Preview Unit Goals

LITERARY ANALYSIS

- Distinguish topic from theme
- Identify theme, including universal and recurring theme
- Compare and contrast themes and characters
- Identify and interpret symbols

READING

- Use reading strategies, including monitoring and setting a purpose for reading
- Make inferences
- Identify and analyze cause and effect and sequence

WRITING AND GRAMMAR

- Write a short story
- Use coordinating conjunctions to join sentences
- Combine dependent and independent clauses

SPEAKING, LISTENING, AND VIEWING

- Compare a film with a play
- Design a DVD cover
- Dramatize a short story

VOCABULARY

- Understand and use denotation and connotation of words
- Use general context clues to understand word meaning

ACADEMIC VOCABULARY

- topic
- theme
- symbol
- cause and effect
- sequence
- make inferences
- compare and contrast
- clauses

UNIT 3

Reader's Workshop

Understanding Theme

The Wizard of Oz could be described as a story about a lost girl who finds her way home. But that description doesn't tell you what the story is really *about.* There is more to a story than what happens and whom it happens to. Often there is a deeper meaning, or theme. A **theme** is a message about life that a writer wants you to understand. A story usually has at least one theme and sometimes more. By figuring out a theme, you can learn a little about human nature.

ALABAMA STANDARDS

LITERATURE STANDARDS

6.a Classifying plot elements including conflict

7 Interpret author's message in literary texts

Part 1: Themes in Literature

It's easy to confuse a story's theme with its topic. Here's a way to tell the difference: A topic can be summed up in a word or two, such as "taking risks." A theme, however, is a writer's message *about* a topic. It usually takes at least one complete sentence to express a theme—for example, "Life's biggest rewards come from taking risks."

Stories can mean different things to different people. Two people reading a story might describe its theme differently or find different themes.

EXAMPLES OF THEMES IN LITERATURE

Thank You, M'am

Unit 1 pages 64–68

PLOT SUMMARY

Mrs. Luella Bates Washington Jones catches Roger trying to steal her purse. She drags him to her home, makes him wash up, and feeds him. Then she gives him the ten dollars he was trying to steal.

TOPIC

- Second chances

POSSIBLE THEMES

- Everyone deserves a second chance.
- An act of kindness can make a difference in a person's life.

Casey at the Bat

Unit 1 pages 130–132

PLOT SUMMARY

When the hometown baseball hero Casey comes to bat, there are two outs and two men on base. Instead of winning the game with a home run, Casey strikes out, and his team loses.

TOPIC

- Baseball

POSSIBLE THEMES

- Even a hero can fail.
- Overconfidence can lead to failure.

MODEL 1: THEME IN A STORY

Fables often convey themes about human nature through the actions of animal characters. What lesson can readers learn from this fable?

The LION and the MOUSE

Fable by **Aesop**

A lion was idling in the sun, pretending to sleep, when he felt a tickle on his nose. He opened one eye and, with a swipe of his huge paw, caught a small mouse trying to run away. The lion roared angrily and tossed the mouse into the air. The mouse cried, "Please don't hurt me! If only you will spare my life, I promise I will repay you." Surprised and amused by the little creature's earnest promise, the lion laughed and let the mouse go.

Time passed, and then one day the lion became ensnared in a trap. As he struggled to free himself, the ropes tightened around him until he couldn't move. The little mouse was close by and heard the lion's roars. She came and set the lion free by gnawing through the ropes. "When you kindly spared my life," said the mouse, "you laughed at the idea that one day I would repay you."

Close Read

1. What does the lion decide to do after capturing the mouse? Explain how the mouse repays the lion.
2. What lesson can readers learn from the way the lion and the mouse treat each other?

MODEL 2: THEME IN A POEM

In this poem, the writer presents a strong message about family.

LiTTLE SiSTER

Poem by **Nikki Grimes**

little sister
holds on tight.
My hands hurt
from all that squeezing,
but I don't mind.
She thinks no one will bother her
when I'm around,
and they won't
if I can help it.
And even when I can't
I try
'cause she believes in me.

Close Read

1. How does the little sister rely on the speaker of the poem? Explain how the speaker feels about his or her sister.
2. Reread the boxed lines. Which statement best expresses the theme?
   a. When family members believe in you, it makes you stronger.
   b. Families should spend more time together.

Part 2: A Closer Look at Theme

Sometimes the theme of a story is stated directly by the narrator or a character. Most often, though, a theme is implied—hinted at but not stated directly. In such a case, you need to **infer** the theme by finding clues in the text. This chart tells you where to look for those clues. Use the questions shown to help you uncover the theme of any story you read.

CLUES TO THEME

TITLE

The title may reflect a story's topic, its theme, or both. Ask

- What does each word in the title mean?
- What ideas does the title emphasize?

PLOT

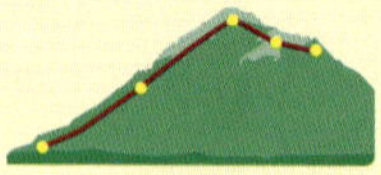

A story's plot often revolves around a conflict that is important to the theme. Ask

- What conflicts do the characters face?
- How are the conflicts resolved?

CHARACTERS

What characters do and learn can reflect a theme. Ask

- What are the main characters like? (Analyze their speech, thoughts, and actions.)
- How do the characters respond to the conflicts?
- How do the characters change?
- What lessons do the characters learn?

SETTING

A setting can suggest a theme because of what it means to the characters. Ask

- How does the setting influence the characters?
- How does the setting affect the conflicts?
- What might the setting represent? (For example, a character's childhood home might represent safety for him or her.)

Part 3: Analyze the Literature

In this story, two brothers respond to a challenge by making very different choices. As you read, use the clues in the story to help you understand what the writer is saying about their choices.

THE TWO BROTHERS

Short story by **Leo Tolstoy**

Two brothers set out on a journey together. At noon they lay down in a forest to rest. When they woke up they saw a stone lying next to them. There was something written on the stone, and they tried to make out what it was.

"Whoever finds this stone," they read, "let him go straight into the forest at sunrise. In the forest a river will appear; let him swim across the river to the other side. There he will find a she-bear and her cubs. Let him take the cubs from her and run up the mountain with them, without once looking back. On the top of the mountain he will see a house, and in that house will he find happiness."

Close Read

1. The title of this story suggests that the two brothers are central to the theme. As you read, think about the differences in the brothers' outlooks on life.

2. What challenge do the brothers face? Predict how they might respond to the challenge.

When they had read what was written on the stone, the younger brother said:

"Let us go together. We can swim across the river, carry off the bear cubs, take them to the house on the mountain, and together find happiness."

"I am not going into the forest after bear cubs," said the elder brother, "and I advise you not to go. In the first place, no one can know whether what is written on this stone is the truth—perhaps it was written in jest. It is even possible that we have not read it correctly. In the second place, even if what is written here is the truth—suppose we go into the forest and night comes, and we cannot find the river. We shall be lost. And if we do find the river, how are we going to swim across it? It may be broad and swift. In the third place, even if we swim across the river, do you think it is an easy thing to take her cubs away from a she-bear? She will seize us, and, instead of finding happiness, we shall perish, and all for nothing. In the fourth place, even if we succeeded in carrying off the bear cubs, we could not run up a mountain without stopping to rest. And, most important of all, the stone does not tell us what kind of happiness we should find in that house. It may be that the happiness awaiting us there is not at all the sort of happiness we would want."

"In my opinion," said the younger brother, "you are wrong. What is written on the stone could not have been put there without reason. And it is all perfectly clear. In the first place, no harm will come to us if we try. In the second place, if we do not go, someone else will read the inscription on the stone and find happiness, and we shall have lost it all. In the third place: if you do not make an effort and try hard, nothing in the world will succeed. In the fourth place: I should not want it thought that I was afraid of anything."

The elder brother answered him by saying: "The proverb says: 'In seeking great happiness small pleasures may be lost.' And also: 'A bird in the hand is worth two in the bush.'"

Close Read

3. Reread the boxed text. The setting—the forest, the river, the bears, and the mountain—all represent danger to the elder brother. What does his reaction to the setting's challenges tell you about him?

4. Reread lines 16–39. How are the brothers' attitudes different? Describe each brother's outlook on life.

The younger brother replied: "I have heard: 'He who is afraid of the leaves must not go into the forest.' And also: 'Beneath a stone no water flows.'"

Then the younger brother set off, and the elder remained behind.

No sooner had the younger brother gone into the forest than he found the river, swam across it, and there on the other side was the she-bear, fast asleep. He took her cubs, and ran up the mountain without looking back. When he reached the top of the mountain the people came out to meet him with a carriage to take him into the city, where they made him their king.

He ruled for five years. In the sixth year, another king, who was stronger than he, waged war against him. The city was conquered, and he was driven out.

Again the younger brother became a wanderer, and he arrived one day at the house of the elder brother. The elder brother was living in a village and had grown neither rich nor poor. The two brothers rejoiced at seeing each other, and at once began telling of all that had happened to them.

"You see," said the elder brother, "I was right. Here I have lived quietly and well, while you, though you may have been a king, have seen a great deal of trouble."

"I do not regret having gone into the forest and up the mountain," replied the younger brother. "I may have nothing now, but I shall always have something to remember, while you have no memories at all."

Close Read

5. How do the brothers resolve their conflict?

6. Reread lines 61–66. How does each brother feel about the choice he made? Explain whether the brothers' attitudes have changed.

7. Consider what the writer might be saying about the choices people make. (Hint: Is there always a right or wrong choice?) Write a statement that expresses the theme of the story.

Amigo Brothers

Short Story by Piri Thomas

What happens when friends COMPETE?

ALABAMA STANDARDS

READING & LIT STANDARDS
1.d Applying self-monitoring strategies
7 Interpret author's message in literary texts

KEY IDEA We face **competition** all the time, whether we are competing for someone's attention or for the best grade. And while some competitions are friendly and even fun, others can be brutal. In "Amigo Brothers," best friends Antonio and Felix find out if their deep friendship can survive an explosive competition.

QUICKWRITE Jot down a list of times when you competed with one or more friends. When you are done, review your list. Decide which of those experiences helped or hurt your friendship. Reflect on one of those experiences in a journal entry.

LITERARY ANALYSIS: THEME VERSUS TOPIC

A story's **theme** is a message about life or human nature that the writer wants readers to understand. Sometimes readers confuse the theme with the subject, or **topic,** of the story. One way to tell topic and theme apart is to remember that a topic can be stated in just one or two words. A theme is often expressed as a sentence.

	Length	Example
Topic	one or two words	growing up
Theme	sentence	Growing up brings new responsibilities.

One topic of "Amigo Brothers" is friendship. As you read the story, you'll find a deeper message as its theme.

READING SKILL: COMPARE AND CONTRAST

Comparing and contrasting characters can help you better understand a story. When you **compare** two or more people or things, you look for ways they are similar. When you **contrast** them, you look for ways they are different. As you read "Amigo Brothers," note similarities and differences between Felix and Antonio in a Venn diagram like the one shown.

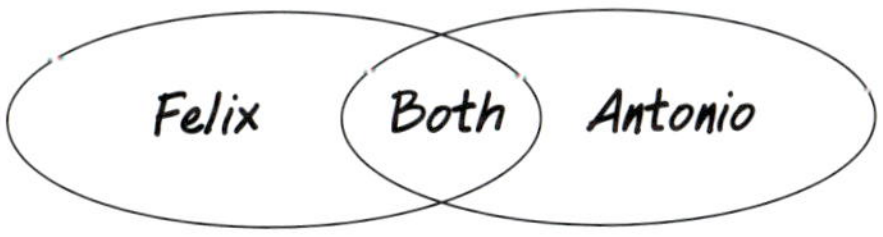

VOCABULARY IN CONTEXT

The boldfaced terms help tell this story about **competition.** Restate each sentence, using a different word or words.

1. He received a **barrage** of criticism for his comments.
2. The report shows the **devastating** effects of the illness.
3. She considered the offer **pensively.**
4. The crowd burst into a **torrent** of laughter.
5. He can't stand her **perpetual** complaining.
6. We were surprised at their **unbridled** enthusiasm.
7. They worked hard to **dispel** my concerns.
8. It was a noisy classroom, where **bedlam** reigned.
9. His arms began to **flail** as he lost his balance.
10. She has remarkable **clarity** for a person her age.

Author Online

A Troubled Beginning
In the 1950s, Piri Thomas realized that he was getting into too much trouble with the law and needed to turn his life around. He said to himself, "Man, where am I at? I got a mind; let's see if I can use it." He says he then "jumped into books." For him, writing became a tool to discover who he really was and to portray his Puerto Rican and African-American heritage.

Piri Thomas
born 1928

A Rich Heritage Thomas's writings are all set where he grew up, in New York City. He writes about neighborhoods that are heavily populated with Puerto Ricans and African Americans, such as Spanish Harlem and the Lower East Side of Manhattan. Thomas's writing celebrates the strength and determination of the people in his community.

MORE ABOUT THE AUTHOR
For more on Piri Thomas, visit the **Literature Center** at **ClassZone.com.**

Background

Golden Gloves In this story, Felix and Antonio compete to participate in a Golden Gloves tournament, a famous amateur boxing competition. Past winners who went on to fame and fortune include Sugar Ray Robinson, George Foreman, and Muhammad Ali.

Amigo BROTHERS

PIRI THOMAS

Antonio Cruz and Felix Vargas were both seventeen years old. They were so together in friendship that they felt themselves to be brothers. They had known each other since childhood, growing up on the lower east side of Manhattan in the same tenement building[1] on Fifth Street between Avenue A and Avenue B.

Antonio was fair, lean, and lanky, while Felix was dark, short, and husky. Antonio's hair was always falling over his eyes, while Felix wore his black hair in a natural Afro style.

Each youngster had a dream of someday becoming lightweight champion of the world. Every chance they had the boys worked out, sometimes at the Boys Club on 10th Street and Avenue A and sometimes at the pro's gym on 14th Street. Early morning sunrises would find them running along the East River Drive, wrapped in sweatshirts, short towels around their necks, and handkerchiefs Apache style around their foreheads. **A**

While some youngsters were into street negatives, Antonio and Felix slept, ate, rapped, and dreamt positive. Between them, they had a collection of *Fight* magazines second to none, plus a scrapbook filled with torn tickets to every boxing match they had ever attended and some clippings of their own. If asked a question about any given fighter, they would immediately zip out from their memory banks divisions,[2] weights, records of fights, knockouts, technical knockouts, and draws or losses.

Each had fought many bouts representing their community and had won two gold-plated medals plus a silver and bronze medallion. The difference was in their style. Antonio's lean form and long reach made him the better boxer, while Felix's short and muscular frame

ANALYZE VISUALS
What do the colors in this painting make you think of?

A COMPARE AND CONTRAST
Reread lines 1–14 and use your Venn diagram to note similarities and differences between the two boys. Add more notes to your diagram as you continue reading.

The Boxers, Roger Coleman. Tempera. Private collection. Photo © The Bridgeman Art Library.

1. **tenement building:** a rundown apartment building in which mostly poor families live.
2. **divisions:** weight groups into which boxers are separated.

made him the better slugger. Whenever they had met in the ring for sparring sessions,[3] it had always been hot and heavy.

Now, after a series of elimination bouts,[4] they had been informed that they were to meet each other in the division finals that were scheduled for the seventh of August, two weeks away—the winner to represent the Boys Club in the Golden Gloves Championship Tournament.

The two boys continued to run together along the East River Drive. But even when joking with each other, they both sensed a wall rising between them.

SOCIAL STUDIES CONNECTION

Antonio and Felix grew up on the Lower East Side of Manhattan.

One morning less than a week before their bout, they met as usual for their daily workout. They fooled around with a few jabs at the air, slapped skin, and then took off, running lightly along the dirty East River's edge.

Antonio glanced at Felix, who kept his eyes purposely straight ahead, pausing from time to time to do some fancy leg work while throwing one-twos followed by upper cuts to an imaginary jaw. Antonio then beat the air with a **barrage** of body blows and short **devastating** lefts with an overhand, jawbreaking right.

barrage (bə-räzh') *n.* a rapid, heavy attack

devastating (dĕv'ə-stā'tĭng) *adj.* very effective in causing pain or destruction **devastate** *v.*

After a mile or so, Felix puffed and said, "Let's stop for awhile, bro. I think we both got something to say to each other."

Antonio nodded. It was not natural to be acting as though nothing unusual was happening when two ace boon buddies were going to be blasting each other within a few short days.

They rested their elbows on the railing separating them from the river. Antonio wiped his face with his short towel. The sunrise was now creating day.

Felix leaned heavily on the river's railing and stared across to the shores of Brooklyn. Finally, he broke the silence.

"Man. I don't know how to come out with it."

Antonio helped. "It's about our fight, right?"

"Yeah, right." Felix's eyes squinted at the rising orange sun.

"I've been thinking about it too, *panín.*[5] In fact, since we found out it was going to be me and you, I've been awake at night, pulling punches[6] on you, trying not to hurt you."

"Same here. It ain't natural not to think about the fight. I mean, we both are *cheverote*[7] fighters, and we both want to win. But only one of us can win. There ain't no draws in the eliminations."

---

3. **sparring sessions:** practice boxing matches.
4. **elimination bouts:** matches to determine which boxers advance in a competition.
5. ***panín*** (pä-nēn') *American Spanish:* pal; buddy.
6. **pulling punches:** holding back in delivering blows.
7. ***cheverote*** (chĕ-vĕ-rô'tĕ) *American Spanish:* great or fantastic.

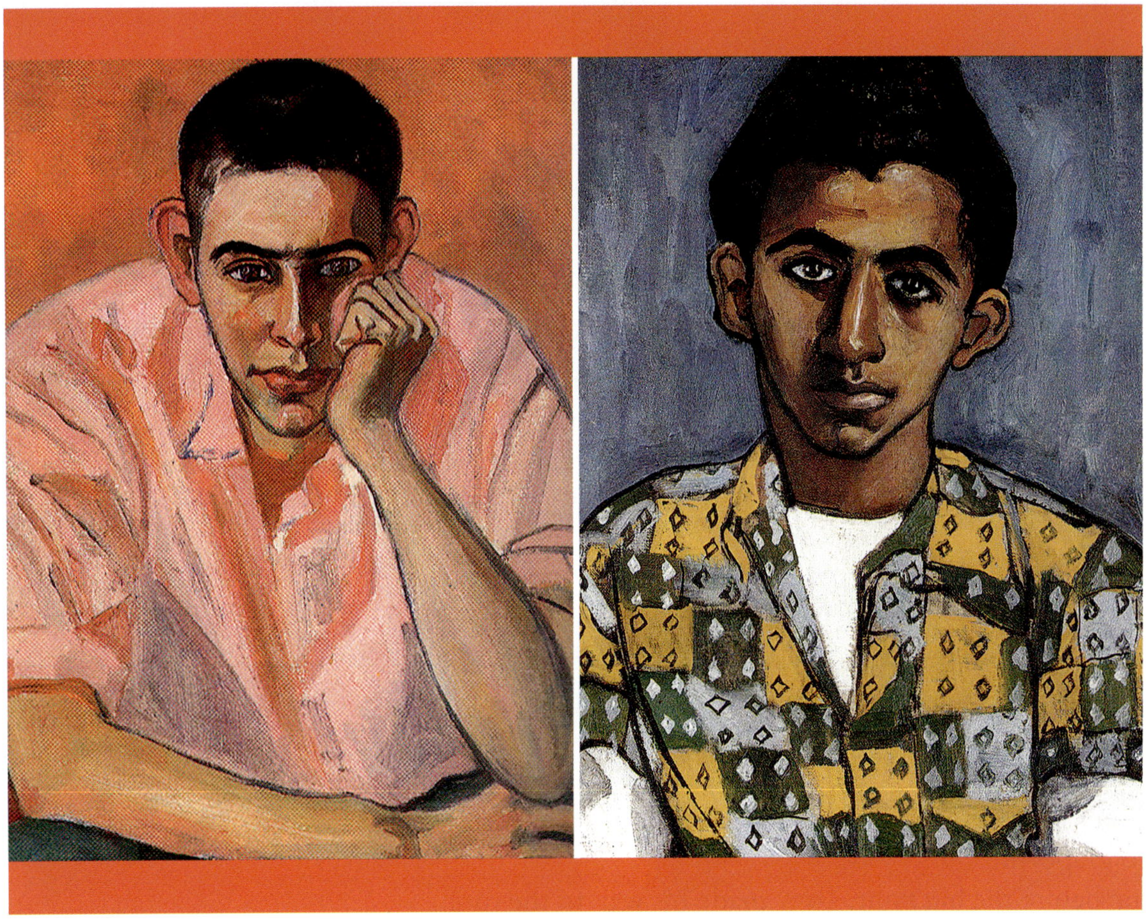

Left, Moose (1956), Alice Neel. © Estate of Alice Neel. Courtesy Robert Miller Gallery, New York. *Right, Call Me Joe* (1955), Alice Neel. Oil on canvas, 34″× 32″. © Estate of Alice Neel. Courtesy Robert Miller Gallery, New York.

Felix tapped Antonio gently on the shoulder. "I don't mean to sound like I'm bragging, bro. But I wanna win, fair and square."

Antonio nodded quietly. "Yeah. We both know that in the ring the better man wins. Friend or no friend, brother or no . . ."

Felix finished it for him. "Brother. Tony, let's promise something right here. Okay?"

"If it's fair, *hermano,*[8] I'm for it." Antonio admired the courage of a tugboat pulling a barge five times its welterweight[9] size.

"It's fair, Tony. When we get into the ring, it's gotta be like we never met. We gotta be like two heavy strangers that want the same thing, and only one can have it. You understand, don'tcha?" **B**

"*Sí,* I know." Tony smiled. "No pulling punches. We go all the way."

"Yeah, that's right. Listen, Tony. Don't you think it's a good idea if we don't see each other until the day of the fight? I'm going to stay with my Aunt Lucy in the Bronx.[10] I can use Gleason's Gym for working out. My manager says he got some sparring partners with more or less your style."

ANALYZE VISUALS
Compare and contrast these pictures with your own mental images of Felix and Antonio.

B THEME
What **characters** say can offer clues about a story's theme. What does the boys' **dialogue,** or conversation, tell you about their friendship?

8. ***hermano*** (ĕr-mä'nô) *Spanish:* brother.
9. **welterweight:** one of boxing's weight divisions, with a maximum weight of 147 pounds.
10. **the Bronx:** a borough of New York City, north of Manhattan.

Tony scratched his nose **pensively.** "Yeah, it would be better for our heads." He held out his hand, palm upward. "Deal?"

"Deal." Felix lightly slapped open skin.

"Ready for some more running?" Tony asked lamely.

"Naw, bro. Let's cut it here. You go on. I kinda like to get things together in my head."

"You ain't worried, are you?" Tony asked.

"No way, man." Felix laughed out loud. "I got too much smarts for that. I just think it's cooler if we split right here. After the fight, we can get it together again like nothing ever happened."

The *amigo*[11] brothers were not ashamed to hug each other tightly.

"Guess you're right. Watch yourself, Felix. I hear there's some pretty heavy dudes up in the Bronx. *Suavecito,*[12] okay?"

"Okay. You watch yourself too, *sabe?*"[13]

Tony jogged away. Felix watched his friend disappear from view, throwing rights and lefts. Both fighters had a lot of psyching up to do before the big fight.

The days in training passed much too slowly. Although they kept out of each other's way, they were aware of each other's progress via the ghetto grapevine.[14]

The evening before the big fight, Tony made his way to the roof of his tenement. In the quiet early dark, he peered over the ledge. Six stories below, the lights of the city blinked, and the sounds of cars mingled with the curses and the laughter of children in the street. He tried not to think of Felix, feeling he had succeeded in psyching his mind. But only in the ring would he really know. To spare Felix hurt, he would have to knock him out, early and quick. **C**

Up in the South Bronx, Felix decided to take in a movie in an effort to keep Antonio's face away from his fists. The flick was *The Champion* with Kirk Douglas, the third time Felix was seeing it.

The champion was getting beat, his face being pounded into raw, wet hamburger. His eyes were cut, jagged, bleeding, one eye swollen, the other almost shut. He was saved only by the sound of the bell.

Felix became the champ and Tony the challenger.

The movie audience was going out of its head, roaring in blood lust at the butchery going on. The champ hunched his shoulders, grunting and sniffing red blood back into his broken nose. The challenger, confident that he had the championship in the bag, threw a left. The champ countered with a dynamite right that exploded into the challenger's brains.

pensively (pĕn′sĭv-lē) *adv.* thoughtfully

C THEME
Understanding a story's **conflict** can help you understand its theme. An **internal conflict** is a struggle within a character's mind. Reread lines 102–104. What is Antonio's internal conflict?

11. ***amigo*** (ä-mē′gô) *Spanish:* friend.
12. ***Suavecito*** (swä-vĕ-sē′tô) *American Spanish:* Take it easy.
13. ***sabe*** (sä′bĕ) *Spanish:* you know.
14. **ghetto grapevine:** the chain of gossip that spreads through the neighborhood.

Felix's right arm felt the shock. Antonio's face, superimposed on the screen, was shattered and split apart by the awesome force of the killer blow. Felix saw himself in the ring, blasting Antonio against the ropes. The champ had to be forcibly restrained. The challenger was allowed to crumble slowly to the canvas, a broken, bloody mess.

When Felix finally left the theatre, he had figured out how to psyche himself for tomorrow's fight. It was Felix the Champion vs. Antonio the Challenger.

He walked up some dark streets, deserted except for small pockets of wary-looking kids wearing gang colors. Despite the fact that he was Puerto Rican like them, they eyed him as a stranger to their turf. Felix did a last shuffle, bobbing and weaving, while letting loose a **torrent** of blows that would demolish whatever got in its way. It seemed to impress the brothers, who went about their own business.

torrent (tôr′ənt) *n.* a violent, rushing stream

Still Open (1994), Douglas Safranek. Egg tempera on panel, 4 5/8′ × 4′. © Museum of the City of New York.

ANALYZE VISUALS
How does this picture **compare** with the description of the **setting** given in lines 98–101?

Finding no takers, Felix decided to split to his aunt's. Walking the streets had not relaxed him, neither had the fight flick. All it had done was to stir him up. He let himself quietly into his Aunt Lucy's apartment and went straight to bed, falling into a fitful sleep with sounds of the gong for Round One.

Antonio was passing some heavy time on his rooftop. How would the fight tomorrow affect his relationship with Felix? After all, fighting was like any other profession. Friendship had nothing to do with it. A gnawing doubt crept in. He cut negative thinking real quick by doing some speedy fancy dance steps, bobbing and weaving like mercury. The night air was blurred with **perpetual** motions of left hooks and right crosses. Felix, his *amigo* brother, was not going to be Felix at all in the ring. Just an opponent with another face. Antonio went to sleep, hearing the opening bell for the first round. Like his friend in the South Bronx, he prayed for victory via a quick, clean knockout in the first round.

perpetual (pər-pĕch'o͞o-əl) *adj.* continual; unending

Large posters plastered all over the walls of local shops announced the fight between Antonio Cruz and Felix Vargas as the main bout.

The fight had created great interest in the neighborhood. Antonio and Felix were well liked and respected. Each had his own loyal following. Betting fever was high and ranged from a bottle of Coke to cold, hard cash on the line.

Antonio's fans bet with **unbridled** faith in his boxing skills. On the other side, Felix's admirers bet on his dynamite-packed fists.

unbridled (ŭn-brīd'ld) *adj.* lacking restraint or control

Felix had returned to his apartment early in the morning of August 7th and stayed there, hoping to avoid seeing Antonio. He turned the radio on to salsa music sounds and then tried to read while waiting for word from his manager.

The fight was scheduled to take place in Tompkins Square Park. It had been decided that the gymnasium of the Boys Club was not large enough to hold all the people who were sure to attend. In Tompkins Square Park, everyone who wanted could view the fight, whether from ringside or window fire escapes or tenement rooftops.

The morning of the fight, Tompkins Square was a beehive of activity with numerous workers setting up the ring, the seats, and the guest speakers' stand. The scheduled bouts began shortly after noon, and the park had begun filling up even earlier.

The local junior high school across from Tompkins Square Park served as the dressing room for all the fighters. Each was given a separate classroom, with desktops, covered with mats, serving as resting tables. Antonio thought he caught a glimpse of Felix waving to him from a room at the far end of the corridor. He waved back just in case it had been him. D

D THEME
What can you **infer** about Antonio's attitude toward Felix on the day of the fight?

The fighters changed from their street clothes into fighting gear. Antonio wore white trunks, black socks, and black shoes. Felix wore sky blue trunks, red socks, and white boxing shoes. Each had dressing gowns to match their fighting trunks with their names neatly stitched on the back.

The loudspeakers blared into the open window of the school. There were speeches by dignitaries, community leaders, and great boxers of yesteryear. Some were well prepared, some improvised on the spot. They all carried the same message of great pleasure and honor at being part of such a historic event. This great day was in the tradition of champions emerging from the streets of the lower east side.

Interwoven with the speeches were the sounds of the other boxing events. After the sixth bout, Felix was much relieved when his trainer, Charlie, said, "Time change. Quick knockout. This is it. We're on."

Waiting time was over. Felix was escorted from the classroom by a dozen fans in white T-shirts with the word FELIX across their fronts.

Antonio was escorted down a different stairwell and guided through a roped-off path.

As the two climbed into the ring, the crowd exploded with a roar. Antonio and Felix both bowed gracefully and then raised their arms in acknowledgment.

Antonio tried to be cool, but even as the roar was in its first birth, he turned slowly to meet Felix's eyes looking directly into his. Felix nodded his head and Antonio responded. And both as one, just as quickly, turned away to face his own corner. **E**

Bong, bong, bong. The roar turned to stillness.

"Ladies and Gentlemen, *Señores y Señoras.*"[15]

The announcer spoke slowly, pleased at his bilingual efforts.

"Now the moment we have all been waiting for—the main event between two fine young Puerto Rican fighters, products of our lower east side."

"*Loisaida,*"[16] called out a member of the audience.

"In this corner, weighing 131 pounds, Felix Vargas. And in this corner, weighing 133 pounds, Antonio Cruz. The winner will represent the Boys Club in the tournament of champions, the Golden Gloves. There will be no draw. May the best man win."

The cheering of the crowd shook the windowpanes of the old buildings surrounding Tompkins Square Park. At the center of the ring, the referee was giving instructions to the youngsters.

"Keep your punches up. No low blows. No punching on the back of the head. Keep your heads up. Understand. Let's have a clean fight. Now shake hands and come out fighting."

E THEME
Reread lines 192–195. How do you think the boys feel at this moment?

15. ***Señores y Señoras*** (sĕ-nyô'rĕs ē sĕ-nyô'räs) *Spanish:* Ladies and Gentlemen.

16. ***Loisaida*** (loi-sī'dä) *American Spanish:* Lower East Side.

Both youngsters touched gloves and nodded. They turned and danced quickly to their corners. Their head towels and dressing gowns were lifted neatly from their shoulders by their trainers' nimble fingers. Antonio crossed himself. Felix did the same.

BONG! BONG! ROUND ONE. Felix and Antonio turned and faced each other squarely in a fighting pose. Felix wasted no time. He came in fast, head low, half hunched toward his right shoulder, and lashed out with a straight left. He missed a right cross as Antonio slipped the punch and countered with one-two-three lefts that snapped Felix's head back, sending a mild shock coursing through him. If Felix had any small doubt about their friendship affecting their fight, it was being neatly **dispelled.**

Antonio danced, a joy to behold. His left hand was like a piston pumping jabs one right after another with seeming ease. Felix bobbed and weaved and never stopped boring in. He knew that at long range he was at a disadvantage. Antonio had too much reach on him. Only by coming in close could Felix hope to achieve the dreamed-of knockout. **F**

Antonio knew the dynamite that was stored in his *amigo* brother's fist. He ducked a short right and missed a left hook. Felix trapped him against the ropes just long enough to pour some punishing rights and lefts to Antonio's hard midsection. Antonio slipped away from Felix, crashing two lefts to his head, which set Felix's right ear to ringing.

Bong! Both *amigos* froze a punch well on its way, sending up a roar of approval for good sportsmanship.

Felix walked briskly back to his corner. His right ear had not stopped ringing. Antonio gracefully danced his way toward his stool none the worse, except for glowing glove burns, showing angry red against the whiteness of his midribs.

"Watch that right, Tony." His trainer talked into his ear. "Remember Felix always goes to the body. He'll want you to drop your hands for his overhand left or right. Got it?"

Antonio nodded, spraying water out between his teeth. He felt better as his sore midsection was being firmly rubbed.

Felix's corner was also busy.

"You gotta get in there, fella." Felix's trainer poured water over his curly Afro locks. "Get in there or he's gonna chop you up from way back."

Bong! Bong! Round two. Felix was off his stool and rushed Antonio like a bull, sending a hard right to his head. Beads of water exploded from Antonio's long hair.

dispel (dĭ-spĕl′) *v.* to get rid of

F COMPARE AND CONTRAST
Reread lines 223–227. Compare and contrast the boys' boxing styles.

ANALYZE VISUALS
Describe the feeling this sculpture conveys.

Seated Fighter (1985), Joseph Sheppard. Bronze, height 21″.

Antonio, hurt, sent back a blurring barrage of lefts and rights that only meant pain to Felix, who returned with a short left to the head followed by a looping right to the body. Antonio countered[17] with his own flurry, forcing Felix to give ground. But not for long.

Felix bobbed and weaved, bobbed and weaved, occasionally punching his two gloves together.

Antonio waited for the rush that was sure to come. Felix closed in and feinted[18] with his left shoulder and threw his right instead. Lights suddenly exploded inside Felix's head as Antonio slipped the blow and hit him with a pistonlike left, catching him flush on the point of his chin.

Bedlam broke loose as Felix's legs momentarily buckled. He fought off a series of rights and lefts and came back with a strong right that taught Antonio respect.

bedlam (bĕd'ləm) *n.* a noisy confusion

Antonio danced in carefully. He knew Felix had the habit of playing possum when hurt, to sucker an opponent within reach of the powerful bombs he carried in each fist.

A right to the head slowed Antonio's pretty dancing. He answered with his own left at Felix's right eye that began puffing up within three seconds.

Antonio, a bit too eager, moved in too close, and Felix had him entangled into a rip-roaring, punching toe-to-toe slugfest that brought the whole Tompkins Square Park screaming to its feet.

Rights to the body. Lefts to the head. Neither fighter was giving an inch. Suddenly a short right caught Antonio squarely on the chin. His long legs turned to jelly, and his arms **flailed** out desperately. Felix, grunting like a bull, threw wild punches from every direction. Antonio, groggy, bobbed and weaved, evading most of the blows. Suddenly his head cleared. His left flashed out hard and straight catching Felix on the bridge of his nose.

flail (flāl) *v.* to wave wildly

Felix lashed back with a haymaker,[19] right off the ghetto streets. At the same instant, his eye caught another left hook from Antonio. Felix swung out, trying to clear the pain. Only the frenzied screaming of those along ringside let him know that he had dropped Antonio. Fighting off the growing haze, Antonio struggled to his feet, got up, ducked, and threw a smashing right that dropped Felix flat on his back.

Felix got up as fast as he could in his own corner, groggy but still game.[20] He didn't even hear the count. In a fog, he heard the roaring of the crowd, who seemed to have gone insane. His head cleared to hear the bell sound at the end of the round. He was very glad. His trainer sat him down on the stool.

---

17. **countered:** gave a blow after receiving or blocking his opponent's blow.
18. **feinted:** made a pretend attack to draw attention from his real purpose.
19. **haymaker:** a powerful blow.
20. **groggy but still game:** unsteady and shaky but willing to proceed.

In his corner, Antonio was doing what all fighters do when they are hurt. They sit and smile at everyone.

The referee signaled the ring doctor to check the fighters out. He did so and then gave his okay. The cold-water sponges brought **clarity** to both *amigo* brothers. They were rubbed until their circulation ran free.

clarity (klăr′ĭ-tē) *n.* clearness of mind

Bong! Round three—the final round. Up to now it had been tick-tack-toe, pretty much even. But everyone knew there could be no draw and that this round would decide the winner.

This time, to Felix's surprise, it was Antonio who came out fast, charging across the ring. Felix braced himself but couldn't ward off the barrage of punches. Antonio drove Felix hard against the ropes.

The crowd ate it up. Thus far the two had fought with *mucho corazón.*[21] Felix tapped his gloves and commenced his attack anew. Antonio, throwing boxer's caution to the winds, jumped in to meet him.

Both pounded away. Neither gave an inch, and neither fell to the canvas. Felix's left eye was tightly closed. Claret red blood poured from Antonio's nose. They fought toe-to-toe.

The sounds of their blows were loud in contrast to the silence of a crowd gone completely mute. The referee was stunned by their savagery.

Bong! Bong! Bong! The bell sounded over and over again. Felix and Antonio were past hearing. Their blows continued to pound on each other like hailstones.

Finally the referee and the two trainers pried Felix and Antonio apart. Cold water was poured over them to bring them back to their senses. G

G **THEME**
Reread lines 313–317. Why do such good friends keep fighting after the bell rings?

They looked around and then rushed toward each other. A cry of alarm surged through Tompkins Square Park. Was this a fight to the death instead of a boxing match?

The fear soon gave way to wave upon wave of cheering as the two *amigos* embraced.

No matter what the decision, they knew they would always be champions to each other.

Bong! Bong! Bong! "Ladies and Gentlemen. *Señores* and *Señoras.* The winner and representative to the Golden Gloves Tournament of Champions is . . ."

The announcer turned to point to the winner and found himself alone. Arm in arm, the champions had already left the ring.

---

21. ***mucho corazón*** (mo͞o′chô kô-rä-sôn′) *Spanish:* a lot of heart; great courage.

Comprehension

ALABAMA STANDARDS

LITERATURE STANDARD
7 Interpret author's message in literary texts

1. **Recall** Why is this fight so important to Felix and Antonio?
2. **Recall** What happens at the end of the fight?
3. **Summarize** Describe how the two boys fight during the boxing match. What strengths does each boy demonstrate?

Literary Analysis

4. **Make Inferences** Felix draws an **analogy,** or point-by-point comparison, between *The Champion* and his upcoming fight with Antonio. How does this analogy help Felix deal with his **internal conflict?**
5. **Compare and Contrast Characters** Look back at the Venn diagram you created as you read "Amigo Brothers." Which are more important, the similarities or the differences? Why?
6. **Draw Conclusions** What effect does the boxing competition have on Felix and Antonio's relationship? Support your answer with examples from the story.
7. **Identify Theme** Draw a graphic organizer like the one shown. Note details from the story about the boys' **friendship.** Then write a theme statement about friendship.
8. **Evaluate** Given that the boys know each other so well, do you think it is easier or harder for them to fight each other? Use examples from the story to support your answer.

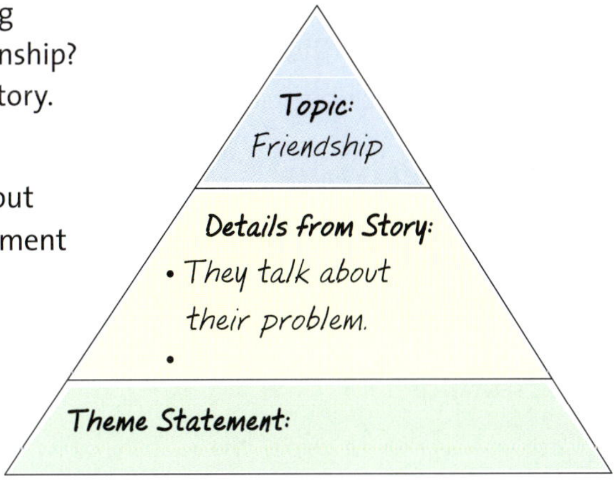

Extension and Challenge

9. **Creative Project: Music** Filmmakers often use music to enhance a movie's **theme.** Suppose you were asked to pick five songs for a film version of "Amigo Brothers." What would they be? Present your list to the class. Explain how each song reflects a theme of the selection.
10. **Inquiry and Research** Find out about the early life of a Golden Gloves champion who later became a professional boxer, such as Oscar de la Hoya or Muhammad Ali. How was the person you researched like Felix and Antonio? Present your findings to the class.

Oscar de la Hoya

RESEARCH LINKS
For more on Golden Glove champions, visit the **Research Center** at **ClassZone.com.**

Vocabulary in Context

VOCABULARY PRACTICE

For each sentence, choose the vocabulary word that is similar in meaning to the boldfaced word or phrase.

barrage, flail, bedlam, pensively, clarity, perpetual, devastating, torrent, dispel, unbridled

1. In the ring, both fighters were **extremely good at causing pain.**
2. Felix was in **continual** motion on his feet.
3. Antonio's fans cheered with **uncontrolled** emotion.
4. The **noise** in the gym was so loud that Felix couldn't hear himself think.
5. The trainer sat **deep in thought.**
6. Antonio began to **wave his arms crazily** about.
7. Felix came at Antonio with a **concentrated attack** of punches.
8. Antonio responded with a **wild, never-ending stream** of blows.
9. At times, both fighters almost lost their **ability to think clearly.**
10. Felix was able to **get rid of** any doubts about his friend.

VOCABULARY IN WRITING

Did the ending of this story surprise you? Write a paragraph explaining your reactions, using three or more of the vocabulary words. You might start like this.

EXAMPLE SENTENCE

*I expected the ending to **dispel** the question of who the better fighter was.*

ALABAMA STANDARDS

READING STANDARD
1.c Using context clues to determine meaning of words

VOCABULARY STRATEGY: THE LATIN ROOT *pel*

The vocabulary word *dispel* contains the Latin root *pel,* which means "drive" or "push." This root, which is sometimes spelled *puls,* is found in many English words. To understand the meaning of words with *pel* or *puls,* use context clues and your knowledge of the root's meaning.

VOCABULARY PRACTICE
For more practice, go to the **Vocabulary Center** at **ClassZone.com.**

PRACTICE Choose the word from the web that best completes each sentence.

1. Use insect _____ before you hike through the woods.
2. A person who is _____ often doesn't think before acting.
3. She threatened to _____ any club member who missed more than two meetings.
4. A plane's _____ helps it move through the air.

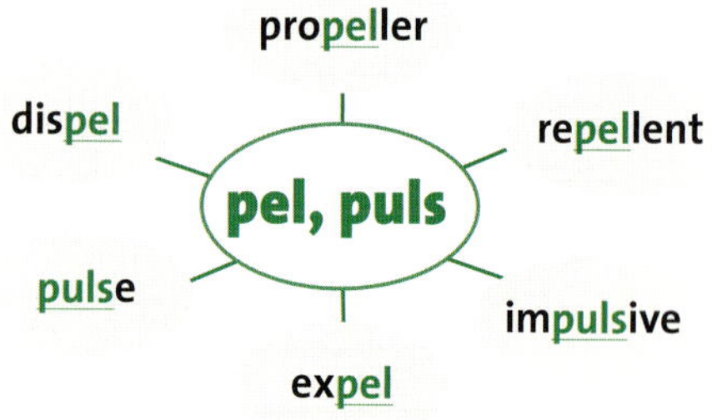

Reading-Writing Connection

Increase your understanding of "Amigo Brothers" by responding to these prompts. Then complete the **Grammar and Writing** exercise.

WRITING PROMPTS	SELF-CHECK
A. Short Response: Analyze the Message Some people believe boxing is too brutal to be an appropriate sport for young people. Others disagree. Which side of this debate is presented in "Amigo Brothers"? Using details and examples from the story, write **one paragraph** explaining your response.	***A strong response will . . .*** • include a clear opening statement • use specific details and examples from the story to support the statement
B. Extended Response: Write Dialogue What do you suppose Antonio and Felix talk about as they walk away from the boxing ring? Keep in mind the big question about **competition** on page 310 and what you know about the boys' friendship. Write their conversation as a **one-page dialogue.**	***An effective dialogue will . . .*** • demonstrate the nature of the boys' friendship • include language that fits each character

GRAMMAR AND WRITING

ALABAMA STANDARDS

WRITING/LANGUAGE STANDARD
10 Apply mechanics in writing

PUNCTUATE DIALOGUE CORRECTLY Dialogue is a conversation between two or more speakers. If you don't punctuate it correctly, readers might be confused about who is speaking. To avoid confusion, use **quotation marks** at the beginning and end of a speaker's words. Place end marks, such as **periods,** inside closing quotation marks. Use **commas** to set off a speaker's words from the rest of a sentence. Notice the placement of the comma and quotation marks in the revised sentence.

Original: Antonio said Felix, you will always be my *amigo* brother.

Revised: Antonio said, "Felix, you will always be my *amigo* brother."

PRACTICE Fix the misplaced punctuation marks in the following dialogue and insert any missing marks.

1. Felix replied, Same here, bro. No way I would let anything come between us.
2. "So, I feel good about our decision", Antonio said.
3. Felix shrugged and said Yeah. Me, too.
4. "Brother, boxing will never mean more to me than our friendship does".

For more help with punctuating dialogue, see page R50 in the ***Grammar Handbook.***

The War of the Wall

Short Story by Toni Cade Bambara

What makes a COMMUNITY?

ALABAMA STANDARDS

READING & LIT STANDARDS
1.d Applying self-monitoring strategies
7 Interpret author's message in literary texts

KEY IDEA Belonging to a **community** can give people feelings of identity and security. What things in the community help contribute to those feelings? In "The War of the Wall," an "outsider" comes to a town and challenges its residents' idea of what it means to be a community.

DISCUSS Think about the different communities, or groups, that you belong to, such as your school, your neighborhood, and your town. With a group of classmates, discuss how you would welcome someone new to your school or town.

LITERARY ANALYSIS: THEME

By paying attention to a story's **theme,** or message, you can learn things about human nature that you might never get a chance to learn from experience. You can determine a story's main theme by

- noting the **setting** of the story and how it might relate to the theme
- making inferences about why the **narrator** and other **characters** say and do things and about how they feel
- noting what **conflicts** arise and how they are resolved

As you read "The War of the Wall," keep these tips in mind in order to identify the story's theme.

READING STRATEGY: MONITOR

Active readers check, or **monitor,** their understanding as they read. One way to monitor your understanding is to pause occasionally and ask yourself questions. Sometimes you'll need to reread to find the answer. Other times you'll want to read on, because your question might be answered later in the story. Either way, asking questions will help you focus on and better understand what you are reading.

As you read "The War of the Wall," record questions and answers about what is happening and why characters act the way they do. Use a chart like the one shown.

My Questions	*Answers*
What is the lady painting on the wall?	

VOCABULARY IN CONTEXT

The following phrases could be newspaper headlines for articles about the artist's painting in "The War of the Wall." Write a definition of each boldfaced word.

1. **Aroma** of Paint Was Promise of Future Beauty
2. Artist's **Masterpiece** Creates Sensation
3. Viewers in **Trance** over Splendid Work
4. Colors and Subject Matter **Beckon** to Wide Audience
5. **Inscription** on Mural Provides Dedication

Author Online

Creative Beginnings

Toni Cade Bambara
1939–1995

Born Miltona Mirkin Cade, Toni Cade Bambara announced at five years old that she was changing her name to Toni. Her mother, who supported all of Bambara's creative efforts, agreed. Bambara began writing as a child and never stopped. She went on to become an award-winning author, teacher, filmmaker, and a leading activist in the African-American community. Although set in a small town, "The War of the Wall" was inspired by Bambara's memories of growing up in the Harlem neighborhood of New York City.

MORE ABOUT THE AUTHOR
For more on Toni Cade Bambara, visit the **Literature Center** at **ClassZone.com.**

Background

Murals A mural is a large picture painted on an interior or exterior wall of a building. Many murals illustrate scenes from history or reflect the people of local communities. In the 1960s, African-American artists began a "wall of respect" movement. They painted murals as symbols of their respect for different groups. Walls of respect appeared everywhere from Eastern cities such as New York to Western cities such as Los Angeles. They were also painted in small Southern towns such as the one in which "The War of the Wall" takes place.

THE WAR OF THE WALL

TONI CADE BAMBARA

Me and Lou had no time for courtesies. We were late for school. So we just flat out told the painter lady to quit messing with the wall. It was our wall, and she had no right coming into our neighborhood painting on it. Stirring in the paint bucket and not even looking at us, she mumbled something about Mr. Eubanks, the barber, giving her permission. That had nothing to do with it as far as we were concerned. We've been pitching pennies against that wall since we were little kids. Old folks have been dragging their chairs out to sit in the shade of the wall for years. Big kids have been playing handball against the wall since so-called integration[1] when the crazies 'cross town poured cement in our pool so we couldn't use it. I'd sprained my neck one time boosting my cousin Lou up to chisel Jimmy Lyons's name into the wall when we found out he was never coming home from the war in Vietnam to take us fishing. **A**

"If you lean close," Lou said, leaning hipshot against her beat-up car, "you'll get a whiff of bubble gum and kids' sweat. And that'll tell you something—that this wall belongs to the kids of Taliaferro Street." I thought Lou sounded very convincing. But the painter lady paid us no mind. She just snapped the brim of her straw hat down and hauled her bucket up the ladder.

"You're not even from around here," I hollered up after her. The license plates on her old piece of car said "New York." Lou dragged me away because I was about to grab hold of that ladder and shake it. And then we'd really be late for school.

When we came from school, the wall was slick with white. The painter lady was running string across the wall and taping it here and there. Me and Lou leaned against the gumball machine outside the pool hall and watched. She had strings up and down and back and forth. Then she began chalking them with a hunk of blue chalk.

ANALYZE VISUALS
Look closely at this picture. What details of **setting** does it include?

A THEME
After reading the first few lines of this story, what do you think the main **conflict** will be? As you continue reading, think about what message this conflict might communicate.

1. **since so-called integration:** from the time in the 1960s when segregation, the separation of the races in public places, was outlawed. The narrator is being sarcastic, suggesting that integration has not been successful.

Harlem Street Scene (1942), Jacob Lawrence. Gouache on paper, 21″ × 20¾″. Private collection. © 2008 The Jacob and Gwendolyn Lawrence Foundation, Seattle/Artists Rights Society (ARS), New York. © Art Resource, New York.

OTEL
MEATS
BAR AND GRILL

The Morris twins crossed the street, hanging back at the curb next to the beat-up car. The twin with the red ribbons was hugging a jug of cloudy lemonade. The one with yellow ribbons was holding a plate of dinner away from her dress. The painter lady began snapping the strings. The blue chalk dust measured off halves and quarters up and down and sideways too. Lou was about to say how hip it all was, but I dropped my book satchel on his toes to remind him we were at war.

Some good **aromas** were drifting our way from the plate leaking pot likker[2] onto the Morris girl's white socks. I could tell from where I stood that under the tinfoil was baked ham, collard greens, and candied yams. And knowing Mrs. Morris, who sometimes bakes for my mama's restaurant, a slab of buttered cornbread was probably up under there too, sopping up some of the pot likker. Me and Lou rolled our eyes, wishing somebody would send us some dinner. But the painter lady didn't even turn around. She was pulling the strings down and prying bits of tape loose.

aroma (ə-rō′mə) *n.* a smell; odor

Side Pocket came strolling out of the pool hall to see what Lou and me were studying so hard. He gave the painter lady the once-over, checking out her paint-spattered jeans, her chalky T-shirt, her floppy-brimmed straw hat. He hitched up his pants and glided over toward the painter lady, who kept right on with what she was doing.

"Whatcha got there, sweetheart?" he asked the twin with the plate.

"Suppah," she said all soft and countrylike.

"For her," the one with the jug added, jerking her chin toward the painter lady's back.

Still she didn't turn around. She was rearing back on her heels, her hands jammed into her back pockets, her face squinched up like the **masterpiece** she had in mind was taking shape on the wall by magic. We could have been gophers crawled up into a rotten hollow for all she cared. She didn't even say hello to anybody. Lou was muttering something about how great her concentration was. I butt him with my hip, and his elbow slid off the gum machine. **B**

masterpiece (măs′tər-pēs′) *n.* a great work of art

B MONITOR
Why do you think the **narrator** says, "We could have been gophers . . . for all she cared"? How is the narrator feeling?

"Good evening," Side Pocket said in his best ain't-I-fine voice. But the painter lady was moving from the milk crate to the step stool to the ladder, moving up and down fast, scribbling all over the wall like a crazy person. We looked at Side Pocket. He looked at the twins. The twins looked at us. The painter lady was giving a show. It was like those old-timey music movies where the dancer taps on the tabletop and then starts jumping all over the furniture, kicking chairs over and not skipping a beat. She didn't even look where she was stepping. And for a minute there, hanging on the ladder to reach a far spot, she looked like she was going to tip right over.

2. **pot likker:** the broth or liquid in which meat or vegetables have been cooked.

"Ahh," Side Pocket cleared his throat and moved fast to catch the ladder. "These young ladies here have brought you some supper."

"Ma'am?" The twins stepped forward. Finally the painter turned around, her eyes "full of sky," as my grandmama would say. Then she stepped down like she was in a **trance.** She wiped her hands on her jeans as the Morris twins offered up the plate and the jug. She rolled back the tinfoil, then wagged her head as though something terrible was on the plate.

trance (trăns) *n.* a condition of daydreaming or being unconscious of one's surroundings

"Thank your mother very much," she said, sounding like her mouth was full of sky too. "I've brought my own dinner along." And then, without even excusing herself, she went back up the ladder, drawing on the wall in a wild way. Side Pocket whistled one of those oh-brother breathy whistles and went back into the pool hall. The Morris twins shifted their weight from one foot to the other, then crossed the street and went home. Lou had to drag me away, I was so mad. We couldn't wait to get to the firehouse to tell my daddy all about this rude woman who'd stolen our wall.

All the way back to the block to help my mama out at the restaurant, me and Lou kept asking my daddy for ways to run the painter lady out of town. But my daddy was busy talking about the trip to the country and telling Lou he could come too because Grandmama can always use an extra pair of hands on the farm.

Later that night, while me and Lou were in the back doing our chores, we found out that the painter lady was a liar. She came into the restaurant and leaned against the glass of the steam table, talking about how starved she was. I was scrubbing pots and Lou was chopping onions, but we could hear her through the service window. She was asking Mama was that a ham hock in the greens, and was that a neck bone in the pole beans, and were there any vegetables cooked without meat, especially pork.

"I don't care who your spiritual leader is," Mama said in that way of hers. "If you eat in the community, sistuh, you gonna eat pig by-and-by, one way or t'other."

Me and Lou were cracking up in the kitchen, and several customers at the counter were clearing their throats, waiting for Mama to really fix her wagon[3] for not speaking to the elders when she came in. The painter lady took a stool at the counter and went right on with her questions. Was there cheese in the baked macaroni, she wanted to know? Were there eggs in the salad? Was it honey or sugar in the iced tea? Mama was fixing Pop Johnson's plate. And every time the painter lady asked a fool question, Mama would dump another spoonful of rice on the pile. She was tapping her foot and heating up in a dangerous way. But Pop Johnson

3. **fix her wagon:** a slang expression meaning "put her in her place; bring about her downfall."

was happy as he could be. Me and Lou peeked through the service window, wondering what planet the painter lady came from. Who ever heard of baked macaroni without cheese, or potato salad without eggs? **C**

"Do you have any bread made with unbleached flour?" the painter lady asked Mama. There was a long pause, as though everybody in the restaurant was holding their breath, wondering if Mama would dump the next spoonful on the painter lady's head. She didn't. But when she set Pop Johnson's plate down, it came down with a bang.

When Mama finally took her order, the starving lady all of a sudden couldn't make up her mind whether she wanted a vegetable plate or fish and a salad. She finally settled on the broiled trout and a tossed salad. But just when Mama reached for a plate to serve her, the painter lady leaned over the counter with her finger all up in the air.

"Excuse me," she said. "One more thing." Mama was holding the plate like a Frisbee, tapping that foot, one hand on her hip. "Can I get raw beets in that tossed salad?"

"You will get," Mama said, leaning her face close to the painter lady's, "whatever Lou back there tossed. Now sit down." And the painter lady sat back down on her stool and shut right up. **D**

All the way to the country, me and Lou tried to get Mama to open fire on the painter lady. But Mama said that seeing as how she was from the North, you couldn't expect her to have any manners. Then Mama said she was sorry she'd been so impatient with the woman because she seemed like a decent person and was simply trying to stick to a very strict diet. Me and Lou didn't want to hear that. Who did that lady think she was, coming into our neighborhood and taking over our wall? **E**

"Wellllll," Mama drawled, pulling into the filling station so Daddy could take the wheel, "it's hard on an artist, ya know. They can't always get people to look at their work. So she's just doing her work in the open, that's all."

Me and Lou definitely did not want to hear that. Why couldn't she set up an easel downtown or draw on the sidewalk in her own neighborhood? Mama told us to quit fussing so much; she was tired and wanted to rest. She climbed into the back seat and dropped down into the warm hollow Daddy had made in the pillow.

All weekend long, me and Lou tried to scheme up ways to recapture our wall. Daddy and Mama said they were sick of hearing about it. Grandmama turned up the TV to drown us out. On the late news was a story about the New York subways. When a train came roaring into the station all covered from top to bottom, windows too, with writings and drawings done with spray paint, me and Lou slapped five. Mama said it was too bad kids in New York had nothing better to do than spray paint all over the trains. Daddy said that in the cities, even grown-ups wrote all over the trains and buildings too. Daddy called it "graffiti." Grandmama called it a shame.

C THEME
Reread lines 96–113. How is the painter different from the people who live in the community?

D MONITOR
What **questions** do you have about what is happening in this scene? Record them in your monitoring chart.

E THEME
Reread lines 130–136. What does the **setting** have to do with the **conflict** between the community and the painter?

We couldn't wait to get out of school on Monday. We couldn't find any black spray paint anywhere. But in a junky hardware store downtown we found a can of white epoxy[4] paint, the kind you touch up old refrigerators with when they get splotchy and peely. We spent our whole allowance on it. And because it was too late to use our bus passes, we had to walk all the way home lugging our book satchels and gym shoes, and the bag with the epoxy.

When we reached the corner of Taliaferro and Fifth, it looked like a block party or something. Half the neighborhood was gathered on the sidewalk in front of the wall. I looked at Lou, he looked at me. We both looked at the bag with the epoxy and wondered how we were going to work our scheme. The painter lady's car was nowhere in sight. But there were too many people standing around to do anything. Side Pocket and his buddies were leaning on their cue sticks, hunching each other. Daddy was there with a lineman[5] he catches a ride with on Mondays. Mrs. Morris had her arms flung around the shoulders of the twins on either side of her. Mama was talking with some of her customers, many of them with napkins still at the throat. Mr. Eubanks came out of the barbershop, followed by a man in a striped poncho, half his face shaved, the other half full of foam.

"She really did it, didn't she?" Mr. Eubanks huffed out his chest. Lots of folks answered right quick that she surely did when they saw the straight razor in his hand. **F**

Mama **beckoned** us over. And then we saw it. The wall. Reds, greens, figures outlined in black. Swirls of purple and orange. Storms of blues and yellows. It was something. I recognized some of the faces right off. There was Martin Luther King, Jr. And there was a man with glasses on and his mouth open like he was laying down a heavy rap. Daddy came up alongside and reminded us that that was Minister Malcolm X. The serious woman with a rifle I knew was Harriet Tubman because my grandmama has pictures

F MONITOR
Reread lines 171–176. Why do people agree with Mr. Eubanks so quickly?

beckon (bĕk'ən) *v.* to summon or call, usually by a gesture or nod

4. **epoxy** (ĭ-pŏk'sē): a plastic used in glues and paints.
5. **lineman:** a person who repairs telephone or power lines.

© Andre Jenny/Alamy.

of her all over the house. And I knew Mrs. Fannie Lou Hamer 'cause a signed photograph of her hangs in the restaurant next to the calendar.

Then I let my eyes follow what looked like a vine. It trailed past a man with a horn, a woman with a big white flower in her hair, a handsome dude in a tuxedo seated at a piano, and a man with a goatee holding a book. When I looked more closely, I realized that what had looked like flowers were really faces. One face with yellow petals looked just like Frieda Morris. One with red petals looked just like Hattie Morris. I could hardly believe my eyes.

SOCIAL STUDIES CONNECTION

Martin Luther King Jr., Malcolm X, Harriet Tubman, and Fannie Lou Hamer (shown here) were all African Americans who fought for freedom and equality.

"Notice," Side Pocket said, stepping close to the wall with his cue stick like a classroom pointer. "These are the flags of liberation," he said in a voice I'd never heard him use before. We all stepped closer while he pointed and spoke. "Red, black and green," he said, his pointer falling on the leaflike flags of the vine. "Our liberation flag.[6] And here Ghana, there Tanzania. Guinea-Bissau, Angola, Mozambique."[7] Side Pocket sounded very tall, as though he'd been waiting all his life to give this lesson.

Mama tapped us on the shoulder and pointed to a high section of the wall. There was a fierce-looking man with his arms crossed against his chest guarding a bunch of children. His muscles bulged, and he looked a lot like my daddy. One kid was looking at a row of books. Lou hunched me 'cause the kid looked like me. The one that looked like Lou was spinning a globe on the tip of his finger like a basketball. There were other kids there with microscopes and compasses. And the more I looked, the more it looked like the fierce man was not so much guarding the kids as defending their right to do what they were doing. G

G THEME

Reread lines 200–208. Here you see the story's main **characters** through the painter's eyes. How does this show that she understands the community?

Then Lou gasped and dropped the paint bag and ran forward, running his hands over a rainbow. He had to tiptoe and stretch to do it, it was so high. I couldn't breathe either. The painter lady had found the chisel marks and had painted Jimmy Lyons's name in a rainbow.

"Read the **inscription,** honey," Mrs. Morris said, urging little Frieda forward. She didn't have to urge much. Frieda marched right up, bent down, and in a loud voice that made everybody quit oohing and ahhing and listen, she read,

inscription (ĭn-skrĭp′shən) *n.* something written, carved, or engraved on a surface

To the People of Taliaferro Street
I Dedicate This Wall of Respect
Painted in Memory of My Cousin
Jimmy Lyons

6. **Red, black and green . . . liberation flag:** a banner of red, black, and green horizontal stripes has been used in the United States as well as Africa to stand for the liberation, or freedom, sought by people of African heritage.

7. **Ghana . . . Tanzania. Guinea-Bissau, Angola, Mozambique** (mō′zəm-bēk′): countries in southern and western Africa.

Comprehension

ALABAMA STANDARDS

READING STANDARD
1.d Applying self-monitoring strategies

1. **Recall** Why is the wall special to the narrator and Lou?
2. **Represent** Who is related to whom in this story? Use web diagrams to show the family relationships mentioned.

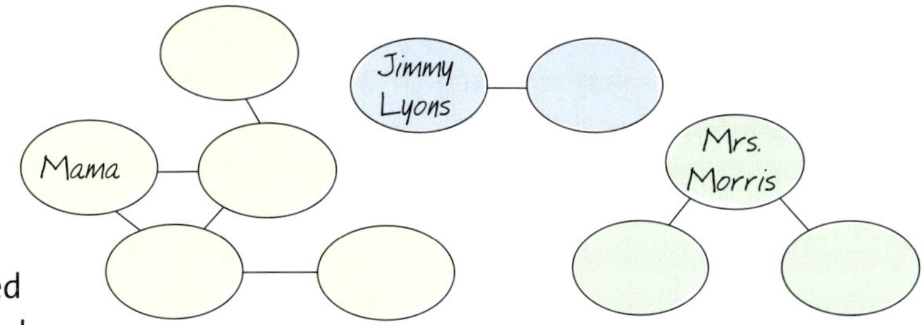

3. **Clarify** Why don't Lou and the narrator carry out their plan to recapture the wall?

Literary Analysis

4. **Monitor** Review the chart you filled in as you read. Which questions and answers were most important for understanding the story? Why?
5. **Make Inferences** Reread lines 209–220. How do you think Lou and the narrator feel about the paint they've bought once they read the inscription on the wall?
6. **Analyze Characters** Mama's reaction to the painter seems to change over the course of the story. Her first impression of the painter seems to be negative. Why does she then defend the painter to the narrator and Lou?
7. **Identify Theme** Given what the **characters** learn about themselves and the painter, what do you think the theme of the story is?
8. **Evaluate** Was the painter an outsider or part of the **community?** Use examples from the story to support your answer.

Extension and Challenge

9. **Readers' Circle** "The War of the Wall" is told from the **first-person point of view.** Everything we learn about the characters and plot comes from what the narrator chooses to tell us. For that reason, we don't know very much about the painter's thoughts and feelings. With a small group of classmates, talk about what the painter may have been thinking about the **community.** Support your responses with evidence from the story.
10. **SOCIAL STUDIES CONNECTION** Read the article "Back to the Wall" on page 337 about the artist Judith Baca's mural restoration project. What are the similarities and differences between Los Angeles's Great Wall and the mural in the story? Think about the subject matter of each mural and the way each was created.

Vocabulary in Context

VOCABULARY PRACTICE

Choose the letter of the situation that you would associate with each boldfaced vocabulary word.

1. **aroma:** (a) arguing with a friend, (b) writing a letter, (c) smelling a rose
2. **masterpiece:** (a) a game of catch, (b) a prize-winning play, (c) a stormy day
3. **trance:** (a) walking a dog, (b) snoring loudly, (c) not paying attention
4. **beckon:** (a) hailing a taxicab, (b) passing a test, (c) eating lunch
5. **inscription:** (a) military service, (b) words on a tombstone, (c) parts of a car

aroma
beckon
inscription
masterpiece
trance

VOCABULARY IN WRITING

What kind of person is the painter? Write a brief character description of her, using two or more vocabulary words. Here is an example of how you might begin.

EXAMPLE SENTENCE

The painter seems to know from the beginning that she is creating a ***masterpiece.***

VOCABULARY STRATEGY: DENOTATIONS AND CONNOTATIONS

A word's **denotation** is its literal meaning—that is, the meaning found in a dictionary definition. A word's **connotation** comes from the shades of meaning it has beyond its definition. For example, a stubborn person could also be described as *strong-willed* or *pig-headed.* But *strong-willed* connotes "independent in thinking and acting," while *pig-headed* connotes "inflexible." Recognizing connotations can improve both your reading and your writing.

PRACTICE Choose the word in each pair that has a positive connotation. Then use the word in a sentence.

1. gathering—mob
2. skinny—slender
3. chuckle—snicker
4. petite—puny
5. inquiring—prying
6. gossip—chat
7. self-confident—arrogant
8. immature—youthful

VOCABULARY PRACTICE
For more practice, go to the **Vocabulary Center** at **ClassZone.com.**

MAGAZINE ARTICLE In "The War of the Wall," a woman paints a mural in a Southern town. In the following article, you'll read about the real-life artist Judith Baca and the people who helped her create and restore a large mural in Los Angeles, California.

Back to the Wall

from **People**

Working in a city known more for freeways than museums, Judith Baca may be the quintessential Los Angeles artist, painting not on canvas but on concrete. Since 1974 she has overseen the creation of roughly 550 murals in public spaces, providing summer work for inner-city kids while she brings color and life to highway underpasses and parks. "I want it to continue," Baca, 58, says of her work. "I want future generations to see it."

One of her most famous pieces is the 13-foot-high, half-mile-long Great Wall, which depicts world and L.A. history on a flood-channel wall. Some 400 youths—many from poor, crime-ridden areas—worked on the mural, and 30 years later, some of their kids worked on its restoration. "People come first for Judy," says Priscilla Becker, 40, who, as a teen from a poor family, worked with Baca for three summers. Now CEO of a software company, Becker adds, "From Judy I learned that dreams are not just dreams."

Baca was teaching art in an inner-city park when she began planning murals to build bridges between rival gangs. She still wants her projects to meet the same goal. "All these people made the wall together," she says. "That's the story what they made together."

What Do Fish Have to Do with Anything?

Short Story by Avi

What is the cure for UNHAPPINESS?

ALABAMA STANDARDS

READING STANDARDS

1.d Applying self-monitoring strategies

2 Relate literary elements and devices to each other

KEY IDEA What helps you through sad times? Is it talking to another person? Is it listening to music by yourself? Everyone deals with **unhappiness** in his or her own way. In "What Do Fish Have to Do with Anything?" a young boy searches for a cure to the unhappiness he sees all around him.

QUICKWRITE With a partner or small group, brainstorm a list of strategies that can help people overcome unhappiness. You may use the list shown to get started. Then record the most effective strategies in your journal.

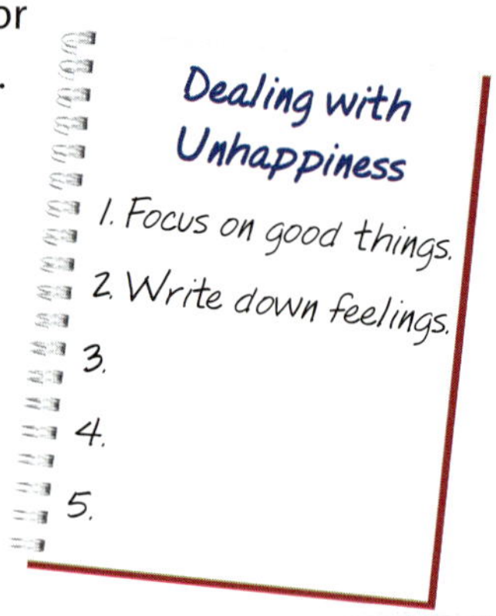

LITERARY ANALYSIS: SYMBOL

When you see a dove, do you think of peace? Many people do, because a dove is a well-known **symbol** for peace. A symbol is a person, place, or thing that stands for something beyond itself. To find symbols in a story, try the following:

- Look for people, places, things, or actions that the writer emphasizes or mentions over and over.
- Think about whether any repeated symbol might be a clue to identifying the overall **theme** of the story.
- Keep the title in mind as you read, because writers often provide clues there.

As you read "What Do Fish Have to Do with Anything?" ask yourself what is being used as a symbol.

READING SKILL: MAKE INFERENCES

An **inference** is a logical guess based on clues in the text plus your own knowledge. Making inferences about characters, what they learn, and how they change will help you understand the message of the story. As you read the story, record each inference you make about the characters in an equation such as the one shown.

Details or Evidence from Story	+	What I Know from Reading or Experience	=	Inference About Character

Review: **Compare and Contrast**

VOCABULARY IN CONTEXT

The words in column A help Avi tell his story about **unhappiness.** Match each word with the word in column B that is closest in meaning.

Column A	Column B
1. contemplate	**a.** unavoidably
2. inevitably	**b.** distracted
3. preoccupied	**c.** reply
4. retort	**d.** necessity
5. threshold	**e.** consider
6. urgency	**f.** entrance

Author Online

Early Challenges Avi Wortis has written over 30 books for children and young adults, but he had to overcome a huge challenge to do so. As a boy, Avi had trouble spelling. But he loved reading—anything from comic books to histories. He later found out that he had a learning disability called dysgraphia, which caused him to reverse letters and misspell words. Although that affected his ability to write, Avi was determined to be a writer. He had no intention of giving up.

Avi
born 1937

Success! Today, Avi is one of the most well-known and respected writers for young adults and has the awards to prove it. His advice to readers: "Don't be satisfied with answers others give you. Don't assume that because everyone believes a thing, it is right or wrong. Reason things out for yourself. Work to get answers on your own." Avi includes this idea in "What Do Fish Have to Do with Anything?"

Homelessness Avi's parents worked to promote civil rights and other social justice issues. As an adult, Avi has shared their concerns. His writing often addresses social problems. In this story, a homeless man plays a positive role in a young boy's life.

MORE ABOUT THE AUTHOR
For more on Avi, visit the **Literature Center** at **ClassZone.com.**

WHAT DO FISH HAVE TO DO WITH ANYTHING?

AVI

Every day at three o'clock Mrs. Markham waited for her son, Willie, to come out of school. They walked home together. If asked why she did it, Mrs. Markham would say, "Parents need to watch their children."

As they left the schoolyard, Mrs. Markham **inevitably** asked, "How was school?"

Willie would begin to talk, then stop. He was never sure his mother was listening. She seemed **preoccupied** with her own thoughts. She had been like that ever since his dad had abandoned them six months ago. No one knew where he'd gone. Willie had the feeling that his mother was lost too. It made him feel lonely.

One Monday afternoon, as they approached the apartment building where they lived, she suddenly tugged at him. "Don't look that way," she said.

"Where?"

"At that man over there."

Willie stole a look over his shoulder. A man, whom Willie had never seen before, was sitting on a red plastic milk crate near the curb. His matted, streaky gray hair hung like a ragged curtain over his dirty face. His shoes were torn. Rough hands lay upon his knees. One hand was palm up. No one seemed to pay him any mind. Willie was certain he had never seen a man so utterly alone. It was as if he were some spat-out piece of chewing gum on the pavement.

"What's the matter with him?" Willie asked his mother in a hushed voice.

Keeping her eyes straight ahead, Mrs. Markham said, "He's sick." She pulled Willie around. "Don't stare. It's rude."

"What kind of sick?"

inevitably
(ĭn-ĕv'ĭ-tə-blē) *adv.* unavoidably; without fail

preoccupied
(prē-ŏk'yə-pīd') *adj.* lost in thought; distracted

ANALYZE VISUALS
What is the first thing you notice about this image? What sense does it give you about the person?

Gregory, Los Angeles, March 31st, 1982, David Hockney. Composite Polaroid, $14\frac{1}{2}'' \times 13\frac{1}{4}''$. Photo © David Hockney/The David Hockney No. 1 U.S. Trust.

Gregory. Los Angeles. March 31st 1982

As Mrs. Markham searched for an answer, she began to walk faster. "He's unhappy," she said.

"What's he doing?"

"Come on, Willie, you know perfectly well. He's begging."

"Do you think anyone gave him anything?"

"I don't know. Now, come on, don't look."

"Why don't you give him anything?"

"We have nothing to spare."

When they got home, Mrs. Markham removed a white cardboard box from the refrigerator. It contained pound cake. Using her thumb as a measure, she carefully cut a half-inch piece of cake and gave it to Willie on a clean plate. The plate lay on a plastic mat decorated with images of roses with diamondlike dewdrops. She also gave him a glass of milk and a folded napkin. She moved slowly.

Willie said, "Can I have a bigger piece of cake?"

Mrs. Markham picked up the cake box and ran a manicured pink fingernail along the nutrition information panel. "A half-inch piece is a portion, and a portion contains the following health requirements. Do you want to hear them?"

"No."

"It's on the box, so you can believe what it says. Scientists study people, then write these things. If you're smart enough you could become a scientist. Like this." Mrs. Markham tapped the box. "It pays well."

Willie ate his cake and drank the milk. When he was done he took care to wipe the crumbs off his face as well as to blot his milk mustache with the napkin. His mother liked him to be neat.

His mother said, "Now go on and do your homework. Carefully. You're in sixth grade. It's important." **A**

A MAKE INFERENCES
Reread lines 34–53. Judging by what Mrs. Markham says and does, how would you describe her?

Willie gathered up his books that lay on the empty third chair. At the kitchen entrance he paused and looked back at his mother. She was staring sadly at the cake box, but he didn't think she was seeing it. Her unhappiness made him think of the man on the street.

"What *kind* of unhappiness do you think he has?" he suddenly asked.

"Who's that?"

"That man."

Mrs. Markham looked puzzled.

"The begging man. The one on the street."

"Oh, could be anything," his mother said, vaguely. "A person can be unhappy for many reasons." She turned to stare out the window, as if an answer might be there.

"Is unhappiness a sickness you can cure?"

"I wish you wouldn't ask such questions."

"Why?"

After a moment she said, "Questions that have no answers shouldn't be asked."

"Can I go out?"

"Homework first."

Willie turned to go again.

"Money," Mrs. Markham suddenly said. "Money will cure a lot of unhappiness. That's why that man was begging. A salesman once said to me, 'Maybe you can't buy happiness, but you can rent a lot of it.' You should remember that."

"How much money do we have?"

"Not enough."

"Is that why you're unhappy?"

"Willie, do your homework." **B**

B SYMBOL
What might money symbolize to Mrs. Markham?

Willie started to ask another question, but decided he would not get an answer. He left the kitchen.

The apartment had three rooms. The walls were painted mint green. Willie walked down the hallway to his room, which was at the front of the building. By climbing up on the windowsill and pressing against the glass he could see the sidewalk five stories below. The man was still there.

It was almost five when he went to tell his mother he had finished his school assignments. He found her in her dim bedroom, sleeping. Since she had begun working the night shift at a convenience store—two weeks now—she took naps in the late afternoon.

For a while Willie stood on the **threshold,** hoping his mother would wake up. When she didn't, he went to the front room and looked down on the street again. The begging man had not moved.

threshold (thrĕsh′ōld′) *n.* a doorway or entrance

Willie returned to his mother's room.

"I'm going out," he announced—softly.

Willie waited a decent interval[1] for his mother to waken. When she did not, he made sure his keys were in his pocket. Then he left the apartment.

By standing just outside the building door, he could keep his eyes on the man. It appeared as if he had still not moved. Willie wondered how anyone could go without moving for so long in the chill October air. Was staying still part of the man's sickness?

During the twenty minutes that Willie watched, no one who passed looked in the beggar's direction. Willie wondered if they even saw the man. Certainly no one put any money into his open hand.

1. **interval:** amount of time.

A lady leading a dog by a leash went by. The dog strained in the direction of the man sitting on the crate. His tail wagged. The lady pulled the dog away. "Heel!" she commanded.

The dog—tail between his legs—scampered to the lady's side. Even so, the dog twisted around to look back at the beggar.

Willie grinned. The dog had done exactly what Willie had done when his mother told him not to stare.

Pressing deep into his pocket, Willie found a nickel. It was warm and slippery. He wondered how much happiness you could rent for a nickel.

Squeezing the nickel between his fingers, Willie walked slowly toward the man. When he came before him, he stopped, suddenly nervous. The man, who appeared to be looking at the ground, did not move his eyes. He smelled bad.

"Here." Willie stretched forward and dropped the coin into the man's open right hand. **C**

C MAKE INFERENCES
Reread lines 113–120. What does Willie's action tell you about his **character?**

"God bless you," the man said hoarsely as he folded his fingers over the coin. His eyes, like high beams on a car, flashed up at Willie, then dropped.

Willie waited for a moment, then went back up to his room. From his window he looked down on the street. He thought he saw the coin in the man's hand, but was not sure.

After supper Mrs. Markham readied herself to go to work, then kissed Willie good night. As she did every night, she said, "If you have regular problems, call Mrs. Murphy downstairs. What's her number?"

"274-8676," Willie said.

"Extra bad problems, call Grandma."

"369-6754."

"Super special problems, you can call me."

"962-6743."

"Emergency, the police."

"911."

"Lay out your morning clothing."

"I will."

"Don't let anyone in the door."

"I won't."

"No television past nine."

"I know."

"But you can read late."

"You're the one who's going to be late," Willie reminded her.

"I'm leaving," Mrs. Markham said.

After she went, Willie stood for a long while in the hallway. The empty apartment felt like a cave that lay deep below the earth. That day in school Willie's teacher had told the class about a kind of fish that lived

At the Aquarium (2003), Jim Macbeth. Digital collage. Photo © Jim Macbeth/SuperStock.

in caves. These fish could not see. They had no eyes. The teacher had said it was living in the dark cave that made them like that.

Willie had raised his hand and asked, "If they want to get out of the cave, can they?"

"I suppose."

"Would their eyes come back?"

"Good question," she said, but did not give an answer. **D**

Before he went to bed, Willie took another look out the window. In the pool of light cast by the street lamp, Willie saw the man.

On Tuesday morning when Willie went to school, the man was gone. But when he came home from school with his mother, he was there again.

"*Please* don't look at him," his mother whispered with some **urgency.**

During his snack, Willie said, "Why shouldn't I look?"

"What are you talking about?"

ANALYZE VISUALS
How do the details in this image connect with the story?

D SYMBOL
Reread lines 145–154. What makes Willie think of the story about the fish with no eyes?

urgency (ûr′jən-sē) *n.* a condition of pressing importance; necessity

"That man. On the street. Begging."

"I told you. He's sick. It's better to act as if you never saw him. When people are that way they don't wish to be looked at."

"Why not?"

Mrs. Markham pondered for a little while. "People are ashamed of being unhappy."

Willie looked thoughtfully at his mother. "Are you sure he's unhappy?"

"You don't have to ask if people are unhappy. They tell you all the time."

"How?"

"The way they look."

"Is that part of the sickness?"

"Oh, Willie, I don't know. It's just the way they are."

Willie **contemplated** the half-inch slice of cake his mother had just given him. A year ago his parents seemed to be perfectly happy. For Willie, the world seemed easy, full of light. Then his father lost his job. He tried to get another but could not. For long hours he sat in dark rooms. Sometimes he drank. His parents began to argue a lot. One day, his father was gone.

contemplate (kŏn'təm-plāt') *v.* to consider carefully and at length

For two weeks his mother kept to the dark. And wept.

Willie looked at his mother. "You're unhappy," he said. "Are *you* ashamed?"

Mrs. Markham sighed and closed her eyes. "I wish you wouldn't ask that."

"Why?"

"It hurts me."

"But are you ashamed?" Willie persisted.

He felt it was urgent that he know. So that he could do something.

She only shook her head.

Willie said, "Do you think Dad might come back?"

She hesitated before saying, "Yes, I think so."

Willie wondered if that was what she really thought.

"Do you think Dad is unhappy?" Willie asked.

"Where do you get such questions?"

"They're in my mind."

"There's much in the mind that need not be paid attention to."

"Fish who live in caves have no eyes."

"What are you talking about?"

"My teacher said it's all that darkness. The fish forget how to see. So they lose their eyes." E

"I doubt she said that."

"She did."

"Willie, you have too much imagination."

E SYMBOL
Reread lines 189–199. What is the connection between the questions Willie is asking his mother and the story about the fish?

After his mother went to work, Willie gazed down onto the street. The man was there. Willie thought of going down, but he knew he was not supposed to leave the building when his mother worked at night. He decided to speak to the man the next day.

That afternoon—Wednesday—Willie stood before the man. "I don't have any money," Willie said. "Can I still talk to you?"

The man lifted his face. It was a dirty face with very tired eyes. He needed a shave.

"My mother," Willie began, "said you were unhappy. Is that true?"

"Could be," the man said.

"What are you unhappy about?"

The man's eyes narrowed as he studied Willie intently. He said, "How come you want to know?"

ANALYZE VISUALS

Compare this man with how you picture the man in the story.

Willie shrugged.

"I think you should go home, kid."

"I am home." Willie gestured toward the apartment. "I live right here. Fifth floor. Where do you live?"

"Around."

"*Are* you unhappy?" Willie persisted.

The man ran a tongue over his lips. His Adam's apple bobbed. "A man has the right to remain silent," he said, and closed his eyes.

Willie remained standing on the pavement for a while before retreating back to his apartment. Once inside he looked down from the window. The man was still there. For a moment Willie was certain the man was looking at the apartment building and the floor where Willie lived.

The next day, Thursday—after dropping a nickel in the man's palm—Willie said, "I've never seen anyone look so unhappy as you do. So I figure you must know a lot about it."

The man took a deep breath. "Well, yeah, maybe."

Willie said, "And I need to find a cure for it."

"A *what?*"

"A cure for unhappiness."

The man pursed his cracked lips and blew a silent whistle. Then he said, "Why?"

"My mother is unhappy."

"Why's that?"

"My dad went away."

"How come?"

"I think because he was unhappy. Now my mother's unhappy too—all the time. So if I found a cure for unhappiness, it would be a good thing, wouldn't it?"

"I suppose. Hey, you don't have anything to eat on you, do you?"

Willie shook his head, then said, "Would you like some cake?"

"What kind?"

"I don't know. Cake."

"Depends on the cake."

On Friday Willie said to the man, "I found out what kind of cake it is."

"Yeah?"

"Pound cake. But I don't know why it's called that."

"Long as it's cake it probably don't matter."

Neither spoke. Then Willie said, "In school my teacher said there are fish who live in caves and the caves are so dark the fish don't have eyes. What do you think? Do you believe that?"

"Sure."

"You do? How come?"

"Because you said so."

"You mean, just because someone *said* it you believe it?"

"Not someone. You." **F**

Willie was puzzled. "But, well, maybe it *isn't* true."

The man grunted. "Hey, do you believe it?"

Willie nodded.

"Well, you're not just anyone. You got eyes. You see. You ain't no fish."

"Oh." Willie was pleased.

"What's your name?" the man asked.

"Willie."

"That's a boy's name. What's your grown-up name?"

"William."

"And that means another thing."

"What?"

"I'll take some of that cake."

Willie started.[2] "You will?" he asked, surprised.

"Just said it, didn't I?"

Willie suddenly felt excited. It was as if the man had given him a gift. Willie wasn't sure what it was except that it was important and he was glad to have it. For a moment he just gazed at the man. He saw the lines on the man's face, the way his lips curved, the small scar on the side of his chin, the shape of his eyes, which he now saw were blue. **G**

"I'll get the cake," Willie cried and ran back to the apartment. He snatched the box from the refrigerator as well as a knife, then hurried back down to the street. "I'll cut you a piece," he said, and he opened the box.

"Hey, that don't look like a pound of cake," the man said.

Willie, alarmed, looked up.

"But like I told you, it don't matter."

Willie held his thumb against the cake to make sure the portion was the right size. With a poke of the knife he made a small mark for the proper width.

Just as he was about to cut, the man said, "Hold it!"

Willie looked up. "What?"

"What were you doing there with your thumb?"

"I was measuring the size. The right portion. A person is supposed to get only one portion."

"Where'd you learn that?"

"It says so on the box. You can see for yourself." He held out the box.

The man studied the box then handed it back to Willie. "That's just lies," he said.

"How do you know?"

"William, how can a box say how much a person needs?"

F COMPARE AND CONTRAST
Why do you think the man believes Willie but his own mother doesn't? How are the man and the mother different?

G MAKE INFERENCES
Reread lines 275–279. What "gift" has the man given Willie?

---

2. **started:** jumped or gave a sudden jerk in surprise.

Celia, Los Angeles, April 10th, 1982, David Hockney. Composite Polaroid, 18″ × 30″. Photo © David Hockney/The David Hockney No. 1 U.S. Trust.

"But it does. The scientists say so. They measured, so they know. Then they put it there."

"Lies," the man repeated.

Willie began to feel that this man knew many things. "Well, then, how much should I cut?" he asked.

The man said, "You have to look at me, then at the cake, and then you're going to have to decide for yourself."

"Oh." Willie looked at the cake. The piece was about three inches wide. Willie looked up at the man. After a moment he cut the cake into two pieces, each an inch and a half wide. He gave one piece to the man and kept the other in the box.

"God bless you," the man said as he took the piece and laid it in his left hand. He began to break off pieces with his right hand and put them in his mouth one by one. Each piece was chewed thoughtfully. Willie watched him eat.

When the man was done, he licked the crumbs on his fingers.

"Now I'll give you something," the man said.

"What?" Willie said, surprised.

"The cure for unhappiness."

"You know it?" Willie asked, eyes wide.

The man nodded.

"What is it?"

"It's this: What a person needs is always more than they say."

"Who's *they?*" Willie asked.

The man pointed to the cake box. "The people on the box," he said.

In his mind Willie repeated what he had been told, then he gave the man the second piece of cake.

The man took it, saying, "Good man," and he ate it.

Willie grinned.

The next day was Saturday. Willie did not go to school. All morning he kept looking down from his window for the man, but it was raining and he did not appear. Willie wondered where he was, but could not imagine it.

Willie's mother woke about noon. Willie sat with her while she ate her breakfast. "I found the cure for unhappiness," he announced.

"Did you?" his mother said. She was reading a memo from the convenience store's owner.

"It's 'What a person needs is always more than they say.'"

His mother put her papers down. "That's nonsense. Where did you hear that?"

ANALYZE VISUALS
Compare the image on page 350 with the one on page 341. What similarities and differences do you see?

"That man."

"What man?"

"On the street. The one who was begging. You said he was unhappy. So I asked him."

"Willie, I told you I didn't want you to even look at that man."

"He's a nice man. . . ."

"How do you know?"

"I've talked to him."

"When? How much?"

Willie shrank down. "I did, that's all."

"Willie, I forbid you to talk to him. Do you understand me? Do you? Answer me!" She was shrill.

"Yes," Willie said, but he'd already decided he would talk to the man one more time. He needed to explain why he could not talk to him anymore.

On Sunday, however, the man was not there. Nor was he there on Monday.

"That man is gone," Willie said to his mother as they walked home from school.

"I saw. I'm not blind."

"Where do you think he went?"

"I couldn't care less. But you might as well know, I arranged for him to be gone."

Willie stopped short. "What do you mean?"

"I called the police. We don't need a nuisance[3] like that around here. Pestering kids."

"He wasn't pestering me."

"Of course he was."

"How do you know?"

"Willie, I have eyes. I can see."

Willie glared at his mother. "No, you can't. You're a fish. You live in a cave." **H**

"Fish?" **retorted** Mrs. Markham. "What do fish have to do with anything? Willie, don't talk nonsense."

"My name isn't Willie. It's William. And I know how to keep from being unhappy. I do!" He was yelling now. "What a person needs is always more than they say! *Always!*" **I**

He turned on his heel and walked back toward the school. At the corner he glanced back. His mother was following. He kept going. She kept following.

H SYMBOL
Reread lines 356–370. Why does Willie compare his mother to the fish living in the cave?

retort (rĭ-tôrt′) *v.* to reply sharply

I MAKE INFERENCES
Reread lines 373–375. Why does Willie now insist that his name is William, not Willie?

3. **nuisance:** someone who is bothersome.

After Reading

Comprehension

1. **Recall** What do Willie and his class learn about a certain kind of fish that lives in caves?
2. **Recall** What does Willie's mother say is wrong with the homeless man?
3. **Retell** Use your own words to retell how the story ends.

ALABAMA STANDARDS

READING STANDARD
2 Relate literary elements and devices to each other

Literary Analysis

4. **Interpret Symbols** The type of fish with no eyes is mentioned many times in this story. What do you think it symbolizes? Now reread lines 34–48 and 286–310. What do you think the pound cake symbolizes?
5. **Make Inferences** Look over the equations you created as you read. What inferences did you make about the **characters** in the story?
6. **Compare and Contrast Characters** The two people in the story who have the greatest influence on Willie are his mom and the homeless man. Compare and contrast how these two characters try to help Willie.
7. **Analyze Theme** Use a chart to help you identify clues the writer provides about the theme of the story. What do you think the theme is?
8. **Evaluate** Willie's mother says, "Parents need to watch their children." Given what you know about her character, do you think she was right or wrong to call the police about the man?

Clues from the Title:	→	*Possible Theme:*
Clues from Symbols:		
Clues from Characters:		
Clues from Plot:		

Extension and Challenge

9. **Big Question Activity** Suppose Willie came to you for a cure for **unhappiness.** Using what you learned about Willie, what advice would you give him? Try giving him advice on specific areas in his life, such as his dad's leaving or his mom's lack of "seeing." Use examples from the story to explain your suggestions. Present your advice to the class.
10. **SOCIAL STUDIES CONNECTION** Find out about organizations and volunteer programs in your community or a nearby city that help people who are homeless or living in poverty. Call or write to one of these organizations to ask for more information about what they do and how young people can help.

Vocabulary in Context

VOCABULARY PRACTICE

Choose *true* or *false* for each statement.

1. If something happens **inevitably,** there is probably no way to avoid it.
2. A **preoccupied** person is one who lives in a house that was previously occupied.
3. A **threshold** can be found at the front of a house.
4. A person walking slowly communicates a feeling of **urgency.**
5. People who **contemplate** art tend to have little respect for culture.
6. If someone **retorts,** he or she is probably irritated or impatient.

contemplate
inevitably
preoccupied
retort
threshold
urgency

VOCABULARY IN WRITING

Using two or more vocabulary words, write a paragraph explaining how Willie came to know the man on the street. You might start like this.

EXAMPLE SENTENCE

Willie began to ***contemplate*** *the man's life while walking home.*

VOCABULARY STRATEGY: GENERAL CONTEXT CLUES

Sometimes you need to figure out the meaning of an unfamiliar word by reading what's around it. You might find **context clues** in the same sentence as the unfamiliar word or in one or more other sentences in the paragraph. For example, a clue to the meaning of *preoccupied* in this story comes in the previous sentence, which says that Willie "was never sure his mother was listening." From this, we know she is often lost in thought, or preoccupied.

PRACTICE Use context clues to determine the definition of each boldfaced word. Then write its definition.

1. Tossing about on their **skiff** in open waters, the passengers got drenched by the thunderstorm.
2. Lola actually made a mistake in counting the election results. She showed that she is **fallible** after all.
3. Mom could not **placate** Peter, no matter how hard she tried. He was determined to remain angry.
4. Wealthy **philanthropists** contribute large sums to charities.
5. Tobias became interested in **philately** once he saw my stamp collection.

ALABAMA STANDARDS

READING STANDARD
1.c Using context clues to determine meaning of words

VOCABULARY PRACTICE
For more practice, go to the **Vocabulary Center** at **ClassZone.com.**

SKILLS PRACTICE

Reading-Writing Connection

Demonstrate your understanding of "What Do Fish Have to Do with Anything?" by responding to these prompts. Then complete the **Grammar and Writing** exercise.

WRITING PROMPTS	SELF-CHECK
A. Short Response: Write a Letter Even though Willie might never see the homeless man again, their brief relationship has made a huge difference in Willie's life. Write a **one-paragraph letter** in which Willie thanks the man for all he did for him.	***A well-written letter will . . .*** • clearly explain why Willie is thanking the man • use details from the story to clarify his reasons
B. Extended Response: Evaluate a Symbol On page 339, you learned that writers often use symbols to help them support ideas they want to share with their readers. Avi chose the fish with no eyes as his main symbol in this story. How does this symbol relate to the idea of **unhappiness?** Write a **two- or three-paragraph response.**	***A strong response will . . .*** • include a clear position statement • use examples from the story to support this position

GRAMMAR AND WRITING

ALABAMA STANDARDS

WRITING/LANGUAGE STANDARD
11.d Using compound sentences

COMBINE SENTENCES You can avoid choppy writing by combining two or more short sentences into one. Use the **coordinating conjunction** *and, but, or, nor, yet, so,* or *for* to join sentences that relate to the same topic. Remember to always put a comma before the coordinating conjunction.

Original: You were friendly. I liked talking to you.

Revised: You were friendly, and I liked talking to you.

PRACTICE Join these sentences by using the correct coordinating conjunctions.

1. You listened to me. You answered my questions.
2. My mom didn't want me to talk to you. I did it anyway.
3. I wanted you to stick around. My mom sent you away.
4. You could come back to stay for good. You could just come for a visit.
5. I miss my conversations with you. I want you to come back.

*For more help with coordinating conjunctions, see page R47 in the **Grammar Handbook.***

Reading for Information

Homeless

Problem-Solution Essay

Use with "What Do Fish Have to Do with Anything?" on page 340.

ALABAMA STANDARDS

READING & LIT STANDARDS
4.d Drawing conclusions
7 Interpret author's message in informational texts

What's the Connection?

In the short story you just read, a mother instructs her son not to look at a homeless man who is begging. In the problem-solution essay you are about to read, Anna Quindlen notes that this is often the way people react to "the homeless," but she recommends a different response.

Skill Focus: Identify Author's Perspective

Your view, or perspective, on a topic is influenced by your experiences, beliefs, and values. For example, if you've had dogs, you might think they're fun. If you haven't, you might be scared of them. Likewise, an **author's perspective**—that is, the way a writer looks at a topic—is influenced by his or her experiences, beliefs, and values.

Here's how to identify Quindlen's perspective on homelessness:

- Notice which parts of the topic Quindlen focuses on.
- Write down direct statements she makes about herself as well as the way she thinks or feels about the topic.
- Note words and details she uses to describe the topic.
- Think about what these elements of her essay tell you about her perspective on being homeless.

As you read Quindlen's essay, use these tips to help you complete a chart like the one started here.

Direct Statements, Descriptive Words, and Other Details	What These Details Tell Me About Quindlen's Perspective
She introduces a homeless woman by name, emphasizing that this woman has a name and is a human being like any one of us.	She views this woman as an individual person first, homeless second.
"I've never been very good at looking at the big picture, taking the global view."	

FOCUS ON FORM "Homeless" is a **problem-solution essay,** a short work of nonfiction in which a writer presents a problem and offers a reasonable solution.

The New York Times B3

Homeless

by Anna Quindlen

Her name was Ann, and we met in the Port Authority Bus Terminal several Januarys ago. I was doing a story on homeless people. She said I was wasting my time talking to her; she was just passing through, although she'd been passing through for more than two weeks. To prove to me that this was true, she rummaged through a tote bag and a manila envelope and finally unfolded a sheet of typing paper and brought out her photographs.

They were not pictures of family, or friends, or even a dog or cat, its eyes brown-red in the flashbulb's light. They were pictures of a house. It was like a thousand houses in a hundred towns, not suburb, not city, but somewhere in between, with aluminum siding and a chainlink fence, a narrow driveway running up to a one-car

garage and a patch of backyard. The house was yellow. I looked on the back for a date or a name, but neither was there. There was no need for discussion. I knew what she was trying to tell me, for it was something I had often felt. She was not adrift, alone, anonymous, although her bags and her raincoat with the grime shadowing its creases had made me believe she was. She had a house, or at least once upon a time had had one. Inside were curtains, a couch, a stove, potholders. You are where you live. She was somebody.

I've never been very good at looking at the big picture, taking the global view, and I've always been a person with an overactive sense of place, the legacy[1] of an Irish grandfather. So it is natural that the thing that seems most wrong with the world to me right now is that there are so many people with no homes. I'm not simply talking about shelter from the elements, or three square meals a day or a mailing address to which the welfare[2] people can send the check—although I know that all these are important for survival. I'm talking about a

1. **legacy** (lĕg′ə-sē): something handed down from an ancestor or from the past.

2. **welfare:** a program of financial aid provided by the government to people in need.

home, about precisely those kinds of feelings that have wound up in cross-stitch and French knots on samplers[3] over the years. **A**

Home is where the heart is. There's no place like it. I love my home with a ferocity totally out of proportion to its appearance or location. I love dumb things about it: the hot-water heater, the plastic rack you drain dishes in, the roof over my head, which occasionally leaks. And yet it is precisely those dumb things that make it what it is—a place of certainty, stability,[4] predictability, privacy, for me and for my family. It is where I live. What more can you say about a place than that? That is everything. **B**

Yet it is something that we have been edging away from gradually during my lifetime and the lifetimes of my parents and grandparents. There was a time when where you lived often was where you worked and where you grew the food you ate and even where you were buried. When that era passed, where you lived at least was where your parents had lived and where you would live with your children when you became enfeebled.[5] Then, suddenly, where you lived was where you lived for three years, until you could move on to something else and something else again.

And so we have come to something else again, to children who do not understand what it means to go to their rooms because they have never had a room, to men and women whose fantasy is a wall they can paint a color of their own choosing, to old people reduced to sitting on molded plastic chairs, their skin blue-white in the lights of a bus station, who pull pictures of houses out of their bags. Homes have stopped being homes. Now they are real estate. **C**

People find it curious that those without homes would rather sleep sitting up on benches or huddled in doorways than go to shelters. Certainly some prefer to do so because they are emotionally ill, because they have been locked in before and they are damned if they will be locked in again. Others are afraid of the violence and trouble they may find there. But some seem to want something that is not available in shelters, and they will not compromise, not for a cot, or oatmeal, or a shower with special soap that kills the bugs. "One room," a woman with a baby who

3. **in cross-stitch and French knots on samplers:** spelled out in fancy stitching and embroidered decorations.

4. **stability:** a condition of being reliable or permanent.

5. **enfeebled:** deprived of strength; made weak.

A AUTHOR'S PERSPECTIVE
What does Quindlen think is most wrong in the world right now? Name two facts she shares about herself to help readers understand her perspective on this issue.

B PROBLEM-SOLUTION ESSAY
Restate the point that Quindlen makes in this paragraph.

C AUTHOR'S PERSPECTIVE
Reread lines 95–109. What does Quindlen say homes have become? What does she mean by this?

was sleeping on her sister's floor, once told me, "painted blue." That was the crux[6] of it; not size or location, but pride of ownership. Painted blue.

This is a difficult problem, and some wise and compassionate people are working hard at it. But in the main I think we work around it, just as we walk around it when it is lying on the sidewalk or sitting in the bus terminal—the problem, that is. It has been customary to take people's pain and lessen our own participation in it by turning it into an issue, not a collection of human beings. We turn an adjective into a noun: the poor, not poor people; the homeless, not Ann or the man who lives in the box or the woman who sleeps on the subway grate. **D**

Sometimes I think we would be better off if we forgot about the broad strokes and concentrated on the details. Here is a woman without a bureau. There is a man with no mirror, no wall to hang it on. They are not the homeless. They are people who have no homes. No drawer that holds the spoons. No window to look out upon the world. My God. That is everything. **E**

6. **crux:** the most important point or element.

D PROBLEM-SOLUTION ESSAY
Reread lines 132–148. How does Quindlen think most people "work around" the problem of homelessness?

E PROBLEM-SOLUTION ESSAY
What does Quindlen recommend that readers do to start addressing the problem she has introduced?

Comprehension

1. **Recall** In Quindlen's opinion, what was Ann trying to tell her by sharing her carefully protected pictures of a house? Explain.
2. **Recall** What do some homeless people want that they cannot get at a shelter? Explain.

Critical Analysis

3. **Analyze Author's Perspective** Review the direct statements and details you noted in your chart. Then pick one and explain what it tells you about Quindlen's perspective on homelessness.
4. **Evaluate a Problem-Solution Essay** A strong problem-solution essay does all of the following: gives a clear picture of the problem, explores its causes and effects, recommends a solution, and explains how to put the solution into effect. Would you say that this essay is a strong problem-solution essay? Why or why not?

Read for Information: Support an Opinion

WRITING PROMPT

In "What Do Fish Have to Do with Anything?" a homeless man tells the main character, "What a person needs is always more than they say" (line 322). Do you think Quindlen would agree with this statement? Why or why not? Support your opinion with evidence from "Homeless."

To answer this prompt, first clarify what the man is saying. You might need to go back to the story to figure this out. Then do as follows:

1. Review your chart to see what you have learned about Quindlen's perspective.
2. Then, keeping her perspective in mind, decide whether she would agree or disagree with the man's statement.
3. Look for evidence in "Homeless" to support your conclusion. For example, you might check whether Quindlen in any way suggests that Ann or the woman with the baby needs more than "they" say.

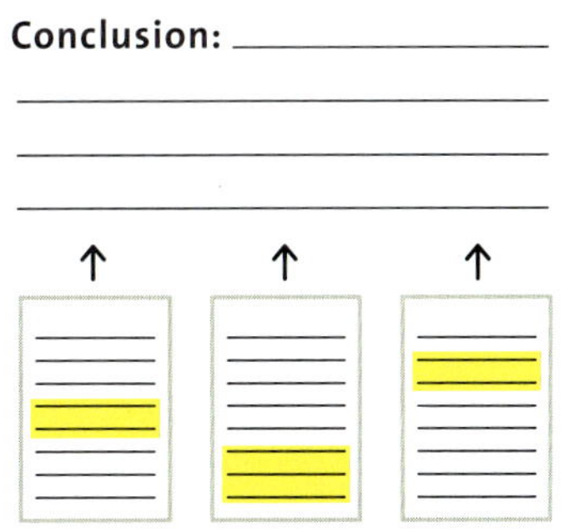

Use evidence from "Homeless" to support your conclusion.

ALABAMA STANDARDS

READING & LIT STANDARDS
4.d Drawing conclusions
7 Interpret author's message in informational texts

A Crush

Short Story by Cynthia Rylant

What makes a GIFT *special?*

ALABAMA STANDARDS

READING & LIT STANDARDS
1.d Applying self-monitoring strategies
7 Interpret author's message in literary texts

KEY IDEA Everyone loves presents, right? Receiving a special **gift** is always a treat, but sometimes giving a gift can be even more rewarding. In the story "A Crush," simple but generous gifts bring about positive changes for both the recipients and the givers.

DISCUSS Gather in a small group to talk about gifts. Consider the following questions: What is the most special gift you have ever received? What is the most special gift you have ever given? How does gift giving make you feel? Do gifts have to cost a lot of money to be special? After your discussion, jot down one or two key points about gifts and giving.

LITERARY ANALYSIS: THEME AND CHARACTER

Paying attention to what **characters** say, do, think, and feel can help you identify a story's **theme,** or message about life. The following questions can guide you:

- What important statements are made by the characters or about the characters?
- What lessons do the characters learn?
- Do any characters change over the course of the story? If so, how do they change?

As you read "A Crush," keep these questions in mind to help you determine the story's theme.

READING SKILL: IDENTIFY CAUSE AND EFFECT

Seeing how things are related can help you understand them. Events in a plot are often related to each other by **cause and effect.** Sometimes, an effect becomes the cause of another event, and so on until the end of the story. This is called a cause-and-effect chain. As you read "A Crush," record events in a chain graphic organizer like the one shown.

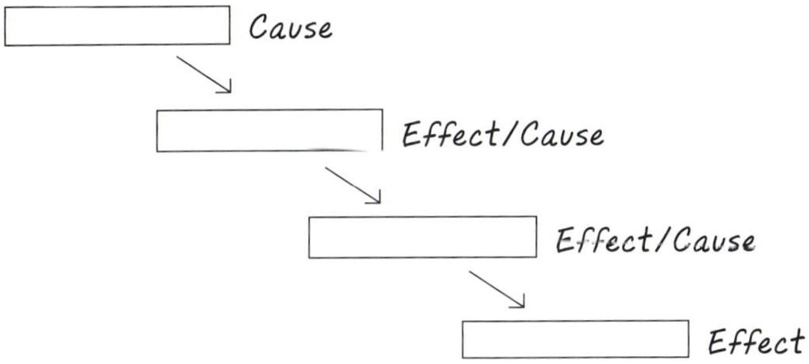

VOCABULARY IN CONTEXT

The words in column A help tell Rylant's story about **giving.** For each word, choose the word or phrase in column B that is related in meaning.

Column A	Column B
1. cherish	**a.** overflow
2. usher	**b.** tall tale
3. improbable	**c.** Valentine card
4. excess	**d.** escort
5. taut	**e.** barely noticed
6. discreetly	**f.** strong knot

Author Online

Humble Beginnings Award-winning author Cynthia Rylant grew up in the mountains of West Virginia. Rylant lived with her grandparents for four years while her mother was in nursing school. Her grandfather was a coal miner, and the family lived in a small house with no plumbing. When Rylant's mother finished school, she found an apartment for herself and her daughter. Rylant says she "felt rich" living there because the building had running water and an indoor bathroom.

Cynthia Rylant
born 1954

MORE ABOUT THE AUTHOR
For more on Cynthia Rylant, visit the **Literature Center** at **ClassZone.com.**

Background

Inspiration In Kent, Ohio, where Cynthia Rylant once lived, a man sometimes brought flowers to the waitresses at a little diner. He was Rylant's inspiration for one of the main characters in "A Crush." Next to the diner was a hardware store. "That's where my imagination found Dolores," said Rylant, referring to another character in the story. Rylant says she enjoys taking "people who don't get any attention in the world and making them really valuable in my fiction—making them absolutely shine with their beauty!"

A CRUSH

CYNTHIA RYLANT

When the windows of Stan's Hardware started filling up with flowers, everyone in town knew something had happened. **Excess** flowers usually mean death, but since these were all real flowers bearing the aroma of nature instead of floral preservative, and since they stood bunched in clear Mason jars[1] instead of impaled on Styrofoam crosses,[2] everyone knew nobody had died. So they all figured somebody had a crush and kept quiet. **A**

There wasn't really a Stan of Stan's Hardware. Dick Wilcox was the owner, and since he'd never liked his own name, he gave his store half the name of his childhood hero, Stan Laurel[3] in the movies. Dick had been married for twenty-seven years. Once, his wife, Helen, had dropped a German chocolate cake on his head at a Lion's Club dance, so Dick and Helen were not likely candidates for the honest expression of the flowers in those clear Mason jars lining the windows of Stan's Hardware, and speculation had to move on to Dolores.

Dolores was the assistant manager at Stan's and had worked there for twenty years, since high school. She knew the store like a mother knows her baby, so Dick—who had trouble keeping up with things like prices and new brands of drywall compound[4]—tried to keep himself busy in the back and give Dolores the run of the floor. This worked fine because the carpenters and plumbers and painters in town trusted Dolores and took her advice to heart. They also liked her tattoo.

excess (ĭk-sĕs') *adj.* too much or too many

A CAUSE AND EFFECT
The first paragraph of this story presents a cause-and-effect relationship. What is the effect of the windows' filling up with flowers?

ANALYZE VISUALS
Why do you think the artist used a "blurry" style for this image?

1. **Mason jars:** glass jars with tight lids, used for canning or preserving foods.
2. **impaled on Styrofoam crosses:** pinned onto crosses made of a lightweight plastic material.
3. **Stan Laurel:** a comedian who with his partner, Oliver Hardy, made comedy films from the 1920s to the 1950s.
4. **drywall compound:** a mixture used to install or repair wallboard, of which the interior walls of many houses are made.

© Bill Firestone.

DAVIS
S. BLADEN
HARDWARE
DAVIS

Dolores was the only woman in town with a tattoo. On the days she went sleeveless, one could see it on the **taut** brown skin of her upper arm: "Howl at the Moon." The picture was of a baying coyote, which must have been a dark gray in its early days but which had faded to the color of the spackling paste[5] Dolores stocked in the third aisle. Nobody had gotten out of Dolores the true story behind the tattoo. Some of the men who came in liked to show off their own, and they'd roll up their sleeves or pull open their shirts, exhibiting bald eagles and rattlesnakes and Confederate flags, and they'd try to coax out of Dolores the history of her coyote. All of the men had gotten their tattoos when they were in the service, drunk on weekend leave and full of the spitfire of young soldiers. Dolores had never been in the service, and she'd never seen weekend leave, and there wasn't a tattoo parlor anywhere near. They couldn't figure why or where any half-sober woman would have a howling coyote ground into the soft skin of her upper arm. But Dolores wasn't telling.

taut (tôt) *adj.* not loose or flabby

That the flowers in Stan's front window had anything to do with Dolores seemed completely **improbable.** As far as anyone knew, Dolores had never been in love, nor had anyone ever been in love with her. Some believed it was the tattoo, of course, or the fine dark hair coating Dolores's upper lip which kept suitors away. Some felt it was because Dolores was just more of a man than most of the men in town, and fellows couldn't figure out how to court someone who knew more about the carburetor of a car or the back side of a washing machine than they did. Others thought Dolores simply didn't want love. This was a popular theory among the women in town who sold Avon and Mary Kay cosmetics. Whenever one of them ran into the hardware for a package of light bulbs or some batteries, she would mentally pluck every one of the black hairs above Dolores's lip. Then she'd wash that grease out of Dolores's hair, give her a good blunt cut, dress her in a decent silk-blend blouse with a nice Liz Claiborne skirt from the Sports line, and, finally, tone down that swarthy, longshoreman look[6] of Dolores's with a concealing beige foundation,[7] some frosted peach lipstick, and a good gray liner for the eyes.

improbable (ĭm-prŏb'ə-bəl) *adj.* not likely

Dolores simply didn't want love, the Avon lady would think as she walked back to her car carrying her little bag of batteries. If she did, she'd fix herself up.

---

5. **spackling paste:** a substance used to repair holes or cracks in plaster.
6. **swarthy, longshoreman look:** darkly tanned skin, like that of a worker who unloads ships all day.
7. **concealing beige foundation:** a liquid makeup that covers skin flaws.

The man who was in love with Dolores and who brought her zinnias and cornflowers and nasturtiums and marigolds and asters and four-o'clocks in clear Mason jars did not know any of this. He did not know that men showed Dolores their tattoos. He did not know that Dolores understood how to use and to sell a belt sander.[8] He did not know that Dolores needed some concealing beige foundation so she could get someone to love her. The man who brought flowers to Dolores on Wednesdays when the hardware opened its doors at 7:00 A.M. didn't care who Dolores had ever been or what anyone had ever thought of her. He loved her, and he wanted to bring her flowers. (B)

(B) THEME AND CHARACTER
How is the man who loves Dolores different from other people in town?

Ernie had lived in this town all of his life and had never before met Dolores. He was thirty-three years old, and for thirty-one of those years he had lived at home with his mother in a small dark house on the edge of town near Beckwith's Orchards. Ernie had been a beautiful baby, with a shock of shining black hair and large blue eyes and a round, wise face. But as he had grown, it had become clearer and clearer that though he was indeed a perfectly beautiful child, his mind had not developed with the same perfection. Ernie would not be able to speak in sentences until he was six years old. He would not be able to count the apples in a bowl until he was eight. By the time he was ten, he could sing a simple song. At age twelve, he understood what a joke was. And when he was twenty, something he saw on television made him cry.

Ernie's mother kept him in the house with her because it was easier, so Ernie knew nothing of the world except this house. They lived, the two of them, in tiny dark rooms always illuminated by the glow of a television set, Ernie's bags of Oreos and Nutter Butters littering the floor, his baseball cards scattered across the sofa, his heavy winter coat thrown over the arm of a chair so he could wear it whenever he wanted, and his box of Burpee[9] seed packages sitting in the middle of the kitchen table.

These Ernie **cherished.** The seeds had been delivered to his home by mistake. One day a woman wearing a brown uniform had pulled up in a brown truck, walked quickly to the front porch of Ernie's house, set a box down, and with a couple of toots of her horn, driven off again. Ernie had watched her through the curtains and, when she was gone, had ventured onto the porch and shyly, cautiously, picked up the box. His mother checked it when he carried it inside. The box didn't have their name on it, but the brown truck was gone, so whatever was in the box was theirs to keep. Ernie pulled off the heavy tape, his fingers trembling, and found inside the box more little packages of seeds than he could count. He lifted them out, one by one, and examined the beautiful photographs of

cherish (chĕr'ĭsh) *v.* to care for deeply

8. **belt sander:** a machine that uses a rough-textured moving belt to smooth surfaces.

9. **Burpee:** W. Atlee Burpee and Co. is the world's largest mail-order seed company.

flowers on each. His mother was not interested, had returned to the television, but Ernie sat down at the kitchen table and quietly looked at each package for a long time, his fingers running across the slick paper and outlining the shapes of zinnias and cornflowers and nasturtiums and marigolds and asters and four-o'clocks, his eyes drawing up their colors. **C**

C THEME AND CHARACTER
Reread lines 98–103. Why do you think the seeds are so interesting to Ernie?

Two months later Ernie's mother died. A neighbor found her at the mailbox beside the road. People from the county courthouse came out to get Ernie, and as they **ushered** him from the home he would never see again, he picked up the box of seed packages from his kitchen table and passed through the doorway.

usher (ŭsh'ər) *v.* to guide in a certain direction

Eventually Ernie was moved to a large white house near the main street of town. This house was called a group home, because in it lived a group of people who, like Ernie, could not live on their own. There were six of them. Each had his own room. When Ernie was shown the room that would be his, he put the box of Burpee seeds—which he had kept with him since his mother's death—on the little table beside the bed, and then he sat down on the bed and cried.

Ernie cried every day for nearly a month. And then he stopped. He dried his tears, and he learned how to bake refrigerator biscuits and how to dust mop and what to do if the indoor plants looked brown. **D**

D CAUSE AND EFFECT
Reread lines 104–118. How does the death of Ernie's mother affect Ernie's life?

Ernie loved watering the indoor plants, and it was this pleasure which finally drew him outside. One of the young men who worked at the group home—a college student named Jack—grew a large garden in the back of the house. It was full of tomato vines and the large yellow blossoms of healthy squash. During his first summer at the house, Ernie would stand at the kitchen window, watching Jack and sometimes a resident of the home move among the vegetables. Ernie was curious but too afraid to go into the garden.

Then one day when Ernie was watching through the window, he noticed that Jack was ripping open several slick little packages and emptying them into the ground. Ernie panicked and ran to his room. But the box of Burpee seeds was still there on his table, untouched. He grabbed it, slid it under his bed, then went back through the house and out into the garden as if he had done this every day of his life.

He stood beside Jack, watching him empty seed packages into the soft black soil, and as the packages were emptied, Ernie asked for them, holding out his hand, his eyes on the photographs of red radishes and purple eggplant. Jack handed the empty packages over with a smile and with that gesture became Ernie's first friend.

Jack tried to explain to Ernie that the seeds would grow into vegetables, but Ernie could not believe this until he saw it come true. And when it did, he looked all the more intently at the packages of zinnias and cornflowers and the rest hidden beneath his bed. He thought more deeply about them, but he could not carry them to the garden. He could not let the garden have his seeds.

That was the first year in the large white house.

The second year, Ernie saw Dolores, and after that he thought of nothing else but her and of the photographs of flowers beneath his bed.

Jack had decided to take Ernie downtown for breakfast every Wednesday morning to ease him into the world outside that of the group home. They left very early, at 5:45 A.M., so there would be few people and almost no traffic to frighten Ernie and make him beg for his room. Jack and Ernie drove to the Big Boy restaurant which sat across the street from Stan's Hardware. There they ate eggs and bacon and French toast among those whose work demanded rising before the sun: bus drivers, policemen, nurses, mill workers. Their first time in the Big Boy, Ernie was too nervous to eat. The second time, he could eat, but he couldn't look up. The third time, he not only ate everything on his plate, but he lifted his head and he looked out the window of the Big Boy restaurant toward Stan's Hardware across the street. There he saw a dark-haired woman in jeans and a black T-shirt unlocking the front door of the building, and that was the moment Ernie started loving Dolores and thinking about giving up his seeds to the soft black soil of Jack's garden.

Love is such a mystery, and when it strikes the heart of one as mysterious as Ernie himself, it can hardly be spoken of. Ernie could not explain to Jack why he went directly to his room later that morning, pulled the box of Burpee seeds from under his bed, then grabbed Jack's hand in the kitchen and walked with him to the garden, where Ernie had come to believe things would grow. Ernie handed the packets of seeds one by one to Jack, who stood in silent admiration of the lovely photographs before asking Ernie several times, "Are you sure you want to plant these?" Ernie was sure. It didn't take him very long, and when the seeds all lay under the moist black earth, Ernie carried his empty packages inside the house and spent the rest of the day spreading them across his bed in different arrangements. (E)

(E) THEME AND CHARACTER
Reread lines 162–173. Why does Ernie suddenly want to grow flowers after he sees Dolores?

That was in June. For the next several Wednesdays at 7:00 A.M. Ernie watched every movement of the dark-haired woman behind the lighted windows of Stan's Hardware. Jack watched Ernie watch Dolores and **discreetly** said nothing.

discreetly (dĭ-skrēt′lē) *adv.* in a manner that shows caution and good judgment

When Ernie's flowers began growing in July, Ernie spent most of his time in the garden. He would watch the garden for hours, as if he expected it suddenly to move or to impress him with a quick trick. The fragile green stems of his flowers stood uncertainly in the soil, like baby colts on their first legs, but the young plants performed no magic for Ernie's eyes. They saved their shows for the middle of the night and next day surprised Ernie with tender small blooms in all the colors the photographs had promised.

The flowers grew fast and hardy, and one early Wednesday morning when they looked as big and bright as their pictures on the empty packages, Ernie pulled a glass canning jar off a dusty shelf in the basement of his house. He washed the jar, half filled it with water, then carried it to the garden, where he placed in it one of every kind of flower he had grown. He met Jack at the car and rode off to the Big Boy with the jar of flowers held tight between his small hands. Jack told him it was a beautiful bouquet.

VISUAL VOCABULARY

Mason jar *n.* a jar with a wide opening and a twist-on lid, used for canning and preserving foods

When they reached the door of the Big Boy, Ernie stopped and pulled at Jack's arm, pointing to the building across the street. "OK," Jack said, and he led Ernie to the front door of Stan's Hardware. It was 6:00 A.M., and the building was still dark. Ernie set the clear Mason jar full of flowers under the sign that read "Closed," then he smiled at Jack and followed him back across the street to get breakfast.

When Dolores arrived at seven and picked up the jar of zinnias and cornflowers and nasturtiums and marigolds and asters and four-o'clocks, Ernie and Jack were watching her from a booth in the Big Boy. Each had a wide smile on his face as Dolores put her nose to the flowers. Ernie giggled. They watched the lights of the hardware store come up and saw Dolores place the clear Mason jar on the ledge of the front window. They drove home still smiling.

All the rest of that summer Ernie left a jar of flowers every Wednesday morning at the front door of Stan's Hardware. Neither Dick Wilcox nor Dolores could figure out why the flowers kept coming, and each of them assumed somebody had a crush on the other. But the flowers had an effect on them anyway. Dick started spending more time out on the floor making conversation with the customers, while Dolores stopped wearing T-shirts to work and instead wore crisp white blouses with the sleeves rolled back off her wrists. Occasionally she put on a bracelet. **F**

By summer's end Jack and Ernie had become very good friends, and when the flowers in the garden behind their house began to wither, and Ernie's face began to grow gray as he watched them, Jack brought home one bright day in late September a great long box. Ernie followed Jack as he carried it down to the basement and watched as Jack pulled a long glass tube from the box and attached this tube to the wall above a table. When Jack plugged in the tube's electric cord, a soft lavender light washed the room.

"Sunshine," said Jack. **G**

Then he went back to his car for a smaller box. He carried this down to the basement, where Ernie still stood staring at the strange light. Jack handed Ernie the small box, and when Ernie opened it, he found more little packages of seeds than he could count, with new kinds of photographs on the slick paper.

"Violets," Jack said, pointing to one of them.

Then he and Ernie went outside to get some dirt.

F CAUSE AND EFFECT
Reread lines 207–214. What effect do the flowers have on Dick and Dolores?

G THEME AND CHARACTER
How is Jack's gift to Ernie like Ernie's gift to Dolores?

© Bill Firestone.

Comprehension

ALABAMA STANDARDS

LITERATURE STANDARD
7 Interpret author's message in literary texts

1. **Recall** How is Ernie different from other people?
2. **Represent** Using stick figures with labels to represent **characters,** draw the scene in which Ernie first gets a crush on Dolores.
3. **Clarify** How does Jack help Ernie at the end of the story?

Literary Analysis

4. **Make Inferences** Reflect on Jack's character. What gifts does he give Ernie in addition to seeds and a light?
5. **Analyze Character** Ernie changes a great deal from the time he receives the box of seeds to the end of the story. Note details about significant changes in his life and his behavior in a diagram such as the one shown. Using your notes, analyze how Ernie's behavior changes.

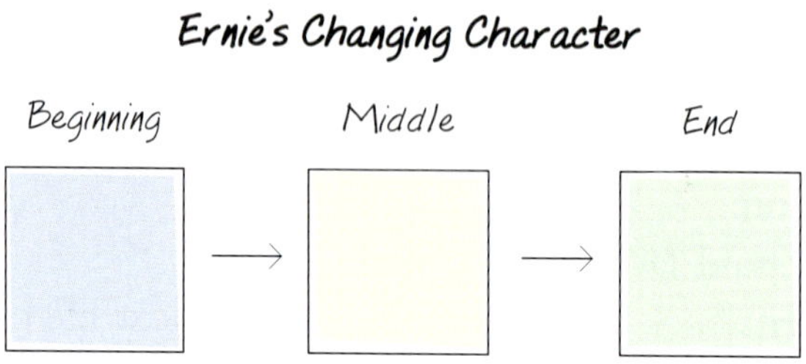

6. **Analyze Cause and Effect** Look at the cause-and-effect chain you created as you read. On the basis of your notes, which event would you say had the most significant effect on Ernie's life? Why?
7. **Identify Theme** Review the questions you asked yourself as you read (see page 363). What did the characters learn in this story? Restate the lesson or lessons as a theme.
8. **Evaluate Point of View** This story is told from a **third-person omniscient point of view,** in which the narrator is an invisible observer who can get into the minds of all the characters. Why is that the best point of view for the author to use in "A Crush"?

Extension and Challenge

9. **Big Question Activity** Newspapers often include stories about local events like those that take place in this story. Write a newspaper article about how Dolores's life changes because of the anonymous gifts of flowers. Think about how she might answer the discussion questions on page 362, about what makes a **gift** special. Remember to include a catchy headline for your article!

THE LOCAL NEWS

STAN'S HARDWARE STORE BLOOMS

Jack B. Nimble

A local woman found herself the focus of a romantic mystery recently when an unidentified person began leaving flowers at her workplace every Wednesday morning. Dolores, who has worked at Stan's Hardware for nearly twenty years, is surprised by all the attention she's been getting since the flowers started arriving. "It's like one day no one noticed me, and the next day everyone did," she commented. "I suddenly feel so special."

Dolores's friends and neighbors say

remarkable change in her since the mystery crush began. "She's a new woman," said Helen Wilcox, the wife of the store's owner. "It's been great to see the changes in her . . . and in my husband."

Dick Wilcox, who was originally believed to be the focus of the anonymous crush, is said to have become much friendlier toward customers. Sales at the hardware store have increased significantly in recent weeks, keeping Wilcox

Vocabulary in Context

VOCABULARY PRACTICE

Use context clues to identify the vocabulary word that best completes each sentence.

1. Dolores was a hard-working woman with _____ muscles.
2. For Ernie to fall in love with Dolores at one glance might seem _____.
3. Nevertheless, he began to _____ her from the first day he saw her.
4. Jack kindly helped to _____ Ernie into the world of gardening.
5. Ernie made a large bouquet of flowers, but he still had _____ flowers in his garden.
6. Not wanting to be noticed, Ernie _____ delivered it early in the morning.

cherish
discreetly
excess
improbable
taut
usher

VOCABULARY IN WRITING

How many people's lives do you think Ernie affected? Write a paragraph explaining your opinion, using two or more vocabulary words. Here is a sample opening sentence.

EXAMPLE SENTENCE

*The way that Ernie **cherished** Dolores affected several people.*

VOCABULARY STRATEGY: FORMS OF THE PREFIX *in-*

As you have learned, the prefix *in-* often means "not." This prefix may have various spellings, depending on the letter that follows it.

- When added to words beginning with *b, m,* or *p,* it is spelled *im-*, as in the vocabulary word *improbable.*
- For words beginning with *l,* it is spelled *il-,* as in the word *illogical.*
- For words beginning with *r,* it is spelled *ir-,* as in the word *irreversible.*

Learning to recognize this prefix with its various spellings can help you figure out the meanings of many words.

PRACTICE Choose the word in each group that contains a correctly spelled prefix meaning "not." Then use the word in a sentence.

1. inproper, inperfect, impossible
2. irresponsible, irelevant, iregular
3. imcapable, imhospitable, intolerant
4. imature, imobile, immortal
5. iladvisable, illegal, inlogical
6. ireparable, irreplaceable, iresistible

VOCABULARY PRACTICE
For more practice, go to the **Vocabulary Center** at **ClassZone.com.**

Great Reads

The Giver

Fantasy Novel by Lois Lowry

Lois Lowry
born 1937

Other Books by Lois Lowry

- *Anastasia Krupnik*
- *Gathering Blue*
- *Messenger*
- *Number the Stars*
- *Rabble Starkey*
- *A Summer to Die*

Meet Lois Lowry

By the time she was three, Lois Lowry had already learned to read, so books played an important role in her childhood. "I was a solitary child who lived in the world of books and my own vivid imagination," she says. "That is how I write—I go back to the child I was and see things through those eyes."

Though she always loved reading and writing stories, Lowry didn't begin writing full-time until after she went to college, married, and raised her four children. She is now the author of over 30 books and has won many awards for her work.

It's no wonder people like Lowry's books so much. To her, there are stories in the most ordinary of life's events. Because of this Lowry's readers find themselves able to identify with the characters she creates and the things that happen to them in her stories.

Try a Fantasy Novel

Many of Lowry's books are a type of literature called **fantasy.** In a fantasy novel, you can travel to a different world where you'll find at least one element that is completely unreal and could exist only in the imagination. The setting might be strange, events might sound impossible, or you might read about characters with superhuman abilities.

Read a Great Book

Lois Lowry puts her astonishing imagination to work in *The Giver,* a novel about a 12-year-old boy named Jonas, who lives in a world without fear of pain, hunger, poverty, or crime. Community leaders control everything, including what indviduals are allowed to say and do. Upon turning 12, children are given specific roles in the community, based on their abilities.

In the following section from the book, the day of assignments has arrived. Jonas anxiously awaits the decision of the Elders.

from the Giver

Now Father sat beside Mother in the audience. Jonas could see them applauding dutifully as the Nines, one by one, wheeled their new bicycles, each with its gleaming nametag attached to the back, from the stage. . . .

Finally the Nines were all resettled in their seats, each having wheeled a bicycle outside where it would be waiting for its owner at the end of the day. Everyone always chuckled and made small jokes when the Nines rode home for the first time. "Want me to show you how to ride?" older friends would call. "I know you've never been on a bike before!" But invariably the grinning Nines, who in technical violation of the rule had been practicing secretly for weeks, would mount and ride off in perfect balance, training wheels never touching the ground.

Then the Tens. Jonas never found the Ceremony of Ten particularly interesting—only time-consuming, as each child's hair was snipped neatly into its distinguishing cut: females lost their braids at Ten, and males, too, relinquished their long childish hair and took on the more manly short style which exposed their ears.

Laborers moved quickly to the stage with brooms and swept away the mounds of discarded hair. Jonas could see the parents of the new Tens stir and murmur, and he knew that this evening, in many dwellings, they would be snipping and straightening the hastily done haircuts, trimming them into a neater line.

Elevens. It seemed a short time ago that Jonas had undergone the Ceremony of Eleven, but he remembered that it was not one of the more interesting ones. By Eleven, one was only waiting to be Twelve. It was simply a marking of time with no meaningful changes. There was new clothing: different undergarments for the females, whose bodies were beginning to change; and longer trousers for the males, with a specially shaped pocket for the small calculator that they would use this year in school; but those were simply presented in wrapped packages without an accompanying speech.

Break for midday meal. Jonas realized he was hungry. He and his groupmates congregated by the tables in front of the Auditorium and took their packaged food. Yesterday there had been merriment at lunch, a lot of teasing, and energy. But today the group stood anxiously separate from the other children. Jonas watched the new Nines gravitate toward their waiting bicycles, each one admiring his or her nametag. He saw the Tens stroking their new shortened hair, the females shaking their heads to feel the unaccustomed lightness without the heavy braids they had worn so long.

"I heard about a guy who was absolutely certain he was going to be assigned Engineer," Asher muttered as they ate, "and instead they gave him Sanitation Laborer. He went out the next day, jumped into the river, swam across, and joined the next community he came to. Nobody ever saw him again."

Jonas laughed. "Somebody made that story up, Ash," he said. "My father said he heard that story when *he* was a Twelve."

But Asher wasn't reassured. He was eyeing the river where it was visible behind the Auditorium. "I can't even swim very well," he said. "My swimming instructor said that I don't have the right boyishness or something."

"Buoyancy," Jonas corrected him.

"Whatever. I don't have it. I sink."

"Anyway," Jonas pointed out, "have you ever once known of anyone—I mean really known for sure, Asher, not just heard a story about it—who joined another community?"

"No," Asher admitted reluctantly. "But you can. It says so in the rules. If you don't fit in, you can apply for Elsewhere and be released. My mother says that once, about ten years ago, someone applied and was gone the next day." Then he chuckled. "She told me that because I was driving her crazy. She threatened to apply for Elsewhere."

"She was joking."

"I know. But it was true, what she said, that someone did that once. She said that it was really true. Here today and gone tomorrow. Never seen again. Not even a Ceremony of Release."

Jonas shrugged. It didn't worry him. How could someone not fit in? The community was so meticulously ordered, the choices so carefully made.

Even the Matching of Spouses was given such weighty consideration that sometimes an adult who applied to receive a spouse waited months or even *years* before a Match was approved and announced. All of the factors—disposition, energy level, intelligence, and interests—had to correspond and to interact perfectly. Jonas's mother, for example, had a higher intelligence than his father, but his father had a calmer disposition. They balanced each other. Their match, which like all Matches had been monitored by the Committee of Elders for three years before they could apply for children, had always been a successful one.

Like the Matching of Spouses and the Naming and Placement of newchildren, the Assignments were scrupulously thought through by the Committee of Elders.

He was certain that his Assignment, whatever it was to be, and Asher's too, would be the right one for them. He only wished that the midday break would conclude, that the audience would reenter the Auditorium, and the suspense would end.

As if in answer to his unspoken wish, the signal came and the crowd began to move toward the doors.

Now Jonas's group had taken a new place in the Auditorium, trading with the new Elevens, so that they sat in the very front, immediately before the stage.

They were arranged by their original numbers, the numbers they had been given at birth. The numbers were rarely used after the Naming. But each child knew his number, of course. Sometimes parents used them in irritation at a child's misbehavior, indicating that mischief made one unworthy of a name. Jonas always chuckled when he heard a parent, exasperated, call sharply to a whining toddler, "That's *enough,* Twenty-three!"

Jonas was Nineteen. He had been the nineteenth newchild born his year. It had meant that at his Naming, he had been already standing and bright-eyed, soon to walk and talk. It had given him a slight advantage the first year or two, a little more maturity than many of his groupmates who had been born in the later months of that year. But it evened out, as it always did, by Three.

After Three, the children progressed at much the same level, though by their first number one could always tell who was a few months older than others in his group. Technically, Jonas's full number was Eleven-nineteen, since there were other Nineteens, of course, in each age group. And today, now that the new Elevens had been advanced this morning, there were *two* Eleven-nineteens. At the midday break he had exchanged smiles with the new one, a shy female named Harriet.

But the duplication was only for these few hours. Very soon he would not be an Eleven but a Twelve, and age would no longer matter. He would be an adult, like his parents, though a new one and untrained still.

Asher was Four, and sat now in the row ahead of Jonas. He would receive his Assignment fourth.

Fiona, Eighteen, was on his left; on his other side sat Twenty, a male named Pierre whom Jonas didn't like much. Pierre was very serious, not much fun, and a worrier and tattletale, too. "Have you checked the rules, Jonas?" Pierre was always whispering solemnly. "I'm not sure that's within the rules." Usually it was some foolish thing that no one cared about—opening his tunic if it was a day with a breeze; taking a brief try on a friend's bicycle, just to experience the different feel of it.

The initial speech at the Ceremony of Twelve was made by the Chief Elder, the leader of the community who was elected every ten years. The speech was much the same each year: recollection of the time of childhood and the period of preparation, the coming responsibilities of adult life, the profound importance of Assignment, the seriousness of training to come.

Then the Chief Elder moved ahead in her speech.

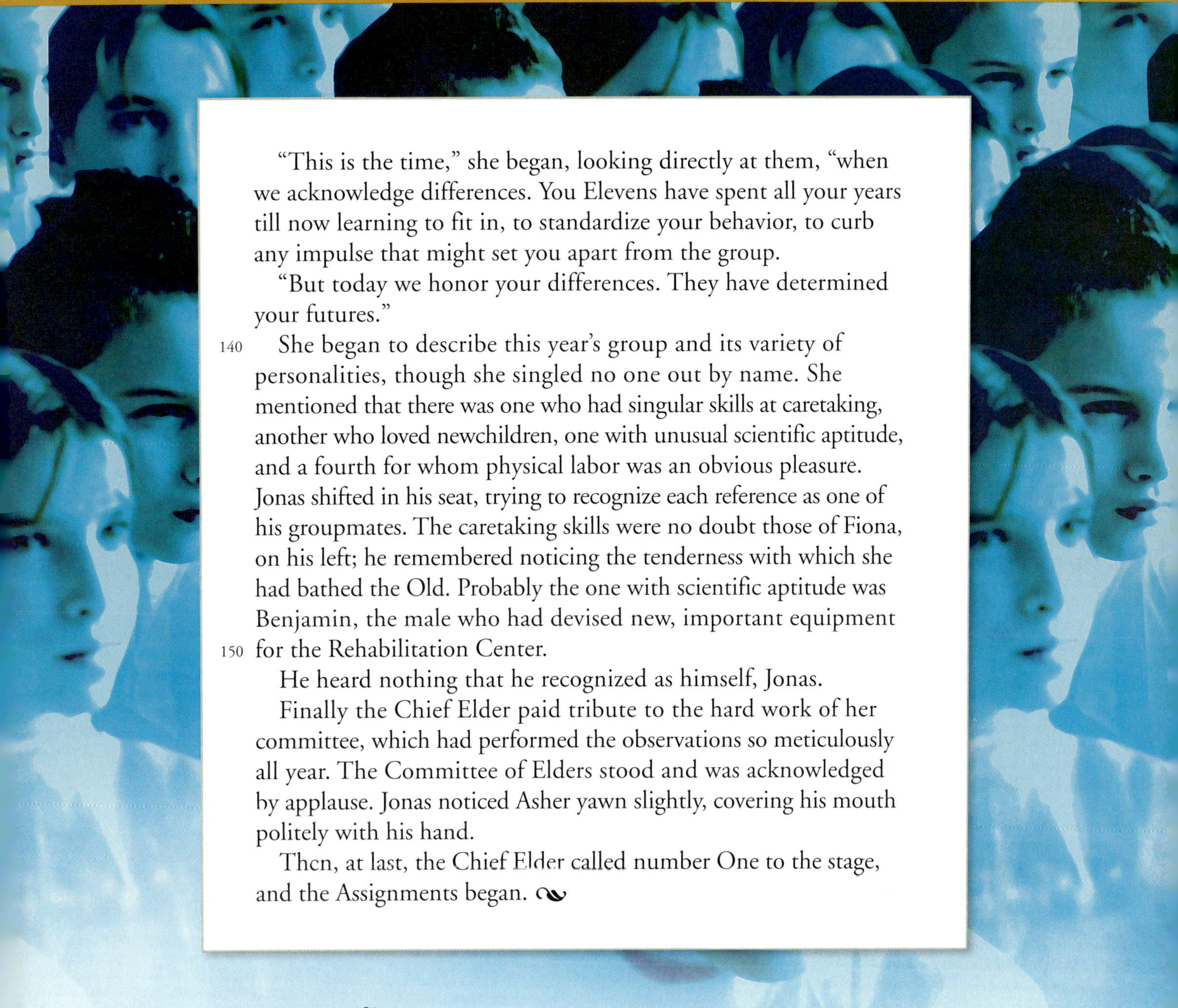

"This is the time," she began, looking directly at them, "when we acknowledge differences. You Elevens have spent all your years till now learning to fit in, to standardize your behavior, to curb any impulse that might set you apart from the group.

"But today we honor your differences. They have determined your futures."

She began to describe this year's group and its variety of personalities, though she singled no one out by name. She mentioned that there was one who had singular skills at caretaking, another who loved newchildren, one with unusual scientific aptitude, and a fourth for whom physical labor was an obvious pleasure. Jonas shifted in his seat, trying to recognize each reference as one of his groupmates. The caretaking skills were no doubt those of Fiona, on his left; he remembered noticing the tenderness with which she had bathed the Old. Probably the one with scientific aptitude was Benjamin, the male who had devised new, important equipment for the Rehabilitation Center.

He heard nothing that he recognized as himself, Jonas.

Finally the Chief Elder paid tribute to the hard work of her committee, which had performed the observations so meticulously all year. The Committee of Elders stood and was acknowledged by applause. Jonas noticed Asher yawn slightly, covering his mouth politely with his hand.

Then, at last, the Chief Elder called number One to the stage, and the Assignments began.

Keep Reading

You've just gotten a sense of the community Jonas lives in. What details about the group seemed strange to you? To learn more about this strange community, read more of *The Giver.* You'll discover how Jonas is assigned to become the new Receiver of Memory for his community and begins training with a man known as The Giver. Once Jonas learns the truth about his society and how it compares to the larger world, he finds that he has some difficult choices to make.

Comparing Themes

Spring Harvest of Snow Peas

Poem by Maxine Hong Kingston

Eating Alone

Poem by Li-Young Lee

Can you be alone and not LONELY?

ALABAMA STANDARDS

LITERATURE STANDARDS

7 Interpret author's message in literary texts

8 Compare selections and their characteristics

KEY IDEA Some people love to be alone. Others get bored or sad when no one else is around or feel **lonely** even when they are with other people. In the two poems you are about to read, the speakers share their thoughts and feelings about being alone.

DISCUSS What advice would you give to someone who is feeling lonely when alone? Work with a partner to list ways to overcome loneliness. Then share your insights with the class to come up with a master list of "loneliness busters."

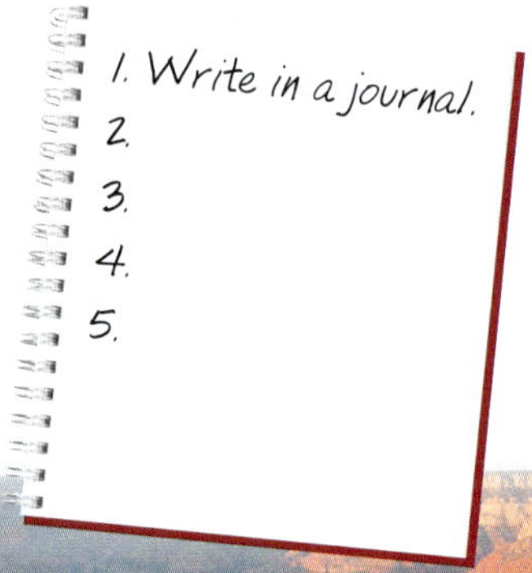

LITERARY ANALYSIS: RECURRING THEME

How many stories and poems have you read that conveyed the message "Love is all you need" or "Growing up is difficult"? You've probably come across these themes fairly often. When the same theme is presented in more than one piece of literature, it is called a **recurring theme.**

The two poems you are about to read have a common theme, but the poets express it differently. As you read each poem, pay attention to the following elements. They will help you find the poems' shared message.

- title
- subjects presented
- words and phrases that describe the speaker's feelings
- **images,** or words and phrases that help you know how things look, feel, smell, sound, or taste

READING STRATEGY: SET A PURPOSE FOR READING

Sometimes your purpose for reading might be to relax with a good book. At other times it might be to get information. In this lesson, your **purpose for reading** the two poems is to identify the recurring theme and compare the ways the poets communicate it.

After you've read "Spring Harvest of Snow Peas" and "Eating Alone," read the poems again. This time, fill in a chart like the one shown. You will be asked to do more with this chart after you finish reading.

	"Spring Harvest of Snow Peas"	"Eating Alone"
What idea is described in the title?		
What subjects are presented?	garden, mother, food	garden, father, food
How is the speaker feeling?		
What important images can you find?		

Author Online

Maxine Hong Kingston: Lifelong Poet Maxine Hong Kingston grew up listening to her mother's bedtime stories and began writing poetry when she was in the fourth grade. She has since become one of the best-known Asian-American writers of nonfiction, fiction, and poetry. As the child of Chinese immigrants, Kingston often focuses her writing on her cultural heritage.

Maxine Hong Kingston
born 1940

Li-Young Lee: Master of Imagery Li-Young Lee's first language was Chinese. He didn't speak English until he moved to the United States in 1964 with his parents. Yet Lee's artistic mastery of English is clear in his award-winning poetry, which has been praised for its imagery and the "brave honesty" of its language.

Li-Young Lee
born 1957

MORE ABOUT THE AUTHOR
For more on Maxine Hong Kingston and Li-Young Lee, visit the **Literature Center** at **ClassZone.com.**

Detail of *Birds XII* (2003), Barbara Weldon. Oil, gold leaf, and wax on canvas, 60″ × 72″.

spring harvest *of* snow peas

Maxine Hong Kingston

They're taller than me.
I taste and eat as I pick along,
choose the flat big ones and baby ones,
and leave the bulging pods for shelling or seed.
The purple and lavender blossoms
and the blue blossoms wave above me
and touch my neck.
I stand on the ledge of the box, reach for more,
and remember my mother and father growing
    snow peas[1] every season. (A)
When she could hardly see anymore, my mother
    showed me
by feel how to plant 3 seeds per mound.
Every day, enough for dinner, and for leaving
    at neighbors' doors.
The birds surround me and eat and sing. I am
    unequivocally happy.

(A) THEME
Reread lines 1–10. How does the speaker seem to feel about being in the garden?

1. **snow peas:** peas of a type having a soft outer pod.

Detail of *Birds III* (2002), Barbara Weldon. Oil, gold leaf, and wax on canvas, 40″ × 40″.

EATING alone

Li-Young Lee

I've pulled the last of the year's young onions.
The garden is bare now. The ground is cold,
brown and old. What is left of the day flames
in the maples at the corner of my
eye. I turn, a cardinal vanishes.
By the cellar door, I wash the onions,
then drink from the icy metal spigot.

Once, years back, I walked beside my father
among the windfall pears. I can't recall
our words. We may have strolled in silence. But
I still see him bend that way—left hand braced
on knee, creaky—to lift and hold to my
eye a rotten pear. In it, a hornet
spun crazily, glazed in slow, glistening juice.

It was my father I saw this morning
waving to me from the trees. I almost
called to him, until I came close enough
to see the shovel, leaning where I had
left it, in the flickering, deep green shade. B

White rice steaming, almost done. Sweet green peas
fried in onions. Shrimp braised in sesame
oil and garlic. And my own loneliness.
What more could I, a young man, want.

B THEME
Reread lines 8–19. Note what the speaker remembers about his father. Are they positive memories?

Comprehension

1. **Recall** Where is the speaker in "Spring Harvest of Snow Peas"?
2. **Recall** What is one reason why the speaker in the second poem is eating alone?
3. **Clarify** How does the last stanza of "Eating Alone" connect with the first stanza?

ALABAMA STANDARDS

LITERATURE STANDARD
8 Compare selections and their characteristics

Literary Analysis

4. **Make Inferences** Reread lines 11–15 of "Spring Harvest of Snow Peas." What do you learn about the speaker's mother?
5. **Draw Conclusions** How do you think the speaker in "Eating Alone" feels about the meal he is fixing? Note the words or phrases that give you clues about his feelings.
6. **Identify Symbols** What does the food in each poem symbolize, or stand for beyond its usual meaning?
7. **Analyze** Note which season it is in each poem. How does the choice of season affect the meaning of each poem?

Comparing Themes

Now that you've read both poems, finish filling in the chart. Then use the answers to the questions to help you identify the **recurring theme** in the poems.

	"Spring Harvest of Snow Peas"	"Eating Alone"
What idea is described in the title?		
What subjects are presented?	garden, mother, food	garden, father, food
How is the speaker feeling?		
What important images can you find?		
What theme do the poems have in common?		

Writing for Assessment

1. READ THE PROMPT

In writing assessments, you will often be asked to compare selections that share a **recurring theme.**

PROMPT

While "Spring Harvest of Snow Peas" and "Eating Alone" share a recurring theme, Maxine Hong Kingston and Li-Young Lee express the theme differently. In four or five paragraphs, compare and contrast the ways the poets get the theme across. Support your response with details from the poems.

STRATEGIES IN ACTION

1. I have to make sure I understand what **message** the poems share.
2. I need to identify the **similarities and differences** in the ways the poets express the message.
3. I should include **details** from the poems to show what I mean.

2. PLAN YOUR WRITING

Using the chart you filled out for the poems, note how each poet develops the theme. Write a position statement that expresses the main similarities and differences you find in the poets' methods. Then decide how you will set up your response.

- Do you want to focus on one poem first and then show how the other poem is similar and different, as shown in the sample outline?
- Do you want to compare each element—title, subject, feelings, and images—in a separate paragraph?

Once you have decided, put your ideas into outline form.

I. Introduction
II. How one poem expresses theme
III. Similarities in how second poem does
IV. Differences in how second poem does
V. Conclusion

3. DRAFT YOUR RESPONSE

Introduction Include the titles and poets' names for the poems you will be comparing, and state the theme that the poems share. Also include your position statement.

Body Paragraphs If using an outline like the one shown, explain everything you want to about the first poem. Then start a new paragraph before you discuss how the second poem is similar or different.

Conclusion Wrap up your response with a restatement of your main idea and a thought about why the theme might appeal to different poets.

Revision Check to see whether adding transitions such as *similarly, unlike,* or *however* can help you make your comparisons and contrasts clearer.

A Christmas Carol

Novel by Charles Dickens

Dramatized by Frederick Gaines

How important is MONEY?

ALABAMA STANDARDS

READING & LIT STANDARDS

1.b Determining sequence of events

7 Interpret author's message in literary texts

KEY IDEA People say, "**Money** makes the world go round," "Show me the money," and "Time is money." But they also say, "You can't buy happiness." There are many sayings about what money can and can't do, about what it is and what it isn't. In *A Christmas Carol,* the main character's opinion about what it means to be wealthy changes drastically by the end of the play.

QUOTE IT Read over the four sayings quoted in the previous paragraph. In a chart, jot down your ideas about what each saying means. Then write your own saying on the last line, expressing your thoughts about money.

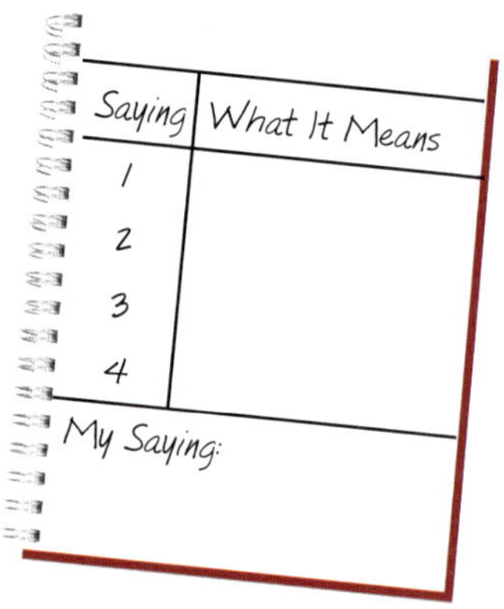

LITERARY ANALYSIS: THEME IN DRAMA

Just as short stories, novels, and poems communicate **themes,** so do dramas. To identify the message in a drama, you can use some of the same methods you use with other works: read closely and think about what larger meaning the writer is suggesting. Also pay special attention to

- descriptions of the setting, events, and characters in the **stage directions**
- **dialogue** between characters

As you read *A Christmas Carol,* try to focus not only on what the characters say and do but also on how and why they say and do those things. Then ask yourself questions about what message the playwright is sharing.

READING SKILL: ANALYZE SEQUENCE

Knowing the order of events in a work of literature helps you better understand the work's theme. Events are not always presented in the order in which they happen. The reader may be taken backward or forward in time.

In a drama, clues about the order, or **sequence,** of events often appear in the stage directions. The titles of the scenes also provide clues about the sequence of events.

As you read *A Christmas Carol,* use a sequence wheel to help you keep track of the unusual sequence of events.

Key Events

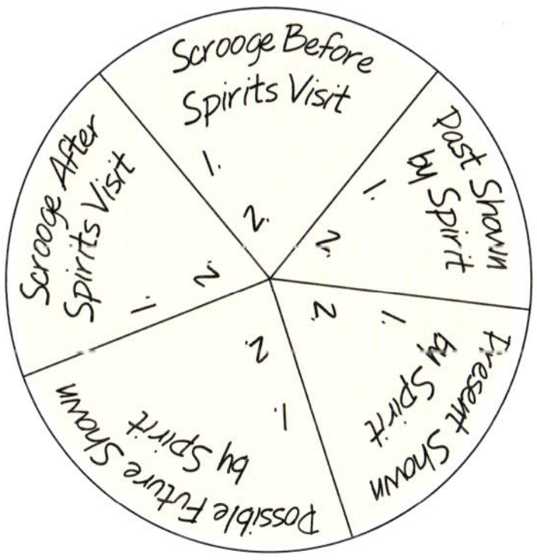

VOCABULARY IN CONTEXT

The following words all help tell the story of a man who is too concerned with **money.** How many words can you match with their definition?

1. accost	**a.** abrupt or blunt in speaking
2. anonymous	**b.** made very angry
3. brusque	**c.** not having one's name known
4. currency	**d.** to approach and speak unpleasantly to
5. incoherent	**e.** money
6. infuriated	**f.** confused

Author Online

Unhappy Childhood

Charles Dickens
1812–1870

Charles Dickens's childhood in England provided material for many of his stories. When Dickens was 12 and living with his family in London, his father was put in prison for not paying his debts. Young Dickens had to leave school to work in a rat-infested factory to help earn money for his family. The hopelessness and shame he felt there affected him deeply.

MORE ABOUT THE AUTHOR
For more on Charles Dickens, visit the **Literature Center** at **ClassZone.com.**

Background

A Plea for the Poor When Frederick Gaines wrote the play you are about to read, he based it on a novel by the same name that Charles Dickens first published in 1843. At that time, about one-third of the people in London were living in poverty and hunger. The city was dirty and overcrowded, and jobs and houses were in short supply. Many children were forced to work instead of staying in school.

Charles Dickens wanted his novel *A Christmas Carol* to be "a plea for the poor." The book was instantly and widely popular, and as Dickens had hoped, it and his other writings did affect how his readers felt about the social conditions of their time.

A CHRISTMAS CAROL

CHARLES DICKENS
DRAMATIZED BY FREDERICK GAINES

CHARACTERS

Carolers, Families, Dancers
First Boy
Second Boy
Third Boy
Girl with a doll
Ebenezer Scrooge
Bob Cratchit, Scrooge's clerk
Fred, Scrooge's nephew
Gentleman Visitor
Warder and Residents of the Poorhouse
Sparsit, Scrooge's servant
Cook
Charwoman
Jacob Marley
Priest
Leper
First Spirit, the Spirit of Christmas Past
Jack Walton
Ben Benjamin
Child Scrooge
Fan, Scrooge's sister
Fezziwig
Young Ebenezer
Dick Wilkins
Sweetheart of Young Ebenezer
Second Spirit, the Spirit of Christmas Present
Poorhouse Children
Mrs. Cratchit
Several Cratchit Children
Tiny Tim
Beggar Children, Hunger and Ignorance
Third Spirit, the Spirit of Christmas Yet to Come
Peter, a Cratchit child
Boy
Butcher
Coachman

© Louisiana Tech University School of Performing Arts.

PROLOGUE

The play begins amid a swirl of street life in Victorian London. Happy groups pass; brightly costumed carolers *and* families *call out to one another and sing "Joy to the World." Three* boys *and a* girl *are grouped about a glowing mound of coal. As the* carolers *leave the stage, the lights dim and the focus shifts to the mound of coals, bright against the dark. Slowly, the children begin to respond to the warmth. A piano plays softly as the children talk.*

First Boy. I saw a horse in a window. (*pause*) A dapple . . . gray and white. And a saddle, too . . . red. And a strawberry mane down to here. All new. Golden stirrups. (*People pass by the children, muttering greetings to one another.*)

Second Boy. Christmas Eve.

Third Boy. Wish we could go.

First Boy. So do I.

Third Boy. I think I'd like it.

First Boy. Oh, wouldn't I . . . wouldn't I!

Second Boy. We're going up onto the roof. (*The* boys *look at him quizzically.*) My father has a glass. Telescope. A brass one. It opens up and it has twists on it and an eyepiece that you put up to look through. We can see all the way to the park with it.

Third Boy. Could I look through it?

Second Boy. Maybe . . . where would you look? (*The* third boy *points straight up.*) Why there?

Third Boy. I'd like to see the moon.

(*The* boys *stand and look upward as the* girl *sings to her doll. One of the* boys *makes a snow angel on the ground.*)

Girl (*singing*).
Christ the King came down one day,
Into this world of ours,
And crying from a manger bed,
Began the Christmas hour.

(*speaking*)
Christ the King, my pretty one,
Sleep softly on my breast,
Christ the King, my gentle one,
Show us the way to rest.

(*She begins to sing the first verse again. As snow starts to fall on the* boy *making the snow angel, he stands up and reaches out to catch a single flake.*)

SCENE I

~ SCROOGE IN HIS SHOP ~

The percussion[1] *thunders.* Scrooge *hurls himself through the descending snowflakes and sends the children scattering. They retreat, watching.* Cratchit *comes in. He takes some coal from the mound and puts it into a small bucket; as he carries it to a corner of the stage, the stage area is transformed from street to office.* Scrooge*'s nephew* Fred *enters, talks with the children, gives them coins, and sends them away with a "Merry Christmas."*

Fred. A Merry Christmas, Uncle! God save you!

Scrooge. Bah! Humbug!

Fred. Christmas a humbug, Uncle? I hope that's meant as a joke.

Scrooge. Well, it's not. Come, come, what is it you want? Don't waste all the day, Nephew.

Fred. I only want to wish you a Merry Christmas, Uncle. Don't be cross.

Scrooge. What else can I be when I live in such a world of fools as this? Merry Christmas! Out with Merry Christmas! What's Christmas to you but a time for paying bills without money, a time for finding yourself a year older and not an hour richer. If I could work my will, every idiot who goes about with "Merry Christmas" on his lips should be boiled with his own pudding and buried with a stake of holly through his heart.

Fred. Uncle!

Scrooge. Nephew, keep Christmas in your own way and let me keep it in mine.

Fred. But you don't keep it.

Scrooge. Let me leave it alone then. Much good may it do you. Much good it has ever done you.

Fred. There are many things from which I might have derived good by which I have not profited, I daresay, Christmas among the rest. And though it has never put a scrap of gold in my pocket, I believe it has done me good and will do me good, and I say, God bless it!

Scrooge. Bah!

Fred. Don't be angry, Uncle. Come! Dine with us tomorrow.

Scrooge. I'll dine alone, thank you.

Fred. But why?

Scrooge. Why? Why did you get married?

Fred. Why, because I fell in love with a wonderful girl.

Scrooge. And I with solitude. Good afternoon.

Fred. Nay, Uncle, but you never came to see me before I was married. Why give it as a reason for not coming now?

Scrooge. Good afternoon.

Fred. I am sorry with all my heart to find you so determined; but I have made the attempt in homage to Christmas, and I'll keep that good spirit to the last. So, a Merry Christmas, Uncle.

Scrooge. Good afternoon!

Fred. And a Happy New Year!

Scrooge. Good afternoon! (Fred *hesitates as if to say something more. He sees that* Scrooge *has gone to get a volume down from the shelf, and so he starts to leave. As he leaves, the doorbell rings.*) Bells. Is it necessary to always have bells? (*The* gentleman visitor *enters, causing the doorbell to ring again.*) Cratchit!

Cratchit. Yes, sir?

Scrooge. The bell, fool! See to it!

Cratchit. Yes, sir. (*He goes to the entrance.*)

---

1. **percussion:** noise made by loudly striking objects, such as drums or cymbals.

© Louisiana Tech University School of Performing Arts.

Scroege (*muttering*). Merry Christmas . . . Wolves howling and a Merry Christmas . . .

Cratchit. It's for you, sir.

Scrooge. Of course it's for me. You're not receiving callers, are you? Show them in.

Cratchit. Right this way, sir. (*The* gentleman visitor *approaches* Scrooge.)

Scrooge. Yes, yes?

Gentleman Visitor. Scrooge and Marley's, I believe. Have I the pleasure of addressing Mr. Scrooge or Mr. Marley?

Scrooge. Marley's dead. Seven years tonight. What is it you want?

Gentleman Visitor. I have no doubt that his liberality is well represented by his surviving partner. Here, sir, my card. (*He hands* Scrooge *his business card.*)

Scrooge. Liberality? No doubt of it? All right, all right, I can read. What is it you want? (*He returns to his work.*)

Gentleman Visitor. At this festive season of the year . . .

Scrooge. It's winter and cold. (*He continues his work and ignores the* gentleman visitor.)

Gentleman Visitor. Yes . . . yes, it is, and the more reason for my visit. At this time of the year it is more than usually desirable to make some slight provision for the poor and destitute[2] who suffer greatly from the cold. Many thousands are in want of common necessaries; hundreds of thousands are in want of common comforts, sir.

Scrooge. Are there no prisons?

Gentleman Visitor. Many, sir.

Scrooge. And the workhouse?[3] Is it still in operation?

Gentleman Visitor. It is; still, I wish I could say it was not.

Scrooge. The poor law is still in full vigor then?

Gentleman Visitor. Yes, sir.

Scrooge. I'm glad to hear it. From what you said, I was afraid someone had stopped its operation.

Gentleman Visitor. Under the impression that they scarcely furnish Christian cheer of mind or body to the multitude, a few of us are endeavoring to raise a fund to buy the poor some meat and drink and means of warmth. We choose this time because it is the time, of all others, when want is keenly felt and abundance rejoices.[4] May I put you down for something, sir?

Scrooge (*retreating into the darkness temporarily*). Nothing.

Gentleman Visitor. You wish to be **anonymous**?

Scrooge. I wish to be left alone. Since you ask me what I wish, sir, that is my answer. I don't make merry myself at Christmas, and I can't afford to make idle people merry. I help support the establishments I have mentioned . . . they cost enough . . . and those who are poorly off must go there.

Gentleman Visitor. Many can't go there, and many would rather die.

Scrooge. If they would rather die, they had better do it and decrease the surplus population. That is not my affair. My business is. It occupies me constantly. (*He talks both to the* gentleman visitor *and to himself while he thumbs through his books.*) Ask a man to give up life and means . . . fine thing. What is it, I want to know? Charity? . . . (*His nose deep in his books, he vaguely hears the dinner bell being rung in the workhouse; he*

2. **destitute:** people lacking the necessities of life.

3. **workhouse:** an establishment in which poor people are housed and required to do work.

4. **abundance rejoices:** those with wealth are happy.

looks up as if he has heard it but never focuses on the actual scene. The warder *of the poorhouse stands in a pool of light at the far left, slowly ringing a bell.*)

Warder. Dinner. All right. Line up. (*The poorly clad, dirty* residents of the poorhouse *line up and file by to get their evening dish of gruel,*[5] *wordlessly accepting it and going back to eat listlessly in the gloom.* Scrooge *returns to the business of his office. The procession continues for a moment, then the image of the poorhouse is obscured by darkness. The dejected* gentleman visitor *exits.*)

Scrooge. Latch the door, Cratchit. Firmly, firmly. Draft as cold as Christmas blowing in here. Charity! (Cratchit *goes to the door, starts to close it, then sees the little* girl *with the doll. She seems to beckon to him; he moves slowly toward her, and they dance together for a moment.* Scrooge *continues to work. Suddenly* carolers *appear on the platform, and a few phrases of their carol, "Angels We Have Heard on High," are heard.* Scrooge *looks up.*) Cratchit! (*As soon as* Scrooge *shouts, the* girl *and the* carolers *vanish and* Cratchit *begins to close up the shop.*) Cratchit!

Cratchit. Yes, sir.

Scrooge. Well, to work then!

Cratchit. It's evening, sir.

Scrooge. Is it?

Cratchit. Christmas evening, sir.

Scrooge. Oh, you'll want all day tomorrow off, I suppose.

Cratchit. If it's quite convenient, sir.

Scrooge. It's not convenient, and it's not fair. If I was to deduct half a crown[6] from your salary for it, you'd think yourself ill-used, wouldn't you? Still you expect me to pay a day's wage for a day of no work.

Cratchit. It's only once a year, sir.

Scrooge. Be here all the earlier the next morning.

Cratchit. I will, sir.

Scrooge. Then off, off.

Cratchit. Yes, sir! Merry Christmas, sir!

Scrooge. Bah! (*As soon as* Cratchit *opens the door, the sounds of the street begin, very bright and loud.* Cratchit *is caught up in a swell of people hurrying through the street. Children pull him along to the top of an ice slide, and he runs and slides down it, disappearing in darkness as the stage suddenly is left almost empty.* Scrooge *goes around the room blowing out the candles, talking to himself.*) Christmas Eve. Carolers! Bah! There. Another day. (*He opens his door and peers out.*) Black, very black. Now where are they? (*The children are heard singing carols for a moment.*) Begging pennies for their songs, are they? Oh, boy! Here, boy! (*The little* girl *emerges from the shadows.* Scrooge *hands her a dark lantern, and she holds it while he lights it with an ember from the pile of coals.*)

© Louisiana Tech University School of Performing Arts.

---

5. **gruel:** a thin, watery food made by boiling ground grain in water or milk.

6. **half a crown:** until 1971, an amount of British money equal to one-eighth of a pound. The pound is the basic unit of British money.

SCENE 2

~ SCROOGE GOES HOME ~

Scrooge (*talking to the little* girl). Hold it quiet! There. Off now. That's it. High. Black as pitch. Light the street, that's it. You're a bright lad! Good to see that. Earn your supper, boy. You'll not go hungry this night. Home. You know the way, do you? Yes, that's the way. The house of Ebenezer Scrooge. (*As the two find their way to Scrooge's house, the audience sees and hears a brief image of a cathedral interior with a living crèche*[7] *and a large choir singing "Amen!"; the image ends in a blackout. The lights come up immediately, and* Scrooge *is at his door.*) Hold the light up, boy, up. (*The* girl *with the lantern disappears.*) Where did he go? Boy? No matter. There's a penny saved. Lantern's gone out. No matter. A candle saved. Yes, here's the key. (*He turns with the key toward the door, and* Marley*'s face swims out of the darkness.* Scrooge *watches, unable to speak. He fumbles for a match, lights the lantern, and swings it toward the figure, which melts away. Pause.* Scrooge *fits the key in the lock and turns it as the door suddenly is opened from the inside by the porter,* Sparsit. Scrooge *is startled, then recovers.*) Sparsit?

Sparsit. Yes, sir?

Scrooge. Hurry, hurry. The door . . . close it.

Sparsit. Did you knock, sir?

Scrooge. Knock? What matter? Here, light me up the stairs.

Sparsit. Yes, sir. (*He leads* Scrooge *up the stairs. They pass the* cook *on the way.* Scrooge *brushes by her, stops, looks back, and she leans toward him.*)

Cook. Something to warm you, sir? Porridge?

Scrooge. Wha . . . ? No. No, nothing.

Cook (*waiting for her Christmas coin*). Merry Christmas, sir. (Scrooge *ignores the request and the* cook *disappears. Mumbling,* Scrooge *follows* Sparsit.)

Scrooge (*looking back after the* cook *is gone*). Fright a man nearly out of his life . . . Merry Christmas . . . bah!

Sparsit. Your room, sir.

Scrooge. Hmmm? Oh, yes, yes. And good night.

Sparsit (*extending his hand for his coin*). Merry Christmas, sir.

Scrooge. Yes, yes . . . (*He sees the outstretched hand; he knows what* Sparsit *wants and is* **infuriated**.) Out! Out! (*He closes the door after* Sparsit, *turns toward his chamber, and discovers the* charwoman *directly behind him.*)

Charwoman. Warm your bed for you, sir?

Scrooge. What? Out! Out!

Charwoman. Aye, sir. (*She starts for the door.* Marley*'s voice is heard mumbling something unintelligible.*)

Scrooge. What's that?

Charwoman. Me, sir? Not a thing, sir.

Scrooge. Then, good night.

Charwoman. Good night. (*She exits, and* Scrooge *pantomimes shutting the door behind her. The voice of* Marley *over an offstage microphone whispers and reverberates:*[8] *"Merry Christmas, Scrooge!" Silence.* Scrooge *hears the voice but cannot account for it. He climbs up to open a window and looks down. A cathedral choir singing "O Come, All Ye Faithful" is heard in the distance.* Scrooge *listens a moment, shuts the window,*

7. **a cathedral interior with a living crèche:** the inside of a large church in which real people pose for the Christmas manger scene.

8. **reverberates** (rĭ-vûr′bə-rāts′): echoes.

© Louisiana Tech University School of Performing Arts.

and prepares for bed. As soon as he has shut the sound out of his room, figures appear; they seem to be coming down the main aisle of a church, bearing gifts to the living crèche. The orchestra plays "O Come, All Ye Faithful" as the procession files out. Scrooge, *ready for bed, warms himself before the heap of coals. As he pulls his nightcap from a chair, a small hand-bell tumbles off onto the floor. Startled, he picks it up and rings it for reassurance; an echo answers it. He turns and sees the little* girl *on the street; she is swinging her doll, which produces the echo of his bell.* Scrooge *escapes to his bed; the* girl *is swallowed up in the darkness. The bell sounds grow to a din,* **incoherent** *as in a dream, then suddenly fall silent.* Scrooge *sits up in bed, listens, and hears the chains of* Marley *coming up the stairs.* Scrooge *reaches for the bell pull to summon* Sparsit. *The bell responds with a gong, and* Marley *appears. He and* Scrooge *face one another.*)

Scrooge. What do you want with me?

Marley (*in a ghostly, unreal voice*). Much.

Scrooge. Who are you?

Marley. Ask who I was.

Scrooge. Who were you?

Marley. In life, I was your partner, Jacob Marley.

Scrooge. He's dead.

Marley. Seven years this night, Ebenezer Scrooge.

Scrooge. Why do you come here?

Marley. I must. It is commanded me. I must wander the world and see what I can no longer share, what I would not share when I walked where you do.

Scrooge. And must go thus?

Marley. The chain? Look at it, Ebenezer, study it. Locks and vaults and golden coins. I forged it, each link, each day when I sat in these chairs, commanded these rooms. Greed, Ebenezer Scrooge, wealth. Feel them, know them. Yours was as heavy as this I wear seven years ago, and you have labored to build it since.

Scrooge. If you're here to lecture, I have no time for it. It is late; the night is cold. I want comfort now.

Marley. I have none to give. I know not how you see me this night. I did not ask it. I have sat invisible beside you many and many a day. I am commanded to bring you a chance, Ebenezer. Heed it!

Scrooge. Quickly then, quickly.

Marley. You will be haunted by three spirits.

Scrooge (*scoffing*). Is that the chance?

Marley. Mark it.

Scrooge. I do not choose to.

Marley (*ominously*). Then you will walk where I do, burdened by your riches, your greed.

Scrooge. Spirits mean nothing to me.

Marley (*slowly leaving*). Expect the first tomorrow, when the bell tolls one, the second on the next night at the same hour, the third upon the next night when the last stroke of twelve has ended. Look to see me no more. I must wander. Look that, for your own sake, you remember what has passed between us.

Scrooge. Jacob . . . Don't leave me! . . . Jacob! Jacob!

Marley. Adieu,[9] Ebenezer. (*At* Marley*'s last words a funeral procession begins to move across the stage. A boy walks in front; a* priest *follows, swinging a censer;*[10] *sounds of mourning and the suggestion of church music are heard.* Scrooge *calls out, "Jacob, don't leave me!" as if talking in the midst of a bad dream. At the end of the procession is the little* girl, *swinging her doll and singing softly.*)

9. **adieu** (ə-dyo͞o'): farewell.

10. **censer:** a container in which incense is burned.

© Louisiana Tech University School of Performing Arts.

Girl.
Hushabye, don't you cry,
Go to sleep, little baby.
When you wake, you shall have
All the pretty little horses,
Blacks and bays, dapples and grays,
All the pretty little horses.

(*She stops singing and looks up at* Scrooge; *their eyes meet, and she solemnly rings the doll in greeting.* Scrooge *pulls shut the bed curtains, and the* girl *exits. The bell sounds are picked up by the bells of a* leper[11] *who enters, dragging himself along.*)

Leper (*calling out*). Leper! Leper! Stay the way! Leper! Leper! Keep away! (*He exits and the clock begins to chime, ringing the hours.* Scrooge *sits up in bed and begins to count the chimes.*)

Scrooge. Eight . . . nine . . . ten . . . eleven . . . it can't be . . . twelve. Midnight? No. Not twelve. It can't be. I haven't slept the whole day through. Twelve? Yes, yes, twelve noon. (*He hurries to the window and looks out.*) Black. Twelve midnight. (*pause*) I must get up. A day wasted. I must get down to the office. (*Two small chimes are heard.*) Quarter past. But it just rang twelve. Fifteen minutes haven't gone past, not so quickly. (*Again two small chimes are heard.*) A quarter to one. The spirit . . . It's to come at one. (*He hurries to his bed as the chimes ring again.*) One.

11. **leper:** a person who has leprosy, a skin disease once thought to be highly contagious.

SCENE 3

~ THE SPIRIT OF CHRISTMAS PAST ~

The hour is struck again by a large street clock, and the first spirit *appears. It is a figure dressed to look like the little girl's doll.*

Scrooge. Are you the spirit whose coming was foretold to me?

First Spirit. I am.

Scrooge. Who and what are you?

First Spirit. I am the Ghost of Christmas Past.

Scrooge. Long past?

First Spirit. Your past.

Scrooge. Why are you here?

First Spirit. Your welfare. Rise. Walk with me.

Scrooge. I am mortal still. I cannot pass through air.

First Spirit. My hand. (Scrooge *grasps the* spirit's *hand tightly, and the doll's bell rings softly.* Scrooge *remembers a scene from his past in which two boys greet each other in the street.*)

First Voice. Halloo, Jack!

Second Voice. Ben! Merry Christmas, Ben!

Scrooge. Jack Walton. Young Jack Walton. Spirits . . . ?

First Voice. Have a good holiday, Jack.

Scrooge. Yes, yes, I remember him. Both of them. Little Ben Benjamin. He used to . . .

First Voice. See you next term, Jack. Next . . . term . . .

Scrooge. They . . . they're off for the holidays and going home from school. It's Christmas time . . . all of the children off home now . . . No . . . no, not all . . . there was one . . . (*The* spirit *motions for* Scrooge *to turn, and he sees a young boy playing with a teddy bear and talking to it.*) Yes . . . reading . . . poor boy.

First Spirit. What, I wonder?

Scrooge. Reading? Oh, it was nothing. Fancy, all fancy and make-believe and take-me-away. All of it. Yes, nonsense.

Child Scrooge. Ali Baba.[12]

Scrooge. Yes . . . that was it . . .

Child Scrooge. Yes, and remember . . . and remember . . . remember Robinson Crusoe?[13]

Scrooge. And the parrot!

Child Scrooge. Yes, the parrot! I love him best.

Scrooge (*imitating the parrot*). With his stripy green body and yellow tail drooping along and couldn't sing—awk—but could talk, and a thing like a lettuce growing out the top of his head . . . and he used to sit on the very top of the tree—up there.

Child Scrooge. And Robinson Crusoe sailed around the island, and he thought he had escaped the island, and the parrot said, the parrot said . . .

Scrooge (*imitating the parrot*). Robinson Crusoe, where you been? Awk! Robinson Crusoe, where you been?

Child Scrooge. And Robinson Crusoe looked up in the tree and saw the parrot and knew he hadn't escaped and he was still there, still all alone there.

Scrooge. Poor Robinson Crusoe.

Child Scrooge (*sadly replacing the teddy bear*). Poor Robinson Crusoe.

Scrooge. Poor child. Poor child.

First Spirit. Why poor?

Scrooge. Fancy . . . fancy . . . (*He tries to mask his feelings by being* **brusque.**) It's his way, a child's

---

12. **Ali Baba:** in the *Arabian Nights,* a poor woodcutter who discovers a treasure.
13. **Robinson Crusoe:** a shipwrecked sailor who survives for years on a small island in the novel *Robinson Crusoe.*

© Louisiana Tech University School of Performing Arts.

way to . . . to lose being alone in . . . in dreams, dreams . . . Never matter if they are all nonsense, yes, nonsense. But he'll be all right, grow out of it. Yes. Yes, he did outgrow it, the nonsense. Became a man and left there, and he became, yes, he became a man and . . . yes, successful . . . rich! (*The sadness returns.*) Never matter . . . never matter. (Fan *runs in and goes to* Child Scrooge.) Fan!

Fan. Brother, dear brother! (*She kisses* Child Scrooge.)

Child Scrooge. Dear, dear Fan.

Fan. I've come to bring you home, home for good and ever. Come with me, come now. (*She takes his hand, and they start to run off, but the* spirit *stops them and signals for the light on them to fade. They look at the* spirit, *aware of their role in the* spirit*'s "education" of* Scrooge.)

Scrooge. Let me watch them go? Let them be happy for a moment! (*The* spirit *says nothing.* Scrooge *turns away from them, and the light goes out.*) A delicate, delicate child. A breath might have withered her.

First Spirit. She died a woman and had, as I remember, children.

Scrooge. One child.

First Spirit. Your nephew.

Scrooge. Yes, yes, Fred, my nephew. (Scrooge *pauses, then tries to bluster through.*) Well? Well, all of us have that, haven't we? Childhoods? Sadnesses? But we grow and we become men, masters of ourselves. (*The* spirit *gestures for music to begin. It is heard first as from a great distance, then* Scrooge *becomes aware of it.*) I've no time for it, Spirit. Music and all of your Christmas folderol.[14] Yes, yes, I've learnt what you have to show me. (Fezziwig, Young Ebenezer, *and* Dick *appear, busily preparing for a party.*)

Fezziwig. Yo ho, there! Ebenezer! Dick!

Scrooge. Fezziwig! It's old Fezziwig that I 'prenticed[15] under.

First Spirit. Your master?

Scrooge. Oh, aye, and the best that any boy could have. There's Dick Wilkins! Bless me. He was very much attached to me was Dick. Poor Dick. Dear, dear.

Fezziwig. Yo ho, my boys! No more work tonight. Christmas Eve, Dick! Christmas, Ebenezer! Let's have the shutters up before a man can say Jack Robinson! (*The music continues. Chandeliers are pulled into position, and mistletoe, holly, and ivy are draped over everything by bustling servants.* Dancers *fill the stage for* Fezziwig*'s wonderful Christmas party. In the midst of the dancing and the gaiety servants pass back and forth through the crowd with huge platters of food. At a pause in the music,* Young Ebenezer, *who is dancing, calls out.*)

Young Ebenezer. Mr. Fezziwig, sir, you're a wonderful master!

Scrooge and Young Ebenezer. A wonderful master!

Scrooge (*echoing the phrase*). A wonderful master! (*The music changes suddenly, and the* dancers *jerk into distorted postures and then begin to move in slow motion. The celebrants slowly exit, performing a macabre dance to discordant sounds.*[16])

First Spirit. Just because he gave a party? It was very small.

Scrooge. Small!

First Spirit. He spent a few pounds of your "mortal" money, three, four at the most. Is that so much that he deserves this praise?

Scrooge. But it wasn't the money. He had the power to make us happy, to make our service light or burdensome. The happiness he gives

14. **folderol** (fŏl'-də-rŏl'): foolishness; nonsense.

15. **'prenticed:** short for *apprenticed,* here meaning "learned a trade while working."

16. **macabre** (mə-kä'brə) **dance to discordant sounds:** a bizarre, ghastly dance with unharmonious music.

is quite as great as if it cost a fortune. That's what . . . a good master is.

First Spirit. Yes?

Scrooge. No, no, nothing.

First Spirit. Something, I think.

Scrooge. I should like to be able to say a word or two to my clerk just now, that's all.

First Spirit. But this is all past. Your clerk, Cratchit, couldn't be here.

Scrooge. No, no, of course not, an idle thought. Are we done?

First Spirit (*motioning for the waltz music to begin*). Nearly.

Scrooge (*hearing the waltz and remembering it*). Surely it's enough. Haven't you tormented me enough? (Young Ebenezer *is seen waltzing with his* Sweetheart.)

First Spirit. I only show the past, what it promised you. Look. Another promise.

Scrooge. Oh. Oh, yes. I had forgotten . . . her. Don't they dance beautifully? So young, so young. I would have married her if only . . .

Sweetheart. Can you love me, Ebenezer? I bring no dowry[17] to my marriage, only me, only love. It is no **currency** that you can buy and sell with, but we can live with it. Can you? (*She pauses, then returns the ring* Scrooge *gave her as his pledge.*) I release you, Ebenezer, for the love of the man you once were. Will that man win me again, now that he is free?

Scrooge (*trying to speak to her*). If only you had held me to it. You should not have let me go. I was young; I did love you.

Sweetheart (*speaking to* Young Ebenezer). We have never lied to one another. May you be happy in the life you have chosen. Good-bye. (*She runs out.* Young Ebenezer *slowly leaves.*)

Scrooge. No, no, it was not meant that way . . . !

First Spirit. You cannot change now what you would not change then. I am your mistakes, Ebenezer Scrooge, all of the things you could have done and did not.

Scrooge. Then leave me! I have done them. I shall live with them. As I have, as I do; as I will.

First Spirit. There is another Christmas, seven years ago, when Marley died.

Scrooge. No! I will not see it. I will not! He died. I could not prevent it. I did not choose for him to die on Christmas Day.

First Spirit. And when his day was chosen, what did you do then?

Scrooge. I looked after his affairs.

First Spirit. His business.

Scrooge. Yes! His business! Mine! It was all that I had, all that I could do in this world. I have nothing to do with the world to come after.

First Spirit. Then I will leave you.

Scrooge. Not yet! Don't leave me here! Tell me what I must do! What of the other spirits?

First Spirit. They will come.

Scrooge. And you? What of you?

First Spirit. I am always with you. (*The little* girl *appears with her doll; she takes* Scrooge*'s hand and gently leads him to bed. Numbed, he follows her. She leans against the foot of the bed, ringing the doll and singing. The* first spirit *exits as she sings.*)

Girl.

When you wake, you shall have
All the pretty little horses,
Blacks and bays, dapples and grays,
All the pretty little horses.

(*She rings the doll, and the ringing becomes the chiming of Scrooge's bell. The* girl *exits.* Scrooge *sits upright in bed as he hears the chimes.*)

Scrooge. A minute until one. No one here. No one's coming. (*A larger clock strikes one o'clock.*)

---

17. **dowry** (dou'rē): money or property brought by a bride to her husband when they marry.

SCENE 4

~ THE SPIRIT OF CHRISTMAS PRESENT ~

A light comes on. Scrooge *becomes aware of it and goes slowly to it. He sees the* second spirit, *the Spirit of Christmas Present, who looks like* Fezziwig.

Scrooge. Fezziwig!

Second Spirit. Hello, Scrooge.

Scrooge. But you can't be . . . not Fezziwig.

Second Spirit. Do you see me as him?

Scrooge. I do.

Second Spirit. And hear me as him?

Scrooge. I do.

Second Spirit. I wish I were the gentleman, so as not to disappoint you.

Scrooge. But you're not . . . ?

Second Spirit. No, Mr. Scrooge. You have never seen the like of me before. I am the Ghost of Christmas Present.

Scrooge. But . . .

Second Spirit. You see what you will see, Scrooge, no more. Will you walk out with me this Christmas Eve?

Scrooge. But I am not yet dressed.

Second Spirit. Take my tails, dear boy, we're leaving.

Scrooge. Wait!

Second Spirit. What is it now?

Scrooge. Christmas Present, did you say?

Second Spirit. I did.

Scrooge. Then we are traveling here? In this town? London? Just down there?

Second Spirit. Yes, yes, of course.

Scrooge. Then we could walk? Your flying is . . . well, too sudden for an old man. Well?

Second Spirit. It's your Christmas, Scrooge; I am only the guide.

Scrooge (*puzzled*). Then we can walk? (*The* spirit *nods.*) Where are you guiding me to?

Second Spirit. Bob Cratchit's.

Scrooge. My clerk?

Second Spirit. You did want to talk to him? (Scrooge *pauses, uncertain how to answer.*) Don't worry, Scrooge, you won't have to.

Scrooge (*trying to change the subject, to cover his error*). Shouldn't be much of a trip. With fifteen bob[18] a week, how far off can it be?

Second Spirit. A world away, Scrooge, at least that far. (Scrooge *and the* spirit *start to step off a curb when a funeral procession enters with a child's coffin, followed by the* poorhouse children, *who are singing. Seated on top of the coffin is the little* girl. *She and* Scrooge *look at one another.*) That is the way to it, Scrooge. (*The procession follows the coffin offstage;* Scrooge *and the* spirit *exit after the procession. As they leave, the lights focus on* Mrs. Cratchit *and her* children. Mrs. Cratchit *sings as she puts* Tiny Tim *and the other* children *to bed, all in one bed. She pulls a dark blanket over them.*)

Mrs. Cratchit (*singing*).
When you wake, you shall have
All the pretty little horses,
Blacks and bays, dapples and grays,
All the pretty little horses.

To sleep now, all of you. Christmas tomorrow. (*She kisses them and goes to* Bob Cratchit, *who is by the hearth.*) How did our little Tiny Tim behave?

Bob Cratchit. As good as gold and better. He told me, coming home, that he hoped the

18. **bob:** a British slang term for shillings. (There were 20 shillings in a pound.)

© Louisiana Tech University School of Performing Arts.

people saw him in church because he was a cripple and it might be pleasant to them to remember upon Christmas Day who made the lame to walk and the blind to see.

Mrs. Cratchit. He's a good boy. (*The* second spirit *and* Scrooge *enter.* Mrs. Cratchit *feels a sudden draft.*) Oh, the wind. (*She gets up to shut the door.*)

Second Spirit. Hurry. (*He nudges* Scrooge *in before* Mrs. Cratchit *shuts the door.*)

Scrooge. Hardly hospitable is what I'd say.

Second Spirit. Oh, they'd say a great deal more, Scrooge, if they could see you.

Scrooge. Oh, they should, should they?

Second Spirit. Oh yes, I'd think they might.

Scrooge. Well, I might have a word for them . . .

Second Spirit. You're here to listen.

Scrooge. Oh. Oh yes, all right. By the fire?

Second Spirit. But not a word.

Bob Cratchit (*raising his glass*). My dear, to Mr. Scrooge. I give you Mr. Scrooge, the founder of the feast.

Mrs. Cratchit. The founder of the feast indeed! I wish I had him here! I'd give him a piece of my mind to feast upon, and I hope he'd have a good appetite for it.

Bob Cratchit. My dear, Christmas Eve.

Mrs. Cratchit. It should be Christmas Eve, I'm sure, when one drinks the health of such an odious,[19] stingy, hard, unfeeling man as Mr. Scrooge. You know he is, Robert! Nobody knows it better than you do, poor dear.

Bob Cratchit. I only know one thing on Christmas: that one must be charitable.

Mrs. Cratchit. I'll drink to his health for your sake and the day's, not for his. Long life to him! A Merry Christmas and a Happy New

---

19. **odious** (ō′dē-əs): causing or deserving strong dislike.

© Louisiana Tech University School of Performing Arts.

Year. He'll be very merry and very happy, I have no doubt.

Bob Cratchit. If he cannot be, we must be happy for him. A song is what is needed. Tim!

Mrs. Cratchit. Shush! I've just gotten him down, and he needs all the sleep he can get.

Bob Cratchit. If he's asleep on Christmas Eve, I'll be much mistaken. Tim! He must sing, dear; there is nothing else that might make him well.

Tiny Tim. Yes, Father?

Bob Cratchit. Are you awake?

Tiny Tim. Just a little.

Bob Cratchit. A song then! (*The* children *awaken and, led by* Tiny Tim, *sit up to sing "What Child Is This?" As they sing,* Scrooge *speaks.*)

Scrooge. (*He holds up his hand; all stop singing and look at him.*) I . . . I have seen enough. (*When the* spirit *signals to the* children, *they leave the stage, singing the carol quietly.* Tiny Tim *remains, covered completely by the dark blanket, disappearing against the black.*) Tiny Tim . . . will he live?

Second Spirit. He is very ill. Even song cannot keep him whole through a cold winter.

Scrooge. But you haven't told me!

Second Spirit (*imitating* Scrooge). If he be like to die, he had better do it and decrease the surplus population. (Scrooge *turns away.*) Erase, Scrooge, those words from your thoughts. You are not the judge. Do not judge, then. It may be that in the sight of heaven you are more worthless and less fit to live than millions like this poor man's child. Oh God! To hear an insect on a leaf pronouncing that there is too much life among his hungry brothers in the dust. Good-bye, Scrooge.

Scrooge. But is there no happiness in Christmas Present?

Second Spirit. There is.

Scrooge. Take me there.

Second Spirit. It is at the home of your nephew . . .

Scrooge. No!

Second Spirit (*disgusted with* Scrooge). Then there is none.

Scrooge. But that isn't enough . . . You must teach me!

Second Spirit. Would you have a teacher, Scrooge? Look at your own words.

Scrooge. But the first spirit gave me more . . . !

Second Spirit. He was Christmas Past. There was a lifetime he could choose from. I have only this day, one day, and you, Scrooge. I have nearly lived my fill of both. Christmas Present must be gone at midnight. That is near now. (*He speaks to two* beggar children *who pause shyly at the far side of the stage. The* children *are thin and wan; they are barefoot and wear filthy rags.*) Come. (*They go to him.*)

Scrooge. Is this the last spirit who is to come to me?

Second Spirit. They are no spirits. They are real. Hunger, Ignorance. Not spirits, Scrooge, passing dreams. They are real. They walk your streets, look to you for comfort. And you deny them. Deny them not too long, Scrooge. They will grow and multiply, and they will not remain children.

Scrooge. Have they no refuge, no resource?

Second Spirit (*again imitating* Scrooge). Are there no prisons? Are there no workhouses? (*tenderly to the* children) Come. It's Christmas Eve. (*He leads them offstage.*)

SCENE 5

~ THE SPIRIT OF CHRISTMAS YET TO COME ~

Scrooge *is entirely alone for a long moment. He is frightened by the darkness and feels it approaching him. Suddenly he stops, senses the presence of the* third spirit, *turns toward him, and sees him. The* spirit *is bent and cloaked. No physical features are distinguishable.*

Scrooge. You are the third. (*The* spirit *says nothing.*) The Ghost of Christmas Yet to Come. (*The* spirit *says nothing.*) Speak to me. Tell me what is to happen—to me, to all of us. (*The* spirit *says nothing.*) Then show me what I must see. (*The* spirit *points. Light illumines the shadowy recesses of Scrooge's house.*) I know it. I know it too well, cold and cheerless. It is mine. (*The* cook *and the* charwoman *are dimly visible in Scrooge's house.*) What is . . . ? There are . . . thieves! There are thieves in my rooms! (*He starts forward to* **accost** *them, but the* spirit *beckons for him to stop.*) I cannot. You cannot tell me that I must watch them and do nothing. I will not. It is mine still. (*He rushes into the house to claim his belongings and to protect them. The two women do not notice his presence.*)

Cook. He ain't about, is he? (*The* charwoman *laughs.*) Poor ol' Scrooge 'as met 'is end.[20] (*She laughs with the* charwoman.)

Charwoman. An' time for it, too; ain't been alive in deed for half his life.

Cook. But the Sparsit's nowhere, is he . . . ?

Sparsit (*emerging from the blackness*). Lookin' for someone, ladies? (*The* cook *shrieks, but the* charwoman *treats the matter more practically, anticipating competition from* Sparsit.)

Charwoman. There ain't enough but for the two of us!

Sparsit. More 'an enough . . . if you know where to look.

Cook. Hardly decent is what I'd say, hardly decent, the poor old fella hardly cold and you're thievin' his wardrobe.

Sparsit. You're here out of love, are ya?

Charwoman. There's no time for that. (Sparsit *acknowledges* Scrooge *for the first time, gesturing toward him as if the living* Scrooge *were the corpse.* Scrooge *stands as if rooted to the spot, held there by the power of the* spirit.)

Sparsit. He ain't about to bother us, is he?

Charwoman. Ain't he a picture?

Cook. If he is, it ain't a happy one. (*They laugh.*)

Sparsit. Ladies, shall we start? (*The three of them grin and advance on* Scrooge.) Cook?

Cook (*snatching the cuff links from the shirt* Scrooge *wears*). They're gold, ain't they?

Sparsit. The purest, madam.

Charwoman. I always had a fancy for that nightcap of his. My old man could use it. (*She takes the nightcap from* Scrooge*'s head.* Sparsit *playfully removes* Scrooge*'s outer garment, the coat or cloak that he has worn in the previous scenes.*)

Sparsit. Bein' a man of more practical tastes, I'll go for the worsted[21] and hope the smell ain't permanent. (*The three laugh.*) Cook, we go round again.

Cook. Do you think that little bell he's always ringing at me is silver enough to sell? (*The three of them move toward the nightstand, and* Scrooge *cries out.*)

---

20. **'as met 'is end:** a dialect pronunciation of "has met his end."

21. **worsted:** a smooth woolen fabric.

© Louisiana Tech University School of Performing Arts.

Scrooge. No more! No more! (*As the* spirit *directs* Scrooge*'s attention to the tableau*[22] *of the three thieves standing poised over the silver bell,* Scrooge *bursts out of the house, clad only in his nightshirt.*) I cannot. I cannot. The room is . . . too like a cheerless place that is familiar. I won't see it. Let us go from here. Anywhere. (*The* spirit *directs his attention to the Cratchit house; the* children *are sitting together near* Mrs. Cratchit, *who is sewing a coat.* Peter *reads by the light of the coals.*)

Peter. "And he took a child and set him in the midst of them."

Mrs. Cratchit (*putting her hand to her face*). The light tires my eyes so. (*pause*) They're better now. It makes them tired to try to see by firelight, and I wouldn't show reddened eyes to your father when he comes home for the world. It must be near his time now.

Peter. Past it, I think, but he walks slower than he used to, these last few days, Mother.

Mrs. Cratchit. I have known him to walk with . . . I have known him to walk with Tiny Tim upon his shoulder very fast indeed. (*She catches herself, then hurries on.*) But he was very light to carry and his father loved him, so that it was no trouble, no trouble. (*She hears* Bob Cratchit *approaching.*) Smiles, everyone, smiles.

Bob Cratchit (*entering*). My dear, Peter . . . (*He greets the other* children *by their real names.*) How is it coming?

Mrs. Cratchit (*handing him the coat*). Nearly done.

---

22. **tableau** (tăb'lō'): a portion of a play where the actors momentarily freeze in their positions for dramatic effect.

© Louisiana Tech University School of Performing Arts.

Bob Cratchit. Yes, good, I'm sure that it will be done long before Sunday.

Mrs. Cratchit. Sunday! You went today then, Robert?

Bob Cratchit. Yes. It's . . . it's all ready. Two o'clock. And a nice place. It would have done you good to see how green it is. But you'll see it often. I promised him that, that I would walk there on Sunday . . . often.

Mrs. Cratchit. We mustn't hurt ourselves for it, Robert.

Bob Cratchit. No. No, he wouldn't have wanted that. Come now. You won't guess who I've seen. Scrooge's nephew, Fred. And he asked after us and said he was heartily sorry and to give his respect to my good wife. How he ever knew that, I don't know.

Mrs. Cratchit. Knew what, my dear?

Bob Cratchit. Why, that you were a good wife.

Peter. Everybody knows that.

Bob Cratchit. I hope that they do. "Heartily sorry," he said, "for your good wife, and if I can be of service to you in any way—" and he gave me his card—"that's where I live"—and Peter, I shouldn't be at all surprised if he got you a position.

Mrs. Cratchit. Only hear that, Peter!

Bob Cratchit. And then you'll be keeping company with some young girl and setting up for yourself.

Peter. Oh, go on.

Bob Cratchit. Well, it will happen, one day, but remember, when that day does come—as it must—we must none of us forget poor Tiny Tim and this first parting in our family.

Scrooge. He died! No, no! (*He steps back and the scene disappears; he moves away from the* spirit.)

SCENE 6

~ SCROOGE'S CONVERSION ~

Scrooge. Because he would not . . . no! You cannot tell me that he has died, for that Christmas has not come! I will not let it come! I will be there . . . It was me. Yes, yes, and I knew it and couldn't look. I won't be able to help. I won't. (*pause*) Spirit, hear me. I am not the man I was. I will not be that man that I have been for so many years. Why show me all of this if I am past all hope? Assure me that I yet may change these shadows you have shown me. Let the boy live! I will honor Christmas in my heart and try to keep it all the year. I will live in the Past, the Present, and the Future. The spirits of all three shall strive within me. I will not shut out the lessons that they teach. Oh, tell me that I am not too late! (*A single light focuses on the little* girl, *dressed in a blue cloak like that of the Virgin Mary. She looks up, and from above a dove is slowly lowered in silence to her; she takes it and encloses it within her cloak, covering it. As soon as she does this, a large choir is heard singing "Gloria!" and the bells begin to ring. Blackout. When the lights come up again,* Scrooge *is in bed. The* third spirit *and the figures in the church have disappeared.* Scrooge *awakens and looks around his room.*) The curtains! They are mine and they are real. They are not sold. They are here. I am here; the shadows to come may be dispelled. They will be. I know they will be. (*He dresses himself hurriedly.*) I don't know what to do. I'm as light as a feather, merry as a boy again. Merry Christmas! Merry Christmas! A Happy New Year to all the world! Hello there! Whoop! Hallo! What day of the month is it? How long did the spirits keep me? Never mind. I don't care. (*He opens the window and calls to a* boy *in the street below.*) What's today?

Boy. Eh?

Scrooge. What's the day, my fine fellow?

Boy. Today? Why, Christmas Day!

Scrooge. It's Christmas Day! I haven't missed it! The spirits have done it all in one night. They can do anything they like. Of course they can. Of course they can save Tim. Hallo, my fine fellow!

Boy. Hallo!

Scrooge. Do you know the poulterers[23] in the next street at the corner?

Boy. I should hope I do.

Scrooge. An intelligent boy. A remarkable boy. Do you know whether they've sold the prize turkey that was hanging up there? Not the little prize; the big one.

Boy. What, the one as big as me?

Scrooge. What a delightful boy! Yes, my bucko!

Boy. It's hanging there now.

Scrooge. It is? Go and buy it.

Boy. G'wan!

Scrooge. I'm in earnest! Go and buy it and tell 'em to bring it here that I may give them the direction where to take it. Come back with the butcher and I'll give you a shilling. Come back in less than two minutes and I'll give you half a crown!

Boy. Right, guv! (*He exits.*)

Scrooge. I'll send it to Bob Cratchit's. He shan't know who sends it. It's twice the size of Tiny Tim and such a Christmas dinner it will make. (Carolers *suddenly appear singing "Hark! The Herald Angels Sing."* Scrooge *leans*

---

23. **poulterers** (pōl′tər-ərz): people who sell poultry, such as chickens and turkeys.

© Louisiana Tech University School of Performing Arts.

out the window and joins them in the song.) I must dress, I must. It's Christmas Day! I must be all in my best for such a day. Where is my China silk shirt? (*The* boy *and the* butcher *run in with the turkey.*) What? Back already? And such a turkey. Why, you can't carry that all the way to Cratchit's. Here, boy, here is your half a crown and here an address in Camden Town. See that it gets there. Here, money for the cab, for the turkey, and for you, good man! (*The* boy *and the* butcher, *delighted, catch the money and run out.* Scrooge *sees the* gentleman visitor *walking by the window.*) Halloo, sir!

Gentleman Visitor (*looking up sadly, less than festive*). Hello, sir.

Scrooge. My dear sir, how do you do? I hope you succeeded yesterday. It was very kind of you to stop by to see me.

Gentleman Visitor (*in disbelief*). Mr. Scrooge?

Scrooge. Yes, that is my name, and I fear it may not be pleasant to you. Allow me to ask your pardon, and will you have the goodness to add this (*throwing him a purse*) to your good work!

Gentleman Visitor. Lord bless me! My dear Mr. Scrooge, are you serious?

Scrooge. If you please, not a penny less. A great many back payments are included in it, I assure you. Will you do me that favor?

Gentleman Visitor. My dear sir, I don't know what I can say to such generosity . . .

Scrooge. Say nothing! Accept it. Come and see me. Will you come and see me?

Gentleman Visitor. I will.

Scrooge. Thank 'ee. I am much obliged to you. I thank you fifty times. God bless you and Merry Christmas!

Gentleman Visitor. Merry Christmas to you, sir!

Scrooge (*running downstairs, out of his house, and onto the street*). Now which is the way to that nephew's house. Girl! Girl!

Girl (*appearing immediately*). Yes, sir?

Scrooge. Can you find me a taxi, miss?

Girl. I can, sir. (*She rings her doll, and a* coachman *appears.*)

Scrooge (*handing the* coachman *a card*). Can you show me the way to this home?

Coachman. I can, sir.

Scrooge. Good man. Come up, girl. (*They mount to the top of the taxi. This action may be stylistically suggested.*) Would you be an old man's guide to a Christmas dinner?

Girl. I would, sir, and God bless you!

Scrooge. Yes, God bless us every one! (*raising his voice almost in song*) Driver, to Christmas! (*They exit, all three singing "Joy to the World." Blackout. The lights come up for the finale*[24] *at Fred's house. The* Cratchits *are there with* Tiny Tim. *All stop moving and talking when they see* Scrooge *standing in the center, embarrassed and humble.*) Well, I'm very glad to be here at my nephew's house! (*He starts to cry.*) Merry Christmas! Merry Christmas!

All (*softly*). Merry Christmas. (*They sing "Deck the Halls," greeting one another and exchanging gifts.* Scrooge *puts* Tiny Tim *on his shoulders.*)

Tiny Tim (*shouting as the carol ends*). God bless us every one!

Scrooge (*to the audience*). Oh, yes! God bless us every one!

---

24. **finale** (fə-năl'ē): conclusion.

Media Literacy: Theme in Movies

Characters need to grow up! As you know from your understanding of *A Christmas Carol* and the character Scrooge, themes are often conveyed through a character's growth and change. To discover a theme in a written story, you look at the words for clues. To identify the theme of a movie, you must focus on the images and sounds. Moviemakers—in particular, the director—use the following techniques to make sure you get the message.

THEME DELIVERY	STRATEGIES FOR VIEWING
The Director's Plan A director makes basic decisions about how to transfer a well-known tale to the screen and what themes to portray.	• Be aware that a director usually presents the same **themes** that appeared in the original work. • Be prepared to find a theme expressed (or repeated) in the key scenes the director presents.
The Director's Tools In presenting certain images important to the theme, a director uses film techniques to highlight the message.	• Study the **camera shots** that show more than one character. These shots bring an audience close enough to see the ways characters react to each other. • The **lighting** of characters can reveal a theme in an indirect way. For example, soft lighting can represent goodness or warm moments beteween characters. • Listen for verbal clues. A director can state a theme directly through **dialogue.** You can also listen to the narration of a **voice-over,** the voice of an unseen narrator who provides important information about the story.
The Actor's Performance An actor can indicate a theme by showing changes in the behavior of his or her character.	• Notice an actor's **body movements.** An actor can portray a character's personality change by using different **gestures** or **facial expressions.** • Focus on the **tone of voice** of the actors. Think of how a voice can change to show surprise, anger, or weariness.

MediaSmart DVD

- **Film Clip:** *A Christmas Carol*
- **Director:** Brian Desmond Hurst
- **Genre:** Fantasy/Drama
- **Running Time:** 12 minutes

Viewing Guide for
A Christmas Carol

Since you've read the play version of *A Christmas Carol,* you already know all that happens to Ebenezer Scrooge. Watch the four movie clips one at a time. Each clip focuses either on Scrooge or on others who are part of his life-changing experience. Try to spot the movie techniques and acting techniques that were carefully designed to deliver Charles Dickens's themes.

View each clip several times and take as much time as you need to observe the events that take place. Keep these questions in mind as you view.

NOW VIEW

FIRST VIEWING: Comprehension

1. **Recall** At what point does Scrooge declare, "I am not the man I was"?
2. **Summarize** What happens to Tiny Tim, according to the voice-over narration at the end?

CLOSE VIEWING: Media Literacy

3. **Compare Lighting Techniques** The lighting in Scrooge's office in clip 1 is dark and dreary. The lighting of Scrooge's home when he awakes in clip 3 is bright and cheerful. What comparison do you think the director is making between Scrooge's old way of looking at the world and his new way?
4. **Interpret Acting** Scrooge goes from being cold-hearted to being softhearted. Beyond his dialogue, how do you know he has changed? Respond by using a chart like the one shown.

Scrooge's Behavior

	Clip 1	Clip 2	Clip 3	Clip 4
Facial expression				
Body movements				
Tone of voice				

Write or Discuss

Compare Play and Film Versions You've read a play version of the Dickens tale and watched scenes from a movie version. What did you enjoy about reading the play as compared to watching the movie scenes? Use evidence from either version to support your answer. Think about

- the portrayal of the character Scrooge in both versions
- how well each version delivers Dickens's basic themes
- the details in the stage directions of the play and the visual representation of the scenes

Produce Your Own Media

Design a DVD Cover Imagine you're part of a team promoting a new, up-to-date version of *A Christmas Carol.* Create a DVD cover that presents the highlights of this retelling. Follow the instructions on the Design Guide to help you position words and pictures on the DVD cover.

HERE'S HOW Use the Design Guide and these tips as you create the cover:

- Think of a modern-day setting and a basic story line that make it clear that this version happens in a very different time and place.
- Who's Scrooge? Brainstorm a cast list.
- Brainstorm what images to use on the cover, where to place them, and what colors to use.
- Write a blurb—a brief description of the version to appear on the back of the cover. Be sure to include within the blurb a statement that reflects a theme of the tale. Also create a rating and a critic's one-line comment about the version.

MEDIA TOOLS

For help with designing a DVD cover, visit the **Media Center** at **ClassZone.com.**

DESIGN GUIDE

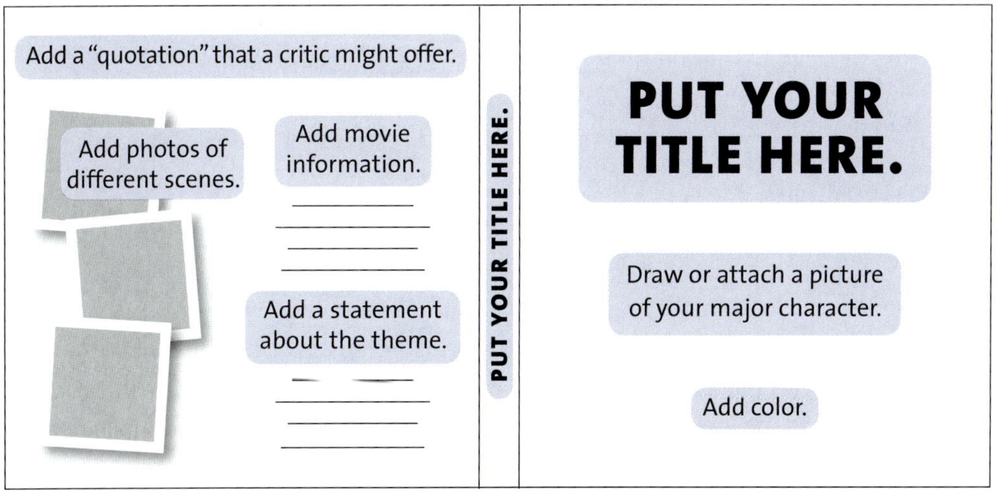

BACK COVER FRONT COVER

Tech Tip

You can choose colored typefaces for your title and other text. Also, try arranging the elements in a unique way. For example, try your title at the bottom.

Writing Workshop

Short Story

Did the stories and characters in this unit surprise you, make you think, or remind you of someone you know? Good stories can draw you into other worlds. In this workshop, you will invent your own combination of characters, setting, and plot. Use the **Writer's Road Map** to guide your creative journey.

WRITER'S ROAD MAP

Short Story

WRITING PROMPT 1

Writing from Your Imagination Write a story that is set in an unusual time or location. Make sure that your story has a plot, a conflict, and one or more characters.

Settings to Consider

- an extreme environment, such as Antarctica or the Sahara
- another time, such as ancient Egypt or the distant future
- a place you have always wanted to visit, such as the Grand Canyon or the Great Wall of China

WRITING PROMPT 2

Writing from Literature Choose a "big question" from this unit that really made you think. Then write a short story related to that question. Create a plot, a conflict, a setting, and one or more characters.

Questions to Make You Think

- What happens when friends compete? ("Amigo Brothers")
- What is the cure for unhappiness? ("What Do Fish Have to Do with Anything?")
- How important is money? (*A Christmas Carol*)

WRITING TOOLS
For prewriting, revision, and editing tools, visit the **Writing Center** at **ClassZone.com.**

KEY TRAITS

1. *IDEAS*

- Has an interesting **plot** and one or more **characters**
- Develops and resolves a **central conflict**
- Includes **descriptive details** that reveal the setting and characters
- Uses **dialogue** to show characters' personalities

2. *ORGANIZATION*

- **Introduces** the characters, the setting, or the action in a way that gets a reader's attention
- Follows a clear **sequence of events**
- Resolves the conflict with a convincing **conclusion**

3. *VOICE*

- Shows the writer's individual **style**

4. *WORD CHOICE*

- Uses **sensory language** to show what fictional characters and places are like

5. *SENTENCE FLUENCY*

- Varies **sentence lengths**

6. *CONVENTIONS*

- Uses **correct grammar, spelling, and punctuation**

WRITING/LANGUAGE STANDARD
9 Compose in narrative mode

Part 1: Analyze a Student Model

Online INTERACTIVE MODEL CLASSZONE.COM

Angela Tressler
Jane Addams Middle School

The Trap

Panic! That's what I was feeling. My friend Jack and I were riding bikes after school. After about an hour I realized that nothing looked familiar anymore.

"Hey, Jack? Any idea where we are?"

"Well," he answered, "it must be a new subdivision or something."

"Must be. Let's see if we can find our way out."

We kept riding. Soon it started getting dark. "Maybe we better ask someone where we are."

The first person we saw was a guy about our age. "Excuse me, how do we get out of this subdivision?" Jack asked him.

"Subdivision?" he asked us. "Funny, I haven't heard that one in a while." Then he started laughing and making fun of us.

Soon we came across this old lady sitting on her front porch with her cats. "Ma'am," I called out, "could you please tell us how to get out of here?"

"Child, you'll have to hurry. Once it gets dark, there's no way of ever leaving."

Suddenly, all the pieces started falling into place. Jack and I had ridden into the Time-To-Relive-Actuality-Permanently area, also called Time Trap for short.

I remember reading about this. As soon as you cross the border of our town, if you're going in the right direction, and the sun is about half set, you'll end up in the Time Trap. Once you're in, you can only get out before the sun sets completely the same day.

KEY TRAITS IN ACTION

Introduces two **characters** in an attention-getting way.

Develops a **central conflict** (being lost).

Has an interesting, unusual **plot.** Writer varies **sentence lengths** throughout story.

Descriptive details add excitement.

"No way, lady, this can't be happening."

"Hush up, child. Only your believing me can save you now. If you get out of here and back to your neighborhood before the sun disappears in the sky, you will have escaped the curse. If you don't make it, every day will be identical for the rest of your immortal life."

Dialogue shows characters' personalities. This writer's **style** is fast-paced and dramatic.

"So all we have to do is go back the way we came?" I asked.

"Not quite. You have to go back by going the exact opposite way you came. It sounds odd, I know, but trust me—it's your only way home."

"So what's the opposite way?" Jack asked.

"Come in. I'll show you on a map."

We followed Yellow Mill to the creek just like she said, but we must have made a wrong turn after that, because we were nowhere near where we should've been. The sun had disappeared almost completely, and we knew that within a half-hour it would be dark.

Follows a clear **sequence of events. Sensory language** adds suspense.

After quite a while we started to see some familiar things, like the lady's house. Sure enough, she was still sitting on her front porch.

"Quick, just tell us what to do after the creek!"

"You turn right, then left at the next stop."

"OK, we've got it now. Come on, Jack, we can still make it!" I cried.

As we rode away, the old lady muttered, "The idiots—don't they realize they've been doing the same thing for 15 years?"

The writer resolves the conflict in a surprising **conclusion.**

2

WRITING/LANGUAGE STANDARD
9.c Using figurative language

Part 2: Apply the Writing Process

PREWRITING

What Should I Do?

1. Brainstorm ideas.
Freewrite about places, people, or "big questions" that interest you. Then circle one or more ideas that might make a good story.

TIP Are you out of ideas? Choose a picture from a book or magazine and freewrite about the person, place, or event shown.

See page 426: Brainstorm Topics

What Does It Look Like?

My friends and I shoot hoops most days after school, and nothing happens.

We ride our bikes around a lot, and it's the same old neighborhood day after day.

What if we went back in time? Or to the future?

2. Focus your ideas.
Identify your characters. The writer of the student model decided to make herself a character in the story. She used **first-person point of view** ("That's what I was feeling" rather than "That's what she was feeling").

Next, decide on your setting. Start to think through what happens to the characters—that is, jot down your first ideas about your **plot.**

Characters	Setting	Plot
me Jack, my friend people we meet on our trip	a strange neighborhood, starting to get dark	We ride our bikes too far and end up getting lost, maybe going to another time or place? Ask the people there for help?

3. Make a story map.
Don't start to write your story until you have mapped out a plot that includes a **conflict** and at least two or three events.

TIP Remember that some ideas will come to you as you write. You can also make changes as you draft.

We realize we're lost.
↓
We ask for directions.
↓
I know we're in the Time Trap.
↓
We have to rush to get out in time.
↓
We find our way out? Or we start over?

DRAFTING

What Should I Do?	What Does It Look Like?
1. Start with a "hook." Right from the first sentence, get your readers' attention. You can do this with **sensory language,** exciting **dialogue, descriptive details,** or a surprising statement.	**Sensory language** *My friend Jack and I rode down street after street, past old houses with peeling paint and some mutt yapping its head off.* **A surprising statement** *Panic! That's what I was feeling.*
2. Develop your characters. Use **dialogue** to make the people in your story seem real.	*"Hey, Jack? Any idea where we are?"* *"Well," he answered, "it must be a new subdivision or something."* *"Must be. Let's see if we can find our way out."*
3. Make sure the sequence of events is clear. Use words and phrases such as *first, next, then, soon,* and *suddenly* to help your reader understand what happens when.	*The first person we saw was a guy about our age. . . .* *Soon we came across this old lady. . . .* *Suddenly, all the pieces started falling into place.*
4. Craft a satisfying ending. Bring your story to a satisfying close. The ending can be happy, sad, or funny. It can teach a lesson. This writer used a surprise ending. **TIP** **Before you revise, look back at the key traits on page 420. Also study the rubric and peer-reader questions on page 426.**	**A dramatic finish** *When it was almost dark, the glowing yellow Time Trap gate appeared. As we rushed through, we heard the old lady yell, "Goodbye, and don't come back!"* **A surprise ending** *As we rode away, the old lady muttered, "The idiots—don't they realize they've been doing the same thing for 15 years?"*

REVISING AND EDITING

What Should I Do?	What Does It Look Like?
1. Match the dialogue to the character. • Ask a peer reader to underline dialogue that seems phony or unnatural. • Revise to include contractions, slang, or exclamations that **match the character's age and personality.** **See page 426:** Ask a Peer Reader	~~"I cannot accept that this is happening."~~ *"No way, lady, this can't be happening."* ~~"Jack, it is time to go."~~ *"Come on, Jack, we can still make it!"*
2. Vary sentence lengths. • If all your sentences are short, they may seem choppy or immature. If all your sentences are long, your writing may be boring or hard to understand. • Revise your story to create **a mix of long and short sentences.**	~~"It sounds odd. I know that. Trust me. It's your only way home."~~ *"It sounds odd, I know, but trust me—it's your only way home."* *After quite a while we started to see some familiar things, like the lady's house. ~~and~~ Sure enough, she was still sitting on her front porch.*
3. Show your style. • Dialogue and word choice are parts of a writer's style. Do you want your style to be fast paced or relaxed, formal or fun filled? • This writer revised her story to make it more dramatic. She added colorful words and phrases (*hush up, save you*) and an important detail (*before the sun disappears in the sky*). You will learn more about style in Unit 4.	~~"If you get out of here, you will escape the curse."~~ *"Hush up, child. Only your believing me can save you now. If you get out of here and back to your neighborhood before the sun disappears in the sky, you will have escaped the curse."*
4. Brainstorm the right title. • Your title should interest a reader but not give away the whole story. If you wish, ask a peer reader for suggestions. • This writer chose a simple, dramatic title.	~~Riding Around Forever~~ **The Trap* ~~Lost in Time~~ ~~Saved Just in Time~~

Preparing to Publish

Short Story

Apply the Rubric

A strong short story . . .

☑ begins in an attention-getting way

☑ includes an interesting plot and at least one character

☑ has a central conflict

☑ uses descriptive details, sensory language, and dialogue to reveal the setting and characters

☑ has its own style

☑ follows a clear sequence of events

☑ uses a variety of sentence lengths

☑ has a satisfying conclusion

Ask a Peer Reader

- What is the conflict in my story?
- How could I make the dialogue more convincing?
- What three words would you use to describe my style?
- What did you like or dislike about the story's ending?

Brainstorm Topics

What if a disaster separated family members in a strange place?

What if a character slipped into another time or reality?

What if enemies had to work together to find their way out of a cave, a jungle, or a forest?

What if characters had to race against time to get to safety?

Check Your Grammar

Make sure each pronoun matches its antecedent (the noun or pronoun to which it refers). In this example, the pronoun *her* matches the antecedent *old lady.*

> *Soon we came across this old lady sitting on ~~their~~ her front porch.*

See page R52: Agreement with Antecedent

Writing Online

PUBLISHING OPTIONS

For publishing options, visit the **Writing Center** at **ClassZone.com.**

ASSESSMENT PREPARATION

For writing and grammar assessment practice, go to the **Assessment Center** at **ClassZone.com.**

COMMUNICATION STANDARD
15 Demonstrate listening skills

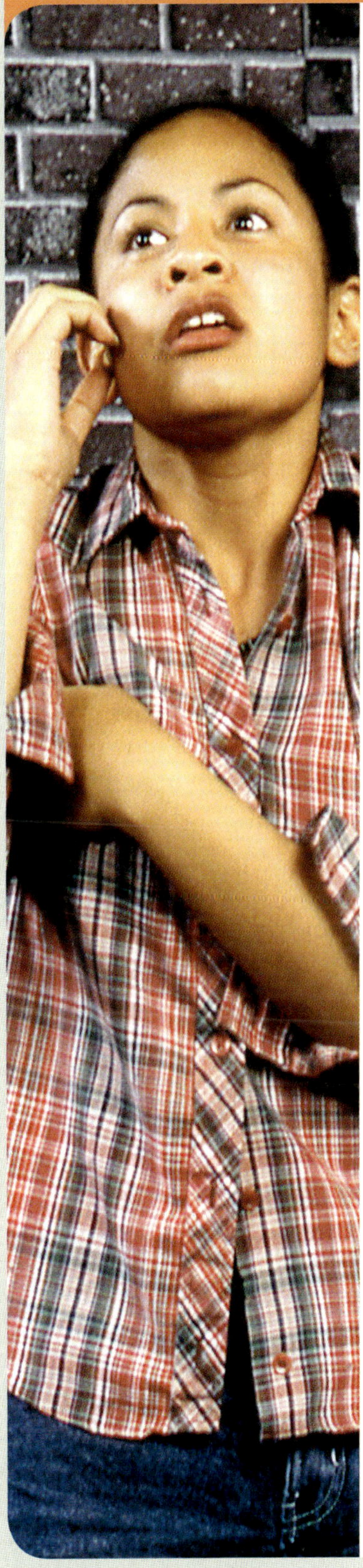

Dramatizing a Short Story

This is your chance to sit in the director's chair. Turn your story, "The Trap," or another story from this unit into a play. Then work with classmates to perform it.

Planning the Dramatization

1. **Identify the mood you want to create.** Should the story make audience members laugh, examine their own lives, feel surprise, or shiver with fear? Keep the mood in mind as you follow the other step.
2. **Write your script.** Dialogue is what moves the action along in most plays, so consider using more of it. You may also want to add a narrator, or even more characters if needed. Remember that a script includes stage directions. You should also add ideas for music and sound effects.

Jack *(fear in his voice). So what's the opposite way?*

Old Lady *(in a serious voice). Come in. I'll show you on a map.*

The three characters walk though a door that creaks. The lights go down. After a moment, the bike riders appear in dim spotlight, stage left.

Narrator. *They followed Yellow Mill to the creek. . . .*

Presenting the Dramatization

1. **Choose your cast and crew.** Decide on the actors. Put other people in charge of music, sound effects, and props. You might also need help with lighting, costumes, and other details.
2. **Rehearse.** Invite someone to listen when you rehearse. Ask for feedback. Actors may need to speak the words more clearly, or you may need to add dialogue.
3. **Act it out.** Present your play to your classmates and/or family members. Soak up the applause! If possible, ask someone to videotape the presentation so you can evaluate its strengths and weaknesses.

See page R80: Evaluate an Oral Interpretation

Assessment Practice

Reading Comprehension

ASSESS

The practice test items on the next few pages match skills listed on the Unit Goals page (page 303) and addressed throughout this unit. Taking this practice test will help you assess your knowledge of these skills and determine your readiness for the Unit Test.

REVIEW

After you take the practice test, your teacher can help you identify any skills you need to review.

- Theme
- Symbol
- Make Inferences
- Cause and Effect
- Compare and Contrast
- Context Clues
- Connotation and Denotation
- Independent and Dependent Clauses
- Coordinating Conjunctions

ASSESSMENT ONLINE

For more assessment practice and test-taking tips, go to the **Assessment Center** at **ClassZone.com.**

DIRECTIONS *Read the selection and answer the questions that follow.*

from The Hummingbird That Lived Through Winter

William Saroyan

There was a hummingbird once which in the wintertime did not leave our neighborhood in Fresno, California.

I'll tell you about it.

Across the street lived old Dikran, who was almost blind. He was past eighty and his wife was only a few years younger. They had a little house that was as neat inside as it was ordinary outside—except for old Dikran's garden, which was the best thing of its kind in the world. Plants, bushes, trees—all strong, in sweet black moist earth whose guardian was old Dikran. All things from the sky loved this spot in our poor neighborhood, and old Dikran loved *them.*

One freezing Sunday, in the dead of winter, as I came home from Sunday School I saw old Dikran standing in the middle of the street trying to distinguish what was in his hand. Instead of going into our house to the fire, as I had wanted to do, I stood on the steps of the front porch and watched the old man. He would turn around and look upward at his trees and then back to the palm of his hand. He stood in the street at least two minutes and then at last he came to me. He held his hand out, and in Armenian he said, "What is this in my hand?"

I looked.

"It is a hummingbird," I said half in English and half in Armenian. Hummingbird I said in English because I didn't know its name in Armenian.

"What is that?" old Dikran asked.

"The little bird," I said. "You know. The one that comes in the summer and stands in the air and then shoots away. The one with the wings that beat so fast you can't see them. It's in your hand. It's dying."

"Come with me," the old man said. "I can't see, and the old lady's at church. I can feel its heart beating. Is it in a bad way? Look again, once."

I looked again. It was a sad thing to behold. This wonderful little creature of summertime in the big rough hand of the old peasant. Here it was in the cold of winter, absolutely helpless and pathetic, not suspended in a shaft of summer light, not the most alive thing in the world, but the most helpless and heartbreaking.

"It's dying," I said.

The old man lifted his hand to his mouth and blew warm breath on the little thing in his hand which he could not even see. "Stay now," he said in Armenian. "It is not long till summer. Stay, swift and lovely."

We went into the kitchen of his little house, and while he blew warm breath on the bird he told me what to do.

"Put a tablespoonful of honey over the gas fire and pour it into my hand, but be sure it is not too hot."

This was done.

After a moment the hummingbird began to show signs of fresh life. The warmth of the room, the vapor of the warm honey—and, well, the will and love of the old man. Soon the old man could feel the change in his hand, and after a moment or two the hummingbird began to take little dabs of the honey.

"It will live," the old man announced. "Stay and watch."

The transformation was incredible. The old man kept his hand generously open, and I expected the helpless bird to shoot upward out of his hand, suspend itself in space, and scare the life out of me—which is exactly what happened. The new life of the little bird was magnificent. It spun about in the little kitchen, going to the window, coming back to the heat, suspending, circling as if it were summertime and it had never felt better in its whole life.

The old man sat on the plain chair, blind but attentive. He listened carefully and tried to see, but of course he couldn't. He kept asking about the bird, how it seemed to be, whether it showed signs of weakening again, what its spirit was, and whether or not it appeared to be restless; and I kept describing the bird to him.

When the bird was restless and wanted to go, the old man said, "Open the window and let it go."

"Will it live?" I asked.

"It is alive now and wants to go," he said. "Open the window."

I opened the window, the hummingbird stirred about here and there,

GO ON

feeling the cold from the outside, suspended itself in the area of the open window, stirring this way and that, and then it was gone.

"Close the window," the old man said.

We talked a minute or two and then I went home.

The old man claimed the hummingbird lived through that winter, but I never knew for sure. I saw hummingbirds again when summer came, but I couldn't tell one from the other.

One day in the summer I asked the old man.

"Did it live?"

"The little bird?" he said.

"Yes," I said. "That we gave the honey to. You remember. The little bird that was dying in the winter. Did it live?"

"Look about you," the old man said. "Do you see the bird?"

"I see humming*birds,*" I said.

"Each of them is our bird," the old man said. "Each of them, each of them," he said swiftly and gently.

Comprehension

DIRECTIONS *Answer the following questions about the selection.*

1. Dikran's garden symbolizes
   - **A** the certainty of death
   - **B** his homeland of Armenia
   - **C** an escape from his house
   - **D** the abundance of nature

2. Seeing Dikran in the street causes the narrator to
   - **A** worry that a car will hit Dikran
   - **B** run to his own house to get warm by the fire
   - **C** watch Dikran to find out what he is doing
   - **D** look for birds suffering from the cold

3. Which action helps cause the hummingbird to revive?
   - **A** keeping the bird inside all winter
   - **B** asking questions about the bird
   - **C** opening the window
   - **D** feeding the bird warm honey

4. Compare and contrast the hummingbird's behavior before and after Dikran takes it inside. Which of the following statements best describes the change in behavior?
   - **A** "It was a sad thing to behold."
   - **B** "The transformation was incredible."
   - **C** "I can feel its heart beating."
   - **D** "I saw hummingbirds again. . . ."

ARMT/ADAW SKILLS PRACTICE

5. Dikran lets the hummingbird go because he knows that
   - **A** it will survive the winter now
   - **B** spring will come soon
   - **C** it is wild and needs to be free
   - **D** he can't take care of it

6. What can you infer about Dikran from the way he cares for the hummingbird?
   - **A** He is unhappy that he can't see very well.
   - **B** He loves caring for living things.
   - **C** He wants to make the narrator feel good.
   - **D** He thinks that this bird is special.

7. What is the most important way in which the narrator and Dikran are similar?
   - **A** They appreciate nature and life.
   - **B** They are Armenian.
   - **C** They live in the same poor neighborhood.
   - **D** They know a lot about nature.

8. What does the hummingbird symbolize to Dikran at the end of the story?
   - **A** death
   - **B** life
   - **C** memories
   - **D** winter

9. Which of the following descriptions best shows what the hummingbird symbolizes?
   - **A** "wonderful little creature of summertime"
   - **B** "absolutely helpless and pathetic"
   - **C** "the most alive thing in the world"
   - **D** "the one with the wings that beat so fast"

10. Which statement best describes a theme of the story?
    - **A** The life force is powerful.
    - **B** Nature is very fragile.
    - **C** Elderly people deserve respect.
    - **D** Life is full of hardships.

11. Which lines from the story best demonstrate its theme?
    - **A** "There was a hummingbird once which in the wintertime did not leave our neighborhood in Fresno, California."
    - **B** "He listened carefully and tried to see, but of course he couldn't."
    - **C** "I saw hummingbirds again when summer came, but I couldn't tell one from the other."
    - **D** "'Each of them is our bird,' the old man said. 'Each of them, each of them,' he said swiftly and gently."

Open-Ended

SHORT ANSWER *Write a short answer to the following question.*

12. Name two things Dikran does to cause the hummingbird to revive.

ESSAY *Write one or two paragraphs to answer this question.*

13. Reread lines 24–33. What is the hummingbird like? Compare its wintertime appearance with how hummingbirds look and act in the summer.

GO ON

Vocabulary

DIRECTIONS *Use context clues to answer the following questions.*

1. Which is the most likely meaning of *distinguish* in line 13?

A hold

B see

C caress

D save

2. Which is the most likely meaning of *pathetic* in line 31?

A pitiful

B lost

C small

D broken

3. Which is the most likely meaning of *suspend* in line 51?

A disappear from sight

B stop breathing for a short time

C hang in the air without falling

D spin out of control

4. Which is the most likely meaning of *spirit* as it is used in line 59?

A a strong loyalty

B the quality that sets something apart

C an emotional tendency

D the energy of a living thing

DIRECTIONS *Use context clues and your knowledge of connotation and denotation to answer the following questions.*

5. The denotation of *ordinary* in line 6 is "usual." Which word below best describes its connotation?

A poor

B small

C plain

D deserted

6. The denotation of *sweet* in line 8 is "free of acid or acidity." Which word below best describes its connotation?

A tasty

B good

C cheap

D perfumed

7. Which connotation does the word *peasant* have in line 30?

A coarseness

B vulgarity

C hostility

D rudeness

ARMT/ADAW SKILLS PRACTICE

Writing & Grammar

DIRECTIONS *Read this passage and then answer the questions that follow.*

(1) Last summer, our family drove to Mexico. (2) Where my mom was born. (3) We saw the places where she played as a little girl and visited her home. (4) Her old neighborhood has narrow streets. (5) That wind past the houses. (6) My mom remembered her friends, although she didn't find any of them living there anymore. (7) She looked for the anthill she had loved to watch as a child. (8) Like her friends, the anthill was gone. (9) Still, Mom was happy we went. (10) We'll probably go back again sometime.

1. Combine sentence 1 and fragment 2 to form one sentence with an independent clause and a dependent clause.

A Last summer, our family drove to Mexico and where my mom was born.

B Last summer, our family drove to Mexico, where my mom was born.

C Last summer, our family drove to Mexico; my mom was born there.

D Our family drove to Mexico last summer to my mom's birthplace.

2. Combine sentence 4 and fragment 5 to form one sentence with an independent clause and a dependent clause.

A Her old neighborhood has narrow streets; that wind past the houses.

B Her old neighborhood has narrow streets that wind past the houses.

C Her old neighborhood has narrow streets—and the streets wind past the houses.

D Her old neighborhood has narrow streets, and furthermore, these streets wind past the houses.

3. Choose the correct coordinating conjunction to combine sentences 7 and 8.

A so

B but

C for

D or

4. Choose the correct coordinating conjunction to combine sentences 9 and 10.

A for

B but

C yet

D and

STOP

UNIT 3

More Great Reads

Ideas for Independent Reading

Which questions from Unit 3 made an impression on you? Continue exploring them with these books.

What happens when friends compete?

Wolf Shadows
by Mary Casanova
As hunting season approaches, 12-year-old Seth finds himself disagreeing with his best friend, Matt, over the protection of wolves. On opening day, Matt wounds a wolf. Can Seth resolve his conflicting emotions before it's too late?

Friends and Enemies
by LouAnn Gaeddert
William and Jim are best friends. But when World War II breaks out, Jim refuses to support the war. Angered by his friend's stance, William joins classmates in attacking Jim. Will Jim ever forgive him?

End of the Race
by Dean Hughes
Two 12-year-olds find their friendship is tested when they represent their school in a track race. Jared feels he has to be the great athlete his dad was, while Davin, who is African American, considers their rivalry a racial conflict.

What is the cure for unhappiness?

Roll of Thunder, Hear My Cry
by Mildred D. Taylor
Cassie Logan, growing up in a loving family, has never had reason to suspect that anyone would wish her harm. All that changes when her community comes under constant threat from "night riders."

Because of Winn-Dixie
by Kate DiCamillo
If you were suddenly uprooted to a distant place, would you be able to adjust? India Opal Buloni's (pronounced "baloney") first summer in the little town of Naomi is action packed—all thanks to a big, ugly dog named Winn-Dixie.

Mick Harte Was Here
by Barbara Park
Can one ever feel happy after the death of a brother or sister? Thirteen-year-old Phoebe describes the stages of grief her family suffers after her brother Mick dies in an accident. Finally, she comes to terms with his death.

Can you be alone and not lonely?

Spider Boy
by Ralph Fletcher
When Bobby Ballenger moves from the Midwest to New York, he has a difficult time adjusting. The cruelty of his classmates makes him long for his former friends. Will he face the bullies and earn a second chance?

Spinners
by Donna Jo Napoli and Richard Tchen
Napoli and Tchen retell a classic tale to give insights into the lives of Rumpelstiltskin and his daughter. Love, pride, avarice, and revenge are all a part of this delightful new version.

The Fire Pony
by Rodman Philbrick
Roy is happiest when he's with his older brother Joe, who has a fiery temper and a special gift for healing horses. All seems well when Joe rescues Roy from a foster home, but before long, Joe reveals a darker side.

UNIT 4

Finding a Voice

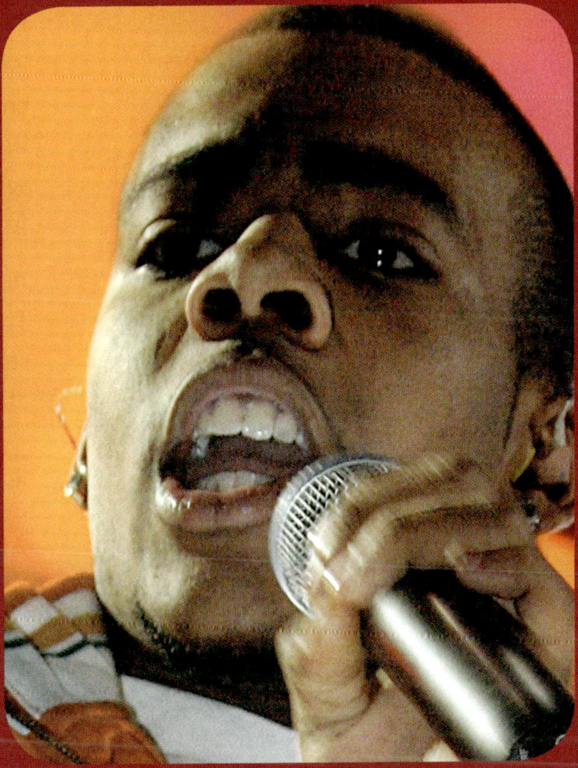

MOOD, TONE, AND STYLE

- In Fiction
- In Nonfiction
- In Poetry
- In Media

UNIT 4 Share What You Know

What's your STYLE?

When we get ready for an important event, we usually start by figuring out what we are going to wear. Why do you think that is? What can our clothing and hairstyle say about us? By making choices about these things, each of us can create a personal style. In things such as writing, filmmaking, and art, **style** refers to the way a person expresses a message. Some people are even known for their unique style.

ACTIVITY Think of three people with distinct personal styles. They can be people you know and admire or people you have seen in movies or on television. Evaluate their styles by thinking about these questions:

- What made you notice each person?
- How do their styles differ?
- Which style is most similar to your own?

After answering these questions, write a description of your own style.

Online LITERATURE CLASSZONE.COM

Literature and Reading Center
Writing Center
Vocabulary and Spelling Center

ALABAMA STANDARDS

Preview Unit Goals

LITERARY ANALYSIS
- Identify and analyze mood, tone, and irony
- Compare and contrast tone
- Identify and analyze elements of style, including word choice, sentence structure, imagery, and dialogue
- Understand form in poetry

READING
- Use reading strategies, including monitoring and setting a purpose for reading
- Summarize a story
- Distinguish fact from opinion

WRITING AND GRAMMAR
- Write a set of instructions
- Write an interpretive essay
- Maintain subject-verb agreement in number
- Maintain subject-verb agreement when using compound subjects

SPEAKING, LISTENING, AND VIEWING
- Analyze visual elements in media
- Produce and edit a video

VOCABULARY
- Identify and use synonyms
- Identify and use literal and figurative meanings of words

ACADEMIC VOCABULARY
- mood
- tone
- style
- monitor
- summarize
- interpretive essay
- subject-verb agreement
- fact
- opinion

UNIT 4

Reader's Workshop

Mood, Tone, and Style

Think of a story as a homemade meal. You've learned about the basic ingredients: plot, characters, setting, and theme. What gives a writer's work a unique flavor? What makes you tear hungrily through one story, while another is hard to digest? The answer is the blend of spices known as mood, tone, and style.

ALABAMA STANDARDS

READING STANDARDS
2 Relate literary devices to each other, including imagery
2.a Determining mood

Part 1: Mood and Tone

Mood is a feeling that a writer creates for readers. **Tone** is a writer's attitude toward his or her subject. What's the difference? Imagine this scenario: You and a friend venture into a haunted house, advertised as "spine-tinglingly scary." As you enter the shadowy house, your stomach tightens. You hear eerie howling. Suddenly, your friend sneers, "Spine-tingling. *Right*. This is as spine-tingling as a laundromat."

The mood of the haunted house was terrifying (at least for you!), but your friend's tone was sarcastic. As a reader, think of mood as the feeling the writer creates—the overall atmosphere. Tone, however, is how you imagine the writer "sounds." Often, you can identify a mood or tone by looking at the writer's choice of words and details.

MOOD

Words to Describe Mood

- cheerful
- romantic
- somber
- wondrous
- eerie
- terrifying
- peaceful
- silly
- thoughtful

Example

The highlighted words and phrases reveal the gloomy setting and create an eerie mood.

A wind had sprung up, driving the dust of the weeks-dry road before it, when they entered the street on which they lived, and the leaves rustled ominously. Lightning flickered.

—from "Rain, Rain, Go Away" by Isaac Asimov

TONE

Words to Describe Tone

- humorous
- sarcastic
- sympathetic
- serious
- sincere
- mocking
- disgusted
- admiring
- angry

Example

The highlighted words and details help you almost "hear" the author's mocking tone.

I went to a British school and every morning we sang "God Save the King." Of course the British children loved singing about their gracious king. Ian Forbes stuck out his chest and sang as if he were saving the king all by himself.

—from *Homesick* by Jean Fritz

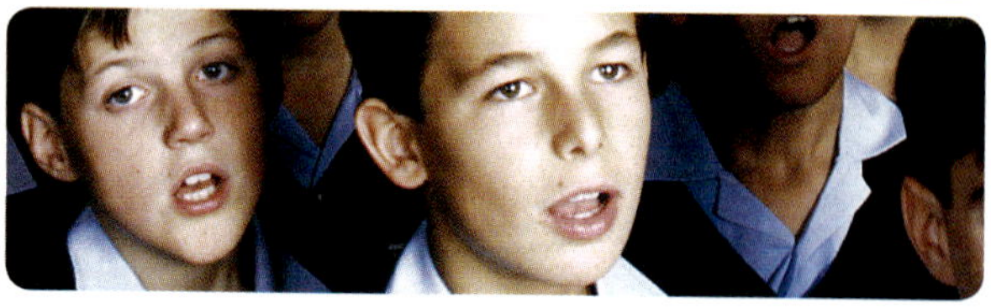

MODEL 1: MOOD

Here, you see a New England autumn through the eyes of a girl from Barbados. Notice the words and details that are used to describe the setting. What mood do they help to create?

from

The Witch of Blackbird Pond

Novel by **Elizabeth George Speare**

. . . The October sun filled the world with mellow warmth. Before Kit's eyes a miracle took place, for which she was totally unprepared. She stood in the doorway of her uncle's house and held her breath with wonder. The maple tree in front of the doorstep burned like a gigantic red torch. The oaks along the roadway glowed yellow and bronze. The fields stretched like a carpet of jewels, emerald and topaz and garnet. Everywhere she walked the color shouted and sang around her. The dried brown leaves crackled beneath her feet and gave off a delicious smoky fragrance. No one had ever told her about autumn in New England. The excitement of it beat in her blood.

Close Read

1. Find two details that the writer uses to describe the setting. Then identify two details that tell you how Kit feels about her surroundings. One of each is boxed.
2. Judging by the details you found, how would you describe the mood?

MODEL 2: TONE

When Roald Dahl was a boy, he spent a lot of time at the local candy shop. In this excerpt from his autobiography, Dahl tells you more than you would ever want to know about the shop's owner, Mrs. Pratchett.

from

BOY: Tales of Childhood

Autobiography by **Roald Dahl**

But by far the most loathsome thing about Mrs. Pratchett was the filth that clung around her. Her apron was grey and greasy. Her blouse had bits of breakfast all over it, toast crumbs and tea stains and splotches of dried egg yolk. It was her hands, however, that disturbed us most. They were disgusting. They were black with dirt and grime. They looked as though they had been putting lumps of coal on the fire all day long. And do not forget, please, that it was these very hands and fingers that she plunged into the sweet jars. . . .

Close Read

1. This excerpt is full of words that have negative **connotations,** or feelings, attached to them. One example has been boxed. Find three more words.
2. Review the words you identified. How would you describe Dahl's tone, or his attitude toward Mrs. Pratchett?

Part 2: What Is Style?

Mood and tone can affect the way you feel about a work of literature. Style, though, is often what brings you back again and again to the writing of a particular author. In literature, **style** is the way something is written—not what is said, but *how* it's said. A writer's style can be chatty, flowery, or overly formal. It all depends on certain elements, such as a writer's tone, sentence structures, and choice of words. Is the tone silly or serious? Does the writer use fancy words, like *expectorate,* or everyday words, like *spit?*

The celebrated author Gary Soto is known for his unique style of writing. Notice how three key elements help to create his one-of-a-kind style.

GARY SOTO'S STYLE

Soto sees himself as "someone who paints a vivid picture." He says, "Most of my writing is descriptive. You come away with clear pictures of the scene. . . ." Notice how Soto's style shines through in the examples from his novel *Taking Sides.*

Word Choice

Style begins with **word choice,** a writer's use of words. With just a few descriptive verbs and adjectives, Soto puts you at the scene of a basketball practice.

Example

Shafts of afternoon sunlight glared on the polished gym floor.

Sentence Structure

Sentence structure refers to whether sentences are short and simple or long and complex. Notice how these sentences reflect the fast pace of a basketball game.

Example

Lincoln passed to James, who passed to Durkins, who took a shot and missed from the top of the key. But Lincoln pulled the ball down, chambered, and shot—*swish.*

Imagery

At the heart of Soto's style is **imagery,** words and phrases that appeal to readers' senses. Here, Soto appeals to the sense of sight with a unique description of a city boy.

Example

Lincoln was a star basketball player, tall but not thin. When he made a fist, his forearm tightened with muscles. His stomach was muscle, his legs muscle. His face was brown, like coffee laced with cream, and his hair black as a chunk of asphalt.

MODEL 1: STYLE IN SCIENCE FICTION

Many writers, including H. G. Wells, have crafted science fiction stories about time travel. Wells, who wrote *The Time Machine* in 1895, is known for his formal style and use of vivid imagery.

from **The Time Machine**

Novel by **H. G. Wells**

. . . I made good my retreat to the narrow tunnel. But I had scarce entered this when my light was blown out, and in the blackness I could hear the Morlocks rustling like wind among leaves, and pattering like the rain, as they hurried after me.

In a moment I was clutched by several hands, and there was no mistaking that they were trying to haul me back. I struck another light, and waved it in their dazzled faces. You can scarce imagine how nauseatingly inhuman they looked—those pale, chinless faces and great, lidless, pinkish-grey eyes!—as they stared in their blindness and bewilderment.

Close Read

1. Certain words and phrases, such as those in the boxed example, contribute to Wells's formal style. Find two more examples.
2. Identify three images that help you see and hear the Morlocks.

MODEL 2: STYLE IN SCIENCE FICTION

Here is an excerpt from another science fiction story, this one by a contemporary author with a much more informal style.

from **Future Tense**

Short story by **Robert Lipsyte**

A half hour later, Mr. Smith called Gary out of Spanish. There was no expression on his regular features. He said, "I'm going to need some help with you."

Cold sweat covered Gary's body as Mr. Smith grabbed his arm and led him to the new vice-principal. She read the composition while they waited. Gary got a good look at her for the first time. Ms. Jones was . . . just there. She looked as though she'd been manufactured to fit her name. Average. Standard. Typical. The cold sweat turned into goose pimples.

How could he have missed the clues? Smith and Jones were aliens!

Close Read

1. Look at the boxed phrases. How does Lipsyte's choice of words compare with Wells's?
2. What is the most striking difference between these two authors' styles? Consider word choice, sentence structure, and imagery.

Part 3: Analyze the Literature

A man goes out for a walk. What situation could be simpler? Both of the following excerpts begin with this setup. However, you will see how a story's mood, tone, and style can make even the most similar situations seem very different.

from

One Ordinary Day, with Peanuts

Short story by **Shirley Jackson**

Mr. John Philip Johnson shut his front door behind him and went down his front steps into the bright morning with a feeling that all was well with the world on this best of all days, and wasn't the sun warm and good, and didn't his shoes feel comfortable after the resoling, and he knew that he had undoubtedly chosen the very precise tie that belonged with the day and the sun and his comfortable feet, and, after all, wasn't the world just a wonderful place? In spite of the fact that he was a small man, and though the tie was perhaps a shade vivid, Mr. Johnson radiated a feeling of well-being as he went down the steps and onto the dirty sidewalk, and he smiled at people who passed him, and some of them even smiled back. He stopped at the newsstand on the corner and bought his paper, saying, "*Good* morning" with real conviction to the man who sold him the paper and the two or three other people who were lucky enough to be buying papers when Mr. Johnson skipped up. He remembered to fill his pockets with candy and peanuts, and then he set out to get himself uptown. He stopped in a flower shop and bought a carnation for his buttonhole, and stopped almost immediately afterward to give the carnation to a small child in a carriage, who looked at him dumbly, and then smiled, and Mr. Johnson smiled, and the child's mother looked at Mr. Johnson for a minute and then smiled, too.

Close Read

1. What words and details in lines 1–7 help to create a cheerful mood?
2. Read the first sentence aloud. How would you describe its length and rhythm? Notice how the sentence structure reflects Mr. Johnson's carefree attitude.
3. Look at the boxed details. Would you describe the author's tone, or attitude toward Mr. Johnson, as mocking or admiring? Explain.

In this excerpt, Rip Van Winkle leaves his nagging wife and goes for a hike with his dog, Wolf. It won't take you long to notice the different "feeling" of this story. Read closely to find out what the author has done to create such a contrasting effect.

from

RIP VAN WINKLE

Short story by **Washington Irving**

. . . He looked down into a deep mountain glen, wild, lonely, and shagged, the bottom filled with fragments from the impending cliffs, and scarcely lighted by the reflected rays of the setting sun. For some time Rip lay musing[1] on this scene; evening was gradually advancing; the mountains began to throw their long blue shadows over the valleys; he saw that it would be dark long before he could reach the village, and he heaved a heavy sigh when he thought of encountering the terrors of Dame Van Winkle.

As he was about to descend, he heard a voice from a distance, hallooing, "Rip Van Winkle! Rip Van Winkle!" He looked around, but could see nothing but a crow winging its solitary flight across the mountain. He thought his fancy[2] must have deceived him, and turned again to descend, when he heard the same cry ring through the still evening air; "Rip Van Winkle! Rip Van Winkle!"—at the same time Wolf bristled up his back, and giving a low growl, skulked[3] to his master's side, looking fearfully down into the glen. Rip now felt a vague apprehension stealing over him; he looked anxiously in the same direction, and perceived a strange figure slowly toiling up the rocks, and bending under the weight of something he carried on his back.

1. **musing:** thinking or reflecting.
2. **fancy:** imagination.
3. **skulked:** moved fearfully.

Close Read

1. Examine the boxed words and details. What mood do they help to create?
2. Read lines 3–8 aloud and try to hear how the author "sounds" while describing Rip's thoughts. Is the author's tone serious or mocking? Explain.
3. Washington Irving is known for his use of formal words and phrases and long, complex sentences. Find two examples of each in this excerpt.

Dark They Were, and Golden-Eyed

Science Fiction by Ray Bradbury

Can where you are CHANGE *who you are?*

ALABAMA STANDARDS

READING & LIT STANDARDS
2.a Determining mood
6 Analyze science fiction for distinguishing characteristics

KEY IDEA Your hobbies, interests, and habits often depend on the climate you are used to and the people and places you encounter every day. If you were to move away from everything you know, how much of who you are would **change,** and how much would stay the same? In "Dark They Were, and Golden-Eyed," a family moves to a very different environment and gets the chance to find out.

DISCUSS With a group, discuss your thoughts about the question at the top of the page. Take turns answering the question and explaining your reasons. Record the group's responses on a chart like the one shown.

Can Where You Are Change Who You Are?		
Name	Yes or No	Why or Why Not?

LITERARY ANALYSIS: MOOD

Has a story ever made you feel hopeful, nervous, or completely terrified? The feeling you get from a story is called the **mood.** Writers create a mood by

- carefully choosing words to describe the **plot, setting,** and **characters**
- showing what characters think and how they talk

Identifying mood can help you understand a story. As you read "Dark They Were, and Golden-Eyed," notice how it makes you feel, and think about which words may have made you feel that way.

READING STRATEGY: READING SCIENCE FICTION

In **science fiction,** writers often explore what life might be like in the future. They do so by blending scientific facts and theories and familiar elements of real life with their own ideas to create imaginary worlds and unique situations.

Science fiction writers often use their stories to comment on present-day problems. As you read Ray Bradbury's story, use a chart to note the elements of science fiction.

Elements of Science Fiction	*Examples in the Story*
known scientific information	
familiar elements of life today	
imaginary worlds and situations	

Review: **Make Inferences**

VOCABULARY IN CONTEXT

Bradbury's **word choice** affects the **mood** of his story. Match each numbered word or phrase with a vocabulary word.

WORD LIST			
convivial	forlorn	recede	
dwindle	muse	subtly	
flimsy	pendulum		

1. friendly
2. indirectly
3. hanging weight
4. decrease
5. become distant
6. daydream
7. lonely
8. breakable

Author Online

An Early Start

Ray Bradbury
born 1920

Ray Bradbury credits his mother for encouraging his imagination. She loved films and started taking her son to see them when he was only 3. By age 8, Bradbury had developed a love for both science fiction and the planet Mars. Bradbury wrote his first Martian stories when he was 12. Just before his 21st birthday, Bradbury sold his first story. That began a career filled with bestsellers, awards, and a lasting love of writing.

Man with a Mission Bradbury believes that one purpose of science fiction is to warn about negative things that might happen in the future if care is not taken in the present. Some of his writing reflects his worries about where our society is headed.

MORE ABOUT THE AUTHOR
For more on Ray Bradbury, visit the **Literature Center** at **ClassZone.com.**

Background

Red Planet Mars has been the setting of many science fiction films and stories, including "Dark They Were, and Golden-Eyed." Films and stories about Mars rarely give a realistic description of the planet, but they often incorporate elements of actual scientific research and developments in space travel.

DARK THEY WERE, AND Golden-Eyed

RAY BRADBURY

The rocket metal cooled in the meadow winds. Its lid gave a bulging *pop.* From its clock interior stepped a man, a woman, and three children. The other passengers whispered away across the Martian meadow, leaving the man alone among his family.

The man felt his hair flutter and the tissues of his body draw tight as if he were standing at the center of a vacuum. His wife, before him, seemed almost to whirl away in smoke. The children, small seeds, might at any instant be sown to all the Martian climes.

The children looked up at him, as people look to the sun to tell what time of their life it is. His face was cold.

"What's wrong?" asked his wife.

"Let's get back on the rocket." **A**

"Go back to Earth?"

"Yes! Listen!"

ANALYZE VISUALS
What can you **infer** about how the person in the painting might be feeling?

A MOOD
How would you describe the man's first impression of Mars? Think about how his feelings affect the mood of the story.

Sugar Sphinx (1933), Salvador Dali. Oil on canvas.
© 2008 Artists Rights Society (ARS), New York.
© Salvador Dali. Gala-Salvador Dali Foundation.

The wind blew as if to flake away their identities. At any moment the Martian air might draw his soul from him, as marrow comes from a white bone. He felt submerged in a chemical that could dissolve his intellect and burn away his past.

They looked at Martian hills that time had worn with a crushing pressure of years. They saw the old cities, lost in their meadows, lying like children's delicate bones among the blowing lakes of grass.

"Chin up, Harry," said his wife. "It's too late. We've come over sixty million miles."

The children with their yellow hair hollered at the deep dome of Martian sky. There was no answer but the racing hiss of wind through the stiff grass. **B**

B MOOD
Reread lines 15–26. On the basis of Bradbury's description of the **setting,** decide whether you have a positive or negative feeling about Mars. What words contribute to your feeling?

He picked up the luggage in his cold hands. "Here we go," he said—a man standing on the edge of a sea, ready to wade in and be drowned.

They walked into town.

Their name was Bittering. Harry and his wife Cora; Dan, Laura, and David. They built a small white cottage and ate good breakfasts there, but the fear was never gone. It lay with Mr. Bittering and Mrs. Bittering, a third unbidden partner at every midnight talk, at every dawn awakening.

"I feel like a salt crystal," he said, "in a mountain stream, being washed away. We don't belong here. We're Earth people. This is Mars. It was meant for Martians. For heaven's sake, Cora, let's buy tickets for home!"

But she only shook her head. "One day the atom bomb will fix Earth. Then we'll be safe here."

"Safe and insane!"

Tick-tock, seven o'clock sang the voice-clock; *time to get up.* And they did.

Something made him check everything each morning—warm hearth, potted blood-geraniums—precisely as if he expected something to be amiss. The morning paper was toast-warm from the 6 A.M. Earth rocket. He broke its seal and tilted it at his breakfast place. He forced himself to be **convivial.** **C**

convivial
(kən-vĭv'ē-əl) *adj.* enjoying the company of others; sociable

C READING SCIENCE FICTION
Reread lines 40–45. What are three examples of how Bradbury brings present-day life into this futuristic **setting?**

"Colonial days all over again," he declared. "Why, in ten years there'll be a million Earthmen on Mars. Big cities, everything! They said we'd fail. Said the Martians would resent our invasion. But did we find any Martians? Not a living soul! Oh, we found their empty cities, but no one in them. Right?"

A river of wind submerged the house. When the windows ceased rattling Mr. Bittering swallowed and looked at the children.

"I don't know," said David. "Maybe there're Martians around we don't see. Sometimes nights I think I hear 'em. I hear the wind. The sand hits my window. I get scared. And I see those towns way up in the mountains where the Martians lived a long time ago. And I think I see things moving around those towns, Papa. And I wonder if those Martians *mind* us living here. I wonder if they won't do something to us for coming here."

"Nonsense!" Mr. Bittering looked out the windows. "We're clean, decent people." He looked at his children. "All dead cities have some kind of ghosts in them. Memories, I mean." He stared at the hills. "You see a staircase and you wonder what Martians looked like climbing it. You see Martian paintings and you wonder what the painter was like. You make a little ghost in your mind, a memory. It's quite natural. Imagination." He stopped. "You haven't been prowling up in those ruins, have you?"

"No, Papa." David looked at his shoes.

"See that you stay away from them. Pass the jam."

"Just the same," said little David, "I bet something happens."

Something happened that afternoon. Laura stumbled through the settlement, crying. She dashed blindly onto the porch.

"Mother, Father—the war, Earth!" she sobbed. "A radio flash just came. Atom bombs[1] hit New York! All the space rockets blown up. No more rockets to Mars, ever!"

"Oh, Harry!" The mother held onto her husband and daughter.

"Are you sure, Laura?" asked the father quietly.

Laura wept. "We're stranded on Mars, forever and ever!"

For a long time there was only the sound of the wind in the late afternoon.

Alone, thought Bittering. Only a thousand of us here. No way back. No way. No way. Sweat poured from his face and his hands and his body; he was drenched in the hotness of his fear. He wanted to strike Laura, cry, "No, you're lying! The rockets will come back!" Instead, he stroked Laura's head against him and said, "The rockets will get through someday." **D**

"Father, what will we do?"

"Go about our business, of course. Raise crops and children. Wait. Keep things going until the war ends and the rockets come again."

The two boys stepped out onto the porch.

"Children," he said, sitting there, looking beyond them, "I've something to tell you."

"We know," they said.

In the following days, Bittering wandered often through the garden to stand alone in his fear. As long as the rockets had spun a silver web

SCIENCE CONNECTION

Robotic equipment sent to Mars to gather data has shown that the planet has no signs of civilization, though there is some evidence of water on its surface.

D MOOD
Reread lines 79–84. Note that Bradbury uses sentence fragments to portray Bittering's thoughts. How does this help create a mood?

1. **atom bombs:** In 1945 the United States dropped atomic bombs over the cities of Hiroshima and Nagasaki, in Japan, killing over 100,000 people and injuring many thousands more.

across space, he had been able to accept Mars. For he had always told himself: Tomorrow, if I want, I can buy a ticket and go back to Earth.

But now: The web gone, the rockets lying in jigsaw heaps of molten girder and unsnaked wire. Earth people left to the strangeness of Mars, the cinnamon dusts and wine airs, to be baked like gingerbread shapes in Martian summers, put into harvested storage by Martian winters. What would happen to him, the others? This was the moment Mars had waited for. Now it would eat them.

He got down on his knees in the flower bed, a spade in his nervous hands. Work, he thought, work and forget.

He glanced up from the garden to the Martian mountains. He thought of the proud old Martian names that had once been on those peaks. Earthmen, dropping from the sky, had gazed upon hills, rivers, Martian seats left nameless in spite of names. Once Martians had built cities, named cities; climbed mountains, named mountains; sailed seas, named seas. Mountains melted, seas drained, cities tumbled. In spite of this, the Earthmen had felt a silent guilt at putting new names to these ancient hills and valleys. **E**

Nevertheless, man lives by symbol and label. The names were given.

Mr. Bittering felt very alone in his garden under the Martian sun, anachronism[2] bent here, planting Earth flowers in a wild soil.

Think. Keep thinking. Different things. Keep your mind free of Earth, the atom war, the lost rockets.

He perspired. He glanced about. No one watching. He removed his tie. Pretty bold, he thought. First your coat off, now your tie. He hung it neatly on a peach tree he had imported as a sapling from Massachusetts.

He returned to his philosophy of names and mountains. The Earthmen had changed names. Now there were Hormel Valleys, Roosevelt[3] Seas, Ford Hills, Vanderbilt Plateaus, Rockefeller[4] Rivers, on Mars. It wasn't right. The American settlers had shown wisdom, using old Indian prairie names: Wisconsin, Minnesota, Idaho, Ohio, Utah, Milwaukee, Waukegan, Osseo. The old names, the old meanings.

Staring at the mountains wildly, he thought: Are you up there? All the dead ones, you Martians? Well, here we are, alone, cut off! Come down, move us out! We're helpless!

The wind blew a shower of peach blossoms.

He put out his sun-browned hand and gave a small cry. He touched the blossoms and picked them up. He turned them, he touched them again and again. Then he shouted for his wife.

"Cora!"

She appeared at a window. He ran to her.

E READING SCIENCE FICTION
Reread lines 107–110. On the basis of these past accomplishments, consider the similarities between Martian and human civilizations. What comment about present-day human civilization might Bradbury be making through this comparison?

2. **anachronism** (ə-năk'rə-nĭz'əm): something placed outside of its proper time period.
3. **Roosevelt:** most likely refers to Franklin Delano Roosevelt, the 32nd president of the United States.
4. **Hormel . . . Ford . . . Vanderbilt . . . Rockefeller:** names of industrial and financial "giants" in American history.

Shellfish Flowers (1929), Max Ernst. Oil on canvas, 129 cm × 129 cm. Inv.: R 19 P. Photo Jean-Francois Tomasian. Musée National d'Art Moderne, Centre Georges Pompidou, Paris. © 2008 Artists Rights Society (ARS), New York/ ADAGP, Paris.

ANALYZE VISUALS
Compare these flowers to the ones on Mars in the story. How are they similar?

"Cora, these blossoms!"

She handled them.

"Do you see? They're different. They've changed! They're not peach blossoms any more!"

"Look all right to me," she said.

"They're not. They're wrong! I can't tell how. An extra petal, a leaf, something, the color, the smell!"

The children ran out in time to see their father hurrying about the garden, pulling up radishes, onions, and carrots from their beds.

"Cora, come look!"

They handled the onions, the radishes, the carrots among them.

"Do they look like carrots?"

"Yes . . . no." She hesitated. "I don't know."

"They're changed."

"Perhaps."

"You know they have! Onions but not onions, carrots but not carrots. Taste: the same but different. Smell: not like it used to be." He felt his heart pounding, and he was afraid. He dug his fingers into the earth. "Cora, what's happening? What is it? We've got to get away from this." He ran across the garden. Each tree felt his touch. "The roses. The roses. They're turning green!" F

F READING SCIENCE FICTION
Think of what you know about plants. Do you think it's possible for plants to change like they do in this story, or is it purely imaginary?

And they stood looking at the green roses.

And two days later Dan came running. "Come see the cow. I was milking her and I saw it. Come on!"

They stood in the shed and looked at their one cow.

It was growing a third horn.

And the lawn in front of their house very quietly and slowly was coloring itself like spring violets. Seed from Earth but growing up a soft purple.

"We must get away," said Bittering. "We'll eat this stuff and then we'll change—who knows to what? I can't let it happen. There's only one thing to do. Burn this food!" G

"It's not poisoned."

"But it is. **Subtly,** very subtly. A little bit. A very little bit. We mustn't touch it."

He looked with dismay at their house. "Even the house. The wind's done something to it. The air's burned it. The fog at night. The boards, all warped out of shape. It's not an Earthman's house any more."

"Oh, your imagination!"

He put on his coat and tie. "I'm going into town. We've got to do something now. I'll be back."

"Wait, Harry!" his wife cried. But he was gone.

In town, on the shadowy step of the grocery store, the men sat with their hands on their knees, conversing with great leisure and ease.

Mr. Bittering wanted to fire a pistol in the air.

What are you doing, you fools! he thought. Sitting here! You've heard the news—we're stranded on this planet. Well, move! Aren't you frightened? Aren't you afraid? What are you going to do?

"Hello, Harry," said everyone.

"Look," he said to them. "You did hear the news, the other day, didn't you?"

They nodded and laughed. "Sure. Sure, Harry."

"What are you going to do about it?"

"Do, Harry, do? What *can* we do?"

"Build a rocket, that's what!"

"A rocket, Harry? To go back to all that trouble? Oh, Harry!"

"But you *must* want to go back. Have you noticed the peach blossoms, the onions, the grass?"

"Why, yes, Harry, seems we did," said one of the men.

"Doesn't it scare you?"

"Can't recall that it did much, Harry." H

"Idiots!"

"Now, Harry."

G MOOD
When he sees that the plants and animals are changing, Mr. Bittering becomes afraid that he and his family will change too. What impact does this **plot** turn have on the mood of the story?

subtly (sŭt′lē) *adv.* not obviously; in a manner hard to notice or perceive

H MOOD
How do the **characters'** reactions to the situation make you feel?

Bittering wanted to cry. "You've got to work with me. If we stay here, we'll all change. The air. Don't you smell it? Something in the air. A Martian virus, maybe; some seed, or a pollen. Listen to me!"

They stared at him.

"Sam," he said to one of them.

"Yes, Harry?"

"Will you help me build a rocket?"

"Harry, I got a whole load of metal and some blueprints. You want to work in my metal shop on a rocket, you're welcome. I'll sell you that metal for five hundred dollars. You should be able to construct a right pretty rocket, if you work alone, in about thirty years."

Everyone laughed.

"Don't laugh."

Sam looked at him with quiet good humor.

"Sam," Bittering said. "Your eyes—"

"What about them, Harry?"

"Didn't they used to be gray?"

"Well now, I don't remember."

"They were, weren't they?"

"Why do you ask, Harry?"

"Because now they're kind of yellow-colored."

"Is that so, Harry?" Sam said, casually.

"And you're taller and thinner—"

"You might be right, Harry."

"Sam, you shouldn't have yellow eyes." **I**

"Harry, what color eyes have *you* got?" Sam said.

"My eyes? They're blue, of course."

"Here you are, Harry." Sam handed him a pocket mirror. "Take a look at yourself."

Mr. Bittering hesitated, and then raised the mirror to his face.

There were little, very dim flecks of new gold captured in the blue of his eyes.

"Now look what you've done," said Sam a moment later. "You've broken my mirror." **J**

I READING SCIENCE FICTION
Are the changes in Sam's appearance realistic according to the laws of science, or is Bradbury using his imagination here?

J MAKE INFERENCES
Why did Sam's mirror break?

Harry Bittering moved into the metal shop and began to build the rocket. Men stood in the open door and talked and joked without raising their voices. Once in a while they gave him a hand on lifting something. But mostly they just idled and watched him with their yellowing eyes.

"It's suppertime, Harry," they said.

His wife appeared with his supper in a wicker basket.

"I won't touch it," he said. "I'll eat only food from our Deepfreeze. Food that came from Earth. Nothing from our garden."

His wife stood watching him. "You can't build a rocket."

"I worked in a shop once, when I was twenty. I know metal. Once I get it started, the others will help," he said, not looking at her, laying out the blueprints.

"Harry, Harry," she said, helplessly.

"We've *got* to get away, Cora. We've got to!"

The nights were full of wind that blew down the empty moonlit sea meadows past the little white chess cities lying for their twelve-thousandth year in the shallows. In the Earthmen's settlement, the Bittering house shook with a feeling of change.

Lying abed, Mr. Bittering felt his bones shifted, shaped, melted like gold. His wife, lying beside him, was dark from many sunny afternoons. Dark she was, and golden-eyed, burnt almost black by the sun, sleeping, and the children metallic in their beds, and the wind roaring **forlorn** and changing through the old peach trees, the violet grass, shaking out green rose petals. K

The fear would not be stopped. It had his throat and heart. It dripped in a wetness of the arm and the temple and the trembling palm.

A green star rose in the east.

A strange word emerged from Mr. Bittering's lips.

"Iorrt. Iorrt." He repeated it.

It was a Martian word. He knew no Martian.

In the middle of the night he arose and dialed a call through to Simpson, the archaeologist.

"Simpson, what does the word *Iorrt* mean?"

"Why that's the old Martian word for our planet Earth. Why?"

forlorn (fər-lôrn′) *adj.* appearing lonely or sad

K MOOD
Reread lines 249–253. Notice Bradbury's **word choice** and unusual **sentence structure.** What word would you use to describe the feeling this paragraph conveys?

ANALYZE VISUALS
If this sculpture had been made specifically for this story, which figure would represent Harry?

The Forest (1950), Alberto Giacometti. Bronze, painted, 22″ × 24″ × 29¼″. Gift of Enid Haupt. © 2008 Artists Rights Society (ARS), New York/ ADAGP, Paris. © National Gallery of Art, Washington, D.C.

"No special reason."

The telephone slipped from his hand.

"Hello, hello, hello, hello," it kept saying while he sat gazing out at the green star. "Bittering? Harry, are you there?"

The days were full of metal sound. He laid the frame of the rocket with the reluctant help of three indifferent men. He grew very tired in an hour or so and had to sit down.

"The altitude," laughed a man.

"Are you *eating,* Harry?" asked another.

"I'm eating," he said, angrily.

"From your Deepfreeze?"

"Yes!"

"You're getting thinner, Harry."

"I'm not!"

"And taller."

"Liar!"

His wife took him aside a few days later. "Harry, I've used up all the food in the Deepfreeze. There's nothing left. I'll have to make sandwiches using food grown on Mars."

He sat down heavily.

"You must eat," she said. "You're weak."

"Yes," he said.

He took a sandwich, opened it, looked at it, and began to nibble at it.

"And take the rest of the day off," she said. "It's hot. The children want to swim in the canals and hike. Please come along."

"I can't waste time. This is a crisis!"

"Just for an hour," she urged. "A swim'll do you good."

He rose, sweating. "All right, all right. Leave me alone. I'll come."

"Good for you, Harry."

The sun was hot, the day quiet. There was only an immense staring burn upon the land. They moved along the canal, the father, the mother, the racing children in their swimsuits. They stopped and ate meat sandwiches. He saw their skin baking brown. And he saw the yellow eyes of his wife and his children, their eyes that were never yellow before. A few tremblings shook him, but were carried off in waves of pleasant heat as he lay in the sun. He was too tired to be afraid. (L)

"Cora, how long have your eyes been yellow?"

She was bewildered. "Always, I guess."

"They didn't change from brown in the last three months?"

She bit her lips. "No. Why do you ask?"

"Never mind."

(L) MOOD
Reread lines 301–304. Note how different Harry's attitude is now than it was before. What effect does this change have on you as a reader?

They sat there.

"The children's eyes," he said. "They're yellow, too."

"Sometimes growing children's eyes change color."

"Maybe *we're* children, too. At least to Mars. That's a thought." He laughed. "Think I'll swim."

They leaped into the canal water, and he let himself sink down and down to the bottom like a golden statue and lie there in green silence. All was water-quiet and deep, all was peace. He felt the steady, slow current drift him easily.

If I lie here long enough, he thought, the water will work and eat away my flesh until the bones show like coral. Just my skeleton left. And then the water can build on that skeleton—green things, deep water things, red things, yellow things. Change. Change. Slow, deep, silent change. And isn't that what it is up *there*?

He saw the sky submerged above him, the sun made Martian by atmosphere and time and space.

Up there, a big river, he thought, a Martian river; all of us lying deep in it, in our pebble houses, in our sunken boulder houses, like crayfish hidden, and the water washing away our old bodies and lengthening the bones and—

He let himself drift up through the soft light.

Dan sat on the edge of the canal, regarding his father seriously.

"*Utha,*" he said.

"What?" asked his father.

The boy smiled. "You know. *Utha's* the Martian word for 'father.'"

"Where did you learn it?"

"I don't know. Around. *Utha!*"

"What do you want?"

The boy hesitated. "I—I want to change my name."

"Change it?"

"Yes."

His mother swam over. "What's wrong with Dan for a name?"

Dan fidgeted. "The other day you called Dan, Dan, Dan. I didn't even hear. I said to myself, That's not my name. I've a new name I want to use."

Mr. Bittering held to the side of the canal, his body cold and his heart pounding slowly. "What is this new name?"

"Linnl. Isn't that a good name? Can I use it? Can't I, please?" **M**

M MAKE INFERENCES
Why does Dan want to change his name?

Mr. Bittering put his hand to his head. He thought of the silly rocket, himself working alone, himself alone even among his family, so alone.

He heard his wife say, "Why not?"

He heard himself say, "Yes, you can use it."

"Yaaa!" screamed the boy. "I'm Linnl, Linnl!"

Racing down the meadowlands, he danced and shouted.

Mr. Bittering looked at his wife. "Why did we do that?"

"I don't know," she said. "It just seemed like a good idea."

They walked into the hills. They strolled on old mosaic paths, beside still pumping fountains. The paths were covered with a thin film of cool water all summer long. You kept your bare feet cool all the day, splashing as in a creek, wading.

They came to a small deserted Martian villa with a good view of the valley. It was on top of a hill. Blue marble halls, large murals, a swimming pool. It was refreshing in this hot summertime. The Martians hadn't believed in large cities.

"How nice," said Mrs. Bittering, "if we could move up here to this villa for the summer."

"Come on," he said. "We're going back to town. There's work to be done on the rocket."

But as he worked that night, the thought of the cool blue marble villa entered his mind. As the hours passed, the rocket seemed less important. **N**

In the flow of days and weeks, the rocket **receded** and **dwindled.** The old fever was gone. It frightened him to think he had let it slip this way. But somehow the heat, the air, the working conditions—

He heard the men murmuring on the porch of his metal shop.

"Everyone's going. You heard?"

"All going. That's right."

Bittering came out. "Going where?" He saw a couple of trucks, loaded with children and furniture, drive down the dusty street.

"Up to the villas," said the man.

"Yeah, Harry. I'm going. So is Sam. Aren't you Sam?"

"That's right, Harry. What about you?"

"I've got work to do here."

"Work! You can finish that rocket in the autumn, when it's cooler."

He took a breath. "I got the frame all set up."

"In the autumn is better." Their voices were lazy in the heat.

"Got to work," he said.

"Autumn," they reasoned. And they sounded so sensible, so right.

"Autumn would be best," he thought. "Plenty of time, then."

No! cried part of himself, deep down, put away, locked tight, suffocating. No! No!

"In the autumn," he said.

"Come on, Harry," they all said.

"Yes," he said, feeling his flesh melt in the hot liquid air. "Yes, in the autumn. I'll begin work again then."

VISUAL VOCABULARY

mosaic (mō-zā′ĭk) *adj.* formed from pieces of stone or glass that are inlaid to make a design

N MAKE INFERENCES
Why is the rocket becoming less important to Harry?

recede (rĭ-sēd′) *v.* to become fainter or more distant

dwindle (dwĭn′dl) *v.* to become less, until little remains

Detail from *Figures Crossing River on Gold Coins*, Andrew Judd. ©Andrew Judd/Masterfile.

"I got a villa near the Tirra Canal," said someone.

"You mean the Roosevelt Canal, don't you?"

"Tirra. The old Martian name."

"But on the map—"

"Forget the map. It's Tirra now. Now I found a place in the Pillan Mountains—"

"You mean the Rockefeller Range," said Bittering.

"I mean the Pillan Mountains," said Sam.

"Yes," said Bittering, buried in the hot, swarming air. "The Pillan Mountains."

Everyone worked at loading the truck in the hot, still afternoon of the next day.

Laura, Dan, and David carried packages. Or, as they preferred to be known, Ttil, Linnl, and Werr carried packages. **O**

The furniture was abandoned in the little white cottage.

"It looked just fine in Boston," said the mother. "And here in the cottage. But up at the villa? No. We'll get it when we come back in the autumn."

Bittering himself was quiet.

"I've some ideas on furniture for the villa," he said after a time. "Big, lazy furniture."

"What about your encyclopedia? You're taking it along, surely?"

ANALYZE VISUALS
What is the **mood** of this painting? Explain what elements help create this mood.

O READING SCIENCE FICTION
Why is it significant that the people are changing the names of the landmarks and themselves?

Mr. Bittering glanced away. "I'll come and get it next week."

They turned to their daughter. "What about your New York dresses?"

The bewildered girl stared. "Why, I don't want them any more."

They shut off the gas, the water, they locked the doors and walked away. Father peered into the truck.

"Gosh, we're not taking much," he said. "Considering all we brought to Mars, this is only a handful!" **P**

P **MOOD**
Reread lines 416–423. What effect does this **dialogue** have on the overall mood of the story?

He started the truck.

Looking at the small white cottage for a long moment, he was filled with a desire to rush to it, touch it, say good-bye to it, for he felt as if he were going away on a long journey, leaving something to which he could never quite return, never understand again.

Just then Sam and his family drove by in another truck.

"Hi, Bittering! Here we go!"

The truck swung down the ancient highway out of town. There were sixty others traveling in the same direction. The town filled with a silent, heavy dust from their passage. The canal waters lay blue in the sun, and a quiet wind moved in the strange trees.

"Good-bye, town!" said Mr. Bittering.

"Good-bye, good-bye," said the family, waving to it.

They did not look back again.

Summer burned the canals dry. Summer moved like flame upon the meadows. In the empty Earth settlement, the painted houses flaked and peeled. Rubber tires upon which children had swung in back yards hung suspended like stopped clock **pendulums** in the blazing air.

pendulum (pĕn′jə-ləm) *n.* a weight hung so that it can swing freely, sometimes used in timing the workings of certain clocks

At the metal shop, the rocket frame began to rust.

In the quiet autumn Mr. Bittering stood, very dark now, very golden-eyed, upon the slope above his villa, looking at the valley.

"It's time to go back," said Cora.

"Yes, but we're not going," he said quietly. "There's nothing there any more."

"Your books," she said. "Your fine clothes."

"Your *llles* and your fine *ior uele rre,*" she said.

"The town's empty. No one's going back," he said. "There's no reason to, none at all."

The daughter wove tapestries and the sons played songs on ancient flutes and pipes, their laughter echoing in the marble villa.

Mr. Bittering gazed at the Earth settlement far away in the low valley. "Such odd, such ridiculous houses the Earth people built."

"They didn't know any better," his wife **mused.** "Such ugly people. I'm glad they've gone."

muse (myo͞oz) *v.* to say thoughtfully

They both looked at each other, startled by all they had just finished saying. They laughed.

"Where did they go?" he wondered. He glanced at his wife. She was golden and slender as his daughter. She looked at him, and he seemed almost as young as their eldest son. **Q**

Q READING SCIENCE FICTION
Reread lines 460–462. Find details that tell you how the Bitterings have changed since they first arrived on Mars. Are they still human?

"I don't know," she said.

"We'll go back to town maybe next year, or the year after, or the year after that," he said, calmly. "Now—I'm warm. How about taking a swim?"

They turned their backs to the valley. Arm in arm they walked silently down a path of clear-running spring water.

Five years later a rocket fell out of the sky. It lay steaming in the valley. Men leaped out of it, shouting.

"We won the war on Earth! We're here to rescue you! Hey!"

But the American-built town of cottages, peach trees, and theaters was silent. They found a **flimsy** rocket frame rusting in an empty shop.

flimsy (flĭm'zē) *adj.* not solid or strong

The rocket men searched the hills. The captain established headquarters in an abandoned bar. His lieutenant came back to report.

"The town's empty, but we found native life in the hills, sir. Dark people. Yellow eyes. Martians. Very friendly. We talked a bit, not much. They learn English fast. I'm sure our relations will be most friendly with them, sir."

"Dark, eh?" mused the captain. "How many?"

"Six, eight hundred, I'd say, living in those marble ruins in the hills, sir. Tall, healthy. Beautiful women."

"Did they tell you what became of the men and women who built this Earth settlement, Lieutenant?"

"They hadn't the foggiest notion of what happened to this town or its people."

"Strange. You think those Martians killed them?"

"They look surprisingly peaceful. Chances are a plague did this town in, sir."

"Perhaps. I suppose this is one of those mysteries we'll never solve. One of those mysteries you read about." **R**

R MAKE INFERENCES
What do you think will happen to the captain and the lieutenant?

The captain looked at the room, the dusty windows, the blue mountains rising beyond, the canals moving in the light, and he heard the soft wind in the air. He shivered. Then, recovering, he tapped a large fresh map he had thumbtacked to the top of an empty table.

"Lots to be done, Lieutenant." His voice droned on and quietly on as the sun sank behind the blue hills. "New settlements. Mining sites, minerals to be looked for. Bacteriological specimens[5] taken. The work, all the work.

5. **bacteriological specimens:** samples of different kinds of single-celled living things.

The Whole City (1935), Max Ernst. Oil on canvas, 60 cm × 81 cm. Kunsthaus, Zurich, Switzerland. © 2008 Artists Rights Society (ARS), New York/ADAGP, Paris.

And the old records were lost. We'll have a job of remapping to do, renaming the mountains and rivers and such. Calls for a little imagination.

"What do you think of naming those mountains the Lincoln Mountains, this canal the Washington Canal, those hills—we can name those hills for you, Lieutenant. Diplomacy. And you, for a favor, might name a town for me. Polishing the apple.[6] And why not make this the Einstein Valley, and farther over . . . are you *listening,* Lieutenant?"

The lieutenant snapped his gaze from the blue color and the quiet mist of the hills far beyond the town.

"What? Oh, *yes,* sir!"

ANALYZE VISUALS
Does the place at the top of the hill look inviting to you? Why or why not?

6. **polishing the apple:** acting in a way to get on the good side of another person.

MAGAZINE ARTICLE As you read this interview, you'll find out how Ray Bradbury views himself as an author, how he writes stories like "Dark They Were, and Golden-Eyed," and what advice he has for beginning writers.

Section 3 THE CHARLOTTE OBSERVER C3

An Interview with RAY BRADBURY

Q: You don't consider yourself a science fiction writer, even though others call you that. How do you see yourself?

A: I am a collector of metaphors. Any idea that strikes me I run with. . . .

I wrote *The October Country,* which is weird fantasy. There is no science fiction there. And *Halloween Tree,* which is a history of Halloween. And *Dandelion Wine,* which is my childhood in Illinois. *Something Wicked This Way Comes,* which is also my childhood plus fantasy. So when you look at the spread of things, there is only one novel that is science fiction. And that's *Fahrenheit 451.* In other words, science fiction is the art of the possible, not the art of the impossible. As soon as you deal with things that can't happen you are writing fantasy.

Q: Walk me through your daily inspiration and writing process.

A: I just wake up with ideas every morning from my subconscious percolating. At 7 in the morning I lie in bed and I watch all the fragments of ideas swarming around in my head and these voices talk to me. And when they get to a certain point, I jump out of bed and run to the typewriter. So I'm not in control. Two hours later I have a new short story or an essay or part of a play. . . .

Q: What kind of advice would you give beginning writers?

A: Explode. Don't intellectualize. Get passionate about ideas. Cram your head full of images. Stay in the library. Stay off the Internet. Read all the great books. Read all the great poetry. See all the great films. Fill your life with metaphors. And then explode. And you're bound to do something good.

After Reading

ALABAMA STANDARDS

READING STANDARD
2.a Determining mood

Comprehension

1. **Recall** Why do the Bitterings settle on Mars?
2. **Recall** Why do the rockets from Earth stop coming to Mars?
3. **Represent** Create a timeline of the main events of the story, including the physical changes Harry notices in the people and things around him.

Literary Analysis

4. **Identify Mood** Before you read the story, you were asked to consider, as you read, how Bradbury's choice of words affected the way you felt. Now think of the story as a whole. What words would you use to describe the overall mood of the story? Cite descriptions of plot elements, setting, or characters and examples of dialogue to support your response.
5. **Interpret Foreshadowing** Writers use foreshadowing to provide hints of what might happen later in the story. Reread lines 15–18. How do Harry's thoughts upon first arriving on Mars foreshadow later events in the story?
6. **Analyze Character** Harry changes throughout the story. Using an organizer like the one shown, record his attitude and appearance at the beginning, middle, and end of the story.

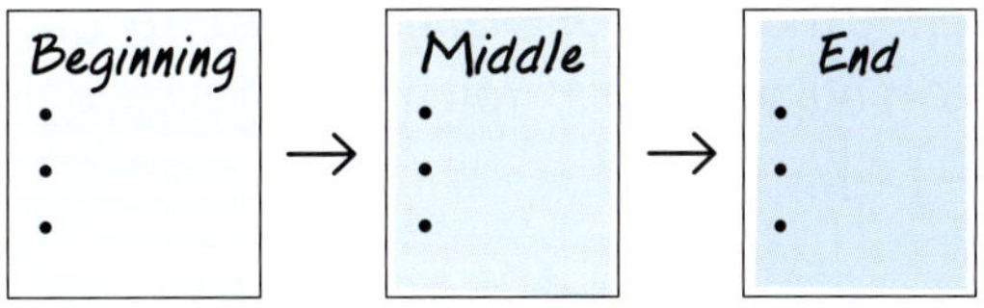

7. **Make Inferences** Who do you think will resist change the most, the captain or the lieutenant? Use examples from the story to support your answer.
8. **Evaluate Science Fiction** Reread Bradbury's first answer from the interview on page 462. Note that he does not consider himself a science fiction writer. In light of this information, do you think it is right to label "Dark They Were, and Golden-Eyed" as science fiction? Explain your answer, using support from the selection, the chart you created as you read, and the interview.

Extension and Challenge

9. **Big Question Activity** Reread the Big Question on page 444. Suppose you are Harry Bittering. Write a journal entry in which you answer the question about **change** from his point of view after he has moved up to the villa.
10. **SCIENCE CONNECTION** Find out more about Mars by visiting the library in your school or neighborhood. What do we now know about the planet? What plans are scientists making to study it further? Focus your research on what interests you most. Report your findings to the class.

RESEARCH LINKS
For more on Mars, visit the **Research Center** at **ClassZone.com.**

Vocabulary in Context

VOCABULARY PRACTICE

Write the letter of the phrase that has a connection to each vocabulary word.

1. **pendulum:** (a) a grandfather clock, (b) a racing motorcycle, (c) a gossiping man
2. **forlorn:** (a) a heavy snowfall, (b) a bitter quarrel, (c) a lonely child
3. **dwindle:** (a) your supply of money, (b) your age, (c) your science textbook
4. **subtly:** (a) a fireworks show, (b) a gradually dimming light, (c) a long bus ride
5. **convivial:** (a) a dog and a squirrel, (b) a friendly crowd, (c) a curving staircase
6. **flimsy:** (a) a stuffed chair, (b) a weak argument, (c) a party in a yard
7. **recede:** (a) a plane flying away, (b) an arriving plane, (c) a plane parked at a gate
8. **muse:** (a) a noisy band, (b) a person considering choices, (c) a windy day

convivial
dwindle
flimsy
forlorn
muse
pendulum
recede
subtly

VOCABULARY IN WRITING

In a paragraph, describe the series of changes that affect the Bitterings. Use three or more vocabulary words. You might start like this.

EXAMPLE SENTENCE

*The changes that gradually overtake the Bitterings begin **subtly**.*

ALABAMA STANDARDS

READING STANDARD
1.c Using context clues to determine word meanings

VOCABULARY STRATEGY: THE LATIN ROOT *pend*

The vocabulary word *pendulum* contains the Latin root *pend,* which means "hang." This root, which is sometimes spelled *pens,* is found in many English words. To understand the meaning of words with *pend* or *pens,* use context clues and your knowledge of the root's meaning.

PRACTICE Choose the word from the web that best completes each sentence. Then explain how the root *pend* relates to the meaning of the word.

1. She wears that _______ around her neck every day.
2. My choice is _______ on what you decide to do.
3. The book was so _______ that he couldn't stop reading it.
4. To hold up his pants, Dad prefers _______ to belts.
5. They could not shake off their feeling of _______ trouble.

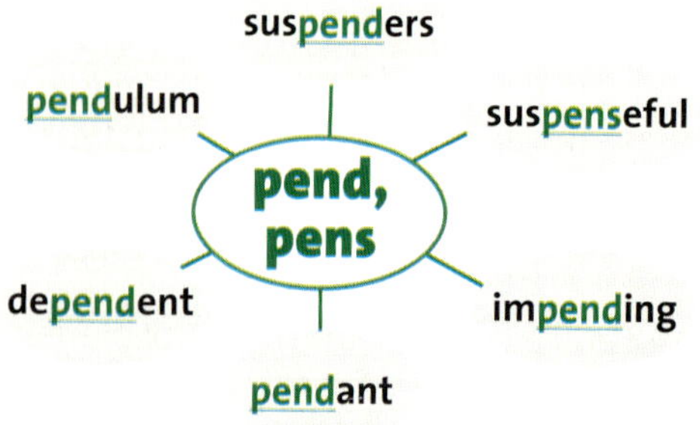

VOCABULARY PRACTICE
For more practice, go to the **Vocabulary Center** at **ClassZone.com.**

Reading-Writing Connection

SKILLS PRACTICE

Increase your understanding of "Dark They Were, and Golden-Eyed" by responding to these prompts. Then complete the **Grammar and Writing** exercise.

WRITING PROMPTS	SELF-CHECK
A. Short Response: Write a Letter Bradbury originally named "Dark They Were, and Golden-Eyed" "The Naming of Names." Which title do you think is more appropriate? Using details and examples from the story, write a **one-paragraph letter** to the author to explain your choice.	***A strong letter will . . .*** • directly address Ray Bradbury • include a well-supported opinion
B. Extended Response: Evaluate Ideas Should all **change** be feared and resisted, or does it depend on the types of changes and why they are happening? Write a **two- or three-paragraph response,** citing examples from the story and from your own experiences.	***An effective response will . . .*** • show an understanding of the question • use evidence from the story as support

GRAMMAR AND WRITING

MAINTAIN SUBJECT-VERB AGREEMENT In any sentence you write, a verb must **agree in number** with its subject. *Number* refers to whether a word is singular or plural. Be especially careful when you form a sentence that is a question or when you use the word *doesn't* or *don't* in a sentence.

Original: The human don't seem to notice the changes.

Revised: The human doesn't seem to notice the changes.
(The subject human *is singular, so the verb should be too.)*

PRACTICE Choose the verb form that agrees in number with each subject.

1. Harry Bittering resists these changes, but he (don't, doesn't) convince the others to resist.
2. Soon the adults and children (starts, start) to use Martian names.
3. How (does, do) Harry and his family cope with these changes?
4. The Bittering family and the other humans (move, moves) into villas on the hill.

For more help with subject-verb agreement in number, see pages R65–R67 in the ***Grammar Handbook.***

ALABAMA STANDARDS

WRITING/LANGUAGE STANDARD
11 Apply grammar conventions to subject-verb agreement

A Day's Wait

Short Story by Ernest Hemingway

Is it BRAVE *to suffer in silence?*

ALABAMA STANDARDS

READING STANDARDS

1.d Applying self-monitoring strategies

2 Relate literary elements and devices to each other

KEY IDEA Whether from an injury or a broken heart, everyone suffers at times. Some people try hard to keep their pain to themselves, while others believe it is better to share their thoughts and feelings with others. In "A Day's Wait," a young boy tries to be **brave** while suffering from an illness.

QUICKWRITE Do you consider it an act of bravery to face pain on your own, or does it take more courage for you to open up to other people? In a journal entry, explain your answers to these questions.

LITERARY ANALYSIS: STYLE

Style is a writer's unique way of communicating ideas. It is often not only what writers say but how they say it that gives stories meaning and makes them memorable. To identify a writer's style, focus on these elements:

- **Word choice,** or the author's choice of language. Hemingway strives to use vivid verbs and precise nouns rather than using many adjectives and adverbs.
- **Sentence structure** and variety. In this story, Hemingway often uses long sentences for descriptions and short sentences when characters are talking.
- **Dialogue,** or conversations between characters. Hemingway relies heavily on realistic dialogue to "tell" his stories.

As you read "A Day's Wait," notice how these elements help create Hemingway's unique writing style.

READING SKILL: UNDERSTAND DIALOGUE

Characters reveal much about themselves by what they say or don't say. When reading **dialogue,** note that

- each speaker's words are framed by quotes
- the line is indented when someone new is speaking

As you read "A Day's Wait," keep track of who's speaking by using a chart like the one shown.

Line	Speaker
"What's the matter, Schatz?"	narrator

VOCABULARY IN CONTEXT

Each of the boldfaced terms reflects Hemingway's **word choice** in "A Day's Wait." How many of these words do you know? Try to figure out the meaning of each.

1. People were there, but he felt **detached** from them.
2. There is a serious flu **epidemic** this winter.
3. He had **slack** muscles from lack of exercise.
4. It was **evidently** too much for him to deal with.
5. The man observed a **covey** of partridges.

Author Online

An Adventurous Life Ernest Hemingway lived a life full of adventure. He was one of a group of writers called the Lost Generation. These writers rejected what they saw as an American focus on acquiring many possessions. Along with being one of America's most famous writers, Hemingway was a fisherman, a hunter, and a fan of bullfighting. He participated in both world wars. Many of his works are based on his experiences in Europe and Cuba.

Ernest Hemingway
1899–1961

An Influential Style Hemingway and other Lost Generation writers, including F. Scott Fitzgerald and Sherwood Anderson, expressed their ideas in writing styles that were new and different. Hemingway's writing style, particularly his method of writing dialogue, has influenced many other writers. He is one of the most often imitated writers of the 1900s.

Fact Becomes Fiction Like much of Hemingway's writing, "A Day's Wait" is based on actual events in Hemingway's life. While Hemingway was living in France, his son came down with a high fever and reacted similarly to the boy in the story you will read.

MORE ABOUT THE AUTHOR
For more on Ernest Hemingway, visit the **Literature Center** at **ClassZone.com.**

A DAY'S WAIT

ERNEST HEMINGWAY

He came into the room to shut the windows while we were still in bed and I saw he looked ill. He was shivering, his face was white, and he walked slowly as though it ached to move.

"What's the matter, Schatz?"[1]

"I've got a headache."

"You better go back to bed."

"No. I'm all right."

"You go to bed. I'll see you when I'm dressed." **A**

But when I came downstairs he was dressed, sitting by the fire, looking a very sick and miserable boy of nine years. When I put my hand on his forehead I knew he had a fever.

"You go up to bed," I said, "you're sick."

"I'm all right," he said.

When the doctor came he took the boy's temperature.

"What is it?" I asked him.

"One hundred and two."

ANALYZE VISUALS
Consider the expression on this boy's face. What **mood** does it convey?

A DIALOGUE
Reread the dialogue in lines 4–8. Notice that Hemingway does not always tell the reader who is speaking. Use your chart to keep track of the different speakers.

1. **Schatz** (shäts): German term of affection meaning "my treasure," used here as a nickname.

Contemplation (1930), Alice Kent Stoddard. Oil on canvas.

Downstairs, the doctor left three different medicines in different-colored capsules with instructions for giving them. One was to bring down the fever, another a purgative,[2] the third to overcome an acid condition. The germs of influenza can only exist in an acid condition, he explained. He seemed to know all about influenza and said there was nothing to worry about if the fever did not go above one hundred and four degrees. This was a light **epidemic** of flu and there was no danger if you avoided pneumonia.

epidemic (ĕp′ĭ-dĕm′ĭk) *n.* an outbreak of a disease that spreads quickly among many people

Back in the room I wrote the boy's temperature down and made a note of the time to give the various capsules.

"Do you want me to read to you?"

"All right. If you want to," said the boy. His face was very white and there were dark areas under his eyes. He lay still in the bed and seemed very **detached** from what was going on.

detached (dĭ-tăcht′) *adj.* separated; disconnected **detach** *v.*

I read aloud from Howard Pyle's *Book of Pirates;*[3] but I could see he was not following what I was reading.

"How do you feel, Schatz?" I asked him.

"Just the same, so far," he said.

I sat at the foot of the bed and read to myself while I waited for it to be time to give another capsule. It would have been natural for him to go to sleep, but when I looked up he was looking at the foot of the bed, looking very strangely.

"Why don't you try to go to sleep? I'll wake you up for the medicine."

"I'd rather stay awake."

After a while he said to me, "You don't have to stay in here with me, Papa, if it bothers you." **B**

"It doesn't bother me."

"No, I mean you don't have to stay if it's going to bother you." **C**

I thought perhaps he was a little lightheaded and after giving him the prescribed capsules at eleven o'clock I went out for a while.

B STYLE
Reread lines 41–42. Hemingway reveals the narrator through dialogue. What does this tell you about his style?

C DIALOGUE
Use your chart to track the speakers in the dialogue in lines 27–44.

It was a bright, cold day, the ground covered with a sleet that had frozen so that it seemed as if all the bare trees, the bushes, the cut brush, and all the grass and the bare ground had been varnished with ice. I took the young Irish setter for a little walk up the road and along a frozen creek, but it was difficult to stand or walk on the glassy surface and the red dog slipped and slithered and I fell twice, hard, once dropping my gun and having it slide away over the ice. **D**

D STYLE
Do the words Hemingway uses to describe the **setting** convey a positive or negative atmosphere? Explain.

---

2. **purgative** (pûr′gə-tĭv): laxative.
3. **Howard Pyle's *Book of Pirates:*** a collection of tales about real and fictional pirates, very popular when it was published in the 1920s.

ANALYZE VISUALS
How does this painting convey the passing of time?

We flushed a **covey** of quail under a high clay bank with overhanging brush and I killed two as they went out of sight over the top of the bank. Some of the covey lit in trees, but most of them scattered into brush piles and it was necessary to jump on the ice-coated mounds of brush several times before they would flush. Coming out while you were poised unsteadily on the icy, springy brush, they made difficult shooting and I killed two, missed five, and started back pleased to have found a covey close to the house and happy there were so many left to find on another day.

covey (kŭv′ē) *n.* a small group or flock of birds, especially partridges or quail

At the house they said the boy had refused to let anyone come into the room.

"You can't come in," he said. "You mustn't get what I have."

I went up to him and found him in exactly the position I had left him, white-faced, but with the tops of his cheeks flushed by the fever, staring still, as he had stared, at the foot of the bed.

I took his temperature.

"What is it?"

"Something like a hundred," I said. It was one hundred and two and four tenths.

"It was a hundred and two," he said.

"Who said so?"

"The doctor."

"Your temperature is all right," I said. "It's nothing to worry about."

"I don't worry," he said, "but I can't keep from thinking."

"Don't think," I said. "Just take it easy."

"I'm taking it easy," he said and looked straight ahead. He was **evidently** holding tight onto himself about something.

evidently (ĕv'ĭ-dənt-lē) *adv.* obviously; clearly

"Take this with water."

"Do you think it will do any good?"

"Of course it will."

I sat down and opened the *Pirate* book and commenced to read, but I could see he was not following, so I stopped.

"About what time do you think I'm going to die?" he asked.

"What?"

"About how long will it be before I die?"

"You aren't going to die. What's the matter with you?"

"Oh, yes, I am. I heard him say a hundred and two."

"People don't die with a fever of one hundred and two. That's a silly way to talk."

"I know they do. At school in France the boys told me you can't live with forty-four degrees. I've got a hundred and two."

He had been waiting to die all day, ever since nine o'clock in the morning.

"You poor Schatz," I said. "Poor old Schatz. It's like miles and kilometers. You aren't going to die. That's a different thermometer. On that thermometer thirty-seven is normal. On this kind it's ninety-eight."

"Are you sure?"

"Absolutely," I said. "It's like miles and kilometers. You know, like how many kilometers we make when we do seventy miles in the car?"

"Oh," he said.

But his gaze at the foot of the bed relaxed slowly. The hold over himself relaxed too, finally, and the next day it was very **slack** and he cried very easily at little things that were of no importance.

SCIENCE CONNECTION

On the Celsius scale, water freezes at 0° and boils at 100°. On the Fahrenheit scale, water freezes at 32° and boils at 212°.

slack (slăk) *adj.* not firm or tight; loose

After Reading

Comprehension

ALABAMA STANDARDS

READING STANDARD
2 Relate literary elements and devices to each other

1. **Recall** Why does the boy think he is going to die?
2. **Clarify** Why does the father spend the afternoon hunting instead of staying with his worried son?
3. **Summarize** How does the story end?

Literary Analysis

4. **Understand Dialogue** Look over the dialogue chart you created as you read. At which points do the father and son not seem to understand each other?
5. **Analyze Character** In what ways does the boy show concern for others?
6. **Draw Conclusions** Why does the boy cry so much the next day?
7. **Make Judgments** Do you think the boy's actions show **bravery?** Why or why not? Support your answer with examples from the story. Use a diagram like the one shown to record your support. Use line numbers when referring to parts of the story.

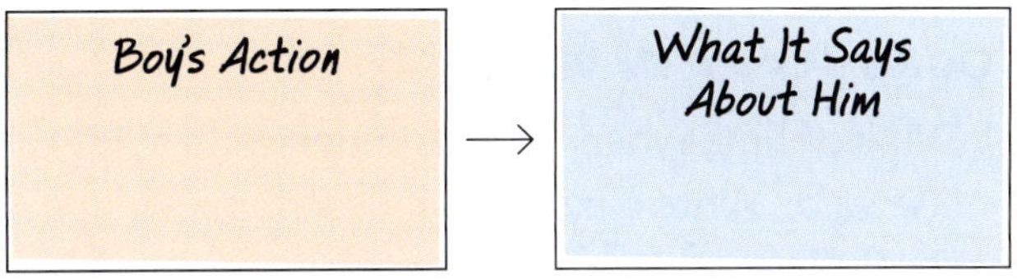

8. **Identify Style** Reread lines 65–83. Note Hemingway's **word choice, sentence structure,** and use of **dialogue.** Why is this passage a good example of Hemingway's style? Explain your answer, using evidence from the passage.

Extension and Challenge

9. **Creative Project: Drama** Most of this story is told through **dialogue** between the father and son. With a partner, choose one of their conversations to act out. Use details from the scene to accurately portray the characters. Practice on your own, and then present the dialogue to the class.
10. **Readers' Circle** With a small group, discuss what clues the story gives you about the relationship between the boy and his father. Consider whether this experience is likely to affect their relationship in any way. If so, how?

Vocabulary in Context

covey

detached

epidemic

evidently

slack

VOCABULARY PRACTICE

Show that you understand the boldfaced words by deciding whether each statement is true or false.

1. If something is **evidently** true, it has been proven through a series of experiments.
2. A **covey** is a place where birds and small mammals go to spend the winter.
3. An **epidemic** generally affects a large number of people.
4. If you are **detached** from a situation, you are probably not very concerned about it.
5. Tightened muscles around someone's lips and jaw are typical of a **slack** expression.

VOCABULARY IN WRITING

Think of time when you misunderstood something important that someone else said. Write a paragraph describing what happened, using at least two vocabulary words. Here is a sample beginning.

EXAMPLE SENTENCE

At camp I thought I heard, "It's time for nights out," but I was ***evidently*** *wrong.*

VOCABULARY STRATEGY: WORDS FOR ANIMAL GROUPS

There are many names for groups of animals. Some, like the vocabulary word *covey,* are used mainly with one or two specific types of animals. Others, like *herd,* are used when describing animals in certain categories, such as large animals that move or feed together (a herd of elephants, a herd of antelope). Knowing the correct word for an animal group can enrich both your reading and your writing.

PRACTICE Match each numbered word for an animal group with the type of animal it is usually associated with. Refer to a dictionary if you need help.

1. pride **a.** cattle
2. swarm **b.** fish
3. drove **c.** wolves
4. pack **d.** birds
5. school **e.** lions
6. flock **f.** bees

VOCABULARY PRACTICE
For more practice, go to the **Vocabulary Center** at **ClassZone.com.**

SKILLS PRACTICE

Reading-Writing Connection

Increase your understanding of "A Day's Wait" by responding to these prompts. Then complete the **Grammar and Writing** exercise.

WRITING PROMPTS	SELF-CHECK
A. Short Response: Evaluate Characterization According to Hemingway, "A writer should create living people; people not characters." Do you think he creates real people in "A Day's Wait"? Write a **one-paragraph response,** using details from the story to support your opinion.	***An effective evaluation will . . .*** • include a clear position statement • use specific details and examples from the story that support the statement
B. Extended Response: Write a Letter Imagine how Schatz would remember this day 20 years later. Write a **two- or three-paragraph letter** from Schatz to his father in which he reminds his father about the misunderstanding and how it affected him.	***A creative response will . . .*** • summarize the events of the story • show an understanding of how the boy felt that day

GRAMMAR AND WRITING

MAINTAIN SUBJECT-VERB AGREEMENT A **compound subject** is made up of two or more subjects joined by a conjunction, such as *and, or,* or *nor.* When you write a sentence with a compound subject joined by *and,* you should usually use a plural verb. When you write a sentence with a compound subject joined by *or* or *nor,* use a verb that agrees in number with the subject closer to it.

Original: Because Schatz is constantly worrying, neither the capsules nor rest seem to help him.

Revised: Because Schatz is constantly worrying, neither the capsules nor rest seems to help him.

PRACTICE Choose the verb form that agrees with each compound subject.

1. Parents and children sometimes (have, has) a problem communicating.
2. Often, the parents or the child (get, gets) confused about some information.
3. In the story, neither the father nor the boy (realize, realizes) the misunderstanding until later on.
4. Once they understand the problem, the boy and his father (relax, relaxes).

For more help with subject-verb agreement with compound subjects, see pages R65–R66 in the ***Grammar Handbook.***

ALABAMA STANDARDS

WRITING/LANGUAGE STANDARD
11 Apply grammar conventions in writing

Reading for Information

How Hemingway Wrote

Informative Article

Use with "A Day's Wait," page 468.

ALABAMA STANDARDS

READING & RESEARCH STANDARDS
4 Distinguish fact from opinion in informational materials
13.a Taking notes to gather and summarize information

What's the Connection?

You've just read a short story by Ernest Hemingway, an author whose style is so distinct and admired that writers often try to copy it. Now you will read an **informative article** that explains how Hemingway approached writing.

Skill Focus: Distinguish Fact from Opinion

An **opinion** is a statement of belief or feeling, such as "I think everyone should read Hemingway's stories." A **fact** is a statement that can be proved, such as "Hemingway wrote many stories."

When you read informative articles, it's important to distinguish facts from opinions. If you mistake an opinion for a fact, you run the risk of basing your conclusions on someone's personal beliefs rather than on provable information. The opinions of experts can be good sources of information, but you should always know whether you are reading a fact or an opinion.

As you read Bruce Rettman's article, list the facts in one column and Rettman's opinions in another. Use the tips on the chart to help you distinguish facts from opinions.

FACT OR OPINION?

Is it a fact?

Watch Out
- Words and phrases often used to state facts: *the fact that, in fact, indeed, the truth is,* and *as a matter of fact.*
- The same words and phrases used to state facts *may* be used to disguise opinions as facts.

Can I prove it by
- consulting a reliable source, such as a print or online encyclopedia?
- interviewing a recognized expert in the field?
- checking the statement against what I observe or know to be true?

If the answer is "yes" . . .

The statement is a **fact.**

Is it an opinion?

Watch Out
Words and phrases often used to express opinions: *I think, I believe, perhaps,* and *maybe.*

Ask yourself:
- Can this statement be debated?
- Might people disagree with the statement?

If the answer is "yes" . . .

The statement is probably an **opinion.**

How Hemingway Wrote. A

by Bruce Rettman

Hemingway is shown here working on a story.

Ernest Hemingway said that the best writing advice he ever got came from the writing guidelines he received as a young reporter working for the *Kansas City Star*. These guidelines began as follows: "Use short sentences. Use short first paragraphs. Use vigorous English, not forgetting to strive for smoothness." Anyone who reads Hemingway's simple and direct sentences built on strong nouns and verbs—not "extravagant adjectives"—can see that he took those guidelines to heart. B

Hemingway's own advice for becoming a good writer is also informative. "When people talk, listen completely," said Hemingway to a young writer. "Don't be thinking what you're going to say. Most people never listen. Nor do they observe." In other words, Hemingway advises young writers to write from life, blending fact and fiction. The short story "A Day's Wait," for example, is based on an actual time when Hemingway's first child had a fever.

FOCUS ON FORM
"How Hemingway Wrote" is an **informative article,** a nonfiction article written to provide information or to explain something about a topic.

A INFORMATIVE ARTICLE
Now that you have read the title, what do you think this informative article will explain?

B DISTINGUISH FACT FROM OPINION
To check whether the statements in lines 1–16 are accurate, who might you contact or what source might you consult?

So, are you getting a sense of how Hemingway approached writing? Well, there's still more to learn from Hemingway's manuscripts. I've studied them to learn how he wrote his stories. I've paid particular attention to his revisions to see how they changed the meaning of a story. What I've discovered is the surprising fact that his revisions were more often additions than cuts. He added details for clarity and depth. Like a painter, Hemingway added to his canvas until the picture was how he wanted it. From this observation I would suggest that to approach writing as Hemingway did, you could start with the bare minimum and build, going back over your writing to see where details might add interest and clarity. **C**

C DISTINGUISH FACT FROM OPINION
Is the last sentence in this paragraph a fact, an opinion, or an expert's opinion? Give reasons for your answer.

There's another piece of information you need to have to begin to understand Hemingway's approach to writing. In Hemingway's stories, dialogue is very important. For example, in "A Day's Wait," after the doctor takes the boy's temperature, the brief exchange that occurs between the doctor and the boy's father is what triggers the boy's day of suffering:

"What is it?" I asked him.
"One hundred and two."

At times Hemingway cut his description of a character's thoughts in order to rely more heavily on dialogue.

You might also want to keep in mind Hemingway's other bit of advice to a young writer: "Get in somebody else's head for a change. If I bawl you out, try to figure what I'm thinking about as well as how you feel about it." In other words, try to see every event from all sides.

Now, perhaps, you are ready to start writing stories of your own. Of course, you have to have something to write about. Hemingway's life experiences were a rich source of material. He was a fisherman and a hunter, went to bullfights, and experienced both World War I and World War II. He lived in Europe, Cuba, and different parts of the United States. I'm not suggesting that you need to do similar things. Just embrace life. Then, maybe, after a time—and if you follow all this advice—you can be a successful writer like Hemingway. **D**

D DISTINGUISH FACT FROM OPINION
Which statement in this paragraph might people disagree about?

Comprehension

1. **Recall** Hemingway is known for writing what kinds of sentences?
2. **Clarify** What actual event in Hemingway's life helped inspire "A Day's Wait"?

Critical Analysis

3. **Distinguish Fact from Opinion** Review the facts and opinions you identified in the informative article. Then identify one of each, and explain why you identified it as you did.
4. **Identify Topic Sentences** A topic sentence is one that tells what a paragraph is about. Not all paragraphs have a topic sentence, but when it is present, it is often the first or second sentence in the paragraph. Identify three topic sentences in this informative article.
5. **Evaluate an Informative Article** A strong informative article is easy to follow, interesting, and useful. Would you say that "How Hemingway Wrote" is a strong informative article? Explain.

Read for Information: Create Instructions for Writers

WRITING PROMPT

In the informative article you just read, Bruce Rettman explains how to approach writing as Ernest Hemingway did. Now use these ideas to create a set of instructions for writers. To help explain your instructions, include examples from "A Day's Wait" or Rettman's article.

To answer this prompt, do as follows:

1. Scan Rettman's article to find six things a person can do to approach writing as Hemingway did.
2. Arrange the six directions in a logical order.
3. Illustrate at least two or three of these directions with examples from "A Day's Wait" or Rettman's article.

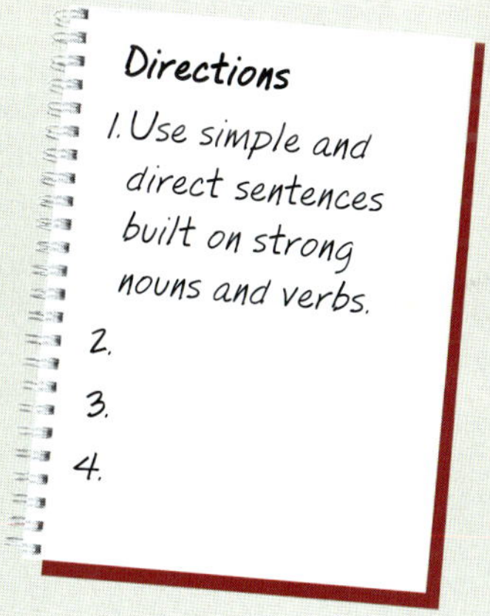

ALABAMA STANDARDS

READING & RESEARCH STANDARDS

4 Distinguish fact from opinion in informational materials

13.a Taking notes to gather and summarize information

The People Could Fly

Folk Tale retold by Virginia Hamilton

Where do people find HOPE?

ALABAMA STANDARDS

READING & LIT STANDARDS

3 Distinguish among subgenres, such as folktales, based on characteristics

6.a Classifying plot elements including conflict and resolution

KEY IDEA What is **hope?** Why do we need it? Where can we find it? How can we give hope to others? In her retelling of "The People Could Fly," Virginia Hamilton shares a story that gave people hope for freedom when little else did.

WEB IT With a partner, discuss the questions posed in the previous paragraph. Record ideas from your conversation in a word web like the one shown, adding to it as necessary.

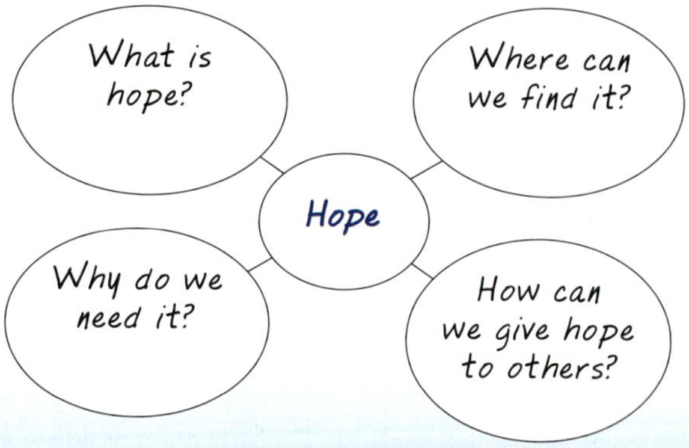

LITERARY ANALYSIS: STYLE IN FOLK TALES

The selection you are about to read is a **folk tale,** a story that has been passed from generation to generation by word of mouth. In writing the folk tale down, Virginia Hamilton chose to use a **style** that reflects how the story would sound if told aloud. That style includes

- nonstandard spellings that match how people might say certain words
- sentence structure that matches how people might talk

As you read, notice how Hamilton uses language to re-create the sound of speech. It may help you to read parts of the story aloud, as it was originally meant to be told.

READING SKILL: SUMMARIZE

One way to check your understanding of what you are reading is to **summarize** it. A summary is a brief retelling, in your own words, of the main ideas of a story. When you summarize a story, include

- the characters, setting, conflict, and resolution
- key details, so that someone who has not read the story understands your summary

As you read "The People Could Fly," collect the information you'll need to give a summary. Note the main elements in a story map like the one shown.

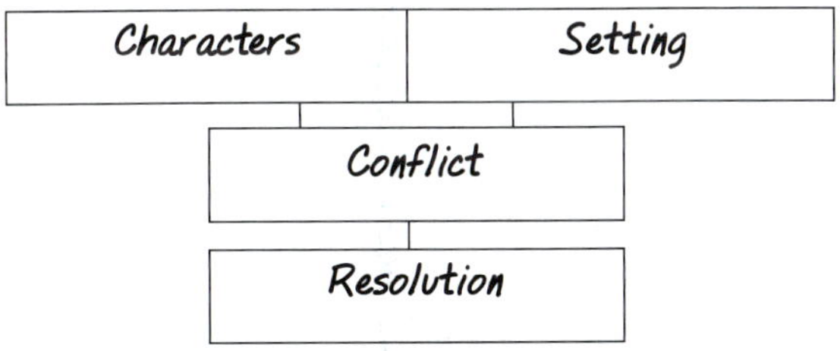

VOCABULARY IN CONTEXT

The boldfaced words all help tell a story of hardship and **hope.** Try to figure out what each word means in the context of the numbered phrases.

1. **croon** a lullaby
2. **snagged** by a tree branch
3. slide and **shuffle** to the left
4. **glinty** diamond

Author Online

A Storytelling Family
Virginia Hamilton grew up listening to her parents, grandparents, and others tell stories of their past. She has since realized that "they were passing along heritage and culture and a pride in their history."

Virginia Hamilton
1936–2002

From Listener to Writer Hamilton put these stories in writing and added some of her own, publishing more than 35 books. Many of her books, including *The People Could Fly*, deal with African-American history and culture.

Background

Slavery Between the 1500s and 1800s, about 12 million Africans were sent to North and South America as enslaved people. Colonists in the Americas wanted a cheap labor force to support their large-scale farming. People were kidnapped in Africa and sent overseas as enslaved people to be sold.

A Hopeful Community Despite the hardships they faced, enslaved people held on to a sense of community and tradition. They passed on stories, folk tales, and legends from generation to generation. The folk tale "The People Could Fly" is one example of these stories of hope and tradition.

MORE ABOUT THE AUTHOR AND BACKGROUND
To learn more about Virginia Hamilton and African-American oral tradition, visit the **Literature Center** at **ClassZone.com.**

The People Could Fly

Virginia Hamilton

They say the people could fly. Say that long ago in Africa, some of the people knew magic. And they would walk up on the air like climbin' up on a gate. And they flew like blackbirds over the fields. Black, shiny wings flappin' against the blue up there.

Then, many of the people were captured for Slavery. The ones that could fly shed their wings. They couldn't take their wings across the water on the slave ships. Too crowded, don't you know. **A**

The folks were full of misery, then. Got sick with the up and down of the sea. So they forgot about flyin' when they could no longer breathe the sweet scent of Africa.

Say the people who could fly kept their power, although they shed their wings. They kept their secret magic in the land of slavery. They looked the same as the other people from Africa who had been coming over, who had dark skin. Say you couldn't tell anymore one who could fly from one who couldn't.

One such who could was an old man, call him Toby. And standin' tall, yet afraid, was a young woman who once had wings. Call her Sarah. Now Sarah carried a babe tied to her back. She trembled to be so hard worked and scorned.

The slaves labored in the fields from sunup to sundown. The owner of the slaves callin' himself their Master. Say he was a hard lump of clay. A hard, **glinty** coal. A hard rock pile, wouldn't be moved. His Overseer[1]

ANALYZE VISUALS
Folk tales often include supernatural elements. What supernatural element does this illustration show?

A STYLE
Reread lines 1–7. Note the sentence fragments. How does Hamilton's use of sentence fragments help make it sound like someone is telling the story out loud?

glinty (glĭn'tē) *adj.* sparkling

1. **Overseer:** a person who directs the work of others; a supervisor. During the time of slavery, the overseer was usually a white man.

From *The People Could Fly* Illustrations © 1985 by Leo and Diane Dillon. Used by permission of Alfred A. Knopf, an imprint of Random House Children's Books, a division of Random House, Inc.

on horseback pointed out the slaves who were slowin' down. So the one called Driver cracked his whip over the slow ones to make them move faster. That whip was a slice-open cut of pain. So they did move faster. Had to. **B**

Sarah hoed and chopped the row as the babe on her back slept.

Say the child grew hungry. That babe started up bawling too loud. Sarah couldn't stop to feed it. Couldn't stop to soothe and quiet it down. She let it cry. She didn't want to. She had no heart to **croon** to it.

"Keep that thing quiet," called the Overseer. He pointed his finger at the babe. The woman scrunched low. The Driver cracked his whip across the babe anyhow. The babe hollered like any hurt child, and the woman fell to the earth. **C**

The old man that was there, Toby, came and helped her to her feet.

"I must go soon," she told him.

"Soon," he said.

Sarah couldn't stand up straight any longer. She was too weak. The sun burned her face. The babe cried and cried, "Pity me, oh, pity me," say it sounded like. Sarah was so sad and starvin', she sat down in the row.

"Get up, you black cow," called the Overseer. He pointed his hand, and the Driver's whip snarled around Sarah's legs. Her sack dress tore into rags. Her legs bled onto the earth. She couldn't get up.

Toby was there where there was no one to help her and the babe.

"Now, before it's too late," panted Sarah. "Now, Father!"

"Yes, Daughter, the time is come," Toby answered. "Go, as you know how to go!"

He raised his arms, holding them out to her. *"Kum . . . yali, kum buba tambe,"* and more magic words, said so quickly, they sounded like whispers and sighs.

The young woman lifted one foot on the air. Then the other. She flew clumsily at first, with the child now held tightly in her arms. Then she felt the magic, the African mystery. Say she rose just as free as a bird. As light as a feather.

The Overseer rode after her, hollerin'. Sarah flew over the fences. She flew over the woods. Tall trees could not **snag** her. Nor could the Overseer. She flew like an eagle now, until she was gone from sight. No one dared speak about it. Couldn't believe it. But it was, because they that was there saw that it was.

Say the next day was dead hot in the fields. A young man slave fell from the heat. The Driver come and whipped him. Toby come over and spoke words to the fallen one. The words of ancient Africa once heard are never remembered completely. The young man forgot them as soon as he heard them. They went way inside him. He got up and rolled over on the air. He rode it awhile. And he flew away.

B SUMMARIZE
Note the **setting** and the names of the **characters** in your story map.

croon (kro͞on) *v.* to sing softly

C SUMMARIZE
What is the **conflict?** Record it in your story map.

snag (snăg) *v.* to catch and tear

Another and another fell from the heat. Toby was there. He cried out to the fallen and reached his arms out to them. *"Kum kunka yali, kum . . . tambe!"* Whispers and sighs. And they too rose on the air. They rode the hot breezes. The ones flyin' were black and shinin' sticks, wheelin' above the head of the Overseer. They crossed the rows, the fields, the fences, the streams, and were away.

"Seize the old man!" cried the Overseer.

"I heard him say the magic *words.* Seize him!"

The one callin' himself Master come runnin'. The Driver got his whip ready to curl around old Toby and tie him up. The slave owner took his hip gun from its place. He meant to kill old black Toby. **D**

But Toby just laughed. Say he threw back his head and said, "Hee, hee! Don't you know who I am? Don't you know some of us in this field?" He said it to their faces. "We are ones who fly!"

And he sighed the ancient words that were a dark promise. He said them all around to the others in the field under the whip, "*. . . buba yali . . . buba tambe . . .*"

There was a great outcryin'. The bent backs straighted up. Old and young who were called slaves and could fly joined hands. Say like they would ring-sing. But they didn't **shuffle** in a circle. They didn't sing. They rose on the air. They flew in a flock that was black against the heavenly blue. Black crows or black shadows. It didn't matter, they went so high. Way above the plantation, way over the slavery land. Say they flew away to *Free-dom.*

And the old man, old Toby, flew behind them, takin' care of them. He wasn't cryin'. He wasn't laughin'. He was the seer. His gaze fell on the plantation where the slaves who could not fly waited. **E**

"Take us with you!" Their looks spoke it, but they were afraid to shout it. Toby couldn't take them with him. Hadn't the time to teach them to fly. They must wait for a chance to run.

"Goodie-bye!" the old man called Toby spoke to them, poor souls! And he was flyin' gone.

So they say. The Overseer told it. The one called Master said it was a lie, a trick of the light. The Driver kept his mouth shut.

The slaves who could not fly told about the people who could fly to their children. When they were free. When they sat close before the fire in the free land, they told it. They did so love firelight and *Free-dom,* and tellin'.

They say that the children of the ones who could not fly told their children. And now, me, I have told it to you.

D STYLE
In line 73 there is an example of **dialect,** a form of language spoken in a certain place or by a certain group of people. Why might Hamilton use dialect in this story?

shuffle (shŭf'əl) *v.* to slide the feet along the ground while walking

E SUMMARIZE
What role does Toby play in the **resolution** of the conflict?

SOCIAL STUDIES CONNECTION

Folk tales and other stories that were first told orally rather than written down make up what is called the **oral tradition** of many cultures throughout the world.

After Reading

Comprehension

1. **Recall** What special power did some of the people in Africa have?
2. **Recall** What does the Driver do to Sarah and her baby?
3. **Clarify** After Toby is gone, who tells the story of the people who could fly?

ALABAMA STANDARDS

READING STANDARD
3 Distinguish among subgenres, such as folktales, based on characteristics

Literary Analysis

4. **Summarize** Use the story map you created as you read to summarize the story. Compare your summary with that of a classmate.
5. **Draw Conclusions** Why do you think the people who first told this **folk tale** did not have all the slaves fly away?
6. **Analyze Theme** What do you think this story meant to the people who first heard it told?
7. **Evaluate Style in a Folk Tale** Reread lines 82–96. In a graphic like the one shown, note examples of Hamilton's style that appear in this section. Do you think this is an effective style for telling this story, or would you prefer to read it with standard spellings and complete sentences? Explain.

Hamilton's Style

Spellings	Sentence Fragments
• ______	• ______
• ______	• ______
• ______	• ______

Extension and Challenge

8. **Big Question Activity** Revisit the Web It activity on page 480. This time, consider how either Toby or Sarah would answer the questions about **hope.** Use details from the folk tale and your own knowledge and experiences to answer the questions as he or she would.
9. **SOCIAL STUDIES CONNECTION** The African-American **oral tradition** has its roots in Africa—particularly West Africa. Research to find out about griots (grē-ōz′) West African storytellers, and their role in the local culture.

RESEARCH LINKS
For more on griots, visit the **Research Center** at **ClassZone.com.**

Vocabulary in Context

VOCABULARY PRACTICE

Use **context clues** to choose a vocabulary word to complete each sentence.

croon
glinty
shuffle
snag

1. Though they tried not to _____ them, people often ripped their clothes while doing hard labor in the fields.
2. They had no money for jewelry or _____ things.
3. They would _____ with their heads down to keep the Overseer from noticing them.
4. At night, the mothers might _____ to their weeping children to comfort them.

VOCABULARY IN WRITING

In your opinion, is this story more about sadness or hope? In a paragraph, tell what you think. Use two or more vocabulary words. You could start this way.

EXAMPLE SENTENCE

*The people in this story had to **shuffle** from one place of hardship to another.*

VOCABULARY STRATEGY: USE THE BEST SYNONYM

One way writers make their stories come alive is by using well-chosen words. Common words like *sing* have many **synonyms,** or words with similar meanings. However, not all synonyms are interchangeable. In this story, for example, the verb *croon* gives a much more precise sense of the scene than the more common verb *sing* would convey. In a **thesaurus**—a book or electronic tool used to find synonyms—*croon* might be grouped with words like *hum, murmur,* and *chant.*

PRACTICE Choose the synonym in parentheses that best replaces each boldfaced word. If you need help, consult a thesaurus or a dictionary.

1. His sleeves got **dirty** from the leaking printer ink. (smudged, dingy)
2. Little children often **frown** if they don't get their way. (glare, pout)
3. Al Capone was a **famous** criminal. (distinguished, notorious)
4. She was so hungry that she **ate** everything in sight. (devoured, dined on)
5. The frightened field mouse **ran** across the kitchen floor. (scampered, jogged)

VOCABULARY PRACTICE
For more practice, go to the **Vocabulary Center** at **ClassZone.com.**

Great Reads

Out of the Dust

Novel in Verse by Karen Hesse

Karen Hesse
born 1952

Other Books by Karen Hesse

- *Aleutian Sparrow*
- *Letters from Rifka*
- *A Light in the Storm*
- *The Music of Dolphins*
- *Phoenix Rising*
- *Stowaway*
- *A Time of Angels*
- *Witness*

Meet Karen Hesse

Karen Hesse has worked as a librarian, teacher, secretary, proofreader, waitress, and nanny, but at heart she's always been a writer. "I love writing," she says. "I can't wait to get to my keyboard every morning." She also loves books and has shared that passion with her two daughters.

Hesse had a troubled childhood, but she feels that her experiences have strengthened her skills as a writer. "My work reflects the bumps and knocks that I've experienced," she explains. "I write the kinds of books that I would've wanted as a child."

Try a Novel in Verse

Most novels are written in prose, the ordinary form of written language, but they can also be written as poetry. Hesse wrote *Out of the Dust* as a series of **free verse** poems, which are poems written without regular rhyme or rhythm. As personal journal entries, these poems provide a window into what the main character is thinking and feeling.

Before Hesse began writing *Out of the Dust,* she spent several months researching the 1930s, the era in U.S. history in which her novel in verse is set. She used real places and events from the era to create her story.

Read a Great Book

Thirteen-year-old Billie Jo and her family of farmers are barely surviving the hardships of the Dust Bowl in Oklahoma in the 1930s. Drought and strong winds have ruined their crops. Dust covers everything, and money is scarce. Every day is a struggle. The only source of joy in Billie Jo's life is her talent for playing the piano.

from

Out of the Dust

Fields of Flashing Light

I heard the wind rise,
and stumbled from my bed,
down the stairs,
out the front door,
into the yard.
The night sky kept flashing,
lightning danced down on its spindly legs.

I sensed it before I knew it was coming.
I heard it,
smelled it,
tasted it.
Dust.

While Ma and Daddy slept,
the dust came,
tearing up fields where the winter wheat,
set for harvest in June,
stood helpless.
I watched the plants,
surviving after so much drought and so much wind,
I watched them fry,
or
flatten,
or blow away,
like bits of cast-off rags.

It wasn't until the dust turned toward the house,
like a fired locomotive,
and I fled,
barefoot and breathless, back inside,
it wasn't until the dust
hissed against the windows,
until it ratcheted the roof,
that Daddy woke.

He ran into the storm,
his overalls half-hooked over his union suit.
"Daddy!" I called. "You can't stop dust."

Ma told me to
cover the beds,
push the scatter rugs against the doors,

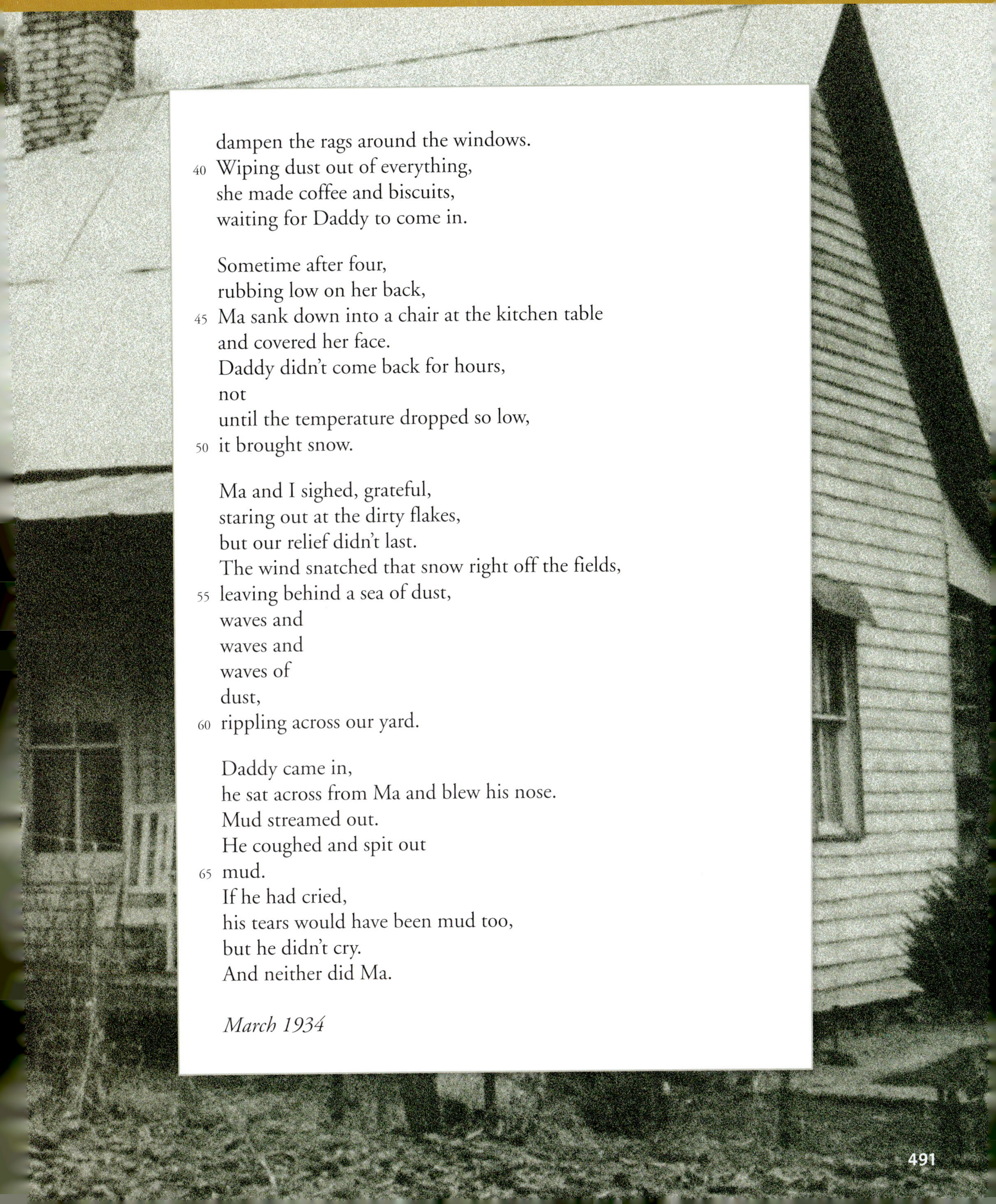

dampen the rags around the windows.
Wiping dust out of everything,
she made coffee and biscuits,
waiting for Daddy to come in.

Sometime after four,
rubbing low on her back,
Ma sank down into a chair at the kitchen table
and covered her face.
Daddy didn't come back for hours,
not
until the temperature dropped so low,
it brought snow.

Ma and I sighed, grateful,
staring out at the dirty flakes,
but our relief didn't last.
The wind snatched that snow right off the fields,
leaving behind a sea of dust,
waves and
waves and
waves of
dust,
rippling across our yard.

Daddy came in,
he sat across from Ma and blew his nose.
Mud streamed out.
He coughed and spit out
mud.
If he had cried,
his tears would have been mud too,
but he didn't cry.
And neither did Ma.

March 1934

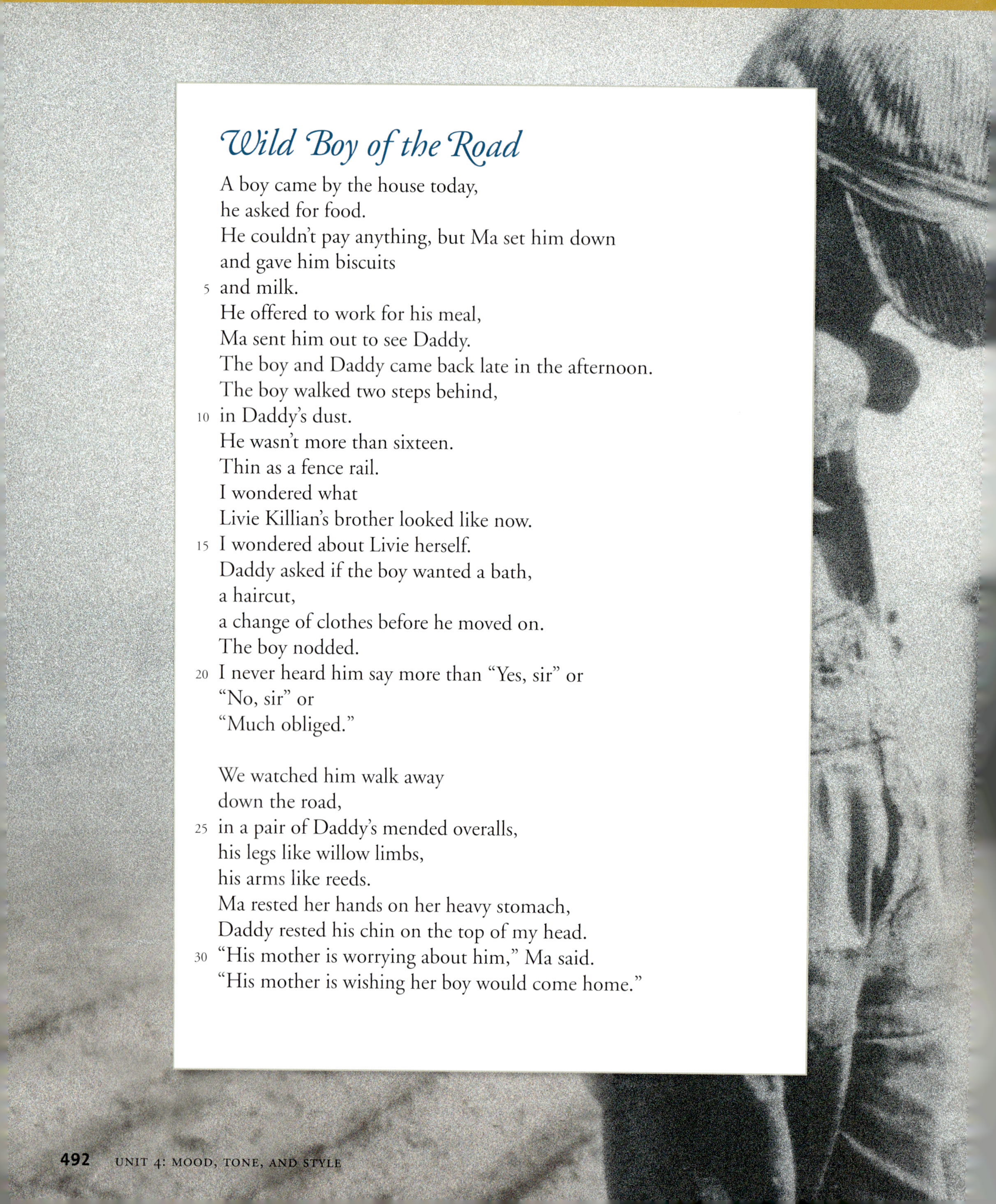

Wild Boy of the Road

A boy came by the house today,
he asked for food.
He couldn't pay anything, but Ma set him down
and gave him biscuits
and milk.
He offered to work for his meal,
Ma sent him out to see Daddy.
The boy and Daddy came back late in the afternoon.
The boy walked two steps behind,
in Daddy's dust.
He wasn't more than sixteen.
Thin as a fence rail.
I wondered what
Livie Killian's brother looked like now.
I wondered about Livie herself.
Daddy asked if the boy wanted a bath,
a haircut,
a change of clothes before he moved on.
The boy nodded.
I never heard him say more than "Yes, sir" or
"No, sir" or
"Much obliged."

We watched him walk away
down the road,
in a pair of Daddy's mended overalls,
his legs like willow limbs,
his arms like reeds.
Ma rested her hands on her heavy stomach,
Daddy rested his chin on the top of my head.
"His mother is worrying about him," Ma said.
"His mother is wishing her boy would come home."

Lots of mothers wishing that these days,
while their sons walk to California,
where rain comes,
and the color green doesn't seem like such a miracle,
and hope rises daily, like sap in a stem.
And I think, some day I'm going to walk there too,
through New Mexico and Arizona and Nevada.
Some day I'll leave behind the wind, and the dust
and walk my way West
and make myself to home in that distant place
of green vines and promise.

July 1934

Keep Reading

This is just a small part of the story about the life of a family during the Great Depression and Dust Bowl of the 1930s. Which descriptions stand out most vividly in your mind? To find out more about Billie Jo and her family, read more of *Out of the Dust*. You'll read about Billie Jo's struggles, why she thinks about running away to a place "where rain comes," and how she finds hope for a better future.

Comparing Tone

The Only Girl in the World for Me

Essay by Bill Cosby

Breaking the Ice

Essay by Dave Barry

What makes us LAUGH?

ALABAMA STANDARDS

READING & LIT STANDARDS

2 Relate literary elements and devices to each other

8 Compare selections and their characteristics

KEY IDEA There have probably been times when you told a joke and nobody laughed. Maybe you heard a joke that made other people laugh but that you didn't think was funny. Each person has a unique sense of **humor,** and everyone has a different way of being funny. The essay writers you are about to read have built careers out of making people laugh.

QUOTE IT "Laughter is the best medicine." "Laugh and the world laughs with you." "Laughter is the closest distance between two people." There are dozens of quotes about laughter. Now it is your turn to add to the list. Think of the kinds of things that make you laugh and how laughing makes you feel. Then write your own quote about laughter.

LITERARY ANALYSIS: TONE

Have you ever been told, "Don't use that tone with me"? If so, the person speaking probably didn't like your attitude. In literature, **tone** is a writer's attitude toward a topic. Tone is part of a writer's **style** and often can be described in one word, such as *sarcastic* or *sentimental*.

The two essays you are about to read relate humorous stories about dating experiences, but each has a different tone. As you read each essay, do the following:

- Identify the topic. Ask: "What is the writer writing about?"
- Notice significant words and phrases. Do most of them convey a similar attitude?
- Notice images and descriptions. Are they exaggerated, silly, or frightening?

These clues will help you identify the tone of each essay.

READING STRATEGY: SET A PURPOSE FOR READING

In this lesson, your **purpose for reading** is to compare tone. As you read, take notes, writing them in a chart like the one shown. You will be asked to add more rows to this chart later.

	"The Only Girl in the World for Me"	"Breaking the Ice"
Topic of the essay		
Words and phrases that display an attitude	"for one golden moment our eyes met"	"Never risk direct contact with the girl in question."
Vivid images and descriptions		

VOCABULARY IN CONTEXT

Descriptive words help Bill Cosby create **humor** in his essay. For each boldfaced word, use context clues to figure out its meaning.

1. I made the **transition** from grade school to junior high.
2. She experienced the **heady** feeling of success.
3. It was an **agonizing** day in the hot, blazing sun.
4. A library is a **reservoir** of information.
5. He was **suppressing** the news and not publicizing it.

Author Online

Bill Cosby: Class Clown

Bill Cosby
born 1937

Bill Cosby began his comedy career long before he was getting paid for it. "I thought that if people laughed at what you said, that meant they liked you," he has said. Cosby was always the class clown. By the time he was in college, he was a professional comedian. He continued his schooling and earned two advanced degrees in education from the University of Massachusetts. Cosby is also a television star, a musician, and an award-winning author.

Dave Barry: Journalism's Funny Man

Dave Barry
born 1947

Pulitzer Prize–winning writer Dave Barry is best known for the columns he has written for the *Miami Herald* newspaper. Barry's columns, including "Breaking the Ice," often exaggerate and poke fun at the daily life of his readers. As one reviewer put it, Barry has a gift for "squeezing every ounce of humor out of a perfectly ordinary experience."

MORE ABOUT THE AUTHOR
For more on Bill Cosby and Dave Barry, visit the **Literature Center** at **ClassZone.com.**

The Only Girl in the World for Me

Bill Cosby

I can't remember where I have left my glasses, but I can still remember the smell of the first girl I ever fell in love with when I was twelve: a blend of Dixie Peach pomade[1] on her hair and Pond's cold cream on her skin; together they were honeysuckle for me. And just as **heady** as her scent was the thought that I was in love with the only girl in the world for me and would marry her and take care of her forever in a palace in North Philadelphia. Because I wanted to make a wondrous impression on this girl, grooming was suddenly important to me. Before puberty, happiness in appearance for me was pants that didn't fall down and a football that stayed pumped; but now I started taking three long baths a day and washing my own belt until it was white and shining my shoes until I could see in them a face that was ready for romance. (A)

heady (hĕd'ē) *adj.* tending to make one feel really happy or excited

The first time I saw her, she was crossing the street to the schoolyard and for one golden moment our eyes met. Well, maybe the moment was closer to bronze because she made no response. But at least she had seen me, just about the way that she saw lampposts, hydrants, and manholes. Or was there something more? I began to dream; and later that day, when I was playing with the boys in the yard, it seemed that she was looking at me and the world was suddenly a better place, especially Twelfth and Girard.

(A) TONE
Reread lines 1–12. On the basis of the title and the first paragraph, what do you think the **topic** of the essay is?

However, we still never talked, but just traded silent unsmiling looks whenever we passed. For several days, just her look was enough of a lift for me; but a higher altitude was coming, for one night at a party, we met and I actually danced with her. Now I was certain that I was in love and was going to win her.

I began my conquest with a combination of sporting skill and hygiene: I made my jump shots and my baths as dazzling as they could be. Oddly enough, however, although I saw her every day at school and on the weekends too, I never spoke to her. I had what was considered one of the faster mouths in Philadelphia, but I still wasn't ready to talk to her because I feared rejection. I feared:

1. **pomade** (pō-mād'): a perfumed ointment for the scalp and hair.

COSBY: I like you very much. Will you be my girlfriend?
GODDESS: *(Doing a poor job of* ***suppressing*** *a laugh)* I'd rather have some cavities filled. **B**

All I did, therefore, was adore her in silent cleanliness. Each Sunday night, I took a bath and then prepared my shirt and pants for display to her. On Monday morning, I took another bath (Bill the Baptist,[2] I should have been called) and then brushed my hair, my shoes, and my eyelashes and went outside to await the pang of another silent passage.

At last, deciding that I could no longer live this way, I sat down one Sunday night and wrote a note that was almost to her. It was to her constant girlfriend and it said:

Please don't tell her, but find out what she thinks of me.
Bill

The following morning, I slipped the note to the girlfriend and began the longest wait of my life.

Two **agonizing** days later, the girlfriend slipped me an answer, but I put it into my pocket unread. For hours, I carried it around, afraid to read it because I didn't happen to be in the mood for crushing rejection that day. At last, however, I summoned the courage to open the note and read:

She thinks you're cute.

Not even malaria[3] could have taken my temperature to where it went. I had been called many things, but cute was never one of them.

An even lovelier fever lay ahead, for the next time I saw her, she smiled at me, I smiled at her, and then I composed my next winged message to her friend:

I think she's cute too. Does she ever talk about me?

The answer to this one came return mail and it sounded like something by Keats:

She talks about you a lot. She knows it when you come around her.

And the angels sang! Imagine: She actually *knew* it when I came around her! The fact that she also knew it when gnats came around her in no way dampened my ecstasy. **C**

And so, we continued to smile as we passed, while I planned my next move. My Western Union[4] style had clearly been charming the pants off her (so to speak) and now I launched my most courageous question yet:

suppressing (sə-prĕ′sĭng) *n.* keeping in; holding back **suppress** *v.*

B TONE
Reread lines 25–33 and think about what makes this passage funny. Why did Cosby use the word "goddess" instead of the girl's real name?

agonizing (ăg′ə-nī′zĭng) *adj.* resulting in great pain or deep sadness **agonize** *v.*

VISUAL VOCABULARY

John Keats (1795–1821), an English Romantic poet

C TONE
Cosby's writing **style** shows us his sense of humor. Reread lines 50–61. Record two examples of funny sentences or phrases that affect the tone of the essay.

2. **Bill the Baptist:** a reference to John the Baptist, a prophet who baptized his followers by submerging them in water.
3. **malaria** (mə-lâr′ē-ə): a disease characterized by chills and fever.
4. **Western Union:** a company that once operated a telegraph service.

Does she have a boyfriend?

When I opened the answer the next day in school, the air left me faster than it left the *Hindenburg:*[5]

Yes.

Trying to recover from this deflation,[6] I told myself that I was still cute. I was the cutest man in second place. But perhaps my beloved wasn't aware of the glory she kept passing by. Once more, I sat down and wrote:

How much longer do you think she'll be going with him? And when she's finished with him, can I be next?

Note the elegance and dignity of my appeal. My dignity, however, did have some trouble with the reply:

She thinks she's going to break up with him in about a week, but she promised Sidney she would go with him next. **D**

Suddenly, my aching heart found itself at the end of a line. But it was like a line at a bank: I knew it was leading to a payoff. I also knew that I could cream Sidney in cuteness.

Once she had made the **transition** to Sidney, I patiently began waiting for her to get sick of him. I had to be careful not to rush the illness because Sidney belonged to a tough gang and there was a chance that I might not be walking around too well when the time came for me to inherit her.

And then, one magnificent morning, I received the magic words:

She would like to talk to you.

I wrote back to see if she would wait until I had finished duty at my post as a school crossing guard. Yes, she would wait; I could walk her home. We were going steady now; and how much more torrid our passion would be when I began to *talk* to her.

At last, the words came and I chose them with care. As I walked her home from school, I reached into my **reservoir** of romantic thoughts, smiled at her soulfully, and said, "How you doing?"

Her response was equally poetic: "All right."

"So we're going steady now?"

"You want to?"

"Yeah. Give me your books."

And now, as if our relationship were not already in the depths of desire, I plunged even deeper by saying, "You wanna go to a movie on Saturday?"

"Why not?"

D TONE
What is Cosby's attitude toward the notes that are being passed around? Identify the words and descriptions that suggest his attitude.

transition (trăn-zĭsh'ən) *n.* change from one place or condition to another

reservoir (rĕz'ər-vwär') *n.* a place where anything is collected and stored

5. ***Hindenburg:*** an airship filled with hydrogen gas that caught fire and blew up following a transatlantic flight in 1937.

6. **deflation** (dĭ-flā'shən): the act or process of losing confidence.

There might have been reasons. Some people were looking at us now because she was so beautiful, people possibly wondering what she was doing with me; but I knew that I was someone special to be the love of a vision like this, no matter how nearsighted that vision might be.

When we reached her door, I said, "Well, I'll see you Saturday."

"Right," she replied as only she could say it.

"What time?"

"One o'clock."

When this day of days finally arrived, I took her to a theater where I think the admission was a dime. As we took our seats for the matinee, two basic thoughts were in my mind: not to sit in gum and to be a gentleman.

Therefore, I didn't hold her hand. Instead, I put my arm around the top of her seat in what I felt was a smooth opening move. Unfortunately, it was less a move toward love than toward gangrene:[7] With my blood moving uphill, my arm first began to tingle and then to ache. I could not, however, take the arm down and let my blood keep flowing because such a lowering would mean I didn't love her; so I left it up there, its muscles full of pain, its fingertips full of needlepoints. **E**

E TONE
Reread lines 113–119. In your chart, record examples of Cosby's unusual descriptive phrases.

Suddenly, this romantic agony was enriched by a less romantic one: I had to go to the bathroom. Needless to say, I couldn't let her know about this urge, for great lovers never did such things. The answer to "Romeo, Romeo, wherefore art thou, Romeo?"[8] was not "In the men's room, Julie."

What a prince of passion I was at this moment: My arm was dead, my bladder was full, and I was out of money too; but I desperately needed an excuse to move, so I said, "You want some popcorn?"

"No," she said.

"Fine, I'll go get some."

When I tried to move, every part of me could move except my arm: It was dead. I reached over and pulled it down with the other one, trying to be as casual as a man could be when pulling one of his arms with the other one.

"What's the matter?" she said.

"Oh, nothing," I replied. "I'm just taking both of my arms with me."

A few minutes later, as I came out of the bathroom, I was startled to meet her: She was coming from the bathroom *too*. How good it was to find another thing that we had in common. With empty bladders and full hearts, we returned to our seats to continue our love. **F**

F TONE
In what way does the last paragraph convey a sense of innocence?

---

7. **gangrene** (găng'grēn'): tissue decay in a part of the body.

8. **"Romeo . . . Romeo?":** approximate quote of a question asked by Juliet in William Shakespeare's play *Romeo and Juliet.*

Comprehension

1. **Recall** How old is Bill Cosby when the events in the essay take place?
2. **Recall** Where do young Cosby and the girl go on their date?
3. **Summarize** Why is he uncomfortable on the date?

ALABAMA STANDARDS

LITERATURE STANDARD
8 Compare selections and their characteristics

Literary Analysis

4. **Make Inferences** Why does Cosby pass notes with the girl's best friend rather than talking to the girl directly? Explain your answer.
5. **Examine Word Choice** Cosby uses formal-sounding phrases such as "and the angels sang" and "this day of days" in this essay. Reread lines 87–94 to find other formal language. How does this language add **humor** to the essay?
6. **Analyze Tone** What seems to be Cosby's attitude toward his first love? Give examples of the words, images, and descriptions that convey this tone.
7. **Draw Conclusions** Why do you think Cosby never names or provides much description about his first love?

Comparing Tone

Now that you've read "The Only Girl in the World for Me," add more information to your chart.

	"The Only Girl in the World for Me"	"Breaking the Ice"
Topic of the essay		
Words and phrases that display an attitude	*"for one golden moment our eyes met"*	*"Never risk direct contact with the girl in question."*
Vivid images and descriptions		
Adjectives that describe the tone		

BREAKING THE ICE

DAVE BARRY

As a mature adult, I feel an obligation to help the younger generation, just as the mother fish guards her unhatched eggs, keeping her lonely vigil day after day, never leaving her post, not even to go to the bathroom, until her tiny babies emerge and she is able, at last, to eat them. "She may be your mom, but she's still a fish" is a wisdom nugget that I would pass along to any fish eggs reading this column.

But today I want to talk about dating. This subject was raised in a letter to me from a young person named Eric Knott, who writes:

ANALYZE VISUALS
As you look at this picture, **predict** what the essay will be about.

I have got a big problem. There's this girl in my English class who is *really* good-looking. However, I don't think she knows I exist. I want to ask her out, but I'm afraid she will say no, and I will be the freak of the week. What should I do? **A**

Eric, you have sent your question to the right mature adult, because as a young person I spent a lot of time thinking about this very problem. Starting in about eighth grade, my time was divided as follows:

Academic Pursuits: 2 percent.
Zits: 16 percent.
Trying to Figure Out How to Ask Girls Out: 82 percent.

The most sensible way to ask a girl out is to walk directly up to her on foot and say, "So, you want to go out? Or what?" I never did this. I knew, as Eric Knott knows, that there was always the possibility that the girl would say no, thereby leaving me with no viable option[1] but to leave Harold C. Crittenden Junior High School forever and go into the woods and become a bark-eating hermit whose only companions would be the gentle and understanding woodland creatures.

"Hey, ZITFACE!" the woodland creatures would shriek in cute little Chip 'n' Dale voices while raining acorns down upon my head. "You wanna DATE? HAHAHAHAHAHA." **B**

So the first rule of dating is: Never risk direct contact with the girl in question. Your role model should be the nuclear submarine, gliding silently beneath the ocean surface, tracking an enemy target that does not even begin to suspect that the submarine would like to date it. I spent the vast majority of 1960 keeping a girl named Judy under surveillance,[2] maintaining a minimum distance of 50 lockers to avoid the danger that I might somehow get into a conversation with her, which could have led to disaster:

JUDY: Hi.
ME: Hi.
JUDY: Just in case you have ever thought about having a date with me, the answer is no.
WOODLAND CREATURES: HAHAHAHAHAHA.

The only problem with the nuclear-submarine technique is that it's difficult to get a date with a girl who has never, technically, been asked. This is why you need Phil Grant. Phil was a friend of mine who had the

A TONE
Reread lines 1–12. What is the **topic** of the essay?

B TONE
Reread lines 26–28. What is Barry's attitude toward his younger self? Note how the **style** of using capital letters helps communicate this attitude.

1. **viable option:** choice that has a possibility of working.
2. **surveillance** (sər-vā'ləns): close observation.

ability to talk to girls. It was a mysterious superhuman power he had, comparable to X-ray vision. So, after several thousand hours of intense discussion and planning with me, Phil approached a girl he knew named Nancy, who approached a girl named Sandy, who was a direct personal friend of Judy's and who passed the word back to Phil via Nancy that Judy would be willing to go on a date with me. This procedure protected me from direct humiliation. . . . C

C TONE
Reread lines 44–51. Note Barry's description of Phil Grant's "superhuman" abilities. How would you describe the tone of this paragraph?

Thus it was that, finally, Judy and I went on an actual date, to see a movie in White Plains, New York. If I were to sum up the romantic ambience[3] of this date in four words, those words would be: "My mother was driving." This made for an extremely quiet drive, because my mother, realizing that her presence was hideously embarrassing, had to pretend she wasn't there. If it had been legal, I think she would have got out and sprinted alongside the car, steering through the window. Judy and I, sitting in the backseat about 75 feet apart, were also silent, unable to communicate without the assistance of Phil, Nancy, and Sandy. D

D TONE
Does Barry seem to enjoy the drive to the movie theater? Note words and phrases that give his description of the ride either a positive or a negative tone.

After what seemed like several years we got to the movie theater, where my mother went off to sit in the Parents and Lepers Section. The movie was called *North to Alaska,* but I can tell you nothing else about it because I spent the whole time wondering whether it would be necessary to amputate my right arm, which was not getting any blood flow as a result of being perched for two hours like a petrified snake on the back of Judy's seat exactly one molecule away from physical contact.

So it was definitely a fun first date, featuring all the relaxed spontaneity of a real-estate closing,[4] and in later years I did regain some feeling in my arm. My point, Eric Knott, is that the key to successful dating is self-confidence. I bet that good-looking girl in your English class would LOVE to go out with you. But YOU have to make the first move. So just do it! Pick up that phone! Call Phil Grant.

3. **ambience** (ăm'bē-əns): atmosphere; environment.

4. **spontaneity of a real-estate closing:** A real-estate closing is a meeting where a piece of property transfers from a seller to a buyer. Many required documents are signed, in a very formal, unspontaneous way.

Comprehension

1. **Recall** How does Dave Barry ask Judy out on a date?
2. **Recall** Where do they go on their date?
3. **Clarify** Why is Barry uncomfortable on the date?

ALABAMA STANDARDS

LITERATURE STANDARD
8 Compare selections and their characteristics

Literary Analysis

4. **Make Inferences** Reread Barry's advice to Eric Knott in lines 70–71. Does Barry himself display self-confidence during his first date? Cite details from the essay to support your answer.
5. **Analyze Style** On the basis of this example of Barry's style, how would you describe his sense of **humor** to someone who hasn't read anything by him?
6. **Compare Descriptions** Compare how Cosby and Barry describe being at a movie with a girl, focusing not only on what each author says about his experience but how he says it. Cite key words and phrases.
7. **Draw Conclusions** Which author seems to have enjoyed his teenage years more? Give clues from each essay that led you to your conclusion.
8. **Evaluate Humor** Consider which essay made you laugh more. What did you think was the most effective part of the funnier essay? Why?

Comparing Tone

Finish filling in your chart with information on "Breaking the Ice." Now add the final question to your chart and try answering it.

	"The Only Girl in the World for Me"	"Breaking the Ice"
Topic of the essay		
Words and phrases that display an attitude	"for one golden moment our eyes met"	"Never risk direct contact with the girl in question."
Vivid images and descriptions		
Adjectives that describe the tone		
In what ways are the essays similar or different in tone?		

Vocabulary in Context

VOCABULARY PRACTICE

In each item, choose the word that differs most in meaning from the other words. Refer to a dictionary or thesaurus if you need help.

1. (a) concealing, (b) suppressing, (c) informing, (d) hiding
2. (a) container, (b) trunk, (c) landscape, (d) reservoir
3. (a) concerned, (b) heady, (c) worried, (d) agitated
4. (a) transition, (b) change, (c) passage, (d) notice
5. (a) painful, (b) tormenting, (c) restoring, (d) agonizing

agonizing
heady
reservoir
suppressing
transition

VOCABULARY IN WRITING

Decide what was the best or the worst part of Cosby's romance as he describes it. Write a paragraph explaining your ideas, using two or more vocabulary words. Here is a sample opening sentence.

EXAMPLE SENTENCE

*The most **agonizing** part of the romance was waiting for it to start.*

VOCABULARY STRATEGY: LITERAL AND FIGURATIVE MEANINGS

Many words have multiple meanings. Some meanings are straightforward, or **literal,** while others are more symbolic, or **figurative.** For example, there are two meanings of the word *reservoir:*

- literal definition: an artificial lake used to collect and store water
- figurative definition: a place where *anything* is collected or stored

When you encounter words that have both a literal and a figurative meaning, it is important to recognize which meaning the writer intends.

PRACTICE For each sentence, tell whether the boldfaced word has a literal or figurative meaning. Then give the meaning of the word as it is used.

1. After the windstorm, a **blanket** of leaves covered the ground.
2. Franklin was **blinded** by bitterness and envy.
3. Mrs. Nelson had to go through a **maze** of confusing letters and bills.
4. When they could no longer make their payments, they went **bankrupt.**
5. Catching a cold just before the debate was one more **hurdle** for Janice.

VOCABULARY PRACTICE
For more practice, go to the **Vocabulary Center** at **ClassZone.com.**

Writing for Assessment

1. READ THE PROMPT

In writing assessments, you might be asked to compare the **tones** of essays—even humorous essays like the ones you just read.

PROMPT

Both "The Only Girl in the World for Me" and "Breaking the Ice" focus on the sometimes amusing, sometimes painful topic of love. However, each author has used a unique tone to present his experience. In four or five paragraphs, describe the tone of each essay, and then compare how each author developed that tone. Support your response with details from the two essays.

STRATEGIES IN ACTION

1. I need to **describe the attitude** each author has toward his subject.
2. I have to show the **similar and different** ways each author makes his attitude known.
3. I should **give examples** from the essays to help explain my ideas.

2. PLAN YOUR WRITING

Review the chart you filled out on page 505. Use the information to help you describe the tone of each essay and identify the similarities and differences in the words, images, and descriptions that convey the tone. Then think about how you will set up your response.

- Do you want to describe the first essay and then point out similarities and differences in the second essay?
- Do you want to compare the words and phrases of both essays in one paragraph and the details of both essays in another paragraph? The sample outline shows this way of organizing.

Once you have decided, outline the order of your paragraphs.

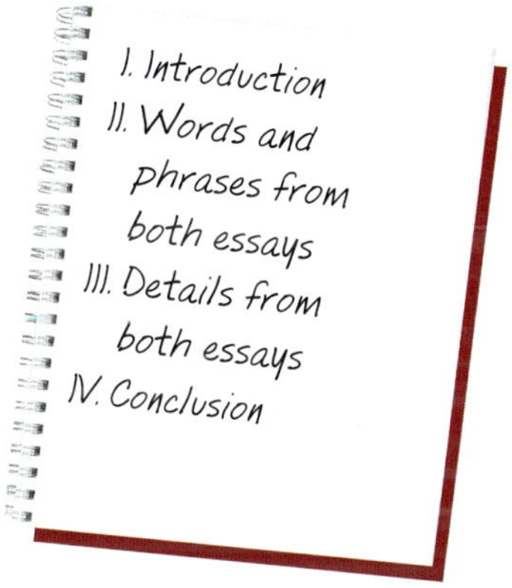

3. DRAFT YOUR RESPONSE

Introduction Include the titles and authors' names for the essays. Identify the tone of each essay, and provide an overview of the similarities and differences in how the authors communicate tone.

Body Stay focused on the points you want to make in each paragraph. Make sure you support each point with an example from one of the essays.

Conclusion Restate your main idea and leave the reader with a final thought about tone and humor.

Revision Check to see that your paragraphs flow smoothly. If they don't, add transitional phrases such as *on the other hand,* or *while both essays.*

One Perfect Rose

Song for an April Dusk

Poems by Dorothy Parker

Does everyone LOVE *being in love?*

ALABAMA STANDARDS

READING STANDARDS

2 Relate literary elements and devices to each other

3 Distinguish among genres, including poetry, based on characteristics

KEY IDEA Love is a popular subject in songs, books, and movies. In fact, romance novels make up nearly half of all adult paperback fiction sales in the United States. But some people prefer things that aren't too "mushy," overly emotional, or **sentimental.** Dorothy Parker's poems give readers a sense of whether she would love being in love.

DISCUSS One of the most popular holidays for cards is Valentine's Day. Why do you think this is so? Talk about the reasons people send Valentine's Day cards. Also, talk about other holidays that are popular for sending cards.

LITERARY ANALYSIS: IRONY

In the two poems you are about to read, the poet uses irony. **Irony** is a contrast between what is expected and what actually happens. Dorothy Parker creates irony in her poetry by

- starting with romantic images
- using form and language to set the poem's **tone,** creating what the reader thinks is Parker's attitude toward the subject
- revealing a different attitude at the end of the poem, taking the reader by surprise

Parker's ironic shifts in attitude add humor to her poems. Her use of irony also allows her to challenge a common assumption. As you read her poems, think about the expectation that women will always respond in the same way. Then notice how the **speaker,** or voice that talks to the reader, responds to romance.

READING STRATEGY: FORM IN POETRY

An important part of understanding poetry comes from understanding its form. A poem's **form** is the way it is laid out on the page. Traditional poems follow regular, or repeated, patterns.

- The length of each **line** in a poem helps create the poem's **rhythm** and meaning.
- Lines might be grouped into **stanzas,** which often express a single idea or **theme.**
- The pattern of lines and stanzas often creates a pattern of **rhyming** words.

Poets choose the form that best suits the intended message of a particular poem. Parker purposely chooses a traditional form for her ironic poems. As you read, make notes about the poems' lines, stanzas, and rhyming words. Use a chart like the one shown.

One Perfect Rose	
Line length	3 the same length, 1 shorter
Number of stanzas	
Rhyming words	

Author On|ine

Harsh Humor After being fired from *Vanity Fair* magazine in New York City for writing reviews that were considered too harsh, Dorothy Parker started writing poetry. With several other writers, she founded a literary group called the Algonquin Round Table. Parker and the rest of the group became known for their humorous and lively conversations.

Dorothy Parker
1893–1967

A New Attitude As a young woman, Parker read the sentimental poetry that was popular in the Victorian era. When writing poetry of her own, Parker blended traditional poetic forms with the "challenge everything" attitude of her time. This new style was a hit. Her first book of poetry, *Enough Rope* (1926), was a bestseller.

Social Critic The 1920s are often symbolized by "flappers"—independent women who challenged what was considered a woman's proper role in society. Parker used her sharp humor to express her independent spirit and to help her comment on issues such as materialism and the limited roles available to women in the 1920s.

MORE ABOUT THE AUTHOR
For more on Dorothy Parker, visit the **Literature Center** at **ClassZone.com.**

One PERFECT *Rose*

Dorothy Parker

A single flow'r he sent me, since we met.
All tenderly his messenger he chose;
Deep-hearted, pure, with scented dew still wet—
One perfect rose. **A**

I knew the language of the floweret;
"My fragile leaves," it said, "his heart enclose."
Love long has taken for his amulet[1]
One perfect rose.

Why is it no one ever sent me yet
One perfect limousine, do you suppose?
Ah no, it's always just my luck to get
One perfect rose. **B**

A FORM IN POETRY
Notice which lines **rhyme** in the first **stanza.** Is the pattern of rhyme the same in stanzas 2 and 3?

B IRONY
In which line does the **tone** of the poem change?

1. **amulet:** an object worn as a magic charm.

Song for an APRIL DUSK

Dorothy Parker

Tell me tales of a lilied pool
Asleep beneath the sun.
Tell me of woodlands deep and cool,
When chuckling satyrs[1] run.
Tell me, in light and tinkling words,
Of rippling, lilting streams.
Tell me of radiant-breasted birds,
Who sing their amorous[2] dreams.
Tell of the doomed butterfly
That flings his hour away.
Fated to live and love and die
Before the death of day. **C**

Tell me tales of the moon-pale sprites[3]
Whose beauty none may know.
Tell me of secret, silver nights
When great red stars are low.
Tell of the virgin Spring, the fair,
Who roams the circling years.
Rain-drops strung in her fragrant hair,
Her eyes a-mist with tears.
Tell me of elves, who leap to kiss,
Who trip the velvet sward.[4]
Tell me stories of things like this,
And, boy, will I be bored! **D**

C FORM IN POETRY
Describe the **rhythm** of this poem. How does **repetition** add to the rhythm?

D IRONY
How does the last line change the meaning of the poem?

1. **satyrs** (sā′tərs): in Greek mythology, woodland spirits in the male form, but with the ears and tail of a horse or goat.
2. **amorous** (ăm′ər-es): filled with love.
3. **sprites:** elves or fairies.
4. **trip the velvet sward:** skip along a smooth lawn.

Comprehension

ALABAMA STANDARDS

READING STANDARD
3 Distinguish among genres, including poetry, based on characteristics

1. **Clarify** In "One Perfect Rose," what gift would the **speaker** prefer to receive?
2. **Summarize** What is the second poem about?
3. **Represent** Choose any pair of lines from "Song for an April Dusk" and illustrate them.

Literary Analysis

4. **Identify Irony** For each poem, complete a chart like the one shown. Record what the first part of the poem leads you to expect, and what actually happens at the end.

Title: ____________	
What We Expect	*What Happens*

5. **Compare and Contrast** In one to three sentences, compare and contrast the attitudes about romance expressed in "One Perfect Rose" and "Song for an April Dusk." How are they similar and different?
6. **Analyze Poetic Form** Look back at the notes you made about the poet's use of **lines, stanzas,** and **rhyme.** Explain how Parker's use of traditional form reinforces the **irony** in her poetry.
7. **Analyze Irony** Did the ending of each poem change your understanding of the poem's meaning? Explain your response, using evidence from the poems. Note which ending you found to be more surprising.
8. **Evaluate Style** Parker is known as a witty and humorous writer. On the basis of these poems, do you think she deserves this reputation? Explain, using examples from the poems.

Extension and Challenge

9. **Creative Project: Poetry** Try writing a short, **ironic** poem about love. You may use Parker's poems as a model, if you wish, or follow a different form.
10. **Inquiry and Research** Research to find out who else was in Parker's literary group, the Algonquin Round Table. Investigate what the group did when they met and how long the group was together. Share your opinion as to how this group may have influenced Parker's writing and style.

RESEARCH LINKS
For more on the Algonquin Round Table, visit the **Research Center** at **ClassZone.com.**

Members of the Algonquin Round Table

maggie and milly and molly and may
who are you,little i
old age sticks

Poems by E. E. Cummings

Are all things CONNECTED?

ALABAMA STANDARDS

READING STANDARDS
1.d Applying self-monitoring strategies
2 Relate literary elements and devices to each other

KEY IDEA A snowflake always has six sides. An insect always has six legs. The moon you see at night is the same moon seen by people in Brazil. In a world of infinite variety, scientists, artists, and writers—including the poet whose work you are about to read—can reveal unexpected **connections**.

WEB IT Think of a plant or an animal, an object, and a very old or very young person that you share connections with. Use a word web to describe each connection. Then compare the connections you noted with those your classmates noted.

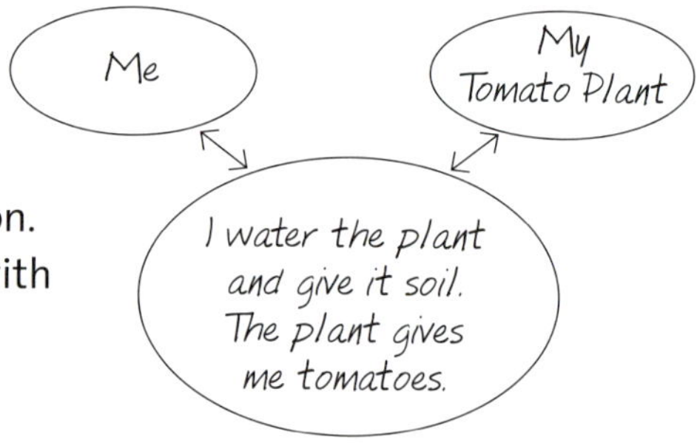

LITERARY ANALYSIS: STYLE IN POETRY

Poet E. E. Cummings has one of the most recognizable **styles** in literature. As with many writers, his style is not in what he says, but in how he says it. To identify the poet's unique style, focus on the following elements:

- **Word Choice** Cummings often invented new words or used familiar words in an unfamiliar way.
- **Form** Cummings often created unusual line breaks in his poetry. Sometimes he even broke a line in the middle of a word. He also arranged the lines of some poems in order to create a visual pattern on the page.
- **Punctuation, Capitalization, and Spacing** Cummings used punctuation in new ways and rarely used capital letters. He sometimes eliminated the space between two words, as well.

As you can see, Cummings broke many "rules." Watch for examples of his style as you read three of his poems.

READING STRATEGY: MONITOR

To get the most meaning out of what you are reading, it is good to occasionally check, or **monitor,** your understanding. One part of monitoring is to **clarify,** or pause to reflect on what you know so far and use clues in the selection to make inferences about meaning. When reading poetry, rephrasing lines in your own words can help make the meaning more clear.

After you read each poem once, read it again. This time, pause to clarify the meaning of the lines as you go. For each poem, it may help you to create a chart like the one shown.

"maggie and milly and molly and may"		
Line Numbers	Poet's Words	My Words
5–6	"milly befriended a stranded star / whose rays five languid fingers were"	Milly discovered a starfish with five arms.

Author Online

An American Original Beginning at age eight, E. E. Cummings wrote a poem a day. While attending Harvard University, he switched from traditional to modern forms of poetry. He frequently traveled to Paris, where he was exposed to modern forms of literature and art.

E. E. Cummings
1894–1962

A Lot of Style Cummings experimented with a writing style that would later make him famous. While the style of Cummings's poems was new and different, his subject matter and themes were often traditional. He frequently wrote about childhood, relationships, and nature. Cummings was also an accomplished visual artist whose work was frequently exhibited at galleries in New York City.

MORE ABOUT THE AUTHOR
For more on E. E. Cummings, visit the **Literature Center** at **ClassZone.com.**

Background

Breaking It Down Cummings wrote during a period of literary and artistic experimentation. He was influenced by writers such as Gertrude Stein and artists such as Pablo Picasso. These writers and artists were trying to break down language and images into their most basic elements. Cummings frequently broke up his poems on the page, with the aim of making their appearance add to their meaning.

maggie and milly and molly and may

E. E. Cummings

maggie and milly and molly and may
went down to the beach(to play one day) **A**

and maggie discovered a shell that sang
so sweetly she couldn't remember her troubles,and

milly befriended a stranded star
whose rays five languid[1] fingers were;

and molly was chased by a horrible thing
which raced sideways while blowing bubbles:and

may came home with a smooth round stone
as small as a world and as large as alone.

For whatever we lose(like a you or a me)
it's always ourselves we find in the sea **B**

A STYLE IN POETRY
In what ways are lines 1–2 both traditional and unusual?

B MONITOR
Clarify by restating the meaning of the last two lines.

1. **languid** (lăng′gwĭd): lacking energy; drooping.

Mural Painting for the Terrace Plaza Hotel, Cincinnati (1947), Joan Miró. Oil on canvas. Cincinnati Art Museum, Cincinnati, Ohio. Gift of Thomas Emery's Sons, Inc. © 2008 Successio Miró/Artists Rights Society (ARS), NY/ADAGP, Paris. Photo by Tony Walsh.

who are you, little i

E. E. Cummings

who are you,little i **C**

(five or six years old)
peering from some high

window;at the gold

of November sunset

(and feeling:that if day
has to become night

this is a beautiful way) **D**

C STYLE IN POETRY
What is the effect of having unusual **line breaks?**

D MONITOR
Clarify what the word *this* refers to in line 8.

Painting (1953), Joan Miró. Oil on canvas, 75 7/8″ × 51″. Collection Mr. and Mrs. Richard K. Weil, St. Louis, Missouri. © 2008 Artists Rights Society (ARS). New York/AGAGP, Paris.

old age sticks

E. E. Cummings

old age sticks
up Keep
Off
signs)&

youth yanks them
down(old
age
cries No

Tres)&(pas)
youth laughs
(sing **E**
old age

scolds Forbid
den Stop
Must
n't Don't **F**

&)youth goes
right on
gr
owing old

E MONITOR
To **clarify,** rephrase what the poet says in lines 1–11.

F STYLE IN POETRY
Note which words are **capitalized** in the poem. Why do you think Cummings chose to capitalize these words?

Comprehension

1. **Recall** According to the poem "maggie and milly and molly and may," what do we find in the sea?
2. **Recall** What does little i see out the window?
3. **Clarify** In lines 9 and 11 of "old age sticks," what familiar word is disguised by Cummings's style?

ALABAMA STANDARDS

READING STANDARD
1.d Applying self-monitoring strategies

Literary Analysis

4. **Monitor** Look back at the charts you created as you read. For each poem, choose one line or one set of lines and explain what clues helped you rephrase it as you did.
5. **Make Inferences** In the poem "who are you,little i," who do you think little i is in relation to the **speaker,** or voice that talks to the reader?
6. **Identify Irony** When what happens in a poem is different than what is expected, the poet has used irony. How is the ending of "old age sticks" ironic?
7. **Identify Recurring Theme** When a similar message, or theme, appears in multiple pieces of writing, it is called a recurring theme. What theme appears in all three of these poems?
8. **Analyze Style** Reread the poems and identify three characteristics of Cummings's style that the poems all share. Using a chart like the one shown, note examples of each characteristic.

Style	*Examples*	*Effects*
Does not use capital letters		

Extension and Challenge

9. **SCIENCE CONNECTION** Cummings's poem "who are you, little i" mentions the connection between day and night. The poem "maggie and milly and molly and may" says "it's always ourselves we find in the sea." What other **connections** or cycles can you see in nature? Brainstorm ideas with a small group of your classmates.
10. **Speaking and Listening** How would Cummings's **punctuation** and line breaks affect a reading of his poetry? Prepare to read one of the poems for the class. Practice different ways of reading the poem until you feel your reading clearly expresses its meaning.

Media Study

Style and Mood in Photographs

Image Collection on *MediaSmart* DVD

When is a PHOTO *more than a picture?*

KEY IDEA The saying "A picture is worth a thousand words" is perhaps the best way to describe the power of **photography.** Photographs create meaning beyond the images they contain. In this lesson, you'll discover how two imaginative photographers use their individual styles to make ordinary subjects extraordinary.

Background

Picture This! Imagine you've just received your first camera. What images would you shoot? Would you take pictures of family and friends or of places in your neighborhood? What would you do to make your photographs special?

The Sicilian photographer Ferdinando Scianna (fär′dĕ-nän′dō shä′nə) is known for capturing people and things in quiet moments. Instead of shooting a subject from the usual direct angle, he sometimes uses unusual points of view. Robert Doisneau (rō-bare′ dwä-no′) is a famous French photographer. He is known for capturing everyday moments in the streets of Paris and for adding a humorous twist to his photographs.

Media Literacy: Style in Photography

Photographers not only take a picture; they create one. Before shooting a picture, photographers decide what they want to include in a frame. The **frame** is what the camera sees. When **composing,** or arranging a subject within a frame, photographers consider the effects of these elements:

- the position of a subject and its background
- the camera angles, such as low and high angles
- the lighting, which can change the way people or objects appear

Study the photographs closely to learn how Ferdinando Scianna experimented with the camera to create his unique style. To see larger versions of these photographs, please access the DVD.

STRATEGIES FOR ANALYZING A PHOTOGRAPH

- Consider how photographs tell a story or convey a message. Once photographers find a subject, they experiment with the subject and its background. They may move closer to or farther away from a subject, depending on the message or mood they want to create. Look at the picture of the balconies. What is your impression of the building?

- Notice how Scianna composed the photographs, shooting from an unusual **angle** or directly to create a dramatic effect. Where do you think the camera was placed?

- Observe the effects of **lighting.** Photographers experiment with lighting to create a **mood** or a dramatic effect, to draw attention to something, or to create a contrast between two or more things. For example, direct sunlight creates shadows that can make a person or object appear mysterious, threatening, or gloomy. What is the effect of the shadows in the second photograph?

MediaSmart DVD

- **Photograph Pair 1:** "Milan" and "Coney Island" by Ferdinando Scianna
- **Photograph Pair 2:** "Musician in the Rain" and "The Cellist" by Robert Doisneau
- **Genre:** Photography

Viewing Guide for

Image Collection

The photographs shown on this page were taken by Robert Doisneau. Doisneau is known for his storytelling talents. His photographs celebrate the daily lives of children, artists, sailors, and others who are willing to tell their stories.

To help you explore the following questions, use the DVD to study larger sizes of the photographs.

NOW VIEW

***FIRST VIEWING:* Comprehension**

1. **Summarize** What is happening in the photographs?
2. **Clarify** What do you think is unusual about the musician's position in "The Cellist"?

***CLOSE VIEWING:* Media Literacy**

3. **Make Inferences** Photographers can create a **mood** that will make viewers feel happy, sad, curious, or even confused. What mood does Doisneau create in these photographs?
4. **Analyze Style** What is the effect of placing an umbrella over the cello in the photograph entitled "Musician in the Rain"?
5. **Analyze Lighting** How do you think the meaning of the photographs would change if they had been taken on a sunny day? How would the meaning change if they had been taken at night?
6. **Analyze Composition** How would the meaning of "The Cellist" change if the photographer had taken a **close-up shot** of the cello player?

Write or Discuss

Analyze Style In this lesson, you've studied two very distinctive photographic styles. On the DVD, you'll find additional photographs taken by Scianna and Doisneau. Choose one photographer. In your own words, describe his style. As you prepare your response, consider the following:

- Whom or what do you see in each photograph?
- What mood do you think the photographs suggest?
- What elements of composition do you see in the photographs?
- How does the composition reflect the photographer's style?

Produce Your Own Media

Experiment with Photography Here's your opportunity to be the next Doisneau or Scianna. Take a few pictures that show your personal style.

HERE'S HOW The sample photograph was taken by a student in the stairwell of her high school. Notice how she experimented with light and shadow. The photograph was taken from an unusual angle to show the photographer's perspective. Before taking your photographs, follow these suggestions:

- Choose a subject that interests you.
- Determine what you want to keep in and leave out of each photograph.
- Experiment with the position of your subject, camera angles, and lighting.

MEDIA TOOLS

For help with taking photographs, visit the **Media Center** at **ClassZone.com.**

STUDENT MODEL

Tech Tip

If you have access to photo-editing software, experiment with shades of color. See how different shades, including black and white tones, change the **mood** of your photographs.

Writing Workshop

Interpretive Essay

In the stories in Unit 4, reality does some shifting, sliding, and squirming. To get a grip on it, you needed to figure out key details as you read. You'll do that same kind of work in this workshop as you interpret, or explain the meaning of, a story. The **Writer's Road Map** will help you.

WRITER'S ROAD MAP

Interpretive Essay

WRITING PROMPT 1

Writing from Literature Interpreting a work of literature involves examining it closely and figuring out meanings that you did not notice at first. Choose a short story and write an interpretive essay that helps the reader find new meanings in it. Examine one or two literary elements in the story, such as plot, characters, conflict, setting, mood, dialogue, or point of view.

Literature to Consider

- conflict in "The People Could Fly"
- character and dialogue in "A Day's Wait"
- setting in "The War of the Wall"

WRITING PROMPT 2

Writing from the Real World Powerful stories are everywhere, not just in literature. Think of a memorable story that you recently viewed or read. Write an essay that briefly summarizes the story and examines its deeper meaning or overall message.

Places to Look

- television dramas with strong characters
- movies that show conflicts
- magazine articles that describe real-life people or settings

WRITING TOOLS

For prewriting, revision, and editing tools, visit the **Writing Center** at **ClassZone.com.**

KEY TRAITS

1. *IDEAS*

- Includes a **thesis statement** that identifies the key points the writer will discuss
- Supports key points with **evidence**—details, examples, or quotations from the story

2. *ORGANIZATION*

- Identifies the author and title of the work in an interesting **introduction**
- Provides **plot details** as needed to help the reader understand the interpretation
- Summarizes the interpretation in a **conclusion** and tells why the story is interesting or important

3. *VOICE*

- Has an appropriate **tone** for the audience and purpose

4. *WORD CHOICE*

- Uses **precise language** to examine and explain the work

5. *SENTENCE FLUENCY*

- Varies **sentence structures**

6. *CONVENTIONS*

- Uses **correct grammar, spelling, and punctuation**

WRITING/LANGUAGE STANDARD
9 Compose in expository mode with thesis sentence

Part 1: Analyze a Student Model

Online INTERACTIVE MODEL CLASSZONE.COM

Erika Herzoff
Concord Regional School

Changed They Were, and Terrified

What if your family decided to live on Mars? What would life be like? Would you ever adjust? Perhaps the move would change you in strange and unexpected ways, as it changes Harry Bittering in "Dark They Were, and Golden-Eyed" by Ray Bradbury. In this story about an Earth family that moves to Mars, Bradbury uses mood and dialogue to tell a chilling tale about how an environment can change a person.

The story sets the mood at the beginning by making Mars seem like an eerie and forbidding place. Bradbury uses the word "alone" to describe the Bitterings' new situation. A strange, unsettling wind blows, creating a mood of uncertainty in the story. It is a wind of change, a wind that makes Harry Bittering feel as if "at any moment the Martian air might draw his soul from him." Later Harry reflects, "We don't belong here. . . . This is Mars. It was meant for Martians." Harry is afraid. The reader feels sympathy because the family is alone and scared. The reader's spine also tingles in fear of what might happen to this Earth family.

In the middle of the story, Harry goes to town, where there are other settlers from Earth. They are "conversing with great leisure and ease." They seem at home on Mars. Harry, however, is jumpy and tense because he can sense an unwanted change coming over him and his family. The mood of unrest increases when Sam says, "You've broken my mirror." The reader knows that the shock of seeing his own golden eyes made Harry drop the mirror. Those golden eyes terrify Harry because the Martians had golden eyes and now he does too. Harry and the others thought they could change Mars to make it like Earth. Instead, Mars is changing them.

KEY TRAITS IN ACTION

Interesting **introduction** states the title and author. The **thesis statement** names two literary elements, mood and dialogue.

Uses quotations and details as **evidence** to support the key points—mood and dialogue.

Includes **plot details** to help the reader understand the interpretation.

Uses **precise language** when interpreting story events.

As the story nears its end and Harry changes, the mood of the story becomes less eerie and less fearful. Harry becomes more relaxed on Mars. The colonists begin to prefer the Martians' old homes, which are "refreshing" and "cool." Harry gives up building the rocket that might take him back to Earth. The narrator explains, "The old fever was gone." After Harry lives in a Martian home for a while, he thinks that Earth people built "such odd, ridiculous houses." Harry has been taken over. Anyone else who comes to Mars will be taken over too.

Varies **sentence structures** so that ideas flow smoothly. Uses a serious **tone** that matches the purpose (to interpret a short story) and the audience (teacher and classmates).

The mood and dialogue in this story help tell how Harry Bittering's environment has changed him. Like so many people, he thought he was in control of everything and could rename and change his new world. Instead, it changed him. At the end of the story, he no longer feels lost and alone, which is how most people feel when they move to a foreign place. His loneliness and fears have been "drawn from him." The reader doesn't know if there's anything left of the real Harry. The environment has changed him in strange and terrifying ways.

Conclusion summarizes the essay and tells why the story is interesting.

2

WRITING/LANGUAGE STANDARD
10 Apply mechanics in writing

Part 2: Apply the Writing Process

PREWRITING

What Should I Do?	What Does It Look Like?
1. Read (or watch) the story again. What did you like about it? What parts really made you think? List some of the story's elements, such as its characters, setting, plot, and conflict. Start breaking the story into parts you can interpret.	**Characters:** *Harry, his family, others* — **Setting:** *house, town, Martians' homes* — **Plot:** *new colony, changes, worries, new people* — **Conflict:** *past vs. present, Earth vs. Mars*
2. Freewrite to find big ideas. Just start writing! Jot down your thoughts and feelings about the story. Ask questions too. Write what comes to mind.	*Harry is really scared about his new world (scared of changing?), but by the end of the story, when he seems to be a Martian, he doesn't even care anymore! What happened to him?*
3. Develop a working thesis. It doesn't have to be perfect, but it should provide a key idea that you can develop. **TIP** **Find your focus by referring to the writing prompt. For prompt 1, your paper must interpret one or two literary elements, so be sure your thesis names them.**	**Working Thesis:** *Harry is afraid of change and worried that something bad will happen, as you can tell from the mood and the dialogue. He wants to change his environment, but the environment may change him instead.*
4. Find evidence to support your thesis. Before you go further, be sure you have some support for your ideas. List examples, details, and quotations from the story that will help you make your point.	**Mood:** *• the wind: weird • Harry's feelings of panic • refreshing, cool Martian homes* — **Dialogue:** *• "We don't belong here." • "odd, ridiculous houses" of settlers*

DRAFTING

What Should I Do?

1. **Plan your essay.**
Create an informal outline before you start drafting. This writer organized her ideas in the order in which events occur in the story (option 1). You can also discuss one literary element at a time (option 2) or discuss the most important ideas first.

What Does It Look Like?

1. STORY ORDER

1. Beginning
- *Mood: strange, unsettling wind*
- *Dialogue: "We don't belong here."*

2. Middle
- *Mood: others calm, Harry tense*
- *Dialogue: "You've broken my mirror."*

3. End
- *Mood: calmer as Harry changes*
- *Dialogue: "odd, ridiculous houses"*

2. ELEMENT BY ELEMENT

1. Mood
- *Beginning: strange, unsettling wind*
- *Middle: others calm, Harry tense*
- *End: calmer as Harry changes*

2. Dialogue
- *Beginning: "We don't belong here."*
- *Middle: "You've broken my mirror."*
- *End: "odd, ridiculous houses"*

2. **Add plot details to help your reader.**
Provide information about the story to help your reader understand your interpretation.

In the middle of the story, Harry goes to town, where there are other settlers from Earth. They are "conversing with great leisure and ease."

3. **Back up your key points with evidence.**
You don't need to discuss every line of the story. You do need to find a few good **details** and **quotations** in the story that support your key ideas.

See page 530: Check Your Grammar

TIP **Before you revise, look back at the key traits on page 524 and the rubric and peer-reader questions on page 530.**

The story sets the mood at the beginning by making Mars seem like an eerie and forbidding place. — Key point

Bradbury uses the word "alone" to describe the Bitterings' new situation. — Support

REVISING AND EDITING

What Should I Do?	What Does It Look Like?
1. Find the right tone. • Remember, the tone has to be right for your audience and purpose. • Read your essay aloud. Underline words that sound too informal or slangy. Instead, choose words that you find in **formal, published writing.**	~~The reader also gets a little freaked out about what's about to go down for these Earth people.~~ *The reader's spine also tingles in fear of what might happen to this Earth family.*
2. Use exact, specific words. • Exact words include strong adverbs and adjectives. Circle *very, really, good, bad, nice,* and other weak and imprecise adverbs and adjectives. • Replace them with **better, bolder modifiers.**	*The story sets the mood at the beginning by making Mars seem like* *an eerie* ~~a very strange~~ *and forbidding* ~~really weird~~ *place.*
3. Vary your sentence structures. • Read your essay aloud again, this time looking for sentences that are short and choppy. • **Combine short sentences** to make them smoother and more sophisticated.	~~The story is coming to an end. Harry is changing. The mood changes too. It becomes less eerie and less fearful.~~ *As the story nears its end and Harry changes, the mood of the story becomes less eerie and less fearful.*
4. Tell why it matters. • Ask a peer reader to draw a box around phrases and sentences that explain why the story is important, interesting, or meaningful. • If there are few or no boxes, add ideas about the story's **significance.** **See page 530:** Ask a Peer Reader	*Like so many people, Harry thought he was in control of everything and could rename and change his new world. Instead, it changed him.* *At the end of the story, he no longer feels lost and alone, which is how most people feel when they move to a foreign place.*

Preparing to Publish

Interpretive Essay

Apply the Rubric

A strong interpretive essay . . .

- ☑ has an attention-getting introduction that identifies the author and title of the work
- ☑ includes a clear thesis statement that lists the key points of the essay
- ☑ uses evidence from the text to support key points
- ☑ provides plot details when needed for clarity
- ☑ uses an appropriate tone for the audience and purpose
- ☑ uses precise language
- ☑ varies sentence structures
- ☑ has a conclusion that summarizes the interpretation and reflects on why the story is important or interesting

Ask a Peer Reader

- How can I make my thesis clearer?
- Where do I need more support or explanation?
- Where in my essay do I explain what makes the story interesting or meaningful?

Check Your Grammar

- Place quotation marks at the beginning and end of any words you copy directly from a story.

They are "conversing with great leisure and ease."

- Periods and commas always go inside the quotation marks.

The colonists begin to prefer the Martians' old homes, which are "refreshing" and "cool."

- Use a comma to separate independent clauses in a compound sentence.

Harry is tense, but the men in town seem calm.

- The comma always comes before—not after—the coordinating conjunction.

Harry cannot control his world, and he is taken over.

See pages R49–R50: Quick Reference: Punctuation

Writing Online

PUBLISHING OPTIONS
For publishing options, visit the **Writing Center** at **ClassZone.com.**

ASSESSMENT PREPARATION
For writing and grammar assessment practice, go to the **Assessment Center** at **ClassZone.com.**

WRITING/LANGUAGE STANDARD
9.b Imitating an author's style, form, and purpose

PUBLISHING WITH TECHNOLOGY

Producing and Editing a Video

Here's how to produce a video that shows style and has style.

Planning the Video

1. **Select story parts.** Go back to the story you just wrote about. If possible, read or view other stories by the same author. Find words, sentences, or sections that show the author's style. Think about choice of words, tone, figurative language, and sentence length.
2. **Find or create images.** For example, if you've chosen a paragraph in which Ray Bradbury describes the Martian landscape, you might make a drawing or collage of the colors, shapes, and feelings that the writing suggests.
3. **Make a plan.** Write a script or storyboard. You might include narration, dramatic readings, onscreen text, music, or sound effects. You may also want to cast actors and create backdrops, costumes, and props.

IMAGE 1: dusty, swirling, sandy landscape of the planet Mars

SFX: eerie, whooshing sounds

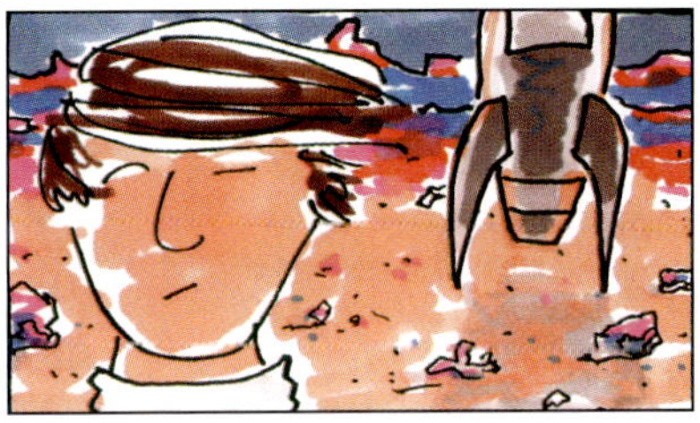

IMAGE 2: man next to spacecraft on this landscape

NARRATOR: "The man felt his hair flutter and the tissues of his body draw tight. . . . His face was cold."

Making the Video

1. **Shoot the video.** Try to include close-ups, medium shots, and long shots. Remember that you are re-creating the author's style, so your video has to sound and look like something that the author created or suggested.
2. **Put it all together.** Use editing software to assemble the video the way you planned it in your script or storyboard.
3. **Show your stuff.** Screen your video for classmates or friends. Ask what they learned about the author's style.

Assessment Practice

Reading Comprehension

DIRECTIONS *Read this selection and answer the questions that follow.*

Mrs. Barrymore and her husband are servants at Baskerville Hall. Sherlock Holmes's friend, Dr. Watson, is describing the couple in a letter to the famous detective.

from The Hound of the Baskervilles

Sir Arthur Conan Doyle

Mrs. Barrymore is of interest to me. She is a heavy, solid person, very limited, intensely respectable, and inclined to be puritanical. You could hardly conceive a less emotional subject. Yet I have told you how, on the first night here, I heard her sobbing bitterly, and since then I have more than once observed traces of tears upon her face. Some deep sorrow gnaws ever at her heart. Sometimes I wonder if she has a guilty memory which haunts her, and sometimes I suspect Barrymore of being a domestic tyrant. I have always felt that there was something singular and questionable in this man's character, but the adventure of last night brings all my suspicions to a head.

And yet it may seem a small matter in itself. You are aware that I am not a very sound sleeper, and since I have been on guard in this house my slumbers have been lighter than ever. Last night, about two in the morning, I was aroused by a stealthy step passing my room. I rose, opened my door, and peeped out. A long black shadow was trailing down the corridor. It was thrown by a man who walked softly down the passage with a candle held in his hand. He was in shirt and trousers, with no covering to his feet. I could merely see the outline, but his height told me that it was Barrymore. He walked very slowly and circumspectly, and there was something indescribably guilty and furtive in his whole appearance.

I have told you that the corridor is broken by the balcony which runs round the hall, but that it is resumed upon the farther side. I waited until he had passed out of sight and then I followed him. When I came round the balcony he had reached the end of the farther corridor, and I could see from the glimmer of light through an open door that he had entered one of the rooms. Now, all these rooms are unfurnished and unoccupied, so that his expedition became more mysterious than ever. The light shone

ASSESS
The practice test items on the next few pages match skills listed on the Unit Goals page (page 437) and addressed throughout this unit. Taking this practice test will help you assess your knowledge of these skills and determine your readiness for the Unit Test.

REVIEW
After you take the practice test, your teacher can help you identify any skills you need to review.

- Mood
- Style
  - Word Choice
  - Sentence Structure
  - Tone
- Summarize
- Synonyms
- Literal and Figurative Meanings
- Subject-Verb Agreement

ASSESSMENT ONLINE
For more assessment practice and test-taking tips, go to the **Assessment Center** at **ClassZone.com.**

steadily as if he were standing motionless. I crept down the passage as noiselessly as I could and peeped round the corner of the door.

Barrymore was crouching at the window with the candle held against the glass. His profile was half turned towards me, and his face seemed to be rigid with expectation as he stared out into the blackness of the moor. For some minutes he stood watching intently. Then he gave a deep groan and with an impatient gesture he put out the light. Instantly I made my way back to my room, and very shortly came the stealthy steps passing once more upon their return journey. Long afterwards when I had fallen into a light sleep I heard a key turn somewhere in a lock, but I could not tell whence the sound came. What it all means I cannot guess, but there is some secret business going on in this house of gloom which sooner or later we shall get to the bottom of. I do not trouble you with my theories, for you asked me to furnish you only with facts. I have had a long talk with Sir Henry this morning, and we have made a plan of campaign founded upon my observations of last night. I will not speak about it just now, but it should make my next report interesting reading.

GO ON

Comprehension

DIRECTIONS *Answer these questions about the excerpt from* The Hound of the Baskervilles.

1. Which word best describes the mood of this passage?

A thrilling

B suspenseful

C peaceful

D comforting

2. Which statement is the best summary of Dr. Watson's impression of Mrs. Barrymore?

A She is intensely moral, sometimes emotional, and not likeable at all.

B She is reliable, trustworthy, and yet unexpectedly severe and cold.

C She wants people to feel sorry for her, so she makes a show of crying at night.

D She gives an appearance of being under control, but something is upsetting her.

3. Which sentence contributes most clearly to the mood of this excerpt?

A "You could hardly conceive a less emotional subject."

B "Last night, about two in the morning, I was aroused by a stealthy step passing my room."

C "He was in shirt and trousers, with no covering to his feet."

D "I do not trouble you with my theories, for you asked me to furnish you only with facts."

4. Which words in lines 18–19 contribute most to the mood of the story?

"He walked very slowly and circumspectly, and there was something indescribably guilty and furtive in his whole appearance."

A walked, slowly

B circumspectly, indescribably

C something, appearance

D guilty, furtive

5. The description of Barrymore's actions in lines 29–31 affects the mood of the story by

A providing relief

B increasing the tension

C making everything clear

D adding hope

6. What is the author's tone toward Watson's investigation in this excerpt?

A vengeful

B ironic

C detached

D suspicious

7. Which words from the excerpt give Watson's report an objective tone?

A heard, observed

B wonder, suspect

C asked, guess

D felt, crept

ARMT/ADAW SKILLS PRACTICE

8. Which one of the following descriptions best characterizes Conan Doyle's style in this excerpt?
   - **A** a formal, flowery style that relies on symbolic language
   - **B** a formal, conversational style that relies on descriptive observations
   - **C** an objective, journalistic style that relies on scientific facts
   - **D** an informal, folksy style that relies on natural speech patterns

9. Which statement is the best summary of Dr. Watson's actions on the morning after he sees Barrymore?
   - **A** Dr. Watson reports what he saw to Sir Henry and they come up with a plan of action.
   - **B** Dr. Watson hears a key turning in a lock, but he doesn't know where.
   - **C** Dr. Watson barely makes it back to his room before he hears steps coming back again.
   - **D** Dr. Watson hears someone weeping miserably in the house.

Open-Ended

SHORT RESPONSE *Write two or three sentences to answer each question.*

10. Briefly summarize Dr. Watson's report to Sherlock Holmes. Identify the characters and the setting in your summary.

11. What is Conan Doyle's attitude toward the character Watson? Give an example from the excerpt to support your answer.

ESSAY *Write a short paragraph to answer this question.*

12. Reread the descriptions of Mr. and Mrs. Barrymore in the excerpt. Describe the author's style based on his words, sentences, and tone.

GO ON

Vocabulary

DIRECTIONS *Use context clues and your knowledge of synonyms to answer the following questions.*

1. Which word is a **synonym** for the underlined word in this sentence from lines 2–3?

"You could hardly conceive a less emotional subject."

A understand **C** plan

B see **D** imagine

2. Which word is a **synonym** for the underlined word in this sentence from lines 3–5?

"Yet I have told you how, on the first night here, I heard her sobbing bitterly, and since then I have more than once observed traces of tears upon her face."

A edges **C** puddles

B streaks **D** shades

3. Which word is a **synonym** for the underlined word in this sentence from line 32?

"For some minutes he stood watching intently."

A angrily **C** carefully

B sadly **D** intelligently

DIRECTIONS *Use context clues and your knowledge of literal and figurative meanings to answer the following questions.*

4. Which expression is the most likely meaning of the underlined words in the following sentence from lines 5–6?

"Some deep sorrow gnaws ever at her heart."

A sickens her **C** angers her

B frightens her **D** troubles her

5. Which expression is the most likely meaning of the underlined term in the following sentence from lines 6–7?

"Sometimes I wonder if she has a guilty memory which haunts her, and sometimes I suspect Barrymore of being a domestic tyrant."

A a strict national ruler

B a local official

C a harsh husband

D a native-born dictator

6. Which word is the most likely meaning of the underlined word in this sentence from lines 37–39?

"What it all means I cannot guess, but there is some secret business going on in this house of gloom which sooner or later we shall get to the bottom of."

A confusion **C** danger

B sadness **D** cruelty

ARMT/ADAW SKILLS PRACTICE

Writing & Grammar

DIRECTIONS *Read this passage and answer the questions that follow.*

(1) Historians tells us that for thousands of years, cultures preserved bodies by embalming them. (2) Ancient Egyptians was among the most well-known embalmers, using a process called mummification. (3) The ancient historian Herodotus and modern archaeologists has taught us much about this process. (4) An embalmer would remove internal organs, dry out the body, and wrap it in linen. (5) Herbs and salt was two ingredients the embalmer would use as part of the drying process. (6) Next, linen or other materials was placed inside the body to fill it out. (7) Such careful preparations shows how important burial was to the Egyptians.

1. To maintain subject-verb agreement in sentence 1, change the underlined words to

A Historian tells

B Historian tell

C Historians tell

D Historians is telling

2. To maintain subject-verb agreement in sentence 2, change the underlined words to

A Egyptian are

B Egyptians were

C Egyptians is

D Egyptian were

3. To maintain subject-verb agreement in sentence 3, change the underlined words to

A Herodotus and modern archaeologists is teaching

B Herodotus and modern archaeologists teaches

C Herodotus and modern archaeologists was teaching

D Herodotus and modern archaeologists have taught

4. To maintain subject-verb agreement in sentence 5, change the underlined words to

A Herb and salts was

B Herbs and salts was

C Herbs and salt were

D Herb and salt was

5. To maintain subject-verb agreement in sentence 6, change the underlined words to

A linen or other material were placed

B linen or other materials were placed

C linens or other materials was placed

D linens or other material were placed

6. To maintain subject-verb agreement in sentence 7, change the underlined words to

A preparations show

B preparation show

C preparation do show

D preparations was showing

STOP

UNIT 4

More Great Reads

Ideas for Independent Reading

Which questions from Unit 4 made an impression on you? Continue exploring them with these books.

Can where you are change who you are?

Skellig
by David Almond
What if you discovered an ailing being in an old garage in your new neighborhood? This happens to Michael, who shares his find with his neighbor, Mina, and the two embark on a secret mission to save Skellig.

Dragonwings
by Laurence Yep
In the early 1900s, a Chinese boy named Moon Shadow travels to San Francisco. There he joins his father, Windrider, whom he has never met. The two survive poverty, loneliness, and an earthquake as they work to fulfill a long-held dream.

Shabanu: Daughter of the Wind
by Suzanne Staples
Shabanu is the 11-year-old daughter of a nomadic family in Pakistan. When it becomes apparent that the family's only chance to survive is to pledge Shabanu in marriage, she has to make a decision. Where will she go?

Is it brave to suffer in silence?

Blackwater
by Eve Bunting
Thirteen-year-old Brodie feels he may have caused the accidental death of Pauline and Otis. It all started out innocently enough, but then there was a fall into the rushing current of the Blackwater River. Should Brodie tell what he knows?

The Window
by Michael Dorris
Rayona, who is part Native American and part African American, has suffered a childhood of neglect and secrets. When her father sends her to live with her grandmother in Kentucky, she finally finds some security and happiness.

The Voices of Silence
by Bel Mooney
When you live in a totalitarian society, keeping silent means staying alive. Does that make you brave? Thirteen-year-old Flora Popescu confronts this question as she comes of age in Communist Romania.

What makes us laugh?

Bud, Not Buddy
by Christopher Curtis
During the Great Depression, ten-year-old Bud escapes from a terrible foster home and hits the road in search of his real dad. The humorous way he tells about his travels across Michigan might make you laugh out loud.

Squashed
by Joan Bauer
Ellie's future prize-winning pumpkin needs to gain 200 pounds in time for the Rock River Pumpkin Weigh-In, and Ellie thinks she needs to lose 20 pounds. Whathallenges she sets for herself is her sense of humor.

A Long Way from Chicago
by Richard Peck
Each summer Joey and his sister, Mary Alice, travel to downstate Illinois for a visit with Grandma Dowdel. This year, her tendency to stretch the truth and hatch wild schemes creates hilarious adventures.

UNIT 5

Picture the Moment

APPRECIATING POETRY

UNIT 5 Share What You Know

What is a POEM?

There are almost as many **poems** as there are people. Some poems are very formal, and others are more playful. Some rhyme, and some don't. Some are published in beautiful books, and others are written on sidewalks. But the thing that makes all poems alike is that each expresses the writer's imagination and feelings in a creative way.

ACTIVITY Think of the poems you've read in the past. Can you remember a particular one that you enjoyed? Now think about the lyrics of your favorite song. With a partner, share the name of the poem and song you chose. Then compare the poem and the song lyrics by considering the following questions:

- What is the most memorable line of the poem or song?
- Are the lines grouped in any particular way?
- Do any of the lines rhyme?

Discuss whether the song lyrics you chose should be considered a poem.

Online LITERATURE CLASSZONE.COM

- Literature and Reading Center
- Writing Center
- Vocabulary and Spelling Center

ALABAMA STANDARDS

Preview Unit Goals

LITERARY ANALYSIS

- Understand form in poetry
- Identify characteristics of free verse, lyric poetry, narrative poetry, ballads, and haiku
- Identify and interpret imagery and figurative language
- Identify and interpret sound devices, such as rhyme, repetition, and alliteration
- Identify and compare mood

READING

- Make inferences
- Use text features to locate and comprehend information
- Use reading strategies, including monitoring and visualizing

WRITING AND GRAMMAR

- Write a personal response to a poem
- Support key points with quotes and details
- Identify and correctly punctuate various types of sentences
- Use active voice

SPEAKING, LISTENING, AND VIEWING

- Give an oral interpretation of a poem

VOCABULARY

- Understand and use connotative meanings of words

ACADEMIC VOCABULARY

- imagery
- figurative language
- sound devices
- form
- personal response
- connotation

UNIT 5

Reader's Workshop

Appreciating Poetry

What makes a song unforgettable? Perhaps it's the rhythm of the music or the catchy lyrics. A song might also speak to you because it reminds you of something in your own life. Like a song, a poem can capture your imagination with what it says and how it sounds. In this workshop, you will learn what gives poetry this special power.

ALABAMA STANDARDS

READING STANDARDS

2 Relate literary devices to each other, including imagery

3 Distinguish among genres, including poetry, based on characteristics

Part 1: The Basics

How does a poem speak to you from the page? Aside from its unique sound, a poem also conveys meaning through its form and its speaker.

Form is the way a poem's words and lines are laid out on the page. Lines may or may not be complete sentences and can vary in length. In some poems, the lines are arranged into groups, called **stanzas.** Each stanza helps to convey a poem's overall message.

Some poems have **traditional,** or **structured,** forms. Traditional poems follow fixed rules; for instance, they might have a certain number of lines or a repeating pattern of rhythm or rhyme. Poems that do not follow set rules are called **free verse.**

A poem's personality depends on its speaker as well as its form. The **speaker** in a poem is the voice that talks to the reader. The speaker may be the poet, or it may be a character created by the poet—a child, for example. In Carl Sandburg's famous poem "Grass," the speaker is actually the grass.

Examine the elements of form and speaker in this traditional poem.

A Minor Bird

Poem by **Robert Frost**

I have wished a bird would fly away,
And not sing by my house all day;

Have clapped my hands at him from the door
When it seemed as if I could bear no more.

The fault must partly have been in me.
The bird was not to blame for his key.

And of course there must be something wrong
In wanting to silence any song.

EXAMINE THE POEM

- Notice that this poem is made up of four two-line stanzas.
- Look at the four pairs of rhyming words.
- Read the poem aloud to hear its singsong rhythm.
- Note that the speaker is the "I" in the poem but may not be the poet. We don't know if the poet shares the speaker's attitude toward the bird.

MODEL: FORM AND SPEAKER

The following poem is written in free verse. Because it has no regular pattern of rhythm or rhyme, the poem sounds like everyday speech. Read it aloud to hear what the speaker is saying about his or her special hiding place.

UNDER THE BACK PORCH

Poem by **Virginia Hamilton**

Our house is two stories high
shaped like a white box.
There is a yard stretched around it
and in back
a wooden porch.

Under the back porch is my place.
I rest there.
I go there when I have to be alone.
It is always shaded and damp.
Sunlight only slants through the slats
in long strips of light,
and the smell of the damp
is moist green,
like the moss that grows here.

My sisters and brothers
can stand on the back porch
and never know
I am here
underneath.
It is my place.
All mine.

Close Read

1. Describe the focus of each stanza. (What do you "see"?) Look at the boxed details for clues.
2. What do you learn about the speaker of this poem? Cite details that help you understand his or her age, personality, and family life.
3. Notice the last four lines of the poem. What effect does their short length help to create? (Hint: Think about where the speaker is at this point in the poem.)

Part 2: Special Effects

You've seen how filmmakers use special effects to transport you to new worlds, affect your emotions, and keep you on the edge of your seat. Poets use special effects too. Sound devices can make a poem seem as peaceful as ocean waves lapping on the shore or as intense as a close race. Imagery and figurative language create word pictures that help you imagine things as vividly as if you were seeing them unfold on a movie screen.

SOUND DEVICES

Sound devices give poems a musical quality, but they can also create a mood and emphasize important ideas or words. Here are a few of the sound devices poets use.

SOUND DEVICES	EXAMPLES
RHYME **the repetition of sounds at the end of words, as in *me* and *see*** **RHYTHM** **the pattern of stressed (´) and unstressed (˘) syllables in each line (A poem with a repeating pattern has what is called a meter.)**	**Notice how the rhythm and rhyme in this poem help to create a playful, upbeat mood.** They came to tell your faults to me, They named them over one by one; I laughed aloud when they were done, I knew them all so well before,— Oh, they were blind, too blind to see Your faults had made me love you more. —"Faults" by Sara Teasdale
REPETITION **the use of a word, phrase, or line more than once** **ALLITERATION** **the repetition of consonant sounds at the beginning of words, such as the *c* in *curved crook***	**The repeated phrases and the alliteration in the last line help to emphasize the moon's shape.** How thin and sharp is the moon tonight! How thin and sharp and ghostly white Is the slim curved crook of the moon tonight! —"Winter Moon" by Langston Hughes

MODEL 1: RHYME AND RHYTHM

As you read this short poem aloud, notice how Emily Dickinson uses rhyme and rhythm to emphasize the most important words.

A word is dead

Poem by **Emily Dickinson**

A word is dead
When it is said,
Some say.

I say it just
Begins to live
That day.

Close Read

1. One pair of rhyming words is boxed. Find the other pair.
2. Stressed and unstressed syllables are marked in the second stanza. How does the rhythm in this stanza compare with that in the first stanza?

MODEL 2: OTHER SOUND DEVICES

This free-verse poem is filled with sound devices: repetition, rhyme, alliteration, and **onomatopoeia**—the use of words (made-up or real) whose sounds suggest their meanings. How do these sound devices help you experience the snow?

Cynthia in the Snow

Poem by **Gwendolyn Brooks**

It SUSHES.
It hushes
The loudness in the road.
It flitter-twitters,
And laughs away from me.
It laughs a lovely whiteness,
And whitely whirs away,
To be
Some otherwhere,
Still white as milk or shirts.
So beautiful it hurts.

Close Read

1. What onomatopoeic words does the poet use to suggest the silencing effect of falling snow?
2. The use of alliteration in the boxed line helps to create a light, joyful mood. Find another example of alliteration.
3. Identify three pairs of rhymes. For one pair, explain what qualities of snow the rhyme helps to emphasize.

IMAGERY AND FIGURATIVE LANGUAGE

Imagery is language that appeals to the five senses—sight, hearing, smell, taste, and touch. "Cynthia in the Snow" focuses on the sense of hearing, but it also helps you see the snow as it "whitely whirs away." With a few vivid images, the poet draws you into the winter scene.

One way poets create imagery is through **figurative language.** Figurative language uses creative comparisons to help readers picture ordinary things in new ways. For example, the snow is not just white but "white as milk or shirts." Here are three types of figurative language.

TYPE	EXAMPLE
SIMILE **a comparison between two unlike things, using the word *like* or *as***	**This simile compares a cat's coloring to spilled milk. The word *as* signals the comparison.** He's white As spilled milk, My cat who sleeps With his belly Turned toward The summer sky. —from "Ode to Mi Gato" by Gary Soto
METAPHOR **a comparison between two unlike things that does not contain the word *like* or *as***	**This metaphor compares fame to a bee. It conveys both the good and the bad side of fame.** Fame is a bee. It has a song— It has a sting— Ah, too, it has a wing. —by Emily Dickinson
PERSONIFICATION **a description of an object, an animal, a place, or an idea as if it were human or had human qualities**	**Here, "proud words" are given human qualities.** Look out how you use proud words. When you let proud words go, it is not easy to call them back. They wear long boots, hard boots; they walk off proud; they can't hear you calling— Look out how you use proud words. —"Primer Lesson" by Carl Sandburg

Part 3: Analyze the Literature

In this poem, the speaker reflects on her mother's courage, a quality that she has missed since her mother died. Use what you've learned in this workshop to analyze the elements—form, speaker, sound devices, figurative language, and imagery—that help to create a picture of a remarkable parent.

The **COURAGE** *That My Mother Had*

Poem by **Edna St. Vincent Millay**

The courage that my mother had
Went with her, and is with her still:
Rock from New England quarried;[1]
Now granite in a granite hill.

The golden brooch[2] my mother wore
She left behind for me to wear;
I have no thing I treasure more:
Yet, it is something I could spare.

Oh, if instead she'd left to me
The thing she took into the grave!—
That courage like a rock, which she
Has no more need of, and I have.

1. **quarried:** dug up from the ground.
2. **brooch:** a piece of jewelry that can be fastened to clothing.

Close Read

1. Describe two characteristics that make this a traditional poem. Think about the number of lines in each stanza and the patterns of rhythm and rhyme.
2. One example of alliteration is boxed. Find another example.
3. Identify the simile in the third stanza. What does it suggest about the mother's personality?
4. How would you describe the speaker of this poem? Think about how she views herself, what she admires about her mother, and what she seems to value.

The Names

Poem by Billy Collins

Why do we need MEMORIALS?

ALABAMA STANDARDS

READING STANDARDS

2 Relate literary devices to each other, including imagery

3 Distinguish among subgenres based on characteristics

KEY IDEA When tragedy strikes, putting the incident behind you as soon as possible might at first seem like the quickest route to recovery. In reality, many people find that creating a **memorial** to remember and reflect on a loss can provide great comfort. Read the memorial poem "The Names" to find out how, in a time of grief, one poet used his work to help others heal.

QUICKWRITE Consider your own experience with loss, or an experience that you've observed. Why do you think remembering a sad event might help the healing process? Reflect on this question in a journal entry.

POETIC FORM: FREE VERSE

The way a poem looks on the page is the poem's **form.** Poetry with no regular pattern of rhyme, rhythm, or line length is written in a form called **free verse.** When poets write free verse, they don't have to follow set rules. They can create whatever lines, rhythms, and rhymes they feel best communicate the ideas they want to express.

LITERARY ANALYSIS: IMAGERY

Imagery consists of words and phrases that appeal to your senses of sight, hearing, smell, taste, and touch. Poets use imagery not only to vividly describe things, but also to communicate feelings and ideas. For example, look at the opening lines of "The Names":

Yesterday, I lay awake in the palm of the night.

A soft rain stole in, unhelped by any breeze,

The images "palm of the night" and "soft rain" appeal to your senses of sight and touch. These phrases also suggest a sense of troubled thoughtfulness and perhaps a feeling of change. As you read "The Names," use a word web to identify these and other examples of imagery.

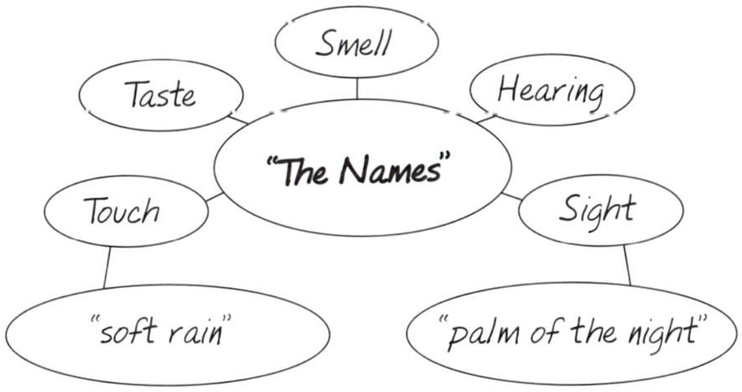

READING SKILL: UNDERSTAND HISTORICAL CONTEXT

Many works of literature seem easier to understand once you know their historical context—the real events and situations that influenced them. Billy Collins wrote "The Names" as a tribute to the more than 3,000 people who died in the terrorist attacks of September 11, 2001. Before you read the poem, read the **Background** on this page. The information can help you better appreciate the imagery Collins uses.

Author Online

A Popular Poet
Poet Billy Collins is a spellbinding performer. His readings have helped spark a renewed hunger for poetry in America. Collins served as the U.S. poet laureate from 2001 to 2003.

Billy Collins
born 1941

Background

A City Grieves Collins was born and raised in New York City. His hometown suffered heavy losses on September 11, 2001, when terrorists flew planes into the World Trade Center, causing its two towers to collapse. In the following days, signs, posters, and photographs showing the dead or missing were posted all over the city and the surrounding area. These postings often turned into memorials, with passersby adding notes, flowers, and mementos as it became clear that few of the missing had survived.

A Poem of Remembrance When asked on the day of the attacks what poem was appropriate to the tragedy, Collins replied, "Any poem." Asked to explain, Collins stated that good poetry affirms life. Collins read "The Names" in a special session of Congress in New York City on September 6, 2002.

MORE ABOUT THE AUTHOR AND BACKGROUND
To learn more about Billy Collins and September 11, 2001, visit the **Literature Center** at **ClassZone.com.**

The NAMES

Billy Collins

Yesterday, I lay awake in the palm of the night.
A soft rain stole in, unhelped by any breeze,
And when I saw the silver glaze on the windows,
I started with A, with Ackerman, as it happened,
Then Baxter and Calabro,
Davis and Eberling, names falling into place
As droplets fell through the dark.

Names printed on the ceiling of the night.
Names slipping around a watery bend.
Twenty-six willows on the banks of a stream.

In the morning, I walked out barefoot
Among thousands of flowers
Heavy with dew like the eyes of tears,
And each had a name—
Fiori inscribed on a yellow petal
Then Gonzalez and Han, Ishikawa and Jenkins. **A**

ANALYZE VISUALS
The towers of light shown in the picture of the New York skyline are turned on each year on September 11. What do you think they **symbolize?**

A IMAGERY
Reread lines 11–16. Which images appeal to your senses of sight and touch? Record the images in your web. Then think about how they affect the poem's meaning.

Names written in the air
And stitched into the cloth of the day.
A name under a photograph taped to a mailbox.
Monogram[1] on a torn shirt,
I see you spelled out on storefront windows
And on the bright unfurled awnings of this city.
I say the syllables as I turn a corner—
Kelly and Lee,
Medina, Nardella, and O'Connor. **B**

When I peer into the woods,
I see a thick tangle where letters are hidden
As in a puzzle concocted for children.
Parker and Quigley in the twigs of an ash,
Rizzo, Schubert, Torres, and Upton,
Secrets in the boughs of an ancient maple.

Names written in the pale sky.
Names rising in the updraft[2] amid buildings.
Names silent in stone
Or cried out behind a door. **C**
Names blown over the earth and out to sea.

In the evening— weakening light, the last swallows.
A boy on a lake lifts his oars.
A woman by a window puts a match to a candle,
And the names are outlined on the rose clouds—
Vanacore and Wallace,
(let X stand, if it can, for the ones unfound)
Then Young and Ziminsky, the final jolt of Z.
Names etched on the head of a pin
One name spanning a bridge, another undergoing a tunnel.
A blue name needled into the skin. **D**

Names of citizens, workers, mothers and fathers,
The bright-eyed daughter, the quick son.
Alphabet of names in green rows in a field.
Names in the small tracks of birds.
Names lifted from a hat
Or balanced on the tip of the tongue.
Names wheeled into the dim warehouse of memory.
So many names, there is barely room on the walls of the heart.

B HISTORICAL CONTEXT
Consider what you learned in the **Background** section on page 549. What can you **infer** about the people Collins is naming?

C FREE VERSE
Reread lines 34–35. Why do you think Collins broke this sentence fragment into two short lines instead of writing it as one line?

D IMAGERY
Reread lines 37–46. Identify images that strike you as particularly powerful. Note what senses they appeal to. What feelings do the images suggest?

---

1. **monogram:** the initials of one's name combined into a design.
2. **updraft:** an upward movement of air.

Comprehension

ALABAMA STANDARDS

READING STANDARD
2 Relate literary devices to each other, including imagery

1. **Recall** According to the poem, what does the letter *X* stand for?
2. **Recall** In what places does the speaker of the poem see the names? Describe three.
3. **Clarify** Whom do the names in the poem belong to?

Literary Analysis

4. **Understand Imagery** Look at the word web you created as you read. Which images from the poem do you consider especially effective? How do these images strengthen the meaning of the poem? Explain your answer.
5. **Identify Theme** The theme of a poem is its basic message about life or human nature. Think about the subject of this poem, the key images, and the words that are emphasized or repeated. What do you think is the overall message about September 11, 2001, that Billy Collins wishes to convey in "The Names"? Collect your thoughts in a graphic like the one shown.

6. **Analyze Historical Context** Recall that Billy Collins read this **memorial** poem when Congress met in New York City nearly one year after the attacks. Choose three lines or sections of the poem and tell why they might have been particularly meaningful to the people hearing them on that day.
7. **Evaluate Free Verse** Read the poem aloud as naturally as you can. Do you think this free verse poem is successful at communicating ideas and emotions? Explain why or why not.

Extension and Challenge

8. **Creative Project: Art** Choose a visual image in the poem that you find particularly powerful. Draw or sketch the image, and explain to the class how the poet's words guided your work.
9. **SOCIAL STUDIES CONNECTION** Read the article "A Nation Mourns" on page 553. Then reread "The Names." In what ways does the information in the article deepen your appreciation of the poem? Share your answer with a small group, being sure to point out at least two specific ways that knowing about the events of September 11 helped to broaden your understanding of the poem.

Reading for Information

ARTICLE Can the worst in humanity bring out the best in humanity? "The Names" reflects on the lives lost on September 11, 2001. Read this article to find out more about that day and the way people responded to the tragedy.

Enemies Attack: *A Nation Mourns*

Between 7:58 A.M. and 8:10 A.M. on September 11, 2001, four passenger planes left the Boston, Newark, and Washington, D.C., airports. In a matter of minutes, each of these planes was hijacked by terrorists. One of the worst attacks on the United States was underway.

Just seconds after 8:46 A.M., Eastern Standard Time, the first of these planes flew into Tower One of the World Trade Center in New York City; about fifteen minutes later, a second plane flew into Tower Two. Both towers collapsed less than two hours after the attacks. A third plane struck the Pentagon just outside of Washington, D.C. The fourth plane crashed in a Pennsylvania field. Its intended target remains unknown. In all, more than 3,000 civilians, firefighters, and police officers were killed that morning, and thousands were wounded.

The nation and most of the world responded with an outpouring of sympathy and good will. Immediately, volunteers in and around New York City and Washington, D.C., arranged services for the survivors and the rescuers. Around the country, people organized charities to aid the families of victims. Improvised memorials sprung up near the sites of the attacks and the victims' homes, and communities held vigils to pay tribute to the dead and comfort the grieving.

Newspapers published profiles of the deceased, revealing people of all ages and professions, from corporate executives to firefighters. The victims included immigrants from more than 80 nations.

Many of the spontaneous memorials that dotted the country in the weeks following the incident have since been replaced by permanent memorials. In Bucks County, Pennsylvania, a Garden of Reflection provides a peaceful place to pay respect. In Sherwood Island State Park in Connecticut, a Living Memorial granite monument and garden now stands. And where the World Trade Center once stood, several different memorials pay tribute to the victims and their families, as well as to the relief workers whose efforts to aid survivors endure as an example of the best in people.

the earth is a living thing

Poem by Lucille Clifton

Sleeping in the Forest

Poem by Mary Oliver

Gold

Poem by Pat Mora

What is our place in NATURE?

ALABAMA STANDARDS

READING STANDARDS

2 Relate literary elements and devices to each other

3 Distinguish among subgenres based on characteristics

KEY IDEA When you left the house to go to school this morning, was the sky clear or cloudy? How did the air feel? Did you hear birds singing or see an insect darting by? **Nature** surrounds us, but sometimes we forget to notice.

SKETCH IT In a small group, discuss how you fit in with the natural world. In what ways does nature affect your life? Do you think people are part of nature or separate from it? Give concrete examples to support your opinion. Then make a sketch that shows your place in nature.

POETIC FORM: LYRIC POETRY

A **lyric poem** is a short poem in which a single speaker expresses personal thoughts and feelings. Lyric poems cover many subjects, from love and death to everyday experiences. Like many other lyric poems, each of those you're about to read creates a strong, unified impression.

LITERARY ANALYSIS: FIGURATIVE LANGUAGE

Literal language is language that reflects the dictionary definition of words. It forms a factual statement, such as "a tree sheds its leaves in autumn." **Figurative language** expesses an idea through a more imaginative use of words: "A tree mourns its lost leaves in autumn."

Here are some types of figurative language poets frequently use:

- **Personification** gives human qualities to an animal, an object, or an idea. (*whispering trees, angrily marching ants*)
- **Similes** compare two unlike things using the word *like* or *as*. (*The stars flamed like torches.*)
- **Metaphors** compare two unlike things without using the word *like* or *as*. (*The stars were torches.*)

READING SKILL: MAKE INFERENCES

To understand poetry, you will have to **make inferences,** or make logical guesses, about images and figurative language. Base these guesses on both the details of the poem and your own knowledge and experience. As you read, use charts like the one shown to record striking or puzzling lines or phrases from each poem. Then record your inferences.

Title: "Sleeping in the Forest"		
Lines and Phrases	What I Know from Reading or Experience	Inference
"I slept/as never before, a stone/on the riverbed"	The speaker compares herself to a stone. Stones are completely still.	The speaker slept soundly, without moving.

Author Online

Lucille Clifton: An Original Voice

Lucille Clifton
born 1936

Though Lucille Clifton was always comfortable when it came to writing, she says, "I had to learn that poetry could sound like me." After writing in traditional forms, Clifton discovered that good poetry could sound like everyday speech.

Mary Oliver: Nature's Poet

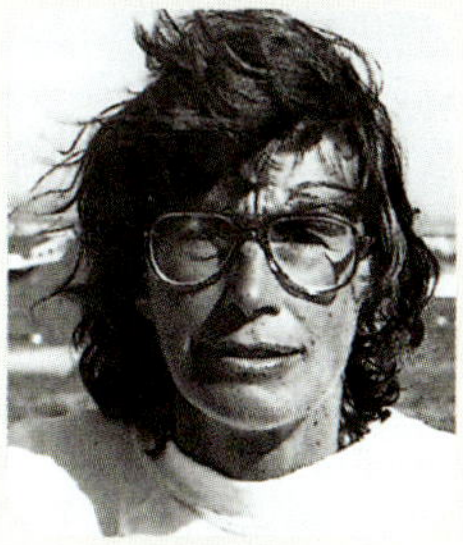
Mary Oliver
born 1935

Mary Oliver finds her inspiration in exploring nature. Oliver describes the writer's life as "an unstoppable urge toward that life of the imagination. I don't think I have been bored one day in my life, you know, or an hour."

Pat Mora: Poetry Pioneer

Pat Mora
born 1942

Pat Mora, who is Mexican American, has helped pioneer poetry about the Mexican-American experience. Since she grew up outside of El Paso, Texas, she also loves to write about the desert.

MORE ABOUT THE AUTHOR
For more on these poets, visit the **Literature Center** at **ClassZone.com.**

the earth is a living thing

Lucille Clifton

is a black shuffling bear
ruffling its wild back and tossing
mountains into the sea

is a black hawk circling
the burying ground circling the bones
picked clean and discarded[1]

is a fish black blind in the belly of water
is a diamond blind in the black belly of coal (A)

is a black and living thing
is a favorite child
of the universe
feel her rolling her hand
in its kinky hair
feel her brushing it clean (B)

(A) FIGURATIVE LANGUAGE
Reread the title and lines 1–8. To what four things is the earth being compared?

(B) FIGURATIVE LANGUAGE
Reread lines 10–14. What relationship between the earth and the universe is suggested by this use of **personification?**

ANALYZE VISUALS
Compare the style of this art with the style of the art on page 559. Which is more realistic?

1. **discarded** (dĭ-skärd′ĕd): thrown away; gotten rid of.

Bear with Houses, Michael Wertz. Pastel. © Michael Wertz.

The Orchard (1997), Peter Davidson. Oil on paper, 37.5 cm × 44 cm. Private collection. Photo © Bridgeman Art Library.

Sleeping in the FOREST

Mary Oliver

I thought the earth
remembered me, she
took me back so tenderly, arranging
her dark skirts, her pockets
full of lichens[1] and seeds. I slept **C**
as never before, a stone
on the riverbed, nothing
between me and the white fire of the stars
but my thoughts, and they floated
light as moths among the branches
of the perfect trees. All night
I heard the small kingdoms breathing
around me, the insects, and the birds
who do their work in the darkness. All night
I rose and fell, as if in water, grappling[2]
with a luminous doom. By morning
I had vanished at least a dozen times
into something better. **D** **E**

C FIGURATIVE LANGUAGE
Reread lines 1–5. What is being **personified?**

D MAKE INFERENCES
Reread the last sentence in the poem. What do you think the speaker means by "something better"?

E LYRIC POETRY
What thoughts and feelings is the speaker conveying in this poem?

1. **lichens** (lī′kənz): fungi that grow together with algae and form crustlike growths on rocks or tree trunks.
2. **grappling:** struggling.

GOLD

Pat Mora

Hacienda (2002), Vanessa Julian. Acrylic on matteboard, 23″ × 19″. © Vanessa Julian.

When Sun paints the desert
with its gold,
I climb the hills.
Wind runs round boulders, ruffles
my hair. I sit on my favorite rock,
lizards for company, a rabbit,
ears stiff in the shade
of a saguaro.[1]
In the wind, we're all
eye to eye. **F**

Sparrow on saguaro watches
rabbit watch us in the gold
of sun setting.
Hawk sails on waves of light, sees
sparrow, rabbit, lizards, me,
our eyes shining,
watching red and purple
sand rivers stream down the hills.

I stretch my arms wide as the sky
like hawk extends her wings
in all the gold light of this, home. **G**

F MAKE INFERENCES
Reread lines 1–10. What can you **infer** about the speaker's connection to nature?

G FIGURATIVE LANGUAGE
Reread lines 19–21. What two **similes** are used to describe the speaker's arms?

---

1. **saguaro** (sə-gwär′ō): a tall, branching cactus found in the southwestern United States and northern Mexico.

Comprehension

ALABAMA STANDARDS

READING STANDARD
3 Distinguish among subgenres based on characteristics

1. **Recall** What living things is the earth compared to in "the earth is a living thing"?
2. **Clarify** What are the "small kingdoms" that the speaker hears in "Sleeping in the Forest"?
3. **Represent** Where, and at what time of day, does the poem "Gold" take place? Make a drawing illustrating the setting described in lines 5–18.

Literary Analysis

4. **Make Inferences** Review the charts you created as you read. Which inferences most helped you understand the poems? Explain your answers.
5. **Examine Figurative Language** What **similes, metaphors,** or examples of **personification** in these poems helped you see **nature** in a fresh way? Give three examples. For each one, tell what type of figurative language was used and why you found it to be effective.
6. **Interpret Meaning** Did the ending of "Sleeping in the Forest" surprise you? Reread lines 14–18. Then tell what feeling you think these lines try to capture.
7. **Compare and Contrast** Use a Venn diagram like the one shown to examine similarities and differences among the three poems. Think about such things as the setting, the speaker, and the **mood,** or feeling, of each poem. Then decide which two poems you think are most similar.

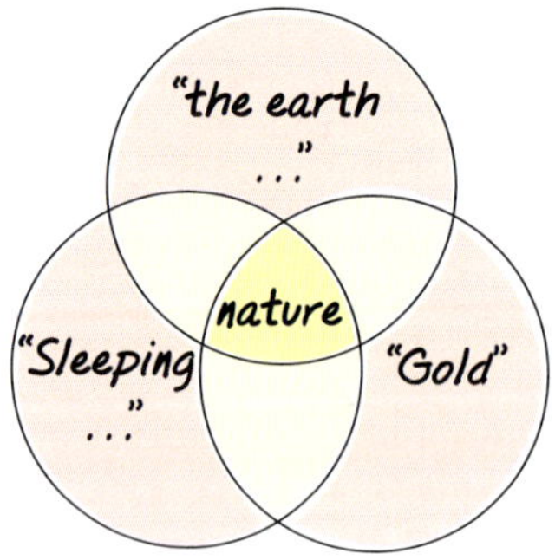

8. **Evaluate Lyric Poetry** Which of the poems do you think was most successful at capturing the speaker's thoughts and feelings? Include specific details from the poem to support your answer.

Extension and Challenge

9. **Big Question Activity** Reread the question on page 554. How would the speaker of each poem answer this question? After you've decided, consider whether the speakers' attitudes have affected how you feel about your own place in nature.
10. **Speaking and Listening** Lyric poems are known for their strong, melodic rhythms. They often use repetition to emphasize emotional experiences. In a group, take turns reading each poem aloud. Which of the poems do you think has an especially appealing sound or rhythm? Discuss your answer.

SKILLS PRACTICE

Reading-Writing Connection

Explore the poems further by responding to these prompts. Then complete the **Grammar and Writing** exercise.

WRITING PROMPTS	SELF-CHECK
A. Short Response: Write a Poem Write a **short poem** about an aspect of **nature** that you find especially inspiring, dramatic, or appealing. Include at least two types of figurative language in your poem.	***A creative poem will . . .*** • use vivid details and imagery to create a strong impression in the reader's mind • use figurative language to enhance the meaning
B. Extended Response: Analyze Metaphors Reread "the earth is a living thing." Select three specific metaphors to explore further. Write **two or three paragraphs** explaining what view of **nature** is suggested by each metaphor.	***An effective analysis will . . .*** • explain how the metaphors relate to the poem's meaning • give reasons and evidence to support the explanation

GRAMMAR AND WRITING

ALABAMA STANDARDS

WRITING/LANGUAGE STANDARD
11.c Identifying sentence patterns

USE CORRECT SENTENCE TYPE In order for your sentences to serve their correct purposes and reflect the emotions you intend, be sure to use the correct sentence type. A **declarative** sentence makes a statement and ends with a period. An **interrogative** sentence asks a question and ends with a question mark. An **imperative** sentence makes a request or gives a command (with the understood subject being *you*) and usually ends with a period. An **exclamatory** sentence shows strong feeling and ends with an exclamation point.

Original: How long has this mountain been here.
I can't believe its beauty.

Revised: How long has this mountain been here?
I can't believe its beauty!

PRACTICE Identify each sentence type and punctuate it correctly.

1. Its peak rises into the clouds like a skyscraper
2. How wonderful it looks
3. Can you hear how the wind whispers around it
4. Listen carefully

For more help with sentence types, see page R60 in the ***Grammar Handbook.***

Scaffolding

Poem by Seamus Heaney

The World Is Not a Pleasant Place to Be

Poem by Nikki Giovanni

Annabel Lee

Poem by Edgar Allan Poe

Whom do you feel CLOSEST *to?*

ALABAMA STANDARDS

READING STANDARDS

1.d Applying self-monitoring strategies

3 Distinguish among genres based on characteristics

KEY IDEA Think about a family member or friend with whom you have a close **relationship.** Chances are you've fought with this person, yet he or she still brings you comfort and joy. Why do you think this is? The poems you're about to read explore the mysteries of strong relationships.

QUICKWRITE What are your two or three most important relationships? Note them in your journal. Then write about what makes each a good relationship. What keeps your bonds strong when difficulties arise?

POETIC FORM: LINE AND STANZA

The **line** is the main unit of a poem. Lines can be organized into **stanzas,** groups of two or more lines that form longer units within a poem. Sometimes, as in this example from "The World Is Not a Pleasant Place to Be," you have to read the whole stanza to learn the speaker's complete thought:

the world is not a pleasant place
to be without
someone to hold and be held by

LITERARY ANALYSIS: RHYME SCHEME

Poets use **sound devices** to convey meaning and create emphasis. One sound device is **rhyme,** the repetition of sounds at the end of words. The **rhyme scheme** is the pattern of rhyme at the ends of lines in a poem. You can track the rhyme by assigning a letter to each line. The first line gets the letter *a.* Each following line that rhymes with it also gets an *a.* The first line that doesn't rhyme gets the letter *b,* as do the other lines that rhyme with that line. Each new rhyme gets a new letter.

And this was the reason that, long ago, — *a*
In this kingdom by the sea, — *b*
A wind blew out of a cloud by night — *c*
Chilling my Annabel Lee; — *b*

As you read "Scaffolding" and "Annabel Lee," use letters to identify each poem's rhyme scheme.

READING SKILL: UNDERSTAND SPEAKER

In poetry, the **speaker** is the voice that "talks" to the reader. To understand a poem, you have to decide who the speaker is and how he or she feels about the subject of the poem. Complete a chart like the one shown as you read each of the selections.

	Poem 1	Poem 2	Poem 3
Who is the speaker?			
How do I know?			
How does he/she feel?			

Author Online

Seamus Heaney: Celebrated Irishman

Seamus Heaney
born 1939

Nobel Prize winner Seamus Heaney's poetry is celebrated throughout the world. Describing how he felt when he wrote his first successful poem, Heaney said, "I felt that I had let down a shaft into real life."

Nikki Giovanni: Storyteller Poet

Nikki Giovanni
born 1943

Nikki Giovanni gained popularity as a poet after the release of an album of her readings, *Truth Is on Its Way.* She says that in her poetry, "I use a very natural rhythm; I want my writing to sound like I talk."

Edgar Allan Poe: Literary Giant

Edgar Allan Poe
1809–1849

Edgar Allan Poe has fascinated generations of readers with his haunting poetry and tales of horror. He and his adored young wife, Virginia, were poor and often sick. "Annabel Lee" is believed to be Poe's tribute to Virginia.

MORE ABOUT THE AUTHOR
For more on these poets, visit the **Literature Center** at **ClassZone.com.**

SCAFFOLDING

SEAMUS HEANEY

Masons,[1] when they start upon a building,
Are careful to test out the scaffolding;

Make sure that planks won't slip at busy points,
Secure all ladders, tighten bolted joints.[2] **A**

And yet all this comes down when the job's done
Showing off walls of sure and solid stone.

So if, my dear, there sometimes seem to be
Old bridges breaking between you and me

Never fear. We may let the scaffolds fall
Confident that we have built our wall. **B**

ANALYZE VISUALS
How does this painting reflect the **title** of the poem?

A LINE AND STANZA
A stanza that consists of two rhyming lines is called a **couplet.** What is being described in this couplet?

B SPEAKER
Reread lines 7–10. Whom is the speaker addressing? In your chart, note how the speaker feels about this person.

1. **masons** (mā′sənz): wallers who build with brick or stone.
2. **joints** (joints): places where two parts or pieces join together.

Stages II, Paul Davis. Oil, 10″ × 8″. Courtesy Coda Gallery. © Paul Davis.

THE WORLD IS NOT A PLEASANT PLACE TO BE

Nikki Giovanni

the world is not a pleasant place
to be without
someone to hold and be held by

a river would stop
its flow if only
a stream were there
to receive it

an ocean would never laugh
if clouds weren't there
to kiss her tears

the world is not
a pleasant place to be without
someone **C**

Detail of *Family in the Park* (1999), Colin Bootman. Oil on canvas. Private collection. Photo © Bridgeman Art Library.

C LINE AND STANZA
Repetition is the repeating of a sound, word, phrase, or line to emphasize an idea. Notice how the last stanza echoes the first with one small difference. What effect is created by this change?

The Seashore (1900), William Henry Margetson. Oil on canvas. Private collection. Photo © The Maas Gallery, London/Bridgeman Art Library.

Annabel Lee

Edgar Allan Poe

It was many and many a year ago,
    In a kingdom by the sea,
That a maiden there lived whom you may know
    By the name of Annabel Lee;—
And this maiden she lived with no other thought
    Than to love and be loved by me. **D**

She was a child and *I* was a child,
    In this kingdom by the sea,
But we loved with a love that was more than love—
    I and my Annabel Lee—
With a love that the wingéd seraphs[1] of Heaven
    Coveted[2] her and me. **E**

D RHYME SCHEME
What rhyme scheme is used in the first stanza?

E SPEAKER
What is the speaker's relationship to Annabel Lee?

1. **seraphs** (sĕr′əfs): any of the highest order of angels.
2. **coveted** (kŭv′ĭ-tĭd): envied.

And this was the reason that, long ago,
In this kingdom by the sea,
A wind blew out of a cloud by night
Chilling my Annabel Lee;
So that her high-born kinsmen came
And bore her away from me,
To shut her up in a sepulcher[3]
In this kingdom by the sea.

The angels, not half so happy in Heaven,
Went envying her and me;
Yes! that was the reason (as all men know,
In this kingdom by the sea)
That the wind came out of the cloud chilling
And killing my Annabel Lee.

But our love it was stronger by far than the love
Of those who were older than we—
Of many far wiser than we—
And neither the angels in Heaven above
Nor the demons down under the sea
Can ever dissever[4] my soul from the soul
Of the beautiful Annabel Lee:— F

For the moon never beams without bringing me dreams
Of the beautiful Annabel Lee;
And the stars never rise but I feel the bright eyes
Of the beautiful Annabel Lee;
And so, all the night-tide, I lie down by the side
Of my darling, my darling, my life and my bride
In her sepulcher there by the sea—
In her tomb by the side of the sea. G

F **LINE AND STANZA** Reread this stanza. Identify words and phrases that are repeated. What emphasis does this **repetition** create?

G **LINE AND STANZA** The last two stanzas are among the longest in the poem. What ideas and emotions does the poet emphasize by ending the poem with long stanzas?

3. **sepulcher** (sĕp′əl-kər): a place for burial; tomb.

4. **dissever** (dĭ-sĕv′ər): separate; tear apart.

ALABAMA STANDARDS

READING STANDARD
3 Distinguish among genres based on characteristics

Comprehension

1. **Recall** Why does the speaker in "Scaffolding" say that the scaffolds in his relationship could be allowed to fall?
2. **Recall** In "The World Is Not a Pleasant Place to Be," what is the relationship between the ocean and the clouds?
3. **Clarify** What happened to Annabel Lee and the person who loved her?

Literary Analysis

4. **Identify Rhyme Scheme** Determine the rhyme scheme in "Scaffolding." Why do you think Seamus Heaney might have chosen this rhyme scheme for a poem about a couple's relationship?
5. **Analyze a Stanza** Reread the first stanza of "The World Is Not a Pleasant Place to Be." How does the meaning of the first line change as you read the rest of the stanza? Find one other example of a line break that you think affects the meaning of the words in an important way.
6. **Draw Conclusions About Speakers** Review the chart you created as you read. Based on the details you recorded and your understanding of the poems, what conclusions can you draw about each speaker's attitude about relationships? Give evidence from the poem to support your conclusions.
7. **Make Judgments** Go back and reread "Annabel Lee." In a chart, note words and details that make the speaker seem romantic and those that make him seem grief stricken. Are his feelings and attitudes understandable? Support your opinion with examples from your chart.

Romantic	Grief Stricken
". . . we loved with a love that was more than love—"	

Extension and Challenge

8. **Big Question Activity** With a partner, role-play an interview between a television reporter and the **speaker** of one of the poems, about what keeps **relationships** strong. Discuss specific details from the poem in your interview.
9. **Creative Project: Art** As you read the poems, which visual images seemed especially beautiful or powerful? Draw a sketch of one of these images, and explain how it helped draw you into the poem.

The Charge of the Light Brigade

Poem by Alfred, Lord Tennyson

The Highwayman

Poem by Alfred Noyes

What is HONOR?

ALABAMA STANDARDS

READING STANDARDS
1.d Applying self-monitoring strategies
3 Distinguish among genres based on characteristics

KEY IDEA When you think of **honor,** who or what comes to mind? Do you picture a person you respect, or do you remember a noble sacrifice that somebody made? In "The Charge of the Light Brigade" and "The Highwayman," the characters give up their lives for very different reasons. It is up to you to decide whether their causes were honorable.

DISCUSS With a small group, discuss people who have acted honorably. On the basis of this conversation, how would you define honor? Be ready to share your definition with the class.

● LITERARY ANALYSIS: RHYTHM AND METER

Rhythm is the pattern of stressed and unstressed syllables in a line of poetry. Rhythm that follows a regular pattern from line to line is called **meter.**

When you "scan" a line of poetry, you analyze its rhythm, marking the syllables that are stressed (´) and those that are unstressed (˘). This system is called scansion. Read these lines from "The Highwayman" out loud. Concentrate on the stressed and unstressed syllables.

The wind was a torrent of darkness among the gusty trees.
The moon was a ghostly galleon tossed upon cloudy seas.

As you read the following selections, notice each poem's rhythm and meter and the effect they create.

Review: **Mood**

■ READING STRATEGY: READING A NARRATIVE POEM

"The Highwayman" and "The Charge of the Light Brigade" are **narrative poems,** which means they tell stories. Like novels and short stories, narrative poems have characters, a setting, and a plot. As you read each poem, keep track of these elements in a story map.

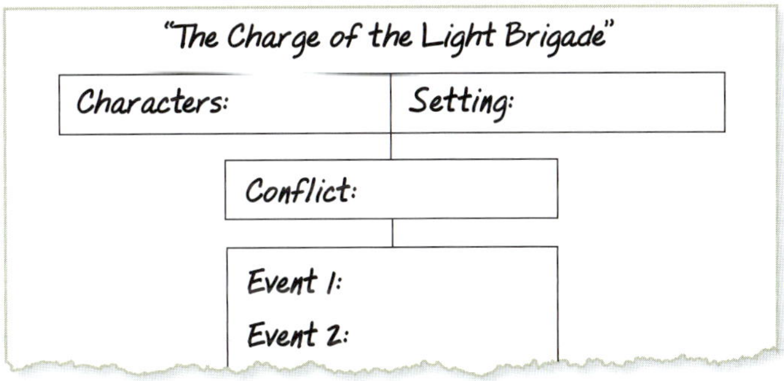

▲ VOCABULARY IN CONTEXT

The boldfaced vocabulary words can help you picture the scenes in these poems. Match each word in Column A to the word or phrase in Column B that is closest in meaning.

Column A	Column B
1. cascade	**a.** twist
2. claret	**b.** tan
3. tawny	**c.** waterfall
4. writhe	**d.** dark red

Author Online

Alfred, Lord Tennyson: Victorian Poet Tennyson's best friend died in 1833, and the shock to Tennyson was severe. However, it was during this time of incredible grief that Tennyson wrote some of his best poetry. These poems were so popular that he was named poet laureate, or court poet, by Queen Victoria.

Alfred, Lord Tennyson
1809–1892

Alfred Noyes: Popular Poet English poet Alfred Noyes wrote "The Highwayman" when he was only 24. Readers loved it, but critics didn't. Regardless of the critics, Noyes still earned his living from poetry.

Alfred Noyes
1880–1958

Background

A Tragic Battle "The Charge of the Light Brigade" was inspired by a real-life battle in the Crimean War between England and Russia (1854–1856). A group of British troops called the Light Brigade, armed only with swords, was ordered to charge a unit of Russian gunners. Though the British lost this battle, they eventually won the war.

MORE ABOUT THE AUTHOR AND BACKGROUND
To learn more about these poets and the Crimean War, visit the **Literature Center** at **ClassZone.com.**

The Charge of the Light Brigade

Alfred, Lord Tennyson

Half a league,[1] half a league,
Half a league onward,
All in the valley of Death
    Rode the six hundred.
"Forward, the Light Brigade!
Charge for the guns!" he said:
Into the valley of Death
    Rode the six hundred. **A**

"Forward, the Light Brigade!"
Was there a man dismay'd?
Not tho' the soldier knew
    Some one had blunder'd:[2]
Theirs not to make reply,
Theirs not to reason why,
Theirs but to do and die:
Into the valley of Death
    Rode the six hundred.

Cannon to right of them,
Cannon to left of them,

A RHYTHM AND METER
Reread lines 1–4, tapping your desk with each stressed syllable. How many stressed syllables are in each line?

ANALYZE VISUALS
How well do the **images** in this painting match the scene described in the poem? Explain your answer.

1. **league:** a distance of three miles.
2. **blunder'd:** made a mistake.

Detail of *The Charge of the Light Brigade.* © Getty Images.

Cannon in front of them
        Volley'd and thunder'd;
Storm'd at with shot and shell,
Boldly they rode and well,
Into the jaws of Death,
Into the mouth of Hell
        Rode the six hundred.

Flash'd all their sabers[3] bare,
Flash'd as they turn'd in air
Sabring the gunners there,
Charging an army, while
        All the world wonder'd:
Plunged in the battery[4] smoke,
Right thro' the line they broke;
Cossack and Russian
Reel'd from the saber-stroke,
        Shatter'd and sunder'd.[5]
Then they rode back, but not,
        Not the six hundred. **B**

Cannon to right of them,
Cannon to left of them,
Cannon behind them
        Volley'd and thunder'd;
Storm'd at with shot and shell,
While horse and hero fell,
They that had fought so well
Came thro' the jaws of Death.
Back from the mouth of Hell,
All that was left of them,
        Left of six hundred. **C**

When can their glory fade?
O, the wild charge they made!
        All the world wonder'd.
Honor the charge they made!
Honor the Light Brigade,
        Noble six hundred!

3. **sabers:** heavy, slightly curved swords.
4. **battery:** related to guns and cannons used together.
5. **sunder'd:** broken apart; split into pieces.

B **READING A NARRATIVE POEM**
Since narrative poems have a plot, they also have a **climax,** or point of greatest excitement. What is the climax of this poem?

C **RHYTHM AND METER**
Reread lines 39–42 aloud. What is happening to the 600 soldiers? Explain how the meter of these lines matches the events being depicted.

Detail of *Equestrian Portrait of a Man with a Page* (1600s), Thomas de Keyser. Oil on canvas, 94.6 cm × 77.2 cm. Private collection. Photo © Bridgeman Art Library.

The Highwayman

Alfred Noyes

Part One

The wind was a torrent of darkness among the gusty trees.
The moon was a ghostly galleon[1] tossed upon cloudy seas.
The road was a ribbon of moonlight over the purple moor,[2]
And the highwayman came riding—
Riding—riding—
The highwayman came riding, up to the old inn-door. **D**

He'd a French cocked-hat on his forehead, a bunch of lace at his chin,
A coat of the **claret** velvet, and breeches of brown doeskin.
They fitted with never a wrinkle. His boots were up to the thigh.
And he rode with a jeweled twinkle,
His pistol butts a-twinkle.
His rapier hilt[3] a-twinkle, under the jeweled sky.

D READING A NARRATIVE POEM
What is the **setting** of this poem? Note the setting and the **characters** in your story map.

claret (klăr′ĭt) *adj.* dark red

1. **galleon** (găl′ē-ən): a large sailing ship.
2. **moor:** a wide, rolling open area, usually covered with low-growing shrubs.
3. **rapier** (rā′pē-ər) **hilt:** sword handle.

Over the cobbles[4] he clattered and clashed in the dark inn-yard.
He tapped with his whip on the shutters, but all was locked and barred.
He whistled a tune to the window, and who should be waiting there
But the landlord's black-eyed daughter,
  Bess, the landlord's daughter,
Plaiting[5] a dark red love-knot into her long black hair.

And dark in the dark old inn-yard a stable wicket[6] creaked
Where Tim the ostler[7] listened. His face was white and peaked.
His eyes were hollows of madness, his hair like moldy hay,
But he loved the landlord's daughter,
  The landlord's red-lipped daughter.
Dumb as a dog he listened, and he heard the robber say—

"One kiss, my bonny sweetheart, I'm after a prize tonight,
But I shall be back with the yellow gold before the morning light;
Yet, if they press me sharply, and harry me through the day,
Then look for me by moonlight,
  Watch for me by moonlight,
I'll come to thee by moonlight, though hell should bar the way."

He rose upright in the stirrups. He scarce could reach her hand,
But she loosened her hair in the casement.[8] His face burnt like a brand
As the black **cascade** of perfume came tumbling over his breast;
And he kissed its waves in the moonlight,
  (O, sweet black waves in the moonlight!)
Then he tugged at his rein in the moonlight, and galloped away to
    the west.

Part Two

He did not come in the dawning. He did not come at noon;
And out of the **tawny** sunset, before the rise of the moon,
When the road was a gypsy's ribbon, looping the purple moor,
A redcoat troop came marching—
  Marching—marching—
King George's men came marching, up to the old inn-door.

SOCIAL STUDIES CONNECTION

With the cry of "Stand and deliver!" highwaymen halted and robbed the carriages of the upper class in 17th- and 18th-century England. Like Robin Hood, highwaymen were admired by ladies and celebrated by the poor, who often felt oppressed by the rich.

cascade (kă-skād') *n.* a waterfall or something that resembles a waterfall

tawny (tô'nē) *adj.* a warm, sandy shade of brownish orange

---

4. **cobbles:** rounded stones used for paving roads.
5. **plaiting:** braiding.
6. **wicket:** a small door or gate.
7. **ostler** (ŏs'-lər): a worker who takes care of horses at an inn.
8. **casement:** a window that opens outward on side hinges.

They said no word to the landlord. They drank his ale instead.
But they gagged his daughter, and bound her, to the foot of her narrow bed.
Two of them knelt at her casement, with muskets at their side!
There was death at every window;
And hell at one dark window;
For Bess could see, through her casement, the road that *he* would ride.

They had tied her up to attention, with many a sniggering jest.
They had bound a musket beside her, with the muzzle beneath her breast!
"Now, keep good watch!" and they kissed her. She heard the doomed man say—
Look for me by moonlight;
Watch for me by moonlight;
I'll come to thee by moonlight, though hell should bar the way! E

She twisted her hands behind her; but all the knots held good!
She **writhed** her hands till her fingers were wet with sweat or blood!
They stretched and strained in the darkness, and the hours crawled by like years,
Till, now, on the stroke of midnight,
Cold, on the stroke of midnight,
The tip of one finger touched it! The trigger at least was hers!

The tip of one finger touched it. She strove no more for the rest.
Up, she stood up to attention, with the muzzle beneath her breast.
She would not risk their hearing; she would not strive again;
For the road lay bare in the moonlight;
Blank and bare in the moonlight;
And the blood of her veins, in the moonlight, throbbed to her love's refrain.

Tlot-tlot; tlot-tlot! Had they heard it? The horse hoofs ringing clear;
Tlot-tlot, tlot-tlot, in the distance? Were they deaf that they did not hear? F
Down the ribbon of moonlight, over the brow of the hill,
The highwayman came riding—
Riding—riding—
The redcoats looked to their priming![9] She stood up, straight and still.

E READING A NARRATIVE POEM
How did the redcoats find out about Bess and the highwayman? Explain how you made this **inference.** Then note the main **conflict** in your story map.

writhe (rīth) *v.* to twist or move painfully

F RHYTHM AND METER
On a piece of paper, scan lines 67–68, noting the stressed and unstressed syllables in each line. Why is this meter perfectly suited to the action that's taking place?

9. **looked to their priming:** prepared their muskets by pouring in the gunpowder used to fire them.

Tlot-tlot, in the frosty silence! *Tlot-tlot,* in the echoing night!
Nearer he came and nearer. Her face was like a light.
Her eyes grew wide for a moment; she drew one last deep breath,
Then her finger moved in the moonlight,
  Her musket shattered the moonlight,
Shattered her breast in the moonlight and warned him—with her death. **G**

G READING A NARRATIVE POEM
What just happened? Note the event on your story map.

He turned. He spurred to the west; he did not know who stood
Bowed, with her head o'er the musket, drenched with her own blood!
Not till the dawn he heard it, his face grew grey to hear
How Bess, the landlord's daughter,
  The landlord's black-eyed daughter,
Had watched for her love in the moonlight, and died in the
    darkness there.

Back, he spurred like a madman, shouting a curse to the sky,
With the white road smoking behind him and his rapier brandished high.
Blood-red were his spurs in the golden noon; wine-red was his velvet coat;
When they shot him down on the highway,
  Down like a dog on the highway,
And he lay in his blood on the highway, with a bunch of lace at
    his throat. **H**

H MOOD
Reread lines 85–90. Note the images that stand out to you. What mood, or feeling, do they help create?

And still of a winter's night, they say, when the wind is in the trees,
When the moon is a ghostly galleon tossed upon cloudy seas,
When the road is a ribbon of moonlight over the purple moor,
A highwayman comes riding—
  Riding—riding—
A highwayman comes riding, up to the old inn-door.

Over the cobbles he clatters and clangs in the dark inn-yard.
He taps with his whip on the shutters, but all is locked and barred.
He whistles a tune to the window, and who should be waiting there
But the landlord's black-eyed daughter,
  Bess, the landlord's daughter,
Plaiting a dark red love-knot into her long black hair.

Comprehension

1. **Clarify** What is the outcome of the Light Brigade's charge?
2. **Recall** Where does Bess wait for the highwayman?
3. **Summarize** In your own words, explain how Bess and the highwayman each die.

ALABAMA STANDARDS

READING STANDARD
3 Distinguish among genres based on characteristics

Literary Analysis

4. **Compare and Contrast Characters** For each poem, make a list of the **character traits** the soldiers display. Are the soldiers in the two poems similar or different? Explain your answer.
5. **Analyze a Ballad** "The Highwayman" is a special type of **narrative poem** called a ballad. Ballads have the same features as narrative poems, but they were originally meant to be sung or read out loud. What elements of "The Highwayman" make it an exciting poem to read aloud? Give examples.
6. **Reading a Narrative Poem** Look back at the story map you created as you read "The Charge of the Light Brigade." How do you think a short story about the same battle might be different from this poem? What added information might the story include, and what effects might be missing?
7. **Evaluate Rhythm and Meter** Choose a few lines from each poem and read them to yourself, exaggerating the emphasis on the stressed syllables. Write the lines in a chart like the one shown and mark the stressed and unstressed syllables in each. Then explain how the rhythm of each line contributes to its overall effect.

"The Charge of the Light Brigade"	
Lines from Poem	**Effect**
Half a league, half a league, Half a league onward,	sounds like a galloping horse

Extension and Challenge

8. **SOCIAL STUDIES CONNECTION** Research the true story behind the legendary Light Brigade. When and where did the battle described in the poem occur? How many soldiers lost their lives? Share your findings with the class.
9. **Big Question Activity** Think back to the discussion of honor on page 570. Who acted with the most **honor**—Bess, the highwayman, or the soldiers of the Light Brigade? Explain your answer.

RESEARCH LINKS
For more on the Light Brigade, visit the **Research Center** at **ClassZone.com.**

Vocabulary in Context

VOCABULARY PRACTICE

Choose the word from the list that best fits each sentence.

1. The hiker looked at the _____ glow of the setting sun and began to worry.
2. Not watching where he was walking, he tripped and fell, which made him _____ in pain.
3. A thin, _____-colored stream of blood trickled down his face.
4. He heard a _____ of water far in the distance and tried not to think about his growing thirst.

cascade

claret

tawny

writhe

VOCABULARY IN WRITING

Which character could you see most clearly in your mind as you read these poems? Write a paragraph describing that character, using at least two vocabulary words. You might start like this.

EXAMPLE SENTENCE

*I pictured Bess most clearly, especially her **cascade** of long black hair.*

VOCABULARY STRATEGY: CONNOTATIONS

Poets use language carefully. They consider not only the dictionary definition of each word, but also its connotation. The connotation of a word includes all the thoughts or feelings the word may bring to people's minds. Words can have a positive, a negative, or a neutral connotation. For example, the vocabulary word *cascade* has a positive connotation that suggests something grand or picturesque.

PRACTICE For each sentence below, tell whether the boldfaced word has a positive, a negative, or a neutral connotation. Then explain the meaning of the word.

1. She didn't like the waiter's **prim** manner and the restaurant's overly formal atmosphere.
2. Because the coach was **decisive,** the players knew exactly what to do.
3. With one look at his **haggard** face, they knew he had been experiencing sleepless nights.
4. She was so interesting and **vivacious** that everyone at the dinner party wanted to sit by her.

VOCABULARY PRACTICE

For more practice, go to the **Vocabulary Center** at **ClassZone.com.**

SKILLS PRACTICE

Reading-Writing Connection

Increase your appreciation of "The Charge of the Light Brigade" and "The Highwayman" by responding to these prompts. Then complete the **Grammar and Writing** excercise.

WRITING PROMPTS	SELF-CHECK
A. Short Response: Write a Dialogue Both Bess and the soldiers of the Light Brigade stand up to something more powerful. Write a **half-page dialogue** between Bess and a soldier of the Light Brigade in which they discuss their ideas of **honor.**	***A realistic dialogue will . . .*** • use language appropriate for each character • include details from the poems that support each character's ideas
B. Extended Response: Write a News Article Pretend you are a reporter writing a front-page story about a recent tragedy. Choose one of the poems and write a journalistic account of its events in **three to five paragraphs.** Include a headline that will grab your readers' attention.	***A successful article will . . .*** • describe all the important events of the poem • use descriptive words and phrases to make the event come alive for the reader

GRAMMAR AND WRITING

USE THE ACTIVE VOICE A verb can be in either the active voice or the passive voice. In a sentence that uses the **active voice,** the subject *performs* the verb's action. In a sentence that uses the **passive voice,** the subject of the sentence *receives* the verb's action.

Active: The officers commanded the British soldiers. *(The subject* officers *performs the action of the verb* commanded.)

Passive: The British soldiers were commanded by the officers. *(The subject* officers *receives the action of the verbs* were commanded.)

PRACTICE Rewrite each of these sentences using the active voice.

1. The officers' commands were obeyed by the Light Brigade.
2. Sabers were the weapons used by the British soldiers.
3. Soldiers and horses alike were killed by the Russians.
4. The Light Brigade will be remembered by the world.

For more help with active and passive voice, see page R57 in the ***Grammar Handbook.***

ALABAMA STANDARDS

WRITING/LANGUAGE STANDARD
11 Apply grammar conventions in writing

Two Haiku

Poems by Matsuo Bashō

Fireflies

Poem by Paul Fleischman

Fireflies in the Garden

Poem by Robert Frost

How do the SEASONS *affect you?*

ALABAMA STANDARDS

READING STANDARDS

2 Relate literary devices to each other, including imagery

3 Distinguish among subgenres based on characteristics

KEY IDEA With shelters, cars, and climate controls of all kinds, it can sometimes be easy to overlook the dramatic changes that occur on the earth each year. But the **seasons** still determine the daily rhythms of our lives. As the poems you're about to read show, the changing seasons can even affect our emotions. How do the seasons make you feel?

SURVEY Conduct a survey of your classmates. Ask them for one or two words or phrases that they associate with each of the four **seasons.** Record their answers in a graphic organizer like the one shown. Review your data when you are done. What patterns do you see?

	Spring	Summer	Fall	Winter
Student 1				
Student 2				

POETIC FORM: HAIKU

Haiku is a form of poetry that originated hundreds of years ago in Japan. In haiku, poets seek to create a clear picture with few words. There are three key points to remember about traditional haiku.

- The entire poem consists of just 17 syllables arranged in three lines.
- The first and third lines each contain 5 syllables, and the second line has 7 syllables.
- Haiku centers on a symbol that instantly reminds its readers of a season.

The haiku by Bashō on page 584 are classics of the form.

LITERARY ANALYSIS: SYMBOL

Are you aware that you are surrounded by symbols? For example, you may have a U.S. flag in your classroom or a company logo on your backpack. A **symbol** is a person, place, object, or activity that stands for something beyond itself.

- Some symbols are unique to certain cultures. In Japan, for example, plum blossoms symbolize early spring. The crow symbolizes late autumn or the coming winter.
- Some symbols are understood across cultures. For instance, in most cultures, a heart represents love.

By using symbols, poets are able to communicate rich and complex ideas quickly. As you read the poems, identify the symbols and think about what ideas they express.

READING STRATEGY: VISUALIZE

Poets create images by using **sensory details**—words and phrases that appeal to the reader's senses of sight, touch, taste, smell, and hearing. Details that appeal to your sense of sight help you **visualize,** or create mental pictures of, the poet's words.

As you read each poem, list the sensory details that help you "see" the pictures created by the poem.

	Sensory Details
"Fireflies"	*1. flickering* *2. glimmering* *3.*

Author Online

Matsuo Bashō: Japan's Master Poet
Matsuo Bashō first pursued a career as a samurai before devoting himself to the poetry that he had loved in his youth. He created a new style that raised haiku to the level of serious literature.

Matsuo Bashō
1644–1694

Paul Fleischman: A Musician of Words
Poet Paul Fleischman gives as much attention to the sound of his words as to their meaning. Fleischman grew up playing piano with his mother and listening to his father, an author, read aloud.

Paul Fleischman
born 1952

Robert Frost: A Legendary Poet
Robert Frost is one of the most beloved poets of the 20th century. As a young man, Frost ran a New Hampshire farm. The New England farmers Frost met were rich sources for his poetry. He won his first of four Pulitzer Prizes in 1924.

Robert Frost
1874–1963

MORE ABOUT THE AUTHOR
For more on these poets, visit the **Literature Center** at **ClassZone.com.**

TWO HAIKU

MATSUO BASHŌ

Plum Garden, Kameido from *One Hundred Views of Famous Places in Edo* (1857), Utagawa Hiroshige. Photo © Christie's Images/Corbis.

On sweet plum blossoms[1]
The sun rises suddenly.
Look, a mountain path! (A)

A crow
has settled on a bare branch—
autumn evening. (B)

(A) HAIKU
Identify at least one symbol in this poem. Also note what season the poem evokes.

(B) SYMBOL
What does the crow's arrival **symbolize?**

1. When haiku is translated from the original Japanese into English, the number of syllables per line sometimes changes slightly.

Fireflies

PAUL FLEISCHMAN

Light	Light
	is the ink we use
Night	Night
is our parchment[1]	
	We're
	fireflies
fireflies	flickering
flitting	
	flashing
fireflies	
glimmering	fireflies
	gleaming **C**
glowing	
Insect calligraphers[2]	Insect calligraphers
practicing penmanship	
	copying sentences
Six-legged scribblers	Six-legged scribblers
of vanishing messages,	
	fleeting[3] graffiti
Fine artists in flight	Fine artists in flight
adding dabs of light	
	bright brush strokes
Signing the June nights	Signing the June nights
as if they were paintings	as if they were paintings **D**
	We're
flickering	fireflies
fireflies	flickering
fireflies.	fireflies.

C VISUALIZE
Reread lines 1–12. What words help you see the fireflies in your mind?

D VISUALIZE
Reread lines 20–24. Notice the **simile** comparing the "June nights" to paintings. What do you picture when you visualize the image presented in lines 20–24?

1. **parchment:** fine-quality paper, usually made from the skin of goats or sheep.
2. **calligraphers** (kə-lĭg′rə-fərz): creators of beautiful, elaborate handwriting.
3. **fleeting:** passing swiftly; soon gone.

Fireflies in the Garden

Robert Frost

Here come real stars to fill the upper skies,
And here on earth come emulating[1] flies,
That though they never equal stars in size,
(And they were never really stars at heart)
Achieve at times a very star-like start.
Only of course they can't sustain[2] the part. **E**

E SYMBOL
Reread the poem and think about what the fireflies might symbolize.

1. **emulating:** imitating.
2. **sustain:** keep up; prolong.

Comprehension

ALABAMA STANDARDS

READING STANDARD
2 Relate literary devices to each other, including imagery

1. **Recall** In the first haiku, what does the rising sun reveal? In the second haiku, where does the crow settle?
2. **Clarify** In "Fireflies," what is the "ink" the fireflies use?
3. **Summarize** In what ways are the fireflies in "Fireflies in the Garden" unlike the stars they try to copy?

Literary Analysis

4. **Visualize** Look back at the list of sensory details that helped you visualize. For each poem, choose the details that most helped you visualize an image from that poem. Sketch one of these images.
5. **Examine Haiku** Which haiku gives you a more hopeful feeling? Explain.
6. **Evaluate Sound Devices** In "Fireflies," Fleischman repeats many words and phrases. What are the words he repeats the most? What other example of **repetition** do you notice? Tell how this repetition reflects the subject of the poem.
7. **Analyze Symbol** In "Fireflies in the Garden," Robert Frost contrasts the stars in the "upper skies" with the fireflies "here on earth." Use a chart like the one shown to explore the comparison more closely. What **theme** or larger idea about life might Frost be trying to express by using the fireflies as a symbol?

Details About the Fireflies	*My Thoughts*
The flies copy the stars.	
The stars are in the sky, and the flies are on earth.	
The flies were "never really stars at heart."	
The flies can shine like stars, but they "can't sustain the part."	

Extension and Challenge

8. **Speaking and Listening** "Fireflies" is written for two voices. Work with a partner and prepare an oral reading of the poem. One of you should read the words in the left column at the same time the other reads the words in the right. Perform your reading for the class. What images in the poem does reading aloud help to reinforce?
9. **Creative Project: Writing** Write a traditional haiku. Pick one **season** and try to express how it affects you. (You might look back at the words and phrases you collected in the survey on page 582 for ideas.)

Reading for Information

Stars with Wings

Science Article

Use with "Fireflies," page 585.

ALABAMA STANDARDS

READING STANDARDS
1.a Distinguishing factual from fictional materials
5 Use textual elements to gain information

What's the Connection?

The more you know about fireflies, the more easily you can spot the clever ways poet Paul Fleischman has imitated them in his poem "Fireflies." Take the time to learn more about these creatures by reading the science article "Stars with Wings."

Skill Focus: Use Text Features

Think about how all of the signs you see each day, even signs such as Do Not Walk on the Grass, communicate important information.

Text features are like signs. They help you figure out where you are in an article, and they tell you what is especially important to know. For example, consider what these text features reveal:

- A **title** identifies the text and its topic.
- An **introductory question** following the title may reveal the writer's focus or main idea.
- A **subheading,** which is a heading within the text, signals the start of a new topic or section and identifies what it will be about
- **Graphic aids**—such as illustrations, maps, and diagrams—help you visualize people, places, things, and ideas.

As you read the science article that follows, look for these text features and notice what you learn from them. Use two-column notes, such as the ones started here, to record your ideas.

Text Feature	What I Learn or Infer
Title and art: "Stars with Wings" with a picture of a firefly	The article will be about fireflies.
Introductory question:	
Subheadings: 1. A Beetle, Actually 2. 3.	 1. Fireflies are not bugs or flies. They are beetles. 2. 3.
Graphic aids:	

Stars with Wings

by Therese Ciesinski

Who needs summer fireworks when you have a backyard display of lightning bugs? **A**

Nature holds many wondrous sights, but few are as magical or close to home as a backyard busy with the luminous meanderings of fireflies. On sultry July evenings, adults ease back in lawn chairs while children race about and capture the pulsating glow of these lightning bugs in a glass jar. "I wonder how many amateur entomologists[1] first became interested in science and insects as the result of collecting fireflies," muses Greg Hoover, an entomologist at Pennsylvania State University in State College, Pennsylvania. Hoover, one of the folks who helped the firefly species Photuris *pennsylvanica* (illustrated here) become the official insect of Pennsylvania, remembers fly-fishing one evening and watching fireflies arise from the woods and reeds along the water's edge. "It was really neat. It looked like the New York City skyline at night," he recalls. Call them fireflies or lightning bugs, these marvelous insects are more than just aesthetic wonders. They're also good for the garden, consuming slugs and other critters who hunger for your vegetables.

- **A Beetle, Actually** **B**

  Neither bug nor fly, a firefly is a soft-bodied beetle belonging to the family Lampyridae, Latin for "shining fire." There are 124 species in North America, mostly in the eastern states and provinces. Lightning bugs are usually brown or black with light-colored markings and grow about an inch in length.

1. **entomologists:** scientists who specialize in the study of insects.

FOCUS ON FORM

A **science article** is a short piece of nonfiction writing on a scientific subject. The **author's purpose** for writing a science article is usually to inform or explain. Science articles often use **text features** to present information clearly.

A USE TEXT FEATURES

What do you learn from the question between the title and first line of this article? Add this information to your chart.

B USE TEXT FEATURES

Preview the rest of the article to identify the other **subheadings** in it. Write these on your chart. Then, as you read the article, jot down what you learn from the text that follows each subheading.

- **Light My Fire**
  A firefly lights up because of *bioluminescence,* a natural glow caused by the chemical reaction of oxygen and *luciferin* and *luciferase,* two substances in the insect's abdomen. Cells within the abdomen reflect and intensify the light. Some frogs love the bitter taste of lightning bugs and ingest so many that they begin to glow themselves.
- **Cool Light**
  A glowing firefly held in the hand won't burn its captor, as the light is "cold." Bioluminescence is 100 percent efficient, giving off no heat. A typical lightbulb, by contrast, emits 10 percent of its energy as light and 90 percent as heat. . . .
- **Hungry for Slugs**
  Juvenile lightning bugs are beneficial insects. The larvae[2] dine on snails, slugs, and aphids.[3]. . . At adulthood, some species don't eat at all; others eat only pollen and nectar.
- **Grounded**
  The light-show portion of a firefly's life—about 3 to 8 weeks—is only a small span of its existence. The life cycle begins when females lay eggs on swampy terrain. The larvae—nicknamed *glowworms* because they give off a faint light—hatch in late summer. After feeding for a few weeks, they burrow underground to escape the winter cold. Emerging in spring, the glowworms feed and later seal themselves within a cell of soil. After 2 weeks they emerge as adult, air-worthy lightning bugs.
- **Time to Shine**
  Lightning bugs are most active in July and August. The light show begins at dusk and usually ends around midnight. In the daytime, you'll find fireflies clinging to tree trunks and branches. "Most people see them in the day but don't realize what they are," says Hoover. "Fireflies like to hang out in crevices in tree bark."
- **Water Lovers**
  Drought and the loss of wetlands impact firefly populations. The beetles need soggy places with low vegetation to breed and thrive. "Soil moisture determines the abundance of fireflies in any given year," Hoover says. "Gardeners may notice a decrease in the amount of fireflies after a drought." **C**

C SCIENCE ARTICLE
What do you think the **author's purpose** was for writing this article?

2. **larvae** (lär′vē): insects at a stage during which they are newly hatched and often wormlike.
3. **aphids** (ā′fĭdz): small, soft-bodied insects of the family Aphididae that have mouthparts specially adapted for feeding on sap from plants.

Comprehension

1. **Recall** What causes fireflies to light up?
2. **Clarify** Why is neither *firefly* nor *lightning bug* an accurate name?

Critical Analysis

3. **Identify Characteristics of a Science Article** What are three characteristics of a science article? Give an example of each one from "Stars with Wings."
4. **Analyze Text Features** Review the chart you completed while reading this science article. What did you learn from the text features? Choose one type of text feature and explain how it was useful to you.

Read for Information: Connect Nonfiction and Poetry

WRITING PROMPT

When poets write about the natural world in their poems, they sometimes relate scientifically accurate details. However, poets might also decide to use imaginative details to create images and express ideas that get at a less literal truth. Explain which poem, "Fireflies" or "Fireflies in the Garden," uses more accurate details.

To answer this prompt, follow these steps:

1. Reread "Fireflies" and "Fireflies in the Garden." Note which lines appear to relate scientifically accurate details.
2. Review "Stars with Wings" and your notes on the article to find out whether the details are accurate. Note passages from the article that support or contradict the lines from the poems.
3. Write a paragraph explaining which poem is more accurate and a paragraph explaining which poem takes more liberties with the facts. Use quotations from the poems as well as the article to support your explanation.

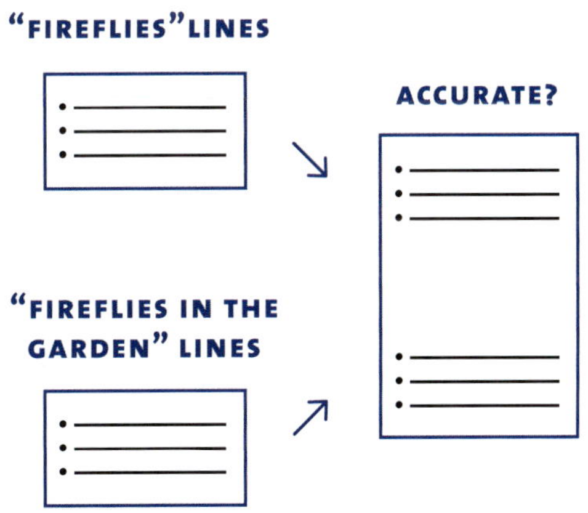

ALABAMA STANDARDS

READING STANDARDS

1.a Distinguishing factual from fictional materials

5 Use textual elements to gain information

Jabberwocky
Poem by Lewis Carroll

Sarah Cynthia Sylvia Stout Would Not Take the Garbage Out
Poem by Shel Silverstein

Two Limericks
Poems by Edward Lear

When does NONSENSE *make sense?*

ALABAMA STANDARDS

READING STANDARDS
1.d Applying self-monitoring strategies
3 Distinguish among subgenres based on characteristics

KEY IDEA Is there a strong feeling that you just can't put into words or a hilarious sight that is impossible to describe? What if you could invent a new word that would capture the idea exactly? A **nonsense** word, like some of those used in the poems that follow, might be just what you need.

BRAINSTORM With a partner, think of something you've never been able to describe clearly. It might be the bouncy movement a squirrel uses when it hops along a fence or the emotion you feel when a bully gets suspended. Invent a nonsense word that captures the idea perfectly, and then write a sentence that uses that word. Share your sentence with the rest of the class, and see if others can guess what it means.

"Ommymay, why do we alktay so unnyfay?"

© Shannon Burns/www.CartoonStock.com

POETIC FORM: HUMOROUS POETRY

The selections you are about to read are examples of **humorous poetry.** This type of poetry is often written for young people and may contain the following:

- sound devices that make the poems fun to read aloud
- descriptions that are exaggerated for comic effect
- elements of fantasy that sweep readers into another world

LITERARY ANALYSIS: SOUND DEVICES

Poets use **sound devices** to make their poems both musical and memorable. As you read these poems, be on the lookout for the following sound devices:

- **Rhyme** is the repetition of the sounds at the end of words. (*baloney* and *macaroni*)
- **Repetition** is the use of a word or phrase more than once.
- **Onomatopoeia** is the use of words that sound like their meanings. (*buzz, whisper, squish*)
- **Alliteration** is the repetition of consonant sounds at the beginning of words. (*twenty tame tigers*)

Think about what these devices add to the poems.

READING STRATEGY: MONITOR

As you read these humorous poems, pause regularly to check, or **monitor,** how well you are understanding them.

- Try rereading confusing lines silently or aloud and discussing your ideas with classmates.
- If you get stuck on an unfamiliar or made-up word, use **context clues,** or information in the surrounding lines, to help you guess the word's meaning.
- As you read each poem, use a chart like the one shown to record notes about language or ideas you clarify.

"Jabberwocky"	
Lines from Poem	*My Notes*
"'Twas brillig, and the slithy toves . . ." (line 1)	*"Brillig" might describe a time of day or the weather. "Slithy" reminds me of "slimy." "Toves" sounds like "toads".*

Author Online

Lewis Carroll: Math Magician Lewis Carroll was an Oxford University mathematician when he began making up children's stories. Before Carroll published his books *Alice's Adventures in Wonderland* and *Through the Looking Glass,* people believed children's books should instruct, not entertain. Carroll, however, offers readers pure delight.

Lewis Carroll
1832–1898

Shel Silverstein: Cartoonist and Poet Shel Silverstein began his artistic career as a child. "I would much rather have been a good baseball player," he says. "But I couldn't play ball. . . . So I started to draw and write."

Shel Silverstein
1932–1999

Edward Lear: Limerick Master The limerick is a type of poem that first appeared in England in the mid-1700s. Edward Lear became a master of the form and helped make limericks popular.

Edward Lear
1812–1888

MORE ABOUT THE AUTHOR
For more on these poets, visit the **Literature Center** at **ClassZone.com.**

JABBERWOCKY

LEWIS CARROLL

'Twas brillig, and the slithy toves
Did gyre[1] and gimble in the wabe:
All mimsy were the borogoves,
And the mome raths outgrabe.

"Beware the Jabberwock, my son!
The jaws that bite, the claws that catch! **A**
Beware the Jubjub bird, and shun
The frumious Bandersnatch!"

He took his vorpal sword in hand:
Long time the manxome foe he sought—
So rested he by the Tumtum tree,
And stood awhile in thought.

And, as in uffish thought he stood,
The Jabberwock, with eyes of flame,
Came whiffling through the tulgey wood,
And burbled as it came! **B**

One, two! One, two! And through and through
The vorpal blade went snicker-snack!
He left it dead, and with its head
He went galumphing back.

"And hast thou slain the Jabberwock?
Come to my arms, my beamish boy!
O frabjous day! Callooh! Callay!"
He chortled in his joy.

'Twas brillig, and the slithy toves
Did gyre and gimble in the wabe:
All mimsy were the borogoves,
And the mome raths outgrabe.

A MONITOR
What do lines 5–6 tell you about the Jabberwock? Using **context clues,** explain what you think a Jabberwock is.

B SOUND DEVICES
Which word in line 16 is an example of **onomatopoeia?** Say the word aloud.

ANALYZE VISUALS
What three **adjectives** best describe the beast on page 595?

1. **gyre** (jīr): whirl.

Dragon, Greg Spalenka. © Greg Spalenka.

Sarah Cynthia Sylvia Stout Would Not Take the Garbage Out

Shel Silverstein

Sarah Cynthia Sylvia Stout
Would not take the garbage out!
She'd scour the pots and scrape the pans,
Candy the yams and spice the hams,
And though her daddy would scream and shout,
She simply would not take the garbage out.
And so it piled up to the ceilings:
Coffee grounds, potato peelings,
Brown bananas, rotten peas,
Chunks of sour cottage cheese. **C**
It filled the can, it covered the floor,
It cracked the window and blocked the door

C SOUND DEVICES
Find two examples of **alliteration** in lines 1–10. What do you think the alliteration adds to this disgusting description?

With bacon rinds and chicken bones,
Drippy ends of ice cream cones,
Prune pits, peach pits, orange peel,
Gloppy glumps of cold oatmeal,
Pizza crusts and withered greens,
Soggy beans and tangerines,
Crusts of black burned buttered toast,
Gristly bits of beefy roasts . . .
The garbage rolled on down the hall,
It raised the roof, it broke the wall . . .
Greasy napkins, cookie crumbs,
Globs of gooey bubble gum,
Cellophane from green baloney,
Rubbery blubbery macaroni,
Peanut butter, caked and dry,
Curdled milk and crusts of pie,
Moldy melons, dried-up mustard,
Eggshells mixed with lemon custard,
Cold french fries and rancid meat,
Yellow lumps of Cream of Wheat. **D**
At last the garbage reached so high
That finally it touched the sky.
And all the neighbors moved away,
And none of her friends would come to play.
And finally Sarah Cynthia Stout said,
"OK, I'll take the garbage out!" **E**
But then, of course, it was too late . . .
The garbage reached across the state,
From New York to the Golden Gate.
And there, in the garbage she did hate,
Poor Sarah met an awful fate,
That I cannot right now relate
Because the hour is much too late.
But children, remember Sarah Stout
And always take the garbage out!

D HUMOROUS POETRY
Silverstein lists 33 types of garbage in this poem. How does this add to the humor of the poem?

E MONITOR
Reread lines 33–38. Why does Sarah finally take the garbage out?

TWO LIMERICKS

EDWARD LEAR

Old Man. Illustration by Alberto Ruggieri.

There was an old man with a light,
Who was dressed in a garment of white;
He held a small candle,
With never a handle,
And danced all the merry long night.

There was an old man who made bold,
To affirm[1] that the weather was cold;
So he ran up and down,
In his grandmother's gown,
Which was woollen, and not very old. F

F SOUND DEVICES
All true limericks have the same **rhyme scheme,** or pattern of rhyming words. What is the pattern?

1. **affirm** (ə-fûrm'): to declare or prove true.

ALABAMA STANDARDS

READING STANDARD
1.d Applying self-monitoring strategies

Comprehension

1. **Recall** How does the Jabberwock die?
2. **Recall** What happens when Sarah finally agrees to take the garbage out?
3. **Recall** In the second limerick, why does the old man run around in his "grandmother's gown"?

Literary Analysis

4. **Monitor** Review the information you recorded as you read "Jabberwocky." Does *frabjous* (line 23) mean "good" or "bad"? How can you tell?
5. **Identify Sensory Details** Silverstein uses sensory details—details that appeal to the five senses—to make you see, smell, and even feel the heaping mass of foul garbage in Sarah's house. Find four sensory details in the poem and explain which sense each appeals to.
6. **Analyze a Limerick** Limericks usually have a specific **rhythm,** or pattern of stressed and unstressed syllables. Reread the first limerick aloud. How many stressed syllables are in each line? Now read the second limerick. How similar is the rhythm to that in the first poem?
7. **Analyze Sound Devices** Reread "Sarah Cynthia Sylvia Stout Would Not Take the Garbage Out." As you read, look for several examples of rhyme, repetition, onomatopoeia, and alliteration. Create a chart like the one shown to record what you find. In your opinion which device most adds to the humor of the piece?

Sound Devices in "Sarah Cynthia . . ."			
Rhyme	Repetition	Onomatopoeia	Alliteration
"Rubbery blubbery" (line 26)			

8. **Evaluate Humorous Poetry** Pick the poem you thought was funniest. Review the characteristics of humorous poetry listed on page 593. Which characteristics helped to make your favorite poem so funny? Give examples to support your answer.

Extension and Challenge

9. **Big Question Activity** Try writing your own **nonsense** poem. Think back to the activity on page 592 and the nonsense word you made up. Write a short, funny poem that explains what your word means.
10. **Inquiry and Research** The word *chortle* didn't exist until Carroll included it in "Jabberwocky." Using a dictionary or the Internet, find this word's definition. Do you think this former nonsense word makes sense?

Comparing Mood

The Delight Song of Tsoai-Talee

Poem by N. Scott Momaday

Four Skinny Trees

Vignette by Sandra Cisneros

How would you DESCRIBE yourself?

ALABAMA STANDARDS

READING & LIT STANDARDS
2.a Determining mood
8 Compare selections and their characteristics

KEY IDEA If someone were to ask you to describe yourself, what would you say? Often, we describe ourselves in **comparison** to something or someone. In the selections you're about to read, people compare themselves to the natural world.

WEB IT Comparing yourself to an element in nature, such as a blooming sunflower or a powerful tiger, can convey a vivid sense of who you are. Create a word web like the one shown. In it show what in nature you would compare yourself to, and why.

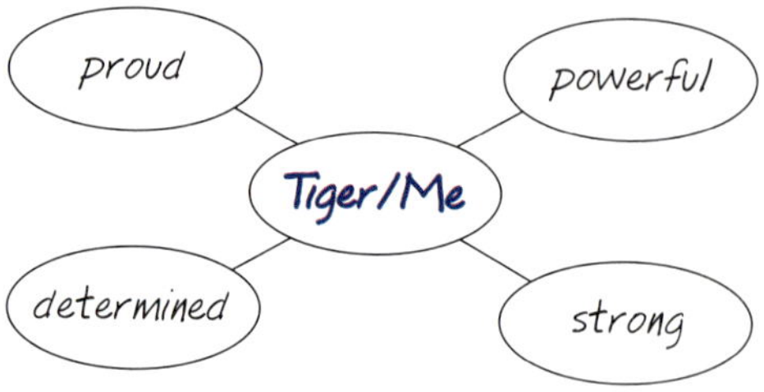

LITERARY ANALYSIS: MOOD AND FIGURATIVE LANGUAGE

Have you ever described a story with a word like *mysterious, creepy, joyful,* or *cheerful?* Then you've described the **mood,** or the feeling that a writer creates for the reader. One way writers create mood is through **figurative language,** which is language used in imaginative ways to express ideas that are not literally true.

- A **metaphor** is a comparison between two unlike things. It does not use the word *like* or *as.* *(I am an antelope.)*
- **Personification** is a comparison that gives human qualities to an object, animal, or idea. *(My shoes punished the pavement.)*

In "The Delight Song of Tsoai-Talee," N. Scott Momaday uses metaphors; in "Four Skinny Trees," Sandra Cisneros uses personification. As you read, notice how the figurative language helps to set the mood of each piece.

Review: **Repetition**

READING STRATEGY: SET A PURPOSE FOR READING

Every time you read something, you read with a purpose. Sometimes that purpose might be just to have fun. Other times it might be to learn specific information.

In this lesson, your **purpose for reading** is to compare the moods of two pieces. To help you do this, look closely at the figurative language in each poem.

After you read "The Delight Song of Tsoai-Talee" and "Four Skinny Trees," read the selections again. You will then be asked to fill in a chart like the one shown.

Figurative Language in "The Delight Song of Tsoai-Talee" (metaphors)	*Figurative Language in "Four Skinny Trees"* (personification)
• • •	• • •
↓	↓
Mood:	*Mood:*

Author Online

N. Scott Momaday: Rock Tree Boy

N. Scott Momaday
born 1934

Pulitzer Prize–winning poet N. Scott Momaday was born to Kiowa and Cherokee parents. He spent his childhood on Native American reservations throughout the Southwest. Momaday's Kiowa name, Tsoai-Talee, means "Rock Tree Boy" and refers to an 865-foot volcanic butte that is sacred to the Kiowa people.

Sandra Cisneros: Writer on the Move

Sandra Cisneros
born 1954

Sandra Cisneros grew up as the only daughter in a large Mexican-American family. The family frequently moved back and forth between the United States and Mexico. "I didn't like school because we moved so much," she says. Despite her awkwardness in class, Cisneros read and wrote a great deal on her own. Around the time she published her first novel, *The House on Mango Street,* she was also teaching and counseling high-school dropouts. The stories her students told her about their lives greatly influenced her writing.

MORE ABOUT THE AUTHOR
For more on N. Scott Momaday and Sandra Cisneros, visit the **Literature Center** at **ClassZone.com.**

The Delight Song of Tsoai-talee

N. Scott Momaday

I am a feather on the bright sky
I am the blue horse that runs in the plain
I am the fish that rolls, shining, in the water
I am the shadow that follows a child
I am the evening light, the lustre of meadows
I am an eagle playing with the wind (A)
I am a cluster of bright beads
I am the farthest star
I am the cold of the dawn
I am the roaring of the rain
I am the glitter on the crust of the snow
I am the long track of the moon in a lake
I am a flame of four colors
I am a deer standing away in the dusk
I am a field of sumac and the pomme blanche[1]
I am an angle of geese in the winter sky
I am the hunger of a young wolf
I am the whole dream of these things

You see, I am alive, I am alive
I stand in good relation to the earth
I stand in good relation to the gods
I stand in good relation to all that is beautiful
I stand in good relation to the daughter of Tsen-tainte[2]
You see, I am alive, I am alive (B)

---

1. **pomme blanche** (pôm bläNsh): a plant with heavy edible roots, also known as breadroot.
2. **Tsen-tainte:** a heroic and respected 19th-century Kiowa chief known for his bold raids on both white and Native American settlements.

ANALYZE VISUALS
List the **images** you see in this collage. Which images portray aspects of nature?

(A) MOOD AND FIGURATIVE LANGUAGE
Reread lines 1–6. Note the first several things that the poet compares himself to. What mood do these **metaphors** create?

(B) REPETITION
Reread lines 19–24. Notice the **repetition** of certain phrases, such as "I stand" and "I am alive." What effect does this repetition create?

Details of *Four Directions* (1995), Jaune Quick-to-See Smith. Lithograph with linocut collage, 44.5″ × 30″. Courtesy The Lawrence Lithography Workshop. © Jaune Quick-to-See Smith.

Camassia quamash
Camas
DO NOT MICROWAVE

Four Skinny Trees

Sandra Cisneros

They are the only ones who understand me. I am the only one who understands them. Four skinny trees with skinny necks and pointy elbows like mine. Four who do not belong here but are here. Four raggedy excuses planted by the city. From our room we can hear them, but Nenny just sleeps and doesn't appreciate these things.

Their strength is secret. They send ferocious roots beneath the ground. They grow up and they grow down and grab the earth between their hairy toes and bite the sky with violent teeth and never quit their anger. This is how they keep. C

Let one forget his reason for being, they'd all droop like tulips in a glass, each with their arms around the other. Keep, keep, keep, trees say when I sleep. They teach.

When I am too sad and too skinny to keep keeping, when I am a tiny thing against so many bricks, then it is I look at trees. When there is nothing left to look at on this street. Four who grew despite concrete. Four who reach and do not forget to reach. Four whose only reason is to be and be. ~ D

C MOOD AND FIGURATIVE LANGUAGE
Reread lines 1–9. What human qualities do the trees have? What emotion is **personified?**

D MOOD AND FIGURATIVE LANGUAGE
Reread lines 13–17. What words and phrases stand out to you? Consider the **mood** and meaning these words and phrases create.

ANALYZE VISUALS
What feeling or emotion do the colors of this image suggest to you?

Detail of *Houses, Trees, Bike,* Anne Lavina Dimeur.
© Anne Lavina Dimeur/Images.com.

After Reading

Comprehension

1. **Recall** In "The Delight Song of Tsoai-Talee," what animals does Tsoai-Talee compare himself to?
2. **Recall** In "Four Skinny Trees," when does the narrator look at the trees?
3. **Represent** What does the narrator's street look like? Make a sketch illustrating the scene.

ALABAMA STANDARDS

READING STANDARD
8 Compare selections and their characteristics

Literary Analysis

4. **Analyze Figurative Language** In "The Delight Song of Tsoai-Talee," what three **metaphors** are especially vivid or imaginative? Explain the feeling you think each metaphor creates.
5. **Interpret Meaning** Reread "The Delight Song of Tsoai-Talee," N. Scott Momaday's biography on page 601, and footnote 2 on page 602. On the basis of this information, how do you interpret the meaning of lines 23–24?
6. **Make Inferences** In "Four Skinny Trees," which details about the trees could also be used to describe the narrator? Explain why the narrator might respond to the trees as she does.
7. **Analyze Mood** Is the overall mood of "Four Skinny Trees" sad, determined, hopeful, or something in between? Explain your opinion by citing three examples of **personification** that contribute to the mood.

Comparing Mood

Now that you've read both selections and answered some questions about them, fill in a chart like the one shown.

Figurative Language in "The Delight Song of Tsoai-Talee" (*metaphors*)	*Figurative Language in "Four Skinny Trees"* (*personification*)
• *"I am a feather on the bright sky"* • •	• • •
↓	↓
Mood: *joyful*	*Mood:*

Writing for Assessment

1. READ THE PROMPT

In writing assessments, you will often be asked to explore how writers use language to create a mood. In this essay, you will focus on figurative language.

PROMPT

The poem "Tsoai-Talee" and the vignette "Four Skinny Trees" convey two very different moods. In four or five paragraphs, contrast the moods and explore how each author uses figurative language to help create that feeling. Support your ideas with details from both selections.

STRATEGY

1. I have to describe the ***feeling*** each selection creates.
2. I need to tell the similarities and differences between the feelings.
3. I should ***give examples*** of the ***figurative language*** that create the different moods.

2. PLAN YOUR WRITING

Referring to your chart, note the figurative language and mood you identified for each selection. Then follow these steps.

- Write a statement that identifies the moods and describes the kinds of figurative language used to create each one.
- Use your chart to collect evidence to support your statement.
- Decide on a logical way to present your ideas, then make an outline. One example of how you might organize your paragraphs is shown here.

I. Introduction
II. Mood of poem and language that creates mood
III. Mood and language of vignette and how it compares to poem
IV. Conclusion

3. DRAFT YOUR RESPONSE

Introduction Introduce the selections and tell why you are comparing them. Include your statement of your main idea.

Body If you're using an outline similar to the one shown, explain how the language of the first selection creates a specific mood. Then start a new paragraph by telling how the second selection is similar or different.

Conclusion Leave your reader with a final thought about the way each author uses figurative language to create a specific mood.

Revision Make sure that the paragraphs after your introduction support the main idea you stated. If they don't, make changes to one or the other.

Writing Workshop

Personal Response to a Poem

When you respond to a poem, you think about its meaning, but your focus is personal. You discuss your own reactions, feelings, or experiences as well as the language and style of the poem. The **Writer's Road Map** will show you how.

WRITER'S ROAD MAP

Personal Response to a Poem

WRITING PROMPT 1

Writing from Literature Choose a poem that caused strong feelings in you. Write a personal response that explains why the poem made you feel the way you did. Briefly describe the poem so that readers unfamiliar with it can understand your response.

Poems to Consider

- "The Highwayman"
- "Sarah Cynthia Sylvia Stout Would Not Take the Garbage Out"

WRITING PROMPT 2

Writing for the Real World Write an essay for a music magazine that describes your response to a song or a type of music. Give readers specific examples to help them understand why the song or type of music is important to you.

Types of Music to Explore

- rap or hip-hop
- rock
- country

WRITING TOOLS
For prewriting, revision, and editing tools, visit the **Writing Center** at **ClassZone.com.**

KEY TRAITS

1. *IDEAS*

- Clearly presents an **overall response** to the work
- Supports key points with **details and quotations**

2. *ORGANIZATION*

- Identifies the title and author of the work in the **introduction**
- Gives enough **information about the work** for readers to understand the response
- Includes **transitional words and phrases**
- Summarizes the response in a **conclusion**

3. *VOICE*

- **Tone** is honest and engaging

4. *WORD CHOICE*

- Uses **literary terms** when describing the work

5. *SENTENCE FLUENCY*

- Varies **sentence beginnings**

6. *CONVENTIONS*

- Uses **correct grammar, spelling, and punctuation**

WRITING/LANGUAGE STANDARD
9 Compose in expository mode

Part 1: Analyze a Student Model

Online INTERACTIVE MODEL CLASSZONE.COM

Kenetha Smithson
Lewiston Middle School

"Sleeping in the Forest"

Some people can't live for even a single night without the Internet or TV. Camping is definitely not for them. For me, though, nothing beats a night outside under the stars. That's why I knew what Mary Oliver was talking about when I read "Sleeping in the Forest." When I go camping, I have some of the same feelings and experiences as the speaker in the poem, even though I don't talk about them in the same way.

Mary Oliver begins her poem by showing the speaker already on the ground, or earth, in the forest. She writes, "I thought the earth / remembered me, she / took me back so tenderly." To Oliver, the earth is a woman with "dark skirts" and pockets full of moss and seeds. Using personification, which means giving human qualities to something that isn't human, Oliver makes the earth seem like an old friend. When I sleep out on the ground, it sometimes feels as if I belong there. Familiar and soft, the earth does feel like a friend.

The speaker says that while sleeping in the forest, there is "nothing / between me and the white fire of the stars / but my thoughts." That's how it is when I'm out in the wilderness. I can think better because there are no interruptions from other people and no music or TVs. The speaker uses the simile "light as moths" to show how thoughts float away. This tells exactly how my own thoughts seem to float away or take off into the air because I feel so calm and peaceful.

KEY TRAITS IN ACTION

Introduction identifies the title and author and clearly presents an **overall response** to the poem.

Gives **information about the work** so readers can understand the response. Varied **sentence beginnings** add sophistication.

Uses **literary terms** when describing the work. A simile is a comparison that uses *like* or *as*.

Another great thing about camping is how quiet it is. In the poem, the speaker hears "the small kingdoms breathing / around me." I believe the speaker is describing all of the new worlds that a camper experiences. Campers hear the little sounds that are hard to hear indoors, such as rustling leaves and hooting owls—"the birds / who do their work in the darkness."

In the last lines of the poem, I think the speaker is talking about dreams or a really deep, great sleep. The poem mentions vanishing "into something better." Maybe the "something better" is a good dream. When I'm camping, I think I sleep more deeply in the fresh air. In the morning, I remember many dreams. Sleeping in the forest is like vanishing into a better place.

I believe that people who don't like camping should read this poem. It can help them understand what it feels like to be outside in nature at night. The poem might even convince some people to go camping. Then maybe they could also sleep "as never before," as Oliver says, and get rid of their worries for a little while. Maybe they could even vanish "into something better."

2

Transitional phrase helps the reader understand how the response is organized.

Details and quotations explain and support the response.

The writer's **tone** is straightforward and thoughtful throughout the essay.

The writer summarizes the response in a satisfying **conclusion.**

WRITING/LANGUAGE STANDARD
9.a Using transitional words and phrases

Part 2: Apply the Writing Process

PREWRITING

What Should I Do?	What Does It Look Like?
1. Create a reading log. Make a two-column chart. On one side, list words and phrases from the work that caught your attention. On the other side, write your reactions, comments, or questions. When you are finished, circle the responses that seem most important to you.	See reading log below.
2. Write down your overall response. Use your circled comments and questions to develop a sentence or two that explains how the work made you feel and why it made you feel that way. **TIP** **Your response statement doesn't have to be perfect. You can change it when you draft and revise.**	***Working Response:*** *I know what Mary Oliver is saying in her poem because I know what it's like to sleep on the ground and dream.*
3. Look for more support. Find more words and phrases that affected your response. Examine the poem for images that helped you see or hear what the poet is describing, unusual word choices, or phrases that made you smile or wonder.	***Images:*** *"nothing / between me and the white fire of the stars / but my thoughts": It's so quiet in the forest—no TVs, no music.* *"small kingdoms": I hear the insects and little animals, and I know there are other worlds out there.*

Reading log for step 1:

Words/Phrases	*My Response*
"she / took me back"	*I belong there. The earth is like a friend that takes me back.*
sleep like "a stone"	*When I go camping, I sleep really well.*
"floated / light as moths"	*What does this mean?*
"something better"	*Sleep is different outside. It's better & deeper, & I have good dreams.*

DRAFTING

What Should I Do?	What Does It Look Like?
1. Develop an informal outline. Making an outline can help you organize your ideas. This writer organized her response from the beginning to the end of the poem. You can organize your response from the most important idea to the least important idea. You can also briefly summarize the work and then explain your reaction to it.	*I. Lines 1–5* *A. The earth "took me back so tenderly."* *B. The earth seems like an old friend to me, too.* *II. Lines 5–11* *A. The speaker describes "the white fire of the stars."* *B. I think the wilderness is calm, peaceful, and beautiful.* *III. Lines 10–14* *A. The speaker hears "small kingdoms breathing."* *B. I hear sounds of nature when camping.* *IV. Lines 14–18* *A. The speaker vanishes "into something better."* *B. I can sleep well in the fresh air.*
2. Make a fresh beginning! Draw your reader in by starting out with a surprising or dramatic statement, an interesting or startling fact, a little bit of humor, or a question.	**A dramatic statement** *Some people can't live for even a single night without the Internet or TV. Camping is definitely not for them.* **A question** *Have you ever slept under the stars?*
3. Clearly explain your response. Don't just say, "I liked this" or "I liked that." Explain your responses. The writer of this essay described the memories the poem triggered in her. **TIP Before you revise, look back at the key traits on page 608 and at the rubric and peer-reader questions on page 614.**	*Maybe the "something better" is a good dream.* — Writer's response *When I'm camping, I think I sleep more deeply in the fresh air. In the morning, I remember many dreams. Sleeping in the forest is like vanishing into a better place.* — Reasons for response

REVISING AND EDITING

What Should I Do?	What Does It Look Like?
1. Be sure to give enough information. • Can your reader understand your reaction to the work? Ask a peer reader to underline parts of your response that lack background information. • Add **details and quotations** that tell about the work. **See page 614:** Ask a Peer Reader	The speaker hears ~~small kingdoms~~ "the breathing / around me." I believe the speaker is describing all of the new worlds that a camper experiences. Campers hear the little sounds that are hard to hear indoors, such as rustling leaves and hooting owls.
2. Be precise: use literary terms. • Circle literary terms, such as *personification, simile,* and *speaker.* • If you have few or no circles, revise to make your response **more specific.**	Using personification, which means giving human qualities to something that isn't human, Oliver makes the earth seem ~~The earth seems~~ like an old friend.
3. Use different sentence beginnings. • Draw a box around words you have repeated at the beginnings of sentences. • Combine, break up, or rewrite these sentences to **change the way they start.**	In ~~I think~~ the last two lines of the poem, I think the speaker is talking ~~talk~~ about dreams or a really deep, great sleep. The poem mentions ~~I think that's what~~ vanishing "into something better." ~~means. I think~~ Maybe the "something better" is a good dream.
4. Show how your response is organized. • Highlight transitional words, phrases, or sentences in your response. • If you have few or no highlights, add **transitions.** These help your reader by specifying which part of the poem you are discussing or by explaining that you are introducing a new idea.	Mary Oliver ~~shows~~ begins her poem by showing the speaker already on the ground . . . — *Tells which part of the poem* Another great thing about camping is how quiet it is. In the poem, the speaker hears . . . — *Introduces new idea*

Preparing to Publish

Personal Response to a Poem

Apply the Rubric

A strong personal response to a poem . . .

- ☑ begins by stating the title, the author, and an overall response
- ☑ contains enough background information for the reader to follow the response
- ☑ has an honest and consistent tone
- ☑ is clearly organized and includes transitions
- ☑ quotes words and phrases from the poem and fully explains the writer's reaction to them
- ☑ includes literary terms to describe the work
- ☑ varies sentence beginnings to make ideas flow smoothly
- ☑ has a conclusion that summarizes the response

Ask a Peer Reader

- Do parts of my response need more background information?
- How could I make my overall response to the poem clearer?
- Where do I need more quotations?

Check Your Grammar

- Avoid dangling modifiers. Make sure that every modifier you use relates to a word in the sentence.

  This phrase dangles. The sentence is missing the word that the phrase should modify.

  Using personification, the earth seems like an old friend.

  This sentence tells who is using personification.

  Using personification, Oliver makes the earth seem like an old friend.

  See page R59: Dangling Modifiers

- Correct fragments—groups of words that are punctuated like sentences but are missing a subject, are missing a predicate, or fail to express complete thought.

  ~~A familiar feeling, like an old friend.~~
  It feels familiar, like an old friend.

  See page R64: Correcting Fragments

Writing Online

PUBLISHING OPTIONS
For publishing options, visit the **Writing Center** at **ClassZone.com.**

ASSESSMENT PREPARATION
For writing and grammar assessment practice, go to the **Assessment Center** at **ClassZone.com.**

COMMUNICATION STANDARD
15 Demonstrate listening skills

SPEAKING AND LISTENING

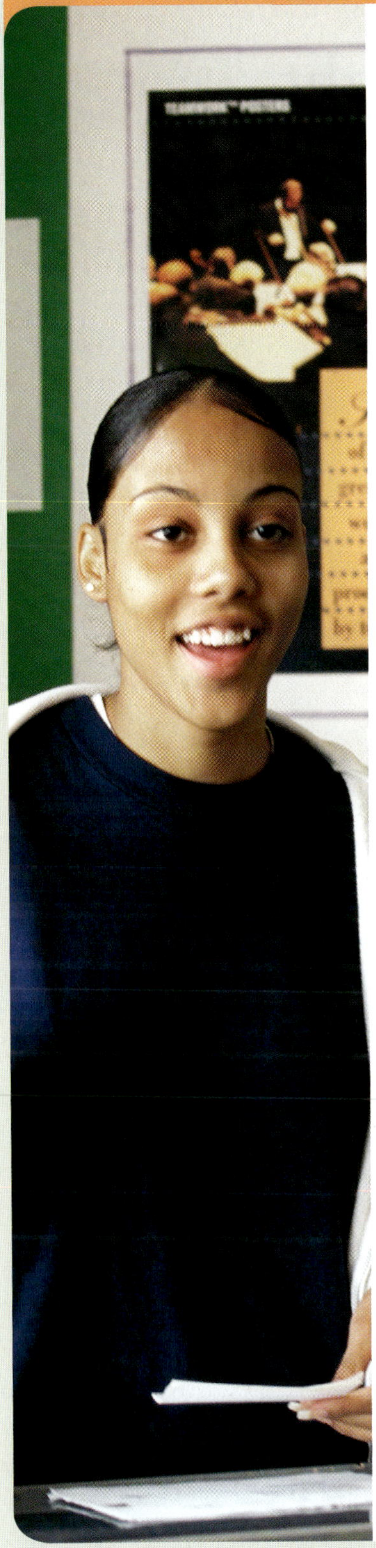

Oral Interpretation of a Poem

Now that you've written about a poem in your own voice, you can perform one in your own voice too.

Planning the Oral Interpretation

1. **Read the poem aloud.** Listen for places to shout or whisper, mourn or celebrate. Decide when the poem should race or crawl. Think about where you can add body language.
2. **Create your own reading guide.** Use capital letters for words you want to say loudly. Underline words you want to say softly. Add slashes for pauses and hyphens to link words that you plan to run together. You might also try stretching out syllables. Add notes for gestures and facial expressions too.

I slept /
as NEVER before, / a stone / (never: shake head)
on the riverbed, /
nothing-between-me /
and the WHITE FIRE of the stars / (white fire: look up)
but my thoughts, /
and they FLOOOATED light as moths (floated: gently wave arm)

3. **Practice to make it perfect.** Read the poem aloud several times. Then practice your performance for a classmate. Get feedback, adjust, and practice some more.

Performing the Oral Interpretation

1. **Don't be nervous!** Instead, think like an actor and get into your performance. If you're nervous about your classmates' reactions, look just over the tops of their heads.
2. **Find out how you did.** Ask a few classmates for feedback on your performance. Were your volume, pacing, and gestures effective? Think about what you might do differently next time.

See page R80: Evaluate an Oral Interpretation

Assessment Practice

Reading Comprehension

ASSESS

The practice test items on the next few pages match skills listed on the Unit Goals page (page 541) and addressed throughout this unit. Taking this practice test will help you assess your knowledge of these skills and determine your readiness for the Unit Test.

REVIEW

After you take the practice test, your teacher can help you identify any skills you need to review.

- Imagery
- Figurative Language
- Sound Devices
- Make Inferences
- Connotation
- Sentence Types
- Active Voice

ASSESSMENT ONLINE

For more assessment practice and test-taking tips, go to the **Assessment Center** at **ClassZone.com.**

DIRECTIONS *Read these poems and answer the questions that follow.*

Ode to enchanted light

Pablo Neruda

Under the trees light
has dropped from the top of the sky,
light
like a green
latticework of branches,
shining
on every leaf,
drifting down like clean
white sand.

A cicada sends
its sawing song
high into the empty air.

The world is
a glass overflowing
with water.

Snow in the Suburbs

Thomas Hardy

Every branch big with it,
Bent every twig with it;
Every fork like a white web-foot;
Every street and pavement mute:
Some flakes have lost their way, and grope back upward, when
Meeting those meandering down they turn and descend again.
The palings are glued together like a wall,
And there is no waft of wind with the fleecy fall.

A sparrow enters the tree,
Whereon immediately
A snow-lump thrice his own slight size
Descends on him and showers his head and eyes,
And overturns him,
And near inurns him,
And lights on a nether twig, when its brush
Starts off a volley of other lodging lumps with a rush.

The steps are a blanched slope,
Up which, with feeble hope,
A black cat comes, wide-eyed and thin;
And we take him in.

GO ON

Comprehension

DIRECTIONS *Answer these questions about "Ode to enchanted light."*

1. The imagery in Neruda's poem appeals primarily to the senses of

A taste and sight

B touch and taste

C sight and hearing

D smell and touch

2. Which one of the following lines contains alliteration?

A "latticework of branches" (line 5)

B "drifting down like clean" (line 8)

C "high into the empty air" (line 12)

D "a glass overflowing" (line 14)

3. Which one of the following images is an example of a simile?

A "light / has dropped from the top of the sky" (lines 1–2)

B "light / like a green / latticework of branches" (lines 3–5)

C "its sawing song" (line 11)

D "The world is / a glass overflowing / with water." (lines 13–15)

4. The image of the light "drifting down like clean / white sand" appeals to the sense of

A hearing

B smell

C sight

D taste

5. Which type of figurative language does the author use in lines 13–15?

A simile

B metaphor

C personification

D onomatopoeia

6. The image in lines 13–15 suggests that the speaker is responding to the world with

A disappointment

B confusion

C wonder

D fear

DIRECTIONS *Answer these questions about "Snow in the Suburbs."*

7. The fork in the simile in line 3 represents

A a spider's web

B an eating utensil

C streets and pavements

D a snow-covered tree branch

8. In line 4, personification is used to create an image of a

A strong wind

B snow-covered tree

C beautiful snowdrift

D quiet setting

ARMT/ADAW SKILLS PRACTICE

9. The alliteration in line 8 emphasizes
   - A speed
   - B softness
   - C coldness
   - D danger

10. Which of the following is a simile that describes a fence covered with snow?
   - A "Every branch big with it" (line 1)
   - B "The palings are glued together like a wall" (line 7)
   - C "A snow-lump thrice his own slight size" (line 11)
   - D "its brush / Starts off a volley of other lodging lumps with a rush" (lines 15–16)

11. Which statement describes the pattern of rhyme in this poem?
   - A Only the first four lines rhyme.
   - B Every other line rhymes.
   - C Every pair of lines rhymes.
   - D Many lines do not rhyme.

12. Which expression is an example of personification?
   - A "Some flakes have lost their way" (line 5)
   - B "A sparrow enters the tree" (line 9)
   - C "The steps are a blanched slope (line 17)
   - D "A black cat comes, wide-eyed and thin" (line 19)

DIRECTIONS *Answer this question about both poems.*

13. The two poems suggest that natural elements such as light and snow can
   - A flood natural habitats
   - B destroy animals' food sources
   - C comfort people who are sad
   - D transform a landscape

Open-Ended

SHORT ANSWER *Write two or three sentences to answer each question.*

14. What can you infer that Neruda is saying about light in "Ode to enchanted light"? Select images from the poem to support your answer.

15. Identify the repetition in lines 13–14 of "Snow in the Suburbs." What is the effect of this repetition?

ESSAY *Write a short paragraph to answer this question.*

16. What inference can you make about each poet's response to nature in these poems? Support your answer with details from the poems.

GO ON

Vocabulary

DIRECTIONS *Use context clues and your knowledge of connotation to answer the following questions.*

1. The word *enchanted* in the title of Neruda's poem suggests that the light is
   - **A** brilliant
   - **B** sinister
   - **C** magical
   - **D** romantic

2. The word *latticework* in line 5 of "Ode to enchanted light" has a connotation of
   - **A** delicacy
   - **B** privacy
   - **C** sturdiness
   - **D** transparency

3. The word *sawing* in line 11 of "Ode to enchanted light" suggests a sound that is
   - **A** loud
   - **B** scratchy
   - **C** soothing
   - **D** musical

4. The word *mute* in line 4 of "Snow in the Suburbs" has a connotation of
   - **A** illness
   - **B** darkness
   - **C** stillness
   - **D** coldness

5. The word *grope* in line 5 of "Snow in the Suburbs" has a connotation of
   - **A** clumsiness
   - **B** certainty
   - **C** elegance
   - **D** aggression

6. The word *meandering* in line 6 of "Snow in the Suburbs" has a connotation of
   - **A** aimlessness
   - **B** orderliness
   - **C** hastiness
   - **D** rashness

7. The word *feeble* in line 18 of "Snow in the Suburbs" has a connotation of
   - **A** sadness
   - **B** oldness
   - **C** sickness
   - **D** weakness

ARMT/ADAW SKILLS PRACTICE

Writing & Grammar

DIRECTIONS *Read this passage and answer the questions that follow.*

> (1) The Declaration of Independence forever changed American history. (2) Did you know the colonists listed their complaints against King George in this important document? (3) Freedom from British rule was declared by them. (4) One year earlier, the colonists had tried to make peace with the king. (5) They outlined their specific pleas in a document known as the Olive Branch Petition. (6) The king's approval of this document was sought by Congress. (7) After he rejected the petition, the king declared the colonists rebels.

1. How might you revise sentence 2 to make it declarative?

A The colonists listed their complaints against King George in this important document.

B The colonists listed their complaints against King George in this important document!

C Read this important document to find out how the colonists listed their complaints against King George.

D Didn't the colonists list their complaints against King George in this important document?

2. Choose the correct way to rewrite sentence 3 by using the active voice.

A They declared freedom from British rule.

B Freedom from British rule was sought by the colonists.

C To gain freedom from British rule was desired by the colonists.

D Freedom from British rule was what was declared by them.

3. Choose the correct way to rewrite sentence 6 by using the active voice.

A Getting this document approved by the king was wanted by Congress.

B An attempt to get this document approved was made by Congress.

C Getting approval of this document by the king was attempted by Congress.

D Congress sought the king's approval of this document.

4. How might you revise sentence 7 to make it exclamatory?

A Did you know that after the king rejected the petition, he declared the colonists rebels?

B After he rejected the petition, the king declared the colonists rebels!

C The king rejected the petition and declared the colonists rebels.

D Find out how the king rejected the petition and declared the colonists rebels.

STOP

UNIT 5

More Great Reads

Ideas for Independent Reading

Which questions from Unit 5 made an impression on you? Continue exploring them with these books.

Why do we need memorials?

The Glory Field
by Walter Dean Myers
The Glory Field chronicles milestones in African-American history from the 1700s to the present day through five generations of the Lewis family. Each generation draws strength from the Glory Field, a hallowed plot of land that represents their cherished heritage.

Bull Run
by Paul Fleischman
In this story, characters memorialize the first battle of the Civil War from 16 different perspectives. Together they add an intimate dimension to our nation's bloodiest conflict.

The Monument
by Gary Paulsen
Can the artist behind a monument change you more than the monument itself? When an artist comes to design a war memorial in Rocky's small Kansas town, he becomes Rocky's mentor and opens her eyes to broader horizons.

Whom do you feel closest to?

Our Only May Amelia
by Jennifer L. Holm
Can time and place have an effect on the strength of family ties? You will enjoy reading 12-year-old May Amelia's diary as she gives a candid account of the joys and pains of pioneer life in the late 1800s.

Pink and Say
by Patricia Polacco
Patricia Polacco tells the story of her great-grandfather during the Civil War. Learn why the friendship of an Ohio farm boy and a freed slave has become a story retold through three generations.

Heaven
by Angela Johnson
When deception backfires, who gets hurt? Fourteen-year-old Marley lives in Heaven, Ohio—a perfect, loving community. Then she learns that her parents are not her real parents and that all her life she's lived with deception.

How would you describe yourself?

Rules of the Road
by Joan Bauer
What measurements could you use to describe your character? *Rules of the Road* follows the independent Jenna Boller as she learns what's important in life.

Buddy Love: Now on Video
by Ilene Cooper
When 13-year-old Buddy Love views his life through a camcorder lens, he gains insight into the lives of his family and friends and into his own character. To his delight, he finds his life is infinitely exciting.

The Crane Wife
by Odds Bodkin
Why do people describe themselves in a certain way, hoping to impress others? In this tale of a poor sail maker who saves the life of a beautiful white crane, greed overcomes virtue, and the sail maker must learn a harsh lesson.

UNIT 6

Sharing Our Stories

MYTHS, LEGENDS, AND TALES

UNIT 6 Share What You Know

What can STORIES teach us?

Many stories do more than simply entertain us. People often tell stories to explain something important or to share different approaches to common experiences. Stories can also express the cultural values of a group of people. Through sharing stories, one generation can teach its values, heritage, and traditions to the next generation.

ACTIVITY Are there any legendary figures in your family line? What stories get passed down from one generation to another or get repeated year after year? In a small group, discuss which family stories mean the most to you and your classmates. Consider the following questions:

- Who told you the story?
- What did you learn from the story?
- Have you told the story to anyone else?

Online LITERATURE CLASSZONE.COM

Literature and Reading Center
Writing Center
Vocabulary and Spelling Center

ALABAMA STANDARDS

Preview Unit Goals

LITERARY ANALYSIS
- Identify and analyze characteristics of myths, legends, folk tales, and tall tales
- Identify cultural values in myths and legends
- Identify and compare universal themes

READING
- Use reading strategies, including predicting, monitoring, and visualizing
- Identify cause-effect relationships and chronological order
- Compare reviewer's reaction to a book to one's own reaction

WRITING AND GRAMMAR
- Write a cause-and-effect essay
- Use correct sentence structure
- Identify simple and compound sentences
- Form complex sentences

SPEAKING, LISTENING, AND VIEWING
- Conduct an interview
- Make a formal presentation

VOCABULARY
- Understand and use homographs
- Understand the meaning of compound words

ACADEMIC VOCABULARY
- myth
- legend
- folk tale
- tall tale
- universal theme
- compound sentences
- complex sentences
- homograph

UNIT 6

Reader's Workshop

Myths, Legends, and Tales

Have you heard or read about the foolish grasshopper that refused to plan ahead, or about the legendary king named Arthur? From ancient Greece to medieval England, every culture has its own stories—myths, legends, and tales that have been handed down from one generation to the next. Part of an oral tradition, these tales continue to entertain and teach us hundreds of years after they were first told. By continuing to read, share, and listen to them, we carry on the tradition and keep the past alive.

ALABAMA STANDARDS

READING STANDARD
3 Distinguish among subgenres, such as myths and fables, based on characteristics

Part 1: Characteristics of Traditional Stories

Traditional stories may be short or long, inspiring or humorous. They might end with the characters learning a lesson or living "happily ever after." In this unit, you will be reading all types of stories, including the ones shown here.

TYPE OF TALE	CHARACTERISTICS
MYTH **A traditional story that was created to explain mysteries of the universe** 	• Often explains how something connected with humans or nature came to be • Reveals the consequences of both good and bad behavior • Features gods or other beings who have supernatural powers as well as certain flaws
LEGEND **A story passed down through many generations that is believed to be based on real people and events** 	• Tells about a hero or heroine who has unusual powers • Focuses on the hero's or heroine's struggle to defeat a powerful force • Highlights a positive quality or way of behaving
FABLE **A brief story that teaches a lesson, or moral, about human nature** 	• Usually includes animal characters that stand for specific human qualities, such as kindness or dishonesty • Has a moral that is directly stated at the end or indirectly communicated through what happens in the fable
TALL TALE **A humorously exaggerated story about impossible events** 	• Stars a hero or heroine who is larger than life—that is, bigger, stronger, and even louder than a regular person • Uses exaggeration to emphasize the abilities and achievements of the hero or heroine

MODEL 1: CHARACTERISTICS OF A FABLE

What human qualities do the fox and the crow display in this fable?

The Fox and the Crow

Fable by **Aesop**

A crow was sitting on a branch of a tree with a piece of cheese in her beak when a fox observed her and set his wits to work to discover some way of getting the cheese. Coming and standing under the tree, he looked up and said, "What a noble bird I see above me! Her beauty is without equal, the hue of her plumage exquisite. If only her voice is as sweet as her looks are fair, she ought without doubt to be Queen of the Birds."

The crow was hugely flattered by this, and, just to show the fox that she could sing, she gave a loud caw. Down came the cheese, of course, and the fox, snatching it up, said, "You have a voice, madam, I see. What you want are wits."

Flattery is the best persuasion.

Close Read

1. Reread the boxed details. What human qualities does each animal stand for?
2. The moral is directly stated in line 11. In your own words, restate the moral. How does the interaction between the fox and the crow illustrate the moral?

MODEL 2: CHARACTERISTICS OF A TALL TALE

Bess Call is the extraordinary heroine of this tall tale. Here, a stranger from England laughs when "big as life" Bess challenges him to a wrestling match. Will the stranger pay the price?

from Bess Call

Tall tale retold by **Robert D. San Souci**

"Humph!" said Bess. "I'll show you a *'real match'*—and no waitin', neither." She rolled up her sleeves and stomped out into the yard.

Back and forth they tussled, making more noise than a boatload of calves on the Hudson. First one, and then the other seemed to get the upper hand, only to find that the edge had slipped over to his or her opponent. The cloud of dust they kicked up covered the sun so that people as far away as Clinton and Cayuga counties reached for their umbrellas thinking unseasonable rain was about to fall.

Their struggles sent them rolling across the yard right up to the fence that separated the farmyard from the road. There Bess took hold of the Englishman one last time and tossed him body, boots, and britches over the fence, where he landed in a muddy ditch.

Close Read

1. In what way is Bess larger than life?
2. One example of humorous exaggeration is boxed. Find another example.

Part 2: Cultural Values in Traditional Stories

One reason for the lasting popularity of many traditional stories is their universal quality. You don't have to be an expert on ancient Greece to understand the moral of an Aesop fable, or know about daily life in 19th-century New York to be amused by "Bess Call."

You can usually appreciate a particular stories without knowing much about the culture or society from which it originally came. But by noticing certain details, you can often draw conclusions about the **cultural values**—the ideals and beliefs—that were honored and upheld by that society or culture. For example, does the story stress the importance of obedience, or does it celebrate those who bend the rules?

Consider the legend of John Henry, a railroad worker and "steel drivin' man" whose job was to drill holes using a hammer and a steel spike. His story was popular among men who worked long days building railroad tracks across the United States after the Civil War. By closely examining the excerpt and asking yourself a few questions, you can learn a great deal about those workers and their concerns.

from

JOHN HENRY

Legend retold by **Mary Pope Osborne**

"I got the best steel driver in the country. His name is John Henry, and he can beat *two* dozen men working together."

"That's impossible," the salesman said. "But if you can prove your hand driller is faster than my steam driller, I'll give you this machine for free."

The boss called to John Henry, "This fellow doubts which of you can drill faster. How about a big contest?"

As John Henry stared at the steam drill, he saw a picture of the future. He saw machines taking over the jobs of the country's finest workers. He saw himself and his friends out of work and begging beside the road. He saw men robbed of their dignity and robbed of their families.

"I'd rather die with my hammer in my hand than let that steam drill run me down," he yelled back. And his boss and friends all cheered.

QUESTIONS TO ASK

Who are the heroes and villains in the story?
The hero is a railroad worker; the villain is a machine.

What attitudes and behaviors are rewarded and admired?
John Henry is rewarded with cheers for taking on the machine. Other workers admire his strength and bravery.

What can you infer about the fears of the country's workers during this time period?
Workers were worried about losing their jobs to machines.

MODEL 1: CULTURAL VALUES IN A MYTH

The Mexican myth of Quetzalcoatl explains how unhappiness came into the world. In this excerpt, the people—the Toltecs—are still happy.

from **Quetzalcoatl**

Mexican myth retold by **Amy Cruse**

But the king-god Quetzalcoatl knew that if his people were to be really happy they must not spend their days in the idle enjoyment of all this loveliness and plenty. They must work, and learn to take a pride in working as well as they possibly could. So he taught them many useful arts—painting and weaving and carving and working in metals. He taught them how to fashion the gold and silver and precious stones which were found in great abundance throughout the country into beautiful vessels and ornaments, and how to make marvelous many-tinted garments and hangings from the feathers of birds. Every one was eager to work, and because each man did his share, there was plenty of leisure for all. No one was in want and no one was unhappy. It seemed as if, for these fortunate Toltecs, the Golden Age had really come.

Close Read

1. What attitudes toward work do you notice in this excerpt? Find specific details to support your answer.
2. Reread lines 4–9. What kinds of skills and products did the people who created this myth value?

MODEL 2: CULTURAL VALUES IN A LEGEND

In this legend, a monster bear called Nyagwahe threatens the peace among the five Iroquois nations. Swift Runner, a weak boy and an unlikely hero, kills the bear. Here, he returns to his village, victorious.

from **Racing the Great Bear**

Iroquois legend retold by **Joseph Bruchac**

Then Swift Runner led his people back to the village. He carried with him the teeth of the Nyagwahe, and those who saw what he carried rejoiced. The trails were safe again, and the Great Peace would not be broken. Swift Runner went to his grandmother's lodge and embraced her.

"Grandson," she said, "you are now the man I knew you would grow up to be. Remember to use your power to help the people."

So it was that Swift Runner ran with the great bear and won the race. Throughout his long life, he used the teeth of the Nyagwahe to heal the sick, and he worked always to keep the Great Peace.

Close Read

1. What traits does Swift Runner's grandmother display in the boxed text? Draw a conclusion about the attitude the Iroquois people have toward their elders.
2. Reread lines 6–9. What traits or qualities are admired in the Iroquois culture? Support your answer.

Part 3: Analyze the Literature

The myths of ancient Greece were first told more than 3,000 years ago. Yet people today still enjoy reading about the powers of mighty gods and goddesses and the daring adventures of heroes. Modern readers can even learn something from these characters' costly mistakes.

In this unit, you will read several Greek myths. Get your first taste of Greek mythology by reading this famous story of unrequited love. What characteristics of a myth do you notice in "Echo"? Through this tale, what do you learn about ancient Greek values?

Echo

Greek myth retold by **Alice Low**

Echo, a beautiful mountain nymph,[1] was a great talker and always had to have the last word. She was a favorite of Artemis, goddess of the hunt. Together they hunted in the woods, swam in mountain pools, and caught fish for meals. But Echo's delightful life was destroyed, all because she tried to protect her friends from Hera's[2] wrath.

One day Hera came spying on a group of nymphs in the woods. She suspected that her husband, Zeus, was in love with one of them and hoped to find out which one he favored.

Echo did not know which nymph was Zeus's favorite, and so she started a conversation with Hera in order to let all the other nymphs escape. "Isn't it lovely here?" she said.

"Yes, indeed," Hera replied, "but I am very busy right now and have no time for talk."

1. **nymph:** in Greek mythology, a godlike being that appears as a beautiful young woman in a natural setting.
2. **Hera's:** belonging to Hera, the wife of Zeus, the supreme ruler of Mount Olympus and all the gods and goddesses who live there.

Close Read

1. The ancient Greeks believed that their gods acted like regular people and even experienced human emotions. Consider Hera's feelings and actions in the boxed lines. In what ways is she like a human being?

"It seems to me you are busy talking," said Echo, "which is the nicest way to be busy, don't you agree?" She went on and on, and every time Hera tried to get away from her, Echo asked another question. By the time Hera got away and ran to the nymphs' pool, all the nymphs had fled.

"This is *your* doing," said Hera to Echo. "*You* kept talking to let them escape. And I shall punish you for that. You shall never be able to speak first, but shall only be able to repeat what others say. You shall always have the last word."

Soon after that, Echo fell in love with a handsome young hunter named Narcissus.[3] She followed him through the woods, hoping to make him notice her. But she could not speak first and had to wait for him to speak to her.

One day her chance came. Narcissus became separated from his friends and called out, "Is anyone here?"

"Here," called Echo.

Narcissus could not see her, for she was behind a bush. He shouted, "Come," thinking she was one of his companions, and she called back, "Come."

"Let us be together," called Narcissus, for he still could not see anybody.

"Let us be together," called Echo, and she ran up to him with her arms open, ready to embrace him. But Narcissus said cruelly, "Do not touch me. I would rather perish than let you have power over me."

"Have power over me," said Echo pleadingly, but Narcissus bounded away, leaving Echo alone and ashamed. Afterward she lived in a cave, and finally, because of her great grief, she shrank to nothing. The only thing left of her was her voice, which echoed through the mountains, repeating the words of anyone who called.

3. **Narcissus:** a handsome but vain boy known for his cruel rejection of the many nymphs who fell in love with him.

Close Read

2. Why does Hera punish Echo?

3. Think about Echo's behavior and actions, as well as her resulting punishment. What can you infer about the kinds of behavior that the Greeks hoped to discourage by telling this myth?

4. Some myths attempt to explain how something in the world came to be. What natural phenomenon is explained by this myth?

Prometheus

Greek Myth Retold by Bernard Evslin

Orpheus and Eurydice

Greek Myth Retold by Olivia Coolidge

Do you THINK *before you act?*

ALABAMA STANDARDS

READING STANDARDS

1.d Applying self-monitoring strategies

3 Distinguish among subgenres, such as myths, based on characteristics

KEY IDEA Did you ever make a decision you wished you could take back? If so, then you know that your actions sometimes have **consequences,** or effects, that you didn't bargain for. You're not alone. As you'll see in the Greek myths you're about to read, people have been acting without thinking since ancient times.

QUICKWRITE Think of a risky decision you might make, such as choosing not to study for a test or choosing to make friends with a person outside your group. What are the possible **consequences** of the decision, both negative and positive? Write a short paragraph explaining whether you would be willing to face these consequences.

LITERARY ANALYSIS: CHARACTERISTICS OF MYTHS

Since ancient times, people have passed down **myths,** or stories that explain mysteries of the universe. Most myths share these characteristics:

- They tell how something came to be, or they reveal the effects of human behavior.
- They feature gods or other beings with supernatural powers. These beings often show such human qualities as anger.

Many famous myths, like the ones you're about to read, were first told in Greece over 3,000 years ago. As you read, note what the myths explain and how the gods act.

READING STRATEGY: MONITOR

The unusual characters, places, and situations in these myths may sometimes distract or confuse you. As you read, try **monitoring,** or checking, your understanding. One way to do this is by asking yourself **questions** about what's going on. If you can't answer, clarify your understanding by reading more slowly, going back, or reading on. Note your questions and the answers in a chart like the one shown.

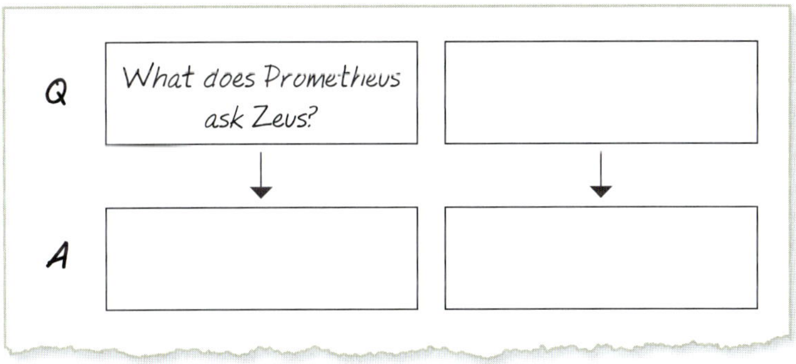

VOCABULARY IN CONTEXT

In the selections, the boldfaced words help tell what happens when the gods are disobeyed. Restate each sentence, using a different word or words for the boldfaced terms.

1. The gods were **infinitely** more powerful than the humans.
2. He had little **aptitude** for following orders.
3. He swore **vengeance** against his enemies.
4. After her son was banished, she was **inconsolable.**
5. She wanted to **ascend** the mountain where the gods lived.

Author Online

Bernard Evslin: Drawn to Myths
In the mid-1960s, Bernard Evslin found his calling retelling myths and legends. His 1986 book *Hercules* won the Washington Irving Children's Book Choice Award.

Bernard Evslin
1922–1993

Olivia Coolidge: Bridging Past and Present
As a child, Olivia Coolidge and her sister made up fairy tales to tell each other. As an adult, Coolidge became a famous reteller of Greek tales and myths.

Olivia Coolidge
born 1908

Background

Zeus, Prometheus, and Hades
The Greek gods were not all equal in power or status. Prometheus was a part of a family of giants, the Titans. Zeus defeated them and became the mighty ruler of all gods. He ordered Prometheus to create humans. Hades, who appears in "Orpheus and Eurydice," was the ruler of the underworld. He, too, answered to Zeus.

MORE ABOUT THE AUTHOR AND BACKGROUND
To learn more about the authors and the Greek gods, visit the **Literature Center** at **ClassZone.com.**

PROMETHEUS

Retold by ***Bernard Evslin***

Prometheus was a young Titan, no great admirer of Zeus. Although he knew the great lord of the sky hated explicit questions, he did not hesitate to beard[1] him when there was something he wanted to know.

One morning he came to Zeus and said, "O Thunderer, I do not understand your design. You have caused the race of man[2] to appear on earth, but you keep him in ignorance and darkness."

"Perhaps you had better leave the race of man to me," said Zeus. "What you call ignorance is innocence. What you call darkness is the shadow of my decree. Man is happy now. And he is so framed that he will remain happy unless someone persuades him that he is unhappy. Let us not speak of this again."

But Prometheus said, "Look at him. Look below. He crouches in caves. He is at the mercy of beast and weather. He eats his meat raw. If you mean something by this, enlighten me with your wisdom. Tell me why you refuse to give man the gift of fire." **A**

ANALYZE VISUALS
Notice the expression on the god's face and the position of his arms. What can you **infer** about the emotion he might be feeling?

A GREEK MYTHS
Based on the conversation between the two gods, what aspect of the natural world do you think this myth will explain? Make a **prediction.**

1. **beard:** to confront or defy.
2. **man:** In older translations, the expression *man* was commonly used to refer to all people.

Prometheus Carrying Fire, Jan Cossiers. Prado, Madrid. © Art Resource, New York.

Zeus answered, "Do you not know, Prometheus, that every gift brings a penalty? This is the way the Fates[3] weave destiny—by which gods also must abide. Man does not have fire, true, nor the crafts which fire teaches. On the other hand, he does not know disease, warfare, old age, or that inward pest called worry. He is happy, I say, happy without fire. And so he shall remain."

"Happy as beasts are happy," said Prometheus. "Of what use to make a separate race called man and endow[4] him with little fur, some wit, and a curious charm of unpredictability? If he must live like this, why separate him from the beasts at all?"

"He has another quality," said Zeus, "the capacity for worship. An **aptitude** for admiring our power, being puzzled by our riddles and amazed by our caprice.[5] That is why he was made."

"Would not fire, and the graces he can put on with fire, make him more interesting?"

"More interesting, perhaps, but **infinitely** more dangerous. For there is this in man too: a vaunting pride that needs little sustenance[6] to make it swell to giant size. Improve his lot, and he will forget that which makes him pleasing—his sense of worship, his humility. He will grow big and poisoned with pride and fancy himself a god, and before we know it, we shall see him storming Olympus. Enough, Prometheus! I have been patient with you, but do not try me too far. Go now and trouble me no more with your speculations."

Prometheus was not satisfied. All that night he lay awake making plans. Then he left his couch at dawn and, standing tiptoe on Olympus, stretched his arm to the eastern horizon where the first faint flames of the sun were flickering. In his hand he held a reed filled with a dry fiber; he thrust it into the sunrise until a spark smoldered. Then he put the reed in his tunic and came down from the mountain. **B**

At first men were frightened by the gift. It was so hot, so quick; it bit sharply when you touched it and for pure spite made the shadows dance. They thanked Prometheus and asked him to take it away. But he took the haunch of a newly killed deer and held it over the fire. And when the meat began to sear and sputter, filling the cave with its rich smells, the people felt themselves melting with hunger and flung themselves on the meat and devoured it greedily, burning their tongues.

"This that I have brought you is called 'fire,'" Prometheus said. "It is an ill-natured spirit, a little brother of the sun, but if you handle

aptitude (ăp'tĭ-to͞od') *n.* natural ability

infinitely (ĭn'fə-nĭt-lē) *adv.* extremely; greatly

SOCIAL STUDIES CONNECTION

Many settings in Greek myths are real places in Greece.

B MONITOR
Make sure you understand the **conflict** between Prometheus and Zeus. What questions do you have about what has already happened and about what will happen next?

---

3. **the Fates:** in Greek mythology, the three goddesses who decide the course of people's lives.
4. **endow** (ĕn-dou'): to provide with a quality or talent
5. **caprice** (kə-prēs'): the quality of acting without planning or thinking beforehand.
6. **vaunting pride that needs little sustenance:** boastful pride that needs little support.

it carefully, it can change your whole life. It is very greedy; you must feed it twigs, but only until it becomes a proper size. Then you must stop, or it will eat everything in sight—and you too. If it escapes, use this magic: water. It fears the water spirit, and if you touch it with water, it will fly away until you need it again."

He left the fire burning in the first cave, with children staring at it wide-eyed, and then went to every cave in the land.

Then one day Zeus looked down from the mountain and was amazed. Everything had changed. Man had come out of his cave. Zeus saw woodmen's huts, farmhouses, villages, walled towns, even a castle or two. He saw men cooking their food, carrying torches to light their way at night. He saw forges[7] blazing, men beating out ploughs, keels, swords, spears. They were making ships and raising white wings of sails and daring to use the fury of the winds for their journeys. They were wearing helmets, riding out in chariots to do battle, like the gods themselves. **C**

C GREEK MYTHS
According to this myth, what event allowed people to build homes, farm, and go to war?

Zeus was full of rage. He seized his largest thunderbolt. "So they want fire," he said to himself. "I'll give them fire—more than they can use. I'll turn their miserable little ball of earth into a cinder." But then another thought came to him, and he lowered his arm. "No," he said to himself, "I shall have **vengeance**—and entertainment too. Let them destroy themselves with their new skills. This will make a long, twisted game, interesting to watch. I'll attend to them later. My first business is with Prometheus."

vengeance (vĕn′jəns) *n.* the infliction of punishment in return for an offense

He called his giant guards and had them seize Prometheus, drag him off to the Caucasus,[8] and there bind him to a mountain peak with great chains specially forged by Hephaestus[9]—chains which even a Titan in agony could not break. And when the friend of man was bound to the mountain, Zeus sent two vultures to hover about him forever, tearing at his belly and eating his liver. **D**

D MONITOR
What does Zeus do to Prometheus, and why? To **clarify** the answer, think about the conflict between the two gods. Then reread lines 77–82.

Men knew a terrible thing was happening on the mountain, but they did not know what. But the wind shrieked like a giant in torment and sometimes like fierce birds.

Many centuries he lay there—until another hero was born brave enough to defy the gods. He climbed to the peak in the Caucasus and struck the shackles from Prometheus and killed the vultures. His name was Heracles.[10]

---

7. **forges** (fôr′jĭz): places where metal is heated and hammered into shape.
8. **Caucasus** (kô′kə-səs): a mountainous region in southeastern Europe.
9. **Hephaestus** (hĭ-fĕs′təs): the Greek god of fire and metalworking.
10. **Heracles** (hĕr′ə-klēz′): another name for Hercules, a son of Zeus who was famous for his great strength and courage.

Orpheus *and* Eurydice

Retold by Olivia Coolidge

In the legend of Orpheus the Greek love of music found its fullest expression. Orpheus, it is said, could make such heavenly songs that when he sat down to sing, the trees would crowd around to shade him. The ivy and vine stretched out their tendrils. Great oaks would bend their spreading branches over his head. The very rocks would edge down the mountainsides. Wild beasts crouched harmless by him, and nymphs[1] and woodland gods would listen to him enchanted. **E**

Orpheus himself, however, had eyes for no one but the nymph, Eurydice.[2] His love for her was his inspiration, and his power sprang from the passionate longing that he knew in his own heart. All nature rejoiced with him on his bridal day, but on that very morning, as Eurydice went down to the riverside with her maidens to gather flowers for a bridal garland, she was bitten in the foot by a snake, and she died in spite of all attempts to save her.

ANALYZE VISUALS
Describe the listeners' expressions. How can you **connect** this ancient scene to your own experience with music?

E GREEK MYTHS
Note what quality makes Orpheus special. According to the first sentence, how much did the Greeks value this quality?

1. **nymphs** (nĭmfs): divine beings represented as beautiful maidens who live in natural places such as trees.
2. **Eurydice** (yo͝o-rĭd′ĭ-sē).

Orpheus in the Underworld (1863), Louis Jacquesson de la Chevreuse. Oil on canvas, 115 cm × 145 cm. Musée des Augustins. © akg-images.

Orpheus was **inconsolable.** All day long he mourned his bride, while birds, beasts, and the earth itself sorrowed with him. When at last the shadows of the sun grew long, Orpheus took his lyre and made his way to the yawning cave which leads down into the underworld, where the soul of dead Eurydice had gone.

inconsolable (ĭn'kən-sō'lə-bəl) *adj.* impossible or difficult to comfort

VISUAL VOCABULARY

lyre (līr) *n.* an ancient stringed instrument resembling a small harp

Even grey Charon, the ferryman of the Styx,[3] forgot to ask his passenger for the price of crossing. The dog, Cerberus, the three-headed monster who guards Hades' gate, stopped full in his tracks and listened motionless until Orpheus had passed. As he entered the land of Hades, the pale ghosts came after him like great, uncounted flocks of silent birds. All the land lay hushed as that marvelous voice resounded across the mud and marshes of its dreadful rivers. In the daffodil fields of Elysium[4] the happy dead sat silent among their flowers. In the farthest corners of the place of punishment, the hissing flames stood still. Accursed Sisyphus,[5] who toils eternally to push a mighty rock uphill, sat down and knew not he was resting. Tantalus,[6] who strains forever after visions of cool water, forgot his thirst and ceased to clutch at the empty air.

The pillared hall of Hades opened before the hero's song. The ranks of long-dead heroes who sit at Hades' board looked up and turned their eyes away from the pitiless form of Hades and his pale, unhappy queen. Grim and unmoving sat the dark king of the dead on his ebony throne, yet the tears shone on his rigid cheeks in the light of his ghastly torches. Even his hard heart, which knew all misery and cared nothing for it, was touched by the love and longing of the music. F

F MONITOR
What **questions** do you have about what the underworld is like? Reviewing what you've read, along with the footnotes, might help you find answers.

At last the minstrel came to an end, and a long sigh like wind in pine trees was heard from the assembled ghosts. Then the king spoke, and his deep voice echoed through his silent land. "Go back to the light of day," he said. "Go quickly while my monsters are stilled by your song. Climb up the steep road to daylight, and never once turn back. The spirit of Eurydice shall follow, but if you look around at her, she will return to me."

Orpheus turned and strode from the hall of Hades, and the flocks of following ghosts made way for him to pass. In vain he searched their ranks for a sight of his lost Eurydice. In vain he listened for the faintest sound behind. The barge of Charon sank to the very gunwales[7] beneath

---

3. **Styx** (stĭks): in Greek mythology, the river across which the souls of the dead are transported.
4. **Elysium** (ĭ-lĭz'ē-əm): the home of the blessed, or those who were judged to have lived well, after death.
5. **Sisyphus** (sĭs'ə-fəs): a cruel king of Corinth condemned forever to roll a huge stone up a hill, only to have it fall down again.
6. **Tantalus** (tăn'tə-ləs): a king who, for his crimes, was condemned to stand in water that receded when he tried to drink.
7. **gunwales** (gŭn'əlz): the upper edge of the side of a vessel.

his weight, but no following passenger pressed it lower down. The way from the land of Hades to the upper world is long and hard, far easier to descend than climb. It was dark and misty, full of strange shapes and noises, yet in many places merely black and silent as the tomb. Here Orpheus would stop and listen, but nothing moved behind him. For all he could hear, he was utterly alone. Then he would wonder if the pitiless Hades were deceiving him. Suppose he came up to the light again and Eurydice was not there! Once he had charmed the ferryman and the dreadful monsters, but now they had heard his song. The second time his spell would be less powerful; he could never go again. Perhaps he had lost Eurydice by his readiness to believe. **G**

Every step he took, some instinct told him that he was going farther from his bride. He toiled up the path in reluctance and despair, stopping, listening, sighing, taking a few slow steps, until the dark thinned out into greyness. Up ahead a speck of light showed clearly the entrance to the cavern.

At that final moment Orpheus could bear no more. To go out into the light of day without his love seemed to him impossible. Before he had quite **ascended,** there was still a moment in which he could go back. Quick in the greyness he turned and saw a dim shade at his heels, as

G GREEK MYTHS
Recall the rule Hades gave to Orpheus. **Predict** whether Orpheus will obey it.

ascend (ə-sĕnd′) *v.* to go or move upward; rise

Orpheus Leading Eurydice from the Underworld (1861), Jean Baptiste Camille Corot. Oil on canvas, 112.3 cm × 137.1 cm. © Museum of Fine Arts, Houston. © The Bridgeman Art Library.

indistinct as the grey mist behind her. But still he could see the look of sadness on her face as he sprung forward saying, "Eurydice!" and threw his arms about her. The shade dissolved in the circle of his arms like smoke. A little whisper seemed to say, "Farewell," as she scattered into mist and was gone. **H**

The unfortunate lover hastened back again down the steep, dark path. But all was in vain. This time the ghostly ferryman was deaf to his prayers. The very wildness of his mood made it impossible for him to attain the beauty of his former music. At last, his despair was so great that he could not even sing at all. For seven days he sat huddled together on the grey mud banks, listening to the wailing of the terrible river. The flitting ghosts shrank back in a wide circle from the living man, but he paid them no attention. Only he sat with his eyes on Charon, his ears ringing with the dreadful noise of Styx.

Orpheus arose at last and stumbled back along the steep road he knew so well by now. When he came up to earth again, his song was pitiful but more beautiful than ever. Even the nightingale who mourned all night long would hush her voice to listen as Orpheus sat in some hidden place singing of his lost Eurydice. Men and women he could bear no longer, and when they came to hear him, he drove them away. At last the women of Thrace, maddened by Dionysus[8] and infuriated by Orpheus' contempt, fell upon him and killed him. It is said that as the body was swept down the river Hebrus, the dead lips still moved faintly and the rocks echoed for the last time, "Eurydice." But the poet's eager spirit was already far down the familiar path.

In the daffodil meadows he met the shade of Eurydice, and there they walk together, or where the path is narrow, the shade of Orpheus goes ahead and looks back at his love. ~ **I**

H MONITOR
Reread lines 66–74. What is the "dim shade" at Orpheus' heels? Why does the shade disappear? If you're not sure, try rereading lines 41–45 and then rereading this passage to **clarify** your understanding.

I MONITOR
How are Orpheus and Eurydice reunited? If you have any **questions**, review this page.

---

8. **women of Thrace** (thrās), **maddened by Dionysus** (dī'ə-nī'səs): Thrace was a Balkan region colonized by the Greeks; Dionysus was the god of wine.

Orpheus (1618), Marcello Provenzale. © Massimo Listri/Corbis.

Song *of* Orpheus

William Shakespeare

Orpheus with his lute[1] made trees,
And the mountain tops that freeze,
Bow themselves when he did sing:
To his music plants and flowers
Ever sprung; as sun and showers
There had made a lasting spring.

Every thing that heard him play,
Even the billows[2] of the sea,
Hung their heads, and then lay by.
In sweet music is such art,
Killing care and grief of heart
Fall asleep, or hearing, die.

---

1. **lute:** a small, stringed musical instrument with a pear-shaped body.
2. **billows:** huge waves.

After Reading

Comprehension

ALABAMA STANDARDS

READING STANDARD
1.d Applying self-monitoring strategies

1. **Recall** When Prometheus gives humans fire, what is their first reaction?
2. **Recall** Why does Zeus decide not to punish the humans for having fire?
3. **Clarify** Why does Hades at first agree to return Eurydice to Orpheus?

Literary Analysis

4. **Monitor** Review the chart you created as you read. Are there questions you are unsure how to answer? Compare your chart with a classmate's. Together, go over the story to answer any remaining questions.
5. **Compare Literary Works** Compare "Orpheus and Eurydice" to William Shakespeare's "Song of Orpheus" on page 643. Identify the part of the myth the poem describes. Which literary work, the myth or the poem, best helps you **visualize** the scene? Explain your answer with details from the selection you choose.
6. **Analyze Characteristics of Greek Myths** Review lines 39–60 of "Prometheus." Why is this passage important in terms of explaining where fire comes from? Give specific details from the passage to support your answer.
7. **Draw Conclusions** What kind of behavior do you think these myths were meant to encourage? Make a chart and go back through the stories, noting which behaviors are rewarded and which are punished. Then give your conclusions about what kind of behavior the Greeks hoped to encourage in people by telling these myths.

Rewarded	*Punished*

Extension and Challenge

8. **Inquiry and Research** Zeus and Hades were part of a group of 12 gods who ruled from Mount Olympus. Do research to find out more about the Olympians. Then create a poster that lists all 12 of these gods and goddesses and tells what they were known for.
9. **Big Question Activity** Imagine you could ask Prometheus or Orpheus the Big Question on page 632. Choose one of these characters and write the answer you think he would give on the basis of his experiences.

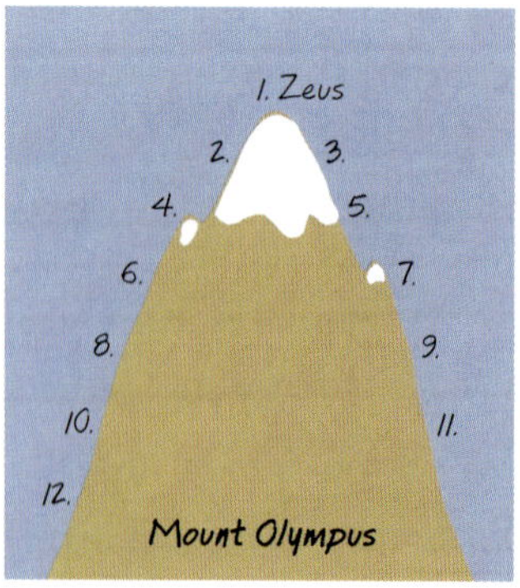

RESEARCH LINKS
For more on the Olympians, visit the **Research Center** at **ClassZone.com.**

Vocabulary in Context

VOCABULARY PRACTICE

Decide whether the words in each pair are synonyms (words that mean the same) or antonyms (words that mean the opposite).

1. aptitude/talent
2. ascend/descend
3. inconsolable/comforted
4. infinitely/barely
5. vengeance/mercy

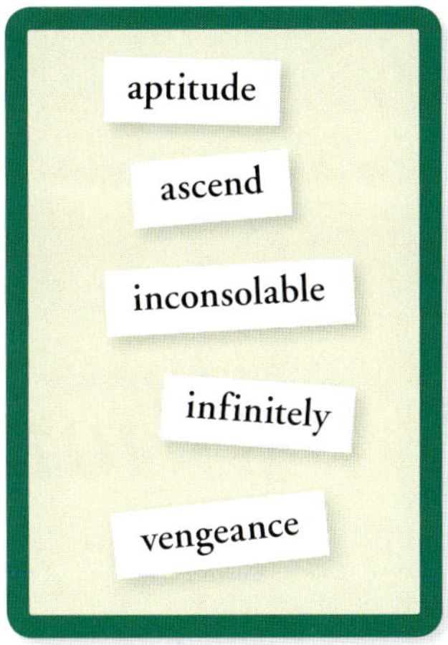

VOCABULARY IN WRITING

In these myths, how do the gods treat people who disobey them? Write a paragraph describing the gods' responses, using two or more vocabulary words. You might start like this.

EXAMPLE SENTENCE

The gods usually act out some form of ***vengeance*** *against those who disobey them.*

VOCABULARY STRATEGY: THE LATIN ROOT *fin*

The vocabulary word *infinitely* contains the Latin root *fin,* which means "end" or "limit." This root occurs in many English words. To understand the meaning of words with *fin,* use context clues and your knowledge of the root's meaning.

PRACTICE Based on context clues and your knowledge of the root *fin,* write a definition for each boldfaced word.

1. Many contestants spelled words wrong, but at the end of the day Mariah was a **finalist.**
2. I can't give you a **definite** answer until I double-check with Andy.
3. We all have a **finite** number of days in our lives.
4. It's hard for the human mind to understand the **infinity** of the universe.
5. All the performers returned to the stage for the **finale.**

ALABAMA STANDARDS

READING STANDARD
1.c Using context clues to determine word meanings

VOCABULARY PRACTICE
For more practice, go to the **Vocabulary Center** at **ClassZone.com.**

Icarus and Daedalus

Greek Myth Retold by Josephine Preston Peabody

Phaëthon, Son of Apollo

Greek Myth Retold by Olivia Coolidge

Should people always REACH *for the stars?*

ALABAMA STANDARDS

READING STANDARDS
1.d Applying self-monitoring strategies
3 Distinguish among subgenres, such as myths, based on characteristics

KEY IDEA Parents, teachers, and others we admire often proclaim that the only **limitations** placed on what we can achieve are those we place on ourselves. But should we always "reach for the stars" and follow our dream, or should we first consider whether the dream is practical or achievable? The characters in the following selections may provide an answer.

CHART IT In the first column of a chart, list dreams or goals that people often mention. In the second column, list the limits that others sometimes put on those dreams. Then tell whether you think the dream is still worth pursuing.

Dream	Limits	Worth Pursuing?
be an actor	not much money at first and few actors are successful	

LITERARY ANALYSIS: CULTURAL VALUES IN MYTHS

Myths of every culture reveal the values of the society in which they were created. These **cultural values** are standards of behavior believed to lead to a good life. In ancient Greece, people entertained one another with stories that celebrated these values:

- Obey your elders.
- Know your place.
- Respect and obey the gods.

Listeners learned important lessons by hearing what happened to characters who upheld—or did not uphold—these values. As you read, notice what happens to each character and decide what values the myth teaches.

READING SKILL: CAUSE AND EFFECT

You'll better understand what happens to characters if you pay attention to the relationship between causes and effects. A **cause** is an event that directly results in a later event, called an **effect.** As you read, record each cause and effect in a graphic. If an effect causes another effect, add squares to your graphic to show the cause-and-effect chain.

VOCABULARY IN CONTEXT

In the selections, the boldfaced words help tell what happens when two boys try to follow their dream. Using context clues, write a definition of each.

1. He had to **veer** to the left to avoid a collision.
2. She tried to **dissuade** him from taking such a risk.
3. They made a **rash** decision to ignore the gods' warnings.
4. The boy has a **cunning** plan to outsmart his opponents.
5. The pathway ended in a **precipitous** drop.
6. Being so high up made the climber's head **reel.**
7. They showed no **deference** to the decision makers.
8. He worked to **sustain** his speed.

Author Online

Josephine Preston Peabody: A Born Writer Josephine Preston Peabody's interest in myths and legends frequently influenced her writing, which included poetry and nonfiction. She published *Old Greek Folk Stories Told Anew* in 1897.

Josephine Preston Peabody
1874–1922

Olivia Coolidge: A Lover of the Classics Olivia Coolidge grew up in England, where she learned to share her family's love of history and the classics. She is now one of the best-loved retellers of Greek myths.

Olivia Coolidge
born 1908

Background

Divine Connections In Greek myths, gods and goddesses frequently have human offspring. Many human, or mortal, heroes are related in some way to the gods.

The Story of the Sun God Apollo, who was also called Phoebus Apollo, was the god of the sun. Daily, he pulled the sun into and out of the sky while riding in his chariot.

MORE ABOUT THE AUTHOR AND BACKGROUND
To learn more about the authors and Greek gods, visit the **Literature Center** at **ClassZone.com.**

ICARUS and DAEDALUS

Retold by Josephine Preston Peabody

Among all those mortals who grew so wise that they learned the secrets of the gods, none was more **cunning** than Daedalus.[1]

He once built, for King Minos of Crete,[2] a wonderful Labyrinth[3] of winding ways so cunningly tangled up and twisted around that, once inside, you could never find your way out again without a magic clue. But the king's favor **veered** with the wind, and one day he had his master architect imprisoned in a tower. Daedalus managed to escape from his cell; but it seemed impossible to leave the island, since every ship that came or went was well guarded by order of the king.

cunning (kŭn'ĭng) *adj.* skillful, clever

veer (vîr) *v.* to change direction; to shift

ANALYZE VISUALS
What might the red shape inside the figure **symbolize?** Explain your thoughts.

1. **Daedalus** (dĕd'l-əs).
2. **Crete:** an island in the Mediterranean Sea, southeast of Greece.
3. **Labyrinth** (lăb'ə-rĭnth'): a maze—that is, a complicated network of paths built to cause confusion.

The Fall of Icarus, (1944), Henri Matisse. Stencil print after a gouache and paper collage. Published in the illustrated book *Jazz,* Editions Tériade, 1947. © 2008 Succession H. Matisse, Paris/ Artists Rights Society (ARS), New York.

At length, watching the sea-gulls in the air—the only creatures that were sure of liberty—he thought of a plan for himself and his young son Icarus,[4] who was captive with him. **A**

Little by little, he gathered a store of feathers great and small. He fastened these together with thread, molded them in with wax, and so fashioned two great wings like those of a bird. When they were done, Daedalus fitted them to his own shoulders, and after one or two efforts, he found that by waving his arms he could winnow the air and cleave it,[5] as a swimmer does the sea. He held himself aloft, wavered this way and that with the wind, and at last, like a great fledgling,[6] he learned to fly.

Without delay, he fell to work on a pair of wings for the boy Icarus, and taught him carefully how to use them, bidding him beware of rash adventures among the stars. "Remember," said the father, "never to fly very low or very high, for the fogs about the earth would weigh you down, but the blaze of the sun will surely melt your feathers apart if you go too near."

For Icarus, these cautions went in at one ear and out by the other. Who could remember to be careful when he was to fly for the first time? Are birds careful? Not they! And not an idea remained in the boy's head but the one joy of escape. **B**

The day came, and the fair wind that was to set them free. The father bird put on his wings, and, while the light urged them to be gone, he waited to see that all was well with Icarus, for the two could not fly hand in hand. Up they rose, the boy after his father. The hateful ground of Crete sank beneath them; and the country folk, who caught a glimpse of them when they were high above the treetops, took it for a vision of the gods—Apollo, perhaps, with Cupid after him.

At first there was a terror in the joy. The wide vacancy of the air dazed them—a glance downward made their brains **reel.**

But when a great wind filled their wings, and Icarus felt himself **sustained,** like a halcyon bird[7] in the hollow of a wave, like a child uplifted by his mother, he forgot everything in the world but joy. He forgot Crete and the other islands that he had passed over: he saw but vaguely that winged thing in the distance before him that was his father Daedalus. He longed for one draft of flight to quench the thirst of his captivity: he stretched out his arms to the sky and made towards the highest heavens.

A CULTURAL VALUES
A character in a myth often represents one human trait, such as goodness. What trait does Daedalus display?

B CAUSE AND EFFECT
Reread lines 26–29. What causes Icarus to forget his father's warning as soon as he hears it?

reel (rēl) *v.* to feel unsteady or dizzy

sustain (sə-stān') *v.* to keep up; to support

---

4. **Icarus** (ĭk'ər-əs).
5. **winnow the air and cleave it:** fan the air, as if with wings, and cut through it.
6. **fledgling:** a young bird.
7. **halcyon** (hăl'sē-ən) **bird:** a bird that, according to legend, built a nest on the sea and thus calmed the water.

Falling Figure (Icarus) (1944), Henri Matisse. Color lithograph after a paper cut-out and gouache. Published on the back cover of the deluxe art review *Verve.* © 2008 Succession H. Matisse, Paris/ Artists Rights Society (ARS), New York.

Alas for him! Warmer and warmer grew the air. Those arms, that had seemed to uphold him, relaxed. His wings wavered, drooped. He fluttered his young hands vainly—he was falling—and in that terror he remembered. The heat of the sun had melted the wax from his wings; the feathers were falling, one by one, like snowflakes; and there was none to help. **C**

He fell like a leaf tossed down the wind, down, down, with one cry that overtook Daedalus far away. When he returned, and sought high and low for his poor boy, he saw nothing but the birdlike feathers afloat on the water, and he knew that Icarus was drowned.

The nearest island he named Icaria, in memory of the child; but he, in heavy grief, went to the temple of Apollo in Sicily, and there hung up his wings as an offering. Never again did he attempt to fly. ~ **D**

C CAUSE AND EFFECT
Why does Icarus fall? Add the cause to your graphic.

D CULTURAL VALUES
Explain what this myth suggests about respecting the warnings of elders.

Phaëthon, Son of Apollo

Retold by Olivia Coolidge

Though Apollo always honored the memory of Daphne,[1] she was not his only love. Another was a mortal, Clymene,[2] by whom he had a son named Phaëthon.[3] Phaëthon grew up with his mother, who, since she was mortal, could not dwell in the halls of Olympus or in the palace of the sun. She lived not far from the East in the land of Ethiopia, and as her son grew up, she would point to the place where Eos,[4] goddess of the dawn, lighted up the sky and tell him that there his father dwelt. Phaëthon loved to boast of his divine father as he saw the golden chariot riding high through the air. He would remind his comrades of other sons of gods and mortal women who, by virtue of their great deeds, had themselves become gods at last. He must always be first in everything, and in most things this was easy, since he was in truth stronger, swifter, and more daring than the others. Even if he were not victorious, Phaëthon always claimed to be first in honor. He could never bear to be beaten, even if he must risk his life in some **rash** way to win. (E)

ANALYZE VISUALS
Is the **mood,** or feeling, of this painting one of tension, exhilaration, or something else? Identify shapes that contribute to the mood.

rash (răsh) *adj.* reckless and careless

(E) CULTURAL VALUES
Reread lines 8–15. What can you **infer** about Phaëthon's personality?

1. **Daphne** (dăf'nē): a wood nymph who did not return Apollo's love. She disappeared, and a laurel tree grew in her place.
2. **Clymene** (klī'mə-nē).
3. **Phaëthon** (fā'ə-thŏn').
4. **Eos** (ē'ŏs').

Study of *Almanach Der Blaue Reiter* (1911), Wassily Kandinsky. Watercolor, gouache, and black ink. Inv. AM 1994–70. Photo by Philippe Migeat. Musée National d'Art Moderne, Centre Georges Pompidou, Paris. © 2008 Artists Rights Society (ARS), New York/ADAGP, Paris.

Most of the princes of Ethiopia willingly paid Phaëthon honor, since they admired him greatly for his fire and beauty. There was one boy, however, Epaphos,[5] who was rumored to be a child of Zeus himself. Since this was not certainly proved, Phaëthon chose to disbelieve it and to demand from Epaphos the **deference** that he obtained from all others. Epaphos was proud too, and one day he lost his temper with Phaëthon and turned on him, saying, "You are a fool to believe all that your mother tells you. You are all swelled up with false ideas about your father."

deference (dĕf'ər-əns) *n.* respect and honor

Crimson with rage, the lad rushed home to his mother and demanded that she prove to him the truth of the story that she had often told. "Give me some proof," he implored her, "with which I can answer this insult of Epaphos. It is a matter of life and death to me, for if I cannot, I shall die of shame."

"I swear to you," replied his mother solemnly, "by the bright orb of the sun itself that you are his son. If I swear falsely, may I never look on the sun again, but die before the next time he mounts the heavens. More than this I cannot do, but you, my child, can go to the eastern palace of Phoebus Apollo—it lies not far away—and there speak with the god himself."

The son of Clymene leaped up with joy at his mother's words. The palace of Apollo was indeed not far. It stood just below the eastern horizon, its tall pillars glistening with bronze and gold. Above these it was white with gleaming ivory, and the great doors were flashing silver, embossed with pictures of earth, sky, and sea, and the gods that dwelt therein. Up the steep hill and the bright steps climbed Phaëthon, passing unafraid through the silver doors, and stood in the presence of the sun. Here at last he was forced to turn away his face, for Phoebus sat in state on his golden throne. It gleamed with emeralds and precious stones, while on the head of the god was a brilliant diamond crown upon which no eye could look undazzled.

Phaëthon hid his face, but the god had recognized his son, and he spoke kindly, asking him why he had come. Then Phaëthon plucked up courage and said, "I come to ask you if you are indeed my father. If you are so, I beg you to give me some proof of it so that all may recognize me as Phoebus' son."

The god smiled, being well pleased with his son's beauty and daring. He took off his crown so that Phaëthon could look at him, and coming down from his throne, he put his arms around the boy, and said, "You are indeed my son and Clymene's, and worthy to be called so. Ask of me whatever thing you wish to prove your origin to men, and you shall have it." **F**

F CAUSE AND EFFECT
Why does Apollo agree to grant Phaëthon proof of his origin?

Phaëthon swayed for a moment and was dizzy with excitement at the touch of the god. His heart leaped; the blood rushed into his face. Now

5. **Epaphos** (ĕp'ə-fəs).

he felt that he was truly divine, unlike other men, and he did not wish to be counted with men any more. He looked up for a moment at his radiant father. "Let me drive the chariot of the sun across the heavens for one day," he said.

Apollo frowned and shook his head. "I cannot break my promise, but I will **dissuade** you if I can," he answered. "How can you drive my chariot, whose horses need a strong hand on the reins? The climb is too steep for you. The immense height will make you dizzy. The swift streams of air in the upper heaven will sweep you off your course. Even the immortal gods could not drive my chariot. How then can you? Be wise and make some other choice."

dissuade (dĭ-swād') *v.* to persuade not to do something

The pride of Phaëthon was stubborn, for he thought the god was merely trying to frighten him. Besides, if he could guide the sun's chariot, would he not have proved his right to be divine rather than mortal? For that he would risk his life. Indeed, once he had seen Apollo's splendor, he did not wish to go back and live among men. Therefore, he insisted on his right until Apollo had to give way. **G**

G CULTURAL VALUES Reread lines 61–73. What does Apollo request of Phaëthon? What is Phaëthon's reaction? Make a **prediction** about whether Phaëthon's decision will turn out to be a wise one.

When the father saw that nothing else would satisfy the boy, he bade the Hours[6] bring forth his chariot and yoke the horses. The chariot was of gold and had two gold-rimmed wheels with spokes of silver. In it there was room for one man to stand and hold the reins. Around the front and sides of it ran a rail, but the back was open. At the end of a long pole there were yokes for the four horses. The pole was of gold and shone with precious jewels: the golden topaz, the bright diamond, the green emerald, and the flashing ruby. While the Hours were yoking the swift, pawing horses, rosy-fingered Dawn hastened to the gates of heaven to draw them open. Meanwhile Apollo anointed his son's face with a magic ointment, that he might be able to bear the heat of the fire-breathing horses and the golden chariot. At last Phaëthon mounted the chariot and grasped the reins, the barriers were let down, and the horses shot up into the air.

At first the fiery horses sped forward up the accustomed trail, but behind them the chariot was too light without the weight of the immortal god. It bounded from side to side and was dashed up and down. Phaëthon was too frightened and too dizzy to pull the reins, nor would he have known anyway whether he was on the usual path. As soon as the horses felt that there was no hand controlling them, they soared up, up with fiery speed into the heavens till the earth grew pale and cold beneath them. Phaëthon shut his eyes, trembling at the dizzy, **precipitous** height. Then the horses dropped down, more swiftly than a falling stone, flinging themselves madly from side to side in panic because they were masterless. Phaëthon dropped the reins entirely and clung with all his might to the chariot rail.

precipitous (prĭ-sĭp'ĭ-təs) *adj.* very steep

6. **the Hours:** attendants of Apollo that represented the various hours of the day.

The Cavalier, Wassily Kandinsky. Staedtische Galerie im Lenbachhaus, Munich, Germany. © 2008 Artists Rights Society (ARS), New York/ADAGP, Paris. Photo © Giraudon/Art Resource, New York.

ANALYZE VISUALS
Is this painting a good representation of Phaëthon's ride? Why or why not?

Meanwhile as they came near the earth, it dried up and cracked apart. Meadows were reduced to white ashes, cornfields smoked and shriveled, cities perished in flame. Far and wide on the wooded mountains the forests were ablaze, and even the snow-clad Alps were bare and dry. Rivers steamed and dried to dust. The great North African plain was scorched until it became the desert that it is today. Even the sea shrank back to pools and caves, until dried fishes were left baking upon the white-hot sands. At last the great earth mother called upon Zeus to save her from utter destruction, and Zeus hurled a mighty thunderbolt at the unhappy Phaëthon, who was still crouched in the chariot, clinging desperately to the rail. The dart cast him out, and he fell flaming in a long trail through the air. The chariot broke in pieces at the mighty blow, and the maddened horses rushed snorting back to the stable of their master, Apollo. H

Unhappy Clymene and her daughters wandered over the whole earth seeking the body of the boy they loved so well. When they found him, they took him and buried him. Over his grave they wept and could not be comforted. At last the gods in pity for their grief changed them into poplar trees, which weep with tears of amber in memory of Phaëthon. I

H CAUSE AND EFFECT
What effects does Phaëthon's chariot ride have on the natural world?

I CULTURAL VALUES
What happens to Phaëthon? Draw a **conclusion** about why the Greeks kept his story alive.

Comprehension

1. **Recall** Why does Daedalus tell Icarus not to fly too high?
2. **Recall** Why does Phaëthon go to Apollo's palace?
3. **Represent** Make a sketch of Phaëthon in Apollo's chariot. Cite at least three details from the selection that you've shown in your sketch.

ALABAMA STANDARDS

READING STANDARD
3 Distinguish among subgenres, such as myths, based on characteristics

Literary Analysis

4. **Analyze Greek Gods** What human qualities do the gods in "Phaëthon" display? In your answer, include concrete details about the gods.
5. **Examine Cause and Effect** Review the graphics you created as you read. Then describe the **limitations** that Daedalus and Apollo tried to place on their sons' plans. What happened when the sons ignored the limitations?
6. **Evaluate a Character** Was Icarus believable to you? Explain whether you think his thoughts and actions are similar to those of a real person. Also tell whether you think people today can relate to someone like Icarus.
7. **Make Inferences** How do you think Daedalus eventually felt about his decision to fly away from Crete? Cite details from the myth in your answer.
8. **Identify Cultural Values** The chart shown lists some of the main values held by the ancient Greeks. Complete a chart like it by citing the line numbers of passages that communicate each value. What other values do you think these myths convey? Add one to your chart, and cite passages to support it.

Values	"Icarus and Daedalus"	"Phaëthon"
Obey your elders.	lines 20–29	
Know your place.		
Respect and obey the gods.		

9. **Draw Conclusions** On the basis of the myths you have read, what conclusions can you draw about the attitude of the ancient Greeks toward human nature? Would you say that their view of people in general is pessimistic, or negative? Explain why or why not, using examples from the selections.

Extension and Challenge

10. **Creative Project: Music** The ancient Greeks often told their myths through songs. Create your own song or rap telling the story of Icarus or Phaëthon. Be sure to base your piece on real details from the myth. Present your piece to the class.

Vocabulary in Context

VOCABULARY PRACTICE

For each item, choose the word that differs most in meaning from the other words. Refer to a dictionary if you need help.

1. (a) cunning, (b) clever, (c) resourceful, (d) wicked
2. (a) discourage, (b) prevent, (c) infuriate, (d) dissuade
3. (a) cooperate, (b) sustain, (c) support, (d) uphold
4. (a) steep, (b) sharp, (c) precipitous, (d) wide
5. (a) rash, (b) hasty, (c) impulsive, (d) distressed
6. (a) shift, (b) veer, (c) stare, (d) swerve
7. (a) esteem, (b) honor, (c) deference, (d) tolerance
8. (a) reel, (b) sway, (c) whisper, (d) totter

cunning
deference
dissuade
precipitous
rash
reel
sustain
veer

VOCABULARY IN WRITING

What role did pride play in the tragedies of Icarus and Phaëthon? Write a paragraph explaining your thoughts. Use at least two vocabulary words. Here is a sample opening.

EXAMPLE SENTENCE

*Neither boy showed **deference** to his father.*

VOCABULARY STRATEGY: HOMOGRAPHS

Homographs are words that are spelled the same but have different meanings and origins. Read these dictionary entries for the word *rash*. Notice that *rash* and *rash,* like other homographs, have different etymologies (histories) as well as different meanings. If you see a word used in a way that is unfamiliar to you, check the dictionary to see if it is a homograph.

rash[1] (răsh) ***adj.*** too hasty and careless [Middle English *rasch,* active]

rash[2] (răsh) ***n.*** an outbreak on the skin [obsolete French *rache,* sore]

ACTIVITY Use a dictionary to find two or three homographs for each listed word. Write simple definitions that show the differences in meaning for each.

1. chop
2. down
3. fluke
4. jam
5. reel
6. shock

VOCABULARY PRACTICE
For more practice, go to the **Vocabulary Center** at **ClassZone.com.**

SKILLS PRACTICE

Reading-Writing Connection

Deepen your understanding of these myths by responding to the prompts. Then complete the **Grammar and Writing** exercise.

WRITING PROMPTS	SELF-CHECK
A. Short Response: Write a Monologue If you were Daedalus or Apollo, would you feel your son deserved his fate for not recognizing his **limitations?** Write a **one-paragraph monologue** describing the events of one of the myths from the perspective of the father.	***A good monologue will . . .*** • include a summary of the myth's plot • give a believable account of the father's feelings
B. Extended Response: Evaluate Descriptions Which of the two myths was better at making you see and feel the terrible descent from the sky? Write **two or three paragraphs** evaluating the description in each myth. Then explain which description was more effective and why.	***A successful evaluation will . . .*** • include a statement that gives your main impression • support the statement by citing specific details

GRAMMAR AND WRITING

USE CORRECT SENTENCE STRUCTURE An **independent clause** is a group of words that contains a subject and a verb and can stand alone as a sentence. A **simple sentence** contains one independent clause, and a **compound sentence** contains two or more independent clauses joined either by a comma and a coordinating conjunction or by a semicolon.

Original: Icarus flew too close to the sun. (*A simple sentence contains one independent clause.*)

Revised: Icarus flew too close to the sun, and he fell to his death. (*Two independent clauses joined with a comma and a coordinating conjunction form a compound sentence.*)

PRACTICE Identify each sentence as simple or compound.

1. I told Icarus not to fly too high or low, but he didn't listen to me.
2. The sun's heat melted the glue in his wings.
3. The wings' feathers fell one by one.
4. He wanted to fly high into the sky; this need for freedom cost him his life.
5. Now I am left without my son.

*For more help with independent clauses, see page R63 in the **Grammar Handbook.** For more help with simple and compound sentences, see pages R63–R64 in the **Grammar Handbook.***

ALABAMA STANDARDS

WRITING/LANGUAGE STANDARD
11.c Identifying sentence patterns

from Young Arthur

Medieval Legend Retold by Robert D. San Souci

Is there a job you were BORN *to do?*

ALABAMA STANDARDS

READING STANDARDS
1.b Determining sequence of events
3 Distinguish among subgenres based on characteristics

KEY IDEA Some people believe that we all have a **destiny,** a predetermined life that we can't change even if we want to. Others think that life is what we make of it. In the legend you're about to read, a kingdom waits to find out which boy is destined to be its king.

DISCUSS With a small group of classmates, discuss whether people are born to do some particular thing. Think of your feelings about your own future, and also consider individuals who have changed history through their dedication to a job or a goal. Be ready to share with the class whether you believe people choose their own destiny or are born to it.

LITERARY ANALYSIS: CHARACTERISTICS OF LEGENDS

A **legend** is a story about heroes or heroines that is handed down from the past. Legends often are based on real people and events. However, as the stories pass through the generations, the characters, setting, and events become more imaginary and less factual. For example, the King Arthur legends are probably based on a real-life chieftain who lived in Britain around A.D. 500. In the course of many retellings, the legends' setting changed to the time of knights, 900 years later.

Because of the courage, honor, and fairness King Arthur displayed, he became a model for others to follow. As you read, notice the conflict young Arthur faces and how he proves his goodness.

READING SKILL: CHRONOLOGICAL ORDER

In a legend, events are often presented in **chronological order,** or the order in which they take place. As you read, look for words and phrases that provide clues to this order, such as *when, eventually, this time,* and *in the days that followed.* Mark the sequence of events on a timeline.

VOCABULARY IN CONTEXT

The words in Column A help recreate the world of medieval England. See how many you know by matching each word to the item in Column B that comes closest to its meaning.

Column A	Column B
1. grievous	**a.** respect
2. homage	**b.** cringing
3. reclaim	**c.** boss
4. dismount	**d.** recover
5. flinching	**e.** climb down
6. upstart	**f.** unhappiness
7. melancholy	**g.** socially climbing
8. taskmaster	**h.** severe

Author Online

Always a Fan One of the first books Robert D. San Souci ever read was a book about King Arthur, and he remembers being fascinated by dragons and knights. In addition to *Young Arthur,* San Souci has written three other books about the Arthurian legend: *Young Guinevere, Young Lancelot,* and *Young Merlin.* San Souci has also retold the tales and legends of groups ranging from the Alaska Natives to the native Australians.

Robert D. San Souci
born 1946

MORE ABOUT THE AUTHOR
For more on Robert D. San Souci, visit the **Literature Center** at **ClassZone.com.**

Background

Pretenders and Kings The Arthur legends paint a vivid picture of the intrigues of medieval life. In the Middle Ages, a king's oldest son was considered the heir to his father's throne. When the enemies of a king wished to take over his kingdom, they might try to kill his son.

Arthurian Legends and Merlin
In the Arthur legends, a magician named Merlin plays an important role. Legends often include unreal or magical people and relate events that could never happen in real life. Some legends also contain magical objects that confer special powers or privileges on their bearers.

Young Arthur

Retold by Robert D. San Souci

King Uther[1] heard the baby's wail and leaped to his feet. There was a sharp rap at the chamber door, and a servant entered grinning happily. "You have a son," he told the king. Uther's joy knew no bounds. When he was ushered into Queen Igerna's[2] bedchamber, Uther looked lovingly at mother and son. "The boy's name shall be Arthur," he declared, "and he shall be a great king. For Merlin [the magician] has foretold that he will one day rule the greatest kingdom under heaven."

But Uther's happiness did not last. His beloved queen died soon after Arthur's birth, and sadness sapped the king's spirit. He lost interest in ruling, and Merlin was unable to rouse him from his **melancholy.**

ANALYZE VISUALS
Examine the main **character** in this illustration. What kind of personality do you think he might have?

melancholy (mĕl′ən-kŏl′ē) *n.* sadness; depression

1. **Uther** (yo͞o′thər).
2. **Igerna** (ē-gĕr′nə).

Illustration by Walter Crane in *King Arthur's Knights* by Henry Gilbert, 1911. © Edwin Wallace/Mary Evans Picture Library.

"Unrest grows throughout the land," Merlin warned. "Your old foes are rising in rebellion. Give the babe into my keeping, for you have enemies even at court." **A**

Anxious for his son's safety, Uther agreed. So Merlin, disguised as a beggar, took the infant Arthur to Sir Ector and his lady, who lived some distance from the court and all its dangers. He told them nothing about the child, save that his name was Arthur. The couple had recently lost their infant son and welcomed Arthur as their own. Soon rebellion divided the kingdom. Uther, **reclaiming** his old spirit, rallied his knights and barons. With Merlin always beside him, he drove back his enemies.

But as Uther celebrated his victory in the town of Verulum,[3] traitors poisoned the town's wells. The king and his loyal followers were stricken. Merlin alone escaped. Though he tried his healing arts on Uther, he was forced to confess, "Sire, there is no remedy."

"Then," said the dying monarch, "I declare that my son shall be king of all this realm after me. God's blessing and mine be upon him." With these words, Uther died.

When the rebels entered Verulum, only Merlin was alive.

"Tell us where Uther's son is hidden," they demanded, "so that we can slay him and end Uther's line."

But Merlin vanished before their eyes.

Young Arthur was raised as a son in Sir Ector's house. He learned to read and write alongside his foster brother, Kay, who was four years older. By the time he was fifteen, Arthur was a tall, handsome, quick-witted lad. Though he had great strength, he also had a gentle manner.

Kay, who had recently been knighted, decided to train Arthur in the knightly arts himself. But Kay was vain and jealous of the favor Arthur found with their father, so he was a harsh **taskmaster.** Arthur came away from his lessons in swordsmanship with many bruises and cuts. When he complained, Kay replied, "A knight must be thick-skinned and ready to bear even **grievous** wounds without **flinching.**" Yet if Arthur so much as pricked his brother, Kay would bellow loudly for the physician. **B**

Eventually Kay appointed Arthur his apprentice. This was an honor the younger boy would happily have forgone. However, seeing that Sir Ector wished it so, Arthur sighed and agreed. But he felt in his heart that he already was a knight, though no lord had dubbed him such.

A CHRONOLOGICAL ORDER
What events have happened so far? Mark the events in order on your timeline.

reclaim (rĭ-klām') *v.* to get back; recover

taskmaster (tăsk'măs'tər) *n.* a person who sets tasks for others to do

grievous (grē'vəs) *adj.* painful; serious

flinching (flĭn'chĭng) *n.* drawing back from difficulty or danger **flinch** *v.*

B LEGENDS
Which of the characters you've met so far represent admirable characteristics and which represent undesirable ones?

3. **Verulum** (vĕr'o͝o-ləm).

Both Arthur and Kay knew it was vital to learn the arts of war. The kingdom was still at the mercy of **upstart** lords who ruled by fire and sword.

upstart (ŭp′stärt′) *adj.* suddenly risen to wealth or power

The story of Uther's lost son, the true heir to the throne, would have been forgotten but for Merlin. One Christmas Eve, the long-absent magician reappeared and summoned the bishops, lords, and common folk to London's square. There he drove a broadsword halfway into a huge stone. Written on the blade in blazing gold letters were the words: "Whoso pulleth out the sword from this stone is born the rightful King of England." **C**

C CHRONOLOGICAL ORDER
What phrase tells you when Merlin put the sword in the stone? Mark the event on your timeline.

In the days that followed, knights and barons, cowherds and bakers, an endless parade of would-be kings eagerly pulled at the sword. But none could loosen it, let alone draw it forth.

When they accused Merlin of trickery, he said, "The rightful king has not yet come. God will make him known at the proper time."

Now it happened that a great tournament[4] was held in London. Among those who came were Sir Ector, Sir Kay, and young Arthur, who served Kay. So eager was the boy to see the jousts[5] that he forgot to pack Kay's sword. There was great upset when the mistake was discovered.

"Woe to you, boy," snarled Kay, "if your error costs me the victory I would otherwise win today!"

Even Sir Ector scolded Arthur and ordered, "Go back directly and fetch the missing sword."

Angry at his carelessness and impatient to see the contests, Arthur started homeward. Then he suddenly reined in his horse.

In the deserted city square was a massive stone with a sword plunged into its center. "Surely that sword is as good as the one left at home," he said. "I will borrow it. When Kay is finished, I will return it to this curious monument."

So saying, he **dismounted,** scrambled up the stone, took the sword handle, and tugged. The sword did not move. Impatient to return to the tournament, he pulled again. This time, the sword slid easily out of the stone. In his haste, he did not notice the words upon the blade. Shoving the weapon into his belt, he remounted and raced to where Sir Kay waited his turn upon the field.

dismount (dĭs-mount′) *v.* to get down or off

The moment he saw the golden words upon the blade, Kay began to tremble with excitement. When Arthur asked what was amiss, Kay shouted, "Go! Get away! You have caused enough trouble." **D**

D LEGENDS
Why does Kay tell Arthur to get away?

But Arthur was curious. So he followed as Kay ran to Sir Ector. "Look, Father!" cried Kay. "Here is the sword of the stone. Therefore, it is I who must be king of all this land!"

4. **tournament:** a medieval sporting event in which groups of armored men fought against each other.

5. **jousts:** competitions or combats between two knights on horseback, using lances.

When Sir Ector and the others saw the sword and read the golden inscription, they began to shout, "The sword from the stone! The king's sword!"

Hearing only this much, Arthur thought that he had stolen a king's weapon. As people hurried excitedly toward Kay, Arthur spurred his horse away, certain he had committed a great crime.

Looking back, he saw Kay and Sir Ector ride off, surrounded by the greatest lords of the realm. Were they taking Kay to trial? he wondered. Had he brought ruin upon Sir Ector's household?

"A true knight would not run away," he said to himself, "and I am a true knight in my heart." Fearful, but determined to do what was right, the boy wheeled his horse around. **E**

The great square was now filled with people. Just how terrible a crime had he committed?

Upon the stone stood Kay, holding the sword. The crowd shouted each time he held the blade aloft. Then silence fell over the throng: Merlin had appeared at the edge of the square. People stood aside to let the magician approach the stone.

"Are you the one who pulled the sword from the stone?" Merlin asked.

"I am holding it, am I not?" Kay replied.

"The rightful king could pull it free a hundred times," said Merlin. "Slip the sword into the groove and pull it out again."

With a shrug, Kay reinserted the sword. But when he tried to jerk it free, it would not budge.

Suddenly all eyes turned toward Arthur, who was pushing his way through the crowd, bellowing at the top of his lungs. "It wasn't Kay's fault! I brought him the sword!" Merlin peered closely at Arthur. Then he smiled and said, "Climb up and draw the sword from the stone." Uncertainly Arthur clambered up beside Kay. Grasping the pommel, he easily pulled the sword out.

Then Merlin cried, "This is Arthur, son of Uther Pendragon,[6] Britain's destined king."

An astonished Sir Ector knelt to pay the boy **homage,** followed by Kay and many others. But all around, there was growing confusion and dispute. Some cried, "It is the will of heaven! Long live the king!" while others cried, "It is Merlin's plot to put a beardless boy, a puppet, on the throne, and so rule the land."

[But] The cries of "Long Live King Arthur!" soon carried the day. **F**

E LEGENDS
What is Arthur thinking? Make an **inference** about his qualities as a person.

VISUAL VOCABULARY

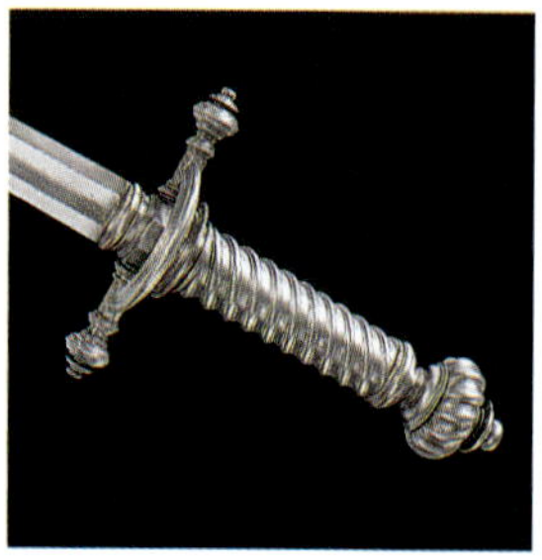

pommel (pŭm′əl) *n.* a knob on the handle of a sword

homage (hŏm′ĭj) *n.* a display of loyalty and respect

F CHRONOLOGICAL ORDER
After Sir Ector pays Arthur homage, who else does? Mark the final events of the story on your timeline.

6. **Pendragon** (pĕn-drăg′ən).

Comprehension

ALABAMA STANDARDS

READING STANDARD
1.b Determining sequence of events

1. **Recall** Why do Uther's enemies want to slay Arthur?
2. **Clarify** Why does Arthur remove the sword from the stone the first time?
3. **Paraphrase** What is written on the sword?

Literary Analysis

4. **Identify Chronological Order** Review the story to make sure you included all its major events on your timeline. Then use your timeline to write a summary of the story.
5. **Examine Characteristics of Legends** Most legends feature a hero or heroine who faces a struggle or conflict. This character often has unusual powers and admirable traits. Note Arthur's conflict, special power, and good traits in a graphic like the one shown.

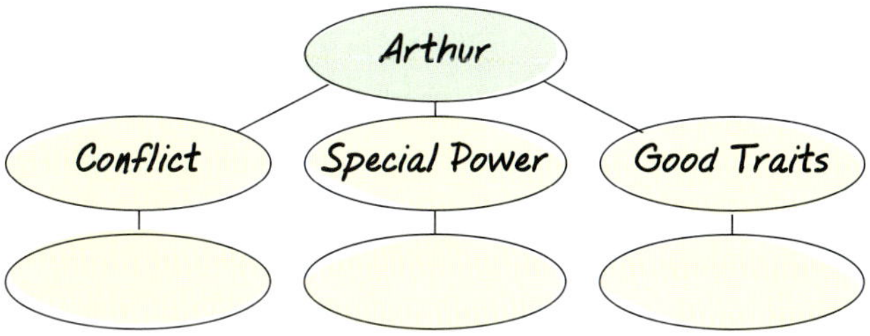

6. **Interpret Theme** Legends communicate their themes not only through the actions of heroes and the consequences the heroes face, but also through the actions of minor characters. Identify the qualities that Kay represents. Then tell whether Kay's behavior pays off in the end. What message about life are readers supposed to learn from Kay's example?
7. **Evaluate a Legend** The story of Arthur has captivated people for generations. What explanation do you have for this? Tell whether you think the legend deserves such wide popularity, and defend your opinion with concrete details from the story.

Extension and Challenge

8. **Big Question Activity** What ideas about **destiny,** or fate, are reflected in this legend? Are they different from or similar to the ideas your group discussed as part of the activity on page 660?
9. **SOCIAL STUDIES CONNECTION** What was life like in Britain during the early Middle Ages? Read "Who Was King Arthur?" on page 669, and then do research on the Internet. Display your answers to the following questions on a poster:
   - How was society organized?
   - Who were the Britons fighting against?
   - What religion was practiced?

RESEARCH LINKS
For more on Britain during the Middle Ages, visit the **Research Center** at **ClassZone.com.**

Vocabulary in Context

VOCABULARY PRACTICE

Show that you understand the vocabulary words by telling whether each statement is true or false.

1. I am **flinching** when I reach out to hug someone.
2. A sad look or a sigh is often a sign of **melancholy.**
3. It is hard to pay **homage** to someone you don't respect.
4. A **grievous** wound is generally easy to recover from.
5. An **upstart** politician is probably serving a second or third term in office.
6. A foreman in a factory is an example of a **taskmaster.**
7. A good time to **dismount** from a horse is when you are galloping on it.
8. A landowner trying to **reclaim** his property wants to get it back.

dismount
flinching
grievous
homage
melancholy
reclaim
taskmaster
upstart

VOCABULARY IN WRITING

In a paragraph, draw on what you learned from this excerpt from *Young Arthur* to describe Arthur's early life. Use two or more vocabulary words. You might start like this.

EXAMPLE SENTENCE

Kay was a hard ***taskmaster,*** *but Arthur's life was not unhappy.*

VOCABULARY STRATEGY: COMPOUND WORDS

Compound words are two or more words combined to have one meaning. Sometimes, as in the word *taskmaster,* the meaning can be inferred from the meanings of the two combined words. Other times, though, as with *upstart,* you may have to look at context clues or even a dictionary.

ACTIVITY Use context clues to figure out the definition of each boldfaced compound word. Then, write the definition. If you have to, consult a dictionary.

1. The actor had never written a book, so he hired a **ghostwriter** to work on his autobiography.
2. The two six-year-old boys love to **roughhouse** when they get together to play.
3. To support the huge building, the contractors excavated all the way down to **bedrock.**
4. The only way Maura will **undertake** this project is with a lot of support from everyone.

ALABAMA STANDARDS

READING STANDARD
1.c Using context clues to determine word meanings

VOCABULARY PRACTICE
For more practice, go to the **Vocabulary Center** at **ClassZone.com.**

MAGAZINE ARTICLE Historians disagree on the facts behind King Arthur legends. This magazine article presents some of the theories about Arthur's true home. Decide whether the information in this article matches your own image of Arthur.

Who Was King Arthur?

by Jerry Dunn

King Arthur and his queen, Guinevere, ruled their kingdom in peace from their castle, Camelot. . . . Camelot represents a lost time of innocence and high adventure during the Dark Ages—the period from A.D. 476 to about A.D. 1000. . . .

But did Arthur and his peaceful Camelot ever really exist? Historians say that around A.D. 410, after the Romans left Britain, fierce invaders called Saxons came from Europe, conquering much of England. In the western part of the country, a local chieftain fought the Saxons. He won a great victory at Badon Hill around A.D. 500. According to some scholars, this real-life brave warrior was Arthur.

His triumph brought 12 years of peace. Could this golden age have been Camelot? Some experts say the real Camelot may have been Cadbury Castle in southern England. Here archaeologists found ruins of a fortified tower and what may have been a great hall of timber, all dating from Arthur's time. Other places around England also lay claim to the noble king. For instance Arthur may have fought his last battle in southwestern England at a place called Camlan.

We may never know all the facts about Arthur. Perhaps it doesn't matter. The legend of King Arthur holds its own timeless truths. This is why people have been reciting stories of King Arthur and his Round Table for at least a thousand years.

THE DARK AGES

- Disorder reigned in most of Europe between A.D. 476 and A.D. 1000, the period called the Dark Ages.
- King Arthur and his knights never wore full suits of armor. They lived in the sixth century; full plate armor didn't show up for another 900 years.
- People who lived in what is now England did not speak English. They probably spoke Latin or British, a language from which Welsh developed.
- Disease, poor diet, and frequent wars meant that most people could not expect to live beyond age 30.
- Only monks and some noblemen learned how to read.

from Sir Gawain and the Green Knight

Medieval Legend Retold by Michael Morpurgo

Is CHIVALRY *dead?*

ALABAMA STANDARDS

READING STANDARDS
1.f Analyzing predictions
3 Distinguish among subgenres based on characteristics

KEY IDEA Back in the ninth century, **chivalry** was a set of rules that gave knights guidance about how to engage in battle, how to serve rulers, and how to behave toward women. Today *chivalry* refers to the personal qualities that were important to knights: bravery, honor, courtesy, and service. In this legend, an act of chivalry gets one knight into a terrible predicament.

SURVEY In our rough-and-tumble modern world, does chivalry still exist? Conduct a survey to find out how often your peers witness people acting chivalrously. Use your results to discuss what modern people are doing well and what they could do better.

	Often	Seldom	Never
Sacrificing for Others			
Keeping Promises			
Being Polite			

LITERARY ANALYSIS: CULTURAL VALUES IN LEGENDS

Most popular movies focus on a hero—a person who is unusually brave. Long before people filmed stories or wrote them down, a hero was often the basis for a legend.

In a legend, the hero's main traits usually reflect the **cultural values** of the society, or the standards of behavior the society wants to promote. In medieval Arthurian legends, knights and their code of chivalry represent these ideals, cherished in the Middle Ages:

- Be loyal to those you serve and be courteous to all.
- Always be truthful and keep your word.
- Face danger with courage and show mercy to the weak.

As you read, look for examples of chivalry.

READING STRATEGY: PREDICT

Predicting is making a reasonable guess about what will happen next in a story. To predict, follow these steps:

- Consider what you know about the characters and plot.
- Combine these thoughts with your own experience, and make a logical guess about what might happen next.
- Adjust your prediction as new information is presented.

As you read, track your predictions on a chart.

Text Evidence	*Prediction*	*What Happens*
King Arthur wishes for a challenge.		

VOCABULARY IN CONTEXT

The words listed help describe a knight and his challenge. Put each word in the appropriate column of a chart. Then write a definition for each word with which you are familiar.

WORD LIST			
	cumbersome	integrity	sever
	daunting	lanky	unperturbed
	demeaning	revere	

Know Well	*Think I Know*	*Don't Know at All*

Author Online

Storyteller with Heart When Michael Morpurgo became a teacher, one of his favorite parts of the job was making up stories for his students. Their interest convinced him that he could become a writer. Now the British author has published over 50 books. In his spare time, Morpurgo runs three farms in England, where kids from the city can stay. In 2003, he was named the third Children's Laureate of England.

Michael Morpurgo
born 1943

Background

The Chivalric Code In the Middle Ages, young men from well-to-do families often became knights. As knights, they served a family of a higher social rank. Knights were expected to be extremely courteous and brave, as well as loyal to their lords.

Knights of the Round Table Stories of Arthur were first told before the age of chivalry, but during the Middle Ages, the stories changed. Arthur and his followers began to be pictured as knights who lived in an ideal kingdom called Camelot. An English writer, Sir Thomas Malory wrote about the Round Table, where the knights sat in perfect equality.

MORE ABOUT THE AUTHOR AND BACKGROUND
To learn more about Michael Morpurgo and the Round Table, visit the **Literature Center** at **ClassZone.com.**

Sir Gawain and the Green Knight

Retold by Michael Morpurgo

It was Christmas time at Camelot, that time of the year when all King Arthur's Knights gathered to celebrate the birth of their Lord and Savior, Jesus Christ. For fifteen joyous days, after holy Mass each morning there was nothing but feasting and dancing and singing, and hunting and jousting too. Jousting was the favorite sport, each Knight striving to unseat the mighty Sir Lancelot—but rarely succeeding of course. And all was done in fun, in a spirit of great comradeship, for they were happy to be all together once more at this blessed time. During the year, these lords were often parted from one another, and from their ladies, as they rode out through the kingdom on their dangerous missions. So this was a time when love and friendship were renewed, a time to celebrate with their young King all their achievements and their great and good purpose: to bring peace to the land, and make of it a kingdom as near to a heaven on earth as had never before been achieved in Britain, or in any other land, come to that. **A**

ANALYZE VISUALS
How does the knight in this painting **compare** with your image of a knight?

A CULTURAL VALUES
Reread lines 10–15. On the basis of this description, what can you **infer** about the kind of behavior people admired during the Middle Ages?

Illustrations © Juan Wijngaard (1981) from *Sir Gawain and the Green Knight* by Selina Hastings. Reproduced by permission of Walker Books, Ltd., London.

On New Year's Eve, after evening Mass had been said in the chapel and generous New Year's gifts exchanged, the High King and Guinevere,[1] his Queen, came at last into the great hall where all the lords and ladies were waiting to dine. No one could begin the feasting until they came, of course, so as you can imagine, the lords and ladies cheered them to the rafters when they saw them. Guinevere had never looked so gloriously beautiful as she did that evening, and there were gasps of admiration from around the hall.

With Arthur on one side of her and Gawain[2] on the other, Guinevere sat down at the high table, which was set on a splendid dais draped all about with silk and richly hung with the finest tapestries from Toulouse[3] and Turkestan.[4] Then, with drummers drumming and pipers piping, the servants came in carrying the food on great silver plates, piling each table high with roasted meat, capons and venison and pork, and fish fresh-baked in sea salt, and baskets of crusty bread, and steaming soups too. Truly there was enough to feed five thousand, but there were only five hundred there to eat it. As they poured out the wine and ale, filling every goblet to the brim, the scents of the feast that lay before them filled the air with succulence,[5] and their nostrils too, so that, their appetites whetted, they were all longing now to begin. But the High King and his Queen sat there, not touching their food, or their drink either. Everyone knew that if they did not begin, then out of respect nor could anyone else. And everyone knew also why it was that the king was refusing to let the feast begin.

The great hall fell silent as Arthur rose to his feet. "You know the custom," he began. "I will not take one mouthful, or one sip of wine, until I am told of some new and stirring tale, some wonderfully outlandish adventure, some extraordinary feat of arms so far unheard of. And it must be true too. I don't want you to go making it up just so you can get at the food—some of you are good at the tall stories." They laughed at that, but as they looked around, it became clear that none of them had a tale to tell. "What?" cried the High King. "What? Not one of you? Well then, I see we must all go hungry. Such a pity. Isn't it strange how food you cannot eat always smells so wonderful? It needn't be a story, of course. It could be some new happening, some weird and wondrous event. If I can't have a story, then you'd better hope, as I do, that maybe

VISUAL VOCABULARY

dais (dā'ĭs) *n.* a raised platform for speakers or honored guests

1. **Guinevere** (gwĭn'ə-vîr').
2. **Gawain** (gə-wän').
3. **Toulouse** (to͞o-lo͞oz').
4. **Turkestan** (tûr'kĭ-stăn'): During the Middle Ages, trade occurred between Britain and many countries in Asia. Tapestries from the historical region Turkestan were prized objects that only the wealthy could afford.
5. **succulence:** juiciness and tastiness.

some stranger will come striding in here right now and challenge us face to face. That would do. I'd be happy with that. Then we could all begin our feasting before the food gets cold." And with that, he sat down. **B**

B PREDICT
Reread lines 40–54. Why does Arthur refuse to let the feast begin? Predict what will happen next.

At that very same moment, just as the High King had finished speaking, they heard a sudden roaring of wind, the rattle of doors and windows shaking, and then outside, the clatter of a horse's hooves on stone. The great doors burst open, and into the hall rode the most awesome stranger anyone there had ever set eyes on. For a start, he was a giant of a man, taller by two heads than any knight there, but not **lanky** and long, not at all. No, shoulder to shoulder he was as broad as any three men stood side by side, and his legs were massive—like tree trunks they were. And you could see the man's arms were about as thick and strong as his legs. But that wasn't all. This giant was green, green from head to toe. Yes, bright green, I tell you, as green as beech leaves in summer when the sun shines through. And when I say the man was green, I don't just mean his clothes. I mean him. His face. Green. His hands. Green. The hair that hung down to his shoulders. Green. Only his eyes, horror of horrors, glowed red, blood red and glaring from under his heavy eyebrows, which were as green as the rest of him. Everyone in that hall simply gaped at him, at his hugeness and his greenness, and at his grimness too, for the man had a thunderous scowl on his face that struck terror into every heart.

lanky (lăng'kē) *adj.* tall and thin

Grim he may have been, but the giant was gorgeous too—if such an apparition can ever be said to be gorgeous. He wore a tunic of green velvet with buttons of gleaming gold. Stirrups and spurs were all of gold, both encrusted with the brightest emeralds of the deepest green. And his horse! His warhorse was a monster of a creature—he had to be, just to carry this giant. The horse was green too, green from nose to hoof, from mane to tail. He was pawing at the ground, tossing his head, foaming at his bit; at least the foam was white. And he looked just as bad-tempered as his master. They suited each other, those two. **C**

C CULTURAL VALUES
Recall what you've learned about knights and chivalry. Does the Green Knight seem like a chivalrous type? As you read, note how chivalry influences his behavior and the reactions of others.

Yet fierce though he seemed, the Knight in green wore no war helmet and no armor either. He held no shield before him, and carried no spear, not even a sword at his side. Instead, the hand clutching the reins held a sprig of holly—green naturally—which might have been laughable had everyone not already noticed what he was carrying in his other hand. It was an ax, but it was no ordinary battle-ax. This weapon was a real head cruncher, yet the handle was most delicately carved—bright green of course, as was the cord that looped about it and the tassels that hung from it. Only the huge blade itself was not green. Curved like a crescent moon at the cutting edge, it was made of polished steel—a hideous widow maker if ever there was one. Even the dogs, usually so fierce with any stranger, shrank back whining under the tables, their tails between their legs.

There came no cheery New Year greeting from this green man, not even a ghost of a smile. In a thunderous, booming voice as terrifying as the man himself, he said, "So, who's in charge here?" No one answered him. "Well, come on. Speak up. Which of you is the King? It's him I've come to talk to, no one else." But as he rode around the hall, his blazing eyes scanning the lords and ladies on every side, no one spoke up. And you can understand why. Many of the knights sitting there in that hushed hall had come across all kinds of astounding and alarming looking creatures on their quests[6]—dragons and monsters, goblins and ghouls—but never anything quite like this. Most sat there stunned to silence. Others kept quiet out of respect for their High King, wanting to hear how he would reply.

No one doubted for a moment that he would have the courage to speak up, and so he did. Indeed, as he rose to his feet, he was smiling broadly. After all, hadn't he just been hoping for such a happening as this? "Welcome to Camelot, Sir Knight," he began. "I am the King you are looking for, I think. My name is Arthur. Believe me, you could not have arrived at a better moment. So please dismount and join our New Year's feasting, and afterward you can tell us perhaps why you have come here to our court." **D**

The knight in green rode toward the dais and spoke directly to the High King, but more courteously now. "My thanks, great King. But I will not stay, or keep you from your feasting. I will speak my purpose plainly. I cannot tell you how honored I am to meet you at last, the great Arthur, High King of all Britain. I have heard, as all the world has heard,

D CULTURAL VALUES
Reread lines 116–127. What can you **infer** about how people in the Middle Ages believed guests should be treated?

6. **quests:** adventurous journeys made by knights.

table. And the blood was not green, as you might have imagined, but bright red like any man's, and it spurted freely from head and body alike.

But instead of toppling over, as everyone expected, that grotesque headless body rose up onto his feet and strode across the floor to where his head lay bleeding, the eyes closed in death. Snatching the baleful[7] head up by the hair, he went straight to his horse, set one foot in the stirrup, and swung himself up easily into his saddle as if nothing at all had happened. Suddenly those eyes opened and glared most horribly around the hall. Everyone was struck dumb with terror.

But worse was still to come, for then the mouth began to speak. "Well struck, Sir Gawain. Now I'm afraid you have your side of the bargain to keep, a promise you made freely and openly, in front of everyone here and in front of your King too. You must seek me out and find me at the Green Chapel, a year and a day from now. There I shall repay you, a blow for a blow, as we agreed. I am known everywhere as

7. **baleful:** foretelling evil.

the Knight of the Green Chapel. Look into the sky as you go and follow where your eyes and your ears lead you. I shall be waiting. Be sure you come, Sir Gawain, or the world will know you forever as a coward." He said nothing more, not one goodbye, but turning his horse about, set spurs to his side and galloped from that hall, sparks flying from the horse's hooves as he went. Where he had come from no one knew. Where he went to no one knew. But as you can well imagine, I think, all were glad to see him gone. **K**

K PREDICT
Did the prediction you made on page 680 come true? Describe what happened after Gawain struck the Green Knight.

It was some time before anyone in the hall found voice to speak, and then it was the High King himself who at last broke the silence. He was as amazed and horrified as everyone else by what they had just witnessed, but he did not like to see his queen and his court so downhearted on this festive evening. "Come on now. Let's not be upset," he said. "After all, this was just such a marvel as we were waiting for, was it not? And marvels like this are as much a part of new year at Camelot as carols and feasting. Like it or not, and I agree it wasn't a very appetizing spectacle, you have to admit we've never seen anything quite like it before, have we? And best of all it means we can now begin our feasting. So hang up your ax, Gawain, somewhere where we can all see it and be reminded of your courage, and come and join us. Let's eat, my friends. Let's drink. Let's be merry." And so they were—all but Gawain, whose thoughts, as ours must now do, ran on ahead of him to New Year's Day a year hence, to the dreaded day when he would meet that Green Knight once again at the Green Chapel. **L**

L CULTURAL VALUES
What reasons does King Arthur have for choosing this moment to invite his knights to the feast?

Eventually, Sir Gawain did indeed set out to find the Green Chapel and fulfill his promise. On his journey, he encountered three temptations that tested his character. By the time he stood before the Green Knight, he had proven himself a worthy, though not perfect, knight. For this reason, the Green Knight injures Gawain slightly but does not take his life.

Comprehension

ALABAMA STANDARDS

READING STANDARD
1.f Analyzing predictions

1. **Clarify** What has to happen before the feast can begin?
2. **Recall** Whom does the Green Knight come looking for?
3. **Represent** What does the scene in the great hall look like before the Green Knight appears? Make a drawing illustrating the description.

Literary Analysis

4. **Predict** Review the chart of predictions you made as you read. What events were the most difficult to predict? Why?
5. **Make Inferences About Culture** What details in this legend reflect what people ate, what they wore, and how they celebrated? Tell what you infer about how the wealthy lived during the Middle Ages.
6. **Analyze Suspense** The growing tension, or excitement, that you feel as you read is called suspense. Which passages in this legend were especially suspenseful? Give the line numbers of at least two passages. Then explain your choices.
7. **Draw Conclusions About Cultural Values** People following the code of **chivalry** were expected to demonstrate the qualities shown in the web. Make a similar web and expand it by giving examples from the legend for each type of behavior. What conclusion can you draw about which of these qualities was most important to the people of the Middle Ages?

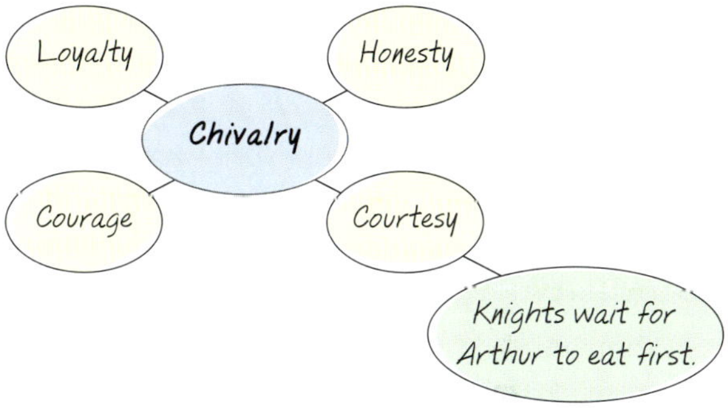

8. **Compare and Contrast Legends** How does the king Arthur portrayed by Michael Morpurgo compare with the young Arthur portrayed by Robert D. San Souci in the legend on page 662? Think about characters' attitude toward others, their confidence in themselves, and the courage they display. Decide whether the young Arthur is more similar to or more different from the adult he becomes.

Extension and Challenge

9. **Readers' Circle** Which character is the true hero of this legend? Discuss your thoughts, giving details from the legend to support your opinion.

Vocabulary in Context

VOCABULARY PRACTICE

Answer the questions to show your understanding of the vocabulary words.

1. Would a large package or one pair of socks more likely be **cumbersome?**
2. In which sport, basketball or football, might it be more important to be **lanky?**
3. If Ann is **unperturbed,** is she sitting calmly or shouting angrily?
4. Would being criticized publicly or being elected class president be more **demeaning?**
5. Would it show respect or disrespect to **revere** a person?
6. Is a telegram sent to **sever** a business deal meant to continue it or cut it off?
7. Who might be a better role model for **integrity,** an honest politician or a popular singer?
8. Which is more **daunting,** climbing a peak or resting in the backyard?

cumbersome
daunting
demeaning
integrity
lanky
revere
sever
unperturbed

VOCABULARY IN WRITING

What happened after Gawain asked to take up the Green Knight's challenge? Describe the events that followed, using three or more vocabulary words. Here is one way you could begin.

EXAMPLE SENTENCE

*Gawain grabbed hold of the **cumbersome** battle-ax.*

VOCABULARY STRATEGY: EASILY CONFUSED WORDS

When you first read the vocabulary word *sever,* did you mistake it for *severe?* The words *sever* and *severe* are easy to confuse, especially in writing. Be sure to choose the correct word from confusing pairs, checking spellings and meanings in a dictionary if you are not sure.

ACTIVITY Choose the word in parentheses that correctly completes each sentence. Refer to a dictionary if necessary.

1. The heavy fog seemed to (envelop, envelope) the entire building.
2. After the team lost its first game by 18 points, (moral, morale) among the players dropped dramatically.
3. To get rid of the cooking smells, we gave the room a (through, thorough) airing.
4. Can you really eat (desert, dessert) after that enormous meal?
5. You can get to our garage by driving down the (ally, alley).

VOCABULARY PRACTICE
For more practice, go to the **Vocabulary Center** at **ClassZone.com.**

Reading-Writing Connection

SKILLS PRACTICE

Explore this legend further by responding to the prompts. Then complete the **Grammar and Writing** exercise.

WRITING PROMPTS	SELF-CHECK
A. Short Response: Write an Explanation Why do you think Gawain accepted the Green Knight's challenge? Write a **one-paragraph explanation** of his motivation.	***A good explanation will . . .*** • show an understanding of Gawain's character and the code of chivalry • explain the causes and effects of his decision
B. Extended Response: Write a Letter If King Arthur could write a letter to the people of today promoting his **chivalrous** ideals, what would he say? Write a **two- or three-paragraph letter** from Arthur telling why chivalrous behavior makes the world a better place.	***A successful letter will . . .*** • be written in the courteous style of a chivalrous leader • present arguments that are convincing to people

GRAMMAR AND WRITING

ALABAMA STANDARDS

WRITING/LANGUAGE STANDARD
11.d Using complex sentences

USE CORRECT SENTENCE STRUCTURE A **dependent clause** is a group of words that contains a subject and a verb but cannot stand alone as a sentence. Dependent clauses begin with words such as *because, if, that, when, while,* and *who.* When a dependent clause and an independent clause are combined, they form a **complex sentence.**

Original: Gawain accepts the Green Knight's challenge. Because he is brave. (*"Because he is brave" is a dependent clause and cannot stand alone as a sentence.*)

Revised: Gawain accepts the Green Knight's challenge because he is brave. (*The clauses now form a complex sentence.*)

PRACTICE Form a complex sentence by combining the dependent clause with the independent clause.

1. The kingdom would fall. If King Arthur died.
2. Gawain still faces the Green Knight. Even though he is frightened.
3. Gawain must face the Green Knight again a year later. Because he promised he would.
4. Gawain proves to be a good nephew. Who sacrifices himself for his uncle.

*For more help with dependent clauses, see page R64 in the **Grammar Handbook.** For more help with complex sentences, see page R64 in the **Grammar Handbook.***

Great Reads

Crispin: The Cross of Lead

Historical Novel by Avi

Avi
born 1937

Other Books by Avi

- *Bright Shadow*
- *The Fighting Ground*
- *The Man Who Was Poe*
- *Midnight Magic*
- *Nothing but the Truth*
- *S.O.R. Losers*
- *The True Confessions of Charlotte Doyle*
- *Wolf Rider*

Meet Avi

Avi notes that reading helped him to become a professional writer: "The more you read, the better your writing can be," he has said. By this measure, it's no surprise Avi is an award-winning writer. He earned a college degree in history and an advanced degree in drama. While working in the New York Public Library's theater collection, he decided to go back to school for an advanced degree in library science.

Avi first wrote plays, but while raising his children, he began writing books for young people. Since then, he has written over 50 books and won many important awards. Avi loves being an author and has said, "To invent the stories that people take to their hearts is, I think, one of the most wonderful things one can do."

Try a Historical Novel

Have you ever wondered what it was like to live in the Middle Ages? Until inventors create a time machine, reading **historical fiction,** or stories that are set in the past, is one of the best ways to find out. Historical fiction can make the past come alive by mixing references to actual people, places, and events with fictional characters and dialogue and other creative details.

Avi's historical fiction has been praised for the accuracy of the historical elements he includes. His 25 years of experience as a research librarian taught him how to find all the details he needs to establish a story's setting in a different time and place.

Read a Great Book

This story is set in England in the year 1377, when nobles ruled the land and their agricultural workers, the serfs, had almost no rights at all. You are about to read a passage about a young serf named Crispin who is on his way home from his mother's funeral. He is attacked by a group of men for reasons he does not yet understand. He narrowly escapes and hides in the woods overnight, then goes to the village priest for advice on what he should do.

from

CRISPIN
THE CROSS OF LEAD

Near the altar the priest genuflected. I did the same. Then we knelt, facing each other. "Speak low," he said. "There's always Judas lurking. Are you hungry?"

"Yes, Father," I murmured.

From behind the tattered altar cloth he produced a loaf of barley bread and gave it to me. "I was hoping you would come," he said.

I took the heavy bread and began to devour it.

"Where have you been?" he asked.

"In the forest."

"Did you know they've been searching for you?"

My mouth full, I nodded.

"Aycliffe claims you stole money from the manor."

"Father," I said, "in all my life, I've never even been there."

"I don't doubt you," the priest said, gently putting his hand to my face to keep me calm. "Most people in the village don't believe the accusation, either. But why does Aycliffe put your name to the crime?"

I told the priest what had happened when I ran from my mother's burial—my fall, my waking to witness the meeting in the clearing, Aycliffe's attempt to kill me.

"He said none of this," the priest said.

"It's true."

"What was the thing the steward read?" the priest asked. "He never mentioned that either."

"I don't know," I said. Then I asked, "Who was the man he met?"

"Sir Richard du Brey," the priest said. "He's brought word that Lord Furnival—God keep him well—has returned from the wars. He's ill and expected to die."

"The stranger said Aycliffe must act immediately."

"About what?"

I shrugged. "He said, 'Are you not her kin? Do you not see the consequences if you don't?' To which Aycliffe replied, 'A great danger to us all.' Then the man said, 'Precisely. There could be those who will see it so and act accordingly. You'll be placed in danger, too.' It made no sense to me," I said.

The priest pondered the words in silence.

"Father," I said, "what will happen if I'm caught?"

The priest put his hand on my shoulder. "The steward," he said, "has declared you a wolf's head."

"A wolf's head!" I gasped, horrified.

"Do you understand what it means?"

"That . . . I'm considered not human," I said, my voice faltering. "That anyone may . . . kill me. Is that why they pulled down our house?"

"I suppose."

"But . . . *why?*"

The priest sat back and gave himself over to thought. In the dim light I studied his face. He seemed distraught, as if the pain of the whole world had settled in his soul.

"Father," I ventured, "is it something about my mother?"

He bowed his head. When he looked up it was to gaze at me. "Asta's son, unless you flee, you won't live long."

"But how can I leave?" I said. "I'm bound to the land. They'll never give me permission to go."

He sighed, reached forward, and placed the side of his frail hand aside my face. "Asta's son, listen to me with the greatest care. When I baptized you, you were named . . . Crispin."

"I was?" I cried.

"It was done in secret. What's more, your mother begged me not to tell you or anyone. She chose to simply call you 'Son.'"

"But . . . why?" I asked.

He took a deep breath and then said, "Did she tell you anything about your father?"

Once again the priest took me by surprise. "My *father?* Only that he died before I was born. In the Great Mortality," I reminded him. "But what has that to do with my name? Or any of this?"

"Dearest boy," the priest said wearily, "I beg you to find your way to some town or city with its own liberties. If you can stay there for a year and a day, you'll gain your freedom."

"Freedom?" I said. "What has that to do with me?"

"You could live by your own choices. As . . . a highborn lord . . . or a king."

"Father," I said, "that's impossible for me. I am what I am. I know nothing but Stromford."

"Even so, you must go. There are cities enough: Canterbury, Great Wexly, Winchester. Even London."

"What . . . what are these places like?"

"They have many souls living there, far more than here. Too many to count. But I assure you they are Christians."

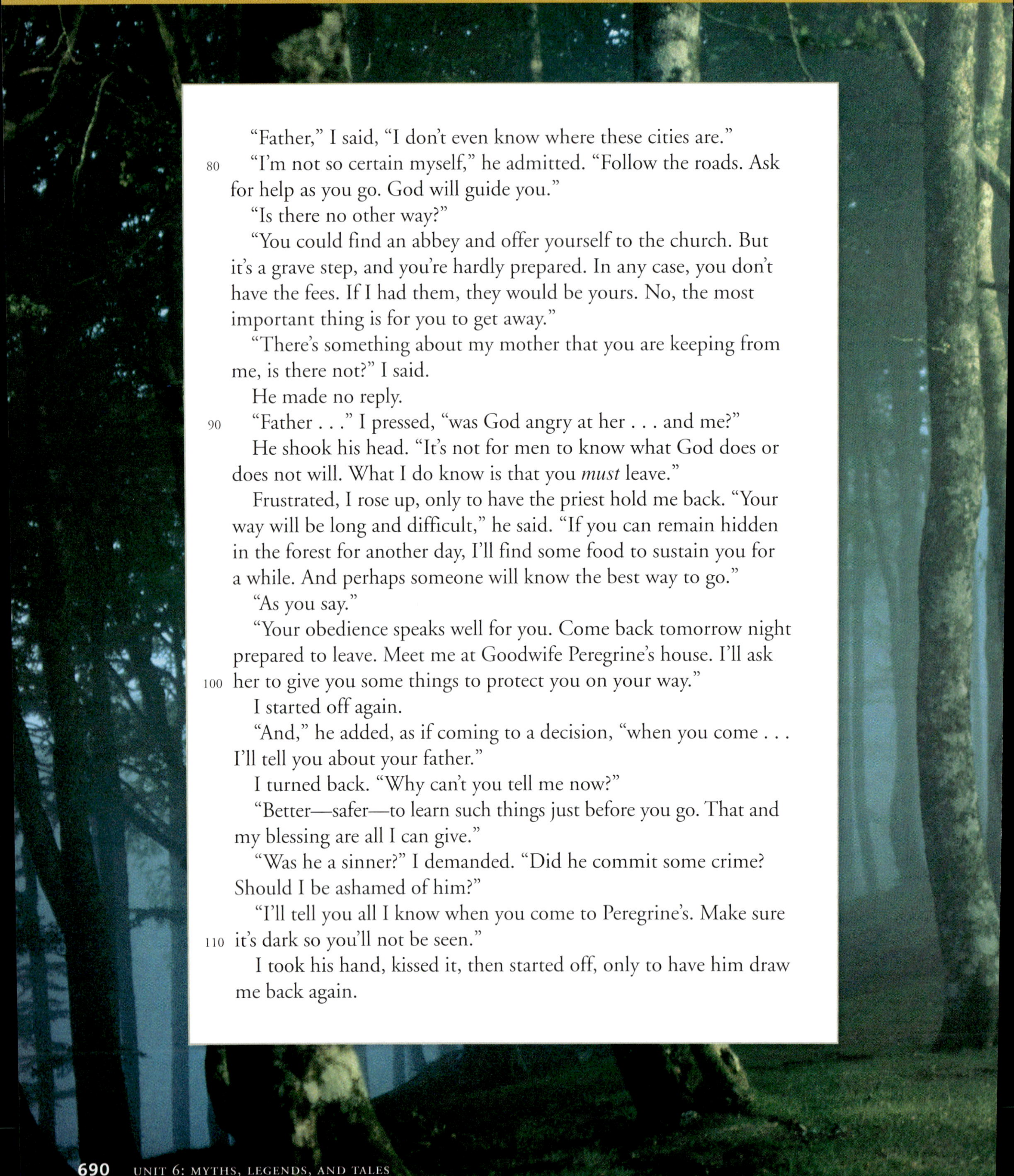

"Father," I said, "I don't even know where these cities are."

"I'm not so certain myself," he admitted. "Follow the roads. Ask for help as you go. God will guide you."

"Is there no other way?"

"You could find an abbey and offer yourself to the church. But it's a grave step, and you're hardly prepared. In any case, you don't have the fees. If I had them, they would be yours. No, the most important thing is for you to get away."

"There's something about my mother that you are keeping from me, is there not?" I said.

He made no reply.

"Father . . ." I pressed, "was God angry at her . . . and me?"

He shook his head. "It's not for men to know what God does or does not will. What I do know is that you *must* leave."

Frustrated, I rose up, only to have the priest hold me back. "Your way will be long and difficult," he said. "If you can remain hidden in the forest for another day, I'll find some food to sustain you for a while. And perhaps someone will know the best way to go."

"As you say."

"Your obedience speaks well for you. Come back tomorrow night prepared to leave. Meet me at Goodwife Peregrine's house. I'll ask her to give you some things to protect you on your way."

I started off again.

"And," he added, as if coming to a decision, "when you come . . . I'll tell you about your father."

I turned back. "Why can't you tell me now?"

"Better—safer—to learn such things just before you go. That and my blessing are all I can give."

"Was he a sinner?" I demanded. "Did he commit some crime? Should I be ashamed of him?"

"I'll tell you all I know when you come to Peregrine's. Make sure it's dark so you'll not be seen."

I took his hand, kissed it, then started off, only to have him draw me back again.

"Can you read?"

"No more than my mother."

"But she could."

"Father, you're greatly mistaken."

"She could write, too."

I shook my head in puzzlement. "These things you say: a name. Reading. Writing. My father . . . Why would my mother keep such things from me?"

The priest became very still. Then, from his pocket, he removed my mother's cross of lead, the one with which she so oft prayed, which was in her hands when she died. I had forgotten about it. He held it up.

"Your mother's."

"I know," I said sullenly.

"Do you know what's on it?"

"Some writing, I think."

"I saw your mother write those words."

I looked at him in disbelief. "But—"

"Tomorrow," he said, cutting me off and folding my fingers over the cross, "I'll explain. Just remember, God mends all. Now go," he said. "And stay well hidden."

Keep Reading

Crispin's life has just changed dramatically. What do you think is unusual about this boy? Why is he on the run? As you read the rest of Avi's book, you'll find that *Crispin: The Cross of Lead* is a suspenseful story from the start, and the action never slows down. You'll be transported to England in the Middle Ages and experience its sights, smells, and sounds as you follow Crispin on his adventures.

Reading for Information

A Medieval Mystery

Book Reviews

Use with *Crispin: The Cross of Lead*, page 687.

ALABAMA STANDARDS

READING STANDARDS

4 Distinguish opinion in informational materials

9 Compose in expository mode

What's the Connection?

Even after reading the scene from *Crispin: The Cross of Lead*, you might not be sure whether you'd like to read the whole book. To reach a decision, read two book reviews of this historical novel.

Skill Focus: Identify Opinions

After you finish a book, how do you pick out the next one? Do you seek out others by the same author, set in the same time period, or of the same genre? One way to find a book you'll love as much as or more than the one before is to read book reviews.

Book reviewers try to provide enough details of a story's setting, characters, and plot to give their readers a sense of what the book offers without giving away the ending. Along the way, and then most strongly toward the end of the review, they sum up their opinions of these elements to explain why they recommend the book—or don't.

As you read the book reviews that follow, keep track of the opinions each reviewer provides in a chart like the one shown.

Opinions About	Review by Rebecca Barnhouse	Review by Cheri Estes
Setting (time and place)	Details about the past are portrayed "accurately and compellingly."	
Character		
Plot		
Other Story Elements		

Book Review

Serf on the Run

by Rebecca Barnhouse

Crispin: The Cross of Lead
by Avi **261 pages**

In 1377 England, mysteries surround thirteen-year-old Crispin, a serf from a rural village who never knows his own name until his mother dies. Nor does he know just who his mother really was—why she was an outcast or how she learned to read and write. Shortly after her burial, Crispin finds himself pursued by men who mean to kill him for reasons he does not understand. He escapes, only to be captured by a huge juggler named Bear. Bear teaches Crispin to sing and play the recorder, and slowly they begin to get to know one another. When they perform in villages and towns, however, they discover that the hunt for Crispin is still in full swing. For Crispin, this situation makes the question of Bear's trustworthiness vital, for Bear has secrets of his own. **A**

The suspense stays taut until the very end of the book, when Crispin uncovers his identity and then must decide how to act on that information. His journey to selfhood recalls Alice's in Karen Cushman's *The Midwife's Apprentice.* Like Alice, Crispin casts off his timidity to make a place for himself within a society that would discard him. As does Cushman, Avi renders the sights, sounds, and smells of medieval England accurately and compellingly. He shows the pervasiveness of the church in medieval society and, in a subplot, weaves in details about John Ball and the Peasants' Rebellion. Exciting and true to the past, this novel is historical fiction at its finest. **B**

FOCUS ON FORM The two selections you are about to read are **book reviews,** short pieces of writing in which a writer describes the main elements of a book and summarizes his or her opinions of the book.

A BOOK REVIEW What details of character, setting, and plot does Rebecca Barnhouse provide?

B IDENTIFY OPINIONS Find the sentences in which Barnhouse states her opinions of *Crispin: The Cross of Lead.* In your own words, write her opinions in the appropriate place in your chart.

BOOK REVIEW

Crispin: The Cross of Lead

by Avi **261 pages**

Medieval Adventures Cheri Estes

As with Karen Cushman's *The Midwife's Apprentice*, the power of a name is apparent in this novel set in 14th-century England. "Asta's son" is all the destitute, illiterate hero has ever been called, but after his mother dies, he learns that his given name is Crispin, and that he is in mortal danger. The local priest is murdered before he can tell him more about his background, and Aycliffe, the evil village steward for Lord Furnival, declares that the boy is a "wolf's head," less than human, and that he should be killed on sight. On the run, with nothing to sustain him but his faith in God, Crispin meets "Bear," a roving entertainer who has ties to an underground movement to improve living conditions for the common people. They make their way to Great Wexly, where Bear has clandestine meetings and Crispin hopes to escape from Aycliffe and his soldiers, who stalk him at every turn. Suspense heightens when the boy learns that the recently deceased Lord Furnival was his father and that Aycliffe is dead set on preventing him from claiming his title. To trap his prey, the villain captures Bear, and Crispin risks his life to save him. C

Avi has done an excellent job of integrating background and historical information, of pacing the plot so that the book is a page-turner from beginning to end, and of creating characters for whom readers will have great empathy. The result is a meticulously crafted story, full of adventure, mystery, and action. D

C BOOK REVIEW
What do you learn about the book's setting, characters, and plot from Estes's review?

D IDENTIFY OPINIONS
What are Estes's opinions of the setting, plot, and characters of *Crispin: The Cross of Lead?* Add these to your chart. Be sure to put quotation marks around any direct quotations you use.

Comprehension

1. **Recall** Which characters are mentioned in Barnhouse's review? Which are mentioned in Estes's review?
2. **Summarize** Summarize the reasons each reviewer gives for recommending *Crispin: The Cross of Lead.*

Critical Analysis

3. **Compare Opinions** Review the chart you created as you read. Which of Barnhouse's and Estes's opinions are similar to each other's? Which, if any, are different?
4. **Evaluate Book Reviews** A good book review gives details of the story without spoiling the story's suspense. Which of these reviews does a better job of this? Explain.

Read for Information: Compare Your Reactions

WRITING PROMPT

Both Rebecca Barnhouse and Cheri Estes recommend *Crispin: The Cross of Lead.* On the basis of what you've read of the novel, do you agree with them? Compare your reactions with theirs, explaining why you agree or disagree.

To answer this prompt, follow these steps:

1. Think about the reactions you had to the setting, characters, and plot you read about in *Crispin: The Cross of Lead* (pages 687–691). Write statements of opinion about each of these elements.
2. Identify each reviewer's opinions of the setting, characters, and plot.
3. Compare your reactions to those of the reviewers to identify which opinions you agree with and which you disagree with.
4. Write an essay in which you compare your reactions to those of the reviewers. Support each comparison with details from the excerpt.

Opinions
- Your opinions
- Barnhouse's opinions
- Estes's opinions

→

Important Points

Points of Agreement
- __________
- __________

Points of Disagreement
- __________
- __________

→

My Essay (with details from excerpts)

____

ALABAMA STANDARDS

READING STANDARDS

4 Distinguish opinion in informational materials

9 Compose in expository mode

Brer Possum's Dilemma

African-American Folk Tale Retold by Jackie Torrence

Waters of Gold

Chinese Folk Tale Retold by Laurence Yep

What can we LEARN *from stories?*

ALABAMA STANDARDS

READING STANDARDS

1.d Applying self-monitoring strategies

3 Distinguish among subgenres based on characteristics

KEY IDEA You've probably been lectured to many times about things you should and shouldn't do. The problem is, it's easy to forget what you hear in a lecture. But what if you happen to learn **lessons** while being entertained by interesting, even unforgettable, characters? Those lessons may be the ones you carry with you for the rest of your life.

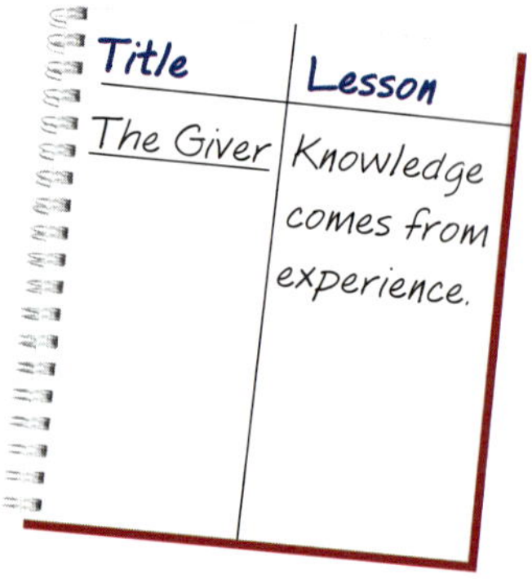

LIST IT On a sheet of notebook paper, list three or four of your favorite stories of all time. What lessons did they teach? Add the lessons to your list, and compare the list to those of your classmates.

LITERARY ANALYSIS: CHARACTERISTICS OF FOLK TALES

Folk tales are stories that have been handed down through generations by being told out loud. Every culture has its own folk tales, but the stories often share certain characteristics.

- Each character usually represents a specific trait, or quality.
- The plot often centers on events that occur in a set of three.
- Many folk tales teach a lesson, or **moral.**

As you read the selections, pay attention to the way the characters and plot work together to teach a lesson.

READING STRATEGY: SUMMARIZE

When you **summarize** what you've read, you briefly retell the story's main points in your own words, focusing only on the most important details. To help you summarize, use a graphic organizer to record key information as you read each selection.

Title and Culture:	Author:	Setting:
Characters:		
Events:		
Lesson or Moral:		

Review: **Predict**

VOCABULARY IN CONTEXT

Each of the vocabulary words here is in these folk tales. Choose the word that completes each sentence.

WORD LIST			
	commence	jostling	prime
	humor	perilously	smugly

1. Don't get ahead in life by _____ others out of the way.
2. Sometimes it's better to _____ someone than to argue with him.
3. For the best results, _____ each day with a good attitude.
4. By wanting it all, she came _____ close to losing what she had.
5. Safety should be a _____ concern for all parents.
6. If you accept praise _____, you won't see much of it.

Author Online

Jackie Torrence: The Story Lady

Jackie Torrence
1944–2004

Jackie Torrence was working as a librarian when one day her boss came looking for help: the library's storyteller hadn't shown up, and children were waiting. Torrence reluctantly took over. She became famous for retelling African-American folk tales, many of which were handed down by her grandfather. Torrence said that "long before TV or radio, all cultures used storytelling to instill values and heritage."

Laurence Yep: Folk Tale Collector

Laurence Yep
born 1948

In addition to being an award-winning writer of books for young people, Laurence Yep researches and collects Chinese folk tales. ("Waters of Gold" came to the United States with Chinese immigrants who settled in California.) He feels that these stories have a "raw power" and mystery that appeal to all ages.

MORE ABOUT THE AUTHOR
For more on Jackie Torrence and Laurence Yep, visit the **Literature Center** at **ClassZone.com.**

Brer Possum's Dilemma

Retold by
Jackie Torrence

Back in the days when the animals could talk, there lived ol' Brer Possum. He was a fine feller. Why, he never liked to see no critters in trouble. He was always helpin' out, a-doin' somethin' for others.

Ever' night, ol' Brer Possum climbed into a persimmon tree, hung by his tail, and slept all night long. And each mornin', he climbed outa the tree and walked down the road to sun 'imself.

One mornin', as he walked, he come to a big hole in the middle of the road. Now, ol' Brer Possum was kind and gentle, but he was also nosy, so he went over to the hole and looked in. All at once, he stepped back, 'cause layin' in the bottom of that hole was ol' Brer Snake with a brick on his back.

Brer Possum said to 'imself, "I best git on outa here, 'cause ol' Brer Snake is mean and evil and lowdown, and if I git to stayin' around 'im, he jist might git to bitin' me."

So Brer Possum went on down the road.

But Brer Snake had seen Brer Possum, and he **commenced** to callin' for 'im.

"Help me, Brer Possum."

Brer Possum stopped and turned around. He said to 'imself, "That's ol' Brer Snake a-callin' me. What do you reckon he wants?"

Well, ol' Brer Possum was kindhearted, so he went back down the road to the hole, stood at the edge, and looked down at Brer Snake.

"Was that you a-callin' me? What do you want?" **A**

ANALYZE VISUALS
What human **traits** do the animals in this image suggest? Tell how the artist creates this impression.

commence (kə-mĕns') *v.* to start or begin

A FOLK TALES
The characters in folktales may be humans or animals with human characteristics. What human characteristics does Brer Possum have?

Brer Snake looked up and said, "I've been down here in this hole for a mighty long time with this brick on my back. Won't you help git it offa me?"

Brer Possum thought.

"Now listen here, Brer Snake. I knows you. You's mean and evil and lowdown, and if'n I was to git down in that hole and git to liftin' that brick offa your back, you wouldn't do nothin' but bite me."

Ol' Brer Snake just hissed.

"Maybe not. Maybe not. Maaaaaaaybe not." **B**

Brer Possum said, "I ain't sure 'bout you at all. I jist don't know. You're a-goin' to have to let me think about it."

So ol' Brer Possum thought—he thought high, and he thought low—and jist as he was thinkin', he looked up into a tree and saw a dead limb a-hangin' down. He climbed into the tree, broke off the limb, and with that ol' stick, pushed that brick offa Brer Snake's back. Then he took off down the road.

Brer Possum thought he was away from ol' Brer Snake when all at once he heard somethin'.

"Help me, Brer Possum."

Brer Possum said, "Oh, no, that's him agin."

But bein' so kindhearted, Brer Possum turned around, went back to the hole, and stood at the edge.

"Brer Snake, was that you a-callin' me? What do you want now?"

Ol' Brer Snake looked up outa the hole and hissed.

"I've been down here for a mighty long time, and I've gotten a little weak, and the sides of this ol' hole are too slick for me to climb. Do you think you can lift me outa here?"

Brer Possum thought.

"Now, you jist wait a minute. If'n I was to git down into that hole and lift you outa there, you wouldn't do nothin' but bite me."

Brer Snake hissed.

"Maybe not. Maybe not. Maaaaaaaybe not."

Brer Possum said, "I jist don't know. You're a-goin' to have to give me time to think about this."

So ol' Brer Possum thought.

And as he thought, he jist happened to look down there in that hole and see that ol' dead limb. So he pushed the limb underneath ol' Brer Snake and he lifted 'im outa the hole, way up into the air, and throwed 'im into the high grass.

Brer Possum took off a-runnin' down the road. **C**

Well, he thought he was away from ol' Brer Snake when all at once he heard somethin'.

B PREDICT
The characters disagree about what will happen if Brer Possum helps Brer Snake. From what you know about the characters so far, what do you predict will happen?

C SUMMARIZE
In your graphic organizer, briefly note the events described so far.

"Help me, Brer Possum."

Brer Possum thought, "That's him agin."

But bein' so kindhearted, he turned around, went back to the hole, and stood there a-lookin' for Brer Snake. Brer Snake crawled outa the high grass just as slow as he could, stretched 'imself out across the road, rared up, and looked at ol' Brer Possum.

Then he hissed. "I've been down there in that ol' hole for a mighty long time, and I've gotten a little cold 'cause the sun didn't shine. Do you think you could put me in your pocket and git me warm?"

Brer Possum said, "Now you listen here, Brer Snake. I knows you. You's mean and evil and lowdown, and if'n I put you in my pocket you wouldn't do nothin' but bite me."

Brer Snake hissed.

"Maybe not. Maybe not. Maaaaaaaybe not."

"No, sireee, Brer Snake. I knows you. I jist ain't a-goin' to do it."

But jist as Brer Possum was talkin' to Brer Snake, he happened to git a real good look at 'im. He was a-layin' there lookin' so pitiful, and Brer Possum's great big heart began to feel sorry for ol' Brer Snake.

"All right," said Brer Possum. "You must be cold. So jist this once I'm a-goin' to put you in my pocket." D

So ol' Brer Snake coiled up jist as little as he could, and Brer Possum picked 'im up and put 'im in his pocket.

Brer Snake laid quiet and still—so quiet and still that Brer Possum even forgot that he was a-carryin' 'im around. But all of a sudden, Brer Snake commenced to crawlin' out, and he turned and faced Brer Possum and hissed.

"I'm a-goin' to bite you."

But Brer Possum said, "Now wait a minute. Why are you a-goin' to bite me? I done took that brick offa your back, I got you outa that hole, and I put you in my pocket to git you warm. Why are you a-goin' to bite me?"

Brer Snake hissed.

"You knowed I was a snake before you put me in your pocket."

And when you're mindin' your own business and you spot trouble, don't never trouble trouble 'til trouble troubles you. E

D FOLK TALES
Note how many times Brer Possum has come to help Brer Snake. What patterns are developing?

E FOLK TALES
Reread lines 99–100. Sometimes you may have to infer the **moral** of a folk tale, but in this case the moral is stated directly. Rephrase it in your own words.

Waters of Gold

Retold by Laurence Yep

Many years ago, there lived a woman whom everyone called Auntie Lily. She was Auntie by blood to half the county and Auntie to the other half by friendship. As she liked to say, "There's a bit of Heaven in each of us." As a result, she was always helping people out.

Because of her many kind acts, she knew so many people that she couldn't go ten steps without meeting someone who wanted to chat. So it would take her half the day to go to the village well and back to her home. **F**

Eventually, though, she helped so many people that she had no more money. She had to sell her fields and even her house to her neighbor, a rich old woman. "If you'd helped yourself instead of others, you wouldn't have to do this," the neighbor said **smugly.** "Where are all those other people when you need them?"

"That isn't why I helped them," Auntie Lily said firmly. She wound up having to pay rent for the house she had once owned. She supported herself by her embroidery; but since her eyes were going bad, she could not do very much.

One day an old beggar entered the village. He was a ragbag of a man—a trash heap, a walking pig wallow. It was impossible to tell what color or what shape his clothes had once been, and his hair was as muddy and matted as a bird's nest. As he shuffled through the village gates, he called out, "Water for my feet. Please, water for my feet. One little bowl of water—that's all I ask."

F **FOLK TALES**
What **trait** do you think Auntie Lily represents?

smugly (smŭg'lē) *adv.* in a self-satisfied way

ANALYZE VISUALS
Compare the village in this picture to the village described in the story. In what ways are they similar?

Orchard (2000), Chen Jia Qi. Watercolor. Red Lantern Folk Art, Mukashi Collection.
© The Mukashi Collection/SuperStock.

Everyone ignored him, pretending to concentrate on their chores instead. One man went on replacing the shaft of his hoe. A woman swept her courtyard. Another woman fed her hens.

The beggar went to each in turn, but they all showed their backs to him.

After calling out a little while longer, the beggar went to the nearest home, which happened to belong to the rich old woman. When he banged at her door, he left the dirty outline of his knuckles on the clean wood. And when the rich woman opened her door, his smell nearly took her breath away.

Now it so happened that she had been chopping vegetables when the beggar had knocked. When the beggar repeated his request, she raised her cleaver menacingly. "What good would one bowl of water be? You'd need a whole river to wash you clean. Go away."

"A thousand pardons," the old beggar said, and shambled on to the next house.

Though Auntie Lily had to hold her nose, she asked politely, "Yes?"

"I'd like a bowl of water to wash my feet." And the beggar pointed one grimy finger toward them.

Her rich neighbor had stayed in her doorway to watch the beggar. She scolded Auntie Lily now. "It's all your fault those beggars come into the village. They know they can count on a free meal."

It was an old debate between them, so Auntie Lily simply said, "Any of us can have bad luck."

"Garbage," the rich old woman declared, "is garbage. They must have done something bad, or Heaven wouldn't have let them become beggars."

Auntie Lily turned to the beggar. "I may be joining you on the road someday. Wait here."

Much to the neighbor's distress, Auntie Lily went inside and poured water from a large jar in her kitchen into a bucket. Carrying it in both hands, she brought it outside to the beggar and set it down.

The beggar stood on one leg, just like a crane, while he washed one callused, leathery sole over the bucket. "You can put mud on any other part of me, but if my feet are clean, then I feel clean."

As he fussily continued to cleanse his feet, Auntie Lily asked kindly, "Are you hungry? I don't have much, but what I have I'm willing to share." **G**

G SUMMARIZE
What happens when Auntie Lily and the rich woman encounter the beggar? Record the events in your graphic organizer.

The beggar shook his head. "I've stayed longer in this village than I have in any other. Heaven is my roof, and the whole world my house."

Auntie Lily stared at him, wondering what she would look like after a few years on the road. "Are you very tired? Have you been on the road for very long?"

"No, the road is on me," the beggar said, and held up his hands from his dirty sides. "But thank you. You're the first person to ask. And you're the first person to give me some water. So place the bucket of water by your bed tonight and do not look into it till tomorrow morning." **H**

As the beggar shuffled out of the village again, Auntie Lily stared down doubtfully at the bucket of what was now muddy water. Then, even though she felt foolish, she picked it up again.

"You're not really going to take that scummy water inside?" laughed the rich neighbor. "It'll probably breed mosquitoes."

"It seemed important to him," she answered. "I'll **humor** him."

"Humoring people," snapped the neighbor, "has got you one step from begging yourself."

However, Auntie Lily carried the bucket inside anyway. Setting it down near her sleeping mat, she covered the mouth of the bucket with an old, cracked plate so she wouldn't peek into it by mistake, and then she got so caught up in embroidering a pair of slippers that she forgot all about the beggar and his bucket of water.

She sewed until twilight, when it was too dark to use her needle. Then, because she had no money for oil or candles, she went to sleep.

The next morning Auntie Lily rose and stretched the aches out of her back. She sighed. "The older I get, the harder it is to get up in the morning."

Detail from *Spring in the Old Village* (2001), Chen Jia Qi. Watercolor. Red Lantern Folk Art, Mukashi Collection. © The Mukashi Collection/SuperStock.

H PREDICT
Reread lines 66–69. From what the beggar has said about Auntie Lily, what kind of thing do you predict will happen if she follows his instructions?

humor (hyo͞o'mər) *v.* to give in to the wishes of

She was always saying something like that, but she had never stayed on her sleeping mat—even when she was sick. Thinking of all that day's chores, she decided to water the herbs she had growing on one side of her house.

Her eyes fell upon the beggar's bucket with its covering plate. "No sense using fresh water when that will do as well. After all, dirt's dirt to a plant."

Squatting down, she picked up the bucket and was surprised at how heavy it was. "I must have filled it fuller than I thought," she grunted.

She staggered out of the house and over to the side where rows of little green herbs grew. "Here you go," she said to her plants. "Drink deep."

Taking off the plate, she upended the bucket; but instead of muddy brown water, there was a flash of reflected light and a clinking sound as gold coins rained down upon her plants.

Auntie Lily set the bucket down hastily and crouched, not trusting her weak eyes. However, where some of her herbs had been, there was now a small mound of gold coins. She squinted in disbelief and rubbed her aching eyes and stared again; but the gold was still there.

She turned to the bucket. There was even more gold inside. Scooping up coins by the handful, she freed her little plants and made sure that the stalks weren't too bent.

Then she sat gazing at her bucket full of gold until a farmer walked by. "Tell me I'm not dreaming," she called to him.

The farmer yawned and came over with his hoe over his shoulder. "I wish I were dreaming, because that would mean I'm still in bed instead of having to go off to work."

Auntie Lily gathered up a handful of gold coins and let it fall in a tinkling, golden shower back into the bucket. "And this is real?"

The farmer's jaw dropped. He picked up one coin with his free hand and bit into it.[1] He flipped it back in with the other coins. "It's as real as me, Auntie. But where did you ever get that?"

So Auntie Lily told him. And as others woke up and stepped outside, Auntie told them as well, for she still could not believe her luck and wanted them to confirm that the gold was truly gold. In no time at all, there was a small crowd around her. **I**

I SUMMARIZE
In your own words, explain what happens to Auntie Lily.

If the bucket had been filled with ordinary copper cash, that would have been more money than any of them had ever seen. In their wildest dreams, they had never expected to see that much gold. Auntie Lily stared at the bucket uncomfortably. "I keep thinking it's going to disappear the next moment."

1. **bit into it:** Gold is soft, so biting it is a way of testing its authenticity.

The farmer, who had been standing there all this time, shook his head. "If it hasn't disappeared by now, I don't think it will. What are you going to do with it, Auntie?"

Auntie Lily stared at the bucket, and suddenly she came to a decision. Stretching out a hand, she picked up a gold coin. "I'm going to buy back my house, and I'm going to get back my land."

The farmer knew the fields. "Those old things? You could buy a valley full of **prime** land with half that bucket. And a palace with the other half."

prime (prīm) *adj.* first in quality or value

"I want what I sweated for." Asking the farmer to guard her bucket, Auntie Lily closed her hand around the gold coin. Then, as the crowd parted before her, she made her way over to her neighbor. **J**

J FOLK TALES
Reread lines 129–139. What does Auntie Lily's decision about how to spend her money say about her?

Now the rich old woman liked to sleep late; but all the noise had woken her up, so she was just getting dressed when Auntie knocked. The old woman yanked her door open as she buttoned the last button of her coat. "Who started the riot? Can't a person get a good night's sleep?"

With some satisfaction, Auntie Lily held up the gold coin. "Will this buy back my house and land?"

"Where did you get that?" the old woman demanded.

"Will it buy them back?" Auntie Lily repeated.

The rich old woman snatched the coin out of Auntie Lily's hand and bit into it just as the farmer had. "It's real," the old woman said in astonishment.

"Will it?" Auntie asked again.

"Yes, yes, yes," the old woman said crabbily. "But where did you ever get that much gold?"

When Auntie Lily told her the story and showed her the bucket of gold, the rich old woman stood moving her mouth like a fish out of water. Clasping her hands together, she shut her eyes and moaned in genuine pain. "And I sent him away. What a fool I am. What a fool." And the old woman beat her head with her fists.

That very afternoon, the beggar—the ragbag, the trash heap, the walking pig wallow—shuffled once more through the village gates with feet as dirty as before. As he went, he croaked, "Water for my feet. Please, water for my feet. One little bowl of water—that's all I ask." **K**

K PREDICT
How do you predict the townspeople will behave now that the beggar has returned?

This time, people dropped whatever they were doing when they heard his plea. Hoes, brooms, and pots were flung down, hens and pigs were kicked out of the way as everyone hurried to fill a bucket with water. There was a small riot by the village well as everyone fought to get water at the same time. Still others rushed out with buckets filled from the jars in their houses.

"Here, use my water," one man shouted, holding up a tub.

A woman shoved in front of him with a bucket in her arms. "No, no, use mine. It's purer."

They surrounded the old beggar, pleading with him to use their water, and in the process of **jostling** one another, they splashed a good deal of water on one another and came **perilously** close to drowning the beggar. The rich old woman, Auntie Lily's neighbor, charged to the rescue.

jostling (jŏs′lĭng) *n.* roughly bumping, pushing, or shoving **jostle** *v.*

perilously (pĕr′ə-ləs-lē) *adv.* dangerously

"Out of the way, you vultures," the rich old woman roared. "You're going to trample him." Using her elbows, her feet, and in one case even her teeth, the old woman fought her way through the mob.

No longer caring if she soiled her hands, the old woman seized the beggar by the arm. "This way, you poor, misunderstood creature."

Fighting off her neighbors with one hand and keeping her grip on the beggar with the other, the old woman hauled him inside her house. Barring the door against the rest of the village, she ignored all the fists and feet thumping on her door and all the shouts.

"I really wasn't myself yesterday, because I had been up the night before tending a sick friend. This is what I meant to do." She fetched a fresh new towel and an even newer bucket and forced the beggar to wash his feet.

When he was done, he handed her the now filthy towel. "Dirt's dirt, and garbage is garbage," he said.

However, the greedy old woman didn't recognize her own words. She was too busy trying to remember what else Auntie Lily had done. "Won't you have something to eat? Have you traveled very far? Are you tired?" she asked, all in the same breath.

The old beggar went to the door and waited patiently while she unbarred it. As he shuffled outside, he instructed her to leave the bucket of water by her bed but not to look into it until the morning.

That night, the greedy old woman couldn't sleep as she imagined the heap of shiny gold that would be waiting for her tomorrow. She waited impatiently for the sun to rise and got up as soon as she heard the first rooster crow.

Hurrying to the bucket, she plunged her hands inside expecting to bring up handfuls of gold. Instead, she gave a cry as dozens of little things bit her, for the bucket was filled not with gold but with snakes, lizards, and ants. **L**

L FOLK TALES
Why do you think the old woman gets this result when she tries to behave like Auntie Lily?

The greedy old woman fell sick—some said from her bites, some claimed from sheer frustration. Auntie Lily herself came to nurse her neighbor. "Take this to heart: Kindness comes with no price."

The old woman was so ashamed that she did, indeed, take the lesson to heart. Though she remained sick, she was kind to whoever came to her door.

Detail from *Sunny Spring* (1999), Zhang Min. Watercolor. Red Lantern Folk Art, Mukashi Collection. © The Mukashi Collection/SuperStock.

One day, a leper[2] came into the village. Everyone hid for fear of the terrible disease. Doors slammed and shutters banged down over windows, and soon the village seemed deserted.

Only Auntie Lily and her neighbor stepped out of their houses. "Are you hungry?" Auntie Lily asked.

"Are you thirsty?" the neighbor asked. "I'll make you a cup of tea."

The leper thanked Auntie Lily and then turned to the neighbor as if to express his gratitude as well; but he stopped and studied her. "You're looking poorly, my dear woman. Can I help?"

With a tired smile, the rich old woman explained what had happened. When she was finished, the leper stood thoughtfully for a moment. "You're not the same woman as before: You're as kind as Auntie Lily, and you aren't greedy anymore. So take this humble gift from my brother, the old beggar."

With that, the leper limped out of the village; and as he left, the illness fell away from the old woman like an old, discarded cloak. But though the old woman was healthy again, she stayed as kind as Auntie Lily and used her own money as well and wisely as Auntie Lily used the waters of gold. M

M **FOLK TALES**
What **moral** does this story convey?

---

2. **leper:** a person suffering from the infectious disease of leprosy, which can result in bodily deformities.

Comprehension

ALABAMA STANDARDS

READING STANDARD
3 Distinguish among subgenres based on characteristics

1. **Recall** Where does Brer Possum meet Brer Snake?
2. **Clarify** Why doesn't Brer Possum want to help Brer Snake at first?
3. **Recall** At the beginning of "Waters of Gold," why does the old woman own Auntie Lily's land?

Literary Analysis

4. **Summarize** Review the graphic organizer you created for each tale. Then summarize one of the folk tales in your own words.
5. **Identify Characteristics of Folk Tales** Use a chart like the one shown to identify how each selection demonstrates the main characteristics of a folk tale.

	"Brer Possum"	"Waters of Gold"
Characters Who Represent a Trait	Brer Snake: Sneaky	
Events That Occur in Sets of Three		
A Moral		

6. **Classify a Tale** A fable is a type of folk tale that uses animal characters to teach a **moral** about human nature or the ways of the world. Which of these stories is a fable? Explain your answer.
7. **Compare and Contrast Characters** The characters in folk tales are often thought of as standing for good or evil. Consider the "good" characters in these two tales. Explain how they are alike and how they differ.
8. **Make Judgments** Which story's **lesson** is more useful in your everyday life? Explain your choice.

Extension and Challenge

9. **Reader's Circle** Jackie Torrence inherited "Brer Possum's Dilemma" from her great-grandfather, who had been enslaved. "Waters of Gold" was told by Chinese immigrant communities during the Great Depression. In a group, choose one of the stories and discuss how it might reflect the culture that created it. Questions to consider include the following:
   - What do you think life was like for the original tellers of the tale?
   - What traits does the story suggest are valuable?
   - What traits does the story seem to warn readers about?
   - Why might these traits have been significant to the original storytellers and their audiences? Why are they significant to you?

Vocabulary in Context

VOCABULARY PRACTICE

Choose the letter of the item you would associate with each vocabulary word as it is used in these selections.

1. **smugly:** (a) carrying a heavy load, (b) looking pleased with oneself, (c) riding an old bike
2. **prime:** (a) an excellent meal, (b) a small family, (c) a necessary decision
3. **commence:** (a) the opening scene, (b) a large rectangle, (c) a long meeting
4. **jostling:** (a) children laughing, (b) dogs barking, (c) crowds pushing
5. **perilously:** (a) singing in a choir, (b) walking on a tightrope, (c) having lunch
6. **humor:** (a) give in, (b) get angry, (c) get better

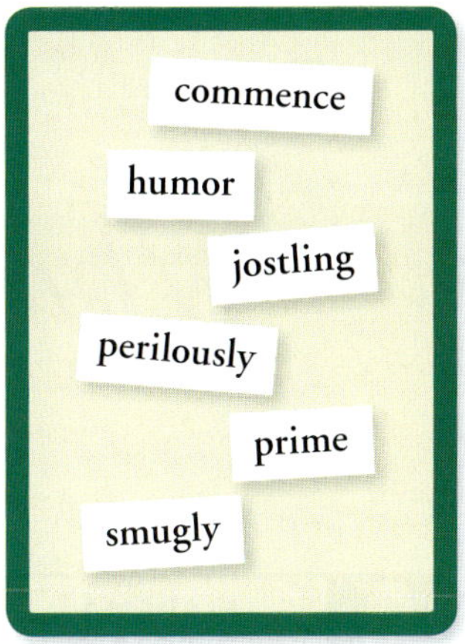

VOCABULARY IN WRITING

Which folk tale character changed more, Brer Possum or the rich old woman in "Waters of Gold"? Using two or more vocabulary words, write several sentences explaining your opinion. Here is a sample opening.

EXAMPLE SENTENCE

*At first, the rich old woman **smugly** assumed that she was right.*

ALABAMA STANDARDS

READING STANDARD
1.c Using context clues to determine word meanings

VOCABULARY STRATEGY: THE LATIN WORD *primus*

The vocabulary word *prime* comes from the Latin word *primus,* which means "first." To determine the meaning of words that come from *primus,* use context clues and your understanding of the root's meaning.

VOCABULARY PRACTICE
For more practice, go to the **Vocabulary Center** at **ClassZone.com.**

ACTIVITY Choose the word from the web that best completes each sentence. If necessary, consult a dictionary.

1. Before they learned to use fire, early people had a fairly _____ way of life.
2. The first three or four grades of school are called the _____ grades.
3. The highest category of mammals, which includes humans and apes, is called _____.
4. The citizens of the town were _____ from German backgrounds.
5. Some say that our solar system developed from a _____ gas cloud.

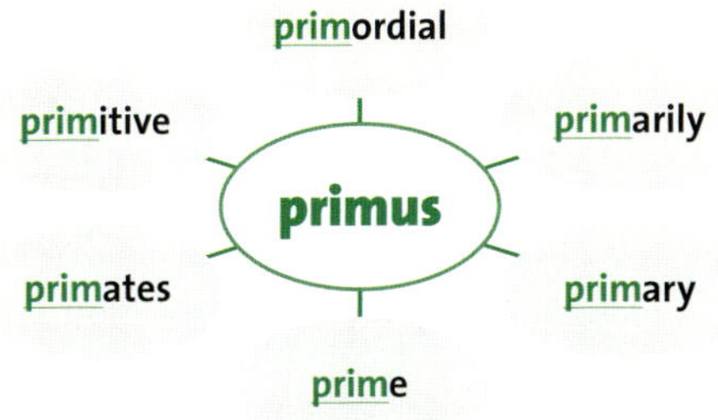

Sally Ann Thunder Ann Whirlwind

American Tall Tale Retold by Mary Pope Osborne

What makes a good COUPLE?

ALABAMA STANDARDS

READING STANDARDS
1.d Applying self-monitoring strategies
3 Distinguish among subgenres based on characteristics

KEY IDEA You know who they are. Couples who just seem so right together that they radiate happiness when they walk down the street. Their **compatibility** might come from having similar personalities or interests, or even from respecting each other's differences. In this selection, a character who is larger than life meets her match.

WEB IT In a small group, create an idea web. Fill it with examples of compatible couples in books and movies, as well as those you know from your own life. Then expand the web by including your ideas about what makes the good couples good.

LITERARY ANALYSIS: CHARACTERISTICS OF TALL TALES

A **tall tale** is a humorously exaggerated story about impossible events. Like other folk tales, tall tales were originally passed along by being told out loud. Tall tales share these characteristics:

- They use exaggeration to make difficult situations seem incredible or funny.
- The hero or heroine is often bigger, stronger, and even louder than an ordinary person.
- The setting is usually the American frontier.

As you read, notice how these characteristics apply to "Sally Ann Thunder Ann Whirlwind."

READING STRATEGY: VISUALIZE

Tall tales are often so exaggerated, funny, and action packed that you might be able to **visualize,** or picture, them as cartoons. To try this, look for descriptive details that appeal to your senses of touch, sound, and especially sight. Then picture the characters and action in your mind. Use a chart like the one shown to record descriptive words and phrases in "Sally Ann Thunder Ann Whirlwind."

Character or Event	Descriptive Words or Phrases

VOCABULARY IN CONTEXT

The words listed help add humor to the tall tale. Place each word in the appropriate column in the chart. Use a dictionary to look up the words you don't know.

WORD LIST

forage	oblige
gigantic	varmint

Know Well	Think I Know	Don't Know

Author Online

Female Heroes

As a child, Mary Pope Osborne says, she was "terrified of little things, like insects and worms and big dogs" and that "it was always a struggle to get over those fears." Now she creates stories with the kind of fearless female heroes that she thinks would have made her "less of a frightened child."

Mary Pope Osborne
born 1949

Background

An American Tradition In trying to claim new lands for building and farming, American settlers faced great challenges. Workers tested their endurance through chopping lumber and building railroads. Pioneers faced wild animals and brutal weather, as well as other difficulties. One way of coping with the difficulties life threw their way was to tell tall tales.

Bigger and Better The heroes and heroines of these tall tales were people like the settlers, but they were larger than life and able to handle any hardship that came along. Paul Bunyan and Pecos Bill are two fictional heroes that came out of this tradition. Others, like Davy Crockett, were real people whose adventures were told so many times that they became legendary.

MORE ABOUT THE AUTHOR AND BACKGROUND

To learn more about Mary Pope Osborne and tall tales, visit the **Literature Center** at **ClassZone.com.**

Sally Ann Thunder Ann Whirlwind

Retold by Mary Pope Osborne

One early spring day, when the leaves of the white oaks were about as big as a mouse's ear, Davy Crockett set out alone through the forest to do some bear hunting. Suddenly it started raining real hard, and he felt **obliged** to stop for shelter under a tree. As he shook the rain out of his coonskin cap, he got sleepy, so he laid back into the crotch of the tree, and pretty soon he was snoring.

Davy slept so hard, he didn't wake up until nearly sundown. And when he did, he discovered that somehow or another in all that sleeping his head had gotten stuck in the crotch of the tree, and he couldn't get it out.

Well, Davy roared loud enough to make the tree lose all its little mouse-ear leaves. He twisted and turned and carried on for over an hour, but still that tree wouldn't let go. Just as he was about to give himself up for a goner, he heard a girl say, "What's the matter, stranger?"

ANALYZE VISUALS
Examine the woman in the painting. What can you **infer** about her personality?

oblige (ə-blīj') *v.* to force; require

Man Leaning on Tree, © 1991 by Michael McCurdy. From *American Tall Tales* by Mary Pope Osborne. Used by permission of Alfred A. Knopf, an imprint of Random House Children's Books, a division of Random House, Inc.

Even from his awkward position, he could see that she was extraordinary— tall as a hickory sapling, with arms as big as a keelboat tiller's. **A**

A VISUALIZE
Reread lines 14–16. What words and phrases help you picture Sally in your mind?

"My head's stuck, sweetie," he said. "And if you help me get it free, I'll give you a pretty little comb."

"Don't call me sweetie," she said. "And don't worry about giving me no pretty little comb, neither. I'll free your old coconut, but just because I want to."

Then this extraordinary girl did something that made Davy's hair stand on end. She reached in a bag and took out a bunch of rattlesnakes. She tied all the wriggly critters together to make a long rope, and as she tied, she kept talking. "I'm not a shy little colt," she said. "And I'm not a little singing nightingale, neither. I can tote a steamboat on my back, outscream a panther, and jump over my own shadow. I can double up crocodiles any day, and I like to wear a hornets' nest for my Sunday bonnet."

As the girl looped the ends of her snake rope to the top of the branch that was trapping Davy, she kept bragging: "I'm a streak of lightning set up edgeways and buttered with quicksilver. I can outgrin, outsnort, outrun, outlift, outsneeze, outsleep, outlie any **varmint** from Maine to Louisiana. Furthermore, *sweetie,* I can blow out the moonlight and sing a wolf to sleep." Then she pulled on the other end of the snake rope so hard, it seemed as if she might tear the world apart. **B**

varmint (vär′mĭnt) *n.* a troublesome person or wild animal

B TALL TALES
Reread lines 30–36. Notice the **metaphor** Sally uses to describe herself, as well as her other figures of speech. What is she saying about herself?

The right-hand fork of that big tree bent just about double. Then Davy slid his head out as easy as you please. For a minute he was so dizzy, he couldn't tell up from down. But when he got everything going straight again, he took a good look at that girl. "What's your name, ma'am?"

"Sally Ann Thunder Ann Whirlwind," she said. "But if you mind your manners, you can call me Sally."

From then on Davy Crockett was crazy in love with Sally Ann Thunder Ann Whirlwind. He asked everyone he knew about her, and everything he heard caused another one of Cupid's arrows to jab him in the gizzard.

"Oh, I know Sally!" the preacher said. "She can dance a rock to pieces and ride a panther bareback!"

"Sally's a good ole friend of mine," the blacksmith said. "Once I seen her crack a walnut with her front teeth."

"Sally's so very special," said the schoolmarm. "She likes to whip across the Salt River, using her apron for a sail and her left leg for a rudder!"

Sally Ann Thunder Ann Whirlwind had a reputation for being funny, too. Her best friend, Lucy, told Davy, "Sally can laugh the bark off a pine tree. She likes to whistle out one side of her mouth while she eats with the other side and grins with the middle!" **C**

C TALL TALES
Reread the peoples' descriptions of Sally, starting with what the preacher says in lines 46–47. Which of her qualities have been exaggerated for humor or emphasis?

According to her friends, Sally could tame about anything in the world, too. They all told Davy about the time she was churning butter and heard something scratching outside. Suddenly the door swung open, and in walked the Great King Bear of the Mud Forest. He'd come to steal one of her smoked hams. Well, before the King Bear could say boo, Sally grabbed a warm dumpling from the pot and stuffed it in his mouth.

The dumpling tasted so good, the King Bear's eyes winked with tears. But then he started to think that Sally might taste pretty good, too. So opening and closing his big old mouth, he backed her right into a corner.

Sally was plenty scared, with her knees a-knocking and her heart a-hammering. But just as the King Bear blew his hot breath in her face, she gathered the courage to say, "Would you like to dance?"

Woman and Bear, © 1991 by Michael McCurdy. From *American Tall Tales* by Mary Pope Osborne. Used by permission of Alfred A. Knopf, an imprint of Random House Children's Books, a division of Random House, Inc.

As everybody knows, no bear can resist an invitation to a square dance, so of course the old fellow forgot all about eating Sally and said, "Love to." **D**

Then he bowed real pretty, and the two got to kicking and whooping and swinging each other through the air, as Sally sang:

We are on our way to Baltimore,
With two behind, and two before:
Around, around, around we go,
Where oats, peas, beans, and barley grow!

And while she was singing, Sally tied a string from the bear's ankle to her butter churn, so that all the time the old feller was kicking up his legs and dancing around the room, he was also churning her butter! **E**

And folks loved to tell the story about Sally's encounter with another stinky varmint—only this one was a *human* varmint. It seems that Mike Fink, the riverboat man, decided to scare the toenails off Sally because he was sick and tired of hearing Davy Crockett talk about how great she was.

One evening Mike crept into an old alligator skin and met Sally just as she was taking off to **forage** in the woods for berries. He spread open his

D VISUALIZE
Reread lines 65–70. Notice the details that help you visualize Sally as she talks with the bear. Which details help you picture this scene as a cartoon?

E TALL TALES
Reread lines 77–79. What can you **infer** about Sally's intelligence from her actions? How is Sally's intelligence exaggerated?

forage (fôr′ĭj) *v.* to search around for food or other supplies

Woman Beating Up Man © 1991 by Michael McCurdy. From *American Tall Tales* by Mary Pope Osborne. Used by permission of Alfred A. Knopf, an imprint of Random House Children's Books, a division of Random House, Inc.

gigantic mouth and made such a howl that he nearly scared himself to death. But Sally paid no more attention to that fool than she would have to a barking puppy dog.

gigantic (jī-găn′tĭk) *adj.* extremely large

However, when Mike put out his claws to embrace her, her anger rose higher than a Mississippi flood. She threw a flash of eye lightning at him, turning the dark to daylight. Then she pulled out a little toothpick and with a single swing sent the alligator head flying fifty feet! And then to finish him off good, she rolled up her sleeves and knocked Mike Fink clear across the woods and into a muddy swamp. **F**

F VISUALIZE
Reread lines 89–94. Pay attention to the descriptive details in this passage. What do they help you see?

When the fool came to, Davy Crockett was standing over him. "What in the world happened to you, Mikey?" he asked.

"Well, I—I think I must-a been hit by some kind of wild alligator!" Mike stammered, rubbing his sore head.

Davy smiled, knowing full well it was Sally Ann Thunder Ann Whirlwind just finished giving Mike Fink the only punishment he'd ever known.

That incident caused Cupid's final arrow to jab Davy's gizzard. "Sally's the whole steamboat," he said, meaning she was something great. The next day he put on his best raccoon hat and sallied forth[1] to see her.

When he got within three miles of her cabin, he began to holler her name. His voice was so loud, it whirled through the woods like a hurricane.

Sally looked out and saw the wind a-blowing and the trees a-bending. She heard her name a-thundering through the woods, and her heart began to thump. By now she'd begun to feel that Davy Crockett was the whole steamboat, too. So she put on her best hat—an eagle's nest with a wildcat's tail for a feather—and ran outside. **G**

G TALL TALES
Reread lines 108–112. Describe Sally's "best hat." Why is the hat so appropriate for a tall-tale heroine like Sally?

Just as she stepped out the door, Davy Crockett burst from the woods and jumped onto her porch as fast as a frog. "Sally, darlin'!" he cried. "I think my heart is bustin'! Want to be my wife?"

"Oh, my stars and possum dogs, why not?" she said.

From that day on, Davy Crockett had a hard time acting tough around Sally Ann Thunder Ann Whirlwind. His fightin' and hollerin' had no more effect on her than dropping feathers on a barn floor. At least that's what *she'd* tell *you.* He might say something else.

---

1. **sallied forth:** set out.

Comprehension

1. **Recall** How does Davy Crockett meet Sally?
2. **Clarify** Why does Sally tie a string to the bear's ankle?
3. **Summarize** What happens when Mike Fink tries to scare Sally?

Literary Analysis

4. **Identify Characteristics of Tall Tales** In what ways is Sally a typical tall-tale character? Cite examples from the story.
5. **Visualize** Look at the visualizing chart you made as you read. Choose the character and event you can picture most clearly and sketch him, her, or it. Explain how the sketch reflects the notes in your chart.
6. **Evaluate Characters** Use a diagram to track the events that help Davy discover how **compatible** he and Sally are. For each event, note what Davy discovers about Sally. Are the characters a good couple? Why?

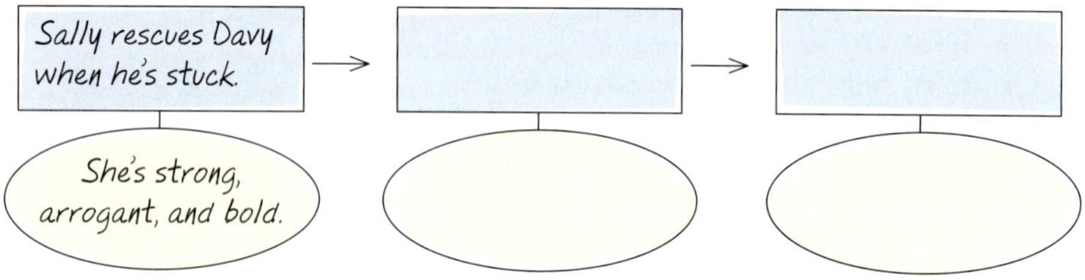

7. **Draw Conclusions** What would make Sally such an appealing character to early American settlers? Explain your answer.

Extension and Challenge

8. **Creative Project: Drama** In groups of two or three, select one of Sally's adventures and write it as a play. Act it out in front of the class. Pay close attention to the vivid and exaggerated details in each incident and find ways to include these details in your performance.
9. **SOCIAL STUDIES CONNECTION** Davy Crockett and Mike Fink are examples of real people whose adventures were turned into tall tales. Research one or two of their real-life accomplishments. Do their real roles in the American West resemble the roles they play in "Sally Ann Thunder Ann Whirlwind"?

RESEARCH LINKS
For more on Davy Crockett and Mike Fink, visit the **Research Center** at **ClassZone.com.**

ALABAMA STANDARDS

READING STANDARD
3 Distinguish among subgenres based on characteristics

Vocabulary in Context

VOCABULARY PRACTICE

Choose the word from the list that best fits the context of each sentence.

1. We saw an ugly-looking _____ digging around in our yard.
2. It seemed to be trying to _____ for acorns.
3. Its tail was extremely long, and its snout was _____ too.
4. Please _____ him and laugh at his jokes.

forage

gigantic

oblige

varmint

VOCABULARY IN WRITING

The exaggeration in this tall tale creates humor. Write several sentences that exaggerate the qualities of one or more of the characters. Use at least two of the vocabulary words. Here is an example.

EXAMPLE SENTENCE

*Davy's hands were so **gigantic** that they looked like whole sides of beef.*

VOCABULARY STRATEGY: DICTIONARY USAGE LABELS

Not all words are appropriate to use in all situations. For example, if you were to look up the vocabulary word *varmint* in a dictionary, you might find the usage label DIALECT at the beginning or end of the entry. This label lets you know that the word is used only in certain regions of the country.

Usage labels may apply to some or all senses of a word. If they relate to only one definition, they are put with that definition. Here are some other usage labels that dictionaries frequently use:

- ARCHAIC or OBSOLETE: a word or meaning that is rarely or never used anymore
- INFORMAL: a word or expression used in everyday speech and writing but not in formal situations
- SLANG: a word or expression that is appropriate in familiar talk with friends

PRACTICE Look up each term in a dictionary and note the usage label you find. If the label applies to only one definition, note that definition as well.

1. legit
2. wishy-washy
3. critter
4. anon
5. lazybones
6. ere

VOCABULARY PRACTICE

For more practice, go to the **Vocabulary Center** at **ClassZone.com.**

Comparing Themes

Two Ways to Count to Ten

Liberian Fable Retold by Frances Carpenter

The Race Between Toad and Donkey

Jamaican Fable Retold by Roger D. Abrahams

Would you rather be CLEVER *or strong?*

ALABAMA STANDARDS

LITERATURE STANDARDS

7 Interpret the author's message in literary texts

8 Compare selections and their characteristics

KEY IDEA In every society, athletes come together to try to outrun, outthrow, and outjump one another. When it comes to sports, strength and speed seem to be the point of the game. Can sheer brainpower ever be enough to win such **contests?** The fables you're about to read explore this question.

QUICKWRITE Put yourself in the place of a professional athlete. What would you say it takes to win a championship? Spend a few minutes writing down what you think an athlete might say. Would the manager or coach of the team have the same answer?

LITERARY ANALYSIS: UNIVERSAL THEME

Throughout the world, people speak different languages and have different customs—yet some feelings and experiences are remarkably similar. The selections you're about to read reflect this. They come from different continents but offer a similar **theme,** or message about life. To identify this theme, pay attention to

- the characters and what traits they represent
- the contests
- who wins the contests
- how they win

When a theme appears in the literature of many cultures across many time periods, it's called a **universal theme. Fables,** which are brief stories that teach a lesson, often contain such themes. As you read these two fables, notice that while they share the same universal theme, their stories are not identical. Each expresses the theme in its own way.

READING STRATEGY: SET A PURPOSE FOR READING

When you **set a purpose for reading,** you choose specific reasons for reading one or more works. Your purpose for reading "Two Ways to Count to Ten" and "The Race Between Toad and Donkey" is to identify the universal theme and to find similarities and differences in how the fables express it. As you read the first fable, begin filling in a chart like the one shown.

	"Two Ways to Count to Ten"	*"The Race Between Toad and Donkey"*
Who are the characters?		
What is the contest and who declares it?		
Who wins the contest? How?		
What do the characters learn?		

LOONEY TUNES characters, names and all related indicia are TM and © Warner Brothers Entertainment Inc. All Rights Reserved.

Author Online

Francis Carpenter: World Traveler

When Frances Carpenter was young, she and her family traversed the world. Africa, where her geographer father traveled for work, was one of their destinations. Carpenter used the information gained on these trips in her writing.

Frances Carpenter
1890–1972

Roger D. Abrahams: Legendary Folklorist

Professor Roger D. Abrahams is one of the most respected scholars in the world of folklore. He has written many books about the folk tales and legends of Africans and African Americans.

Roger D. Abrahams
born 1933

Living Traditions One place Abrahams collected folk tales is Jamaica. This island nation in the West Indies is home to a rich cultural tradition. Many Jamaicans are descendants of enslaved Africans who were taken to the island to work on plantations. The Africans brought their music, stories, and way of life with them. Jamaican life continues to reflect an African influence.

MORE ABOUT THE AUTHOR
For more on the authors, visit the **Literature Center** at **ClassZone.com.**

Two *Ways to Count to* Ten

Retold by
Frances Carpenter

"Old Tanko has come! The Teller of Good Tales is here!"

The news spread quickly through the Liberian village and in the faraway back country. Men, women, and children came running to the Palaver House, the big "talky-talk" hut which had room for them all. **A**

A UNIVERSAL THEME
What is the **setting** of this fable?

Everyone in that village knew Old Tanko, the Teller of Good Tales. Everyone there enjoyed his exciting stories. Whenever he wandered into their cluster of grass-roofed huts, they made him welcome.

"Ai, I'll sing you a story," Tanko said that day when he had finished the bowl of soup they set before him. "It will be a strange tale from the long ago." He arranged his white robe and settled himself cross-legged on the earth floor.

The old man placed a very small gourd drum in his lap. And with his bony brown fingers, he began to tap lightly, lightly upon it.

"I had this tale from my grandfather," he began. "He, too, was a great teller of tales."

"What will the tale say to us, Tanko?" The headman of the village was speaking. He had squatted down on the ground, close to the old man.

"It will say there is more than one way to count to ten. It will also tell how, if you can guess the right way, you can even get yourself a king's daughter for your wife."

The people in the talky-talk house nodded to one another. They smiled. It was as if they were thinking, "This will be another good tale." But no one spoke. In silence, they waited for Old Tanko to tell his story.

ANALYZE VISUALS
The animals in this tale are **personified,** or given human characteristics. What human traits are suggested by this picture of the antelope?

The little drum on the old man's knees soon began to whisper. "Tap! Tap! Tap-tap-tap!" And Tanko in his soft singing voice told this strange tale.

In the long, long ago, animals were not so different, one from the other. Oh, they had different shapes, just as they do today. But they lived together in friendship and peace. Like people, those of one animal tribe sometimes took their wives from those of a different tribe. Like you and me, in those times beasts could talk. And, like people, they had a king to rule over them.

In the place of this story, the leopard was king. Rich he was, beyond telling. Mighty was he in his power over the other beasts. All the animals obeyed him.

"Whom shall I name to rule after me when I shall die?" King Leopard said one day to his pretty daughter. "I must find one who is wise enough so that he can rule well. Yes, my dear daughter, I must seek out the cleverest beast in our jungle land. I shall make him a prince. He shall have you for his bride. And to me he shall be a son."

King Leopard was pleased with his idea, and he planned a great feast. His royal drums carried word of it far and wide through the jungle. And all the animals came.

There were good things to eat. There was plenty to drink. The drums beat. And the guests at King Leopard's feast danced for three days.

At last the king called them to make a huge circle. Stepping into its center, he called his pretty daughter to come to his side. Then he spoke in a loud voice.

"Listen to my words, friends!" he cried. "Someday I must die. Someday another king must rule in my place. I will choose him now from among you, so that he will be ready."

There was a murmur of wonder all through the crowd. The King had to order them to be quiet.

"I shall seek the cleverest among you, for your king must be wise. I shall name him Prince. He shall be to me a son and to my dear daughter a husband. He shall share all my riches. And when I die he shall be your king."

Shouts came from the eager guests at the King's feast. No doubt each animal hoped that the good fortune would be his.

Then King Leopard held up his hunting spear. "Look at this, my people! Watch!" And he flung the spear far up into the air.

"With this spear will I test you," he went on. "He who would be our prince must throw the spear toward the sky. He must send it so high that he can count to ten before it drops down to earth again." **B**

SOCIAL STUDIES CONNECTION

Liberia, a country on the west coast of Africa, is home to rain forests filled with elephants, chimpanzees, bush oxen, and antelopes. Leopards, once common there, are in danger of disappearing.

B UNIVERSAL THEME
Why is King Leopard setting up a contest? In your chart, write down how the contest works.

There was a buzz of talk among all the animals then. This would not be so hard to do, they thought.

One after another, they came forward to try their skill. Each jungle beast danced before King Leopard and his pretty daughter. Each one sang a song that told how well he would rule, if he were chosen.

First to try his luck was the elephant. He was so big that he could push all the other beasts out of his way.

"I must be first," he said to himself. "This task is too easy. Almost any one of us can do it."

The elephant danced clumsily. He was very big and his body was heavy. Then, with his trunk in the air, he trumpeted all the fine deeds he would perform if he were prince. **C**

C UNIVERSAL THEME
In fables, animal characters often represent human traits. What trait might the elephant represent?

The great beast threw King Leopard's spear up into the air.

"One! Two! Three!" he began counting. But he spoke slowly, as he did everything else. An elephant cannot easily hurry, you know.

Before the elephant had said, "Four!" the King's spear had dropped to earth. The proud beast hung his head so low that the tip of his trunk dragged on the ground. He knew he had failed.

Next came the bush ox. His wide gray horns swept the other beasts to the side.

"I'll throw the spear up to the sun," the huge animal sang while he danced. "I'll be a strong husband for King Leopard's daughter." **D**

D UNIVERSAL THEME
Why does the bush ox think he would make a good husband?

The bush ox picked the spear up in his mouth. With a mighty toss of his great head, he flung it far, far above his spreading horns.

"One! Two! Three! Four!" the bush ox counted more quickly than the elephant. But he, too, was slow. Before he could say "Five," the spear was down on the ground. He went off, ashamed, into the deep jungle.

The chimpanzee was third. He jumped up and down in a merry dance, and King Leopard's daughter laughed at his antics. He beat his hairy chest with his two fists, and he sang of how much he would like to be king in the leopard's place.

The young ape rose up straight on his hind legs. He held the spear in one hand, just like a man. With a twist of his long arm, he threw it up toward the sky.

"One-two-three-four-five-six-seven!" He chattered as fast as he could. The watching animals held their breaths. Surely, with such a quick tongue, the chimpanzee would make the count.

But he did not! He had not even said, "Eight!" before he had caught the spear once more in his hand.

One by one, other animals tried to count to ten while the spear was still up in the air. One by one, they all failed.

"It seems I must look somewhere else for a prince to rule when I am gone," King Leopard spoke sadly.

Then out from the crowd stepped an antelope.

Beside the elephant, the bush ox, and even the chimpanzee, the young deerlike antelope seemed puny and weak. His legs were long, yet so slender that it was almost a wonder that they would hold up his body. But the antelope spoke bravely.

"Let me try to throw your spear, O King," he cried. "I would like well to marry your pretty daughter."

"Ho! Ho!" The other animals burst into laughter. How could such a weak creature fling the King's spear high enough to say more than two or three words? However could he hope to count up to ten? **E**

But the antelope would not be turned aside.

"I wish to try," he insisted. And King Leopard nodded his head. He had promised a fair trial for all who wished to take part in this contest.

"Who can say what any creature can do until he has tried?" The King spoke to the crowd. "The antelope may throw the spear." So the other beasts were moved back to give him room. **F**

When the antelope, on his slender legs, danced before the King, the leopard's daughter cried out with pleasure. No one could deny that his steps were more graceful than those of the elephant, or of the bush ox, or the chimpanzee.

Then the antelope threw the spear. With a toss of his head, he flung it far up into the air. Before it could fall to earth, the clever beast called out two words. "Five! Ten!" he cried. "I have counted to ten. King Leopard did not say how the count should be made."

The leopard laughed then. He nodded his royal head.

"No, I did not say how the count was to be made," he agreed. "And as everyone knows, one can count by fives as well as by ones. The antelope has won the contest. He has proved he is the cleverest of you all. He shall wed my dear daughter. He shall be king when I am gone."

The other animals stared stupidly at the winner. They did not understand yet what had happened. But they could see that the antelope had outwitted the King.

At the wedding feast that King Leopard gave for his daughter, they all cheered for the antelope, their new prince.

Old Tanko put his drum down in his lap.

"Remember this tale, friends," he said to the crowd in the talky-talk hut. "Do not forget that it is not always the biggest nor the strongest, but sometimes the cleverest who wins the prize."

E UNIVERSAL THEME
Why do the other animals laugh at the antelope?

F UNIVERSAL THEME
Reread lines 118–122. What do you learn about King Leopard based on his treatment of the antelope?

Comprehension

1. **Recall** To whom does Old Tanko tell the fable?
2. **Clarify** Why does King Leopard want a clever husband for his daughter? Describe the contest he creates to find the husband.
3. **Summarize** Summarize what happens when each of the following animals competes: the elephant, the bush ox, the chimpanzee, and the antelope.

Literary Analysis

4. **Analyze Characters** Which character in the fable do you think represents wisdom, or good judgment? Which character represents cleverness, or quick, original thinking? Cite evidence from the fable to support your answer.
5. **Identify Theme** Sometimes the theme of a selection must be inferred. Other times, as with this selection, the theme is directly stated. What lines state the theme? Restate the theme in your own words.
6. **Make Judgments** Was King Leopard's contest a good way to find the next king? Explain why.

Comparing Universal Themes

Finish filling in the chart column under "Two Ways to Count to Ten." Add information that helped you understand how the fable expresses its theme.

	"Two Ways to Count to Ten"	"The Race Between Toad and Donkey"
Who are the characters?	*Old Tanko, King Leopard, King Leopard's daughter, the elephant, the bush ox, the chimpanzee, and the antelope*	
What is the contest and who declares it?		
Who wins the contest? How?		
What do the characters learn?		

ALABAMA STANDARDS

LITERATURE STANDARD
8 Compare selections and their characteristics

The RACE Between TOAD and DONKEY

Retold by
Roger D. Abrahams

One day, Master King decided to have a race and he would give a big prize to whoever won. Both Toad and Donkey decided to enter, but Toad got Donkey angry with all his boasting about how he'd win.

Now, the race was to be for twenty miles. So when Donkey looked at Toad he wondered out loud how any animal so small and powerless could hope to keep up with him. "I have very long legs, you know, as well as long ears and tail. Just measure our legs, and you'll see why you can't possibly hope to win this race." But Toad was stubborn—and he was smart, too—and he said that he was going to win the race. That just got Donkey more vexed. (A)

ANALYZE VISUALS
On the basis of this image, which character would you **infer** is the cleverer of the two? Why?

(A) UNIVERSAL THEME
Note the character who will compete with Donkey. Why does Donkey think he'll win the race?

So Donkey told the king that he was ready to start, but the king said that he had to make the rules first. At each mile every racer had to sing out to indicate he had gotten that far—for the king wanted to know what was happening in the race, you know.

Now Toad is a smart little fellow, and he said to the king that he needed a little time to take care of business, so would he let him have a day or two. And the king said to the two of them, "You must come here first thing tomorrow." Donkey objected, for he knew that Toad was a very trickifying creature, but the king wouldn't listen. **B**

B UNIVERSAL THEME
Why does Donkey object to Toad's request for more time?

Now the toad had twenty children, and they all looked exactly alike. And while Donkey was sleeping, Toad took his twenty children along the racing ground, and at every milepost Toad left one of them. He told them that they must listen for Mr. Donkey, and whenever they heard him cry out, they should do so too. And Toad hid one of his children there behind each of those mileposts. **C**

C UNIVERSAL THEME
How does Toad plan to win the race? As you read, notice how Toad's plan affects Donkey.

So the race began the next day. Donkey looked around, and he was so sure in his heart that he was going to beat Toad that he sucked his teeth, *Tche,* to show everyone there how little he thought of Toad. "That little bit of a fellow Toad can't keep up with me. I'll even have a little time to eat some grass along the way. *Tche.*"

So he just went a little way down the road and he stopped and ate some grass. He poked his head through the fence where he saw some good-looking sweet-potato tops and had a taste of some gungo peas. He took more than an hour to get to the first milepost. And as he got there, he bawled out, "Ha, ha, I'm better than Toad." And the first child heard this, and he called, like all toads do:

Jin-ko-ro-ro, Jin-kok-kok-kok.

The sound really surprised Donkey, who of course thought he had gotten there first. Then he thought, "I delayed too long eating that grass. I must run quicker this next mile." So he set off with greater speed, this time stopping only for a minute to drink some water along the way. And as he got to the next post, he bawled out:

Ha! Ha! Ha! I'm better than Toad.

And then the second child called out:

Jin-ko-ro-ro, Jin-kok-kok-kok.

And Donkey said, "Lord, Toad can really move, for sure. Never mind, there are a lot more miles." So he started, and when he reached the third milepost, he bawled:

Ha! Ha! Ha! I'm better than Toad.

And the third child sang:

Jin-ko-ro-ro, Jin-kok-kok-kok.

Now Donkey got very angry when he heard Toad answer him, and he started to smash the toad, but Toad, being a little fellow, hid himself in the grass.

Donkey was then determined to get to the next milepost before Toad, and he took his tail and he switched it like a horsewhip and he began to gallop. And he got to the fourth milepost and he bawled:

Ha! Ha! Ha! I'm better than Toad.

And out came the answer from the fourth child.

When he heard that, he stood there and began to tremble, and he said, "My goodness, what am I going to do? I'm going to have to run so fast I really kick that hard, hard dirt." And he galloped off faster than he ever had before, until he reached the fifth milepost. And now he was very tired, and out of breath. He just barely had enough wind to bawl:

Ha! Ha! Ha! I'm better than Toad.

And then he heard:

Jin-ko-ro-ro, Jin-kok-kok-kok.

This time he was really angry, and he raced on harder than ever. But at each milepost he bawled out the same thing, and at each he heard the same answer. And Donkey got so sad in his mind that he just gave up after a while, sad because he knew he had lost that race.

So through Toad's smartness, Donkey can never be a racer again. **D**

Jack Mandora me no choose one.[1]

SOCIAL STUDIES CONNECTION

Many Jamaicans speak Creole, which combines elements of English, Spanish, French, and a variety of African languages.

D UNIVERSAL THEME
Draw a **conclusion** about the lesson or theme of the fable.

1. **Jack Mandora me no choose one:** Traditionally, Jamaican storytellers make this statement at the end of a tale. In Creole, it means "Don't blame me for the story I've just told."

Comprehension

ALABAMA STANDARDS

LITERATURE STANDARD
8 Compare selections and their characteristics

1. **Recall** What are the rules of the race between Toad and Donkey?
2. **Clarify** What do Toad's children do to help him?
3. **Represent** Draw three profiles of Donkey. Complete each by showing Donkey's expression at the beginning, middle, and end of the race.

Literary Analysis

4. **Identify Characteristics of Fables** What human abilities or traits does Donkey represent? What traits does Toad represent? Give examples from the story to support your answers.
5. **Make Judgments** In your view, did Toad win the contest fairly? Explain.
6. **Evaluate Theme** Recall the theme you identified for this fable. Then think of two other fables, stories, or personal experiences from which you have taken this same message. Why do you think this message has been repeated throughout history and all over the world?

Comparing Universal Themes

Now that you have read both fables, finish filling in your chart. Then state the universal theme the selections share.

	"Two Ways to Count to Ten"	*"The Race Between Toad and Donkey"*
Who are the characters?	*Old Tanko, King Leopard, King Leopard's daughter, the elephant, the bush ox, the chimpanzee, and the antelope*	*Master King, Toad, Donkey, Toad's 20 children*
What is the contest and who declares it?		
Who wins the contest? How?		
What do the characters learn?		
What's the universal theme?		

Writing for Assessment

1. READ THE PROMPT

In writing assessments, you will often be asked to compare and contrast two works that are similar in some way, such as the two fables with a similar theme.

PROMPT

While the fables "Two Ways to Count to Ten" and "The Race Between Toad and Donkey" communicate the same universal theme, they express this theme in different ways. In four or five paragraphs, compare and contrast the ways in which the fables convey their message. Cite details from the fables to support your response.

STRATEGIES IN ACTION

1. I have to make sure I understand the **message** both fables share.
2. I need to identify the **similarities and differences** in how the fables express the message.
3. I should give examples from the fables to help explain my ideas.

2. PLAN YOUR WRITING

Using your chart, identify the ways each fable conveys the theme. Then think about how you will set up your response.

- Do you want to focus on each fable in a separate paragraph and then write a paragraph comparing them, as shown in the sample outline?
- Do you want to compare each element—characters, contests, and theme—in a separate paragraph and then point out the differences between the stories in another paragraph?

Once you have decided, outline the order of your paragraphs.

I. Introduction
II. How first fable conveys theme
III. How second fable conveys theme
IV. Comparison of fables
V. Conclusion

3. DRAFT YOUR RESPONSE

Introduction Introduce the fables and tell what universal theme they share. Then state your main idea, which should include an overview of the similarities and differences in the ways the fables convey the theme.

Body Use your chart and outline as a guide to the key points of your comparison. If you're using an outline that's similar to the sample, make sure you discuss the characters, contests, and theme for each selection.

Conclusion Wrap up with a restatement of your main idea and a reminder about how stories from different cultures can have the same theme.

Revision Make sure your sentences vary in structure.

Writing Workshop

Cause-and-Effect Essay

One sure lesson in the literature of this unit is that actions have consequences. Make a choice, and results—intended or otherwise—follow. When one thing brings about the next, in literature or in life, that's a cause-and-effect relationship. The **Writer's Road Map** will guide you in writing a cause-and-effect essay.

WRITER'S ROAD MAP

Cause-and-Effect Essay

WRITING PROMPT 1

Writing from the Real World Write an essay about a cause-and-effect relationship that you think is important or interesting. Make sure you can show clearly how one event caused another event to happen.

Topics to Consider

- an event in your life, such as changing schools or moving
- a community development, such as a curfew or a new community center
- a new school policy, such as removing lockers or adding a lounge

WRITING PROMPT 2

Writing from Literature The literature in this unit is full of cause-and-effect relationships. Write an essay that traces a cause-and-effect relationship in a literary work.

Topics to Consider

- failure to heed warnings ("Orpheus and Eurydice," "Icarus and Daedalus," "Phaëthon")
- the consequences of war ("Young Arthur," *Sir Gawain and the Green Knight*)

WRITING TOOLS

For prewriting, revision, and editing tools, visit the **Writing Center** at **ClassZone.com.**

KEY TRAITS

1. *IDEAS*

- Identifies a true **cause-and-effect relationship**
- Presents a **thesis statement** that explains the connection between causes and effects
- Includes **facts, examples,** and other **details** to **support** each cause and effect

2. *ORGANIZATION*

- Presents causes and effects in a sensible **order**
- Shows the relationship between causes and effects by using **transitions**
- Has an interesting **introduction** and a **conclusion** that summarizes the cause-and-effect relationship

3. *VOICE*

- Has a **tone** that is appropriate for the audience and purpose

4. *WORD CHOICE*

- Explains each cause and effect with **precise language**

5. *SENTENCE FLUENCY*

- Varies **sentence lengths** to add interest and sophistication

6. *CONVENTIONS*

- Uses **correct grammar, spelling, and punctuation**

WRITING/LANGUAGE STANDARD
9 Compose in expository mode with thesis sentence

Part 1: Analyze a Student Model

Online INTERACTIVE MODEL CLASSZONE.COM

Zachary Eckler
Robbins Park Charter School

Our Dog Chip

"This is a big decision," my mother said, looking at me with her best mother look. "A dog is a lot of work. For this reason alone, it's going to change your life!"

Because I could see how serious she was, I said, "I know, Mom. You're right." The truth is, however, I didn't know what was ahead. As it turned out, getting our dog Chip caused us a ton of trouble, a whole load of work, and a lot of joy, too.

The trouble came first. We adopted Chip from the nearby shelter when he was two. The woman there told us Chip had had "a couple of failed adoptions." That was code for "trouble," but we didn't know it. Because my sister and I liked Chip, we brought him home. The first night, we learned that Chip didn't care if we called him or not. Accordingly, when he got loose the first time, there was no getting him back. He ran around as long as he wanted. Worse, he found my neighbors' pet rabbit and knocked over its cage. Then he started running down that poor bunny. Dad got there about one second before it was too late. My neighbors weren't too happy. The first week, we also found out how much Chip liked the taste of carpets. Actually, he didn't like the ones that cost $4.98 at Save-a-Buck—no way! He preferred the new living-room carpet. A few days later, he also showed us another great talent he had—he could take bites out of our sofa. For these reasons, I thought Chip might have one more "failed adoption," but somehow we kept him.

KEY TRAITS IN ACTION

Introduction uses dialogue to hook readers.

Thesis statement identifies a true **cause-and-effect relationship** (dog caused trouble, work, and joy).

Transitions signal cause and effect.

Includes **examples** to **support** the first effect (that Chip caused trouble). Uses a variety of **sentence lengths.**

Chip caused us a lot of work, too. He has so much energy, and we have a small apartment. So Mom said he had to be walked or run three times a day. Worse, I had to carry a scoop, gloves, and bags with me. I had to take Chip out during rainstorms, in baking heat, and in the snow and ice. When it was late and I just wanted to lie on the sofa, there was still the evening walk to do.

Uses **precise language** to describe the second effect (that Chip caused the writer to work hard).

Luckily, Chip turned out to be more than a lot of trouble and work. He actually turned out to be good for our family. In a funny kind of way, he brought my sister and me together. Because I'm all sports and guy stuff and she's all ballet and girl stuff, we used to avoid each other. With the dog, though, we had to work out plans for taking care of him. We played with him together, too. As a result, Chip helped me figure out that my sister isn't as weird as I thought she was. Also, everybody in the house loved Chip once he calmed down, because he gave us all such great greetings. He could also tell when we were upset and liked to snuggle up and help.

Presents all three effects in a sensible **order.** The writer uses a friendly, conversational **tone** as he describes the third effect (that Chip brought joy to the family).

As it turned out, getting Chip did change my whole life. He made it harder sometimes and better many other times. Now I know that when people say that dogs are a lot of work, they're right. Still, because of the pleasure that results, having a dog is worth it.

Conclusion summarizes the cause-and-effect relationship.

2

WRITING/LANGUAGE STANDARD
9.a Using transitional words and phrases

Part 2: Apply the Writing Process

PREWRITING

What Should I Do?	What Does It Look Like?

1. Brainstorm to find a topic.

Review the prompts on page 736 and choose the one you prefer. Create a cluster map with a bulleted item from the prompt in the center. Then think of experiences that you have had or read about that relate to that item. Don't edit. Just write!

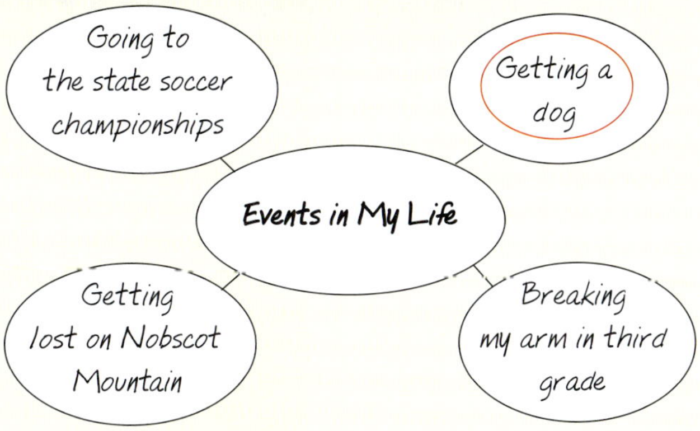

2. Chart the causes and effects.

You might show one cause with several effects or several causes that led to one effect. But remember, just because one event follows another doesn't mean that one event caused the other. "Stacie went out in the rain and caught the flu" is an example of a **false cause.** Not everyone who goes out in the rain gets sick.

Causes		Effects
Dog misbehaves.	→	Trouble
Dog needs to go out.	→	Work
Dog gives great greetings.	→	Joy

3. Write a thesis statement.

Base your thesis on your chart. Zachary Eckler's thesis has three key points: his dog (1) caused him trouble and (2) led to lots of work but (3) made him happy.

Working thesis statement:

Our dog Chip caused trouble at first, and he still needs lots of walks and attention. But he is fun to be around, so I wouldn't trade him for anything.

4. Collect evidence to support each key point.

Evidence is anything that explains, demonstrates, or otherwise clarifies your point. You might include facts, reasons, examples, or other details.

Key point 1: *trouble*

Evidence:

- *almost killed the Hansens' pet rabbit*
- *chewed our new carpet*
- *ruined the arm of the living-room sofa*

DRAFTING

What Should I Do?	What Does It Look Like?
1. Choose an organizational pattern. This writer described each effect first and then explained its cause. Another option is to describe the cause or causes first and then describe one or more effects.	*I. Introduction A. Mom said having a dog would be lots of work. B. Thesis: Dog brought us trouble, work, and joy. II. Trouble A. Chip almost killed the neighbors' pet rabbit. B. He chewed on the carpet and sofa. III. Work A. He has to be walked or run three times a day. B. He needs to go out even if I'm tired or the weather is bad. IV. Joy A. My sister and I play with Chip. B. He gives everyone great greetings. V. Conclusion A. Chip changed my life. B. Having a dog is worth all the hard work.*
2. Tell how and why. Don't include examples, facts, and other details just to fill up space. Instead, help your reader understand how and why something happened.	*The trouble came first. The first night, we learned that Chip didn't care if we called him or not. Accordingly, when he got loose the first time, there was no getting him back. He ran around as long as he wanted. Worse, he found my neighbors' pet rabbit and knocked over its cage.*
3. End powerfully. Your conclusion should clearly summarize the cause-and-effect relationship, but it should go further too. It might reflect on the events, show how the topic is important, or include a call to action. **TIP Before you revise, look back at the key traits on page 736 and at the rubric and peer-reader questions on page 742.**	*As it turned out, getting Chip did change my whole life. He made it harder sometimes and better many other times.* — Summary *Now I know that when people say that dogs are a lot of work, they're right. Still, because of the pleasure that results, having a dog is worth it.* — Significance

REVISING AND EDITING

What Should I Do?	What Does It Look Like?
1. Start out strong. • Use a **hook**—something special or surprising, like humor, drama, a question, or a quotation—to draw the reader in. • Underline your first sentence or two. If these lines seem ordinary or boring, add **fresh details,** a **question,** or a bit of **dialogue.**	My mother said getting a dog was a big decision. "This is a big decision," my mother said, looking at me with her best mother look. "A dog is a lot of work. For this reason alone, it's going to change your life!"
2. Don't be vague. • Make sure you **support each key point** with evidence. • Don't just state the evidence. **Explain** it. • Circle your evidence and explanations. If you don't have many circles, see what you can do to **tell your reader more.**	He has so much energy, and we have a small apartment. So, Mom said he had to be walked or run three times a day. Worse, I had to carry a scoop, gloves, and bags with me. I had to take Chip out during rainstorms, in baking heat, and in the snow and ice.
3. Connect your ideas. • Draw a box around each transition you used. • Ask a peer reader to point out places where the order or organization is unclear. • **Add transitions** where you need them. **See page 742:** Cause-Effect Transitions	My sister and I used to avoid each other. With the dog, though, we had to work out plans for taking care of him. We played with him together, too. As a result, Chip helped me figure out that my sister isn't as weird as I thought she was.
4. Use long, short, and medium sentences. • Find and [bracket] your longest sentence. Also, look for several short sentences in a row. • Does your essay have too many long, confusing sentences? Does your essay have too many short, immature-sounding sentences? • Revise your essay to **vary sentence lengths.**	[~~The first week, we also found out how much Chip liked the taste of carpets, but not the kind of carpets that cost $4.98 at Save-a-Buck, no way, he preferred the new living room carpet.~~] The first week, we also found out how much Chip liked the taste of carpets. Actually, he didn't like the ones that cost $4.98 at Save-a-Buck—no way! He preferred the new living-room carpet.

Preparing to Publish

Cause-and-Effect Essay

Apply the Rubric

A strong cause-and-effect essay . . .

- ☑ introduces and discusses a true cause-and-effect relationship
- ☑ has a thesis statement that connects causes and effects
- ☑ includes precise facts or examples to support each cause and effect
- ☑ is sensibly organized
- ☑ links causes and effects with transitions
- ☑ varies sentence lengths
- ☑ uses a tone that matches the audience and purpose
- ☑ concludes with a summary of the cause-and-effect relationship

Ask a Peer Reader

- What cause-and-effect relationship does my essay explain?
- Where should I add transitions?
- How could I strengthen my introduction and conclusion?
- Where should I improve my explanations or support?

Cause-Effect Transitions

accordingly	for this reason
as a result	if . . . then
because	so
consequently	therefore

Check Your Grammar

- Remember, *it's* means "it is." The word *its* (without the apostrophe) is a possessive pronoun; *its* shows ownership.

  He found my neighbors' pet rabbit and knocked over ~~it's~~ its cage.

  See page R52: Pronouns

- Be sure elements in your sentences are parallel. For example, when you have items in a series, present them all in the same types of phrases or clauses.

  I had to carry a scoop, gloves, and ~~bring~~ bags with me.

  See page R64: Parallel Structure

Writing Online

PUBLISHING OPTIONS
For publishing options, visit the **Writing Center** at **ClassZone.com.**

ASSESSMENT PREPARATION
For writing and grammar assessment practice, go to the **Assessment Center** at **ClassZone.com.**

COMMUNICATION STANDARD
14 Present findings using a variety of resources

Making a Formal Presentation

Now that you have thoroughly explained a cause-and-effect relationship in writing, it's time to educate others.

Planning the Presentation

1. **Decide on your subject.** You might use your essay as the basis of your presentation. If you prefer, you may research a different subject. Your audience will notice your level of enthusiasm, so choose a subject that truly interests you.
2. **Plan the points of your presentation.** Reread your essay or research your topic. Decide which points are most important, and restate them accurately in simple, clear language. You will be talking to audience members, not reading to them. If you include information from books, magazines, newspapers, or other research sources, be sure to cite those sources.
3. **Find or create visuals.** Think about which visuals would make the cause-and-effect relationship clear and intriguing. Consider using photographs, maps, diagrams, charts, graphs, video clips, or music. The writer of the student model included home video footage of his dog, Chip. Audience members saw for themselves how Chip's behavior changed over time.
4. **Develop an outline.** Write down a few words about each of your main points. Note when you will introduce visuals.
5. **Make some practice presentations.** Ask audience members: Was any part of my presentation unclear? Do my pacing, facial expressions, and gestures match my subject matter?

Making the Presentation

1. **Be calm and confident.** If you forget which point is next, glance at your outline. Make sure that everyone can see the visuals.
2. **Reflect.** Think about how well the presentation went and why. Decide what you will do differently next time.

See page R78: Evaluate an Informative Speech

Assessment Practice

ASSESS

The practice test items on the next few pages match skills listed on the Unit Goals page (page 625) and addressed throughout this unit. Taking this practice test will help you assess your knowledge of these skills and determine your readiness for the Unit Test.

REVIEW

After you take the practice test, your teacher can help you identify any skills you need to review.

- Characteristics of Myths and Tales
- Cultural Values
- Chronological Order
- Cause and Effect
- Compound Words
- Homographs
- Compound Sentences
- Complex Sentences

ASSESSMENT ONLINE

For more assessment practice and test-taking tips, go to the **Assessment Center** at **ClassZone.com.**

Reading Comprehension

DIRECTIONS *Read these selections and answer the questions that follow.*

King Midas had pleased the god Dionysus, and so Dionysus promised to give Midas anything he wished. Midas wished that everything he touched would turn to gold.

from The King Who Wished for Gold

retold by **Anne Rockwell**

As soon as he reached his palace, the king ordered a grand and extravagant feast to be set before him. All kinds of rare and expensive delicacies were prepared because Midas thought, After all, if I am so rich, why should I spare any expense?

And then he sat down to eat.

But the piece of bread he picked up hardened in his hand and turned to gold. Slices of meat became slabs of glimmering gold. He picked up his cup of wine, and slippery liquid gold gagged him so that he could not drink.

Poor King Midas realized that for all his newfound wealth he would soon starve to death if he could not eat or drink. Suddenly he hated the gift that he had wanted so much. He lifted his hands toward the sky and said, "Please, Lord Dionysus, forgive me for making such a foolish wish. I beg you, set me free from my own greed and stupidity!"

Dionysus was full of pity for the situation Midas had created for himself. Because he was a kindly and forgiving god, he immediately canceled the charm that had made everything King Midas touched turn to gold.

But he said to him, "Just to be sure that no trace of this charm remains, I want you to go and wash yourself at the source of the River Sardis. Where the spring spouts forth in clouds of spray, scrub your entire body and hair and beard until you wash all the gold away."

King Midas did as the god had told him. Dionysus had been right, for sprinkles of gold spangled the stream when he washed himself in it. To this day, gold flows through that river—the very gold that King Midas washed from himself.

From then on, King Midas was content with his rose garden and never again wished for gold and great wealth.

from The Three Wishes

Ricardo E. Alegría

Many years ago, there lived a woodsman and his wife. They were very poor but very happy in their little house in the forest. Poor as they were, they were always ready to share what little they had with anyone who came to their door. They loved each other very much and were quite content with their life together. Each evening, before eating, they gave thanks to God for their happiness.

One day, while the husband was working far off in the woods, an old man came to the little house and said that he had lost his way in the forest and had eaten nothing for many days. The woodsman's wife had little to eat herself, but, as was her custom, she gave a large portion of it to the old man. After he had eaten everything she gave him, he told the woman that he had been sent to test her and that, as a reward for the kindness she and her husband showed to all who came to their house, they would be granted a special grace. This pleased the woman, and she asked what the special grace was.

The old man answered, "Beginning immediately, any three wishes you or your husband may wish will come true."

When she heard these words, the woman was overjoyed and exclaimed, "Oh, if my husband were only here to hear what you say!"

The last word had scarcely left her lips when the woodsman appeared in the little house with the ax still in his hands. The first wish had come true.

The woodsman couldn't understand it at all. How did it happen that he, who had been cutting wood in the forest, found himself here in his house? His wife explained it all as she embraced him. The woodsman just stood there, thinking over what his wife had said. He looked at the old man who stood quietly, too, saying nothing.

Suddenly he realized that his wife, without stopping to think, had used one of the three wishes, and he became very annoyed when he remembered all of the useful things she might have asked for with the first wish. For the first time, he became angry with his wife. The desire

GO ON

for riches had turned his head, and he scolded his wife, shouting at her, among other things, "It doesn't seem possible that you could be so stupid! You've wasted one of our wishes, and now we have only two left! May you grow ears of a donkey!"

He had no sooner said the words than his wife's ears began to grow, and they continued to grow until they changed into the pointed, furry ears of a donkey!

When the woman put her hand up and felt them, she knew what had happened and began to cry. Her husband was very ashamed and sorry, indeed, for what he had done in his temper, and he went to his wife to comfort her.

The old man, who had stood by silently, now came to them and said, "Until now, you have known happiness together and have never quarreled with each other. Nevertheless, the mere knowledge that you could have riches and power has changed you both. Remember, you have only one wish left. What do you want? Riches? Beautiful clothes? Servants? Power?"

The woodsman tightened his arm about his wife, looked at the old man, and said, "We want only the happiness and joy we knew before my wife grew donkey's ears."

No sooner had he said these words than the donkey ears disappeared. The woodsman and his wife fell upon their knees to ask forgiveness for having acted, if only for a moment, out of covetousness and greed. Then they gave thanks for all their happiness.

Comprehension

DIRECTIONS *Answer these questions about the excerpt from "The King Who Wished for Gold."*

1. Why does Midas order a large feast?

- **A** He wants to eat like the gods.
- **B** He thinks he is wealthy enough to spend as much as he wants.
- **C** He hopes to see the food and drink become gold treasures.
- **D** He wants to share his fortune.

2. What happens after Midas sits down to eat?

- **A** Dionysus sends him to the river.
- **B** He wishes to be wealthy.
- **C** No one attends his feast.
- **D** Food turns to gold in his hand.

3. What causes King Midas to hate the gift he had wanted so much?

- **A** He wants to please Dionysus.
- **B** He realizes he cannot eat or drink.
- **C** He remembers that he loves his roses.
- **D** He is bored with all of the gold.

ARMT/ADAW SKILLS PRACTICE

4. Why is Dionysus' behavior in lines 15–18 characteristic of a Greek myth?

A He shows supernatural power.

B He becomes extremely angry.

C He proves that he is an immortal.

D He knows that Midas is a fool.

5. Which aspect of the natural world does this myth explain?

A how gold came to be in the river

B why rose gardens became popular

C why rivers have springs

D how thunder forms in the sky

6. Which words in lines 1–9 are clues to the order of events in this myth?

A after all, became

B ordered, turned

C before, but

D as soon as, then

DIRECTIONS *Answer these questions about the excerpt from "The Three Wishes."*

7. Which event causes the woodsman to become angry with his wife?

A The wife gives food to the old man.

B The woodsman is suddenly home.

C The wife wastes one of the wishes.

D The old man rewards the wife.

8. Which quality does the woodsman stand for in this tale?

A simplicity

B laziness

C honesty

D foolishness

9. After the wife grows donkey ears, the

A old man grants three wishes

B woodsman comforts his sad wife

C wife shares her food

D old man knocks on the door

DIRECTIONS *Answer this question about both selections.*

10. Which value is most likely prized by the cultures that gave us these two stories?

A Respect your elders.

B Be kind to strangers.

C Appreciate what you have.

D Work steadily toward a goal.

Open-Ended

SHORT ANSWER *Write two or three sentences to answer the following question.*

11. On the basis of "The King Who Wished for Gold," what human traits do you think the ancient Greeks valued?

ESSAY *Write a short paragraph to answer this question.*

12. What lessons do King Midas and the couple in "The Three Wishes" learn about happiness and wealth?

GO ON

Vocabulary

DIRECTIONS *Use context clues and your knowledge of compound words to answer the following questions.*

1. Which is the likely definition of the compound word *newfound* in line 10 of "The King Who Wished for Gold"?

"Poor King Midas realized that for all his newfound wealth he would soon starve to death if he could not eat or drink."

A unexpectedly returned

B recently acquired

C up-to-date

D earned

2. In line 1 of "The Three Wishes," the compound word *woodsman* refers to someone who

A works in the forest

B lives outdoors

C loves nature

D plants trees

3. Which is the likely definition of the compound word *overjoyed* in line 18 of "The Three Wishes"?

"When she heard these words, the woman was overjoyed and exclaimed, 'Oh, if my husband were only here to hear what you say!'"

A almost happy

B too happy

C unhappy

D extremely happy

DIRECTIONS *Use context clues and your knowledge of homographs to answer the following questions.*

The last word had scarcely left her lips when the woodsman appeared in the little house with the ax still in his hands.

4. Which sentence uses *last* as it is used in line 20 of "The Three Wishes"?

A She was the last one out of the pool.

B I wonder if that new worker will last.

C He is the last person I want to see.

D At long last, you may all go home.

5. Which sentence uses *left* as it is used in line 20 of "The Three Wishes"?

A According to the map, we turn left.

B Liberal groups are sometimes called "the left."

C She left the room hastily.

D They left the lights on all night.

6. Which sentence uses *still* as it is used in line 21 of "The Three Wishes"?

A It felt hotter when the wind died and the air became still.

B Still, I can't go shopping until the car is repaired.

C The play is still being performed at the 6th Street Theater.

D They used a still photograph to promote the movie.

ARMT/ADAW SKILLS PRACTICE

Writing & Grammar

DIRECTIONS *Read this passage and answer the questions that follow.*

(1) One of the most famous magicians was Harry Houdini. (2) Whose original name was Erich Weisz. (3) Houdini was born in Hungary in 1874. (4) He later moved to America. (5) Houdini did not get very far in his education. (6) But he loved to read. (7) One day, he read a book by Robert-Houdin, a famous magician. (8) He decided he would be a magician too. (9) He named himself "Houdini" after Robert-Houdin.

1. How might you combine sentence 1 and fragment 2 to form a complex sentence?

A One of the most famous magicians was Harry Houdini; Houdini's original name was Erich Weisz.

B Harry Houdini's original name was Erich Weisz, and he was one of the most famous magicians.

C One of the most famous magicians was Harry Houdini, whose original name was Erich Weisz.

D Harry Houdini was one of the most famous magicians, and his original name was Erich Weisz.

2. How might you combine sentences 3 and 4 to form a compound sentence?

A Houdini, who was born in Hungary in 1874, later moved to America.

B After he was born in Hungary in 1874, Houdini moved to America.

C Although he was born in Hungary in 1874, Houdini later moved to America.

D Houdini was born in Hungary in 1874; he later moved to America.

3. How might you combine sentences 5 and 6 to form a complex sentence?

A Although Houdini did not get very far in his education, he loved to read.

B Houdini did not get very far in his education; still, he loved to read.

C Houdini did not get very far in his education, but he loved to read.

D He loved to read; however, Houdini did not get very far in his education.

4. How might you combine sentences 8 and 9 to form a compound sentence?

A Because he decided he would be a magician too, he named himself "Houdini" after Robert-Houdin.

B After he decided he would be a magician too, he named himself "Houdini" after Robert-Houdin.

C He named himself "Houdini" after Robert-Houdin when he decided he would be a magician too.

D He decided he would be a magician too, and he named himself "Houdini" after Robert-Houdin.

STOP

UNIT 6

More Great Reads

Ideas for Independent Reading

Which questions from Unit 6 made an impression on you? Continue exploring them with these books.

Do you think before you act?

Nothing but the Truth
by Avi

In this "documentary novel," 13-year-old Philip Malloy faces dire consequences when he defends his right to freedom of speech. The story is presented through fictional memos, letters, diary entries, and official school documents.

When JFK Was My Father
by Amy Gordon

When 13-year-old Georgia Hughes's family life is changed drastically, she creates a fantasy family in which President Kennedy is her father. What will she do when the time comes to consider reality and leave her fantasies behind?

Honus and Me
by Dan Gutman

Are you willing to risk a guilty conscience? Twelve-year-old Joe Stoshack discovers a baseball card worth half a million dollars—in someone else's attic. As he wrestles with his conscience, will he decide to keep the card?

Should people always reach for the stars?

Purely Rosie Pearl
by Patricia Cochrane

Two young girls—one an optimist and one a pessimist—help each other endure the hardships of the Great Depression. Is either philosophy right, or is the answer somewhere in between?

Through My Eyes
by Ruby Bridges

Could you be optimistic about your future in the face of awful experiences? Learn how Ruby Bridges kept her dreams alive as the only African-American first grader in a newly desegregated school in 1960.

Jazmin's Notebook
by Nikki Grimes

Fourteen-year-old Jazmin has been passed along from one foster home to another. When she is finally given a chance to realize her dream of becoming a writer, will she achieve her goal despite the obstacles?

Is there a job you were born to do?

Zack
by William Bell

During a tough year at his new school, Zack discovers that a distant relative of his was a former slave who fought in the American Revolution. What he finds when he researches his family history will surprise you.

Promises to the Dead
by Mary Downing Hahn

Twelve-year-old Jesse promises Lydia, a dying runaway slave, that he will bring her young son Perry to relatives in Baltimore. Along the way, Jesse learns young Perry's true heritage and has to reevaluate everything he's ever known.

Trouble River
by Betsy Byars

Dewey Martin, a 12-year-old boy living in the 1800s, is left behind to tend the family farm while his parents go to Hunter City. Fearing an Indian raid, Dewey, his grandmother, and their dog, Charlie, set off on a small raft on the uncharted Trouble River—the only escape!

UNIT 7

Writing a Life

BIOGRAPHY AND AUTOBIOGRAPHY

- In Nonfiction
- In Media
- In Drama
- In Poetry

UNIT 7 Share What You Know

How do we share OUR STORIES?

Have you ever put together a photo album or scrapbook to help you tell others about an important event in your life? If someone looked through the book without you there to explain it, what would they learn about you? Sharing stories from our lives can help us better understand each other.

ACTIVITY Using words, pictures, or a mix of both, tell your class about a great day you had. As you share your story and listen to the stories told by your classmates, think about the following questions:

- In what ways are other stories similar to yours?
- In what ways are they different?
- What does each story teach you about the person telling it?
- What do your classmates learn about you from your story?

Online LITERATURE CLASSZONE.COM

Literature and Reading Center
Writing Center
Vocabulary and Spelling Center

ALABAMA STANDARDS

Preview Unit Goals

LITERARY ANALYSIS

- Identify form and characteristics of biography, autobiography, personal essay, and historical drama
- Read and identify characteristics of primary sources and newspaper articles

READING

- Identify chronological order
- Make inferences and draw conclusions
- Summarize
- Identify treatment and scope
- Evaluate texts for usefulness

WRITING AND GRAMMAR

- Write a personal narrative
- Punctuate titles with italics and quotation marks

SPEAKING, LISTENING, AND VIEWING

- Present a personal narrative
- Analyze a documentary
- Plan and conduct an interview

VOCABULARY

- Recognize base words
- Understand and use Latin roots

ACADEMIC VOCABULARY

- biography
- autobiography
- personal essay
- historical drama
- primary sources
- personal narrative

UNIT 7

Reader's Workshop

Biography and Autobiography

What was it like to be the first person to set foot on the moon? How did World War II soldiers deal with the horrors of combat while so far away from home? What is an athlete thinking the moment he or she crosses the finish line? We are all curious about other people—about what they do, why they do it, and how they feel. You can satisfy this curiosity by reading biographies and autobiographies.

ALABAMA STANDARDS

READING & LIT STANDARDS

3 Distinguish among genres, including biographies and autobiographies

6 Analyze nonfiction for distinguishing characteristics

7.a Comparing various types of informational texts

Part 1: Understanding the Basics

A **biography** is a story of a person's life told by someone else and written from the third-person point of view. The writer, or **biographer,** usually gets information about the subject by doing detailed research using a number of sources. Sometimes, the biographer might even interview the subject directly.

An **autobiography** is also the story of a person's life, but it is told by that person and is written from the first-person point of view. Although most of the information is from the subject's mind and memories, he or she may still consult others for help in remembering details about his or her life.

Usually, when people talk about biographies or autobiographies, they are referring to whole books about people's lives. However, biographical and autobiographical writing also includes other forms, shown in the chart.

BIOGRAPHY

SOURCES

- letters to and from the subject
- interviews with the subject and/or others
- books about the subject
- diaries or journals

FORMS

- biographical books
- encyclopedia entries
- feature articles in newspapers and magazines or on Web sites

AUTOBIOGRAPHY

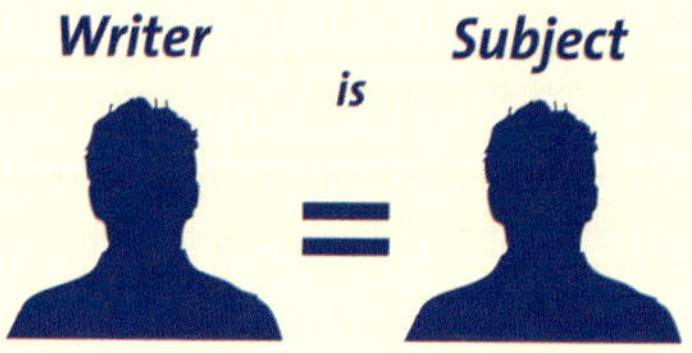

SOURCES

- memories
- thoughts and feelings
- family, friends, or associates
- memorabilia

FORMS

- autobiographical books
- diaries and journals
- personal essays
- memoirs

MODEL 1: BIOGRAPHY

This excerpt is from a biography about Wilbur and Orville Wright, two brothers who invented and flew the first machine-powered airplane.

from

THE WRIGHT BROTHERS

Biography by **Russell Freedman**

Orville was more impulsive, "bubbling over with ideas," according to his niece. Among family and friends, he had a reputation as a tease and a practical joker. Among strangers, however, he seemed uncomfortably shy. He would clam up and fade silently into the background.

Orville's greatest pleasure was to take something apart, see how it worked, and put it back together. Wilbur was more of a visionary, fascinated by the big picture rather than its individual parts. He was the one who first dreamed of building an airplane. . . .

Close Read

1. What clues tell you that this is a biography rather than an autobiography?
2. How were Wilbur and Orville different? Cite details to support your answer. Also note who provided the author with some of these details.

MODEL 2: AUTOBIOGRAPHY

Now read this excerpt from the autobiography of a Japanese-American author. What do you learn about her thoughts and feelings?

from

THE INVISIBLE THREAD

Autobiography by **Yoshiko Uchida**

I was born in California, recited the Pledge of Allegiance to the flag each morning at school, and loved my country as much as any other American—maybe even more.

Still, there was a large part of me that was Japanese simply because Mama and Papa had passed on to me so much of their own Japanese spirit and soul. Their own values of loyalty, honor, self-discipline, love, and respect for one's parents, teachers, and superiors were all very much a part of me.

There was also my name, which teachers couldn't seem to pronounce properly even when I shortened my first name to Yoshi. And there was my Japanese face, which closed more and more doors to me as I grew older. How wonderful it would be, I used to think, if I had blond hair and blue eyes like Marian and Solveig.

Close Read

1. What clues in the boxed sentences signal that this is an autobiography?
2. Name two things you learn about Uchida from her description of her own thoughts and feelings.

Part 2: Reading Biographies and Autobiographies

Picture yourself standing in front of a shelf at the library, a book in each hand. One is an autobiography of somebody who interests you—perhaps your favorite musician or a former president. The other is a biography of the same person. From which book would you learn more?

You might think that an autobiography is the better source. After all, who knows more about a person's life experiences than that person? Actually, though, each form has strengths and limitations that readers should consider. (Of course, if you want to get a well-rounded picture of a person—and his or her accomplishments and flaws—you should read both forms.)

BIOGRAPHY

When you read a biography, you . . .

- get information from a variety of sources
- discover how other people view the subject
- might get a more objective picture of the subject's life

Eleanor Roosevelt
by William Jay Jacobs
pages 762–773

However, you should ask

- How does the writer feel about the subject? A writer's tone or choice of words can reveal his or her personal bias.
- Who are the writer's sources—historians, people close to the subject, the subject, or people who barely knew him or her? A biography is only as reliable as its sources.
- When was this work written? A biography written halfway through the subject's life would be very different from one written 100 years later.

AUTOBIOGRAPHY

When you read an autobiography, you . . .

- get the subject's own interpretation of events
- learn the subject's private thoughts and feelings
- hear the subject's voice and get a sense of his or her personality

The Noble Experiment
by Jackie Robinson as told to Alfred Duckett
pages 810–819

However, you should ask

- Is there another side to the story? Other people in the subject's life might have different recollections or opinions of events.
- Have any details been left out? The subject may have forgotten something or might be leaving out certain details to make himself- or herself look better.
- At what point in the subject's life did he or she write the autobiography? When the subject wrote the work affects what experiences he or she writes about.

MODEL 1: READING A BIOGRAPHY

The actor Christopher Reeve was famous for his 1978 movie role as Superman. This article was published in 1982.

from

CHRISTOPHER REEVE

Feature article in *Current Biography*

Another outstanding quality is that he [Reeve] brings the same energy and enthusiasm to his recreations that he does to acting: he owns both a $350,000 private plane and a glider; he is an accomplished sailor who, upon completing *Superman,* gathered a six-man crew and sailed a boat from Connecticut to Bermuda; and he has played classical piano since adolescence, usually practicing ninety minutes every day, and also composes music. His hobbies, moreover, include skiing, ice-skating, and playing tennis. But nothing takes precedence over his work, as Aljean Harmetz told readers of the *New York Times* (August 20, 1979), "He thrives on acting. . . ." According to her, Reeve admitted: ". . . [I am] still at the stage where I'm taking care of myself, my career, first."

Close Read

1. Look at the boxed details. How would you describe the author's attitude toward Reeve?
2. What source does the author use for quotes by and about Reeve?
3. Based on this article, how would you describe Reeve?

MODEL 2: READING AN AUTOBIOGRAPHY

In 1995, a fall from a horse left Reeve paralyzed from the neck down, and he died in 2004. In this essay, Reeve reminds people not to let fear take over their lives. Reeve conquered his own fears when he participated in research for spinal cord injuries.

from

LIVING WITHOUT FEAR

Personal essay by **Christopher Reeve**

Of course, the greater difficulty lies in being fearless in surrendering and in giving. I don't want to sound too noble, but I really have been able to say, All right, I've had some setbacks, but look at the other people who have benefited.

I recommend you do the same thing because being fearless is not always going to get you exactly where you expect to go. It might take you in a completely different direction. It might not give you what you want, but it can satisfy you to know you did something for the world, for the planet, or even just for your family or your neighbors. And that's enough.

Close Read

1. Describe Reeve's personality at this point in his life. In your opinion, has his attitude toward life changed or stayed the same?
2. What picture do you get of Reeve's life as a whole? Explain how this picture would be different if you had only read one of these excerpts.

Part 3: Analyze the Literature

In 1955, a 42-year-old African-American woman in Montgomery, Alabama, refused to give up her seat on a public bus. Her action sparked a citywide bus boycott and helped break down the barriers of racial segregation in the South. Her name was Rosa Parks.

The first excerpt is from a biography of Parks; the second is from her autobiography. What do you learn about Parks from each excerpt?

from

ROSA  PARKS

Biography by **Mary Hull**

The driver [J. F. Blake] repeated his order: "Look, woman, I told you I wanted the seat. Are you going to stand up?"

In a firm, steady voice, Parks questioned him. "Why should I have to get up and stand? Why should we have to be pushed around?" The driver slammed on the brakes and pulled the bus over to the curb. He walked back to her seat and stood over her. He asked her if she was going to move, and Parks said, "No." He told her he would call the police if she did not move. "Go ahead. You may do that," Parks answered. Blake left the bus angrily and went for the police. Several passengers—all of them black—followed, reluctant to become involved in an incident that invited trouble with whites. While everyone else aboard the bus waited to see what would happen next, Parks looked out the window at Montgomery.

Parks had a right to be scared, for she recognized the driver. Twelve years earlier, she had refused to enter a bus through the rear door and had been evicted from the bus by this same driver. Although Parks had seen him before while waiting at bus stops, she never boarded a bus if she knew he was driving. In all these years she had never forgotten his face. That evening, Parks had not looked at the driver when she boarded, but when he stood over her, there was no mistaking who he was.

Parks's mother and grandparents had always taught her not to regard herself as inferior to whites because she was black, but she admitted that until that fateful December day on the bus "every part of my life pointed to the white superiority and negro inferiority." She was uncertain about what exactly had provoked her not to move on the bus driver's order, but her feet certainly hurt, her shoulders ached, and suddenly everything became too much. "I had had enough," Parks later said. She was tired of giving in. "I wanted to be treated like a human being."

Close Read

1. How can you tell that this excerpt is from a biography? Cite details to support your answer.
2. Consider how the author describes Parks's words and actions in lines 3–13. How does the author seem to feel about Parks?
3. What do you learn about Parks's upbringing from this biography?
4. One of the sources for this biography was Rosa Parks's own autobiography. As a result, the author was able to include details about Parks's thoughts and feelings. One example is boxed. Find one more.

Now read this excerpt from the beginning of Parks's autobiography. Pay attention to how Parks describes the incident on the bus. Also notice what she reveals about her thoughts and feelings at that time in her life.

from

Rosa Parks: My Story

Autobiography by **Rosa Parks**
(with Jim Haskins)

One evening in early December 1955 I was sitting in the front seat of the colored section of a bus in Montgomery, Alabama. The white people were sitting in the white section. More white people got on, and they filled up all the seats in the white section. When that happened, we black people were supposed to give up our seats to the whites. But I didn't move. The white driver said, "Let me have those front seats." I didn't get up. I was tired of giving in to white people.

"I'm going to have you arrested," the driver said.

"You may do that," I answered.

Two white policemen came. I asked one of them, "Why do you all push us around?"

He answered, "I don't know, but the law is the law and you're under arrest."

For half of my life there were laws and customs in the South that kept African Americans segregated from Caucasians and allowed white people to treat black people without any respect. I never thought this was fair, and from the time I was a child, I tried to protest against disrespectful treatment. But it was very hard to do anything about segregation and racism when white people had the power of the law behind them.

Somehow we had to change the laws. And we had to get enough white people on our side to be able to succeed. I had no idea when I refused to give up my seat on that Montgomery bus that my small action would help put an end to the segregation laws in the South. I only knew that I was tired of being pushed around. I was a regular person, just as good as anybody else.

Close Read

1. Reread the boxed sentences. Would you say that this autobiography was written in the 1950s, or later? Explain.

2. How can you tell that the author of the biography used Parks's autobiography as a source? Cite similar details in both excerpts to support your answer.

3. By revealing her thoughts and beliefs in lines 13–25, Parks gives readers a real sense of her personality. How would you describe her? In your opinion, do you get this same sense from reading the biography about her? Support your answer.

Eleanor Roosevelt

Biography by William Jay Jacobs

What is your DUTY to others?

ALABAMA STANDARDS

READING STANDARDS
3 Distinguish among genres, including biographies
4.a Determining sequence of events

KEY IDEA There are probably times when you wish you didn't owe anything to anyone. However, like most people, you have responsibilities to many different people. Family members, teachers, classmates, and the teams and other groups you belong to all need you in one way or another. In "Eleanor Roosevelt," you'll learn how a famous first lady's commitment to her **duties** changed history.

QUICKWRITE Make a list of your duties to others. Which of these do you think will most influence the adult you will become? Explore that question in a journal entry, considering career possibilities and other life choices you will be making.

● LITERARY ANALYSIS: BIOGRAPHY

A **biography** is the story of a person's life told by another person, a biographer. Biographers often reveal their personal opinions of their subject. However, they also balance their opinions with facts and details that

- provide information about the person's life
- reveal important aspects of his or her personality
- show us what others thought of the person
- explain the importance of his or her life and work

As you read "Eleanor Roosevelt," notice how a biography can make you feel about a historical figure.

■ READING SKILL: IDENTIFY CHRONOLOGICAL ORDER

A biography usually presents events in **chronological order,** or the order in which they happened. Words and phrases such as *then, next, within 18 months, meanwhile, by spring,* and *the first few years* may signal the order of events in this type of work.

As you read "Eleanor Roosevelt," keep track of the order of events on a timeline like the one shown.

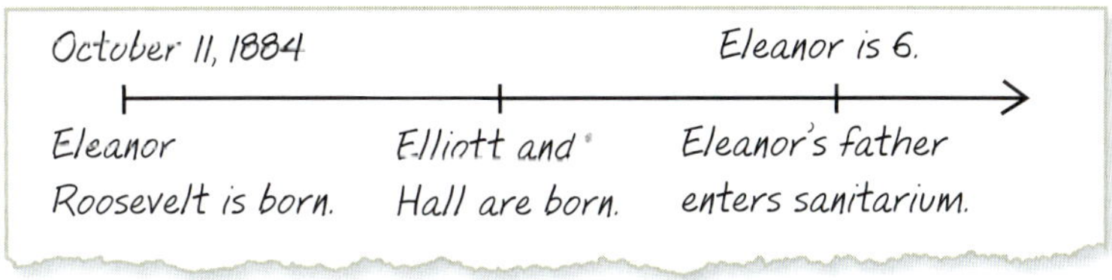

▲ VOCABULARY IN CONTEXT

These headlines describe important moments in Eleanor Roosevelt's life. Use context clues to figure out the meaning of each boldfaced word.

1. Woman from **Prominent** Family Leads by Example
2. First Lady Is **Compassionate** Toward Others
3. **Impoverished** Families Going Hungry in America
4. **Migrant** Workers Search for Jobs
5. Roosevelt Feels **Grave** Obligation to Help
6. Women **Dominate** at Home-Front Meeting
7. **Wavering** Members Convinced to Support War Effort
8. Country **Brooding** at Death of President

Author Online

The Biographer
As an author who wrote more than 30 biographies, William Jay Jacobs said that he was "able to reach a very special audience: young people searching for models. . . ."

William Jay Jacobs
1933–2004

A Strong Role Model Jacobs admired Eleanor Roosevelt for her strength of character. He noted, "The more I learned about Eleanor Roosevelt, the more I saw her as a woman of courage. She turned her pain to strength."

MORE ABOUT THE AUTHOR
For more on William Jay Jacobs, visit the **Literature Center** at **ClassZone.com.**

Background

Hard Times Eleanor Roosevelt was first lady of the United States from 1933 to 1945. Her husband, Franklin D. Roosevelt, took office during the Great Depression, a worldwide economic crisis that lasted through most of the 1930s. Millions of Americans were unemployed, penniless, and suffering.

Help on the Way To encourage recovery, the Roosevelt administration introduced programs—such as Social Security and a minimum wage—that still provide relief today. Many of the First Lady's ideas were incorporated into her husband's New Deal programs.

Eleanor Roosevelt

WILLIAM JAY JACOBS

Eleanor Roosevelt was the wife of President Franklin Delano Roosevelt. But Eleanor was much more than just a president's wife, an echo of her husband's career.

Sad and lonely as a child, Eleanor was called "Granny" by her mother because of her seriousness. People teased her about her looks and called her the "ugly duckling.". . .

Yet despite all of the disappointments, the bitterness, the misery she experienced, Eleanor Roosevelt refused to give up. Instead she turned her unhappiness and pain to strength. She devoted her life to helping others. Today she is remembered as one of America's greatest women. (A)

Eleanor was born in a fine townhouse in Manhattan. Her family also owned an elegant mansion along the Hudson River, where they spent weekends and summers. As a child Eleanor went to fashionable parties. A servant took care of her and taught her to speak French. Her mother, the beautiful Anna Hall Roosevelt, wore magnificent jewels and fine clothing. Her father, Elliott Roosevelt, had his own hunting lodge and liked to sail and to play tennis and polo. Elliott, who loved Eleanor dearly, was the younger brother of Theodore Roosevelt, who in 1901 became president of the United States. The Roosevelt family, one of America's oldest, wealthiest families, was respected and admired.

ANALYZE VISUALS
What can you **infer** about Eleanor Roosevelt from this 1957 photograph taken at her home?

(A) BIOGRAPHY
Why might Jacobs have chosen to begin with an overview of Mrs. Roosevelt's life?

To the outside world it might have seemed that Eleanor had everything that any child could want—everything that could make her happy. But she was not happy. Instead her childhood was very sad.

Almost from the day of her birth, October 11, 1884, people noticed that she was an unattractive child. As she grew older, she could not help but notice her mother's extraordinary beauty, as well as the beauty of her aunts and cousins. Eleanor was plain looking, ordinary, even, as some called her, homely. For a time she had to wear a bulky brace on her back to straighten her crooked spine. **B**

B CHRONOLOGICAL ORDER
Jacobs begins his use of chronological order with Eleanor's birth date. Start adding events to your timeline.

When Eleanor was born, her parents had wanted a boy. They were scarcely able to hide their disappointment. Later, with the arrival of two boys, Elliott and Hall, Eleanor watched her mother hold the boys on her lap and lovingly stroke their hair, while for Eleanor there seemed only coolness, distance.

Feeling unwanted, Eleanor became shy and withdrawn. She also developed many fears. She was afraid of the dark, afraid of animals, afraid of other children, afraid of being scolded, afraid of strangers, afraid that people would not like her. She was a frightened, lonely little girl.

The one joy in the early years of her life was her father, who always seemed to care for her, love her. He used to dance with her, to pick her up and throw her into the air while she laughed and laughed. He called her "little golden hair" or "darling little Nell."

Then, when she was six, her father left. An alcoholic, he went to live in a sanitarium[1] in Virginia in an attempt to deal with his drinking problem. Eleanor missed him greatly.

Next her mother became ill with painful headaches. Sometimes for hours at a time Eleanor would sit holding her mother's head in her lap and stroking her forehead. Nothing else seemed to relieve the pain. At those times Eleanor often remembered how her mother had teased her about her looks and called her "Granny." But even at the age of seven Eleanor was glad to be helping someone, glad to be needed—and noticed.

The next year, when Eleanor was eight, her mother, the beautiful Anna, died. Afterward her brother Elliott suddenly caught diphtheria[2] and he, too, died. Eleanor and her baby brother, Hall, were taken to live with their grandmother in Manhattan.

A few months later another tragedy struck. Elliott Roosevelt, Eleanor's father, also died. Within eighteen months Eleanor had lost her mother, a brother, and her dear father. **C**

C CHRONOLOGICAL ORDER
Reread lines 52–58. What words and phrases in these paragraphs help you understand the order of events and the passage of time?

---

1. **sanitarium** (săn′ĭ-târ′ē-əm): an institution for the care of people with a specific disease or with other health problems.
2. **diphtheria** (dĭf-thîr′ē-ə): a serious infectious disease.

Eleanor Roosevelt with her father, Elliott Roosevelt

For the rest of her life Eleanor carried with her the letters that her father had written to her from the sanitarium. In them he had told her to be brave, to become well educated, and to grow up into a woman he could be proud of, a woman who helped people who were suffering.

Only ten years old when her father died, Eleanor decided even then to live the kind of life he had described—a life that would have made him proud of her. D

D BIOGRAPHY
Reread lines 60–62. According to Jacobs, how did Eleanor's father influence her goals and values?

Few things in life came easily for Eleanor, but the first few years after her father's death proved exceptionally hard. Grandmother Hall's dark and gloomy townhouse had no place for children to play. The family ate meals in silence. Every morning Eleanor and Hall were expected to take cold baths for their health. Eleanor had to work at better posture by walking with her arms behind her back, clamped over a walking stick.

Instead of making new friends, Eleanor often sat alone in her room and read. For many months after her father's death she pretended that he was still alive. She made him the hero of stories she wrote for school. Sometimes, alone and unhappy, she just cried.

Some of her few moments of happiness came from visiting her uncle, Theodore Roosevelt, in Oyster Bay, Long Island. A visit with Uncle Ted meant playing games and romping outdoors with the many Roosevelt children.

Once Uncle Ted threw her into the water to teach her how to swim, but when she started to sink, he had to rescue her. Often he would read to the children old Norse[3] tales and poetry. It was at Sagamore Hill, Uncle Ted's home, that Eleanor first learned how much fun it could be to read books aloud.

For most of the time Eleanor's life was grim. Although her parents had left plenty of money for her upbringing, she had only two dresses to wear to school. Once she spilled ink on one of them, and since the other was in the wash, she had to wear the dress with large ink stains on it to school the next day. It was not that Grandmother Hall was stingy. Rather, she was old and often confused. Nor did she show much warmth or love for Eleanor and her brother. Usually she just neglected them.

ANALYZE VISUALS
What **mood** does this photograph of a teenage Eleanor Roosevelt convey?

Just before Eleanor turned fifteen, Grandmother Hall decided to send her to boarding school in England. The school she chose was Allenswood, a private academy for girls located on the outskirts of London.

It was at Allenswood that Eleanor, still thinking of herself as an "ugly duckling," first dared to believe that one day she might be able to become a swan.

At Allenswood she worked to toughen herself physically. Every day she did exercises in the morning and took a cold shower. Although she did not like competitive team sports, as a matter of self-discipline she tried out for field hockey. Not only did she make the team but, because she played so hard, also won the respect of her teammates.

They called her by her family nickname, "Totty," and showed their affection for her by putting books and flowers in her room, as was the custom at Allenswood. Never before had she experienced the pleasure of having schoolmates actually admire her rather than tease her.

At Allenswood, too, she began to look after her health. She finally broke the habit of chewing her fingernails. She learned to eat nutritious foods, to get plenty of sleep, and to take a brisk walk every morning, no matter how miserable the weather.

Under the guidance of the school's headmistress, Mademoiselle Souvestre (or "Sou"), she learned to ask searching questions and think for herself instead of just giving back on tests what teachers had said.

3. **Norse** (nôrs): coming from ancient Scandinavia, the area that is now Norway, Sweden, and Denmark.

She also learned to speak French fluently, a skill she polished by traveling in France, living for a time with a French family. Mademoiselle Souvestre arranged for her to have a new red dress. Wearing it, after all of the old, worn dresses Grandmother Hall had given her, made her feel very proud.

Eleanor was growing up, and the joy of young womanhood had begun to transform her personality.

In 1902, nearly eighteen years old, she left Allenswood, not returning for her fourth year there. Grandmother Hall insisted that, instead, she must be introduced to society as a debutante—to go to dances and parties and begin to take her place in the social world with other wealthy young women.

Away from Allenswood, Eleanor's old uncertainty about her looks came back again. She saw herself as too tall, too thin, too plain. She worried about her buckteeth, which she thought made her look horselike. The old teasing began again, especially on the part of Uncle Ted's daughter, "Princess" Alice Roosevelt, who seemed to take pleasure in making Eleanor feel uncomfortable.

Eleanor, as always, did as she was told. She went to all of the parties and dances. But she also began working with poor children at the Rivington Street Settlement House[4] on New York's Lower East Side. She taught the girls gymnastic exercises. She took children to museums and to musical performances. She tried to get the parents interested in politics in order to get better schools and cleaner, safer streets. E

E BIOGRAPHY
Reread lines 131–142. Note that Jacobs chooses details that reveal various aspects of Eleanor's personality. What are some of her strengths and weaknesses?

Meanwhile Eleanor's life reached a turning point. She fell in love! The young man was her fifth cousin, Franklin Delano Roosevelt.

Eleanor and Franklin had known each other since childhood. Franklin recalled how once he had carried her piggyback in the nursery. When she was fourteen, he had danced with her at a party. Then, shortly after her return from Allenswood, they had met by chance on a train. They talked and almost at once realized how much they liked each other.

For a time they met secretly. Then they attended parties together. Franklin—tall, strong, handsome—saw her as a person he could trust. He knew that she would not try to **dominate** him. F

F CHRONOLOGICAL ORDER
Reread lines 143–152. What words and phrases help you understand the order in which Eleanor and Franklin's relationship progressed?

But did he really love her? Would he always? She wrote to him, quoting a poem she knew: "Unless you can swear, *'For life, for death!'* . . . Oh, never call it loving!"

Franklin promised that his love was indeed "for life," and Eleanor agreed to marry him. It was the autumn of 1903. He was twenty-one. She was nineteen.

On March 17, 1905, Eleanor and Franklin were married. "Uncle Ted," by then president of the United States, was there to "give the bride away."

dominate (dŏm′ə-nāt′) *v.* to have control over

4. **settlement house:** a place in a poor, neglected neighborhood where services are provided for residents.

It was sometimes said that the dynamic, energetic Theodore Roosevelt had to be "the bride at every wedding and the corpse at every funeral." And it was certainly true that day. Wherever the president went, the guests followed at his heels.

Before long Eleanor and Franklin found themselves standing all alone, deserted. Franklin seemed annoyed, but Eleanor didn't mind. She had found the ceremony deeply moving. And she stood next to her husband in a glow of idealism—very serious, very **grave,** very much in love.

grave (grāv) *adj.* solemn and dignified

In May 1906 the couple's first child was born. During the next nine years Eleanor gave birth to five more babies, one of whom died in infancy. Still timid, shy, afraid of making mistakes, she found herself so busy that there was little time to think of her own drawbacks.

Still, looking back later on the early years of her marriage, Eleanor knew that she should have been a stronger person, especially in the handling of Franklin's mother, or, as they both called her, "Mammá." Too often Mammá made the decisions about such things as where they would live, how their home would be furnished, how the children would be disciplined. Eleanor and Franklin let her pay for things they could not afford—extra servants, vacations, doctor bills, clothing. She offered, and they accepted.

Before long, trouble developed in the relationship between Eleanor and Franklin. Serious, shy, easily embarrassed, Eleanor could not share Franklin's interests in golf and tennis. He enjoyed light talk and flirting with women. She could not be lighthearted. So she stayed on the sidelines. Instead of losing her temper, she bottled up her anger and did not talk to him at all. As he used to say, she "clammed up." Her silence only made things worse, because it puzzled him. Faced with her coldness, her **brooding** silence, he only grew angrier and more distant.

brooding (bro͞o'dĭng) *adj.* full of worry; troubled **brood** *v.*

Meanwhile Franklin's career in politics advanced rapidly. In 1910 he was elected to the New York State Senate. In 1913 President Wilson appointed him Assistant Secretary of the Navy—a powerful position in the national government, which required the Roosevelts to move to Washington, D.C. **G**

G CHRONOLOGICAL ORDER
The word *meanwhile* indicates that something else happened at the same time. In what ways are the early years of their marriage different for Eleanor and Franklin?

In 1917 the United States entered World War I as an active combatant. Like many socially **prominent** women, Eleanor threw herself into the war effort. Sometimes she worked fifteen and sixteen hours a day. She made sandwiches for soldiers passing through the nation's capital. She knitted sweaters. She used Franklin's influence to get the Red Cross to build a recreation room for soldiers who had been shell-shocked[5] in combat. . . .

prominent (prŏm'ə-nənt) *adj.* well-known; widely recognized

In 1920 the Democratic Party chose Franklin as its candidate for vice-president of the United States. Even though the Republicans won

5. **shell-shocked:** affected with a nervous or mental disorder resulting from the strain of battle.

the election, Roosevelt became a well-known figure in national politics. All the time, Eleanor stood by his side, smiling, doing what was expected of her as a candidate's wife.

She did what was expected—and much more—in the summer of 1921 when disaster struck the Roosevelt family. While on vacation Franklin suddenly fell ill with infantile paralysis—polio—the horrible disease that each year used to kill or cripple thousands of children, and many adults as well. When Franklin became a victim of polio, nobody knew what caused the disease or how to cure it.

Franklin lived, but the lower part of his body remained paralyzed. For the rest of his life he never again had the use of his legs. He had to be lifted and carried from place to place. He had to wear heavy steel braces from his waist to the heels of his shoes.

His mother, as well as many of his advisers, urged him to give up politics, to live the life of a country gentleman on the Roosevelt estate at Hyde Park, New York. This time, Eleanor, calm and strong, stood up for her ideas. She argued that he should not be treated like a sick person, tucked away in the country, inactive, just waiting for death to come.

Franklin agreed. Slowly he recovered his health. His energy returned. In 1928 he was elected governor of New York. Then, just four years later, he was elected president of the United States. (H)

(H) **BIOGRAPHY**
Why was Franklin's illness a turning point for Eleanor?

President Franklin Delano Roosevelt and First Lady Eleanor Roosevelt, April 17, 1938

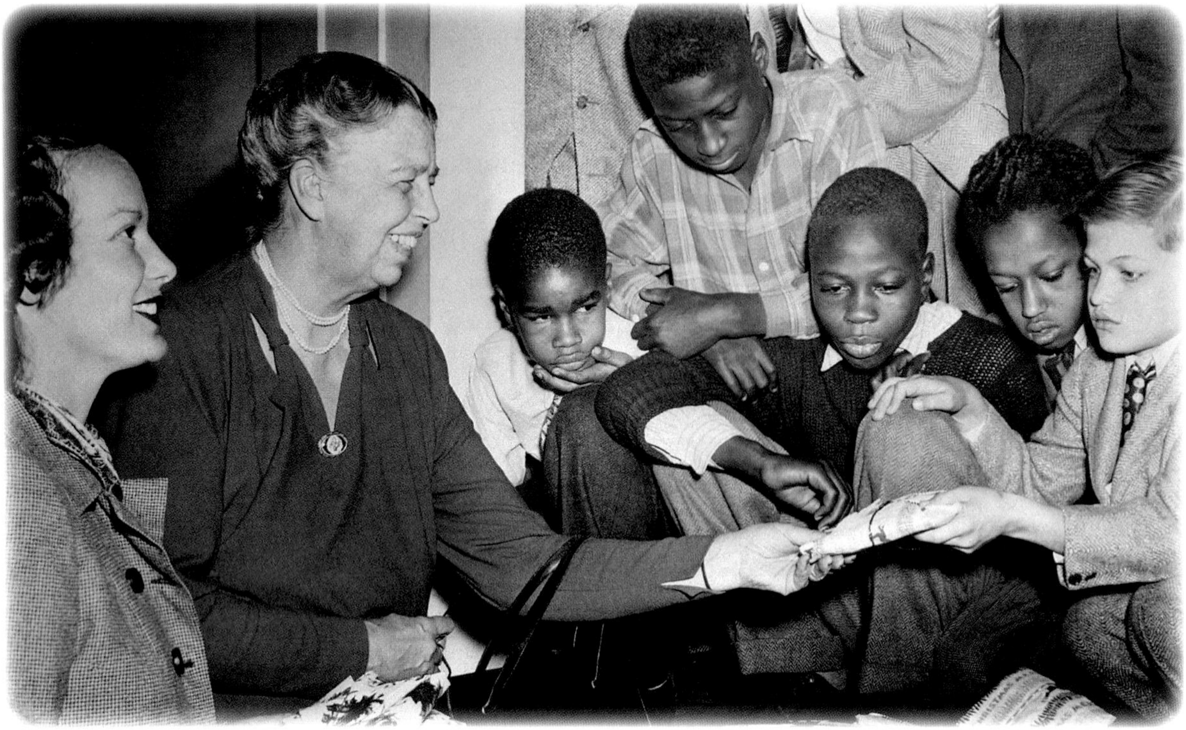

By visiting places such as this school for underprivileged boys, Eleanor Roosevelt raised public awareness of social problems.

Meanwhile Eleanor had changed. To keep Franklin in the public eye while he was recovering, she had gotten involved in politics herself. It was, she thought, her "duty." From childhood she had been taught "to do the thing that has to be done, the way it has to be done, when it has to be done."

With the help of Franklin's adviser Louis Howe, she made fund-raising speeches for the Democratic Party all around New York State. She helped in the work of the League of Women Voters, the Consumer's League, and the Foreign Policy Association. After becoming interested in the problems of working women, she gave time to the Women's Trade Union League (WTUL).[6]

It was through the WTUL that she met a group of remarkable women—women doing exciting work that made a difference in the world. They taught Eleanor about life in the slums. They awakened her hopes that something could be done to improve the condition of the poor. She dropped out of the "fashionable" society of her wealthy friends and joined the world of reform—social change.

For hours at a time Eleanor and her reformer friends talked with Franklin. They showed him the need for new laws: laws to get children out of the factories and into schools; laws to cut down the long hours that women worked; laws to get fair wages for all workers.

6. **Women's Trade Union League:** an organization founded in 1903 to promote laws to protect the rights of women working in factories and to help establish labor unions for women.

By the time that Franklin was sworn in as president, the nation was facing its deepest depression. One out of every four Americans was out of work, out of hope. At mealtimes people stood in lines in front of soup kitchens for something to eat. Mrs. Roosevelt herself knew of once-prosperous families who found themselves reduced to eating stale bread from thrift shops or traveling to parts of town where they were not known to beg for money from house to house.

Eleanor worked in the charity kitchens, ladling out soup. She visited slums. She crisscrossed the country learning about the suffering of coal miners, shipyard workers, **migrant** farm workers, students, housewives—Americans caught up in the paralysis of the Great Depression. Since Franklin himself remained crippled, she became his eyes and ears, informing him of what the American people were really thinking and feeling.

Eleanor also was the president's conscience, personally urging on him some of the most **compassionate,** forward-looking laws of his presidency, including, for example, the National Youth Administration (NYA), which provided money to allow **impoverished** young people to stay in school.

She lectured widely, wrote a regularly syndicated[7] newspaper column, "My Day," and spoke frequently on the radio. She fought for equal pay for women in industry. Like no other First Lady up to that time, she became a link between the president and the American public.

Above all she fought against racial and religious prejudice. When Eleanor learned that the DAR (Daughters of the American Revolution) would not allow the great black singer Marian Anderson to perform in their auditorium in Washington, D.C., she resigned from the organization. Then she arranged to have Miss Anderson sing in front of the Lincoln Memorial.

Similarly, when she entered a hall where, as often happened in those days, blacks and whites were seated in separate sections, she made it a point to sit with the blacks. Her example marked an important step in making the rights of blacks a matter of national priority.

On December 7, 1941, Japanese forces launched a surprise attack on the American naval base at Pearl Harbor, Hawaii, as well as on other American installations in the Pacific. The United States entered World War II, fighting not only against Japan but against the brutal dictators who then controlled Germany and Italy.

Eleanor helped the Red Cross raise money. She gave blood, sold war bonds. But she also did the unexpected. In 1943, for example, she visited barracks and hospitals on islands throughout the South Pacific. When she visited a hospital, she stopped at every bed. To each soldier she said something special, something that a mother might say. Often, after she left, even battle-hardened men had tears in their eyes. Admiral Nimitz,

migrant (mīʹgrənt) *adj.* moving from place to place

compassionate (kəm-păshʹə-nĭt) *adj.* wanting to help those who suffer

impoverished (ĭm-pŏvʹər-ĭsht) *adj.* very poor **impoverish** *v.*

SOCIAL STUDIES CONNECTION

At the Lincoln Memorial, Marian Anderson performed in front of 75,000 people. Later, in 1943, Anderson performed at Constitution Hall, where she had been denied.

7. **syndicated** (sĭnʹdĭ-kātʹĭd): sold to many newspapers for publication.

who originally thought such visits would be a nuisance, became one of her strongest admirers. Nobody else, he said, had done so much to help raise the spirits of the men. **I**

By spring 1945 the end of the war in Europe seemed near. Then, on April 12, a phone call brought Eleanor the news that Franklin Roosevelt, who had gone to Warm Springs, Georgia, for a rest, was dead.

As Eleanor later declared, "I think that sometimes I acted as his conscience. I urged him to take the harder path when he would have preferred the easier way. In that sense, I acted on occasion as a spur, even though the spurring was not always wanted or welcome.

"Of course," said Eleanor, "I loved him, and I miss him."

After Franklin's funeral, every day that Eleanor was home at Hyde Park, without fail, she placed flowers on his grave. Then she would stand very still beside him there.

With Franklin dead, Eleanor Roosevelt might have dropped out of the public eye, might have been remembered in the history books only as a footnote to the president's program of social reforms. Instead she found new strengths within herself, new ways to live a useful, interesting life—and to help others. Now, moreover, her successes were her own, not the result of being the president's wife. **J**

I BIOGRAPHY
What does Admiral Nimitz's change in attitude suggest about the quality of the First Lady's work?

J BIOGRAPHY
Reread lines 297–302. What words and phrases does Jacobs use that give important details about Eleanor?

In December 1945 President Harry S. Truman invited her to be one of the American delegates going to London to begin the work of the United Nations. Eleanor hesitated, but the president insisted. He said that the nation needed her; it was her duty. After that, Eleanor agreed.

In the beginning some of her fellow delegates from the United States considered her unqualified for the position, but after seeing her in action, they changed their minds.

It was Eleanor Roosevelt who, almost single-handedly, pushed through the United Nations General Assembly a resolution giving refugees from World War II the right *not* to return to their native lands if they did not wish to. The Russians angrily objected, but Eleanor's reasoning convinced **wavering** delegates. In a passionate speech defending the rights of the refugees she declared, "We [must] consider first the rights of man and what makes men more free—not governments, but man!"

wavering (wā′vər-ĭng) *adj.* hesitating between two choices **waver** *v.*

Next Mrs. Roosevelt helped draft the United Nations Declaration of Human Rights. The Soviets wanted the declaration to list the duties people owed to their countries. Again Eleanor insisted that the United Nations should stand for individual freedom—the rights of people to free speech, freedom of religion, and such human needs as health care and education. In December 1948, with the Soviet Union and its allies refusing to vote, the Declaration of Human Rights won approval of the UN General Assembly by a vote of forty-eight to zero.

As a delegate to the United Nations, Eleanor Roosevelt defended people's rights and freedoms.

Even after retiring from her post at the UN, Mrs. Roosevelt continued to travel. In places around the world she dined with presidents and kings. But she also visited tenement slums[8] in Bombay, India; factories in Yugoslavia; farms in Lebanon and Israel. K

Everywhere she met people who were eager to greet her. Although as a child she had been brought up to be formal and distant, she had grown to feel at ease with people. They wanted to touch her, to hug her, to kiss her.

Eleanor's doctor had been telling her to slow down, but that was hard for her. She continued to write her newspaper column, "My Day," and to appear on television. She still began working at seven-thirty in the morning and often continued until well past midnight. Not only did she write and speak, she taught retarded children and raised money for health care of the poor.

As author Clare Boothe Luce put it, "Mrs. Roosevelt has done more good deeds on a bigger scale for a longer time than any woman who ever appeared on our public scene. No woman has ever so comforted the distressed or so distressed the comfortable."

Gradually, however, she was forced to withdraw from some of her activities, to spend more time at home.

On November 7, 1962, at the age of seventy-eight, Eleanor died in her sleep. She was buried in the rose garden at Hyde Park, alongside her husband.

Adlai Stevenson, the American ambassador to the United Nations, remembered her as "the First Lady of the World," as the person—male or female—most effective in working for the cause of human rights. As Stevenson declared, "She would rather light a candle than curse the darkness." L

And perhaps, in sum, that is what the struggle for human rights is all about.

K CHRONOLOGICAL ORDER
Reread lines 303–328. Note the accomplishments that Mrs. Roosevelt achieved after her husband's death. What words and phrases help you figure out the order of the events?

L BIOGRAPHY
Reread lines 338–350. Why might Jacobs quote two famous people and their thoughts about Mrs. Roosevelt in these last paragraphs?

---

8. **tenement** (tĕn′ə-mənt) **slums:** parts of a city where poor people live in crowded, shabby buildings.

Comprehension

ALABAMA STANDARDS

READING STANDARD
4.a Determining sequence of events

1. **Recall** Tell how Eleanor felt about herself as a young girl.
2. **Summarize** What are some examples of ways Mrs. Roosevelt helped society?
3. **Clarify** How did Mrs. Roosevelt act as her husband's "eyes and ears" when he was president?

Literary Analysis

4. **Examine Chronological Order** Review the timeline you made. What period do you think contains the most important events in Eleanor Roosevelt's life?
5. **Make Inferences** Reread the quotation by Clare Boothe Luce in lines 338–341. Who were the "comfortable" people, and how did Mrs. Roosevelt "distress" them?
6. **Analyze Cause and Effect** How do you think Eleanor's childhood affected the choices she made later in life? Create a chart to show the effects of these experiences, or causes. Some causes will have more than one effect.

Cause	Effect	Effect
Eleanor's father told her to help people who were suffering.	She worked with poor children.	
Eleanor was teased and made fun of.		

7. **Make Judgments** Adlai Stevenson referred to Mrs. Roosevelt as the "First Lady of the World." Do you agree with this statement? Explain.
8. **Evaluate Biography** Review the bulleted list at the top of page 761. In your opinion, did Jacobs achieve his purpose as a biographer? Provide examples from the text that support your opinion.

Extension and Challenge

9. **Big Question Activity** On page 770, Jacobs writes that Eleanor Roosevelt was taught "'to do the thing that has to be done, the way it has to be done, when it has to be done.'" Think about how this view had an impact on her life. Then reread the journal entry you wrote as part of the **Quickwrite** activity on page 760. Compare your generation's attitude toward **duty** to Eleanor Roosevelt's attitude.
10. **SOCIAL STUDIES CONNECTION** In addition to arranging for Marian Anderson to sing at the Lincoln Memorial, Mrs. Roosevelt supported civil rights in other ways. Research to find two more examples of how the First Lady promoted women's rights or racial equality.

RESEARCH LINKS
For more on Eleanor Roosevelt's support of civil rights, visit the **Research Center** at **ClassZone.com.**

Vocabulary in Context

VOCABULARY PRACTICE

Note the letter of the item you might associate with each boldfaced word.

1. **prominent:** (a) an unexplored cave, (b) a well-known lawyer, (c) a narrow valley
2. **brooding:** (a) an unhappy person, (b) a late-model car, (c) a small garden
3. **migrant:** (a) a successful business, (b) a bad headache, (c) a traveling worker
4. **grave:** (a) a loud party, (b) a serious illness, (c) a reunion between two brothers
5. **impoverished:** (a) a brick sidewalk, (b) a large grocery store, (c) a poor family
6. **wavering:** (a) a nosy neighbor, (b) a tough decision, (c) the beginning of winter
7. **dominate:** (a) a poorly planned event, (b) an undefeated team, (c) a serious drought
8. **compassionate:** (a) two children playing, (b) an angry crowd, (c) a kind nurse

brooding
compassionate
dominate
grave
impoverished
migrant
prominent
wavering

VOCABULARY IN WRITING

Use three or more vocabulary words to write a paragraph about what Eleanor Roosevelt taught the world. Here is a sample opening sentence.

EXAMPLE SENTENCE

*Eleanor Roosevelt taught the world that it is important to be **compassionate**.*

ALABAMA STANDARDS

READING STANDARD
1.c Using context clues to determine word meanings

VOCABULARY STRATEGY: THE LATIN ROOT *domin*

The vocabulary word *dominate* contains the Latin root *domin,* which means "master" or "rule." This root is found in many English words. To understand the meaning of words with *domin,* you can often use context clues and your knowledge of the root's meaning.

VOCABULARY PRACTICE
For more practice, go to the **Vocabulary Center** at **ClassZone.com.**

PRACTICE Choose a word from the web that best completes each sentence. Use context clues or, if necessary, a dictionary.

1. The king ruled his ______ with fairness and justice.
2. Our boss is very ______ and expects his orders to be taken seriously.
3. In this county, voters for the New Party ______.
4. ______ traits or characteristics may be inherited from one or both parents.
5. The warlord's intent was to gain complete ______ of the country's ports.

domin
- predominate
- dominant
- domineering
- dominion
- domination

Reading for Information

A First Lady Speaks Out

Letter, page 777

Autobiography, page 778

Use with "Eleanor Roosevelt," page 762.

ALABAMA STANDARDS

READING & RESEARCH STANDARDS
4.d Drawing conclusions
13.a Taking notes to gather, summarize information

What's the Connection?

In "Eleanor Roosevelt," you read William Jay Jacobs's description of Eleanor's life growing up and then as the wife of the president. Now you will have the chance to hear from Mrs. Roosevelt herself as you read a letter she wrote to the Daughters of the American Revolution (DAR) and part of her autobiography.

Skill Focus: Synthesize

Have you ever formed an idea about someone from what one person told you? If so, perhaps your opinion changed once you met him or her for yourself.

When you put together information from more than one source, you **synthesize.** As a result, you gain a better understanding of a subject.

After you read the following letter and autobiography excerpt, you will synthesize the information about Eleanor Roosevelt. Take a moment to think about the impression of the First Lady you formed from Jacobs's biography. Then, as you learn more about her from the following selections, notice whether your idea of Mrs. Roosevelt changes. Doing the following can help:

- Summarize what you learned about Mrs. Roosevelt from reading the biography of her.
- Jot down any additional information you gather about her as you read her letter and autobiography. Feel free to note your own impressions or opinions of her as well.

Record your notes in a chart like the one shown.

Source	*Strengths, Weaknesses, Accomplishments, and Other Information*
"Eleanor Roosevelt"	*She was a sad and lonely child.* *She devoted her life to helping others.*
Letter to the DAR	
Autobiography	

Letter to the President General of the Daughters of the American Revolution

Eleanor Roosevelt

Eleanor Roosevelt wrote this letter after the Daughters of the American Revolution barred Marian Anderson's performance at Constitution Hall in Washington, D.C. Mrs. Roosevelt further protested their actions by organizing a performance for Marian Anderson in front of 75,000 people at the Lincoln Memorial.

FOCUS ON FORM
A **letter** is a handwritten or printed text addressed to a particular person or organization and usually sent by mail. Letters from historical figures help you better understand their private thoughts, feelings, opinions, and daily concerns.

THE WHITE HOUSE
WASHINGTON

February 28, 1939

My dear Mrs. Henry M. Robert Jr.:

I am afraid that I have never been a very useful member of the Daughters of the American Revolution, so I know it will make very little difference to you whether I resign, or whether I continue to be a member of your organization.

However, I am in complete disagreement with the attitude taken in refusing Constitution Hall to a great artist. You have set an example which seems to me unfortunate, and I feel obliged to send in to you my resignation. You had an opportunity to lead in an enlightened way and it seems to me that your organization has failed. A

I realize that many people will not agree with me, but feeling as I do this seems to me the only proper procedure to follow. B

Very sincerely yours,

Eleanor Roosevelt

A SYNTHESIZE
What event prompted Mrs. Roosevelt to write this letter? In your chart, note what you learn about her from her response to this event.

B LETTER
From Mrs. Roosevelt's closing remark, what do you learn about her personality? Add this to your chart.

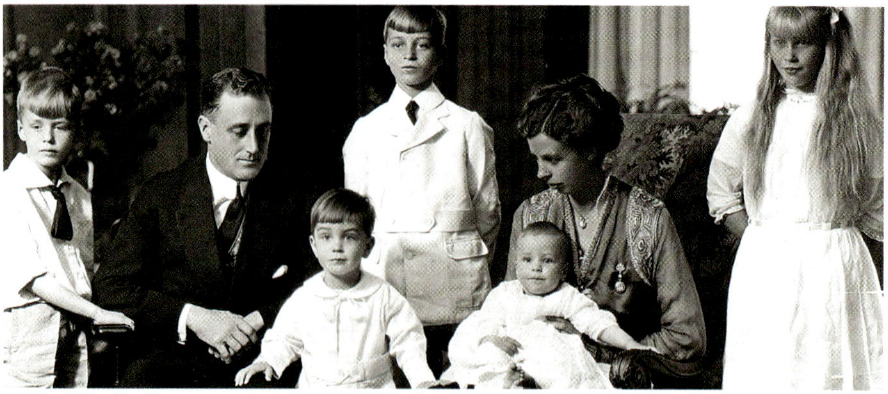

~ FROM ~

The Autobiography of Eleanor Roosevelt

by Eleanor Roosevelt

In the beginning, because I felt, as only a young girl can feel it, all the pain of being an ugly duckling, I was not only timid, I was afraid. Afraid of almost everything, I think: of mice, of the dark, of imaginary dangers, of my own inadequacy. My chief objective, as a girl, was to do my duty. This had been drilled into me as far back as I could remember. Not my duty as I saw it, but my duty as laid down for me by other people. It never occurred to me to revolt. Anyhow, my one overwhelming need in those days was to be approved, to be loved, and I did whatever was required of me, hoping it would bring me nearer to the approval and love I so much wanted. **C**

C SYNTHESIZE
In "Eleanor Roosevelt," you learned that Eleanor was a lonely child. In your chart, write down additional information about her childhood that you learn from her autobiography.

As a young woman, my sense of duty remained as strict and rigid as it had been when I was a girl, but it had changed its focus. My husband and my children became the center of my life, and their needs were my new duty. I am afraid now that I approached this new obligation much as I had my childhood duties. I was still timid, still afraid of doing something wrong, of making mistakes, of not living up to the standards required by my mother-in-law, of failing to do what was expected of me.

As a result, I was so hidebound by duty that I became too critical, too much of a disciplinarian. I was so concerned with bringing up my children properly that I was not wise enough just to love them. Now, looking back, I think I would rather spoil a child a little and have more fun out of it. **D**

D SYNTHESIZE
What new information and insights does Mrs. Roosevelt share about her adulthood? Add these to your chart.

Comprehension

1. **Recall** Why does Mrs. Roosevelt write to Mrs. Henry M. Robert Jr.?
2. **Recall** As a child, why was Eleanor so concerned with doing her duty?

Critical Analysis

3. **Identify Primary Sources** A primary source on Mrs. Roosevelt could be anything she wrote that provides information about her. It could also be a photograph of her or something written about her by someone who knew her. Are the autobiography and letter you just read primary sources on Eleanor Roosevelt? Explain why or why not.
4. **Draw Conclusions from a Letter** What do you learn about Mrs. Roosevelt's character from her letter to Mrs. Henry M. Robert Jr.? Use evidence from the letter to support your answer.
5. **Synthesize** Review the notes in your chart. How did Eleanor's attitude toward duty change over the course of her life? Support your answer.

Read for Information: Draw Conclusions

WRITING PROMPT

In a paragraph, state and support a conclusion about one of these topics:

- the way Eleanor Roosevelt changed over time
- the kind of person Eleanor Roosevelt was
- what motivates people to do great things

As you may recall, a **conclusion** is a judgment or belief about something. Following the numbered steps can help you reach and support a conclusion about one of the three topics given above.

1. Review your notes about Mrs. Roosevelt. What do they lead you to conclude? Jot down a conclusion for each topic. Then pick one you think you can best support.
2. Reread the three selections to find details that support your conclusion. If you can't find much support, consider revising your conclusion or picking a different one.
3. Once you have a conclusion you can support well, state it in a topic sentence. Then present the reasons and evidence that support this conclusion.

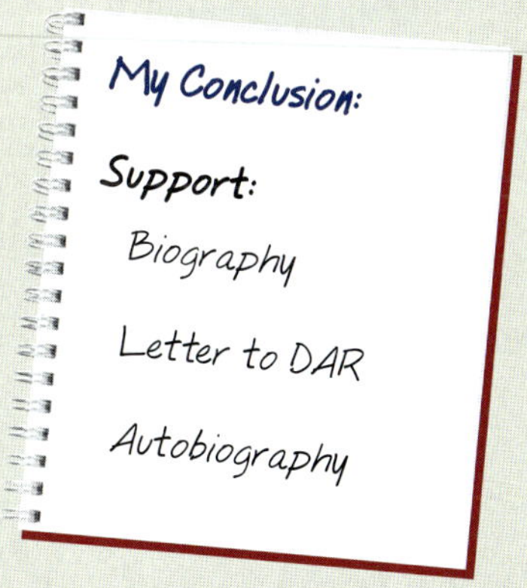

ALABAMA STANDARDS

READING & RESEARCH STANDARDS
4.d Drawing conclusions
13.a Taking notes to gather, summarize information

Names/Nombres

Personal Essay by Julia Alvarez

What does your NAME *really mean?*

ALABAMA STANDARDS

READING & LIT STANDARDS

4.c Applying self-monitoring strategies

6 Analyze nonfiction for distinguishing characteristics

KEY IDEA Parents may choose a **name** for their child because its original meaning is important to them. They might name a new baby after a relative or a famous person. Sometimes parents select a name just because they like the way it sounds. But when it comes to nicknames, adults don't always have control. In "Names/Nombres," author Julia Alvarez writes about how her many nicknames affected her.

WEB IT Create an idea web with your name in the middle. Write down all the names and nicknames you have had throughout your life. Who uses each name and what does that name mean to you?

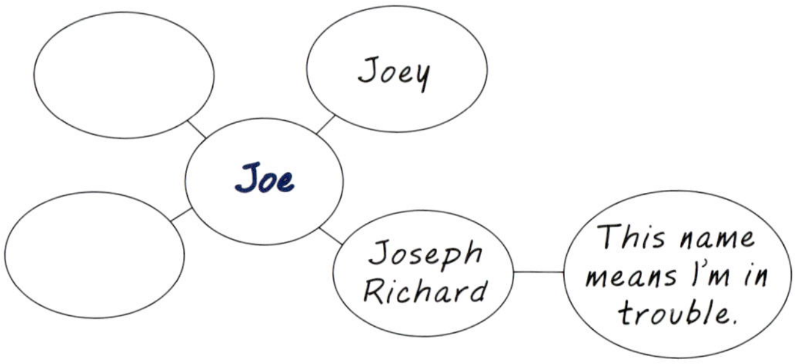

LITERARY ANALYSIS: PERSONAL ESSAY

A **personal essay** is a form of nonfiction that expresses the writer's thoughts and feelings about one subject. You can understand the **writer's message,** or main point, by paying close attention to the writer's

- use of **anecdotes,** or short accounts of events
- choice of words
- descriptions of thoughts and feelings

As you read "Names/Nombres," pay attention to the anecdotes, thoughts, and feelings Alvarez shares about her name.

READING STRATEGY: CONNECT

Think about the many talks and discussions you have had with your friends. It probably comes naturally to relate to what they're saying. Similarly, you can **connect** with someone's writing by comparing the events described with your own experiences. Connecting can help you better understand both the things you read and your own world.

As you read "Names/Nombres," keep a log to record any connections that you have with the essay.

Julia	Me
Her parents call her "Hoo-lee-tah."	My family calls me "Little Joe."

VOCABULARY IN CONTEXT

The boldfaced words help Julia Alvarez convey her feelings and experiences. Use context clues to figure out what each word means.

1. She noted **ironically** that rain made her think of her former home.
2. Leaving one home for another was exciting but **chaotic.**
3. His **convoluted** answers to my simple questions were frustrating.
4. We wanted to **specify** our choices on the questionnaire.
5. The students wanted to **merge** into their new culture.

Author Online

A Tale of Two Countries
Although Julia Alvarez was born in New York City, she lived in the Dominican Republic until she was ten. When the family returned to New York in 1960 to escape the Dominican dictatorship, Alvarez felt out of place—a foreigner with a different language, name, and way of life.

Julia Alvarez
born 1950

A World of Words Alvarez's first years back in New York were tough, but she soon found a way to cope. She started to write stories and poetry. "I could save what I didn't want to lose—memories and smells and sounds, things too precious to put anywhere else," she explained. Alvarez's writings continue to draw on her early memories and immigrant experiences.

MORE ABOUT THE AUTHOR
For more on Julia Alvarez, visit the **Literature Center** at **ClassZone.com.**

Background

A Troubled History The Dominican Republic is a nation that covers about two-thirds of the island of Hispaniola in the Caribbean Sea. A dictator, General Rafael Trujillo, ruled the nation from 1930 to 1961. Many Dominicans came to the United States—especially New York City—during this violent, unsettling period in Dominican history.

Names/ Nombres

Julia Alvarez

When we arrived in New York City, our names changed almost immediately. At Immigration, the officer asked my father, *Mister Elbures,* if he had anything to declare.[1] My father shook his head no, and we were waved through. I was too afraid we wouldn't be let in if I corrected the man's pronunciation, but I said our name to myself, opening my mouth wide for the organ blast of the *a,* trilling my tongue[2] for the drumroll of the *r, All-vah-rrr-es!* How could anyone get *Elbures* out of that orchestra of sound? (A)

At the hotel my mother was *Missus Alburest,* and I was *little girl,* as in, "Hey, little girl, stop riding the elevator up and down. It's *not* a toy."

When we moved into our new apartment building, the super[3] called my father *Mister Alberase,* and the neighbors who became mother's friends pronounced her name *Jew-lee-ah* instead of *Hoo-lee-ah.* I, her namesake, was known as *Hoo-lee-tah* at home. But at school I was *Judy* or *Judith,* and once an English teacher mistook me for *Juliet.*

ANALYZE VISUALS
What **mood** do the colors, images, and brushstrokes create in this painting?

(A) PERSONAL ESSAY
Reread lines 1–8. Consider Alvarez's choice of words and her thoughts at Immigration. Do you think Julia is proud of her last name?

---

1. **At Immigration . . . declare:** Immigration is the place where government officials check the documents of people entering a country. People must acknowledge, or declare, certain goods or moneys that they are carrying.
2. **trilling my tongue:** rapidly vibrating the tongue against the roof of the mouth, as in pronouncing a Spanish *r.*
3. **super:** superintendent, or building manager.

West 17th Street, New York City (20th century), Patti Mollica. © Patti Mollica/SuperStock.

It took a while to get used to my new names. I wondered if I shouldn't correct my teachers and new friends. But my mother argued that it didn't matter. "You know what your friend Shakespeare said, 'A rose by any other name would smell as sweet.'"[4] My family had gotten into the habit of calling any literary figure "my friend" because I had begun to write poems and stories in English class.

By the time I was in high school, I was a popular kid, and it showed in my name. Friends called me *Jules* or *Hey Jude,*[5] and once a group of troublemaking friends my mother forbade me to hang out with called me *Alcatraz.*[6] I was *Hoo-lee-tah* only to Mami and Papi and uncles and aunts who came over to eat *sancocho*[7] on Sunday afternoons—old world folk whom I would just as soon go back to where they came from and leave me to pursue whatever mischief I wanted to in America. JUDY ALCATRAZ: the name on the wanted poster would read. Who would ever trace her to me? **B**

B CONNECT
You might have listed a nickname for the activity on page 780. Compare how this nickname makes you feel with how Julia's nicknames make her feel.

My older sister had the hardest time getting an American name for herself because *Mauricia* did not translate into English. **Ironically,** although she had the most foreign-sounding name, she and I were the Americans in the family. We had been born in New York City when our parents had first tried immigration and then gone back "home," too homesick to stay. My mother often told the story of how she had almost changed my sister's name in the hospital.

ironically (ī-rŏn'ĭk-lē) *adv.* in a way that is contrary to what is expected or intended

After the delivery, Mami and some other new mothers were cooing over their new baby sons and daughters and exchanging names and weights and delivery stories. My mother was embarrassed among the Sallys and Janes and Georges and Johns to reveal the rich, noisy name of *Mauricia,* so when her turn came to brag, she gave her baby's name as *Maureen.*

"Why'd ya give her an Irish name with so many pretty Spanish names to choose from?" one of the women asked her.

My mother blushed and admitted her baby's real name to the group. Her mother-in-law had recently died, she apologized, and her husband had insisted that the first daughter be named after his mother, *Mauran.* My mother thought it the ugliest name she had ever heard, and she talked my father into what she believed was an improvement, a combination of *Mauran* and her own mother's name, *Felicia.*

"Her name is Mao-ree-shee-ah," my mother said to the group.

"Why, that's a beautiful name," the new mothers cried. "*Moor-ee-sha, Moor-ee-sha,*" they cooed into the pink blanket. *Moor-ee-sha* it was when

4. **'A rose . . . smell as sweet':** In Shakespeare's *Romeo and Juliet,* the main characters' families are enemies. But when Romeo and Juliet fall in love, Juliet uses almost these words to say that Romeo is precious to her no matter what his family name is.
5. ***Hey Jude:*** the title of a hit song by the Beatles in 1968.
6. ***Alcatraz*** (ăl'kə-trăz'): the name of an island in San Francisco Bay that was once the site of a prison.
7. ***sancocho*** (säng-kô'chô) *Spanish:* a traditional Caribbean stew of meat and vegetables.

we returned to the States eleven years later. Sometimes, American tongues found even that mispronunciation tough to say and called her *Maria* or *Marsha* or *Maudy* from her nickname *Maury.* I pitied her. What an awful name to have to transport across borders! **C**

C PERSONAL ESSAY
Why do you think Alvarez included this **anecdote** in her personal essay?

My little sister, Ana, had the easiest time of all. She was plain *Anne*—that is, only her name was plain, for she turned out to be the pale, blond "American beauty" in the family. The only Hispanic-seeming thing about her was the affectionate nicknames her boyfriends sometimes gave her. *Anita,* or as one goofy guy used to sing to her to the tune of the banana advertisement, *Anita Banana.*

Later, during her college years in the late 60's, there was a push to pronounce Third World[8] names correctly. I remember calling her long distance at her group house and a roommate answering.

"Can I speak to Ana?" I asked, pronouncing her name the American way.

"Ana?" The man's voice hesitated. "Oh! You must mean *Ah-nah!*"

Our first few years in the States, though, ethnicity was not yet "in." Those were the blond, blue-eyed, bobby-sock years of junior high and high school before the 60's ushered in peasant blouses, hoop earrings, *sarapes.*[9] My initial desire to be known by my correct Dominican name faded. I just wanted to be Judy and **merge** with the Sallys and Janes in my class. But, inevitably, my accent and coloring gave me away.

merge (mûrj) *v.* to blend together

"So where are you from, Judy?"

"New York," I told my classmates. After all, I had been born blocks away at Columbia Presbyterian Hospital.

"I mean, *originally.*"

"From the Caribbean," I answered vaguely, for if I **specified,** no one was quite sure what continent our island was located on.

specify (spĕs′ə-fī′) *v.* to make known or identify

"Really? I've been to Bermuda. We went last April for spring vacation. I got the worst sunburn! So, are you from Portoriko?"

"No," I shook my head. "From the Dominican Republic."

"Where's that?"

"South of Bermuda."

They were just being curious, I knew, but I burned with shame whenever they singled me out as a "foreigner," a rare, exotic friend.

"Say your name in Spanish, oh, please say it!" I had made mouths drop one day by rattling off my full name, which, according to Dominican custom, included my middle names, Mother's and Father's surnames[10] for four generations back.

SOCIAL STUDIES CONNECTION

The Dominican Republic

8. **Third World:** from the developing nations of Latin America, Africa, and Asia.
9. ***sarapes*** (sə-rä′pāz) *Spanish*: long, blanketlike shawls.
10. **surnames:** last names.

"Julia Altagracia María Teresa Álvarez Tavares Perello Espaillat Julia Pérez Rochet González." I pronounced it slowly, a name as **chaotic** with sounds as a Middle Eastern bazaar or market day in a South American village.

chaotic (kā-ŏt'ĭk) *adj.* confused; disordered

I suffered most whenever my extended family attended school occasions. For my graduation, they all came, the whole noisy, foreign-looking lot of fat aunts in their dark mourning dresses and hair nets, uncles with full, droopy mustaches and baby-blue or salmon-colored suits and white pointy shoes and fedora hats, the many little cousins who snuck in without tickets. They sat in the first row in order to better understand the Americans' fast-spoken English. But how could they listen when they were constantly speaking among themselves in florid-sounding phrases, rococo consonants, rich, rhyming vowels? Their loud voices carried.

Introducing them to my friends was a further trial to me. These relatives had such complicated names and there were so many of them, and their relationships to myself were so **convoluted.** There was my Tía Josefina, who was not really an aunt but a much older cousin. And her daughter, Aída Margarita, who was adopted, *una hija de crianza.*[11] My uncle of affection, Tío José, brought my *madrina* Tía Amelia and her *comadre* Tía Pilar.[12] My friends rarely had more than their nuclear family[13] to introduce, youthful, glamorous-looking couples ("Mom and Dad") who skied and played tennis and took their kids for spring vacations to Bermuda. **D**

convoluted (kŏn'və-lo͞o'tĭd) *adj.* difficult to understand; complicated

D CONNECT
Think about how Julia feels when she introduces her family to her friends. What situation have you experienced or read about that can help you understand her feelings?

After the commencement ceremony, my family waited outside in the parking lot while my friends and I signed yearbooks with nicknames which recalled our high school good times: "Beans" and "Pepperoni" and "Alcatraz." We hugged and cried and promised to keep in touch.

Sometimes if our goodbyes went on too long, I heard my father's voice calling out across the parking lot. "*Hoo-lee-tah! Vámonos!*"[14] **E**

E PERSONAL ESSAY
Reread lines 112–115. Do you think Julia likes her nickname by the time she graduates from high school? Tell what clues helped you answer this question.

Back home, my tíos and tías and *primas*, Mami and Papi, and *mis hermanas* had a party for me with *sancocho* and a store-bought *pudín,* inscribed with *Happy Graduation, Julie.*[15] There were many gifts—that was a plus to a large family! I got several wallets and a suitcase with my initials and a graduation charm from my godmother and money from my uncles. The biggest gift was a portable typewriter from my parents for writing my stories and poems.

Someday, the family predicted, my name would be well-known throughout the United States. I laughed to myself, wondering which one I would go by.

---

11. ***una hija de crianza*** (o͞o'nä ē'hä dĕ krē-än'sä) *Spanish*: a child raised as if one's own.
12. **My uncle of affection . . . Tía Pilar:** My favorite uncle, Uncle José, brought my godmother Aunt Amelia and her close friend Aunt Pilar.
13. **nuclear family:** a family unit consisting of a mother, a father, and their children.
14. ***Vámanos*** (bä'mä-nôs) *Spanish:* Let's go.
15. **Back home . . . *Julie:*** Back home, my uncles and aunts and cousins, Mami and Papi, and my sisters had a party for me with a stew and a store-bought pudding, inscribed with *Happy Graduation, Julie.*

After Reading

ALABAMA STANDARDS

LITERATURE STANDARD
6 Analyze nonfiction for distinguishing characteristics

Comprehension

1. **Clarify** Why does Julia say it is a "trial" to introduce her family?
2. **Summarize** Explain what happens in the hospital when Mauricia is born.
3. **Represent** Review "Names/Nombres" to find all of Julia's names and nicknames. Arrange her names into three categories: (1) those used by her family and friends, (2) those used by strangers, and (3) those used by both.

Literary Analysis

4. **Examine Connections** Review the notes you made in your log while reading "Names/Nombres." What can you learn from Alvarez about your own experiences?
5. **Make Inferences** Reread lines 1–15. Why do you think Alvarez chooses to refer to the mispronunciation of her and her family's names as a changing of their names?
6. **Draw Conclusions** How would you describe Julia's mother, Mrs. Alvarez, on the basis of her words and actions?
7. **Interpret a Personal Essay** In a graphic like the one shown, note clues that contribute to Alvarez's message about **names** and identities. What is the writer's message in "Names/Nombres"? Explain your reasoning based on the information in your graphic.

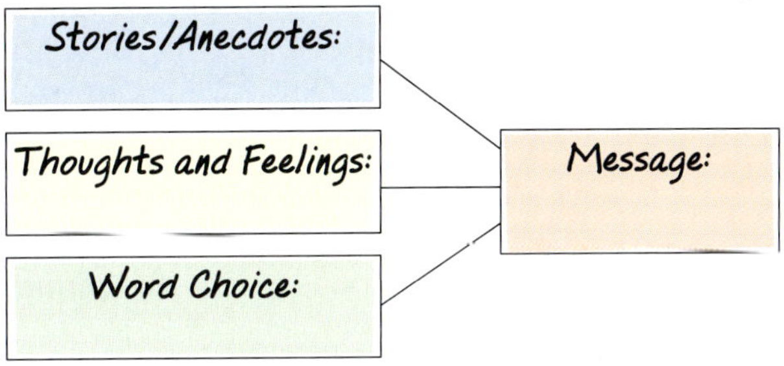

Extension and Challenge

8. **Creative Project: Drama** With a partner, role-play a conversation between Eleanor Roosevelt and Julia Alvarez about their experiences with nicknames. Start by reviewing "Eleanor Roosevelt" and "Names/Nombres" to find the nicknames each woman had. Then have them discuss what they think of their nicknames, how their names influenced them, and what advice they have about nicknames.
9. **SOCIAL STUDIES CONNECTION** Julia Alvarez divided her childhood between the United States and the Dominican Republic. Write three questions about the Dominican Republic and research to find the answers. Share the information with the class.

RESEARCH LINKS
For more on the Dominican Republic, visit the **Research Center** at **ClassZone.com.**

Vocabulary in Context

VOCABULARY PRACTICE

Decide whether the words in each pair are synonyms (words that have the same meaning) or antonyms (words that have opposite meanings).

1. chaotic/orderly
2. ironically/predictably
3. specify/identify
4. merge/join
5. convoluted/simple

chaotic
convoluted
ironically
merge
specify

VOCABULARY IN WRITING

How did Julia Alvarez initially want to relate to classmates in the United States? Write a brief paragraph about this, using two or more vocabulary words. Here is an example of how you might begin.

EXAMPLE SENTENCE

Julia just wanted to ***merge*** *into classes and everyday activities.*

VOCABULARY STRATEGY: CONNOTATIONS AND MEANING

A word's **connotations** are the shades of meaning the word may take on beyond a dictionary definition. For example,

- *exotic* means "unusual," but it carries a positive connotation of fascination or wonder
- *bizarre* also means "unusual," but it has a negative connotation of strangeness or weirdness

When choosing words in writing, consider their possible connotations. They can affect the way your message is understood.

PRACTICE For each of the following words, tell whether the connotation is positive or negative. Then write a sentence using the word correctly. You may need to use a dictionary.

1. cottage
2. cheap
3. mysterious
4. sincere
5. reckless
6. peculiar
7. funny
8. casual
9. modern
10. strong-willed

VOCABULARY PRACTICE
For more practice, go to the **Vocabulary Center** at **ClassZone.com.**

SKILLS PRACTICE

Reading-Writing Connection

Now that you've read "Names/Nombres," explore the importance of names by responding to these prompts. Then complete the **Grammar and Writing** exercise.

WRITING PROMPTS	SELF-CHECK
A. Short Response: Explore Connections Write **one paragraph** about one of your **names** or nicknames. Using Alvarez's essay as a model, relate an anecdote, or story, that shows how you got the name or that explores your thoughts and feelings about your name.	***A strong response will . . .*** • include specific details to describe a revealing event • provide a clear message about your thoughts and feelings toward your name
B. Extended Response: Track Changes Julia Alvarez has had many different names in her life, but she hasn't always felt the same way about them. Write a **two- or three-paragraph explanation** of how her attitude about having different names changes from the beginning to the end of the essay.	***A successful explanation will . . .*** • identify Julia's attitude about being called different names • explain why her attitude changes

GRAMMAR AND WRITING

ALABAMA STANDARDS

WRITING/LANGUAGE STANDARD
10 Apply mechanics in writing

CAPITALIZE CORRECTLY A common noun is a general name for a person, a place, a thing, or an idea *(sister, country, park)* and is usually not capitalized. A **proper noun** is the name of a particular person, place, thing, or idea *(Kathy, Spain, Central Park)* and is always capitalized. Words that indicate family relationships are only capitalized when they are used as names or before names.

Original: When Julia first arrived in new york, she was known by many different names.

Revised: When Julia first arrived in New York, she was known by many different names. (*New York* is a proper noun.)

PRACTICE Correct the capitalization in each of the following sentences.

1. Julia was known as *Hoo-lee-tah* only to her parents and Aunts and Uncles.
2. Mauricia, Julia's Sister, also had many nicknames.
3. Julia knew she had to listen to mother's advice.
4. Julia probably wanted uncle José and aunt Amelia to call her Judy.

For more help with capitalization, see page R51 in the ***Grammar Handbook.***

from It's Not About the Bike

Autobiography by Lance Armstrong
with Sally Jenkins

from 23 Days in July

Nonfiction Account by John Wilcockson

What is a WINNER?

ALABAMA STANDARDS

READING & LIT STANDARDS
4.c Applying self-monitoring strategies
6 Analyze nonfiction for distinguishing characteristics

KEY IDEA You might normally associate a **winner** with a contest, a game, or a sport. But can you also be a winner when you're not competing with other people? If so, how? In the selections you're about to read, you will find out how Lance Armstrong faced two very different challenges and came out a winner in both.

SKETCH IT Do you remember a time in your life when you felt like a winner? Maybe you won a spelling bee or achieved something that no one else ever had. Perhaps you faced a fear or a challenge. Create a sketch of the moment and include a title that describes what is happening. Share your sketch with the class.

● ELEMENTS OF NONFICTION: QUOTATIONS

Sometimes writers decide that it is best to present information straight from the source. In that case, they use **quotations,** or direct statements from others, which are set off with quotation marks. Quotations can provide

- a clear picture of what a person is like
- an expert opinion to support the writer's ideas
- an eyewitness account that makes a scene come alive

As you read the selections from *It's Not About the Bike* and *23 Days in July,* note how the authors use quotations to help the reader better understand the subjects, setting, and events.

■ READING SKILL: MAKE INFERENCES

People have many reasons for doing what they do. To understand the behavior of people you read about or encounter in life, it helps to **make inferences,** or make logical guesses based on new clues and what you already know. As you read, make equations to record your inferences about Lance Armstrong.

Clue	+	What I Know	=	Inference

▲ VOCABULARY IN CONTEXT

The following words help tell about Lance Armstrong's victories. See how many you know by choosing the word that best completes each sentence.

WORD LIST			
	culminate	prestigious	stance
	perception	recessed	terse

1. The athlete's comeback will _____ in a prized medal.
2. His _____, with his feet firmly planted, was one that showed determination.
3. She gave _____, one-word answers to some of his questions.
4. The winner received a _____ award befitting a hero.
5. Special features on the bicycle are _____ in order to aid the cyclist.
6. His nurse spoke with wisdom and _____.

Author Online

Against All Odds Lance Armstrong was a rising star in the world of professional cycling when his life was turned upside down. In 1996, he was diagnosed with cancer and given less than a 50 percent chance of survival. He underwent difficult chemotherapy treatments that made him very ill and did not guarantee success. However, Armstrong returned to professional bicycling and won his first Tour de France in 1999. He went on to win again in 2000, 2001, 2002, 2003, and 2004. John Wilcockson captured the moments of the history-making sixth Tour de France win of 2004 in *23 Days in July.*

Lance Armstrong born 1971

Then in 2005, Armstrong did the unbelievable once again—he won a seventh Tour de France. After his 2005 win, he announced that he would devote his time and energy to a different kind of challenge: cancer research.

Background

The Tour de France The Tour de France is a 3-week bicycling race that covers about 2,500 miles in France and other European countries.

MORE ABOUT THE AUTHOR AND BACKGROUND
To learn more about Lance Armstrong and the Tour de France, visit the **Literature Center** at **ClassZone.com.**

It's Not About the Bike

LANCE ARMSTRONG

After his cancer diagnosis, Lance Armstrong launched a relentless attack against his disease with the help of the doctors and nurses at Indiana University Medical Center in Indianapolis. The photo on the right shows Armstrong after chemotherapy treatment.

There are angels on this earth and they come in subtle forms, and I decided LaTrice Haney was one of them. Outwardly, she looked like just another efficient, clipboard-and-syringe-wielding[1] nurse in a starched outfit. She worked extremely long days and nights, and on her off hours she went home to her husband, Randy, a truck driver, and their two children, Taylor, aged seven, and Morgan, four. But if she was tired, she never seemed it. She struck me as a woman utterly lacking in ordinary resentments, sure of her responsibilities and blessings and unwavering in her administering of care, and if that wasn't angelic behavior, I didn't know what was.

Often I'd be alone in the late afternoons and evenings except for LaTrice, and if I had the strength, we'd talk seriously. With most people I was shy and **terse,** but I found myself talking to LaTrice, maybe because she was so gentle-spoken and expressive herself. LaTrice was only in her late 20s, a pretty young woman with a coffee-and-cream complexion, but she had self-possession and **perception** beyond her years. While other people our age were out nightclubbing, she was already the head nurse for the oncology research unit.[2] I wondered why she did it. "My satisfaction is to make it a little easier for people," she said. Ⓐ

She asked me about cycling, and I found myself telling her about the bike with a sense of pleasure I hadn't realized I possessed. "How did you start riding?" she asked me. I told her about my first bikes, and the early sense of liberation, and that cycling was all I had done since I was 16. I talked about my various teammates over the years, about their humor and selflessness, and I talked about my mother, and what she had meant to me.

I told her what cycling had given me, the tours of Europe and the extraordinary education, and the wealth. I showed her a picture of

terse (tûrs) *adj.* speaking little; communicating in few words

perception (pər-sĕp′shən) *n.* insight; ability to understand people and situations

Ⓐ QUOTATIONS
Reread lines 18–19. What does this quotation tell you about LaTrice?

1. **syringe-wielding** (sə-rĭnj′ wēl′dĭng): holding and using an instrument for giving patients injections.
2. **oncology** (ŏn-kŏl′ə-jē) **research unit:** in a hospital or clinic, the division or section dedicated to the study of cancer.

my house, with pride, and invited her to come visit, and I showed her snapshots of my cycling career. She leafed through images of me racing across the backdrops of France, Italy, and Spain, and she'd point to a picture and ask, "Where are you here?" **B**

B MAKE INFERENCES
Why might LaTrice ask Lance specific questions about his bicycling career?

I confided that I was worried about my sponsor, Cofidis,[3] and explained the difficulty I was having with them. I told her I felt pressured. "I need to stay in shape, I need to stay in shape," I said over and over again.

"Lance, listen to your body," she said gently. "I know your mind wants to run away. I know it's saying to you, 'Hey, let's go ride.' But listen to your body. Let it rest."

I described my bike, the elegant high performance of the ultralight tubing and aerodynamic wheels. I told her how much each piece cost, and weighed, and what its purpose was. I explained how a bike could be broken down so I could practically carry it in my pocket, and that I knew every part and bit of it so intimately that I could adjust it in a matter of moments.

I explained that a bike has to fit your body, and that at times I felt melded to it. The lighter the frame, the more responsive it is, and my racing bike weighed just 18 pounds. Wheels exert centrifugal force[4] on the bike itself, I told her. The more centrifugal force, the more momentum. It was the essential building block of speed. "There are 32 spokes in a wheel," I said. Quick-release levers allow you to pop the wheel out and change it quickly, and my crew could fix a flat tire in less than 10 seconds.

"Don't you get tired of leaning over like that?" she asked.

Yes, I said, until my back ached like it was broken, but that was the price of speed. The handlebars are only as wide as the rider's shoulders, I explained, and they curve downward in half-moons so you can assume an aerodynamic **stance** on the bike.

stance (stăns) *n.* posture; position

"Why do you ride on those little seats?" she asked.

The seat is narrow, contoured to the anatomy, and the reason is that when you are on it for six hours at a time, you don't want anything to chafe your legs. Better a hard seat than the torture of saddle sores. Even the clothes have a purpose. They are flimsy for a reason: to mold to the body because you have to wear them in weather that ranges from hot to hail. Basically, they're a second skin. The shorts have a chamois padded[5] seat, and the stitches are **recessed** to avoid rash. **C**

recessed (rē'sĕst') *adj.* set-in or set back **recess** *v.*

C MAKE INFERENCES
Why is Lance able to talk so enthusiastically about his bike even though he is seriously ill?

When I had nothing left to tell LaTrice about the bike, I told her about the wind. I described how it felt in my face and in my hair. I told her about being in the open air, with the views of soaring Alps, and the

---

3. **Cofidis:** the sponsor of the French cycling team that Armstrong then rode for.
4. **centrifugal** (sĕn-trĭf'yə-gəl) **force:** the force that seems to cause a revolving object to move away from the point it revolves around.
5. **chamois** (shăm'ē) **padded:** padded with soft leather made from the skin of goats, sheep, or deer.

glimmer of valley lakes in the distance. Sometimes the wind blew as if it were my personal friend, sometimes as if it were my bitter enemy, sometimes as if it were the hand of God pushing me along. I described the full sail of a mountain descent, gliding on two wheels only an inch wide. **D**

"You're just out there, free," I said.

"You love it," she said.

"Yeah?" I said.

"Oh, I see it in your eyes," she said.

D MAKE INFERENCES
Reread lines 63–69. What can you infer about why Lance rides his bike?

I understood that LaTrice was an angel one evening late in my last cycle of chemo.[6] I lay on my side, dozing on and off, watching the steady, clear drip-drip of the chemo as it slid into my veins. LaTrice sat with me, keeping me company, even though I was barely able to talk.

"What do you think, LaTrice?" I asked, whispering. "Am I going to pull through this?"

"Yeah," she said. "Yeah, you are."

"I hope you're right," I said, and closed my eyes again.

LaTrice leaned over to me.

"Lance," she said softly, "I hope someday to be just a figment of your imagination.[7] I'm not here to be in your life for the rest of your life. After you leave here, I hope I never see you ever again. When you're cured, hey, let me see you in the papers, on TV, but not back here. I hope to help you at the time you need me, and then I hope I'll be gone. You'll say, 'Who was that nurse back in Indiana? Did I dream her?'" **E**

It is one of the single loveliest things anyone has ever said to me. And I will always remember every blessed word.

E QUOTATIONS
Reread lines 83–88. Why do you think Armstrong chooses to quote LaTrice here?

---

6. **chemo** (kē′mō): short for *chemotherapy.*

7. **figment of your imagination:** something not real; a fantasized or made-up image.

Lance Armstrong and LaTrice Haney

23 DAYS IN JULY

JOHN WILCOCKSON

Although Armstrong went on to win a seventh Tour de France in 2005, the 2004 race was especially meaningful since no other cyclist had ever won a sixth Tour.

Paris is looking magnificent. Her golden domes and eagles and gilded gates are all glowing in the late-afternoon sunshine. The dark-green plane trees along the Champs-Élysées have been newly trimmed. Rainbows shimmer in the spray from the crystal fountains of the Place de la Concorde.[1] And across the Seine River, the thousand-foot-high Eiffel Tower stands starkly regal against an opaque blue sky.

Another Tour de France has just ended, this one **culminating** in a historical sixth consecutive victory for a long-jawed young man from the lone star state of Texas. He stands now on the top step of the podium, at the finish line on the Champs-Élysées. Dressed in a golden tunic, Lance Armstrong holds a yellow LiveStrong[2] cap over his heart as a full-blooded rendition of the "Star Spangled Banner" rings out, resounding proudly over the russet-brown cobblestones of these Elysian Fields. . . .[3]

At the foot of the yellow steps of the canopied, most **prestigious** viewing stand, Armstrong's coach Chris Carmichael reminds me: "I told you back in March, it wasn't even going to be close. You gotta know the intensity of this guy. Nobody has got his intensity. Nobody. It's just phenomenal." **F**

ANALYZE VISUALS
Look back at the picture of Lance Armstrong on page 793. What comes to mind as you **contrast** the two pictures?

culminate (kŭl'mə-nāt') *v.* to reach the highest point or degree

prestigious (prĕ-stē'jəs) *adj.* having a high reputation

F QUOTATIONS
Why might Wilcockson quote Chris Carmichael?

1. **Champs-Élysées** (shäN-zā-lē-zā') . . . **Place de la Concorde** (pläs' də lä kôN-kôrd'): a famous boulevard and a large plaza in Paris.
2. **LiveStrong:** livestrong.org is the official Web site for the Lance Armstrong Foundation.
3. **Elysian** (ĭ-lĭzh'ən) **Fields:** the English translation of *Champs-Élysées.* In Greek mythology, the Elysian Fields were where good people went after death.

CREDIT
LYONNAIS
2004
UNITED STATES
POSTAL SERVICE
BERRY FLOOR
TREK
LYONNAIS

Armstrong said on the eve of this day, "Winning in '99 was a complete shock and surprise for me. Not that I've gotten used to winning the Tour de France, but I do know what it means and I know what it feels like to ride into the Champs-Élysées. . . . This one is very, very special for me. They're all special, but this one is something that in '99 I never believed possible. I never thought I'd win a second one, or a third, or however many. This one is incredibly special. I'm humbled by it. A lot of people just one month ago thought it wouldn't be possible for me to do it. We tried to stay calm, the team tried to stay calm . . . and we were confident that we had a good chance."

I think back to December, and remember something Armstrong told me in Austin: "I'm doing three or four hours of exercise every day right now. Yesterday I was in DC, so I got up early—I'd just come back from Europe and had jetlag[4]—and I went down to the gym for an hour and a half . . . yes, lifting weights. It was pouring with freezing rain outside, so I went back to the room, and rode my bike for an hour on the rollers. It's not easy to ride rollers. I hate that." G

But he doesn't hate this: homage from a half-million people lining the most glorious boulevard in the world. When he and his U.S. Postal team are introduced by race announcer Daniel Mangeas, as the last team to start their lap of honor around the Champs-Élysées, the modern "anthem" of the British rock group Queen thumps into the balmy Paris air:

G QUOTATIONS
Reread lines 30–35. What do you learn about Armstrong from this quotation?

4. **jet lag:** tiredness and other effects that may be caused by a long flight through several time zones.

Armstrong, in yellow, takes a victory lap with his teammates along the Champs-Élysées in Paris.

"*We are the champions, my friend. . . . We are the champions. We are the champions. We are the champions . . . of the world.*"

Girlfriends perch on boyfriends' shoulders to get a better view. Banners unfurl, one saying, "The eyes of Texas are upon you." Thousands of fans from all over the United States line the barriers, most dressed in yellow. Two guys from Texas in the crowd say, "We did it. And next year we'll come again!" . . . **H**

H MAKE INFERENCES
Why are the fans dressed in yellow?

Now they're playing another song over the loudspeakers. Its words float down the boulevard backed by the thumping guitar chords of the champion's gal: "All I want to *do* . . . is have some fun . . ." And Lance *is* having fun. The celebrations will continue all night, maybe for the rest of his life. A life that almost ended in 1996. Six Tour de France wins have come along since then, since his chemo nurse LaTrice gave him that silver cross.

"I really love this event," Armstrong says. "I think it's an epic sport. It's something I will sit around the TV and watch in ten years, and in twenty years." He will always be a fan of the Tour, but right now he's the champion. *Le patron.*[5]

It's after 7 p.m. and the crowds are starting to leave. One of the last to go is a friendly, middle-aged American. He rolls up his Texas flag, grabs his wife's hand, and, before he walks down the stone steps into the Metro,[6] proclaims to the world, "He's the man!"

---

5. ***le patron*** (lə pä-trôN) *French*: the boss.
6. **Metro:** the Paris subway.

After Reading

ALABAMA STANDARDS

LITERATURE STANDARD
6 Analyze nonfiction for distinguishing characteristics

Comprehension

1. **Recall** In the excerpt from *It's Not About the Bike,* why is Armstrong in the hospital?
2. **Clarify** Why does Armstrong call his head nurse, LaTrice, an "angel"?
3. **Clarify** Reread lines 22–25 in the excerpt from *23 Days in July.* Armstrong says winning the 2004 Tour de France was "incredibly special" to him. Why was it so special?

Literary Analysis

4. **Make Inferences** Review the inference equations that you made while reading. Which, if any, of your inferences have changed? Explain your reasons for either changing an inference or keeping an original inference.
5. **Interpret Meaning** Reread LaTrice's quotation in lines 83–88 of the excerpt from *It's Not About the Bike.* Why does Armstrong say, "It is one of the single loveliest things anyone has ever said to me"?
6. **Compare and Contrast** The autobiography *It's Not About the Bike* shows the private side of Lance Armstrong. On the other hand, John Wilcockson's account portrays Armstrong in public. Use a Y chart like the one shown to compare and contrast the private and public man.

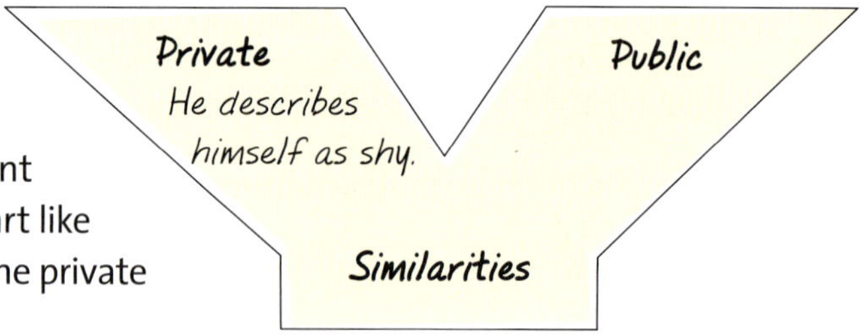

7. **Analyze Quotations** On the basis of the quotations in the excerpt from *23 Days in July,* what do you think Wilcockson wants the reader to remember about Armstrong? Cite three quotations to support your opinion.
8. **Draw Conclusions** In 1996, Armstrong beat cancer. In 2004, he became a six-time winner of the Tour de France. Considering what you learned from the selections that you just read, what qualities helped Armstrong win such big victories?

Extension and Challenge

9. **Inquiry and Research** Research the Tour de France and create a tourist's guide to the race. Provide the reader with some historical information, explain the rules of the race, and include a map of the upcoming race.

RESEARCH LINKS
For more on the Tour de France, visit the **Research Center** at **ClassZone.com.**

Vocabulary in Context

VOCABULARY PRACTICE

For each item, choose the word that differs most in meaning from the other words. Refer to a dictionary if you need help.

1. chatty, talkative, terse, gossipy
2. culminate, top, begin, crown
3. awkward, hidden, recessed, inset
4. pose, posture, worry, stance
5. intuition, ignorance, understanding, perception
6. prestigious, notable, honorable, unworthy

culminate
perception
prestigious
recessed
stance
terse

VOCABULARY IN WRITING

Write a paragraph describing how you might have felt if you had been Armstrong entering Paris. Use two or more vocabulary words. You could start like this.

EXAMPLE SENTENCE

*Riding into Paris with my team as the winners of this **prestigious** race was the highlight of my career.*

VOCABULARY STRATEGY: RECOGNIZING BASE WORDS

You already know that to understand an unfamiliar word with affixes, it helps to identify the base word first. Sometimes, though, the spelling of base words is different when affixes are present. The vocabulary word *perception,* for example, is related to *perceive.* In cases where you do not recognize a base word, you may have to rely on context clues to figure out the meaning.

PRACTICE Define each boldfaced word. Then give the base word that each one is related to. Use a dictionary if necessary.

1. Mr. Lewis resented the **intrusion** of noisy neighborhood children into his privacy.
2. The doctor recommended a complete **renunciation** of his patient's lifestyle if she was to become healthy.
3. The severe earthquake did **irreparable** damage to many homes.
4. **Consumption** of several glasses of water a day is a healthy habit.
5. Far from being forced, the audience's loud applause had real **spontaneity.**

ALABAMA STANDARDS

READING STANDARD
4.b Using context clues to determine word meanings

VOCABULARY PRACTICE
For more practice, go to the **Vocabulary Center** at **ClassZone.com.**

Great Reads

Malcolm X: By Any Means Necessary

Biography by Walter Dean Myers

Walter Dean Myers
born 1937

Other Books by Walter Dean Myers

Nonfiction

- *Bad Boy: A Memoir*
- *The Greatest: Muhammad Ali*

Fiction

- *Crystal*
- *The Glory Field*
- *Monster*
- *Scorpions*
- *Somewhere in the Darkness*

Meet Walter Dean Myers

Walter Dean Myers knows what it's like to rise above difficult circumstances. His mother died before he was two years old, and his father, who was very poor, had to give Walter away. Walter's foster mother, Florence Dean, taught him to read, and books soon became a welcome escape for Walter. One of his teachers suggested that he write down his thoughts in the form of poems and stories. Walter began writing then and has never stopped.

Many of the stories Myers writes are based on his childhood in Harlem, on the Upper West Side of Manhattan in New York City. He is also interested in history, which often leads him to write nonfiction books about people or events that grab his attention.

Try a Biography

People are naturally curious about the lives of important, fascinating people. A **biography** is a story of a person's life that is written by someone else. Most biographies are about famous people who changed history or made an impact in other ways. Biographies are often told in chronological order, beginning with the person's childhood and ending with his or her death. The introduction and conclusion of a biography usually highlight the lasting importance of the person.

Read a Great Book

Malcolm X was an important figure in the struggle for equal rights for African Americans. The following section from Myers's award-winning biography provides an overview of Malcolm X's life and legacy. You'll read about how Malcolm's experiences shaped him into a leader of the 20th century.

from

Malcolm X: By Any Means Necessary

Who was Malcolm X, and what is his legacy?

Malcolm's life seems so varied, he did so many things over the far too short thirty-nine years of his life, that it almost appears that there was not one Malcolm at all, but four distinct people. But in looking at Malcolm's life, in examining the expectations against what he actually did, we see a blending of the four Malcolms into one dynamic personality that is distinctively American in its character. For only a black man living in America could have gone through what Malcolm went through.

The first Malcolm was Malcolm the child, who lived in Nebraska and Michigan. He lived much like a million other black boys born in the United States. He was loved by two parents, Earl and Louise Little. From them he learned about morality, and decency, and the need to do well in school. His parents gave him a legacy of love, but also a legacy of pride.

Malcolm saw his father, a Baptist minister, at the meetings of the Universal Negro Improvement Association, saw him speaking about the black race, and about the possibility of justice. From what the young Malcolm saw, from what he experienced as a young child, one might have expected him, upon reaching maturity, to become a religious man and an activist for justice, as was his father.

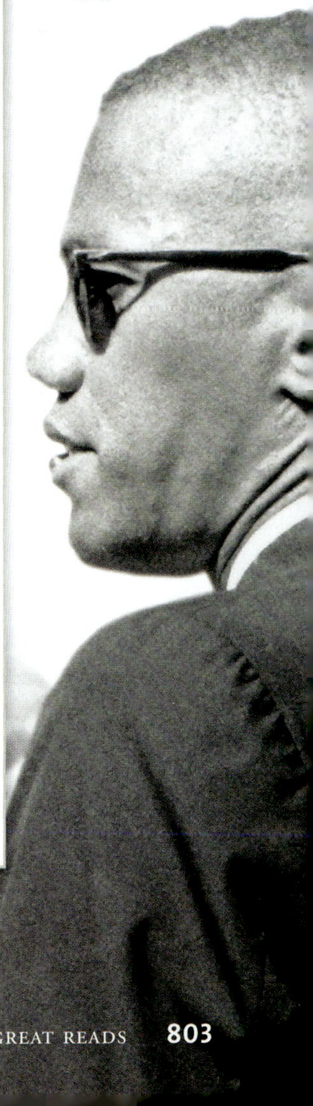

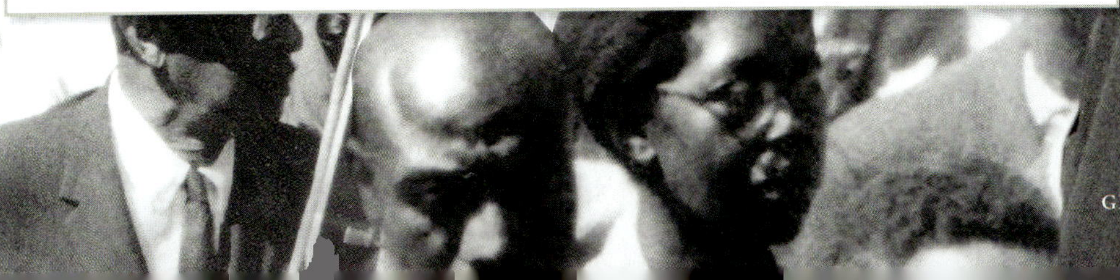

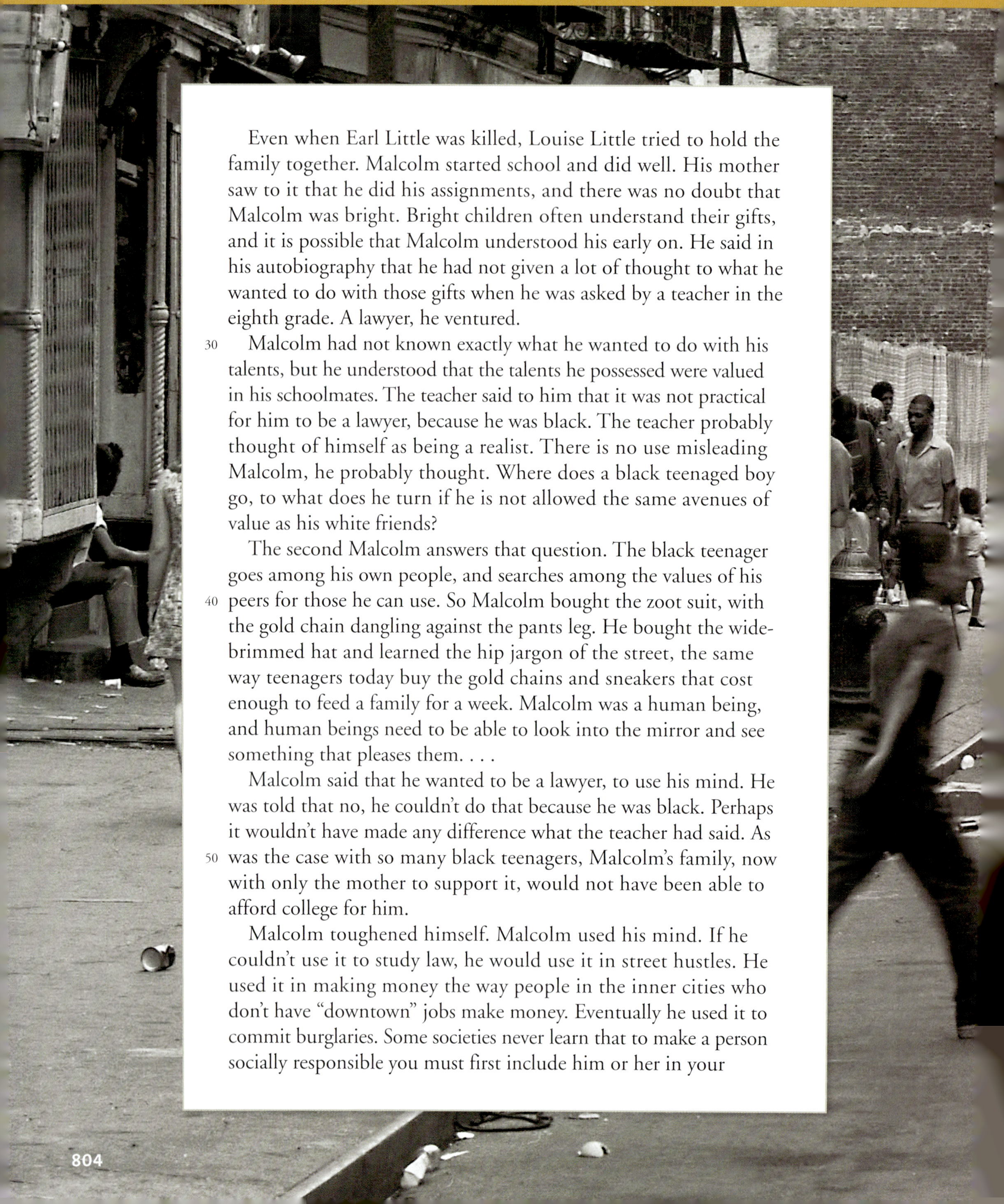

Even when Earl Little was killed, Louise Little tried to hold the family together. Malcolm started school and did well. His mother saw to it that he did his assignments, and there was no doubt that Malcolm was bright. Bright children often understand their gifts, and it is possible that Malcolm understood his early on. He said in his autobiography that he had not given a lot of thought to what he wanted to do with those gifts when he was asked by a teacher in the eighth grade. A lawyer, he ventured.

Malcolm had not known exactly what he wanted to do with his talents, but he understood that the talents he possessed were valued in his schoolmates. The teacher said to him that it was not practical for him to be a lawyer, because he was black. The teacher probably thought of himself as being a realist. There is no use misleading Malcolm, he probably thought. Where does a black teenaged boy go, to what does he turn if he is not allowed the same avenues of value as his white friends?

The second Malcolm answers that question. The black teenager goes among his own people, and searches among the values of his peers for those he can use. So Malcolm bought the zoot suit, with the gold chain dangling against the pants leg. He bought the wide-brimmed hat and learned the hip jargon of the street, the same way teenagers today buy the gold chains and sneakers that cost enough to feed a family for a week. Malcolm was a human being, and human beings need to be able to look into the mirror and see something that pleases them. . . .

Malcolm said that he wanted to be a lawyer, to use his mind. He was told that no, he couldn't do that because he was black. Perhaps it wouldn't have made any difference what the teacher had said. As was the case with so many black teenagers, Malcolm's family, now with only the mother to support it, would not have been able to afford college for him.

Malcolm toughened himself. Malcolm used his mind. If he couldn't use it to study law, he would use it in street hustles. He used it in making money the way people in the inner cities who don't have "downtown" jobs make money. Eventually he used it to commit burglaries. Some societies never learn that to make a person socially responsible you must first include him or her in your

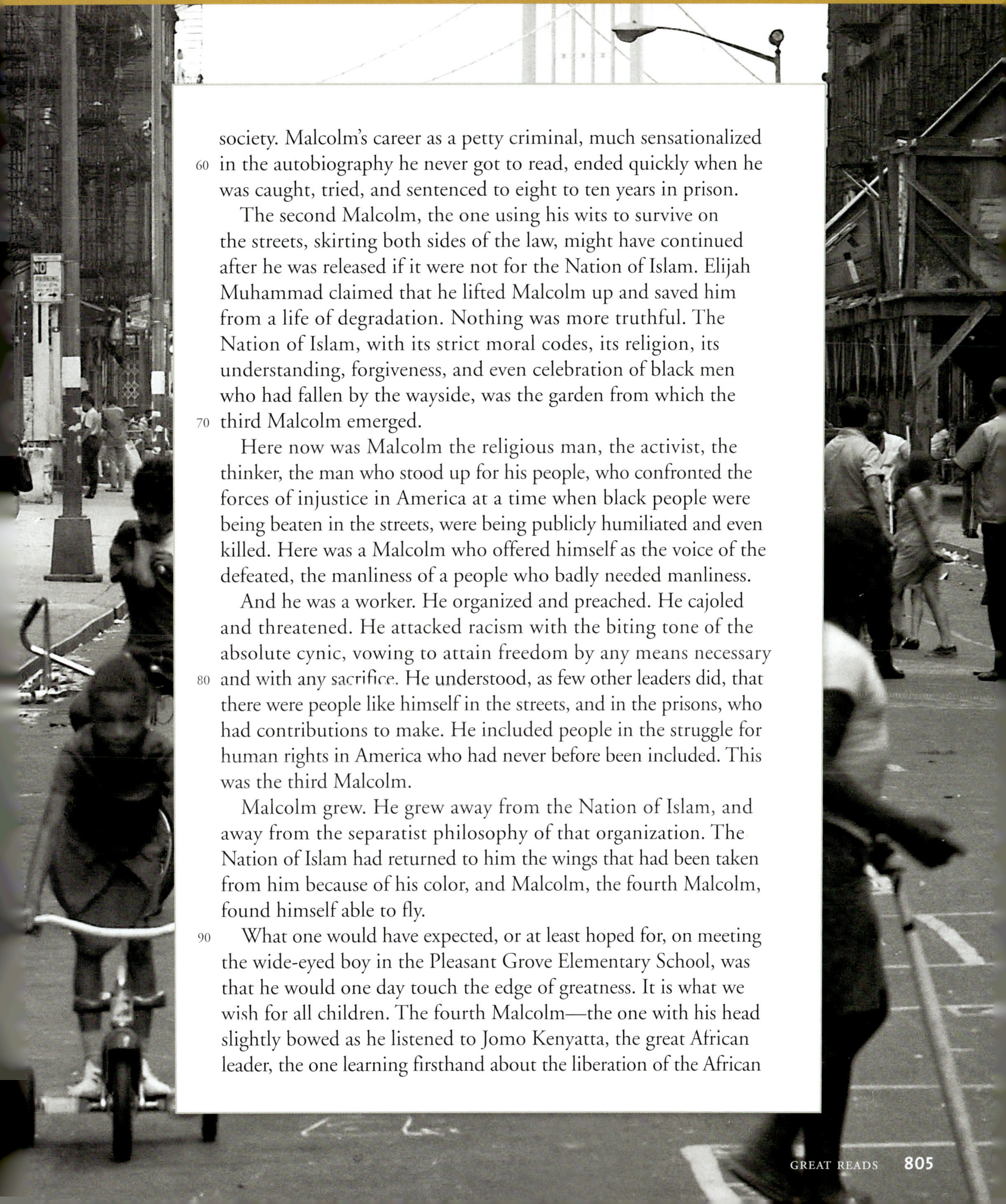

society. Malcolm's career as a petty criminal, much sensationalized in the autobiography he never got to read, ended quickly when he was caught, tried, and sentenced to eight to ten years in prison.

The second Malcolm, the one using his wits to survive on the streets, skirting both sides of the law, might have continued after he was released if it were not for the Nation of Islam. Elijah Muhammad claimed that he lifted Malcolm up and saved him from a life of degradation. Nothing was more truthful. The Nation of Islam, with its strict moral codes, its religion, its understanding, forgiveness, and even celebration of black men who had fallen by the wayside, was the garden from which the third Malcolm emerged.

Here now was Malcolm the religious man, the activist, the thinker, the man who stood up for his people, who confronted the forces of injustice in America at a time when black people were being beaten in the streets, were being publicly humiliated and even killed. Here was a Malcolm who offered himself as the voice of the defeated, the manliness of a people who badly needed manliness.

And he was a worker. He organized and preached. He cajoled and threatened. He attacked racism with the biting tone of the absolute cynic, vowing to attain freedom by any means necessary and with any sacrifice. He understood, as few other leaders did, that there were people like himself in the streets, and in the prisons, who had contributions to make. He included people in the struggle for human rights in America who had never before been included. This was the third Malcolm.

Malcolm grew. He grew away from the Nation of Islam, and away from the separatist philosophy of that organization. The Nation of Islam had returned to him the wings that had been taken from him because of his color, and Malcolm, the fourth Malcolm, found himself able to fly.

What one would have expected, or at least hoped for, on meeting the wide-eyed boy in the Pleasant Grove Elementary School, was that he would one day touch the edge of greatness. It is what we wish for all children. The fourth Malcolm—the one with his head slightly bowed as he listened to Jomo Kenyatta, the great African leader, the one learning firsthand about the liberation of the African

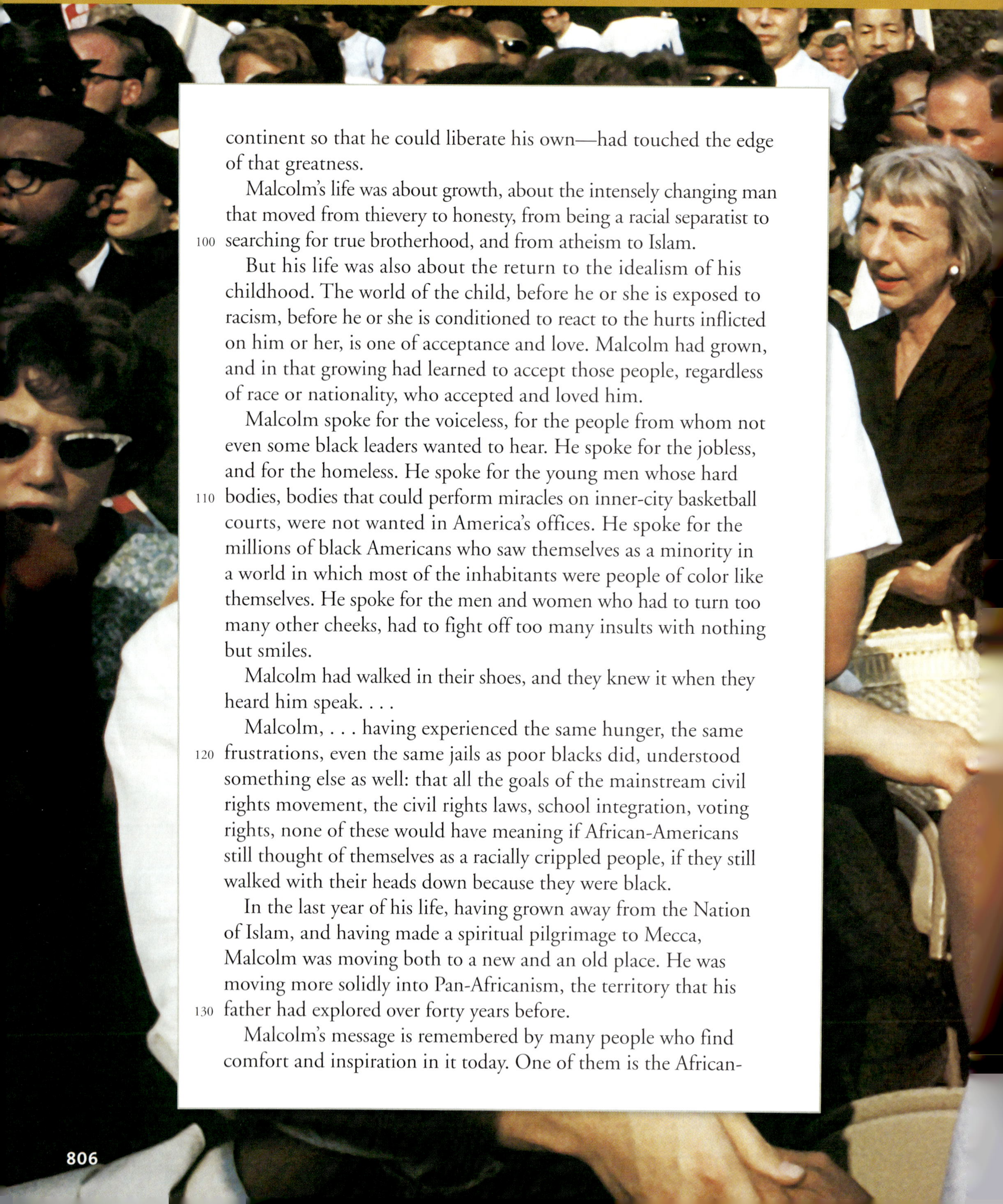

continent so that he could liberate his own—had touched the edge of that greatness.

Malcolm's life was about growth, about the intensely changing man that moved from thievery to honesty, from being a racial separatist to searching for true brotherhood, and from atheism to Islam.

But his life was also about the return to the idealism of his childhood. The world of the child, before he or she is exposed to racism, before he or she is conditioned to react to the hurts inflicted on him or her, is one of acceptance and love. Malcolm had grown, and in that growing had learned to accept those people, regardless of race or nationality, who accepted and loved him.

Malcolm spoke for the voiceless, for the people from whom not even some black leaders wanted to hear. He spoke for the jobless, and for the homeless. He spoke for the young men whose hard bodies, bodies that could perform miracles on inner-city basketball courts, were not wanted in America's offices. He spoke for the millions of black Americans who saw themselves as a minority in a world in which most of the inhabitants were people of color like themselves. He spoke for the men and women who had to turn too many other cheeks, had to fight off too many insults with nothing but smiles.

Malcolm had walked in their shoes, and they knew it when they heard him speak. . . .

Malcolm, . . . having experienced the same hunger, the same frustrations, even the same jails as poor blacks did, understood something else as well: that all the goals of the mainstream civil rights movement, the civil rights laws, school integration, voting rights, none of these would have meaning if African-Americans still thought of themselves as a racially crippled people, if they still walked with their heads down because they were black.

In the last year of his life, having grown away from the Nation of Islam, and having made a spiritual pilgrimage to Mecca, Malcolm was moving both to a new and an old place. He was moving more solidly into Pan-Africanism, the territory that his father had explored over forty years before.

Malcolm's message is remembered by many people who find comfort and inspiration in it today. One of them is the African-

American poet Wopashitwe Mondo Eyen we Langa, who wrote the poem "Great Bateleur." A bateleur is a reddish-brown eagle found in Africa. It is notable for its acrobatic flying style and its ferocious cry as it dives to capture its prey.

from **Great Bateleur**
(In Tribute to Malcolm)

We were those who begged, Malcolm
who could not find courage
nor faith in ourselves
who could not peer into reflecting pools
nor look each other in the face
and see the beauty that was ours
but for you, Malcolm
but for you, Great Bateleur
Eagle of Africa
still your spirit flies.

Perhaps history will tell us that there were no wrong strategies in the civil rights movement of the sixties. That all factors involved, the pray-ins, the legal cases, the marches, the militancy, were all vital to the time, that each had its place. Undoubtedly, too, as current needs color memories of distant events, we will bring different concepts from that period of American history, and voices. One voice that we will not forget is that of El Hajj Malik el Shabazz, the man we called Malcolm.

Keep Reading

Which part of this overview of Malcolm X's dramatic life sparked your curiosity? In other parts of Myers's biography, you'll read more about the hard times Malcolm faces as a child, how he gets into trouble with the law, why he makes some people angry while inspiring others, and the tragic way his life comes to an end.

The Noble Experiment

From the Autobiography *I Never Had It Made* by Jackie Robinson as Told to Alfred Duckett

When is there DIGNITY in silence?

ALABAMA STANDARDS

READING & RESEARCH STANDARDS
3 Distinguish among genres, including autobiographies
13.a Taking notes to summarize information

KEY IDEA What do you do when someone yells at you? Some people choose to yell back. Some people explain themselves calmly. But there are times when silence is the most effective response. When does silence give you **dignity,** or make you worthy of respect? In the selection you're about to read, Jackie Robinson tells why he needed to find strength in silence.

DISCUSS With a group, decide the best response to each scenario listed. Should you yell back, explain calmly, or simply stay silent?

Scenario	Response
The principal accuses you of something you didn't do.	
A younger sibling calls you names to make you angry.	
The referee makes a call you think is unfair.	
A friend yells at you for calling a play against him.	

LITERARY ANALYSIS: AUTOBIOGRAPHY

An **autobiography** is the story of a person's life as written by that person. The writer

- uses the first-person point of view
- often introduces people who influenced him or her
- shares thoughts and feelings about his or her experiences

Autobiographies not only help you understand a person, but they also help you understand the society in which the person lived. As you read "The Noble Experiment," note what you learn about Jackie Robinson and his times.

READING STRATEGY: SUMMARIZE

When you **summarize,** you briefly restate in your own words the main ideas and important details of something you've read. As you read "The Noble Experiment," note important people and events in a log. Later you can use the log to help you identify the main ideas and summarize the selections.

Important Characters

- *Branch Rickey—Ohio Wesleyan baseball coach*
- *Charley Thomas—Player for Ohio Wesleyan*
-

Important Events

-

VOCABULARY IN CONTEXT

The listed words all help tell about a dramatic turning point in Jackie Robinson's life. See which ones you know well, think you know, or don't know at all. Then place each word in the correct column of a chart like the one shown.

WORD LIST	camouflage	insinuation	speculate
	capitalize	integrated	taunt
	disillusionment	retaliate	
	eloquence	shrewdly	

Know Well	*Think I Know*	*Don't Know*

Author Online

National Hero
Jackie Robinson was the first man at the University of California, Los Angeles, to earn varsity letters in four sports. He then went on to play professional baseball in 1945 in the Negro Leagues. His talent and extraordinary character were quickly noticed.

Jackie Robinson
1919–1972

In 1947, he joined the Brooklyn Dodgers. Robinson was honored as Rookie of the Year in 1947 and National League Most Valuable Player in 1949. He was inducted into the Baseball Hall of Fame in 1962. With the help of his wife, Rachel, Jackie paved the way for African-American athletes.

Cowriter and Fan Robinson worked on his autobiography with Alfred Duckett, a writer and baseball fan. Active in the civil rights movement, Duckett was a speechwriter for Dr. Martin Luther King Jr.

MORE ABOUT THE AUTHOR
For more on Jackie Robinson, visit the **Literature Center** at **ClassZone.com.**

Background

Segregated National Pastime In the 1940s, African Americans faced many barriers. Segregation kept African Americans separate from whites in every part of society, including sports. In baseball the Negro League was completely separate from the all-white teams of the Major League. Jackie Robinson would help change that.

THE NOBLE EXPERIMENT

Jackie Robinson
as Told to Alfred Duckett

In 1910 Branch Rickey was a coach for Ohio Wesleyan. The team went to South Bend, Indiana, for a game. The hotel management registered the coach and team but refused to assign a room to a black player named Charley Thomas. In those days college ball had a few black players. Mr. Rickey took the manager aside and said he would move the entire team to another hotel unless the black athlete was accepted. The threat was a bluff because he knew the other hotels also would have refused accommodations to a black man. While the hotel manager was thinking about the threat, Mr. Rickey came up with a compromise. He suggested a cot be put in his own room, which he would share with the unwanted guest. The hotel manager wasn't happy about the idea, but he gave in. A

Years later Branch Rickey told the story of the misery of that black player to whom he had given a place to sleep. He remembered that Thomas couldn't sleep.

"He sat on that cot," Mr. Rickey said, "and was silent for a long time. Then he began to cry, tears he couldn't hold back. His whole body shook with emotion. I sat and watched him, not knowing what to do until he began tearing at one hand with the other—just as if he were trying to scratch the skin off his hands with his fingernails. I was alarmed. I asked him what he was trying to do to himself.

"'It's my hands,' he sobbed. 'They're black. If only they were white, I'd be as good as anybody then, wouldn't I, Mr. Rickey? If only they were white.'"

"Charley," Mr. Rickey said, "the day will come when they won't have to be white."

ANALYZE VISUALS
What might you **infer** from the cover of this 1951 special edition comic book?

A AUTOBIOGRAPHY
What does Robinson want the reader to know about the society in which Branch Rickey was coaching?

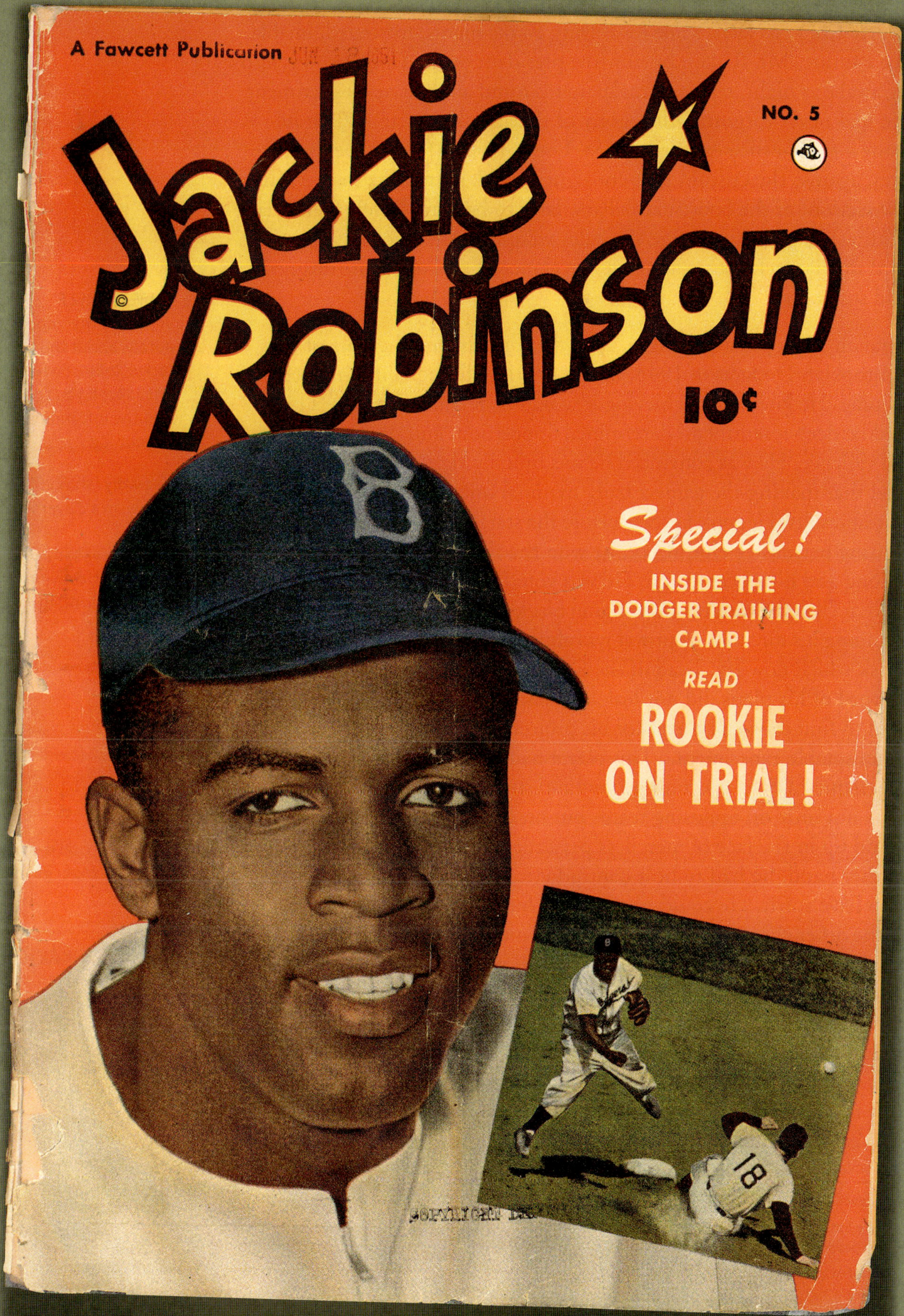
A Fawcett Publication
Jackie Robinson
NO. 5
10¢
Special!
INSIDE THE DODGER TRAINING CAMP!
READ
ROOKIE ON TRIAL!
18

Thirty-five years later, while I was lying awake nights, frustrated, unable to see a future, Mr. Rickey, by now the president of the Dodgers, was also lying awake at night, trying to make up his mind about a new experiment.

He had never forgotten the agony of that black athlete. When he became a front-office executive in St. Louis, he had fought, behind the scenes, against the custom that consigned black spectators to the Jim Crow section[1] of the Sportsman's Park, later to become Busch Memorial Stadium. His pleas to change the rules were in vain. Those in power argued that if blacks were allowed a free choice of seating, white business would suffer. **B**

Branch Rickey lost that fight, but when he became the boss of the Brooklyn Dodgers in 1943, he felt the time for equality in baseball had come. He knew that achieving it would be terribly difficult. There would be deep resentment, determined opposition, and perhaps even racial violence. He was convinced he was morally right, and he **shrewdly** sensed that making the game a truly national one would have healthy financial results. He took his case before the startled directors of the club, and using persuasive **eloquence,** he won the first battle in what would be a long and bitter campaign. He was voted permission to make the Brooklyn club the pioneer in bringing blacks into baseball.

Winning his directors' approval was almost insignificant in contrast to the task which now lay ahead of the Dodger president. He made certain that word of his plans did not leak out, particularly to the press. Next, he had to find the ideal player for his project, which came to be called "Rickey's noble experiment." This player had to be one who could take abuse, name-calling, rejection by fans and sportswriters and by fellow players not only on opposing teams but on his own. He had to be able to stand up in the face of merciless persecution and not **retaliate.** On the other hand, he had to be a contradiction in human terms; he still had to have spirit. He could not be an "Uncle Tom."[2] His ability to turn the other cheek had to be predicated[3] on his determination to gain acceptance. Once having proven his ability as player, teammate, and man, he had to be able to cast off humbleness and stand up as a full-fledged participant whose triumph did not carry the poison of bitterness. **C**

Unknown to most people and certainly to me, after launching a major scouting program, Branch Rickey had picked me as that player. The Rickey talent hunt went beyond national borders. Cuba, Mexico, Puerto Rico, Venezuela, and other countries where dark-skinned people lived

B SUMMARIZE
What are the important details about the people Jackie Robinson has introduced you to so far? Add the information to your log.

shrewdly (shro͞od′lē) *adv.* wisely; in a clever way

eloquence (ĕl′ə-kwəns) *n.* forceful, convincing speech or writing

retaliate (rĭ-tăl′ē-āt′) *v.* to get revenge; get even

C AUTOBIOGRAPHY
Why does Jackie Robinson choose to tell you so much about Branch Rickey's thoughts on the qualities the first major-league black baseball player will have to have?

1. **consigned . . . to the Jim Crow section:** directed African Americans to sit in a separate section.
2. **"Uncle Tom":** an offensive term for an African-American person seen as trying overly hard to please white people; originally from the novel *Uncle Tom's Cabin,* written in 1851 by Harriet Beecher Stowe.
3. **predicated** (prĕd′ĭ-kā′tĭd): based.

Jackie Robinson in his Kansas City Monarchs uniform shortly before he met Branch Rickey, 1945

had been checked out. Mr. Rickey had learned that there were a number of black players, war veterans mainly, who had gone to these countries, despairing of finding an opportunity in their own country. The manhunt had to be **camouflaged.** If it became known he was looking for a black recruit for the Dodgers, all hell would have broken loose. The gimmick he used as a cover-up was to make the world believe that he was about to establish a new Negro league. In the spring of 1945 he called a press conference and announced that the Dodgers were organizing the United States League, composed of all black teams. This, of course, made blacks and prointegration whites indignant. He was accused of trying to uphold the existing segregation and, at the same time, **capitalize** on black players. Cleverly, Mr. Rickey replied that his league would be better organized than the current ones. He said its main purpose, eventually, was to be absorbed into the majors. It is ironic that by coming very close to telling the truth, he was able to conceal that truth from the enemies of **integrated** baseball. Most people assumed that when he spoke of some distant goal of integration, Mr. Rickey was being a hypocrite on this issue as so many of baseball's leaders had been. **D**

camouflage (kăm′ə-fläzh′) *v.* to disguise or portray falsely in order to conceal

capitalize (kăp′ĭ-tl-īz′) *v.* to take advantage of

integrated (ĭn′tĭ-grā′tĭd) *adj.* open to people of all races and groups **integrate** *v.*

D SUMMARIZE
What challenges will face Rickey and any African-American player he chooses?

Black players were familiar with this kind of hypocrisy. When I was with the Monarchs, shortly before I met Mr. Rickey, Wendell Smith, then sports editor of the black weekly Pittsburgh *Courier,* had arranged for me and two other players from the Negro league to go to a tryout with the Boston Red Sox. The tryout had been brought about because a Boston city councilman had frightened the Red Sox management. Councilman Isadore Muchneck threatened to push a bill through banning Sunday baseball unless the Red Sox hired black players. Sam Jethroe of the Cleveland Buckeyes, Marvin Williams of the Philadelphia Stars, and I had been grateful to Wendell for getting us a chance in the Red Sox tryout, and we put our best efforts into it. However, not for one minute did we believe the tryout was sincere. The Boston club officials praised our performance, let us fill out application cards, and said, "So long." We were fairly certain they wouldn't call us, and we had no intention of calling them.

Incidents like this made Wendell Smith as cynical as we were. He didn't accept Branch Rickey's new league as a genuine project, and he frankly told him so. During this conversation, the Dodger boss asked Wendell whether any of the three of us who had gone to Boston was really good major league material. Wendell said I was. I will be forever indebted to Wendell because, without his even knowing it, his recommendation was in the end partly responsible for my career. At the time, it started a thorough investigation of my background. E

E AUTOBIOGRAPHY
Reread lines 96–103. Notice that Robinson uses first-person pronouns such as *I* and *we*. To whom does the *we* refer?

In August 1945, at Comiskey Park in Chicago, I was approached by Clyde Sukeforth, the Dodger scout. Blacks have had to learn to protect themselves by being cynical but not cynical enough to slam the door on potential opportunities. We go through life walking a tightrope[4] to prevent too much **disillusionment.** I was out on the field when Sukeforth called my name and beckoned. He told me the Brown Dodgers were looking for top ballplayers, that Branch Rickey had heard about me and sent him to watch me throw from the hole. He had come at an unfortunate time. I had hurt my shoulder a couple of days before that, and I wouldn't be doing any throwing for at least a week.

disillusionment
(dĭs'ĭ-lo͞o'zhən-mənt) *n.*
disappointment; loss of hope

VISUAL VOCABULARY

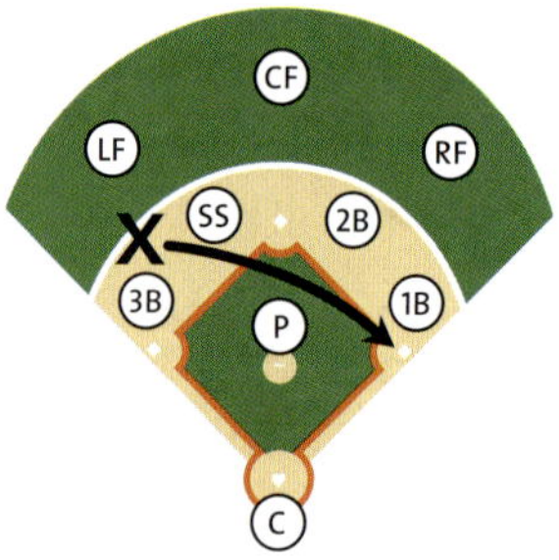

throw from the hole *v.* to throw from deep in the infield (**X**) to first base (**1B**)

Sukeforth said he'd like to talk with me anyhow. He asked me to come to see him after the game at the Stevens Hotel.

Here we go again, I thought. Another time-wasting experience. But Sukeforth looked like a sincere person, and I thought I might as well listen. I agreed to meet him that night. When we met, Sukeforth got right to the point. Mr. Rickey wanted to talk to me about the possibility of becoming a Brown Dodger. If I could get a few days off and go to Brooklyn, my fare and expenses would be paid. At first I said that I couldn't leave my team and go to Brooklyn just like that. Sukeforth wouldn't take no for an answer. He pointed out that I couldn't play for a few days anyhow because of my bum arm. Why should my team object?

4. **walking a tightrope:** maintaining a narrow balance.

Jackie Robinson and Branch Rickey on signing day

I continued to hold out and demanded to know what would happen if the Monarchs fired me. The Dodger scout replied quietly that he didn't believe that would happen.

I shrugged and said I'd make the trip. I figured I had nothing to lose.

Branch Rickey was an impressive-looking man. He had a classic face, an air of command, a deep, booming voice, and a way of cutting through red tape and getting down to basics. He shook my hand vigorously and, after a brief conversation, sprang the first question.

"You got a girl?" he demanded.

It was a hell of a question. I had two reactions: why should he be concerned about my relationship with a girl; and, second, while I thought, hoped, and prayed I had a girl, the way things had been going, I was afraid she might have begun to consider me a hopeless case. I explained this to Mr. Rickey and Clyde. F

F AUTOBIOGRAPHY
Reread lines 135–139. What can you **infer** about Jackie Robinson's personal life and feelings?

Mr. Rickey wanted to know all about Rachel. I told him of our hopes and plans.

"You know, you *have* a girl," he said heartily. "When we get through today, you may want to call her up because there are times when a man needs a woman by his side."

My heart began racing a little faster again as I sat there **speculating.** First he asked me if I really understood why he had sent for me. I told him what Clyde Sukeforth had told me.

speculate
(spĕk'yə-lāt') *v.* to view or consider different possibilities; to guess what might happen

"That's what he was supposed to tell you," Mr. Rickey said. "The truth is you are not a candidate for the Brooklyn Brown Dodgers. I've sent for you because I'm interested in you as a candidate for the Brooklyn National League Club. I think you can play in the major leagues. How do you feel about it?"

My reactions seemed like some kind of weird mixture churning in a blender. I was thrilled, scared, and excited. I was incredulous. Most of all, I was speechless.

"You think you can play for Montreal?"he demanded.

I got my tongue back. "Yes," I answered.

Montreal was the Brooklyn Dodgers' top farm club. The players who went there and made it had an excellent chance at the big time.

I was busy reorganizing my thoughts while Mr. Rickey and Clyde Sukeforth discussed me briefly, almost as if I weren't there. Mr. Rickey was questioning Clyde. Could I make the grade?

Abruptly, Mr. Rickey swung his swivel chair in my direction. He was a man who conducted himself with great drama. He pointed a finger at me.

"I know you're a good ballplayer," he barked. "What I don't know is whether you have the guts."

I knew it was all too good to be true. Here was a guy questioning my courage. That virtually amounted to him asking me if I was a coward. Mr. Rickey or no Mr. Rickey, that was an **insinuation** hard to take. I felt the heat coming up into my cheeks. **G**

insinuation
(ĭn-sĭn'yo͞o-ā'shən) *n.*
a suggestion or hint intended to insult

G AUTOBIOGRAPHY
Reread lines 153–170. What words and phrases help you understand how Robinson felt during his interview with Branch Rickey?

Before I could react to what he had said, he leaned forward in his chair and explained.

I wasn't just another athlete being hired by a ball club. We were playing for big stakes. This was the reason Branch Rickey's search had been so exhaustive. The search had spanned the globe and narrowed down to a few candidates, then finally to me. When it looked as though I might be the number-one choice, the investigation of my life, my habits, my reputation, and my character had become an intensified study.

"I've investigated you thoroughly, Robinson," Mr. Rickey said.

One of the results of this thorough screening were reports from California athletic circles that I had been a "racial agitator"[5] at UCLA. Mr. Rickey had not accepted these criticisms on face value. He had demanded and received more information and came to the conclusion that if I had been white, people would have said, "Here's a guy who's a contender, a competitor."

After that he had some grim words of warning. "We can't fight our way through this, Robinson. We've got no army. There's virtually nobody on our side. No owners, no umpires, very few newspapermen. And I'm afraid

5. **"racial agitator":** negative term used for someone who tries to stir up trouble between the races.

that many fans will be hostile. We'll be in a tough position. We can win only if we can convince the world that I'm doing this because you're a great ballplayer and a fine gentleman."

He had me transfixed as he spoke. I could feel his sincerity, and I began to get a sense of how much this major step meant to him. Because of his nature and his passion for justice, he had to do what he was doing. He continued. The rumbling voice, the theatrical gestures were gone. He was speaking from a deep, quiet strength.

"So there's more than just playing," he said. "I wish it meant only hits, runs, and errors—only the things they put in the box score. Because you know—yes, you would know, Robinson, that a baseball box score is a democratic thing. It doesn't tell how big you are, what church you attend, what color you are, or how your father voted in the last election. It just tells what kind of baseball player you were on that particular day." **H**

H SUMMARIZE
What does Branch Rickey really want to find out about Jackie Robinson during this interview? Include these details in your log.

Jackie Robinson crosses the plate after one of his many home-run hits for the Montreal Royals.

I interrupted. "But it's the box score that really counts—that and that alone, isn't it?"

"It's all that *ought* to count," he replied. "But it isn't. Maybe one of these days it *will* be all that counts. That is one of the reasons I've got you here, Robinson. If you're a good enough man, we can make this a start in the right direction. But let me tell you, it's going to take an awful lot of courage."

He was back to the crossroads question that made me start to get angry minutes earlier. He asked it slowly and with great care.

"Have you got the guts to play the game no matter what happens?"

"I think I can play the game, Mr. Rickey," I said.

The next few minutes were tough. Branch Rickey had to make absolutely sure that I knew what I would face. Beanballs[6] would be thrown at me. I would be called the kind of names which would hurt and infuriate any man. I would be physically attacked. Could I take all of this and control my temper, remain steadfastly loyal to our ultimate aim?

He knew I would have terrible problems and wanted me to know the extent of them before I agreed to the plan. I was twenty-six years old, and all my life—back to the age of eight when a little neighbor girl called me names—I had believed in payback, retaliation. The most luxurious possession, the richest treasure anybody has, is his personal dignity. I looked at Mr. Rickey guardedly, and in that second I was looking at him not as a partner in a great experiment, but as the enemy—a white man. I had a question, and it was the age-old one about whether or not you sell your birthright. ❶

❶ AUTOBIOGRAPHY
Reread lines 218–222. What is most important to Jackie Robinson?

"Mr. Rickey," I asked, "are you looking for a Negro who is afraid to fight back?"

I never will forget the way he exploded.

"Robinson," he said, "I'm looking for a ballplayer with guts enough not to fight back."

After that, Mr. Rickey continued his lecture on the kind of thing I'd be facing.

He not only told me about it, but he acted out the part of a white player charging into me, blaming me for the "accident" and calling me all kinds of foul racial names. He talked about my race, my parents, in language that was almost unendurable.

"They'll **taunt** and goad you," Mr. Rickey said. "They'll do anything to make you react. They'll try to provoke a race riot in the ballpark. This is the way to prove to the public that a Negro should not be allowed in the major league. This is the way to frighten the fans and make them afraid to attend the games."

taunt (tônt) *v.* to make fun of

6. **beanballs:** pitches thrown purposely at a batter's head.

Jackie makes the big time with the Brooklyn Dodgers.

If hundreds of black people wanted to come to the ballpark to watch me play and Mr. Rickey tried to discourage them, would I understand that he was doing it because the emotional enthusiasm of my people could harm the experiment? That kind of enthusiasm would be as bad as the emotional opposition of prejudiced white fans.

Suppose I was at shortstop. Another player comes down from first, stealing, flying in with spikes high, and cuts me on the leg. As I feel the blood running down my leg, the white player laughs in my face.

"How do you like that, boy?" he sneers. J

Could I turn the other cheek? I didn't know how I would do it. Yet I knew that I must. I had to do it for so many reasons. For black youth, for my mother, for Rae, for myself. I had already begun to feel I had to do it for Branch Rickey.

I was offered, and agreed to sign later, a contract with a $3,500 bonus and $600-a-month salary. I was officially a Montreal Royal. I must not tell anyone except Rae and my mother.

J SUMMARIZE
How does Branch Rickey test Jackie Robinson to make sure he is strong enough to succeed with dignity?

Comprehension

1. **Recall** Branch Rickey was searching for a special person to help him integrate baseball. What qualities did he believe this player needed to have?
2. **Clarify** Why was Rickey's search for an African-American player kept secret?
3. **Clarify** Why was Jackie Robinson suspicious of Clyde Sukeforth's invitation to meet with Branch Rickey?

Literary Analysis

4. **Summarize** Review the log you created while reading and cross out details that don't seem as important now. Use the remaining information to write a summary of the selection.
5. **Draw Conclusions** What general statement can you make in regard to the society Jackie Robinson writes about? Cite details to support your answer.
6. **Interpret Autobiography** How does Robinson feel about Branch Rickey? Cite passages from the autobiography that show Robinson's impressions of Rickey.
7. **Analyze Author's Purpose** Why do you think Robinson wanted to share his experience with the public?
8. **Evaluate Title** Do you think "The Noble Experiment" is an appropriate title for this selection? Why or why not?

Extension and Challenge

9. **Readers' Circle** During Jackie Robinson's conversation with Branch Rickey, Robinson asks, "But it's the box score that really counts—that and that alone, isn't it?" Do you agree that the box score is all that counts? With a group, discuss whether we should expect professional athletes to be role models and act with **dignity,** or whether we should only judge them on their athletic performance. Use examples from the selection to support your opinion.
10. **SOCIAL STUDIES CONNECTION** The 1940s, when Jackie Robinson entered professional baseball, were a dramatic decade. Create a timeline of the era that gives the events in the autobiography and also those in the Eleanor Roosevelt biography beginning on page 762. Then research to find four other events that were happening in the world at the same time. Add these other events to your timeline.

1943

Branch Rickey becomes the boss of the Brooklyn Dodgers.

ALABAMA STANDARDS

RESEARCH STANDARD
13.a Taking notes to summarize information

RESEARCH LINKS
For more on world events in the 1940s, visit the **Research Center** at **ClassZone.com.**

Vocabulary in Context

VOCABULARY PRACTICE

Choose the word from the box that is the best substitute for each boldfaced word or term.

1. Branch Rickey **cleverly** devised a cover story to mislead the press.
2. He was accused of trying to **gain advantage** on African Americans.
3. The **lack of hope** African-American baseball players felt about joining the major leagues was based on past experience.
4. Robinson took time to **think** about the outcome of his actions.
5. The true goal of Rickey's plan was to have **desegregated** major leagues.
6. Some players on other teams would **make fun of** Robinson.
7. Robinson was not allowed to **get even.**
8. A sportswriter made a **suggestion** intended to insult Robinson.
9. The minister spoke with **great verbal skill** about the evils of prejudice.
10. Branch Rickey had to **conceal** his plan.

camouflage
capitalize
disillusionment
eloquence
insinuation
integrated
retaliate
shrewdly
speculate
taunt

VOCABULARY IN WRITING

What challenges did Branch Rickey expect Robinson to face during his early baseball career? Using three or more vocabulary words, write a paragraph about them. You could start this way.

EXAMPLE SENTENCE

*Rickey warned Robinson that spectators might **taunt** him.*

ALABAMA STANDARDS

READING STANDARD
1.c Using context clues to determine word meanings

VOCABULARY STRATEGY: THE LATIN ROOT *spec*

The vocabulary word *speculate* contains the Latin root *spec,* which means "to see" or "to look." This root, which may also be spelled *spect,* is found in many English words. To understand the meaning of words with *spec* or *spect,* you can often use context clues and your knowledge of the root's meaning.

VOCABULARY PRACTICE
For more practice, go to the **Vocabulary Center** at **ClassZone.com.**

PRACTICE Choose a word from the web that best completes each sentence. Use context clues or, if necessary, a dictionary.

1. The ______ fireworks show thrilled everyone.
2. Interview the witness to get a better ______ on the accident.
3. The health ______ makes sure that all local restaurants are clean.
4. The ______ of speaking before an audience makes me nervous.
5. The police officer carefully removed the blood ______ from the crime scene.

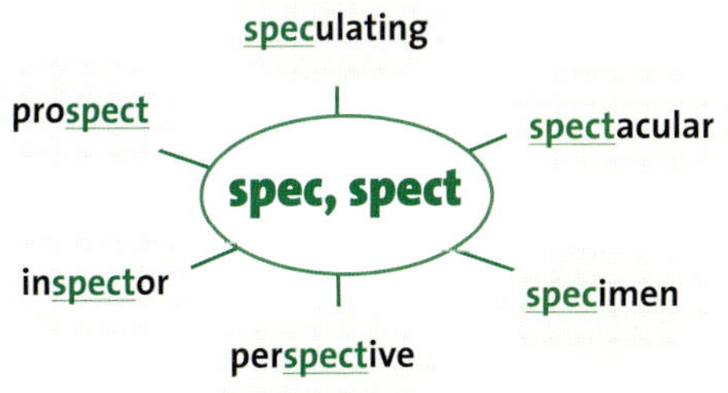

Reading for Information

Jackie Robinson Makes Headlines

Historical Sports Articles

Use with "The Noble Experiment," page 810.

ALABAMA STANDARDS

LIT & RESEARCH STANDARDS
7.a Comparing informational texts
13 Apply steps in the research process

What's the Connection?

You have just read Jackie Robinson's autobiography. Now read what newspaper reporters had to say about him during his career.

Skill Focus: Identify Treatment and Scope

Even when the same writing topic is assigned to everyone in your class, each student's paper will be different. This happens because you each make different decisions about how to cover the topic.

The way a topic is handled is called its **treatment.** Treatment includes the form the writer chooses to use, as well as the writer's purpose. Treatment also includes tone, or the writer's attitude toward the subject. For example, here are two ways to treat the same topic: movie ratings.

Movie Ratings	Form	Purpose	Tone
Treatment A	news article	to inform	serious
Treatment B	editorial	to persuade	lighthearted

Another thing that makes each piece of writing different is the writer's **scope**—what he or she focuses on. For example, even two serious articles about movie ratings can still be very different in scope. One might focus on how movie ratings have changed over the years. The other could focus on how inaccurate ratings hurt good movies.

As you read the articles that follow, identify their treatment and scope by answering the questions in this chart.

Element	Questions to Answer	"Montreal Signs Negro Shortstop"	"Robinson Steals Home in Fifth"
Treatment	What form does the writing take?	sports article	sports article
	What is the purpose?		
	What is the tone?		
Scope	What is the topic?		
	What aspects of the topic are covered in the article?		
	How much detail is provided?		

MONTREAL SIGNS NEGRO SHORTSTOP

Organized Baseball Opens Its Ranks to Negro Player

Jackie Robinson signs with the Montreal Royals. Looking on are Hector Racine, Royals president; Branch Rickey Jr.; and Romeo Gauvreau, Royals vice president.

Robinson Gets Bonus to Sign Ⓐ

MONTREAL, Oct. 23 (AP)—The first Negro player ever to be admitted to organized baseball, Jack Robinson, today put his signature on a contract calling not only for a player's salary, but also a bonus for signing.

Product of a three-year search and $25,000 hunt for Negro diamond talent by the Dodgers, Robinson signed up in a history-making huddle with Hector Racine and Lieut. Col. Romeo Gauvreau, Royals' president and vice president respectively, and Branch Rickey Jr., who heads the Brooklyn farm system.

"Mr. Racine and my father," said young Rickey, "will undoubtedly be severely criticized in some sections of the United States where racial prejudice is rampant. They are not inviting trouble, but they won't avoid it if it comes. Jack Robinson is a fine type of young man, intelligent and college bred, and I think he can take it, too."

FOCUS ON FORM

A **sports article** is a newspaper account of a sports event. Sports articles typically have the following elements:

- a **headline**, which often sums up the article. Sometimes there is a second headline in smaller print.
- a **subtitle**, which adds a "teaser," a prompt to make you want to read
- **photographs**
- **captions**
- a **lead**, the attention-grabbing first few sentences
- **information** about *who, what, when, where, why,* and *how*

Ⓐ **SPORTS ARTICLE**

What do you learn from the **subtitle** of this article that you don't learn from the **headline?**

Robinson, himself, had little to say. "Of course, I can't begin to tell you how happy I am that I am the first member of my race in organized ball," he declared. "I realize how much it means to me, to my race and to baseball. I can only say I'll do my very best to come through in every manner."

Robinson is seen here as he takes a practice swing.

Implications Are Realized

With sports writers and photographers assembled, young Rickey and Racine made the announcement here. Rickey Jr. went on to explain that both he and his father—who was not present—realized the implications and possible reactions in other quarters of the diamond world. B

"It may cost the Brooklyn organization a number of ball players," he said. "Some of them, particularly if they come from certain sections of the South, will steer away from a club with colored players on its roster. Some players now with us may even quit, but they'll be back in baseball after they work a year or two in a cotton mill."

Rickey Sr.'s hunt for Negro talent has produced some twenty-five others he expects to sign to contracts for double-A ball, with the intention of developing them into big leaguers.

On Aug. 29 Robinson was quietly taken to Brooklyn. Rickey Sr. told him what he had in mind, and the broad-shouldered Pasadena, Calif., Negro agreed to sign a contract by Nov. 1.

"Robinson is a good ball player and comes to us highly recommended by our scouts," Racine said. "He will join us at our training camp in Florida next spring." C

B TREATMENT AND SCOPE
Would you describe the writer's **tone** as respectful, humorous, or something else? Add this description to your chart.

C TREATMENT AND SCOPE
Identify the **topic** of this article. What aspects of this topic does the reporter focus on? Add this information to your chart.

The New York Times

WEDNESDAY, JUNE 25, 1947 SPORTS 33

ROBINSON STEALS HOME IN FIFTH

by ROSCOE McGOWEN

Robinson slides home to win the ball game against Pittsburgh. D

PITTSBURGH, June 24—They're never too old to learn something. The 40-year-old Fritz Ostermueller learned tonight at Forbes Field, before 35,331 distressed witnesses, that it is unwise to wind up with Jackie Robinson on third base. E

The Negro flash stole home with two out in the fifth inning while Fritz was going through his full motion to pitch a third ball to Dixie Walker—and that run was enough to win the ball game, although the Brooks went on to outscore the Pirates, 4–2.

At the time Robinson committed his larceny the score was tied, both teams having scored twice in the second inning. Dixie Walker

D SPORTS ARTICLE
Based on the **headline, photo,** and **caption,** what does the article focus on?

E TREATMENT AND SCOPE
Reread lines 2–8. What **tone** does a phrase like "They're never too old to learn something" convey?

opened the second with a long triple to left center and Pee Wee Reese, catching a three-and-one pitch on the fat part of his bat, walloped the ball far over the outer left field barrier for his eighth homer of the campaign.

The Box Score

PITTSBURGH

		ab.	r.	h.	po.	a.	e.
Rikard	rf	3	0	1	3	0	0
Wiet'nn	2b	4	0	0	3	1	0
Gustine	3b	4	0	0	0	2	0
Kiner	lf	3	1	1	1	0	0
Cox.	ss	3	1	2	2	3	0
Fletcher	1b	4	0	1	5	1	0
W'lake	cf	4	0	0	2	0	0
Howell	c	4	0	1	8	1	0
Oster'ler	p	3	0	1	3	1	0
Sullivan		1	0	0	0	0	0
Total		33	2	7	27	9	0

BROOKLYN

		ab.	r.	h.	po.	a.	e.
Stanky	2b	4	0	1	1	4	0
Gionfriddo	lf	4	1	0	3	0	0
Robinson	1b	4	1	1	11	0	0
Furillo	cf	4	0	2	2	0	1
Walker	rf	3	1	1	1	0	0
Reese	ss	4	1	1	3	3	0
Jorgens'n	3b	4	0	2	0	2	0
Hodges	c	3	0	0	5	0	0
Branca	p	4	0	0	1	1	0
Total		34	4	8	27	10	1

Brooklyn	0	2	0	0	1	0	1	0	0	—	4
Pittsburgh	0	2	0	0	0	0	0	0	0	—	2

Runs batted in—Reese 2, Fletcher, Furillo
Two-base hit—Rikard. Three-base hit—Walker. Home run—Reese. Stolen bases—Furillo, Robinson, Gionfriddo. Double play—Stanky, Reese and Robinson. Left on bases—Brooklyn 7. Pittsburgh 7. Bases on balls—Off Branca 3. Ostermueller 4. Struck out—By Ostermueller 7. Branca 4. Umpires—Stewart, Ballanfant and Henline. Time of game—2:41. Attendance—35,331. F

F SPORTS ARTICLE
A **box score** is a **graphic aid** that uses abbreviations to show at a glance the number of times a player

- was at bat **(ab.)**
- scored a run **(r.)**
- got a hit **(h.)**
- put out another player **(po.)**
- assisted in a play **(a.)**
- made an error **(e.)**

What else can you learn from this box score?

Comprehension

1. **Recall** What was Jackie Robinson the first African-American person to do?
2. **Summarize** In the article "Montreal Signs Negro Shortstop," Branch Rickey Jr. says that he and his father realize what the reactions to signing Robinson may be. Summarize these possible reactions.

Critical Analysis

3. **Analyze the Lead** Explain what a lead is. Identify the lead in either one of the two sports articles you just read. Then explain how that lead gets its readers' attention.
4. **Compare Treatment and Scope** Using the chart you completed, compare the treatment and scope of the two articles.

Read for Information: Evaluate Texts for Usefulness

ALABAMA STANDARDS

LIT & RESEARCH STANDARDS
7.a Comparing informational texts
13 Apply steps in the research process

WRITING PROMPT

Imagine you have chosen one of the following topics for a report:

- box scores and how they have changed over the years
- attitudes toward African-American athletes in the 1940s
- sports reporting

Explain which article you would use as a source of information for this topic and why. If both articles would be useful to you, be sure to explain what each would provide.

To answer this prompt, first identify the topic you would want to focus on. Then follow these steps:

1. Review the chart you filled in. What information does each article provide?
2. In a paragraph, identify the topic you picked, the article(s) you would use for a report on that topic, and a brief explanation as to why the article(s) would be useful to you.

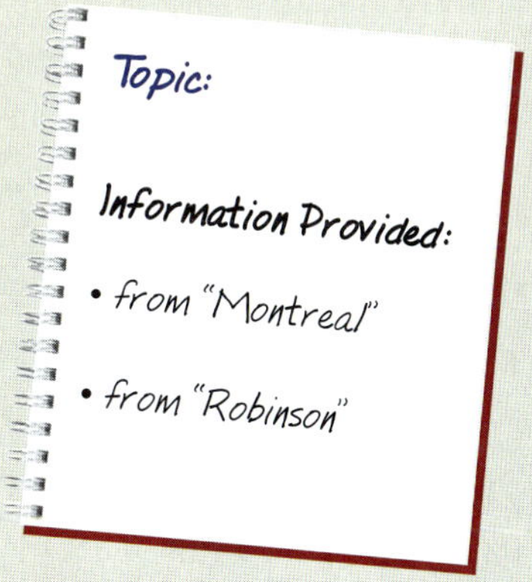

Media Study

from Jackie Robinson

Documentary on MediaSmart DVD

What makes a person a TRAILBLAZER?

ALABAMA STANDARDS

COMMUNICATION STANDARD
15 Demonstrate listening skills

KEY IDEA Jackie Robinson did more than play baseball. He helped pave the way for racial equality in professional sports. You've read about the key moment in his **remarkable career.** Now watch a documentary that shows the obstacles Jackie Robinson overcame to pave a new path for baseball.

Background

Retiring Number 42 It's common for a professional team to retire the jersey number of an outstanding player. It's quite uncommon to retire a number throughout an entire league. This happened in 1997, when Jackie Robinson's number, 42, was retired to mark the 50th anniversary of breaking the color barrier in baseball. Many baseball greats were at the ceremony to pay tribute to this trailblazer.

This documentary from the A&E Channel's *Biography* series shows how Robinson's courage won him the respect of his teammates and earned him admiration nationwide.

Media Literacy: Documentary

A **documentary** is a nonfiction film or television production that tells about important people, historic places, or major events. The purpose of a documentary may be to inform, to explain, or to persuade. A documentary that is biographical presents the factual details of a person's life, focusing on major events. Most documentaries use interesting visuals and sounds and are edited to make the information easy to follow.

BASIC FEATURES	STRATEGIES FOR VIEWING
Visuals To bring a subject to life, a documentary uses **photographs, film, interviews,** or **graphics.**	• Look for **footage** that helps you understand the subject. Footage can include photographs, letters, interviews, news reports, film clips, and even home video movies. Documentary filmmakers use footage to show key information or details about a person, a place, or an event and to give a sense of a particular time. • Pay attention to **interviews.** People who are interviewed can be experts on a topic, or people who are directly involved with the subject of the documentary.
Sound Many documentaries include **voice-over narration,** which is the voice of an unseen speaker who is heard as the documentary plays. Other sounds include **music, sound effects,** and **dialogue.**	• Listen carefully to the **voice-over narrator.** The voice-over tells viewers why the subject is important and provides clues about how the information is organized. The voice-over may also summarize key scenes or events. • Follow **musical cues.** Music can be used simply to entertain viewers. It can also signal a change in the documentary's setting or changes in mood.
Editing **Editing** is the process of selecting and arranging visuals and sounds in a way that makes sense and is interesting for viewers.	Pay attention to how the information is presented and **edited.** Most documentaries will show events from beginning to end in a chronological, or time-order, sequence.

MediaSmart DVD

- **Video Clip:** *Jackie Robinson*
- **Genre:** Documentary
- **Running Time:** 8 minutes

Viewing Guide for

Jackie Robinson

Today, all athletes have an equal chance to play in professional sports, but there was a time when Jackie Robinson was the only African-American athlete out in the field. As you view the documentary, pay attention to the comments of those who knew and worked with Robinson. They will help you understand why he is considered a hero by so many people.

To continue exploring the features of a documentary, answer the following questions.

NOW VIEW

FIRST VIEWING: Comprehension

1. **Recall** Who is the player who became Jackie Robinson's friend during Robinson's first year with the Dodgers?
2. **Clarify** The documentary ends with this quotation from Jackie Robinson: "A life is not important except in the impact it has on other lives." In your own words, explain what this means.

CLOSE VIEWING: Media Literacy

3. **Examine Musical Cues** Describe the music that is used during the footage of the 1947 World Series. What kind of **mood,** or feeling, does the music create?
4. **Analyze Interviews** Andrew Young, a civil rights leader, explains why he admires Jackie Robinson. Based on the interview, what do you think Young wants today's viewers to admire about Jackie Robinson?
5. **Evaluate Footage** The documentary uses such footage as interviews, photographs, and video. Which of these features helped you understand most about the impact of "The Noble Experiment"? Explain.

Write or Discuss

Analyze the Documentary The television documentary clip you've just viewed shows highlights of Jackie Robinson's life and baseball career. What new information did you learn about Jackie Robinson from the documentary? Think about

- the interviews with Rachel Robinson, Andrew Young, Branch Rickey, and Jackie Robinson himself
- the film footage that shows Jackie Robinson as a player, the Brooklyn fans, and the 1947 World Series
- the voice-over narration that provides details of key events in Robinson's life

Produce Your Own Media

Record an Interview Imagine you're creating a documentary about someone you think is an everyday hero. Make plans for an **interview.** If you don't have direct contact with a hero, create a list of jobs that you think involve heroism and courage. Then get permission to find and interview someone whose job you have listed.

HERE'S HOW Use the tips and the student model to help you prepare for and carry out an interview session.

- Do some research about your interview subject. Then contact the person and arrange an interview. Arrange to have an adult accompany you for this session.
- Make a list of questions you'd like to ask. Organize those questions into a key word outline. For example, questions about the subject's childhood and education could be listed under the key word "Background."
- During the interview, listen to the person's responses and ask follow-up questions. Refer to your key-word outline for question ideas.

MEDIA TOOLS

For help with interviewing, visit the **Media Center** at **ClassZone.com.**

STUDENT MODEL

QUESTIONS

Background

Where did you grow up?
Who was your hero when you were young?

Earliest Success

What was the first project you really felt successful doing?
How did you feel about being given greater responsibility?

Favorite Activities

What do you like to do most in your spare time?
Do you have a favorite book?

Tech Tip

If available, use an audio or video recorder to tape the interview.

Lucy Stone: Champion of Women's Rights

Drama by Claire Boiko

How can we CHANGE what's wrong?

ALABAMA STANDARDS

READING STANDARDS

1.d Applying self-monitoring strategies

3 Distinguish among genres based on characteristics

KEY IDEA It's not easy to **change** what is wrong or unfair. Those people who fought to end slavery, those who helped women get the right to vote, and those who protected children from harmful working conditions were considered troublemakers by many in their day. Yet their victories made the world a better place. In this play, you'll learn about one such person.

DISCUSS List people who fought for change in order to make the world a better place. Discuss whether these people might have achieved the same results if they hadn't upset anyone.

LITERARY ANALYSIS: HISTORICAL DRAMA

Historical dramas are plays that take place in the past and are based on real events. In many of these plays, like the one you're about to read, the characters are also based on real historical figures. The dialogue and the action, however, are mostly created by the playwright. As you read *Lucy Stone: Champion of Women's Rights,* look for details and dialogue that tell you about Lucy and the time in which she lived.

READING STRATEGY: VISUALIZE

When you watch a play being performed, you can see the stage, the costumes, and the actors' movements. When you read a play, **visualizing** these elements, or forming a mental picture of them, can help you understand the setting and the action.

As you read, examine the **stage directions** carefully. These instructions to the actors, director, and reader are in parentheses and contain details that help you create mental pictures. Record the details in a chart. Then sketch the pictures you form in your mind.

Details from Stage Directions	Mental Picture
"Two Women, wearing shabby farm clothing with aprons, enter, followed by Man, wearing somber clothes of the early 1800s."	

VOCABULARY IN CONTEXT

The boldfaced words help describe the feelings of Lucy Stone and her family. To see how many of the words you know, substitute a different word or words for each term.

1. He was **aghast** at what he heard.
2. She was seen as the **agitator** in the family.
3. She was **bemused** by her friend's sudden secretiveness.
4. The grandfather was the **patriarch** of the whole clan.
5. He bowed his head **piously** to pray.
6. Don't **squander** your money on unnecessary things.
7. She didn't want to be **subservient** to anyone.
8. "No way!" Lucy cried **vehemently.** "I won't do it!"

Author Online

On Stage and Off

Claire Boiko
born 1925

Claire Boiko has been performing in, producing, and writing plays since she earned a drama degree in 1946. For two years during the Korean War, she served as an entertainment and music technician for the U.S. Army. Many of the historical pageants Boiko has written were coauthored by her husband, a history teacher.

MORE ABOUT THE AUTHOR
For more on Claire Boiko, visit the **Literature Center** at **ClassZone.com.**

Background

Fighting for Her Rights Lucy Stone was born in Massachusetts in 1818. At that time, women did not have the same rights as men. They were not allowed to vote or own property. In many places, they were not allowed to attend college. However, Stone was determined to fight for women's rights, even as a young woman. She attended Oberlin College, the first college in the United States to admit both men and women.

A Vision for Change Stone married Henry Blackwell, an antislavery activist, in 1855, but she did not take his last name. This was a radical idea for a woman at that time. In 1869, Stone helped create the American Woman Suffrage Association, which fought for women's right to vote.

LUCY STONE

CHAMPION OF WOMEN'S RIGHTS

Claire Boiko

CHARACTERS

Two Women, narrators
Man, narrator
Hannah Stone
Francis Stone
Lucy Stone, their daughter, 16
Aunt Sally
Bowman, Lucy's brother
Eliza, Lucy's sister
Rhoda, Lucy's sister
Luther, Lucy's brother
Sarah, Lucy's sister
Henry Brown Blackwell

In the early 1800s, women were considered inferior to men. Women did not enjoy the rights they have today, such as the right to vote. It was difficult for them to get an education. But times were starting to change. Women began to go to college. They also began to organize to demand more equality. This play is about Lucy Stone, a pioneer of the women's rights movement.

The Girl I Left Behind Me (1870–1875), Eastman Johnson. Smithsonian American Art Museum, Washington, D.C. Photo © Smithsonian American Art Museum, Washington, D.C./Art Resource, New York.

Before rise:[1] Two Women, *wearing shabby farm clothing with aprons, enter, followed by* Man, *wearing somber clothes of the early 1800s.*

1st Woman. We come from the shadows of time to remind you—men and women both—of how things used to be.

2nd Woman. If the world is a better place for women now, it is because of the courage and persistence of one young girl—Lucy Stone.

1st Woman. In the early nineteenth century, when Lucy was growing up, girls weren't educated beyond the sixth grade.

2nd Woman. A husband had the legal right to beat his wife.

1st Woman. And women had *no* legal rights!

Man (***vehemently***). Education? Legal rights? For women? Never! Why, they are the inferior sex. A woman must be **subservient** to her husband in all things. 'Twas ever thus and shall always be so. Subject closed!

2nd Woman. Subject closed. Until Lucy Stone.

1st Woman. Lucy Stone, champion of women's rights.

Man (*shaking head*). Lucy Stone. She's nothing but an **agitator**! A disturber of the natural order! (*They exit.*)

Time: *a summer evening, 1834.*

Setting: *the parlor of the Stone farmhouse, West Brookfield, Massachusetts. A settle*[2] *stands in front of large fireplace, up center. Behind settle is a metal oil can. A table with oil lamp and three chairs stand left, before curtained window. An easy chair stands up right, beside which is a knitting basket. Against wall right is a small settle. Exit down right leads outside, exit down left leads to rest of house.*

Detail of *Old Homestead* (about 1877), George Inness. Oil on canvas. The Haggin Museum, Stockton, California (1943.56.10).

At rise:[3] Aunt Sally *is seated in easy chair knitting. After a moment she yawns, rubs her eyes, and puts down her knitting.* Lucy, *a bright, lively, 16-year-old girl, runs in right, followed by her older brother* Luther, *who limps.* Lucy *stops center, turns to* Luther.

Lucy (*laughing*). Slowpoke. I beat you again.

Luther (*whining*). It's not fair, Lucy. I stubbed my toe.

Lucy. You always have an excuse, Luther. Why don't you admit I'm a faster runner?

Luther. Because it's not right for a girl to run faster than a boy. You're a freak, Lucy Stone.

Lucy (*shrugging*). I'd rather be a freak than a bad loser.

Aunt Sally. Here now, you two. Stop your quarreling.

Luther (*complaining*). I'm going to soak my poor sore toe. It's all swollen. I'll never race with you again, Lucy.

---

1. **before rise:** before the curtain rises.
2. **settle:** a long wooden bench with a high back.
3. **at rise:** as the curtain rises.

Lucy (*laughing*). Well, don't, then. Go race with the other slowpokes—the *boys.* (Luther *scowls and limps off left.*)

Aunt Sally (*shaking her head*). Lucy, Lucy. What's to become of you? Look at you, all tousled like a dog caught in the brambles.

Lucy (*tossing her head*). I like being tousled, Aunt Sally. It makes me feel alive—not like a wax dummy of a girl in a frilly dress.

Aunt Sally. I've been meaning to speak to you. You're sixteen years old, no longer a child. Young men'll be looking you over soon, for marriage.

Lucy (*defiantly*). Looking me over? You mean like a prize cow? (*opens her mouth wide*) Checking to see if my teeth are good, and if I'm strong enough to work the fields?

Aunt Sally (*briskly*). Don't be pert[4] with me, young lady. You've got to start thinking about marriage. It's the only way for a woman.

Lucy (*sharply*). Well, it's not the way for *this* woman. I've seen the mean way men treat their wives around here. They work them until they're ready to drop, and then complain that they aren't young and pretty anymore. Why, if a man did that to his hired hand, he'd be brought up on charges.

Aunt Sally (*sighing*). That's the way of the world. You can't change it.

Lucy. I can change it for me. (*tossing her head*) I just won't marry.

Aunt Sally (*firmly*). Oh, yes, you will. You don't want to end up an old maid, like me. A left-over person of no use to anyone. (Lucy *runs to her.*)

Lucy (*hugging her*). Aunt Sally, don't say that! You're not a left-over person. Why, I don't know what we'd do without you. You have character!

Aunt Sally (***bemused***). Where do you get your notions, child? I declare there's not another like you in the state of Massachusetts. All that fire and spunk is wasted on a girl. What a pity you weren't a boy!

Lucy (*defiantly*). I like being a girl. I wouldn't be a boy for all the tea in China.

Aunt Sally (*sighing*). Be that as it may— (*She rises, crosses to window, and peers out.*) The sun's going down. You'd best fill the lamp. Your father wants everyone gathered here at sundown. He has something to tell us. (*shivering*) It's a bit cold. I'll get my shawl. (*She exits left.* Lucy *takes metal oil can from behind settle, fills the lamp on table, and lights it.* Bowman *enters left, carrying a Bible. He approaches* Lucy *hesitantly.*)

Bowman. Lucy?

Lucy (*looking up*). Yes, Bowman? (*spying Bible*) Ah—you want a little help with your Bible lesson again?

Bowman. I'd be obliged, Lucy. I'm to read the lesson this Sunday and I don't want to make a fool of myself. You're the only one in the family who can help me. Pa's too busy, and Ma doesn't know much.

Lucy (*hotly*). Ma knows a good deal, Bowman, even if it's not from books. If you had to work from sunup to sundown and raise children to boot, you wouldn't have much time for book learning either.

Bowman (*taken aback*). I suppose not. I never thought about it. (*opens Bible and indicates place*) I've tried to read these words, but I stumble on them.

Lucy (*reading clearly*). "Then came the daughters of Zelophehad, the son of Hepher, the son of Gilead, the son of Machir, the son of Manasseh, of the families of Manasseh the son

4. **pert:** too bold in speech or action.

of Joseph; and these are the names of his daughters: Mahlah, Noah, and Hoglah, and Milcah, and Tirzah." There. That's not so hard, is it?

Bowman (*admiringly*). You read that every bit as well as Reverend Blagdon. You'd make a mighty fine preacher—if only you were a boy.

Lucy (*angrily*). I could do a thousand wonderful things, if only I were a boy. Why shouldn't I go to school, learn a profession—even preach, if I want to? Answer me that, Bowman!

Bowman (*backing away, alarmed*). Don't take it out on me, Lucy. I didn't make the world the way it is.

(Hannah Stone *enters left, carrying a handbell.*)

Hannah. Oh, there you are, Bowman. Will you please go out to the barn and ring the bell to call the other children? Your father has something to tell everyone. And Bowman—tell them to hurry. You know how your father hates to be kept waiting. (*She hands the bell to* Bowman.)

Bowman. I'll make them hustle, Ma. Don't worry. (*He exits right.*)

Hannah (*to Lucy*). Thank you for lighting the lamp, Lucy dear. (*offstage sound of bell ringing*)

Lucy (*thoughtfully*). Mama—I've been thinking . . .

Hannah (*sighing*). Oh, Lucy. I wish you wouldn't. . . . Every time you think, it means trouble.

Lucy (*insistently*). But that's just it, Mama. I must think. My mind won't let me stop. Here on the farm I feel as if I'm starving. (*firmly*) Mama—is it true that a woman must submit to her husband in all things? (*pause, then dreamily*) If I could only go to college, I could study Greek and Latin and decide for myself.

Hannah (***aghast***). Oh, Lucy! What a notion. Your father would never hear of it.

Lucy. But what if I approached him in a calm, logical manner? I would say, "Father, you must be aware that I am the equal of any of the boys in this family. Do you not conclude that I am worthy of an education?" (Hannah, *shaking her head, puts her arm around* Lucy's *shoulder.*)

Hannah (*gently*). When you were first born, I looked at your sweet face, so like a flower, and I wept. Yes, I wept because you were a girl, and a woman's life is so hard. Why must you make it even harder by defying the way things are?

Lucy. Because all around me I see bright women with fine minds reduced to a kind of slavery. (*fiercely*) It isn't right, Mama! It just isn't fair!

Hannah (*reasoning with her*). But my dear child, it isn't your burden. It isn't up to you to turn the world upside down.

Lucy (*strongly*). But somebody must. Why shouldn't I be the one? (Bowman *enters, followed by* Eliza, Rhoda, Luther, *and* Sarah. *They ad lib boisterously.*)[5]

Bowman. Here they are, Ma. (*smiling*) They were frisky as spring lambs, but I brought them into the fold. (*The girls and* Lucy *sit on settle right; the boys sit on chairs at table left.* Hannah *sits on settle upstage.* Aunt Sally *enters, adjusting her shawl.*)

Aunt Sally (*anxiously*). Am I late?

Hannah. Not at all, Sally.

Eliza. What do you reckon Papa wants to tell us?

Luther (*sourly*). He's probably got a complaint about how we did the haying.

Rhoda (*teasingly*). Well, Luther, you did lean on your pitchfork more than usual.

Bowman. Seemed to me, Papa was almost happy when I saw him in the field. He nearly smiled at me.

---

5. **ad lib boisterously:** make up dialogue on the spot, in a loud manner.

Detail of *A Musical Evening* (19th century), Thomas Webster. Oil on canvas, 50.5 cm × 60.5 cm. Private collection. © Phillips, The International Fine Art Auctioneers/Bridgeman Art Library.

Sarah (*in mock surprise*). Pa nearly smiled? Sakes alive. The world is coming to an end! (*All laugh uproariously.*)

Hannah. Hush, children. (*looks off left*) Here comes your father, now. (*Laughter stops abruptly. Children rise, as* Francis Stone, *a stern* ***patriarch,*** *enters left, crosses to stand in front of the upstage settle. Girls curtsey, boys bow and are seated.*)

Francis (*clearing his throat*). I'm a man of few words, and I'll not make a book of the matter at hand. This concerns Bowman and Luther—and the rest of you as well.

Bowman and Luther (*exchanging worried looks*). Us?

Francis. It seems that Bowman and Luther have high ambitions. They want to go to college. (*All buzz with excitement.* Francis *holds up his hand for silence.*) I have taken the matter under consideration. (*pauses*) They may go, even though it means you girls will have to double up on the work. I expect we can do without the boys while they get their education.

(*Girls groan.* Francis *looks at them sharply.*)

Bowman (*excitedly*). Thank you, Papa, thank you.

Luther (*happily*). That is mighty good news, Papa. Will you pay for the books, too?

Francis. I reckon so. It's worth the expense to have educated men in the family.

Aunt Sally (*aside*). Humph. Educated "men," is it?

Lucy (*rising*). Papa! (Hannah *tries to hush her.*)

Francis (*impatiently*). Not now, Lucy. Whatever it is can wait. It's time for you to do the evening chores, now.

Lucy (*persistently*). But, Papa—(Francis *waves her aside.*)

Hannah (*nervously*). Come along, children. There are things for us to do. Lucy, dear. Do come with me. (Lucy *shakes her head. All exit left, except* Lucy, *who faces her father with determination.*)

Francis (*sternly*). Well, Lucy? What is it?

Lucy. Papa, I will do the evening chores. But the matter I wish to discuss cannot wait.

Francis (*annoyed*). I declare, girl, you are like a burr under my hide. Very well, speak up.

Lucy (*taking a deep breath*). Papa, you hate waste, don't you?

Francis (***piously***). Waste not, want not. That is what I always say.

Lucy. Well, if there were someone in this family brighter by far than Bowman and Luther, wouldn't it be a waste for that person not to go to college?

Francis (*briskly*). Yes, but there is no such person. What is your point?

Lucy (*firmly*). But there *is* such a person . . . Me!

Francis (*astonished*). You?

Lucy. If you'd paid attention, Papa, you'd know that I learn faster, read better, and think more clearly than the boys. (*pleading*) Oh, Papa. I want to go to college so much. There's a college in Ohio, called Oberlin, that will admit women. Please, Papa, please let me go there!

Francis (*furiously*). Are you daft?[6] You want me to **squander** my money on a girl? Why, the minute you get yourself a husband—if ever a flibbertigibbet[7] like you could get one—you'll turn your back on your so-called education and where will I be? Shortchanged by a mere female.

Lucy (*firmly*). No, Papa. I would never do such a thing.

Francis (*angrily*). I will not spend a penny to educate a girl. It's unnatural. I'd be a laughingstock. Go now—do your chores. (*He starts to exit down left.* Lucy *buries her face in her hands, then takes a deep breath and speaks with calm determination.*)

Lucy. Papa—I have a proposition for you.

Francis (*turning back*). Have you, now? And what sort of proposition could *you* possibly have?

Lucy. Don't the banks lend money upon a note for security? If I were to give *you* a note stating that I would pay you back every penny for my education, would you lend me the money?

Francis (*in disbelief*). Lend you money? And how, pray tell, would you ever pay me back?

Lucy. I could teach the lower grades.

Francis (*scornfully*). At a dollar a week, it would take you years to repay me.

Lucy (*defiantly*). If it takes me till I'm ninety—so be it. I will repay you every cent.

Francis (*impatiently*). You are the most pestiferous[8] girl ever born. You never let a man be. It would be worth my while to give you a loan just to get you from this house. (*thinks for a moment.*) Very well. You'll get your tuition and not a penny more. Nothing for books, nor for food, nor for any of your female fripperies.[9] I'll draw up the note in the morning.

Lucy (*with deliberate irony*). Thank you, Papa. It is more than generous of you.

Francis. Go do your chores. And blow out the lamp. I'll not have oil wasted in this house. (*He stalks off left.*)

Lucy (*crossing to table, aside*). I'll teach every minute the sun shines. I'll rise at five and gather nuts and berries to sell for my books. I'll work till midnight sewing and mending. I'll work and study until my eyes grow dim. (*drawing lamp close*) I'll snuff this flame,

---

6. **daft:** crazy.
7. **flibbertigibbet** (flĭb'ər-tē-jĭb'ĭt): a silly, scatterbrained person.
8. **pestiferous** (pĕ-stĭf'ər-əs): troublesome.
9. **fripperies** (frĭp'ə-rēz): showy clothes.

Papa. But inside my mind there is a flame glowing more radiant by the hour. And that flame, Papa, I promise you, will *never* go out! (*She blows out lamp, and as stage darkens, spotlight shines on* Lucy, *who faces audience with a triumphant smile.* Two Women *enter.*)

1st Woman. Lucy Stone kept her promise and more. She graduated from Oberlin College and was the first woman in the state of Massachusetts to earn a college degree.

2nd Woman. She sounded a trumpet call for the women's rights movement, lecturing to all who would hear her.

1st Woman. She founded her own paper, the *Woman's Journal,* in Boston, and called for the First National Woman's Rights Convention in 1850. (Henry Brown Blackwell *enters, bows.*)

Henry. And she was the first married woman to keep her own name. Oh, yes. Despite Aunt Sally's fears, Lucy was married. For there were men in those days who appreciated such a rare and beautiful spirit, men who wanted their wives to be equal partners in every way. I know, because I am the man who married Lucy Stone—Henry Brown Blackwell. (*He crosses to* Lucy *and takes her arm.* Two Women *cross to stand beside* Lucy *and* Henry. *Other female cast members enter and join them.*)

1st Woman. And now, because of Lucy Stone and others inspired by her example, the Nineteenth Amendment to the Constitution of the United States of America, passed by Congress in 1919, declares . . .

All (*together*). "The rights of citizens of the United States to vote shall not be denied or abridged by the United States or by any state on account of sex."

2nd Woman. And the words of Thomas Jefferson in the Declaration of Independence now include the other half of the human race.

All (*together*). "We hold these truths to be self-evident . . .

Henry. That all men—

All Women. And women—

All. Are created equal, that they are endowed by their Creator with certain unalienable rights;[10] that among these are life, liberty—

Lucy (*proudly*). And the pursuit of happiness!"

(*curtain*)

Lucy Stone, about 1875

10. **endowed . . . rights:** given, by God, certain rights that cannot be taken away.

Comprehension

ALABAMA STANDARDS

READING STANDARD
3 Distinguish among genres based on characteristics

1. **Clarify** Why does Lucy say that she will never marry?
2. **Recall** What deal does Lucy make with her father?
3. **Summarize** What did Lucy go on to do after she finished college? In your own words, summarize her accomplishments.

Literary Analysis

4. **Visualize** Look over the sketches you made as you read. Which were you able to visualize more clearly, the play's characters or its setting? Which words and phrases helped you to form such a vivid mental picture?
5. **Draw Conclusions** Reread lines 181–183. In light of how women were treated in the early 1800s, what does Lucy mean when she says that women were "reduced to a kind of slavery"?
6. **Compare Characters** How does each member of Lucy's family respond to her? Create a spider map like the one shown to explore how each character reacts to Lucy's confidence, strength, and intelligence.

7. **Analyze Historical Drama** Historical drama is usually a mix of fact and fiction. Facts can be confirmed by a reliable source, such as an encyclopedia. Find one example of factual information in the play and one example of a conversation or situation that was probably created by the playwright.
8. **Evaluate** Several characters in the play state that it is better to be a boy than a girl. How does that thinking affect Lucy's mother and aunt? How does it affect Lucy?

Extension and Challenge

9. **Creative Project: Drama** Lucy discusses the role of girls and women with various people in this play. Work with a partner to choose one of these conversations and act it out for the class.
10. **SOCIAL STUDIES CONNECTION** Lucy Stone founded the American Woman Suffrage Association (AWSA). Research AWSA's history. What **change** was it fighting for? Did it succeed? Share your findings with the class.

RESEARCH LINKS
For more on AWSA, visit the **Research Center** at **ClassZone.com.**

SKILLS PRACTICE

Reading-Writing Connection

Demonstrate your understanding of *Lucy Stone: Champion of Women's Rights* by responding to these prompts. Then complete the **Grammar and Writing** exercise.

WRITING PROMPTS	SELF-CHECK
A. Short Response: Analyze Issues If Lucy Stone were alive today, which national or world issues might concern her? In **one paragraph,** describe one or two current problems Stone might work to **change.**	***An effective analysis will . . .*** • identify a problem Stone might fight to solve • use examples from the play to explain why the issues would bother Stone
B. Extended Response: Write a Letter Write a **two- or three-paragraph letter** to Lucy Stone, updating her on the progress the women's rights movement has made. Make sure to clearly describe how things are different for American women today.	***A strong letter will . . .*** • address Stone directly and clearly explain your purpose • tell the rights women have and give details of what has changed

GRAMMAR AND WRITING

PUNCTUATE TITLES CORRECTLY The punctuation you use in titles shows what kind of work you are writing about. Use **quotation marks** to set off the titles of shorter works, such as short stories, tall tales, essays, articles, and poems. Use **italics** (or underlining) for titles of longer works, such as books, plays, magazines, newspapers, movies, and TV series.

Original: The poem Jabberwocky is my favorite.

Revised: The poem "Jabberwocky" is my favorite.

PRACTICE Correctly punctuate the titles in the following sentences.

1. Little Women is an example of a book with strong women characters.
2. Mary Pope Osborne's tall tale Sally Ann Thunder Ann Whirlwind also features a strong woman.
3. Newspapers, such as the Chicago Tribune, often devote whole sections to news about women.
4. Oprah Winfrey, who hosts The Oprah Winfrey Show, is one of the wealthiest entertainers in the world.

For more help with punctuating titles, see page R50 in the ***Grammar Handbook.***

ALABAMA STANDARDS

WRITING/LANGUAGE STANDARD
10.a Punctuating titles correctly

My Mother Enters the Work Force

Poem by Rita Dove

Washington Monument by Night

Poem by Carl Sandburg

Why should you keep TRYING?

ALABAMA STANDARDS

READING STANDARDS

1.d Applying self-monitoring strategies

2 Relate literary elements and devices to each other

KEY IDEA Heroes are not necessarily people who are perfect or who never fail. Often they are the people who keep trying until they are successful. This quality is called **perseverance,** and the people in the poems you're about to read share it. Their successes can show us the value of trying over and over again.

WEB IT Create an **idea web** that shows some people you consider heroes. Expand the web by adding the challenges they have faced and the successes they have achieved.

LITERARY ANALYSIS: SPEAKER

The **speaker** of a poem is the voice who "talks" to the reader through the poem's words. The speaker and the poet aren't necessarily the same person.

You might think of the speaker as a character in a very short play. The speaker walks onto a dark stage, says his or her lines (the poem), and exits. There are no props, scenery, or lighting. The speaker's words provide everything you need to know about the feelings, ideas, and experiences he or she is sharing. As you read "My Mother Enters the Work Force" and "Washington Monument by Night," watch for clues that tell you who the speaker is and what he or she thinks of the subject of the poem.

READING STRATEGY: UNDERSTAND FIGURATIVE LANGUAGE

Poems often use **figurative language,** or words that mean something other than their "real" meaning. For example, in "Washington Monument by Night," Sandburg describes the monument this way:

A lean swimmer dives into night sky,

Sandburg does not really mean a person is leaping into the sky. Instead, he's using words in an imaginative way. The words create a dramatic effect and emphasize how the monument soars above everything else.

If you restate figurative language in your own words, or **paraphrase** it, you can often better understand a poem's main ideas. As you read each poem, keep a chart of the figurative language in the poem and your paraphrases.

Figurative Language	Paraphrase
Lines 1–3: "The path to ABC Business School / was paid for by a lucky sign: / ALTERATIONS, QUALIFIED SEAMSTRESS INQUIRE WITHIN."	The mother just happened to see a sign for a job that gave her money to go to business school.

Author Online

Rita Dove: People's Poet Rita Dove served as poet laureate, or the representative poet, of the United States from 1993 to 1995. Her poems reflect experiences of the many whose stories haven't always been heard.

Rita Dove
born 1952

Carl Sandburg: People's Voice Carl Sandburg, recognized as a poet to use the language of the people, honored both the great heroes of U.S. history and the everyday heroes who make the country work.

Carl Sandburg
1878–1967

MORE ABOUT THE AUTHOR
For more on these poets, visit the **Literature Center** at **ClassZone.com.**

Background

An Eight-Year Conflict One of the poems you are about to read refers to the Revolutionary War, which lasted from 1775 to 1783. A low point for the American troops occurred during the winter of 1777 and 1778. Led by General George Washington, the ragtag soldiers camped out at Valley Forge, Pennsylvania. They had little food or warm clothing, and disease was widespread.

MY MOTHER **ENTERS** THE
WORK FORCE

RITA DOVE

The path to ABC Business School
was paid for by a lucky sign:
ALTERATIONS, QUALIFIED SEAMSTRESS INQUIRE WITHIN.
Tested on sleeves, hers
never puckered—puffed or sleek,
leg-o'-mutton or raglan—[1]
they barely needed the damp cloth
to steam them perfect. **A**

Those were the afternoons. Evenings
she took in piecework,[2] the treadle machine
with its locomotive whir
traveling the lit path of the needle
through quicksand taffeta
or velvet deep as a forest.
And now and now sang the treadle,
I know, I know. . . . **B**

And then it was day again, all morning
at the office machines, their clack and chatter
another journey—rougher,
that would go on forever
until she could break a hundred words
with no errors—ah, and then

no more postponed groceries,
and that blue pair of shoes!

A SPEAKER
The title of the poem gives a good clue about the speaker. Who is "telling" this poem?

B UNDERSTAND FIGURATIVE LANGUAGE
In your own words, restate what the speaker is describing in lines 9–16.

ANALYZE VISUALS
How does the woman in this painting **compare** with your mental image of the mother in the poem?

---

1. **leg-o'-mutton or raglan:** types of sleeves. A leg-of-mutton sleeve is wide at the top and narrow at the bottom. A raglan sleeve is cut so that it continues up to the collar.
2. **piecework:** work paid for according to the amount done, not the time it takes.

Alma Sewing (about 1935), Francis Criss. Oil on canvas, 33″ × 45″. High Museum of Art, Atlanta, Georgia.

Francis Criss

WASHINGTON MONUMENT BY NIGHT

CARL SANDBURG

1
The stone goes straight.
A lean swimmer dives into night sky,
Into half-moon mist.

2
Two trees are coal black.
This is a great white ghost between.
It is cool to look at.
Strong men, strong women, come here. **C**

3
Eight years is a long time
To be fighting all the time.

4
The republic is a dream.
Nothing happens unless first a dream.

5
The wind bit hard at Valley Forge one Christmas.
Soldiers tied rags on their feet.
Red footprints wrote on the snow . . .
. . . and stone shoots into stars here
. . . into half-moon mist tonight.

6
Tongues wrangled dark at a man.
He buttoned his overcoat and stood alone.
In a snowstorm, red hollyberries, thoughts,
he stood alone.

7
Women said: He is lonely
. . . fighting . . . fighting . . . eight years . . .

8
The name of an iron man goes over the world.
It takes a long time to forget an iron man. **D**

9
. . . .
. . . .

C UNDERSTAND FIGURATIVE LANGUAGE
In your chart, tell what surrounds the monument and what color the monument is.

D SPEAKER
Is the speaker someone who lived during Washington's time or someone who lives in the present time of the poem? Tell how you know.

Comprehension

ALABAMA STANDARDS

READING STANDARD
2 Relate literary elements and devices to each other

1. **Recall** How does the mother in "My Mother Enters the Work Force" pay for business school?
2. **Clarify** How does the mother's life change in lines 21–24 of "My Mother Enters the Work Force"?
3. **Clarify** Who is the "man" in stanzas 6, 7, and 8 in "Washington Monument by Night"?

Literary Analysis

4. **Understand Figurative Language** Compare the paraphrases you wrote with those of a partner. How are your paraphrases similar or different?
5. **Analyze Speaker** What is the speaker's opinion of her mother in "My Mother Enters the Work Force"? Support your answer with words and phrases from the poem.
6. **Interpret** What does the last stanza in "Washington Monument by Night" suggest about the "iron man"?
7. **Compare and Contrast Character** Both the mother in "My Mother Enters the Work Force" and the man in "Washington Monument by Night" **persevered** in the face of huge obstacles. What other similarities do they share? What are their differences? Use a Venn diagram like the one shown to compare and contrast the two people.

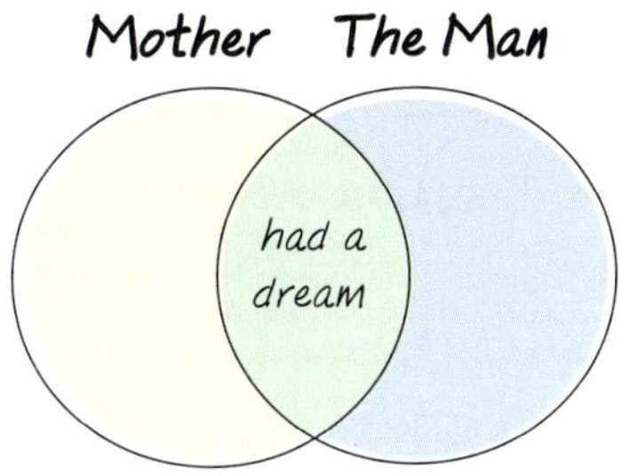

8. **Evaluate Figurative Language** Is line 5 of "Washington Monument by Night" a good description of the Washington Monument? Refer to evidence in the poem and to the photograph on page 848 to support your opinion.

Extension and Challenge

9. **Big Question Activity** Review the Big Question on page 844 and the idea web that you made as part of the **Web It** activity. Write a journal entry that explains how you think each hero in your web would answer the Big Question. Then write a response for the mother in "My Mother Enters the Work Force" and the man in "Washington Monument by Night."
10. **Creative Project: Art** Carl Sandburg's poem describes a monument to the man in the poem. Now sketch a monument in honor of the speaker's mother in "My Mother Enters the Work Force." List the materials you would use to make the monument. In a short dedication speech, explain your reasons for the monument's design, why you chose the colors you did, and how the materials reflect the mother's personality.

Writing Workshop

Personal Narrative

Although few people have a life story like Jackie Robinson's or Eleanor Roosevelt's, every life is filled with stories to share. You have them too, and chances are you tell them every day, informally or in bits and pieces. Follow the **Writer's Road Map** to learn how to turn these stories into personal narratives.

WRITER'S ROAD MAP

Personal Narrative

WRITING PROMPT 1

Writing from Your Life Write a narrative that describes a special event in your life. Include details that help your reader understand what the event was like. Be sure to explain why the event was important to you.

Events to Consider

- your first day in a new place
- going to a different school or to camp
- winning a game or learning a skill

WRITING PROMPT 2

Writing from Literature Choose a literary work that reminded you of an event in your life. Write a narrative that identifies the title and author of the work and describes the similar event that you experienced. Explain why the event was important to you.

Events and Literary Works to Consider

- a time when you felt different or out of place ("Names/Nombres")
- an accomplishment by a family member ("My Mother Enters the Work Force")

WRITING TOOLS

For prewriting, revision, and editing tools, visit the **Writing Center** at **ClassZone.com.**

KEY TRAITS

1. *IDEAS*

- Focuses on a **single experience**
- Re-creates the event with **descriptive details** and **dialogue**

2. *ORGANIZATION*

- Gets the reader's attention with an interesting **introduction**
- Makes the **order of events** clear by using transitional words and phrases
- Concludes by summarizing the **significance** of the event

3. *VOICE*

- Uses the **active voice**

4. *WORD CHOICE*

- Brings the event alive for the reader by using **sensory language**

5. *SENTENCE FLUENCY*

- Uses a variety of **sentence types** (statements, questions, commands, and exclamations)

6. *CONVENTIONS*

- Uses **correct grammar, spelling, and punctuation**

Part 1: Analyze a Student Model

WRITING/LANGUAGE STANDARD
9 Compose in narrative mode

Online INTERACTIVE MODEL CLASSZONE.COM

Michelle Gruneisen
St. Columban School

The Secret Kitten

"So how exactly are we going to do this?" I asked.

My friend Amy and I were sitting in the front room of her house, bored stiff. It was a hot summer day, and Amy's bellyaching about giving up her cute, cuddly, purring kittens had gotten her wheels turning.

"I don't know how," said Amy, "but we have to hide at least one kitten."

Amy's parents had decided to give her last two of the original five kittens away, claiming that Amy already had two cats and that was enough. Amy, however, was determined to keep at least one.

"I know! How about underground?" I suggested playfully.

"No!" she replied passionately. "Cave-ins would be bad! What about in my shed?"

"Amy, dear, sharp objects and kittens don't mix," I shot back.

"Okay," she said meekly. "How about in my closet?"

"Now that's an idea!" I said with enthusiasm.

Straightaway, we went to work. We cleared out old toys and games and made room for the litter box and food dishes. Next, we made sure that every shelf was stable, and we made a soft bed for the kitten. We even spread out Amy's clothes to muffle any sound the kitten emitted. In addition, we made a schedule to exercise and groom the kitten. We cleaned off the rust from the screen latch and oiled the window crank, making it easy to get the kitten from Amy's room to Amy's yard without being noticed.

KEY TRAITS IN ACTION

Introduction grabs the reader's attention by introducing characters and including **descriptive details.**

Uses realistic **dialogue** and a variety of **sentence types.**

Focuses on a **single experience** (trying to hide the kitten).

By the following week, all that was left to do was choose the kitten. Amy decided on a female kitten with white paws, smoky black and gray fur, and eyes like deep pools of crystal-clear water. It was that same day that her parents made the announcement.

Order of events is clear. **Sensory language** helps the reader imagine the kitten.

I was over at her house in the front room; we were plotting about our secret kitten when her parents came in. Her mom had an expression of suppressed joy, and her dad looked quite proud of himself.

"Well, Amy," her mom started. "We've made a decision."

Had they found out about our plan? Did they find homes for both kittens already? So many thoughts raced through my head. It seemed as though the moment would never end.

Uses the **active voice.** Dramatic questions help make the narrative suspenseful.

Her dad continued, "We've decided that you may keep one more kitten!"

Amy and I looked at each other in wonderment. Amy was happy, sad, and frustrated all at once. Somehow she managed a smile. I felt like crying and laughing at once.

We had done all that work and planning for nothing, but Amy got what she wanted. Looking back, I realize that our plan never would have worked, but it would have been fun trying!

Concludes with a reflection on the event's **significance**.

2

WRITING/LANGUAGE STANDARD
9.a Using transitional words and phrases

Part 2: Apply the Writing Process

PREWRITING

What Should I Do? | **What Does It Look Like?**

1. Analyze the prompt.
Read the prompt carefully. Circle the word that names the type of writing you must produce. Underline words and phrases that tell what you must include.

WRITING PROMPT Write a narrative that describes a special event in your life. Include details that help your reader understand what the event was like. Be sure to explain why the event was important to you.

2. Think of an event to share.
This writing has to come from your own past, so make a list of memory triggers: people, places, times, and events that might bring back the stories of your life.

Memory Triggers	Specific Memory
summers at Camp Far Winds	learning to swim
my best friend, Amy	our secret kitten
baseball teams	my grand slam
our family pets	when Muffin ran away

3. Consider your audience and purpose.
Make a chart to show who you think will read your narrative, what your purpose for writing is (stated in the prompt), and what the event meant to you.

TIP Is the event you chose too personal to share with your teacher or classmates? Choose a new event from the list you generated in Step 2.

Audience	Purpose	Significance
classmates, teacher	describe a special event	seemed so important at the time, but didn't matter in the end

4. Use your descriptive powers.
Use descriptive words and phrases to help your reader understand important parts of your narrative.

DRAFTING

What Should I Do?	What Does It Look Like?
1. Plan your narrative. An engaging personal narrative often has many of the same elements as a terrific short story, such as plot, characters, dialogue, and suspense. To make sure that your narrative is well organized, make a story map. Be sure it includes your characters and the setting. Be sure, too, that you have a clear sequence of events. Most narratives are told in **chronological order,** also called time order. If you want, you can work in a **flashback** (an event that took place before the start of the story). **See page 26:** Plot at a Glance	***Title:*** *The Secret Kitten* ***Setting:*** *Amy's house* ***Characters:*** *Amy, her parents, me* ***Plot Summary:*** *Amy and I make plans to hide a kitten, and then her parents give her the kitten after all.* ***Sequence of Events:*** *1. We decide to hide one kitten in the closet.* *2. We clean and prepare.* *3. We decide which kitten to keep.* *4. Amy's parents announce she can have one more kitten.* ***Significance:*** *We couldn't believe that we had done all that for nothing!*
2. Set the scene in your introduction. Use your introduction to tell basic information, such as who, where, and when. Every reader requires a little background, but not every story has to give the same kind of background. Here the writer vividly relates how Amy came up with the idea of the secret kitten.	From prewriting notes . . . *My friend Amy got an idea.* . . . to draft *My friend Amy and I were sitting in the front room of her house, bored stiff. It was a hot summer day, and Amy's bellyaching about giving up her cute, cuddly, purring kittens had gotten her wheels turning.*
3. Tell who said what to whom. Be sure to include dialogue to make your characters sound like real people taking part in real events. **TIP Before revising, look back at the key traits on page 850 and at the rubric and peer-reader questions on page 856.**	From prewriting notes . . . *We talked over places to keep the kitten.* . . . to draft *"I know! How about underground?" I suggested playfully.* *"No!" she replied passionately. "Cave-ins would be bad! What about in my shed?"*

REVISING AND EDITING

What Should I Do?	What Does It Look Like?
1. Make sure the sequence is clear. • Ask a peer reader to underline parts of your narrative that are out of order or that do not lead clearly from one step to the next. • Add transitions, move text, or revise the narrative to make the sequence clear. **See page 856:** Ask a Peer Reader	*Her mom had an expression of suppressed joy.* *I was over at her house in the front room; we were plotting about our secret kitten when* *Her parents came in.*
2. Add sensory language or other descriptive details. • Circle words that tell how something looked, sounded, felt, tasted, or smelled. • If you have few or no circles, revise to make your response more detailed.	*Amy decided on ~~the~~ a female kitten ~~she wanted~~. with white paws, smoky black and gray fur, and eyes like deep pools of crystal-clear water.*
3. Use the active voice. • Draw a box around sentences in the passive voice (*The kitten was hidden by us*). • Change inappropriate uses of the passive voice to the active voice (*We hid the kitten*).	*We cleared out* *Old toys and games ~~got cleared out~~.* *We made* *A schedule to exercise and groom the kitten ~~was made~~.* *Had they found out about our plan?* *~~Had our plan been found out about by them?~~*
4. Reflect on the experience. • [Bracket] parts of your narrative that tell what you learned from the experience, why you chose it, or even why—as the writer of the student model concluded—it seemed more important than it really was. • Be sure that your narrative explains what the experience meant to you.	*We had done all that work and planning for nothing, but [Amy got what she wanted.] Looking back, I realize that our plan never would have worked, but it would have been fun trying!*

Preparing to Publish

Personal Narrative

Apply the Rubric

A strong personal narrative . . .

- ☑ captures the reader's attention with an interesting introduction
- ☑ focuses on a single experience
- ☑ makes the order of events clear by using transitional words and phrases
- ☑ re-creates the event with dialogue, sensory language, and descriptive details
- ☑ uses the active voice
- ☑ uses a variety of sentence types (statements, questions, commands, and exclamations)
- ☑ concludes by reflecting on the significance of the experience

Ask a Peer Reader

- What kinds of descriptive details or dialogue should I add?
- What could I do to make the sequence clearer?
- Where in my conclusion do I reflect on why the experience is important to me?

Check Your Grammar

- When you write dialogue, enclose each speaker's exact words in quotation marks. Begin a new paragraph each time the speaker changes.

> *"Amy, dear, sharp objects and kittens don't mix," I shot back.*
>
> *"Okay," she said meekly. "How about in my closet?"*

- Use a comma to separate a speaker's words from a description of who is speaking. If the speaker's words end with a question mark or an exclamation point, no comma is needed.

> *"Well, Amy," her mom started.*
>
> *"Now that's an idea!" I said.*

See pages R49–R50: Quick Reference: Punctuation

- Use the same verb tense to show two or more actions that occur at the same time.

> *We cleared out old toys and ~~make~~ made room for the litter box and food dishes.*

See page R56: Verb Tense

Writing Online

PUBLISHING OPTIONS

For publishing options, visit the **Writing Center** at **ClassZone.com.**

ASSESSMENT PREPARATION

For writing and grammar assessment practice, go to the **Assessment Center** at **ClassZone.com.**

SPEAKING AND LISTENING

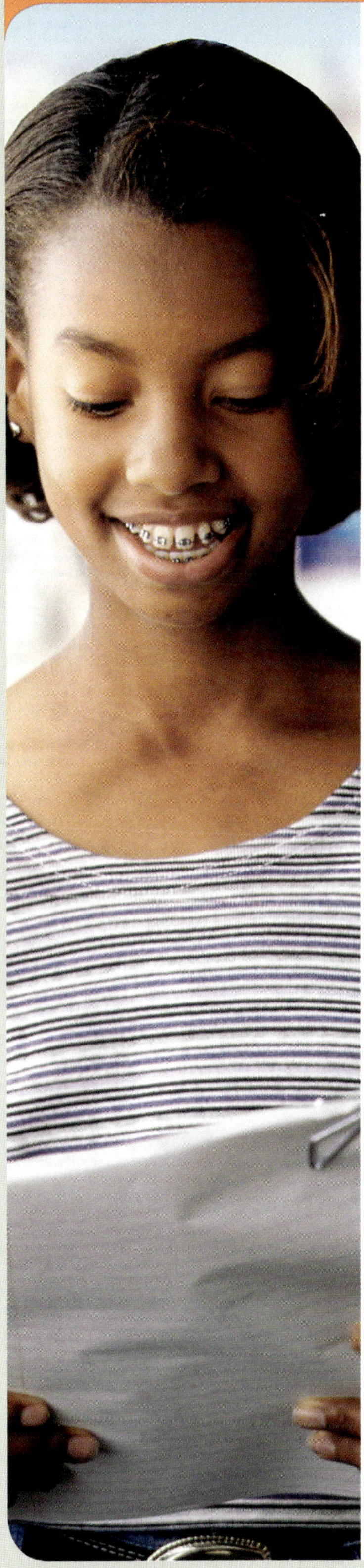

Presenting an Anecdote

In this unit, you've read some big stories about fascinating lives. Now it's your turn to tell a little story, or anecdote, from your own life.

Preparing the Anecdote

1. **Choose part of your narrative to share.** Find the best part of your personal narrative—the part that's funniest, liveliest, most dramatic, or most surprising. Pull it out for shaping into an anecdote, which is a brief story that you might tell a friend.
2. **Add and subtract.** Decide what you need to add, such as humor or drama, to punch up your story for a face-to-face audience. Alternatively, you may want to shorten or tighten your story. Be sure that your anecdote clearly specifies the setting—where and when the event took place. Remember, your audience is listening, not reading. They can't slow down your pace or go back and reread.
3. **Consider your tone.** You might want to make formal language more conversational, long sentences shorter, or complicated descriptions simpler.
4. **Practice and refine.** Consider learning your anecdote by heart so that you don't have to rely on notes. Tell your anecdote to a friend or family member, and get feedback on how to improve your performance.

Presenting the Anecdote

1. **Act out the parts.** Create a different voice for each character. Consider changing stances, gestures, and facial expressions for each character.
2. **Watch your pacing.** You might pause once or twice to make your anecdote suspenseful. If possible, have a friend in the audience signal to let you know whether to speed things up or slow them down.
3. **Take a bow.** Don't just trail off at the end. Finish with confidence. Afterward, ask audience members whether any parts of your anecdote were unclear.

See page R80: Evaluate a Descriptive Speech

Assessment Practice

ASSESS

The practice test items on the next few pages match skills listed on the Unit Goals page (page 753) and addressed throughout this unit. Taking this practice test will help you assess your knowledge of these skills and determine your readiness for the Unit Test.

REVIEW

After you take the practice test, your teacher can help you identify any skills you need to review.

- Biography
- Chronological Order
- Make Inferences
- Summarize
- Latin Words and Roots
- Base Words
- Proper Nouns
- Italics and Quotation Marks

ASSESSMENT ONLINE

For more assessment practice and test-taking tips, go to the **Assessment Center** at **ClassZone.com.**

Reading Comprehension

DIRECTIONS *Read the following selection and then answer the questions.*

The world-famous pilot Amelia Earhart worked as a volunteer nurse in Toronto, Canada, during World War I. There, she developed her lifelong interest in flying.

from East to the Dawn: The Life of Amelia Earhart

Susan Butler

When Amelia had spare time, she headed for the stables, and it was through her riding that she got her first exposure to airplanes. She was riding a horse named Dynamite, whom she had "gentled" with a combination of horsemanship and apples, when she was joined by three air force officers. They were so impressed by how well she controlled her mount—famous for bucking off a colonel—that they asked her to go out to Armour Heights, an airfield at the edge of the city, to watch how they controlled their planes.

Amelia had seen planes before. She saw her first at a fair in Des Moines when she was ten, but "it was a thing of rusty wire and wood and looked not at all interesting." The chances are, it was the same first plane that Clarence Chamberlin, who also grew up to be a crack pilot, saw in his home town of Denison, Iowa, at about the same time—an old-style pusher, with the pilot sitting out front "on a sort of birdcage seat," and the propeller and engine in the rear. He too had been "frankly unimpressed . . . quite willing to let anyone take such fool chances who would."

But ten years had passed. These planes were a different generation; now they were beautiful: "They were full sized birds that slid on the hard-packed snow and rose into the air with an extra roar that echoed from the evergreens that banked the edge of the field." She stood close to them—so close that the propellers threw snow in her face, and "I felt a first urge to fly." She tried to get permission to go up, but failed—"not even a general's wife could do so—apparently the only thing she couldn't do." So she did "the next best thing" and got to know the fliers.

One day she had a chance to test her faith in planes, not by flying but by standing in the path of one. It was at a Toronto fair, and the pilots, war aces, were giving exhibitions of stunt flying. She and a girlfriend were standing in the middle of a clearing off by themselves in order to see better. The pilot began diving at the crowd. She would never forget what happened next.

"He was bored. He had looped and rolled and spun and finished his little bag of tricks, and there was nothing left to do but watch the people on the ground running as he swooped close to them." Then he started diving at the two girls off in the clearing. "I remember the mingled fear and pleasure which surged over me as I watched that small plane at the top of its earthward swoop. Common sense told me that if something went wrong with the mechanism, or if the pilot lost control, he, the airplane and I would be rolled up in a ball together. I did not understand it at the time but I believe that little red airplane said something to me as it swished by." Her friend ran off. Amelia didn't; she was fascinated.

GO ON

Comprehension

DIRECTIONS *Answer these questions about the excerpt from* East to the Dawn: The Life of Amelia Earhart.

1. Which statement is a clue that this is a biography and not an autobiography?
   - **A** The author reveals the thoughts and feelings of Amelia Earhart.
   - **B** The author uses the word *she* to refer to Amelia Earhart.
   - **C** The author reveals the thoughts and feelings of other people.
   - **D** The author includes dialogue throughout the excerpt.

2. Which statement best summarizes lines 1–8?
   - **A** Embarrassed that Earhart could tame a wild horse better than they could, three air force officers showed off their flying skills.
   - **B** Impressed with Earhart's ability to control a wild horse, three air force officers invited her to watch them fly.
   - **C** Earhart tamed a wild horse so that she might be invited to see the newest planes.
   - **D** Earhart was afraid of airplanes and decided to tame a wild horse to prove that she was brave.

3. Events in this excerpt are presented in
   - **A** random order
   - **B** mostly chronological order
   - **C** the order of their importance to Earhart
   - **D** the order in which the author learned about them

4. Which words or phrases in the excerpt help you understand the order in which events happen?
   - **A** spare time, first exposure, one day
   - **B** chances, different generation, next best thing
   - **C** stood close, in order to, also
   - **D** before, ten years had passed, what happened next

5. Which quotation from the excerpt gives you an important clue about Amelia Earhart's future?
   - **A** "She was riding a horse named Dynamite, whom she had 'gentled' with a combination of horsemanship and apples. . . ."
   - **B** "Amelia had seen planes before. She saw her first at a fair in Des Moines when she was ten. . . ."
   - **C** "She stood close to them—so close that the propellers threw snow in her face, and 'I felt a first urge to fly.'"
   - **D** "She and a girlfriend were standing in the middle of a clearing off by themselves in order to see better."

6. You learn about Amelia Earhart's thoughts and feelings in this excerpt mostly from
   - **A** direct quotations from her
   - **B** the author's opinions of her
   - **C** facts about her accomplishments
   - **D** quotations from people who knew her

ARMT/ADAW SKILLS PRACTICE

7. Which statement best summarizes lines 17–24?
   - **A** Ten years after she first fell in love with airplanes, Amelia Earhart saw the beautiful new airplanes and enjoyed the way they roared off the field.
   - **B** The latest airplanes were beautiful, large machines that roared when they took off, kicked up snow with the propellers, and slid on snow when they landed.
   - **C** Although she was fascinated with the latest airplanes, Amelia Earhart knew she could never fly them because even a general's wife could not get permission to fly.
   - **D** Amelia Earhart loved watching the beautiful new planes and wanted to fly; when she was unable to get permission to go up in them, she befriended the fliers instead.

8. Which statement best summarizes lines 31–40?
   - **A** The pilot was bored, so he started to do more tricks and scared the two young women in the field.
   - **B** The pilot lost control of the plane and it started to swoop down toward Earhart, who did not move.
   - **C** After the pilot had run out of stunts and started diving at people, he dove at the two girls; Earhart stood watching, spellbound, and her friend ran away.
   - **D** Earhart's friend ran away after the pilot of the stunt plane threatened the crowd at the fair, but Earhart froze in fear as the plane dove at her.

9. Which qualities can you infer Earhart has from her reaction to the diving plane?
   - **A** pride and defiance
   - **B** foolishness and immaturity
   - **C** level-headedness and reliability
   - **D** curiosity and courageousness

10. Which list presents the main events in this excerpt in chronological order?
   - **A** Earhart met air force pilots; she saw her first plane; she stood in the path of a diving plane.
   - **B** Earhart tamed a horse; she saw her first plane; she watched stunt flying.
   - **C** Earhart saw her first plane; she watched air force pilots; she stood in the path of a diving plane.
   - **D** Earhart tamed a horse; she went to a fair; she met war pilots.

Open-Ended

SHORT ANSWER *Write two or three sentences to answer this question.*

11. What can you infer about the biographer's opinion of Amelia Earhart?

ESSAY *Write a short paragraph to answer this question.*

12. What can you infer from Earhart's explanation in lines 38–40 that, "I did not understand it at the time but I believe that little red airplane said something to me as it swished by"?

GO ON

Vocabulary

DIRECTIONS *Use context clues and the definitions of the Latin words and roots to answer the following questions.*

1. The prefix *im-* means "into," and the Latin word *premere* means "to press." What is the most likely meaning of *impressed* as it is used in line 5?

A amazed

B influenced

C annoyed

D pressured

2. The Latin root *gen* means "to be produced." What is the most likely meaning of the word *generation* as it is used in line 17?

A a group of people born at about the same time

B new technology developed from earlier models

C a stage in the life cycle of an organism

D time between the birth of parents and the birth of their children

3. The Latin word *surgere* means "to rise." What is the most likely meaning of *surged* as it is used in line 35?

A marched in columns

B increased suddenly

C settled gradually

D flowed in waves

DIRECTIONS *Use your knowledge of base words to answer the following questions.*

4. The word *exposure* is used in line 2. What is the base word of *exposure?*

A espouse

B explode

C expound

D expose

5. The word *combination* is used in line 4. What is the base word of *combination?*

A combine

B combat

C combust

D comb

6. The word *permission* is used in line 22. What is the base word of *permission?*

A mission

B permeate

C permit

D permissive

7. The word *pleasure* is used in line 35. What is the base word of *pleasure?*

A please

B plausible

C plead

D play

ARMT/ADAW SKILLS PRACTICE

Writing & Grammar

DIRECTIONS *Read the passage and answer the questions that follow.*

(1) Throughout the years, women have excelled in the field of aviation. (2) In 1912, harriet quimby became the first woman to fly across the english channel. (3) Nine years later, Bessie Coleman became the world's first licensed African-American aviator. (4) In 1935, amelia earhart became the first person to fly solo across the Pacific ocean. (5) Women reached another milestone on june 17, 1983, when astronaut Sally Ride became the first U.S. woman in space. (6) The book At the Controls: Women in Aviation has more on this subject. (7) Also check Aviation History magazine for an article entitled Lady Lindy: The Remarkable Life of Amelia Earhart.

1. Which nouns should be capitalized in sentence 2?

A harriet, quimby

B harriet, quimby, woman

C english channel

D harriet, quimby, english channel

2. Which nouns should be capitalized in sentence 4?

A amelia, earhart, person

B amelia, earhart, ocean

C amelia

D person, ocean

3. Which noun should be capitalized in sentence 5?

A june

B woman

C astronaut

D space

4. Choose the correct way to punctuate the title in sentence 6.

A *At the Controls: Women in Aviation*

B "At the Controls: Women in Aviation"

C "At the Controls": *Women in Aviation*

D *"At the Controls: Women in Aviation"*

5. Choose the correct use of italics and quotation marks for the titles in sentence 7.

A *Aviation History* and *Lady Lindy: The Remarkable Life of Amelia Earhart*

B *Aviation History* and "Lady Lindy: The Remarkable Life of Amelia Earhart."

C "Aviation History" and "Lady Lindy: The Remarkable Life of Amelia Earhart"

D "Aviation History" and *Lady Lindy: The Remarkable Life of Amelia Earhart*

STOP

UNIT 7

More Great Reads

Ideas for Independent Reading

Which questions from Unit 7 made an impression on you? Continue exploring them with these books.

What is your duty toward others?

Lyddie
by Katherine Paterson
When her family loses their farm, 14-year-old Lyddie Worthen risks everything and takes a job in a Massachusetts mill. Under the worst possible working conditions, she succeeds in overcoming adversity through the strength of her character.

Across Five Aprils
by Irene Hunt
This historical novel centers on the divided loyalties of the Creightons during the Civil War. Jethro is left behind to run the family farm, but he is not spared the horrors of war as experienced from the home front.

The Greatest: Muhammad Ali
by Walter Dean Myers
This biography traces the life of boxer Muhammad Ali from his childhood through his present-day struggles with Parkinson's disease. Along the way, he fights racism, stands up for his beliefs, and becomes a hero to millions.

When is there dignity in silence?

Touching Spirit Bear
by Ben Mikaelsen
Families have rules, schools have rules, and societies have rules. Fifteen-year-old Cole Matthews has always had trouble with those rules. Can he change his destructive path while living alone on a remote island?

On the Way Home
by Laura Ingalls Wilder
Finding strength in writing, Laura Ingalls Wilder captures in her diary the landscapes, cultures, and people she encounters as her family travels from South Dakota to Missouri in the late 1800s.

Homeless Bird
by Gloria Whelan
What is it like to live in a society where how you are treated depends on your gender? In modern-day India, 13-year-old Koly must marry a 16-year-old boy from a distant village. When he dies, Koly is alone in an unfamiliar city.

How can we change what's wrong?

Beyond the Burning Time
by Kathryn Lasky
What would it take to make you stand alone? In a New England village during colonial times, 12-year-old Mary Chase must defend her mother against the community's accusations of witchcraft.

The Golden Compass
by Philip Pullman
Fairy tales and legends allow you to imagine yourself saving the world. In the first book of a trilogy, the adventurer Lyra holds the future of the world and all of its inhabitants in her hands.

Under the Blood-Red Sun
by Graham Salisbury
Life is normal for 13-year-old Tomi Nakaji. Then, on December 7, 1941, Japanese planes bomb Pearl Harbor and Tomi's world turns into a nightmare.

UNIT 8

Face the Facts

INFORMATION, ARGUMENT, AND PERSUASION

- In Nonfiction
- In Media

UNIT 8 **Share What You Know**

Can you BELIEVE *everything you read?*

All around you are sources of information—newspapers, books, magazines, and the Internet, to name a few. You may also get information from television, radio, billboards, product labels, and people you know. But can you **believe** all of it? It is important to learn to evaluate the information you receive so that you can know what to believe and what not to believe.

ACTIVITY What do you know? How did you come to know it? Think about all the sources of information you encounter in a day. Make a list of the sources, and then answer the following questions:

- How useful is the information you get from each source?
- Which source do you depend on most often?
- Is the information from that source always accurate?

After answering these questions, write a paragraph encouraging people to use your favorite source for information.

Dog Enrolls in College

August 9 Dr. Zachary Lynch, veterinarian at Zach's General Store, thought that someone had made a mistake when he was asked to help conduct physicals for incoming freshmen at the local communit

Two-Headed Turtle Talks Twice As Much

August 9 In recent weeks scientists have been observing the language habits of the recently discovered two-headed turtle. The turtle, which was found nesting on a small island off the coast of Bora Bora, seemed somewhat disoriente

Online LITERATURE CLASSZONE.COM

Literature and Reading Center
Writing Center
Vocabulary and Spelling Center

ALABAMA STANDARDS

Preview Unit Goals

READING
- Identify main idea and supporting details
- Identify fact and opinion
- Identify and use text features to locate and comprehend information
- Understand elements of an argument
- Analyze persuasive techniques
- Evaluate reasoning

WRITING AND GRAMMAR
- Write a persuasive essay
- Use commas and colons correctly

SPEAKING, LISTENING, AND VIEWING
- Deliver a persuasive speech
- Compare how different media cover the same event
- Recognize and analyze persuasive techniques in television advertising
- Identify target audience

VOCABULARY
- Use word roots and prefixes to help determine the meanings of words
- Use context clues to understand idioms

ACADEMIC VOCABULARY
- fact
- opinion
- text features
- argument
- persuasive techniques
- reasoning

UNIT 8

Reader's Workshop

Reading for Information

In today's information age, knowledge is power. Facts and figures on just about any subject, from consumer products to Jupiter's moons, are virtually at your fingertips. How do you find the information you're looking for? What are the best ways to understand and remember what you read? Learning a few simple strategies now can give you an edge and empower you for a lifetime.

ALABAMA STANDARDS

READING & RESEARCH STANDARDS

5 Use textual elements, including main idea and supporting details, to gain information

13.a Taking notes to gather, summarize information

Part 1: Get the Big Picture

Flipping through a newspaper or surfing the Web can be an overwhelming experience. That's because information overload can keep you from knowing where to begin. To help readers get their bearings and quickly see what a text is about, many writers use **text features,** or special design elements. Text features include headings, subheadings, boldfaced type, and captions. These elements all serve as road signs, guiding you through a text and pointing out key ideas.

Just as you would look at a road map before driving to a new place, you may also find it helpful to **preview** a text before you start to read it carefully. Notice how much you can tell about this article by scanning the text features.

The **title** reveals the topic of the article—the Dust Bowl.

Graphic aids, such as this map, present detailed information in an easy-to-read format.

Captions clarify information in the graphic aid.

Headings state the main idea of each paragraph.

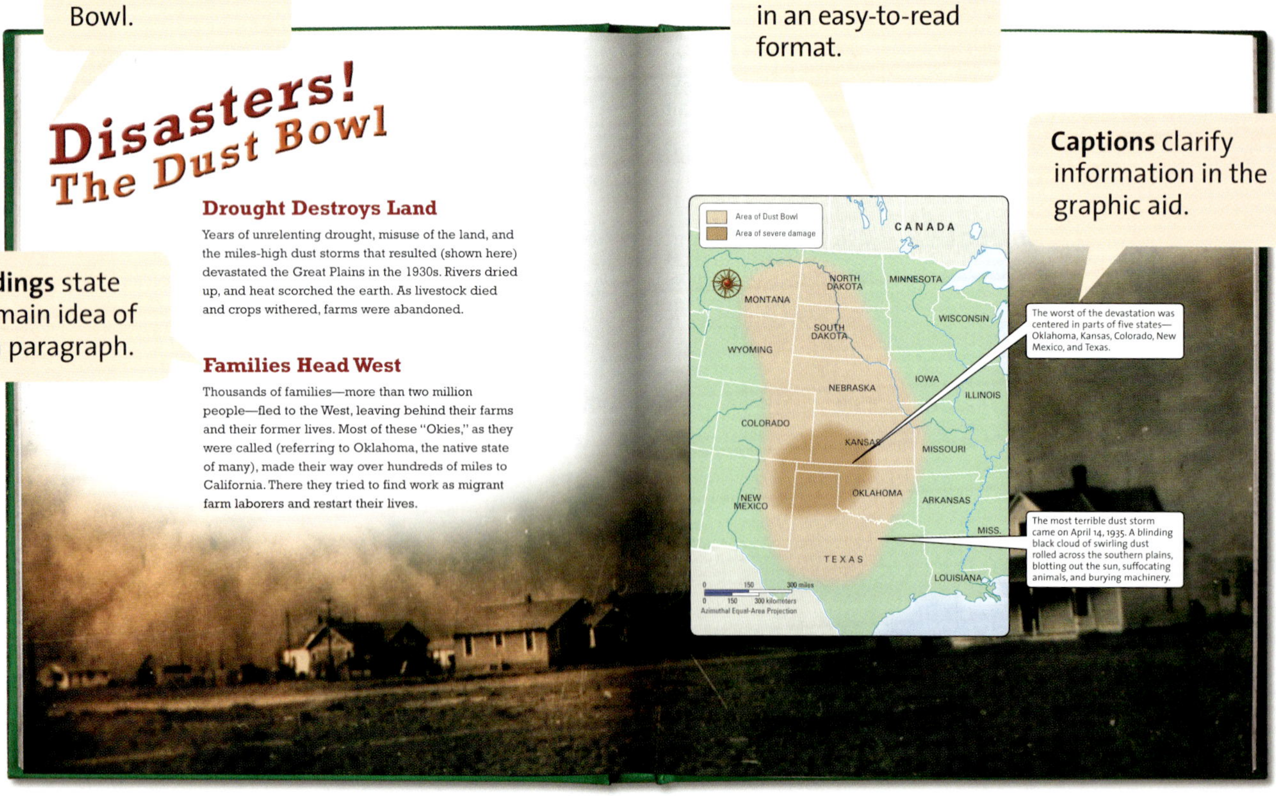

MODEL: TEXT FEATURES

Quickly skim the text features of this article. After seeing these features, what information do you think the article will provide? Now read the passage closely and answer the questions.

from **EARTHQUAKES**

Reference article in ***Popular Science Almanac***

. . . Earth's crust isn't just one solid piece, like an eggshell. Instead, it's broken up into different pieces, called plates. . . .

. . . Plate movement is responsible for earthquakes as well as volcanoes. See, Earth's plates are constantly growing at one end, getting consumed at the other, shifting alongside other plates, and pushing headlong into others. All of this causes a tremendous amount of pressure build-up. Rocks are rigid. Since they don't break easily, they resist this pressure for a long, long time. But after a while, something's got to give. Rapid movement of massive blocks of rock releases the tension . . . at least for the time being.

The San Andreas Fault in California falls at the boundary of two tectonic plates. The slipping of these plates is often the cause of earthquakes in the region.

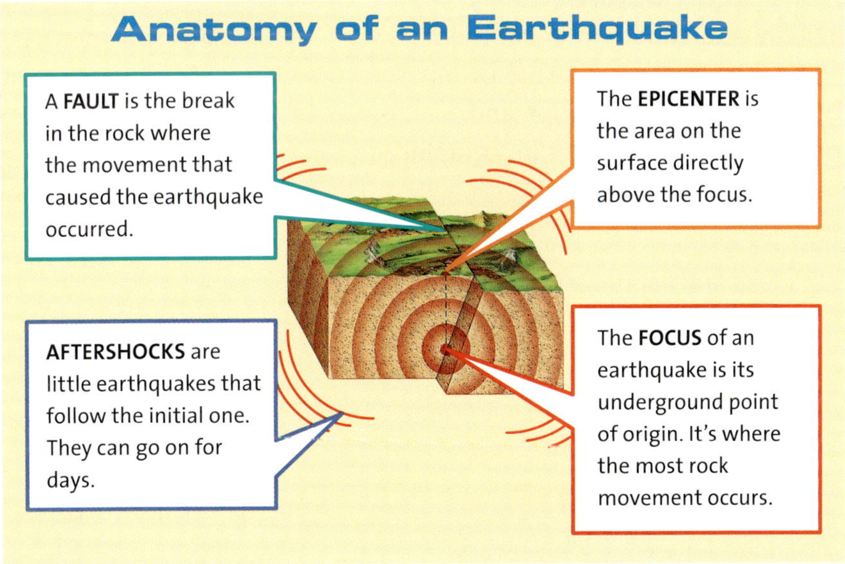

Close Read

1. If you were doing a report on the parts of an earthquake, would this article help you? Explain your answer.
2. Name two things you learn about earthquakes from the caption and the photograph.
3. Review the graphic aid at the bottom of this article. In your own words, describe the information it presents.

Part 2: Read for Understanding

Text features may be the road signs guiding you through a text, but your final destination is not just the end of the selection or page. It's arriving at an understanding of what you've read. The following strategies can help you reach that destination without running into roadblocks:

IDENTIFY THE MAIN IDEAS

To really understand a text, you first need to know how to find its main ideas. **Main ideas** are the most important ideas about a topic that a writer wants to communicate to readers. **Supporting details,** such as facts and examples, help to explain or elaborate on the main ideas. Most of the time, the main idea of a paragraph is directly stated in a **topic sentence,** which is usually located at the beginning or end of that paragraph. Consider this example from the article you just read.

> . . . Plate movement is responsible for earthquakes as well as volcanoes. See, Earth's plates are constantly growing at one end, getting consumed at the other, shifting alongside other plates, and pushing headlong into others. . . .

This **topic sentence** states the main idea of one paragraph in the article: the cause of earthquakes.

This **supporting detail** further explains what plate movement is and how it can cause earthquakes.

Sometimes the main idea is **implied**—suggested but not directly stated. In such a case, you have to **infer** it by asking yourself: What do all the supporting details add up to?

TAKE NOTES

Taking notes as you read can help you identify the main ideas and supporting details in a text and remember them after you've finishing reading. The key to good note taking is learning to zero in on the important information and restate it in your own words. You can take notes in a **graphic organizer,** an **outline,** or a variety of other formats.

To create a formal outline like this one, use Roman numerals to label the main ideas and capital letters to label the supporting points.

Earthquakes

I. Caused by movement of plates (pieces of the earth's crust)
A. Plates hit each other.
B. Movement causes pressure on rocks.
C. Tension is released when rock shifts.

II. Anatomy of an earthquake
A. Focus is the point where rock shifts underground.
B. Epicenter is the point on surface above focus.

Part 3: Analyze the Text

Read this article about the *Titanic,* the famous ship that sank in 1912. Preview the article and answer the first **Close Read** question. Then read the article more closely, using the other questions to help you take notes.

SCIENCE WATCH

What's Eating the *Titanic?*

The world's most famous sunken wreck becomes a gift for deep-sea scientists.

Oceanographer Robert Ballard is returning to the *Titanic,* but it's not the same sunken ship he found in 1985. The deep ocean has been steadily destroying the once-great cruise liner, and scientists say the process is unlike any they've ever seen. "Even if we could stop it, I wouldn't," says scientist Charles Pellegrino. "The *Titanic* is becoming something that belongs to biology."

The ship has attracted all kinds of hungry deep-sea life. Other critters (including tourists) are steadily chomping away at the ship too. Here's your guide to the wreck's undoing.

THE CULPRITS	THE DESTRUCTION	AN END IN SIGHT?
Mollusks and microorganisms that stirred up from the ocean floor when the ship first hit bottom	Worms munched on softer woods, while microorganisms ate some clothes and other fabrics. By the time scientists arrived to survey the ship, only the hard woods, such as mahogony, remained.	The worms moved on—the worst is done.
Bacteria from the ocean floor	Living off the sulfur in steel, bacteria also remove iron for housing and get rid of the rest. Bacteria have sucked over 1,000 tons of iron from the ship.	The bacterial colonies are growing, and half the steel could be gone by 2204.
The elements, such as water pressure, salt, and icebergs	Water pressure damaged parts of the ship when it sank. Salt slowly eats away at the hull, while gravel from icebergs overhead rains down on the deck.	Some suggest saving specific parts of the *Titanic* by bringing them on shore.
Tourists, pirates, and explorers attracted by profit and the popularity of *Titanic* TV specials	Small submarines are used to explore the site of the wreck. Careless piloting of these submarines has caused some damage to the hull and the deck.	The government has rules for protecting sunken ships, but it does not have the power to enforce them.

Close Read

1. Preview the title, the subtitle, and the headings in the chart. What do you think this article will be about?
2. The main idea of the first paragraph is listed in the outline shown. In your notebook, record two supporting details.

I. Scientists see the *Titanic's* destruction as an opportunity for study.
   A.
   B.

3. The second paragraph and the chart present another main idea listed by Roman numeral II. One supporting detail has been filled in. Complete the outline by adding other details.

II. Many culprits are causing the destruction.
   A. Mollusks and microorganisms
      1. Worms ate softer woods
      2. Microorganisms ate fabrics
      3. Worst damage is done

What Do You Know About Sharks?

Magazine Article by Sharon Guynup

Can appearances DECEIVE?

ALABAMA STANDARDS

READING STRATEGIES SKILLS

5 Use textual elements, including main idea and supporting details, to gain information

13.a Taking notes to gather, summarize information

KEY IDEA Cute doesn't always mean cuddly, and frightening doesn't always mean vicious. Appearances can **deceive,** as you will find out when you read "What Do You Know About Sharks?"

DISCUSS How much do you really know about sharks? Copy the chart shown here, and decide whether each statement is true or false. Then gather with others in a small group and share your answers. Does everyone agree on the "facts"?

Statement	True or False?
1. The great white is the largest shark.	
2. Most sharks are dangerous to humans.	
3. Sharks lived at the time of dinosaurs.	

ELEMENTS OF NONFICTION: TEXT FEATURES

Writers use design elements called **text features** to organize text and to point out key ideas and important information. Some of the most common text features include

- titles
- sidebars
- captions
- subheadings
- graphic aids
- bulleted lists

As you read, use the notes in the margins as a guide to help you identify these features. Ask yourself how each text feature helps you understand what you are reading.

READING SKILL: OUTLINE

To help yourself keep track of the **main ideas** and **supporting details** in a text, create an **outline.** To take notes in outline form, follow these guidelines:

- Use the text features to identify the article's main ideas.
- Use a roman numeral to label each main idea.
- Under each main idea, add supporting details. Label each with a capital letter.

"What Do You Know About Sharks?"
I. Protection
A. Sharks could vanish from ocean.
B. Without sharks, other species would overpopulate.
II. Kinds of Sharks

VOCABULARY IN CONTEXT

The boldfaced words helped Sharon Guynup share her knowledge of sharks and the sea. Use context clues to figure out what each word means.

1. Fish and whales are **aquatic** creatures.
2. The ocean is one kind of **ecosystem.**
3. A terrible disease can **decimate** a species.
4. The **carcass** of a half-eaten sea lion washed ashore.
5. Light will **diffuse** as it enters the water.
6. A life jacket increases a swimmer's **buoyancy.**

Author Online

Animal Lover
Sharon Guynup (gī′nəp) has found a way to combine her two loves, writing and the environment. She completed a master's degree in journalism from New York University's Science and Environmental Reporting program and continues to write articles about animals and the environment. Her work has appeared in national science magazines, in newspapers, and on the Web. Guynup also produces *State of the Wild,* a yearly review of the condition of the world's wildlife and lands.

Sharon Guynup
born 1958

MORE ABOUT THE AUTHOR
To learn more about Sharon Guynup, visit the **Literature Center** at **ClassZone.com.**

Background

An Ocean of Knowledge How do we know so much about sharks? People who study fish and how they live and grow in their environment are called ichthyologists (ĭk′thē-ŏl′ə-jĭsts). Their work in laboratories, in museums, at universities, and on research ships provides information about over 300 species of sharks. "What Do You Know About Sharks?" gives information about sharks in general, as well as facts about specific species.

Ⓐ TEXT FEATURES
The **title** often helps readers identify an article's main idea. What kind of information do you think this article will present?

aquatic (ə-kwăt'ĭk) *adj.* growing or living in the water

ecosystem (ē'kō-sĭs'təm) *n.* a physical environment, such as an ocean, and the community of things that live in it

decimate (dĕs'ə-māt') *v.* to kill or destroy a large part of

WHAT DO YOU KNOW ABOUT SHARKS? Ⓐ

SHARON GUYNUP

They're ferocious predators. They haunt us in nightmares. But the scariest thing about sharks may be that they're vanishing from the world's oceans. . . .

Why do sharks need protection? Sharks are top predators in the <u>aquatic</u> food chain—a web that interconnects all organisms, in which smaller creatures become food for larger predators. Without sharks, the ocean's delicate <u>ecosystem</u> would be disrupted. Species that sharks devour, like seals, for example, would overpopulate and in turn <u>decimate</u> other species, like salmon. Read the following questions and answers to learn more about the world's most fear-inspiring fish.

Nurse Shark
Nurse sharks are sluggish bottom dwellers found in the Atlantic Ocean. They're usually not dangerous and are one of the few sharks that breathe by pumping water through their gills while lying motionless. They sometimes suck in prey as well.

Wobbegong Shark
Wobbegongs are found resting on the sea floor in shallow waters of the Indo-Pacific and the Red Sea. The barbels, or fringe of flesh around their mouths, are feelers that act as camouflage.

What Are Sharks? B

Sharks are fish with skeletons made of rubbery cartilage (tough, flexible tissue) instead of bone. They're cold-blooded (unable to generate their own body heat), breathe through gills (respiratory organs), and have a two-chambered heart. Though most live in warm seas, the Greenland shark thrives in frigid Arctic seas. C

What's the Largest Shark? The Smallest?

Weighing in at 15 tons and stretching up to 14 meters (46 feet) long, the whale shark is the world's largest fish—bigger than a school bus! Nine hundred meters (2,953 feet) below the ocean surface lives the smallest shark: the dwarf shark. An adult measures only 25 centimeters (10 inches) long!

Are All Sharks Dangerous to People?

Most sharks are harmless. "Out of 375 shark species, only two dozen are in any way really dangerous to us," says Robert Hueter, director of the Center for Shark Research at Mote Marine Laboratory. Still, scientists don't know for sure why sharks sometimes attack humans. One theory: sharks may mistake the sound of swimming humans for that of injured fish—which are easy prey.

Goblin Shark

Goblin sharks feature needle-like teeth. They're rarely spotted—only 36 specimens have been counted—most found in waters deeper than 1,150 feet. Scientists think they inhabit seas from Europe to Australia.

Hammerhead Shark

Hammerheads inhabit shorelines and deep seas worldwide. The head, or cephalofoil, provides greater maneuverability—and enlarged nostrils and eyes at the ends of their "hammer" receive more information giving them a hunting advantage. D

B OUTLINE
Each orange question is a **subheading** that introduces a new main idea. State each main idea as a phrase and add it to your outline.

C OUTLINE
What are the important details in this paragraph? Add them to your outline.

D TEXT FEATURES
Sidebars are set off from the main article—usually on the side or bottom of the page—and provide additional information. You can read sidebars at any time. What information does this sidebar give you?

E TEXT FEATURES
Preview the **subheadings** on these pages. Which section will tell you where swimmers are most at risk?

Which Shark Is the Most Dangerous to Humans? E

"In terms of fatal attacks, it's a tossup between the great white, the tiger, and the bull shark," Hueter says. People fear the massive great white the most because of its size—up to 6.4 meters (21 feet) long—and its large razor-like teeth, not to mention the terror stirred up by *Jaws* flicks. But great whites usually inhabit deep seas—not shallow waters where people swim. Worldwide, fewer than 100 human attacks by all shark species are reported each year.

Where Do Most Shark Attacks Happen?

Florida leads the world in shark bites, with 22 to 25 reported incidents each year. But, claims Hueter, they're not repeated shark attacks—usually a single bite. . . . "Most really bad attacks occur off the coasts of California, Hawaii, Australia, and South Africa," Hueter says.

Just How Powerful Is a Shark's Bite?

Scientists built a "shark-bite meter" that measures the jaw strength of one species, the dusky shark. It exerts 18 tons of pressure per square inch on a victim. That's like being crushed beneath the weight of ten cars!

Whale Shark
The largest fish in the sea—whale sharks—are very docile. They feed on plankton, tiny drifting animals. They swim with their enormous mouths open, filtering food from the water with 15,000 tiny teeth.

Leopard Shark
Leopard sharks are commonly found near shore, often in large schools along the Pacific coast from Oregon to Mexico. They feed on small fish and crustaceans and are generally harmless.

What Do Sharks Eat?

Sharks chow down on what they can when they can—usually smaller animals from shrimp and fish to turtles and seabirds. Some, like the bull shark, consume large mammals like sea lions or dolphins; others, like the whale shark, eat only plankton, tiny drifting animals. And tiger sharks devour just about anything—mammal **carcasses**, tin cans, plastic bags, coal, and even license plates have been found inside their stomachs! F

carcass (kär'kəs) *n.* the dead body of an animal

F OUTLINE
How many details about what sharks eat have you included in your outline? Remember, you can include as many lettered details as you need.

How Do Sharks Find Prey?

Sharks can hear a wide range of sounds but are attracted by bursts of sound—like those made by an injured fish—or occasionally humans romping in water. At close range, sharks also sense vibration with their lateral line, a sensory system that runs from head to tail on each side of a shark's body. Inside the lateral line, which helps a shark maintain balance as well as detect sound, are canals filled with fluid and tiny "hair cells." Sound causes the liquid to vibrate, alerting the shark to the presence of another creature. This sense allows sharks to hunt even in total darkness.

Brushing and Flossing

Sharks continually lose their teeth, but some species grow new teeth as often as every week to replace worn or lost ones. During their lifetime, some species shed 30,000 teeth. Shark teeth vary according to what's on the menu:

top: nurse shark teeth, which chew up shellfish

middle: tiger shark teeth, which crunch everything from fish and birds to tin cans and other garbage

bottom: mako shark teeth, which grind up squid and big fish like tuna and mackerel G

G TEXT FEATURES
Graphic aids are visuals, such as graphs, photographs, and maps, that provide more information on a topic. What information do you get from looking at these photographs that you don't get from the text?

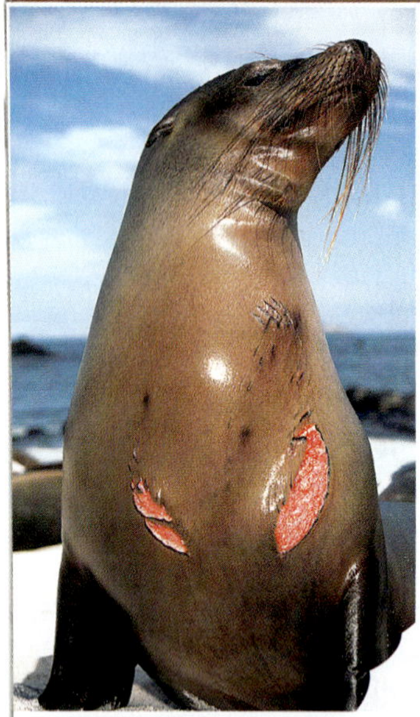

Shark Attack

This sea lion managed to survive a vicious shark attack. **H**

What's a "Feeding Frenzy"?

Sharks usually travel solo, but if one finds easy prey, an excited, competitive swarm of sharks may join in the feast, biting anything that lies in its path.

How Do Sharks Breathe?

A shark usually swims with its mouth open to force oxygen-rich water to pass over a set of gills housed in a cavity behind its head—a process known as ramjet ventilation. Gill flaps called lamellae absorb and help **diffuse** oxygen into the shark's bloodstream. Lamellae also help sharks expel carbon dioxide, a gaseous waste product of breathing, from the bloodstream.

diffuse (dĭ-fyōōz′) *v.* to spread out or through

H TEXT FEATURES
A **caption** is the text that provides information about a graphic aid. How does this caption support your understanding of the photo and reinforce the article?

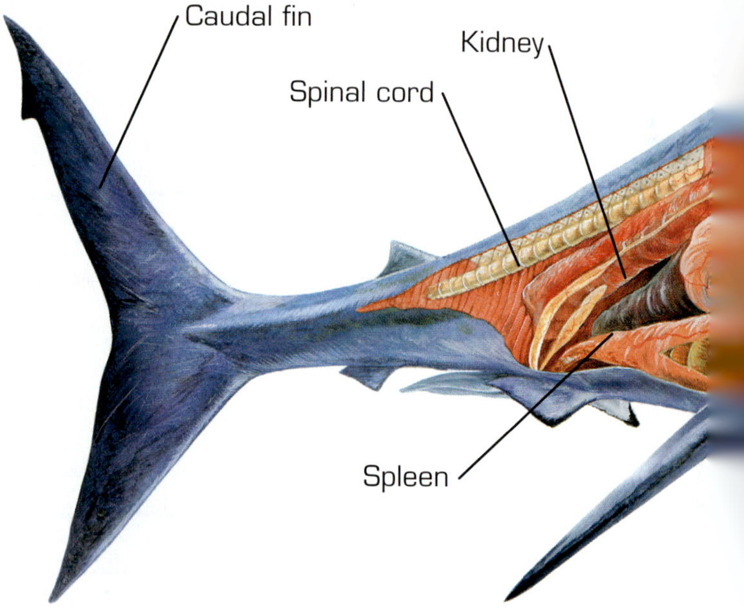

Top-Powerful Tail

Since its upper lobe is larger than the lower one, the great white's thrashing tail movements drive the shark forward and push its head down. This nosedive is countered by the fish's wedge-shaped head and its pectoral fins, which lift the front end.

Are Sharks Smart?

Experiments show that sharks recognize and remember shapes and patterns. Using shark snacks as rewards, scientists have taught lemon sharks to swim through mazes, ring bells, and press targets. "Although we learn new things about sharks every day, there's still a lot we don't know about them," says Hueter.

Great White Shark

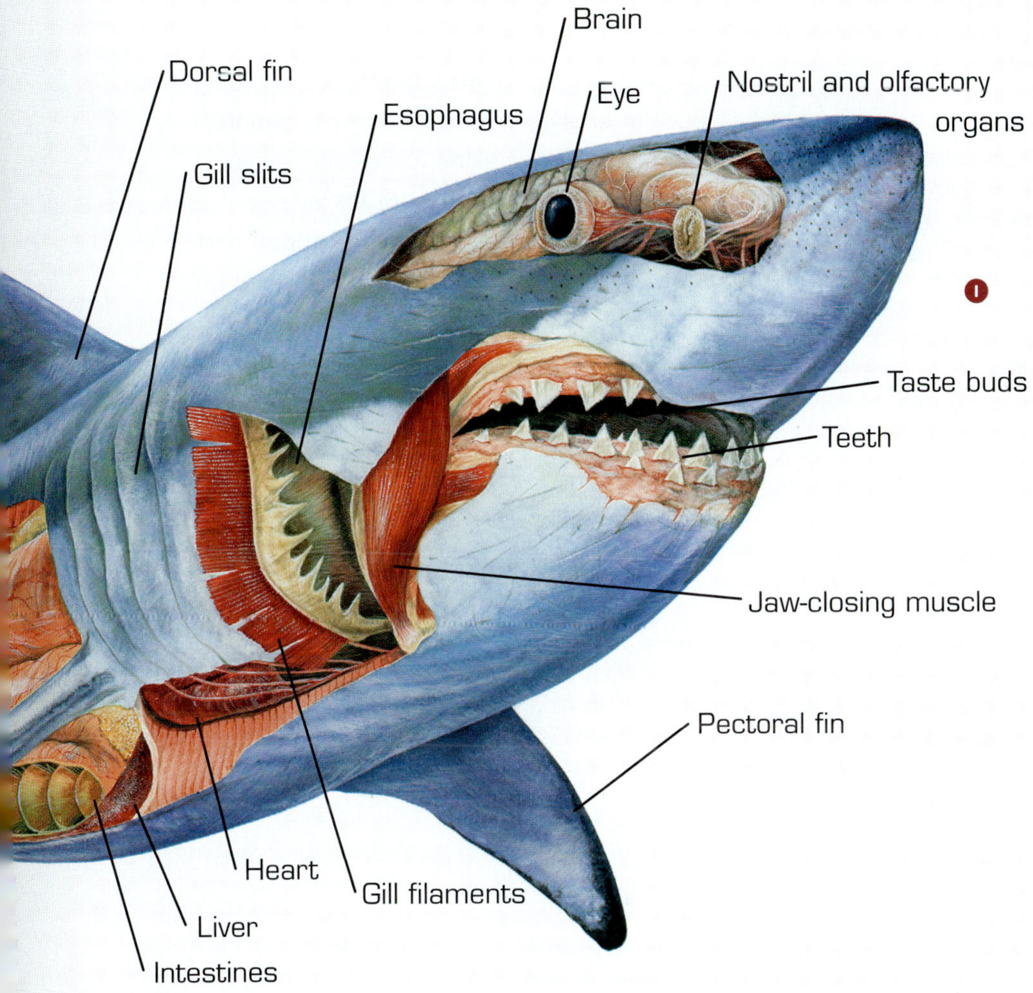

1 TEXT FEATURES
Use the **labels** on the illustration to identify the spinal cord, kidney, and brain.

Sandpaper Skin

Rough and tough, shark skin is made of hard, platelike scales, like tiny teeth pointing backward.

Gills

Water flows in the mouth and over blood-rich gill filaments. Some dissolved oxygen passes into the bloodstream before the water flows out through gill slits.

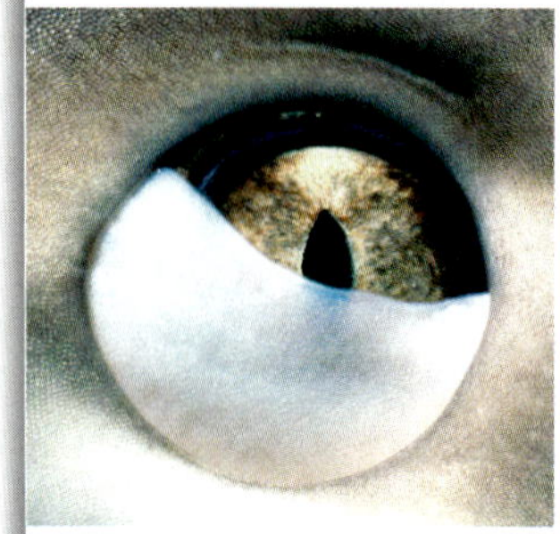

Shark Eyes

Sharks have good eyesight and can see colors. Their eyes are protected by a nictitating (nĭk'tĭ-tā'tĭng) membrane that moves up and down like an eyelid.

What Are Sharks' Natural Enemies?

Large sharks sometimes eat smaller sharks, and killer whales also dine on sharks. But the shark's greatest enemy is people. Humans kill sharks for food, use their skins for leather, make medicine from their liver oil, and use shark teeth for jewelry. Many sharks are killed senselessly for sport or get trapped and die in fishing nets. And it takes a long time for shark populations to rebound. Most shark species take ten years to reach reproductive age and produce small litters of less than a dozen pups.

Bite-Size Facts

- The first sharks appeared in the ancient oceans about 400 million years ago—200 million years before the dinosaurs!
- Sharks are carnivores (meat-eaters). Most gobble their prey whole or rip it into large, shark-size bites.
- Most sharks are found in the ocean but some, like the bull shark, also swim in lakes and rivers. Most shark attacks occur in warm waters—20° to 30°C (68° to 86°F).
- Sharks lack the inflatable swim bladder that allows bony fish to control **buoyancy**. Most sharks must swim endlessly. If they stop, they sink to the bottom and may drown from a lack of water flowing over the gills. (J)

buoyancy (boi'ən-sē) *n.* the ability to remain afloat in liquid

(J) TEXT FEATURES
The Bite-Size Facts are organized in a **bulleted list.** Why do you think writers use bulleted lists to present information?

Comprehension

ALABAMA STANDARDS

READING STANDARD
5 Use textual elements, including main idea and supporting details, to gain information

1. **Recall** What does the author think is the scariest thing about sharks?
2. **Clarify** What place do sharks hold in the aquatic food chain?
3. **Represent** Draw a simple illustration of a shark. Label its tail, dorsal fin, pectoral fins, and gill slits.

Critical Analysis

4. **Identify Text Features** Locate the photograph of the shark's eye on page 880 and the text features that are used with it. What do you learn from the photograph alone? What does the text add to your understanding of the photograph?
5. **Compare Outlines** Compare the outline you made while reading this article to one created by a classmate. Which main ideas and supporting details did you both have? Which were different?
6. **Analyze Author's Purpose** What do you think is the author's main purpose for writing "What Do You Know About Sharks?" Explain how the text features help Guynup achieve this purpose.
7. **Draw Conclusions** Do appearances **deceive** when it comes to sharks? Use a chart like the one shown to list facts supporting both of the opinions given. Use information from your outline, or return to the article if necessary. Be prepared to defend your conclusion in class.

Opinion 1: Sharks Are Very Dangerous	*Opinion 2: Sharks Are Mostly Harmless*
A dusky shark's bite is like being crushed beneath the weight of ten cars.	

Extension and Challenge

8. **Creative Project: Art** Work with a partner to create a poster illustrating the truth about sharks. Use your outline to help you remember the information that is important to include.
9. **Big Question Activity** Review the chart you made as part of the **Discuss** activity on page 872. After reading "What Do You Know About Sharks?" have you changed your mind about whether any of the statements are true or false? Next to each answer you want to change, record the information from the article that supports your new view.

Vocabulary in Context

VOCABULARY PRACTICE

Answer the questions to show your understanding of the vocabulary words.

1. Which is an example of an **ecosystem,** a desert or a gymnasium?
2. Which would be more likely to **decimate** a species, overhunting or rain?
3. If you wanted to **diffuse** air in a room, would you use a vacuum or a fan?
4. Which has **buoyancy,** a boulder or a raft?
5. If something is a **carcass,** is it alive or dead?
6. Would a person who liked **aquatic** things more likely own a fish tank or a cactus?

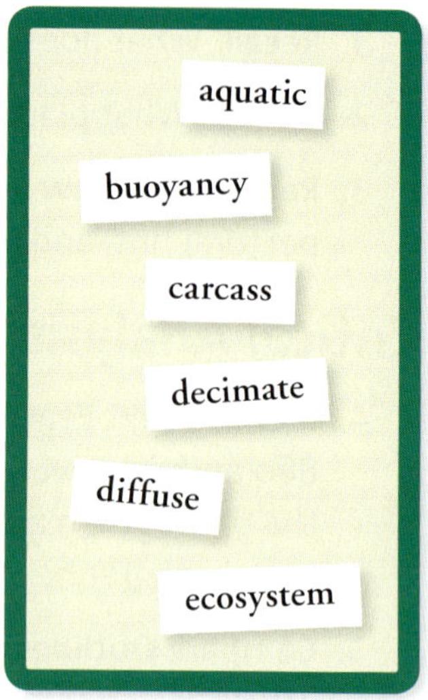

VOCABULARY IN WRITING

What else do you want to know about sea animals? Write several questions, using at least three vocabulary words. Here is an example.

EXAMPLE SENTENCE

*How do animals in the shark's **ecosystem** protect themselves?*

VOCABULARY STRATEGY: CONTENT-SPECIFIC WORDS

Whenever you study a specific subject or explore an area of interest, you are likely to encounter new words that are directly related to that subject. For example, in this article about sharks, you learned that the word *aquatic* refers to things that grow or live in the water. By learning content-specific words, you'll be better able to understand, discuss, and write about the subject yourself.

PRACTICE Match the word in the first column with its definition in the second column. Refer to a dictionary or science textbook if you need help.

1. tsunami	**a.** having to do with the sea or the things in it
2. current	**b.** animals with soft bodies and often hard shells
3. mollusks	**c.** large brown seaweed
4. marine	**d.** ocean stream that moves continuously in one direction
5. kelp	**e.** hard-shelled animals with jointed body and legs
6. crustaceans	**f.** destructive wave caused by an underwater earthquake

VOCABULARY PRACTICE
For more practice, go to the **Vocabulary Center** at **ClassZone.com.**

SKILLS PRACTICE

Reading-Writing Connection

Increase your understanding of "What Do You Know About Sharks?" by responding to these prompts. Then complete the **Grammar and Writing** exercise.

WRITING PROMPTS	SELF-CHECK
A. Short Response: Write Informational Text Rewrite the information in the caption for "Shark Eyes" on page 880 so that it is organized in a question-answer format. Use the organization of the article as a model.	***Strong informational text will . . .*** • include a subheading in the form of a question • provide a clear main idea and at least two details
B. Extended Response: Write a Summary When you write a summary, you restate the main ideas and the most important details of a selection in your own words. Use your outline to help you write a **two- or three-paragraph summary** of "What Do You Know About Sharks?"	***A successful summary will . . .*** • provide a one-sentence overview of the article • include only the most important details

GRAMMAR AND WRITING

USE COMMAS CORRECTLY **Commas** are used to make the meanings of sentences clear by setting off certain elements. One such element is an **appositive.** An appositive is a noun or pronoun that explains, identifies, or renames the noun or pronoun it follows. Sometimes the appositive has a modifier. This is called an **appositive phrase.**

Original: The tiger shark a ferocious predator will eat just about anything.

Revised: The tiger shark, a ferocious predator, will eat just about anything. (*Insert a comma before and after the appositive phrase "a ferocious predator."*)

PRACTICE In the following sentences, add commas where necessary.

1. Great white sharks the most fearsome fish usually live in deep seas.
2. The whale shark the world's largest fish eats plankton.
3. Humans the shark's greatest enemy kill sharks for leather.
4. The nurse shark a slow bottom dweller is not usually dangerous.

For more help with punctuating appositive phrases, see page R61 in the ***Grammar Handbook.***

ALABAMA STANDARDS

WRITING/LANGUAGE STANDARD
10.d Using commas to set off appositives

Great White Sharks

Magazine Article by Peter Benchley

Can you tell FACT *from fiction?*

ALABAMA STANDARDS

READING & LIT STANDARDS

4 Distinguish fact from opinion in informational materials

7 Interpret the author's message

KEY IDEA Artists and writers often use what they know to be true about the world to create imaginary scenerios that can seem more real than life itself. But how do you know when a work of fiction is technically **accurate** and when it's not? Peter Benchley has made a name for himself by dealing in both facts and fiction about great white sharks.

LIST IT Choose a movie you have seen or a book you have read that features animals or natural events. For each movie or book, make a list of some of the details that were included, explaining whether they're true or not.

Homeward Bound

1. Animals can find their way home across hundreds of miles.
2.
3.
4.

● ELEMENTS OF NONFICTION: FACT AND OPINION

Even informational text can include opinions. Be sure you can tell the difference between facts and opinions.

- A **fact** is a statement that can be proved. To prove, or verify, a fact, you might use personal observations, eyewitness accounts, a reliable print or online source, a scientific experiment, or a discussion with an expert.
- An **opinion** is a statement that can't be proved because it expresses a person's beliefs, feelings, or thoughts.

As you read Peter Benchley's article, decide which of his statements are facts and which are opinions.

● READING SKILL: RECOGNIZE AUTHOR'S BIAS

Writers' experiences and beliefs often affect their attitude about their topic. This creates a **bias** for or against what they're writing about. One way writers reveal their bias is through **loaded language,** or words that suggest a strong positive or negative feeling. As you read, record the loaded language in a chart like the one shown. Use the clues the language provides to identify the author's bias.

Loaded Language	*Possible Author's Bias*
"most wonderful of natural-born killers"	*Benchley is impressed by sharks' survival instincts.*

Review: **Compare-and-Contrast Organization**

▲ VOCABULARY IN CONTEXT

The boldfaced words help Peter Benchley share facts and feelings about great white sharks. Use context clues to figure out the meaning of each word.

1. Humans **demonize** an innocent creature out of fear.
2. The tourist gave **anecdotal** evidence instead of hard facts.
3. We finally reached a **consensus** after a loud debate.
4. The evidence was subject to close **scrutiny.**
5. Most scary movies are based on our **visceral** fears.
6. The scientist interviewed two **prospective** assistants.
7. The test errors were caused by **inadvertence** to detail.
8. The trial was a **travesty** because the jury was biased.

Author Online

The *Jaws* Sensation Peter Benchley is best known for his novel *Jaws,* which is about the hunt for a great white shark that killed several people in a beach community. *Jaws* stayed on the bestseller list for 40 weeks. In 1975, Steven Spielberg turned it into one of the top-grossing movies at the time. It was also nominated for an Academy Award for Best Picture. Benchley went on to write other novels and screenplays with the ocean as the setting, as well as nonfiction works about the ocean.

Peter Benchley
1940–2006

Regrets In the 1970s, when Benchley wrote *Jaws,* little was known about great white sharks. His description of them as vicious man-eaters frightened many people out of the water and triggered an aggressive shark hunt. Benchley, always fascinated by the ocean, spent a great deal of his life exploring it. He came to discover that much of what he wrote was incorrect. He was outspoken in his regrets for helping to create this hysteria. Benchley noted, "For every human being killed by a shark, roughly ten million sharks are killed by humans."

MORE ABOUT THE AUTHOR
For more on Peter Benchley, visit the **Literature Center** at **ClassZone.com.**

ANALYZE VISUALS
What might you **infer** about the great white shark from this photograph?

Considering the knowledge accumulated about great whites in the past 25 years, I couldn't possibly write *Jaws* today—not in good conscience anyway. Back then, it was generally accepted that great whites were anthropophagous—they ate people by choice. Now we know that almost every attack on a human is an accident. The shark mistakes the human for its normal prey.

Back then, we thought that once a great white scented blood, it launched a feeding frenzy that inevitably led to death. Now we know that nearly three-quarters of all bite victims survive, perhaps because the shark recognizes that it has made a mistake and doesn't return for a second bite.

Back then, we believed that great whites attacked boats. Now we know that their sensory systems detect movement, sound, and electrical fields, such as those caused by metal and motors, in water, and when they approach a boat, they're merely coming to investigate. Granted, investigation by a 3,000-pound animal can wreak havoc.[1]

Finally, back then, it was OK to **demonize** an animal, especially a shark, because man had done so since the beginning of time, and, besides, sharks appeared to be infinite in number. **A**

No longer. Today we know that these most wonderful of natural-born killers, these exquisite creatures of evolution, are not only *not* villains, they are victims in danger of—if not extinction quite yet—serious, perhaps even catastrophic, decline. Much of the evidence is **anecdotal.** Fishermen and naturalists are seeing fewer great whites, and in most places those they are seeing are younger and smaller. **B**

---

1. **wreak havoc:** bring about great destruction.

demonize (dē′mə-nīz′) *v.* to give evil, demonic qualities to

A COMPARE AND CONTRAST
What is Benchley comparing and contrasting in the previous four paragraphs?

anecdotal (ăn′ĭk-dōt′l) *adj.* based on observations rather than scientific analysis

B RECOGNIZE AUTHOR'S BIAS
Reread lines 23–27. What examples of **loaded language** do you find here? Record them in your chart.

consensus (kən-sĕn'səs) *n.* general agreement

C FACT AND OPINION Reread lines 30–37. Which statements can be verified, or proved? Where do you see evidence of bias?

Scientists estimate that, worldwide, populations of some species of sharks have dropped by 80 percent. Though precise numbers of white sharks aren't known, there is a growing **consensus** that they are not reproducing at a rate sufficient to maintain the population. What *is* known now is that great white sharks—scarce by nature and growing scarcer thanks to contact with man—are, for all their grace and power and manifest menace, remarkably fragile. . . . C

Nowadays more people are coming to respect and appreciate sharks for what they are: beautiful, graceful, efficient, and, above all, integral members of the ocean food chain. In large measure the change is due to television and the abundance of films documenting not only the glories from sharks but also the dangers to them from longlines, nets, and the odious practice of finning—slicing the fins off sharks to sell in Asian markets, then tossing the living animals overboard to die. Gradually governments and individuals are learning that while a dead shark may bring ten or twenty or even fifty dollars to a single fisherman, a live shark can be worth thousands of dollars more in tourist revenue to a community. Divers will fly halfway around the world to see white sharks.

Shark finning in the Pacific Ocean

This 17-foot great white shark was caught in the Atlantic Ocean. It weighed a record-breaking 3,500 pounds.

Immodestly I claim some credit for the change in attitude. For while the *Jaws* phenomenon was blamed for distorting the public's view of sharks and causing sporadic outbreaks of macho mayhem,[2] it also generated a fascination with and, over time, an affection for sharks that had not existed before.

2. **sporadic outbreaks of macho mayhem:** occasional wild flare-ups of people trying to show their superiority over sharks by attacking and killing them.

These days I receive more than a thousand letters a year from youngsters who were not alive when *Jaws* appeared, and all of them, without exception, want to know more about sharks in general and great whites in particular.

A great white shark in South Africa jumps out of the water to attack a seal.

Great white sharks are among the true apex predators in the ocean. The largest predatory fish in the world, they have few natural enemies. And so, in balanced nature, there are not very many great whites, and the number grows or shrinks depending on availability of food. They breed late in life and pup relatively few. Again, nobody knows exactly how many, but seven or eight seems to be a safe average. The youngsters appear alive, four or five feet long, weighing 50–60 pounds, fully armed and ready to rumble. Still, many don't survive the first year because other sharks, including great whites, will eat them. **D**

Of all the infuriating unknowns about great white sharks, none is more controversial than size. How big can they grow to be? Fishermen from Nova Scotia to South Australia, from Cape Town to Cape Cod claim to have encountered 25-footers, 30-footers, even 36-footers. Usually the proof offered is that the beast was "bigger than the boat." There have been reports of a 23-footer in the waters off Malta and a 21-foot, 7,000-pounder off Cuba, but none has held up under **scrutiny.** The largest

D FACT AND OPINION
Reread lines 72–82. What methods would you use to verify these facts?

scrutiny (skro͞ot'n-ē) *n.* close examination or study

generally accepted catch—made by lasso, of all things—was a shark 19.5 feet long. The largest great white shark ever caught on rod and reel weighed 2,664 pounds.

According to British biologist Ian Fergusson, chairman of the Shark Trust, no great white shark longer than 19.5 feet has ever been validated, and in a widely circulated e-mail, he expressed irritation at "this stubborn reluctance by some elements of the media to accept the facts and even more of a reluctance to accept that a 16-foot, 4500-pound white shark is big, very big, and should need no further exaggeration to impress even the most discerning of viewers when seen up close." **E**

E FACT AND OPINION Notice that Benchley quotes an expert in this paragraph. But even experts communicate both facts and opinions. Reread lines 94–101. What part of Fergusson's statement is a fact and what part is an opinion?

I can attest that underwater, cruising toward you out of the gloom with the serene confidence of the invincible, a 12-foot great white looks like a locomotive with malice in mind. . . .

At the moment science accepts about 400 species of sharks, but the number changes as new species are discovered. Of all known species, only four attack human beings with any frequency: bull sharks, tiger sharks, oceanic whitetips, and great whites.

In Australia, between 1876 and 1999, 52 attacks by great whites were recorded, and of them 27 were fatal. In the Mediterranean Sea since 1900 there have been 23 reliably recorded encounters with great whites, including one in 1909 in which the remains of two adults and a child were found inside a single 15-foot-long female shark caught off Augusta, Sicily.

The old adage is true: A swimmer has a better chance of being struck by lightning than killed by a shark. And around the world many, many more people die every year from bee stings, snakebites, falling off ladders, or drowning in bathtubs than from shark attack. None of which, to be sure, detracts from the ghastly, **visceral** horror of being eaten by a huge fish, but all of which should give some comfort to the recreational swimmer. . . .

visceral (vĭs'ər-əl) *adj.* instinctive

More and more these days it is the naturalists and field operators, guides and dive masters who are contributing to the accumulation of practical knowledge about great whites. To cite just one example: Until recently scientists thought that the scars that mar nearly every mature shark were acquired either from prey that fought back or from ritual biting by **prospective** mates. Now there is eyewitness testimony of aggressive social interaction[3] between sharks and also of spectacular threat displays that take the place of major—potentially fatal—encounters with other white sharks. **F**

A caged diver in South Australia comes face to face with a great white shark.

So we are learning—bit by bit, anecdote by anecdote—more and more about these magnificent predators. We must hope that we're learning enough to save them before, through ignorance and **inadvertence,** we destroy them.

Great white sharks have survived, virtually unchanged, for millions of years. They are as perfectly in tune with their environment as any living thing on the planet. For them to be driven to extinction by man, a relative newcomer, would be more than an ecological tragedy; it would be a moral **travesty.** **G**

3. **aggressive social interaction:** contact that is combative even though there is no actual intent to fight.

prospective (prə-spĕk′tĭv) *adj.* likely to be or become

F RECOGNIZE AUTHOR'S BIAS
Reread lines 130–134. What does the word *spectacular* reveal about Benchley's attitude toward sharks' behavior?

inadvertence (ĭn′əd-vûr′tns) *n.* a lack of attention; carelessness

travesty (trăv′ĭ-stē) *n.* a degraded or grotesque likeness

G RECOGNIZE AUTHOR'S BIAS
Identify the **loaded language** in the last two paragraphs. Why do you think Benchley uses loaded language here?

Comprehension

1. **Recall** How many years passed between the time the author wrote *Jaws* and the time he wrote the article?
2. **Clarify** Why are there naturally so few great white sharks?
3. **Summarize** What are two facts about great white sharks?

Critical Analysis

4. **Identify Fact** Statistics are facts expressed in numbers. Reread lines 110–115 and identify the statistics. On the basis of the statistics in this paragraph, what factual statement can you make about the likelihood of a great white shark fatally attacking a human?
5. **Examine Opinion** A **prediction** is an opinion about something that will happen in the future. Reread lines 135–143. What does Benchley predict will happen to the great white shark if something isn't done?
6. **Analyze Author's Bias** Review the chart you made while reading. Identify Benchley's attitude toward his subject. On the basis of the information in the chart and what you know from the biography on page 885, why do you think Benchley feels as he does about great whites?
7. **Compare and Contrast Articles** Review "Great White Sharks" and "What Do You Know About Sharks?" to find ways they are similar and different. Then use a Venn diagram like the one shown to record your answers.

Extension and Challenge

8. **SCIENCE CONNECTION** Review the article and choose three facts about great white sharks. For each fact, find two reliable sources, such as an encyclopedia, an atlas, or an almanac, that verify it. Present your findings to the class.
9. **Creative Response: Screenplay** Benchley compares and contrasts the beliefs about great white sharks at the time he wrote *Jaws* with the knowledge available now. Use the facts that are now known to write a movie scene that features an accurate portrayal of a great white shark.

ALABAMA STANDARDS

READING STANDARD
4 Distinguish fact from opinion in informational materials

Vocabulary in Context

VOCABULARY PRACTICE

Decide whether the words in each pair are synonyms (words with the same meaning) or antonyms (words with opposite meanings).

1. consensus/disagreement
2. inadvertence/inattention
3. visceral/analytical
4. demonize/praise
5. travesty/distortion
6. scrutiny/observation
7. anecdotal/scientific
8. prospective/unexpected

VOCABULARY IN WRITING

Review your list from the activity on page 884. Using three or more vocabulary words, describe one of the movies or books. Here is a sample beginning.

EXAMPLE SENTENCE

The spider's ***visceral*** *needs caused it to bite Peter Parker.*

VOCABULARY STRATEGY: PREFIXES AND THE LATIN ROOT *vert*

The vocabulary word *inadvertence* contains the Latin root *vert,* which means "turn." This root, sometimes spelled *vers(e),* is combined with various prefixes to form simple English words. To understand the meanings of words with *vert* or *vers(e),* use the meaning of the root and the prefixes it is used with.

PRACTICE Combine a prefix from the chart with *vert* or *vers(e)* to form words to complete each of these sentences. Note that some prefix spellings vary.

1. If you back up a car, you put it in ______.
2. A person who is very outgoing is known as a(n) ______.
3. If you don't want to watch a scary movie, you can ______ your eyes.
4. To cross a desert, you must ______ a lot of sand.

Prefixes Used with *vert, vers(e)*	Meaning
ab-, a-	away from
extra-, extro-	outside
re-	again; back
trans-, tra-	across

VOCABULARY PRACTICE
For more practice, go to the **Vocabulary Center** at **ClassZone.com.**

Comparing Organization

Like Black Smoke: The Black Death's Journey

Magazine Article by Diana Childress

A World Turned Upside Down: How the Black Death Affected Europe

Magazine Article by Mary Morton Cowan

How do we fight DISEASE?

ALABAMA STANDARDS

READING & LIT STANDARDS

4 Apply strategies that include setting purposes for reading

7.a Comparing informational texts

KEY IDEA Each year, doctors and scientists learn more about how communities can stay healthy and prevent **disease.** But people didn't always know what we know now. The articles you are about to read tell about a time during the Middle Ages when the bubonic plague affected so many people that it changed a society.

LIST IT What can each of us do to encourage good health for ourselves and others? Make a list of at least five guidelines that people can follow to prevent contagious diseases from spreading. Be ready to explain why you included each guideline.

● ELEMENTS OF NONFICTION: PATTERNS OF ORGANIZATION

Nonfiction writers use a **pattern of organization** to help them explain key points. Here are two common patterns:

- **Cause-and-effect organization** points out the relationship between an event and its cause or effect. Signal words and phrases, such as *caused, because,* and *led to,* may indicate a cause or an effect.
- **Chronological order** organizes events according to when they happened. Signal words include *after* and *the following* and phrases that give specific times or dates.

As you read, decide how each article's pattern of organization helps the author explain her main points.

■ READING STRATEGY: SET A PURPOSE FOR READING

As you read these two articles, look for similarities and differences in the information the articles contain and the ways they are organized. A chart like the one shown can help you identify these similarities and differences.

	"Like Black Smoke"	"A World Turned Upside Down"
Purpose		
Main Idea and Supporting Details		
Type of Organization		

Review: **Interpret Graphic Aids**

▲ VOCABULARY IN CONTEXT

The following words help provide information about the bubonic plague. See which ones you already know. Place each word in the correct column of a chart like the one shown.

WORD LIST			
	artisan	cope	rampage
	bacterium	disarray	recurrence
	chronicle	hierarchy	

Know Well	Think I Know	Don't Know at All

Author Online

Diana Childress: History Lover Award-winning author Diana Childress has written numerous books and articles for young people, most of them based on her favorite subject—history.

Diana Childress
born 1940

Mary Morton Cowan: Many Talents Articles aren't the only thing Mary Morton Cowan writes for young people. She also writes folk tales, historical plays, photo essays, and puzzles.

Mary Morton Cowan
born 1939

MORE ABOUT THE AUTHOR
For more on the authors, visit the **Literature Center** at **ClassZone.com.**

Background

Devastation in the Middle Ages The Middle Ages lasted from about A.D. 500 to A.D. 1500. One of the most significant events of this time period was the spread of the bubonic plague, or the Black Death. Those who caught the disease suffered fever and painful swellings, called buboes, in the lymph glands. The buboes, from which the disease gets its name, were followed by black spots on the skin. Next came a severe, bloody cough, and after that—death. At the time, no one knew what caused the disease.

ANALYZE VISUALS
What are the individuals in this image doing?

Burying plague victims in coffins at Tournai in 1349. Illumination from the *Annals of Gilles de Muisit* (1352). The Granger Collection, New York.

Like Black Smoke

The Black Death's Journey **A**

Diana Childress

A SET A PURPOSE FOR READING
Read the title and scan the **subheadings.** What do you expect to learn from this article?

"We see death coming into our midst like black smoke," wrote the poet Jeuan Gethin,[1] when plague invaded Wales in March 1349. This "rootless phantom which has no mercy" was especially frightening for those who witnessed it because they knew it was somehow contagious, but no one could halt or explain its relentless spread across Europe.

Eastern Beginnings

The earliest evidence of the Black Death lies in a cemetery in what was once a prosperous town near Lake Issyk-Kul[2] on the fabled Silk Road[3] in Central Asia. An unusually large number of graves there are dated 1338 and 1339. Three headstones mentioning the cause of death provide a clue about why so many people died: the plague.

Did the Black Death originate near Issyk-Kul? No one knows for sure. Most medieval writers say that the plague began in the East. They name places like Cathay (China), India, and Turkey. Modern historians agree that

1. **Jeuan Gethin** (yā'ən gĕth'ĭn).
2. **Lake Issyk-Kul** (ĭ'sĭk-kŭl').
3. **Silk Road:** an important trade route on which both goods and ideas were exchanged between China and the countries of western Europe.

the epidemic started in Asia—more specifically, somewhere on the central steppes[4] or in the Himalayan lowlands on the border of India and China. In both regions, the plague **bacterium,** *Yersinia pestis,*[5] has long thrived among wild marmots, ground squirrels, and gerbils.

On the Move

How did the disease travel from wild rodents to humans? According to early accounts, before the Black Death broke out, earthquakes, floods, and famines devastated Asia. One theory is that these disasters drove wild animals into villages and towns in search of food. Fleas then spread plague germs to rats. . . .

When rats died of the plague, their fleas hunted for new hosts. Since rats nested in the adobe (sun-dried brick) walls and thatched roofs of medieval houses, the next meal for these fleas often came from people. . . .

The disease spread more easily if an infected person's lungs started filling up with plague bacteria. Then, every cough and sneeze spewed germs into the air, spreading pneumonic plague[6] directly to others.

If they are not among the lucky few who recover, people and rats soon die of the plague, but infected fleas can lurk in a rat's nest, barnyard manure, or bedding and clothing for many months without eating. A medieval writer was not far wrong when he wrote that "even the houses or clothes of the victims could kill."

Fleas infect rats with *Yersinia pestis,* the plague bacterium. Rats spread the disease to humans. Once human lungs fill with plague bacteria, the germ becomes airborne every time a person coughs or sneezes.

. . . Cloth, grain, furs, and hides kept in rat-infested warehouses soon became delayed-action "plague bombs" waiting to go off. An account tells

4. **steppes:** treeless plains in southeastern Europe and in Asia.
5. ***Yersinia pestis*** (yər-sĭn'ē-ə pĕst'ĭs).
6. **pneumonic** (no͞o-mŏn'ĭk) **plague:** the most contagious and deadly form of the Black Death.

bacterium (băk-tîr'ē-əm) *n.* the singular form of *bacteria,* microscopically small living things that may cause disease

B INTERPRET GRAPHIC AIDS
How does this illustration **clarify** your understanding of how people caught the disease?

how four soldiers learned the hard way about contaminated goods. Looting houses in a deserted town, they stole a fleece off a bed and later slept under it. They were dead by morning.

Commercial caravans, Mongol armies, and other wayfarers[7] "carried" the Black Death in their baggage as they crisscrossed Asia. By 1345, it had traveled from Issyk-Kul to Sarai and Astrakhan,[8] the major cities of the Golden Horde[9] (a part of the Mongol Empire that is today southwestern Russia).

From Asia to the Mediterranean

At the time, Italian merchants from Genoa and Venice had established trading posts at Kaffa, a city on the Crimean Peninsula that juts out into the Black Sea. Since the mid-1200s, their galleys had transported Asian horses, furs, and slaves to Syria and Egypt and silks and spices to Italy. When plague began to spread to the Crimea, many of the Europeans tried to escape by sea, but the Black Death sailed with them.

---

7. **commercial caravans . . . wayfarers:** Commercial caravans are bands of merchants or traders traveling together for safety. Mongols had a large empire covering most of Asia and eastern Europe. Wayfarers are generally people who travel on foot.
8. **Sarai** (sä-rī′) . . . **Astrakhan** (ăs′trə-kăn′).
9. **Golden Horde:** a name for the Mongol army.

C INTERPRET GRAPHIC AIDS
According to the map, in what direction did the Black Death first travel? Note how many continents were affected.

The following summer, plague broke out in Constantinople. From there, it crossed the Mediterranean region. That fall, ships brought the plague to Alexandria, Egypt, one arriving with only 45 of its original crew of 332 men still alive. Another fleet came to Messina, Sicily, its crew so ill that a **chronicle** reports that the men had "sickness clinging to their very bones." D

The epidemic reached Genoa on New Year's Eve 1347 aboard three galleys laden with spices from the East. On discovering that many seamen were sick, the Genoese chased the ships from the port with "burning arrows and engines of war." Plague-ridden rats, however, had already jumped ship. The galleys sailed off along the coast of France, still hoping to find a place to sell their deadly merchandise.

Following the Trade Routes

Following 14th-century trade routes, the Black Death swept across Europe, North Africa, and the Middle East. After it assaulted the seaports, smaller boats carried it to neighboring towns and to river ports far inland. It could not be stopped. Although some towns refused entry to travelers from infected areas, and people learned to mistrust "plague goods," few noticed the dead rats, and no one thought of the fleas.

Reports of plague in 1348 show how the circles of infection widened. In the east, it hit Cyprus, Aleppo, Damascus, Jerusalem, and even pilgrims

chronicle (krŏn′ĭ-kəl) *n.* a record of historical events in the order in which they took place

D PATTERNS OF ORGANIZATION
Reread lines 64–69. What phrases help you follow this paragraph's pattern of organization?

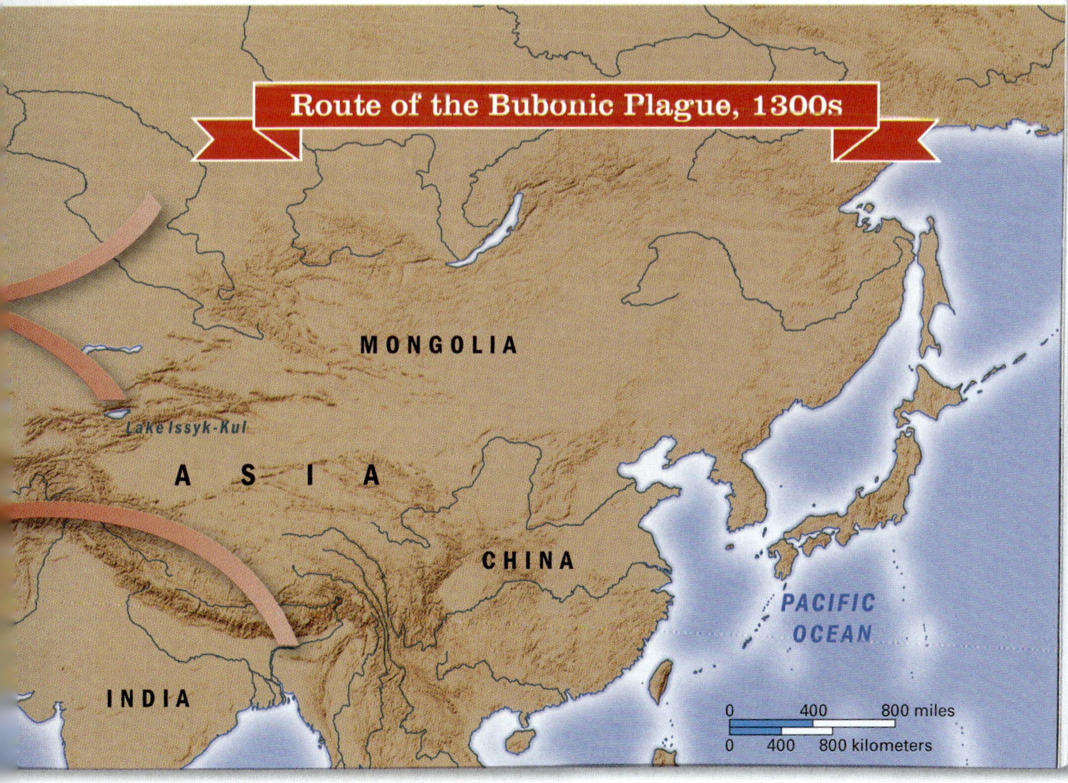

visiting Mecca. From Genoa and Venice it crept down the Italian boot toward Florence and Rome. Going west, it struck Marseilles, Tunis, and Barcelona. By June, the epidemic was storming Paris, causing the French royal family to flee to Rouen,[10] where it soon followed. That summer, it overran Germany, Poland, and Hungary and crossed the channel to southern England.

Winter did not slow its progress. The weather was unusually mild and wet, perhaps warm enough for fleas living on house rats to remain active. Huddled indoors, people were also exposed to air contaminated both by those suffering from pneumonic plague and by the dust from rodent droppings.

As the disease moved northward through England, citizens of Lincoln wrote wills at 30 times the normal annual rate. At first, the Scots avoided the plague, but when they assembled troops to invade England, pestilence[11] struck, perhaps imported by soldiers from France.

The Black Death landed in Scandinavia on a ship carrying wool from London to Norway. The ship had run aground near Bergen because all the crew had died. From there, plague spread across Norway, into Sweden, and across the Baltic Sea to Russia.

The Journey Ends

In 1350, plague peaked in Scotland and Scandinavia, while in southern Spain, it killed King Alfonso XI of Castile. The following year, it stretched to Greenland, where it helped wipe out the Norwegian colony, and to Yemen, at the tip of the Arabian peninsula. In 1353, it closed in on Moscow, killing both the patriarch of the Russian church and the grand duke of Muscovy.

Finally, the Black Death petered out somewhere in Kiev, having come almost full circle back to Kaffa. During its long **rampage,** between one-third and one-half of the population of Europe, North Africa, and the Middle East died. No natural disaster before or since has caused such devastation of human life over such a large area. It was one of the greatest catastrophes in human history. **E**

A priest blesses plague-infected monks. Illumination from *Omne Bonum* (about 1370), Jacobus Anglicus. Ms. Royal 6, E VI, fol. 301. © British Library/akg-images.

rampage (răm′pāj′) *n.* a wild or violent outbreak

E PATTERNS OF ORGANIZATION
Reread lines 103–119. Which words signal the pattern of organization? How does the final subheading reinforce this organization?

10. **Rouen** (ro͞o-än′): a city in France, about 84 miles northwest of Paris.
11. **pestilence** (pĕs′tə-ləns): any disease that spreads rapidly and causes many deaths.

ALABAMA STANDARDS

LITERATURE STANDARD
7.a Comparing informational texts

Comprehension

1. **Recall** Where do most historians think the Black Death started?
2. **Recall** How did boats spread the disease?
3. **Summarize** Summarize how the plague spread from rodents to people.

Critical Analysis

4. **Identify Fact or Opinion** Reread the last statement in the article. Is this sentence a fact or an opinion? Explain why you think so.
5. **Examine Cause and Effect** Reread lines 49–52. Which of the soldiers' actions probably led to their deaths? Explain.
6. **Analyze Author's Purpose** What do you think are the main points Childress wants readers to learn from this article? Explain your reasoning.
7. **Evaluate Events** Create a timeline of the key events that contributed to the spread of the Black Death. Which event do you think was most critical? Support your choice with details from the article.

Comparing Patterns of Organization

In your chart complete the column labeled "Like Black Smoke." Add information that helps you understand how the article is organized.

	"Like Black Smoke"	"A World Turned Upside Down"
Purpose		
Main Idea and Supporting Details	*Black Death travels from the East.*	
Type of Organization		

Detail of *Triumph of Death* (1597), Jan Brueghel. Oil on canvas, 119 cm × 164 cm. Steiermärk. Landesmuseum Johanneum. © akg-images.

A WORLD TURNED UPSIDE DOWN: HOW THE BLACK DEATH AFFECTED EUROPE

Mary Morton Cowan

A SET A PURPOSE FOR READING
Reread lines 1–4. **Paraphrase** the main idea that this article will explore.

hierarchy (hī'ə-rär'kē) *n.* an organization of people according to rank

Substantial changes in population often have dramatic effects on society. The bubonic plague, which in just four years killed up to one-third of the people in Europe, almost literally turned Europe's social structure upside down. **A**

Life in the Middle Ages centered around a **hierarchy** called the feudal system. Noble lords lived in castles or manors, which were surrounded by acres of land. The nobles depended on peasants to farm their land. In turn, peasants received protection, shelter, and a small plot of land to plant their own crops. According to the Christian church, the feudal system was God's plan, and no one questioned the authority of the church.

In the 300 years before the Black Death, the European population tripled. Additional land was cultivated, but food was still scarce. Some peasants left

for a better life in the city, where merchants and craftsmen were beginning to thrive. The now-crowded cities, however, could not handle the overflow of unskilled laborers.

After gunpowder was invented, the lords had found it harder to defend their castles. They also experienced some bad harvests, and many had to **cope** with the consequences of a war between France and England. Yet, they remained in control.

Then, without warning, the Black Death swept through Western Europe, killing 25 million people. Some families were wiped out. Large estates were left without heirs. Survivors moved in and claimed any property they could find. Cities and towns lost people by the thousands. Monasteries,[1] which previously had as many as 150 monks, now had only seven or eight. In all, thousands of villages were abandoned. B

Agriculture was also in **disarray**. The tools and land were there, but suddenly the workers were missing. Food prices dropped, and there was even a surplus of food where once many had barely had enough to stay alive.

Because workers were scarce, peasants who survived the plague now had bargaining power for the first time. Resentment among the working class led to violence and revolt in the centuries that followed, as Europe teetered between the old feudal system and a new economic system.

1. **monasteries:** buildings where religious men called monks live, work, and pray together.

ANALYZE VISUALS
What might the skeletons in this painting **symbolize,** or stand for?

cope (kōp) *v.* to struggle with and act to overcome

B PATTERNS OF ORGANIZATION
Reread lines 20–25. What effects of the Black Death does the author give?

disarray (dĭs'ə-rā') *n.* a state of disorder; confusion

artisan (är'tĭ-zən) *n.* a person who is skilled in a trade

C PATTERNS OF ORGANIZATION
Reread lines 30–45. What clue words help you recognize the pattern of organization?

recurrence (rĭ-kûr'əns) *n.* the act of happening again; return

D INTERPRET GRAPHIC AIDS
What was the population of western Europe in the early 1300s?

The shortage of skilled craftsmen caused an industrial crisis. Unlike agricultural workers, craftsmen require long apprenticeships, and now there were few replacements when any skilled **artisan** died. Reduced production forced prices of saddles, farm tools, and other goods to soar. **C**

This depopulation crisis, however, encouraged technological developments. The most notable labor-saving invention was the printing press, developed around 1450. One such press replaced hand-copying by hundreds of scribes.[2]

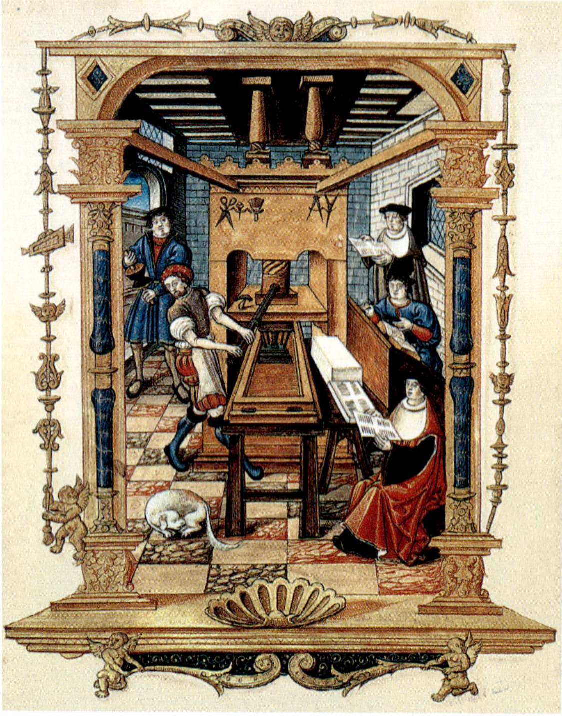

Survivors of the plague use a printing press to copy manuscript.

Illumination from *Chants royaux* (about 1500). Bibliothèque Nationale. © akg-images/VISIOARS.

The Black Death affected the entire medieval social structure. When the pestilence returned a few years later, people were even more terrified. Its unpredictable **recurrence** in the following decades was enough to keep Europeans in constant fear. A mood of gloom swept across Europe, and many began to question the authority of the church. In fact, they began to have doubts about their entire world view. Yet, it was this questioning that led to far-reaching reforms in religion, art, medicine, and science. Without a doubt, the Black Death forever changed Europe's economic and social structure.

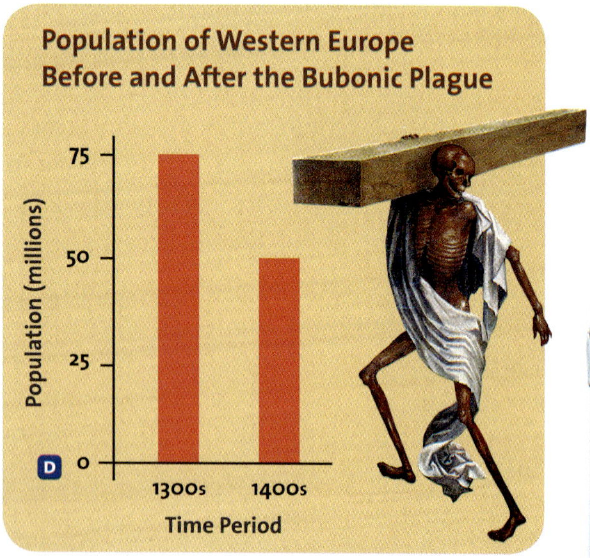

Detail of *Danse Macabre. Pope* (1500s), Bernt Notke. Oil on canvas, 160 cm × 750 cm. St. Nicholas' Church, Art Museum of Estonia, Tallinn, Estonia. © Bridgeman Art Library.

2. **scribes:** people whose job was to copy manuscripts.

Comprehension

1. **Recall** How long did it take for the bubonic plague to wipe out one-third of Europe's population?
2. **Recall** Why did the depopulation of Europe encourage technological developments?
3. **Summarize** What was life like in Europe in the Middle Ages before the Black Death swept through?

ALABAMA STANDARDS

LITERATURE STANDARD
7.a Comparing informational texts

Critical Analysis

4. **Identify Author's Main Idea** Writers choose the details that will best support the main idea they want to convey. What main idea is Cowan supporting in this article?
5. **Examine Cause and Effect** Why did food prices drop after the Black Death swept through western Europe?
6. **Analyze Graphic Aids** What information does the bar graph on page 904 give you that the text does not?
7. **Evaluate** What were some positive changes caused by the spread of this deadly disease?

Comparing Patterns of Organization

Now that you've read both articles, finish filling in your chart. Then use the chart to help you identify each article's pattern of organization.

	"Like Black Smoke"	"A World Turned Upside Down"
Purpose		
Main Idea and Supporting Details	Black Death travels from the East.	Plague reversed Europe's social structure.
Type of Organization		

Vocabulary in Context

VOCABULARY PRACTICE

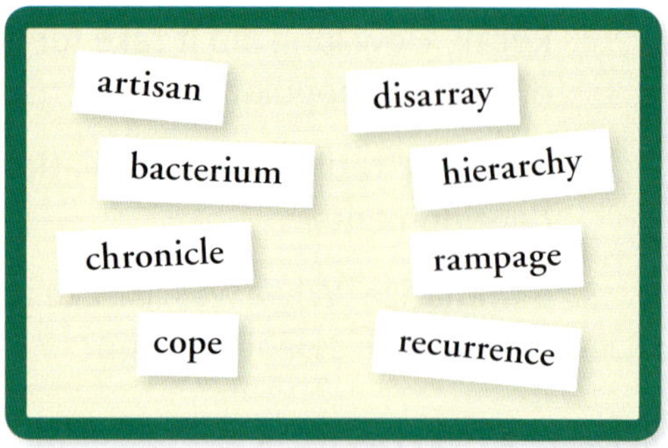

In each item, choose the word that differs most in meaning from the other words. Refer to a dictionary if you need help.

1. (a) record, (b) listing, (c) chronicle, (d) clock
2. (a) artisan, (b) police officer, (c) firefighter, (d) sanitation worker
3. (a) turmoil, (b) commotion, (c) caretaker, (d) disarray
4. (a) hierarchy, (b) anarchy, (c) chaos, (d) disorganization
5. (a) class, (b) frenzy, (c) rampage, (d) uproar
6. (a) bacterium, (b) germ, (c) pandemonium, (d) microorganism
7. (a) reappearance, (b) renounce, (c) repetition, (d) recurrence
8. (a) instruct, (b) teach, (c) cope, (d) educate

VOCABULARY IN WRITING

Pretend you are a survivor of the Black Death. Using three or more vocabulary words, write about how your life has changed. You could start like this.

EXAMPLE SENTENCE

*I survived the plague, but my whole life is in **disarray**.*

VOCABULARY STRATEGY: SPECIALIZED VOCABULARY

Recognizing a word that is often associated with disease or its prevention or treatment can help you better understand issues related to health.

PRACTICE Match the word in the first column with its definition in the second column. Refer to a dictionary or a science textbook if you need help.

1. virus	**a.** medicine for treating infections caused by bacteria
2. antibiotic	**b.** free from germs
3. pandemic	**c.** substance used to build immunity to a disease
4. inoculation	**d.** process of administering a vaccine
5. vaccine	**e.** decrease or disappearance of symptoms of a disease
6. remission	**f.** very small particle that can cause many types of disease
7. sterile	**g.** a very widespread or worldwide epidemic

VOCABULARY PRACTICE
For more practice, go to the **Vocabulary Center** at **ClassZone.com.**

Writing for Assessment

1. READ THE PROMPT

In writing assessments, you might be asked to compare and contrast two informational texts that have a similar subject but differ in other ways.

PROMPT

In four or five paragraphs, compare and contrast "Like Black Smoke" and "A World Turned Upside Down." Be sure to identify the purpose, the main idea, and the pattern of organization of each article. Support your response with details from the two articles.

STRATEGIES IN ACTION

1. I have to note **similarities** and **differences** between the two articles.
2. I must **tell** each **author's point** and **reason** for writing. I must **tell** how the ideas are organized.
3. I should **give examples** from each article to prove my points.

2. PLAN YOUR WRITING

Review the chart you filled out on page 905. Use the chart to help you identify how the articles are alike and different. Write a position statement that conveys your main idea about how the articles compare. Then think about how to best present and support the similarities and differences.

- Review the articles to find examples and details that support the similarities and differences.
- Create an outline to organize your ideas. The sample outline shows one way to organize your paragraphs.

I. Introduction
II. Purpose of each article
III. Main idea of each article
IV. Organization of each article
V. Conclusion

3. DRAFT YOUR RESPONSE

Introduction Introduce the topic mentioned in the prompt. Include your position statement.

Body Use your chart and outline as guides to writing the key points of your comparison. Support your points with details from the selections.

Conclusion Leave your readers with a final thought about why the authors used different patterns of organization when writing about a similar subject.

Revision Use words that make your ideas clear. Proofread your response.

Media Study

News Reports

TV Newscast Clip / Web News Report on MediaSmart DVD

What DECISIONS *shape the news?*

ALABAMA STANDARDS

COMMUNICATION STANDARD
15 Demonstrate listening skills

KEY IDEA The news is a flow of information that doesn't stop. Today's fresh news reports compete for space with updated details of news that happened yesterday. What helps journalists choose what to publish each day? You'll examine two news forms to discover who **decides** what news is reported and why.

Background

Uneasy Seasons The hurricane seasons of 2004 and 2005 were difficult ones for millions of people who live along the Atlantic and Gulf coastal regions of the United States. In two of the most dangerous and destructive seasons on record, Florida, Louisiana, Mississippi, Texas, and other coastal states suffered major damage. The TV newscast in this lesson deals with Hurricane Charley, the first of four major hurricanes that battered Florida in 2004. The Web news report deals with Hurricane Frances.

Media Literacy: Newsworthiness

Newsworthiness is the importance of an event or action that makes it worthy of media reporting. Each day, journalists such as news editors decide which news stories will appear in newspapers, on newscasts, and online. Certain factors guide journalists in choosing a report and in shaping its details.

KEY FACTORS OF NEWSWORTHINESS

Timeliness is the quality of being current. The public is always eager for the latest news reports.

Proximity is the nearness of an event to a particular city, region, or country. Most people are more interested in stories that take place locally.

Widespread impact is said to belong to any event with a far-reaching effect. The more people the event could affect, the more likely it is to be newsworthy.

Uniqueness is a quality of news reports about very uncommon events or circumstances.

Human interest characterizes stories that cause readers or viewers to feel emotions such as happiness, anger, or sadness. People are interested in learning news about other people.

Compelling video and **photographs** grab people's attention. In a sense, visual images can place viewers right at the scene of an event.

STRATEGIES FOR VIEWING

In general, understand that the more factors of newsworthiness that a story has, the more attention-getting and long lasting the news report might be.

- Consider the **purposes** behind a report. The primary purpose of news is to inform. Another purpose is to present the advertisements that pay for published or broadcast news.
- Ask yourself: What people or groups are affected by the report? Does the report appeal to the emotions? How does this news affect my world?
- Be aware that the dramatic, attention-getting wording often appears in the **lead,** the opening sentences of a news story.

![MediaSmart DVD]

MediaSmart DVD

- **News Format 1:** "Hurricane Charley"
- **Genre:** TV newscast
- **Running Time:** 3.5 minutes
- **News Format 2:** "Florida and Georgia Recover After Frances"
- **Genre:** Web news report

Viewing Guide for

News Reports

The ABC network news report was first broadcast shortly after Hurricane Charley had struck a Florida town called Punta Gorda. The Web news report was published three weeks later, when Florida was struck by Hurricane Frances.

Watch the TV newscast clip and read the Web report a few times. Keep in mind the time that each report was first published. This can help you figure out what factors of newsworthiness were operating at the time. Use these questions to help you.

NOW VIEW

FIRST VIEWING: Comprehension

1. **Recall** Describe conditions in the town of Punta Gorda, Florida, on the basis of the images from the TV news report.
2. **Recall** According to the Web news report, how much damage (in dollars) did Hurricane Frances cause?

CLOSE VIEWING: Media Literacy

3. **Identify Newsworthiness** Each report gives an account of a hurricane and its effects. Quickly review the key factors of newsworthiness on page 909. If you had been a reporter living in Florida during these times, which one of the key factors would have been most important to you? Give a reason for your choice.
4. **Analyze Newsworthiness** Near the end of the TV newscast, one amazed-looking hurricane survivor states, "I have never seen anything like this, period. Never." What factor of news-worthiness might the news editor have had in mind when he or she chose to include statements from those directly affected by the hurricane? Support your choice.

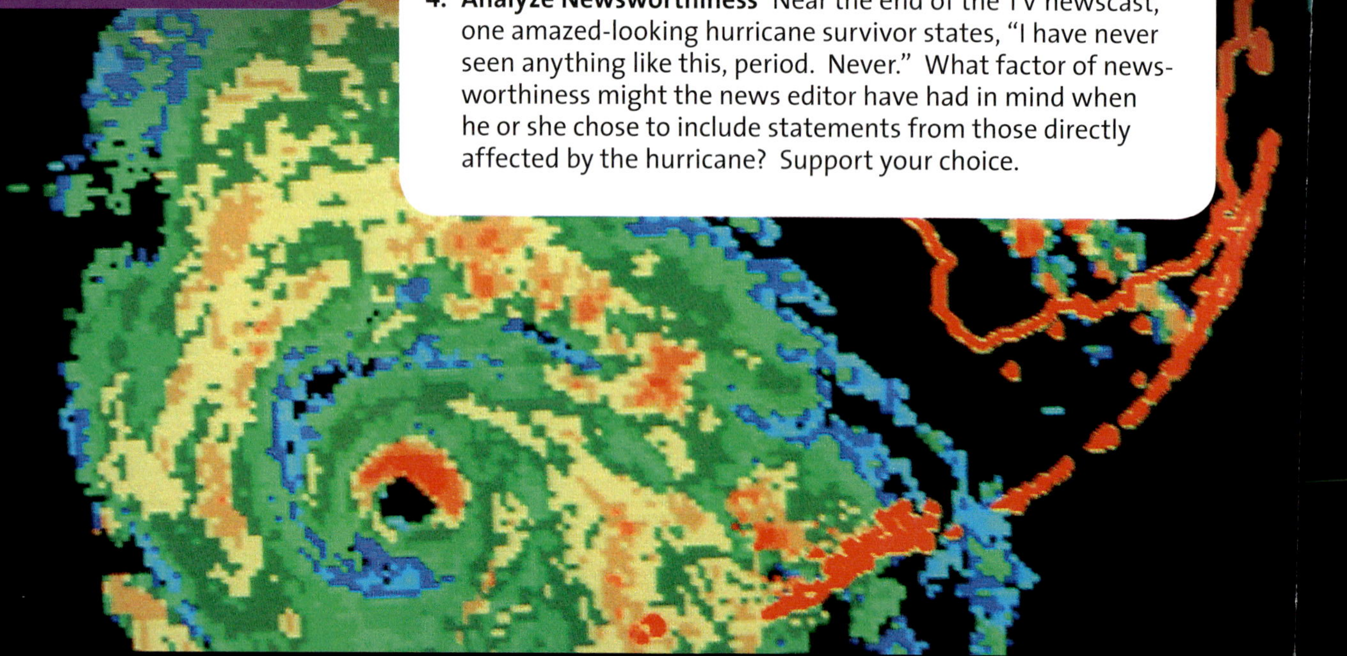

Write or Discuss

Compare Newsworthiness Now that you've examined two news reports about hurricanes, think about how the two are alike or different. Which of the key factors of newsworthiness do you think might have led journalists to publish each report? Briefly explain the reasons for your choices. Think about the factors that make a news event worth reporting.

- Timeliness
- Widespread impact
- Human interest
- Proximity
- Uniqueness
- Compelling video or photographs

Produce Your Own Media

Make a Reporter's Guidebook Use recent news reports and photographs to present what you've learned about the key factors of newsworthiness. Begin by gathering three days' worth of newspaper clippings and Web news reports. (Be sure you have permission to take clippings and to make copies.) Skim the reports. Using sticky notes, label the stories (or photographs) with the factors you find, such as timeliness, widespread impact, and so on.

HERE'S HOW In a small group, follow these steps to assemble the guidebook:
- Use construction paper and paper fasteners to form the basic booklet. Choose a different color to represent each factor of newsworthiness.
- Start each section with a cover sheet that presents a key factor and its definition.
- Look over the clippings and photographs more carefully. Select the best examples for each section of the guide.
- Paste the clippings into the appropriate sections.

MEDIA TOOLS

For help with creating a reporter's guidebook, visit the **Media Center** at **ClassZone.com.**

STUDENT MODEL

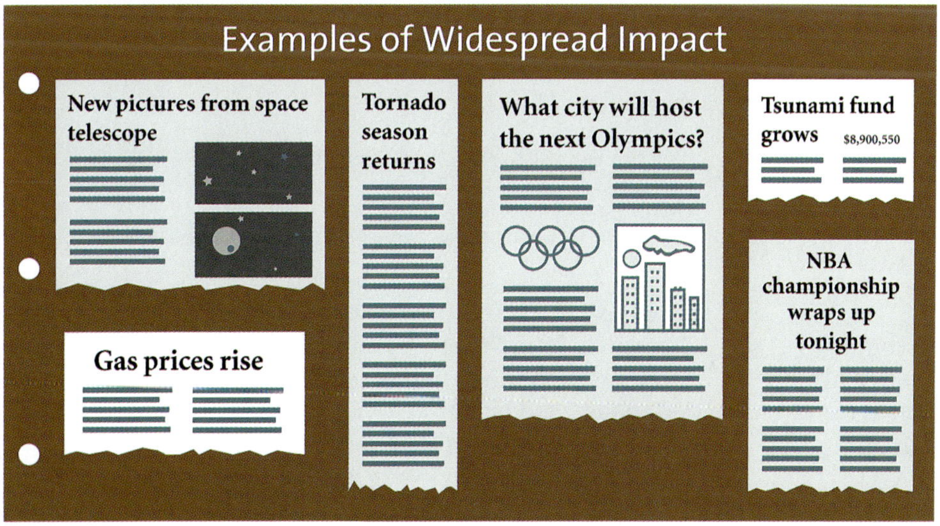

Tech Tip

You can use a word-processing program to create cover sheets for the key factors.

UNIT 8

Reader's Workshop

Argument and Persuasion

Have you ever tried to count the number of persuasive messages you see and hear each day? Letters to the editor, billboards, slogans on the back of your cereal box—persuasive messages are everywhere. In this workshop, you will learn how to analyze the arguments at the heart of these messages and recognize the techniques that are used to persuade you. Armed with this knowledge, you can make up your own mind about messages and ideas that matter.

ALABAMA STANDARDS

READING & LIT STANDARDS
5 Recognize the use of textual elements
7 Interpret author's message in informational texts

Part 1: What Is an Argument?

When you hear the word *argument,* you might think of a fight between two people, complete with differences of opinion, angry shouting, and hurt feelings. In formal speaking and writing, however, an argument is not emotional. It is a claim supported by reasons and evidence.

A **claim** is a writer's position on a problem or an issue. A claim might be stated directly, as in this example: "Crunchy Puffs are an important part of a nutritious breakfast." Sometimes a writer's claim is implied, as in this slogan: "Juan for Student Council—Let the Good Times Roll." The slogan suggests that if Juan is elected, everyone at school will have more fun.

The strength of an argument depends not on the claim but on the **support,** or the reasons and evidence that are used to prove the claim. Evidence can take many forms, including facts, statistics, and examples.

Look closely at the elements of an argument in this example.

CLAIM
All students in the United States should learn a foreign language.

Reason 1
Students in other countries learn foreign languages.

Evidence
In a study of 20 countries, 17 countries required all students to learn at least one foreign language.

Reason 2
Studying a language helps students excel in other subjects.

Evidence
One study found that students who took foreign languages had higher grade point averages than those who didn't.

Reason 3
Knowing other languages is important in the business world.

Evidence
Companies are often international; employees must be able to communicate with customers and with each other.

MODEL: THE ELEMENTS OF AN ARGUMENT

As you read this article about the importance of exercise, try to identify the claim. What is the author urging you to do or believe? What reasons and evidence help the author make her case?

Why Work Out?

Magazine article by **Erica Cheng**

"You don't need to exercise—you look fine the way you are."

You've probably heard comments like this one before. Maybe you yourself have even reassured a friend or an acquaintance with these words of encouragement. After all, the message we see and hear constantly is that exercise is the key to looking like the models on the covers of fitness magazines. So if you are generally happy with the way you look, why bother working out?

Exercise does burn calories and help you build stronger, more defined muscles. Changes in your physical appearance may be the easiest to see, but they are certainly not the most important. Here are a few *real* reasons to work up a sweat:

Raw power. You don't have to be an action hero to find out how satisfying it feels to push yourself and achieve more than you ever thought you could. Regular exercise pays off in greater strength, endurance, and agility—whether your goal is to swim faster, pedal farther, or cross the finish line in record time.

Mood enhancement. When you exercise, your body generates endorphins—chemicals that help you feel content and peaceful, even if you had previously been feeling down. In fact, in one recent study, people who were anxious, lonely, or depressed got the biggest boost from a good workout.

Pure fun. Exercising does not have to be a chore, especially since there are so many exciting activities that you can choose from. Snowboarding. Judo. Trampoline. Hip-hop. Kickboxing. Dodge ball. If you find something you love to do, you'll be more likely to stick with it. And when you're strong, happy, and having a good time, who even cares about how you look?

Close Read

1. Think about the title of this article and reread lines 9–12. What claim is the author making?
2. In the boxed paragraph, the author explains that exercise can have a positive effect on a person's mood. What evidence does she offer to support this reason?
3. In your own words, summarize the other two reasons that the author uses to support her position, or claim.

Part 2: What Really Persuades You?

Do you wear a brand of jeans because they're comfortable, or because everyone else is wearing them? Did you donate money to an animal shelter because you have a passion for saving animals, or because the photograph of a puppy on the shelter's brochure captured your heart?

People aren't always logical. Emotion can play a key role in decision-making. That's why writers and speakers use **persuasive techniques,** or methods that are intended to sway people's feelings and actions. The following techniques can give a strong argument extra punch. Be aware, however, that they are often used to disguise flaws in a weak argument.

Appeals by Association

Link an idea or a product to something or someone positive or influential

Bandwagon Appeal

Taps into people's desire to belong

See the movie and discover the surprise ending that everybody's talking about.

Testimonial

Uses celebrities or satisfied customers to persuade

As an Olympic athlete, I need all the energy I can get. That's why I drink Quench-Ade.

Transfer

Connects a product, a candidate, or a cause with a positive image or idea

A vote for Proposition 43 is a vote for freedom.

Emotional Appeals

Use strong feelings, rather than facts, to persuade

Appeal to Pity

Taps into people's compassion for others

Won't you give this abandoned puppy a home?

Appeal to Fear

Preys upon people's fear for their safety

Is your home safe? ProAlarm Systems—because you shouldn't take any chances.

Appeal to Vanity

Uses flattery to win people over

Bring your creativity and intelligence to our team. Join the yearbook staff!

Loaded Language

Uses words with strongly positive or negative associations

Words with Positive Associations

Call up favorable images, feelings, or experiences

Start your day with Morning Glory's refreshing, all-natural juice.

Words with Negative Associations

May bring to mind unpleasant images, feelings, or experiences; often create a sense of distrust or unease

Who wants to hear the same tired, stale ideas? We need a candidate with a fresh vision.

MODEL 1: PERSUASION IN TEXT

The author of this editorial argues that playing video games can have some significant harmful effects. What techniques does the author use to persuade you to adopt his position?

from

Break the Addiction!

Editorial by **Ethan Flemming**

Hours disappear, and you don't notice. You spend all your money buying more. You think it's an effective way to relieve stress but you end up cutting yourself off from family, friends, and reality.

What started in living rooms across the country as a few hours here and there has become an alarming widespread problem—a population addicted to video games. In fact, the average eighth-grade boy spends 23 hours a week playing video games, while the average eighth-grade girl spends 12 hours.

You may think that video games are just harmless fun, but studies tell a more disturbing story. Some studies have concluded that excessive playing can decrease attention spans, dull imaginations, and create serious social problems. At least 60 percent of games are violent, and most teenagers cite those as their favorites. Repeatedly seeing violent situations unfold on a TV screen can take its toll. After all, such games glamorize violent behavior and paint an unrealistic picture of the world.

Close Read

1. What emotion is the author appealing to in this editorial? Explain how the author might want readers to react to his message.
2. One example of loaded language is boxed. Find two additional examples.

MODEL 2: PERSUASION IN ADVERTISING

If you've turned on the television or skimmed a magazine recently, you know that persuasive techniques are used to sell all kinds of products, from soap to video games. What techniques do you notice in this ad?

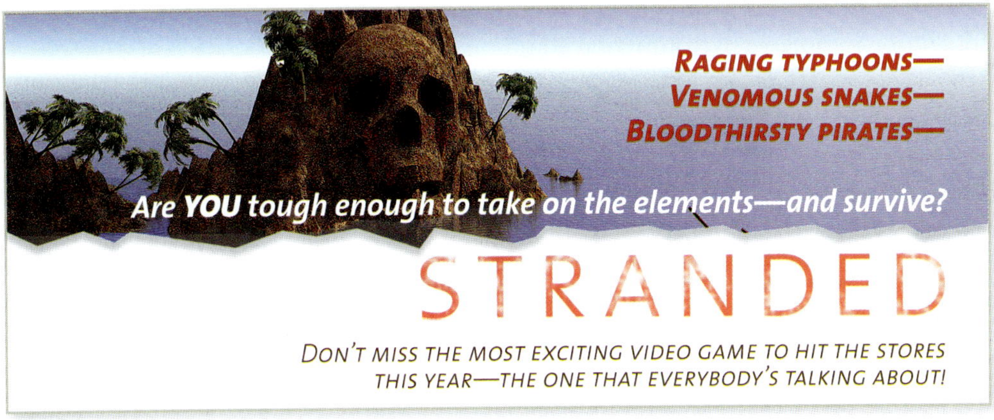

Close Read

1. Explain how this ad tries to appeal to your vanity.
2. Name at least one other persuasive technique used in the ad. Support your answer with details.

Part 3: Analyze the Text

In this essay, British scientist Jane Goodall shares her outlook on the future of the earth. Originally famous for studying the behaviors of chimpanzees in Africa, Goodall now travels around the world, speaking to people about the importance of protecting the environment. Read Goodall's essay, and then examine the public service ad that follows. What argument does each text present? What techniques does each use to persuade you?

THE PROMISE

Nonfiction article by **Jane Goodall**

As we begin the 21st century, it is easy to be overwhelmed by feelings of hopelessness. We humans have destroyed the balance of nature: forests are being destroyed, deserts are spreading, there is terrible pollution and poisoning of air, earth, water. Climate is changing, people are starving. There are too many humans in some parts of the world, overconsumption in others. There is human cruelty to "man" and "beast" alike; there is violence and war. Yet I do have hope. Let me share my four reasons.

Firstly, we have at last begun to understand and face up to the problems that threaten the survival of the earth. And we are problem-solving creatures. Our amazing brains have created modern technology, much of which has greatly benefited millions of people around the globe. Sadly, along with our tendency to overreproduce, it has also resulted in massive destruction and pollution of the natural world. But can we not use our awesome problem-solving ability to now find more environmentally friendly ways to conduct our business? Good news—it's already happening as hundreds of industries and businesses adopt new "green" ethics.[1] And we must play our part—in our billions we must adopt less-harmful lifestyles. Refuse to buy products from companies, corporations, that do not conform to new environmental standards. We *can* change the world.

Second, nature is amazingly resilient.[2] Given the chance, poisoned rivers can live again. Deforested land can be coaxed—or left—to blossom again. Animal species, on the verge of extinction, can sometimes be bred and saved from a few individuals.

1. **"green" ethics:** rules and guidelines that require businesses to use resources, machines, and procedures that are not harmful to the environment.
2. **resilient:** flexible.

Close Read

1. Reread the first paragraph. What is Goodall's claim?
2. In the boxed examples of loaded language, Goodall uses negative words to describe the world's problems. However, she also uses positive words to explain why she still has hope. Find four examples.
3. Goodall's first reason for hope is that humans have already begun to solve some of the problems affecting our environment. What evidence does she give to back up this reason?

My third reason for hope lies in the tremendous energy, enthusiasm, and commitment of young people around the world. Young people want to fight to right the wrongs, for it will be their world tomorrow—they will be the ones in leadership positions, and they themselves will be parents. . . .

My fourth reason for hope lies in the indomitable[3] nature of the human spirit. There are so many people who have dreamed seemingly unattainable dreams and, because they never gave up, achieved their goals against all the odds, or blazed a path along which others could follow.

So let us move into the next millennium with hope—with faith in ourselves, in our intelligence, in our indomitable spirit. Let us develop respect for all living things. Let us try to replace violence and intolerance with understanding and compassion and love.

---

3. **indomitable:** incapable of being defeated; unconquerable.

Close Read

4. Summarize the other reasons that Goodall gives to support her claim.

Close Read

1. Examine the text and the photographs at the top of this ad. What emotional appeal is being used?

2. How does this ad use the technique of transfer?

3. What claim is being made in this ad? (Think about what the ad is trying to convince you to do.)

Pro Athletes' Salaries Aren't Overly Exorbitant

Editorial by Mark Singletary

Do Professional Athletes Get Paid Too Much?

Editorial by Justin Hjelm

Are people paid FAIRLY?

ALABAMA STANDARDS

READING & LIT STANDARDS
4.c Applying self-monitoring strategies
7 Interpret author's message in informational texts

KEY IDEA The president of the United States earns $400,000 a year. A Wall Street stock trader can earn even more, while a first-year New York City policeman earns less than $20,000. Is this fair? In the editorials that follow, two writers offer opposite opinions about the multimillion-dollar **salaries** today's professional athletes make.

DISCUSS With a group of classmates, examine this chart of average annual salaries. If it were up to you, how would the salaries be different? Talk about who you think deserves more, who could do with a little less, who is paid the right amount, and why.

AVERAGE ANNUAL SALARIES

Retail Salesperson $22,540	**Firefighter** $38,810
Kindergarten Teacher $43,530	**Registered Nurse** $52,810
Computer Programmer $65,170	**Airline Pilot** $129,230
Surgeon $182,690	**Major League Baseball Player** $2,376,580

Source: "November 2003 National Occupational Employment and Wage Estimates," U.S. Department of Labor: Bureau of Labor Statistics

ELEMENTS OF NONFICTION: ARGUMENT

An **argument** expresses a position on an issue or problem and provides support for that position. Strong arguments have the following elements:

- a **claim,** which is the writer's main idea or position
- **support,** or reasons and evidence that back up the claim
- **counterarguments,** which are arguments made to address points that someone with an opposing view might raise

As you read, identify the elements in each argument.

READING SKILL: EVALUATE REASONING

When you analyze an argument, it is important to look for fallacies, or **errors in reasoning,** like those explained below:

- An **overgeneralization** is a statement about a group of people or things that is much too broad to be true. "All teenagers love to listen to loud music" is an overgeneralization, because not all teenagers do.
- A **single-cause fallacy** suggests there is only one cause for something when there are actually several. "The only reason people go to the beach is to swim" is a single-cause fallacy. People might go to sunbathe or to hang out with friends.

As you read, use a chart to record errors in reasoning.

Example of Error	*Type of Error/Explanation*
". . . the players are selfish . . ." (line 10)	*Overgeneralization*

VOCABULARY IN CONTEXT

The boldfaced words help these authors construct their arguments. To see how many you know, substitute a different word or phrase for each boldfaced term.

1. Star Player's **Compensation** Shoots Up to $15 Million
2. **Brevity** of Pitcher's Career Caused by Arm Injury
3. Umpire Call Challenged by **Dissenter**
4. Coach's **Entitlement** to Special Treatment Questioned
5. **Appalling** Brawl in Bleachers Injures 20
6. **Voracious** Fans Can't Get Enough of Home Team

Author Online

Mark Singletary: Veteran Publisher

Mark Singletary
born 1952

Mark Singletary is president and publisher of New Orleans Publishing Group, which prints business-related journals. What does Singletary say about professional athletes' salaries? "More power to 'em."

Justin Hjelm: Student Journalist

Justin Hjelm
born 1983

While attending Westmont College in California, Justin Hjelm (yĕlm) knew that the best way to make his views known was to write about them. Hjelm's editorial is an example of how students can make their voices heard.

MORE ABOUT THE AUTHOR
For more on the authors, visit the **Literature Center** at **ClassZone.com.**

Background

Weighing In on Heavy Salaries Frequently when athletes' salaries make the news, editorials start appearing in many publications. "Pro Athletes' Salaries Aren't Overly Exorbitant" appeared in *New Orleans CityBusiness.* "Do Professional Athletes Get Paid Too Much?" was published in Westmont College's campus newspaper, the *Horizon.*

New Orleans CITYBUSINESS

A player signs autographs for die-hard fans before the 75th Major League Baseball All-Star Game.

Pro Athletes' Salaries Aren't Overly Exorbitant[1] (A)

MARK SINGLETARY

(A) ARGUMENT
You can immediately identify the author's claim by reading the editorial's title. **Paraphrase** the title, or restate it in your own words.

I am going to try and make a point about the salaries that professional athletes get to play their games. I think I'm moving into a very solid "more power to 'em" position. I guess until recently I've thought the players were a bit selfish and their salaries would lead to the failure of professional sports.

Of course, the players are selfish and ultimately professional sports will fail or have to be restructured significantly. Who knows when that time will come? (B)

(B) EVALUATE REASONING
What **overgeneralization** does Singletary make in lines 10–13? Explain why his statement is too broad.

But the players are no more selfish than the owners who pay the salaries. And the owners are no more selfish than the television and radio networks that pay outlandish sums to broadcast the games.

All of us are looking for something. The games work best when those willing to pay match up evenly with what the others have to sell.

I've always thought of myself as the kind of guy who would give his left arm or eye or big toe to have a chance to play any of the major league sports. Now I think I can honestly say that I would give up a lot, but

1. **exorbitant** (ĭg-zôr′bĭ-tənt): exceeding all bounds of custom or fairness.

not everything, to have the chance to play one big game.

Pause and reflection make me think now that it would still be awesome to train hard, make a major league roster and spend an entire season with the team, but at some point the fun might turn into work.

I would probably begin to think that if I was good enough to make the squad, then I would deserve to be paid the same as my teammates. And if by chance I would happen to be star quality and could reasonably assume that coming to see me play was a big deal, then I might end up asking for a little more than the average player gets.

Also, when I read the sports or business pages of the newspaper, I see that television networks pay huge sums to broadcast my games. When I go to work, I realize that other companies want to name our stadium, promote our schedule and decorate our arena with their advertisements.

The historical argument for paying exorbitant salaries to athletes is the **brevity** of their careers. All of these athletes are a busted knee, concussion or torn rotator cuff[2] away from the end of their career, and very few sports offer guaranteed contracts that go beyond the season when the injury occurs.

Our fans are important to the economic health of our ball club. My teammates and I are responsible for finding and keeping fans. If I am a star, it can rightly be assumed the fans come to see me play. **C**

When the fans come to see the stars perform, the value of the franchise[3] increases. I'm pretty smart and understand all this and how it relates to me. I also know what I make and how that relates to others that play my game.

So, it seems to me that even though I love the game, even though just playing the game is huge **compensation** and very, very satisfying, I want things to be fair.

Fair is fair. And fair is that the athletes deserve what the fans are willing to pay.

The owners probably don't care what the athletes make, as long as they can pass the cost on to sponsors and ticket buyers. The intelligence in sports ownership is the ability to predict exactly where the fans and sponsors lose interest.

Until that time, it seems fair to allocate as much as possible to the players that make the games entertaining. It's also the only way to win consistently in modern, major league sports. The smartest in all the groups are not only taking as much and passing along as much as possible, but they are also looking toward the future to see when it all ends. **D**

So, everyone benefits right up until the time that no one benefits.

2. **concussion . . . rotator cuff:** A concussion is an injury to the brain caused by a fall or a blow to the head. A rotator cuff is the muscle and tendon that support the shoulder joint, a place of common injury among baseball pitchers.

3. **franchise:** a team that is a member of a professional sports league.

C EVALUATE REASONING
Reread lines 64—69. Do you think Singletary's statement is a **single-cause fallacy?** Explain.

compensation (kŏm'pən-sā'shən) *n.* payment

brevity (brĕv'ĭ-tē) *n.* shortness

D ARGUMENT
Reread lines 91–100, which contain Singletary's main **claim.** Paraphrase, or restate, his claim.

The Horizon

WESTMONT COLLEGE SANTA BARBARA, CALIFORNIA

DO PROFESSIONAL ATHLETES GET PAID TOO MUCH?

JUSTIN HJELM

Staff Reporter

YES. When asked in the early twenties what justified him making more money than the President of the United States, Babe Ruth[1] replied "Well, I had a better year."

For nearly a century, superstar athletes have demanded and received salaries grossly out of proportion with the average income of their times. What makes modern times different and more disturbing is that even the role players in professional sports are pulling in an exorbitant amount of money.

Fifty years ago, only the 40-home-run outfielder would make a huge salary. Now, however, the utility infielder who comes in as a defensive replacement three times a week makes ten times more than the average working man. **E**

E ARGUMENT
"Athletes have always made a lot of money"—that's the argument Hjelm anticipates in lines 6–21. What is his **counterargument?**

Nolan Ryan[2] broke ground in 1979, becoming the first athlete to receive a $1-million-a-year contract. It took over a century for baseball to reach this milestone income figure, and just 25 years later a $1 million contract offer is considered an insult.

1. **Babe Ruth:** a baseball player from 1914 to 1935, considered by many to be the best baseball player in the history of the sport.
2. **Nolan Ryan:** a baseball pitcher from 1966 to 1993 who held over 50 major-league records.

The contracts of professional athletes have gone unchecked for too long, and now athletes are among the wealthiest people in our nation.

Athletes are paid far too much for simply playing games. Essentially, as anyone can tell you, sports are entertainment. We pay to see these athletes perform at the highest level. **F**

It is a sad commentary on our societal values that these entertainers are raking in seven-figure salaries while teachers, police officers, and fire fighters make less than one percent of the income of some athletes. Entertainment is a necessary thing, but it is not needed nearly as much as countless other occupations are.

What kind of message are we sending our children with these backward values?

From the perspective of a young person, sports seem like the better and easier path. Would a child rather play basketball and make millions or go to school for years and end up making $50,000 a year?

Dissenters will say that it is not that cut and dried,[3] and they are probably right. Making a professional sporting league is exceptionally difficult. But fewer and fewer kids are realizing this.

One only needs to look as far as the NBA draft[4] for proof of this.

Athlete: Babe Ruth
Sport: Baseball
Team: New York Yankees
Contract Year: 1921
Contracted Salary: $39,638
Salary Adjusted to 2004 Dollars: $418,303

Athlete: Jackie Robinson
Sport: Baseball
Team: Brooklyn Dodgers
Contract Year: 1947
Contracted Salary: $8,500
Salary Adjusted to 2004 Dollars: $72,002

Athlete: Bill Russell
Sport: Basketball
Team: Boston Celtics
Contract Year: 1956
Contracted Salary: $19,500
Salary Adjusted to 2004 Dollars: $135,425

Athlete: Nolan Ryan
Sport: Baseball
Team: Houston Astros
Contract Year: 1979
Contracted Salary: $1,100,000
Salary Adjusted to 2004 Dollars: $2,862,121

F ARGUMENT
Reread lines 33–38. What is Hjelm's **claim** about the salaries of professional athletes? As you continue to read, note how Hjelm **supports** his claim.

dissenter (dĭ-sĕn′tər) *n.* one who disagrees or holds a different opinion

3. **cut and dried:** simple
4. **NBA draft:** the process by which teams in the National Basketball Association select, or draft, players. Generally, the teams with the worst records from the preceding year get the top draft choices.

MATH CONNECTION
How much more was Alex Rodriguez's contracted salary in 2004 than Kenny Anderson's was in 1999?

Athlete: Kenny Anderson
Sport: Basketball
Team: Boston Celtics
Contract Year: 1999
Contracted Salary: $5,845,000
Salary Adjusted to 2004 Dollars: $6,627,374

Athlete: Alex Rodriguez
Sport: Baseball
Team: New York Yankees
Contract Year: 2004
Contracted Salary: $21,726,881

A decade ago, a high school player skipping college was a rarity. In 1994, you could count the early entrants on one hand. Now, however, there are numerous high schoolers declaring for the draft every year, some of whom do not even get drafted. These players forfeit their college eligibility and will struggle for years to make an NBA team. After that, without a college education, they struggle to find a decent job.

Also troubling are the egos of the athletes receiving these giant paychecks. They have no ability to relate to the public. During the NBA lockout in 1998-99, players were crying poverty. **G**

Kenny Anderson, then a guard for the Boston Celtics, complained of not being able to afford the insurance on his eight cars. The sense of **entitlement** that these athletes have is **appalling.** They play a game that many would play for meal money and get paid like royalty, and then have the gall to whine that they are not paid enough.

It's startling that people have blasé[5] attitudes about $100 million contracts. Eight-figure deals are not something to be yawned at, but with their current frequency, it is becoming that way. Athletes are paid far too much for what they do, but I believe that society is more at fault for this than the athletes themselves are.

We simply put too much importance on entertainment, and with this statement I condemn myself and the rabidity[6] with which I follow sports. The once tightly controlled finances of the sporting world have been torn apart and the winds of greed and America's **voracious** thirst for entertainment have scattered the pieces so that they can never be put together again.

G EVALUATE REASONING
Reread lines 77–82. What **overgeneralization** does Hjelm make about professional athletes? Explain.

entitlement (ĕn-tĭt'l-mənt) *n.* the state of having a right or claim to something

appalling (ə-pô'lĭng) *adj.* outrageous; terrible
appall *v.*

voracious (vô-rā'shəs) *adj.* possessing an insatiable desire; greedy

5. **blasé** (blä-zā'): unconcerned; uninterested.
6. **rabidity:** craziness or unreasonable extremeness.

After Reading

Comprehension

1. **Recall** What does Singletary believe about the future of professional sports?
2. **Clarify** Why does Hjelm place some of the blame for athletes' high salaries on himself as a sports fan and on society as a whole?

ALABAMA STANDARDS

LITERATURE STANDARD
7 Interpret author's message in informational texts

Critical Analysis

3. **Identify a Counterargument** Reread lines 10–20 of the first editorial. What counterargument does Singletary offer to oppose the notion that pro athletes are selfish?
4. **Analyze an Argument** Think about the **claim** that Hjelm presents in "Do Professional Athletes Get Paid Too Much?" Complete the graphic by listing three reasons or examples Hjelm uses to **support** his claim.

5. **Evaluate Reasoning** Examine the errors in reasoning you noted as you read. Suggest how Singletary and Hjelm might each reword his statements to correct these errors and make his argument stronger.
6. **Make Judgments** Which of these editorials did you find more convincing? Explain your answer, citing specific lines you found especially effective.

Extension and Challenge

7. **Speaking and Listening** Work with classmates to set up a panel discussion about the **salaries** of professional athletes. Each panelist should play the role of a different character: a team owner, a professional athlete, a sports broadcaster, and a fan. A moderator can take questions from the audience, and the panelists should respond as they think their characters would.
8. **MATH CONNECTION** Using Babe Ruth's salary adjusted to 2004 dollars, how much more money did Alex Rodriguez make in 2004 than Babe Ruth did in 1921? What percentage increase is this? You can find these numbers in the sidebars on pages 923 and 924.

$$\%\text{ increase} = \frac{\text{amount of increase}}{\text{lower salary in 2004 dollars}}$$

Vocabulary in Context

VOCABULARY PRACTICE

Decide whether each statement is true or false.

1. A **dissenter** is usually a person who goes along with what others think.
2. Someone with a **voracious** appetite for sports often goes to several games a week.
3. An **appalling** situation is one that shocks and depresses you.
4. If you do volunteer work, you don't expect **compensation** for your services.
5. The author of a 3,400-page book should be praised for her **brevity.**
6. Meek, humble people usually feel a strong sense of **entitlement.**

appalling
brevity
compensation
dissenter
entitlement
voracious

VOCABULARY IN WRITING

Choose an athlete or other professional who you think either deserves or does not deserve a high salary. Write a paragraph explaining your opinion, using two or more vocabulary words. You might start like this.

EXAMPLE SENTENCE

Since she was voted Most Valuable Player three years in a row, this player's ***compensation*** *makes sense.*

VOCABULARY STRATEGY: IDIOMS

Idioms are common expressions that mean something different from the meaning of the individual words in them. For example, the expression *cut and dried,* which appears on page 923, means "simple," not "sliced into pieces and dried."

PRACTICE Define the italicized idiom in each sentence.

1. To get along with Madeline, you need to learn to *hold your tongue.*
2. All those compliments are *going to Sam's head.*
3. After he lost his job, Mr. Murphy looked a bit *down at the heels.*
4. I can't quite *put my finger on* why she makes me so angry.
5. It is a good idea for business partners to *see eye to eye* on most things.
6. The rumor is that Jake *paid through the nose* for that car.

VOCABULARY PRACTICE
For more practice, go to the **Vocabulary Center** at **ClassZone.com.**

SKILLS PRACTICE

Reading-Writing Connection

Demonstrate your understanding of these editorials by responding to the prompts. Then complete the **Grammar and Writing** exercise.

WRITING PROMPTS	SELF-CHECK
A. Short Response: Write a Letter Write a **one-paragraph letter** to the editor of *New Orleans CityBusiness* or the *Horizon* in response to one of the selections. Explain whether you agree or disagree with the writer's opinion. Remember to keep your audience in mind as you write.	***A strong letter will . . .*** • point out any errors in reasoning • provide one more claim to support the argument or one brief counterargument
B. Extended Response: Explore the Key Idea Select one of the athletes listed in the sidebar on pages 923 and 924. In a **two- or three-paragraph response,** construct an argument that expresses why you think that person's **salary** is fair or unfair.	***A successful response will . . .*** • have one primary claim • use adequate support, including factual examples • include a counterargument

GRAMMAR AND WRITING

USE COMMAS CORRECTLY Be sure to use commas correctly after **introductory words and phrases** and when listing **items in a series.** Place commas immediately after introductory words such as *Finally* and *Afterwards* and after introductory phrases that contain prepositional phrases. Also place a comma after every item in a series except the last one. (A series consists of three or more items.)

Original: During their careers athletes face injuries stiff competition and a lot of pressure to prove themselves.

Revised: During their careers, athletes face injuries, stiff competition, and a lot of pressure to prove themselves.

PRACTICE In each sentence, add commas where they are needed.

1. In recent years athletes' salaries have greatly increased.
2. Babe Ruth Jackie Robinson and Nolan Ryan deserved good salaries.
3. Within the sports community it is well known how much money owners make from sponsors.
4. The owners the networks and the sponsors are all making money.

*For more help with punctuating introductory words and phrases and items in a series, see page R49 in the **Grammar Handbook.***

ALABAMA STANDARDS

WRITING/LANGUAGE STANDARD
10 Apply mechanics in writing, including commas following introductory phrases

Why We Shouldn't Go to Mars

Magazine Article by Gregg Easterbrook

Do we have our PRIORITIES *straight?*

ALABAMA STANDARDS

LIT & RESEARCH STANDARDS

7 Interpret author's message in informational texts

13.a Taking notes to gather, summarize information

KEY IDEA As a seventh grader, you may have many obligations to juggle—homework, sports or hobbies, time with friends and family, and maybe even an afterschool job. Deciding on **priorities,** or what is most important, can be a difficult task. Setting priorities can be tough for nations and societies too. You're about to read one writer's ideas of what our national priorities should and should not be.

ROLE-PLAY With a group, create a panel discussion in which each student represents a different demand on one seventh grader's time. (The list of obligations in the paragraph above can give you ideas.) Each person should argue why his or her demand deserves to be a priority. Then decide as a group which two demands should be at the top of the priority list.

● ELEMENTS OF NONFICTION: COUNTERARGUMENT

A strong counterargument is an important part of any argument. A **counterargument** anticipates what "the other side" might say and answers possible objections with reasons and evidence.

As you can probably guess from this article's title, author Gregg Easterbrook believes that sending astronauts on a mission to Mars is a mistake. Rather than ignoring those who disagree with him, Easterbrook states his opponents' views and then tells why he disagrees. As you read, search for examples of this technique.

■ READING SKILL: TAKE NOTES

When you **take notes,** you record a text's most important information in a way that is easy to refer to later. The form your notes take will depend on what you're reading and why you're reading it.

In an article like this one, where the author states his opinion in the title, you can expect the main ideas to be the reasons for his opinion. The evidence he gives for this opinion are the details. As you read, note the main reasons and evidence as shown.

Why Easterbrook Thinks We Shouldn't Go to Mars

- *It's too expensive.*
  - *—It would cost $600 billion in today's money.*

▲ VOCABULARY IN CONTEXT

The boldfaced words help Easterbrook make his case for not sending people to Mars. To see how many you know, match each vocabulary word in Column A to the word or phrase in Column B that is closest in meaning.

Column A	Column B
1. amenable	**a.** tempting
2. exhilarating	**b.** agreeable
3. tantalizing	**c.** self-running
4. automated	**d.** reasonableness
5. proponent	**e.** supporter
6. rationality	**f.** thrilling

Author Online

A Wide World of Writing Before he became a full-time writer and editor, Gregg Easterbrook worked as a bus driver and a used-car salesman. Now a senior editor of *The New Republic,* Easterbrook has contributed to *Time, Newsweek,* and ESPN.

Gregg Easterbrook
born 1953

Background

The Red Planet The United States and the former Soviet Union began attempting flights to Mars in the early 1960s. In 1965, the first successful mission was completed when a U.S. spacecraft flew by Mars and sent 22 photos back to Earth. Since then, extensive space missions have revealed that Mars is rocky, cold, and sterile. Humans have never gone to Mars, and scientists still aren't sure if there has ever been life there.

Mission to Mars? In 2004, President George W. Bush announced a new space exploration program. Gregg Easterbrook responded to this announcement by writing the article "Why We Shouldn't Go to Mars" for *Time* magazine.

MORE ABOUT THE AUTHOR AND BACKGROUND
To learn more about Gregg Easterbrook and the space exploration program, visit the **Literature Center** at **ClassZone.com.**

ANALYZE VISUALS
This picture of the planets combines photographs taken by different spacecraft. Pluto is not shown because no spacecraft has yet visited it. As a whole, what **mood** does this image convey?

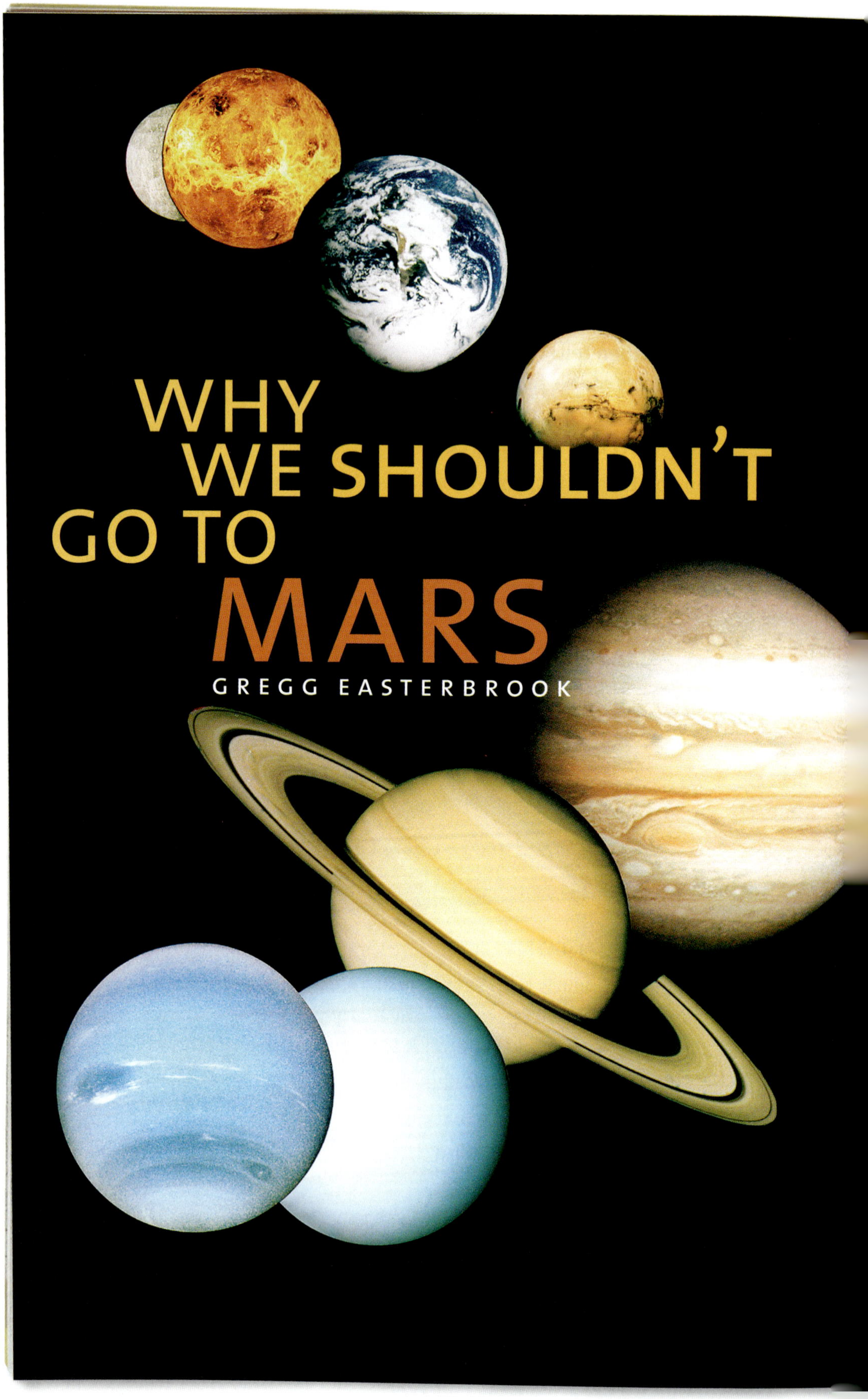

WHY WE SHOULDN'T GO TO MARS

GREGG EASTERBROOK

"Two centuries ago, Meriwether Lewis and William Clark left St. Louis to explore the new lands acquired in the Louisiana Purchase,"[1] George W. Bush said, announcing his desire for a program to send men and women to Mars. "They made that journey in the spirit of discovery. . . . America has ventured forth into space for the same reasons."

Yet there are vital differences between Lewis and Clark's expedition and a Mars mission. First, Lewis and Clark were headed to a place **amenable** to life; hundreds of thousands of people were already living there. Second, Lewis and Clark were *certain* to discover places and things of immediate value to the new nation. Third, the Lewis and Clark venture cost next to nothing by today's standards. In 1989 NASA estimated that a people-to-Mars program would cost $400 billion, which inflates to $600 billion today. The Hoover Dam cost $700 million in today's money, meaning that sending people to Mars might cost as much as building about 800 new Hoover Dams. A Mars mission may be the single most expensive nonwartime undertaking in U.S. history. (A)

The thought of travel to Mars is **exhilarating.** Surely men and women will someday walk upon that planet, and surely they will make wondrous discoveries about geology[2] and the history of the solar system, perhaps even about the very origin of life. Many times I have stared up at Mars in the evening sky—in the mountains, away from cities, you can almost see the red tint—and wondered what is there, or was there.

But the fact that a destination is **tantalizing** does not mean the journey makes sense, even considering the human calling to explore. And Mars as a destination for people makes absolutely no sense with current technology.

1. **Louisiana Purchase:** an area extending from the Mississippi River to the Rocky Mountains, purchased from France in 1803.
2. **geology:** the scientific study of the history and structure of the earth.

amenable (ə-mē′nə-bəl) *adj.* open; agreeable

(A) COUNTERARGUMENT
A **false analogy** is a comparison that doesn't hold up because of an important difference between the two subjects. How does Easterbrook prove that likening a Mars mission to Lewis and Clark's expedition is a false analogy?

exhilarating (ĭg-zĭl′ə-rā′tĭng) *adj.* stimulating; making one feel thrilled or inspired **exhilarate** *v.*

tantalizing (tăn′tə-lī′zĭng) *adj.* tempting but out of reach **tantalize** *v.*

Left, NASA artist's concept of the Mars Exploration Rover, which landed on Mars in 2004; *right,* computer-generated image of the surface of Mars.

Present systems for getting from Earth's surface to low-Earth orbit[3] are so fantastically expensive that merely launching the 1,000 tons or so of spacecraft and equipment a Mars mission would require could be accomplished only by cutting health-care benefits, education spending or other important programs—or by raising taxes. Absent some remarkable discovery, astronauts, geologists and biologists once on Mars could do little more than analyze rocks and feel awestruck beholding the sky of another world. Yet rocks can be analyzed by **automated** probes without risk to human life, and at a tiny fraction of the cost of sending people. **B**

automated (ô'tə-mā'tĭd) *adj.* able to function with little or no assistance from people **automate** *v.*

B TAKE NOTES
In this paragraph, what are the main reasons Easterbrook gives for not sending a person to Mars? Jot them down in your notes.

It is interesting to note that when President Bush unveiled his proposal, he listed these recent major achievements of space exploration: pictures of the rings of Saturn and the outer planets, evidence of water on Mars and the moons of Jupiter, discovery of more than 100 planets outside our solar system and study of the soil of Mars. All these accomplishments came from automated probes or automated space telescopes. Bush's proposal, which calls for "reprogramming" some of NASA's present budget into the Mars effort, might actually lead to a reduction in such unmanned science—the one aspect of space exploration that's working really well.

Rather than spend hundreds of billions of dollars to hurl tons toward Mars using current technology, why not take

3. **low-Earth orbit:** a region roughly 200 to 500 miles above Earth, the easiest area to reach in space and the area from which scientists hope to launch future space missions.

Mars, the Red Planet

a decade—or two decades, or however much time is required—researching new launch systems and advanced propulsion? If new launch systems could put weight into orbit affordably, and if advanced propulsion could speed up that long, slow transit to Mars, then the dream of stepping onto the Red Planet might become reality. Mars will still be there when the technology is ready.

Space-exploration **proponents** deride as lack of vision the mention of technical barriers or the insistence that needs on Earth come first. Not so. The former is **rationality,** the latter the setting of priorities. If Mars proponents want to raise $600 billion privately and stage their own expedition, more power to them; many of the great expeditions of the past were privately mounted. If Mars proponents expect taxpayers to foot their bill, then they must make their case against the many other competing needs for money. And against the needs for health care, education, poverty reduction, reinforcement of the military and reduction of the federal deficit,[4] the case for vast expenditures to go to Mars using current technology is very weak. C

The drive to explore is part of what makes us human, and exploration of the past has led to unexpected glories. Dreams must be tempered by realism, however. For the moment, going to Mars is hopelessly unrealistic.

proponent (prə-pō′nənt) *n.* a person who supports something

rationality (răsh′ə-năl′ĭ-tē) *n.* reasonableness

C **COUNTERARGUMENT**
Easterbrook's opponents could claim that he has a "lack of vision" because he is against a Mars mission. Reread lines 63–75. What is his counterargument to this possible criticism?

---

4. **federal deficit:** a shortage of funds caused by the government's spending more than it collects in taxes.

Comprehension

ALABAMA STANDARDS

LITERATURE STANDARD
7 Interpret author's message in informational texts

1. **Recall** How does the cost of a Mars mission compare to the cost of the Hoover Dam?
2. **Recall** In what areas does Easterbrook suggest that "wondrous discoveries" might one day be made on Mars?
3. **Clarify** What national issues does Easterbrook suggest are more important than sending U.S. astronauts to Mars?

Critical Analysis

4. **Summarize Notes** What are three main reasons Easterbrook gives for believing that the government should not send people to Mars? If you can't find the answer in your notes, look for it in the article. Then revise your notes so that they include this important information.
5. **Identify a Counterargument** Reread lines 43–53. Easterbrook's opponents argue that sending astronauts on missions is necessary in order to make achievements in space exploration. What counterargument does Easterbrook offer in response?
6. **Evaluate Support** Easterbrook supports his argument with evidence. Which pieces of evidence did you find most, or least, convincing? Pick at least two and list them in a chart. Then describe your reaction to the evidence.

Evidence	My Reaction
Lewis and Clark's expedition cost very little, while a Mars mission will cost $600 billion.	I think $600 billion seems like way too much money! We could put that money to better use.

Extension and Challenge

7. **Readers' Circle** When deciding about how to spend taxpayers' money, Easterbrook says, "needs on Earth come first." Discuss whether you agree with Easterbrook's opinion about what our national **priorities** should be.
8. **SCIENCE CONNECTION** Do some research on past automated Mars missions. Consider the following questions:
   - What was the name of the spacecraft that first orbited Mars?
   - What year did a U.S. craft first land on the planet?
   - What do you think is the best thing that Mars probes have discovered?

RESEARCH LINKS
For more on Mars, visit the **Research Center** at **ClassZone.com.**

Vocabulary in Context

VOCABULARY PRACTICE

Choose the letter of the item most closely associated with each vocabulary word.

1. **tantalizing:** (a) an old pair of tennis shoes, (b) the smell of chocolate-chip cookies baking, (c) a statement about an overdue bill
2. **amenable:** (a) an easygoing person, (b) a dilapidated car, (c) a protest march
3. **automated:** (a) a soccer ball, (b) a robot, (c) a birthday party
4. **exhilarating:** (a) a brisk walk on a beach, (b) a large herd of cattle, (c) a low hedge
5. **proponent:** (a) part of an airplane, (b) leader of a voting drive, (c) carton of unworn gloves
6. **rationality:** (a) a new shopping center, (b) a letter from an old friend, (c) a well thought-out plan

amenable
automated
exhilarating
proponent
rationality
tantalizing

VOCABULARY IN WRITING

What issues or projects do you think our government should invest money in? Choose one and explain your opinion about it, using at least two vocabulary words. You might start like this.

EXAMPLE SENTENCE

*I am a strong **proponent** of our government's working to eliminate hunger around the world.*

ALABAMA STANDARDS

READING STANDARD
4.b Using context clues to determine word meaning

VOCABULARY STRATEGY: THE GREEK ROOT *aut*

The vocabulary word *automated* contains the Greek root *aut,* which means "self." This root, and the related prefix *auto-*, is found in a number of English words. Use your understanding of the root's meaning, as well as context clues, to figure out the meanings of words formed from *aut*.

VOCABULARY PRACTICE
For more practice, go to the **Vocabulary Center** at **ClassZone.com.**

PRACTICE Choose a word from the web that best completes each sentence. If you need help, check a dictionary.

1. A genuine _____ by Abraham Lincoln is worth a lot of money.
2. How often are planes flown on _____?
3. Because of _____, many jobs can be done more quickly and with less effort.
4. Countries that are _____ are governed by their own people.
5. _____ limits its sufferers' ability to communicate with others.

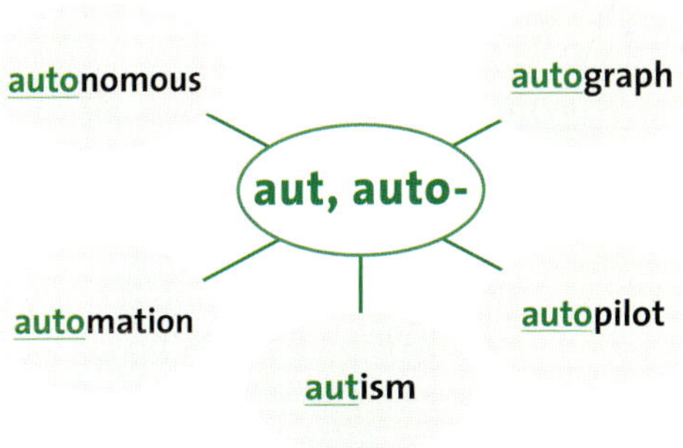

Remarks at the Dedication of the Aerospace Medical Health Center

Speech by John F. Kennedy

What INSPIRES *people?*

ALABAMA STANDARDS

READING STANDARDS

2 Relate literary elements and devices to each other

4 Apply strategies to comprehend informational materials

KEY IDEA It's sometimes hard to do the right thing, especially if you feel as if you're doing it all alone. Every once in a while, a leader emerges who can **inspire** people to break through their fear and preoccupation to make our society the best it can be. You're about to read a speech by one such leader—President John F. Kennedy.

QUICKWRITE Think about a time when someone convinced you to make a change or take an action. Write a journal entry telling why you felt inspired.

● ELEMENTS OF NONFICTION: PERSUASIVE TECHNIQUES

Advertisers, politicians, and writers often try to influence or persuade us to support their product, beliefs, or position on an issue. Common **persuasive techniques** include

- referring to the opinion of an expert (appeal to authority)
- appealing to common sense (logical appeal)
- appealing to the desire to belong (appeal by association)
- evoking strong feelings (emotional appeal)

As you read President Kennedy's speech, identify the persuasive techniques he uses.

■ READING STRATEGY: READING A SPEECH

After reading the **speech** silently, read it aloud. If you listen closely, you will be able to hear the techniques and strategies Kennedy uses to keep the listeners' interest. Use a chart to note examples of the strategies.

Strategies	*Examples from the Speech*
Sound devices such as rhythm, repetition, and alliteration	*first paragraph: repeats "era" three times*
Organization that makes the speech easy to follow	
Concrete examples that connect to the audience's lives	

▲ VOCABULARY IN CONTEXT

The boldfaced words helped Kennedy communicate the importance of space research. Restate each sentence using a different word or words for the boldfaced term.

1. It is a **partisan** law that only benefits the rich.
2. This is a noble **endeavor** that will eventually succeed.
3. The pilot observed the spacecraft on **radar.**
4. She experienced **disorientation** in the space lab.
5. Exercise helped the patient increase his **metabolism.**
6. He has a temporary **impairment** and needs to use crutches.
7. Cheap land was a great **impetus** for the new settlers.
8. Studying the chart is a **tedious** task.

Author Online

U.S. President John F. Kennedy, the 35th president of the United States, set out to lead the way into a future filled with scientific discoveries and improvements in society. Wanting to bring democracy and freedom to the world, Kennedy asked that all American citizens join him in this New Frontier.

John F. Kennedy
1917–1963

A Race to Space In 1957, the country then known as the Soviet Union launched *Sputnik I*, the first satellite to orbit the earth. The Soviet Union and the United States were bitter enemies, and after becoming president in 1961, Kennedy was determined to equal and even surpass the Soviets' knowledge of space. He said, "No nation which expects to be the leader of other nations can expect to stay behind in this race for space." In a session before Congress in 1961, Kennedy called for plans to send astronauts to the moon. The United States achieved this goal on July 20, 1969.

An Inspirational Speaker A line from Kennedy's inaugural address is often quoted: "Ask not what your country can do for you—ask what you can do for your country." You are about to read the speech he made on November 21, 1963. The following day, November 22, 1963, John F. Kennedy was assassinated.

MORE ABOUT THE AUTHOR
For more on John F. Kennedy, visit the **Literature Center** at **ClassZone.com.**

Remarks at the Dedication of the Aerospace Medical Health Center

President John F. Kennedy

Mr. Secretary, Governor, Mr. Vice President, Senator, Members of the Congress, members of the military, ladies and gentlemen:

For more than 3 years I have spoken about the New Frontier. This is not a **partisan** term, and it is not the exclusive property of Republicans or Democrats. It refers, instead, to this Nation's place in history, to the fact that we do stand on the edge of a great new era, filled with both crisis and opportunity, an era to be characterized by achievement and by challenge. It is an era which calls for action and for the best efforts of all those who would test the unknown and the uncertain in every phase of human **endeavor**. It is a time for pathfinders and pioneers. **A**

partisan (pär′tĭ-zən) *adj.* relating to or in support of one political party

endeavor (ĕn-dĕv′ər) *n.* purposeful or serious activity; enterprise

A READ A SPEECH
Reread lines 3–10. Speech writers often use **repetition** and **alliteration,** or the repetition of consonant sounds at the beginning of words, to create memorable phrases. Find an example of both.

I have come to Texas today to salute an outstanding group of pioneers, the men who man the Brooks Air Force Base School of Aerospace Medicine and the Aerospace Medical Center. It is fitting that San Antonio should be the site of this center and this school as we gather to dedicate this complex of buildings. For this city has long been the home of the pioneers in the air. It was here that Sidney Brooks, whose memory we honor today, was born and raised. It was here that Charles Lindbergh and Claire Chennault,[1] and a host of others, who, in World War I and World War II and Korea, and even today have helped demonstrate American mastery of the skies, trained at Kelly Field and Randolph Field,[2] which form a major part of aviation history. And in the new frontier of outer space, while headlines may be made by others in other places, history is being made every day by the men and women of the Aerospace Medical Center, without whom there could be no history.

Many Americans make the mistake of assuming that space research has no values here on earth. Nothing could be further from the truth. Just as the wartime development of **radar** gave us the transistor, and all that it made possible, so research in space medicine holds the promise of

radar (rā′där) *n.* a method of detecting distant objects through the use of radio waves

1. **Sidney Brooks . . . Charles Lindbergh . . . Claire Chennault** (shən′ôlt): Sidney Brooks was a young flyer killed in a training accident. Charles Lindbergh was the first transatlantic solo pilot, and Claire Chennault was an important figure in the development of air-war theories.
2. **Kelly Field and Randolph Field:** airfields in the San Antonio area where many military pilots were trained.

substantial benefit for those of us who are earthbound. For our effort in space is not, as some have suggested, a competitor for the natural resources that we need to develop the earth. It is a working partner and a coproducer of these resources. And nothing makes this clearer than the fact that medicine in space is going to make our lives healthier and happier here on earth.

I give you three examples: first, medical space research may open up new understanding of man's relation to his environment. Examinations of the astronaut's physical, and mental, and emotional reactions can teach us more about the differences between normal and abnormal, about the causes and effects of **disorientation**, about changes in **metabolism** which could result in extending the life span. When you study the effects on our astronauts of exhaust gases which can contaminate their environment, and you seek ways to alter these gases so as to reduce their toxicity, you are working on problems similar to those we face in our great urban centers which themselves are being corrupted by gases and which must be clear. B

And second, medical space research may revolutionize the technology and the techniques of modern medicine. Whatever new devices are created, for example, to monitor our astronauts, to measure their heart activity, their breathing, their brain waves, their eye motion, at great distances and under difficult conditions, will also represent a major advance in general medical instrumentation. Heart patients may even be able to wear a light monitor which will sound a warning if their activity exceeds certain limits. An instrument recently developed to record automatically the impact of acceleration upon an astronaut's eyes will also be of help to small children who are suffering miserably from eye defects, but are unable to describe their **impairment**. And also by the use of instruments similar to those used in Project Mercury, this Nation's private as well as public nursing services are being improved, enabling one nurse now to give more critically ill patients greater attention than they ever could in the past. C

And third, medical space research may lead to new safeguards against hazards common to many environments. Specifically, our astronauts will need fundamentally new devices to protect them from the ill effects of

disorientation
(dĭs-ôr'ē-ĕn-tā'shən) *n.* mental confusion or impaired awareness

metabolism
(mĭ-tăb'ə-lĭz'əm) *n.* all the processes a living thing uses to continue to grow and live

B READ A SPEECH
In lines 38–50, President Kennedy supports the **claim** he made in lines 34–37. What words introduce his first example? Watch for where he repeats the phrase in later paragraphs.

impairment
(ĭm-pâr'mənt) *n.* the condition of being damaged, injured, or harmed

C PERSUASIVE TECHNIQUES
Reread lines 58–61. Notice President Kennedy refers to "small children who are suffering." What persuasive technique is he using?

D READ A SPEECH
What three **concrete examples** does President Kennedy give to connect the technical issues of space exploration to people's everyday lives?

impetus (ĭm′pĭ-təs) *n.* a driving force; a motivation

tedious (tē′dē-əs) *adj.* tiresome; boring

E READ A SPEECH
What words or phrases are repeated in this paragraph?

F PERSUASIVE TECHNIQUES
In this paragraph, President Kennedy appeals to people's desire to belong. To what group does he hope people feel an association or loyalty?

radiation which can have a profound influence upon medicine and man's relations to our present environment. **D**

Here at this center we have the laboratories, the talent, the resources to give new **impetus** to vital research in the life centers. I am not suggesting that the entire space program is justified alone by what is done in medicine. The space program stands on its own as a contribution to national strength. And last Saturday at Cape Canaveral I saw our new Saturn C-1 rocket booster,[3] which, with its payload,[4] when it rises in December of this year, will be, for the first time, the largest booster in the world, carrying into space the largest payload that any country in the world has ever sent into space.

I think the United States should be a leader. A country as rich and powerful as this which bears so many burdens and responsibilities, which has so many opportunities, should be second to none. And in December, while I do not regard our mastery of space as anywhere near complete, while I recognize that there are still areas where we are behind—at least in one area, the size of the booster—this year I hope the United States will be ahead. And I am for it. We have a long way to go. Many weeks and months and years of long, **tedious** work lie ahead. There will be setbacks and frustrations and disappointments. There will be, as there always are, pressures in this country to do less in this area as in so many others, and temptations to do something else that is perhaps easier. But this research here must go on. This space effort must go on. The conquest of space must and will go ahead. That much we know. That much we can say with confidence and conviction. **E**

Frank O'Connor, the Irish writer, tells in one of his books how, as a boy, he and his friends would make their way across the countryside, and when they came to an orchard wall that seemed too high and too doubtful to try and too difficult to permit their voyage to continue, they took off their hats and tossed them over the wall—and then they had no choice but to follow them.

This Nation has tossed its cap over the wall of space, and we have no choice but to follow it. Whatever the difficulties, they will be overcome. Whatever the hazards, they must be guarded against. With the vital help of this Aerospace Medical Center, with the help of all those who labor in the space endeavor, with the help and support of all Americans, we will climb this wall with safety and with speed—and we shall then explore the wonders on the other side. **F**

Thank you.

---

3. **booster:** a rocket used to launch a spacecraft.
4. **payload:** the load carried by a rocket or other vehicle.

Comprehension

1. **Recall** Who is in the audience that President Kennedy is speaking to?
2. **Clarify** Why does President Kennedy believe the United States needs to be a leader?
3. **Summarize** According to President Kennedy, what are three ways that medical research in space can make life on Earth better?

ALABAMA STANDARDS

READING STANDARD
4 Apply strategies to comprehend informational materials

Critical Analysis

4. **Identify Audience** Reread lines 11–23. What does President Kennedy say to the audience members to make a strong connection with them?
5. **Identify a Counterargument** Reread lines 24–37. President Kennedy anticipates that his opponents will argue that research in space medicine competes for the natural resources we need to develop the earth. What counterargument does President Kennedy give?
6. **Examine Persuasive Techniques** Which of the four persuasive techniques listed on page 937 do you think President Kennedy uses most successfully? Give an example of how he uses this technique to **inspire** people.
7. **Evaluate a Speech** Review the chart that you made while you read. Explain the effect each strategy had on you. Was President Kennedy successful in keeping your interest? Why or why not?
8. **Compare Nonfiction** Both Gregg Easterbrook, author of "Why We Shouldn't Go To Mars," and President Kennedy try to influence people's beliefs about funding space-related programs. Use a Y chart to compare and contrast Easterbrook's and President Kennedy's reasons for their differing opinions.

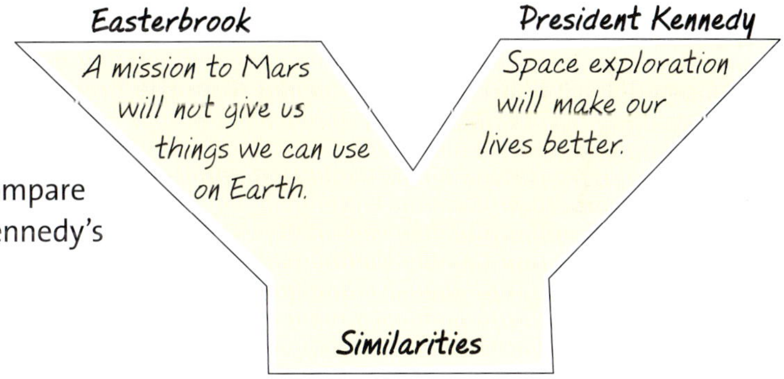

Extension and Challenge

9. **SCIENCE CONNECTION** Search the Internet for three everyday products that resulted from space-related research. Share your findings with the class.

RESEARCH LINKS
For more on space research, visit the **Research Center** at **ClassZone.com.**

Vocabulary in Context

VOCABULARY PRACTICE

Choose the word from the list that best completes each sentence.

1. Sending people to the moon was a difficult _____ .
2. I would rather do anything else than that _____ job.
3. The wrestler used his _____ as an excuse to forfeit the match.
4. The senator was not reelected because of his _____ voting record.
5. The quest for advancement in medicine was a(n) _____ for space research.
6. The plane flew under the _____.
7. The astronaut's _____ grew worse as the rocket disappeared into space.
8. It is important to have a healthy _____ to live and grow.

disorientation
endeavor
impairment
impetus
metabolism
partisan
radar
tedious

VOCABULARY IN WRITING

Which of President Kennedy's reasons for continuing the space program did you think was most convincing? Write a paragraph explaining your opinion, using at least three vocabulary words. You might begin this way.

EXAMPLE SENTENCE

*I think improving the health of people on Earth is a great **impetus** for space research.*

VOCABULARY STRATEGY: ACRONYMS

Acronyms are words that are formed from the first letters or syllables of other words. The vocabulary word *radar,* for example, is formed from the opening letters of *radio detection and ranging.* As time passes and an acronym takes on its own meaning, its origin in many cases becomes less important.

PRACTICE Using a dictionary, match each acronym with the description of what it stands for. Then provide the actual words from which each acronym is formed.

1. OPEC	a. a safeguard to protect people's identity
2. laser	b. group that helps children around the world
3. NASA	c. group that works on aerospace development
4. UNICEF	d. group of countries that produce and sell oil
5. PIN	e. a very intense beam of light

VOCABULARY PRACTICE
For more practice, go to the **Vocabulary Center** at **ClassZone.com.**

SKILLS PRACTICE

Reading-Writing Connection

Explore the ideas presented in President Kennedy's speech by responding to these prompts. Then complete the **Grammar and Writing** exercise.

WRITING PROMPTS	SELF-CHECK
A. Short Response: Write a Letter Write a **one-paragraph letter** to a congressional representative or senator arguing your position on funding space research with tax dollars.	***A strong letter will . . .*** • clearly state your opinion and give specific reasons • use a persuasive technique • address opposing views
B. Extended Response: Write a Speech Imagine that not long from now you're asked to give a speech at your class's graduation ceremony. Write a **two- or three-paragraph speech** to **inspire** your classmates to rise to a challenge.	***A strong response will . . .*** • explain a challenge and its importance • use a persuasive technique to inspire your audience

GRAMMAR AND WRITING

ALABAMA STANDARDS

WRITING/LANGUAGE STANDARD
10 Apply mechanics in writing

USE COLONS CORRECTLY Colons have many uses. They indicate that a **list** follows (*I need to get the following groceries: bread, milk, and butter*). They are used after a **formal greeting** in a business letter (*Dear Madam:*). They also are used **between numerals** in expressions of time (*5:45*). When using a colon to introduce a list, avoid placing the colon directly after a verb or a preposition.

Original: Our new school provides: better opportunities, newer computers, and many activities.

Revised: Our new school provides the following: better opportunities, newer computers, and many activities. (*Inserting* the following *makes use of the colon correct.*)

PRACTICE In the following sentences, insert or delete colons where needed.

1. Some of the activities include the following an art club and a school newspaper.
2. We will meet at 11 00 A.M. today to discuss more of these activities.
3. We should be proud of: the support we've received, the high quality of our students, and the new facilities.
4. Please join me at 1 30 P.M. tomorrow to celebrate our new school.

*For more help with using colons correctly, see page R50 in the **Grammar Handbook.***

Media Study

Persuasive Techniques in Commercials

TV Commercials on MediaSmart DVD

How do you SELL *an idea?*

ALABAMA STANDARDS

COMMUNICATION STANDARD
15 Demonstrate listening skills

KEY IDEA From the latest gadgets to the trendiest pair of shoes, advertisers want you to buy their products. They will use many persuasive tools to get your attention. In this lesson, you'll watch two TV commercials that will help you explore the techniques advertisers use to **sell** practically everything.

Background

To Buy or Not to Buy Ads are everywhere. They're on trains, buses, buildings, and even stadium walls. Think about the **logos,** the symbols or names of companies, that appear on your clothes and shoes. Right now, you may be a walking advertisement.

Each year, companies spend billions of dollars on TV commercials that showcase products and services. The first TV commercial you'll view is for Mountain Dew, a popular soft drink. The second commercial is for Kibbles 'n Bits, a well-known brand of dog food.

Media Literacy: Persuasion in Advertising

Advertisers carefully design TV ads with a specific audience in mind. A **target audience** is one that sponsors want to persuade. Members of a target audience share certain features, such as age, gender, ethnic background, values, or lifestyle. Advertisers rely on certain **persuasive techniques,** which are methods used to convince a target audience to buy products. Here are some things to think about when you're analyzing TV commercials.

STRATEGIES FOR ANALYZING TV COMMERCIALS

Persuasive Techniques

- Notice how some ads use words to appeal to your sense of reason, while other ads appeal to your emotions. **Emotional appeals** create strong feelings, such as happiness, sadness, or excitement. For example, if a commercial makes you laugh, chances are you'll remember the product and the commercial.
- Watch for ads that tell viewers that everyone is using their product. The **bandwagon** technique appeals to people's desire to fit in or be accepted.
- Listen for **repetition.** Repeated words help viewers remember a product.

Visual Techniques

- Notice the use of **color.** Colors can create certain feelings about a product. For example, blue is often used to create a fresh or peaceful feeling.
- Think about how commercials are **edited.** Each shot is carefully selected and arranged to create a persuasive effect. The **pace,** or length of time each shot stays on the screen, is often designed to express excitement.

Sound Techniques

- Pay attention to the **music.** For example, an upbeat, popular song might be used to make a product seem exciting.
- Listen for **sound effects,** such as the screeching of tires, the sizzling of a burger, or the popping and fizzing of a soft drink. Sound effects are often used to make a product more appealing or to grab viewers' attention.
- Listen closely to what the voice in the commercial (called a **voice-over**) is saying. The details that viewers hear about a product are just as important as the carefully designed images.

MediaSmart DVD

- **Commercial 1:** "Mountain Dew"
- **Commercial 2:** "Kibbles 'n Bits"
- **Genre:** Advertisement

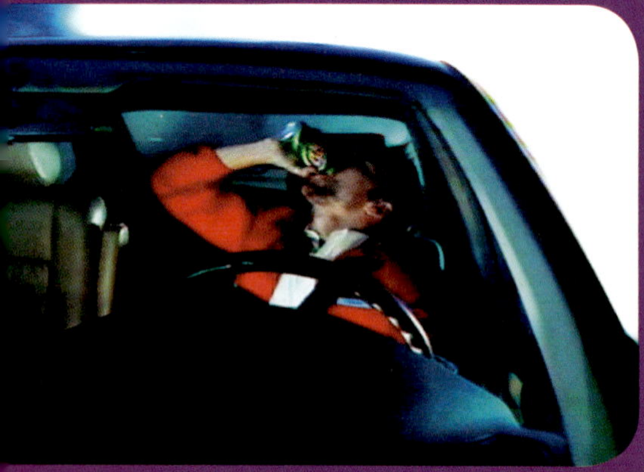

Viewing Guide for

TV Commercials

The first TV commercial is a Mountain Dew ad that begins at the entrance of a parking lot. As you view the ad, pay attention to music and sound effects. The second commercial is entitled "Spike and Speck II." The ad follows two dogs on their way to dinner. Notice persuasive techniques that help make this commercial memorable.

To help you analyze how persuasive techniques are used in TV commercials, view each ad more than once and answer the following questions.

NOW VIEW

FIRST VIEWING: Comprehension

1. **Summarize** Describe what happens in each commercial.
2. **Recall** Describe the music and sound effects that are used in the Mountain Dew ad.

CLOSE VIEWING: Media Literacy

3. **Analyze Visual Techniques** The Mountain Dew ad uses fast-paced **editing.** What is the effect of using this technique?
4. **Analyze Sound Techniques** Music is often used to create an image for a product. For example, the use of classical music can create an image of elegance and class. What kind of image do you think the **music** creates in the Mountain Dew ad?
5. **Evaluate Persuasive Techniques** Do you think the technique of **repetition** is effective in the Kibbles 'n Bits commercial? Why or why not? Think about the following:
   - how repetition may affect viewers' memories
   - the kind of emotional appeal advertisers might be making by using a repeated word or phrase.

Write or Discuss

Evaluating TV Commercials Consider the commercials in this lesson. Which one do you think is more effective at grabbing your attention and helping you remember the product? As part of your response think about

- how the visual elements help the product stand out
- how the sound techniques trigger certain emotions
- how the persuasive techniques influence how you feel about the product

Produce Your Own Media

Designing a Print Ad Imagine that you are part of an advertising team whose job it is to create a magazine **print ad** for a major company. In small groups, choose one product from the list and create your own print ad.

- Turbo Racer (video game)
- Raisin Oatbran O's (healthy cereal)
- Zoom (running shoes)
- Dazzle (toothpaste)
- Pep (energy snack bar)
- Essence (bottled water)

HERE'S HOW Before you create your ad, consider where you will place the product and how much space it will take up on the page. To help you create the ad, think about the following suggestions:

- Determine who will be the target audience—for example, teens, athletes, parents, or young children.
- Use persuasive techniques that will make your ad more appealing.
- Use visual techniques, such as color, that will draw attention to your product.

MEDIA TOOLS

For help with designing print ads, visit the **Media Center** at **ClassZone.com.**

STUDENT MODEL

Tech Tip

Search the Internet for clip art and other images that can be used in your ad.

Writing Workshop

Persuasive Essay

The writers in this unit have explored real-life issues and taken firm, clear positions on them. Taking a stand, however, was only the beginning of what they did. To persuade, they also gave reasons, explained and supported their ideas, and used logical arguments. The **Writer's Road Map** will show you how to do the same.

WRITER'S ROAD MAP

Persuasive Essay

WRITING PROMPT 1

Writing for the Real World Have you ever been treated unfairly? Have you noticed injustices you want to speak up about? Choose an issue you feel strongly about. Write a persuasive essay in which you explain the issue and attempt to persuade your reader to agree with your point of view.

Issues to Explore

- school locker searches
- discrimination in various forms
- banning junk food on school property

WRITING PROMPT 2

Writing from Literature Sometimes you read something that gives you a whole new way to think about an issue. Using a selection in this unit as a springboard, write a persuasive essay about an issue that interests you.

Issues to Explore

- salaries of professional athletes ("Do Professional Athletes Get Paid Too Much?")
- funding for space travel ("Why We Shouldn't Go to Mars")

WRITING TOOLS
For prewriting, revision, and editing tools, visit the **Writing Center** at **ClassZone.com.**

KEY TRAITS

1. *IDEAS*

- Presents a **thesis statement** that makes a **claim** about a clearly identified issue
- Uses convincing details to **support** the position
- Answers **opposing arguments** and counterclaims

2. *ORGANIZATION*

- Explains the issue in a memorable **introduction**
- Uses **transitions** to create a consistent **organizational pattern**
- Concludes by **summarizing** the position or issuing a **call to action**

3. *VOICE*

- Reflects the writer's **commitment** to his or her ideas

4. *WORD CHOICE*

- Uses **persuasive language** effectively

5. *SENTENCE FLUENCY*

- Varies **sentence lengths** and **structures**

6. *CONVENTIONS*

- Uses **correct grammar, spelling, and punctuation**

WRITING/LANGUAGE STANDARD
9 Compose in persuasive mode with thesis sentence

Part 1: Analyze a Student Model

Online INTERACTIVE MODEL CLASSZONE.COM

Mehmet Alzein
Rockland Junior High School

Homework: Let's Do One Thing at a Time

My literature book weighs almost five pounds. My social studies book weighs three pounds. Carrying home a stack of books each night is hard work. I also have so many assignments that I have trouble keeping track of them all. That is why teachers in English, math, science, and social studies should each give homework only once every four nights. That way, backpacks will be lighter, students can give their full attention to just one subject per night, and teachers can assign more in-depth work.

The most obvious reason for giving homework in just one subject per night is the weight of textbooks. Studies have shown that heavy backpacks can be painful and harmful. Overloaded packs can even cause students to fall. Our school nurse says that children are having back pain at earlier and earlier ages because of heavy backpacks. She recommends using bags with wheels instead, but they are expensive. If teachers rotated nights for homework, each student would carry home materials for just one subject per night. Students would avoid back injuries and pain.

A second reason for giving homework in just one subject per night is that students can focus all their attention on that subject. Students shouldn't race through four or more assignments. Instead, they should concentrate on just one. Students who have more time are able to do better work. They can plan, research, review, revise, or double-check their assignments.

KEY TRAITS IN ACTION

Introduction is unusual and memorable.

Thesis statement presents a **claim** (also called an opinion or a position) on a clearly defined issue.

Convincing details **support** each reason and show the writer's **commitment** to his idea.

Transitions help the reader see the **organizational pattern.**

A third reason for limiting homework to just one subject per night is that teachers can give longer, more in-depth assignments. For example, a student might read a whole chapter of a science textbook instead of just one section. Reading everything at once will help students see how the material is related from section to section. A student might also read, outline, and answer questions on the same night.

Another **transition** introduces the third reason.

Some people argue that students should have several assignments each night. They say students will have to juggle many assignments in college and in the working world. These skills, however, do not need to be taught in junior high; there is time for that in high school. Also, are these skills worth the cost of injuring a student's back?

The writer answers **opposing arguments** and counterclaims that opponents might have. He also varies **sentence lengths** and **structures** effectively.

Another argument against rotating assignments is that it is better to review material every night. If teachers always expect nightly reviews of every subject, however, students will never learn to concentrate on just one thing for a long time. As it is, students are always flipping channels. They instant-message several kids at once. Students already know how to bounce from one thing to the next. Let's focus on one class at a time so we learn to concentrate, too.

The writer uses **persuasive language,** including lively words (*flipping, bounce, focus, concentrate*) and examples from his everyday life.

For all these reasons, teachers should start rotating homework assignments immediately. Rotating assignments in the four major subject areas will result in healthier students and better thinkers.

A strongly stated **call to action** and a brief **summary** conclude the essay.

2

WRITING/LANGUAGE STANDARD
10 Apply mechanics in writing

Part 2: Apply the Writing Process

PREWRITING

What Should I Do?	What Does It Look Like?
1. Analyze the prompt. Read the prompt carefully. Circle the type of writing you must do. Underline other important details, such as information about your purpose and audience. Make notes to help you understand and interpret the prompt.	***WRITING PROMPT*** Choose an issue you feel strongly about. Write a persuasive essay in which you explain the issue and attempt to persuade your reader to agree with your point of view. *The audience is not specified, so I must be writing for my teacher and classmates.*
2. List issues that matter to you. You must show your strong commitment to your ideas, so write about an issue you truly care about. **TIP Be sure there are two sides to the topic you choose. You can't write a persuasive essay if everybody already agrees with you.**	*Issues I Care About* *price of tickets for sports events* ***too much homework every night and too many books to carry*** *school starting way too early* *~~cheating~~ (one-sided issue: nobody supports cheating)*
3. Write a thesis statement. In persuasive writing, your thesis is the claim you are making, and it belongs in your introduction. You can revise your thesis as you draft and edit your essay.	*Working thesis statement:* *We should rotate homework so we have assignments in English, math, science, and social studies once every four nights.*
4. Decide on your reasons and support. You need strong, clear reasons for your opinion. Reasons aren't enough to persuade, though. In addition, you need explanations, evidence, facts, or statistics that help your reader understand why, how, and what for.	(see table below)

Reason	*Support*
heavy textbooks	*all books + all notebooks = back pain, injuries, falls*
concentrate on one thing	*more time to research, study, review, revise*
teachers able to give longer, tougher assignments	*helps students see how ideas are related*

DRAFTING

What Should I Do?	What Does It Look Like?
1. Plan your organization. You can organize your ideas by explaining all your reasons and then dealing with the opposing reasons (pattern 1). Another approach is to discuss both sides of each point or reason as you present it (pattern 2).	**PATTERN 1** **A. Arguments for** 1. lighter backpacks 2. longer, more in-depth assignments **B. Arguments against** 1. juggling assignments prepares kids for college, work 2. important to review material every night **PATTERN 2** **A. Lighter backpacks** 1. for: avoid injuries 2. against: use wheeled bags to avoid injuries **B. In-depth assignments** 1. for: can see how ideas are related 2. against: important to review teaching every night
2. Use persuasive language. No one needs to shout to persuade, but your sentences should sound firm and strong. They should say, between the lines, "I'm sure" or "I know." Notice how the writer states his ideas with confidence and certainty.	*If teachers rotated nights for homework, each student would carry home materials for just one subject per night. Students would avoid back injuries and pain.* *For all these reasons, teachers should start rotating homework assignments immediately.*
3. Provide supporting evidence. Explain your reasons. You can use examples, statistics, quotations, and facts. You can quote or describe the ideas of experts.	*Studies have shown that heavy backpacks can be painful and harmful. Our school nurse says that children are having back pain at earlier and earlier ages because of heavy backpacks.*
4. Answer each opposing argument fully and completely. Explain why you disagree with opposing viewpoints. Help your reader dismiss the ideas that might cause disagreement.	***Opposing argument: Kids have to learn to organize.*** *These skills do not need to be taught in junior high. There is time for that in high school.*

REVISING AND EDITING

What Should I Do?	What Does It Look Like?
1. Correct circular reasoning. Circular reasoning is supporting a statement by merely repeating it in different words. Ask a peer reader to point out examples of circular reasoning. Add facts and reasons to support your statements. **See page 954:** More Errors in Reasoning	*A third reason for limiting homework to just one subject per night is that ~~limited homework is better.~~ teachers can give longer, more in-depth assignments.*
2. Make sure your support makes sense and is fully explained. • Circle the facts, examples, and other details you used to support each reason. • If you don't have many circles, decide what you can do to **tell your reader more.**	*Another argument against rotating assignments is that it is better to review material every night. If teachers always expect nightly reviews of every subject, however, students will never learn to concentrate on just one thing for a long time. As it is, students are always flipping channels. They instant-message several kids at once. Students already know how to bounce from one thing to the next. Let's focus on one class at a time so we learn to concentrate, too.*
3. Revise for more persuasive language. • Use **precise words** instead of vague ones, such as *really* and *very*. • Hold your reader's attention by asking a **question** or making a **suggestion.**	*~~Maybe these skills aren't really that important.~~ Are these skills worth the cost of injuring a student's back?*
4. Craft a strong ending. • Include a **call to action** that tells your reader what he or she should do. • You may also want to make your point one more time in a brief **summary statement.**	*For all these reasons, teachers should ~~maybe think about what I'm saying here,~~ start rotating homework assignments immediately.* *Rotating assignments in the four major subject areas ~~is the best idea for students and teachers.~~ will result in healthier students and better thinkers.*

Preparing to Publish

Persuasive Essay

Apply the Rubric

A strong persuasive essay . . .

- ☑ has a thesis statement that takes a clear stand on an issue
- ☑ presents reasons and convincing details that support the thesis
- ☑ organizes points clearly and links them with transitions
- ☑ answers opponents' arguments and counterclaims
- ☑ reflects the writer's strong beliefs
- ☑ uses persuasive and accurate language
- ☑ varies sentence lengths and structures
- ☑ concludes with a summary or a call to action

Ask a Peer Reader

- How can I state my thesis more clearly?
- How could I make my arguments more persuasive?
- Where have I made mistakes in reasoning?

More Errors in Reasoning

False cause: thinking that one event led to another just because the second event followed the first ("Draper School rotates assignments, and they beat us in the spelling bee.")

Either/or fallacy: a statement that suggests there are only two choices available ("Either we accept my plan, or students will suffer.")

Check Your Grammar

The pronouns *who* and *whom* can be confusing. If you can substitute the subject pronoun *he, she,* or *they* for the interrogative word, use *who.*

> *Who wants to carry such a heavy backpack?*
> *She wants to carry such a heavy backpack.*

If you can answer a question with the object pronoun *him, her,* or *them,* use *whom,* not *who.*

> *Whom do you know with back pain?*
> *I know her.*

See page R54: Interrogative Pronouns

Writing Online

PUBLISHING OPTIONS

For publishing options, visit the **Writing Center** at **ClassZone.com.**

ASSESSMENT PREPARATION

For writing and grammar assessment practice, go to the **Assessment Center** at **ClassZone.com.**

COMMUNICATION STANDARD
15 Demonstrate listening skills

SPEAKING AND LISTENING

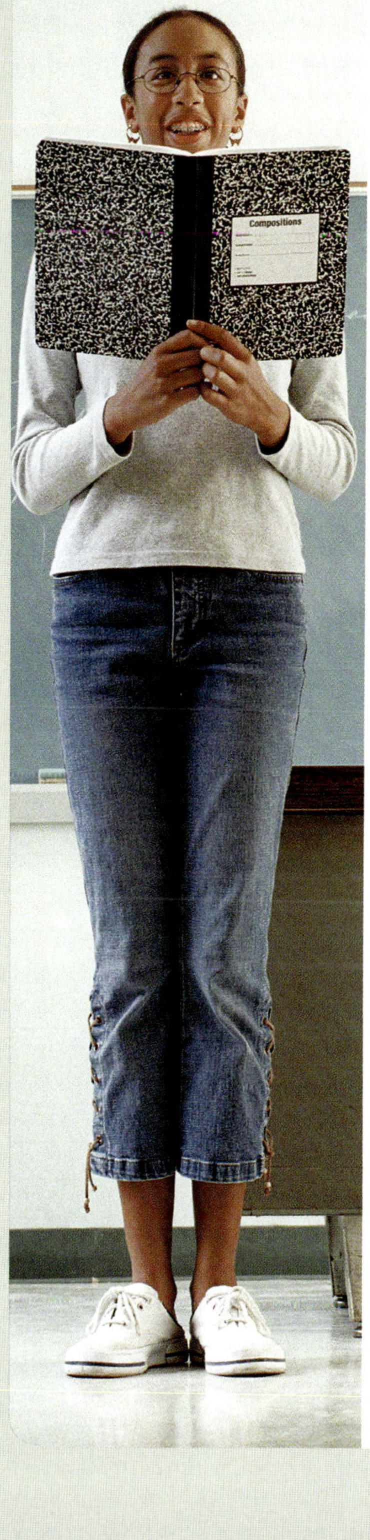

Delivering a Persuasive Speech

Follow these steps to turn your essay into a persuasive speech.

Planning the Speech

1. **Make notes on your essay.** Mark the points you want to make in your speech. Try out different ways of stating them persuasively.
2. **Write your script.** Start with a strong introduction. Begin with an interesting little story, some startling statistics, or a bit of humor. Then state your opinion. Continue with strong, well-supported reasons. Wrap it up with a brief summary and a powerful call to action.
3. **Create a visual aid.** Put your main points on a poster—or prepare transparencies or screens for use with an overhead projector or a power presentation. Remember that as you display each point, you'll need to present the information that explains and supports it.

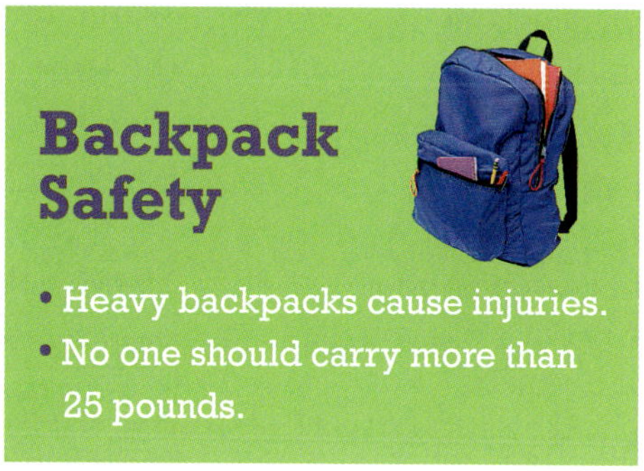

4. **Use strong, positive language.** Your audience should know how you feel about the topic, why you feel that way, and what you want others to do.

Delivering the Speech

1. **Show your commitment.** As much as possible, look your audience in the eye. Use a tone that shows you are confident and serious.
2. **Use pauses and a varied pace.** Add more power to your speech by pausing briefly after important points or slowing down to deliver your most important lines.

See page R79: Evaluate a Persuasive Speech

Assessment Practice

ASSESS

The practice test items on the next few pages match skills listed on the Unit Goals page (page 867) and addressed throughout this unit. Taking this practice test will help you assess your knowledge of these skills and determine your readiness for the Unit Test.

REVIEW

After you take the practice test, your teacher can help you identify any skills you need to review.

- Elements of an Argument
- Fact and Opinion
- Text Features
- Main Idea and Supporting Details
- Idioms
- Prefixes and Latin Roots and Words
- Commas
- Colons

ASSESSMENT ONLINE

For more assessment practice and test-taking tips, go to the **Assessment Center** at **ClassZone.com.**

Reading Comprehension

DIRECTIONS *Read these selections and answer the questions that follow.*

Teen Reading Survey

***SmartGirl.org* online magazine**

Reading Habits: Respondent Behavior and Opinion

The survey showed that

- Many teens enjoy reading and often do read for pleasure; 43% of teens surveyed said that most often they read for the fun of it.
- There was a significant difference, however, between boys and girls; 50% of girls said they read for pleasure, while only 32% of boys did.

While teens appear to enjoy reading, they find that they often do not have the time to do so. Other reasons given for not reading or not reading more: they found reading boring and prefer watching television or movies; they lack good reading materials.

Survey Results

SmartGirl asked: Which statement below do you agree with most?

Statement	Total	Girls	Boys
I read constantly for my own satisfaction, and I love it.	26%	31%	18%
I don't have much time to read for pleasure, but I like to when I get a chance.	46%	49%	40%
I only read what I'm supposed to for school.	16%	12%	22%
I don't read books much at all.	7%	4%	11%
No answer	6%	4%	9%

SmartGirl asked: Most often, the reason I read is . . . (Please choose the best answer from this selection).

Statement	Total	Girls	Boys
Just for the fun of it	43%	50%	32%
Because I have to for school	19%	17%	22%
Because I get bored and have nothing else to do	12%	13%	11%
To learn new things on my own	12%	10%	15%
I don't really read much	5%	3%	8%
Because my parents encourage me to	4%	3%	4%

Take a Book Wherever You Go

Joan Aiken

If you were going to sail round the world alone in a small boat, and could take only one of these things to amuse you, which would you choose: a big iced cake, a beautiful picture, a book, a pack of cards, a paintbox (and paper), a pair of knitting needles and wool, a musical box, a harmonica . . . ? It would be a hard choice. Myself, I wouldn't want the cake; I'd eat it too fast. Nor the cards; they might blow away. Nor the wool; in case it got wet. The harmonica would be better than the musical box, for one could make up one's own tunes. I wouldn't take the picture, for I could look at the sea. Nor the paintbox, because in the end I'd use up all the paper. So the last choice would be between the harmonica and the book. And I'm pretty sure I'd choose the book.

One book! I can hear someone say. But if you were sailing round the world, you'd have read it a hundred times before the trip was over. You'd know it by heart.

And I'd answer, Yes, I might read it a hundred times; yes, I might know it by heart. *That wouldn't matter.* You don't refuse to see your friend, or your mother, or your brother, because you have met them before. You don't leave home because you know what's there.

A book you love is like a friend. It is like home. You meet your friend a hundred times. On the hundred-and-first meeting you can still say, "Well, I never realized you knew that!" You go home every day; after ten years you can still say, "I never noticed how beautiful the light is, when it shines on that corner."

There is always something new to find in a book, however often you read it.

When you read a story you do something that no animal can, however well trained; only man can do it; you are stepping out of your own mind into someone else's. You are listening to the thoughts of another person. While doing this, you are making your own mind work. And making your own mind work is the most interesting thing there is to do.

So I'd sit in my boat and read that book over and over. First I'd think about the people in the story, why they acted the way they did. Then I

GO ON

might wonder why the writer wrote that particular story. Then I might carry on the story in my mind, after the end. Then I'd go back and read all my favorite bits and wonder why I liked them best. Then I'd read all the rest and look for things that I hadn't noticed before. Then I'd list the things I'd learned from the book. Then I'd try to imagine what the writer was like, from the way he's written his story. . . . It would be like having another person in the boat.

A book you love is a friend; it's a familiar place where you can go when you choose. It's something of your own, for no two people read the same book in the same way.

If every single person in the world had a book, just one book (they'd have to be able to read it, of course) we'd have a lot less trouble, I'm sure.

Just one book apiece. That shouldn't be too hard to manage.

How shall we start?

Comprehension

DIRECTIONS *Answer these questions about "Teen Reading Survey."*

1. The title "Teen Reading Survey" tells you that this selection will most likely

A compare books and movies for teens

B analyze book sales in the teen market

C list teens' favorite interests and activities

D present statistics about teens' reading habits

2. Which statement from lines 1–10 expresses the main idea of the survey results?

A "Many teens enjoy reading and often do read for pleasure."

B "They lack good reading materials."

C "50% of girls said they read for pleasure, while only 32% of boys did."

D "They found reading boring and prefer watching television or movies."

3. Which statement is an opinion based on information gathered in the survey?

A Many teens think that they have little time to read for pleasure.

B Boys should spend more time reading.

C Ten percent of girls read to learn new things on their own.

D More boys than girls read only what is required for school.

4. Which statement is a fact based on information from the survey?

A Many teens do not read because there are few good books written for them.

B Teens should not wait for an adult to encourage them to read.

C Of the teens who responded, 4% read because their parents encourage them to.

D Parents need to be more involved in getting their teens to read.

ARMT/ADAW SKILLS PRACTICE

5. Which text feature introduces the two charts?
   - A the title of the article
   - B the subheading in line 1
   - C a bulleted list
   - D the subheading in line 11

DIRECTIONS *Answer these questions about "Take a Book Wherever You Go."*

6. By choosing to take a book on her trip, the author is making which claim?
   - A A book is easy to carry on a trip.
   - B There are many kinds of books that appeal to different people.
   - C A book will provide the most satisfaction and pleasure.
   - D Books are inexpensive to replace.

7. Which reason does the author give to support her claim?
   - A Every time you read a book, you can discover something new.
   - B Reading a book would make the trip seem shorter.
   - C By reading, you could learn how to write your own book.
   - D You could learn a book so well that you could discuss it later with your friends.

8. Which statement from the essay is a fact?
   - A "It would be a hard choice."
   - B "A book you love is like a friend."
   - C "And making your own mind work is the most interesting thing there is to do."
   - D "When you read a story you do something that no animal can. . . ."

9. What counterargument does the author address in lines 12–18?
   - A She would probably stop reading the book before she got to the end of it.
   - B She would have to read the book over and over again on such a long trip.
   - C The book would probably fall apart before the trip was done.
   - D She would regret her choice and wish she had the harmonica.

DIRECTIONS *Answer this question about both selections.*

10. Which idea about reading do both selections convey?
    - A Reading is enjoyable.
    - B Reading is necessary to succeed.
    - C Reading is unlike any other activity.
    - D Reading is like talking to a friend.

Open-Ended

SHORT ANSWER *Write two or three sentences to answer this question.*

11. Read the subheading in line 1 of "Teen Reading Survey." Which two categories of reading habits are covered in the survey? Which chart covers which category?

ESSAY *Write a short paragraph to answer this question.*

12. Discuss the main idea of "Take a Book Wherever You Go." What details does the author use to support this idea?

GO ON

Vocabulary

DIRECTIONS *Use context clues and your knowledge of idioms to answer the following questions.*

1. In line 18 of "Teen Reading Survey," the idiom "at all" means

A often

B to any extent

C considering everything

D to the degree expected

2. In line 26 of "Teen Reading Survey," the idiom "on my own" means

A in a short time

B by one's own efforts

C at one's own house

D with guidance

3. In line 9 of "Take a Book Wherever You Go," the idiom "in the end" means

A somewhere

B soon

C eventually

D maybe

4. In lines 14 and 16 of "Take a Book Wherever You Go," the idiom "by heart" means

A learned to read

B felt deeply

C memorized word for word

D understood meanings

DIRECTIONS *Use context clues and your knowledge of prefixes and Latin words to answer the following questions.*

5. The Latin prefix *super-* means "over," and the Latin word *videre* means "to look." What is the meaning of the word *survey* as it is used in the title "Teen Reading Survey"?

A a careful inspection

B the determination of an area's boundaries

C a collection of data or viewpoints

D an outline of a subject

6. The Latin prefix *ad-* means "toward," and the Latin word *parere* means "to show." The most likely meaning of *appear* as it is used in line 7 of "Teen Reading Survey" is

A show up

B exist

C seem

D intend

7. The word *manage* comes from the Latin word *manus,* which means "hand." The most likely meaning of *manage* as it is used in line 45 of "Take a Book Wherever You Go" is to

A continue to get along

B direct business affairs

C control the use of

D succeed in accomplishing

ARMT/ADAW SKILLS PRACTICE

Writing & Grammar

DIRECTIONS *Read this section from a letter and answer the questions that follow.*

> Dear Student
>
> (1) This Friday is the last day of school. (2) As a result we will be having a small party. (3) The party a hot dog lunch will be held in the cafeteria. (4) However, when school lets out at 335 p.m., please behave. (5) Do not run, push, or yell. (6) Students who violate these rules are subject to the following a call to parents a meeting with the principal or other disciplinary action.

1. Choose the correct way to punctuate the formal greeting.

A Dear Student! **C** Dear Student:

B Dear Student; **D** Dear Student.

2. Choose the correct way to punctuate sentence 2 with a comma.

A As a result we will be having a small, party.

B As a result we will, be having a small party.

C As a result we will be having a small party.

D As a result, we will be having a small party.

3. Choose the correct way to punctuate the appositive phrase in sentence 3.

A The party a hot, dog lunch, will be held in the cafeteria.

B The party, a hot dog lunch, will be held in the cafeteria.

C The party a hot dog lunch will be held, in the cafeteria.

D The party a hot dog lunch, will be held in the cafeteria.

4. Chose the correct place to insert a colon in sentence 4.

A 335 P.M.: **C** please:

B 3:35 P.M. **D** However:

5. Choose the correct way to punctuate sentence 6 with a colon and commas.

A Students who violate these rules are subject to the following: a call, to parents, a meeting with the principal or other disciplinary action.

B Students who violate these rules are subject to: the following a call to parents, a meeting with the principal, or other disciplinary action.

C Students who violate these rules are: subject to the following, a call to parents, a meeting with the principal, or other disciplinary action.

D Students who violate these rules are subject to the following: a call to parents, a meeting with the principal, or other disciplinary action.

STOP

UNIT 8

More Great Reads

Ideas for Independent Reading

Which questions from Unit 8 made an impression on you? Continue exploring them with these books.

Can appearances deceive?

Buffalo Gals: Women of the Old West
by Brandon Marie Miller
This book makes history "come alive" through journal entries, letters, and songs. Learn about the many experiences of these strong, fearless women and the difficulties they faced as they took care of their children and homes.

The Contender
by Robert Lipsyte
An African-American high-school dropout living in Harlem in the 1960s, during the civil rights movement, struggles to prove himself through the rigor and discipline of boxing. He wonders whether he has the heart of a contender—inside and outside the ring.

The Tulip Touch
by Anne Fine
Who might deceive you? Advertisers? Friends? When Natalie meets her neighbor, a girl named Tulip, she becomes a willing pawn in Tulip's wicked deceits. When the lies turn dangerous, can Natalie escape?

How do we fight disease?

Fever 1793
by Laurie Halse Anderson
In this novel, 14-year-old Mattie Cook's day in 18th-century Philadelphia begins with her coffeehouse chores and ends with an epidemic of yellow fever. Does Mattie become a statistic of this outbreak?

Lost in the War
by Nancy Antle
Events like war are often a kind of disease. Thirteen-year-old Lisa Grey is too young to remember her father, who was killed in Vietnam. But she relives the war every day through her mom, who suffers from posttraumatic stress disorder.

Snake Dreamer
by Priscilla Galloway
Disease can be physical or mental. Sixteen-year-old Dusa suffers from nightmares of writhing snakes. When her mother takes her to a sleep-disorder clinic in Greece, things become even more frightening.

What inspires people?

Walks Alone
by Brian Burks
It's how we overcome challenges that can make us heroes. It's 1879, and 15-year-old Walks Alone watches the massacre of her tribe during a raid. Her loss and the challenges that follow teach her courage and hope.

Passage to Freedom
by Ken Mochizuki
Japanese diplomat Chiune Sugihara watched Nazi forces invade Europe at the start of World War II. Jewish citizens were applying for visas in order to leave, but for many there were no visas. Inspired to help, Sugihara risked much to grant visas to as many as 10,000 Jews.

Bound for the North Star: True Stories of Fugitive Slaves
by Dennis Brindell Fradin
The former slaves described in these 12 stories of heroic escapes have inspired movies and books. These stories continue to inspire readers to fight against cruelty worldwide.

UNIT 9

The Power of Research

RESEARCH WORKSHOPS

- Research Strategies
- Writing Research Reports

UNIT 9

Share What You Know

How can I find ANSWERS?

You do research every day. You find out the weather report, movie times, and game scores. Maybe you also locate the lowest price for an item or the best Web site for keeping up with music. Every time you track down information, even in the phone book or on TV, you are doing research. In this unit, you'll learn to sharpen your skills to answer harder questions.

ACTIVITY List some research questions you answer at home, at school, and in other places. Tell where you get answers.

	Questions	Where I Find Answers
Home		
School		
Other places		

Online LITERATURE CLASSZONE.COM

Literature and Reading Center
Writing Center
Vocabulary and Spelling Center

ALABAMA STANDARDS

Preview Unit Goals

DEVELOPING RESEARCH SKILLS

- Plan research
- Develop research questions
- Use library and media center resources
- Evaluate information and sources, including nonfiction books, periodicals, and Web sites
- Collect your own data

WRITING

- Write a research report
- Narrow your research topic
- Locate and evaluate sources
- Take notes
- Make source cards
- Summarize and paraphrase
- Quote directly and avoid plagiarism
- Document sources
- Prepare a Works Cited list
- Format your paper

SPEAKING, LISTENING, AND VIEWING

- Create a multimedia report

ACADEMIC VOCABULARY

- research topic
- research report
- sources
- source cards
- plagiarism
- documentation
- Works Cited
- multimedia report

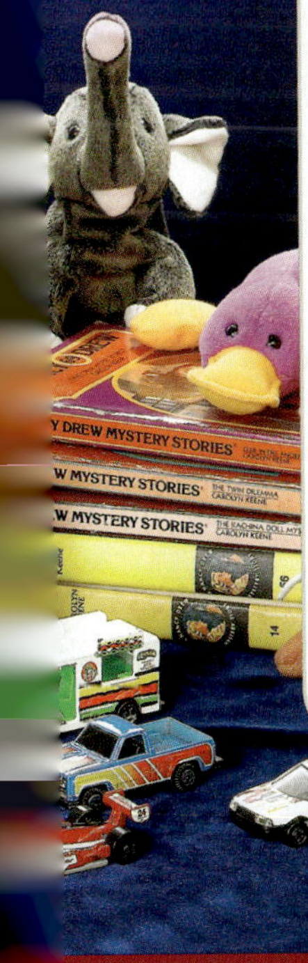

UNIT 9

Research Strategies Workshop

Where do I look for INFORMATION?

ALABAMA STANDARDS

RESEARCH/INQUIRY STANDARD
13 Apply steps in the research process

KEY IDEA Finding answers isn't always easy, especially since many questions have more than one answer. This unit will help you answer **research** questions in efficient and reliable ways. You will learn how and where to look, as well as how to look critically at everything you find.

QUICKWRITE In this unit, you will follow a group of students as they look for information about different kinds of collections. Begin by putting yourself in the same situation. Imagine that your school puts on a collectors' show each year. You want to participate, but what will you display? Working alone or with a partner, list several types of collections that you would like to learn more about.

Planning Your Research

Good research begins with a reading and thinking stage. Don't just jump in. Stop and think about what you want to accomplish.

SET A GOAL

What do you want to learn from your research? Start by listing your general and specific goals.

> ***General goal:*** *How can I figure out something I would like to collect?*
>
> ***Questions:***
>
> - ***What especially interests me?*** *I like baseball, bugs, rocks, and camping.*
> - ***Do any of my interests lead to collections?*** *I could collect baseball cards, certain kinds of bugs, or different kinds of rocks.*
>
> ***Specific goal:*** *I want to learn more about collecting baseball cards.*

GET AN OVERVIEW

After you set a goal, it's time to understand your topic better.

- **Talk to people.** Look for a person who knows about your topic. Talking to him or her may give you lots of ideas.
- **Use the Internet.** For example, if you type the words *baseball cards* into a search engine, you will probably get a few million hits. Look at the first ten entries or so. They may give you ideas for more specific terms to use.
- **Visit the library.** Is there a reference book or an encyclopedia article on your topic? These sources will give you an overview.
- **Talk with a librarian.** He or she may be able to suggest books, magazines, and online sources.

NARROW YOUR FOCUS

Big topics are harder to manage than smaller, more specific ones. Once you decide on a specific topic, you might brainstorm ways to narrow it. The result of your brainstorm might look like this.

Topic	***More Specific***	***Even More Specific***
baseball cards	*baseball cards from a specific time period*	*baseball cards of a specific team or player*

WRITE RESEARCH QUESTIONS

Let's say you have a narrow topic—for example, Seattle Mariners baseball cards. A good next step is to develop questions to guide your research.

Research questions are big questions about your topic. They can't be answered with just a yes or a no. They sum up what you want to know about your topic. After you write your research questions, highlight key terms in them.

- *When did people first start collecting Seattle Mariners baseball cards?*
- *What determines the prices and values of these cards?*
- *What are some interesting stories about collectors and Mariners cards?*

Use the questions and the terms to focus your research.

GET READY TO TAKE NOTES

As you get started on your research, the more organized you are, the better off you will be. When you do research for a class assignment, one of the best ways to take notes is by using note cards. You will learn more about note cards on page 991.

For other kinds of research, you might use different note-taking tools, such as charts or lists. Think about the kinds of information you need and the format that would work best to keep you organized. For instance, you might create a chart of terms used by baseball card collectors.

Term	Meaning
Star cards	cards of the best-known players—can be expensive
Common cards	cards of lesser-known players—cheaper, but very important to collectors who want all the cards of a certain team
Insert cards	cards with special designs that are placed into some packs
Memorabilia cards	insert cards that either are autographed by the players or contain fragments of equipment used by the players, such as pieces of bats, jerseys, or caps

Using the Internet

When you use the World Wide Web, you are also using the Internet, a huge system of linked computers. The Web includes hundreds of millions of Web sites and billions of Web pages.

SEARCH THE WEB

Begin your search by going to one or more search engines. **Search engines** are Web sites that locate information based on titles, keywords, and content. There are many to choose from, and each yields different information.

USE KEYWORDS

A **keyword** is the term or phrase that you enter into a search engine. The best keywords are very specific, like those you highlighted on page 968.

Suppose you want to learn more about collecting bracelets that people wear to show their support for a cause. Here's what may happen if you use a search engine.

YOU TYPE IN...	YOU GET...	THIS IS...
bracelet	4,120,000 results	too broad, but perhaps you see the word *awareness* a lot
+bracelet +awareness	324,000 results	still too broad, but now you see *nonprofit,* so you try *+bracelets +nonprofit*

ADVANCED SEARCHES

Some search engines let you make a search more specific by using the word *AND, NOT,* or *OR*. Other search engines let you use plus and minus signs. Here are some examples:

- *bracelet NOT charm* (This eliminates results about charm bracelets.)
- *+bracelet +nonprofit +"Lance Armstrong"* (This finds only pages that mention all three terms.)
- *bracelet AND "Race for the Cure"* (This finds only pages that mention both terms.)

LIBRARY CATALOG SEARCHES

Library search engines tend to be different from commercial search engines. A good way to get started searching on them is to explain your topic to a reference librarian and ask for help in identifying key terms.

ACADEMIC VOCABULARY FOR THE INTERNET

Here are terms that you will use when discussing the Internet:

- World Wide Web
- Web site
- keyword
- home page
- URL (uniform resource locator, also called a Web address)
- search engine
- menu
- hyperlink
- icon

TIP Use quotation marks to enclose words that go together as one term. For example, instead of *Lance Armstrong*, type in *"Lance Armstrong."*

EXAMINE SEARCH ENGINE RESULTS

One search can bring up millions of results. For example, a rock collector who types in *rocks* could get information on everything from Red Rocks Community College to a database of rock music downloads. A more manageable search might begin with *"rock collecting"* or *rock NOT music* or *+collecting +rocks +minerals.*

Follow these guidelines for examining the results that pop up:

1. Don't just click on the first result. The page that the search engine lists first may not be the most useful source for you.
2. Read the description of each page, including the Web address. The abbreviation at the end of the domain name in the Web address tells you about the page's source. For example, names of U.S. government domains end in *.gov.* Names of school sites contain *.edu.*
3. If a description seems to match your goal or keywords, click on it. If not, either go to the next description or think of ways to make your search terms better and try again.

TIP The most common ending in domain names is *.com.* Sites with *.com* in their names are generally personal sites or product sites. Domains with names that end in *.org* often belong to nonprofit organizations, including some libraries.

TRY IT OUT! *Select Search Engine Results*

Entering *"rock collecting"* in a search engine led to these results (and more than 30,000 others). Which ones would you click on? Why?

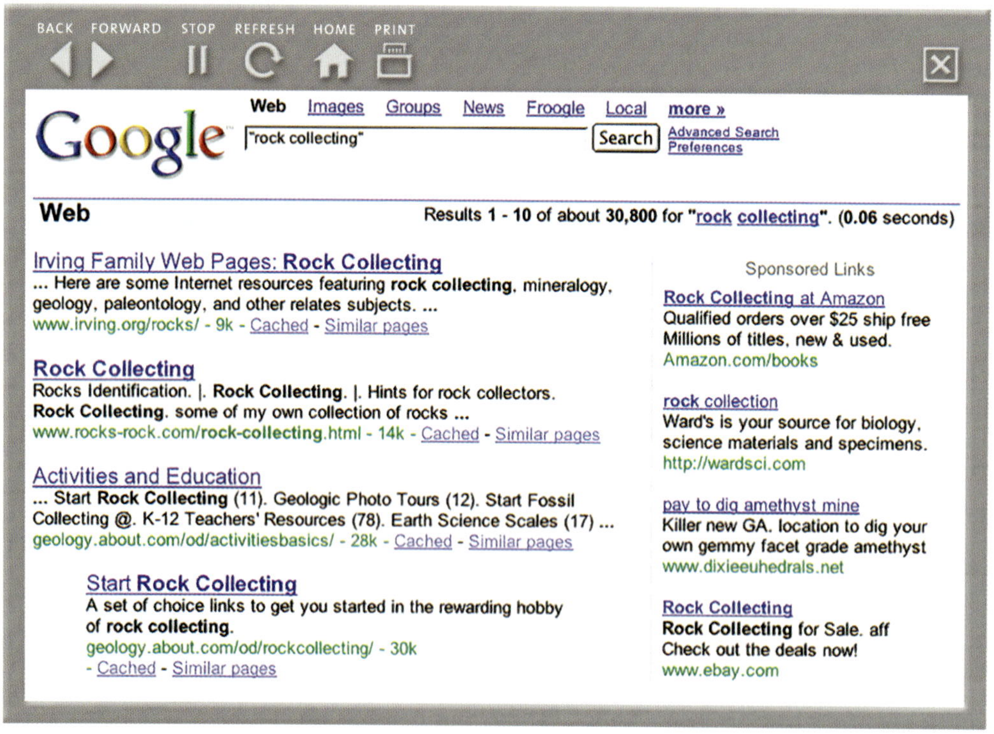

Close Read

1. What term was used in this search? How could you narrow the search even more?
2. Which of these results would you click on first? Why?
3. The "sponsored links" are paid for by businesses. They want to sell their products on the Web. Predict what you would find at one of the sponsored links on this page.

EXPLORE A WEB SITE

Web sites have many special features.

- **Home page** A home page is the "first" page of a Web site—a title page and table of contents all in one. It welcomes you to the site, provides general information, and helps you get where you want to go.
- **Menus** These can run across the top, along the sides, or across the bottom of pages. They tell you what pages or sections the site has and can keep you from getting lost as you explore the site. Many sites also include **hyperlinks** (underlined or boldfaced words) and **icons** (small pictures or symbols). Clicking on any of these takes you to other pages or to different sites.
- **Sponsor or creator** A site should tell you who created it.
- **Credits** Many sites include information about who created them and when they were last updated.

TRY IT OUT! ***Navigate a Web Site***

Look at the information on this Web page about collecting.

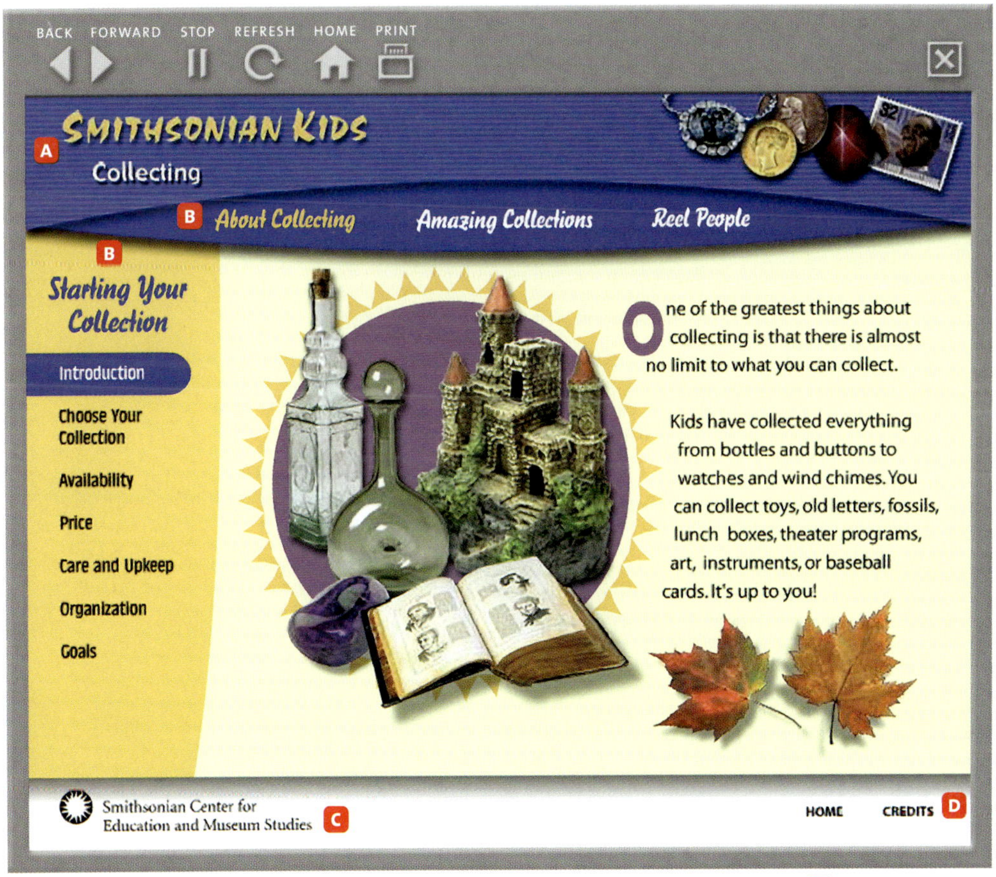

A Home page **B** Menus **C** Sponsor/creator **D** Credits

Close Read

1. Where are the menus on this page?
2. What would you click on to get ideas about different kinds of collections?
3. Where would you click to find out who created this site and when it was last updated? Why is that information important?

Evaluating Information

Not all sources of information are created equal. To be sure the sources you choose are trustworthy, you must evaluate them first. That means asking and answering questions about each source you find. These evaluation guidelines apply to all sources—books, magazines, newspapers, Web sites, and even personal interviews.

WHAT TO ASK	WHY IT MATTERS
What is the date of the information?	For some topics—especially in science, medicine, technology, and sports—up-to-the-minute information is especially important. Even when an event happened long ago, up-to-date sources often contain the latest findings and insights.
Who is the author?	Some authors are experts on their topics. Some aren't. Look for information on the author's other books, education, job or profession, and awards. Is he or she an authority on this topic?
Who is the publisher?	Some publishers are more reliable and careful than others. For example, university presses tend to produce reliable books. Tabloid newspapers such as the *National Enquirer* can be far less reliable. A reference librarian can help you find reliable sources.
What is the purpose?	Some publications are one-sided or biased. For example, if a model-train company publishes a book about model trains, its purpose may be to sell its own brand. Look for information about the publisher and the author. Draw conclusions about purpose.
Is this information use-ful to me?	Check the menu or the table of contents for subjects that interest you. Also, make sure you can understand the source. Is it written at a level that's right for you?

EVALUATE A WEB SITE

Publishing a book usually involves an author and editors. Many books are fact-checked and updated regularly. The Web is different. A personal Web site is usually the work of just one individual. Not all personal Web sites are unreliable, but be cautious. Ask yourself these questions:

- **Who created the site?** Is there a way to contact that person or group?
- **Why was the site created?** Is the site designed to give you information, to entertain you, or to sell you something? Some sites are created for more than one purpose.
- **Does the site contain problems?** Do you notice misspelled words, grammatical errors, or broken hyperlinks?
- **Does the author of the site seem knowledgeable about the topic?** Could you find more or better information in another source, such as an encyclopedia?

See page 982: Checklist for Evaluating a Source

TIP Even reputable publishers and Web sites sometimes publish incorrect information. Use a variety of sources when you do research.

TRY IT OUT! *Examine a Web Site*

This is an example of a personal Web site. What do you think is useful here? What problems do you see?

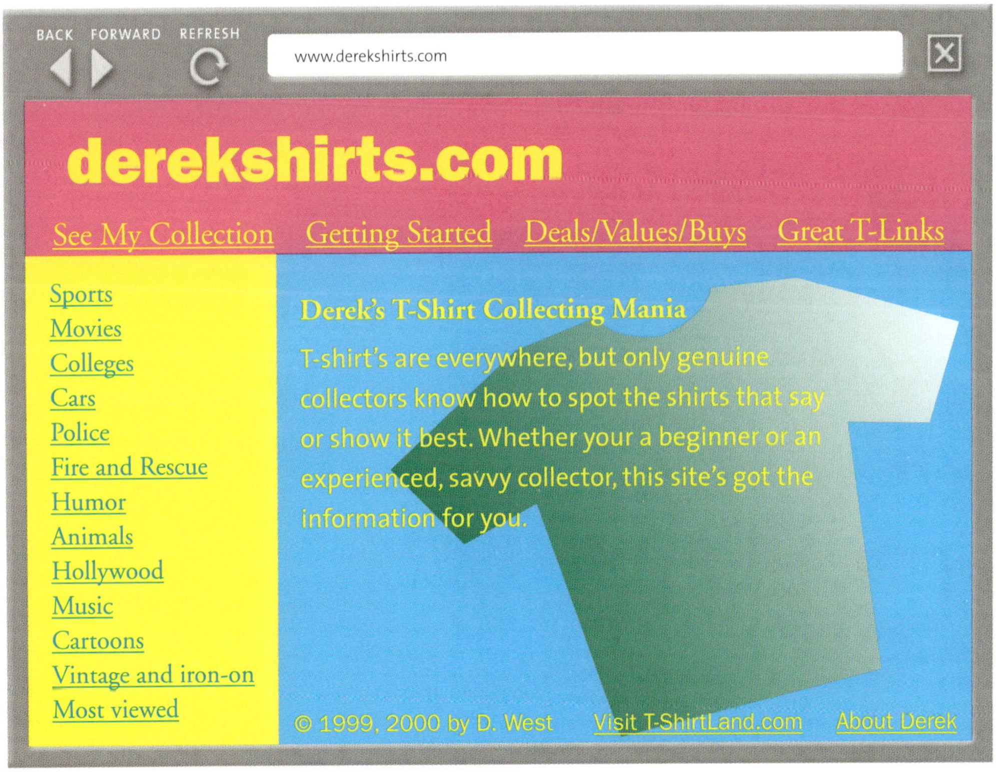

Close Read

1. Who created this site?
2. What is the purpose of this site?
3. When was the site last updated? How do you know?
4. What problems do you notice?

ACADEMIC VOCABULARY FOR THE LIBRARY

You will use these terms when doing research in the library or media center:

- reference section
- primary source
- secondary source
- table of contents
- bibliography
- index
- catalog
- database

Using the Library or Media Center

Libraries have sections for adults, for children, and often for young adults or teens. In addition, most libraries have several other areas:

- meeting and study rooms
- special sections (such as ones for business, local history, and genealogy)
- special resources (such as maps)
- computer terminals

LIBRARY AND MEDIA CENTER RESOURCES

BOOKS

Fiction: Works of fiction come from writers' imaginations, although the writers may base their works on real people and events. Novels and short stories are works of fiction.

Nonfiction: Nonfiction is writing that tells about real people, places, and events. Biographies, diaries, newspaper and magazine articles, essays, and true-life adventure stories are examples of nonfiction.

REFERENCE

Reference desk: a place to ask for help with your research

Reference materials: encyclopedias, almanacs, atlases, and similar works, which usually cannot be checked out

NEWSPAPERS AND PERIODICALS

Magazines and newspapers: current issues, plus past issues in print or on microfilm

AUDIO AND VIDEO RESOURCES

DVDs: documentaries and other films and television shows

Audio resources: audio recordings of speeches and other events, audio books, and audio CDs

E-RESOURCES

Electronic collections: databases, CD-ROMs, e-books, and MP3s

THE LIBRARY CATALOG

An online library **catalog** is a complete index of a library's or library network's holdings. If you have questions about accessing the catalog, or if you want tips on more efficient searching, ask a reference librarian.

There are at least four ways to search a library catalog:

- **Author** Check to see whether you should type the first name first (for example, *Juan Gutierrez*) or the last name first (*Gutierrez, Juan*).
- **Title** You do not need to type in beginning words such as *A, An,* or *The.*
- **Subject** You may need to try a variety of words to get to your subject. For example, some systems may not respond to the subject word *seashells.* Instead, they may use *shells.*
- **Keyword** You can try various keywords, or you can ask a reference librarian for help.

TRY IT OUT! *Search a Library Catalog*

To get to a catalog page, you might do a subject search for the term *shells.* That search would probably give you a list of subcategories, such as "Shells—Caribbean Sea" and "Shells in Art." The catalog page below is for the subcategory "Shells—Collection and Preservation."

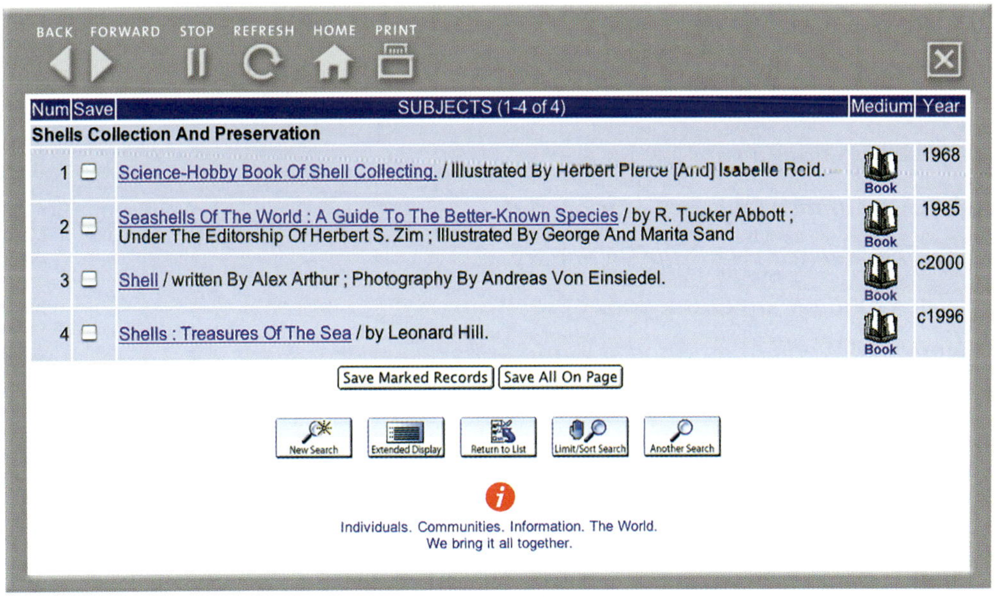

Close Read

1. Which book has information about both shells and collecting? How do you know?
2. Are these books or periodicals? How do you know?

Choosing and Evaluating Sources

The many different departments and resources in your local library can seem confusing. Be sure to ask a librarian for guidance.

PRIMARY AND SECONDARY SOURCES

All sources are either primary or secondary. This chart shows the difference.

PRIMARY SOURCES	SECONDARY SOURCES
Definition: firsthand accounts created by people who took part in or witnessed events	**Definition:** records of events created by people who were not directly involved in or present at the events
Examples: letters, diaries, photographs, autobiographies, interviews, speeches, birth certificates, census reports, first-person newspaper and magazine articles	**Examples:** textbooks, reference books, biographies, third-person newspaper and magazine articles

REFERENCE WORKS

The best place to get an overview of a topic is often a library's reference section. Reference works are available in print, on CD-ROM, and online. Here are some types of reference works:

- **Encyclopedias:** *Britannica Student Encyclopedia*
- **Dictionaries:** *The American Heritage Dictionary*
- **Almanacs:** *The World Almanac and Book of Facts*
- **Atlases:** *Hammond World Atlas, Goode's World Atlas*

DATABASES

Databases are electronic collections of information. A database may be specific to one subject, such as human health, or to one publication, such as the *Los Angeles Times*. Some databases, like the Internet Movie Database, are free. Many others, including InfoTrac, require paid subscriptions. Your school media center or your local library probably subscribes to many databases, which you can browse for free.

NONFICTION BOOKS

One of the best ways to get in-depth information about a topic is to check out a nonfiction book. Certain parts of a book can help you decide whether the book is right for your research.

1. Read the **title** and **subtitle** to get a general idea of the subject matter.
2. Check out the **copyright page** for the copyright date. The latest date is the one you should focus on. Is the book recent enough for your topic?
3. Read the **table of contents** for an overview. This page can also tell you whether the book contains a **bibliography** (a list of the sources used) or a list of **further reading.** Another useful feature in many books is a **glossary,** which is an alphabetical list of specialized terms, with definitions.
4. Look in the **index** for specific terms and topics that interest you. See how many pages include your topic. If the index lists just a page or two, the book may only mention your topic rather than explain it.

TIP Are there whole books written on your exact topic? Then your topic may be too broad.

TRY IT OUT! *Examine the Parts of a Book*

Which parts of a book are shown here?

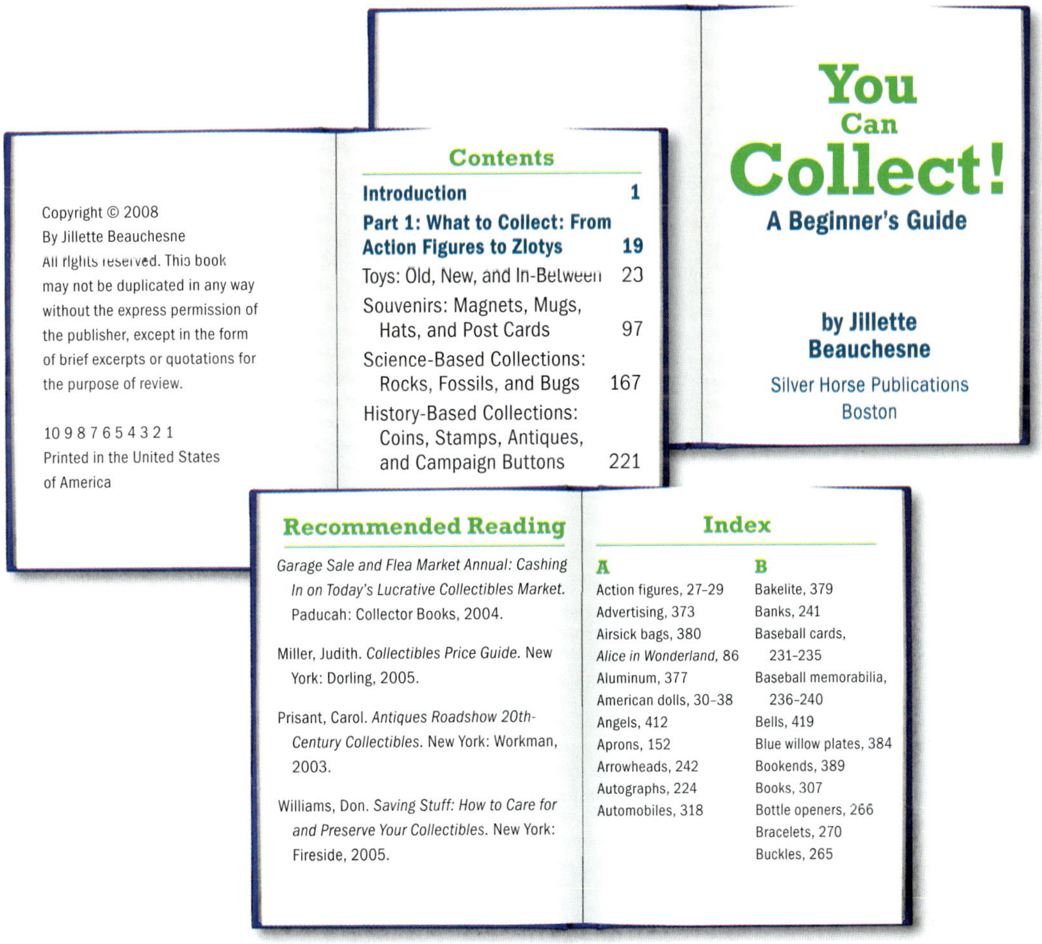

Close Read

1. How does the subtitle help you understand what the book is about?
2. Does this book contain information about collecting post cards? How about autographs? How do you know?
3. How up-to-date is this information? How do you know?

EVALUATE NONFICTION BOOKS

To be sure a nonfiction book is right for your purposes, ask these questions:

- **What is the most recent copyright date?** Check the **copyright notice,** which is usually on the back side of the title page. Have there been many updates and printings? That is often a sign that the book is reliable.
- **Is this a well-researched book?** Look for the author's sources. Is there a **bibliography,** a list of works the author consulted? Are there **footnotes, endnotes,** or **cross-references** that help you understand how the author got information? Is there an **appendix** of additional material, such as maps, tables, or charts?
- **What does the book say about the author?** Look for information about the author on the book jacket, at the beginning of the book, and at the end. Check the **preface** too. In this short introductory essay you may find clues to the author's background and a statement of his or her purpose.

TRY IT OUT! *Examine a Nonfiction Book*

Use what you have learned about nonfiction books to decide whether this book is a good source for someone who wants to learn more about collecting buttons.

Close Read

1. What is this book about?
2. Why is the author qualified or not qualified to write about the topic?
3. How recent is the information in the book? How do you know?
4. What other parts of the book should someone look at to be sure it's suitable for his or her research? (Hint: See page 977.)

NEWSPAPERS AND PERIODICALS

Newspapers are publications that contain news and advertising and that are published very frequently, in most cases daily or weekly. Publications that are issued on a regular basis of more than one day apart are called **periodicals.** Magazines are a common type of periodical.

- **Newspapers** *Seattle Times, Boston Globe, St. Louis Post-Dispatch, Houston Chronicle, Miami Herald, Sacramento Bee*
- **Magazines** *Time, Teen Ink, Next Step, Skateboarder, Newsweek, Odyssey, New York Times Upfront*

One of the best ways to search for articles on your topic is by using a database of newspaper and magazine articles, such as InfoTrac. The page below comes from InfoTrac Junior Edition, a database aimed at students in grades 5–12.

TRY IT OUT! *Finding a Newspaper or Magazine Article*

A keyword search for *collecting autographs* brought up these results on InfoTrac Junior Edition. Clicking on the title of a document or on the "Check Out" link brings up the text of the entire article.

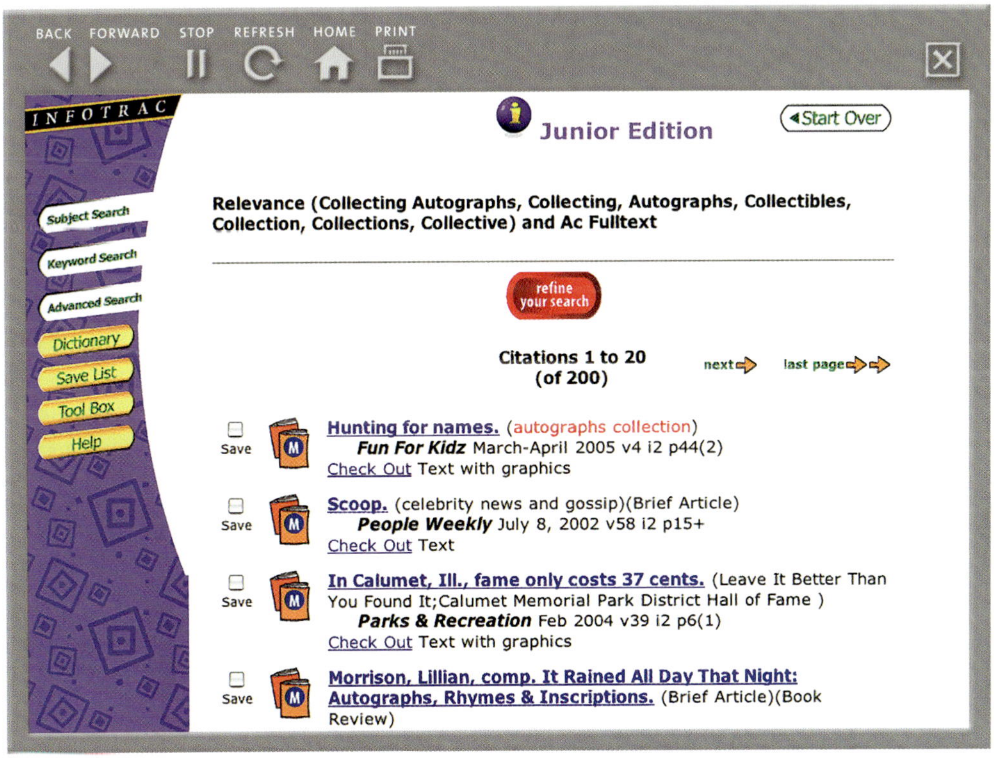

Close Read

1. If you were hunting for information on collecting autographs, which result would you click on first? Why?
2. These results are arranged by relevance, or how well they are related to the user's search terms. What does that tell you about the entries near the end of the list?
3. What could you click on to improve your search?

EVALUATE NEWSPAPERS AND PERIODICALS

Newspaper and magazine articles can be a good source of concise information. Your library may offer some of them in hard copies and many others online, on microfilm, or on microfiche. Once you find an article, you should evaluate it before you use it. Ask yourself these questions:

- **Is the source well-known and respected?** Most large-circulation newspapers and many national magazines are reliable. Avoid newspapers and magazines that cover mostly celebrity gossip, fad diets, UFOs, and similar topics.
- **When was it published?** Up-to-date is great, but not always best. For example, if you're researching the first moon landing, a newspaper article from 1969 could be your best source.
- **Who is the author?** Staff writers and contributing editors for major newspapers and magazines tend to be reliable. Some articles include notes about the authors' qualifications and previous publications.
- **Can the facts be verified?** Does the author give sources for the facts?

TRY IT OUT! ***Examine a Newspaper Article***

Ask questions about the author and about the facts and other content to evaluate this article.

from the Springfield Courier

Autograph Show Opens

Exhibit features the rich, the famous, and the faded

BY TAISHA JACKSON, STAFF WRITER

The autographs of John F. Kennedy, Rosa Parks, and Tiger Woods will be on display for the next six weeks at the Ritter Museum's first-ever autograph show. Visitors will see those signatures and almost 1,200 others on letters, photographs, books, and documents.

Other highlights include a football signed by Joe Montana, a movie poster signed by Harrison Ford, and a very rare document with George Washington's signature.

Museum director Marcia Fiore calls this show a must for anyone interested in collecting. "There's a ton of stuff here for the beginning collector," she adds.

Among the displays for beginners are a timeline of collecting history, tips

See AUTOGRAPHS, page A6

WHAT MAKES AN AUTOGRAPH VALUABLE?

Age/rareness

Popularity/"fickle factor"

Quality/condition

Close Read

1. How well is this article related to the research topic "collecting autographs"? Give reasons for your answer.
2. Would you call the information in this article reliable? Why or why not?
3. How could you check the facts in this article?
4. Although they are not shown here, the newspaper's and museum's e-mail addresses appear at the end of the article. Why is this important?

Collecting Your Own Data

Although the library and the Internet are good resources, they are not the only places to get information. When you conduct an interview or learn by observation, you are doing original research.

INTERVIEWS

Interviews can be excellent means of gathering information. First, they provide primary-source information. Second, they can give you new insights into your topic or even whole new ways of looking at it.

You might interview someone who has in-depth knowledge of your topic. An interview can take place in person, or it can be conducted by telephone, e-mail, or letter. The most important part of an interview is preparing for it. Specific questions, prepared and thought through in advance, are a must.

See pages R81–R82: Conducting an Interview

FIELD RESEARCH AND OBSERVATION

When you observe with a research goal in mind, you are doing **field research.** For example, if you want to know more about teddy bear collecting, you might do field research at a flea market that attracts teddy bear collectors. In that case, your field research might include creating a chart of available items and their prices. Or you might visit a museum if you want to learn about certain kinds of butterflies or about life during the European Middle Ages. Observations that you make and carefully record in these places are also field research.

Notes on Visit to Winston County Flea Market, 5/21/2008

- *132 booths/tables/displays, only 4 with teddy bears*
- *military-themed bears: army, navy, marines, air force*
- *teddy bears with brand-name labels; also teddy bears that are sold along with children's books*
- *koala, panda, and other "bears"*
- *prices ranging from $1 to $1,500 (for a teddy bear from the 1950s)*
- *bears vary by clothing, ribbons, other accessories; some bears for holidays (Valentine's Day) or occasions (graduation)*

Research Tips and Strategies

Web Know-How

To search the Web, you have to know what tools to use. Keep these options in mind.

Search Engines

You can and should use more than one search engine. Here are a few to try:

- Ask Jeeves for Kids (ajkids.com)
- Google (google.com)
- Yahoo! (search.yahoo.com)

Metasearch Tools

A metasearch engine combines results from a number of search engines.

- Dogpile (dogpile.com)
- Metacrawler (go2net.com)

Directories

Directories arrange Internet resources into subject categories.

- LookSmart directory (looksmart.com)
- Yahoo! Directory (dir.yahoo.com)

Virtual Libraries

Use a virtual library to find information in encyclopedias, directories, and indexes.

- Internet Public Library (ipl.org)
- Librarians' Index to the Internet (lii.org)

Other Web Resources

- Our Nation's Library: The Library of Congress (loc.gov)
- Databases: ProQuest K-12, InfoTrac Junior Edition

Checklist for Evaluating a Source

- ☑ The information is clearly related to your topic.
- ☑ The author is qualified to write about the topic.
- ☑ The information is up-to-date.
- ☑ The information is trustworthy because it has been reviewed and/or updated or it has been developed and posted by a reliable institution, such as a U.S. government agency.
- ☑ The facts can be verified in at least one other source.
- ☑ The writing is at your level. It isn't for little kids, and it isn't for scholars.

Understanding Web Addresses

The abbreviations in Web addresses give clues about who created the site and why.

WEB ABBREVIATIONS AND MEANINGS

.COM	commercial—information about products; some personal sites; some combinations of products and information, such as World Book Online
.EDU	education—information about schools, classes, schedules, and campus life; may also include students' personal sites
.GOV	U.S. government—official sites of the White House, the Library of Congress, and many government agencies
.MIL	U.S. military—official sites of the armed forces and related agencies
.NET	network—product information and sales
.ORG	organizations—charities, libraries, and other nonprofit organizations; also political parties

Library Literacy

Almost all libraries and media centers arrange **fiction** by authors' last names. In general, for **nonfiction,** school media centers and public libraries use the Dewey decimal system, and university and research libraries use the Library of Congress system.

DEWEY DECIMAL SYSTEM

000–099	General works
100–199	Philosophy and psychology
200–299	Religion
300–399	Social sciences
400–499	Language
500–599	Natural sciences and mathematics
600–699	Technology (applied sciences)
700–799	Arts and recreation
800–899	Literature and rhetoric
900–999	Geography and history

LIBRARY OF CONGRESS SYSTEM

A	General works
B	Philosophy, psychology, religion
C–D	History
E–F	American history
G	Geography, anthropology, recreation
H	Social sciences
J	Political science
K	Law
L	Education
M	Music
N	Fine arts
P	Language and literature
Q	Science
R	Medicine
S	Agriculture
T	Technology
U	Military science
V	Naval science
Z	Bibliography and library science

Writing Workshop

Research Report

When you write a formal research report, you draw information from many sources and put it together in a way that is your own. In the process, you show what you have learned about a topic and present your own ideas about it. The **Writer's Road Map** will show you how.

WRITER'S ROAD MAP

Research Report

WRITING PROMPT 1

Writing from Literature Develop a specific question about a work of fiction or nonfiction that you read this year. Write a research report that explores that question in detail. Your report should present information from at least three sources as well as your own ideas. Include a list of the sources you used.

Topics to Consider

- How did Jackie Robinson change baseball? ("The Noble Experiment")
- What was it like to be a knight? (*Sir Gawain and the Green Knight*)

WRITING PROMPT 2

Writing from the Real World Is there a question or topic that you have always wanted to know more about? Write a research report that investigates it. Your report should present information from at least three sources. It should also include your own ideas. Finish with a list of the sources you used.

Topics to Consider

- How does the human brain store information?
- Can tsunamis be predicted and prevented?

RESEARCH TOOLS
For research tools and citation guidelines, go to the **Research Center** at **ClassZone.com.**

KEY TRAITS

1. *IDEAS*

- Presents a **thesis statement** that identifies the controlling idea of the report
- Supports the thesis with **evidence,** such as facts, statistics, examples, and expert opinions
- Combines information from **multiple sources** and includes **quotations** and **paraphrases**
- Includes the **writer's own ideas**

2. *ORGANIZATION*

- Follows a clear **organizational pattern**
- Connects ideas with **transitions**
- Includes a strong **introduction** and a satisfying **conclusion**

3. *VOICE*

- Maintains a serious, formal **tone**

4. *WORD CHOICE*

- Uses **precise words** to explain ideas

5. *SENTENCE FLUENCY*

- Varies the **lengths of sentences**

6. *CONVENTIONS*

- Uses **correct grammar, spelling, and punctuation**
- **Credits sources**
- Uses **correct formats and style**

WRITING/LANGUAGE STANDARD
9 Compose in expository mode with thesis sentence

Part 1: Analyze a Student Model

Latushkin 1

Alex Latushkin
Ms. Tokoyuni
English 7
12 March 2008

A Short, Hard Life

What was it like to be alive during the Middle Ages? Movies and television shows have led many people to imagine handsome young knights dodging swords, arrows, and axes as they storm a castle. However, most Europeans of the time were peasants, not knights, and their lives were anything but glamorous. Peasants were at the bottom of the social order during the European Middle Ages, so they struggled to survive, had few comforts, and lived short lives.

For the typical peasant, each day was a struggle. Peasants had to grow or raise their own food and make everything they needed to live, including their clothes, blankets, and tools. In addition, in return for protection, they had to grow grain for their lord, or landowner. Farming was backbreaking work in the Middle Ages because peasants had only basic tools, such as plows and pitchforks, instead of machinery (Hackett 254). If there was a flood or drought, if some crops froze, or if pests ate the crops, the peasants didn't have enough to eat. Sometimes, when there was war, invaders burned their fields and homes.

A peasant's struggle to survive did not end with growing crops. Peasants "had few rights and were almost completely at the mercy of their lords" (Deliyannis). Besides growing food for their lord, they had to do services for him. For example, they might have to build roads or cut wood for him. They even had to fight sometimes, although they

KEY TRAITS IN ACTION

Uses headers and margins required by teacher.

Exciting **introduction** grabs the reader's attention.

Clear **thesis statement** gives the most important idea and shows how the report will be organized.

Uses **precise words** and varies **sentence lengths** throughout.

Latushkin 2

did not have training or good weapons. Peasants also had to make other payments to their lord, such as for using his mill to grind their grain. Finally, peasants had to pay one-tenth of everything they produced to the church (Singman 100). All this work and all these costs made life hard. No wonder Hackett says that peasants "worked from sunrise to sunset" (158).

Transitions show how ideas are related.

Even though some peasants earned a little money through their labor, they still struggled. According to Singman, in England in the late 1200s, some peasants could earn about 1 d. (one English penny) per day (59). As this chart shows, that didn't buy much.

Some Thirteenth-Century Prices			
1 loaf of bread	1/4 d.	1 dozen eggs	1/2 d.
1 ax	4 d.	1 pound of candles	6 d.

Source: Singman 60.

This student used a chart to show a large amount of information in a small space.

In other words, a peasant could work all day for just four loaves of bread.

Peasants who survived had few comforts, because "most medieval homes were cold, damp, and dark" ("Middle Ages"). A peasant's home was just a hut with a place for a fire in the middle (Hackett 158). Pigs and chickens might live in the house with the family. The floor was dirt or clay, and there was not much light or heat. People didn't have beds. Instead, they slept on sacks of straw on the floor. For furniture, there might have been a stool, a bench, and maybe a table (Singman 84-85). A peasant's diet was simple: bread, beans, chicken, eggs, vegetables (such as cabbage and onions), and perhaps milk and cheese (Deliyannis; "Middle Ages"; Singman 70). Only "the fortunate peasant" might have a cow (Hackett 159).

Weaves together information from **multiple sources** and **credits** each one properly.

Latushkin 3

Compared with today, people in the Middle Ages had short lives. They faced "malnutrition, poor hygiene, parasitic infections, and disease" (Hackett 158). Singman explains that during the 1200s, one child out of every six died before his or her first birthday (18). Many others died before they became adults. Deliyannis says the average life span was 30 years in the 900s. Old age was especially hard on peasants. Singman believes that many old peasants had to beg to survive (31). After a lifetime of hard work, it must have been terrible to beg for a crust of bread.

Although many films and television shows make life in the European Middle Ages seem exciting and glamorous, the peasants probably had a different view of things. Their lives were short and hard, and their crops meant far more to them than any castle did.

Provides a direct **quotation** and an expert opinion as **evidence.** The serious **tone** is appropriate for the subject matter.

Writer reflects on what he has learned and includes **his own idea** about it.

Thoughtful **conclusion** refers back to the introduction and summarizes what the writer learned.

Latushkin 4

Works Cited

Deliyannis, Deborah Mauskopf. "Middle Ages." World Book Online Reference Center. 2005. World Book. 25 Feb. 2008 <http://www.worldbookonline.com/wb/Article?id=ar360060>.

Hackett, Jeremiah, ed. Medieval Europe, 814-1350. World Eras 4. Detroit: Gale, 2002.

"The Middle Ages: Homes." Learner.org. Annenberg/CPB. 6 Mar. 2008 <http://www.learner.org/exhibits/middleages/homes.html>.

Singman, Jeffrey L. Daily Life in Medieval Europe. Westport: Greenwood, 1999.

Online encyclopedia

Reference book

Reliable Web site

Book

RESEARCH/INQUIRY STANDARD
12 Cite sources used in research

Part 2: Apply the Writing Process

PREWRITING

What Should I Do?

What Does It Look Like?

1. Find a topic.
Make a list of topics that you want to research and write about. If your teacher has assigned you a specific subject area, generate ideas and questions based on that. If your teacher has told you to choose your own topic, think about what you have learned this year in school or on your own. For example, you may want to explore a topic or idea from literature, science, or social studies. Circle the most interesting words and ideas on your list.

I liked learning about medieval Europe in social studies class and English class this year.
kinds of weapons that knights used
kings and queens, knights, archers, monks, peasants
Crispin: The Cross of Lead is about a peasant accused of murder.
What was it like to live in a medieval village?
What did everyday people eat, drink, and wear?
TV shows and movies make medieval times seem exciting. Were they?

2. Narrow the topic.
Most topics that leap to mind are too broad. Keep "reducing" your topic until you have something that you can cover in the number of pages your teacher has assigned.

See page 967: Narrow Your Focus

LIVING IN THE MIDDLE AGES
THE FEUDAL SYSTEM
Classes of Feudal Society
Peasants/Commoners
daily life of peasants

3. Ask research questions.
What do you want to know about your topic? List some questions that will help guide your research.

My Research Questions
1. *What work did peasants do?*
2. *Were they more like slaves or more like farmers?*
3. *What were their homes like?*
4. *What did they do besides work?*

RESEARCHING

What Should I Do?

1. **Find possible sources.**
One of the best places to start is an encyclopedia, whether in print, online, or in CD-ROM form. You may have to look up a broad topic, such as "Middle Ages," in order to find a subsection about a narrow topic, such as "peasants." Ask a librarian for help.

After you have examined some reference materials, you will have a better idea of what **keywords** to type into an online catalog or search engine. Specific keywords will help you find just the right books, Web sites, and other sources.

What Does It Look Like?

Sources	My Comments
General Encyclopedias	
"Middle Ages" *World Book Online*	interesting; good facts
"Middle Ages" *World Book* (print)	not a lot about peasants
Library Reference Books	
Encyclopedia of the Middle Ages (Ref 940.1 ENC)	really hard to understand!
Medieval Europe, 814–1350 (Ref 940.14 MED)	good info; I can understand this
Other Library Materials	
Life in the Middle Ages: The Serf (J VIDEO 909.07 SERF)	video from children's room
Daily Life in Medieval Europe (940.1 S617)	terrific source: lots of facts, illustrations, explanation
Web Sites	
"The Middle Ages"	terrific; I bookmarked this
"The Middle Ages: Life of a Medieval Peasant"	easy to read; reliable?

2. **Evaluate each source.**
Decide whether each source is worth using or has a problem. Sources with problems might include
   - a Web site that does not show who created it
   - a book or Web site that is too simple or too complicated for your needs

See pages 973 and 976–980 for evaluation guidelines.

Rejected Sources

Encyclopedia of the Middle Ages: too specific for my topic

Life in the Middle Ages video: for younger students; should use sources from Teen and Adult Nonfiction sections instead

"The Middle Ages: Life of a Medieval Peasant" Web site: no author given, so information may not be reliable

RESEARCHING

What Should I Do?

3. Make source cards.
Write the information below on each card. Then number the card in the top right-hand corner.

Online encyclopedia
- author (if given) and title of article
- date of publication or posting (if given)
- publisher and date accessed
- URL

Print or CD-ROM encyclopedia
- author (if given) and title of article
- name and year of encyclopedia
- if a CD-ROM, the term *CD-ROM* and place of publication and publisher

World Wide Web site
- author (if given) and title of Web page or article
- publication information for a print version (if there is one)
- date created or posted (if given)
- name of institution or organization responsible for the site
- date accessed
- URL

Book
- author or editor and title
- place of publication and publisher
- year of publication
- library call number

See page 998: Citing Other Types of Sources

What Does It Look Like?

Online encyclopedia

(1)

Deliyannis, Deborah Mauskopf. "Middle Ages." World Book Online Reference Center. 2005. World Book. 25 Feb. 2008 <http://www.worldbookonline.com/wb/Article?id=ar360060>.

Print encyclopedia

(2)

Lyon, Bryce. "Middle Ages." The World Book Encyclopedia. 2000 ed.

World Wide Web site

(3)

"The Middle Ages: Homes." Learner.org. Annenberg/CPB. 6 Mar. 2008 <http://www.learner.org/exhibits/middleages/homes.html>.

Book

(4)

Singman, Jeffrey L. Daily Life in Medieval Europe. Westport: Greenwood, 1999.
940.1 S617

RESEARCHING

What Should I Do?	What Does It Look Like?
4. Take notes. As you read your sources, look for information that answers your questions and makes you think of new questions. Use this information to create note cards. Each card should include the following: • a specific heading • the source number (from its source card) • the fact or idea that you want to include in your report • a page number if one is available	*What peasants ate* (1) *"black bread, eggs, poultry, and such vegetables as cabbage and turnips" (online, no page number)* *How long people lived* (1) *In the 900s, the average life span was just 30 years (online, no page number).*
5. Record information accurately. There are three different ways to capture a piece of information: • You can **quote** the text, which means **copying it exactly.** Put quotation marks around what you write. • You can **paraphrase** the text, which means **restating the ideas in your own words.** A paraphrase captures all the ideas of the original passage and is about the same length as it. • You can **summarize** the text, which means **recording only the most basic ideas** in it. Because a summary does not include unnecessary details, it is shorter than the original passage.	**Original source** Each house was a simple single-room, single-story, high-roofed structure. At the center of the room was an open-hearth fire on the packed-earth floor; it vented through a hole in the roof. Hackett, Jeremiah, ed., Medieval Europe, 814–1350 **Paraphrase** *Peasants' homes* (5) *A peasant's home was just one room with high walls, a roof, and a dirt floor. Each home had a fireplace in the middle and an opening in the roof to let the smoke out (158).* **Summary** *Peasants' homes* (5) *A peasant's home was just a hut with a place for a fire in the middle (158).*

RESEARCHING

What Should I Do?

6. Avoid plagiarism.
Plagiarism is the use of other people's words and ideas without an explanation of where these words and ideas came from. It is a way of taking credit for learning, research, and thinking that you didn't do—and that's dishonest. Here are some ways to avoid plagiarizing:

- **Summarize and paraphrase often when taking notes.** This will help you avoid lifting other people's words and ideas when you draft.
- **Don't rely heavily on one source.** The more you read from many authors, the more likely you are to see a bigger picture—and start developing your own ideas and opinions.
- **Put all your sources away when you draft.** At that time, use only your note cards.

TIP When you use specific phrases that someone else wrote, you must credit the source. For example, if your source uses the phrase "the fortunate peasant" and you use that phrase without citing the source, you are plagiarizing.

What Does It Look Like?

Original source

Children have weak immune systems, and the high incidence of disease and limited medical knowledge of the period meant that many children never reached adulthood. During the thirteenth century, about one child in six may have died in the first year, one in four by age five; perhaps two-thirds lived to age twenty.
Singman, Jeffrey L., Daily Life in Medieval Europe

Plagiarized

In the thirteenth century, about one child in six may have died in its first year.

Correctly documented

Singman explains that during the 1200s, one child out of every six died before his or her first birthday (18).

Original source

The fortunate peasant might have a cow tethered at the base of the garden grazing on the naturally growing grasses.
Hackett, Jeremiah, ed., Medieval Europe, 814–1350

Plagiarized

The fortunate peasant might have a cow tied up at the edge of the garden.

Correctly documented

Only "the fortunate peasant" might have a cow (Hackett 159).

RESEARCHING

What Should I Do?	What Does It Look Like?
7. Write your thesis. Ask yourself: What are the answers to my research questions? What main point do I want to make about my topic? Remember, your thesis doesn't have to be perfect right now. You can revise it later. **TIP Your thesis is the governing idea of your whole report. In other words, the thesis tells your reader what information you will discuss and how the parts of your discussion will be arranged.**	***Answers to Some of My Research Questions*** • *Peasants didn't have a life of their own. They had to do what their lord wanted.* • *They farmed—long, hard work!* • *Their homes were small and basic and had farm animals in them (yuck).* • *Peasants didn't live long.* ↓ ***Working thesis statement:*** *Peasants had to do what their lord wanted, worked hard, had bad homes, and didn't live long.*
8. Organize and outline your report. Sort your note cards into piles, with each pile having a similar main idea. Next, put the piles in a logical order—maybe from earliest event to latest or from simplest idea to most complicated. The key ideas you have discovered and organized will be the basic entries in your outline. **TIP You can create a formal outline, as shown here. Or if you prefer, you can create a graphic organizer or group the ideas into questions and answers.**	***The Hard Lives of Peasants*** *I. Introduction* *A. Interesting "hook"* *B. My thesis* *II. Body* *A. Peasants had to grow or make everything.* *B. They had to do extra jobs for their lord.* *C. They could earn money but couldn't buy much.* *D. They had terrible homes.* *E. They didn't live long.* *III. Conclusion* *A. It was tough to be a peasant.* *B. People don't know what it was really like.*

DRAFTING

What Should I Do?	What Does It Look Like?
1. Begin your first draft. Use your outline and note cards to tell your reader what you learned.	*Peasants were at the bottom of the social order in the Middle Ages. They had to grow or raise their own food and make everything they needed to live. Farming was very hard work in the Middle Ages (Hackett 254). Sometimes there was too much rain. Other times there wasn't enough.*
2. Weave in sources as you draft. Don't just plop ideas from your note cards straight into your paper. Instead, introduce them with phrases such as "Singman believes," "Deliyannis says," and "According to Hackett." Another way to weave in sources is to follow them with comments or conclusions of your own.	*According to Singman,* *In England in the late 1200s, some peasants could earn about 1 d. (one English penny) per day (~~Singman~~ 59).* *Deliyannis says* *The average life span was 30 years in the 900s. Old age was especially hard on peasants.* *Singman believes that* *Many old peasants had to beg to survive (~~Singman~~ 31). After a lifetime of hard work, it must have been terrible to beg for a crust of bread.*
3. Consider creating a graphic. A chart, a graph, a diagram, or another graphic organizer can give your reader a great deal of information in a small space. **TIP Add a source line that tells where you found any facts or figures that you are using.**	**Some Thirteenth-Century Prices** 1 loaf of bread: 1/4 d. 1 dozen eggs: 1/2 d. 1 ax: 4 d. 1 pound of candles: 6 d. Source: Singman 60.

DRAFTING

What Should I Do?	What Does It Look Like?
4. Document your sources. Show the source of each idea in parentheses at the end of the sentence. This is called **parenthetical documentation** and usually includes an author's last name and a page number, like this: (Hackett 254). Here are some exceptions: • **Author already mentioned in sentence**—use only the page number: (158) • **Web site (no page numbers)**—use only the author's name: (Deliyannis) • **Web site, article, or book with no author named**—use a short form of the title: ("Middle Ages") • **More than one source supporting an idea**—separate the citations of the sources with semicolons: (Deliyannis; "Middle Ages"; Singman 70)	*Finally, peasants had to pay one-tenth of everything they produced to the church (Singman 100).* — Basic documentation: author and page number *All this work and all these costs made life hard. No wonder Hackett says that peasants "worked from sunrise to sunset" (158).* — Author mentioned in sentence *A peasant's diet was simple: bread, beans, chicken, eggs, vegetables (such as cabbage and onions), and perhaps milk and cheese (Deliyannis; "Middle Ages"; Singman 70).* — Information from three sources
5. Make a Works Cited list. Put your source cards in alphabetical order by the authors' last names. (If there is no author, alphabetize by title.) Follow the examples shown here. For situations not shown, see page 998 of this book or the *MLA Handbook for Writers of Research Papers*.	**Works Cited** Deliyannis, Deborah Mauskopf. "Middle Ages." World Book Online Reference Center. 2005. World Book. 25 Feb. 2008. <http://www.worldbookonline.com/wb/Article?id=ar360060>. Hackett, Jeremiah. Medieval Europe, 814–1350. World Eras 4. Detroit: Gale, 2002. "The Middle Ages: Homes." Learner.org. Annenberg/CPB. 6 Mar. 2008 <http://www.learner.org/exhibits/middleages/homes.html>.

REVISING AND EDITING

What Should I Do?	What Does It Look Like?
1. Improve your introduction. • Highlight your introduction. • Ask yourself: Will this beginning interest my reader? Why or why not? • Consider starting with a vivid **description,** a surprising **question,** or a short and thought-provoking **quotation.**	*What was it like to be alive during the Middle Ages? Movies and television shows have led many people to imagine handsome young knights dodging swords, arrows, and axes as they storm a castle. However, most Europeans of the time were peasants, not knights, and their lives were anything but glamorous. Peasants were at the bottom of the social order in the Middle Ages.*
2. Use transitions to connect ideas. • Because a research report is longer than an essay or a narrative, it's especially important to have a clear organizational pattern. • Circle the transitional words, phrases, and sentences in your report. If you don't have very many circles, add some transitions to help your reader **understand how ideas are related.**	*For example,* *Besides growing food for their lord, peasants had to do services for him. They might have to build roads or cut wood for him. They even had to fight sometimes, although they did not have training or good weapons.* *also* *Peasants had to make other payments to their lord, such as for using his mill to grind their grain.*
3. Delete unnecessary information. • Reread your report. Are there parts that are unrelated to your thesis? • Revise or delete these passages to make your report **clear and to the point.**	*They even had to fight sometimes, although they did not have training or good weapons.* ~~*I saw a movie once that showed peasants using clubs and pitchforks as weapons, which was pretty gross. It was a good movie because it was very exciting, and also I learned some things about medieval times.*~~

REVISING AND EDITING

What Should I Do?	What Does It Look Like?
4. Strengthen your support. • Ask a peer reader to read your draft and [bracket] parts that lack support. • Add facts, details, and examples where they are needed. Be sure to document where each came from. **See page 998:** Ask a Peer Reader	*, including their clothes, blankets, and tools.* *[Many peasants struggled to survive. They had to grow or raise their own food and make everything they needed to live. Farming was very hard work in the Middle Ages] because peasants had only basic tools, such as plows and pitchforks, instead of machinery (Hackett 254).*
5. Improve sentence quality. • Skim your report again, this time looking at sentence lengths. Do you have many short sentences in a row? Do you have long sentences that are hard to understand? • Combine choppy sentences and break up droning sentences to make your report smooth and easy to read.	*~~Sometimes there was too much rain. Other times there wasn't enough. Some years the weather was too cold. Other years there were lots of bugs. During those times, there wasn't enough food.~~* *If there was a flood or drought, if some crops froze, or if pests ate the crops, the peasants didn't have enough to eat.*
6. Craft a strong ending. Don't waste your conclusion by repeating what you have already written. Even though you don't need new ideas at this point, you do need fresh words. TIP **One way to create a strong ending is to return to an image or idea from the beginning of the report.**	*~~The Middle Ages was not a great time to be a peasant. The lives of peasants were short and hard. All they did was farm and work for the lord.~~* *Although many films and television shows make life in the European Middle Ages seem exciting and glamorous, the peasants probably had a different view of things. Their lives were short and hard, and their crops meant far more to them than any castle did.*

Preparing to Publish — Research Report

Apply the Rubric

A strong research report . . .

- ☑ has an exciting or thought-provoking introduction
- ☑ has a clear thesis statement
- ☑ supports the thesis with evidence
- ☑ follows a logical pattern of organization and uses transitions
- ☑ uses information from three or more sources and credits them completely and correctly
- ☑ includes the writer's own ideas
- ☑ is appropriately serious and formal
- ☑ employs precise words and varied sentence lengths
- ☑ has a fresh, interesting conclusion

Ask a Peer Reader

- Where should I add support?
- How can I do a better job of weaving in my supporting information?
- Where have I made mistakes in documenting my sources?

Citing Other Types of Sources

When writing your source cards and Works Cited list, you may need to use these formats.

CD-ROM encyclopedia

"Middle Ages." Britannica Student Encyclopedia. 2004 ed. CD-ROM. Chicago: Encyclopaedia Britannica, 2004.

Magazine or newspaper article

Hilton, R. H. "The Ties That Bound: Peasant Families in Medieval England." History Today Dec. 1986: 52.

Interview you conducted with an expert

Kurland, Sari. Personal interview. 1 Mar. 2008.

Book with editor

Schetter, Daniela, ed. Everyday Life in Medieval Times. Westport: Greenwood, 2005.

Film or documentary

The Merchant. Dir. Ashleigh V. Denneth. Videocassette. Schlessinger Media, 2002.

For more citation guidelines, see the *MLA Handbook for Writers of Research Papers.*

Writing Online

PUBLISHING OPTIONS
For publishing options, visit the **Writing Center** at **ClassZone.com.**

ASSESSMENT PREPARATION
For writing and grammar assessment practice, go to the **Assessment Center** at **ClassZone.com.**

PUBLISHING WITH TECHNOLOGY

Creating a Multimedia Report

Now that you're an expert on the subject you researched, you can create a multimedia report that will inform and educate others.

Planning the Presentation

1. **Review your report with an eye for sights and sounds.** Mark parts of your findings that would lend themselves to pictures, photographs, drawings, musical accompaniment, or sound effects.
2. **Make a rough outline.** This should be an ordered list of what your audience will see and hear, including narration.
3. **Create a storyboard.** Sketch out, screen by screen, what your audience will see and hear.

Producing the Presentation

1. **Create or collect the parts of your show.** Gather images or draw them. Scan or download them into a computer. Record or download your music and sound effects too.
2. **Put it together.** Use an editing software program to put the parts of your multimedia presentation into sequence. Create a title screen that includes your name. Include a final screen that credits the sources of your words, sounds, and images.

Reading any text—short story, poem, magazine article, newspaper, Web page—requires the use of special strategies. For example, you might plot the events of a short story on a diagram, while you may use text features to spot main ideas in a magazine article. You also need to identify patterns of organization in the text. Using such strategies can help you read different texts with ease and also help you understand what you're reading.

1 Reading Literary Texts

Literary texts include short stories, novels, poems, and dramas. Literary texts can also be biographies, autobiographies, and essays. To appreciate and analyze literary texts, you will need to understand the characteristics of each type of text.

1.1 READING A SHORT STORY

Strategies for Reading

- Read the title. As you read the story, you may notice that the title has a special meaning.
- Keep track of events as they happen. Plot the events on a diagram like this one.

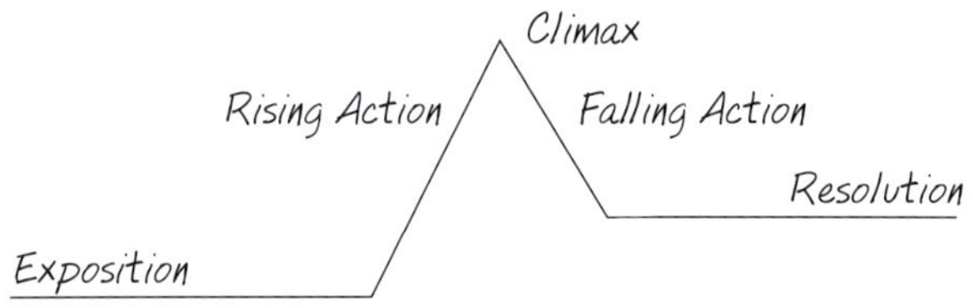

- From the details the writer provides, **visualize** the characters. **Predict** what they might do next.
- Look for specific adjectives that help you visualize the **setting**—the time and place in which events occur.

1.2 READING A POEM

Strategies for Reading

- Notice the **form** of the poem, or the number of its lines and their arrangement on the page.
- Read the poem aloud a few times. Listen for **rhymes** and **rhythms.**
- **Visualize** the images and comparisons.
- **Connect** with the poem by asking yourself what message the poet is trying to send.
- Create a word web or another **graphic organizer** to record your reactions and questions.

1.3 READING A PLAY

Strategies for Reading

- Read the stage directions to help you **visualize** the setting and characters.
- **Question** what the title means and why the playwright chose it.
- Identify the main conflict (struggle or problem) in the play. To **clarify** the conflict, make a chart that shows what the conflict is and how it is resolved.
- **Evaluate** the characters. What do they want? How do they change during the play? You may want to make a chart that lists each character's name, appearance, and traits.

1.4 READING LITERARY NONFICTION

Strategies for Reading

- If you are reading a biography, an autobiography, or another type of biographical writing, such as a diary, a memoir, or letters, use a family tree or word web to keep track of the people mentioned.
- When reading an essay, **evaluate** the writer's ideas. Is there a clear main idea? Does the writer use appropriate details to support a main idea?

2 Reading Informational Texts: Text Features

An **informational text** is writing that provides factual information. Informational materials, such as chapters in textbooks and articles in magazines, encyclopedias, and newspapers, usually contain elements that help the reader recognize their purpose, organization, and key ideas. These elements are known as **text features.**

2.1 UNDERSTANDING TEXT FEATURES

Text features are design elements of a text that indicate its organizational structure or otherwise make its key ideas and information understandable. Text features include titles, headings, subheadings, boldface type, bulleted and numbered lists, and graphic aids, such as charts, graphs, illustrations, and photographs. Notice how the text features help you find key information on the textbook page shown.

A The **title** identifies the topic.

B A **subheading** indicates the start of a new topic or section and identifies the focus of that section.

C **Questions** may be used to focus your understanding of the text.

D A **bulleted list** shows items of equal importance.

E **Graphic aids,** such as illustrations, photographs, charts, diagrams, maps, and timelines, often make ideas in the text clearer.

F **A caption,** or the text that accompanies a graphic aid, gives information about the graphic aid that isn't necessarily obvious from the image itself.

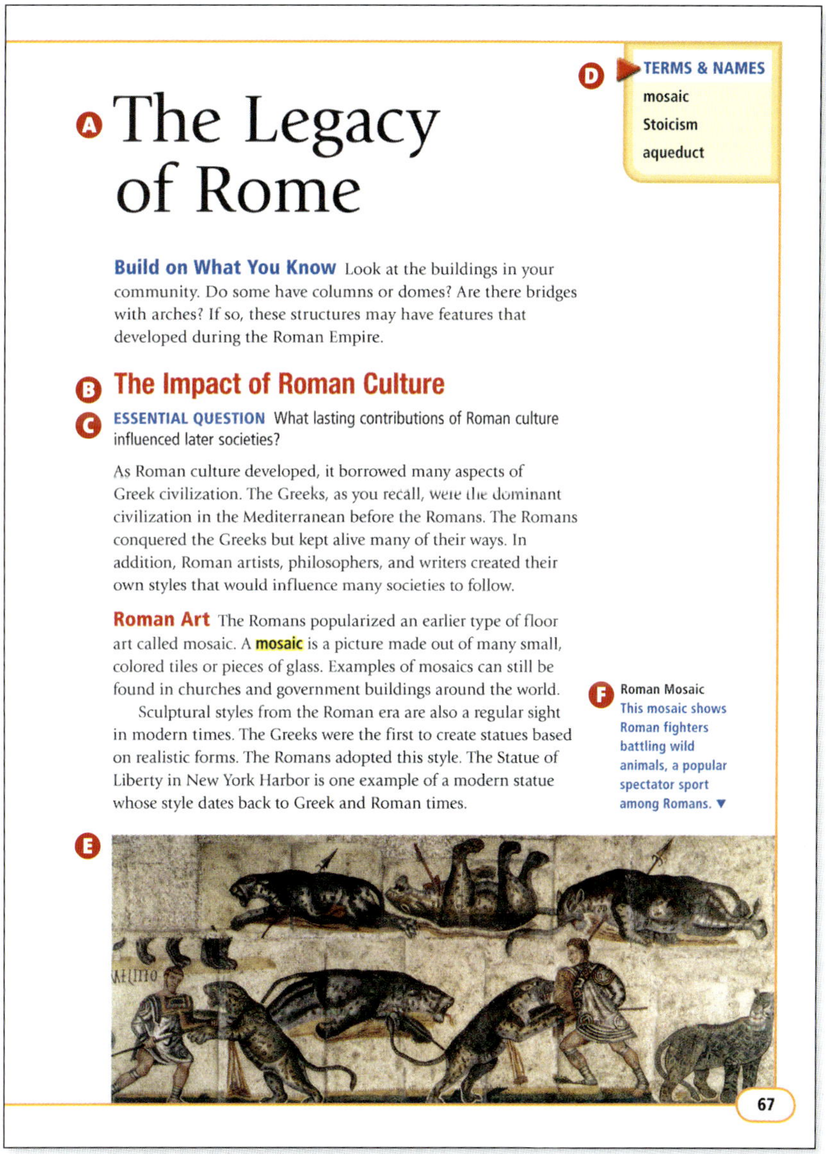
A The Legacy of Rome

D TERMS & NAMES
mosaic
Stoicism
aqueduct

Build on What You Know Look at the buildings in your community. Do some have columns or domes? Are there bridges with arches? If so, these structures may have features that developed during the Roman Empire.

B The Impact of Roman Culture

C ESSENTIAL QUESTION What lasting contributions of Roman culture influenced later societies?

As Roman culture developed, it borrowed many aspects of Greek civilization. The Greeks, as you recall, were the dominant civilization in the Mediterranean before the Romans. The Romans conquered the Greeks but kept alive many of their ways. In addition, Roman artists, philosophers, and writers created their own styles that would influence many societies to follow.

Roman Art The Romans popularized an earlier type of floor art called mosaic. A **mosaic** is a picture made out of many small, colored tiles or pieces of glass. Examples of mosaics can still be found in churches and government buildings around the world.

Sculptural styles from the Roman era are also a regular sight in modern times. The Greeks were the first to create statues based on realistic forms. The Romans adopted this style. The Statue of Liberty in New York Harbor is one example of a modern statue whose style dates back to Greek and Roman times.

F Roman Mosaic
This mosaic shows Roman fighters battling wild animals, a popular spectator sport among Romans. ▼

E

67

PRACTICE AND APPLY

1. What is the first subhead following the title?
2. Reread the Essential Question. Identify one lasting contribution of Roman culture.
3. What activity does the mosaic portray? What do you learn from the caption?

2.2 USING TEXT FEATURES

You can use text features to locate information, to help you understand it, and to take notes. Just use the following strategies when you encounter informational text.

Strategies for Reading

- **Preview** the text by looking at the title, headings, and subheadings to get an idea of the main concepts and the way the text is organized.
- Before you begin reading the text more thoroughly, **skim** it—read it quickly—to get an overview.
- Read any **questions** that appear at the end of a lesson or chapter. Doing this will help you set a purpose for your reading.
- Turn subheadings into questions. Then use the text below the subheadings to answer the questions. Your answers will be a **summary** of the text.
- **Take notes** by turning headings and subheadings into main ideas. You might use a chart like the following.

The Legacy of Rome	
Impact of Roman culture	Notes: 1. borrowed from Greeks 2. created their own styles 3. example is mosaic

Main heading

Subheading

- As you read to locate particular facts or details, **scan** the text. Look for key words and phrases as you move slowly down the page.

2.3 TURNING TEXT HEADINGS INTO OUTLINE ENTRIES

After you have read a selection at least once, you can use text features to take notes in outline form. The following outline shows how one student used text headings from the sample page on page R3. Study the outline and use the strategies that follow to create an outline based on text features.

I. Legacy of Rome
  A. Impact of Roman culture
    1. Roman Art
      a. mosaic
      b. sculpture
  B.
    1.
    2.

Main heading roman numeral entry

Subheading capital letter entry

Detail number entry

Strategies for Using Text Headings

- Preview the headings and subheadings in the text to get an idea of what different kinds there are and what their positions might be in an outline.
- Be consistent. Note that subheadings that are the same size and color should be used consistently in Roman-numeral or capital-letter entries in the outline. If you decide that a chapter heading should appear with a Roman numeral, then that's the level at which all other chapter headings should appear.
- Write the headings and subheadings that you will use as your Roman-numeral and capital-letter entries first. As you read, fill in numbered details from the text under the headings and subheadings in your outline.

PRACTICE AND APPLY

Reread "Like Black Smoke: The Black Death's Journey," pages 896–900. Use text features in the selection to take notes in outline form.

Preview the subheadings in the text to get an idea of the different kinds. Write the headings and subheadings you are using as your Roman-numeral and capital-letter entries first. Then fill in the details.

2.4 GRAPHIC AIDS

Information is communicated not only with words but also with graphic aids. **Graphic aids** are visual representations of verbal statements. They can be charts, webs, diagrams, graphs, photographs, or other visual representations of information. Graphic aids usually make complex information easier to understand. For that reason, graphic aids are often used to organize, simplify, and summarize information for easy reference.

Graphs

Graphs are used to illustrate statistical information. A **graph** is a drawing that shows the relative values of numerical quantities. Different kinds of graphs are used to show different numerical relationships.

Strategies for Reading

- **A** Read the title.
- **B** Find out what is being represented or measured.
- **C** In a circle graph, compare the sizes of the parts.
- **D** In a line graph, study the slant of the line. The steeper the line, the faster the rate of change.
- **E** In a bar graph, compare the lengths of the bars.

A **circle graph,** or **pie graph,** shows the relationships of parts to a whole. The entire circle equals 100 percent. The parts of the circle represent percentages of the whole.

MODEL: CIRCLE GRAPH

Line graphs show changes in numerical quantities over time and are effective in presenting trends such as world population growth. A line graph is made on a grid. Here, the vertical axis indicates quantity, and the horizontal axis shows years. Points on the graph indicate data. The line that connects the points highlights a trend or pattern.

MODEL: LINE GRAPH

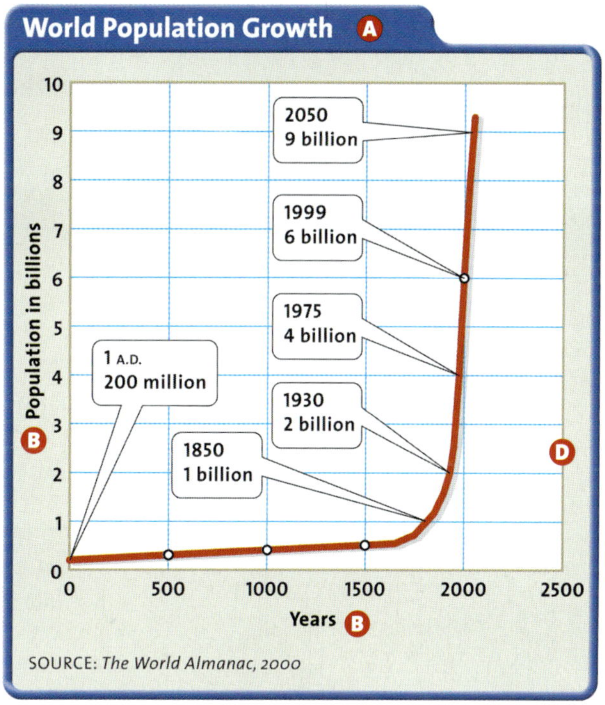

In a **bar graph,** vertical or horizontal bars are used to show or compare categories of information, such as voting trends. The lengths of the bars indicate the quantities.

MODEL: BAR GRAPH

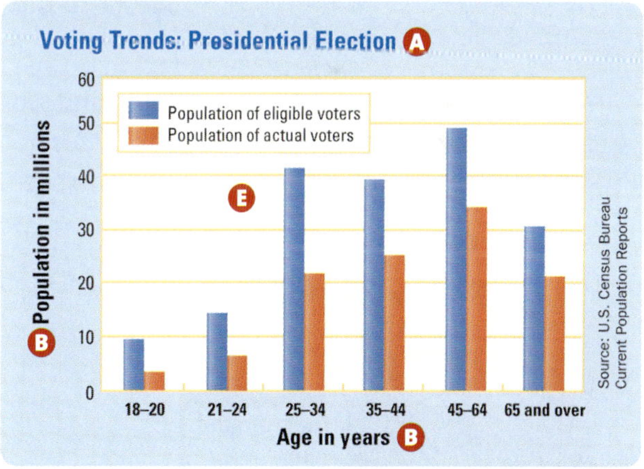

WATCH OUT! Evaluate carefully the information presented in graphs. For example, circle graphs show major factors and differences well but tend to reduce the importance of smaller factors and differences.

Diagrams

A **diagram** is a drawing that shows how something works or how its parts relate to one another.

A **picture diagram** is a picture or drawing of the subject being discussed.

Strategies for Reading

A Read the title.

B Read each label and look at the part it identifies.

C Follow any arrows or numbers that show the order of steps in a process, and read any captions.

MODEL: PICTURE DIAGRAM

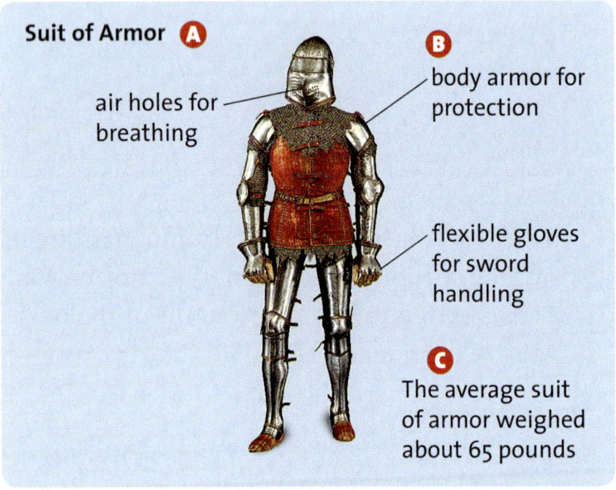

In a **schematic diagram,** lines, symbols, and words are used to help readers visualize processes or objects they wouldn't normally be able to see.

MODEL: SCHEMATIC DIAGRAM

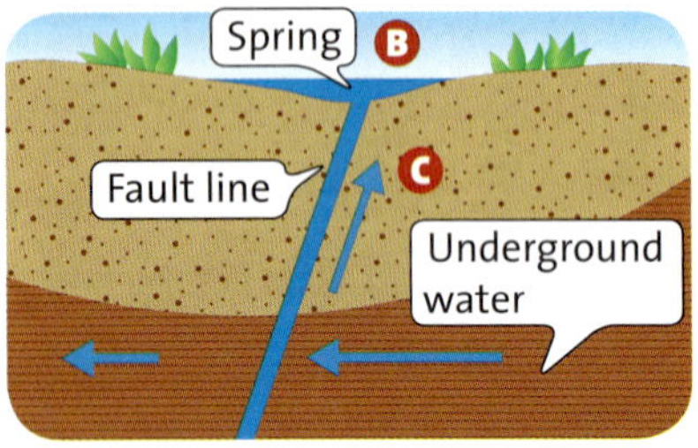

Oasis A
An oasis is a fertile or green spot in the midst of a desert.

Charts and Tables

A **chart** presents information, shows a process, or makes comparisons, usually in rows or columns.

A **table** is a specific type of chart that presents a collection of facts in rows and columns and shows how the facts relate to one another.

Strategies for Reading

A Read the title to learn what information the chart or table covers.

B Study column headings and row labels to determine the categories of information presented.

C Look down columns and across rows to find specific information.

MODEL: CHART

Size of Selected Civilizations A

Civilization	B Dates	Size (est.) millions of sq. miles
Persia	559–330 B.C.	C 2.0
Rome	27 B.C.–A.D. 476	3.40
Mongol	1206–1368	11.7
Aztec	1325–1521	0.2
United States	1776	3.7

MODEL: TABLE

The Beaufort Scale of Wind Strength A

Wind B	Wind Speed	Effect of Wind
Calm (0)	Less than 1 kph	smoke rises straight up.
Light air (1)	1 to 5 kph	Smoke drifts. C
Light breeze (2)	6 to 11 kph	Wind felt on face.
Gentle breeze (3)	12 to 19 kph	Leaves and twigs move.
Moderate breeze (4)	20 to 28 kph	Flags flap.
Fresh breeze (5)	29 to 38 kph	Small trees sway.
Strong breeze (6)	39 to 49 kph	Large branches move.
Moderate gale (7)	50 to 61 kph	Whole trees sway.
Fresh gale (8)	62 to 74 kph	Twigs break off trees.
Strong gale (9)	75 to 88 kph	Branches break off trees.
Whole gale (10)	89 to 102 kph	Trees uprooted.
Storm (11)	103 to 117 kph	Widespread damage.
Hurricane (12)	More than 117 kph	Destruction.

Maps

A **map** visually represents a geographic region, such as a state or country. It provides information about areas through lines, colors, shapes, and symbols. There are different kinds of maps.

- **Political maps** show political features, such as national borders.
- **Physical maps** show the landforms in areas.
- **Road or travel maps** show roads and highways.
- **Thematic maps** show information on a specific topic, such as climate, weather, or natural resources.

Strategies for Reading

A Read the title to find out what kind of map it is.

B Read the labels to get an overall sense of what the map shows.

C Look at the **key** or **legend** to find out what the symbols and colors on the map stand for.

MODEL: PHYSICAL MAP

MODEL: THEMATIC MAP

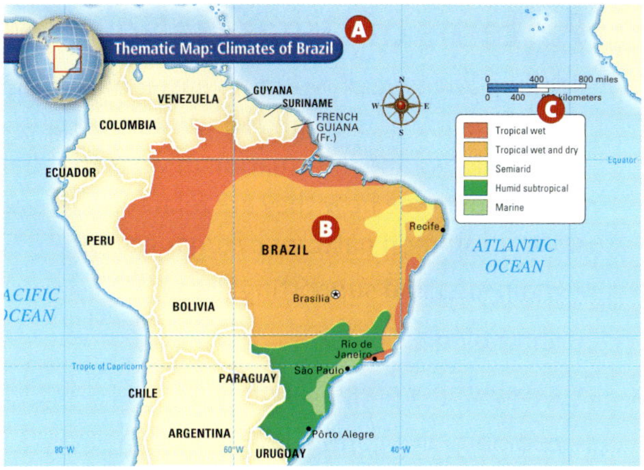

PRACTICE AND APPLY

Use the graphic aids shown on pages R5–R7 to answer the following questions:

1. According to the circle graph, were there more elephants than lions at the game preserve?
2. How many years did it take to double the world population from 1 billion to 2 billion?
3. According to the bar graph, does the number of actual voters equal the number of eligible voters in any age group?
4. What important feature is part of the helmet of a suit of armor?
5. According to the diagram of an oasis, how does water get to the surface of the ground?
6. Which civilization controlled the largest amount of territory according to the chart?
7. Using the table, find the wind speed that is strong enough to make whole trees sway.
8. Are there mountains over 13,000 feet high in Brazil?
9. Using the key on the climate map of Brazil, determine whether the driest area is in the eastern or western part of the country.

3 Reading Informational Texts: Patterns of Organization

Reading any type of writing is easier once you recognize how it is organized. Writers usually arrange ideas and information in ways that best help readers see how they are related. There are several common patterns of organization:

- main idea and supporting details
- chronological order
- cause-effect organization
- compare-and-contrast organization

3.1 MAIN IDEA AND SUPPORTING DETAILS

Main idea and supporting details is a basic pattern of organization in which a central idea about a topic is supported by details. The **main idea** is the most important idea about a topic that a particular text or paragraph conveys. **Supporting details** are words, phrases, or sentences that tell more about the main idea. The main idea may be directly stated at the beginning and then followed by supporting details, or it may be merely implied by the supporting details. It may also be stated after it has been implied by supporting details.

Strategies for Reading

- To find a stated main idea in a paragraph, identify the paragraph's topic. The topic is what the paragraph is about and can usually be summed up in one or two words. The word, or synonyms of it, will usually appear throughout the paragraph. Headings and subheadings are also clues to the topics of paragraphs.
- Ask: What is the topic sentence? The topic sentence states the most important idea, message, or information the paragraph conveys about this topic. It is often the first sentence in a paragraph; however, it may appear at the end.
- To find an implied main idea, ask yourself: Whom or what did I just read about? What do the details suggest about the topic?
- Formulate a sentence stating this idea and add it to the paragraph. Does your sentence convey the main idea?

Notice how the main idea is expressed in each of the following models.

MODEL: MAIN IDEA AS THE FIRST SENTENCE

When the nomads of Africa began using camels around 300 A.D., trade across the Sahara became easier. The donkeys, horses, and oxen that had been used previously could not travel far without stopping for food and water. Camels, on the other hand, could cover 25 miles in a day and often go for two weeks without water.

Main idea

Supporting details

MODEL: MAIN IDEA AS THE LAST SENTENCE

The new trade routes passed through lands occupied by the Soninke people. These farming people referred to their chief as ghana. Soon the land came to be known as the kingdom of Ghana. The tribal chiefs taxed the goods that traveled across their territory. By the eighth century, trade had made Ghana a rich kingdom.

Supporting details

Main idea

MODEL: IMPLIED MAIN IDEA

The West African savannas and forests south of the savanna were rich in gold. No salt was available there, though. In the Sahara, on the other hand, there was abundant salt but no gold. Traders brought salt south through the desert and traded it for gold mined from the forests.

Implied main idea: Gold and salt were two important items that were traded in West Africa.

PRACTICE AND APPLY

Read each paragraph, and then do the following:

1. Identify the main idea in the paragraph, using one of the strategies discussed on the previous page.
2. Identify whether the main idea is stated or implied in the paragraph.

Home is where the heart is. There's no place like it. I love my home with a ferocity totally out of proportion to its appearance or location. I love dumb things about it: the hot-water heater, the plastic rack you drain dishes in, the roof over my head, which occasionally leaks. And yet it is precisely those dumb things that make it what it is—a place of certainty, stability, predictability, privacy, for me and for my family. It is where I live. What more can you say about a place than that? That is everything.

—Anna Quindlen, "Homeless"

Some boys taught me to play football. This was fine sport. You thought up a new strategy for every play and whispered it to the others. You went out for a pass, fooling everyone. Best, you got to throw yourself mightily at someone's running legs. Either you brought him down or you hit the ground flat out on your chin, with your arms empty before you. It was all or nothing. If you hesitated in fear, you would miss and get hurt: you would take a hard fall while the kid got away, or you would get kicked in the face while the kid got away. But if you flung yourself wholeheartedly at the back of his knees—if you gathered and joined body and soul and pointed them diving fearlessly—then you likely wouldn't get hurt, and you'd stop the ball. Your fate, and your team's score, depended on your concentration and courage. Nothing girls did could compare with it.

—Annie Dillard, *An American Childhood*

3.2 CHRONOLOGICAL ORDER

Chronological order is the arrangement of events in the order in which they happen. This type of organization is used in short stories and novels, historical writing, biographies, and autobiographies. To show the order of events, writers use order words such as *before, after, next,* and *later* and time words and phrases that identify specific times of day, days of the week, and dates, such as *the next morning, Tuesday,* and *on July 4, 1776.*

Strategies for Reading

- Look in the text for headings and subheadings that may indicate a chronological pattern of organization.
- Look for words and phrases that identify times, such as *in a year, three hours earlier, in 202 B.C.,* and *the next day.*
- Look for words that signal order, such as *first, afterward, then, during,* and *finally,* to see how events or steps are related.
- Note that a paragraph or passage in which ideas and information are arranged chronologically will have several words or phrases that indicate time order, not just one.
- Ask yourself: Are the events in the paragraph or passage presented in time order?

Notice the words and phrases that signal time order in the first two paragraphs of the following model.

MODEL

A Butterfly Gets Its Wings

How does a butterfly get its wings? During its life, the butterfly goes through different growth stages. There are four main stages altogether: 1) the egg, 2) the caterpillar, 3) the pupa, and 4) the adult. The ancient Greeks called this whole process *metamorphosis*, a word we still use today.

Events

At first, the butterfly is a single slimy egg, no larger than a fingertip. The baby insect grows within the egg until it is ready to hatch. For most types of butterflies, this first stage lasts about 10 days. When the egg cracks open, a caterpillar crawls out.

Order words and phrases

Time words and phrases

In the second stage, the caterpillar spends most of its time eating and growing. As the caterpillar becomes bigger, it sheds its spiky or fuzzy skin. This process is called *molting.* A caterpillar molts several times during its life. Once the caterpillar has shed its skin for the last time, it becomes a pupa.

In the third stage, the pupa immediately grows a hard shell called a *chrysalis.* Then, inside the chrysalis, the pupa goes through the changes that will make it a butterfly. The pupa's hormones turn its body into wings, antennas, and other butterfly parts. After all the changes are complete, the shell splits open. A butterfly is ready to make its entrance.

Finally, the adult butterfly breaks from the chrysalis. Its body, however, doesn't look quite right. It's all soft and wrinkly. As air and blood are pumped through the butterfly's body, it starts to look more like its usual self. In a short time, the butterfly is ready to try out its new wings. With a few flutters, it's off and away!

PRACTICE AND APPLY

Refer to the preceding model to do the following:

1. List at least six words in the last three paragraphs that indicate time or order.
2. What does the writer call the four main parts in the life of a butterfly?
3. In what form does a butterfly begin its life?

3.3 CAUSE-EFFECT ORGANIZATION

Cause-effect organization is a pattern of organization that shows causal relationships between events, ideas, and trends. Cause-effect relationships may be directly stated or merely implied by the order in which the information is presented. Writers often use the cause-effect pattern in historical and scientific writing. Cause-effect relationships may have several forms.

One cause with one effect

Cause ▶ Effect

One cause with multiple effects

Cause ▶ Effect
▶ Effect

Multiple causes with a single effect

Cause ▶
Cause ▶ Effect

A chain of causes and effects

Cause ▶ Effect (Cause) ▶ Effect

Strategies for Reading

- Look for headings and subheadings that indicate a cause-effect pattern of organization, such as "Effects of Food Allergies."
- To find the effect or effects, read to answer the question, What happened?
- To find the cause or causes, read to answer the question, Why did it happen?
- Look for words and phrases that help you identify specific relationships between events, such as *because, since, had the effect of, led to, as a result, resulted in, for that reason, due to, therefore, if . . . then,* and *consequently.*
- Look closely at each cause-effect relationship. Do not assume that because one event happened before another, the first event caused the second event.
- Use graphic organizers like the diagrams shown to record cause-effect relationships as you read.

Notice the words that signal causes and effects in the following model.

MODEL

How a Tsunami Forms

Tsunami is a word that brings fear to people who live near the sea. Also known in English as a tidal wave, a tsunami is a huge ocean wave caused by an underwater volcanic eruption or earthquake.

An earthquake or the explosion of a volcano on the ocean floor creates massive waves of energy. These energy waves spread out in widening circles, like waves from a pebble dropped into a pond.

Effect
Signal words
Cause
Cause
Effect

As the tsunami nears the shore, it begins to scrape along the ocean bottom. This friction causes the waves in the front to slow down. As a result, the waves traveling behind begin piling up and growing higher. This increase in height can happen very quickly—by as much as 90 feet in 10 or 15 minutes.

The effects of a tsunami can include the death of many people and the destruction of ships, buildings, and land along the shore. An especially dangerous situation may occur when the first part of a tsunami to hit the shore is the trough, or low point, rather than the crest of a wave. This trough sucks all the water away from the shore and may attract curious people on the beach. Within a few minutes, however, the crest of the wave will hit and may drown the onlookers. The most destructive tsunami ever recorded struck the Indonesian island of Sumatra, in 2004. It left more than 200,000 people dead.

PRACTICE AND APPLY

1. Use the pattern of a chain of causes and effects, illustrated on page R10, to make a graphic organizer showing the causes and effects described in the text.
2. List three words that the writer uses to signal cause and effect in the last two paragraphs.

3.4 COMPARE-AND-CONTRAST ORGANIZATION

Compare-and-contrast organization is a pattern of organization that provides a way to look at similarities and differences in two or more subjects. A writer may use this pattern of organization to compare the important points or characteristics of two or more subjects. These points or characteristics are called **points of comparison.** The compare-and-contrast pattern of organization may be developed in either of two ways:

Point-by-point organization—The writer discusses one point of comparison for both subjects, then goes on to the next point.

Subject-by-subject organization—The writer covers all points of comparison for one subject and then all points of comparison for the next subject.

Strategies for Reading

- Look in the text for headings, subheadings, and sentences that may suggest a compare-and-contrast pattern of organization, such as "Plants Share Many Characteristics," to help you identify where similarities and differences are addressed.
- To find similarities, look for words and phrases such as *like, similarly, both, all, every, also,* and *in the same way.*
- To find differences, look for words and phrases such as *unlike, but, on the other hand, more, less, in contrast,* and *however.*
- Use a graphic organizer, such as a Venn diagram or a compare-and-contrast chart, to record points of comparison and similarities and differences.

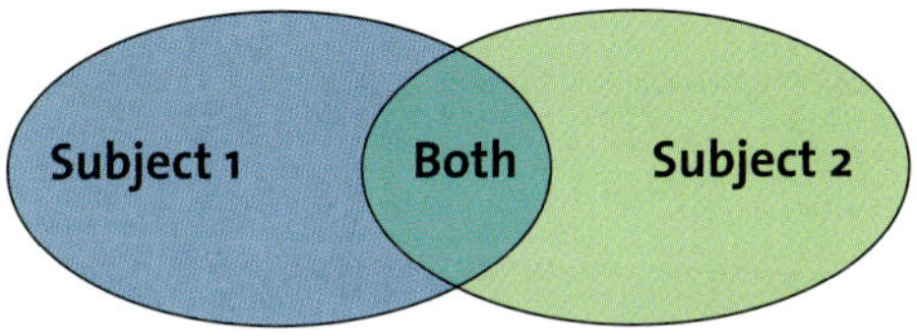

	Subject 1	Subject 2
Point 1		
Point 2		
Point 3		

Read the following models. As you read, use the signal words and phrases to identify the similarities and differences between the subjects and how the details are organized in each text.

MODEL 1

Living in Outer Space

Ten . . . nine . . . eight . . . The date is December 21, 1968.

Seven . . . six . . . five . . . Alongside a launch gantry at Cape Kennedy, Florida, a huge Saturn V rocket stands fueled and ready for blastoff, hydrogen vapor steaming from its rocket motors.

Four . . . three . . . two . . . At the top of the rocket sits the *Apollo 8* command module, the capsule that will ferry astronauts Frank Borman, James A. Lovell Jr., and William A. Anders to the moon and back.

One . . . zero . . . Liftoff! The Saturn's powerful engines roar to life, and another exciting chapter in the history of the United States space program begins.

Today, that same *Apollo 8* command module is one of the most popular attractions at the Henry Crown Space Center at the Museum of Science and Industry in Chicago. For six days in 1968, this cone-shaped capsule was home to the first humans to leave the security of Earth's orbit and venture out to visit another heavenly body.

Museum visitors, especially young people accustomed to space travel in the shuttle era, are often amazed at the cramped quarters within the capsule, and they wonder just how three adults lived for six days in such a compact environment. Space travel has come a long way since those pioneering days of the 1960s. Some of the main similarities and differences relate to living quarters and food.

Comparison words and phrases

Today's shuttle crews have both a flight deck and a lower crew-quarters deck in which to move around. The Apollo crews, however, were pretty much confined to their metal-and-fabric flight couches, although there was a little stretching room beneath the couches and around the hatch area that led to the Lunar Excursion Module.

Contrast words and phrases

Subjects

Mealtime is a highlight of anyone's day, including every astronaut's. Early space travelers were limited to puréed foods squeezed out of toothpaste tubes and juices in plastic bags. Shuttle crews, on the other hand, enjoy a much more appetizing diet. It's still not exactly fine dining, but at least the food is served on trays, is eaten with utensils, and includes healthy snacks, like fresh fruit.

At the end of a working "day" in space, all astronauts are ready for some rest. In *Apollo,* the crew simply drifted off to sleep on their couches. Aboard the shuttle, crew members sleep in special sleep restraints. Some sleep horizontally, while others opt for a vertical snooze. In zero gravity, position doesn't matter!

The United States has continued to develop the space program. The lessons learned during the first three decades of space flight are making life in the alien environment beyond Earth's atmosphere much more pleasant for a new generation of space explorers.

MODEL 2

To compare the two types of energy, we must first understand what energy is. Energy is the ability to do work. That doesn't just mean work as in homework or yard work. Energy comes in many forms, such as a rock falling off a cliff, a moving bicycle, or the stored energy in food. With all these forms, there are only two main types of energy, potential and kinetic. These are the energies of rest and motion.

Subjects

Potential energy is the energy an object has stored up based on how high up it is or how much it weighs. For instance, suppose two kids weigh the same and climb a tree. If they are on different branches, the kid on the higher branch has more potential energy than the kid on the lower branch. However, if one kid weighs more than the other, and they both sit at the same height, the heavier kid has more potential energy than the lighter kid.

Comparison words and phrases

Contrast words and phrases

If the kids jump out of the tree, their potential energy becomes kinetic energy. This kind comes from the motion of an object. Kinetic energy increases with the speed of an object. When the kids jump, their speed increases as they fall. They have more kinetic energy when they are falling faster than they do when they first jump and are falling more slowly. Also, the more mass an object has, the more kinetic energy it has. Even if both kids jump at the exact same time, the one with more mass will always have more kinetic energy.

These two kids probably knew they were using a lot of energy, but they would probably be surprised to know how much work they had been doing.

PRACTICE AND APPLY

Refer to the preceding models to answer the following questions:

1. Which model is organized by subject? Which model is organized by points of comparison?
2. Identify two words or phrases in each model that signal a compare-and-contrast pattern of organization.
3. List two points that the writer of each model compares and contrasts.
4. Use a Venn diagram or a compare-and-contrast chart to identify two or more points of comparison and the similarities and differences shown in one of the two models.

3.5 PROBLEM-SOLUTION ORDER

Problem-solution order is a pattern of organization in which a problem is stated and analyzed and then one or more solutions are proposed and examined. This pattern of organization is often used in persuasive writing, such as editorials or proposals.

Strategies for Reading

- Look for an explanation of the problem in the first or second paragraph.
- Look for words, such as *problem* and *reason,* that may signal an explanation of the problem.
- To find the solution, ask: What suggestion does the writer offer to solve the problem?
- Look for words, such as *propose, conclude,* and *answer,* that may signal a solution.

MODEL

I love baseball, but I won't be going to any major-league games, and I won't be rooting for the local major-league team. The reason is simple. There is no local major-league team in North Dakota. There's none in South Dakota or in Montana or even in Wyoming. The closest major-league team is the Minnesota Twins, and that's over 240 miles away!

The problem is that getting a major-league team costs money. Any city that wants a team has to have enough money to build a stadium. The city also has to have a big enough population to support the team. Fargo is the biggest city in North Dakota, and it only has about 91,484 people. That's not enough to support a major-league franchise. Sports stadiums often hold more people than Fargo has!

Even though the towns around here aren't exactly huge, there are a lot of die-hard baseball fans like my friends and me. So here's my plan. Why couldn't a couple of towns get together to build a stadium and start a team? For example, Moorhead, Minnesota, is right next to Fargo. They already share the same airport, and the metropolitan area has about 174,367 people. That might be enough to support a team. If it's not, then maybe Grand Forks, or even Aberdeen, could join in too.

People might say that there would be a problem naming a team that is supported by cities in two or three different states. I think baseball fans would be so happy to have a team, they wouldn't really care what it was called.

If enough people wrote to the Fargo and Moorhead city governments, maybe the idea could be put on the ballot. Major-league baseball is supposed to be our national pastime. Shouldn't we be a part of it too?

PRACTICE AND APPLY

Reread the model and then answer the following questions:

1. According to the model, what is the cause of the problem?
2. What solution does the writer offer? What words are a clue?

4 Reading Informational Texts: Forms

Magazines, newspapers, Web pages, and consumer, public, and workplace documents are all examples of informational materials. To understand and analyze informational texts, pay attention to text features and patterns of organization.

4.1 READING A NEWSPAPER ARTICLE

Because people often skim newspapers, newspaper publishers use devices to attract attention to articles.

Strategies for Reading

A "Teen Rap" is the name of a **column,** a type of article that appears regularly in a newspaper and is usually written by the same person.

B Notice whether **graphic aids** or **quotations** attract your attention.

C Once you decide that you're interested in the article, read the **title** and other **headings** to find out more about its topic and organization.

D Notice whether the article has a **byline,** a line naming the author.

E A **caption** accompanying a graphic aid may provide information or examples that add to the meaning of the article.

PRACTICE AND APPLY

1. How does the circle graphic relate to the title?
2. Who wrote the article?
3. What does the photograph with its caption tell you?

A TEEN RAP

Source: The *Boston Herald*

by Lauren Beckham D

C

The Difference a City Year Makes

What kind of person gets up at the break of dawn, spends all day tutoring teenagers, cleaning up former crack houses, or teaching kids to read and write—all in the name of community service?

The kind who joins City Year.

Hundreds of young adults come together in Boston for CYZYGY, City Year's Annual Convention of Idealism, to show community leaders, business people and—most importantly—other young adults that community service, though difficult, is rewarding to both those who give and those who receive.

B CITY YEAR

B

"Young people are coming together and giving back"

When Anthony Samuels of Dorchester graduated from Melrose High School last year, he had a specific plan.

"I was ready to give back to my community," Samuels, 19, said. "When I learned about City Year, I jumped right in."

Samuels spends his days at the Umana Barnes Middle School in East Boston, mentoring and tutoring at-risk boys in a remedial class.

Two participants in a Winter Wonderland camp for young children displaced by Hurricane Katrina. E

"I could say that it was a challenge but that's what I needed," said the Dorchester teen. "And they needed me. I'm proud to be part of their accomplishments."

Samuels plans to attend Bunker Hill Community College next year and then pursue a bachelor's degree in child psychology. Meanwhile, he is looking forward to the CYZYGY conference.

"Hopefully in the next five years we'll have, instead of eight City Year sites, 15 to 20," he said. "CYZYGY will show Boston that young people are coming together and giving back."

4.2 READING A TEXTBOOK

Each textbook that you use has its own system of organization based on the content in the book. Often an introductory unit will explain the book's organization and special features. If your textbook has such a unit, read it first.

Strategies for Reading

A Before you begin reading the lesson or chapter, read any **questions** that appear at the end of it. Then use the questions to set your purpose for reading.

B **Read slowly and carefully** to better understand and remember the ideas presented in the text. When you come to an unfamiliar word, first try to figure out its meaning from **context clues.** If necessary, find the meaning of the word in a **glossary** in the textbook, or in a dictionary. Avoid interrupting your reading by constantly looking up words in a dictionary.

For more information on context clues and glossaries, see the ***Vocabulary and Spelling Handbook,*** *pages R68 and R72.*

C Use the book's special features, such as sidebars, to increase your understanding of the text. A **sidebar** is a short presentation of additional information. It is usually set off in a box on the page.

D Take notes as you read. Use text features such as **subheadings** and boldfaced terms to help you organize your notes. Record your notes in graphic organizers, such as cause-effect charts, to help you clarify relationships among ideas.

Primary Source **C**

Background: One of the most important Stoic thinkers of the Roman era was the scholar and politician Marcus Tullius Cicero (106–43 B.C.). He stressed the importance of citizenship and believed that Romans should work for the good of each other and Rome.

from "On Duty"
By Marcus Tullius Cicero
Translated by Walter Miller

As the Stoics hold, everything that the earth produces is created for man's use; and as men, too, are born for the sake of men, that they may be able mutually to help one another . . . we ought to . . . contribute to the general good by an interchange of acts of kindness, by giving and receiving, and thus by our skill, our industry, and our talents to cement human society more closely together, man to man.

DOCUMENT-BASED QUESTION
What are ways that people can demonstrate good citizenship, according to Cicero?

B **Philosophy and Citizenship** The Romans borrowed much of their philosophy from the Greeks. The philosophy of **Stoicism** was especially influential in Rome. It was developed by the Greek philosopher Zeno. Stoicism stressed the importance of virtue, duty, and endurance in life. These were all values that many Romans prized.

The beliefs of Stoicism helped create a strong sense of citizenship in Rome. Citizenship refers to the relationship individuals have with their country. As part of this relationship, a country provides protection and security for its citizens. In return, citizens are expected to take an active part in society in order to strengthen their country. Today, these aspects of Stoicism are viewed by many as necessary qualities for being a good citizen.

D **Roman Language** Another lasting aspect of Roman culture was its language, known as Latin. Because the Romans conquered most of Europe, Latin is the basis for several European languages. These include Spanish, Italian, French, Portuguese, and Romanian. In addition, more than half of the words in English have a basis in Latin. What's more, Latin was the official language of the Roman Catholic Church into the 20th century.

A REVIEW What influence did Latin have on the larger world?

PRACTICE AND APPLY

Reread the textbook page and answer the following questions:

1. How would you find the definition of *philosophy?*
2. How does the sidebar add to the text?
3. Use the text to answer the Review question.

4.3 READING A CONSUMER DOCUMENT

Consumer documents are printed materials that accompany products and services. They usually provide information about the use, care, operation, or assembly of the products they accompany. Some common consumer documents are contracts, warranties, manuals, instructions, and schedules.

Strategies for Reading

A Read the heading to see what information the document covers. Read the **subheadings** to learn what process each section of the instructions explains.

B Read the directions all the way through at least once.

C Look for **numbers** or **letters** that indicate the order in which the steps should be followed. Or look for signal words such as *first* and *finally* to see the order in which the steps should be followed.

D Words that appear in **all capital letters** are often names or labels that appear on the device you are being shown how to use. If there is an illustration or diagram, try to match the words in the instructions to words or symbols in the graphic aid.

E Look for **verbs that describe actions** you should take, such as *plug, touch, enter,* and *press.*

F Pay attention to **warnings** or **notes** that describe problems.

PRACTICE AND APPLY

Reread the microwave instructions and explain how to solve the following problems:

1. The clock needs to be reset after a power outage.
2. The clock was incorrectly set at 14:30.

MICROWAVE INSTRUCTIONS

A **Before Operating**

B **1.** Plug the power cord into a three-pronged electrical outlet.

C **2.** Display panel will light up and flash 00:00. Touch STOP/CLEAR pad.

3. Set the clock.

D Touch STOP/CLEAR pad when the oven is first plugged in, or after the electrical power has been interrupted.

A **Setting the Clock**

Procedure

E **1.** Touch TIMER CLOCK pad.

2. Enter the time of day. For example, if it is 10:30, touch the number pads 1030 and "10:30" will appear.

3. Press the TIMER CLOCK pad again to set the time.

Note You can select any time of the day from 1:00–12:59. To reset Clock, repeat steps 1 through 3 above. If incorrect time (for example, 8:61 or 13:00, etc.) is entered, "EE" will appear on display. Touch STOP/CLEAR pad and program correctly.

Canceling a Program

- To reset, or cancel, a cooking program as it is being entered, touch STOP/CLEAR pad once.
- To stop the oven while it is operating, touch STOP/CLEAR pad once. Do not open the door without pressing STOP/CLEAR pad.
- An entire cooking program (one stage or multiple stages) can be canceled after the oven has started cooking. This can be done by touching STOP/CLEAR pad twice.

F **Note** See page 10 to create your own cooking programs.

Power Levels

Most foods can be cooked at full power (P-HI). However, for best results, some foods require a lower cooking power. Some foods such as tender cuts of meat can be cooked only with a lower power. Before setting any power level, the POWER LEVEL pad must be touched, followed by desired number. See chart.

POWER	Touch POWER LEVEL pad, then	Display
100%	Touch Power Level pad once more.	P-HI
90%	Touch number pad 9.	P-90
80%	Touch number pad 8.	P-80
70%	Touch number pad 7.	P-70
60%	Touch number pad 6.	P-60
50%	Touch number pad 5.	P-50
40%	Touch number pad 4.	P-40
30%	Touch number pad 3.	P-30
20%	Touch number pad 2.	P-20
10%	Touch number pad 1.	P-10

Note Choose P.30 for thawing or defrosting foods.

4.4 READING A PUBLIC DOCUMENT

Public documents are documents that are written for the public to provide information that is of public interest or concern. These documents are often free. They can be federal, state, or local government documents. They can be speeches or historical documents. They may even be laws, posted warnings, signs, or rules and regulations.

Strategies for Reading

A The **shapes** of signs help convey their messages.

- circle—railroad
- diamond—warning
- square—information
- rectangle (vertical)—regulations, such as speed limits, lane markings, parking restrictions

B The **colors** of signs have specific meaning.

- yellow—warning
- orange—construction
- green—information
- white—regulations

C The **symbols,** or pictures, used on signs give specific information that anyone can usually understand.

SIGNS IN A DRIVER EDUCATION PAMPHLET

Signs

PRACTICE AND APPLY

Refer to the signs shown to answer the following questions:

1. How do you know that the first sign is a warning sign as well as a railroad sign? What warning does it give?
2. If you had just moved to a new town, how would the second sign help you?
3. What does the third sign tell a driver?
4. If you are walking on the right side of a path and see the fourth sign, what should you do?

4.5 READING A WORKPLACE DOCUMENT

Workplace documents are materials that are produced or used within a workplace, usually to aid in the functioning of a business. These may be documents generated by a business to monitor itself, such as minutes of a meeting or a sales report. These documents may also explain company policies, organizational structures, and operating procedures. Workplace documents include memos, business letters, job applications, and résumés.

Strategies for Reading

A Read the title and any subtitles to see what information the document covers.

B Determine who needs to read the document. Look for clues to see if it applies to you.

C Look for subheadings to identify main ideas and topics and to determine how the document is organized.

D Read the document slowly and carefully, as it may contain details that should not be overlooked.

E Notice how to contact the creator of the document. You will need this information to clear up anything you don't understand.

F Take notes to help you remember what actions are required.

PRACTICE AND APPLY

Reread the document and answer the questions:

1. What organization created the document?
2. Who needs to read the document?
3. Who should accompany children onto the playground?
4. If there is a fire, what should you do before opening a door?
5. What three things should you do before leaving for the day?

OPERATING PROCEDURES

"Little Folks" Play Group **A**

Middleton Park District

Notice to Volunteers
Safety Guidelines **B**

We're glad you have volunteered to help with our Saturday morning play group for children ages 2–5. To keep our space clean and safe and our children happy, we all must follow these safety rules.

Staffing **C**

- An adult must be in the playroom at all times.
- Children who go outside to the playground must be accompanied by an adult.

Emergencies **C**

- In case of emergency, dial 911 on the phone in the kitchen.
- In case of fire, evacuate the children through the main door or the emergency exit. Before opening a door, touch it to see if it is hot. A fire extinguisher is located next to the emergency exit.

Cleanup **C**

- Make sure the playroom is clean at the end of the day. Put all toys in the toy chests.
- Wipe tabletops clean with a damp sponge.
- Turn off the lights as you leave.

This document was prepared by the Middleton Park District. If you have questions or concerns, contact the Program Coordinator. **E**

4.6 READING ELECTRONIC TEXT

Electronic text is any text that is in a form that a computer can store and display on a screen. Electronic text can be part of Web pages, CD-ROMs, search engines, and documents that you create with your computer software. Like books, Web pages often provide aids for finding information. However, each Web page is designed differently, and information is not in the same location on each page. It is important to know the functions of different parts of a Web page so that you can easily find the information you want.

Strategies for Reading

A Look at the **title** of a page to determine what topics it covers.

B For an online source, such as a Web page or search engine, note the **Web address,** known as a **URL** (Universal Resource Locator). You may want to make a note of it if you need to return to that page.

C Look for a **menu bar** along the top, bottom, or side of a Web page. Clicking on an item in a menu bar will take you to another part of the Web site.

D Notice any hyperlinks to related pages. **Hyperlinks** are often underlined or highlighted in a contrasting color. You can click on a hyperlink to get to another page—one that may or may not have been created by the same person or organization.

E For information that you want to keep for future reference, save documents on your computer or print them. For online sources, you can pull down the **Favorites** or **Bookmarks** menu and bookmark pages so that you can easily return to them or print the information you need. Printing the pages will allow you to highlight key ideas on a hard copy.

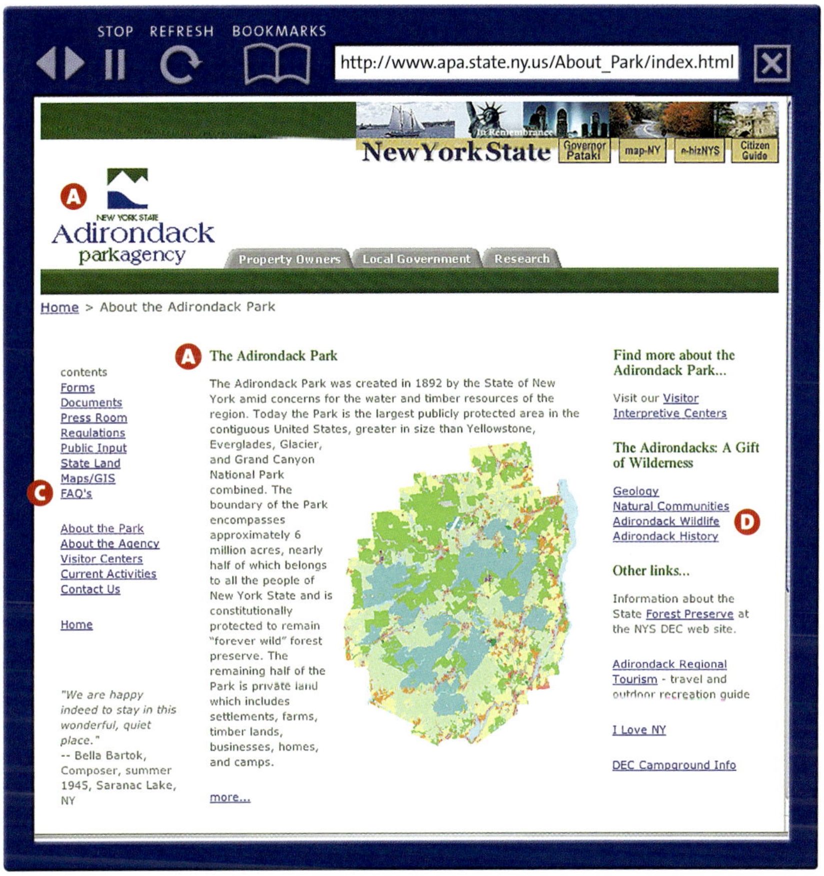

PRACTICE AND APPLY

1. What is the URL of the Web page shown?
2. Which links would you click on to find out about recreation in the park?
3. What would you do if you had questions that weren't answered by information on the site?

5 Reading Persuasive Texts

5.1 ANALYZING AN ARGUMENT

An **argument** expresses a position on an issue or problem and supports it with reasons and evidence. Being able to analyze and evaluate arguments will help you distinguish between claims you should accept and those you should not. A sound argument should appeal strictly to reason. However, arguments are often used in texts that also contain other types of persuasive devices. An argument includes the following elements:

- A **claim** is the writer's position on an issue or problem.
- **Support** is any material that serves to prove a claim. In an argument, support usually consists of reasons and evidence.
- **Reasons** are declarations made to justify an action, decision, or belief—for example, "My reason for thinking we will be late is that we can't make it to the appointment in five minutes."
- **Evidence** can be the specific references, quotations, facts, examples, and opinions that support a claim. Evidence may also consist of statistics, reports of personal experience, or the views of experts.
- A **counterargument** is an argument made to oppose another argument. A good argument anticipates the opposition's objections and provides counterarguments to disprove or answer them.

Claim	I think I should be allowed to watch more TV.
Reason	TV can provide opportunities for learning and enjoyment.
Evidence	TV can take you to faraway places and can bring art, music, and science right into your home.
Counterargument	Some people think TV is really bad for kids, but those people are looking at only the worst part of TV, not the best.

PRACTICE AND APPLY

Read the following editorial and use a chart like the one shown to identify the claim, reason, evidence, and counterargument.

Important Hours
by Gina Maraini

"The Golden Years." That is what some people call old age. They think it is a time of peace and relaxation. But many old people spend time alone. Some cannot get out of their homes because of illness. "What can I do?" you ask. You can do more than you think to make an important contribution to an older person's life. Even spending an hour a week can mean a lot to an older neighbor who lives alone.

Some kids might say that they can only do good for an older person if they have lots of time and lots of patience. It's easy to talk yourself out of volunteering your time by saying, "I only have an hour a week. What good would that do?" Never underestimate just how much good you can do even in a little bit of time.

Sometimes things happen that seem unimportant to a kid but can really be a problem to an old person. If a small object like a pen or pencil slides under furniture, an older person often is not able to stoop down and pick it up. But they feel embarrassed to ask for help. So, the pen stays there. Sometimes it gets forgotten about and becomes lost. You can help that older person find these things. And by helping, you are reminding that person that he or she is not forgotten about either.

Sometimes it is hard for an older person to reach up high. Putting things away, like groceries, becomes a problem. Often the older person gets tired and gives up. You can help to put groceries and other heavy objects away. And by doing that, you are helping that older person feel like he or she can still keep up with life's challenges.

One of the most important things you can do for a senior citizen who lives alone is to give that person someone to talk to. Old people, who have lived long lives and had many experiences, have stories to tell that you can learn a lot from. And it is important for you to say so, too. That way, you can show the older person that he or she is contributing to your life.

You can make a real contribution to an older person's life. Even if you only have an hour to spend, you can help an older person feel cared about and important. Find ways to reach out, whether through volunteer organizations or just by being aware of who is alone in your neighborhood. And always remember: as much as you give, you get back so much more, simply by knowing the difference that you have made.

5.2 RECOGNIZING PERSUASIVE TECHNIQUES

Persuasive texts typically rely on more than just the **logical appeal** of an argument to be convincing. They also rely on ethical and emotional appeals and other **persuasive techniques**—devices that can convince you to adopt a position or take an action.

Ethical appeals establish a writer's credibility and trustworthiness with an audience. When a writer links a claim to a widely accepted value, the writer not only gains moral support for that claim but also establishes a connection with readers. For example, with the following appeal, the writer reminds readers of a value they should accept and links a claim to it: "Most of us agree that we should protect our natural resources, but we don't invest a lot of time or money to preserve them."

The chart shown here explains several other means by which a writer may attempt to sway you to adopt his or her position. Learn to recognize these techniques, and you are less likely to be influenced by them.

Persuasive Technique	Example
Appeals by Association	
Bandwagon appeal Suggests that a person should believe or do something because "everyone else" does	Every day more buyers are enjoying the conveniences of catalog shopping.
Testimonial Relies on endorsements from well-known people or satisfied customers	Todd Marshall, star of stage and screen, buys his shoes at Fine Footwear. Shouldn't you?
Snob appeal Taps into people's desire to be special or part of an elite group	Be among the first to enjoy the upgraded facilities at Spring Lake Fitness Center.
Appeal to loyalty Relies on people's affiliation with a particular group	Say *Yes!* to your community—support the campaign to build a new library!
Emotional Appeals	
Appeals to pity, fear, or vanity Use strong feelings, rather than facts, to persuade	We need to keep the homeless shelter open—think how you would feel if you had no place to go.
Word Choice	
Glittering generality A generalization that includes a word or phrase with positive connotations, to promote a product, person, or idea.	Buying handmade jewelry from the Hang Up helps support small-town America.

PRACTICE AND APPLY

Identify the persuasive techniques used in this model.

Vote for Velazquez!

Whom do you want to represent you in Congress—a dinosaur who's stuck in the past or someone who's courageously facing the future? Why settle for Jill Jolsen, who hasn't lifted a finger to help this community? Don't let her slick ads fool you. Instead, join the leaders in the community and many of your neighbors who have already put their support behind Victor Velazquez. Local businesswoman Janice Wu is behind Velazquez all the way—she says he will bring new jobs and fresh ideas that will really work. Don't miss this once-in-a-lifetime chance to change this town. Vote for Velazquez!

5.3 ANALYZING LOGIC AND REASONING

While persuasive techniques may sway you to side with a writer, they should not be enough to convince you that an argument is sound. To determine the soundness of an argument, you really need to examine the argument's claim and support and the logic or reasoning that links them. To do this, it is helpful to identify the writer's mode of reasoning.

The Inductive Mode of Reasoning

When a writer leads from specific evidence to a general principle or generalization, that writer is using **inductive reasoning.** Here is an example of inductive reasoning.

SPECIFIC FACTS

Fact 1 Turtles are the only reptiles that have a shell.

Fact 2 The green turtle, a sea turtle, can swim almost 20 miles an hour.

Fact 3 Snapping turtles have powerful, sharp-edged jaws and are aggressive when attacked.

GENERALIZATION

Turtles have a variety of protective strategies.

Strategies for Determining the Soundness of Inductive Arguments

Ask yourself the following questions to evaluate an inductive argument:

- **Is the evidence valid and sufficient support for the conclusion?** Inaccurate facts lead to inaccurate conclusions.
- **Does the conclusion follow logically from the evidence?** From the facts listed above, the conclusion that *all* turtles have a wide variety of protective strategies would be too broad a generalization.
- **Is the evidence drawn from a large enough sample?** Even though there are only three facts listed above, the sample is large enough to support the claim. If you wanted to support the conclusion that only turtles have a variety of protective strategies, the sample is not large enough.

The Deductive Mode of Reasoning

When a writer arrives at a conclusion by applying a general principle to a specific situation, the writer is using **deductive reasoning.** Here's an example.

Being exposed to loud noise over a long period will damage a person's hearing.	General principle or premise
▼	
I listen to my stereo at its highest setting for hours every day.	Specific situation
▼	
I will have some hearing loss.	Specific conclusion

Strategies for Determining the Soundness of Deductive Arguments

Ask yourself the following questions to evaluate a deductive argument:

- **Is the general principle actually stated, or is it implied?** Note that writers often use deductive reasoning in arguments without stating the general principles. They just assume that readers will recognize and agree with the principles. So you may want to identify the general principle for yourself.
- **Is the general principle sound?** Don't just assume the general principle is sound. Ask yourself whether it is really true.
- **Is the conclusion valid?** To be valid, a conclusion in a deductive argument must follow logically from the general principle and the specific situation.

The following chart shows two conclusions drawn from the same general principle.

All seventh-graders are going to the zoo next week.	
Accurate Deduction	**Inaccurate Deduction**
Laura is in the seventh grade; therefore, Laura is going to the zoo next week.	Laura is going to the zoo next week; therefore, Laura is in the seventh grade.

Laura may be going to the zoo with her family or friends.

PRACTICE AND APPLY

Identify the mode of reasoning used in the following paragraph.

> In science class, I learned what different substances do for the human body. Protein aids growth and repairs muscles. Fruits and vegetables provide critical vitamins, and calcium strengthens bones. Carbohydrates supply energy to the body. Clearly, a balanced diet is important for good health.

Identifying Faulty Reasoning

Sometimes an argument at first appears to make sense but isn't valid because it is based on a fallacy. A **fallacy** is an error in logic. Learn to recognize these common fallacies.

TYPE OF FALLACY	DEFINITION	EXAMPLE
Circular reasoning	Supporting a statement by simply repeating it in different words	I'm tired because **I don't have any energy.**
Either/or fallacy	A statement that suggests that there are only two choices available in a situation that really offers more than two options	**Either** we raise taxes, **or** we close the parks.
Oversimplification	An explanation of a complex situation or problem as if it were much simpler than it is	Getting a good grade in Mrs. Raimi's class depends on **whether she likes you.**
Overgeneralization	A generalization that is too broad. You can often recognize overgeneralizations by the use of words such as *all, everyone, every time, anything, no one,* and *none.*	You **never** get me anything I want.
Hasty generalization	A conclusion drawn from too little evidence or from evidence that is biased	She left after fifteen minutes. **She must not like us.**
Stereotyping	A dangerous type of overgeneralization. Stereotypes are broad statements about people on the basis of their gender, ethnicity, race, or political, social, professional, or religious group.	**All rock stars** are self-centered.
Attacking the person or name-calling	An attempt to discredit an idea by attacking the person or group associated with it. Candidates often engage in name-calling during political campaigns.	The **narrow-minded** senator opposes recycling.
Evading the issue	Responding to an objection with arguments and evidence that do not address its central point	Yes, I broke my campaign promise not to raise taxes, **but higher taxes have led to increases in police patrols and paved highways.**
False cause	The mistake of assuming that because one event occurred after another event in time, the first event caused the second one to occur	John didn't get his homework done because he had to take the dog for a walk.

PRACTICE AND APPLY

Look for examples of logical fallacies in the following argument. Identify each one and explain why you identified it as such.

> Dear Editors:
>
> There has been a lot of talk about students' lack of concern for the appearance of our school. Nobody gets rid of his or her trash properly and everyone writes graffiti on the walls. But if the school seemed more worth caring about, students would take better care of it. Most of the school is very old. The halls are dark and the walls are dingy because the maintenance staff has been on strike for several weeks. The old-fashioned school board said that an entirely new building wasn't needed. So only a new gym was added. It is clean and bright because students have kept it that way. Either we build a new school, or it will be destroyed in three years.

5.4 EVALUATING PERSUASIVE TEXTS

Learning how to evaluate persuasive texts and identify bias will help you become more selective when doing research and also help you improve your own reasoning and arguing skills. **Bias** is an inclination for or against a particular opinion or viewpoint. A writer may reveal a strongly positive or negative opinion on an issue by presenting only one way of looking at it or by heavily weighting the evidence on one side of the argument. The presence of the following is often a sign that a writer is biased:

Loaded language consists of words with strongly positive or negative connotations that are intended to influence a reader's attitude.

EXAMPLE: *Barbara Larsen is the best choice for student council president because she has fresh ideas and fantastic people skills.* (*Fresh* and *fantastic* have very positive connotations.)

Propaganda is any form of communication that is so distorted that it conveys false or misleading information. Some politicians create and distribute propaganda. Many logical fallacies, such as name-calling, the either/or fallacy, and false causes, are often used in propaganda. The following example shows an oversimplification. The writer uses one fact to support a particular point of view but does not reveal another fact that does not support that viewpoint.

EXAMPLE: *Since the new park opened, vandalism in the area has increased by 10 percent. Clearly, the park has had a negative impact on the area.* (The writer does not include the fact that the vandalism was caused by people who were not drawn into the area by the park.)

For more information on logical fallacies, see ***Identifying Faulty Reasoning****, page R24.*

Strategies for Evaluating Evidence

It is important to have a set of standards by which you can evaluate persuasive texts. Use the questions below to help you critically assess facts and opinions that are presented as evidence.

- **Are the facts presented verifiable?** Facts can be proved by eyewitness accounts, authoritative sources such as encyclopedias and almanacs, experts, or research.
- **Are the opinions presented well informed?** Any opinions offered should be supported by facts, be based on research or eyewitness accounts, or be the opinions of experts on the topic.
- **Is the evidence thorough?** Thorough evidence leaves no reasonable questions unanswered. If a choice is offered, background for making the choice should be provided. If taking a side is called for, all sides of the issue should be presented.
- **Is the evidence biased?** Be alert to evidence that contains loaded language or other signs of bias.
- **Is the evidence authoritative?** The people, groups, or organizations that provided the evidence should have credentials that support their authority.

- **Is it important that the evidence be current?** Where timeliness is crucial, as in the areas of medicine and technology, the evidence should reflect the latest developments in the areas.

PRACTICE AND APPLY

Read the argument below. Identify the facts, opinion, and elements of bias.

Let your voice be heard. The Students' League is hosting a demonstration against U.S Representative Sharon Bullhorn on Saturday. Just last week, Representative Bullhorn voted against raising the minimum wage. Obviously Representative Bullhorn doesn't care about young people. If she did, she would have helped pass the much-needed minimum wage increase, so that preteens and teens could earn the money they deserve.

Strategies for Determining a Strong Argument

Make sure that all or most of the following statements are true:

- The argument presents a claim or thesis.
- The claim is connected to its support by a general principle that most readers would readily agree with. Valid general principle: *It is the job of a school to provide a well-rounded physical education program.* Invalid general principle: *It is the job of a school to produce healthy, physically fit people.*
- The reasons make sense.
- The reasons are presented in a logical and effective order.
- The claim and all reasons are adequately supported by sound evidence.
- The evidence is adequate, accurate, and appropriate.
- The logic is sound. There are no instances of faulty reasoning.
- The argument adequately anticipates and addresses reader concerns and counterclaims with counterarguments.

PRACTICE AND APPLY

Use the preceding criteria to evaluate the strength of the following proposal.

MODEL

Summary of Proposal

I propose that our school install video cameras in halls, lunchrooms, and other public areas to monitor students' activities.

Need

The halls and public areas of our school are not well supervised because of a shortage of security staff. Last month, three students were hurt in fights on school property.

Proposed Solution

Installing video monitors in the halls and public areas of the school will create a safe environment for students at a reasonable cost.

There is good evidence that video monitoring works. Westview School has monitored its students for over a year. In that time there has not been one incident of fighting or damage to property.

People who are against video monitoring don't agree. They say that monitoring violates students' rights to privacy.

In my opinion, junior high students need to act like responsible adults. We need guidelines and monitoring to show us where the limits are and to help us learn to act responsibly on our own.

Not only does video monitoring work, but installing the equipment can lower supervisory costs in the long run. Only eight cameras would be needed, installed in the two main hallways, the lunchroom, and the auditorium. The total cost would be around $16,000. I believe the money can be found in the general school budget.

What idiot would not support video monitoring of students?

It would be a crime not to have video monitoring.

Most school officials only care about their jobs and not what's good for students. I say to those school officials who do care: Either install video cameras or wait for more students to be injured.

6 Adjusting Reading Rate to Purpose

You may need to change the way you read certain texts in order to understand what you read. To adjust the way you read, you first need to be aware of what you want to get out of what you are reading. Then you can adjust the speed at which you read in response to your purpose and the difficulty of the material.

Determine Your Purpose for Reading

You read different types of materials for different purposes. You may read a novel for enjoyment. You may read a textbook unit to learn a new concept or to master the content for a test. When you read for enjoyment, you naturally read at a pace that is comfortable for you. When you read for information, you need to read material more slowly and thoroughly. When you are being tested on material, you may think you have to read fast, especially if the test is being timed. However, you can actually increase your understanding of the material if you slow down.

Determine Your Reading Rate

The rate at which you read most comfortably is called your **independent reading level.** It is the rate that you use to read materials that you enjoy. To learn to adjust your reading rate to read materials for other purposes, you need to be aware of your independent reading level. You can figure out your reading level by following these steps:

1. Select a passage from a book or story you enjoy.
2. Have a friend or classmate time you as you begin reading the passage silently.
3. Read at the rate that is most comfortable for you.
4. Stop when your friend or classmate tells you one minute has passed.
5. Determine the number of words you read in that minute and write down the number.
6. Repeat the process at least two more times, using different passages.
7. Add the numbers and divide the sum by the number of times your friend timed you.

Reading Techniques for Informational Material

You can use the following techniques to adapt your reading for informational texts, to prepare for tests, and to better understand what you read:

- **Skimming** is reading quickly to get the general idea of a text. To skim, read only the title, headings, graphic aids, highlighted words, and first sentence of each paragraph. Also, read any introduction, conclusion, or summary. Skimming can be especially useful when taking a test. Before reading a passage, you can skim questions that follow it in order to find out what is expected and better focus on the important ideas in the text.

  When researching a topic, skimming can help you decide whether a source has information that is related to your topic.
- **Scanning** is reading quickly to find a specific piece of information, such as a fact or a definition. When you scan, your eyes sweep across a page, looking for key words that may lead you to the information you want. Use scanning to review for tests and to find answers to questions.
- **Changing pace** is speeding up or slowing down the rate at which you read parts of a particular text. When you come across familiar concepts, you might be able to speed up without misunderstanding them. When you encounter unfamiliar concepts or material presented in an unpredictable way, however, you may need to slow down to understand the information.

WATCH OUT! Reading too slowly can affect your ability to understand what you read. Make sure you aren't just reading one word at a time. Practice reading phrases.

PRACTICE AND APPLY

Find an article in a magazine or textbook. Skim the article. Then answer the following questions:

1. What did you notice about the organization of the article from skimming it?
2. What is the main idea of the article?

Writing is a process, a journey of discovery in which you can explore your thoughts, experiment with ideas, and search for connections. Through writing, you can explore and record your thoughts, feelings, and ideas for yourself alone or you can communicate them to an audience.

WRITING TOOLS
Go to the **Writing Center** at **ClassZone.com** for interactive models, publishing ideas, and other support.

1 The Writing Process

The writing process consists of the following stages: prewriting, drafting, revising and editing, proofreading, and publishing. These are not stages that you must complete in a set order. Rather, you may return to an earlier stage at any time to improve your writing.

1.1 PREWRITING

In the prewriting stage, you explore what you want to write about, what your purpose for writing is, whom you are writing for, and what form you will use to express your ideas. Ask yourself the following questions to get started.

Topic	• Is my topic assigned, or can I choose it? • What would I be interested in writing about?
Purpose	• Am I writing to entertain, to inform, to persuade, or for some combination of these purposes? • What effect do I want to have on my readers?
Audience	• Who is the audience? • What might the audience members already know about my topic? • What about the topic might interest them?
Format	• Which format will work best? Essay? Poem? Speech? Short story? Article? Research paper?

Find Ideas for Writing

- Browse through magazines, newspapers, and Web sites.
- Start a file of articles you want to save for future reference.
- With a group, brainstorm as many ideas as you can. Compile your ideas into a list.
- Write down anything that comes into your head.
- Interview someone who is an expert on a particular topic.
- Use a cluster map to explore subordinate ideas that relate to a general topic.

Organize Ideas

Once you've chosen a topic, you will need to compile and organize your ideas. If you are writing a description, you may need to gather sensory details. For an essay or a research paper, you may need to record information from different sources. To record notes from sources you read or view, use any or all of these methods:

- **Summarize:** Briefly retell the main ideas of a piece of writing in your own words.
- **Paraphrase:** Restate all or almost all of the information in your own words.
- **Quote:** Record the author's exact words.

Depending on what form your writing takes, you may also need to arrange your ideas in a certain pattern.

For more information, see the ***Writing Handbook,*** *pages R34–R41.*

1.2 DRAFTING

In the drafting stage, you put your ideas on paper and allow them to develop and change as you write. You don't need to worry about correct grammar and spelling at this stage. There are two ways that you can draft:

Discovery drafting is a good approach when you are not quite sure what you think about your subject. You just start writing and let your feelings and ideas lead you in developing the topic.

Planned drafting may work better if you know that your ideas have to be arranged in a certain way, as in a research paper. Try making a writing plan or an informal outline before you begin drafting.

1.3 REVISING AND EDITING

The revising and editing stage allows you to polish your draft and make changes in its content, organization, and style. Use the questions that follow to spot problems and determine what changes would improve your work:

- Does my writing have a **main idea** or central focus? Is my thesis clear?
- Have I used **precise** nouns, verbs, and modifiers?
- Have I included **adequate detail** and **evidence?** Where might I include a telling detail, revealing statistic, or vivid example?
- Is my writing **unified?** Do all ideas and supporting details help explain my main idea?
- Is my writing clear and **coherent?** Do sentences connect to one another smoothly and logically?
- Have I used a consistent **point of view?**
- Do I need to add **transitional words, phrases,** or sentences to explain relationships among ideas?
- Have I used a **variety of sentence types?** Are they well constructed? What sentences might I combine to improve the rhythm of my writing?
- Have I used a **tone** appropriate for my audience and purpose?

1.4 PROOFREADING

When you are satisfied with your revision, proofread your paper for mistakes in grammar, usage, and mechanics. You may want to do this several times, looking for a different type of mistake each time. Use the following questions to help you correct errors:

- Have I corrected any errors in **subject-verb agreement** and **pronoun-antecedent agreement?**
- Have I double-checked for errors in **confusing word pairs,** such as *it's/its, than/then,* and *too/to?*
- Have I corrected any **run-on sentences** and **sentence fragments?**
- Have I followed rules for **correct capitalization?**
- Have I used **punctuation marks** correctly?
- Have I checked the **spellings of all unfamiliar words** in the dictionary?

TIP If possible, don't begin proofreading just after you've finished writing. Put your work away for at least a few hours. When you return to it, you will find it easier to identify and correct mistakes.

For more information, see the ***Grammar Handbook*** *and the* ***Vocabulary and Spelling Handbook****, pages R46–R75.*

Use the proofreading symbols in the chart to mark changes on your draft.

Proofreading Symbols	
∧ Add letters or words.	/ Make a capital letter lowercase.
⊙ Add a period.	¶ Begin a new paragraph.
≡ Capitalize a letter.	↯ Delete letters or words.
⁐ Close up space.	∿ Switch the positions of letters or words.
∧ Add a comma.	

1.5 PUBLISHING AND REFLECTING

Always consider sharing your finished writing with a wider audience. Reflecting on your writing is another good way to finish a project.

Publishing Ideas

- Post your writing on a Weblog.
- Create a multimedia presentation and share it with classmates.
- Publish your writing in a school newspaper, local newspaper, or literary magazine.
- Present your work orally in a report, speech, reading, or dramatic performance.

Reflecting on Your Writing

Think about your writing process and whether you would like to add what you have written to your writing portfolio. You might attach a note in which you answer questions like these:

- Which parts of the process did I find easiest? Which parts were more difficult?
- What was the biggest problem I faced during the writing process? How did I solve the problem?
- What changes have occurred in my writing style?
- Have I noticed any features in the writing of published authors or my peers that I can apply to my own work?

1.6 PEER RESPONSE

Peer response consists of the suggestions and comments you make about the writing of your peers and also the comments and suggestions they make about your writing. You can ask a peer reader for help at any time in the writing process.

Using Peer Response as a Writer

- Indicate whether you are more interested in feedback about your ideas or about your presentation of them.
- Ask questions that will help you get specific information about your writing. Open-ended questions that require more than yes-or-no answers are more likely to give you information you can use as you revise.
- Give your readers plenty of time to respond thoughtfully to your writing.
- Encourage your readers to be honest.

Being a Peer Reader

- Respect the writer's feelings.
- Offer positive reactions first.
- Make sure you understand what kind of feedback the writer is looking for, and then respond accordingly.

*For more information on the writing process, see the **Introductory Unit**, pages 16–19.*

2 Building Blocks of Good Writing

Whatever your purpose in writing, you need to capture your reader's interest and organize your thoughts clearly.

2.1 INTRODUCTIONS

An introduction should present a thesis statement and capture your reader's attention.

Kinds of Introductions

There are a number of ways to write an introduction. The one you choose depends on who the audience is and on your purpose for writing.

Make a Surprising Statement Beginning with a startling statement or an interesting fact can arouse your reader's curiosity about a subject, as in the following model.

MODEL

Bats may seem like a nuisance, but not as much as the many pounds of insects a colony of bats can eat in one night. Despite their ugly faces and all the scary stories about them, bats are very important and useful animals.

Provide a Description A vivid description sets a mood and brings a scene to life for your reader.

Here, details about wild geese swimming in an unfrozen river during the winter set the tone for an essay about water pollution.

MODEL

The temperature is 15 degrees. Drifts of snow hide picnic tables and swings. In the middle of the park, however, steam rises from a lake where Canada geese swim. It sounds beautiful, but the water is warm because it has been heated by a chemical plant upriver. In fact, the geese should have migrated south by now.

Ask a Question Beginning with a question can make your reader want to read on to find out the answer. The following introduction asks what two seemingly different things have in common.

MODEL

What do billiard balls and movie film have in common? It was in an effort to find a substitute for ivory billiard balls that John Hyatt created celluloid. This plastic substance was also used to make the first movies.

Relate an Anecdote Beginning with an anecdote, or brief story, can hook your reader and help you make a point in a dramatic way. The following anecdote introduces a humorous story about a childhood experience.

MODEL

When I was younger, my friends and I would rub balloons in our hair and make them stick to our clothes. Someone once said, "I get a charge out of this," not knowing that we were really generating static electricity.

Address the Reader Speaking directly to your reader establishes a friendly, informal tone and involves the reader in your topic.

MODEL

Learn the latest dances from a famous video choreographer. Come to the community center for a free dance lesson on Saturday night at 6 P.M.

Begin with a Thesis Statement A thesis statement expressing a main idea may be woven into both the beginning and the end of a piece of nonfiction writing.

MODEL

Unlike the strategically planned warfare in today's world, warfare in medieval times was unsophisticated and included many primitive weapons.

TIP To write the best introduction for your paper, you may want to try more than one of the methods and then decide which is the most effective for your purpose and audience.

2.2 PARAGRAPHS

A paragraph is made up of sentences that work together to develop an idea or accomplish a purpose. Whether or not it contains a topic sentence stating the main idea, a good paragraph must have unity and coherence.

Unity

A paragraph has unity when all the sentences support and develop one stated or implied idea. Use the following technique to create unity in your paragraphs:

Write a Topic Sentence A topic sentence states the main idea of the paragraph; all other sentences in the paragraph provide supporting details. A topic sentence is often the first sentence in a paragraph, as shown in the model that follows. However, it may also appear later in a paragraph or at the end, to summarize or reinforce the main idea.

MODEL

Flying a hot-air balloon looks fun, but it requires a good mathematician to fly one safely. Since a balloon is controlled by heating and cooling the air inside the balloon, the pilot must know the temperature of the air outside it and how high he or she plans to fly in order to calculate the maximum weight the balloon can carry. If the pilot doesn't do the math correctly, the balloon could crash.

TIP Paying attention to topic sentences when you read literature can help you craft your own topic sentences. Notice the use of strong topic sentences in "The Noble Experiment" on pages 810–819. For example, the fourth paragraph on page 812 begins, "Winning his directors' approval was almost insignificant in contrast to the task which now lay ahead of the Dodger president." The rest of the paragraph then explains that task in detail.

Coherence

A paragraph is coherent when all its sentences are related to one another and each flows logically to the next. The following techniques will help you achieve coherence in paragraphs:

- Present your ideas in the most logical order.
- Use pronouns, synonyms, and repeated words to connect ideas.
- Use transitional words to show relationships among ideas.

In the model shown here, the writer used several techniques to create a coherent paragraph.

MODEL

Before you buy a backpack, you should make sure it fits you and will last a long time. First, check the seams to be sure they are zigzag stitched and not single-row stitched. Next, check that the zippers are covered by flaps so your homework doesn't get wet when it rains. Finally, make sure that the bottom of the backpack rests comfortably on your hips.

2.3 TRANSITIONS

Transitions are words and phrases that show connections between details. Clear transitions help show how your ideas relate to one another.

Kinds of Transitions

The types of transitions you choose depend on the ideas you want to convey.

Time or Sequence Some transitions help to clarify the sequence of events over time. When you are telling a story or describing a process, you can connect ideas with such transitional words as *first, second, always, then, next, later, soon, before, finally, after, earlier, afterward,* and *tomorrow.*

MODEL

Long before mountain bikes were made, bicycles were much less comfortable. The first cycle, which actually had four wheels, was made in 1645 and had to be walked. Later, two-wheeled cycles with pedals were called boneshakers because of their bumpy ride.

Spatial Order Transitional words and phrases such as *in front, behind, next to, along, nearest, lowest, above, below, underneath, on the left,* and *in the middle* can help your reader visualize a scene.

MODEL

The audience entered the theater from the back. The stage was in front, and fire exits were located to the right and left of the stage.

Degree of Importance Transitional words such as *mainly, strongest, weakest, first, second, most important, least important, worst,* and *best* may be used to rank ideas or to show degrees of importance.

MODEL

My strongest reason for going on the canoeing trip would be not hearing my little brother and sister squabbling over the TV. My weakest reason for going is that there is nothing better to do.

Compare and Contrast Words and phrases such as *similarly, likewise, also, like, as, neither . . . nor,* and *either . . . or* show similarity between details. *However, by contrast, yet, but, unlike, instead, whereas,* and *while* show difference. Note the use of transitions showing contrast in the model.

MODEL

While my local public library is a quieter place to study than home, I don't always get much done in the library. I'm so used to the cheerful chatter of my baby brother that, by contrast, the stillness of the library makes me sleepy.

TIP Both *but* and *however* can be used to join two independent clauses. When *but* is used as a coordinating conjunction, it is preceded by a comma. When *however* is used as a conjunctive adverb, it is preceded by a semicolon and followed by a comma.

EXAMPLE

A greenbottle fly is small, but its eyes contain many lenses.

You can try to quietly sneak up on a fly with a swatter; however, the fly, with its compound eyes, will still be able to see the motion of the swatter.

Cause-Effect When you are writing about a cause-effect relationship, use transitional words and phrases such as *since, because, thus, therefore, so, due to, for this reason,* and *as a result* to help explain that relationship and make your writing coherent.

MODEL

Because we missed seven days of school as a result of snowstorms, the school year will be extended. Therefore, we will be in school until June 17.

2.4 CONCLUSIONS

A conclusion should leave readers with a strong final impression.

Kinds of Conclusions

Good conclusions sum up ideas in a variety of ways. Here are some techniques you might try.

Restate Your Thesis A good way to conclude an essay is by restating your thesis, or main idea, in different words. The following conclusion restates the thesis introduced on page R31.

MODEL

It may be hard to imagine that ladders, bows, and catapults were once used in battle; yet these primitive weapons accomplished the attackers' main goal—to get a castle's inhabitants to surrender.

Ask a Question Try asking a question that sums up what you have said and gives your reader something new to think about. This question concludes a piece of persuasive writing and suggests a course of action.

MODEL

If tutoring a student in writing, reading, or math can help you do better in these subjects yourself, shouldn't you take advantage of the opportunities to tutor at Western Elementary School?

Make a Recommendation When you are persuading your audience to take a position on an issue, you can conclude by recommending a specific course of action.

MODEL

Since learning a foreign language gives you a chance to expand your world view and make new friends, register for one of the introductory courses that start next fall.

Offer an Opinion Leave your reader with something to think about by offering your personal opinion on the topic. The following model offers an opinion about medieval warfare.

MODEL

Even though the tools used in medieval times seem primitive today, warfare is serious and deadly business, no matter what century you're in.

End with the Last Event If you're telling a story, you may end with the last thing that happens. Here, the ending includes an important moment for the narrator.

MODEL

As I raced down the basketball court in the final seconds of the game, I felt as alone as I did on all those nights practicing by myself in the driveway. My perfect lay-up drew yells from the crowd, but I was cheering for myself on the inside.

2.5 ELABORATION

Elaboration is the process of developing an idea by providing specific supporting details that are relevant and appropriate to the purpose and form of your writing.

Facts and Statistics A fact is a statement that can be verified, and a statistic is a fact expressed as a number. Make sure the facts and statistics you supply are from reliable, up-to-date sources.

MODEL

Rhode Island is the smallest state in area; however, it is not the smallest in population. According to the U.S. Census Bureau, its population was estimated to be 1,080,632 in 2004. There are fewer people living in Alaska, Delaware, Montana, North Dakota, South Dakota, Vermont, and Wyoming.

Sensory Details Details that show how something looks, sounds, tastes, smells, or feels can enliven a description, making readers feel they are actually experiencing what you are describing. Which senses does the writer appeal to in the following model?

MODEL

I was nervous during my math test last week. Chewing on my pencil left my mouth feeling dry and flaky. My palms were sweating so much, they left stains on the pages. The ticking of the clock seemed like the beating of a drum inside my head.

Incidents From our earliest years, we are interested in hearing "stories." One way to illustrate a point powerfully is to relate an incident or tell a story, as shown in the example.

MODEL

People who are afraid of heights tend to panic even in perfectly safe situations. When my friend Jill and I rode to the top floor of a shopping mall, I enjoyed the view from the glass-enclosed elevator, but Jill's face was pale and her hands trembled.

Examples An example can help make an abstract idea concrete or can serve to clarify a complex point for your reader.

MODEL

The origins of today's professional sporting events in the United States can be traced to countries all over the world. For example, hockey is believed to have been influenced by the Irish game of hurling which included a stick and a square wooden block.

Quotations Choose quotations that clearly support your points, and be sure that you copy each quotation word for word. Remember always to credit the source.

MODEL

After the tragic events that come to pass in Rod Serling's teleplay *The Monsters Are Due on Maple Street,* the narrator says to the audience, "The tools of conquest do not necessarily come with bombs and explosions and fallout. There are weapons that are simply thoughts, attitudes, prejudices—to be found only in the minds of men. For the record, prejudices can kill and suspicion can destroy."

3 Descriptive Writing

Descriptive writing allows you to paint word pictures about anything, from events of global importance to the most personal feelings. It is an essential part of almost every piece of writing.

RUBRIC: Standards for Writing

Successful descriptive writing should

- have a clear focus and sense of purpose
- use sensory details and precise words to create a vivid image, establish a mood, or express emotion
- present details in a logical order

For more information, see ***Writing Workshop: Descriptive Essay,*** *pages 158–165.*

3.1 KEY TECHNIQUES

Consider Your Goals What do you want to accomplish with your description? Do you want to show why something is important to you? Do you want to make a person or scene more memorable? Do you want to explain an event?

Identify Your Audience Who will read your description? How familiar are they with your subject? What background information will they need? Which details will they find most interesting?

Think Figuratively What figures of speech might help make your description vivid and interesting? What simile or metaphor comes to mind? What imaginative comparisons can you make? What living thing does an inanimate object remind you of?

Gather Sensory Details Which sights, smells, tastes, sounds, and textures make your subject come alive? Which details stick in your mind when you observe or recall your subject? Which senses does it most strongly affect?

You might want to use a chart like the one shown here to collect sensory details about your subject.

Sights	Sounds	Textures	Smells	Tastes

Organize Your Details Details that are presented in a logical order help the reader form a mental picture of the subject. Descriptive details may be organized chronologically, spatially, by order of impression, or by order of importance.

3.2 OPTIONS FOR ORGANIZATION

Option 1: Spatial Order Choose one of these options to show the spatial order of elements in a scene you are describing.

For more information, see ***Transitions,*** *page R32.*

EXAMPLE 1 Top → Bottom

EXAMPLE 2 Left → Right

EXAMPLE 3 Outside / Inside

EXAMPLE 4 Near → Far

MODEL

The room was quiet—too quiet. To my left loomed the big white refrigerator. To my right squatted the gas stove, blue pilots glowing. Straight ahead sat the huge island. Cutting board, knife, and half-chopped carrot lay abandoned upon it now. Stepping cautiously to the right of the island, I came in view of the oven. That's where I froze. The oven door was open. A faint, white light pulsed and flickered high in one corner.

Option 2: Order of Impression Order of impression is the order in which you notice details.

What first catches your attention → What you notice next → What you see after that → What you focus on last

MODEL

As she lost her balance on the slippery pebbles, her first thought was that she was going to sprain her ankle and be swept away by the surf. Her heart beat rapidly, but before she knew it, she was sitting in the sand while the warm surf rolled in, almost covering her. She realized that the water was not going to reach beyond her shoulders and that she was safe. Then, suddenly, she felt the tug of the water in the other direction as the undertow flowed back, sweeping the sand from under her as it went. As soon as the water had receded she scrambled to her feet.

TIP Use transitions that help readers understand the order of the impressions you are describing. Some useful transitions are *after, next, during, first, before, finally,* and *then.*

Option 3: Order of Importance You can use order of importance as the organizing structure for a description.

Least important → More important → Most important

MODEL

I think our school should offer karate as part of the gym program. There are several reasons this is a good idea. First, karate is fun, and anyone can learn to do it. Many students who want to learn martial arts can't afford to because private lessons are so expensive. Karate is also a great form of exercise. It improves strength, coordination, and grace. The most important reason, though, is that learning karate makes students more confident and gives them skills that can help them throughout life.

For more information, see ***Transitions,*** *page R32.*

Option 4: Chronological Order You can use chronological order as the organizing structure for a description. See section 4.2 on page R36 for an example of how this is done.

4 Narrative Writing

Narrative writing tells a story. If you write a story from your imagination, it is a fictional narrative. A true story about actual events is a nonfictional narrative. Narrative writing can be found in short stories, novels, news articles, personal narratives, and biographies.

RUBRIC: Standards for Writing

A successful narrative should

- hook the reader's attention with a strong introduction
- include descriptive details and dialogue to develop the characters, setting, and plot
- have a clear beginning, middle, and end
- have a logical organization, with clues and transitions that help the reader understand the order of events
- maintain a consistent tone and point of view
- use language that is appropriate to the audience
- demonstrate the significance of events or ideas

*For more information, see **Writing Workshop: Short Story,** pages 420–427, and **Writing Workshop: Personal Narrative,** pages 850–857.*

4.1 KEY TECHNIQUES

Identify the Main Events What are the most important events in your narrative? Is each event needed to tell the story?

Describe the Setting When do the events occur? Where do they take place? How can you use setting to create mood and to set the stage for the characters and their actions?

Depict Characters Vividly What do your characters look like? What do they think and say? How do they act? What details can show what they are like?

TIP Dialogue is an effective means of developing characters in a narrative. As you write dialogue, choose words that express your characters' personalities and that show how the characters feel about one another and about the events in the plot.

4.2 OPTIONS FOR ORGANIZATION

Option 1: Chronological Order One way to organize a piece of narrative writing is to arrange the events in chronological order, as shown.

EXAMPLE

Roger walked into the store where he had seen the fancy new bikes.

"Can I help you?" the salesperson asked. Roger pointed toward the bikes against a wall.

As his hand glided over the handlebars on the bike, he barely heard the salesperson ask if he had money.

Roger ran for the door, knowing he had to find the old woman who had given him the money.

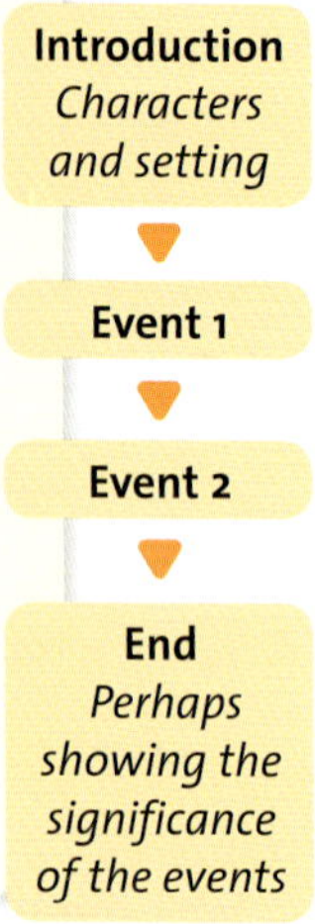

Option 2: Flashback In narrative writing, it is also possible to introduce events that happened before the beginning of the story. You may want to hook your reader's interest by opening a story with an exciting event. After your introduction, you can use a flashback to show how past events led up to the present situation or to provide background about a character or event. Use clue words such as *last summer, as a young girl, the previous school year,* and *his earliest memories* to let your reader know that you are interrupting the main action to describe earlier events.

Notice how the flashback interrupts the action in the model.

MODEL

At the trials for the first big meet of the school year, Shayna was eager to prove to the coach that she could be a leader on the track team. During warm-ups, her mind drifted back to her disastrous showing in the final meet last year, when she had dropped a baton in a relay race.

Option 3: Focus on Conflict When a fictional narrative focuses on a central conflict, the story's plot may be organized as in the following example.

EXAMPLE

A kind stranger gives Roger money he doesn't really deserve. Roger decides he will buy a bike with the money. In the store the bikes are lined up in a row, beautiful, shiny, and bright.

Describe main characters and setting.

Roger is struggling with spending the stranger's money on a fancy bike that he really doesn't need.

Present conflict.

- A salesperson walks up to Roger.
- Roger explains that he is looking at a 12-speed, super-lightweight bike.
- The salesperson tells Roger that the bike is very expensive and asks if he has enough money.

Relate events that make conflict complex and cause characters to change.

Roger realizes that he shouldn't spend the money needlessly and runs out of the store in search of the stranger. He plans to return the money.

Present resolution or outcome of conflict.

5 Expository Writing

Expository writing informs and explains. You can use it to explain how to cook spaghetti, to explore the origins of the universe, or to compare two pieces of literature. There are many types of expository writing. Think about your topic and select the type that presents the information most clearly.

5.1 COMPARISON AND CONTRAST

Compare-and-contrast writing examines the similarities and differences between two or more subjects. You might, for example, compare and contrast two short stories, the main characters in a novel, or two movies.

RUBRIC: Standards for Writing

Successful compare-and-contrast writing should

- hook the reader's attention with a strong introduction
- clearly identify the subjects that are being compared and contrasted
- include specific, relevant details
- follow a clear plan of organization
- use language and details appropriate to the audience
- use transitional words and phrases to clarify similarities and differences

For more information, see ***Writing Workshop: Comparison-Contrast Essay,*** *pages 286–293,* ***Writing Workshop: Interpretive Essay,*** *pages 524–531,* ***Writing Workshop: Personal Response to a Poem,*** *pages 608–615, and* ***Writing Workshop: Cause-and-Effect Essay,*** *pages 736–743.*

Options for Organization

Compare-and-contrast writing can be organized in different ways. The examples that follow demonstrate point-by-point organization and subject-by-subject organization.

Option 1: Point-by-Point Organization

EXAMPLE

I. Similarities in Appearance — **Point 1**

Subject A. Domestic honeybees are about five-eighths of an inch long.

Subject B. Africanized bees, contrary to rumor, are about the same size.

II. Differences in Temperament — **Point 2**

Subject A. Domestic honeybees are bred to be gentle.

Subject B. The Africanized bee is a "wild" bee that is quick-tempered around animals and people.

Option 2: Subject-by-Subject Organization

EXAMPLE

I. Domestic Honeybees — **Subject A**

Point 1. Domestic honey-bees are about five-eighths of an inch long.

Point 2. Domestic honeybees are bred to be gentle.

II. Africanized Bees — **Subject B**

Point 1. Africanized bees are about five-eighths of an inch long.

Point 2. The Africanized bee is a "wild" bee that is quick-tempered around animals and people.

*For more information, see **Writing Workshop: Comparison-Contrast Essay,** pages 286–293.*

5.2 CAUSE AND EFFECT

Cause-effect writing explains why something happened, why certain conditions exist, or what resulted from an action or a condition. You might use cause-effect writing to explain a character's actions, the progress of a disease, or the outcome of a war.

RUBRIC: Standards for Writing

Successful cause-effect writing should

- hook the reader's attention with a strong introduction
- clearly state the cause-and-effect relationship
- show clear connections between causes and effects
- present causes and effects in a logical order and use transitions effectively
- use facts, examples, and other details to illustrate each cause and effect
- use language and details appropriate to the audience

*For more information, see **Writing Workshop: Cause-and-Effect Essay,** pages 736–743.*

Options for Organization

Your organization will depend on your topic and your purpose for writing.

Option 1: Effect-to-Cause Organization If you want to explain the causes of an event, such as the threat of Africanized bees to commercial beekeeping, you might first state the effect and then examine its causes.

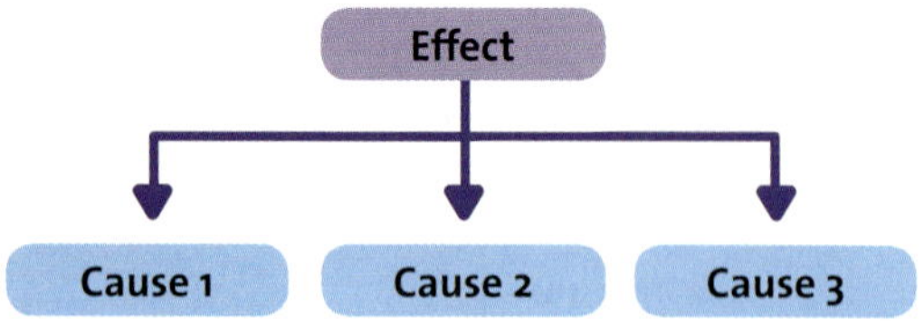

Option 2: Cause-to-Effect Organization If your focus is on explaining the effects of an event, such as the appearance of Africanized bees in the United States, you might first state the cause and then explain the effects.

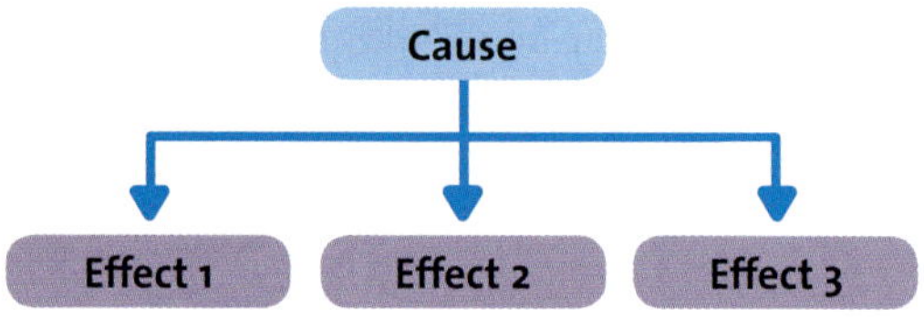

Option 3: Cause-Effect Chain Organization
Sometimes you'll want to describe a chain of cause-and-effect relationships to explore a topic such as the myths about the Africanized honeybee.

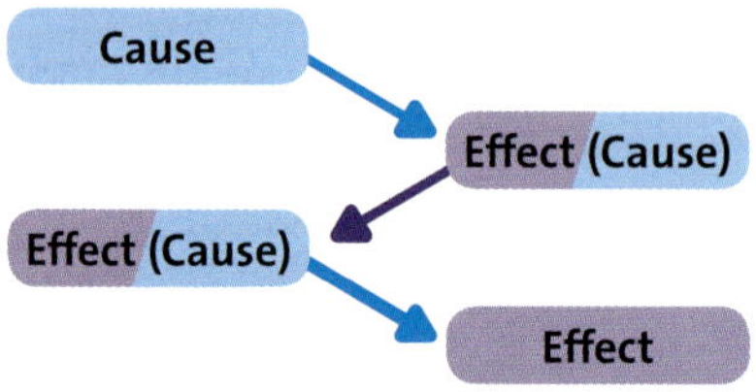

TIP Don't assume that a cause-effect relationship exists just because one event follows another. Look for evidence that the later event could not have happened if the first event had not caused it.

5.3 PROBLEM-SOLUTION

Problem-solution writing clearly states a problem, analyzes the problem, and proposes a solution to the problem. It can be used to identify and solve a conflict between characters, investigate global warming, or tell why the home team keeps losing.

RUBRIC: Standards for Writing

Successful problem-solution writing should

- hook the reader's attention with a strong introduction
- identify the problem and help the reader understand the issues involved
- analyze the causes and effects of the problem
- include quotations, facts, and statistics
- explore possible solutions to the problem and recommend the best one(s)
- use language, details, and a tone appropriate to the audience

Options for Organization

Your organization will depend on the goal of your problem-solution piece, your intended audience, and the specific problem you have chosen to address. The organizational methods that follow are effective for different kinds of problem-solution writing.

Option 1: Simple Problem-Solution

Description of problem and why it needs to be solved

▼

Recommended solution

▼

Explanation of solution

▼

Conclusion

Option 2: Deciding Between Solutions

Description of problem and why it needs to be solved

▼

Solution A
Pros
Cons

▼

Solution B
Pros
Cons

▼

Recommendation

5.4 ANALYSIS

In writing an analysis, you explain how something works, how it is defined, or what its parts are.

RUBRIC: Standards for Writing

A successful analysis should

- hook the reader's attention with a strong introduction
- clearly define the subject and its parts
- use a specific organizing structure to provide a logical flow of information
- show connections among facts and ideas through transitional words and phrases
- use language and details appropriate for the audience

Options for Organization

Organize your details in a logical order appropriate to the kind of analysis you're writing. Use one of the following options:

Option 1: Process Analysis A process analysis is usually organized chronologically, with steps or stages in the order in which they occur. You might use a process analysis to explain how to program a cell phone or prepare for a test, or to explain the different stages of development in an insect's life.

MODEL

Insect metamorphosis

Many insects grow through a four-step cycle.

Step 1 egg
Step 2 larva
Step 3 pupa
Step 4 adult

Introduce process.

Give background.

Explain steps.

Option 2: Definition Analysis You can organize the details of a definition analysis in order of importance or impression. Use a definition analysis to explain a quality (such as excellence), the characteristics of a limerick, or the characteristics of insects.

MODEL

What is an insect?

An insect is a small animal with an external skeleton, three body segments, and three pairs of legs.

Feature 1: external skeleton

Feature 2: three body segments

Feature 3: three pairs of legs

Introduce term and definition.

Explain features.

Option 3: Parts Analysis The following parts analysis explains the main parts of an insect..

MODEL

An insect's body is divided into three main parts.

Part 1: The head includes eyes, mouth, and antennae.

Part 2: The thorax has the legs and wings attached to it.

Part 3: The abdomen contains organs for digesting food, eliminating waste, and reproducing.

Introduce subject.

Explain parts.

6 Persuasive Writing

Persuasive writing allows you to use the power of language to inform and influence others. It includes speeches, persuasive essays, newspaper editorials, advertisements, and critical reviews.

RUBRIC: Standards for Writing

Successful persuasive writing should

- hook the reader's attention with a strong introduction
- state the issue and the writer's position
- give opinions and support them with facts or reasons
- have a reasonable and respectful tone
- answer opposing views
- use sound logic and effective language
- conclude by summing up reasons or calling for action

For more information, see ***Writing Workshop: Persuasive Essay,*** *pages 948–955.*

6.1 KEY TECHNIQUES

Clarify Your Position What do you believe about the issue? How can you express your opinion most clearly?

Know Your Audience Who will read your writing? What do they already know and believe about the issue? What objections to your position might they have? What additional information might they need? What tone and approach would be most effective?

Support Your Opinion Why do you feel the way you do about the issue? What facts, statistics, examples, quotations, anecdotes, or expert opinions support your view? What reasons will convince your readers? What evidence can answer their objections?

Ways to Support Your Argument	
Statistics	facts that are stated in numbers
Examples	specific instances that explain points
Observations	events or situations you yourself have seen
Anecdotes	brief stories that illustrate points
Quotations	direct statements from authorities

For more information, see ***Identifying Faulty Reasoning,*** *page R24.*

Begin and End with a Bang How can you hook your readers and make a lasting impression? What memorable quotation, anecdote, or statistic will catch their attention at the beginning or stick in their minds at the end? What strong summary or call to action can you conclude with?

MODEL

Beginning

If you want to spend an evening with your neighbors, seeing a live performance or shopping for homemade crafts, will you come to the community center? Probably not. It's too hot!

End

Many people put hours and weeks into providing our town with entertainment. Often only a few people attend these events at the community center because the building is too hot on summer evenings. One "cool" solution would be to purchase an air-conditioning system.

6.2 OPTIONS FOR ORGANIZATION

In a two-sided persuasive essay, you want to show the weaknesses of other opinions as you explain the strengths of your own.

Option 1: Reasons for Your Opinion

Introduction states issue and your position on it.
↓
Reason 1 with evidence and support
↓
Reason 2 with evidence and support
↓
Reason 3 with evidence and support
↓
Objections to whole argument
↓
Response to objections
↓
Conclusion includes restatement of your position and recommended action.

Option 2: Point-by-Point Basis

Introduction states issue and your position on it.
↓
Reason 1 with evidence and support
↓
Objections and responses for reason 1
↓
Reason 2 with evidence and support
↓
Objections and responses for reason 2
↓
Reason 3 with evidence and support
↓
Objections and responses for reason 3
↓
Conclusion includes restatement of your position and recommended action.

7 Workplace and Technical Writing

Business writing is writing done in a workplace to support the work of a company or business. You may need to do business writing to request information or complain about a product or service. Several types of formats, such as memos, letters, e-mails, and applications, have been developed to make communication easier.

RUBRIC: Standards for Writing

Successful business writing should

- be courteous
- use language that is geared to its audience
- state the purpose clearly in the opening sentences or paragraph
- have a formal tone and not contain slang, contractions, or sentence fragments
- use precise words
- present only essential information
- present details in a logical order
- conclude with a summary of important points

7.1 KEY TECHNIQUES OF WORKPLACE WRITING

Think About Your Purpose Why are you doing this writing? Do you want to order or complain about a product?

Identify Your Audience Who will read your writing? What background information will they need? What tone or language is appropriate?

Use a Pattern of Organization That Is Appropriate to the Content If you have to compare and contrast two products in a letter, you can use the same compare-and-contrast organization that you would use in an essay.

Support Your Points What specific details might clarify your ideas? What reasons do you have for your statements?

Finish Strongly How can you best sum up your statements? What is your main point? What action do you want the recipients to take?

Revise and Proofread Your Writing Just as you are graded on the quality of an essay you write for a class, you will be judged on the quality of your writing in the workplace.

7.2 MATCHING THE FORMAT TO THE OCCASION

E-mail messages, memos, and letters have similar purposes but are used in different situations. The chart shows how each format can be used.

Format	Occasion
Memo	Use to send correspondence **inside** the workplace only.
E-mail message	Use to send correspondence **inside or outside** the company.
Letter	Use to send correspondence **outside** the company.

TIP Memos are often sent as e-mail messages in the workplace. Remember that both require formal language and standard spelling, capitalization, and punctuation.

Technical writing is used for detailed instructions or descriptions of items and processes. It is important to a variety of fields, such as science, government, and industry. Technical writing is used to present information in such a way that the reader can use it to complete a task, such as performing an experiment, assembling an object, or using a tool.

At work, at school, or in everyday life you may have to use technical writing to leave instructions for another person.

RUBRIC: Standards for Writing

Instructions should

- present only essential information
- present steps in a logical order
- include sentences that are short and simple
- include definitions of unfamiliar terms if necessary
- use transitions and/or numbered steps
- use verbs that describe actions
- use the present tense

7.3 KEY TECHNIQUES OF TECHNICAL WRITING

Think About Your Organization As you write, make sure you are presenting your information in a sensible order. For example, you would probably list any necessary tools and materials early on. Then you would present the steps in the order in which they should be followed.

Keep Your Audience in Mind Make sure you explain to readers unfamiliar with the activity or process what they need to know. Sometimes making a comparison to something the reader is familiar with can help. Graphics, such as pictures and maps, can also help make instructions easier to understand.

Use Transitions as Needed Transitions such as *first, next, after,* and *last* and numbered steps can make the order of steps clear and guide your reader from one step to the next.

Review Your Ending You can simply end with the last step, or you can end by describing the result or outcome of following the directions.

Evaluate Your Instructions Have a friend follow your instructions to make sure they are clear.

7.4 FORMATS

Business letters usually have a formal tone and a specific format as shown below. The key to writing a business letter is to get to the point as quickly as possible and to present your information clearly.

MODEL: BUSINESS LETTER

180 Nemic Street
Boston, MA 02118

June 1, 2010

Heading *Where the letter comes from and when*

Joe Naglar
PBG Music Club
1 Beach Place
Stamford, CT 06904

Inside address *To whom the letter is being sent*

Dear Mr. Naglar:

Salutation *Greeting*

I'm writing to ask you about five CDs I ordered but never received. I ordered these selections over four months ago. My parents' credit card has been charged for them, but they have still not arrived.

If there is some problem with the availability of these selections, or some other problem with my order, please let me know. As it is now, it looks like I've been charged for things I never received and then I've been forgotten about.

I hope that whatever the problem was, it has been cleared up and that I will soon receive my CDs, or that my parents' card will be credited.

Body *Text of the message*

Sincerely,
Charles Terhune
Charles Terhune

Closing

PRACTICE AND APPLY

1. Draft a response to the letter. Then revise your letter as necessary according to the rubric at the beginning of page R42. Make sure you have included the necessary information and have written in an appropriate tone. Proofread your letter for grammatical errors and spelling mistakes. Follow the format of the model and use appropriate spacing between each part.

Memos are often used in workplaces as a way of sending information in a direct and concise manner. They can be used to announce or summarize meetings and to request actions or specific information.

MODEL: MEMO

To: Grace Brodsky
From: Joe Naglar
Subject: customer complaint
Date: June 10, 2010

Please read the attached letter. Then review the original order from Charles Terhune. Send a letter of apology and the CDs he ordered as soon as possible. Do not charge him for two of the CDs, and credit his parents' account.

Heading
Receiver's name
Sender's name
Topic of memo
Complete date

Body

TIP Don't forget to write the topic of your memo in the subject line. This will help the receiver determine the importance of your memo.

PRACTICE AND APPLY

Write a memo in response to the memo shown here. Tell the receiver what actions you have taken. Follow the format of the model.

MODEL: INSTRUCTIONS

How to Prove That Rusting Is a Chemical Reaction That Causes Heat

You can do a simple experiment that shows that rusting is a chemical reaction that produces heat.

You will need:

- a pad of steel wool
- vinegar
- a small bowl
- a thermometer
- a large glass jar with a lid

1. Place the thermometer in the jar and put the lid on the jar.
2. After five minutes, record the temperature while the thermometer is still in the jar.
3. Fill the small bowl with vinegar.
4. Soak the steel-wool pad in the vinegar for two minutes.
5. Remove the lid from the jar, and wrap the steel-wool pad around the bulb of the thermometer. Put the lid back on the jar.
6. After five more minutes, record the temperature again while the thermometer is still in the jar.

Notice that the temperature has risen a few degrees. The vinegar removes a coating from the steel wool. As a result the iron in the steel-wool pad starts to rust. The rusting is caused by the interaction of iron and oxygen. This chemical reaction releases heat, causing the temperature reading on the thermometer to rise.

PRACTICE AND APPLY

Think about something you might want someone else to do because you won't be at home, such as do laundry or prepare dinner. Use the rubric at the bottom of page R42 to write instructions. Be sure to include the following:

- an opening statement that describes what needs to be done
- a list of tools and materials needed to perform the task
- the steps needed to perform the task
- transition words and/or numbered steps if order is important
- any special notes or warnings about a tool or step in the process

Writing that has a lot of mistakes can confuse or even annoy a reader. A business letter with a punctuation error might lead to a miscommunication and delay a reply. Or a sentence fragment might lower your grade on an essay. Paying attention to grammar, punctuation, and capitalization rules can make your writing clearer and easier to read.

Quick Reference: Parts of Speech

PART OF SPEECH	FUNCTION	EXAMPLES
Noun	names a person, a place, a thing, an idea, a quality, or an action	
Common	serves as a general name, or a name common to an entire group	poet, novel, love, journey
Proper	names a specific, one-of-a-kind person, place, or thing	Jackson, Pleasant Street, Statue of Liberty
Singular	refers to a single person, place, thing, or idea	shark, planet, flower, truth
Plural	refers to more than one person, place, thing, or idea	sharks, planets, flowers, truths
Concrete	names something that can be perceived by the senses	snake, path, Philadelphia, damage
Abstract	names something that cannot be perceived by the senses	intelligence, fear, joy, loneliness
Compound	expresses a single idea through a combination of two or more words	girlfriend, father-in-law, Christmas Eve
Collective	refers to a group of people or things	army, flock, class, species
Possessive	shows who or what owns something	Strafford's, Bess's, children's, witnesses'
Pronoun	takes the place of a noun or another pronoun	
Personal	refers to the person making a statement, the person(s) being addressed, or the person(s) or thing(s) the statement is about	I, me, my, mine, we, us, our, ours, you, your, yours, she, he, it, her, him, hers, his, its, they, them, their, theirs
Reflexive	follows a verb or preposition and refers to a preceding noun or pronoun	myself, yourself, herself, himself, itself, ourselves, yourselves, themselves
Intensive	emphasizes a noun or another pronoun	(same as reflexives)
Demonstrative	points to one or more specific persons or things	this, that, these, those
Interrogative	signals a question	who, whom, whose, which, what
Indefinite	refers to one or more persons or things not specifically mentioned	both, all, most, many, anyone, everybody, several, none, some
Relative	introduces an adjective clause by relating it to a word in the clause	who, whom, whose, which, that

PART OF SPEECH	FUNCTION	EXAMPLES
Verb	expresses an action, a condition, or a state of being	
Action	tells what the subject does or did, physically or mentally	run, reaches, listened, consider, decides, dreamed
Linking	connects the subject to something that identifies or describes it	am, is, are, was, were, sound, taste, appear, feel, become, remain, seem
Auxiliary	precedes the main verb in a verb phrase	be, have, do, can, could, will, would, may, might
Transitive	directs the action toward someone or something; always has an object	The storm **sank** the ship.
Intransitive	does not direct the action toward someone or something; does not have an object	The ship **sank.**
Adjective	modifies a noun or pronoun	**strong** women, **two** epics, **enough** time
Adverb	modifies a verb, an adjective, or another adverb	walked **out, really** funny, **far** away
Preposition	relates one word to another word	at, by, for, from, in, of, on, to, with
Conjunction	joins words or word groups	
Coordinating	joins words or word groups used the same way	and, but, or, for, so, yet, nor
Correlative	used as a pair to join words or word groups used the same way	both . . . and, either . . . or, neither . . . nor
Subordinating	introduces a clause that cannot stand by itself as a complete sentence	although, after, as, before, because, when, if, unless
Interjection	expresses emotion	wow, ouch, hurrah

Quick Reference: The Sentence and Its Parts

The diagrams that follow will give you a brief review of the essentials of a sentence and some of its parts.

The builder used steel beams for the house.

The **complete subject** includes all the words that identify the person, place, thing, or idea that the sentence is about.

The **complete predicate** includes all the words that tell or ask something about the subject.

builder

The **simple subject** tells exactly whom or what the sentence is about. It may be one word or a group of words, but it does not include modifiers.

used

The **simple predicate,** or **verb,** tells what the subject does or is. It may be one word or several, but it does not include modifiers.

Every word in a sentence is part of a complete subject or a complete predicate.

The house will give its inhabitants a high level of comfort and convenience.

subject

Verbs often have more than one part. A verb may be made up of a **main verb,** like *give,* and one or more **auxiliary,** or **helping, verbs,** like *will.*

A **direct object** is a word or group of words that tells who or what receives the action of the verb.

An **indirect object** is a word or group of words that tells to whom or for whom or to what or for what the verb's action is performed. A sentence can have an indirect object only if it has a direct object. The indirect object always comes before the direct object.

A **prepositional phrase** consists of a preposition, its object, and any modifiers of the object. In this phrase, *of* is the preposition and *comfort and convenience* is its object.

Quick Reference: Punctuation

MARK	FUNCTION	EXAMPLES
End Marks period, question mark, exclamation point	ends a sentence	We can start now. When would you like to leave? What a fantastic hit!
period	follows an initial or abbreviation **Exception:** postal abbreviations of states	Mrs. Dorothy Parker, McDougal Littell Inc., C. P. Cavafy, P.M., A.D., lb., oz., Blvd., Dr. NE (Nebraska), NV (Nevada)
period	follows a number or letter in an outline	I. Volcanoes A. Central-vent 1. Shield
Comma	separates part of a compound sentence	I had never disliked poetry, but now I really love it.
	separates items in a series	She is brave, loyal, and kind.
	separates adjectives of equal rank that modify the same noun	The slow, easy route is best.
	sets off a term of address	Maria, how can I help you? You must do something, soldier.
	sets off a parenthetical expression	Hard workers, as you know, don't quit. I'm not a quitter, believe me.
	sets off an introductory word, phrase, or dependent clause	Yes, I forgot my key. At the beginning of the day, I feel fresh. While she was out, I was here. Having finished my chores, I went out.
	sets off a nonessential phrase or clause	Ed Pawn, the captain of the chess team, won. Ed Pawn, who is the captain, won. The two leading runners, sprinting toward the finish line, finished in a tie.
	sets off parts of dates and addresses	Mail it by May 14, 2010, to the Hauptman Company, 321 Market Street, Memphis, Tennessee.
	follows the salutation and closing of a letter	Dear Jim, Sincerely yours,
	separates words to avoid confusion	By noon, time had run out. What the minister does, does matter. While cooking, Jim burned his hand.
Semicolon	separates items that contain commas in a series	We spent the first week of summer vacation in Chicago, Illinois; the second week in St. Louis, Missouri; and the third week in Albany, New York.
	separates parts of a compound sentence that are not joined by a coordinating conjunction	The last shall be first; the first shall be last. I read the Bible; however, I have not memorized it.
	separates parts of a compound sentence when the parts contain commas	After I ran out of money, I called my parents; but only my sister was home, unfortunately.

MARK	FUNCTION	EXAMPLES
Colon	introduces a list	Those we wrote were the following**:** Dana, John, and Will.
	introduces a long quotation	Abraham Lincoln wrote**:** "Four score and seven years ago, our fathers brought forth on this continent a new nation. . . ."
	follows the salutation of a business letter	To Whom It May Concern**:** Dear Leonard Atole**:**
	separates certain numbers	1**:**28 P.M., Genesis 2**:**5
Dash	indicates an abrupt break in thought	I was thinking of my mother**—**who is arriving tomorrow**—**just as you walked in.
Parentheses	enclose less important material	It was so unlike him **(**John is always on time**)** that I began to worry. The last World Series game **(**did you see it?**)** was fun.
Hyphen	joins parts of a compound adjective before a noun	The not**-**so**-**rich taxpayer won't stand for this!
	joins parts of a compound with *all-*, *ex-*, *self-*, or *-elect*	The ex**-**firefighter helped rescue him. Our president**-**elect is self**-**conscious.
	joins parts of a compound number (to ninety-nine)	Today, I turned twenty**-**one.
	joins parts of a fraction	My cup is one**-**third full.
	joins a prefix to a word beginning with a capital letter	Which Pre**-**Raphaelite painter do you like best? It snowed in mid**-**October.
	indicates that a word is divided at the end of a line	How could you have any reasonable expect**-** ations of getting a new computer?
Apostrophe	used with *s* to form the possessive of a noun or an indefinite pronoun	my friend**'**s book, my friends**'** books, anyone**'**s guess, somebody else**'**s problem
	replaces one or more omitted letters in a contraction or numbers in a date	don**'**t (omitted *o*), he**'**d (omitted *woul*), the class of **'**99 (omitted *19*)
	used with *s* to form the plural of a letter	I had two A**'**s on my report card.
Quotation Marks	set off a speaker's exact words	Sara said, **"**I'm finally ready.**"** **"**I'm ready,**"** Sara said, **"**finally.**"** Did Sara say, **"**I'm ready**"**? Sara said, **"**I'm ready!**"**
	set off the title of a story, an article, a short poem, an essay, a song, or a chapter	I like Paulsen's **"**Dirk the Protector**"** and Poe's **"**Annabel Lee.**"** I like Ritchie Valens's **"**La Bamba.**"**
Ellipses	replace material omitted from a quotation	"When in the course of human events **. . .** and to assume among the powers of the earth. **. . .**"
Italics	indicate the title of a book, a play, a magazine, a long poem, an opera, a film, or a TV series, or the name of a ship	***Holes, The Monsters Are Due on Maple Street, Newsweek,*** the ***Odyssey, Madame Butterfly, Gone with the Wind, Seinfeld, Titanic***

Quick Reference: Capitalization

CATEGORY	EXAMPLES
People and Titles	
Names and initials of people	Amy Tan, W. H. Auden
Titles used before a name	Professor Holmes, Senator Long
Deities and members of religious groups	Jesus, Allah, Buddha, Zeus, Baptists, Roman Catholics
Names of ethnic and national groups	Hispanics, Jews, African Americans
Geographical Names	
Cities, states, countries, continents	Philadelphia, Kansas, Japan, Europe
Regions, bodies of water, mountains	the South, Lake Baikal, Mount Everest
Geographic features, parks	Great Basin, Yellowstone National Park
Streets and roads, planets	318 East Sutton Drive, Charles Court, Jupiter, Pluto
Organizations, Events, Etc.	
Companies, organizations, teams	Ford Motor Company, Boy Scouts of America, St. Louis Cardinals
Buildings, bridges, monuments	Empire State Building, Eads Bridge, Washington Monument
Documents, awards	Declaration of Independence, Stanley Cup
Special named events	Mardi Gras, World Series
Government bodies, historical periods and events	U.S. Senate, House of Representatives, Middle Ages, Vietnam War
Days and months, holidays	Thursday, March, Thanksgiving, Labor Day
Specific cars, boats, trains, planes	Porsche, *Carpathia, Southwest Chief,* Concorde
Proper Adjectives	
Adjectives formed from proper nouns	French cooking, Spanish omelet, Edwardian age, Western movie
First Words and the Pronoun *I*	
First word in a sentence or quotation	This is it. He said, "Let's go."
First word of sentence in parentheses that is not within another sentence	The spelling rules are covered in another section. (Consult that section for more information.)
First words in the salutation and closing of a letter	Dear Madam, Very truly yours,
First word in each line of most poetry Personal pronoun *I*	Then am I A happy fly If I live Or if I die.
First word, last word, and all important words in a title	*The Call of the Wild,* "Take Me Out to the Ball Game"

1 Nouns

A **noun** is a word used to name a person, a place, a thing, an idea, a quality, or an action. Nouns can be classified in several ways.

For more information on different types of nouns, see ***Quick Reference: Parts of Speech,*** *page R46.*

1.1 COMMON NOUNS

Common nouns are general names, common to entire groups.

1.2 PROPER NOUNS

Proper nouns name specific, one-of-a-kind people, places, and things.

Common	Proper
leader, park, forest, mountain	Sequoya, Sierra Nevada, Giant Forest, Mount Whitney

For more information, see ***Quick Reference: Capitalization,*** *page R51.*

1.3 SINGULAR AND PLURAL NOUNS

A noun may take a singular or a plural form, depending on whether it names a single person, place, thing, or idea or more than one. Make sure you use appropriate spellings when forming plurals.

Singular	Plural
tourist, city, mouse	tourists, cities, mice

For more information, see ***Forming Plural Nouns,*** *page R74.*

1.4 POSSESSIVE NOUNS

A **possessive noun** shows who or what owns something.

For more information, see ***Forming Possessives,*** *page R74.*

2 Pronouns

A **pronoun** is a word that is used in place of a noun or another pronoun. The word or word group to which the pronoun refers is called its **antecedent.**

2.1 PERSONAL PRONOUNS

Personal pronouns change their form to express person, number, gender, and case. The forms of these pronouns are shown in the following chart.

	Nominative	Objective	Possessive
Singular			
First person	I	me	my, mine
Second person	you	you	your, yours
Third person	she, he, it	her, him, it	her, hers, his, its
Plural			
First person	we	us	our, ours
Second person	you	you	your, yours
Third person	they	them	their, theirs

2.2 AGREEMENT WITH ANTECEDENT

Pronouns should agree with their antecedents in number, gender, and person.

If an antecedent is singular, use a singular pronoun.

EXAMPLE: *Rachel wrote a* ***detective story.*** *It has a surprise ending.*

If an antecedent is plural, use a plural pronoun.

EXAMPLES: *The* ***characters*** *have their motives for murder.*

Javier loves ***mysteries*** *and reads them all the time.*

The gender of a pronoun must be the same as the gender of its antecedent.

EXAMPLE: *The* ***man*** *has to use all his wits to stay alive and solve the crime.*

The person of the pronoun must be the same as the person of its antecedent. As the chart in Section 2.1 shows, a pronoun can be in first-person, second-person, or third-person form.

EXAMPLE: ***You*** *want a story to grab your attention.*

GRAMMAR PRACTICE

Rewrite each sentence so that the underlined pronoun agrees with its antecedent.

1. The story "Dark They Were, and Golden-Eyed" tells about a man who travels to Mars and its life.
2. Harry has a feeling of dread, but he ignores them.
3. The colonists began to change, but he didn't notice anything odd.
4. Harry's fears were coming true, and it was hard to ignore.
5. When you finish this story, we might wonder if it could really happen.

2.3 PRONOUN FORMS

Personal pronouns change form to show how they function in sentences. The three forms are the subject form, the object form, and the possessive form. For examples of these pronouns, see the chart in Section 2.1.

A **subject pronoun** is used as a subject in a sentence.

EXAMPLE: A Christmas Carol *tells about Ebenezer Scrooge. He visits his past.*

Also use the subject form when the pronoun follows a linking verb.

EXAMPLE: *The first ghost was he.*

An **object pronoun** is used as a direct object, an indirect object, or the object of a preposition.

SUBJECT OBJECT

He will lead them to us.

OBJECT OF PREPOSITION

A **possessive pronoun** shows ownership. The pronouns *mine, yours, hers, his, its, ours,* and *theirs* can be used in place of nouns.

EXAMPLE: *This money is mine.*

The pronouns *my, your, her, his, its, our,* and *their* are used before nouns.

EXAMPLE: *Scrooge thanked the spirits for their help.*

WATCH OUT! Many spelling errors can be avoided if you watch out for *its* and *their.* Don't confuse the possessive pronoun *its* with the contraction *it's,* meaning "it is" or "it has." The homonyms *they're* (a contraction of *they are*) and *there* ("in that place" or an expletive) are often mistakenly used for *their.*

TIP To decide which pronoun to use in a comparison, such as "He tells better tales than (I *or* me)," fill in the missing word(s): *He tells better tales than I tell.*

GRAMMAR PRACTICE

Write the correct pronoun form to complete each sentence.

1. Charles Dickens wrote *A Christmas Carol* when (he, him) was 31 years old.
2. This work of (him, his) was written in only a few weeks.
3. Dickens wrote other novels about Christmas. All of (their, his) dates of composition are from the 1840s.
4. (Them, They) have rather serious themes mixed with some humor.
5. When William Makepeace Thackeray, a fellow writer, reviewed *A Christmas Carol,* he said that (its, his) publication was a national benefit.

2.4 REFLEXIVE AND INTENSIVE PRONOUNS

These pronouns are formed by adding *-self* or *-selves* to certain personal pronouns. Their forms are the same, and they differ only in how they are used.

A **reflexive pronoun** follows a verb or preposition and reflects back on an earlier noun or pronoun.

EXAMPLES: *He likes himself too much.*

She is now herself again.

Intensive pronouns intensify or emphasize the nouns or pronouns to which they refer.

EXAMPLES: *They themselves will educate their children.*

You did it yourself.

WATCH OUT! Avoid using *hisself* or *theirselves.* Standard English does not include these forms.

NONSTANDARD: *Alex dedicated hisself to learning the magician's secrets.*

STANDARD: *Alex dedicated himself to learning the magician's secrets.*

2.5 DEMONSTRATIVE PRONOUNS

Demonstrative pronouns point out things and persons near and far.

	Singular	Plural
Near	this	these
Far	that	those

2.6 INDEFINITE PRONOUNS

Indefinite pronouns do not refer to specific persons or things and usually have no antecedents. The chart shows some commonly used indefinite pronouns.

Singular	Plural	Singular or Plural	
another	both	all	none
anybody	few	any	some
no one	many	more	most
neither			

TIP Indefinite pronouns that end in *one, body,* or *thing* are always singular.

INCORRECT: *Did everybody play their part well?*

If the indefinite pronoun might refer to either a male or a female, *his or her* may be used to refer to it, or the sentence may be rewritten.

CORRECT: *Did everybody play his or her part well?*

Did all the students play their parts well?

2.7 INTERROGATIVE PRONOUNS

An **interrogative pronoun** tells a reader or listener that a question is coming. The interrogative pronouns are *who, whom, whose, which,* and *what.*

EXAMPLES: *Who is going to rehearse with you?*

From whom did you receive the script?

TIP *Who* is used as a subject; *whom,* as an object. To find out which pronoun you need to use in a question, change the question to a statement.

QUESTION: *(Who/Whom) did you meet there?*

STATEMENT: *You met (?) there.*

Since the verb has a subject (*you*), the needed word must be the object form, *whom.*

EXAMPLE: *Whom did you meet there?*

WATCH OUT! A special problem arises when you use an interrupter, such as *do you think,* within a question.

EXAMPLE: *(Who/Whom) do you think will win?*

If you eliminate the interrupter, it is clear that the word you need is *who.*

2.8 RELATIVE PRONOUNS

Relative pronouns relate, or connect, adjective clauses to the words they modify in sentences. The noun or pronoun that a relative clause modifies is the antecedent of the relative pronoun. Here are the relative pronouns and their uses.

	Subject	Object	Possessive
Person	who	whom	whose
Thing	which	which	whose
Thing/Person	that	that	whose

Often, short sentences with related ideas can be combined by using a relative pronoun to create a more effective sentence.

SHORT SENTENCE: *Poe wrote "Annabel Lee."*

RELATED SENTENCE: *"Annabel Lee" is a well-known poem in American literature.*

COMBINED SENTENCE: *Poe wrote "Annabel Lee," which is a well-known poem in American literature.*

GRAMMAR PRACTICE

Write the correct form of each incorrect pronoun.

1. Whom has read "Dark They Were, and Golden-Eyed"?
2. Colonists whom travel to Mars realize they can't go home.
3. Nobody knows what they will do.
4. Each person is changing, but they don't worry about it.
5. Harry hisself doesn't believe what is happening.

2.9 PRONOUN REFERENCE PROBLEMS

The referent of a pronoun should always be clear. Avoid problems by rewriting sentences.

An **indefinite reference** occurs when the pronoun *it, you,* or *they* does not clearly refer to a specific antecedent.

UNCLEAR: *My aunt hugged me in front of my friends, and it was embarrassing.*

CLEAR: *My aunt hugged me in front of my friends, and I was embarrassed.*

A **general reference** occurs when the pronoun *it, this, that, which,* or *such* is used to refer to a general idea rather than a specific antecedent.

UNCLEAR: *Jenna takes acting lessons. This has improved her chances of getting a part in the school play.*

CLEAR: *Jenna takes acting lessons. The lessons have improved her chances of getting a part in the school play.*

Ambiguous means "having more than one possible meaning." An **ambiguous reference** occurs when a pronoun could refer to two or more antecedents.

UNCLEAR: *Tony talked to Fred and said that he could meet us later.*

CLEAR: *Tony talked to Fred and said that Fred could meet us later.*

GRAMMAR PRACTICE

Rewrite the following sentences to correct indefinite, ambiguous, and general pronoun references.

1. During the *Titanic*'s maiden voyage, they hit an iceberg and sank in less than three hours.
2. Jack Thayer talked to Milton Long and said that he was traveling home to the States.
3. The *Titanic* split in two in its last moments. This made each half plunge to the bottom of the ocean.
4. In the article, it said that many lifeboats were only half full.

3 Verbs

A **verb** is a word that expresses an action, a condition, or a state of being.

For more information, see ***Quick Reference: Parts of Speech,*** *page R47.*

3.1 ACTION VERBS

Action verbs express mental or physical activity.

EXAMPLE: *Mr. Cho slept with the window open.*

3.2 LINKING VERBS

Linking verbs join subjects with words or phrases that rename or describe them.

EXAMPLE: *When he awoke the next morning, his bed was wet from the rain.*

3.3 PRINCIPAL PARTS

Action and linking verbs typically have four principal parts, which are used to form verb tenses. The principal parts are the **present,** the **present participle,** the **past,** and the **past participle.**

Action verbs and some linking verbs also fall into two categories: regular and irregular. A **regular verb** is a verb that forms its past and past participle by adding *-ed* or *-d* to the present form.

Present	Present Participle	Past	Past Participle
jump	(is) jumping	jumped	(has) jumped
solve	(is) solving	solved	(has) solved
grab	(is) grabbing	grabbed	(has) grabbed
carry	(is) carrying	carried	(has) carried

An **irregular verb** is a verb that forms its past and past participle in some other way than by adding *-ed* or *-d* to the present form.

Present	Present Participle	Past	Past Participle
begin	(is) beginning	began	(has) begun
break	(is) breaking	broke	(has) broken
go	(is) going	went	(has) gone

3.4 VERB TENSE

The **tense** of a verb indicates the time of the action or the state of being. An action or state of being can occur in the present, the past, or the future. There are six tenses, each expressing a different range of time.

The **present tense** expresses an action or state that is happening at the present time, occurs regularly, or is constant or generally true. Use the present part.

NOW: *That snow looks deep.*

REGULAR: *It snows every day.*

GENERAL: *Snow falls.*

The **past tense** expresses an action that began and ended in the past. Use the past part.

EXAMPLE: *The storyteller finished his tale.*

The **future tense** expresses an action or state that will occur. Use *shall* or *will* with the present part.

EXAMPLE: *They will attend the next festival.*

The **present perfect tense** expresses an action or state that (1) was completed at an indefinite time in the past or (2) began in the past and continues into the present. Use *have* or *has* with the past participle.

EXAMPLE: *Poetry has inspired many readers.*

The **past perfect tense** expresses an action in the past that came before another action in the past. Use *had* with the past participle.

EXAMPLE: *He had built a fire before the dog ran away.*

The **future perfect tense** expresses an action in the future that will be completed before another action in the future. Use *shall have* or *will have* with the past participle.

EXAMPLE: *They will have read the novel before they see the movie version of the tale.*

TIP A past-tense form of an irregular verb is not used with an auxiliary verb, but a past-participle main irregular verb is always used with an auxiliary verb.

INCORRECT: *I have saw her somewhere before.* (*Saw* is the past-tense form of an irregular verb and shouldn't be used with *have*.)

CORRECT: *I have seen her somewhere before.*

INCORRECT: *I seen her somewhere before.* (*Seen* is the past participle of an irregular verb and shouldn't be used without an auxiliary verb.)

3.5 PROGRESSIVE FORMS

The progressive forms of the six tenses show ongoing actions. Use forms of *be* with the present participles of verbs.

PRESENT PROGRESSIVE: *She is rehearsing her lines.*

PAST PROGRESSIVE: *She was rehearsing her lines.*

FUTURE PROGRESSIVE: *She will be rehearsing her lines.*

PRESENT PERFECT PROGRESSIVE: *She has been rehearsing her lines.*

PAST PERFECT PROGRESSIVE: *She had been rehearsing her lines.*

FUTURE PERFECT PROGRESSIVE: *She will have been rehearsing her lines.*

WATCH OUT! Do not shift from tense to tense needlessly. Watch out for these special cases.

- In most compound sentences and in sentences with compound predicates, keep the tenses the same.

INCORRECT: *His boots freeze, and he shook with cold.*

CORRECT: *His boots freeze, and he shakes with cold.*

- If one past action happens before another, do shift tenses.

  INCORRECT: *They wished they started earlier.*

  CORRECT: *They wished they had started earlier.*

GRAMMAR PRACTICE

Rewrite each sentence, using a form of the verb in parentheses. Identify each form that you use.

1. Some medical developments (begin) with the space age—for example, laparoscopy and robotics.
2. Both of these areas (grow) and (advance) the field of surgery.
3. In the 1990s "robotic assistants" (help) in surgery.
4. People (come) to expect simpler procedures because of these new techniques.
5. Some day other procedures that avoid cutting into tissue (develop).

Rewrite each sentence to correct an error in tense.

1. I seen a movie about the cobra and its natural enemy, the mongoose.
2. Most snakes hide and avoided people.
3. The cobra raised its head when it seeks out its next victim.
4. Both the male and female protected their eggs and will attack an approaching intruder.
5. The venom of a cobra was deadly and kills a human being within a few hours.

3.6 ACTIVE AND PASSIVE VOICE

The voice of a verb tells whether its subject performs or receives the action expressed by the verb. When the subject performs the action, the verb is in the **active voice.** When the subject is the receiver of the action, the verb is in the **passive voice.**

Compare these two sentences:

ACTIVE: *Lois Lowry wrote* The Giver.

PASSIVE: The Giver *was written by Lois Lowry.*

To form the passive voice, use a form of *be* with the past participle of the verb.

WATCH OUT! Use the passive voice sparingly. It can make writing awkward and less direct.

AWKWARD: The Giver *is a novel that was written by Lois Lowry.*

BETTER: *Lois Lowry wrote the novel* The Giver.

There are occasions when you will choose to use the passive voice because

- you want to emphasize the receiver: *The king was shot.*
- the doer is unknown: *My books were stolen.*
- the doer is unimportant: *French is spoken here.*

4 Modifiers

Modifiers are words or groups of words that change or limit the meanings of other words. Adjectives and adverbs are common modifiers.

4.1 ADJECTIVES

Adjectives modify nouns and pronouns by telling which one, what kind, how many, or how much.

WHICH ONE: *this, that, these, those*

EXAMPLE: *That bird is a scarlet ibis.*

WHAT KIND: *small, sick, courageous, black*

EXAMPLE: *The sick bird sways on the branch.*

HOW MANY: *some, few, ten, none, both, each*

EXAMPLE: *Both brothers stared at the bird.*

HOW MUCH: *more, less, enough*

EXAMPLE: *The bird did not have enough strength to remain perched.*

4.2 PREDICATE ADJECTIVES

Most adjectives come before the nouns they modify, as in the examples above. A **predicate adjective,** however, follows a linking verb and describes the subject.

EXAMPLE: *My friends are very intelligent.*

Be especially careful to use adjectives (not adverbs) after such linking verbs as *look, feel, grow, taste,* and *smell.*

EXAMPLE: *The bread smells wonderful.*

4.3 ADVERBS

Adverbs modify verbs, adjectives, and other adverbs by telling where, when, how, or to what extent.

WHERE: *The children played outside.*

WHEN: *The author spoke yesterday.*

HOW: *We walked slowly behind the leader.*

TO WHAT EXTENT: *He worked very hard.*

Adverbs may occur in many places in sentences, both before and after the words they modify.

EXAMPLES: *Suddenly the wind shifted.*

The wind suddenly shifted.

The wind shifted suddenly.

4.4 ADJECTIVE OR ADVERB?

Many adverbs are formed by adding *-ly* to adjectives.

EXAMPLES: *sweet, sweetly; gentle, gently*

However, *-ly* added to a noun will usually yield an adjective.

EXAMPLES: *friend, friendly; woman, womanly*

4.5 COMPARISON OF MODIFIERS

Modifiers can be used to compare two or more things. The form of a modifier shows the degree of comparison. Both adjectives and adverbs have **comparative** and **superlative** forms.

The **comparative form** is used to compare two things, groups, or actions.

EXAMPLES: *His father's hands were stronger than his own.*

His father was more courageous than the other man.

The **superlative form** is used to compare more than two things, groups, or actions.

EXAMPLES: *His father's hands were the strongest in the family.*

His father was the most courageous of them all.

4.6 REGULAR COMPARISONS

Most one-syllable and some two-syllable adjectives and adverbs have comparatives and superlatives formed by adding *-er* and *-est*. All three-syllable and most two-syllable modifiers have comparatives and superlatives formed with *more* or *most*.

Modifier	Comparative	Superlative
small	smaller	smallest
thin	thinner	thinnest
sleepy	sleepier	sleepiest
useless	more useless	most useless
precisely	more precisely	most precisely

WATCH OUT! Note that spelling changes must sometimes be made to form the comparatives and superlatives of modifiers.

EXAMPLES: *friendly, friendlier* (Change *y* to *i* and add the ending.)

sad, sadder (Double the final consonant and add the ending.)

4.7 IRREGULAR COMPARISONS

Some commonly used modifiers have irregular comparative and superlative forms. They are listed in the following chart. You may wish to memorize them.

Modifier	Comparative	Superlative
good	better	best
bad	worse	worst
far	farther *or* further	farthest *or* furthest
little	less *or* lesser	least
many	more	most
well	better	best
much	more	most

4.8 PROBLEMS WITH MODIFIERS

Study the tips that follow to avoid common mistakes:

Farther* and *Further Use *farther* for distances; use *further* for everything else.

Double Comparisons Make a comparison by using *-er/-est* or by using *more/most*. Using *-er* with *more* or using *-est* with *most* is incorrect.

INCORRECT: *I like her more better than she likes me.*

CORRECT: *I like her better than she likes me.*

Illogical Comparisons An illogical or confusing comparison results when two unrelated things are compared or when something is compared with itself. The word *other* or the word *else* should be used when comparing an individual member to the rest of a group.

ILLOGICAL: *The narrator was more curious about the war than any student in his class.* (implies that the narrator isn't a student in the class)

LOGICAL: *The narrator was more curious about the war than any other student in his class.* (identifies that the narrator is a student)

Bad* vs. *Badly *Bad,* always an adjective, is used before a noun or after a linking verb. *Badly,* always an adverb, never modifies a noun. Be sure to use the right form after a linking verb.

INCORRECT: *Ed felt badly after his team lost.*

CORRECT: *Ed felt bad after his team lost.*

Good* vs. *Well *Good* is always an adjective. It is used before a noun or after a linking verb. *Well* is often an adverb meaning "expertly" or "properly." *Well* can also be used as an adjective after a linking verb when it means "in good health."

INCORRECT: *Helen writes very good.*

CORRECT: *Helen writes very well.*

CORRECT: *Yesterday I felt bad; today I feel well.*

Double Negatives If you add a negative word to a sentence that is already negative, the result will be an error known as a double negative. When using *not* or *-n't* with a verb, use *any-* words, such as *anybody* or *anything,* rather than *no-* words, such as *nobody* or *nothing,* later in the sentence.

INCORRECT: *We haven't seen nobody.*

CORRECT: *We haven't seen anybody.*

Using *hardly, barely,* or *scarcely* after a negative word is also incorrect.

INCORRECT: *They couldn't barely see two feet ahead.*

CORRECT: *They could barely see two feet ahead.*

Misplaced Modifiers Sometimes a modifier is placed so far away from the word it modifies that the intended meaning of the sentence is unclear. Prepositional phrases and participial phrases are often misplaced. Place modifiers as close as possible to the words they modify.

MISPLACED: *We found the child in the park who was missing.*

CLEARER: *We found the child who was missing in the park.* (The child was missing, not the park.)

Dangling Modifiers Sometimes a modifier doesn't appear to modify any word in a sentence. Most dangling modifiers are participial phrases or infinitive phrases.

DANGLING: *Looking out the window, his brother was seen driving by.*

CLEARER: *Looking out the window, Josh saw his brother driving by.*

GRAMMAR PRACTICE

Choose the correct word or words from each pair in parentheses.

1. When Ellis Island opened, it was the (larger, largest) port of entry to the United States.
2. In the 1980s, the facility underwent the (greatest, most greatest) restoration ever performed.
3. The restoration project (bad, badly) needed funds.
4. The project didn't have (no, any) funding until fundraising efforts began in 1982.
5. In 1990, the (grandly, grand) reopening was received (good, well.)

GRAMMAR PRACTICE

Rewrite each sentence that contains a misplaced or dangling modifier. Write "correct" if the sentence is written correctly.

1. We traveled to Yellowstone Park with many tourists.
2. Driving our car, the mother bear growled.
3. We took pictures of the bears in the camper.
4. My brother and I went for a hike, but we got lost.
5. Taping our adventures, we had lots of film.

5 The Sentence and Its Parts

A **sentence** is a group of words used to express a complete thought. A complete sentence has a subject and a predicate.

For more information, see ***Quick Reference: The Sentence and Its Parts,*** *page R48.*

5.1 KINDS OF SENTENCES

There are four basic types of sentences.

Type	Definition	Example
Declarative	states a fact, a wish, an intent, or a feeling	Gary Soto understands youths.
Interrogative	asks a question	Did you read "Seventh Grade"?
Imperative	gives a command or direction	Read the story.
Exclamatory	expresses strong feeling or excitement	The story is great!

5.2 COMPOUND SUBJECTS AND PREDICATES

A compound subject consists of two or more subjects that share the same verb. They are typically joined by the coordinating conjunction *and* or *or.*

EXAMPLE: *A short story or novel will keep you engaged.*

A compound predicate consists of two or more predicates that share the same subject. They too are usually joined by a coordinating conjunction: *and, but,* or *or.*

EXAMPLE: *The class finished all the poetry but did not read the short stories.*

5.3 COMPLEMENTS

A **complement** is a word or group of words that completes the meaning of the sentence. Some sentences contain only a subject and a verb. Most sentences, however, require additional words placed after the verb to complete the meaning of the sentence. There are three kinds of complements: direct objects, indirect objects, and subject complements.

Direct objects are words or word groups that receive the action of action verbs. A direct object answers the question *what* or *whom.*

EXAMPLES: *The students asked many questions.* (Asked what?)

The teacher quickly answered the students. (Answered whom?)

Indirect objects tell to whom or what or for whom or what the actions of verbs are performed. Indirect objects come before direct objects. In the examples that follow, the indirect objects are highlighted.

EXAMPLES: *My sister usually gave her friends good advice.* (Gave to whom?)

Her brother sent the store a heavy package. (Sent to what?)

Subject complements come after linking verbs and identify or describe the subjects. A subject complement that names or identifies a subject is called a **predicate nominative.** Predicate nominatives include **predicate nouns** and **predicate pronouns.**

EXAMPLES: *My friends are very hard workers.*

The best writer in the class is she.

A subject complement that describes a subject is called a **predicate adjective.**

EXAMPLE: *The pianist appeared very energetic.*

6 Phrases

A **phrase** is a group of related words that does not contain a subject and a predicate but functions in a sentence as a single part of speech.

6.1 PREPOSITIONAL PHRASES

A **prepositional phrase** is a phrase that consists of a preposition, its object, and any modifiers of the object. Prepositional phrases that modify nouns or pronouns are called **adjective phrases.** Prepositional phrases that modify verbs, adjectives, or adverbs are **adverb phrases.**

ADJECTIVE PHRASE: *The central character of the story is a villain.*

ADVERB PHRASE: *He reveals his nature in the first scene.*

6.2 APPOSITIVES AND APPOSITIVE PHRASES

An **appositive** is a noun or pronoun that identifies or renames another noun or pronoun. An **appositive phrase** includes an appositive and modifiers of it. An appositive usually follows the noun or pronoun it identifies.

An appositive can be either **essential** or **nonessential.** An **essential appositive** provides information that is needed to identify what is referred to by the preceding noun or pronoun.

EXAMPLE: *The book is about the author Dave Barry.*

A **nonessential appositive** adds extra information about a noun or pronoun whose meaning is already clear. Nonessential appositives and appositive phrases are set off with commas.

EXAMPLE: *The book, an autobiography, tells how he began writing.*

7 Verbals and Verbal Phrases

A **verbal** is a verb form that is used as a noun, an adjective, or an adverb. A **verbal phrase** consists of a verbal along with its modifiers and complements. There are three kinds of verbals: **infinitives, participles,** and **gerunds.**

7.1 INFINITIVES AND INFINITIVE PHRASES

An **infinitive** is a verb form that usually begins with *to* and functions as a noun, an adjective, or an adverb. An **infinitive phrase** consists of an infinitive plus its modifiers and complements.

NOUN: *To know her is my only desire.* (subject)
I'm planning to walk with you. (direct object)
Her goal was to promote women's rights. (predicate nominative)

ADJECTIVE: *We saw his need to be loved.* (adjective modifying *need*)

ADVERB: *She wrote to voice her opinions.* (adverb modifying *wrote*)

Because *to,* the sign of the infinitive, precedes infinitives, it is usually easy to recognize them. However, sometimes *to* may be omitted.

EXAMPLE: *Let no one dare [to] enter this shrine.*

7.2 PARTICIPLES AND PARTICIPIAL PHRASES

A **participle** is a verb form that functions as an adjective. Like adjectives, participles modify nouns and pronouns. Most participles are present-participle forms, ending in *-ing,* or past-participle forms ending in *-ed* or *-en.* In the examples below, the participles are highlighted.

MODIFYING A NOUN: *The dying man had a smile on his face.*

MODIFYING A PRONOUN: *Frustrated, everyone abandoned the cause.*

Participial phrases are participles with all their modifiers and complements.

MODIFYING A NOUN: *The dogs searching for survivors are well trained.*

MODIFYING A PRONOUN: *Having approved your proposal, we are ready to act.*

7.3 DANGLING AND MISPLACED PARTICIPLES

A participle or participial phrase should be placed as close as possible to the word that it modifies. Otherwise the meaning of the sentence may not be clear.

MISPLACED: *The boys were looking for squirrels searching the trees.*

CLEARER: *The boys searching the trees were looking for squirrels.*

A participle or participial phrase that does not clearly modify anything in a sentence is called a **dangling participle.** A dangling participle causes confusion because it appears to modify a word that it cannot sensibly modify. Correct a dangling participle by providing a word for the participle to modify.

DANGLING: *Running like the wind, my hat fell off.* (The hat wasn't running.)

CLEARER: *Running like the wind, I lost my hat.*

7.4 GERUNDS AND GERUND PHRASES

A **gerund** is a verb form ending in *-ing* that functions as a noun. Gerunds may perform any function nouns perform.

SUBJECT: *Running is my favorite pastime.*

DIRECT OBJECT: *I truly love running.*

INDIRECT OBJECT: *You should give running a try.*

SUBJECT COMPLEMENT: *My deepest passion is running.*

OBJECT OF PREPOSITION: *Her love of running keeps her strong.*

Gerund phrases are gerunds with all their modifiers and complements.

SUBJECT: *Wishing on a star never got me far.*

OBJECT OF PREPOSITION: *I will finish before leaving the office.*

APPOSITIVE: *Her avocation, flying airplanes, finally led to full-time employment.*

GRAMMAR PRACTICE

Rewrite each sentence, adding the type of phrase shown in parentheses.

1. I read Jackie Robinson's autobiography. (infinitive phrase)
2. I found several books and articles about him. (participial phrase)
3. Opposition to Robinson died down. (prepositional phrase)
4. Robinson played his entire major-league career with the same team. (appositive phrase)
5. Robinson went on to become one of the most popular Dodger players. (gerund phrase)

8 Clauses

A **clause** is a group of words that contains a subject and a predicate. There are two kinds of clauses: independent clauses and subordinate clauses.

8.1 INDEPENDENT AND SUBORDINATE CLAUSES

An **independent clause** can stand alone as a sentence, as the word *independent* suggests.

INDEPENDENT CLAUSE: *I read "Amigo Brothers."*

A sentence may contain more than one independent clause.

EXAMPLE: *I finished dinner, and I read the story.*

In the preceding example, the coordinating conjunction *and* joins two independent clauses.

For more information, see ***Coordinating Conjunction,*** *page R47.*

A **subordinate (dependent) clause** cannot stand alone as a sentence. It is subordinate to, or dependent on, an independent clause.

EXAMPLE: *After I finished dinner, I read "Amigo Brothers."*

The highlighted clause cannot stand by itself.

8.2 ADJECTIVE CLAUSES

An **adjective clause** is a subordinate clause used as an adjective. It usually follows the noun or pronoun it modifies.

EXAMPLE: *Felix and Antonio are the boys who are the main characters in "Amigo Brothers."*

Adjective clauses are typically introduced by the relative pronouns *who, whom, whose, which,* and *that.*

For more information, see ***Relative Pronouns,*** *page R54.*

EXAMPLE: *The story, which takes place in New York, is about a boxing tournament.*

An adjective clause can be either essential or nonessential. An **essential adjective clause** provides information that is necessary to identify the preceding noun or pronoun.

EXAMPLE: *The boys had to make a decision that might change their lives.*

A **nonessential adjective clause** adds additional information about a noun or pronoun whose meaning is already clear. Nonessential clauses are set off with commas.

EXAMPLE: *The boys, who fought each other, wanted to remain friends.*

8.3 ADVERB CLAUSES

An **adverb clause** is a subordinate clause that is used to modify a verb, an adjective, or an adverb. It is introduced by a subordinating conjunction.

For examples of subordinating conjunctions, see ***Noun Clauses,*** *page R63.*

Adverb clauses typically occur at the beginning or end of sentences.

MODIFYING A VERB: *When we need you, we will call.*

MODIFYING AN ADVERB: *I'll stay here where there is shelter from the rain.*

MODIFYING AN ADJECTIVE: *Roman felt as good as he had ever felt.*

TIP An adverb clause should be followed by a comma when it comes before an independent clause. When an adverb clause comes after an independent clause, a comma may not be needed.

8.4 NOUN CLAUSES

A **noun clause** is a subordinate clause that is used as a noun. A noun clause may be used as a subject, a direct object, an indirect object, a predicate nominative, or the object of a preposition. Noun clauses are introduced either by pronouns, such as *that, what, who, whoever, which,* and *whose,* or by subordinating conjunctions, such as *how, when, where, why,* and *whether.*

For more subordinating conjunctions, see ***Quick Reference: Parts of Speech,*** *page R47.*

TIP Because the same words may introduce adjective and noun clauses, you need to consider how a clause functions within its sentence. To determine if a clause is a noun clause, try substituting *something* or *someone* for the clause. If you can do it, it is probably a noun clause.

EXAMPLES: *I know whose woods these are.*

("I know something." The clause is a noun clause, direct object of the verb *know.*)

Give a copy to whoever wants one. ("Give a copy to someone." The clause is a noun clause, object of the preposition *to.*)

GRAMMAR PRACTICE

Add descriptive details to each sentence by writing the type of clause indicated in parentheses.

1. Some students volunteer at animal shelters. (adjective clause)
2. They help take care of dogs and cats. (adverb clause)
3. The veterinarian tries to explain to the students. (noun clause)
4. Many people appreciate the students. (adjective clause)
5. I plan to work at the shelter. (adverb clause)

9 The Structure of Sentences

When classified by their structure, there are four kinds of sentences: simple, compound, complex, and compound-complex.

9.1 SIMPLE SENTENCES

A **simple sentence** is a sentence that has one independent clause and no subordinate clauses.

EXAMPLES: *Sam ran to the theater.*

Max waited in front of the theater.

A simple sentence may contain a compound subject or a compound verb.

EXAMPLES: *Sam and Max went to the movie. (compound subject)*

They clapped and cheered at their favorite parts. (compound verb).

9.2 COMPOUND SENTENCES

A **compound sentence** consists of two or more independent clauses. The clauses in compound sentences are joined with commas and coordinating conjunctions (*and, but, or, nor, yet, for, so*) or with semicolons. Like simple sentences, compound sentences do not contain any subordinate clauses.

EXAMPLES: *Sam likes action movies, but Max prefers comedies.*

The actor jumped from one building to another; he barely made the final leap.

WATCH OUT! Do not confuse compound sentences with simple sentences that have compound parts.

EXAMPLE: *The actor knew all the lines but didn't play the part well.*
(Here *but* joins parts of a compound predicate, not a compound sentence.)

9.3 COMPLEX SENTENCES

A **complex sentence** consists of one independent clause and one or more subordinate clauses.

EXAMPLES: *One should not complain unless one has a better solution.*
Mr. Neiman, who is an artist, sketched pictures until the sun went down.

9.4 COMPOUND-COMPLEX SENTENCES

A **compound-complex sentence** contains two or more independent clauses and one or more subordinate clauses. Compound-complex sentences are, simply, both compound and complex. If you start with a compound sentence, all you need to do to form a compound-complex sentence is add a subordinate clause.

COMPOUND: *All the students knew the answer, yet they were too shy to volunteer.*

COMPOUND-COMPLEX: *All the students knew the answer that their teacher expected, yet they were too shy to volunteer.*

9.5 PARALLEL STRUCTURE

When you write sentences, make sure that coordinate parts are equivalent, or **parallel,** in structure.

NOT PARALLEL: *Erin loved basketball and to play hockey.* (*Basketball* is a noun; *to play hockey* is a phrase.)

PARALLEL: *Erin loved basketball and hockey.* (*Basketball* and *hockey* are both nouns.)

NOT PARALLEL: *He wanted to rent an apartment, a new car, and traveling around the country.* (*To rent* is an infinitive, *car* is a noun, and *traveling* is a gerund.)

PARALLEL: *He wanted to rent an apartment, to drive a new car, and to travel around the country.* (*To rent, to drive,* and *to travel* are all infinitives.)

10 Writing Complete Sentences

Remember, a sentence is a group of words that expresses a complete thought. In writing that you wish to share with a reader, try to avoid both sentence fragments and run-on sentences.

10.1 CORRECTING FRAGMENTS

A **sentence fragment** is a group of words that is only part of a sentence. It does not express a complete thought and may be confusing to a reader or listener. A sentence fragment may be lacking a subject, a predicate, or both.

FRAGMENT: *Waited for the boat to arrive.* (no subject)

CORRECTED: *We waited for the boat to arrive.*

FRAGMENT: *People of various races, ages, and creeds.* (no predicate)

CORRECTED: *People of various races, ages, and creeds gathered together.*

FRAGMENT: *Near the old cottage.* (neither subject nor predicate)

CORRECTED: *The burial ground is near the old cottage.*

In your writing, fragments may be a result of haste or incorrect punctuation. Sometimes fixing a fragment will be a matter of attaching it to a preceding or following sentence.

FRAGMENT: *We saw the two girls. Waiting for the bus to arrive.*

CORRECTED: *We saw the two girls waiting for the bus to arrive.*

10.2 CORRECTING RUN-ON SENTENCES

A **run-on sentence** is made up of two or more sentences written as though they were one. Some run-ons have no punctuation within them. Others may have only commas where conjunctions or stronger punctuation marks are necessary. Use your judgment in correcting run-on sentences, as you have choices. You can change a run-on to two sentences if the thoughts are not closely connected. If the thoughts are closely related, you can keep the run-on as one sentence by adding a semicolon or a conjunction.

RUN-ON: *We found a place for the picnic by a small pond it was three miles from the village.*

MAKE TWO SENTENCES: *We found a place for the picnic by a small pond. It was three miles from the village.*

RUN-ON: *We found a place for the picnic by a small pond it was perfect.*

USE A SEMICOLON: *We found a place for the picnic by a small pond; it was perfect.*

ADD A CONJUNCTION: *We found a place for the picnic by a small pond, and it was perfect.*

WATCH OUT! When you form compound sentences, make sure you use appropriate punctuation: a comma before a coordinating conjunction, a semicolon when there is no coordinating conjunction. A very common mistake is to use a comma alone instead of a comma and a conjunction. This error is called a **comma splice.**

INCORRECT: *He finished the job, he left the village.*

CORRECT: *He finished the job, and he left the village.*

11 Subject-Verb Agreement

The subject and verb in a clause must agree in number. Agreement means that if the subject is singular, the verb is also singular, and if the subject is plural, the verb is also plural.

11.1 BASIC AGREEMENT

Fortunately, agreement between subjects and verbs in English is simple. Most verbs show the difference between singular and plural only in the third person of the present tense. In the present tense, the third-person singular form ends in *-s.*

Present-Tense Verb Forms

Singular	Plural
I sleep	we sleep
you sleep	you sleep
she, he, it sleeps	they sleep

11.2 AGREEMENT WITH *BE*

The verb *be* presents special problems in agreement, because this verb does not follow the usual verb patterns.

Forms of *Be*

Present Tense		Past Tense	
Singular	Plural	Singular	Plural
I am	we are	I was	we were
you are	you are	you were	you were
she, he, it is	they are	she, he, it was	they were

11.3 WORDS BETWEEN SUBJECT AND VERB

A verb agrees only with its subject. When words come between a subject and a verb, ignore them when considering proper agreement. Identify the subject, and make sure the verb agrees with it.

EXAMPLES: *A story in the newspapers tells about the 1890s.*

Dad as well as Mom reads the paper daily.

11.4 AGREEMENT WITH COMPOUND SUBJECTS

Use plural verbs with most compound subjects joined by the word *and.*

EXAMPLE: *My father and his friends play chess everyday.*

To confirm that you need a plural verb, you could substitute the plural pronoun *they* for *my father and his friends.*

If a compound subject is thought of as a unit, use a singular verb. Test this by substituting the singular pronoun *it.*

EXAMPLE: *Peanut butter and jelly [it] is my brother's favorite sandwich.*

Use a singular verb with a compound subject that is preceded by *each, every,* or *many a.*

EXAMPLE: *Each novel and short story seems grounded in personal experience.*

When the parts of a compound subject are joined by *or, nor,* or the correlative conjunctions *either . . . or* or *neither . . . nor,* make the verb agree with the noun or pronoun nearest the verb.

EXAMPLES: *Cookies or ice cream is my favorite dessert.*

Either Cheryl or her friends are being invited.

Neither ice storms nor snow is predicted today.

11.5 PERSONAL PRONOUNS AS SUBJECTS

When using a personal pronoun as a subject, make sure to match it with the correct form of the verb *be.* (See the chart in Section 11.2.) Note especially that the pronoun *you* takes the forms *are* and *were,* regardless of whether it is singular or plural.

WATCH OUT! *You is* and *you was* are nonstandard forms and should be avoided in writing and speaking. *We was* and *they was* are also forms to be avoided.

INCORRECT: *You was a good student.*

CORRECT: *You were a good student.*

INCORRECT: *They was starting a new school.*

CORRECT: *They were starting a new school.*

11.6 INDEFINITE PRONOUNS AS SUBJECTS

Some indefinite pronouns are always singular; some are always plural.

Singular Indefinite Pronouns			
another	either	neither	one
anybody	everybody	nobody	somebody
anyone	everyone	no one	someone
anything	everything	nothing	something
each	much		

EXAMPLES: *Each of the writers was given an award.*

Somebody in the room upstairs is sleeping.

Plural Indefinite Pronouns			
both	few	many	several

EXAMPLES: *Many of the books in our library are not in circulation.*

Few have been returned recently.

Still other indefinite pronouns may be either singular or plural.

Singular or Plural Indefinite Pronouns		
all	more	none
any	most	some

The number of the indefinite pronoun *any* or *none* often depends on the intended meaning.

EXAMPLES: *Any of these topics has potential for a good article.* (any one topic)

Any of these topics have potential for good articles. (all of the many topics)

The indefinite pronouns *all, some, more, most,* and *none* are singular when they refer to quantities or parts of things. They are plural when they refer to numbers of individual things. Context will usually give a clue.

EXAMPLES: *All of the flour is gone.* (referring to a quantity)

All of the flowers are gone. (referring to individual items)

11.7 INVERTED SENTENCES

A sentence in which the subject follows the verb is called an **inverted sentence.** A subject can follow a verb or part of a verb phrase in a question, a sentence beginning with *here* or *there,* or a sentence in which an adjective, an adverb, or a phrase is placed first.

EXAMPLES: *There clearly are far too many cooks in this kitchen.*

What is the correct ingredient for this stew?

Far from the embroiled cooks stands the master chef.

TIP To check subject-verb agreement in some inverted sentences, place the subject before the verb. For example, change *There are many people* to *Many people are there.*

11.8 SENTENCES WITH PREDICATE NOMINATIVES

In a sentence containing a predicate noun (nominative), the verb should agree with the subject, not the predicate noun.

EXAMPLES: *The speeches of Martin Luther King Jr. are a landmark in American civil rights history.* (*Speeches* is the subject—not *landmark*—and it takes the plural verb *are.*)

One landmark in American civil rights history is the speeches of Martin Luther King Jr. (The subject is *landmark*—not *speeches*—and it takes the singular verb *is.*)

11.9 *DON'T* AND *DOESN'T* AS AUXILIARY VERBS

The auxiliary verb *doesn't* is used with singular subjects and with the personal pronouns *she, he,* and *it.* The auxiliary verb *don't* is used with plural subjects and with the personal pronouns *I, we, you,* and *they.*

SINGULAR: *She doesn't know Martin Luther King's famous "I Have a Dream" speech.*

Doesn't the young woman read very much?

PLURAL: *We don't have the speech memorized.*

Don't speakers usually memorize their speeches?

11.10 COLLECTIVE NOUNS AS SUBJECTS

Collective nouns are singular nouns that name groups of persons or things. *Team,* for example, is the collective name of a group of individuals. A collective noun takes a singular verb when the group acts as a single unit. It takes a plural verb when the members of the group act separately.

EXAMPLES: *Our team usually wins.* (The team as a whole wins.)

Our team vote differently on most issues. (The individual members vote.)

11.11 RELATIVE PRONOUNS AS SUBJECTS

When the relative pronoun *who, which,* or *that* is used as a subject in an adjective clause, the verb in the clause must agree in number with the antecedent of the pronoun.

SINGULAR: *I didn't read the* ***poem*** *about fireflies that was assigned.*

The antecedent of the relative pronoun *that* is the singular *poem;* therefore, *that* is singular and must take the singular verb *was.*

PLURAL: ***Mary Oliver and Pat Moran,*** *who are very different from each other, are both outstanding poets.*

The antecedent of the relative pronoun *who* is the plural compound subject *Mary Oliver and Pat Moran.* Therefore *who* is plural, and it takes the plural verb *are.*

GRAMMAR PRACTICE

Locate the subject of each verb in parentheses in the sentences below. Then choose the correct verb form.

1. In "Zebra" one (learn, learns) how John Wilson and Adam become friends.
2. John (tell, tells) Adam that he has an idea for a summer art class.
3. Many of Adam's classmates (think, thinks) that the summer art class will be fun.
4. Some (go, goes) to camp during the summer months, while others just (hang, hangs) around.
5. Among psychologists, many (believe, believes) that making art is good therapy.
6. Even you (has, have) a chance to be a good artist.
7. Does anyone else (want, wants) to take this class?
8. Objects in the attic, such as a broken umbrella, (is, are) good materials for making sculptures.
9. There (is, are) many beautiful objects made from old things.
10. Each of the students (leave, leaves) the class having learned something special.

The key to becoming an independent reader is to develop a tool kit of vocabulary strategies. By learning and practicing the strategies, you'll know what to do when you encounter unfamiliar words while reading. You'll also know how to refine the words you use for different situations—personal, school, and work.

Being a good speller is important when communicating your ideas in writing. Learning basic spelling rules and checking your spelling in a dictionary will help you spell words that you may not use frequently.

VOCABULARY PRACTICE
For more practice, go to the **Vocabulary Center** at **ClassZone.com.**

1 Using Context Clues

The context of a word is made up of the punctuation marks, words, sentences, and paragraphs that surround the word. A word's context can give you important clues about its meaning.

1.1 GENERAL CONTEXT

Sometimes you need to determine the meaning of an unfamiliar word by reading all the information in a passage.

The sweater was of inferior quality. It was torn and had several buttons missing.

You can figure out from the context that *inferior* means "poor or low."

1.2 SPECIFIC CONTEXT CLUES

Sometimes writers help you understand the meanings of words by providing specific clues such as those shown in the chart.

1.3 IDIOMS, SLANG, AND FIGURATIVE LANGUAGE

An **idiom** is an expression whose overall meaning is different from the meaning of the individual words. **Slang** is informal language in which made-up words and ordinary words are used to mean something different from their meanings in formal English. **Figurative language** is language that communicates meaning beyond the literal meaning of the words. Use context clues to figure out the meanings of idioms, slang, and figurative language.

Button your lip about the party. (idiom; means "keep quiet")

That's a really bad jacket; I want one. (slang: means "good-looking, excellent")

My brother had tried to make dinner. The kitchen was a battleground of dirty dishes, stains, spills, and potato peels. (figurative language; battleground, dirty dishes, stains, spills, and potato peels represent a messy scene)

Specific Context Clues

Type of Clue	Key Words/ Phrases	Example
Definition or restatement of the meaning of the word	or, which is, that is, in other words, also known as, also called	Most chemicals are *toxic*, or **poisonous.**
Example following an unfamiliar word	such as, like, as if, for example, especially, including	*Amphibians*, such as **frogs and salamanders**, live in the pond by our house.
Comparison with a more familiar word or concept	as, like, also, similar to, in the same way, likewise	Like the rest of my *frugal* family, I always **save** most of the money I earn.
Contrast with a familiar word or experience	unlike, but, however, although, on the other hand, on the contrary	I wish I had more *ingenuity* in making money instead of simply relying on the **same old** baby-sitting jobs.
Cause-and-effect relationship in which one term is familiar	because, since, when, consequently, as a result, therefore	Because the chemicals are *flammable*, the scientists wear special **fire-resistant** clothing.

For more information, see ***Vocabulary Strategy: Context Clues,*** *pages 225 and 354,* ***Vocabulary Strategy: Idioms,*** *page 278, and* ***Vocabulary Strategy: Literal and Figurative Meanings,*** *page 506.*

2 Analyzing Word Structure

Many words can be broken into smaller parts. These word parts include base words, roots, prefixes, and suffixes.

2.1 BASE WORDS

A **base word** is a word part that by itself is also a word. Other words or word parts can be added to base words to form new words.

For more information, see ***Vocabulary Strategy: Recognizing Base Words,*** *page 801.*

2.2 ROOTS

A **root** is a word part that contains the core meaning of the word. Many English words contain roots that come from older languages such as Greek, Latin, Old English (Anglo-Saxon), and Norse. Knowing the meaning of the word's root can help you determine the word's meaning.

Root	Meaning	Example
photo (Greek)	light	photography
therm (Greek)	heat	thermometer
cred (Latin)	believe	credit
mot (Latin)	move	motion
hēadfod (Old English)	head, top	headfirst

For more information, see ***Vocabulary Strategy: Word Roots,*** *pages 40, 90, 256, 324, 464, 645, 775, 821, 893, and 935.*

2.3 PREFIXES

A **prefix** is a word part attached to the beginning of a word. Most prefixes come from Greek, Latin, or Old English.

Prefix	Meaning	Example
mal-	bad or wrong	**mal**function
micro-	small or short	**micro**scope
semi-	half	**semi**circle

For more information, see ***Vocabulary Strategy: Prefixes,*** *pages 70, 373, 893.*

2.4 SUFFIXES

A **suffix** is a word part that appears at the end of a root or base word to form a new word. Some suffixes do not change word meaning. These suffixes are

- added to nouns to change the number of persons or objects
- added to verbs to change the tense
- added to modifiers to change the degree of comparison

Suffix	Meaning	Examples
-s, -es	to change the number of a noun	lock + s = locks
-d, -ed, -ing	to change verb tense	stew + ed = stewed
-er, -est	to indicate comparison in modifiers	mild + er = milder soft + est = softest

Other suffixes can be added to the root or base to change the word's meaning. These suffixes can also determine a word's part of speech.

Suffix	Meaning	Example
-er	one who does	teacher
-able	capable of	readable
-ly	in what manner	slowly

For more information, see ***Vocabulary Strategy: Suffixes That Form Adjectives,*** *page 127.*

2.5 CONTENT-AREA VOCABULARY

Knowing the meaning of Greek, Latin, and Anglo-Saxon word parts can help you figure out the meaning of content-area vocabulary.

Word Part	Meaning	Example
derm	skin	dermatologist
logy	study of	astrology
bio	life	biography
hydr	water	hydrant
hypo	below, beneath	hypodermic
vid/vis	to see	visual
fract	to break	fraction

3 Understanding Word Origins

Strategies for Understanding Unfamiliar Words

- Look for any prefixes or suffixes. Remove them so that you can concentrate on the base word or the root.
- See if you recognize any elements—prefix, suffix, root, or base—of the word. You may be able to guess its meaning by analyzing one or two elements.
- Think about the way the word is used in the sentence. Use the context and the word parts to make a logical guess about the word's meaning.
- Look in a dictionary to see whether you are correct.

PRACTICE AND APPLY

Use the strategies in this section and the vocabulary lessons in this book to help you figure out the meanings of the following content-area words.

forefathers	vision	microfilm
biology	fracture	import
auditory	ecology	hypothermia

3.1 ETYMOLOGIES

Etymologies show the origin and historical development of a word. When you study a word's history and origin, you can find out when, where, and how the word came to be.

> **ge•om•e•try** (jē-ŏm′ĭ-trē) *n., pl.* **-tries** **1.** The mathematics of the properties, measurement, and relationships of points, lines, angles, surfaces, and solids. **2.** Arrangement. **3.** A physical arrangement suggesting geometric lines and shapes. [from Greek *geōmetriā,* from *geōmetrein,* to measure land].

3.2 WORD FAMILIES

Words that have the same root make up a word family and have related meanings. The following chart shows a common Greek and a common Latin root. Notice how the meanings of the example words are related to the meanings of their roots.

Latin Root	*sens: "sense or feel"*
English	**sensory** relating to the senses **sensitive** responsive to sensations **sensation** a perception or feeling
Greek Root	***ast(e)r:* "star"**
English	**asteroid** a small object in outer space **asterisk** a star-shaped punctuation mark **astronomy** the study of outer space

3.3 FOREIGN WORDS

The English language includes words from diverse languages, such as French, Dutch, Spanish, Italian, and Chinese. Many words have stayed the way they were in their original languages.

French	Dutch	Spanish	Italian
ballet	boss	canyon	diva
vague	caboose	rodeo	cupola
mirage	dock	bronco	spaghetti

4 Synonyms and Antonyms

4.1 SYNONYMS

A **synonym** is a word with a meaning similar to that of another word. You can find synonyms in a thesaurus or a dictionary. In a dictionary, synonyms are often given as part of the definition of the word. The following word pairs are synonyms:

satisfy/please	occasionally/sometimes
rob/steal	schedule/agenda

For more information, see ***Vocabulary Strategy: Use the Best Synonym,*** *page 487.*

4.2 ANTONYMS

An **antonym** is a word with a meaning opposite that of another word. The following word pairs are antonyms:

accurate/incorrect	similar/different
fresh/stale	unusual/ordinary

For more information, see ***Vocabulary Strategy: Antonyms As Context Clues,*** *page 59.*

5 Denotation and Connotation

5.1 DENOTATION

A word's dictionary meaning is called its **denotation.** For example, the denotation of the word *thin* is "having little flesh; spare; lean."

5.2 CONNOTATION

The images or feelings you connect to a word add a finer shade of meaning, called **connotation.** The connation of a word goes beyond its basic dictionary definition. Writers use connotations of words to communicate positive or negative feelings.

Positive	Negative
slender	scrawny
thrifty	cheap
young	immature

Make sure you understand the denotation and connotation of a word when you read it or use it in your writing.

For more information, see ***Vocabulary Strategy: Denotations and Connotations,*** *pages 336, 580, and 788.*

6 Analogies

An **analogy** is a comparison between two things that are similar in some way but are otherwise not alike. Analogies are sometimes used in writing when unfamiliar subjects or ideas are explained in terms of familiar ones. Analogies often appear on tests as well. In an analogy problem, the analogy is expressed using two groups of words. The relationship between the first pair of words is the same as the relationship between the second pair of words. Some analogy problems are expressed like this:

love : hate :: war: _______________
a. soldier b. peace c. battle d. argument

Follow these steps to determine the correct answer:

- Read the problem as "*love* is to *hate* as ***war*** is to. . . ."
- Ask yourself how the words *love* and *hate* are related. (*Love* and *hate* are antonyms.)
- Ask yourself which answer choice is an antonym of *war*. (*Peace* is an antonym of *war,* therefore *peace* is the best answer.)

For more information, see ***Vocabulary Strategy: Analogies,*** *page 116.*

7 Homonyms, Homographs, and Homophones

7.1 HOMONYMS

Homonyms are words that have the same spelling and sound but have different meanings.

The snake shed its skin in the shed behind the house.

Shed can mean "to lose by natural process," but an identically spelled word means "a small structure."

Sometimes only one of the meanings of a homonym may be familiar to you. Use context clues to help you figure out the meaning of an unfamiliar word.

7.2 HOMOGRAPHS

Homographs are words that are spelled the same but have different meanings and origins. Some are also pronounced differently, as in these examples.

Please close the door. (clōz)
That was a close call. (clōs)

If you see a word used in a way that is unfamiliar to you, check a dictionary to see if it is a homograph.

For more information, see ***Vocabulary Strategy: Homographs,*** *page 658.*

7.3 HOMOPHONES

Homophones are words that sound alike but have different meanings and spellings. The following homophones are frequently misused:

it's/its	they're/their/there
to/too/two	stationary/stationery

Many misused homophones are pronouns and contractions. Whenever you are unsure whether to write *your* or *you're* and *who's* or *whose,* ask yourself if you mean *you are* and *who is/has.* If you do, write the contraction. For other homophones, such as *fair* and *fare,* use the meaning of the word to help you decide which one to use.

8 Words with Multiple Meanings

Some words have acquired additional meanings over time that are based on the original meaning.

I had to be replaced in the cast of the play because of the cast on my arm.

These two uses of *cast* have different meanings, but both of them have the same origin. You will find all the meanings of *cast* listed in one entry in the dictionary.

For more information, see ***Vocabulary Strategy: Words with Multiple Meanings,*** *page 238.*

9 Specialized Vocabulary

Specialized vocabulary is special terms suited to a particular field of study or work. For example, science, mathematics, and history all have their own technical or specialized vocabularies. To figure out specialized terms, you can use context clues and reference sources, such as dictionaries on specific subjects, atlases, or manuals.

For more information, see ***Vocabulary Strategy: Specialized Vocabulary,*** *page 906.*

10 Using Reference Sources

10.1 DICTIONARIES

A **general dictionary** will tell you not only a word's definitions but also its pronunciation, parts of speech, and history and origin.

(1) **tangible** (2) (tăn′jə-bəl) (3) *adj.* **1a.** (4) Discernible by the touch; palpable. **b.** Possible to touch. **c.** Possible to be treated as fact; real or concrete. **2.** Possible to understand or realize. **3.** Law that can be valued monetarily [Late Latin *tangibilis,* from Latin *tangere,* to touch] (5)

(1) Entry word
(2) Pronunciation
(3) Part of speech
(4) Definitions
(5) Etymology

A **specialized dictionary** focuses on terms related to a particular field of study or work. Use a dictionary to check the spelling of any word you are unsure of in your English class and other classes as well.

For more information, see ***Vocabulary Strategy: Dictionary Usage Labels,*** *page 721.*

10.2 THESAURI

A **thesaurus** (plural, *thesauri*) is a dictionary of synonyms. A thesaurus can be especially helpful when you find yourself using the same modifiers over and over again.

10.3 SYNONYM FINDERS

A **synonym finder** is often included in word-processing software. It enables you to highlight a word and be shown a display of its synonyms.

10.4 GLOSSARIES

A **glossary** is a list of specialized terms and their definitions. It is often found in the back of a book and sometimes includes pronunciations. Many textbooks contain glossaries. In fact, this textbook has three glossaries: the **Glossary of Literary Terms,** the **Glossary of Reading & Informational Terms,** and the **Glossary of Vocabulary in English & Spanish.** Use these glossaries to help you understand how terms are used in this textbook.

For more information, see ***Vocabulary Strategy: Using Reference Aids,*** *page 266.*

11 Spelling Rules

11.1 WORDS ENDING IN A SILENT *E*

Before adding a suffix beginning with a vowel or ***y*** to a word ending in a silent ***e,*** drop the ***e*** (with some exceptions).

amaze + -ing = amazing
love + -able = lovable
create + -ed = created
nerve + -ous = nervous

Exceptions: *change + -able = changeable; courage + -ous = courageous*

When adding a suffix beginning with a consonant to a word ending in a silent ***e,*** keep the ***e*** (with some exceptions).

late + -ly = lately
spite + -ful = spiteful
noise + -less = noiseless
state + -ment = statement

Exceptions: *truly, argument, ninth, wholly, awful,* and others

When a suffix beginning with ***a*** or ***o*** is added to a word with a final silent ***e,*** the final ***e*** is usually retained if it is preceded by a soft ***c*** or a soft ***g.***

bridge + -able = bridgeable
peace + -able = peaceable
outrage + -ous = outrageous
advantage + -ous = advantageous

When a suffix beginning with a vowel is added to words ending in ***ee*** or ***oe,*** the final silent ***e*** is retained.

agree + -ing = agreeing **free + -ing = freeing**
hoe + -ing = hoeing **see + -ing = seeing**

11.2 WORDS ENDING IN *Y*

Before adding most suffixes to a word that ends in ***y*** preceded by a consonant, change the ***y*** to ***i.***

easy + -est = easiest
crazy + -est = craziest
silly + -ness = silliness
marry + -age = marriage

Exceptions: *dryness, shyness,* and *slyness*

However, when you add ***-ing,*** the ***y*** does not change.

empty + -ed = emptied but
empty + -ing = emptying

When adding a suffix to a word that ends in ***y*** preceded by a vowel, the ***y*** usually does not change.

play + -er = player
employ + -ed = employed
coy + -ness = coyness
pay + -able = payable

11.3 WORDS ENDING IN A CONSONANT

In one-syllable words that end in one consonant preceded by one short vowel, double the final consonant before adding a suffix beginning with a vowel, such as ***-ed*** or ***-ing.*** These are sometimes called 1+1+1 words.

dip + -ed = dipped **set + -ing = setting**
slim + -est = slimmest **fit + -er = fitter**

The rule does not apply to words of one syllable that end in a consonant preceded by two vowels.

feel + -ing = feeling **peel + -ed = peeled**
reap + -ed = reaped **loot + -ed = looted**

In words of more than one syllable, double the final consonant when (1) the word ends with one consonant preceded by one vowel and (2) when the word is accented on the last syllable.

be•gin´ per•mit´ re•fer´

In the following examples, note that in the new words formed with suffixes, the accent remains on the same syllable:

be•gin´ + -ing = be•gin´ning = beginning
per•mit´ + -ed = per•mit´ted = permitted

Exceptions: In some words with more than one syllable, though the accent remains on the same syllable when a suffix is added, the final consonant is nevertheless not doubled, as in the following examples:

tra´vel + er = tra´vel•er = traveler
mar´ket + er = mar´ket•er = marketer

In the following examples, the accent does not remain on the same syllable; thus, the final consonant is not doubled:

re•fer´ + -ence = ref´er•ence = reference
con•fer´ + -ence = con´fer•ence = conference

11.4 PREFIXES AND SUFFIXES

When adding a prefix to a word, do not change the spelling of the base word. When a prefix creates a double letter, keep both letters.

dis- + approve = disapprove
re- + build = rebuild
ir- + regular = irregular
mis- + spell = misspell
anti- + trust = antitrust
il- + logical = illogical

When adding ***-ly*** to a word ending in ***l,*** keep both ***l***'s. When adding ***-ness*** to a word ending in ***n,*** keep both ***n***'s.

careful + -ly = carefully
sudden + -ness = suddenness
final + -ly = finally
thin + -ness = thinness

11.5 FORMING PLURAL NOUNS

To form the plural of most nouns, just add ***-s.***

prizes dreams circles stations

For most singular nouns ending in ***o,*** add ***-s.***

solos halos studios photos pianos

For a few nouns ending in ***o,*** add ***-es.***

heroes tomatoes potatoes echoes

When the singular noun ends in ***s, sh, ch, x,*** or ***z,*** add ***-es.***

waitresses brushes ditches
axes buzzes

When a singular noun ends in ***y*** with a consonant before it, change the ***y*** to ***i*** and add ***-es.***

army—armies candy—candies
baby—babies diary—diaries
ferry—ferries conspiracy—conspiracies

When a vowel (***a, e, i, o, u***) comes before the ***y,*** just add ***-s.***

boy—boys way—ways
array—arrays alloy—alloys
weekday—weekdays jockey—jockeys

For most nouns ending in ***f*** or ***fe,*** change the ***f*** to ***v*** and add ***-es*** or ***-s.***

life—lives calf—calves knife—knives
thief—thieves shelf—shelves loaf—loaves

For some nouns ending in ***f,*** add ***-s*** to make the plural.

roofs chiefs reefs beliefs

Some nouns have the same form for both singular and plural.

deer sheep moose salmon trout

For some nouns, the plural is formed in a special way.

man—men goose—geese
ox—oxen woman—women
mouse—mice child—children

For a compound noun written as one word, form the plural by changing the last word in the compound to its plural form.

stepchild—stepchildren firefly—fireflies

If a compound noun is written as a hyphenated word or as two separate words, change the most important word to the plural form.

brother-in-law—brothers-in-law
life jacket—life jackets

11.6 FORMING POSSESSIVES

If a noun is singular, add ***'s.***

mother—my mother's car Ross—Ross's desk

Exception: The ***s*** after the apostrophe is dropped after *Jesus', Moses',* and certain names in classical mythology *(Zeus').* These possessive forms can thus be pronounced easily.

If a noun is plural and ends with ***s,*** just add an apostrophe.

parents—my parents' car
the Santinis—the Santinis' house

If a noun is plural but does not end in ***s,*** add ***'s.***

people—the people's choice
women—the women's coats

11.7 SPECIAL SPELLING PROBLEMS

Only one English word ends in ***-sede:*** *supersede.* Three words end in ***-ceed:*** *exceed, proceed,* and *succeed.* All other verbs ending in the sound "seed" are spelled with ***-cede.***

concede precede recede secede

In words with **ie** or **ei,** when the sound is long ***e*** (as in *she*), the word is spelled ***ie*** except after ***c*** (with some exceptions).

i* before *e	**thief**	**relieve**	**field**
	piece	**grieve**	**pier**
except after *c*	**conceit**	**perceive**	**ceiling**
	receive	**receipt**	
Exceptions:	**either**	**neither**	**weird**
	leisure	**seize**	

12 Commonly Confused Words

WORDS	DEFINITIONS	EXAMPLES
accept/except	The verb *accept* means "to receive or believe"; *except* is usually a preposition meaning "excluding."	Did the teacher **accept** your report? Everyone smiled for the photographer **except** Jody.
advice/advise	*Advise* is a verb; *advice* is a noun naming that which an *adviser* gives.	I **advise** you to take that job. Whom should I ask for **advice?**
affect/effect	As a verb, *affect* means "to influence." *Effect* as a verb means "to cause." If you want a noun, you will almost always want *effect.*	How deeply did the news **affect** him? The students tried to **effect** a change in school policy. What **effect** did the acidic soil produce in the plants?
all ready/already	*All ready* is an adjective meaning "fully ready." *Already* is an adverb meaning "before or by this time."	He was **all ready** to go at noon. I have **already** seen that movie.
desert/dessert	*Desert* (dĕz′ərt) means "a dry, sandy, barren region." *Desert* (dĭ-zûrt′) means "to abandon." *Dessert* (dĭ-zûrt′) is a sweet, such as cake.	The Sahara, in North Africa, is the world's largest **desert.** The night guard did not **desert** his post. Alison's favorite **dessert** is chocolate cake.
among/between	*Between* is used when you are speaking of only two things. *Among* is used for three or more.	**Between** ice cream and sherbet, I prefer the latter. Gary Soto is **among** my favorite authors.
bring/take	*Bring* is used to denote motion toward a speaker or place. *Take* is used to denote motion away from such a person or place.	**Bring** the books over here, and I will **take** them to the library.
fewer/less	*Fewer* refers to the number of separate, countable units. *Less* refers to bulk quantity.	We have **less** literature and **fewer** selections in this year's curriculum.
leave/let	*Leave* means "to allow something to remain behind." *Let* means "to permit."	The librarian will **leave** some books on display but will not **let** us borrow any.
lie/lay	To *lie* is "to rest or recline." It does not take an object. *Lay* always takes an object.	Rover loves to **lie** in the sun. We always **lay** some bones next to him.
loose/lose	*Loose* (lo͞os) means "free, not restrained"; *lose* (lo͞oz) means "to misplace or fail to find."	Who turned the horses **loose?** I hope we won't **lose** any of them.
passed/past	*Passed* is the past tense of *pass* and means "went by." *Past* is an adjective that means "of a former time." *Past* is also a noun that means "time gone by."	We **passed** through the Florida Keys during our vacation. My **past** experiences have taught me to set my alarm. Ebenezer Scrooge is a character who relives his **past.**
than/then	Use *than* in making comparisons; use *then* on all other occasions.	Ramon is stronger **than** Mark. Cut the grass and **then** trim the hedges.
two/too/to	*Two* is the number. *Too* is an adverb meaning "also" or "very." Use *to* before a verb or as a preposition.	Meg had **to** go **to** town, **too.** We had **too** much reading **to** do. **Two** chapters is **too** many.
their/there/they're	*Their* means "belonging to them." *There* means "in that place." *They're* is the contraction for "they are."	**There** is a movie playing at 9 P.M. **They're** going to see it with me. Sakara and Jessica drove away in **their** car after the movie.

For more information, see ***Vocabulary Strategy: Easily Confused Words,*** *page 684.*

Effective oral communication occurs when the audience understands a message the way the speaker intends it. Good speakers and listeners do more than just talk and hear. They use specific techniques to present their ideas effectively, and they are attentive and critical listeners.

1 Speech

In school, in business, and in community life, a speech is one of the most effective means of communicating.

1.1 AUDIENCE, PURPOSE, AND OCCASION

Delivering a speech is an opportunity to share your ideas. Before you begin to prepare a speech, you will need to know *why* you are making the presentation and to *whom* you are presenting it. Understanding your purpose, the background and interests of your audience, and the occasion will help you select an appropriate focus and organizational structure for your speech.

- **Know Your Audience** What kind of group are you presenting to? Fellow classmates? A group of teachers? What are their interests and backgrounds? Understanding their different points of view can help you organize the information so that they understand and are interested in it.
- **Understand Your Purpose** Keep in mind your purpose for speaking. Are you trying to persuade the audience to do something? Perhaps you simply want to entertain them by sharing a story or experience. Your purpose directly affects your tone. Decide whether you'll best accomplish your purpose by being serious or humorous.
- **Know the Occasion** Are you speaking at a special event? Is it formal? Will others be giving speeches besides you? Knowing what the occasion is will help you choose the proper language and the right length for the event.

1.2 WRITING YOUR SPEECH

Once you understand your purpose and audience, you are ready to write your speech. Use the following guidelines to help you:

- **Create a Unified Speech** Do this first by organizing your speech into paragraphs, each of which develops a single main idea. Then make sure that just as all the sentences in a paragraph support the main idea of the paragraph, all the paragraphs in your speech support the main idea of the speech.
- **Clarify Your Ideas** Make sure that you show clear relationships between ideas. Transition words can help listeners follow your ideas.

*For more information on transitions, see the **Writing Handbook,** page R32.*

- **Use Appropriate Language** The subject of your speech—and the way you choose to present it—should match your audience, your purpose, and the occasion. You can use informal language, such as slang, to share a story with your classmates. For a persuasive speech in front of a school assembly, use formal, standard American English. If you are giving an informative presentation, be sure to explain any terms that the audience may not be familiar with.
- **Provide Evidence** Include relevant facts, statistics, and incidents; quote experts to support your ideas and opinions. Elaborate—provide specific details, perhaps with visual or media displays—to clarify what you are saying.
- **Arrange Details and Evidence Effectively** In a good presentation, your main thesis statement should be supported by clearly stated evidence. The evidence can be presented as details, reasons, descriptions, or examples. Use the following chart to help you arrange your ideas.

Introduction	• Focus on one strong example or statistic. • Make sure your evidence is intense or even surprising, so that it grabs the audience's attention.
Main Body	• Try to provide at least one piece of evidence for every new idea you introduce. • Define unfamiliar terms clearly. • When possible, include well-labeled diagrams or illustrations.
Conclusion	• Leave your audience with one strong piece of evidence or a powerful detail.

- **Use Figurative Language** To help your audience follow the main ideas of your speech, be sure to draw attention to important points with similes, metaphors, and sensory images.
- **Use Precise Language** Use precise language to convey your ideas, and vary the structure and length of your sentences. You can keep the audience's attention with a word that brings out strong emotion. You can use a question or interjection to make a personal connection with the audience.
- **Start Strong, Finish Strong** As you begin your speech, consider using a "hook"—an interesting question or statement to capture your audience's attention. At the end of the speech, restate your main ideas simply and clearly. Perhaps conclude with a powerful example or anecdote to reinforce your message.
- **Revise Your Speech** After you write your speech, revise, edit, and proofread it as you would a written report. Use a variety of sentence structures to achieve a natural rhythm. Check for correct subject-verb agreement and consistent verb tense. Correct run-on sentences and sentence fragments. Use parallel structure to emphasize ideas. Make sure you use complete sentences and correct punctuation and capitalization, even if no one else will see it. Your written speech should be clear and error free. If you notice an error in your notes during the speech, you may not remember what you actually wanted to say.

1.3 DELIVERING YOUR SPEECH

Confidence is the key to a successful presentation. Use these techniques to help you prepare and present your speech:

Prepare

- **Review Your Information** Reread your notes and review any background research. You'll feel more confident during your speech.
- **Organize Your Notes** Some people prefer to write down only key points. Others prefer the entire script. Write each main point, or each paragraph, of your speech on a separate numbered index card. Be sure to include your most important evidence and examples.
- **Plan Your Visual Aids** If you are planning on using visual aids, such as slides, posters, charts, graphs, video clips, overhead transparencies, or computer projections, now is the time to design them and decide how to work them into your speech.

Practice

- **Rehearse** Rehearse your speech several times, possibly in front of a practice audience. Maintain good posture by standing with your shoulders back and your head up. If you are using visual aids, arrange them in the order in which you will use them. Adapt your rate of speaking, pitch, and tone of voice to your audience and setting. Glance at your notes to refresh your memory, but avoid reading them word for word. Your style of performance should express the purpose of your speech. Use the following chart to help you.

Purpose	Pace	Pitch	Tone
To persuade	fast but clear	even	urgent
To inform	using plenty of pauses	even	authoritative
To entertain	usually building to a "punch"	varied to create characters or drama	funny or dramatic

- **Use Audience Feedback** If you had a practice audience, ask them specific questions about your delivery: Did I use enough eye contact? Was my voice at the right volume? Did I stand straight, or did I slouch? Use the audience's comments to evaluate the effectiveness of your delivery and to set goals for future rehearsals.
- **Evaluate Your Performance** When you have finished each rehearsal, evaluate your performance. Did you pause to let an important point sink in or use gestures for emphasis? Make a list of the aspects of your presentation that you will try to improve for your next rehearsal.

Present

- **Begin Your Speech** Try to look relaxed and smile.
- **Make Eye Contact** Try to make eye contact with as many audience members as possible. This will establish personal contact and help you determine if the audience understands your speech.
- **Remember to Pause** A slight pause after important points will provide emphasis and give your audience time to think about what you're saying.
- **Speak Clearly** Speak loud enough to be heard clearly, but not so loud that your voice is overwhelming. Use a conversational tone.
- **Maintain Good Posture** Stand up straight and avoid nervous movements that may distract the audience's attention from what you are saying.
- **Use Expressive Body Language** Use facial expressions to show your feelings toward your topic. Lean forward when you make an important point; move your hands and arms for emphasis. Use your body language to show your own style and reflect your personality.
- **Watch the Audience for Responses** If they start fidgeting or yawning, speak a little louder or get to your conclusion a little sooner. Use what you learn to evaluate the effectiveness of your speech and to decide what areas need improvement for future presentations.

Respond to Questions

Depending on the content of your speech, your audience may have questions. Follow these steps to make sure that you answer questions in an appropriate manner:

- Think about what your audience may ask and prepare answers before your speech.
- Tell your audience at the beginning of your speech that you will take questions at the end. This helps avoid audience interruptions that may make your speech hard to follow.
- Call on audience members in the order in which they raise their hands.
- Repeat each question before you answer it to ensure that everyone has heard it. This step also gives you time to prepare your answer.

2 Different Types of Oral Presentations

2.1 INFORMATIVE SPEECH

When you deliver an informative speech, you give the audience new information, provide a better understanding of information, or enable the audience to use the information in a new way. An informative speech is presented in an objective way.

*For more information, see **Speaking and Listening: Making a Formal Presentation**, page 743.*

Use the following questions to evaluate the presentation of a peer or a public figure, or your own presentation.

Evaluate an Informative Speech

- Did the speaker explain the purpose of the presentation?
- Did the speaker take the audience's previous knowledge into consideration?
- Did the speaker cite a variety of sources for the information?
- Did the speaker communicate the information objectively?
- Did the speaker explain technical terms?
- Did the speaker use visual aids effectively?

2.2 PERSUASIVE SPEECH

When you deliver a persuasive speech, you offer a thesis or clear statement on a subject, you provide relevant evidence to support your position, and you attempt to convince the audience to accept your point of view.

For more information, see ***Speaking and Listening: Delivering a Persuasive Speech,*** *page 955.*

Use the following questions to evaluate the presentation of a peer or a public figure, or your own presentation.

Evaluate a Persuasive Speech

- Did the speaker present a clear thesis or argument?
- Did the speaker anticipate and address audience concerns, biases, and counterarguments?
- Did the speaker use sound logic and reasoning in developing the argument?
- Did the speaker support the argument with convincing evidence, examples, facts, expert opinions, and quotations?
- Did the speaker hold the audience's interest with an effective voice, facial expressions, and gestures?
- Is your reaction to the speech similar to other audience members'?

2.3 DEBATE

A debate is a balanced argument covering both sides of an issue. In a debate, two teams compete to win the support of the audience. In a formal debate, two teams, each with two members, present their arguments on a given proposition or policy statement. One team argues for the proposition or statement and the other argues against it. Each debater must consider the proposition closely and must research both sides of it. To argue persuasively either for or against a proposition, a debater must be familiar with both sides of the issue.

Use the following guidelines to evaluate a debate.

Evaluate a Team in a Debate

- Did the team prove that a significant problem does or does not exist?
- How did the team convince you that the proposition is or is not the best solution to the problem?
- How effectively did the team present reasons and evidence supporting the case?
- How effectively did the team respond to arguments made by the opposing team?
- Did the speakers maintain eye contact and speak at an appropriate rate and volume?
- Did the speakers observe proper debate etiquette?

PRACTICE AND APPLY

View a political debate for a school, local, state, or national election. Use the preceding criteria to evaluate it.

2.4 NARRATIVE SPEECH

When you deliver a narrative speech, you tell a story or present a subject using a story-type format. A good narrative keeps an audience informed and entertained. It also allows you to deliver a message in a creative way.

Use the following guidelines to evaluate a speaker or your own presentation.

Evaluate a Narrative Speech

- Did the speaker choose a setting that makes sense and contributes to a believable narrative?
- Did the speaker locate incidents in specific places?
- Does the plot flow well?
- Did the speaker use words that convey the appropriate mood and tone?
- Did the speaker use sensory details that allow the audience to experience the sights, sounds, and smells of a scene and the specific actions, gestures, and thoughts of the characters?
- Did the speaker use a range of narrative devices to keep the audience interested?
- Is your reaction to the presentation similar to other audience members'?

2.5 DESCRIPTIVE SPEECH

Description is part of most presentations. In a descriptive speech, you describe a subject that you are personally involved with.

Use the following questions to evaluate a speaker or your own presentation.

Evaluate a Descriptive Speech

- Did the speaker make clear his or her point of view toward the subject being described?
- Did the speaker use sensory details, figurative language, and factual details?
- Did the speaker use tone and pitch to emphasize important details?
- Did the speaker use facial expressions to emphasize his or her feelings toward the subject?

For more information, see ***Speaking and Listening: Presenting an Anecdote,*** *page 857.*

2.6 ORAL INTERPRETATION

When you read a poem, play, or story aloud, your voice can bring the literature to life.

Oral Reading

An oral reading can be a monologue, during which you assume the voice of a character, the narrator, or the speaker in a poem. Or it may be a dialogue, during which you take the roles of two or more characters. Use the following techniques when giving an oral reading:

- **Speak Clearly** As you speak, pronounce your words carefully and clearly.
- **Control Your Volume** Make sure that you are loud enough to be heard but do not shout.
- **Pace Yourself** Read at a moderate rate, but vary your pace if it seems appropriate to the emotions of the character or to the action.
- **Vary Your Voice** Use a different voice for each character. Stress important words and phrases. Use your voice to express different emotions.

For more information, see ***Speaking and Listening: Producing a Radio Dramatization,*** *page 165, and* ***Speaking and Listening: Oral Interpretation of a Poem,*** *page 615.*

Dramatic Reading

In a dramatic reading, several speakers participate in the reading of a play or other work. Use the following techniques in your dramatic reading:

- **Prepare** Rehearse your material several times. Become familiar with the humorous and serious parts of the script. Develop a special voice that fits the personality of the character you portray.
- **Project** As you read your lines, aim your voice toward the back of the room to allow everyone to hear you.
- **Perform** React to the other characters as if you were hearing their lines for the first time. Deliver your own lines with the appropriate emotion. Use not only hand gestures and facial expressions but also other body movements to express your emotions.

For more information, see ***Speaking and Listening: Dramatizing a Short Story,*** *page 427.*

Use the following questions to evaluate an artistic performance by a peer or public presenter, a media presentation, or your own performance.

Evaluate an Oral Interpretation

- Did the speaker speak clearly?
- Did the speaker maintain eye contact with the audience?
- Did the speaker project his or her voice without shouting?
- Did the speaker vary the rate of speech appropriately to express emotion, mood, and action?
- Did the speaker use a different voice for the character(s)?
- Did the speaker stress important words or phrases?
- Did the speaker use voice, tone, and gestures to enhance meaning?

PRACTICE AND APPLY

Listen to an oral reading by a classmate or view a dramatic performance in a theater or on television. Use the preceding criteria to evaluate it.

2.7 ORAL SUMMARY

An oral summary includes the main ideas of a book or article. It also includes the most important details or evidence.

Use the following questions to evaluate a speaker or your own presentation.

Evaluate an Oral Summary

- Did the speaker introduce the subject clearly?
- Did the speaker present the main ideas early in the presentation?
- Did the speaker discuss the supporting details?
- Did the speaker show the audience that he or she really understood the piece?

PRACTICE AND APPLY

Listen as a classmate delivers an oral summary of a book or an article. Use the preceding criteria to evaluate the presentation.

3 Other Types of Communication

3.1 CONVERSATION

Conversations are informal, but they are important means of communicating. When two or more people exchange messages, it is equally important that each person contribute and actively listen.

3.2 GROUP DISCUSSION

Successful groups assign a role to each member. These roles distribute responsibility among the members and help keep discussions focused.

Role	Responsibilites
Chairperson	• Introduces topic • Explains goal or purpose • Participates in discussion and keeps it on track • Helps resolve conflicts • Helps group reach goal
Recorder	• Takes notes on discussion • Reports on suggestions and decisions • Organizes and writes up notes • Participates in discussion
Participants	• Contribute relevant facts or ideas to discussion • Respond constructively to one another's ideas • Reach agreement or vote on final decision

Guidelines for Discussion

- Be informed about the topic.
- Participate in the discussion.
- Ask questions and respond appropriately to questions.
- Don't talk while someone else is talking.
- Support statements and opinions with facts and examples.
- Listen attentively; be courteous and respectful of others' viewpoints.
- Work toward the goal; avoid getting sidetracked by unrelated topics.

3.3 INTERVIEW

An **interview** is a formal type of conversation with a definite purpose and goal. To conduct a successful interview, use the following guidelines:

Prepare for the Interview

- Select your interviewee carefully. Identify who has the kind of knowledge and experience you are looking for.
- Set a time, a date, and a place. Ask permission to tape-record the interview.
- Learn all you can about the person you will interview or the topic you want information on.

- Prepare a list of questions. Create questions that encourage detailed responses instead of yes-or-no answers. Arrange your questions in order from most important to least important.
- Arrive on time with everything you need.

Conduct the Interview

- Ask your questions clearly and listen to the responses carefully. Give the person whom you are interviewing plenty of time to answer.
- Be flexible; follow up on any responses you find interesting.
- Avoid arguments; be tactful and polite.
- Even if you tape an interview, take notes on important points.
- Thank the person for the interview, and ask if you can call with any follow-up questions.

Follow Up on the Interview

- Summarize your notes or make a written copy of the tape recording as soon as possible.
- If any points are unclear or if information is missing, call and ask more questions while the person is still available.
- Select the most appropriate quotations to support your ideas.
- If possible, have the person you interviewed review your work to make sure you haven't misrepresented what he or she said.
- Send a thank-you note to the person in appreciation of his or her time and effort.

For more information, see ***Speaking and Listening: Conducting an Interview,*** *page 293.*

Evaluate an Interview

You can determine how effective your interview was by asking yourself these questions:

- Did you get the type of information you were looking for?
- Were your most important questions answered to your satisfaction?
- Were you able to keep the interviewee focused on the subject?

4 Active Listening

Active listening is the process of receiving, interpreting, evaluating, and responding to a message. Whether you listen to a class discussion or a formal speech, use the following strategies to get as much as you can from the message.

Listening with a Purpose

Situation	Reason for Listening	How to Listen
A friend tells a funny story.	enjoyment	Maintain eye contact; react to the joke.
You're watching a TV show called "Wolves of the Tundra."	for enjoyment, to learn something new	Listen for ideas that interest you or add to your knowledge.

Before Listening

- Learn what the topic is beforehand. You may need to read background information about the topic or learn new terms in order to understand the speaker's message.
- Think about what you know or want to know about the topic.
- Have a pen and paper to take notes.
- Establish a purpose for listening.

While Listening

- Focus your attention on the speaker. Your facial expressions and body language should demonstrate your interest in hearing the topic. Try to ignore uncomfortable room temperature and noise.
- Listen for the speaker's purpose (usually stated at the beginning), which alerts you to main ideas.
- To help you understand the speaker's message, listen for words or phrases that signal important points, such as *to begin with, in addition, most important, finally,* and *in conclusion.*
- Listen carefully for explanations of unfamiliar terms. Use these terms to help you understand the speaker's message.
- Listen for ideas that are repeated for emphasis.

- Take notes. Write down only the most important points.
- If possible, use an outline or list format to organize main ideas and supporting points.
- Note comparisons and contrasts, causes and effects, or problems and solutions.
- As you take notes, use phrases, abbreviations, and symbols to keep up with the speaker.
- To aid your understanding, note how the speaker uses word choice, voice pitch, posture, and gestures to convey meaning.

After Listening

- Ask questions to clarify anything that was unclear or confusing.
- Review your notes right away to make sure you understand what was said.
- Summarize and paraphrase the speaker's ideas.
- You may also wish to compare your interpretation of the speech with the interpretations of others who listened to it.

4.1 CRITICAL LISTENING

Critical listening involves evaluating a spoken message to judge its accuracy and reliability. You can use the following strategies as you listen to messages from public speakers:

- **Determine the Speaker's Purpose** Think about the background, viewpoint, and possible motives of the speaker. Separate facts from opinions. Listen carefully to details and evidence that a speaker uses to support the message.
- **Listen for the Main Idea** Figure out the speaker's main message before allowing yourself to be distracted by seemingly convincing facts and details.
- **Recognize the Use of Persuasive Techniques** Pay attention to a speaker's choice of words. Speakers may present information in a particular way to persuade you to buy a product or accept an idea. Persuasive devices such as glittering generalities, either/or reasoning, and bandwagon or snob appeal may represent faulty reasoning and provide misleading information.

*For more information, see **Recognizing Persuasive Techniques,** page R21.*

- **Observe Nonverbal Messages** A speaker's gestures, facial expressions, and tone of voice should reinforce the message. If they don't, you should doubt the speaker's sincerity and his or her message's reliability.
- **Give Appropriate Feedback** An effective speaker looks for verbal and nonverbal cues from you, the listener, to see how the message is being received. For example, if you understand or agree with the message, you might nod your head. If possible, during or after a presentation, ask questions to check your understanding.

4.2 VERBAL FEEDBACK

At times you will be asked to give direct feedback to a speaker. You may be asked to evaluate the way the speaker delivers the presentation as well as the content of the presentation.

Evaluate Delivery

- Did the speaker articulate words clearly and distinctly?
- Did the speaker pronounce words correctly?
- Did the speaker vary his or her rate?
- Did the speaker's voice sound natural and not strained?
- Was the speaker's voice loud enough?

Evaluate Content

Here's how to give constructive suggestions for improvement:

Be Specific Don't make statements like "Your charts need work." Offer concrete suggestions, such as "Please make the type bigger so we can read the poster from the back of the room."

Discuss Only the Most Important Points Don't overload the speaker with too much feedback about too many details. Focus on important points, such as

- Is the topic too advanced for the audience?
- Are the supporting details well organized?
- Is the conclusion weak?

Give Balanced Feedback Tell the speaker not only what didn't work but also what did work: "Consider dropping the last two slides, since you covered those points earlier. The first two slides got my attention."

Every day you are exposed to hundreds of images and messages from television, radio, movies, newspapers, and the Internet. What is the effect of all this media? What do you need to know to be a smart media consumer? Being media literate *means that you know what media products are, who created them, and what they mean. It means that you are able to analyze and evaluate media messages and how they influence you and your world. To become media literate, you'll need the tools to study media messages.*

MEDIA TOOLS
For more information, visit the **Media Center** at **ClassZone.com.**

1 Five Core Concepts in Media Literacy

from The Center for Media Literacy

The five core concepts of media literacy provide you with the basic ideas you can consider when examining media messages.

All media messages are "constructed." All media messages are made by someone. In fact, they are carefully thought out and researched and have attitudes and values built into them. Much of the information that you use to make sense of the world comes from the media. Therefore, it is important to know how a medium is put together so you can better understand the message it conveys.

Media messages are constructed using a creative language with its own rules. Each means of communication—whether it is film, television, newspapers, magazines, radio, or the Internet—has its own language and design. Therefore, the message must use the language and design of the medium that delivers the message. Thus, the medium actually shapes the message. For example, a horror film may use music to heighten suspense, or a newspaper may use a big headline to signal the importance of a story. Understanding the language of each medium can increase your enjoyment of it as well as help you recognize any subtle attempt to persuade you.

Different people experience the same media messages differently. Personal factors such as age, education, and experience will affect the way a person responds to a media message. How many times has your interpretation of a film or book differed from that of a friend? Everyone interprets media messages differently.

Media have embedded values and points of view. Media messages carry underlying values, which are purposely built into them by the creators of the message. For example, a commercial's main purpose may be to persuade you to buy something, but the commercial may also aim to convince you that the product is important to a particular way of life. Understanding not only the main message but also any other points of view will help you decide whether to accept or reject the message.

Most media messages are constructed to gain profit and/or power. The creators of media messages often provide a commodity, such as information or entertainment, in order to make money. The bigger the audience, the more the media outlet can charge for advertising. Consequently, media outlets want to build large audiences in order to bring in more revenue from advertising. For example, a television network will create programming to appeal to the largest audience possible, in the hope that the viewer ratings will attract more advertising dollars.

2 Media Basics

2.1 MESSAGE

When a film or TV show is created, it becomes a media product. Each media product is created to send a **message,** or an expression of a belief or opinion, that serves a specific purpose. In order to understand the message, you will need to deconstruct it.

Deconstruction is the process of analyzing a media presentation. To analyze a media presentation you will need to ask why and how it was created, who created it, and whom it is trying to influence.

2.2 AUDIENCE

A **target audience** is the specific group of people that a product or presentation is aimed at. The members of a target audience usually share certain characteristics, such as age, gender, ethnic background, values, or lifestyle. For example, a target audience may be kids ages 11 to 14 who like to eat hamburgers.

Demographics are the characteristics of a population, including age, gender, profession, income, education, ethnicity, and geographical location. Media decision makers use demographics to shape their content to suit the needs and tastes of a target audience.

2.3 PURPOSE

The **purpose,** or intent, of a media presentation is the reason it was made. All media products—from news programs to video games—are created for a specific purpose. Identifying why a media product was invented is the first step in understanding how it can influence you. The following chart shows purposes of different media products.

Purposes of Media Products

Purpose	Example
Inform	news reports and articles, public service announcements, some Web sites
Persuade	advertisements, editorials, reviews, political cartoons
Entertain	most TV shows, films, recorded music; video games; most talk shows

Most media products have more than one purpose. For example, TV commercials are often entertaining, but their main purpose is to persuade you to buy something. If you aren't aware of all of a media products' purposes, you may become influenced without knowing it. This chart shows some examples.

Main and Other Purposes in Media

Media Product	Main Purpose	Other Purposes
Sports coverage	To entertain	To inform you about sports or athletes
Advertisement	To persuade	To entertain you; to inform you about a product
News broadcast	To inform	To persuade you that an issue or idea is important

2.4 TYPES AND GENRES OF MEDIA

The term ***media*** refers to television, newspapers, magazines, radio, movies, and the Internet. Each is a **medium** or means for carrying information, entertainment, and advertisements to a large audience.

Each type of media has different characteristics, strengths, and weaknesses. The following chart shows how several types of media deliver their messages.

Type of Media	Characteristics
Newspaper Article	• Provides detailed information and dramatic photographs • Use **headlines** and **subheads** to give main ideas • Can't be updated until next edition or next day
Television News Report	• Uses an **announcer,** or "anchor," to guide viewers through the news report • Uses **video footage** to bring news to life or clarify what happened • Uses **graphics** to give information at a glance • Can be updated quickly
Documentary	• Tells about historic people and places, major events, and important social, political, or environmental issues • Uses **footage,** or shots of photographs, interviews, news reports, and film clips, to help viewers understand the subject • Features **interviews** of experts or people directly involved with the subject • Uses a **voice-over narrator,** the voice of an unseen speaker, who tells viewers why the subject is important and how the information about the subject is organized
Web Site	• Gives in-depth information on specialized subjects • Uses **text, still images,** and **video** • Allows users to select the information they want to receive by clicking on links • Allows users to see when the site was last updated • Can be updated quickly

For more information, see ***Types of Media****, page 10.*

2.5 PRODUCERS AND CREATORS

People who control the media are known as **gatekeepers.** Gatekeepers decide what information to share with the public and the ways it will be presented. The following diagram gives some examples.

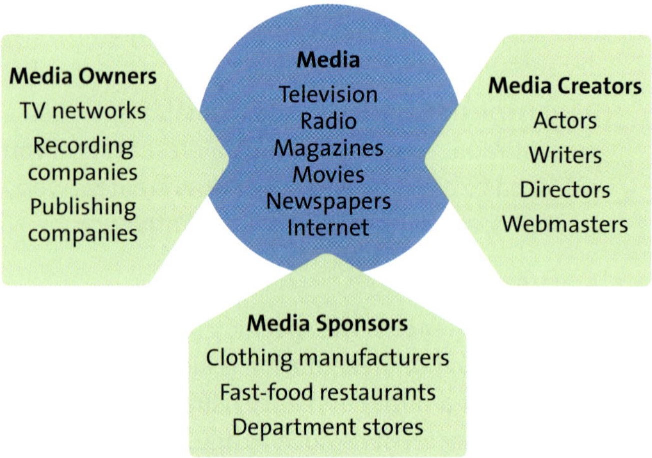

Media sponsors are companies that pay for their products to be advertised. It's important to be aware of sponsors and other gatekeepers, because they control much of what you see and hear. For example, if a soft-drink company sponsors a TV show, you probably won't see or hear about competing brands of soft drinks on that show.

2.6 INFLUENCE OF MEDIA

Everywhere you go, you're bombarded by the media—advertisements, newspapers, magazines, radio, and television. Different kinds of media are all competing for your attention, telling you, "Buy this product. Listen to this music. Read this story. Look at this image. Think about this opinion." The creators of these media products are selling messages. But they may also be sending subtle messages about values that they want you to believe in. For example, a car ad is meant to sell a car, but if you look closer, you will see that it is using a set of values, such as a luxurious lifestyle, to make the car attractive to the target audience. One message of the ad is that if you buy the car, you'll have the luxurious lifestyle. The other message is that the luxurious lifestyle is good and desirable. TV shows, movies, and news programs also convey values and beliefs.

Media can also shape your opinions about the world. For example, news about crime shapes our understanding about how much and what type of crime is prevalent in the world around us. TV news items, talk show interviews, and commercials may shape what we think of a political candidate, a celebrity, an ethnic group, a country, or a regional area. As a result, our knowledge of someone or someplace could be completely based on the information we receive from the television.

3 Film and TV

Films and television programs come in a variety of types. Films include comedies, dramas, documentaries, and animated features. Televison programs cover dramas, sitcoms, talk shows, reality shows, newscasts, and so on. Producers of films and producers of television programs rely on many of the same elements to make the action and settings seem real and to also affect the emotions of their audiences. Among these elements are scripts, visual and sound elements, special effects, and editing.

3.1 SCRIPT AND WRITTEN ELEMENTS

The writer and editor develop a story for television or film using a script and storyboard. A **script** is the text or words of a film or television show. A **storyboard** is a device used to plan the shooting of a movie or TV show. A storyboard is made up of drawings and brief descriptions of what is happening in each shot of a scene. The drawings of a storyboard help a director visualize how a finished scene might look before the scene is filmed. The following storyboard shows some scenes that a student created.

Shot 1
Marty is speeding down the street.

Shot 2
The hand moves on the clock.

For more information, see ***Media Study: Produce Your Own Media,*** *page 153.*

3.2 VISUAL ELEMENTS

Visual elements in film and television include camera shots and angles. A **camera shot** is a single, continuous view taken by a camera. A **camera angle** is the angle at which the camera is positioned during the recording of a shot or image. Each azis carefully planned to create an effect. The chart shows what different shots are used for.

Camera Shot/Angle	Effect
Establishing shot introduces viewers to the location of a scene, usually by presenting a wide view of an area	establishes the setting of a film
Close-up shot shows a close view of a person or object	helps to create emotion and make viewers feel as if they know the character
Medium shot shows a view wider than a close-up but narrower than an establishing or long shot	shows part of an object, or a character from the knees or waist up
Long shot gives a wide view of a scene, showing the full figure(s) of a person or group and the surroundings	allows the viewer to see the "big picture" and shows the relationship between characters and the environment
Reaction shot shows in some way what he or she sees	allows the viewer to see how the subject feels in order to create empathy in the viewer
Low-angle shot looks up at an object or person	makes a character, object, or scene appear more important or threatening
High-angle shot looks down on an object or person	makes a character, object, or scene seem weak or unimportant
Point-of-view (POV) shot shows a part of the story through a character's eyes	helps viewers identify with that character

3.3 SOUND ELEMENTS

Sound elements in film and television include music, voice-over, and sound effects.

Music may be used to set the mood and atmosphere in a scene. Music can have a powerful effect on the way viewers feel about a story. For example, fast-paced music helps viewers feel excited during an action scene.

Voice-over is the voice of the unseen commentator or narrator of a film, TV program, or commercial.

Sound effects are the sounds added to films, TV programs, and commercials during the editing process. Sound effects, such as laugh tracks or the sounds of punches in a fight scene, can create humor, emphasize a point, or contribute to the mood.

3.4 SPECIAL EFFECTS

Special effects include computer-generated animation, manipulated video images, and fast- or slow-motion sequences in films, TV programs, and commercials.

Animation on film involves the frame-by-frame photography of a series of drawings or objects. When these frames are projected—at a rate of 24 per second—the illusion of movement is achieved.

A **split screen** is a special-effects shot in which two or more separate images are shown in the same frame. One example is when two people, actually a distance apart, are shown talking to each other.

3.5 EDITING

Editing is the process of selecting and arranging shots in a sequence. Moviemakers put shots together in ways that help you follow the action of a story. The editor decides which scenes or shots to use, as well as the length of each shot, the number of shots, and their sequence.

Cut is the transition from one shot to another. To create excitement, editors often use quick cuts, which are a series of short shots strung together.

Dissolve is a device in which one scene fades into another.

Fade-in is a device in which a white or black shot fades in to reveal the beginning of a new scene.

Fade-out is a device in which a shot fades to darkness to end a scene.

Jump cut is an abrupt and jarring change from one shot to another. A jump cut shows a break in time.

Pace is the length of time each shot stays on the screen and the rhythm that is created by the transitions between shots. Short, quick cuts create a fast pace in a story. Long cuts slow down a story.

4 News

The **news** is information on events, people, and places in your community, the region, the nation, and the world. It can be found in local newspapers, newscasts, online wire services, magazines, and documentaries. Because it's impossible to publish all the news that happens in one day in any one source, journalists have to make decisions about which stories will appear in newspapers and on newscasts. They use several factors to help them choose stories.

4.1 CHOOSING THE NEWS

Newsworthiness is the importance of an event or action that makes it worthy of media reporting. Journalists and their editors often use the following criteria in determining which stories should make the news:

Timeliness is the quality of being very current. Timely events usually take priority over previously reported events. For example, a car accident with deaths will be timely on the day it occurs. Because of its timeliness it may be on the front page of a newspaper or may be the lead story on a newscast.

Widespread impact is a characteristic of an event that could affect a number of people. The more widespread the impact of an event, the more likely it is to be newsworthy.

Proximity measures the nearness of an event to a particular city, region, or country. People tend to be more interested in stories that take place close to where they live and that thus may affect them directly.

Human interest is a quality of stories that cause readers or listeners to feel emotions such as happiness, anger, or sadness. People are interested in reading stories about other people.

Uniqueness is the condition of being the only one of a kind. Unique or uncommon events or circumstances are likely to be interesting to an audience.

Compelling video and **photographs** grab people's attention and stay in their minds.

4.2 REPORTING THE NEWS

While developing a news story, a journalist makes a variety of decisions about how to construct the story, such as what information to include and how to organize it. The following elements are commonly used in news stories:

5 *W*'s and *H* are the six questions reporters answer when writing news stories—*who, what, when, where, why,* and *how.* It is a journalist's job to answer these questions in any type of news report. These questions also provide a structure for writing and editing a story.

Inverted pyramid is the means of organizing information according to importance. In the inverted-pyramid diagram below, the most important information (the answers to the 5 *W*'s and *H*) appears at the top of the pyramid. The less important details appear at the bottom. Not all stories are reported using the inverted-pyramid form. The form remains popular, however, because it helps a reader to get the important information without reading the entire story. Notice the following example.

Angle or slant is the point of view from which a story is written. Even an objective report must have an angle.

Consider these two headlines that describe the same house fire.

The first headline focuses on a fact. The second headline focuses on an opinion and has a negative slant.

Standards for News Reporting

The ideal of journalism is to present news in a way that is objective, accurate, and thorough. The best news stories contain the following elements:

- **Objectivity** The story takes a balanced point of view on the issues. It is not biased, nor does it reflect a specific attitude or opinion.
- **Accuracy** The story presents factual information that can be verified.
- **Thoroughness** The story presents all sides of an issue. It includes background information, telling *who, what, when, where, why,* and *how.*

Balanced Versus Biased Reporting

Objectivity in news reporting can be measured by how balanced or biased the story is.

Balanced reporting represents all sides of an issue equally and fairly.

A balanced news story

- represents people and subjects in a neutral light
- treats all sides of an issue equally
- does not include inappropriate questions, such as "Will you seek counseling after this terrible tragedy?"

- does not show stereotypes or prejudice toward people of a particular race, gender, age, religion, or other group
- does not leave out important background information that is needed to establish a context or perspective

Biased reporting is reporting in which one side is favored over another or in which the subject is unfairly represented. Biased reporting may show an overly negative view of a subject, or it may encourage racial, gender, or other stereotypes and prejudices. Sometimes biased reporting is apparent in the journalist's choice of sources.

Sources are the people interviewed for the news report and also any written materials and documents the journalist used for background information. From each source, the journalist gets a different point of view. To decide whether news reporting is balanced or biased, you will need to pay attention to the sources. Consider a news story on a new snack food, for instance. If the journalist's only source is a representative from the company that made the snack, the report may be biased. But if the journalist also includes the perspective of someone neutral, such as a scientist who is studying the nutritional value of the snack, the report may be more balanced. The following chart shows which sources are reliable.

Sources for News Stories

Reliable Sources	Weak Sources
• experts in a field • people directly affected by the reported event (eyewitnesses) • published reports that are specifically mentioned or shown	• unnamed or anonymous sources • people who are not involved in the reported event (for example, people who heard about a story from a friend) • research, data, or reports that are not specifically named or are referred to only in vague terms (for example, "Research shows that . . .")

5 Advertising

Advertising is a sponsor's paid use of various media to promote products, services, or ideas. Some common forms of advertising are shown in the chart.

Type of Ad	Description
Billboard	a large outdoor advertising sign
Print ad	typically appears in magazines and newspapers; uses eye-catching graphics and persuasive copy
Flyer	a print ad that is circulated by hand or mail
Infomercial	an extended ad on TV that usually includes detailed product information, demonstrations, and testimonials
Public service announcement	a message aired on radio or TV to promote ideas that are considered to be in the public interest
Political ad	broadcast on radio or TV to promote political candidates
Trailer	a short film promoting an upcoming movie, TV show, or video game

Marketing is the process of transferring products and services from producer to consumer. It involves determining the packaging and pricing of a product, how it will be promoted and advertised, and where it will be sold. One way companies market their products is by becoming media sponsors.

Sponsors pay for their products to be advertised. These companies hire advertising agencies to create and produce specific campaigns for their products. They then buy television or radio airtime or magazine, newspaper, or billboard space to feature ads where the target audience is sure to see them. Because selling time and space to advertisers produces much of the income the media need to function, the media need advertisers just as much as advertisers need the media.

Product placement is the intentional and identifiable featuring of brand-name products in movies, television shows, video games, and other media. The intention is to have viewers feel positive about a product because they see a favorite character using it. Another purpose may be to promote product recognition.

5.1 PERSUASIVE TECHNIQUES

Persuasive techniques are the methods used to convince an audience to buy a product or adopt an idea. Advertisers use a combination of visuals, sound, special effects, and words to persuade their target audience. Recognizing the following techniques can help you evaluate persuasive media messages and identify misleading information:

Emotional appeals use strong feelings, such as fear and pity, rather than facts to persuade consumers. An example is, "Is your home safe? ProAlarm Systems will make sure it is."

Bandwagon appeals use the argument that a person should believe or do something because "everyone else" does. These appeals take advantage of people's desire to be socially accepted by other people. An example of a bandwagon appeal is "More and more people are making the switch to Discountline long-distance service."

Slogans are memorable phrases used in advertising campaigns. Slogans substitute catchy phrases for facts.

Logical appeals rely on logic and facts, appealing to a consumer's reason and his or her respect for authority. Two examples of logical appeals are expert opinions and product comparison.

Celebrity ads use one of the following two categories of spokesperson:

- **Celebrity authorities** are experts in a particular field. Advertisers hope that audiences will transfer the respect or admiration they have for the person to the product. For example, a famous chef may endorse a particular brand of cookware. The manufacturers of the cookware want you to think that it is a good product because a cooking expert wouldn't endorse pots and pans that didn't perform well.
- **Celebrity spokespeople** are famous people who endorse a product. Advertisers hope that audiences will associate the product with the celebrity.

Product comparison is comparing between a product and its competition. Often mentioned by name, the competing product is portrayed as inferior. The intended effect is for people to question the quality of the competing product and to believe the featured product is better.

6 Elements of Design

The design of a media message is just as important as the words are in conveying the message. Like words, visuals are used to persuade, inform, and entertain.

Graphics and images, such as charts, diagrams, maps, timelines, photographs, illustrations, and symbols, present information that can be quickly and easily understood. The following basic elements are used to give meaning to visuals:

Color can be used to highlight important elements such as headlines and subheads. It can also create mood, because many colors have strong emotional or psychological impacts on the reader or viewer. For example, warm colors are often associated with happiness and comfort. Cool colors are often associated with feelings of peace and contentment or sometimes with sadness.

Lines—strokes or marks—can be thick or thin, long or short, and smooth or jagged. They can focus attention and create a feeling of depth. They can frame an object. They can also direct a viewer's eye or create a sense of motion.

Texture is the surface quality or appearance of an object. For example, an object's texture can be rough, wet, or shiny. Texture can be used to create contrast. It can also be used to make an object look "real." For example, a pattern on wrapping paper can create a feeling of depth even though the texture is only visual and cannot be felt.

Shape is the external outline of an object. Shapes can be used to symbolize living things or geometric objects. They can emphasize visual elements and add interest. Shapes can symbolize ideas.

Notice how this movie poster uses design elements.

Lines The reader's eyes are led upward from the main image by the top hat, to the smaller images at the top of the poster.

Color Bright pinks, blues, and yellows suggest that the film may tell a happy story.

Shape The circles at the top of the poster add interest and also help to tell who the other characters in the movie are.

7 Evaluating Media Messages

By looking closely at media products, you can see how their messages influence your opinions and your buying habits. Here are six questions to ask about any media message:

Who made—and who sponsored—this message, and for what purpose? The source of the message is a clue to its purpose. If the source of the message is a private company, that company may be trying to sell you a product. If the source is a government agency, that agency may be trying to promote a program or particular point of view. To discover the purpose, think about why its creator paid for and produced the message.

Who is the target audience and how is the message specifically tailored to it? Think about the age group, ethnic group, gender, and/or profession the message is targeting. Decide how it relates to you.

What are the different techniques used to inform, persuade, entertain, and attract attention? Analyze the elements, such as humor, music, special effects, and graphics, that have been used to create the message. Think about how visual and sound effects, such as symbols, color, photographs, words, and music, support the purpose behind the message.

What messages are communicated (and/or implied) about certain people, places, events, behaviors, lifestyles, and so forth? The media try to influence who we are, what we believe in, how we view things, and what values we hold. Look or listen closely to determine whether certain types of behavior are being depicted and if judgments or values are communicated through those behaviors. What are the biases in the message?

How current, accurate, and believable is the information in this message? Think about the reputation of the source. Note the broadcast or publication date of the message and whether the message might change quickly. If a report or account is not supported by facts, authoritative sources, or eyewitness accounts, you should question the message.

What is left out of this message that might be important to know? Think about what the message is asking you to believe. Also think about what questions come to mind as you watch, read, or listen to the message.

Strategies and Practice for State and Standardized Tests

The test items in this section are modeled after test formats that are used on many state and standardized tests. The strategies presented here will help you prepare for these tests. This section offers general test-taking strategies and tips for answering multiple-choice items, as well as short-response and extended-response questions in critical reading and writing. It also includes guidelines and samples for essay writing. For each test, read the tips in the margin. Then apply the tips to the practice items. You can also apply the tips to Assessment Practice Tests in this book.

1 General Test-Taking Strategies

- Arrive on time and be prepared. Be sure to bring either sharpened pencils with erasers or pens—whichever you are told to bring.
- If you have any questions, ask them before the test begins. Make sure you understand the test procedures, the timing, and the rules.
- Read the test directions carefully. Look at the passages and questions to get an overview of what is expected.
- Tackle the questions one at a time rather than thinking about the whole test.
- Look for main ideas as you read passages. They are often stated at the beginning or the end of a paragraph. Sometimes the main idea is implied.
- Refer back to the reading selections as needed. For example, if a question asks about an author's attitude, you might have to reread a passage for clues.
- If you are not sure of your answer, make a logical guess. You can often arrive at the correct answer by reasoning and eliminating wrong answers.
- As you fill in answers on your answer sheet, make sure you match each test item to its numbered space on the answer sheet.
- Don't look for patterns in the positions of correct choices.
- Only change an answer if you are sure your original choice is incorrect. If you do change an answer, erase your original choice neatly and thoroughly.
- Check your answers and reread your essay.

2 Critical Reading

As you advance through middle school and into high school, you will be exposed to different types of writing, both fiction and nonfiction. You will read novels, persuasive essays, poems, historical documents, and scientific or technical information. Tests will measure your ability to read and analyze these kinds of writings. Test selections can range in length from 100 words to 500 or 600 words.

Directions: Read the selection and then answer the questions on the following page.

SELECTION

On Friday I had my last day at Happy Valley Elementary School. On Saturday the moving truck came and took all our stuff to Hoboken, New Jersey, and we left our house in Happy Valley forever. On Sunday, our first day in the new house, the temperature was one hundred degrees Fahrenheit—the beginning of the hottest heat wave ever recorded in Hoboken in the month of June for 120 years.

One hundred and twenty years ago was when our Hoboken house had been built. This is what my parents did. They gave up a modern house in Happy Valley, New Jersey—a house with a front yard, a backyard, and trees, on a street with similar houses and similar trees—to move to a brick house with no front yard, practically no backyard, and no trees, on a street with guys sitting on the steps and spitting on the sidewalk, and cars and buses running right past our door. And the Hoboken house was in rotten condition and cost three times as much as we got for our Happy Valley house.

My parents said we were going to fix up the house and have an "urban lifestyle." This is what an urban lifestyle is: My bike was stolen the first hour we were in town. And it was one hundred degrees Fahrenheit. My mother said she didn't want me growing up in a suburb. She said life was real in cities. I went upstairs to sit in my crummy 120-year-old room.

My father climbed the stairs to my room. "Egad! It's hot as an oven in here, old pal," he said.

My father says things like "egad" and "odds bodkin." They have no meaning. I simply tolerate these weirdnesses, along with so many things my parents do.

"Sorry about your bike, old man," my father said.

He calls me *old man,* also *old chap.* There is no explanation for this.

"We'll get you another bike, I promise," he said. "But could you possibly wait until your birthday? There are a lot of expenses fixing up the new house."

This was great. I could have a bike for my birthday, instead of some other present, which I would have gotten if I was not to get a bike, which I would not be getting if the one I already had hadn't been stolen, which it probably would not have been if we had not moved to Hoboken, which was not my idea in the first place. . . .

Tips: Reading Text

1. Before you begin reading a passage, skim the questions that follow it to focus your reading.
2. Look for key ideas as you read. Change is a key idea in this passage. It is expressed in the opening lines.
3. Pay attention to the connotation of words. The examples that the narrator uses to define an "urban lifestyle" give the expression a negative connotation.
4. Draw conclusions. The narrator isn't happy with the move, but he tells his father that everything is fine. He probably doesn't want to hurt his father's feelings.

"That will be fine, Dad," I said.

"Good show, old man," my father said. "Now about this room. I don't see how you can stand it. Maybe you'd like us to drag your mattress into our room, where it's nice and cool." [4]

My parents' bedroom had a little dinky air conditioner that puffed air about three degrees cooler than what was outside. It was pathetic.

"I'll be fine here, Dad," I said.

"Good lad. Now do you want to help us scrape paint off the woodwork or just explore around?"

"I think I'll do some exploring," I said.

—from *Looking for Bobowicz*
Daniel Pinkwater

Directions: Answer these questions about the selection from *Looking for Bobowicz.*

[1] stem

1. What can you infer about the narrator from his description of the two houses in lines 8–19?

- **A** He is unhappy about moving.
- **B** He wants to run away.
- **C** He is spoiled.
- **D** He likes city life. [4]

2. Which statement best describes the *theme* of this passage? [2]

- **A** Suburban life is better than city life.
- **B** Parents don't listen to their children.
- **C** Crime is a big part of urban life.
- **D** Change is difficult to accept.

3. In this passage, the narrator and his parents have different feelings about

[3] choices

- **A** household chores
- **B** the benefits of city life
- **C** the importance of honesty
- **D** family finances

4. The summer heat wave in this passage symbolizes the [5]

- **A** danger of the city
- **B** narrator's intense feelings
- **C** run-down house
- **D** father's enthusiasm

Tips: Multiple Choice

A multiple-choice question consists of a stem and a set of choices. The stem is in the form of a question or an incomplete sentence. One of the choices correctly answers the question or completes the sentence. Many tests offer four answer choices, but no matter how many choices are given, you can use the same strategies to guide you to the best answer.

1. Read the stem carefully and try to answer the question before you look at the choices.
2. Pay attention to key words in the stem. They may direct you to the correct answer. Note that question 2 is looking for the *theme,* or main idea, of the passage.
3. Don't jump to conclusions about the correct answer until you've read all of the choices. In question 3, you might decide to stop at choice A, because the narrator does talk about the modern house he moved out of and the 120-year-old house he lives in now, but that is not the correct answer.
4. After reading all of the choices, eliminate any that you know are incorrect. In question 1, you can safely eliminate choice D, because the narrator expresses his strong dislike of city life throughout the passage.
5. Some questions ask you to interpret a symbol.

Answers: **1.** A, **2.** D, **3.** B, **4.** B

3 Vocabulary

Most standardized tests include items that ask about the meanings of words. Some questions might refer to a passage you just read, while others might provide a sentence or paragraph of context followed by the answer choices.

1. Which of the following words from the passage on pages R94–R95 has a negative connotation? ❶

A stuff (line 2)
B modern (line 8)
C egad (line 20)
D dinky (line 37)

2. Which word from the passage comes from the Latin root meaning "city"?

A house (line 3)
B street (line 10)
C sidewalk (line 12)
D urban (line 15) ❷

3. Which line from the passage contains a simile? ❸

A "She said life was real in cities." (lines 18–19)
B "It's hot as an oven in here, old pal" (lines 20–21)
C "Good show, old man" (line 34)
D "It was pathetic." (line 38)

4. Read this dictionary entry for the word *chap*. Which noun definition represents the meaning of *chap* as used in line 25 of the passage?

> **DEFINITION**
>
> *n.* **1.** The roughening of the skin caused especially by cold. **2.** (*Chiefly Brit.*) fellow. **3.** The face.

A *n.* meaning 1
B *n.* meaning 2
C *n.* meaning 3
D *v.* meaning 1 ❹

Tips: Word Meaning

❶ Connotation is the suggestion or feeling a word carries beyond its literal meaning. *Small* is a neutral word. *Compact* is a more positive word for small, but the word *dinky* has a negative connotation.

❷ If you don't know the exact meaning of a word, look for clues in nearby sentences. For the word *urban* in line 15, read the description in the preceding paragraph and ask yourself where you will find houses with small yards and busy streets with buses. *Urban,* choice C, is the best answer to that question. *Urban* means "relating to the city."

❸ A simile is a figure of speech. The words *like* and *as* are clues that a comparison is a simile.

❹ Eliminate any answers that are not the same part of speech as the meaning of the word in the passage. *Chap* is used as a noun in the passsage, so you can rule out answer choice D.

Answers: 1. D, **2.** D, **3.** B, **4.** B

4 Writing and Grammar

You will be asked to write essays and even research papers in middle school. When it comes to writing, good ideas aren't enough. You need to know how to express them. That requires knowledge of English grammar, sentence structure, and usage. To measure that skill, many standardized tests ask you to identify errors or to improve sentences and paragraphs.

Directions: Read this passage and then answer the questions.

PASSAGE

1 (1) On May 1 and October 1 you might see two or three moving trucks on a single city block. (2) These are the busiest moving days of the year. (3) The longest trucks are usually from companies that supply movers and sturdy packing boxes. (4) You have to reserve these trucks weeks in advance. (5) They won't be available. (6) Professional movers use thick pads <u>for furniture protection from scratches</u>. (7) Sometimes people try to save money by renting a truck and moving himself. (8) Their things often get broken because they aren't packed properly.

1. The correct coordinating conjunction to join sentences 4 and 5 is

3
- **A** but
- **B** for
- **C** or
- **D** while

2. What is the best way to rewrite the underlined part of sentence 6?

2
- **A** to protect furniture from scratches
- **B** for scratch protection on furniture
- **C** for the protection of furniture from scratches
- **D** in order to protect from scratches on furniture

4 **3.** What change, if any, should be made to sentence 7?

- **A** Change *try* to *trying*
- **B** Change *renting* to *getting*
- **C** Change *himself* to *themselves*
- **D** Make no change 6

5 **4.** What change, if any, should be made to sentence 8?

- **A** Change *their* to *there*
- **B** Change *broken* to *broke*
- **C** Change *aren't* to *are'nt*
- **D** Make no change 6

Tips: Grammar

1. Read the entire passage to grasp its overall meaning. Pay particular attention to any underlined parts.
2. Before choosing a revision, read through all of the choices to decide which one is best. Your selection should produce a sentence that is grammatically correct.
3. If you are asked to combine sentences, think about how the ideas relate to each other. When you understand the connection between the thoughts, you will know how to join them. The word *but* (choice A) can be used to show how two different ideas are related, but it is not the right word to use to join sentences 4 and 5.
4. Some items will test your knowledge of language conventions. Make sure that pronouns agree with antecedents and that verbs agree with subjects.
5. Some items will also test your knowledge of commonly confused words. In test item 4, choice A is a possible revision. Read sentences carefully to determine how each word is used before deciding which choice is best.
6. In test items 3 and 4, choice D says, "Make no change." Choose this answer only if the sentence is correct as it is originally written.

Answers: 1. C, **2.** A, **3.** C, **4.** D

5 Responding to Writing Prompts

Not all tests are multiple choice. Sometimes you have to develop your ideas into a paragraph or a short essay. You might be asked to interpret, summarize, or react to a reading selection.

Directions: Reread the selection from *Looking for Bobowicz* on pages R94–R95 and follow the directions for the short and extended responses.

SHORT RESPONSE

Write a well-organized paragraph comparing and contrasting the narrator's old and new homes.

SAMPLE SHORT RESPONSE

The narrator's two homes are very different. (1) In Happy Valley he lived on a tree-lined street in a quiet suburb. In Hoboken he lives in a noisy urban neighborhood where bicycles get stolen. The house in Happy Valley was modern and was surrounded by greenery. The house in Hoboken is an old, run-down building surrounded by busy streets. (2) The name Happy Valley suggests a cool, rural locale that is free from the stifling heat and close quarters of Hoboken.

EXTENDED RESPONSE

Discuss in two or three paragraphs what the narrator's mother means when she says life is "real" in cities.

SAMPLE EXTENDED RESPONSE

When the narrator's mother says life is real in cities, she probably means that the city is a reflection of life itself. (3)

Variety is what makes a city real. As you travel through a big city you can hear many languages being spoken, and you can sample foods from different parts of the world. (4) You can rub shoulders with executives on one street and panhandlers on the next. You find people living in penthouses, modest homes, and public housing. You see mosques, churches, and synagogues.

The challenges of urban life are also very real. (3) People in cities, including children, learn to cope with overcrowding, noise, air pollution, traffic, and crime. (5)

Tips: Responding to Writing Prompts

1. Short-response prompts are often fact based rather than interpretive. Get right to the point in your answer, and stick to the facts.
2. Make sure that you write about the assigned topic. Support your answer with details from the passage, such as a quotation, a paraphrase, or an example.
3. When you are writing an extended response, build your paragraphs around clear topic sentences that will pull your ideas together.
4. If you are asked to interpret a passage, don't just copy the author's words. Try to express the ideas in your own words. Express your ideas clearly so that the reader understands your viewpoint.
5. Proofread your response for errors in capitalization, punctuation, spelling, or grammar.

6 Writing an Essay

Many tests will ask you to read a prompt and write an essay in response to it. You might be asked to write a narrative, persuasive, or expository essay. You might be asked to write a story, summarize an article, or respond to a piece of writing. It is important to read the prompt carefully and look for direction words that tell you what to write about. Because of the time constraints, an impromptu essay will not be polished. It will represent a first draft. Even so, it should be complete. Essays are scored on the following criteria:

- **Focus** Establish a point of view in the opening paragraph. Stay with that topic throughout the essay.
- **Organization** Maintain a logical progression of ideas.
- **Support for ideas** Use details and examples to develop an argument or line of thinking.
- **Style/word choice** Use words accurately and vary sentences.
- **Grammar** Use standard English and proofread for errors.

Writing Prompt

In 2004, a bill was introduced to the California legislature that proposed lowering the voting age to 14. Under the "Training Wheels for Citizenship" concept, votes cast by 14- and 15-year-olds would be counted as one-fourth of a full vote, and those cast by 16- and 17-year-olds would be counted as one-half. Write a persuasive essay of four or five paragraphs supporting or rejecting this idea.

SAMPLE PERSUASIVE ESSAY

Lowering the voting age is not a good idea, especially if our votes wouldn't count as full votes. A lot of high school students aren't interested in politics. (1) It seems that many adults aren't either, because less than half of them vote in most elections. Teenagers are focused on getting into college. Events on Capitol Hill seem a long way off. Most of us probably wouldn't vote even if we could. (2)

Voter independence is another issue. I generally listen to my parents, but sometimes they have their ideas and I have mine. If I were allowed to vote, I'm afraid they would try to influence my decision. Voting is supposed to be private, but my mom can always get the truth out of me.

As for counting our votes as fractions of a vote, that is an insult. For teenagers to have an impact on an election, four times as many of us would have to vote. It's almost un-American, because our nation was founded on the idea that everyone's vote has the same weight, whether we are rich or poor.

A lot of political issues affect young people. Most of the people living in poverty, for example, are kids. And of course the government pays more attention to the needs of people who vote. (3) But money also influences government policies, and money is one thing young people don't have.

In conclusion, young people lack the interest, the independence, and the economic power to make a difference in the voting booth. (4)

Tips: Writing an Essay

Before you begin writing, take a minute or two to gather your thoughts. You don't need to prepare a complete outline, but write the main points you want to make. In the essay here on lowering the voting age, the lack of interest, independence, and equality of voters are key issues.

1. When writing a persuasive essay, state your point of view in the introduction.
2. Facts and examples make your writing come to life, no matter what the topic is. Use them in the body of your essay to clarify your points and to strengthen your arguments. The writer of this essay uses statistics to demonstrate voter apathy among adults.
3. Try to consider the opposing point of view and respond to it. In the sample essay, the student notes that "the government pays more attention to the needs of people who vote."
4. Make sure your essay has a conclusion, even if it's just a single sentence. A conclusion pulls your ideas together and lets the reader know you have finished.
5. Allow time to reread what you have written. If you have to make a correction, do so neatly and legibly.

Act An act is a major division within a play, similar to a chapter in a book. Each act may be further divided into smaller sections, called scenes. Plays can have as many as five acts. *The Monsters Are Due on Maple Street* by Rod Serling has two acts.

Adventure Story An adventure story is a literary work in which action is the main element. An **adventure novel** usually focuses on a main character who is on a mission and is facing many challenges and choices.

Alliteration Alliteration is the repetition of consonant sounds at the beginning of words. Note the repetition of the *b* sound in these lines.

> **Crusts of black burned buttered toast,**
> **Gristly bits of beefy roasts . . .**
> **—Shel Silverstein, "Sarah Cynthia Sylvia Stout Would Not Take the Garbage Out"**

See pages 544, 594.

Allusion An allusion is a reference to a famous person, place, event, or work of literature. In the essay "The Only Girl in the World for Me," Bill Cosby makes an allusion to the poet John Keats.
See page 496.

Analogy An analogy is a point-by-point comparison between two things that are alike in some respect. Often, writers use analogies in nonfiction to explain unfamiliar subjects or ideas in terms of familiar ones.
See also **Extended Metaphor; Metaphor; Simile.**

Anecdote An anecdote is a short account of an event that is usually intended to entertain or make a point. In "Names/Nombres," Julia Alvarez uses an anecdote about arriving at the immigration office to show how her name began changing once she entered the United States.
See page 781.

Antagonist The antagonist is a force working against the protagonist, or main character, in a story, play, or novel. The antagonist is usually another character but can be a force of nature, society itself, or an internal force within the main character. In Michael Morpurgo's retelling of "Sir Gawain and the Green Knight," the Green Knight is the antagonist.
See page 671.
See also **Protagonist.**

Assonance Assonance is the repetition of vowel sounds within nonrhyming words. An example of assonance is the repetition of the *i* sound in the following line.

> **is a diamond blind in the black belly of coal**
> **—Lucille Clifton, "the earth is a living thing"**

Author's Perspective An author's perspective is the unique combination of ideas, values, feelings, and beliefs that influences the way the writer looks at a topic. **Tone,** or attitude, often reveals an author's perspective. Peter Benchley writes "Great White Sharks" from a perspective that reflects his fascination with the sea and his regret that his novel *Jaws* caused misconceptions about sharks.
See page 885.
See also **Author's Purpose; Tone.**

Author's Purpose A writer usually writes for one or more of these purposes: to express thoughts or feelings, to inform or explain, to persuade, and to entertain. For example, in his "Remarks at the Dedication of the Aerospace Medical Health Center," President John F. Kennedy's purpose was to persuade Americans that the United States should lead the world in space research.
See also **Author's Perspective.**

Autobiography An autobiography is a writer's account of his or her own life. In almost every case, it is told from the first-person point of view. Generally, an autobiography focuses on the most significant events and people in the writer's life over a period of time. Lance Armstrong's *It's Not About the Bike* is an autobiography.
See pages 8, 754, 792.
See also **Memoir.**

Ballad A ballad is a type of narrative poem that tells a story and was originally meant to be sung or recited. Because it tells a story, a ballad has a setting, a plot, and characters. **Folk ballads** were composed orally and handed down by word of mouth from generation to generation. "The Highwayman" by Alfred Noyes is an example of a **literary ballad,** which takes its form from the folk ballad but is not composed orally.

Biography A biography is the true account of a person's life, written by another person. As such, biographies are usually told from a third-person point of view. The writer of a biography usually researches his or her subject in order to present accurate information. The best biographers strive for honesty and balance in their accounts of their subjects' lives. William Jay Jacobs's "Eleanor Roosevelt" is an example of a biography.

Cast of Characters In the script of a play, a cast of characters is a list of all the characters in the play, usually in order of appearance. It may include a brief description of each character.

Character Characters are the people, animals, or imaginary creatures who take part in the action of a work of literature. Like real people, characters display certain qualities, or **character traits,** that develop and change over time, and they usually have **motivations,** or reasons, for their behaviors.

Main character: Main characters are the most important characters in literary works. Generally, the plot of a short story focuses on one main character, but a novel may have several main characters.

Minor characters: The less important characters in a literary work are known as minor characters. The story is not centered on them, but they help carry out the action of the story and help the reader learn more about the main character.

Dynamic character: A dynamic character is one who undergoes important changes as a plot unfolds. The changes occur because of the character's actions and experiences in the story. The changes are usually internal and may be good or bad. Main characters are usually, though not always, dynamic.

Static character: A static character is one who remains the same throughout a story. The character may experience events and have interactions with other characters, but he or she is not changed because of them.

See pages 5, 24, 176, 183.
See also **Characterization; Character Traits.**

Characterization The way a writer creates and develops characters is known as characterization. There are four basic methods of characterization:

- The writer may make direct comments about a character through the voice of the narrator.
- The writer may describe the character's physical appearance.
- The writer may present the character's own thoughts, speech, and actions.
- The writer may present thoughts, speech, and actions of other characters.

See pages 178, 241, 255, 259.
See also **Character; Character Traits.**

Character Traits Character traits are the qualities shown by a character. Traits may be physical (brown eyes) or expressions of personality (shyness). Writers reveal the traits of their characters through methods of characterization. Sometimes writers directly state a character's traits, but more often readers need to infer traits from a character's words, actions, thoughts, appearance, and relationships. Examples of words that describe traits include *courageous, humble, generous,* and *wild.*

Climax The climax stage is the point of greatest interest in a story or play. The climax usually occurs toward the end of a story, after the reader has understood the **conflict** and become emotionally involved with the characters. At the climax, the conflict is resolved and the outcome of the plot usually becomes clear.

See pages 26, 574.
See also **Plot.**

Comedy A comedy is a dramatic work that is light and often humorous in tone, usually ending happily with a peaceful resolution of the main conflict.

Conflict A conflict is a struggle between opposing forces. Almost every story has a main conflict—a conflict that is the story's focus. An **external conflict** involves a character who struggles against a force outside him- or herself, such as nature, a physical obstacle, or another character. An **internal conflict** is one that occurs within a character.

Examples: In Rudyard Kipling's "Rikki-tikki-tavi," the mongoose Rikki is in conflict with the cobras Nag and Nagaina. In Robert D. San Souci's retelling of *Young Arthur,* Arthur is torn between wanting to escape punishment when he thinks he has stolen the king's sword and wanting to accept responsibility as a true knight should.

See pages 5, 24, 63, 74, 661.
See also **Plot.**

Connotation A word's connotations are the ideas and feelings associated with the word, as opposed to its dictionary definition. For example, the word *mother,* in addition to its basic meaning ("a female parent"), has connotations of love, warmth, and security.

Couplet A couplet is a rhymed pair of lines. A couplet may be written in any rhythmic pattern.

> **Masons, when they start upon a building,**
> **Are careful to test out the scaffolding;**
> **—Seamus Heaney, "Scaffolding"**

See also **Stanza.**

Critical Essay *See* **Essay.**

Denotation A word's denotation is its dictionary definition.

See also **Connotation.**

Description Description is writing that helps a reader to picture events, objects, and characters. To create descriptions, writers often use **imagery**—words and phrases that appeal to the reader's senses.

Dialect A dialect is a form of a language that is spoken in a particular place or by a particular group of people. Dialects may feature unique pronunciations, vocabulary, and grammar. For example, when Antonio and Felix speak to each other in Piri Thomas's story "Amigo Brothers," they use dialect that reflects their Puerto Rican community in New York. Their dialect includes informal grammar and slang words drawn from both American Spanish and English.

> **"Same here. It ain't natural not to think about the fight. I mean, we both are *cheverote* fighters, and we both want to win."**

Dialogue Dialogue is written conversation between two or more characters. Writers use dialogue to bring characters to life and to give readers insights into the characters' qualities, traits, and reactions to other characters. In fiction, dialogue is usually set off with quotation marks. In drama, stories are told primarily through dialogue.

Diary A diary is a daily record of a writer's thoughts, experiences, and feelings. As such, it is a type of autobiographical writing. The terms *diary* and *journal* are often used synonymously.

Drama A drama, or play, is a form of literature meant to be performed by actors in front of an audience. In a drama, the characters' dialogue and actions tell the story. The written form of a play is known as a script. A script usually includes dialogue, a cast of characters, and stage directions that give instructions about performing the drama. The person who writes the drama is known as the playwright or dramatist.

Dynamic Character *See* **Character.**

Epic Poem An epic poem is a long narrative poem about the adventures of a hero whose actions reflect the ideals and values of a nation or a group of people.

Essay An essay is a short work of nonfiction that deals with a single subject. There are many types of essays. An **expository essay** presents or explains information and ideas. A **personal essay** usually reflects the writer's experiences, feelings, and personality. A **persuasive essay** attempts to convince the reader to adopt a certain viewpoint. A **critical essay** evaluates a situation or a work of art.

See pages 8, 494, 757.

Exaggeration An extreme overstatement of an idea is called an exaggeration. It is often used for purposes of emphasis or humor. In "Sally Ann Thunder Ann Whirlwind," Mary Pope Osborne exaggerates Sally's size, strength, and cleverness to create a humorous, memorable impression of the character.

Exposition Exposition is the first stage of a typical story plot. The exposition provides important background information and introduces the setting and the important characters. The conflict the characters face may also be introduced in the exposition, or it may be introduced later, in the rising action.

See pages 26, 31.

See also **Plot.**

Expository Essay *See* **Essay.**

Extended Metaphor An extended metaphor is a figure of speech that compares two essentially unlike things at some length and in several ways. It does not contain the word *like* or *as*.

See also **Metaphor.**

External Conflict *See* **Conflict.**

Fable A fable is a brief tale told to illustrate a moral or teach a lesson. Often the moral of a fable appears in a distinct and memorable statement near the tale's beginning or end. "The Race Between Toad and Donkey" by Roger D. Abrahams is an example of a fable from Jamaica.

See also **Moral.**

Falling Action The falling action is the stage of the plot in which the story begins to draw to a close. The falling action comes after the climax and before the resolution. Events in the falling action show the results of the important decision or action that happened at the climax. Tension eases as the falling action begins; however, the final outcome of the story is not yet fully worked out at this stage.

See page 26.

See also **Climax; Plot.**

Fantasy Fantasy is a type of fiction that is highly imaginative and portrays events, settings, or characters that are unrealistic. The setting might be a nonexistent world, the plot might involve magic or the supernatural, and the characters might have superhuman powers.

Farce Farce is a type of exaggerated comedy that features an absurd plot, ridiculous situations, and humorous dialogue. The main purpose of a farce is to keep an audience laughing. Comic devices typically used in farces include mistaken identity, wordplay (such as puns and double meanings), and exaggeration.

Fiction Fiction is prose writing that tells an imaginary story. The writer of a fictional work might invent all the events and characters or might base parts of the story on real people and events. The basic elements of fiction are plot, character, setting, and theme. Fiction includes both short stories and novels.

See also **Novel; Short Story.**

Figurative Language In figurative language, words are used in an imaginative way to express ideas that are not literally true. "Tasha's money is burning a hole in her pocket" is an example of figurative language. The sentence does not really mean that Tasha's pocket is on fire. Instead, it means that Tasha is anxious to spend her money. Figurative language is used for comparison, emphasis, and emotional effect.

See pages 546, 555, 601.

See also **Metaphor; Onomatopoeia; Personification; Simile.**

First-Person Point of View *See* **Point of View.**

Flashback In a literary work, a flashback is an interruption of the action to present events that took place at an earlier time. A flashback provides information that can help a reader better understand a character's current situation.

Example: In "The Last Dog," Katherine Paterson uses flashback to explain how Brock became interested in the "ancient fictions" and the world outside the dome.

Foil A foil is a character who provides a striking contrast to another character. By using a foil, a writer can call attention to certain traits possessed by a main character or simply enhance a character by contrast. In Avi's "What Do Fish Have to Do with Anything?" the mother acts as a foil to the main character, Willie.

Folklore The traditions, customs, and stories that are passed down within a culture are known as its folklore. Folklore includes various types of literature, such as legends, folk tales, myths, trickster tales, and fables.

See **Fable; Folk Tale; Myth.**

Folk Tale A folk tale is a story that has been passed from generation to generation by word of mouth. Folk tales may be set in the distant past and involve supernatural events. The characters in them may be animals, people, or superhuman beings. "Waters of Gold" is an example of a folk tale.

Foreshadowing Foreshadowing occurs when a writer provides hints that suggest future events in a story. Foreshadowing creates suspense and makes readers eager to find out what will happen. For example, in the myth "Icarus and Daedalus," Daedalus' warnings about flying close to the sun hint at Icarus' fate.

Form The structure or organization of a work of writing is often called its form. The form of a poem includes the arrangement of its words and lines on the page.

Free Verse Poetry without regular patterns of rhyme and rhythm is called free verse. Some poets use free verse to capture the sounds and rhythms of ordinary speech. The poem "The Names" by Billy Collins is written in free verse.

> **Yesterday, I lay awake in the palm of the night.**
> **A soft rain stole in, unhelped by any breeze,**
> **And when I saw the silver glaze on the windows,**
> **I started with A, with Ackerman, as it happened,**
> **Then Baxter and Calabro, . . .**
>
> **—Billy Collins, "The Names"**

See pages 542, 549.

See also **Rhyme.**

Genre The term *genre* refers to a category in which a work of literature is classified. The major genres in literature are fiction, nonfiction, poetry, and drama.

Haiku Haiku is a form of Japanese poetry in which 17 syllables are arranged in three lines of 5, 7, and 5 syllables. The rules of haiku are strict. In addition to following the syllabic count, the poet must create a clear picture that will evoke a strong emotional response in the reader. Nature is a particularly important source of inspiration for Japanese haiku poets, and details from nature are often the subjects of their poems.

> **On sweet plum blossoms**
> **The sun rises suddenly.**
> **Look, a mountain path!**
>
> **—Bashō**

Hero A hero is a main character or protagonist in a story. In older literary works, heroes tend to be better than ordinary humans. They are typically courageous, strong, honorable, and intelligent. They are protectors of society who hold back the forces of evil and fight to make the world a better place. In modern literature, a hero may simply be the most important character in a story. Such a hero is often an ordinary person with ordinary problems.

Historical Dramas Historical dramas are plays that take place in the past and are based on real events. In many of these plays, the characters are also based on real historical figures. The dialogue and the action, however, are mostly created by the playwright.

Historical Fiction A short story or a novel can be called historical fiction when it is set in the past and includes real places and real events of historical importance. The novel *Crispin: The Cross of Lead* by Avi is an example of historical fiction.

See page 686.

Humor Humor is a quality that provokes laughter or amusement. Writers create humor through exaggeration, amusing descriptions, irony, and witty and insightful dialogue. In his essay "The Only Girl in the World for Me," Bill Cosby uses humor to tell the story of the absurd things he did to impress his first girlfriend.

See pages 496, 593.

Hyperbole Hyperbole is a figure of speech in which the truth is exaggerated for emphasis or humorous effect.

Idiom An idiom is an expression that has a meaning different from the meaning of its individual words. For example, "to go to the dogs" is an idiom meaning "to go to ruin."

Imagery Imagery consists of words and phrases that appeal to a reader's five senses. Writers use sensory details to help the reader imagine how things look, feel, smell, sound, and taste.

> **When the sun paints the desert**
> **with its gold,**
> **I climb the hills.**
> **Wind runs round boulders, ruffles**
> **my hair. . . .**
>
> **—Pat Mora, "Gold"**

See pages 546, 549, 559.

Internal Conflict *See* **Conflict.**

Interview An interview is a conversation conducted by a writer or reporter, in which facts or statements are elicited from another person, recorded, and then broadcast or published. This book includes an interview with Ray Bradbury.

See page 462.

Irony Irony is a contrast between what is expected and what actually exists or happens. The last line of Dorothy Parker's "Song for an April Dusk," which changes the meaning of the poem, is an example of irony.

See page 509.

Journal *See* **Diary.**

Legend A legend is a story handed down from the past about a specific person, usually someone of heroic accomplishments. Legends usually have some basis in historical fact. *Young Arthur* by Robert D. San Souci is an example of a legend.

Limerick A limerick is a short, humorous poem composed of five lines. It usually has the rhyme scheme *aabba,* created by two rhyming couplets followed by a fifth line that rhymes with the first couplet. A limerick typically has a sing-song rhythm.

> **There was an old man with a light,** *a*
> **Who was dressed in a garment of white;** *a*
> **He held a small candle,** *b*
> **With never a handle,** *b*
> **And danced all the merry long night.** *a*
>
> **—Edward Lear**

Lyric Poetry Lyric poetry is poetry that presents the personal thoughts and feelings of a single speaker. Most poems, other than narrative poems, are lyric poems. Lyric poetry can be in a variety of forms and cover many subjects, from love and death to everyday experiences. Mary Oliver's "Sleeping in the Forest" is an example of a lyric poem.

Memoir A memoir is a form of autobiographical writing in which a writer shares his or her personal experiences and observations of significant events or people. Often informal or even intimate in tone, memoirs usually give readers insight into the impact of historical events on people's lives. *An American Childhood* by Annie Dillard is a memoir.

See page 119.

See also **Autobiography.**

Metaphor A metaphor is a comparison of two things that are basically unlike but have some qualities in common. Unlike a simile, a metaphor does not contain the word *like* or *as.* In "The Delight Song of Tsoai-Talee," the speaker of the poem compares himself to different things in nature, including "a feather on the bright sky" and "the hunger of a young wolf."

See pages 546, 601.

See also **Extended Metaphor; Figurative Language; Simile.**

Meter In poetry, meter is the regular pattern of stressed (´) and unstressed (˘) syllables. Although poems have rhythm, not all poems have regular meter. Each unit of meter is known as a **foot** and is made up of one stressed syllable and one or two unstressed syllables. Notice the meter marked in the following lines.

> The wind was a torrent of darkness among the gusty
> trees.
> The moon was a ghostly galleon tossed upon cloudy
> seas.
>
> —Alfred Noyes, "The Highwayman"

See pages 544, 571.

See also **Rhythm.**

Minor Character *See* **Character.**

Mood Mood is the feeling or atmosphere that a writer creates for the reader. Descriptive words, imagery, and figurative language all influence the mood of a work. In "Dark They Were, and Golden-Eyed," Ray Bradbury creates a mood of fearfulness and dread.

See pages 438, 445, 601.

See also **Tone.**

Moral A moral is a lesson that a story teaches. A moral is often stated at the end of a fable. For example, the stated moral of the Liberian fable "Two Ways to Count to Ten" is "It is not always the biggest nor the strongest, but sometimes the cleverest who wins the prize."

See also **Fable.**

Motivation *See* **Character.**

Myth A myth is a traditional story that attempts to answer basic questions about human nature, origins of the world, mysteries of nature, and social customs. For example, "Prometheus" is a Greek myth that explains how humans received the gift of fire.

Narrative Nonfiction Narrative nonfiction is writing that reads much like fiction, except that the characters, setting, and plot are real rather than imaginary. Narrative nonfiction includes autobiographies, biographies, and memoirs. *Exploring the Titanic* by Robert D. Ballard is an example of narrative nonfiction.

Narrative Poetry Poetry that tells a story is called narrative poetry. Like fiction, a narrative poem contains characters, a setting, and a plot. It might also contain such elements of poetry as rhyme, rhythm, imagery, and figurative language. Ernest Lawrence Thayer's "Casey at the Bat" is a narrative poem.

Narrator The narrator is the voice that tells a story. Sometimes the narrator is a character in the story. At other times, the narrator is an outside voice created by the writer. The narrator is not the same as the writer.

An **unreliable narrator** is one who tells a story or interprets events in a way that makes readers doubt what he or she is saying. An unreliable narrator is usually a character in the story. The narrator may be unreliable for a number of different reasons. For example, the narrator may not have all the facts or may be too young to understand the situation.

See also **Point of View.**

Nonfiction Nonfiction is writing that tells about real people, places, and events. Unlike fiction, nonfiction is mainly written to convey factual information. Nonfiction includes a wide range of writing—newspaper articles, letters, essays, biographies, movie reviews, speeches, true-life adventure stories, advertising, and more.

Novel A novel is a long work of fiction. Like a short story, a novel is the product of a writer's imagination. Because a novel is considerably longer than a short story, a novelist can develop the characters and story line more thoroughly.

See also **Fiction.**

Ode An ode is a type of lyric poem that deals with serious themes, such as justice, truth, or beauty.

Onomatopoeia Onomatopoeia is the use of words whose sounds echo their meanings, such as *buzz, whisper, gargle,* and *murmur.* In "Amigo Brothers," the word *bong* is used to indicate the bell sounding at the beginning and end of each round of the boxing match.

> *Bong! Bong! Bong!* The bell sounded over and over again.
> —Piri Thomas, "Amigo Brothers"

Oral Literature Oral literature consists of stories that have been passed down by word of mouth from generation to generation. Oral literature includes folk tales, legends, and myths. In more recent times, some examples of oral literature have been written down or recorded so that the stories can be preserved.

Personal Essay *See* **Essay.**

Personification The giving of human qualities to an animal, object, or idea is known as personification. In "Rikki-tikki-tavi," for example, the animals are personified. They have conversations with each other as if they were human.

> "Don't kill me," said Chuchundra, almost weeping. "Rikki-tikki, don't kill me!"
> "Do you think a snake killer kills muskrats?" said Rikki-tikki scornfully.
> —Rudyard Kipling, "Rikki-tikki-tavi"

See pages 74, 546.

See also **Figurative Language.**

Persuasive Essay *See* **Essay.**

Play *See* **Drama.**

Playwright *See* **Drama.**

Plot The series of events in a story is called the plot. The plot usually centers on a **conflict,** or struggle, faced by the main character. The action that the characters take to solve the problem builds toward a climax in the story. At this point, or shortly afterward, the problem is solved and the story ends. Most story plots have five stages: exposition, rising action, climax, falling action, and resolution.

See pages 5, 26, 31.

See also **Climax; Exposition; Falling Action; Rising Action.**

Poetry Poetry is a type of literature in which words are carefully chosen and arranged to create certain effects. Poets use a variety of sound devices, imagery, and figurative language to express emotions and ideas.

See also **Alliteration; Assonance; Ballad; Free Verse; Imagery; Meter; Narrative Poetry; Rhyme; Rhythm; Stanza.**

Point of View Point of view refers to how a writer chooses to narrate a story. When a story is told from the **first-person** point of view, the narrator is a character in the story and uses first-person pronouns, such as *I, me,* and *we.* In a story told from the **third-person** point of view, the narrator is not a character. Third-person narration makes use of pronouns such as *he, she, it,* and *they.* A writer's choice of narrator affects the information readers receive.

It is also important to consider whether a writer is writing from a **subjective** or an **objective** point of view. When writing from a subjective point of view, the writer includes personal opinions, feelings, and beliefs. When writing from an objective point of view, the writer leaves out personal opinions and instead presents information in a straightforward, unbiased way.

See pages 176, 217, 227.

See also **Narrator.**

Prop The word *prop,* originally an abbreviation of the word *property,* refers to any physical object that is used in a drama. In the play based on Charles Dickens's *A Christmas Carol,* the props include a turkey and a dove.

Prose The word *prose* refers to all forms of writing that are not in verse form. The term may be used to describe very different forms of writing—short stories as well as essays, for example.

Protagonist A protagonist is the main character in a story, play, or novel. The protagonist is involved in the main conflict of the story. Usually, the protagonist undergoes changes as the plot runs its course. In "A Retrieved Reformation" by O. Henry, Jimmy Valentine is the protagonist.

Radio Play A radio play is a drama that is written specifically to be broadcast over the radio. Because the audience is not meant to see a radio play, sound effects are often used to help listeners imagine the setting and the action. The stage directions in the play's script indicate the sound effects.

Recurring Theme *See* **Theme.**

Refrain A refrain is one or more lines repeated in each stanza of a poem.

See also **Stanza.**

Repetition Repetition is a technique in which a sound, word, phrase, or line is repeated for emphasis or unity. Repetition often helps to reinforce meaning and create an appealing rhythm. Note how the use of repetition in the following lines emphasizes the rhythm of battle.

> **Cannon to right of them,**
> **Cannon to left of them,**
> **Cannon in front of them**
> **—Alfred, Lord Tennyson, "The Charge of the Light Brigade"**

See page 129.

See also **Alliteration; Sound Devices.**

Resolution *See* **Falling Action.**

Rhyme Rhyme is the repetition of sounds at the end of words. Words rhyme when their accented vowels and the letters that follow have identical sounds. *Cat* and *hat* rhyme, as do *feather* and *leather.* The most common type of rhyme in poetry is called **end rhyme,** in which rhyming words come at the ends of lines. Rhyme that occurs within a line of poetry is called **internal rhyme.** The following lines include examples of end rhyme.

> **'Twas brillig, and the slithy toves**
> **Did gyre and gimble in the wabe:**
> **All mimsy were the borogroves,**
> **And the mome raths outgrabe.**
> **—Lewis Carroll, "Jabberwocky"**

See pages 129, 544, 571, 592.

Rhyme Scheme A rhyme scheme is a pattern of end rhymes in a poem. A rhyme scheme is noted by assigning a letter of the alphabet, beginning with *a,* to each line. Lines that rhyme are given the same letter.

> **It was many and many a year ago,** *a*
> **In a kingdom by the sea,** *b*
> **That a maiden there lived whom you may know** *a*
> **By the name of Annabel Lee;** *b*
> **—Edgar Allan Poe, "Annabel Lee"**

See pages 563, 567.

Rhythm Rhythm is a pattern of stressed and unstressed syllables in a line of poetry. Poets use rhythm to bring out the musical quality of language, to emphasize ideas, and to create moods. Devices such as alliteration, rhyme, assonance, and consonance often contribute to creating rhythm.

See pages 129, 544.

See also **Meter.**

Rising Action The rising action is the stage of the plot that develops the **conflict,** or struggle. During this stage, events occur that make the conflict more complicated. The events in the rising action build toward a **climax,** or turning point.

See page 26.

See also **Plot.**

Scene In drama, the action is often divided into acts and scenes. Each scene presents an episode of the play's plot and typically occurs at a single place and time.

See also **Act.**

Scenery Scenery is a painted backdrop or other structures used to create the setting for a play.

Science Fiction Science fiction is fiction in which a writer explores unexpected possibilities of the past or the future, using known scientific data and theories as well as his or her creative imagination. Most science fiction writers create believable worlds, although some create fantasy worlds that have familiar elements. Ray Bradbury, the author of "Dark They Were, and Golden-Eyed," is a famous writer of science fiction.

See also **Fantasy.**

Screenplay A screenplay is a play written for film.

Script The text of a play, film, or broadcast is called a script.

Sensory Details Sensory details are words and phrases that appeal to the reader's senses of sight, hearing, touch, smell, and taste. Note the sensory details in the following line. These details appeal to the senses of touch and smell.

> **There was a cool breeze blowing and a sweet smell of mesquite fruit in the air, but I didn't appreciate it.**
> **—Marta Salinas, "The Scholarship Jacket"**

See also **Imagery.**

Setting The setting of a story, poem, or play is the time and place of the action. Sometimes the setting is clear and well-defined. At other times, it is left to the reader's imagination. Elements of setting include geographic location, historical period (past, present, or future), season, time of day, and culture.

See pages 5, 24, 43.

Short Story A short story is a work of fiction that centers on a single idea and can be read in one sitting. Generally, a short story has one main conflict that involves the characters and keeps the story moving.

See also **Fiction.**

Simile A simile is a figure of speech that makes a comparison between two unlike things using the word *like* or *as.*

> **The fingers were all there, but <u>like dead leaves that never fell</u>, the ring and little fingers were rigid and curled, the others barely moved.**
>
> **—Chaim Potok, "Zebra"**

See pages 184, 546.

See also **Figurative Language; Metaphor.**

Sonnet A sonnet is a poem that has a formal structure, containing 14 lines and a specific rhyme scheme and meter. The sonnet, which means "little song," can be used for a variety of topics.

See also **Rhyme Scheme.**

Sound Devices Sound devices are ways of using words for the sound qualities they create. Sound devices can help convey meaning and mood in a writer's work. Some common sound devices include **alliteration, assonance, meter, onomatopoeia, repetition, rhyme,** and **rhythm.**

See pages 544, 563, 593.

See also **Alliteration; Assonance; Meter; Onomatopoeia; Repetition; Rhyme; Rhythm.**

Speaker In poetry the speaker is the voice that "talks" to the reader, similar to the narrator in fiction. The speaker is not necessarily the poet. For example, in Carl Sandburg's "Washington Monument by Night," the experiences described may or may not have happened to the poet.

See pages 509, 542, 563, 845.

Speech A speech is a talk or public address. The purpose of a speech may be to entertain, to explain, to persuade, to inspire, or any combination of these purposes. President John F. Kennedy's speech "Remarks at the Dedication of the Aerospace Medical Health Center" was written and delivered in order to persuade his audience.

See pages 8, 937.

Stage Directions In the script of a play, the instructions to the actors, director, and stage crew are called the stage directions. Stage directions might suggest scenery, lighting, sound effects, and ways for actors to move and speak. Stage directions often appear in parentheses and in italic type.

> (*As soon as* Scrooge *shouts, the* girl *and the* carolers *vanish and* Cratchit *begins to close up the shop.*)
>
> —Frederick Gaines, *A Christmas Carol*

See pages 7, 387.

Stanza A stanza is a group of two or more lines that form a unit in a poem. Each stanza may have the same number of lines, or the number of lines may vary.

See also **Couplet; Form; Poetry.**

Static Character *See* **Character.**

Stereotype In literature, characters who are defined by a single trait are known as stereotypes. Such characters do not usually demonstrate the complexities of real people. Familiar stereotypes in popular literature include the absent-minded professor and the busybody.

Structure The structure of a work of literature is the way in which it is put together. In poetry, structure involves the arrangement of words and lines to produce a desired effect. One structural unit in poetry is the stanza. In prose, structure involves the arrangement of such elements as sentences, paragraphs, and events. "Dark They Were, and Golden-Eyed," for example, has a circular structure, in which the end mirrors the beginning.

Style A style is a manner of writing. It involves how something is said rather than what is said. For example, "A Day's Wait" by Ernest Hemingway is written in a style that makes use of vivid verbs, precise nouns, long descriptive sentences, and realistic dialogue.

Surprise Ending A surprise ending is an unexpected plot twist at the end of a story. The surprise may be a sudden turn in the action or a piece of information that gives a different perspective to the entire story. The short story writer O. Henry is famous for using this device.

See page 228.

Suspense Suspense is a feeling of growing tension and excitement felt by a reader. Suspense makes a reader curious about the outcome of a story or an event within a story. A writer creates suspense by raising questions in the reader's mind. The use of **foreshadowing** is one way that writers create suspense.

See pages 73, 89, 99.

See also **Foreshadowing.**

Symbol A symbol is a person, a place, an object, or an activity that stands for something beyond itself. For example, a flag is a colored piece of cloth that stands for a country. A white dove is a bird that represents peace.

Example: In "What Do Fish Have to Do with Anything?" by Avi, money represents happiness, opportunity, and freedom to Willie's mother.

See pages 339, 583.

Tall Tale A tall tale is a humorously exaggerated story about impossible events, often involving the supernatural abilities of the main character. Stories about folk heroes such as Pecos Bill and Paul Bunyan are typical tall tales.

Teleplay A teleplay is a play written for television. In a teleplay, scenes can change quickly and dramatically. The camera can focus the viewer's attention on specific actions. The camera directions in teleplays are much like the stage directions in stage plays.

See page 135.

Theme A theme is a message about life or human nature that the writer shares with the reader. In many cases, readers must infer what the writer's message is. One way of figuring out a theme is to apply the lessons learned by the main characters to people in real life. For example, a theme of "A Crush" by Cynthia Rylant is that simple acts of kindness can make a positive difference in people's lives.

Recurring themes are themes found in a variety of works. For example, authors from different backgrounds might express similar themes having to do with the importance of family values. **Universal themes** are themes that are found throughout the literature of all time periods. For example, *The Lord of the Rings* contains a universal theme relating to the hero's search for truth, goodness, and honor.

See pages 5, 304, 327, 364.

See also **Moral.**

Third-Person Point of View *See* **Point of View.**

Title The title of a piece of writing is the name that is attached to it. A title often refers to an important aspect of the work. For example, the title "The War of the Wall" refers to Lou and the narrator's conflict with the "painter lady."

Tone The tone of a literary work expresses the writer's attitude toward his or her subject. Words such as *angry, sad,* and *humorous* can be used to describe different tones. For example, the tone of Dave Barry's essay "Breaking the Ice" is humorous.

See pages 438, 495.

See also **Author's Perspective; Mood.**

Tragedy A tragedy is a dramatic work that presents the downfall of a dignified character or characters who are involved in historically or socially significant events. The events in a tragic plot are set in motion by a decision that is often an error in judgment on the part of the hero. Succeeding events are linked in a cause-and-effect relationship and lead inevitably to a disastrous conclusion, usually death. William Shakespeare's *Romeo and Juliet* is a famous tragedy.

Traits *See* **Character.**

Turning Point *See* **Climax.**

Understatement Understatement is a technique of creating emphasis by saying less than is actually or literally true. It is the opposite of **hyperbole,** or exaggeration. Understatement is often used to create a humorous effect.

Universal Theme *See* **Theme.**

Unreliable Narrator *See* **Narrator.**

Voice The term *voice* refers to a writer's unique use of language that allows a reader to "hear" a human personality in the writer's work. Elements of style that contribute to a writer's voice can reveal much about the author's personality, beliefs, and attitudes.

See page 18.

Word Choice The success of any writing depends on the writer's choice of words. Words not only communicate ideas but also help describe events, characters, settings, and so on. Word choice can make a writer's work sound formal or informal, serious or humorous. A writer must choose words carefully depending on the goal of the piece of writing. For example, a writer working on a science article would probably use technical, formal words; a writer trying to establish the setting in a short story would probably use more descriptive words.

See also **Style.**

Glossary of Reading and Informational Terms

Almanac *See* **Reference Works.**

Analogy An analogy is a comparison between two things that are alike in some way. Often, writers use analogies in nonfiction to explain an unfamiliar subject or idea by showing how it is like a familiar one.

Argument An argument is speaking or writing that expresses a position on a problem and supports it with reasons and evidence. An argument often takes into account other points of view, anticipating and answering objections that opponents might raise.
See also **Claim; Counterargument; Evidence.**

Assumption An assumption is an opinion or belief that is taken for granted. It can be about a specific situation, a person, or the world in general. Assumptions are often unstated.

Author's Message An author's message is the main idea or theme of a particular work.
See also **Main Idea; Theme,** *Glossary of Literary Terms, page R109.*

Author's Perspective *See Glossary of Literary Terms, page R100.*

Author's Position An author's position is his or her opinion on an issue or topic.
See also **Claim.**

Author's Purpose *See Glossary of Literary Terms, page R100.*

Autobiography *See Glossary of Literary Terms, page R100.*

Bias In a piece of writing, the author's bias is the side of an issue that he or she favors. Words with extremely positive or negative connotations are often a signal of an author's bias.

Bibliography A bibliography is a list of related books and other materials used to write a text. Bibliographies can be good sources for further study on a subject.
See also **Works Consulted.**

Biography *See Glossary of Literary Terms, page R100.*

Business Correspondence Business correspondence is written business communications such as business letters, e-mails, and memos. In general, business correspondence is brief, to the point, clear, courteous, and professional.

Cause and Effect Two events are related by cause and effect when one event brings about, or causes, the other. The event that happens first is the **cause;** the one that follows is the **effect.** Cause and effect is also a way of organizing an entire piece of writing. It helps writers show the relationships between events or ideas.
See also **False Cause,** *Reading Handbook, page R24.*

Chronological Order Chronological order is the arrangement of events by their order of occurrence. This type of organization is used in fictional narratives and in historical writing, biography, and autobiography.

Claim In an argument, a claim is the writer's position on an issue or problem. Although an argument focuses on supporting one claim, a writer may make more than one claim in a text.

Clarify Clarifying is a reading strategy that helps readers understand or make clear what they are reading. Readers usually clarify by rereading, reading aloud, or discussing.

Classification Classification is a pattern of organization in which objects, ideas, and/or information are presented in groups, or classes, based on common characteristics.

Cliché A cliché is an overused expression. "Better late than never" and "hard as nails" are common examples. Good writers generally avoid clichés unless they are using them in dialogue to indicate something about a character's personality.

Compare and Contrast To compare and contrast is to identify the similarities and differences of two or more subjects. Compare and contrast is also a pattern of organizing an entire piece of writing.

Conclusion A conclusion is a statement of belief based on evidence, experience, and reasoning. A valid conclusion is one that logically follows from the facts or statements upon which it is based.

Connect Connecting is a reader's process of relating the content of a text to his or her own knowledge and experience.

Consumer Documents Consumer documents are printed materials that accompany products and services. They usually provide information about the use, care, operation, or assembly of the product or service they accompany. Some common consumer documents are applications, contracts, warranties, manuals, instructions, labels, brochures, and schedules.

Context Clues When you encounter an unfamiliar word, you can often use context clues to understand it. Context clues are the words or phrases surrounding the word that provide hints about the word's meaning.

Counterargument A counterargument is an argument made to oppose another argument. A good argument anticipates opposing viewpoints and provides counterarguments to disprove them.

Credibility Credibility is the believability or trustworthiness of a source and the information it provides.

Critical Review A critical review is an evaluation or critique by a reviewer, or critic. Types of reviews include film reviews, book reviews, music reviews, and art show reviews.

Database A database is a collection of information that can be quickly and easily accessed and searched and from which information can be easily retrieved. It is frequently presented in an electronic format.

Debate A debate is basically an argument—but a very structured one that requires a good deal of preparation. In school settings, debate usually is a formal contest in which two opposing teams defend and attack a proposition.

See also **Argument.**

Deductive Reasoning Deductive reasoning is a way of thinking that begins with a generalization, presents a specific situation, and then moves forward with facts and evidence toward a logical conclusion. The following passage has a deductive argument embedded in it: "All students in the math class must take the quiz on Friday. Since Lana is in the class, she had better show up." This deductive argument can be broken down as follows: generalization: All students in the math class must take the quiz on Friday; specific situation: Lana is a student who is in the math class; conclusion: Therefore, Lana must take the math quiz.

See also **Analyzing Logic and Reasoning,** *Reading Handbook, pages R22–R25.*

Dictionary *See* **Reference Works.**

Draw Conclusions To draw a conclusion is to make a judgment or arrive at a belief based on evidence, experience, and reasoning.

Editorial An editorial is an opinion piece that usually appears on the editorial page of a newspaper or as part of a news broadcast. The editorial section of the newspaper presents opinions rather than objective news reports.

See also **Op/Ed Piece.**

Either/Or Fallacy An either/or fallacy is a statement that suggests that there are only two choices available in a situation when in fact there are more than two.

See also **Identifying Faulty Reasoning,** *Reading Handbook, page R24.*

Emotional Appeals Emotional appeals are messages that create strong feelings to make a point. An appeal to fear is a message that taps into people's fear of losing their safety or security. An appeal to pity is a message that taps into people's sympathy and compassion for others to build support for an idea, a cause, or a proposed action. An appeal to vanity is a message that attempts to persuade by tapping into people's desire to feel good about themselves.

See also **Recognizing Persuasive Techniques,** *Reading Handbook, pages R21–R22.*

Encyclopedia *See* **Reference Works.**

Essay *See Glossary of Literary Terms, page R102.*

Evaluate To evaluate is to examine something carefully and to judge its value or worth. Evaluating is an important skill. A reader can evaluate the actions of a particular character, for example. A reader can also form opinions about the value of an entire work.

Evidence Evidence is a specific piece of information that supports a claim. Evidence can take the form of a fact, a quotation, an example, a statistic, or a personal experience, among other things.

Expository Essay *See* **Essay,** *Glossary of Literary Terms, page R102.*

Fact Versus Opinion A **fact** is a statement that can be proved, or verified. An opinion, on the other hand, is a statement that cannot be proved because it expresses a person's beliefs, feelings, or thoughts.

See also **Generalization; Inference.**

Fallacy A fallacy is an error of reasoning. Typically, a fallacy is based on an incorrect inference or a misuse of evidence.

See also **Either/Or Fallacy, Logical Appeal; Overgeneralization.**

See also **Identifying Faulty Reasoning,** *Reading Handbook, page R24.*

Faulty Reasoning *See* **Fallacy.**

Feature Article A feature article is a main article in a newspaper or a cover story in a magazine.

Generalization A generalization is a broad statement about a class or category of people, ideas, or things based on a study of, or a belief about, some of its members.
See also **Overgeneralization; Stereotyping.**

Government Publications Government publications are documents produced by government organizations. Pamphlets, brochures, and reports are just some of the many forms these publications take. Government publications can be good resources for a wide variety of topics.

Graphic Aid A graphic aid is a visual tool that is printed, handwritten, or drawn. Charts, diagrams, graphs, photographs, and maps are examples of graphic aids.
See also **Graphic Aids**, *Reading Handbook, pages R4–R7.*

Graphic Organizer A graphic organizer is a "word picture"—a visual illustration of a verbal statement—that helps a reader understand a text. Charts, tables, webs, and diagrams can all be graphic organizers. Graphic organizers and graphic aids can look the same. However, graphic organizers and graphic aids do differ in how they are used. Graphic aids help deliver important information to students using a text. Graphic organizers are actually created by students themselves. They help students understand the text or organize information.

Historical Documents Historical documents are writings that have played a significant role in human events. The Declaration of Independence, for example, is a historical document.

How-To Book A how-to book explains how to do something—usually an activity, a sport, or a household project.

Implied Main Idea *See* **Main Idea.**

Index The index of a book is an alphabetized list of important topics covered in the book and the page numbers on which they can be found. An index can be used to quickly find specific information about a topic.

Inductive Reasoning Inductive reasoning is the process of logical reasoning that starts with observations, examples, and facts and moves on to a general conclusion or principle.
See also **Analyzing Logic and Reasoning,** *Reading Handbook, pages R22–R25.*

Inference An inference is a logical guess that is made based on facts and one's own knowledge and experience.

Informational Text Informational text is writing that provides factual information. It often explains an idea or teaches a process. Examples include news reports, a science textbook, software instructions, and lab reports.

Internet The Internet is a global, interconnected system of computer networks that allows for communication through e-mail, listservs, and the World Wide Web. The Internet connects computers and computer users throughout the world.

Journal A journal is a periodical publication issued by a legal, medical, or other professional organization. The term may also be used to refer to a diary or daily record.

Loaded Language Loaded language consists of words with strongly positive or negative connotations, intended to influence a reader's or listener's attitude.

Logical Appeal A logical appeal is a way of writing or speaking that relies on logic and facts. It appeals to people's reasoning or intellect rather than to their values or emotions. Flawed logical appeals—that is, errors in reasoning—are called logical fallacies.
See also **Fallacy.**

Logical Argument A logical argument is an argument in which the logical relationship between the support and claim is sound.

Main Idea The main idea is the central or most important idea about a topic that a writer or speaker conveys. It can be the central idea of an entire work or of just a paragraph. Often, the main idea of a paragraph is expressed in a topic sentence. However, a main idea may just be implied, or suggested, by details. A main idea is typically supported by details.

Make Inferences *See* **Inference.**

Monitor Monitoring is the strategy of checking your comprehension as you read and modifying the strategies you are using to suit your needs. Monitoring often includes the following strategies: questioning, clarifying, visualizing, predicting, connecting, and rereading.

Narrative Nonfiction *See Glossary of Literary Terms, page R105.*

News Article A news article is writing that reports on a recent event. In newspapers, news articles are usually brief and to the point, presenting the most important facts first, followed by more detailed information.

Nonfiction *See Glossary of Literary Terms, page R105.*

Op/Ed Piece An op/ed piece is an opinion piece that typically appears opposite ("op") the editorial page of a newspaper. Unlike editorials, op/ed pieces are written and submitted by readers.

Organization *See* **Pattern of Organization.**

Overgeneralization An overgeneralization is a generalization that is too broad. You can often recognize overgeneralizations by the appearance of words and phrases such as *all, everyone, every time, any, anything, no one,* or *none.* An example is "None of the city's workers really cares about keeping the environment clean." In all probability, there are many exceptions. The writer can't possibly know the feelings of every city worker.

See also **Identifying Faulty Reasoning,** *Reading Handbook, page R24.*

Overview An overview is a short summary of a story, a speech, or an essay.

Paraphrase Paraphrasing is the restating of information in one's own words.

See also **Summarize.**

Pattern of Organization The term *pattern of organization* refers to the way ideas and information are arranged and organized. Patterns of organization include cause-and-effect, chronological, compare-and-contrast, classification, and problem-solution, among others.

See also **Cause and Effect; Chronological Order; Classification; Compare and Contrast; Problem-Solution Order; Sequential Order.**

See also **Reading Informational Texts: Patterns of Organization,** *Reading Handbook, pages R8–R13.*

Periodical A periodical is a magazine or other publication that is issued on a regular basis.

Personal Essay *See* **Essay,** *Glossary of Literary Terms, page R102*

Persuasion Persuasion is the art of swaying others' feelings, beliefs, or actions. Persuasion normally appeals to both the mind and the emotions of readers.

See also **Emotional Appeals; Loaded Language; Logical Appeal.**

See also **Recognizing Persuasive Techniques,** *Reading Handbook, pages R21–R22.*

Predict Predicting is a reading strategy that involves using text clues to make a reasonable guess about what will happen next in a story.

Primary Source *See* **Sources.**

Prior Knowledge Prior knowledge is the knowledge a reader already possesses about a topic. This information might come from personal experiences, expert accounts, books, films, and other sources.

Problem-Solution Order Problem-solution order is a pattern of organization in which a problem is stated and analyzed and then one or more solutions are proposed and examined.

Propaganda Propaganda is a form of communication that may use false or misleading information.

Public Documents Public documents are documents that were written for the public to provide information that is of public interest or concern. They include government documents, speeches, signs, and rules and regulations.

See also **Government Publications.**

Reference Works Reference works are sources that contain facts and background information on a wide range of subjects. Most reference works are good sources of reliable information because they have been reviewed by experts. The following are some common reference works: encyclopedias, dictionaries, thesauri, almanacs, atlases, and directories.

Review *See* **Critical Review.**

Rhetorical Questions Rhetorical questions are those that have such obvious answers that they do not require a reply. Writers often use them to suggest that their claim is so obvious that everyone should agree with it.

Scanning Scanning is the process used to search through a text for a particular fact or piece of information. When you scan, you sweep your eyes across a page, looking for key words that may lead you to the information you want.

Secondary Source *See* **Sources.**

Sequential Order Sequential order is a pattern of organization that shows the order of steps or stages in a process.

Setting a Purpose The process of establishing specific reasons for reading a text is called setting a purpose. Readers can look at a text's title, headings, and illustrations to guess what it might be about. They can then use these guesses to figure out what they want to learn from reading the text.

Sidebar A sidebar is additional information set in a box alongside or within an article. Popular magazines often make use of sidebars.

Signal Words In a text, signal words are words and phrases that help show how events or ideas are related. Some common examples of signal words are *and, but, however, nevertheless, therefore,* and *in addition.*

Sources A source is anything that supplies information. **Primary sources** are materials written by people who witnessed or took part in an event. Letters, diaries, autobiographies, and speeches are primary sources. Unlike primary sources, **secondary sources** are made by people who were not directly involved in an event or present when it occurred. Encyclopedias, textbooks, biographies, and most newspaper and magazine articles are examples of secondary sources.

Speech *See Glossary of Literary Terms, page R108.*

Stereotyping Stereotyping is a dangerous type of overgeneralization. It can lead to unfair judgments of people based on their ethnic background, beliefs, practices, or physical appearance.

Summarize To summarize is to briefly retell the main ideas of a piece of writing in one's own words.
See also **Paraphrase.**

Support Support is any information that helps to prove a claim.

Supporting Detail *See* **Main Idea.**

Synthesize To synthesize information means to take individual pieces of information and combine them in order to gain a better understanding of a subject.

Text Features Text features are elements of a text, such as boldface type, headings, and subheadings, that help organize and call attention to important information. Italic type, bulleted or numbered lists, sidebars, and graphic aids such as charts, tables, timelines, illustrations, and photographs are also considered text features.

Thesaurus *See* **Reference Works.**

Thesis Statement A thesis statement is the main proposition that a writer attempts to support in a piece of writing.

Topic Sentence The topic sentence of a paragraph states the paragraph's main idea; all other sentences in the paragraph provide supporting details.

Visualize Visualizing is the process of forming a mental picture based on written or spoken information.

Web Site A Web site is a collection of "pages" on the World Wide Web, usually devoted to one specific subject. Pages are linked together and accessed by clicking hyperlinks or menus, which send the user from page to page within a Web site. Web sites are created by companies, organizations, educational institutions, branches of the government, the military, and individuals.

Workplace Documents Workplace documents are materials that are produced or used within a work setting, usually to aid in the functioning of the workplace. They include job applications, office memos, training manuals, job descriptions, and sales reports.

Works Cited The term *works cited* refers to a list of all the works a writer has referred to in his or her text. This list often includes not only books and articles but also Internet sources.

Works Consulted The term *works consulted* refers to a list of all the works a writer consulted in order to create his or her text. It is not limited just to those cited in the text.
See also **Bibliography.**

accommodations (ə-kŏm′ə-dā′shənz) *n.* rooms and food, especially in a hotel or on a ship or train
alojamiento *s.* habitaciones para que duerman y coman viajeros en hoteles, barcos o trenes

accost (ə-kôst′) *v.* to approach a person and speak unpleasantly or aggressively
importunar *v.* acercarse a una persona y hablarle de modo desagradable o agresivo

adjoining (ə-joi′nĭng) *adj.* next to or in contact with **adjoin** *v.*
colindante *adj.* al lado; contiguo **colindar** *v.*

aghast (ə-găst′) *adj.* struck by terror or amazement
aterrado *adj.* espantado; sobresaltado

agile (ăj′əl) *adj.* quick and light in movement
ágil *adj.* que puede moverse con facilidad

agitator (ăj′ĭ-tā′tər) *n.* someone who stirs up people to support a cause
agitador *s.* persona que exhorta a apoyar una causa

agonizing (ăg′ə-nī′zĭng) *adj.* resulting in great pain or deep sadness **agonize** *v.*
angustioso *adj.* que produce mucho dolor o tristeza **angustiar** *v.*

amenable (ə-mē′nə-bəl) *adj.* open; agreeable
dispuesto *adj.* que está de acuerdo

anecdotal (ăn′ĭk-dōt′l) *adj.* based on observations rather than scientific analysis
anecdótico *adj.* basado en observaciones más que en análisis científico

anonymous (ə-nŏn′ə-məs) *adj.* having an unknown or withheld name
anónimo *adj.* de nombre desconocido u oculto

antagonism (ăn-tăg′ə-nĭz′əm) *n.* hostility; unfriendliness
antagonismo *s.* hostilidad; oposición

appalling (ə-pô′lĭng) *adj.* outrageous; terrible **appall** *v.*
terrible *adj.* espantoso; atroz

aptitude (ăp′tĭ-to͞od′) *n.* natural ability
aptitud *s.* habilidad natural

aquatic (ə-kwăt′ĭk) *adj.* growing or living in the water
acuático *adj.* que crece o vive en el agua

aroma (ə-rō′mə) *n.* a smell; odor
aroma *s.* olor, generalmente agradable

artisan (är′tĭ-zən) *n.* a person who is skilled in a trade
artesano *s.* persona que hace objetos a mano siguiendo un método tradicional

ascend (ə-sĕnd′) *v.* to go or move upward; rise
ascender *v.* subir

assent (ə-sĕnt′) *n.* agreement
asentimiento *s.* acuerdo

automated (ô′tə-mā′tĭd) *adj.* able to function with little or no assistance from people **automate** *v.*
automatizado *adj.* que funciona por su cuenta con poca ayuda humana **automatizar** *v.*

bacterium (băk-tîr′ē-əm) *n.* the singular form of *bacteria,* microscopically small living things that may cause disease
bacteria *s.* organismo microscópico que puede causar enfermedades

balk (bôk) *v.* to refuse to move or act
resistirse *v.* rehusarse

barrage (bə-räzh′) *n.* a rapid, heavy attack
descarga *s.* sucesión rápida de golpes o balas

barren (băr′ən) *adj.* empty; lacking interest or charm
estéril *adj.* vacío; sin interés o encanto

beckon (bĕk′ən) *v.* to summon or call, usually by a gesture or nod
llamar *v.* atraer con un gesto

bedlam (bĕd′ləm) *n.* a noisy confusion
pandemonio *s.* confusión y ruido

bemused (bĭ-myo͞ozd′) *adj.* confused
desconcertado *adj.* confuso

brevity (brĕv′ĭ-tē) *n.* shortness
brevedad *s.* concisión

brooding (bro͞o′dĭng) *adj.* full of worry; troubled **brood** *v.*
inquietante *adj.* pertubador; preocupante **inquietar** *v.*

brusque (brŭsk) *adj.* abrupt or blunt in speaking
brusco *adj.* abrupto o contundente al hablar

buoyancy (boi′ən-sē) *n.* the ability to remain afloat in liquid
flotabilidad *s.* capacidad de flotar en un líquido

camouflage (kăm′ə-fläzh′) *v.* to disguise or portray falsely in order to conceal
camuflar *v.* disfrazar o disimular

capitalize (kăp′ĭ-tl-īz′) *v.* to take advantage of
capitalizar *v.* sacar provecho

carcass (kär′kəs) *n.* the dead body of an animal
cadáver *s.* esqueleto de animal muerto

cascade (kă-skād′) *n.* a waterfall or something that resembles a waterfall
cascada *s.* caída de agua

chafe (chāf) *v.* to irritate by rubbing
rozar *v.* frotar e irritar

chaotic (kā′ŏt′ĭk) *adj.* confused; disordered
caótico *adj.* confuso; desordenado

cherish (chĕr′ĭsh) *v.* to care for deeply
apreciar *v.* querer; valorar

chronicle (krŏn′ĭ-kəl) *n.* a record of historical events in the order in which they took place
crónica *s.* registro de sucesos históricos en el orden en que se dan

claret (klăr′ĭt) *adj.* dark red
granate *adj.* color vino tinto

clarity (klăr′ĭ-tē) *n.* clearness of mind
claridad *s.* lucidez

cohort (kō′hôrt′) *n.* a companion or associate
compinche *s.* compañero o socio

commence (kə-mĕns′) *v.* to start or begin
comenzar *v.* empezar

compassionate (kəm-păsh′ə-nĭt) *adj.* wanting to help those who suffer
compasivo *adj.* que siente pena por los que sufren y desea ayudar

compensation (kŏm′pən-sā′shən) *n.* payment
remuneración *s.* pago

compulsory (kəm-pŭl′sə-rē) *adj.* forced; required
obligatorio *adj.* forzoso

consensus (kən-sĕn′səs) *n.* general agreement
consenso *s.* acuerdo general

consolation (kŏn′sə-lā′shən) *n.* a comfort
consuelo *s.* alivio

contemplate (kŏn′təm-plāt′) *v.* to consider carefully and at length
contemplar *v.* considerar con atención

contorted (kən-tôr′tĭd) *adj.* twisted or strained out of shape **contort** *v.*
contorsionado *adj.* torcido **contorsionar** *v.*

contour (kŏn′to͝or′) *n.* the outline of a figure or body
contorno *s.* conjunto de líneas que limitan una figura

conventional (kən-vĕn′shə-nəl) *adj.* usual; traditional
convencional *adj.* usual; tradicional

converge (kən-vûrj′) *v.* to come together
convergir *v.* unirse

convivial (kən-vĭv′ē-əl) *adj.* enjoying the company of others; sociable
cordial *adj.* sociable; simpático

convoluted (kŏn′və-lo͞o′tĭd) *adj.* difficult to understand; complicated
enrollado *adj.* difícil de entender; complicado

cope (kōp) *v.* to struggle with and overcome
superar *v.* hacer frente y vencer

copious (kō′pē-əs) *adj.* more than enough; plentiful
copioso *adj.* abundante

covey (kŭv′ē) *n.* a small group or flock of birds, especially partridges or quail
nidada *s.* grupo de aves, especialmente de perdices o codornices

cower (kou′ər) *v.* to crouch or shrink down in fear
encogerse *v.* doblarse con miedo

croon (kro͞on) *v.* to sing softly
canturrear *v.* cantar suavemente

culminate (kŭl′mə-nāt′) *v.* to reach the highest point or degree
culminar *v.* llegar a su momento o grado más alto

cumbersome (kŭm′bər-səm) *adj.* awkward; hard to manage
incómodo *adj.* pesado y díficil de manejar

cunning (kŭn′ĭng) *adj.* skillful, clever
astuto *adj.* ingenioso, listo

cunningly (kŭn′ĭng-lē) *adv.* in a clever way that is meant to trick or deceive
astutamente *adv.* de modo ingenioso con el fin de engañar

currency (kûr′ən-sē) *n.* money
moneda *s.* dinero

cynically (sĭn′ĭ-kəl-lē) *adv.* in a way that shows mistrust in the motives of others
cínicamente *adv.* con desconfianza de los motivos ajenos

daunting (dôn′tĭng) *adj.* frightening; intimidating **daunt** *v.*
sobrecogedor *adj.* desalentador; asustador **sobrecoger** *v.*

decimate (dĕs′ə-māt′) *v.* to kill or destroy a large part of
diezmar *v.* matar o destruir una gran parte

decoy (dē′koi′) *n.* a person or thing used to distract others or lead them in a different direction
señuelo *s.* persona o cosa que se usa para distraer o desviar

deference (dĕf′ər-əns) *n.* respect and honor
deferencia *s.* respeto y honor

defiant (dĭ-fī′ənt) *adj.* willing to stand up to opposition; bold
desafiante *adj.* que confronta oposición

demeaning (dĭ-mē′nĭng) *adj.* lowering one's dignity or standing **demean** *v.*
degradante *adj.* que reduce la dignidad o posición de una persona **degradar** *v.*

demonize (dē′mə-nīz′) *v.* to give evil, demonic qualities to
demonizar *v.* atribuir características muy negativas

despair (dĭ-spâr′) *v.* to lose hope
desesperar *v.* perder la esperanza

detached (dĭ-tăcht′) *adj.* separated; disconnected **detach** *v.*
separado *adj.* alejado; distanciado **separar** *v.*

devastating (dĕv′ə-stā′tĭng) *adj.* very effective in causing pain or destruction **devastate** *v.*
devastador *adj.* que causa gran dolor o destrucción **devastar** *v.*

diffuse (dĭ-fyo͞oz′) *v.* to spread out or through
difundir *v.* difuminar; diseminar

disarray (dĭs′ə-rā′) *n.* a state of disorder; confusion
desorganización *s.* desorden; confusión

disciplinarian (dĭs′ə-plə-nâr′ē-ən) *n.* someone who enforces strict discipline, or rules
ordenancista *s.* persona que impone reglas estrictas de orden y disciplina

discreetly (dĭ-skrēt′lē) *adv.* in a manner that shows caution and good judgment
discretamente *adv.* de modo moderado y sensato

disembodied (dĭs′ĕm-bŏ′dēd) *adj.* separated from or lacking a body **disembody** *v.*
incorpóreo *adj.* que no tiene cuerpo

disillusionment (dĭs′ĭ-lo͞o′zhən-mənt) *n.* disappointment; loss of hope
desilusión *s.* decepción; pérdida de la esperanza

dismay (dĭs-mā′) *n.* distress caused by trouble or something unexpected
consternación *s.* angustia por problemas o por sucesos inesperados

dismount (dĭs-mount′) *v.* to get down or off
desmontarse *v.* bajarse

disorientation (dĭs-ôr′ē-ĕn-tā′shən) *n.* mental confusion or impaired awareness
desorientación *s.* confusión mental

dispel (dĭ-spĕl′) *v.* to get rid of
disipar *v.* hacer desaparecer

dissenter (dĭ-sĕn′tər) *n.* one who disagrees or holds a different opinion
disidente *s.* el que no está de acuerdo o tiene una opinión distinta

dissuade (dĭ-swād′) *v.* to persuade not to do something
disuadir *v.* convencer de no hacer algo

dominate (dŏm′ə-nāt′) *v.* to have control over
dominar *v.* mandar

dwindle (dwĭn′dl) *v.* to become less, until little remains
disminuir *v.* reducir hasta que no queda casi nada

eavesdrop (ēvz′drŏp′) *v.* to listen secretly to a private conversation of others
fisgonear *v.* escuchar en secreto conversaciones privadas

ecosystem (ē′kō-sĭs′təm) *n.* a physical environment, such as an ocean, and the community of things that live in it
ecosistema *s.* ambiente físico, como un océano, y las comunidades que viven en él

eloquence (ĕl′ə-kwəns) *n.* forceful, convincing speech or writing
elocuencia *s.* facultad de hablar o escribir de modo convincente

elusive (ĭ-lo͞o′sĭv) *adj.* tending to elude capture
evasivo *adj.* escurridizo; difícil de capturar

eminent (ĕm′ə-nənt) *adj.* famous; well-respected
eminente *adj.* muy famoso

endeavor (ĕn-dĕv′ər) *n.* purposeful or serious activity; enterprise
empeño *s.* esfuerzo serio y resuelto

entitlement (ĕn-tīt′l-mənt) *n.* the state of having a right or claim to something
derecho *s.* prerrogativa o atribución

epidemic (ĕp′ĭ-dĕm′ĭk) *n.* an outbreak of a disease that spreads quickly among many people
epidemia *s.* enfermedad que ataca a mucha gente al mismo tiempo

evasive (ĭ-vā′sĭv) *adj.* tending or trying to avoid
evasivo *adj.* que tiende a evitar

evidently (ĕv′ĭ-dənt-lē) *adv.* obviously; clearly
evidentemente *adv.* obviamente; claramente

excess (ĭk-sĕs′) *adj.* too much or too many
excesivo *adj.* que tiene demasiado

exhilarating (ĭg-zĭl′ə-rā′tĭng) *adj.* stimulating; making one feel thrilled or inspired **exhilarate** *v.*
estimulante *adj.* tonificante; que hace sentir entusiasmo **estimular** *v.*

exuberantly (ĭg-zo͞o′bər-ənt-lē) *adv.* in a manner showing enthusiasm or joy
exuberantemente *adv.* con mucho entusiasmo o alegría

falsify (fôl′sə-fī′) *v.* to make false by adding to or changing
falsificar *v.* falsear

ferocity (fə-rŏs′ĭ-tē) *n.* fierceness; extreme intensity
ferocidad *s.* fiereza; extrema intensidad

fester (fĕs′tər) *v.* to become an increasing source of irritation or poisoning
enconarse *v.* volverse más irritante o venenoso

feverishly (fē′vər-ĭsh-lē) *adv.* in a way marked by intense emotion or activity
febrilmente *adv.* con intensa emoción o actividad

flail (flāl) *v.* to wave wildly
agitar *v.* ondear fuertemente

fledgling (flĕj′lĭng) *n.* a young bird that has recently grown its flight feathers
polluelo *s.* pichón que acaba de echar plumas

flimsy (flĭm′zē) *adj.* not solid or strong
ligero *adj.* insubstancial; débil

flinching (flĭn′chĭng) *n.* drawing back from difficulty or danger **flinch** *v.*
reculada *s.* titubeo; vacilación **recular** *v.*

forage (fôr′ĭj) *v.* to search around for food or other supplies
hurgar *v.* buscar lo que se necesita, especialmente alimento

foray (fôr′ā′) *n.* a trip into an unknown area
incursión *s.* viaje a un territorio desconocido

forerunner (fôr′rŭn′ər) *n.* person or thing that came before
precursor *s.* persona o cosa que precede algo que se desarrollará más tarde

foresighted (fôr′sī′tĭd) *adj.* having the ability to anticipate the future and prepare for it
visionario *adj.* que anticipa el futuro y se prepara

forlorn (fər-lôrn′) *adj.* appearing lonely or sad
desdichado *adj.* de aspecto triste y solo

frail (frāl) *adj.* delicate; weak and fragile
frágil *adj.* delicado; débil

fray (frā) *n.* a fight; a heated dispute
refriega *s.* lucha

gait (gāt) *n.* a manner of walking or moving on foot
paso *s.* modo de andar

gaunt (gônt) *adj.* thin and bony
enjuto *adj.* delgado y huesudo

genially (jēn′yəl-lē) *adv.* in a pleasant, friendly manner
cordialmente *adv.* de modo amistoso

ghastly (găst′lē) *adj.* terrifyingly horrible
espantoso *adj.* horrendo

gigantic (jī-găn′tĭk) *adj.* extremely large
gigantesco *adj.* enorme

glinty (glĭn′tē) *adj.* sparkling
destellante *adj.* brillante

grave (grāv) *adj.* solemn and dignified
grave *adj.* solemne y digno

grievous (grē′vəs) *adj.* painful; serious
penoso *adj.* doloroso; serio

grimace (grĭm′ĭs) *v.* to twist one's face to show pain or disgust
hacer una mueca *v.* retorcer la cara de dolor o desagrado

heady (hĕd′ē) *adj.* tending to make one feel really happy or excited
embriagador *adj.* emocionante; vertiginoso

hierarchy (hī′ə-rär′kē) *n.* an organization of people according to rank
jerarquía *s.* organización por rango

homage (hŏm′ĭj) *n.* a display of loyalty and respect
homenaje *s.* demostración de lealtad y respeto

humor (hyo͞o′mər) *v.* to give in to the wishes of
llevar la corriente *v.* acceder; satisfacer

hustle (hŭs′əl) *v.* to gain by energetic effort
conseguir *v.* obtener con mucho esfuerzo

impairment (ĭm-pâr′mənt) *n.* the condition of being damaged, injured, or harmed
deterioro *s.* daño o herida

impasse (ĭm′păs′) *n.* a situation in which no progress can be made; a deadlock
impasse *s.* situación en que no se avanza; punto muerto

impetus (ĭm′pĭ-təs) *n.* a driving force; a motivation
ímpetu *s.* fuerza motriz; motivación

impoverished (ĭm-pŏv′ər-ĭsht) *adj.* very poor **impoverish** *v.*
empobrecido *adj.* muy pobre **empobrecer** *v.*

improbable (ĭm-prŏb′ə-bəl) *adj.* not likely
improbable *adj.* poco probable

improvise (ĭm′prə-vīz′) *v.* to make up on the spur of the moment, without preparation
improvisar *v.* inventar en el momento

inadvertence (ĭn′əd-vûr′tns) *n.* a lack of attention; carelessness
inadvertencia *s.* descuido; omisión

incoherent (ĭn′kō-hîr′ənt) *adj.* confused; lacking logical connections
incoherente *adj.* confuso; carente de conexiones lógicas

inconsolable (ĭn′kən-sō′lə-bəl) *adj.* impossible or difficult to comfort
inconsolable *adj.* que no se puede consolar

incredulously (ĭn-krĕj′ə-ləs-lē) *adv.* in a way that shows doubt or disbelief
incrédulamente *adj.* con incredulidad

incriminate (ĭn-krĭm′ə-nāt′) *v.* to cause to appear guilty
incriminar *v.* hacer parecer culpable

indefinitely (ĭn-dĕf′ə-nĭt-lē) *adv.* for an unlimited length of time
indefinidamente *adv.* por un tiempo ilimitado

inevitably (ĭn-ĕv′ĭ-tə-blē) *adv.* unavoidably; without fail
inevitablemente *adv.* que no se puede evitar; sin falta

infinitely (ĭn′fə-nĭt-lē) *adv.* extremely; greatly
infinitamente *adv.* sumamente; enormemente

infuriated (ĭn-fyo͝or′ē-ā′tĭd) *adj.* very angry **infuriate** *v.*
enfurecido *adj.* furioso **enfurecer** *v.*

inscription (ĭn-skrĭp′shən) *n.* something written, carved, or engraved on a surface
inscripción *s.* cosa escrita, tallada o gravada en una superficie

insinuation (ĭn-sĭn′yo͞o-ā′shən) *n.* a suggestion or hint intended to insult
insinuación *s.* manera sutil de insultar

insolently (ĭn′sə-lənt-lē) *adv.* boldly and insultingly
insolentemente *adv.* de modo grosero

integrated (ĭn′tĭ-grā′tĭd) *adj.* open to people of all races and groups **integrate** *v.*
integrado *adj.* abierto a personas de todas las razas o grupos étnicos **integrar** *v.*

integrity (ĭn-tĕg′rĭ-tē) *n.* honesty or sincerity
integridad *s.* honestidad o sinceridad

intricate (ĭn′trĭ-kĭt) *adj.* arranged in a complex way; elaborate
intrincado *adj.* presentado de una manera compleja; elaborado

ironically (ī-rŏn′ĭk-lē) *adv.* in a way that is contrary to what is expected or intended
irónicamente *adv.* de manera contraria a lo esperado

jauntily (jôn′tə-lē) *adv.* in a light and carefree way
gallardamente *adv.* de manera ligera y despreocupada

jostling (jŏs'ə-lĭng) *n.* roughly bumping, pushing, or shoving **jostle** *v.*
empujón *s.* empellón **empujar** *v.*

languish (lăng'gwĭsh) *v.* to remain unattended or be neglected
languidecer *v.* debilitarse o perder fuerza por abandono

lanky (lăng'kē) *adj.* tall and thin
largirucho *adj.* alto y flaco

linger (lĭng'gər) *v.* to continue to stay; delay leaving
vacilar *v.* quedarse; tardar en partir

masterpiece (măs'tər-pēs') *n.* a great work of art
obra maestra *s.* obra de arte magistral

melancholy (mĕl'ən-kŏl'ē) *n.* sadness; depression
melancolía *s.* tristeza; depresión

merge (mûrj) *v.* to blend together
combinarse *v.* unirse

metabolism (mĭ-tăb'ə-lĭz'əm) *n.* all the processes a living thing uses to continue to grow and live
metabolismo *s.* conjunto de procesos que se producen en las células de los seres vivos

migrant (mī'grənt) *adj.* moving from place to place
migratorio *adj.* que se muda de un sitio a otro

mistrust (mĭs-trŭst') *v.* to think of without confidence or trust
desconfiar *v.* no tener confianza

moderate (mŏd'ər-ĭt) *adj.* not excessive or extreme; average
moderado *adj.* mediano; módico

muse (myo͞oz) *v.* to say thoughtfully
contemplar *v.* decir de modo pensativo

novelty (nŏv'əl-tē) *n.* something new, original, or unusual
novedad *s.* algo nuevo, original o inusual

oblige (ə-blīj') *v.* to force; require
obligar *v.* forzar; requerir

optimistic (ŏp'tə-mĭs'tĭk) *adj.* hopeful about the future
optimista *adj.* con esperanzas del futuro

partisan (pär'tĭ-zən) *adj.* relating to or in support of one political party
partidario *adj.* que apoya un partido político

patriarch (pā'trē-ärk') *n.* a male head of a family
patriarca *s.* hombre jefe de familia

pendulum (pĕn'jə-ləm) *n.* a weight hung so that it can swing freely, sometimes used in timing the workings of certain clocks
péndulo *s.* cuerpo que oscila libremente usado para regular el movimiento de las manecillas de los relojes

pensively (pĕn'sĭv-lē) *adv.* thoughtfully
pensativamente *adv.* reflexivamente

perception (pər-sĕp'shən) *n.* insight; ability to understand people and situations
percepción *s.* comprensión; capacidad de entender personas y situaciones

perfunctorily (pər-fŭngk'tə-rĭ-lē) *adv.* in a mechanical or unconcerned way
mecánicamente *adv.* superficialmente; como por obligación

perilously (pĕr'ə-ləs-lē) *adv.* dangerously
arriesgadamente *adv.* peligrosamente

perpetual (pər-pĕch'o͞o-əl) *adj.* continual; unending
perpetuo *adj.* eterno; sin fin

piously (pī'əs-lē) *adv.* religiously; in a manner showing reverence or respect
piadosamente *adv.* devotamente; de modo reverente y respetuoso

portly (pôrt'lē) *adj.* stout or overweight
corpulento *adj.* grueso o con exceso de peso

posterity (pŏ-stĕr'ĭ-tē) *n.* future generations
posteridad *s.* generaciones futuras

precipitous (prĭ-sĭp'ĭ-təs) *adj.* very steep
escarpado *adj.* muy pendiente

predatory (prĕd'ə-tôr'ē) *adj.* given to stealing from or hurting others for one's own gain
rapaz *adj.* propenso a robar o hacer daño por beneficio propio

preoccupied (prē-ŏk'yə-pīd') *adj.* lost in thought; distracted
absorto *adj.* ensimismado; distraído

presentable (prĭ-zĕn'tə-bəl) *adj.* fit to be seen by people
presentable *adj.* en condiciones de ser visto

prestigious (prĕ-stē'jəs) *adj.* having a high reputation
prestigioso *adj.* que tiene renombre o importancia

prime (prīm) *adj.* first in quality or value
óptimo *adj.* de primera calidad o valor

prominent (prŏm'ə-nənt) *adj.* well-known; widely recognized
prominente *adj.* bien conocido; reconocido en muchas partes

prophecy (prŏf'ĭ-sē) *n.* a prediction of the future
profecía *s.* predicción del futuro

proponent (prə-pō'nənt) *n.* a person who supports something
defensor *s.* el que apoya una posición

prospective (prə-spĕk'tĭv) *adj.* likely to be or become
potencial *adj.* posible

punctual (pŭngk'cho͞o-əl) *adj.* on time; prompt
puntual *adj.* a tiempo

puny (pyo͞o'nē) *adj.* weak and small
enclenque *adj.* débil y raquítico

quiver (kwĭv'ər) *v.* to shake with a slight, rapid movement
temblar *v.* vibrar con un movimiento rápido y sutil

radar (rā'där) *n.* a method of detecting distant objects through the use of radio waves
radar *s.* método de detectar objetos distantes por medio de ondas de radio

rampage (răm'pāj') *n.* a wild or violent outbreak
alboroto *s.* tumulto violento

rash (răsh) *adj.* reckless and careless
precipitado *adj.* impetuoso e imprudente

rationality (răsh'ə-năl'ĭ-tē) *n.* reasonableness
racionalidad *s.* lógica; conformidad con la razón

raucous (rô'kəs) *adj.* loud and harsh-sounding
escandaloso *adj.* fuerte y estridente

recede (rĭ-sēd') *v.* to become fainter or more distant
desvanecerse *v.* alejarse

recessed (rē'sĕst') *adj.* set-in or set back **recess** *v.*
empotrado *adj.* metido en la pared **empotrar** *v.*

reclaim (rĭ-klām') *v.* to get back; recover
recuperar *v.* recobrar

recurrence (rĭ-kûr'əns) *n.* the act of happening again; return
reaparición *s.* repetición; regreso

redeem (rĭ-dēm') *v.* to set free
redimir *v.* liberar

redundant (rĭ-dŭn'dənt) *adj.* not needed; more than necessary
redundante *adj.* más de lo necesario

reel (rēl) *v.* to feel unsteady or dizzy
tambalearse *v.* sentirse mareado

rehabilitate (rē'hə-bĭl'ĭ-tāt') *v.* to restore to useful life, as through therapy and education
rehabilitar *v.* restaurar a través de terapia y educación

renounce (rĭ-nouns') *v.* to give up
renunciar *v.* dejar o abandonar

reproof (rĭ-pro͞of') *n.* criticism for a fault
reprobación *s.* crítica por una falta

reservoir (rĕz'ər-vwär') *n.* a place where anything is collected and stored
depósito *s.* lugar de almacenamiento

retaliate (rĭ-tăl'ē-āt') *v.* to get revenge; get even
vengarse *v.* tomar represalias

retort (rĭ-tôrt') *v.* to reply sharply
replicar *v.* contestar con brusquedad

retribution (rĕt'rə-byo͞o'shən) *n.* punishment for bad behavior
castigo *s.* pena al que ha cometido una falta

revelation (rĕv'ə-lā'shən) *n.* something made known
revelación *s.* algo que se da a conocer

revere (rĭ-vîr') *v.* to honor or worship
venerar *v.* honrar o adorar

revert (rĭ-vûrt') *v.* to return to a former condition
revertir *v.* regresar a una condición anterior

revive (rĭ-vīv') *v.* to return to life or consciousness
revivir *v.* recobrar la conciencia; despertarse

righteous (rī'chəs) *adj.* based on one's sense of what is right
recto *adj.* correcto; honrado

saunter (sôn′tər) *v.* to stroll in a casual manner
pasear *v.* caminar lentamente

scrutiny (skro͞ot′n-ē) *n.* close examination or study
examen *s.* estudio detallado

sever (sĕv′ər) *v.* to cut off or apart
cortar *v.* separar

shanty (shăn′tē) *n.* a rundown house; a shack
choza *s.* casucha

sheepishly (shē′pĭsh-lē) *adv.* with a bashful or embarrassed look
tímidamente *adv.* con una expresión tímida o avergonzada

shrewdly (shro͞od′lē) *adv.* wisely; in a clever way
astutamente *adv.* inteligentemente; con astucia

shuffle (shŭf′əl) *v.* to slide the feet along the ground while walking
arrastrar los pies *v.* rozar el suelo con los pies al caminar

simultaneously (sī′məl-tā′nē-əs-lē) *adv.* at the same time
simultáneamente *adv.* al mismo tiempo

singe (sĭnj) *v.* to burn lightly
chamuscar *v.* quemar en la superficie

slack (slăk) *adj.* not firm or tight; loose
flojo *adj.* fláccido

smugly (smŭg′lē) *adv.* in a self-satisfied way
presumidamente *adv.* con satisfacción vanidosa

snag (snăg) *v.* to catch and tear
enganchar *v.* agarrarse y romperse

somber (sŏm′bər) *adj.* serious; gloomy
sombrío *adj.* serio; triste

specify (spĕs′ə-fī′) *v.* to make known or identify
especificar *v.* detallar o identificar

speculate (spĕk′yə-lāt′) *v.* to view or consider different possibilities; to guess what might happen
especular *v.* pensar en distintas posibilidades; imaginar lo que puede pasar

spherical (sfîr′ĭ-kəl) *adj.* having the shape of a sphere or round ball
esférico *adj.* con forma de esfera o de pelota

squander (skwŏn′dər) *v.* to waste
derrochar *v.* malgastar

stance (stăns) *n.* posture; position
postura *s.* posición

subservient (səb-sûr′vē-ənt) *adj.* humble and obedient
obsequioso *adj.* humilde y obediente

subtly (sŭt′lē) *adv.* not obviously; in a manner hard to notice or perceive
sutilmente *adv.* veladamente; con discreción

suppressing (sə-prĕ′sĭng) *n.* keeping in; holding back
suppress *v.*
inhibidor *s.* supresor **inhibir** *v.*

sustain (sə-stān′) *v.* to keep up; to support
sustentar *v.* preservar; mantener

tantalizing (tăn′tə-lī′zĭng) *adj.* tempting but out of reach
tantalize *v.*
tentador *adj.* que inspira interés sin satisfacer **tentar** *v.*

taskmaster (tăsk′măs′tər) *n.* a person who sets tasks for others to do
supervisor *s.* persona que reparte tareas

taunt (tônt) *v.* to make fun of
burlar *v.* provocar con burlas; ridiculizar

taut (tôt) *adj.* not loose or flabby
tirante *adj.* tenso; terso

tawny (tô′nē) *adj.* a warm, sandy shade of brownish orange
leonado *adj.* color pardo rojizo

tedious (tē′dē-əs) *adj.* tiresome; boring
tedioso *adj.* aburrido

terse (tûrs) *adj.* speaking little; communicating in few words
seco *adj.* lacónico; que se comunica con pocas palabras

threshold (thrĕsh′ōld′) *n.* a doorway or entrance
umbral *s.* entrada

torrent (tôr′ənt) *n.* a violent, rushing stream
torrente *s.* corriente rápida y veloz

trance (trăns) *n.* a condition of daydreaming or being unconscious of one's surroundings
trance *s.* ensoñación; ensimismamiento

transition (trăn-zĭsh′ən) *n.* change from one place or condition to another
transición *s.* cambio de un lugar o situación a otros

translucent (trăns-lo͞o′sənt) *adj.* allowing light to pass through
translúcido *adj.* que deja pasar la luz

travesty (trăv′ĭ-stē) *n.* a degraded or grotesque likeness
parodia *s.* imitación burlesca de una cosa seria; distorsión

unbridled (ŭn-brīd′ld) *adj.* lacking restraint or control
desenfrenado *adj.* sin restricciones

unison (yo͞o′nĭ-sən) *n.* harmony or agreement; as with one voice
unísono *s.* armonía o acuerdo; dicho con una voz

unperceived (ŭn-pər-sēvd′) *adj.* not seen or noticed
desapercibido *adj.* no visto

unperturbed (ŭn′pər-tûrbd′) *adj.* not troubled or distressed
impasible *adj.* que no se molesta

upstart (ŭp′stärt′) *adj.* suddenly risen to wealth or power
advenedizo *adj.* arribista

urgency (ûr′jən-sē) *n.* a condition of pressing importance; necessity
urgencia *s.* gran necesidad

usher (ŭsh′ər) *v.* to guide in a certain direction
conducir *v.* llevar en cierta dirección

valiant (văl′yənt) *adj.* brave; courageous
valiente *adj.* valeroso

varmint (vär′mĭnt) *n.* a troublesome person or wild animal
alimaña *s.* persona o animal que causa problemas

veer (vîr) *v.* to change direction; to shift
virar *s.* cambiar de dirección; dar un viraje

vehemently (vē′ə-mənt-lē) *adv.* forcefully
vehementemente *adv.* de modo apasionado

venerable (vĕn′ər-ə-bəl) *adj.* deserving respect because of age, character, or importance
venerable *adj.* que merece respeto por edad, carácter o importancia

vengeance (vĕn′jəns) *n.* the infliction of punishment in return for an offense
venganza *s.* imposición de castigo por una ofensa

vile (vīl) *adj.* disgusting; unpleasant
repugnante *adj.* desagrable; asqueroso

virtuous (vûr′cho͞o-əs) *adj.* morally good; honorable
virtuoso *adj.* de buen carácter moral; honorable

visceral (vĭs′ər-əl) *adj.* instinctive
visceral *adj.* instintivo

voracious (vô-rā′shəs) *adj.* possessing an insatiable desire; greedy
voraz *adj.* que tiene un deseo insaciable; glotón

wavering (wā′vər-ĭng) *adj.* hesitating between two choices **waver** *v.*
vacilante *adj.* que duda entre dos alternativas **vacilar** *v.*

wince (wĭns) *v.* to draw back, as in pain or distress
estremecerse *v.* encogerse o contraerse por dolor

writhe (rīth) *v.* to twist or move painfully
retorcerse *v.* contorsionarse de dolor

Pronunciation Key

Symbol	Examples
ă	**a**t, g**a**s
ā	**a**pe, d**ay**
ä	f**a**ther, b**a**rn
âr	f**air**, d**are**
b	**b**ell, ta**b**le
ch	**ch**in, lun**ch**
d	**d**ig, bore**d**
ĕ	**e**gg, t**e**n
ē	**e**vil, s**ee**, m**ea**l
f	**f**all, lau**gh**, **ph**rase
g	**g**old, bi**g**
h	**h**it, in**h**ale
hw	**wh**ite, every**wh**ere
ĭ	**i**nch, f**i**t
ī	**i**dle, m**y**, tr**ie**d
îr	d**ear**, h**ere**
j	**j**ar, **g**em, ba**dge**
k	**k**eep, **c**at, lu**ck**
l	**l**oad, rattl**e**

Symbol	Examples
m	**m**an, see**m**
n	**n**ight, mitte**n**
ng	si**ng**, ha**ng**er
ŏ	**o**dd, n**o**t
ō	**o**pen, r**oa**d, gr**ow**
ô	**aw**ful, b**ough**t, h**o**rse
oi	c**oi**n, b**oy**
o͝o	l**oo**k, f**u**ll
o͞o	r**oo**t, gl**ue**, thr**ough**
ou	**ou**t, c**ow**
p	**p**ig, ca**p**
r	**r**ose, sta**r**
s	**s**it, fa**ce**
sh	**sh**e, ma**sh**
t	**t**ap, hopp**ed**
th	**th**ing, wi**th**
th	**th**en, o**th**er
ŭ	**u**p, n**u**t
ûr	**fur**, **ear**n, b**ir**d, w**or**m

Symbol	Examples
v	**v**an, sa**ve**
w	**w**eb, t**w**ice
y	**y**ard, law**y**er
z	**z**oo, rea**s**on
zh	trea**s**ure, gara**ge**
ə	**a**wake, ev**e**n, penc**i**l, pil**o**t, foc**u**s
ər	p**er**form, lett**er**

Sounds in Foreign Words

KH	*German* i**ch**, au**ch**; *Scottish* lo**ch**
N	*French* e**n**tre, bo**n**, fi**n**
œ	*French* f**eu**, c**œu**r; *German* sch**ö**n
ü	*French* **u**tile, r**ue**; *German* gr**ü**n

Stress Marks

′ This mark indicates that the preceding syllable receives the primary stress. For example, in the word *language*, the first syllable is stressed: lăng′gwĭj.

′ This mark is used only in words in which more than one syllable is stressed. It indicates that the preceding syllable is stressed, but somewhat more weakly than the syllable receiving the primary stress. In the word *literature*, for example, the first syllable receives the primary stress, and the last syllable receives a weaker stress: lĭt′ər-ə-cho͝or′.

Adapted from *The American Heritage Dictionary of the English Language,* fourth edition. Copyright ©2000 by Houghton Mifflin Company. Used with the permission of Houghton Mifflin Company.

INDEX OF FINE ART

Index of Skills

D

G

H

M

Q

R

S

T

U

V

W

INDEX OF TITLES & AUTHORS

Page numbers that appear in italics refer to biographical information.

ACKNOWLEDGMENTS

UNIT 1

Hill and Wang: "The Last Cover," from *The Pride of Lions and Other Stories* by Paul Annixter. Copyright © 1960 by Hill and Wang, renewed copyright © 1988 by Hill and Wang. Reprinted by permission of Hill and Wang, a division of Farrar, Straus and Giroux, LLC.

Brandt & Hochman: Excerpt from "The Third Wish," from *Not What You Expected: A Collection of Short Stories* by Joan Aiken. Copyright © 1974 by Joan Aiken. Reprinted by permission of Brandt & Hochman, Inc.

Harcourt: "Seventh Grade," from *Baseball in April and Other Stories* by Gary Soto. Copyright © 1990 by Gary Soto. Reprinted by permission of Harcourt, Inc.

Scholastic: "The Last Dog" by Katherine Paterson. Copyright © 1999 by Minna Murra, Inc. Published in *Tomorrowland: 10 Stories about the Future* compiled by Michael Cart. Copyright © 1999 by Michael Cart. Reprinted by permission of Scholastic, Inc.

ABC: Excerpts from "'Spot' Goes High-Tech" by Jackie Judd, from ABCNEWS.com. Copyright © 2002 by ABCNews Internet Ventures. Courtesy of ABCNEWS.com.

Hill and Wang: "Thank You, M'am," from *Short Stories* by Langston Hughes. Copyright © 1996 by Ramona Bass and Arnold Rampersad. Reprinted by permission of Hill and Wang, a division of Farrar, Straus and Giroux, LLC.

Harvard University Press: "If I can stop one heart from breaking," from *The Poems of Emily Dickinson*, edited by Thomas H. Johnson. Copyright © 1951, 1955, 1979, 1983 by the President and Fellows of Harvard College. Reprinted by permission of the publishers and the Trustees of Amherst College.

Farrar, Straus and Giroux: Excerpt from *Holes* by Louis Sachar. Copyright © 1998 by Louis Sachar. Jacket design by Vladimir Radunsky from *Holes* by Louis Sachar. Jacket art and design copyright © 1998 by Vladimir Radunsky. Reprinted by permission of Farrar, Straus and Giroux, LLC.

Scholastic: Excerpts from *Exploring the Titanic* by Robert D. Ballard. Copyright © 1988 by Ballard & Family. Reprinted by permission of Scholastic, Inc.

HarperCollins Publishers: Excerpt from *An American Childhood* by Annie Dillard. Copyright © 1987 by Annie Dillard. Reprinted by permission of HarperCollins Publishers.

The Estate of Rod Serling: "The Monsters Are Due on Maple Street" by Rod Serling. Copyright © 1960 by Rod Serling. Copyright © 1988 by Carolyn Serling, Jody Serling, and Anne Serling Sutton. Reprinted by permission of Code Entertainment and Carol Serling, on behalf of the Estate of Rod Serling.

Daniel Briney: Excerpts from "The Unnatural Course of Time" by Daniel Briney, from CultureDose.net. Copyright © 2002 by Daniel Briney. Reprinted with permission.

UNIT 2

Scholastic: Excerpt from "An Hour with Abuelo," from *An Island Like You: Stories of the Barrio* by Judith Ortiz Cofer. Copyright © 1995 by Judith Ortiz Cofer. Reprinted by permission of Scholastic, Inc.

Gish Jen: Excerpt from "The White Umbrella" by Gish Jen. Copyright © 1984 by Gish Jen. First published in *the Yale Review.* Reprinted by permission of the author.

Random House Children's Books: Excerpt from "Kitty and Mack: A Love Story," from *145th Street: Short Stories* by Walter Dean Myers. Copyright © 2000 by Walter Dean Myers. Used by permission of Random House Children's Books, a division of Random House, Inc.

Curtis Brown: "Birthday Box" by Jane Yolen, from *Birthday Surprises: Ten Great Stories to Unwrap*, published by Morrow Junior Books. Copyright © 1995 by Jane Yolen. Reprinted by permission of Curtis Brown, Ltd.

Alfred A. Knopf: "Zebra," from *Zebra and Other Stories* by Chaim Potok. Copyright © 1998 by Chaim Potok. Used by permission of Alfred A. Knopf, an imprint of Random House Children's Books, a division of Random House, Inc.

Naomi Shihab Nye: "The Rider" by Naomi Shihab Nye, first published in *Invisible.* Reprinted by permission of the author.

The Washington Post: Excerpts from "The Collected Grief of a Nation; An Exhibit of Mementos from the Vietnam Wall" by Judith Weinraub, from *the Washington Post.* Copyright © 1992 by the Washington Post. Reprinted with permission.

National Park Service: Mrs. Eleanor Wimbish Letter to Her Son, William "Billy" Stocks. Reprinted by permission of the National Park Service, Vietnam Veterans Memorial Collection.

Bilingual Press/Editorial Bilingüe: "The Scholarship Jacket" by Marta Salinas, from *Nosotras: Latina Literature Today* (1986), edited by María del Carmen Boza, Beverly Silva, and Carmen Valle. By permission of Bilingual Press/Editorial Bilingüe, Arizona State University, Tempe, AZ.

Philomel Books: "The Three-Century Woman" by Richard Peck, from *Second Sight: Stories for a New Millennium.* Copyright © 1999 by Richard Peck. Reprinted by permission of Philomel Books, a division of Penguin Putnam Books for Young Readers.

Farrar, Straus and Giroux: "Charles," from *The Lottery* by Shirley Jackson. Copyright © 1948, 1949 by Shirley Jackson, renewed © 1976, 1977 by Laurence Hyman, Barry Hyman, Mrs. Sarah Webster, and Mrs. Joanne Schnurer. Reprinted by permission of Farrar, Straus and Giroux, LLC.

Random House: Excerpt from *The Heart of a Woman* by Maya Angelou. Copyright © 1981 by Maya Angelou. Used by permission of Random House, Inc.

Estate of Martin Luther King Jr.: Excerpt from Crusade for Citizenship Mass Meeting, February 12, 1958. Copyright © 1958 by Martin Luther King Jr. Copyright renewed © 1991 by Coretta Scott King. Reprinted by arrangement with the Estate of Martin Luther King Jr., c/o Writers House as agent for the proprietor New York, NY.

Wylie Agency: "It Was a Long Time Before," from *Storyteller* by Leslie Marmon Silko. Copyright © 1981 by Leslie Marmon Silko. Reprinted with permission of the Wylie Agency, Inc.

Susan Bergholz Literary Services: "Abuelito Who," from *My Wicked Wicked Ways* by Sandra Cisneros. Copyright © 1987 by Sandra Cisneros. Published by Third Woman Press and in hardcover by Alfred

A. Knopf. Reprinted by permission of Susan Bergholz Literary Services, New York and Third Woman Press. All rights reserved.

UNIT 3

HarperCollins Publishers: "The Lion and the Mouse," from *Fables of Aesop* retold by Frances Barnes-Murphy. Copyright © 1994 by Frances Barnes-Murphy. Used by permission of HarperCollins Publishers.

Curtis Brown: "Little Sister" by Nikki Grimes. First appeared in *Something On My Mind* published by Peter Smith Publisher. Copyright © 1978 by Nikki Grimes. Reprinted by permission of Curtis Brown, Ltd.

Piri Thomas: Excerpt from *Stories from El Barrio* by Piri Thomas. Copyright © 1978 by Piri Thomas. Reprinted by permission of the author.

Pantheon Books: "The War of the Wall," from *Deep Sightings and Rescue Missions* by Toni Cade Bambara. Copyright © 1996 by the Estate of Toni Cade Bambara. Used by permission of Pantheon Books, a division of Random House, Inc.

Time: "Back to the Wall," from *People Weekly,* May 27, 2004. Copyright © 2004 by People Weekly. Used by permission of Time, Inc. All rights reserved.

Candlewick Press: "What Do Fish Have to Do With Anything?" from *What Do Fish Have to Do With Anything? and Other Stories* by Avi. Copyright © 1994 by Avi. Used by permission of Candlewick Press.

Random House: "Homeless," from *Living Out Loud* by Anna Quindlen. Copyright © 1987 by Anna Quindlen. Used by permission of Random House, Inc.

Scholastic: "A Crush," from *A Couple of Kooks and Other Stories About Love* by Cynthia Rylant. Copyright © 1990 by Cynthia Rylant. Published by Orchard Books/Scholastic, Inc. Used by permission.

Houghton Mifflin Company: Excerpt from *The Giver* by Lois Lowry. Copyright © 1993 by Lois Lowry. Reprinted by permission of Houghton Mifflin Company. All rights reserved.

Harvard University Press: "Spring Harvest of the Snow Peas," from *To Be the Poet* by Maxine Hong Kingston, pp. 86–87, Cambridge, Mass., Harvard University Press. Copyright © 2002 by Maxine Hong Kingston. Reprinted by permission of the publisher.

BOA Editions: "Eating Alone," from *Rose* by Li-Young Lee. Copyright © 1986 by Li-Young Lee. Reprinted with the permission of the author and BOA Editions, Ltd., www.BOAEditions.org.

University of Minnesota Press: *A Christmas Carol* by Charles Dickens, adapted by Frederick Gaines, from *Five Plays from the Children's Theatre Company of Minneapolis,* published by the University of Minnesota Press. Copyright © 1975 by Frederick Gaines. All rights reserved.

David A. Perdue: *A Christmas Carol Review* by David A. Perdue, from the Charles Dickens Page. Used by permission of the author.

UNIT 4

Bantam Books: Excerpt from "One Ordinary Day, with Peanuts," from *Just An Ordinary Day: The Uncollected Stories* by Shirley Jackson. Copyright © 1979 by the Estate of Shirley Jackson. Used by permission of Bantam Books, a division of Random House, Inc.

Don Congdon Associates: "Dark They Were, and Golden-Eyed" as "The Naming of Names," from *Thrilling Wonder Stories* by Ray Bradbury. Copyright © 1949 by Standard Magazines, renewed 1976 by Ray Bradbury. Reprinted by permission of Don Congdon Associates, Inc.

The Charlotte Observer: Excerpt from "Ray Bradbury, Science Fiction Supernova, Has Little Use for the Internet" by Sandy Hill, the *Charlotte Observer,* October 12, 1997. Copyright © 1997 by the *Charlotte Observer.* Reprinted with permission of the *Charlotte Observer.*

Scribner: "A Day's Wait," from *The Short Stories of Ernest Hemingway.* Copyright 1933 by Charles Scribner's Sons. Copyright © 1961 by Mary Hemingway. Reprinted with permission of Scribner, an imprint of Simon & Schuster Adult Publishing Group.

Alfred A. Knopf Children's Books: Excerpt from *The People Could Fly: American Black Folktales* by Virginia Hamilton. Text copyright © 1985 by Virginia Hamilton. Reprinted by permission of Alfred A. Knopf Children's Books, a division of Random House, Inc.

Scholastic: "Fields of Flashing Light" and "Wild Boy of the Road," from *Out of the Dust* by Karen Hesse. Copyright © 1997 by Karen Hesse. Published by Scholastic Press/Scholastic, Inc. Reprinted by permission.

Doubleday: Excerpt from *Love and Marriage* by Bill Cosby. Copyright © 1989 by Bill Cosby. Used by permission of Doubleday, a division of Random House, Inc.

Crown Publishers: "Breaking the Ice," from *Dave Barry Is Not Making This Up* by Dave Barry. Copyright © 1994 by Dave Barry. Used by permission of Crown Publishers, a division of Random House, Inc.

Viking Penguin: "One Perfect Rose" by Dorothy Parker, from *The Portable Dorothy Parker,* edited by Brendan Gill. Copyright © 1926, copyright renewed © 1954 by Dorothy Parker. Used by permission of Viking Penguin, a division of Penguin Group (USA), Inc.

National Association for the Advancement of Colored People: "Song for an April Dusk" by Dorothy Parker, from *Dorothy Parker: Complete Poems.* Copyright © 1999 by The NAACP. The publisher wishes to thank the National Association for the Advancement of Colored People for this use of Dorothy Parker's work.

Liveright Publishing: "maggie and milly and molly and may," from *Complete Poems: 1904–1962* by E. E. Cummings, edited by George J. Firmage. Copyright © 1956, 1984, 1991 by the Trustees for the E. E. Cummings Trust. 1904 "who are you,little i?" from *Complete Poems: 1904–1962* by E. E. Cummings, edited by George J. Firmage. Copyright © 1963, 1991 by the Trustees for the E. E. Cummings Trust. "old age sticks," from *Complete Poems: 1904–1962* by E. E. Cummings, edited by George J. Firmage. Used by permission of Liveright Publishing Corporation.

UNIT 5

Henry Holt and Company: Excerpt from "A Minor Bird," from *The Poetry of Robert Frost,* edited by Edward Connery Lathem. Copyright © 1956 by Robert Frost. Copyright © 1928, 1969 by Henry Holt and Company. Reprinted by permission of Henry Holt and Company, LLC.

Arnold Adoff: "Under the Back Porch" by Virginia Hamilton. Copyright © 1992, 1999 by Virginia Hamilton Adoff. Copyright © 2006 by Arnold Adoff, Executor of the Estate of Virginia Hamilton Adoff. Used by permission.

Scribner: "Faults" by Sara Teasdale, from *The Collected Poems of Sara Teasdale.* Copyright © 1937 by the Macmillan Company. Reprinted with the permission of Scribner, an imprint of Simon & Schuster Adult Publishing Group.

Harvard University Press: "A word is dead" and "Fame is a bee," from *The Poems of Emily Dickinson*, edited by Thomas H. Johnson. Copyright © 1951, 1955, 1979, 1983 by the President and Fellows of Harvard College. Reprinted by permission of the publishers and the Trustees of Amherst College.

HarperCollins Publishers: "Cynthia in the Snow," from *Bronzeville Boys and Girls* by Gwendolyn Brooks. Copyright © 1956 by Gwendolyn Brooks Blakely. Used by permission of HarperCollins Publishers.

Harcourt: Excerpt from "Ode to Mi Gato," from *Neighborhood Odes* by Gary Soto. Copyright © 1992 by Gary Soto. Reprinted by permission of Harcourt, Inc. This material may not be reproduced in any form or by any means without the prior written permission of the publisher.

Harcourt: "Primer Lesson," from *Slabs of the Sunburnt West* by Carl Sandburg. Copyright © 1922 by Harcourt, Inc., and renewed 1950 by Carl Sandburg. Reprinted by permission of the publisher. This material may not be reproduced in any form or by any means without the prior written permission of the publisher.

Sterling Lord Literistic: "The Names" by Billy Collins. Copyright © 2002 by Billy Collins. Reprinted by permission of SII/Sterling Lord Literistic, Inc.

Copper Canyon Press: "the earth is a living thing," from *The Book of Light* by Lucille Clifton. Copyright © 1993 by Lucille Clifton. Reprinted with the permission of Copper Canyon Press, P.O. Box 271, Port Townsend, WA 98368-0271.

Little, Brown and Company: "Sleeping in the Forest," from *Twelve Moons* by Mary Oliver. Copyright © 1972, 1973, 1974, 1976, 1977, 1978, 1979 by Mary Oliver. By permission of Little, Brown and Company, Inc.

Curtis Brown: "Gold" by Pat Mora, first appeared in *Home: A Journey Through America*, published by Silver Whistle Books. Copyright © 1998 by Pat Mora. Reprinted by permission of Curtis Brown, Ltd.

Faber and Faber: "Scaffolding," from *Death of a Naturalist* by Seamus Heaney. Copyright © 1966 by Seamus Heaney. Reprinted by permission of Faber and Faber, Ltd.

HarperCollins: "The World Is Not a Pleasant Place to Be," from *My House* by Nikki Giovanni. Copyright © 1972 by Nikki Giovanni. Reprinted by permission of HarperCollins Publishers.

Hugh Noyes: "The Highwayman," by Alfred Noyes. Reprinted by permission of Hugh Noyes for the Society of Authors as the Literary Representative of the Estate of Alfred Noyes.

HarperCollins Publishers: One haiku by Basho, from *The Essential Haiku: Versions of Basho, Buson & Issa*, edited and with an introduction by Robert Hass. Copyright © 1994 by Robert Hass. Reprinted by permission of HarperCollins Publishers.

HarperCollins Publishers: "Fireflies," from *Joyful Noise* by Paul Fleischman. Text copyright © 1988 by Paul Fleischman. Used by permission of HarperCollins Publishers.

Henry Holt and Company: "Fireflies in the Garden," from *The Poetry of Robert Frost* edited by Edward Connery Lathem. Copyright 1956 by Robert Frost. Copyright 1928, 1969 by Henry Holt and Company. Reprinted by permission of Henry Holt and Company, LLC.

HarperCollins Children's Books: "Sarah Cynthia Sylvia Stout Would Not Take the Garbage Out," from *Where the Sidewalk Ends* by Shel Silverstein. Copyright © 2004 by Evil Eye Music, Inc. Reprinted with permission from the Estate of Shel Silverstein and HarperCollins Children's Books.

N. Scott Momaday: "The Delight Song of Tsoai-talee," from *The Gourd Dancer* by N. Scott Momaday. Copyright © 1976 by N. Scott Momaday. Reprinted by permission of the author.

Susan Bergholz Literary Services: "Four Skinny Trees," from *The House on Mango Street* by Sandra Cisneros. Copyright © 1984 by Sandra Cisneros. Published by Vintage Books, a division of Random House, Inc., and in hardcover by Alfred A. Knopf in 1994. Reprinted by permission of Susan Bergholz Literary Services, New York. All rights reserved.

UNIT 6

Philomel Books: "Bess Call," from *Cut From the Same Cloth* by Robert D. San Souci. Copyright © 1993 by Robert D. San Souci. Used by permission of Philomel Books, a division of Penguin Young Readers Group, a member of Penguin Group (USA) Inc., 345 Hudson Street, New York, NY 10014. All rights reserved.

Scholastic: "Racing the Great Bear," from *Flying with the Eagle, Racing the Great Bear* by Joseph Bruchac. Copyright © 1993 by Joseph Bruchac. Reprinted by permission of Scholastic Inc.

Simon & Schuster Books for Young Readers: "Echo," from *The Macmillan Book of Greek Gods and Heroes* by Alice Low. Copyright © 1985 by Macmillan Publishing Company. Reprinted with the permission of Simon & Schuster Books for Young Readers, an imprint of Simon & Schuster Children's Publishing Division.

Scholastic: Excerpt from *The Greek Gods* by Bernard Evslin. Copyright © 1966 by Scholastic, Inc. Reprinted by permission of Scholastic, Inc.

Houghton Mifflin Company: "The Great Musician" and "Phaëthon, Son of Apollo," from *Greek Myths* by Olivia E. Coolidge. Copyright © 1949 by Olivia E. Coolidge. Copyright renewed © 1977 by Olivia E. Coolidge. Adapted by permission of Houghton Mifflin Company. All rights reserved.

Barbara S. Kouts Literary Agent: *Young Arthur* by Robert D. San Souci. Copyright © 1977 by Robert D. San Souci. Reprinted by permission of Barbara S. Kouts Literary Agent.

National Geographic Society: Excerpts from "Looking for King Arthur" by Jerry Dunn, from *National Geographic World*, March 1997. Copyright © 1997 by National Geographic. Reprinted with permission from the National Geographic Society.

Candlewick Press: *Sir Gawain and the Green Knight* by Michael Morpurgo. Text copyright © 2004 by Michael Morpurgo. Reproduced by permission of the publisher Candlewick Press, Inc., Cambridge, MA., on behalf of Walker Books Ltd., London.

Hyperion: Excerpt from *Crispin: The Cross of Lead* by Avi. Copyright © 2002 by Avi. Reprinted by permission of Hyperion, an imprint of Disney Children's Book Group, LLC.

Rowman & Littlefield Publishing Group: "Crispin: The Cross of Lead" book review by Rebecca Barnhouse, from *Voya*, Vol. 25, No. 2, June 2002. Copyright © 2002 by Rowman & Littlefield Publishing Group. Reprinted with permission.

Reprint Management Services: "Crispin: The Cross of Lead" book review by Cheri Estes, from *School Library Journal*, Vol. 48, No. 6, June 2002. Copyright © 2002 by School Library Journal. Reprinted with permission.

Lori Seals: "Brer Possum's Dilemma" by Jackie Torrence. Copyright © by Jackie Torrence. Used by permission of Lori Seals for the Estate of Jackie Torrence.

Curtis Brown: "Waters of Gold," from *Tongues of Jade* by Laurence Yep, published by HarperCollins. Text copyright © 1991 by Laurence Yep. Reprinted by permission of the author.

Alfred A. Knopf: "Sally Ann Thunder Ann Whirlwind," from *American Tall Tales* by Mary Pope Osbourne. Copyright © 1991 by Mary Pope Osbourne. Illustrations copyright © 1991 by Michael McCurdy. Used by permission of Alfred A. Knopf, an imprint of Random House Children's Books, a division of Random House, Inc.

Doubleday: "Two Ways to Count to Ten," from *African Wonder Tales* by Frances Carpenter Huntington. Copyright © 1963 by Frances Carpenter Huntington. Used by permission of Doubleday, a division of Random House, Inc.

Pantheon Books: "The Race Between Toad and Donkey," from *Afro-American Folktales,* edited by Roger D. Abrahams. Copyright © 1985 by Roger D. Abrahams. Used by permission of Pantheon Books, a division of Random House, Inc.

UNIT 7

Holiday House: Excerpt from *The Wright Brothers: How They Invented the Airplane* by Russell Freedman. Copyright © 1991 by Russell Freedman. Reprinted by permission of Holiday House, Inc.

Simon & Schuster Books for Young Readers: Excerpt from *The Invisible Thread* by Yoshiko Uchida. Copyright © 1991 by Yoshiko Uchida. Reprinted with the permission of Simon & Schuster Books for Young Readers, an imprint of Simon & Schuster Children's Publishing Division.

H. W. Wilson Company: Excerpt from "Christopher Reeve," from *Current Biography.* Copyright © 1982 by the H. W. Wilson Company. Reprinted by special arrangement with the H. W. Wilson Company.

Dial Books for Young Readers: Excerpt from *Rosa Parks: My Story* by Rosa Parks with Jim Haskins. Copyright © 1992 by Rosa Parks. Used by permission of Dial Books for Young Readers, a division of Penguin Young Readers Group, a Member of Penguin Group (USA), Inc., 345 Hudson Street, New York, NY 10014. All rights reserved.

Atheneum Books for Young Readers: Excerpts from "Eleanor Roosevelt," from *Great Lives: Human Rights* by William Jay Jacobs. Copyright © 1990 by William Jay Jacobs. Reprinted with the permission of Atheneum Books for Young Readers, an imprint of Simon & Schuster Children's Publishing Division.

Susan Bergholz Literary Services: "Names/Nombres" by Julia Alvarez, first published in *Nuestro,* March 1985. Copyright © 1985 by Julia Alvarez. Reprinted by permission of Susan Bergholz Literary Services, New York. All rights reserved.

G. P. Putnam's Sons: "Chemo," from *It's Not About the Bike* by Lance Armstrong. Copyright © 2000 by Lance Armstrong. Used by permission of G. P. Putnam's Sons, a division of Penguin Group (USA), Inc.

Da Capo Press: Excerpt from *23 Days in July* by John Wilcockson. Copyright © 2004 by John Wilcockson. Reprinted by permission of Da Capo Press, a member of Perseus Books, LLC.

CMG Worldwide: Excerpt from *I Never Had It Made* by Jackie Robinson as told to Alfred Duckett. Copyright © 1972 by Jackie Robinson and Alfred Duckett. Copyright © Rachel Robinson by CMG Worldwide, www.JackieRobinson.com. Reprinted by permission of CMG Worldwide.

Excerpt from *Malcolm X: By Any Means Necessary* by Walter Dean Myers. Copyright © 1993 by Walter Dean Myers. TM 2005 Malcolm X by CMG Worldwide, Inc. www.CMGWorldwide.com.

The New York Times: Excerpt from "Montreal Signs Negro Shortstop," from *the New York Times.* Copyright © 1945 by the New York Times Co. Reprinted by permission.

The New York Times: Excerpts from "Robinson Steals Home in Fifth" by Roscoe McGowen, from *the New York Times.* Copyright © 1947 by the New York Times Co. Reprinted with permission.

PLAYS: "Lucy Stone, Champion of Women's Rights" by Claire Boiko, from *Plays of Great Achievers.* Reproduced with the permission of PLAYS, the Drama Magazine for Young People/Sterling Partners, Inc., P.O. Box 600160, Newton, MA 02460.

W. W. Norton & Company: "My Mother Enters the Work Force," from *On the Bus with Rosa Parks* by Rita Dove. Copyright © 1999 by Rita Dove. Used by permission of W. W. Norton & Company, Inc.

Harcourt: "Washington Monument by Night," from *Slabs of the Sunburnt West* by Carl Sandburg. Copyright © 1922 by Harcourt, Inc., and renewed 1950 by Carl Sandburg. Reprinted by permission of the publisher. This material may not be reproduced in any form or by any means without the prior written permission of the publisher.

UNIT 8

Popular Science: Adaptation of "What's Eating the Titanic?" by Gregory Mone, from *Popular Science,* July 2004. Copyright © 2004 by Popular Science. Reprinted with permission.

Sharon Guynup: Excerpts from "What Do You Know About Sharks?" by Sharon Guynup, from *Science World.* Copyright © 2001 by Scholastic, Inc. Reprinted by permission of the author.

National Geographic Society: Excerpts from "Great White Sharks" by Peter Benchley, from *National Geographic,* April 2000. Copyright © 2000 by National Geographic. Reprinted with permission from the National Geographic Society.

Cobblestone Publishing: "Like Black Smoke—The Black Death's Journey" by Diana Childress, from *CALLIOPE,* March 2001. Copyright © 2001 by Cobblestone Publishing, 30 Grove Street, Suite C, Peterborough, NH 03458. All rights reserved. Used by permission of Carus Publishing Company.

Cobblestone Publishing: "A World Turned Upside Down: How the Black Death Affected Europe" by Mary Morton Cowan, from *CALLIOPE,* March 2001. Copyright © 2001 by Cobblestone Publishing, 30 Grove Street, Suite C, Peterborough, NH 03458. All rights reserved. Used by permission of Carus Publishing Company.

D. Mark Singletary: "Pro Athletes' Salaries Aren't Overly Exorbitant" by Mark Singletary, from *New Orleans CityBusiness,* March 25, 2002. Copyright © 2002 by D. Mark Singletary. Reprinted with permission.

Justin Hjelm: "Do Professional Athletes Get Paid Too Much?" by Justin Hjelm, from *the Horizon.* Copyright © 2004 by Justin Hjelm. Used by permission of the author.

Time: "Why We Shouldn't Go to Mars" by Gregg Easterbrook, from *Time,* January 26, 2004. Copyright © 2004 by TIME, Inc. Reprinted by permission.

The editors have made every effort to trace the ownership of all copyrighted material found in this book and to make full acknowledgment for its use. Omissions brought to our attention will be corrected in a subsequent edition.

ART CREDITS

CONSULTANTS

Title page © Getty Images; Photo © Duane McCubrey; Photo © Mark Schmidt; Photo © Bruce Forrester; Photo © McDougal Littell; Photo © Howard Gollub; Photo © Tamra Stallings; Photo © Mark Schmidt; Photo © Robert J. Marzano; Photo © McDougal Littell; Photo © Dawson & Associates Photography; Photo © Gitchell's Studio; Photo © Michael Romeo; Photo © Monica Ani; Photo © William McBride; Photo © Bill Caldwell; Photo © Gabriel Pauluzzi; Photo © Steven Scheffler.

TABLE OF CONTENTS

Contents in Brief verso *top* An Imprint of HarperCollins Publishers. Illustration © 1997 by Jerry Pinkney; *bottom* From *The People Could Fly* Illustrations © 1985 by Leo and Diane Dillon. Used by permission of Alfred A. Knopf, an imprint of Random House Children's Books, a division of Random House, Inc.; **recto** *top* © Detlev Van Ravensway/Photo Researchers, Inc.; *bottom, top center left, and bottom right- on right book page* © Siede Preis/Getty Images; *all other images* © Jupiterimages Corporation; **Unit 1 verso** *left* Illustration by Erika O'Rourke/ Elm Studios; *right* right © Artville; **recto** *top* Courtesy American Library Association; *bottom* © PunchStock; **Unit 2 verso** *left* Library of Congress; *right, Boy with Orange,* Murray Kimber. © Murray Kimber/Illustrationworks.com; **recto** © PunchStock; **Unit 3 verso** *left* © Adrian Arbib/Alamy Images; *right* Detail of *Birds XII* (2003), Barbara Weldon. Oil, gold leaf, and wax on canvas; **recto** *top* Courtesy American Library Association; *bottom* © PunchStock; **Unit 4 verso** *right* © Andrew Judd/Masterfile; *left* © Ferdinando Scianna/Magnum Photos; **recto** © PunchStock; **Unit 5 verso** *left* © The Image Bank/Getty Images; *right, Dragon,* Greg Spalenka. © Greg Spalenka; **recto** © PunchStock; **Unit 6 verso** *left, Falling Figure (Icarus)* (1944), Henri Matisse. Color lithograph after a paper cut-out and gouache. Published on the back cover of the deluxe art review *Verve* © 2007 Succession H. Matisse, Paris/Artists Rights Society (ARS), New York; *right* Illustration © Juan Wijngaard (1981) from *Sir Gawain and the Green Knight* by Selina Hastings. Reproduced by permission of Walker Books, Ltd., London; **recto** *top* Courtesy American Library Association; *bottom* © PunchStock; **Unit 7 verso** *left* © Marvin Koner/Corbis; *right* AP/Wide World Photos; **recto** *top* Courtesy American Library Association; *bottom* © PunchStock; **Unit 8 verso** *left* © Jeff Rotman/Alamy Images; *right* © Stephen Frink Collection/Alamy Images; **recto** © PunchStock; **Unit 9** *left* © Photo courtesy of Seattle Public Library; *right, top center left, and bottom right- on right book page* © Siede Preis/Getty Images; *all other images* © Jupiterimages Corporation.

THE POWER OF IDEAS

1 *left* From *The People Could Fly* Illustrations © 1985 by Leo and Diane Dillon. Used by permission of Alfred A. Knopf, an imprint of Random House Children's Books, a division of Random House, Inc.; *top right* © 2008 by Universal Studios Licensing LLLP. Courtesy of Universal Studios Licensing LLLP. All rights reserved; *bottom right* © Joseph Sohm; Visions of America/Corbis; **2** *left* An Imprint of HarperCollins Publishers. Illustration © 1997 by Jerry Pinkney; *right* © Alan Powdrill/Getty Images; **7** *left* © Images.com/Corbis; *right* AP/Wide World Photos; **8** *top to bottom* © Bettmann/Corbis; © Bill Pierce/Time Life Pictures/Getty Images; © Corbis; Courtesy Westmont College (Santa Barbara) Student Newspaper, *The Horizon*; © Photographer's Choice/Getty Images; © Judith Collins/Alamy; **10** *top to bottom* © 2008 by Universal Studios Licensing LLLP. Courtesy of Universal Studios Licensing LLLP. All rights reserved; Courtesy of ABC NEWS; © CBS Photo Archive; *Kibbles n' Bits Commercial* © Del Monte corporation; The Granger Collection, New York; **11** © Garry Hunter/Getty Images; **16** *left* © Jose Luis Pelaez, Inc./Corbis; *center* © Yellow Dog Productions/Getty Images; *right, inset left* © Time Life Pictures/ Getty Images; *right, inset right* © 2005 The Summer Northwestern; **17** © Siede Preis/Photodisc Green/Getty Images; **18** © Sam Barricklow/Workbookstock.com; **19** *left* © Image Source/Getty Images; *center* © Rob Brimson/Getty Images; *right* © Flying Colours, Ltd./Getty Images.

UNIT 1

21 *left* © William Low; *right* © Galen Rowell/Corbis; **22–23** © Paul Edmondson/Corbis; **22** *left* From *The Black Stallion* by Walter Farley. Cover art © 2002 by John Rowe. Used by permission of Random House; *right* © Kelly Reno/Photofest; **30** © Ed Bock/Corbis; **31** Courtesy of Gary Soto; **33** © Lisa Pines/Getty Images; **35** © Elizabeth Knox/Masterfile; **36** *left* © Jose Luis Pelaez, Inc./Corbis; *center* © Royalty-Free/PictureQuest; **42** *background* © Doug Wilson/ Corbis; *center* © PhotoDisc; **43** © Samantha Loomis Paterson; **45** Illustration by Erika O'Rourke/Elm Studios; **46** © Javier Larrea/Age Fotostock America, Inc.; **49–57** Illustrations by Erika O'Rourke/Elm Studios; **62** © David M. Grossman/ Workbookstock.com; **63** © Corbis; **67** *Gamin* (1929), Augusta Savage. Painted plaster, 9 × 5 3/4″ × 4 3/8″. Gift of Benjamin and Olya Margolin © Smithsonian American Art Museum, Washington, D.C./Art Resource, New York; **72** *center* © Marc Romanelli/Getty Images; *background* © Artbeats; **73** © Getty Images; **75** An Imprint of HarperCollins Publishers. Illustration © 1997 by Jerry Pinkney **76** © Jeremy Horner/Corbis; **77** *top* © GeoNova, LLC; *bottom* An Imprint of HarperCollins Publishers. Illustration © 1997 by Jerry Pinkney; **78, 82, 85, 86** An Imprint of HarperCollins Publishers. Illustration © 1997 by Jerry Pinkney; **92** *top* © Les Cunliffe/Age Fotostock America, Inc.; *center* © Carla Sachar; **92–93** © Jeff Hunter/Getty Images; **93** *top* Courtesy American Library Association; *bottom* From *Holes* by Louis Sachar. Cover illustration by Vladimir Radunsky. Reprinted by permission of Yearling Books, a division of Random House, Inc.; **94–95** © Royalty-Free/Corbis; **96–97** © Digital Vision/Getty Images; **98** *background* © C. Lee/Photolink/Getty Images; *center* © Richard Cummins/ Corbis; **99** © Bettmann/Corbis; **103** *top* © Don Lynch Collection; *frame* © Kimbell Art Museum/Corbis; *bottom* © From the Collections of the University of Pennsylvania Archives; *frame* © Kimbell Art Museum/Corbis; **106** Museum of Science and Industry, Chicago; **107** *top right* The Granger Collection, New York, *frame* © Kimbell Art Museum/Corbis; **111** © The National Archives of the United Kingdom; **115** 20th Century Fox/Paramount © Photofest; **118** © S. Beaudet/zefa; **119** © Jerry Bauer; **124** © Helen Norman/Corbis; **128** © Joe Robbins/Getty Images; **129** HUP Thayer, Ernest L. (1), Courtesy of the Harvard University Archives; **133** © Bettmann/Corbis; **134** © Enrique Algarra/Age Fotostock America, Inc.; **135** © Bettmann/Corbis; **137** *Empire of Lights* (1954), René Magritte. Oil on canvas, 146 cm × 114 cm. Musée d'Art Moderne, Brussels. © Phototheque R. Magritte/ADAGP, Paris/Art Resource, New York © 2008 C. Herscovici, Brussels/Artists Rights Society (ARS), New York; **139, 140, 143, 144, 147** © CBS Photo Archive; **150** © MCA/Universal Pictures/Courtesy Everett Collection; **151** *top* © 2008 by Universal Studios Licensing LLLP. Courtesy of Universal Studios Licensing LLLP. All rights reserved; *center* © MCA/Universal Pictures/Courtesy Everett Collection; *bottom* © 2008 by Universal Studios Licensing LLLP. Courtesy of Universal Studios Licensing LLLP. All rights reserved; **152** *top left, bottom left* © 2008 by Universal Studios Licensing LLLP. Courtesy of Universal Studios Licensing LLLP. All rights reserved; *background* © A & J Verkaik/Corbis; **154** *left* © MCA/Universal Pictures/Courtesy Everett Collection; *top right* © 2008 by Universal Studios Licensing LLLP. Courtesy of Universal Studios Licensing LLLP. All rights reserved; *center right* © MCA/Universal Pictures/Courtesy Everett Collection; *bottom right* © 2008 by Universal Studios Licensing LLLP. Courtesy of Universal Studios Licensing LLLP. All rights reserved; **155** © MCA/Universal Pictures/ courtesy The Everett Collection; **158, 164** © Craig Aurness/Corbis; **165** © Jim Cummins/Corbis; **172** © Siede Preis/Photodisc/Getty Images.

UNIT 2

173 *left, Bernadita* (1922), Robert Henri. Oil on canvas, 24 1/8″ × 20 1/8″. Gift of the San Diego Wednesday Club. © San Diego Museum of Art (1926:138); *right* © Michael Goldman/Taxi/Getty Images; **174–175** © 20th Century Fox/ ZUMA/Lucasfilm Ltd./Photofest; **182** *background* © Getty Images/Royalty Free; *center* © Alexander Walter/Getty Images; **183** © Bettmann/Corbis; **185** *background* © James Gritz/Getty Images /www.jamesgritz.com; *center* © Joshua Sheldon/Getty Images; **189** © Alan Powdrill/Getty Images; **192** © Peter Finger/ Corbis; **195** © GeoNova, LLC; **197** *background* © Joe Raedle/Getty Images; *center left, center right* AP/Wide World Photos; **199** © Royalty-Free/Corbis; **203** © Alamy Images; **204** © Thinkstock/Getty Images; **205** AP/Wide World Photos; **208** *collaged* © James Gritz/Getty Images /www.jamesgritz.com; © Joshua Sheldon/Getty Images; **209** AP/Wide World Photos; **210, 211** © Nathan Benn/Corbis; **214** *top* © David J. and Janice L. Frent Collection/ Corbis; *bottom, left* © Leif Skoogfors/Corbis; *bottom right* © Corbis Sygma; **216** © Alan Schein Photography/Corbis; **217** © David H. Wells; **226** AP/ Wide World Photos; **227** © Bettmann/Corbis; **229** *Tides of Memory* (1936), Norman Rockwell. Oil on board, 18 3/4″ × 15 1/4″. Collection of Mr. and Mrs. Norman Rockwell. Reproduced by permission of the Norman Rockwell Family Agency, Inc. Photo courtesy of the Norman Rockwell Museum at Stockbridge, Massachusetts; **234** *Hill, Main Street, Gloucester* (1916), John Sloan. Oil on canvas, 25 3/4″× 39 7/8″. Littlejohn Collection, The Parrish Art Museum, Southampton, New York, 1961.3.208; **240** © Reuters/Corbis; **241** *top, bottom* AP/Wide World Photos; **246** Library of Congress, Prints and Photographs Division; **247** © Beth Reitmeyer/McDougal Littell; **248** © Photodisc Blue/ Getty Images; **250** © Images.com/Corbis; **258** Louis Lanzano/AP/Wide World Photos; **259** © Frederick M. Brown/Getty Images; **261** *inset* © Bettmann/ Corbis; *background* © Reg Lancaster/Express/Getty Images; **262** *left, right* Library of Congress; *center* © Bettmann/Corbis; **263** *left, right* © Bettmann/ Corbis; *center* Library of Congress; **268** Photo by Sharon Hoogstraten; **269** © C.E. Mitchell/stockphoto.com; **274** © Peter Weimann/Animals Animals–Earth Scenes; **280** © Walter Hodges/Corbis; **281** *top* © Nancy E. Crampton; *bottom* © Gene Blevins/Corbis; **284** © Chris Dyball/Getty Images; **286, 292** © Joseph Sohm; ChromoSohm Inc./Corbis; **293** © Jeff Greenberg/Age Fotostock America, Inc.; **300** © Siede Preis/Photodisc/Getty Images.

UNIT 3

301 *left* Detail of *Birds XII* (2003), Barbara Weldon. Oil, gold leaf, and wax on canvas; *right* © Adrian Arbib/Alamy Images; **302** *left* Cover from *The Wonderful Wizard of Oz,* 100th Anniversary Edition by L. Frank Baum. Illustrated by W. W. Denslow. © 2000 HarperCollins Publishers, Inc.; *right* © MGM/The Kobal Collection; **304** *left, Faith Ringgold* (1977), Alice Neel. Oil on canvas, 48″ × 36″. Private collection. © 2004 Estate of Alice Neel/Courtesy Robert Miller Gallery, New York/Philadelphia Museum of Art, Special Exhibition (Accession: *The Art of Alice Neel,* Page 150, Plate 70); *right, Mighty Casey Advancing to the Bat* (1912), Dan Sayre Groesbeck. From illustration series for *Casey at the Bat* by Phineas Thayer. Mary Evans Picture Library; **310** *background* © Getty Images; *front* © Corbis; **311** © Nic Paget-Clarke; **314** © GeoNova, LLC; **323** AP/Wide World Photos; **326** © Jim West/The Image Works, Inc.; **327** © Schomburg Center for Research in Black Culture, New York Public Library/Art Resource, New York; **329** *Harlem Street Scene* (1942), Jacob Lawrence. Gouache on paper, 21″ × 20 3/4″. Private collection. © Art Resource, New York © 2008 The Jacob and Gwendolyn Lawrence Foundation, Seattle/Artists Rights Society (ARS), New York; **334** © Bettmann/Corbis; **337** *top, World Wall: A Vision of the Future Without Fear.* With Judith Baca. © SPARC www.sparcmurals.org; *bottom* © by People Weekly. Used by permission of Time Inc. All rights reserved; **338** © Alex James Photographic/Getty Images; **339** Photo by Russ Wright/Courtesy of the author; **341** *Gregory. Los Angeles, March 31st 1982* (1982), David Hockney. Composite Polaroid. 14 1/2″ × 13 1/4″. © David Hockney/The David Hockney No. 1 U.S. Trust; **347** © 2002 Gueorgui Pinkhassov/Magnum Photos; **350** *Celia. Los Angeles, April 10th 1982* (1982), David Hockney. Composite Polaroid. 18″ × 30″. © David Hockney/The David Hockney No. 1 U.S. Trust; **357** © Bill Pierce/Time Life Pictures/Getty Images; **356** *Gregory. Los Angeles, March 31st 1982* (1982), David Hockney. Composite Polaroid. 14 1/2″ × 13 1/4″. © David Hockney/ The David Hockney No. 1 U.S. Trust; **357** *top* The New York Times Company; *bottom* © Bill Pierce/Time Life Pictures/Getty Images; **358** *top* The New York Times Company; *bottom* © Jeff Dunn/PictureQuest; **359** The New York Times Company; **360** *top* The New York Times Company; *bottom* Gloria H. Chomica/Masterfile; **362** © Cassy Cohen/PhotoEdit; **363** © Margaret Miller/Courtesy Simon & Schuster; **365** © Bill Firestone; **368** *left* © Comstock Images/Alamy Images; *center* © John McAnulty/Corbis; *right* © Richard Cummins/Corbis; **371** © Bill Firestone; **374** *top* © Les Cunliffe/Age Fotostock America, Inc.; *bottom* © Lois Lowry; **374–375** © Hulton-Deutsch Collection/ Corbis; **375** *top* Courtesy American Library Association; *bottom* © McDougal Littell; **376–377** © Horace Bristol/Corbis; **378–379** © Laurence Mouton/ PhotoAlto; **380** © Al Petteway /National Geographic Image Collection; **381** *top* © Christopher Felver/Corbis; *bottom* © 2002 Margaretta K. Mitchell; **386** © Thierry Dosogne/iconica Limited; **387** The Granger Collection, New York; **388, 389, 391, 393, 395, 397, 403, 404, 407, 408, 409, 411** © 2003 Michael Rasbury/Louisiana Tech University School of Performing Arts; **413, 414** The Granger Collection, New York; **416** © Bettmann/Corbis; **417** *top* © Bettmann/Corbis; *center* © John Springer Collection/Corbis; *bottom* © MGM/The Kobal Collection; **418** *top* © The Everett Collection; *center* © United Artists/Photofest; **420, 426** © Daryl Benson/Masterfile; **427** © Will Hart/PhotoEdit; **434** © Siede Preis/Photodisc/Getty Images.

UNIT 4

435 *left, Mural Painting for the Terrace Plaza Hotel, Cincinnati* (1947), Joan Miró. Oil on canvas. Cincinnati Art Museum, Cincinnati, Ohio. Gift of Thomas Emery's Sons, Inc. Photo by Tony Walsh. © 2008 Successio Miró/ Artists Rights Society (ARS), New York/ADAGP, Paris; *right* © John Stanton/ Getty Images; **436** *left* © Shuji Kobayashi/Getty Images; **436–437** *background* © PhotoDisc; *foreground* © Getty Images; **437** *right* © Ben Edwards/Getty Images; **438** *left* © Joel Sartore/National Geographic Image Collection; *right* © Micheline Pelletier/Corbis; **440** Courtesy of Gary Soto; **444** © Image Bank/Getty Images; **445** © Bassouls Sophie/Corbis Sygma; **447** *Sugar Sphinx* (1933), Salvador Dali. Oil on canvas. © Salvador Dali. Gala-Salvador Dali Foundation © 2008 Artists Rights Society (ARS), New York; **449** NASA/JPL/ Caltech; **451** *Shellfish Flowers* (1929), Max Ernst. Oil on canvas, 129 cm × 129 cm. Inv.: R 19 P. Photo Jean-Francois Tomasian. Musée National d'Art Moderne, Centre Georges Pompidou, Paris. Photo © CNAC/MNAM/Dist. Réunion des Musées Nationaux/ Art Resource, New York © 2008 Artist Rights Society (ARS), New York/ADAGP, Paris; **454** *The Forest* (1950), Alberto Giacometti. Bronze, painted, 22″ x 24″ x 29 1/4″. Gift of Enid Haupt. © National Gallery of Art, Washington, D.C. © 2008 Artists Rights Society (ARS), New York/ADAGP, Paris; **457** © Araldo de Luca/Corbis; **458** © Andrew Judd/Masterfile; **461** *The Whole City* (1935), Max Ernst. Oil on canvas, 60 cm x 81 cm. Kunsthaus, Zurich, Switzerland © 2008 Artists Rights Society (ARS), New York/ADAGP, Paris; **462** *top* © the Charlotte Observer. Reprinted by permission of the Charlotte Observer; *bottom* AP/Wide World Photos; **463** NASA; **466** © Thinkstock/Getty Images; **467** © Time Life Pictures/Getty Images; **471** *The Rocker* (2000), Pam Ingalls © Pam Ingalls/Corbis; **472** © Dave King/Dorling Kindersley Images; **476** *Contemplation* (1930), Alice Kent Stoddard, Oil on canvas. © SuperStock; **477** © Cornell Capa Photos by Robert Capa © 2001/Magnum Photos; **480** © G. Rossenbach/zefa; **481** © Ron Rovtar; **485** Photo by Gordon Lewis; **486** © David C. Conrad 1975; **488** *top left* © Les Cunliffe/Age Fotostock America, Inc.; *center left* Courtesy of the author; **488–489** *bottom* © Three Lions/Getty Images; **489** *top right* Courtesy American Library Association;

Courtesy American Library Association; *center right* From *Out of the Dust* by Karen Hesse. Published by Scholastic Press, a division of Scholastic, Inc. Jacket illustration © 1997 by Scholastic, Inc. Used by permission. Jacket photo courtesy of Library of Congress Prints and Photographs division, Farm Security Administration; **490–491** © Time Life Pictures/Getty Images; **492–493** © American Stock/Getty Images; © Getty Images; **494** © Yellow Dog Productions/Getty Images; **495** *top* © Stephen J. Boitano/Getty Images; *bottom* © Bob Daemmrich/Corbis; **497** © Cheryl Himmelstein/Getty Images; **498** The Granger Collection, New York; **502** © Diana Ong/SuperStock; **508** © Royalty- Free/Corbis; **509** The Granger Collection, New York; **511** © Matthias Kulka/Corbis; **512** © Robert Stahl/Getty Images; **513** © Bettmann/Corbis; **514** © Topham/The Image Works, Inc.; **515** © Bettmann/Corbis; **516-517** *Mural Painting for the Terrace Plaza Hotel, Cincinnati* (1947), Joan Miró. Oil on canvas. Cincinnati Art Museum, Cincinnati, Ohio. Gift of Thomas Emery's Sons, Inc. Photo by Tony Walsh. © 2008 Successio Miró/ Artists Rights Society (ARS), New York/ADAGP, Paris; **518** *Painting* (1953), Joan Miró. Oil on canvas, 75 7/8″ × 51″. Collection Mr. and Mrs. Richard K. Weil, St. Louis, Missouri. © 2008 Artists Rights Society (ARS), New York/AGAGP, Paris; **520** © Laura Ciapponi/Getty Images; **521** *top, bottom* © Ferdinando Scianna/Magnum Photos; **522** *top left, Musician in the Rain,* Robert Doisneau. © Estate of Robert Doisneau/Rapho; *bottom left, The Cellist,* 1957, Robert Doisneau. © Estate of Robert Doisneau/ Rapho; *background* © Peter Jon Hamann/Getty Images; **523** © Corinne Mudge; **524, 530** © Richard Sisk/PictureQuest; **531** © Michael Pole/Corbis; **538** © Siede Preis/Photodisc/Getty Images.

UNIT 5

539 *left, Hacienda* (2002), Vanessa Julian. Acrylic on matboard, 23″ × 19″. © Vanessa Julian; *right* © The Image Bank/Getty Images; **540** © Alex Webb/Magnum Photos; **548** © Photorush/Corbis; **549** © Christopher Felver/ Corbis; **550** © Joseph Sohm; Visions of America/Corbis; **552** © Ruth Fremson/ Pool/Reuters/Corbis; **553** © Joe Raedel/Getty Images; **554** © Paula Borchardt/ Age Fotostock America, Inc.; **555** *top* © Michael Glaser/St. Mary's College of Maryland; *center* © Barbara Savage Cheresh/Molly Malone Cook Literary Agency; *bottom* Courtesy Pat Mora/Photo by Cheron Bayna; **562** © Peter Byron/ PhotoEdit; **563** *top* © David Levenson/Getty Images; *center* © Mike Simons/ Getty Images; *bottom* © Bettmann/Corbis; **569** Todd Davidson © Images.com/ Corbis; **570** AP/Wide World Photos; **571** *top* © Bettmann/Corbis; *bottom* The Granger Collection, New York; **573** © Time Life Pictures/Getty Images; **582** © Steve Satushek/Getty Images; **583** *top* National Archives; *center* © Dana Fleischman; *bottom* Detail of *Portrait of Basho.* Suzuki Nanbei, Kameda Bosai. Hanging scroll in ink and color on paper. © New Orleans Museum of Art: Gift of an anonymous donor, 80.181; **586, 588** Stephen Alvarez/National Geographic Image Collection; **589** © Ken Oliver/The Art Agency; **592** © Shannon Burns/ www.CartoonStock.com; **593** *top* © Bettmann/Corbis; *center* © Jeff Albertson/ Corbis; *bottom, Edward Lear* (1863), Schier and Schoefft. Albumen carte-de-visite, 3¾″ × 2¼″. Photo © National Portrait Gallery, United Kingdom; **596** © Richard Downs; **600** © Owen Franken/Corbis; **601** *top* © N. Scott Momaday/ Royce Carlton, Inc.; *bottom* © Gene Blevins/Corbis; **608, 614** © Daryl Benson/ Masterfile; **615** © Mary Kate Denny/PhotoEdit; **622** © Siede Preis/Photodisc/ Getty Images.

UNIT 6

623 *left* Study of *Almanach Der Blaue Reiter* (1911), Wassily Kandinsky. Watercolor, gouache, and black ink. Inv. AM 1994-70. Photo by Philippe Migeat. Musée National d'Art Moderne, Centre Georges Pompidou, Paris. © CNAC/MNAM/Dist. Réunion des Musées Nationaux/Art Resource, New York © 2008 Artists Rights Society (ARS), New York/ADAGP, Paris; *right* © Jim Zuckerman/Corbis; **624** © Tom Smart/Liaison/Getty Images; **632** © Paul A. Souders/Corbis; **633** *top* Courtesy of the author; *bottom* Courtesy of Julian Coolidge; **636** © GeoNova, LLC; **640** Museo della Civilta Romana, Rome. © Dagli Orti/The Art Archive; **646** © JupiterImages/Creatas/Royalty-Free; **647** *top* © The Schlesinger Library, Radcliffe Institute, Harvard University. http://www.radcliffe.edu/schles; *bottom* Courtesy of Julian Coolidge; **649** *The Fall of Icarus* (1944),Henri Matisse. Stencil print after a gouache and paper collage. © 2008 Succession H. Matisse, Paris/Artists Rights Society (ARS), New York; **651** *Falling Figure (Icarus)* (1944), Henri Matisse. Color lithograph after a paper cut-out and gouache. Published on the back cover of the deluxe art review *Verve.* © 2008 Succession H. Matisse, Paris/Artists Rights Society (ARS), New York; **653** *Study of Almanach Der Blaue Reiter* (1911), Wassily Kandinsky. Watercolor, gouache, and black ink. Inv. AM 1994-70. Photo by Philippe Migeat. Musée National d'Art Moderne, Centre Georges Pompidou, Paris. © CNAC/MNAM/Dist. Réunion des Musées Nationaux/Art Resource, New York © 2008 Artists Rights Society (ARS), New York/ADAGP, Paris; **656** *The Cavalier*, Wassily Kandinsky. Staedtische Galerie im Lenbachhaus, Munich, Germany © Giraudon/Art Resource, New York © 2008 Artists Rights Society (ARS), New York/ADAGP, Paris; **660** © Mason Morfit/Workbookstock/ Jupiterimages Corporation; **661** © Robert D. San Souci; **666** © Arte & Immagini srl/Corbis; **669** © Francis G. Mayer/Corbis; **670** © Kelvin Murray/ Getty Images; **671** © David Levenson/Getty Images; **674** © Heritage-Images/ The Image Works, Inc.; **686** *top left* © Les Cunliffe/Age Fotostock America, Inc.; *bottom left* Photo by Russ Wright; courtesy of the author; **686–687** © Robert Estall/Corbis; **687** *top* Courtesy American Library Association; *bottom* Cover image from *Crispin, The Cross of Lead* by Avi. © 2002. Reprinted with permission of Hyperion Books for Children, New York, New York; **688–689** © Bruno Morandi/Age Fotostock America, Inc.; **690–691** © Santiago Yaniz/Age Fotostock America, Inc.; **692** *top left* © Les Cunliffe/Age Fotostock America, Inc.; *center left* Photo by Russ Wright; courtesy of the author; *bottom* © Robert Estall/Corbis; *top right* Courtesy American Library Association; *lower right* Cover image from *Crispin, The Cross of Lead* by Avi. © 2002. Reprinted with permission of Hyperion Books for Children, New York, New York; **693** Dover Publications; **694** Cover image from *Crispin, The Cross of Lead* by Avi. © 2002. Reprinted with permission of Hyperion Books for Children, New York, New York; **696** © Digital Vision/Getty Images; **697** *top* Courtesy of the author; *bottom* Courtesy of Laurence Yep; **699** Illustration by Ingrid Hess; **712** *foreground* © Eric and David Hosking/Corbis; *background* © PhotoDisc; **713** © 2003 Paul Coughlin; **723** *top* Detail of photograph of Frances Carpenter with statue of Buddha, n.d., by Smithsonian Institution, Museum of Natural History (Neg #: 12520). Used in *The Elephant's Bathtub*. Record 2121/Sophia Smith Collection, Smith College; *bottom* University of Pennsylvania Center for Folklore and Ethnography; **725** Collage created by Celia Jordan; *background* © Gallo Images/Corbis; *center* © Paul A. Souders/Corbis; **726** © GeoNova, LLC; **731** *background* © David Reddick/Workbookstock.com; *left* © Tracy Kahn Photography, Inc./Workbookstock.com; *right* © Image Source/Workbookstock. com; **733** © GeoNova, LLC; **736, 742** © J. David Andrews/Masterfile; **743** © Zigy Kaluzny/Getty Images; **750** © Siede Preis/Photodisc/Getty Images.

UNIT 7

751 *left,* Detail of *Alma Sewing* (about 1935), Francis Criss. Oil on canvas, 33″ × 45″. High Museum of Art, Atlanta, Georgia. Purchase with funds from the Fine Art Collectors, Mr. and Mrs. Henry Schwob, the Director's Circle, Mr. and Mrs. John L. Huber, High Museum of Art Enhancement Fund, Stephen and Linda Sessler, the J.J. Haverty Fund, and through prior acquisitions. 2002.70; *right* © Jim Cornfield/Corbis; **752** girls Photos © Amy Carneghi; daisies © Bezkorovayny Dmitry/ShutterStock; peanuts © Neil Webster/ShutterStock; glove © PhotoDisc; popcorn © Scott Rothstein/ShutterStock; **752–753** Photo by Sharon Hoogstraten; grass © Donna Middlemiss/ShutterStock; boys Photo © Erik Koelle; **753** baseball, bat © PhotoDisc; **756** *left* © Marvin Koner/Corbis; *right* © Bettmann/Corbis; **759** © Reuters/Corbis; **760** © Viviane Moos/Corbis; **761** Reprinted with the permission of Atheneum Books for Young Readers, an imprint of Simon and Schuster Children's Publishing Division from the author photograph in *Great Lives: Human Rights* by William Jay Jacobs. Charles Scribner's Sons, New York, 1990; **763** © Marvin Koner/Corbis; **765, 766** © Corbis; **769, 770** © Bettmann/Corbis; **771** © Hulton Archive/Getty Images; **773** The Granger Collection, New York; **776** © Marvin Koner/Corbis; **777, 778** © Bettmann/Corbis; **780** *left, center* © SuperStock, Inc./SuperStock; *right* © Michael Rougier/Getty Images; **781** AP/Wide World Photos; **785** © GeoNova, LLC; **790** South Bend Tribune/AP/Wide World Photos; **791** © Duomo/Corbis; **793** © James Startt; **795** Courtesy LaTrice Haney; **797, 798–799** AP/Wide World Photos; **800** © AFP/Getty Images; **802** *top left* © Les Cunliffe/Age Fotostock America, Inc.; *center left* © Jerry Bauer; **802–803** AP/Wide World Photos; **803** *left* From *By Any Means Necessary* by Malcolm X. Cover photograph © John Launois/Black Star. Used with permission of the publisher Scholastic, Inc., New York; *right* Courtesy American Library Association; **804–805** © Bruce Davidson/Magnum Photos; **806–807** © James P. Blair/National Geographic Image Collection; **808** AP/Wide World Photos; **809** © Bettmann/Corbis; **811** Library of Congress Serial and Government Publications Division; **813** *left* Library of Congress Prints and Photographs Division; *right* © Barros & Barros/Getty Images; **815** *left* National Archives; *right* © Lake County Museum/Corbis; **817** *left* © Bettmann/Corbis; *right* © PhotoDisc/Getty Images; **819** *left* © Bettmann/Corbis; *right* © Blank Archives/Getty Images; *inset* Library of Congress, Prints and Photographs Division; **822** Library of Congress Serial and Government Publications Division; **823, 824** AP/Wide World Photos; **825** *top* The New York Times Company; *bottom* © Bettmann/Corbis; **826** The New York Times Company; **828** © Getty Images; **829** *top* © Bettmann/Corbis; *center, bottom* Footage from *Biography: Jackie Robinson,* A & E Television Networks; **830** *top left, bottom left* Footage from *Biography: Jackie Robinson,* A & E Television Networks; *background* © Jerry Driendl/Getty Images; **832** AP/Wide World Photos; **833** © Patricia Boiko/Winning Pictures LLC; **841** © The Schlesinger Library, Radcliffe Institute, Harvard University; *frame* © 1996 Image Farm, Inc. All rights reserved; **844** © Bettmann/Corbis; **845** *top* © Fred Viebahn; *bottom* © Bettmann/Corbis; **847** *Alma Sewing* (about 1935), Francis Criss. Oil on canvas, 33″ × 45″. High Museum of Art, Atlanta, Georgia. Purchase with funds from the Fine Art Collectors, Mr. and Mrs. Henry Schwob, the Director's Circle, Mr. and Mrs. John L. Huber, High Museum of Art Enhancement Fund, Stephen and Linda Sessler, the J.J. Haverty Fund, and through prior acquisitions. 2002.70; **848** © Sylvia Offe/Getty Images; **850, 856** © Jason Ernst/Age Fotostock America, Inc.; **857** Hunter Freeman/Getty Images; **864** © Siede Preis/Photodisc/Getty Images.

UNIT 8

865 *left* © Detlev Van Ravensway/Photo Researchers, Inc.; *right* NASA Dryden Flight Research Center (NASA-DFRC); **866** *left* © Cynthia Pringle/Corbis; *right* © Steve Cole/Getty Images; **866–867** © Artbeats; **868** *background* NOAA George E. Marsh Album/AP/Wide World Photos; *right* © GeoNova, LLC; **869** *top* © D. Parker/Photo Researchers, Inc.; *bottom* Illustration by Raymond Turvey; **871** Raul Touzon/Getty Images; **872** © Ralph A. Clevenger/Corbis; **873** Courtesy of the author; **874** *left* © Jeff Rotman/Alamy Images; *right* © Gary Bell/oceanwideimages.com; **874–875** *bottom* © Raul Touzon/Getty Images; **875** *left* © David Shen/SeaPics.com; *right* © Fred Bavendam/Minden Pictures; **876** *left* © Douglas D. Seifert/Getty Images; *right* © Kelvin Aitken/marinethemes.com; *bottom* © Raul Touzon/Getty Images; **877** *top* © Bob Cranston/SeaPics.com; *center, bottom* © Kelvin Aitken/marinethemes.com; **878** *top* © Tui De Roy/Minden Pictures; **878–879** Illustration by Stuart Jackson-Carter/The Art Agency; **880** © Jeff Rotman/Alamy Images; **884** © James O'Mara/Getty Images; **885** © Yvonne Hemsey/Getty Images; **886** © Stephen Frink Collection/Alamy Images; **888** *top* © Brandon Cole/www.brandoncole.com; *bottom* © Bettmann/Corbis; **889** © C. and M. Fallows/oceanwideimages.com; **891** © Jeff Rotman/Getty Images; **894** © Steve Mason/Getty Images; **895** *top* Photo by Stephen Childress © Diana Childress; *bottom* © Carl Cowan; **897** Illustration by Stephen R. Wagner; **898–899** © GeoNova, LLC; **908** AP/Wide World Photos; **909** *left, right* Courtesy of ABC NEWS; **910** *top* Courtesy of ABC NEWS; *background* AP/Wide World Photos; **910** *center* © 2005 Time Inc.; *inset* © Jose Jimenez/Getty Images; **913** © Rick Gomez/Masterfile; **915** © Corbis; **917** *top* © Bruce Forster/Getty Images; *center* © James P. Blair/Getty Images; *bottom* © Kelvin Murray/Getty Images; **918** © Big Cheese Photo/PictureQuest; **919** *top* Courtesy of Mark Singletary; *bottom* Courtesy of Justin Hjelm; **920** *top* Courtesy New Orleans City Business *bottom* © Getty Images; **922** *top* Courtesy Westmont College (Santa Barbara) Student Newspaper, *The Horizon*; *bottom* © Photographer's Choice/Getty Images; **923** *top* © Getty Images; *top center* © MLB Photos via Getty Images; **923** *bottom center* © NBAE 2002 Photo by NBAP/NBAE/Getty Images; *bottom* © Focus on Sport/Getty Images; **924** *left* © Nat Butler/NBAE/Getty Images; *right* AP/Wide World Photos; **928** © Patrick Olear/PhotoEdit; **929** © Courtesy of Random House; **930** NASA Jet Propulsion Laboratory; **932** *left* NASA Jet Propulsion Laboratory; *right* © Detlev Van Ravensway/Photo Researchers, Inc.; **933** *left* © U.S. Geological Survey/Photo Researchers, Inc.; *right* © NASA/Roger Ressmeyer/Corbis; **936** AP/Wide World Photos; **937** © Bettmann/Corbis; **938** The Granger Collection, New York; **939** © Corbis; **945** Mountain Dew's *Parking Attendant* © Pepsi-Cola Company; **946** *top left* Mountain Dew's *Parking Attendant* © Pepsi-Cola Company; *bottom left, Kibbles n' Bits Commercial* © Del Monte corporation; **948, 954** © Alain Choisnet/Getty Images; **955** *left* © Sean Justice/Getty Images; *right* © Getty Images; **962** © Siede Preis/Photodisc/Getty Images.

UNIT 9

963 *left* © George Grall/National Geographic Image Collection; *right, top center left, and bottom right- on right book page* © Siede Preis/Getty Images; *all other images* © Jupiterimages Corporation; **964** Photo by Sharon Hoogstraten; **966** © Brand X Pictures/Alamy Images; **970** © Google; **971** Smithsonian Institution, www.SmithsonianEducation.org; **975** Courtesy of Minuteman Library Network; **978** © Richard Levine/Alamy Images; **979** From *InfoTrac,* by Gale Group. Reprinted by permission of the Gale Group; **983** © Photo courtesy of Seattle Public Library; **984, 998** © Sam Barricklow/Workbookstock.com; **999** © Ian Shaw/Getty Images.

STUDENT RESOURCE BANK

R3 Mosaic with circus scene: fight with leopards. Galleria Borghese, Rome, Italy. © Scala/Art Resource, New York; **R6** *Armor* (1400 or later). Italian. Steel, brass, textile, H. 66.5 in. (168.9 cm.). Bashford Dean Memorial Collection. Gift of Helen Fahnestock Hubbard, in memory of her father, Harris C. Fahnestock, 1929. (29.154.3) © Metropolitan Museum of Art/Art Resource, New York; **R7** GeoNova, LLC; **R14** *left* © City Year; *right* AP/Wide World Photos; **R15** Bust of Cicero (0-100). © Araldo de Luca/Corbis; **R19** © 2003 New York State Adirondack Park Agency. All rights reserved; **R85** © Stockbyte Photography/Veer; **R92** © Warner Bros./The Kobal Collection.

BACK COVER

© Photodisc/Getty Images

ARS Electronic Restrictions

The multimedia product and its contents are protected under copyright law. Any theatrical, televised, or public display or performance, including transmission of any image over a network, excepting a local area network is prohibited by law, as is the preparation of any derivative work, including the extraction in whole or in part of any images without the permission of Artists Rights Society (ARS), New York.

Reproduction, including downloading of Ernst, Miro, Dali, Matisse, Kandinsky, Lawrence, and Giacometti works is prohibited by copyright laws and international conventions without the express written permission of Artists Rights Society (ARS), New York.

McDougal Littell has made every effort to locate the copyright holders of all copyrighted material in this book and to make full acknowledgment for its use. Omissions brought to our attention will be corrected in a subsequent edition.

ALABAMA COURSE OF STUDY FOR ENGLISH LANGUAGE ARTS GRADE 7

Reading

1. Apply strategies appropriate to the type of reading material, including setting purposes for reading and making generalizations, to comprehend seventh-grade recreational reading materials.
   - 1.a Distinguishing factual from fictional materials
   - 1.b Determining sequence of events
   - 1.c Using specific context clues to determine meaning of unfamiliar words
   - 1.d Applying self-monitoring strategies for text understanding
   - 1.e Drawing conclusions to interpret unstated intent
   - 1.f Analyzing predictions, including confirming and refuting
2. Relate literary elements and devices to each other, including main idea and supporting details, climax, point of view, and imagery.
   - 2.a Determining mood
   - 2.b Recognizing use of flashback
3. Distinguish among the major genres, including poetry, short stories, novels, plays, biographies, and autobiographies, and subgenres, such as folktales, myths, parables, fables, and science fiction, based on their characteristics.
4. Apply strategies that include setting purposes for reading, distinguishing fact from opinion, making generalizations, and reviewing to comprehend informational and functional reading materials.
   - 4.a Determining sequence of events to enhance text understanding
   - 4.b Using specific context clues to determine meaning of unfamiliar words
   - 4.c Applying self-monitoring strategies for text understanding
   - 4.d Drawing conclusions to determine unstated intent
5. Recognize the use of textual elements, including main idea and supporting details, to gain information from various text formats, including graphs.

Literature

6. Analyze nonfiction, science fiction, mystery or suspense, fantasy, and adventure for distinguishing characteristics.
   - 6.a Classifying plot elements as exposition or hook, conflict, rising action, climax, falling action, or resolution
7. Interpret the author's message in various literary, informational, and functional texts.
   - 7.a Comparing various types of informational and functional texts
8. Compare selections of culturally diverse literature and their characteristics.

Writing and Language

9. Compose in descriptive, narrative, expository, and persuasive modes with a thesis sentence and introductory, supporting, and concluding paragraphs when appropriate.
   - 9.a Using transitional words and phrases for coherence
   - 9.b Composing various genres of literature by imitating an author's style, form, and purpose
   - 9.c Using figurative language when writing in various genres
10. Apply mechanics in writing, including commas to set off nouns of address and following introductory phrases and clauses.
    - 10.a Punctuating titles correctly using quotation marks, underlining, or italics
    - 10.b Using semicolons, conjunctive adverbs, and commas to join two independent clauses or to correct run-on sentences
    - 10.c Demonstrating correct sentence structure by avoiding comma splices
    - 10.d Using commas to set off nonessential clauses and appositives

11. Apply grammar conventions in writing to pronoun-antecedent agreement and to subject-verb agreement with inverted word order and with indefinite pronouns as subjects.
  - **11.a** Identifying gerunds, infinitives, and participles in writing
  - **11.b** Using degrees of comparison in writing
  - **11.c** Identifying sentence patterns in writing
  - **11.d** Using compound and complex sentences in writing

Research and Inquiry

12. Cite sources used in the research process.
13. Apply steps in the research process to identify a problem or issue, locate resources and information, and present findings.
  - **13.a** Taking notes to gather and summarize information

Oral and Visual Communication

14. Present findings from inquiry and research using a variety of resources.
15. Demonstrate listening skills, including identifying the main idea, detail, purpose, and bias in group discussions, public speeches, and media messages.

ALABAMA DIRECT ASSESSMENT OF WRITING: GRADE SEVEN

Focused Holistic Rubric

Level I—Does not meet standard

Responses at **Level I** indicate little understanding of the writing task. There is little or no sense of audience and purpose. The writing exhibits little or no organizational plan and gives little or no attention to topic development. Level I responses at the seventh grade are characterized by the following:

Purpose	• Indicates little understanding of the writing task.
Content	• Descriptive: Attempts to describe someone or something. Presents limited information/details in vague, general terms. • Narrative: Presents an unclear sequence of events that tells what happened in a poorly organized manner. May present a vaguely defined time frame. • Expository: Attempts to present reasons, explanations, or steps in a process. Displays little or no attention to appropriate sequencing of steps or ideas. Presents few details and a vague main idea. • Persuasive: Contains an opinion and presents limited persuasive details, reasons, and/or examples supporting the position.
Audience	• Displays little or no sense of audience and purpose in word choice (tone and language).
Organization/ Clarity	• Displays little or no evidence of an organizational plan or strategy. • Displays little or no sense of author involvement. • Presents one or more weak, unclear controlling idea(s). • Gives little or no attention to topic development. • May present irrelevant ideas. • May commit many obvious errors in sentence formation, grammar, usage, and mechanics that interrupt the flow of communication.

ALABAMA DIRECT ASSESSMENT OF WRITING: GRADE SEVEN

Focused Holistic Rubric

Level II—Partially meets standard

Responses at **Level II** indicate some understanding of the writing task. The writers may drift off mode and/or off topic. The writers display some sense of audience and purpose but more author involvement than author control. Some success is evident with an organizational plan, but ideas are loosely organized. The writers introduce the topic but may wander from it or may develop it minimally with basic/functional vocabulary. Level II responses at the seventh grade are characterized by the following:

Purpose	• Indicates some understanding of the writing task.
Content	• Descriptive: Describes someone or something. Presents general information/details. • Narrative: Presents a sequence of events that tells what happened in a poorly organized manner. Presents a vaguely defined time frame. • Expository: Presents reasons, explanations, or steps in a process. Displays some attention to appropriate sequencing of steps or ideas. Presents incomplete development, with limited details. May include a stated or implied main idea. • Persuasive: Contains an opinion and presents some persuasive details, reasons, and/or examples supporting the position.
Audience	• Displays some sense of audience and purpose in word choice (tone and language).
Organization/ Clarity	• Displays some evidence of an organizational plan or strategy, although ideas are loosely organized. • Displays some sense of author involvement but weak author control. • Uses a controlling idea but may wander from it or uses several controlling ideas. • Introduces the topic and develops it minimally. • Presents ideas with minimal attention to their flow. • Uses basic-functional vocabulary. • May commit some errors in sentence formation, grammar, usage, and/or mechanics that interrupt the flow of communication.

ALABAMA DIRECT ASSESSMENT OF WRITING: GRADE SEVEN

Focused Holistic Rubric

Level III—Meets standard

Responses at **Level III** indicate a good understanding of the writing task. A sense of audience and purpose is evident. The writers display a sense of author control, using one controlling idea with only minimal wandering from it. The organization of these sufficiently developed responses and the use of meaningful, precise vocabulary set the Level III responses apart from the Level II responses. Level III responses at the seventh grade are characterized by the following:

Purpose	• Indicates a good understanding of the writing task.
Content	• Descriptive: Describes someone or something. Presents specific information/details. Includes other relevant details. • Narrative: Presents clearly a sequence of events, telling what happened. Establishes a time frame. • Expository: Presents reasons, explanations, or steps in a process. Displays logical order: appropriate sequencing of steps or ideas. Contains a main idea and supporting details and may provide a conclusion. • Persuasive: Contains a clearly stated opinion and presents sufficiently persuasive details, reasons, and/or examples supporting the position.
Audience	• Displays a sense of audience and purpose in word choice (tone and language).
Organization/ Clarity	• Displays an organizational plan or strategy. • Displays a sense of author control. • Uses one controlling idea with only minimal wandering from it. • Introduces the topic and develops it sufficiently. • Presents ideas so that they flow smoothly from one to the next with clarity. • May provide a conclusion. • Makes occasional errors in grammar, usage, and mechanics that do not interrupt the flow of communication. • Uses a variety of sentence structures. • Uses meaningful, precise vocabulary. • May display creativity in presenting information.

ALABAMA DIRECT ASSESSMENT OF WRITING: GRADE SEVEN

Focused Holistic Rubric

Level IV—Exceeds standard

Responses at **Level IV** indicate a thorough understanding of the writing task. The writers successfully address and control the writing task with a strong sense of audience and purpose. These thoroughly developed responses are precise, consistent, and elaborated. The responses display clear and coherent ideas that flow smoothly. The use of vivid and precise vocabulary sets these responses apart from the Level III responses. Level IV responses at the seventh grade are characterized by the following:

Purpose	• Indicates a thorough understanding of the writing task.
Content	• Descriptive: Describes clearly someone or something. Uses precise, vivid sensory details. Includes other relevant details. • Narrative: Presents clearly a sequence of events, telling explicitly what happened. Provides a definite time frame. • Expository: Presents reasons, explanations, or steps in a process. Uses logical order and the appropriate sequencing of steps or ideas. Contains a main idea, supporting details, and a conclusion. • Persuasive: Contains a clearly stated opinion and presents persuasive details, reasons, and/or examples that thoroughly support the position.
Audience	• Displays a strong sense of audience and purpose in word choice (tone and language).
Organization/ Clarity	• Displays a strong organizational plan or strategy with overall completeness. • Displays a strong sense of author control. • Uses one clear controlling idea and does not wander from it. • Introduces the topic and develops it thoroughly. • Presents clear ideas so that they flow smoothly from one to the next with clarity and coherence, using appropriate transitions. • May provide a conclusion. • Displays limited minor errors in grammar, usage, and mechanics. • Uses a variety of sentence structures appropriately. • Uses vivid and precise vocabulary. • May display creativity in presenting information.

ALABAMA DIRECT ASSESSMENT OF WRITING: GRADE SEVEN

Alabama Analytic Rubric

WRITING MECHANICS	
Level IV	• Few if any errors in mechanics and • Success with use of advanced techniques
Level III	• Few errors in mechanics and • Some use of advanced techniques
Level II	• Some or no errors in mechanics and • No use of advanced techniques
Level I	• Frequent, serious errors in mechanics and • No use of advanced techniques
SENTENCE FORMATION	
Level IV	• Few if any errors in sentence formation and • Success in the use of varied and advanced sentence structure or formation
Level III	• Few errors in sentence formation and • Some use of varied and/or advanced sentence structure or formation
Level II	• Some or no errors in sentence formation and • No variety in sentence structure or formation
Level I	• Frequent, serious errors in sentence formation and • No variety in sentence structure or formation
GRAMMAR AND USAGE	
Level IV	• Few if any errors in grammar and usage and • Expressive, powerful, creative word choice
Level III	• Few errors in grammar and usage and • Meaningful, precise word choice
Level II	• Some or no errors in grammar and usage and • Appropriate, basic-functional word choice
Level I	• Frequent and/or serious errors in grammar and usage and • Inappropriate, repetitive, vague word choices